Machine Learning Foundations

Volume I: Supervised Learning

Roi Yehoshua, PhD

✦ Addison-Wesley

Hoboken, New Jersey

Library of Congress Control Number: 2025938817

ISBN-13: 978-0-13-533786-8
ISBN-10: 0-13-533786-0

1 2026

Contents

Preface

Machine learning has rapidly evolved over the past few decades from a niche academic pursuit into a driving force behind many of today's most transformative technologies. From personalized recommendations and real-time language translation to self-driving cars and large language models, cutting-edge AI systems powered by machine learning are reshaping the way we work, communicate, and understand the world.

Amid this rapid progress, the study of machine learning has never been more exciting—or more essential. Yet for many students and practitioners, the journey can feel overwhelming. The field is vast and fast-moving, with a conceptual depth that is often matched by its practical complexity.

This book was born out of the need for a clear, rigorous, and comprehensive guide to machine learning—one that not only teaches the underlying theory but also emphasizes hands-on implementation and practical considerations.

As a teaching professor of machine learning and data science at Northeastern University, I had long been searching for a textbook that could serve as the primary resource for my courses. Yet time and again, I found that existing resources fell short. Some books are too theoretical, rich in mathematical rigor but lacking practical examples or code. Others are too hands-on, offering quick tutorials on machine learning libraries without explaining the principles behind the methods. Additionally, many books focus on a specific area of machine learning (e.g., probabilistic models or deep learning), leaving students with an incomplete view of the discipline. Inconsistent definitions and notations across texts further make it difficult for learners to build a cohesive understanding as they progress.

This textbook aims to address these gaps by providing broad and integrated coverage of machine learning, unifying notation and terminology, and balancing rigorous theoretical foundations with practical implementations and real-world examples. Readers will gain not only a deep understanding of the mathematical underpinnings of machine learning models but also the ability to implement them from scratch and apply them effectively to real-world problems using modern libraries such as Scikit-Learn, PyTorch, and Hugging Face Transformers. This unified approach makes the book suitable for a wide range of learners, including students seeking a solid foundation and practitioners aiming to apply these techniques effectively in real-world settings.

In addition to classical models, the book also explores recent advances in the field, including generative AI, large language models, and active areas of research. By combining foundational knowledge with modern developments, the book aims to equip students, instructors, and practitioners with both the conceptual understanding and practical tools needed to engage with today's machine learning landscape.

Organization of the Book

This textbook provides a comprehensive guide to both the theoretical foundations and practical applications of machine learning. It covers the full spectrum of the field, including supervised, unsupervised, and semi-supervised learning, as well as reinforcement learning, deep learning, and recent advances such as generative AI and large language models.

Beyond covering a wide range of topics, the book emphasizes all key aspects of machine learning models: their theoretical foundations, mathematical derivations, algorithmic implementations, and practical considerations such as feature engineering, model selection, hyperparameter tuning, model evaluation, interpretability, and deployment.

To reflect the breadth and depth of the field, the content is organized into three volumes:

1. **Volume I: Supervised Learning**. This volume introduces the core concepts of machine learning, including generalization, model capacity, the bias–variance tradeoff, regularization, and the typical workflow for building and evaluating models. It also familiarizes readers with essential libraries for implementing and experimenting with machine learning models, including Scikit-Learn and XGBoost. The volume covers foundational supervised learning algorithms such as linear and logistic regression, k-nearest neighbors, naive Bayes, decision trees, ensemble methods, and support vector machines, while discussing their assumptions, mathematical foundations, training procedures, and practical applications.

2. **Volume II: Unsupervised and Deep Learning**. This volume explores learning from unlabeled data, including topics such as clustering, dimensionality reduction, density estimation, anomaly detection, and semi-supervised learning. It also provides a rigorous treatment of deep learning, covering fundamental architectures such as feedforward neural networks, convolutional neural networks (CNNs), recurrent neural networks (RNNs), autoencoders, transformers, and graph neural networks (GNNs). The volume combines theoretical depth with practical insights, showcasing applications in diverse areas such as computer vision, medical diagnosis, natural language processing, and recommender systems.

3. **Volume III: Advanced Topics**. This volume covers advanced and emerging areas in machine learning, including deep reinforcement learning, generative AI, and large language models (LLMs). It also delves into foundational principles from statistical learning theory, offering deeper insights into the theoretical guarantees and limitations of learning algorithms. Additional chapters address practical and ethical aspects of machine learning, including model deployment and serving, interpretability, bias and fairness, and adversarial robustness. The volume concludes with a comprehensive survey of current research directions and open questions, preparing the reader for independent investigation and further exploration of this vast field.

Who This Book Is For

This book is designed to serve a broad and diverse audience, including students, academic researchers, data science practitioners, and engineers. Its comprehensive coverage and modular structure make it flexible enough to support different learning paths, allowing readers to tailor their journey according to their goals and background. As such, the book can be used both as a textbook in academic courses and as a self-study resource or reference guide for professionals seeking to deepen their understanding of machine learning.

- **Undergraduate students** are encouraged to read the entire book to build a solid foundation in both the theory and practice of machine learning. Depending on their background, they may find it helpful to review the mathematical appendices before or alongside the main chapters. More advanced sections, marked with an asterisk (*), can be skimmed or revisited later as their understanding deepens.

- **Graduate students and researchers** will benefit from studying all the material in depth, including the starred sections. Throughout the book, references to research papers and advanced textbooks support deeper exploration and engagement with current research.

- **Practitioners and industry professionals** can focus on the conceptual explanations, algorithmic intuition, and hands-on implementation aspects. Most mathematical proofs can be safely skipped without loss of continuity. Practical examples, illustrations, and Python code using libraries like Scikit-Learn, XGBoost, and PyTorch make the book especially useful for applying machine learning techniques to real-world problems.

- **Instructors** will find the book well-suited for undergraduate and graduate courses in machine learning, data science, and artificial intelligence. More specifically:

  - **Volume I** can serve as a textbook for a full-semester course on supervised machine learning or introduction to machine learning. For example, it aligns well with courses such as *CS 6140: Machine Learning* and *EECE 5644: Introduction to Machine Learning and Pattern Recognition* at Northeastern University.

  - **Volume II** is suitable for full-semester courses dedicated to unsupervised learning (e.g., Northeastern's *DS 5230: Unsupervised Machine Learning and Data Mining*) or deep learning (e.g., *CS 7150: Deep Learning*).

  - **Volume III** can support advanced electives on topics such as reinforcement learning (e.g., *CS 4180/5180: Reinforcement Learning*), large language models (e.g., *EECE 5668: Large Language Models*), or learning theory (e.g., *15-854: Machine Learning Theory* at Carnegie Mellon).

About the First Volume

The first volume focuses on the core principles of machine learning and foundational supervised learning algorithms. It begins by introducing fundamental concepts that form the backbone of machine learning, including model capacity, the bias–variance tradeoff, regularization, and optimization techniques. Building on these foundations, it presents a wide range of classical supervised learning algorithms, including linear regression, decision trees, ensemble methods, and support vector machines, and demonstrates how these methods can be applied across diverse data types such as tabular data, images, and text. Throughout the volume, essential Python libraries such as Scikit-Learn, NLTK, and XGBoost, are introduced to equip readers with practical tools for implementing these approaches in hands-on projects.

For each topic, I have taken care to:

- Clearly explain the intuition behind the method or concept.

- Demonstrate the method or technique on a simple toy problem.

- Provide rigorous mathematical derivations and proofs where appropriate.

- Show how to implement the algorithm in Python, either from scratch or using libraries such as Scikit-Learn.

- Discuss practical considerations, including data preprocessing, model evaluation, hyperparameter tuning, and deployment best practices.

- Compare the advantages and limitations of each method relative to others.

- Provide both theoretical and programming exercises to reinforce understanding and encourage active learning.

The book is organized into 12 chapters that progressively increase in depth and complexity, starting with foundational models such as linear regression and advancing to more complex models such as gradient boosting and support vector machines. While some chapters focus on specific algorithms, the book is intended to be read sequentially, as many of the more advanced models build on concepts and techniques introduced earlier in the book.

The following provides a brief overview of the contents of each chapter:

1. **Introduction to Machine Learning**: Introduces the field of machine learning, defines core paradigms (supervised, unsupervised, reinforcement learning), discusses applications and limitations, and provides historical context, ethical considerations, and an overview of popular libraries and datasets.

2. **Supervised Machine Learning**: Introduces the supervised learning paradigm, starting with formal definitions of learning and the distinction between regression and classification tasks. The chapter presents key model components, including parameters, hyperparameters, loss functions, optimization methods, and evaluation metrics, as well as fundamental statistical principles such as maximum likelihood estimation and Bayesian inference. It concludes with a discussion of the supervised learning pipeline and practical challenges commonly encountered in real-world applications.

3. **Introduction to Scikit-Learn**: Introduces Scikit-Learn as the primary tool for building machine learning models in Python, covering its API and the end-to-end process of building, tuning, and evaluating models. The chapter provides an extensive discussion of data preprocessing techniques, including handling missing values, categorical encoding, outliers,

skewed data, and feature scaling. It also presents hyperparameter tuning methods such as grid search, random search, and Bayesian optimization, and includes complete hands-on examples using real datasets.

4. **Linear Regression**: Develops linear regression from first principles, covering ordinary least squares, model assumptions, evaluation metrics, and practical implementation. The chapter presents optimization techniques for training linear regression models, including the normal equations, gradient descent and its variants, as well as regularization methods such as ridge, lasso, and elastic net. It also explores extensions to nonlinear regression using polynomial and basis function models, and concludes with Bayesian linear regression. Numerous worked examples and Python implementations are provided throughout.

5. **Logistic Regression**: Introduces logistic regression as an extension of linear models to classification tasks, covering the model assumptions, training objective, decision boundaries, and optimization techniques such as gradient descent and Newton's method, along with a practical implementation in Python. It also presents a wide range of classification metrics, including precision, recall, F1 score, and ROC curves, and discusses methods for handling imbalanced datasets such as SMOTE. The chapter then extends logistic regression to multi-class problems through softmax regression and the cross-entropy loss, and concludes with a brief introduction to generalized linear models.

6. **K-Nearest Neighbors**: Presents the k-nearest neighbors algorithm for both classification and regression, covering distance-weighted voting, hyperparameter selection, and implementation in Python. The chapter discusses a variety of distance and similarity metrics, including Minkowski, Hamming, Jaccard, and cosine similarity. It also introduces efficient data structures such as KD-trees and ball trees for scalable neighbor search, and examines the challenges posed by high-dimensional spaces, known as the curse of dimensionality.

7. **Naive Bayes**: Presents the naive Bayes algorithm and its main variants—Bernoulli, Categorical, Multinomial, and Gaussian naive Bayes—illustrated through detailed numerical examples and demonstrations using Scikit-Learn. It then applies a naive Bayes model to a text classification task, introducing a typical natural language processing (NLP) pipeline that includes text preprocessing and feature extraction using libraries such as NLTK and spaCy. The chapter concludes with an introduction to Bayesian networks and probabilistic graphical models.

8. **Decision Trees**: Covers the construction of decision trees for both classification and regression, including impurity measures such as information gain and Gini index. The chapter also discusses handling continuous features, missing values, and multi-output problems, as well as pre-pruning and post-pruning techniques to avoid overfitting. Tree visualization and feature importance analysis are demonstrated using Scikit-Learn. The chapter concludes with oblique decision trees, which generalize standard decision trees by allowing splits based on linear combinations of features.

9. **Ensemble Methods**: Introduces the concept of ensembles and motivates their use as a means to improve the accuracy and robustness of machine learning models. It explores key ensemble learning techniques—including voting, bagging, boosting, and stacking—and covers commonly used algorithms such as random forests, extra trees, AdaBoost, and gradient boosting. Illustrative numerical and coding examples using Scikit-Learn are provided throughout the chapter.

10. **Gradient Boosting Libraries**: Provides in-depth coverage of popular gradient boosting libraries, including XGBoost, LightGBM, and CatBoost. The chapter covers their API usage, algorithmic innovations such as histogram-based and ordered boosting, and system-level optimizations including parallelization, GPU acceleration, and out-of-core computation. The chapter concludes with a detailed comparative evaluation of these libraries on the large-scale Higgs Boson dataset.

11. **Support Vector Machines**: Introduces the theory and intuition behind support vector machines (SVMs), covering both linear and nonlinear classification, hard-margin and soft-margin formulations, Lagrange duality, KKT conditions, hinge loss, and the kernel trick. Kernel methods are further discussed, including commonly used kernel functions and Mercer's theorem. The chapter also explores support vector regression (SVR) and efficient training methods for large-scale datasets, such as the Sequential Minimal Optimization (SMO) algorithm.

12. **Summary and Additional Resources**: Recaps the key concepts covered throughout the book and offers practical guidance on selecting algorithms, designing experiments, participating in machine learning competitions, and conducting research. It also provides a curated list of recommended resources for further study and a comprehensive set of integrative exercises to reinforce and connect concepts across the entire volume.

The book also includes six comprehensive appendices[1] covering both essential mathematical topics for machine learning—including linear algebra, calculus, probability, statistics, and optimization—as well as an overview of Python's core scientific libraries, such as NumPy, Matplotlib, and Pandas:

1. **Appendix A: Linear Algebra**. Reviews essential linear algebra concepts for machine learning, including vectors, vector spaces, linear transformations, and matrix operations. It also covers more advanced topics such as eigenvalues and eigendecomposition, the spectral theorem, matrix definiteness, ill-conditioned matrices, matrix factorizations, and tensor operations—key tools for understanding many machine learning algorithms. Clear definitions, geometric interpretations, and practical exercises are included throughout to reinforce understanding.

2. **Appendix B: Calculus**. Reviews fundamental topics in single-variable and multivariable calculus, including functions, limits, continuity, derivatives, integrals, and infinite series. It

---

1. These appendices are available as supplemental online material; go to informit.com/mlfoundations.

also provides detailed coverage of gradients, directional derivatives, Jacobians, Hessians, and matrix calculus, which simplifies derivative computations in multivariable settings. A dedicated section on convex analysis introduces convex sets and functions, first- and second-order conditions for convexity, Jensen's inequality, and subgradients, forming a solid foundation for convex optimization—a central tool in machine learning.

3. **Appendix C: Probability**. Covers the fundamental principles of probability theory, including basic axioms, random variables, and probability distributions. It presents both discrete and continuous distributions, highlighting key families such as Bernoulli, Binomial, Poisson, Gaussian, Exponential, Gamma, Beta, and Student's t-distribution. The appendix also covers joint, marginal, and conditional distributions; expectations, variances, and higher-order moments; covariance and correlation; moment-generating functions; and multivariate distributions. It concludes with the fundamental limit theorems—the Law of Large Numbers and the Central Limit Theorem—which provide the theoretical basis for understanding sampling behavior and approximation in probabilistic models.

4. **Appendix D: Statistics**. Provides a comprehensive introduction to statistical inference, bridging probability theory with data analysis. Topics include random sampling, descriptive statistics, point estimation, and the bias–variance tradeoff. The appendix also covers maximum likelihood estimation (MLE), methods for constructing confidence intervals, and the framework of hypothesis testing, including test statistics, p-values, and decision rules. It then presents specific tests for means, proportions, categorical data, nonparametric methods, ANOVA, and A/B testing. The appendix concludes with Bayesian inference, including MAP estimation, conjugate priors, posterior analysis, and credible intervals.

5. **Appendix E: Optimization**. Provides a comprehensive overview of optimization methods essential for training machine learning models. The appendix begins with formal definition of optimization problems and key concepts such as global and local optima, feasibility, and convergence rates. It then covers first-order methods such as gradient descent, stochastic gradient descent, conjugate gradient, and coordinate descent along with their convergence analyses and practical considerations. Second-order methods such as Newton's method and quasi-Newton approaches are also discussed. Lastly, constrained optimization is explored through the method of Lagrange multipliers, KKT conditions, and Lagrange duality.

6. **Appendix F: Python Libraries**. Provides a practical introduction to Python libraries widely used in data science and machine learning, including NumPy for numerical computing, Matplotlib and Seaborn for data visualization, Pandas for data manipulation and analysis, and SciPy for scientific computation. Topics include array operations, broadcasting, data selection and aggregation, statistical functions, visualization techniques, data cleaning, time series handling, numerical algorithms, and performance tips for working with large datasets.

As such, the appendices collectively cover much of the material typically taught in undergraduate mathematics courses (e.g., Calculus I–III, Linear Algebra, and Probability Theory), thereby making the book self-contained and accessible to readers from diverse academic and professional backgrounds.

Beyond reviewing prerequisite material, the appendices also address two important challenges in bridging traditional mathematical education with the demands of modern machine learning:

- Undergraduate courses often focus on functions of one, two, or three variables and low-dimensional matrices, while modern machine learning frequently involves high-dimensional data and vector-valued functions. The appendices therefore emphasize general formulations that extend to arbitrary dimensions and multivariate settings, including multivariable calculus, matrix-based representations of functions, and multivariate probability distributions.

- The appendices also introduce advanced topics essential for machine learning that are typically not covered in standard curricula. These include matrix calculus, subgradients, moment-generating functions, random vectors, maximum likelihood estimation, Bayesian inference, stochastic gradient descent, momentum methods, convex optimization, and Lagrange duality, among others.

Readers are encouraged to engage with the appendices according to their background and learning goals. Those with strong mathematical background may choose to skim or selectively review topics as needed, while others are encouraged to study the material more thoroughly. Some foundational topics are best reviewed early to support the main text, whereas more advanced topics—such as convex optimization and Lagrange duality—can be studied later as they arise in specific chapters (e.g., in the chapter on support vector machines).

About the Exercises

To truly master the material in this book, active engagement with the exercises is essential. Machine learning is best learned through practice ("learning by doing") and this includes both mathematical reasoning and hands-on programming.

Each chapter concludes with a comprehensive set of exercises designed to reinforce key concepts and develop both theoretical understanding and practical skills. The exercises fall into three main categories:

- **Multiple-choice questions (MCQs)**: Designed to review and assess understanding of the core concepts introduced in the chapter.

- **Theoretical exercises**: Include a variety of tasks such as manual computations, dry runs of algorithms on toy datasets, and more advanced problems involving proofs or theoretical analysis. Some exercises also involve reading research papers related to the chapter and answering conceptual or technical questions based on them.

- **Programming exercises**: These exercises vary in scope and complexity, from implementing algorithms from scratch to applying standard libraries such as Scikit-Learn to real-world problems. Some exercises involve building full machine learning pipelines—including data exploration, preprocessing, model training, hyperparameter tuning, and evaluation—using both synthetic and real-world datasets from a variety of domains such as image classification, document analysis, gene expression analysis, and credit card fraud detection.

The exercises follow the sequence of topics presented in the chapter and progress gradually from basic to more challenging problems. Advanced problems are marked with an asterisk (*). Readers can work through the exercises alongside the corresponding sections or use them for review after completing the chapter. Some exercises include hints or step-by-step instructions to support learning while encouraging independent problem-solving. A companion solutions supplement with selected answers will be made available at `https://roiyeho.com/ml-book`.

I strongly encourage you to attempt the exercises independently before consulting the solutions or using AI tools. Solving problems on your own helps build intuition, deepen understanding, and develop the problem-solving skills essential for applying machine learning methods in real-world scenarios.

About the Code

All code examples presented in this book are available on GitHub at `https://github.com/roiyeho/ml-book`. Most examples are provided as Jupyter notebooks to support interactive exploration, while larger projects—such as implementing XGBoost or the backpropagation algorithm from scratch—are organized into folders containing `.py` files.

The code is thoroughly commented and closely integrated with the main text to help readers understand not only how it works, but also the reasoning behind each implementation choice and its connection to the theoretical concepts introduced in the chapter. Readers are encouraged to experiment with the code, modify it, and extend it as part of their learning process.

All code examples can be executed on a standard laptop, making it easy for readers to follow along and explore variations. For deep learning and large language model (LLM) examples, access to a machine with a GPU is recommended for faster training and inference. Alternatively, these notebooks can be run using free GPU resources on platforms such as Google Colab (`https://colab.research.google.com`).

The code is released under the permissive MIT License, allowing you to use, modify, and distribute it, provided that the original copyright notice is retained.

About the Datasets

All datasets used in this book are open source and publicly available. Most are hosted on well-known platforms such as the UCI Machine Learning Repository (`https://archive.ics.uci.edu`), Kaggle (`https://www.kaggle.com`), or Hugging Face (`https://huggingface.co/docs/datasets`).

For each dataset, clear instructions are provided for downloading it or loading it directly into a Jupyter notebook using Python libraries such as Scikit-Learn or Pandas. This ensures that readers can easily reproduce all examples and complete the exercises on their own machines.

Notation and Conventions

To help readers follow the material more easily, the following conventions are used throughout the book:

- **Bold font** is used to highlight important terms and concepts when they are introduced for the first time.

- Sections, subsections, and exercises marked with an asterisk (*) indicate more advanced material that may be skipped on a first reading. These are intended for readers seeking a deeper understanding or additional challenges.

- Inline code, file paths, and Python objects are written in `monospace font`.

- Mathematical notation is introduced when new concepts appear for the first time. For example, the convention of using bold lowercase letters for vectors (e.g., $\mathbf{x}$) and uppercase italic letters for matrices (e.g., A) is explained in Appendix A (Linear Algebra), where these objects are formally defined.

- Objects and functions from Python libraries (e.g., `LinearRegression`) are linked to their official documentation when first introduced, giving readers easy access to their full API and parameter details (key parameters are explained directly in the text).

- In the PDF version of the book, references to sections, equations, and exercises are hyperlinked and highlighted in magenta, allowing readers to click and navigate directly to the corresponding content.

Acknowledgments

Writing this book has been a deeply rewarding journey, bringing together many years of teaching, research, and writing. I am grateful to my students and colleagues, whose support and inspiration have been invaluable along the way.

I would also like to thank the professors and academic mentors who shaped my academic path—especially Mireille Avigal, Ron Unger, Gal Kaminka, Noa Agmon, Christopher Amato, and David Kaeli. Their teaching, passion for learning, and dedication to research left a lasting impression and influenced my own approach to education.

I am also deeply grateful to my editor at Pearson, Kim Spenceley, for her patience, encouragement, and steady guidance throughout the writing process. I would also like to thank the production team at Pearson, and especially Julie Nahil, for their professional work, careful attention to detail, and dedication to producing a high-quality book.

Finally, I want to thank my family—most of all my parents, Nissim and Haya—for their unwavering support and encouragement at every stage. They have always been my greatest champions, and I am endlessly grateful for that.

Support and Feedback

I sincerely hope that you, the reader, will find this book helpful—whether you are a student encountering machine learning for the first time, an instructor teaching it, or a professional applying it to real-world problems.

If you have questions, comments, or suggestions, I would be happy to hear from you. Readers are welcome to send feedback by email to mlbook.feedback@gmail.com, and I will do my best to review all messages and respond where appropriate. Your feedback helps improve future editions of the book and ensures that the material remains clear, accurate, and relevant.

Thank you for being part of this learning journey.

Register your copy of *Machine Learning Foundations, Volume I: Supervised Learning*, on the InformIT site for convenient access to updates and/or corrections as they become available. To start the registration process, go to informit.com/mlfoundations and log in or create an account. The product ISBN (9780135337868) will already be populated. Click Submit. Look on the Registered Products tab for an Access Bonus Content link next to this product, and follow that link to access any available bonus materials. If you would like to be notified of exclusive offers on new editions and updates, please check the box to receive email from us.

About the Author

Roi Yehoshua is a teaching professor in the Department of Electrical and Computer Engineering at Northeastern University, where he develops and teaches graduate-level courses in machine learning and data science. He brings over two decades of experience in both academia and industry, spanning roles in software development, machine learning research, and robotics.

Roi earned his PhD in computer science from Bar-Ilan University, where he developed efficient coverage algorithms for robots operating in adversarial environments. His research has been published in leading AI and robotics venues, including *IJRR*, *AAMAS*, *IROS*, and *ECAI*. Following his doctoral studies, he conducted postdoctoral research at Northeastern's Khoury College of Computer Sciences, focusing on decentralized reinforcement learning methods for multi-drone search and detection tasks.

As a teaching professor at Northeastern, Roi has designed and taught a broad range of machine learning courses, covering both supervised and unsupervised learning. He also launched the university's first graduate course on Large Language Models (LLMs), offering students an in-depth exploration of their foundations, training techniques, and real-world applications. The course quickly became one of the most popular electives in the department, consistently drawing high enrollment and outstanding student feedback.

Beyond the classroom, Roi is passionate about making machine learning education accessible to a wider audience. He writes for popular platforms such as *Medium* and *Towards Data Science*, where his articles have reached thousands of readers worldwide. He also contributes to the public understanding of AI by authoring and editing Wikipedia pages related to machine learning.

Drawing on his extensive teaching and research experience, Roi has created this comprehensive textbook to provide students and practitioners with a solid foundation in the theory and practice of machine learning.

Chapter 1

Introduction to Machine Learning

Machine learning (ML) is a central branch of artificial intelligence that enables computers to learn from data, predict outcomes, and make decisions autonomously. Rather than relying on explicit programming of task-specific rules, machine learning algorithms discover patterns and statistical trends within the data to make informed predictions and decisions. From diagnosing medical conditions using image data to powering autonomous vehicles, machine learning transforms the way we interact with the world.

This chapter provides a comprehensive introduction to the field of machine learning. It is organized as follows. Section 1.1 presents a formal definition of machine learning and contrasts it with traditional programming as a tool to solve computational problems. Section 1.2 explores the diverse landscape of machine learning types, focusing on supervised, unsupervised, and reinforcement learning. Section 1.3 examines the interplay between machine learning and other fields in computer science, data science, and statistics. Section 1.4 presents historical milestones and breakthroughs that have led to the sophisticated algorithms we have today. Section 1.5 explores practical applications of machine learning across various industries, including healthcare, finance, and manufacturing. Section 1.6 discusses what kind of problems can be solved by machine learning and the challenges of applying machine learning to real-world problems. Section 1.7 considers the ethical implications of machine learning applications. Section 1.8 introduces popular software libraries that are used for building machine learning models. Section 1.9 provides an overview of commonly used datasets in machine learning research. Section 1.10 discusses emerging trends and future directions in machine learning. Section 1.11 concludes with a summary.

Let's embark on this journey through the fascinating and dynamic world of machine learning!

1.1 Formal Definition

A widely accepted definition of machine learning, attributed to Tom Mitchell [426], states: "A computer program is said to learn from experience E with respect to some task T and some performance measure P, if its performance on T, as measured by P, improves with experience E."

This definition underscores three essential components of machine learning:

- **Task** (T): The specific problem the learning algorithm is designed to solve, such as classification (assigning inputs to predefined categories) or regression (predicting continuous values).

- **Experience** (E): The data or interactions from which the algorithm learns.

- **Performance measure** (P): The criterion used to evaluate how well the algorithm performs the task.

For example, consider the problem of classifying emails as spam or not spam. The task (T) is binary classification, the experience (E) consists of previously labeled emails, and the performance measure (P) could be the classification accuracy on new, unseen emails.

A machine learning model is considered to be "learning" if its performance on the task improves with more experience, typically by processing additional data. This contrasts with traditional programming, where developers manually specify explicit rules to map inputs to outputs.

For example, in spam detection, a traditional program might classify emails based on hand-crafted rules, such as the presence of certain keywords or phrases commonly associated with spam. In machine learning, by comparison, the algorithm automatically learns these patterns from data. Instead of writing rules manually, we provide the algorithm with a labeled dataset and allow it to infer a model that can generalize to new, unseen examples. This data-driven approach often results in systems that are more concise, adaptable, and easier to maintain. Figure 1.1 illustrates the key differences between traditional programming and machine learning approaches.

Machine learning particularly excels at solving complex problems that traditional programming cannot easily address, such as object detection in images under varied conditions (e.g., different backgrounds, lighting, or angles). Traditional methods would require specifying the pixel configurations for each object across all variations, a nearly impossible task given the vast diversity of visual appearances. In contrast, machine learning, particularly deep learning and convolutional neural networks, learns the essential features of each object from extensive examples under varied

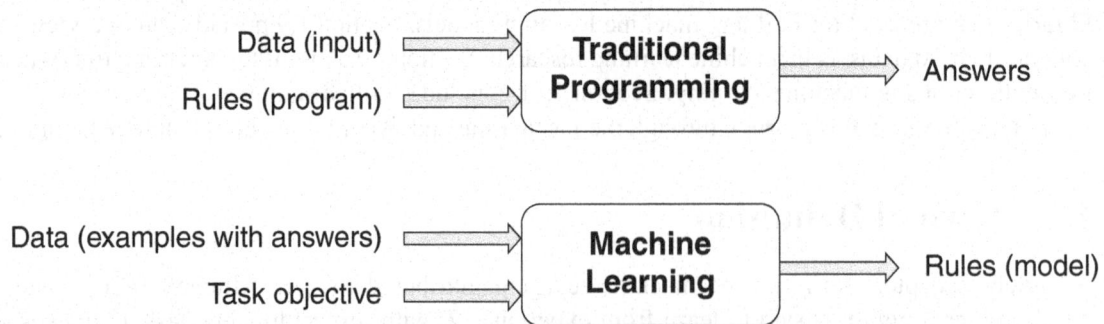

Figure 1.1: Traditional programming versus machine learning. While traditional programming directly transforms data into answers using human-crafted rules, machine learning uses data and answers to generate models (or rules) that can be applied to future data.

conditions, enabling it to recognize these objects in new, unseen images. With sufficient data and training, the machine learning model can achieve high accuracy, far surpassing what a traditional algorithm could achieve on this task.

1.2   Types of Machine Learning

Machine learning can be broadly categorized into three main types:

- **Supervised Learning**: Supervised learning is a fundamental paradigm in machine learning, where models are trained on **labeled datasets** [596, 54, 258]. These datasets consist of pairs of input features (e.g., words in an email) and their corresponding output labels (e.g., spam or ham). The primary objective is to learn a mapping from the input features to the output labels, which allows the model to make accurate predictions on new, unseen data.

  Supervised learning tasks are typically categorized into **classification**, where the goal is to assign inputs to predefined classes (e.g., object detection in images), and **regression**, where the goal is to predict a continuous numerical value (e.g., estimating house prices based on various features). Supervised learning is the main focus of the first volume of this book.

- **Unsupervised Learning**: Unsupervised learning involves training models on data without explicit labels. The primary goal is to uncover hidden structure, patterns, or meaningful representations within the data. Common techniques in unsupervised learning include **clustering** [291], which groups similar data points together, and **dimensionality reduction** [304], which seeks to identify and retain the most significant features of the data. Unsupervised learning methods will be covered in detail in the second volume of this book.

- **Reinforcement Learning**: In reinforcement learning, an agent learns to make decisions and solve problems by interacting with an environment, where it receives rewards or penalties based on its actions [569, 428, 552]. The agent's goal is to learn a policy that maximizes its cumulative reward over time. This type of learning is particularly relevant in fields such as robotics, autonomous vehicles, game playing, and financial trading, where explicit labeled examples are not available. Reinforcement learning and its diverse applications will be explored in the third volume of this book.

Other notable areas and subfields of machine learning include:

- **Deep Learning**: Deep learning is a subfield of machine learning that leverages multilayer neural networks to automatically extract patterns and features from large datasets, thereby reducing the need for manual feature engineering [346, 231]. Over the last decade, deep learning has led to significant advancements in various fields such as image classification, speech recognition, and natural language processing. Deep learning is covered in depth in the second volume of this book.

- **Semi-Supervised Learning**: This approach leverages both labeled and unlabeled data to build models, making it particularly useful when labeled data is scarce or expensive to obtain, but large amounts of unlabeled data are available [105, 593]. Semi-supervised learning is covered in the second volume of the book.

- **Generative AI**: This class of algorithms is designed to generate new content, such as text, images, sound, and video, by learning the patterns and structures of their input data. Key techniques include **variational autoencoders (VAEs)**, which provide a framework for learning latent representations [319]; **generative adversarial networks (GANs)**, known for producing high-quality, photo-realistic images [232]; and **diffusion models**, which generate high-quality images by gradually converting random noise into structured patterns [271].

- **Large Language Models (LLMs)**: Large language models are powerful AI systems capable of understanding and generating human-like text by learning from massive corpora of text data [667]. Recent models such as OpenAI's ChatGPT [78, 455], Google's Gemini [234], and Anthropic's Claude [19] have set new benchmarks in language understanding, conversational ability, and reasoning, reshaping the field of artificial intelligence and machine learning. Large language models and their applications will be covered in detail in the third volume of this book.

1.3   Related Fields

Machine learning is deeply interconnected with various other disciplines, both contributing to and benefiting from its advancements. The following are some of the most influential fields related to machine learning:

- **Artificial Intelligence (AI)**: AI is the overarching field that encompasses machine learning along with other areas such as robotics, knowledge representation, and expert systems [513]. While AI aims to create machines capable of performing tasks that would typically require human intelligence, machine learning focuses on algorithms that learn from data to improve performance on those tasks.

- **Statistics**: A branch of applied mathematics focused on analyzing data and drawing inferences about populations from samples [610]. Core statistical techniques, such as maximum likelihood estimation, Bayesian inference, and regression analysis are fundamental to many machine learning methods. Refer to Appendix D for a detailed overview of key concepts and tools from statistics.

- **Information Theory**: A branch of applied mathematics that studies the quantification, transmission, and storage of information [134]. Concepts from information theory, such as entropy and the Kullback-Leibler divergence, have found applications in machine learning algorithms, particularly in areas like model evaluation and feature selection.

- **Decision Theory**: Decision theory provides a formal framework for making informed decisions under uncertainty. Its principles are integral to many machine learning algorithms, which aim to make data-driven decisions by optimizing expected outcomes under a probabilistic model [42].

- **Data Science**: A multidisciplinary field that combines statistical methods, machine learning algorithms, and domain-specific knowledge to extract insights and information from data [487]. While machine learning provides the key tools and techniques for data science, data science is a broader field that deals with the entire data processing pipeline, including data collection, preprocessing, exploration, analysis, and visualization.

- **Computer Vision**: A subfield of AI that enables machines to derive meaningful information from visual data such as images and videos, often leveraging machine learning algorithms to enhance its capabilities and accuracy [571].

- **Natural Language Processing (NLP)**: A branch of AI dedicated to the understanding and generation of human language, frequently employing machine learning techniques to analyze, interpret, and produce text and speech [306].

- **Robotics**: Robotics is an interdisciplinary branch of computer science and engineering that deals with the design, construction, operation, and application of robots [551]. By incorporating machine learning algorithms, robots can learn from their environment, adapt to it, and make decisions autonomously.

- **Neuroscience**: Machine learning models, particularly neural networks, are inspired by the structure and function of biological neurons and the brain [257, 458]. Conversely, neuroscience leverages machine learning techniques to analyze vast amounts of neural data, uncover brain activity, and model cognitive processes [502].

1.4   Brief History

The history of machine learning is marked by pivotal milestones that have significantly shaped the field. Here is a concise list of the major breakthroughs:

- 1763: Thomas Bayes formulated Bayes' theorem, foundational for Bayesian learning [34].

- 1805: Legendre and Gauss formalized the method of least squares, laying the foundation for linear regression [349, 217].

- 1943: McCulloch and Pitts introduced a computational model of biological neurons, the basis for neural networks [405].

- 1950: Alan Turing proposed the Turing Test to determine whether or not a computer is capable of human-like intelligence, based on its ability to simulate a conversation indistinguishable from that of a human being [588].

- 1951: The k-nearest neighbors (KNN) algorithm was introduced by Evelyn Fix and Joseph Hodges as a nonparametric method for classification [194].

- 1956: The term "Artificial Intelligence" was coined at the Dartmouth workshop, marking the official birth of the AI field [403].

- 1957: Frank Rosenblatt proposed the perceptron, an early model of neural networks that could learn from data by adjusting its weights based on classification errors [506].

- 1959: Arthur Samuel developed a self-learning program to play checkers, which was one of the earliest examples of reinforcement learning [521].

- 1965: Vladimir Vapnik and Alexey Chervonenkis introduced the concept of the Vapnik–Chervonenkis (VC) dimension [598], which later became a cornerstone of Statistical Learning Theory. This theory provides a rigorous framework for analyzing the capacity, generalization ability, and performance guarantees of learning algorithms [596].

- 1969: Minsky and Papert's book "Perceptrons" exposed limitations of preceptron models, casting doubt on the potential of neural networks and leading to the first AI winter [425].

- 1969: John Holland introduced genetic algorithms, optimization techniques inspired by the process of natural selection [275].

- 1979: Hans Moravec and his team at Stanford developed the Stanford Cart, an early robotic vehicle capable of navigating autonomously in a room filled with obstacles [431].

- 1986: Ross Quinlan developed the ID3 algorithm for constructing decision trees, a foundational model in machine learning [489].

- 1986: The backpropagation algorithm for training multi-layer perceptrons was introduced by Rumelhart, Hinton, and Williams, rekindling interest in neural networks [511].

- 1989: Yann LeCun and colleagues designed the first convolutional neural network, LeNet, for handwritten digit recognition. [347]

- 1992: Bernhard Boser, Isabelle Guyon, and Vladimir Vapnik introduced Support Vector Machine (SVM), a powerful classification method backed by robust theoretical foundations [61].

- 1995: Yoav Freund and Robert Schapire introduced AdaBoost, one of the earliest and most influential boosting algorithms, which combines multiple weak learners into a strong ensemble [197].

- 1996: Leo Breiman introduced Bagging, an ensemble method that reduces variance by aggregating predictions from multiple models trained on bootstrap samples [67].

- 1999: Jerome Friedman introduced gradient boosting, a powerful method that enhances predictive accuracy by iteratively training weak learners to correct residual errors [201].

- 2006: Geoffrey Hinton coined the term "deep learning" to describe learning through deep layered neural networks [268].

- 2006: Netflix announced a $1 million prize for improving its movie recommendation system by 10% [39], spurring major advances in research and development of recommender systems.

- 2012: AlexNet, a deep convolutional neural network, halved the error rate in the ImageNet competition, sparking renewed interest in deep learning [334].

- 2014: Ian Goodfellow developed Generative Adversarial Networks (GANs), which introduced a novel way of training generative models through adversarial learning [232].

- 2014: Tianqi Chen and Carlos Guestrin introduced XGBoost, a highly efficient gradient boosting algorithm that gained widespread adoption in both industry and research [109].

- 2014: Facebook developed DeepFace, a facial recognition system capable of recognizing faces with human-level accuracy [572].

- 2016: DeepMind's AlphaGo defeated the 18-time world champion Lee Sedol in the game of Go, demonstrating superior strategy and tactical play [552].

- 2017: The Transformer architecture was introduced in the seminal paper "Attention is All You Need" by Vaswani et al., revolutionizing natural language processing and sequence modeling [599].

- 2020: OpenAI released GPT-3, a highly advanced language model with 175 billion parameters, demonstrating outstanding text generation capabilities [78].

- 2022: OpenAI introduced ChatGPT, an advanced conversational model based on GPT-3.5, which can engage in detailed and coherent dialogues and assist with a wide range of tasks [454].

- 2022: Stable Diffusion, an open-source text-to-image model, was released, enabling high-quality image generation and fostering widespread innovation in digital art, design, and creative applications [505].

- 2023: OpenAI released GPT-4, a large multimodal model demonstrating significant improvements in reasoning, instruction-following, and factual accuracy across a wide range of tasks [455].

- 2023: Google introduced Gemini, an advanced multimodal model that integrates text, image, audio, and video data, setting new benchmarks in AI performance across multiple domains [234].

- 2024: OpenAI unveiled Sora, a groundbreaking text-to-video model capable of generating coherent and realistic videos up to one minute in length from textual prompts [456].

- 2024: DeepMind released AlphaFold 3, extending protein structure prediction to complexes with DNA, RNA, ligands, and ions, achieving 65% accuracy in benchmark tests—well above the previous state-of-the-art of 28% [6].

- 2025: Anthropic released Claude 3.7, an advanced language model that achieved PhD-level performance on benchmarks such as AIME for mathematical reasoning and GPQA for graduate-level science questions, marking a substantial leap in AI's problem-solving capabilities [18].

- 2025: DeepMind introduced AlphaEvolve, a Gemini-powered coding agent capable of autonomously designing advanced algorithms. Notably, it discovered an algorithm for multiplying 4×4 complex matrices using only 48 scalar multiplications, improving on Strassen's 1969 algorithm—the best-known solution for over 50 years [150].

1.5   Machine Learning Applications

Machine learning has become integral to nearly every industry, improving business processes and enhancing the capabilities of existing systems. Key examples include:

- **Healthcare**: Machine learning algorithms analyze medical images, assist radiologists in detecting tumors in X-rays and MRI images, recommend treatments to patients, and analyze DNA sequences to advance personalized medicine [182, 241].

- **Finance**: Financial institutions leverage machine learning for fraud detection, credit scoring, personal finance advisory, and enhancing algorithmic trading strategies [379, 111, 631].

- **Marketing and Retail**: Machine learning is used for customer segmentation [308], sales forecasting [86], and recommending products to users based on their past purchases [9].

- **Real Estate**: Machine learning models predict property prices with high accuracy based on features such as location, size, and amenities, providing valuable insights for buyers and sellers [467].

- **Agriculture**: Machine learning plays a pivotal role in modernizing agriculture, from predicting crop yields to automating irrigation systems and identifying potential diseases or pests [363].

- **Energy**: Machine learning is used to optimize grid management in real-time, predict equipment failures, and improve overall energy efficiency [327, 573].

- **Manufacturing**: Predictive maintenance, enabled by machine learning, anticipates equipment failures and optimizes manufacturing processes, minimizing downtime and costs [348].

- **Social Media**: Social media platforms utilize machine learning for tasks such as content suggestion, ad targeting, and fake news detection, enhancing user engagement and experience [329, 135].

- **Autonomous Vehicles**: Self-driving cars leverage machine learning to process vast amounts of sensor data, allowing them to navigate complex terrains, detect obstacles, and make driving decisions [88, 59].

- **Chatbots and Conversational AI**: Chatbots powered by large language models, such as ChatGPT [454] and Google's Gemini [234], have revolutionized the field of conversational AI by enabling natural, human-like dialogue and helping users with various tasks such as customer support, mental health assistance, creative content generation, tutoring, coding help, and task automation.

1.6   Limitations of Machine Learning

Although machine learning has demonstrated remarkable capabilities, not all computational tasks are well-suited to be framed as learning tasks or solved efficiently with learning-based approaches. This can be due to the nature of the task itself or inherent limitations of machine learning models. Here are some examples:

- **Deterministic algorithm tasks**: Problems that have deterministic, algorithmic solutions generally do not benefit from learning-based approaches. For example, tasks like sorting a list of numbers or computing the greatest common divisor of two integers can be solved efficiently and exactly using traditional algorithms.

- **Tasks with undefined goals**: When the objective is not clearly defined, it is difficult to frame the problem as a learning task. For example, in data science, exploratory data analysis (EDA) involves examining datasets to understand their main attributes, often through visual inspection [587]. While specific techniques, such as outlier detection, can be automated, the overall process is typically open-ended and lacks a clearly defined learning objective.

- **Tasks without patterns**: Machine learning excels when there are discernible patterns and regularities in the data. If the data is purely random or lacks structure, learning-based methods are ineffective. For example, the outcome of flipping a fair coin is inherently unpredictable and offers no pattern to learn from.

- **Highly dynamic environments**: Environments that change faster than a model can adapt may be inappropriate for standard machine learning approaches. For example, the stock market is a highly dynamic environment with conditions that change instantaneously. While machine learning models can capture historical trends, real-time stock price prediction is challenging due to rapid and unpredictable market fluctuations, rendering learned patterns obsolete.

- **Ethical decisions**: Questions of ethics, morality, and value often do not have definitive right answers, and vary across cultures and individuals [605]. Using machine learning to make ethical decisions can be problematic, especially when the training data may encode and perpetuate biases.

- **Tasks requiring common sense**: Some tasks rely on profound human insight or general understanding, which can be hard to convert into data for training a model [145]. Examples for such tasks include recognizing sarcasm or hidden emotions in conversations, or interpreting ambiguous instructions.

- **Safety-critical systems**: Safety remains a pivotal concern in machine learning applications [14]. By their nature, machine learning models deal with probabilities and uncertainties, and must generalize from limited training data to unseen situations. This can lead to errors when the model is faced with novel or rare conditions, as was tragically illustrated in 2018 when an Uber self-driving car failed to recognize a pedestrian, resulting in a fatal accident [503].

  Although machine learning algorithms cannot guarantee error-free operation—no more than humans can—the goal is to achieve safety levels that are comparable to, if not superior to, those of human capabilities. Through extensive testing, redundant safety mechanisms, and continuous improvements, the aim is to achieve a level of safety that not only matches but ultimately surpasses human performance—even if absolute perfection remains unattainable.

- **Tasks with low data quality**: The effectiveness of machine learning models is heavily dependent on the quantity and quality of the training data, often more than the specific algorithm used to build them [249, 567, 497]. The adage "Garbage in, garbage out" (GIGO) aptly highlights this dependency: models that are trained on noisy and incomplete data tend to underperform and produce inaccurate predictions when applied to new, unseen data.

1.7   Ethical Considerations

As machine learning models increasingly influence critical decisions in areas such as healthcare, finance, and law enforcement, ethical aspects such as fairness, accountability, and transparency are becoming ever more important. Some of the main ethical challenges faced by machine learning systems include:

- **Bias and Fairness**: Machine learning models can inadvertently amplify social biases when their training data reflect historical prejudices [412]. For example, facial recognition systems have been criticized for higher error rates among underrepresented ethnic groups, reflecting biases in their training datasets [84]. Similarly, large language models (LLMs), which are trained on vast collections of text from the internet, often mirror societal biases and stereotypes present in their training data [613, 56].

- **Privacy Concerns**: As machine learning often relies on vast amounts of personal data, it poses significant risks to user privacy. A notable instance occurred during the 2006 "Netflix Prize" competition, where Netflix released 100 million anonymous movie ratings to improve its recommendation system. Researchers from the University of Texas later showed that parts of this supposedly anonymized data could be re-identified by correlating it with public IMDB ratings [437]. More recently, researchers have shown that it is possible to recover personally identifiable information (PII), such as names, phone numbers, and email addresses, from the training data of large language models by carefully crafting input queries [94].

- **Accountability**: Determining responsibility for decisions made by machine learning systems is challenging [164]. For example, if an autonomous vehicle is involved in an accident, it is difficult to ascertain whether the fault lies with the manufacturer, the software, or the vehicle owner.

- **Transparency**: Many machine learning models, such as deep neural networks, operate as "black boxes" in which the decision-making process is not visible [256]. This lack of transparency can be problematic in high-stack domains, such as credit scoring or medical diagnoses, where clear explanations are often required for accountability and trust.

Addressing these ethical challenges involves rigorous testing, transparent model development, privacy protection measures, and methods that promote fairness and impartiality [301, 247]. Ethical machine learning is essential for safely integrating AI into society and continues to be an active area of research.

1.8 Software Libraries

As machine learning has grown in popularity and complexity, its ecosystem of software libraries and frameworks has also evolved significantly, facilitating everything from data preprocessing to model training and evaluation. These libraries offer implementations of common algorithms and techniques through user-friendly interfaces, making them indispensable tools for researchers and practitioners alike.

The main machine learning libraries featured in this book are:

- **Scikit-Learn**: A popular machine learning library in Python that offers a broad range of supervised and unsupervised learning algorithms, as well as tools for data preprocessing, model selection, and evaluation [473]. Scikit-Learn and its main features are introduced in Chapter 3.

- **XGBoost (Extreme Gradient Boosting)**: A high-performance, scalable open-source library for gradient boosting [109]. XGBoost consistently achieves state-of-the-art results in supervised learning tasks on structured (tabular) data and is a favored tool in machine learning competitions. XGBoost and other gradient boosting libraries are covered in Chapter 10.

- **PyTorch**: The most widely used deep learning framework, known for its Pythonic design, intuitive interface, and training efficiency [468]. It is supported by a rich ecosystem of tools—such as PyTorch Lightning, TorchServe, and ONNX—that streamline model training, scaling, and deployment.

- **NLTK (Natural Language Toolkit)**: A comprehensive toolkit for symbolic and statistical natural language processing [53]. NLTK provides easy access to over 50 corpora and lexical resources, and includes tools for common text processing tasks such as tokenization, stemming, tagging, parsing, and semantic reasoning. NLTK is introduced in Chapter 7.

- **Hugging Face Transformers**: An open-source library for building and fine-tuning Transformer-based models, including large language models (LLMs), across a variety of tasks in natural language processing, computer vision, and beyond [628]. The Hugging Face

Hub hosts a vast collection of pre-trained models, featuring prominent architectures such as BERT, GPT, T5, and LLaMA.

In addition, we will frequently use the following Python libraries for numerical computations, data analysis, and visualization, which are essential for developing machine learning applications in Python:

- **NumPy**: A foundational library for numerical computations, known for its efficient handling of arrays and matrices, and its wide range of mathematical operations [452].

- **Matplotlib**: A versatile plotting library used for creating a wide range of graphs and visualizations, such as histograms, scatter plots, and bar charts [285].

- **Pandas**: A powerful library for data manipulation and analysis, providing extensive tools for indexing, cleaning, grouping, and performing statistical operations on data [408].

Refer to Appendix F for a more detailed overview of these libraries.

1.9   Common Datasets

In machine learning research, datasets can generally be categorized into two types: synthetic and real-world datasets. Each type serves a different purpose and offers distinct advantages:

- **Synthetic Datasets**: These are artificially created rather than collected from real-world observations. They are often generated using mathematical functions or simulations, allowing price control over factors such as noise levels, number of features, or the degree of non-linearity. This level of control is valuable for systematically evaluating the robustness, efficiency, and accuracy of algorithms under varied conditions.

- **Real-world Datasets**: These datasets reflect the complexity and variability encountered in natural settings. They are collected from actual events, behaviors, or observations, providing essential insights into how algorithms perform in practical scenarios and deal with challenges such as noise, missing values, and class imbalance.

Below is a list of commonly used datasets in machine learning, widely adopted as benchmarks for evaluating new algorithms and used throughout this book:

- **Iris Dataset**: A classic dataset introduced by the statistician Ronald Fisher in the 1930s, consisting of 150 samples from three species of Iris flowers [192]. It is often used as a benchmark for testing classification algorithms due to its simplicity and well-structured class boundaries.

- **Adult Dataset**: Also known as the "Census Income" dataset, it includes data from the 1994 US Census Bureau and is used to predict whether an individual earns over $50,000 a year based on features like age, education, and marital status [35]. It is more challenging to handle than the Iris dataset due to its mix of continuous and categorical data types and the presence of missing values in some features.

- **California Housing Dataset**: Commonly used for regression tasks, this dataset contains data on housing prices across California districts, derived from the 1990 US census [462]. It includes attributes like median house value, household income, number of bedrooms, and block population.

- **Credit Card Fraud Detection Dataset**: A widely referenced dataset in the domain of fraud detection [144]. It comprises transactions made by European cardholders over two days in September 2013. The dataset is highly unbalanced, with only 492 fraudulent transactions out of 284,807 total transactions, making it ideal for studying anomaly detection techniques.

- **MNIST**: Often described as the "hello world" of machine learning, this dataset contains 70,000 images of handwritten digits and is used as a standard benchmark for evaluating image recognition algorithms [155].

- **CIFAR-10 and CIFAR-100**: These datasets consist of 60,000 32×32 color images collected from the web, each categorized into 10 and 100 classes, respectively [333]. They are commonly used for evaluating deep learning models, particularly convolutional neural networks (CNNs) and vision transformers (ViTs).

- **IMDB Reviews Dataset**: A dataset with 50,000 movie reviews from the Internet Movie Database along with their sentiment labels (either a positive or a negative review) [387]. It is widely used for benchmarking sentiment analysis and text classification models.

Many additional machine learning datasets are available from the following websites:

- The UCI Machine Learning Repository[1] hosts a large collection of datasets widely used for empirical studies and algorithm benchmarking.

- OpenML[2] is an open platform for sharing datasets, algorithms, and experiments.

- Kaggle Datasets[3] offers a variety of datasets used in Kaggle, a popular platform for data science and machine learning competitions.

- Google Dataset Search[4] is a search engine for datasets.

- Papers with Code[5] links research papers, primarily in machine learning, to their code implementations (typically hosted on GitHub) and associated datasets.

- Hugging Face Datasets[6] provides a wide range of datasets, primarily used for training and fine-tuning large language models.

---

1. https://archive.ics.uci.edu
2. https://www.openml.org
3. https://www.kaggle.com/datasets
4. https://datasetsearch.research.google.com
5. https://paperswithcode.com
6. https://huggingface.co/datasets

1.10   Current Trends and Future Directions

Machine learning is rapidly advancing toward the ambitious goal of developing **Artificial General Intelligence (AGI)**—a form of intelligence capable of performing any intellectual task that a human can do [226, 62].

Recent models in machine learning have already surpassed human performance in various domains, including image recognition [261, 182], speech recognition [637], language understanding [455], and complex game environments [553]. Large language models such as OpenAI's GPT [455] and Google's Gemini [234] have demonstrated the ability to solve novel and difficult tasks across diverse fields including natural language, commonsense reasoning, coding, and mathematics. In many cases, their performance matches or even exceeds that of human experts, signaling early steps toward AGI [80].

The rapid evolution from GPT-2 to GPT-4 within just four years illustrates the dramatic progress in AI capabilities—from preschool-level abilities to college-level proficiency. These developments have led some researchers to speculate that AGI may be achievable in the near future, with some forecasts suggesting a timeline as early as 2027 [1].

It is anticipated that future AI systems will be able to contribute to AI research itself—developing new models and algorithms in an increasingly automated cycle. In a recent development, Sakana AI, in collaboration with researchers from the universities of Oxford and British Columbia, introduced "The AI Scientist" [382]. This system autonomously conducts end-to-end scientific research: generating innovative ideas, writing code, executing experiments, visualizing results, drafting papers, and even peer-reviewing its own work. Impressively, it has made original contributions to machine learning in areas such as diffusion modeling, novel Transformer architectures, and the study of learning dynamics.

The future of machine learning is undeniably exciting, with the coming years poised to bring significant advancements. I am thrilled to guide you on this transformative journey through the pages of this book, as we explore the forefront of machine learning and its vast possibilities.

1.11   Summary

In this introductory chapter, we began with a formal definition of machine learning, contrasting its principles with traditional programming. We introduced the main types of learning, including supervised, unsupervised, semi-supervised, and reinforcement learning. We then traced the historical evolution of the field, highlighting influential figures, key algorithms, and transformative milestones. We presented practical applications of machine learning across diverse industries, demonstrating its widespread impact on nearly every aspect of our lives. We also examined the limitations of machine learning, including safety concerns and ethical implications. The chapter concluded with an overview of essential machine learning libraries, widely used datasets, and current trends shaping the future of the field.

Chapter 2

Supervised Machine Learning

Supervised machine learning is a subfield of machine learning focused on building models from labeled data in order to make predictions for new, unseen examples. It is the most widely studied and applied branch of machine learning.

In supervised learning, we are given a dataset that consists of examples paired with their correct outputs—much like a student learning from a teacher who provides questions along with the correct answers. For example, we can use supervised learning to build a spam filter by training on a collection of emails labeled as spam or non-spam. This data-driven approach typically yields filters that are more effective and robust than manually crafted rule-based systems, which tend to become outdated as spamming strategies evolve.

Supervised machine learning is widely applied across many domains, such as:

- Fraud detection systems protect financial institutions from malicious activity.

- Medical diagnosis systems are able to detect a wide range of diseases, often with precision that rivals that of medical professionals.

- Speech recognition systems translate voice to text more accurately and faster than humans.

This chapter introduces the key principles and foundational theories of supervised machine learning, setting the stage for a deeper exploration of learning algorithms and their applications in subsequent chapters. The chapter is organized as follows. Section 2.1 formally defines the supervised machine learning problem and distinguishes between its main types, such as regression and classification. Section 2.2 explores the key components of a machine learning model, including parameters, hyperparameters, loss functions, optimization methods, and evaluation metrics. Section 2.3 discusses the probabilistic framework underlying supervised learning, introducing the concepts of the data-generating process and Bayes error, which defines the theoretical limit of classification accuracy. Section 2.4 formalizes the learning objective through the principle of empirical risk minimization, explaining how learning algorithms approximate the expected prediction error using finite training data. Section 2.5 presents two fundamental approaches to parameter estimation in supervised learning: maximum likelihood estimation (MLE) and Bayesian inference. Section 2.6 explores the bias–variance tradeoff, a key concept for understanding the relationship between model capacity and generalization performance. It also discusses strategies for controlling model capacity, including regularization techniques. Section 2.7 outlines the practical steps involved in constructing a supervised learning model, from data preparation to model selection and evaluation. Section 2.8 discusses common challenges in supervised learning, such as data quality issues, imbalanced classes, and overfitting. The chapter concludes with a summary of key concepts and a set of exercises designed to reinforce understanding.

2.1   Formal Definition

In supervised machine learning problems, we are given a dataset of n labeled **samples** (also called **examples**, **instances**, **observations**, or **data points**). Each sample in the dataset is a pair consisting of a vector x, which contains the **features** (or **attributes**) of that sample, and its corresponding **label** (or **target**) y.

For example, in a spam filter application, x consists of the email attributes, such as its subject, sender, recipients, and the words in its body, and y is a binary label that indicates whether the email is a spam ($y = 1$) or a ham ($y = 0$). In an image classification task, x is a vector that contains all the raw pixels of the image, and y is the class to which the image belongs (e.g., $y = 0$ represents a car, $y = 1$ indicates a flower, etc.).

If we denote by d the number of features in the dataset (d stands for dimensionality), then x is a d-dimensional vector[1]:

$$\mathbf{x} = (x_1, \ldots, x_d)^T .$$ (2.1)

Collectively, we denote the given dataset by D:

$$D = \{(\mathbf{x}_1, y_1), (\mathbf{x}_2, y_2), \ldots, (\mathbf{x}_n, y_n)\}.$$ (2.2)

The feature vectors are often stored together in a matrix called a **design matrix** (or **feature matrix**) and denoted by X:

$$X = \begin{pmatrix} x_{11} & x_{12} & \cdots & x_{1d} \\ x_{21} & x_{22} & \cdots & x_{2d} \\ \vdots & \vdots & \ddots & \vdots \\ x_{n1} & x_{n2} & \cdots & x_{nd} \end{pmatrix}.$$ (2.3)

The rows of X represent the samples and the columns represent the features, such that x_{ij} is the value of the j-th feature associated with the i-th sample. For example, the Iris dataset, which contains 150 samples with four features each, can be represented by a design matrix $X \in \mathbb{R}^{150 \times 4}$. The design matrix allows the learning algorithm to apply algebraic operations on the dataset as a single entity. For example, solving linear regression problems typically involves computing the inverse of $X^T X$ (see Section 4.4).

---

1. We assume that all vectors are column vectors, unless stated otherwise.

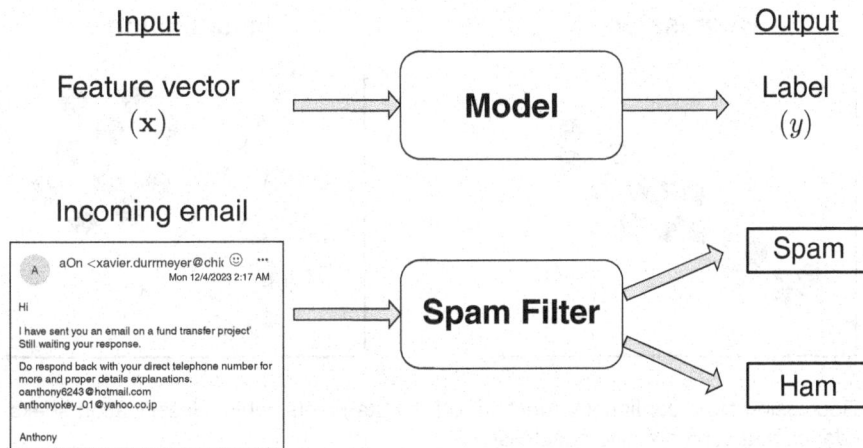

Figure 2.1: Illustration of supervised learning using a spam filter model. The model takes an input feature vector x, derived from incoming emails, and predicts a label y indicating whether an email is "Spam" or "Ham" (non-spam).

The goal in supervised learning is to find a function $f\colon \mathcal{X} \to \mathcal{Y}$ that accurately maps feature vectors $\mathbf{x}$ in the input space $\mathcal{X}$ to their corresponding labels y in the output space $\mathcal{Y}$ (see Figure 2.1). The exact form of the true mapping f is usually unknown to us, and must be inferred from a limited number of samples $D = \{(\mathbf{x}_i, y_i)\}_{i=1}^{n}$, which are often noisy and cover only a small part of the input space.

Since our learning is based on a finite and imperfect set of training samples, we can only obtain an approximation of the true mapping $f(\mathbf{x})$. This approximation is known as a **hypothesis**, denoted by $h(\mathbf{x})$. The model's hypothesis is an element in some **hypothesis space** H, which contains the set of all functions that the learning algorithm can choose from as possible solutions. For example, in linear regression, H consists of all linear functions of $\mathbf{x}$, while in decision trees, H includes all functions that can be represented as a sequence of binary decisions.

2.1.1   Regression versus Classification

We distinguish between two types of supervised learning problems:

- In **regression problems**, the label y is a continuous value ($y \in R$). For example, in a house price prediction task, y is a real positive value that represents the price of the house. Regression models are often referred to as **regressors**.

- In **classification problems**, the label y is discrete, i.e., it can take one of k values ($y \in 1, \ldots, k$), representing the class to which the sample belongs. Classification models are often referred to as **classifiers**.

Regression   **Classification**

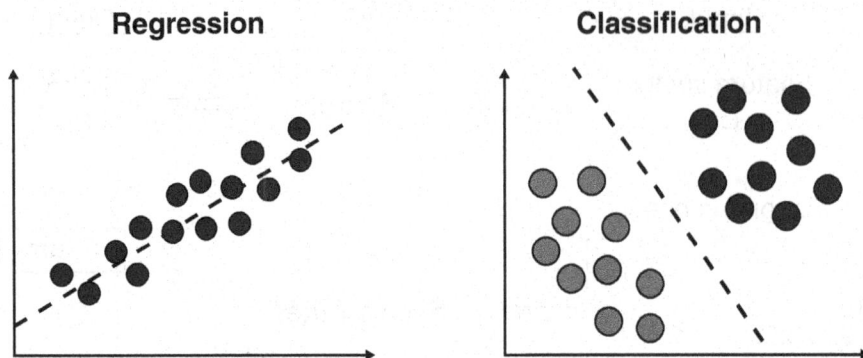

Figure 2.2: Regression fits a continuous function to the data points, while classification seeks to establish distinct boundaries that separate different classes.

We further distinguish between two subtypes of classification problems:

 – In **binary classification**, there are only two classes ($k = 2$). For example, spam detection is a binary classification problem, in which the label can be either $y = 1$ (spam) or $y = 0$ (ham).

 – In **multi-class classification**, there are more than two classes ($k > 2$). For example, a handwritten digit recognition task is a multi-class problem with $k = 10$ classes (one for each possible digit 0–9).

Beyond the way labels are defined, regression and classification also differ in the structure of their outputs. Regression models predict continuous values by fitting a function that closely approximates the observed data points, whereas classification models learn decision boundaries that partition the input space into distinct regions, each corresponding to a different class (see Figure 2.2).

2.1.2   Deterministic versus Probabilistic Classification

Classification methods are often classified into two main types:

 • **Deterministic classifiers** output a specific class label for a given input (a *hard label*), without providing a measure of uncertainty or confidence for their predictions. For example, a deterministic spam filter would classify a given email as either spam or non-spam, without indicating any uncertainty or probability.

 • **Probabilistic classifiers** provide probability estimates $P(y = k|\mathbf{x})$ for each of the k possible classes the input can belong to (a *soft label*). These probabilities reflect the model's confidence in its predictions. For example, a probabilistic spam filter might say that an email has a 80% chance of being spam and 20% chance of being ham.

In general, probabilistic classifiers are harder to implement, but they provide valuable insights into the model's uncertainty, making them especially useful in domains such as medical diagnosis and financial forecasting, where understanding the confidence of a prediction is crucial.

2.2 Machine Learning Models

Machine learning models are programs or systems that learn from data in order to make predictions. They are built using machine learning algorithms that fit the model parameters to the observed data. The main components of a machine learning model include:

- **Data**: The dataset used to train and evaluate the model. It is typically divided into three subsets:
  - The **training set** is used to train the model.
  - The **validation set** helps in tuning and validating the model's performance.
  - The **test set** provides an unbiased evaluation of the final model.

- **Learning algorithm**: The method used to train the model. The choice of algorithm depends on the type of task (e.g., classification or regression) and the nature of the data. Learning algorithms are discussed in Section 2.2.1.

- **Model parameters**: Parameters are the components of the model that are learned from the training data, e.g., the coefficients in a linear regression model (see Section 2.2.2).

- **Loss function**: The loss function measures how well the model's predictions match the actual data. The goal of training is to minimize this function. Loss functions are discussed in Section 2.2.3.

- **Learning process**: This process involves using a learning algorithm to optimize the model parameters in order to best fit the training data, according to the chosen loss function.

- **Optimization techniques**: Methods that are used to find the optimal parameters of the model by minimizing the loss function, such as gradient descent (see Section 2.2.4).

- **Hyperparameters**: Unlike parameters, hyperparameters are not learned from the data. They are set prior to the learning process and control the model's structure or learning behavior (see Section 2.2.5).

- **Evaluation metrics**: Metrics that are used to assess the model's performance after training (see Section 2.2.6).

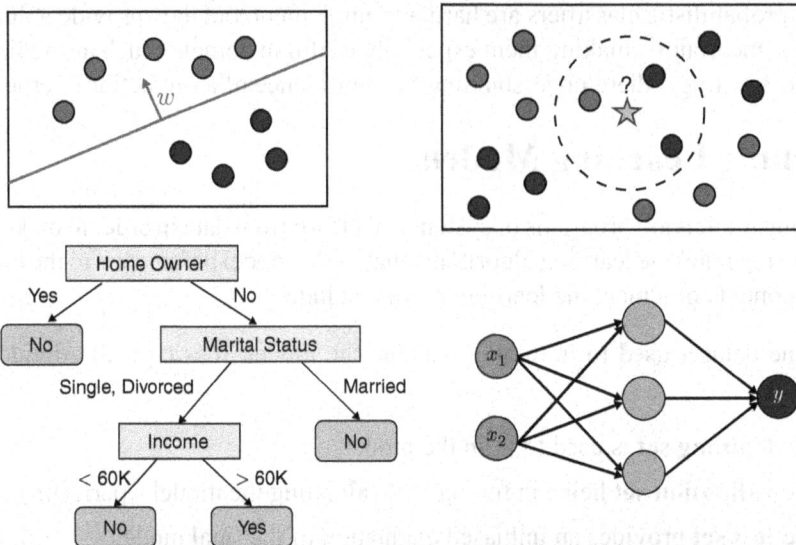

Figure 2.3: Commonly used supervised machine learning algorithms. Starting from top-left and going clockwise: Logistic regression, k-nearest neighbors, neural networks, and decision trees.

2.2.1 Learning Algorithms

A wide range of supervised learning algorithms are available, each with its own strengths and weaknesses (see Figure 2.3). The most commonly used supervised learning algorithms are:

- Linear regression (Chapter 4)

- Logistic regression (Chapter 5)

- K-nearest neighbors (Chapter 6)

- Naive Bayes (Chapter 7)

- Decision trees (Chapter 8)

- Support vector machines (Chapter 11)

- Neural networks (covered in Volume II)

Some of these algorithms can handle both regression and classification tasks, while others can handle only one type of problems (e.g., Naive Bayes can only handle classification problems). Ensemble methods (see Chapter 9), such as random forests and gradient boosting, combine together multiple algorithms to create more powerful models.

The **no free lunch theorem** [630] states that no single learning algorithm is the best for all problems. More specifically, any two learning algorithms perform equally well when their performance is averaged over all possible data distributions. This theorem underscores the importance of choosing algorithms that are well-suited to the specific characteristics of the problem at hand.

Another general principle known as **Occam's razor** [57] suggests that if two models have similar performance and they explain the known observations equally well, the simpler model should be preferred (e.g., the model with fewer parameters or less assumptions on the domain). This principle, which is widely adopted in various scientific disciplines, emphasizes simplicity and parsimony in explanatory models.

2.2.2 Model Parameters

Many machine learning models are **parametric models**, i.e., they have a set of learnable parameters that are optimized to best fit the training data. This set of parameters is typically denoted by θ or $\mathbf{w}$, and the model's hypothesis, which depends on these parameters, is often written as $h(\mathbf{x}; \theta)$ or $h_\theta(\mathbf{x})$.

For example, in linear regression, the model's hypothesis is a function of the form $h(\mathbf{x}) = w_0 + w_1 x_1 + \ldots + w_d x_d$, and the model parameters are the coefficients (or weights) of the features: $\mathbf{w} = (w_0, \ldots, w_d)^T$. In neural networks, the parameters are the weights of the connections between neurons in the network and the neuron biases.

The number of parameters is strongly correlated with the **model complexity**. If a model has too few parameters, it may fail to capture the complexity of the data, resulting in poor performance. On the other hand, a model that has too many parameters or its parameters are too finely tuned to the training data may perform very well on the training data but poorly on new, unseen data (a phenomenon known as **overfitting**).

Nonparametric models, such as k-nearest neighbors and decision trees, do not have a fixed number of parameters. This flexibility allows them to adapt more freely to the intricacies of the data and capture complex patterns that parametric models might miss. On the other hand, these models usually require more data to make accurate predictions and tend to be more prone to overfitting.

2.2.3 Loss Functions

An important part of building a supervised learning model is selecting an appropriate loss function. A **loss function**, denoted by $L(y, \hat{y})$, measures the error between the model's output for a given input $\hat{y} = h(\mathbf{x})$ and the true label $y = f(\mathbf{x})$. For parametric models with a parameter vector θ, it is common to denote the loss function as $L(y, h(\mathbf{x}); \theta)$, or $L(\theta)$ for short, to underscore the function's dependence on the model parameters.

The loss function guides the optimization process of the model and determines how it adjusts its parameters during training to minimize the prediction error. Consequently, different loss functions can lead to different behaviors of the model. For example, some loss functions prioritize overall accuracy, while others focus on robustness to outliers or improved performance on underrepresented classes.

Desirable properties of a loss function include:

- Task-specific relevance: The loss function should align with the specific objective of the task the model is trying to solve. For example, in regression tasks, a common loss function is the squared loss $(y - h(\mathbf{x}))^2$, which penalizes the squared difference between the predicted value and the actual value (see Section 4.2).

- Symmetry: The loss should be the same for an error above or below the target value.

- Differentiability: Most optimization algorithms used in machine learning require the loss function to be continuous and differentiable, with some requiring it to be twice differentiable.

- Convexity: Convex functions (see Section B.11.2) have the desirable property that any local minimum is also a global minimum, which makes them easier to optimize.

- Computationally efficient: The loss function should be fast to compute, especially when dealing with large datasets.

2.2.4   Optimization

In supervised learning, the learning process typically involves finding the set of model parameters θ that minimizes the error on the training set. This turns the learning task into an **optimization problem** whose objective is to minimize a **cost function**—typically defined as the average loss over all training samples.

Most machine learning models do not admit closed-form solutions for this optimization problem, especially when the loss function is non-convex or the model is complex. In such cases, optimization is usually performed using iterative algorithms that update the parameters incrementally to reduce the error. The choice of optimization method plays a crucial role in the efficiency and success of the learning process.

Gradient-based methods, such as **gradient descent** and its variants, are among the most widely used optimization techniques in machine learning. These methods iteratively adjust the parameters in the direction of the negative gradient of the loss function. In some cases, second-order methods like **Newton's method**, which leverage curvature information via second derivatives, can achieve faster convergence. **Constrained optimization** techniques are also used when the learning task involves additional constraints, as in the case of support vector machines.

These and other optimization methods are discussed in detail in Appendix E. Readers unfamiliar with optimization are strongly encouraged to review this appendix to gain a deeper understanding of the mathematical tools that underpin many of the algorithms described in this book.

Optimization by itself is a challenging problem with no single method that works best in all situations. In machine learning, this challenge is further compounded by the fact that the true objective is not merely to minimize the training error, but to reduce the **generalization error**, that is, the model's performance on unseen data. Unlike the training error, which can be directly measured, generalization error is inherently unobservable during training, adding an additional layer of complexity to the learning process.

2.2.5   Hyperparameters

Hyperparameters are configurable settings of the learning algorithm that define and control its behavior. They are set prior to the training process, in contrast to model parameters, which are learned from the data during training. Common examples of hyperparameters include the learning rate in gradient-based algorithms, and the number of hidden layers and neurons in neural networks.

Hyperparameter tuning is the search for the combination of hyperparameter values that yield the best performance of the model. This process is a critical step in the machine learning pipeline, as improperly tuned hyperparameters can lead to models that either perform poorly or overfit to the training data. For example, setting a learning rate that is too high in gradient descent can cause the model to oscillate around the minimum point without converging.

Hyperparameter tuning techniques range from manual trial-and-error experimentation to more principled methods such as grid search or random search, which systematically explore the hyperparameter space in order to find the most effective configuration settings (see Section 3.8).

When tuning hyperparameters, it is essential to evaluate the model's performance on an independent dataset, separate from the training and test sets. Using the test set for repeated evaluations during model development or hyperparameter tuning can *contaminate* the test data, leading the model to become overfitted to it. As a result, the model may end up working well on the test set, but not on truly unseen data.

Therefore, it is a common practice to divide the available training data into two disjoint subsets: a training set and a validation set. The model is trained on the training set using the chosen hyperparameters, and then its performance is evaluated on the validation set. The model's performance on the validation set provides an estimate of how the model will perform on unseen data, guiding the selection of the best hyperparameters.

A common split for dividing the dataset is a 70-20-10 split, where 70% of the data is used for training the model, 20% is used for validation, and 10% is reserved for testing the model after training and tuning (see Figure 2.4). However, these percentages may vary based on the size and characteristics of the dataset.

Using a single validation set can sometimes result in a biased evaluation, especially if this set is small or not representative of the overall data. **Cross-validation** is a technique that addresses this issue by dividing the training data into multiple subsets (or folds) [79]. The model is then trained and validated multiple times, each time using a different subset as the validation set and the rest as the training set. This process yields multiple performance metrics (such as accuracy or error rate), which are averaged to get a more reliable estimate of the model's performance. Cross-validation is discussed in more detail in Section 3.7.

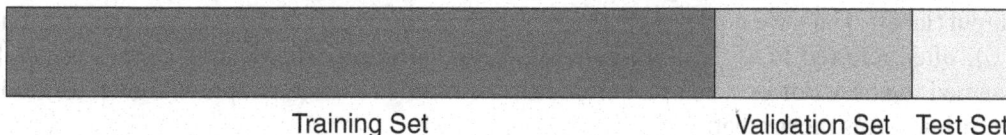

Training Set   Validation Set   Test Set

Figure 2.4: A typical 70-20-10 partition of the dataset into training, validation, and test sets. The training set is used to fit the model, the validation set helps tune hyperparameters and select the best model, and the test set provides an unbiased evaluation of the final model's performance.

2.2.6 Evaluation Metrics

Evaluation metrics are used to evaluate the performance of the model after training. In contrast to cost functions that define the model's training objective and guide its optimization process, evaluation metrics are applied post-training to evaluate the model's performance on the validation or test sets. Evaluation metrics allow us to compare the performance of different models or assess the same model under varying hyperparameters. Different machine learning tasks use different evaluation metrics:

- For regression tasks, common metrics include root mean squared error (RMSE), mean absolute error (MAE), and the R^2 score (see Section 4.5). These metrics evaluate the difference between the predicted values and the actual target values.

- For classification tasks, metrics like accuracy, precision, recall, F1 score, and the area under the ROC curve (AUC) are widely used (see Section 5.5). These metrics provide different insights into the classifier's performance, such as its overall correctness or its ability to minimize false positives or false negatives.

In addition to the standard metrics, it is often necessary to develop custom metrics tailored to the specific requirements or business objectives of the problem domain. For example, when developing a recommender system for an e-commerce website, we may be interested in evaluating not only the accuracy of the system's recommendations, but also how much these recommendations lead to increased sales. In this case, we may develop a custom metric such as sales conversion rate of recommended products, which measures the percentage of recommended products that resulted in a purchase.

2.3   The Data-Generating Process

In machine learning, we commonly assume that the observed data represents a **random sample** drawn from some underlying population. Formally, a random sample is a collection of random variables $X_1, X_2, \ldots, X_n$ that are independent and identically distributed (i.i.d.), each having the same distribution as a population variable X (see Section D.2).[2]

In supervised machine learning, each observation consists of both an input (feature vector) and an output (label). Thus, we model each observation as a pair $(\mathbf{x}, y)$ drawn from a joint distribution $p(\mathbf{x}, y)$, often referred to as the **data-generating distribution**. The dataset $D = \{(\mathbf{x}_i, y_i)\}_{i=1}^n$ is assumed to consist of i.i.d. samples from this distribution—an assumption known as the **i.i.d. assumption**.[3] This means that:

---

2. In machine learning, the term "sample" typically refers to an individual observation or data point, while in statistics, a "random sample" refers to the entire collection of such observations drawn i.i.d. from a population. Throughout this book, we will use "sample" to refer to individual data points unless otherwise specified.

3. The i.i.d. assumption may not hold in many real-world scenarios. For example, in time series data, successive observations are often correlated rather than independent. Similarly, concept drift may occur when the data-generating distribution changes over time, violating the assumption that training and test samples are drawn from the same distribution. Such cases are addressed by specialized techniques, which will be covered in later chapters of this book.

- Each pair $(\mathbf{x}_i, y_i)$ is independent of the others, and

- All pairs are drawn from the same joint distribution $p(\mathbf{x}, y)$.

For example, in spam detection, each observation consists of an email represented by features $\mathbf{x}$ (such as word frequencies or sender information) and a label y indicating whether the email is spam ($y = 1$) or not ($y = 0$). The data-generating process in this context refers to the probabilistic mechanism that produces such pairs $(\mathbf{x}, y)$ according to a joint distribution $p(\mathbf{x}, y)$, which models both the characteristics of emails and the likelihood of being spam. Under the i.i.d. assumption, the dataset $D = \{(\mathbf{x}_i, y_i)\}_{i=1}^{n}$ consists of independent samples from this distribution, providing the training data from which the model learns to classify new emails.

This probabilistic framing of the learning problem is fundamental in machine learning. It allows us to apply probabilistic tools and techniques to define learning objectives, analyze algorithm performance, and study the relationship between training error and generalization error, under the assumption that both the training and test data are sampled from the same distribution.

Some machine learning algorithms make explicit assumptions about the form of the data-generating distribution. For example, logistic regression assumes that the target label is drawn from a Bernoulli distribution, and Gaussian naive Bayes assumes that each feature is independently drawn from a normal distribution. Other algorithms avoid specifying a particular distribution and instead attempt to learn its underlying structure directly from the data.

In practice, however, the data-generating process may be complex, involving hidden variables or latent factors that are not directly observed. Additionally, the training dataset may not perfectly reflect the true data-generating distribution due to factors such as selection bias, measurement error, or missing data. When such mismatches occur, the model may fail to generalize well to new, unseen data.

2.3.1 Discriminative versus Generative Models

Depending on how they model the data-generating process, classification models are commonly grouped into two broad categories: **discriminative models**, which directly model the boundaries between classes, and **generative models**, which model the joint distribution of inputs and labels to capture how the data is generated (see Figure 2.5).

Discriminative models aim to find a function that discriminates between the different classes by either directly learning the relationship between the input features and the labels $y = f(\mathbf{x})$, or by estimating the conditional probability distribution $p(y|\mathbf{x})$, which provides the likelihood for each class given the input. These models focus on identifying the decision boundary that separates different classes in the input space, rather than modeling the distribution of the input data itself. Examples include logistic regression, k-nearest neighbors, and support vector machines (SVMs).

In contrast, generative models aim to model the data-generating process itself. They estimate the class-conditional distributions $p(\mathbf{x}|y)$ and the class prior $p(y)$, capturing how the data is generated in each class. When used for classification, Bayes' theorem (see Section C.8.5) can then be applied to compute the class posterior probabilities:

$$p(y|\mathbf{x}) = \frac{p(\mathbf{x}|y)p(y)}{p(\mathbf{x})}. \tag{2.4}$$

Discriminative   **Generative**

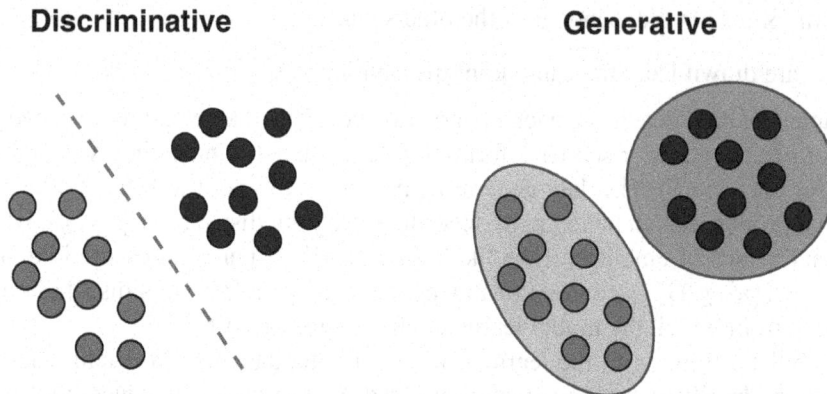

Figure 2.5: Discriminative models learn the decision boundaries between the classes, while generative models learn the input distributions in each class.

Alternatively, generative models can estimate the joint probability distribution $p(\mathbf{x}, y)$ directly, and then normalize it (by dividing it by $p(\mathbf{x})$) to obtain the posterior probabilities $p(y|\mathbf{x})$.

For example, consider an image classification task, where we need to distinguish between images of dogs ($y = 1$) and images of cats ($y = 0$). A generative model would first build a model of what dogs look like $p(\mathbf{x}|y = 1)$ and what cats look like $p(\mathbf{x}|y = 0)$. Then, to classify a new image, it would compare the new image against both these models to determine if it more closely resembles the dog or the cat images seen during training.

In general, generative models provide more information compared to discriminative models, as they learn not only the class probabilities but also the input distribution. This allows them to be used both for classification tasks and for generating new data samples that resemble the training data. For example, in the previous scenario, we could generate new images of dogs by sampling from the learned distribution $p(\mathbf{x}|y = 1)$.

On the downside, generative models are more complex to build and train due to the difficulty in learning the densities $p(\mathbf{x}|y)$. For example, if the input vector $\mathbf{x}$ consists of d binary features, in order to learn $p(\mathbf{x}|y)$ we need to estimate 2^d conditional probabilities for each class from the data. To mitigate this problem, some assumptions are usually made about the input distribution. For example, naive Bayes models (Chapter 7) assume that the features are conditionally independent given the class.

More advanced machine learning models, such as neural networks, can function as both discriminative and generative models. Generative AI models, such as Generative Adversarial Networks (GANs) and Variational Autoencoders (VAEs), utilize deep neural network architectures for generating new content such as images, video, and audio.

2.3.2   Bayes Error

The ideal machine learning model would have a complete knowledge of the true probability distribution generating the data. However, even such a model may still suffer from some level of error

Figure 2.6: Coyote (left) and grey wolf (right). (Images: Denis Pepin/Shutterstock, left; Agnieszka Bacal/ Shutterstock, right)

due to inherent noise in that distribution. This is because the mapping from $\mathbf{x}$ to y may be inherently stochastic, or y might depend on other variables that are not included in $\mathbf{x}$. The error incurred by a model making predictions from the true distribution $p(\mathbf{x}, y)$ is referred to as the **Bayes error** or **irreducible error**. This error represents the optimal error rate that could be achieved by any model, even if an infinite amount of data samples is available.

For example, imagine that we need to distinguish between wolves and coyotes based only on their height (see Figure 2.6). The shoulder height of adult grey wolves can be modeled by a normal distribution with a mean of 80 cm and a standard deviation of 8 cm, denoted by $\mathcal{N}(80, 8)$. On the other hand, the shoulder height of coyotes can be modeled by a normal distribution with a mean of 60 cm and a standard deviation of 10 cm, denoted by $\mathcal{N}(60, 10)$. Figure 2.7 shows the two distributions.

Even a model with perfect knowledge of both distributions will still make errors due to the inherent overlap between them. Let x^* be the intersection point of the two distributions (in this example $x^* = 70.227$). The optimal classification model would classify any animal with a height lower than x^* as a coyote and any animal with a height larger than x^* as a wolf. Therefore, the Bayes error in this case is represented by the area where the two distributions overlap, which can be computed by integrating the conditional probability densities on either side of the intersection point:

$$E^* = \int_{-\infty}^{x^*} p(\text{Wolf}|x)\, dx + \int_{x^*}^{\infty} p(\text{Coyote}|x)\, dx. \tag{2.5}$$

The first integral quantifies the probability of misclassifying a wolf as a coyote for all heights below x^*, while the second integral quantifies the probability of misclassifying a coyote as a wolf for heights above x^*.

More generally, we can write the Bayes error as follows:

$$E^* = \int_{\mathcal{X}} \left(1 - \max_i p(C_i|\mathbf{x})\right) p(\mathbf{x})\, d\mathbf{x}, \tag{2.6}$$

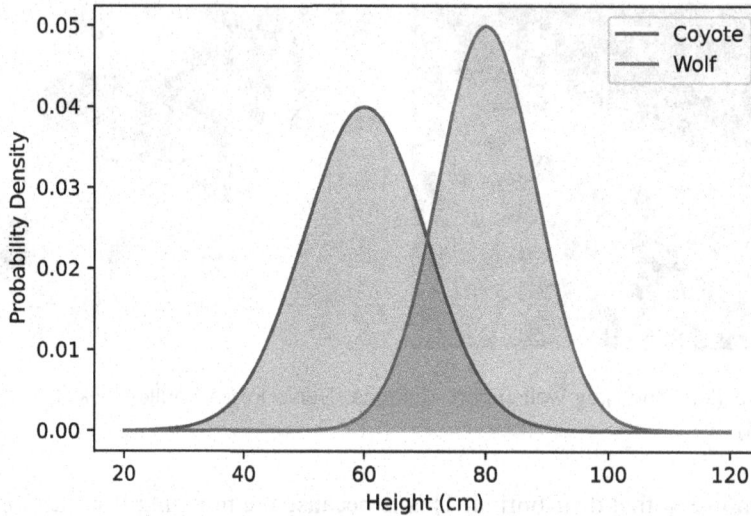

Figure 2.7: Probability density functions for the heights of coyotes and wolves. The overlapping region represents the Bayes error—the irreducible error that arises from the inherent ambiguity in distinguishing between the two species based on height alone.

which represents the expected probability of misclassification under the optimal (Bayes) classifier. For each input $\mathbf{x}$, the classifier selects the most probable class, and the error is the total probability of all other classes at that point.

2.4   Generalization Error and Empirical Risk Minimization

Building on the probabilistic framework introduced in the previous section, we can now formally define the objective of supervised learning: finding a model that minimizes the expected prediction error on data drawn from the underlying data-generating distribution. This quantity is known as the **expected risk** and also referred to as the **true risk**, **generalization error**, or **out-of-sample error**.

Formally, the expected risk of a hypothesis h, denoted by $R(h)$, is defined as the expected value of the loss function with respect to the joint distribution $p(\mathbf{x}, y)$ of inputs and labels:

$$R(h) = \mathbb{E}_{(\mathbf{x},y)\sim p(\mathbf{x},y)}[L(y, h(\mathbf{x}))] = \int_{\mathcal{X}\times\mathcal{Y}} L(y, h(\mathbf{x}))p(\mathbf{x}, y)\, d\mathbf{x}\, dy. \qquad (2.7)$$

The ultimate goal in supervised learning is to find a hypothesis $h^*(\mathbf{x})$ that minimizes the expected risk:

$$h^* = \operatorname*{argmin}_{h \in H} R(h). \qquad (2.8)$$

However, since the data-generating distribution $p(\mathbf{x}, y)$ is typically unknown, we cannot compute the expected risk directly. Instead, we approximate it using the **empirical risk** (also referred to as the **training error** or **cost function**), which is calculated by averaging the loss function over the given training set:

$$R_{\text{emp}}(h) = \frac{1}{n} \sum_{i=1}^{n} L(y_i, h(\mathbf{x}_i)), \qquad (2.9)$$

where n is the number of samples in the training set.

The empirical risk serves as a practical surrogate for the theoretical generalization error, providing an estimate of how well the hypothesis h performs on the observed data. When the model is parameterized by a vector $\boldsymbol{\theta}$, the training error is often denoted by $J(\boldsymbol{\theta})$.

In **empirical risk minimization (ERM)**, the supervised learning algorithm aims to find a function h that minimizes the empirical risk:

$$\min_{h \in H} R_{\text{emp}}(h). \qquad (2.10)$$

This approach minimizes the observed discrepancies between predicted and actual outcomes within the training dataset, using the empirical risk as a proxy for the true risk.

A learning algorithm is said to **generalize well** if the hypothesis it produces performs well not only on the training data but also on new, unseen data drawn from the same distribution. In other words, a model that generalizes well achieves a small generalization error, indicating strong predictive performance beyond the training set.

A related but stronger concept is known as **consistency**. A learning algorithm is said to be **consistent** if, as the number of training samples grows large, the empirical risk converges to the true risk:

$$\lim_{n \to \infty} R(h_n) - R_{\text{emp}}(h_n) = 0, \qquad (2.11)$$

where h_n denotes the hypothesis produced by the algorithm when trained on a dataset of size n. Consistency ensures that, given enough data, minimizing the empirical risk will also minimize the generalization error.[4]

2.5 Parameter Estimation

In parameterized models, our goal is to estimate the parameters that best explain the relationship between inputs and outputs while minimizing the generalization error. Two fundamental approaches to parameter estimation are **maximum likelihood estimation (MLE)** and **Bayesian inference**. While these methods are discussed in detail in the Statistics appendix (see Sections D.5 and D.8), we focus here on their application to supervised learning.

2.5.1 Maximum Likelihood Estimation (MLE)

Maximum likelihood estimation seeks to determine the model parameters that maximize the probability of the observed data under the assumed probabilistic model.

---

4. Consistency can be formally proven for many classical algorithms, such as linear regression, k-nearest neighbors, and decision trees, providing theoretical justification for their use with sufficient data.

The training dataset is given by $D = \{(\mathbf{x}_1, y_1), \ldots, (\mathbf{x}_n, y_n)\}$, where each pair is assumed to be drawn i.i.d. from the data-generating distribution $p(\mathbf{x}, y)$. We further assume that the labels y are generated by a conditional distribution $p(y|\mathbf{x}; \boldsymbol{\theta})$, where $\boldsymbol{\theta}$ represents the model parameters. Under this assumption, the joint distribution factorizes as $p(\mathbf{x}, y; \boldsymbol{\theta}) = p(y|\mathbf{x}; \boldsymbol{\theta})p(\mathbf{x})$.

The objective of maximum likelihood estimation is to find the parameter values that maximize the **likelihood** of observing the given labels in the training data:

$$\boldsymbol{\theta}_{ML} = \underset{\boldsymbol{\theta}}{\arg\max} \prod_{i=1}^{n} p(y_i|\mathbf{x}_i; \boldsymbol{\theta}). \tag{2.12}$$

In practice, we often maximize the **log-likelihood** instead of the likelihood itself to simplify computations:

$$\ell(\boldsymbol{\theta}) = \sum_{i=1}^{n} \log p(y_i|\mathbf{x}_i; \boldsymbol{\theta}). \tag{2.13}$$

A common practice in supervised learning is to define the loss function as the **negative log-likelihood (NLL)** of the observed labels under the model. Given an assumed conditional probability distribution $p(y|\mathbf{x}; \boldsymbol{\theta})$, the NLL loss for a single training example is defined as:

$$L(y, h(\mathbf{x}); \boldsymbol{\theta}) = -\log p(y|\mathbf{x}; \boldsymbol{\theta}). \tag{2.14}$$

The empirical risk is then computed as the average of the NLL over the training set:

$$J(\boldsymbol{\theta}) = -\frac{1}{n} \sum_{i=1}^{n} \log p(y_i|\mathbf{x}_i; \boldsymbol{\theta}). \tag{2.15}$$

This formulation directly connects empirical risk minimization to maximum likelihood estimation, as minimizing the average NLL is equivalent to maximizing the log-likelihood of the training data.

Many common loss functions in supervised learning can be interpreted as instances of this negative log-likelihood framework. For example, the squared loss in regression corresponds to assuming that the labels are generated by a Gaussian distribution (see Section 4.2.1), while the cross-entropy loss in classification arises from modeling the labels with a Bernoulli or categorical distribution (see Section 5.3.1).

2.5.2 Bayesian Inference

The Bayesian approach offers a different perspective: instead of seeking a single best estimate for the parameters, it treats the parameters $\boldsymbol{\theta}$ as random variables and computes a **posterior distribution** over them using Bayes' theorem:

$$p(\boldsymbol{\theta}|D) = \frac{p(D|\boldsymbol{\theta})\, p(\boldsymbol{\theta})}{p(D)}, \tag{2.16}$$

where D is the training set, $p(\theta)$ is the prior distribution expressing prior beliefs about the parameters, and $p(D|\theta)$ is the likelihood of the data given those parameters.

The Bayesian framework allows for integrating prior knowledge into the learning process and provides a full distribution over the parameters rather than just point estimates. This can be particularly useful when data is limited or noisy, or when quantifying uncertainty in predictions is important.

On the other hand, Bayesian inference also presents several challenges: computing the posterior distribution can be computationally intensive, especially for complex models; the choice of appropriate priors can be subjective; and the probabilistic nature of Bayesian methods may feel less intuitive to those used to point estimates in frequentist approaches.

2.5.3 Example: Medical Diagnosis

To illustrate these two approaches, consider the task of predicting whether a patient has a particular disease based on diagnostic test results and patient characteristics. Under the MLE framework, we might assume that the labels (disease present or not) are drawn from a Bernoulli distribution, where the parameter represents the probability of the disease being present. The model parameters are then estimated by maximizing the likelihood of the observed labels in the training data, without incorporating any prior assumptions.

In contrast, the Bayesian approach allows us to introduce prior knowledge about the disease prevalence in the population, informed by epidemiological studies or expert knowledge. The likelihood is again determined by how well the model explains the observed data, such as the results of diagnostic tests or patient risk factors. Based on this likelihood, the Bayesian model updates its posterior distribution over the model parameters. As more patient data becomes available, the influence of the initial prior diminishes, and the posterior distribution becomes increasingly shaped by the observed data.

In summary, MLE and Bayesian inference provide two complementary approaches to parameter estimation in supervised learning. MLE seeks the parameter values that maximize the likelihood of the observed data, while Bayesian inference combines prior beliefs with observed data to produce a posterior distribution over the parameters. Both approaches recur throughout this book, as they form the foundation of many machine learning methods.

2.6 The Bias–Variance Tradeoff

The bias–variance tradeoff is a fundamental concept in machine learning, representing the balance between the model's ability to accurately capture the training set (its **bias**) versus its ability to generalize well to unseen data (its **variance**) [220].

In general, the generalization error of a model can be decomposed into three components:

- **Bias**: The systematic error caused by incorrect or overly simplistic model assumptions, which leads to consistent deviations between the model's predictions and the true values. A model with high bias is unable to capture the complexities and underlying patterns in the data, resulting in poor performance on both the training set and unseen data. Such a model is said to be **underfitting** the training data.

- **Variance**: The error due to the model's sensitivity to fluctuations in the training data, reflecting how much the model's predictions change when trained on different datasets. A model with high variance adapts too closely to the specific details of the training data (including the noise), which often results in poor generalization to new data. Such a model is said to be **overfitting** the training data.

- **Irreducible error**: The portion of error caused by the inherent noise in the data, arising from factors such as measurement inaccuracies, data entry mistakes, or other unpredictable influences. This error cannot be eliminated by any model, regardless of its complexity.

Theorem 2.1 establishes the relationship between these three components.

Theorem 2.1. *Generalization Error = Bias^2 + Variance + Noise*

First, we introduce a lemma necessary for the proof of Theorem 2.1.

Lemma 1. *If A and B are two independent random variables and $\mathbb{E}[B] = 0$, then $\mathbb{E}[(A+B)^2] = \mathbb{E}[A^2] + \mathbb{E}[B^2]$.*

Proof. Since A and B are independent, we have $\mathbb{E}[AB] = \mathbb{E}[A]\mathbb{E}[B] = 0$ (see Section C.9.5). The proof now follows from expanding the square and using the linearity of expectation:

$$\mathbb{E}[(A+B)^2] = \mathbb{E}[A^2 + 2AB + B^2] = \mathbb{E}[A^2] + \mathbb{E}[B^2] + 2\mathbb{E}[AB] = \mathbb{E}[A^2] + \mathbb{E}[B^2]$$

$\square$

With the lemma established, we now prove Theorem 2.1, focusing on regression problems[5]:

Proof. We consider the following setup:

1. The targets are generated by an unknown function $f(\mathbf{x})$ combined with some random noise ϵ, where ϵ has a mean of 0 and a standard deviation of σ. This noise represents the irreducible error, capturing the randomness inherent in the data:

$$y = f(\mathbf{x}) + \epsilon. \tag{2.17}$$

2. We train our model on a randomly drawn training set $D = \{\mathbf{x}_i, y_i\}_{i=1}^n$.

3. The generalization error is measured as the expected squared error of the model's prediction on a test sample $(\mathbf{x}, y)$, averaged over the random draw of the training set D:

$$\text{MSE}(\mathbf{x}) = \mathbb{E}_D\left[(y - h_D(\mathbf{x}))^2\right]. \tag{2.18}$$

Here, h_D is the hypothesis of the model that was trained on D, y is the true label, and $\mathbb{E}_D$ represents the expectation over all possible training sets. The expected MSE (Mean Squared Error) on a given sample $\mathbf{x}$ quantifies the model's average performance considering variability in the training data selection.

---

5. The bias–variance decomposition for classification is less definitive than for regression, with various proposed formalisms but no consensus on the most appropriate or useful approach.

We now decompose the MSE into bias and variance terms:

$$
\begin{aligned}
\text{MSE}(\mathbf{x}) &= \mathbb{E}_D\left[(y - h_D(\mathbf{x})^2)\right] && \text{(definition of MSE)}\\
&= \mathbb{E}_D\left[(f(\mathbf{x}) + \epsilon - h_D(\mathbf{x}))^2\right] && \text{(Equation (2.17))}\\
&= \mathbb{E}_D\left[\left[(f(\mathbf{x}) - h_D(\mathbf{x})) + \epsilon\right]^2\right] && \text{(rearranging terms)}\\
&= \mathbb{E}_D\left[(f(\mathbf{x}) - h_D(\mathbf{x}))^2\right] + \mathbb{E}_D[\epsilon^2] && \text{(Using Lemma 1)}\\
&= \mathbb{E}_D\left[(f(\mathbf{x}) - h_D(\mathbf{x}))^2\right] + \sigma^2 && (\mathbb{E}_D[\epsilon^2] = \text{Var}(\epsilon) = \sigma^2)\\
&= (\mathbb{E}_D\left[f(\mathbf{x}) - h_D(\mathbf{x})\right])^2 + \text{Var}_D\left(f(\mathbf{x}) - h_D(\mathbf{x})\right) + \sigma^2 && (\mathbb{E}[X^2] = \mathbb{E}[X]^2 + \text{Var}(X))\\
&= \underbrace{(\mathbb{E}_D\left[f(\mathbf{x}) - h_D(\mathbf{x})\right])^2}_{\text{Bias}^2} + \underbrace{\text{Var}_D(h_D(\mathbf{x}))}_{\text{Variance}} + \underbrace{\sigma^2}_{\text{Noise}} && (\text{Var}(a + bX) = b^2\,\text{Var}(X))
\end{aligned}
$$

$\square$

The bias term represents the expected deviation between the true underlying function and the model's hypothesis, averaged over all the possible training datasets. Essentially, the bias quantifies the portion of generalization error caused by the model's limited ability to capture the true data-generating process. Conversely, the variance term measures the model's sensitivity to fluctuations in the training data, indicating how much its predictions change with different training sets. Lastly, the irreducible error represents the noise intrinsically present in the problem itself, which no model can eliminate.

Adjusting the model to decrease the bias, e.g., by adding more parameters or employing a more complex architecture, tends to increase its variance. Similarly, reducing the variance, often by simplifying the model, tends to increase the bias. This reciprocal relationship between bias and variance is referred to as the **bias–variance tradeoff**.

2.6.1 Model Capacity

A primary way to control the bias–variance tradeoff is by adjusting the model's **capacity**, also known as its complexity, expressive power, or flexibility.

A model that is too simple to capture the underlying patterns in the data will have high bias and low variance (Figure 2.8, left). Such models tend to perform poorly on both the training and test sets. This situation is analogous to a novice zoologist who identifies animals based on only one or two traits—such as assuming that all animals with feathers are birds—leading to errors like misclassifying bats or other non-avian species.

Conversely, a complex model with excessively high capacity may overfit the training data, leading to low bias but high variance (Figure 2.8, right). These models tend to memorize the specific details of the training data rather than learning the general patterns, resulting in excellent performance on the training set but poor generalization to new data. This is similar to a zoologist with a photographic memory who, when encountering a new bird species, concludes it is not a bird simply because its tail feathers have a unique pattern not previously observed.

Underfitting	Appropriate fitting	Overfitting

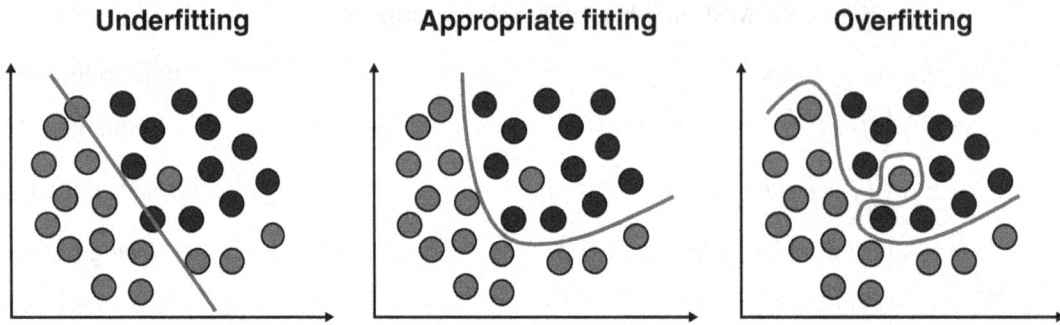

Figure 2.8: Illustration of the bias–variance tradeoff across different model complexities in supervised learning. Underfitting is depicted on the left with a simple linear curve, indicating high bias and low variance, failing to capture the complexity of the data. In the middle, an appropriately fitting model is shown using a quadratic curve, balancing bias and variance to effectively model the underlying data trend. On the right, overfitting is represented by a highly complex curve, which closely follows all data points, including the noisy ones, resulting in low bias but high variance.

The ideal model strikes the right balance between bias and variance (Figure 2.8, middle). Such a model typically has a training error that is slightly lower than its test error, indicating a good fit to the data without overfitting.

Models with insufficient capacity struggle to handle complex tasks, whereas those with high capacity can solve complex tasks, but if their capacity exceeds what is necessary for the task, they risk overfitting. The optimal model is the one whose capacity matches the true complexity of the task and the amount of available training data (see Figure 2.9).

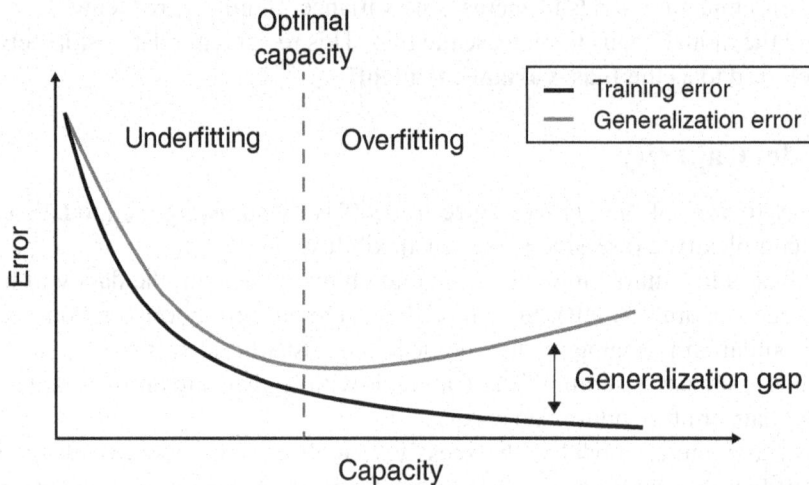

Figure 2.9: The relationship between model capacity and error. Initially, when we increase capacity, both the training and generalization errors decrease. When the capacity becomes too large, the generalization error starts increasing while the training error keeps decreasing. This is where we move from the underfitting zone to the overfitting zone.

Adjusting the capacity of a model can be done in several ways. One way is to modify the model's hypothesis space. For example, in a linear regression model, the hypothesis space consists of linear functions of the input. Expanding this space to include polynomial functions increases the model's capacity. Another way to control the model capacity is by applying regularization techniques, which penalize complex models and help prevent overfitting (see Section 2.6.2).

Statistical learning theory, developed by Vapnik and Chervonenkis in the late 1960s [596], provides a theoretical foundation for understanding the tradeoff between model complexity and generalization in machine learning. It introduces concepts such as the **Vapnik-Chervonenkis (VC) dimension**, which measures a model's capacity to fit a wide range of functions. This theory justifies minimizing the empirical risk (training error) rather than the expected risk (generalization error) when the hypothesis class H is sufficiently restricted. These advanced topics, essential for a deeper understanding of machine learning, will be further explored in Volume III of this book series.

2.6.2 Regularization

Regularization is a widely used technique in machine learning to control the model capacity and prevent overfitting. A common form of regularization involves adding a penalty term to the cost function that increases with the model's complexity:

$$J(h) = R_{\text{emp}}(h) + \lambda C(h) \tag{2.19}$$

Here, $R_{\text{emp}}(h)$ is the empirical risk (the model's error on the training set), $C(h)$ is a penalty term, and λ is a **regularization coefficient** that controls the bias–variance tradeoff. Increasing λ imposes a greater penalty on model complexity, leading to simpler models with higher bias and lower variance. The optimal value of λ is typically determined empirically via cross-validation.

The complexity of the model can be measured in various ways. For example, in parametric models, it is common to use the norm of the parameter vector $\|\boldsymbol{\theta}\|$ as a measure of complexity, where different norms lead to different types of penalties (see Section 4.11).

Minimizing the regularized function $J(h)$ is known as **structural risk minimization**, as opposed to empirical risk minimization, which focuses only on minimizing the training error. Structural risk minimization aims to achieve a balance between fitting the training data well (minimizing empirical risk) and keeping the model simple enough to ensure good generalization to unseen data (through regularization).

To summarize, strategies to reduce underfitting (high bias) include:

- Increasing the model complexity: Introduce more parameters or use more complex algorithms to capture subtle patterns in the data.

- Adding more features: Incorporate additional predictors to provide the model with more information and improve its predictive power.

- Reducing regularization: Decrease the strength of regularization to allow the model to fit the training data more closely.

Strategies to reduce overfitting (high variance) include:

- Simplifying the model: Use fewer parameters or simpler algorithms to prevent the model from capturing noise as signal.

- Using more training data: More samples provide more information, which helps the model to generalize better rather than memorizing the training data.

- Applying regularization: Introduce regularization or increase its strength to penalize overly complex models and promote simpler solutions.

Overall, striking the right balance between bias and variance is a central challenge in model development and a key focus area in machine learning research.

2.7 Building a Machine Learning Model

Having outlined the basic components and objectives of a machine learning model, we are now ready to present a typical workflow of building such a model (see Figure 2.10). The process generally involves the following steps:

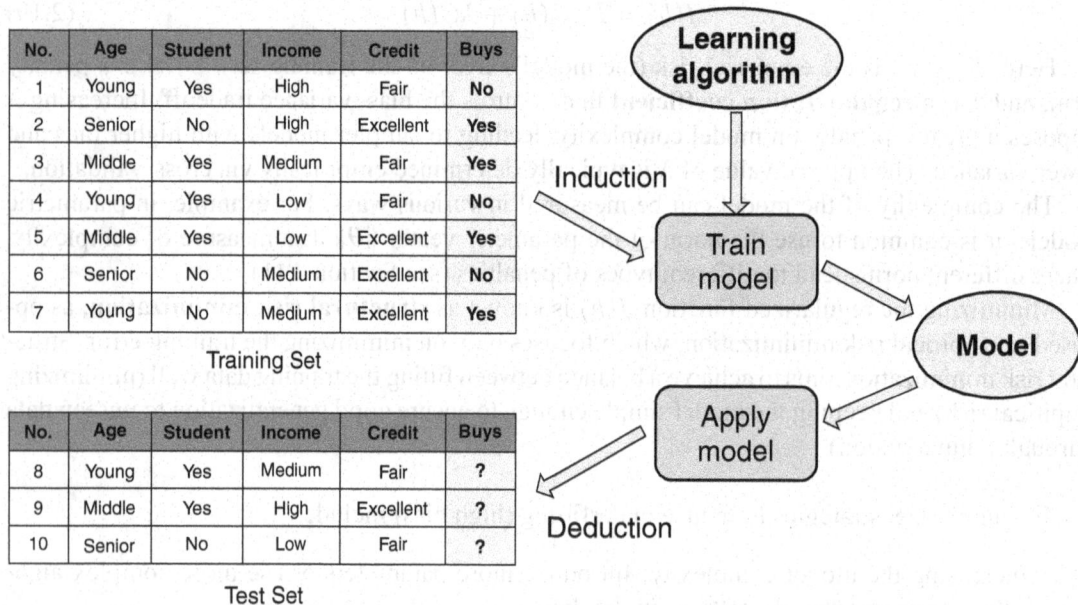

No.	Age	Student	Income	Credit	Buys
1	Young	Yes	High	Fair	No
2	Senior	No	High	Excellent	Yes
3	Middle	Yes	Medium	Fair	Yes
4	Young	Yes	Low	Fair	No
5	Middle	Yes	Low	Excellent	Yes
6	Senior	No	Medium	Excellent	No
7	Young	No	Medium	Excellent	Yes

Training Set

No.	Age	Student	Income	Credit	Buys
8	Young	Yes	Medium	Fair	?
9	Middle	Yes	High	Excellent	?
10	Senior	No	Low	Fair	?

Test Set

Learning algorithm

Induction

Train model

Model

Apply model

Deduction

Figure 2.10: The main stages in building a supervised machine learning model. The initial phase involves using a learning algorithm to develop a model from a set of labeled training examples. The trained model is then applied to a test set of new samples to make predictions, and these predictions are compared to their actual labels in order to evaluate the model's ability to generalize to new, unseen data. In practice, each of these stages consists of multiple steps; refer to the main text for more details.

1. **Problem Definition**:

   (a) Define the problem you want to solve. Is it a classification problem, regression, clustering, or other?

   (b) Clearly specify the inputs and desired outputs. For example, in a handwritten zip code recognition task, the input might be a single digit, the entire zip code, or even an image of the envelope containing the zip code.

   (c) Choose an appropriate performance metric to evaluate the model, such as accuracy, F1 score, mean squared error, etc.

2. **Data Collection**:

   (a) Acquire data relevant to the problem—e.g., from databases, web scraping, or third-party sources. The dataset needs to be representative of the real-world domain of the problem.

   (b) For supervised learning tasks, you also need to collect labels for the data, either from human experts or derived from measurements.

3. **Data Cleaning and Preprocessing**:

   (a) Handle missing values by imputation or removal.

   (b) Encode categorical data into numerical format, using techniques like one-hot encoding or ordinal encoding.

   (c) Detect and remove outliers, or determine how to handle them.

   (d) Normalize or standardize features when required by the algorithm.

4. **Data Exploration**:

   (a) Compute descriptive statistics to summarize the distribution of each feature.

   (b) Visualize the data to understand patterns, relationships, and anomalies.

5. **Feature Engineering**:

   (a) Create new features that could improve model performance.

   (b) Reduce dimensionality if needed using techniques like PCA or t-SNE.

6. **Train-Test Split**:

   (a) Divide your data into training and test sets. Typically, 70%-80% of the data is used for training and the rest for testing.

   (b) Consider using a validation set or cross-validation for model selection and hyperparameter tuning.

7. **Model Selection**:

   (a) Choose a suitable algorithm for the task. Different algorithms are suited for different types of data and problems:

   - For structured (tabular) data, gradient boosting methods such as XGBoost and LightGBM are often the go-to choice.
   - For text data, models such as naive Bayes and, more recently, transformer-based architectures are commonly used.
   - For image data, convolutional neural networks (CNNs) and vision transformers usually give the best results.

   (b) Start with a simple model as a **baseline** to quickly assess the problem's difficulty and identify any issues in the data:

   - For regression tasks, you might start with linear regression (Chapter 4).
   - For classification tasks, logistic regression (Chapter 5) or a simple decision tree (Chapter 8) can be a good starting point.

   (c) If the baseline underfits (performs poorly on the training set), consider switching to more complex algorithms. These algorithms typically require more data and computation.

   (d) Be cautious of overfitting as model complexity increases. Techniques such as regularization or early stopping can help mitigate this.

   (e) Model selection is typically iterative: train a model, evaluate it on the validation set (or via cross-validation), and revise based on the results or new insights about the data.

8. **Model Training**:

   (a) Train the selected model on the training set.

9. **Model Evaluation and Hyperparameter Tuning**:

   (a) Evaluate the trained model on the validation set (if available) or using cross-validation.

   (b) Tune the hyperparameters using techniques such as grid search, random search, or Bayesian optimization (see Section 3.8).

   (c) Check for overfitting: if the model performs well on the training set but poorly on the validation set, consider applying regularization, choosing a simpler model, or adjusting the hyperparameters.

   (d) This step is typically iterative: tune the hyperparameters, train a new model, evaluate it on the validation set (or via cross-validation), and revise based on the results.

10. **Final Model Training and Evaluation**:

    (a) Once the best model and hyperparameters are selected, retrain the model on the full training data (including the validation set).

    (b) Evaluate the final model on the test set to obtain an unbiased estimate of its performance. Report the result as is, and avoid further tuning of the model.

11. **Model Deployment**:

    (a) Deploy the model to a production environment or make it accessible via APIs.

    (b) Continuously monitor the model's performance in production. Due to **concept drift**—changes in the statistical properties of the data over time—the model may become outdated, requiring retraining or other adjustments.

Implementation of the entire workflow in Python is demonstrated in Section 3.4.

2.8   Challenges in Supervised Learning

Key challenges to address in supervised machine learning include the following:

- Insufficient training data: Complex models with many parameters require large, labeled datasets, which are often costly and difficult to obtain. Strategies like data augmentation and semi-supervised learning can help mitigate this issue of data scarcity.

- Dealing with large datasets: This is a complementary issue to the previous one. Processing large datasets requires extensive computational resources, and some are too large to fit into the memory of a single machine. Such datasets are often handled using specialized algorithms, such as distributed or online algorithms.

- High dimensionality: Working with high-dimensional data poses significant challenges, often referred to as the **curse of dimensionality** (see Section 6.6). As the number of dimensions increases, data points become increasingly sparse and less informative, causing standard distance metrics to lose their effectiveness. These issues are commonly addressed through feature selection and dimensionality reduction techniques.

- Overfitting and underfitting: Achieving the optimal balance between underfitting and overfitting is a key challenge in model development (see Section 2.6).

- Heterogeneity of the data: Handling diverse data types (continuous, categorical, ordinal, counts, etc.) and formats (tabular, graph, text, image, etc.) presents significant challenges. Most machine learning algorithms can only work with numerical input, so data preprocessing is needed to convert non-numerical data types into a numerical format (see Section 3.10).

- Data quality issues: Issues such as noisy data, missing values, and redundancy can severely degrade model performance and must be addressed through proper data cleaning and preprocessing.

- Complex objective functions: Many learning tasks have complex, nonlinear objective functions with multiple local optima, making optimization difficult. Common methods such as gradient descent generally converge to locally optimal solutions, which may be far inferior to the global optimum.

- No theoretical guarantees: Most machine learning algorithms do not provide theoretical guarantees on their performance (i.e., their generalization error). As a result, it is usually impossible to know in advance which algorithm will work best for a given problem, requiring empirical comparison across multiple methods.

- Interpretability of the model: Interpretability refers to how well a human can understand the decisions made by the model. Some machine learning models, such as neural networks, behave like "black boxes," where the decision-making process is not easily explainable. Interpretability is particulary important in critical domains such as finance or healthcare, where model decisions can have a profound impact.

- Concept drifts: In dynamic environments, models must continuously adapt to remain accurate, as data distributions may shift due to changing conditions. For example, spam filters adapt over time to detect new forms of unwanted emails as spammers continually change their strategies.

2.9   Summary

To summarize the main points discussed in this chapter:

- Supervised learning is the task of inferring a function from labeled training data that can accurately predict the output label for new, unseen inputs.

- The main two types of supervised learning problems are classification, where the goal is to predict to which class a sample belongs, and regression, where the goal is to predict a continuous value for a target variable.

- The model's hypothesis is a function learned from the training data that approximates the true mapping from features to labels.

- A loss function measures the error of the model's predictions on the training data and is used to guide the optimization process of the model.

- Generative models learn the joint probability distribution of inputs and labels, while discriminative models focus on learning the decision boundary between classes.

- Two common methods for estimating model parameters are maximum likelihood estimation (MLE) and Bayesian inference. MLE seeks to find the parameter values that maximize the likelihood of the observed data, whereas Bayesian inference combines beliefs with the observed data to produce a posterior distribution over the parameters.

- The bias–variance tradeoff represents the tension between a model's ability to perform well on the training set (bias) and its ability to generalize to unseen data (variance).

- Regularization is a common technique to combat overfitting by penalizing complex models.

- A typical machine learning pipeline includes data collection and preparation, model selection, training, hyperparameter tuning, performance evaluation, and deployment.

- Supervised machine learning involves navigating a complex landscape of challenges, ranging from data quality and quantity to model complexity and interpretability.

2.10 Exercises

2.10.1 Multiple-Choice Questions

Circle all the correct choices. There may be more than one correct choice, but there is always at least one correct choice.

2.1. What does the data-generating distribution represent?

    (a) The real-world process by which the data is generated

    (b) The probability distribution from which the training data is drawn

    (c) The distribution of features in the training set

    (d) The distribution used by generative models to create new data samples

2.2. What does the generalization error of a model represent?

    (a) The error rate of the model on the test data

    (b) The variance of the model's predictions on the test data

    (c) The expected value of the error on new input

    (d) The difference in error between training and testing data

2.3. Maximum Likelihood Estimation (MLE) in supervised learning is used to:

    (a) Maximize the probability of observing the given data under the model parameters

    (b) Minimize the error between the predicted and actual values

    (c) Estimate the probability of the model being correct given the data

    (d) Update the model parameters based on prior beliefs and the likelihood of the observed data

2.4. Generative models:

   (a) model the boundary between classes.

   (b) model the input distribution in individual classes.

   (c) can be used for classification tasks.

   (d) can only be used with continuous data, not categorical data.

2.5. Bayesian statistics in supervised learning is used for what purpose?

   (a) To reduce the amount of data needed for model training

   (b) To model uncertainty in predictions by producing probability distributions over outcomes

   (c) To estimate the parameters of a model probabilistically

   (d) To incorporate prior knowledge into the model

2.6. Which of the following statements are true about gradient descent?

   (a) Gradient descent is used to minimize the cost function in machine learning models.

   (b) When the function is convex, gradient descent is guaranteed to find the global minimum.

   (c) Choosing a high learning rate causes gradient descent to converge more rapidly.

   (d) Gradient descent requires the function to be twice differentiable.

2.7. The bias–variance tradeoff in machine learning suggests that:

   (a) As bias decreases, variance tends to increase, and vice versa.

   (b) Low bias is usually preferable to low variance.

   (c) Reducing variance leads to better model performance on unseen data.

   (d) High bias can lead to underfitting, while high variance can lead to overfitting.

   (e) A perfect model has neither bias nor variance.

2.8. Reducing the regularization strength λ will lead to:

   (a) lower bias

   (b) lower variance

   (c) higher bias

   (d) higher variance

2.9. Which of the following strategies help to reduce overfitting?

   (a) Increase the size of the training set.

   (b) Use a more complex model.

(c) Perform feature selection to reduce the number of input variables.

(d) Use cross-validation to ensure the model performs well on unseen data.

2.10. Which of the plots in Figure 2.11 shows a hypothesis that underfits the training data?

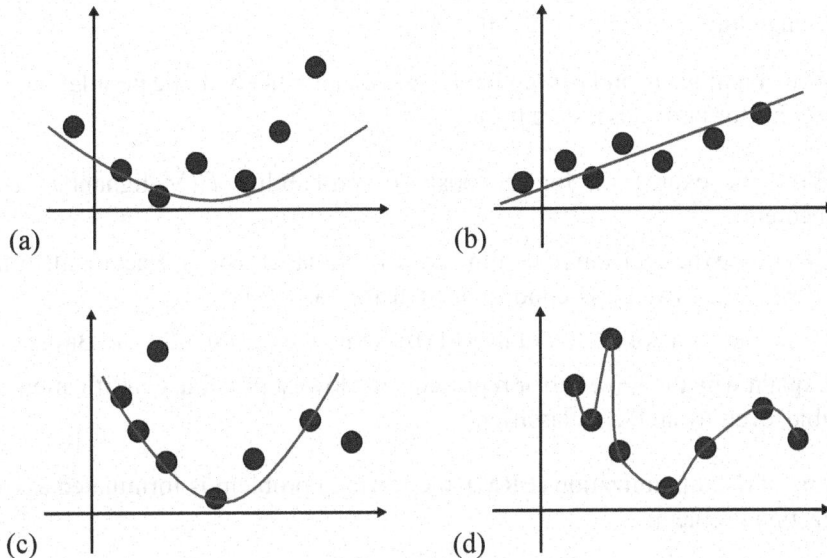

Figure 2.11: Four models with different levels of model complexity. Which one underfits the data?

2.10.2 Theoretical Exercises

2.11. Identify which of the following problems can be framed as a supervised machine learning problem. For each such problem, clearly state what are the inputs and the outputs (labels), and whether it is a classification or a regression problem.

(a) Build a medical diagnosis application that recommends treatments to patients based on their symptoms and their characteristics such as gender, age, blood pressure, and outcomes of various tests.

(b) Build a chatbot application that provides customer support to the user.

(c) Flag offensive content in a social media application.

(d) Learn to play chess.

(e) Detect the locations of ships in satellite images.

(f) Build a movie recommendation system that suggests new movies to users based on their favorite movies from the past.

2.12. Consider the problem of classifying tumors as either benign or malignant based on their measured size (in millimeters). The sizes of tumors from the two classes are modeled as follows:

- Malignant tumors: size $x \sim \mathcal{N}(40, 8^2)$
- Benign tumors: size $x \sim \mathcal{N}(20, 6^2)$

Assume that malignant and benign tumors are equally likely in the population (i.e., the prior probabilities for both classes are 0.5).

(a) Write the expression for the posterior probability $P(\text{Malignant}|x)$ using Bayes' theorem.

(b) Determine the decision rule of the Bayes optimal classifier. Specifically, find the value x^* where the two class-conditional densities are equal.

(c) Using the value of x^* found in part (b), write the formula for the Bayes error E^*.

(d) Explain why the Bayes error represents the lowest possible classification error achievable, even by an ideal classifier.

2.13. In empirical risk minimization (ERM), the learning problem is formulated as the following optimization problem:

$$\min_{h \in H} R_{\text{emp}}(h),$$

where $R_{\text{emp}}(h)$ is the empirical risk, defined as the average loss over the training set.

(a) Explain why this problem is considered an optimization problem. Specify what constitutes the objective function, the variables, and the feasible set.

(b) What properties of the loss function and the hypothesis space H would ensure that the empirical risk minimization problem has a unique global minimum?

(c) Why are iterative optimization methods (such as gradient descent) commonly used in practice to solve ERM problems, even when the optimization objective is well-defined?

2.14. In binary classification, each label $y \in \{0, 1\}$ is often assumed to be generated from a Bernoulli distribution[6] with success probability p, where p represents the probability of the label being 1.

(a) Write the likelihood function for a single labeled data point $(\mathbf{x}, y)$, assuming the model predicts the probability of class 1 as p.

(b) Suppose we have n independent data points $(\mathbf{x}_1, y_1), \ldots, (\mathbf{x}_n, y_n)$, where the model assigns probability p_i to class 1 for input $\mathbf{x}_i$. Write the likelihood function for the dataset.

---

6. See Section C.5.6.1 for a review of the Bernoulli distribution.

    (c) Derive the log-likelihood function for the dataset.

    (d) Write down the negative log-likelihood (NLL) for the dataset.

2.15. Consider a binary classification problem where the goal is to detect fraudulent transactions. Assume that:

- Only 2% of the transactions in the population are actually fraudulent.
- The classifier has 90% sensitivity (i.e., the probability of correctly identifying a fraudulent transaction).
- The classifier has 85% specificity (i.e., the probability of correctly identifying a legitimate transaction).

    (a) Calculate the probability that a transaction is actually fraudulent given that the classifier predicts it as fraudulent.

    (b) How does this probability change if the prevalence of fraud in the population increases from 2% to 10%? Explain intuitively why the prevalence affects the result.

    (c) Calculate the false positive rate of the classifier (i.e., the probability that the classifier predicts fraud when the transaction is actually legitimate).

2.16. In supervised learning, model parameters θ are often estimated by either maximum likelihood estimation (MLE) or Bayesian inference.

    (a) Write down the expression for the posterior distribution $p(\theta|D)$ of the model parameters given the training data $D = \{(x_i, y_i)\}_{i=1}^{n}$, according to Bayes' theorem.

    (b) Show that if the prior distribution $p(\theta)$ is uniform, maximizing the posterior probability is equivalent to maximizing the likelihood function $p(D|\theta)$, and hence equivalent to maximum likelihood estimation.

    (c) Briefly explain what this result means in the context of supervised learning.

2.17. Which of the following is likely to decrease the bias of a model and increase its variance? Justify your answer in each case.

    (a) Add more training data.

    (b) Add more features.

    (c) Use a more complex model architecture.

    (d) Train the model for longer time.

    (e) Remove outliers from the dataset.

    (f) Decrease regularization strength.

2.18. (*) Read the foundational paper on the No Free Lunch (NFL) theorem by Wolpert and Macready (1997) [630] and answer the following questions based on your understanding:

   (a) What is the No Free Lunch theorem, and how does it challenge the notion of a universally best model in machine learning?

   (b) Provide a real-world example that illustrates the impact of the No Free Lunch theorem on model selection.

   (c) How does the NFL theorem influence the approach to algorithm design and evaluation in practice?

2.10.3   Programming Exercises

2.19. (Maximum Likelihood Estimation) Implement maximum likelihood estimation to estimate the parameters of a Gaussian distribution (mean and standard deviation) given a dataset. Use the following steps:

   (a) Generate a synthetic dataset of $n = 100$ data points by sampling from a Gaussian distribution with a true mean of $\mu = 50$ and a true standard deviation of $\sigma = 5$. *Hint*: Use the function np.random.normal[7] to sample from a normal distribution.

   (b) Calculate the MLE estimates for the mean and standard deviation of your dataset. *Hint*: The MLE for the mean is the sample mean, and the MLE for the standard deviation is the sample standard deviation.

   (c) Compare the estimated parameters with the true parameters used to generate the data.

   (d) Plot an histogram of your sampled dataset. Overlay the probability density function of the Gaussian distribution with the estimated parameters on the same plot. *Hint*: Use the scipy.stats.norm[8] object and its pdf method.

   (e) Explore the effect of sample size on the accuracy of the MLE estimates. Repeat the process with different sample sizes (e.g., $n = 10, 50, 100, 500, 1000$) and plot how the estimates of the mean and standard deviation vary with sample size.

2.20. (Bayes Error) Write a program to estimate the Bayes error rate for a classification task involving two classes with overlapping distributions. Follow these steps:

   (a) Define two normal distributions: $\mathcal{N}_1(0, 0.5)$ and $\mathcal{N}_2(1, 1)$, and plot their probability density functions (PDFs) on the same graph.

   (b) Find the intersection point of the two PDFs, corresponding to the decision boundary of the Bayes optimal classifier. *Hint*: Use scipy.optimize.fsolve[9] to solve for the points where the two PDFs are equal.

---

7. https://numpy.org/doc/stable/reference/random/generated/numpy.random.normal.html
8. https://docs.scipy.org/doc/scipy/reference/generated/scipy.stats.norm.html
9. https://docs.scipy.org/doc/scipy/reference/generated/scipy.optimize.fsolve.html

(c) Estimate the Bayes error rate by calculating the area under the curve of each distribution up to the intersection point. *Hint*: Use `scipy.integrate.quad`[10] to compute these integrals.

2.21. (Gradient Descent) In this exercise you will implement the gradient descent algorithm (Algorithm E.1), starting from a simple univariate function and then extending it to more complex multivariate functions.

(a) Implement the gradient descent algorithm for univariate functions. *Hint:* The gradient at point x can be approximated using the finite difference $\nabla f(x) \approx \frac{f(x+h)-f(x)}{h}$, where h is a small number.

(b) Use your implementation to find the minimum of $f(x) = x^2 + 10 \sin x$ starting from a random point.

(c) Plot the function $f(x)$ and overlay on it the path gradient descent took towards the minimum.

(d) Explore the effect of various learning rates (e.g., $1, 0.1, 0.01, 0.001$) on the convergence of the algorithm. Discuss your observations.

(e) Extend your implementation to multivariate functions. For this, modify the gradient computation and update steps to handle vectors instead of scalar values. *Hint:* You can use the function scipy.optimize.approx_fprime() for finite difference approximation.

(f) Use the extended implementation to find the minimum of the function $f(x, y) = x^2 + y^2 + 10 \sin(xy)$, starting from a random point in two-dimensional space.

(g) Plot the function $f(x, y)$ in 3D space and overlay on it the path gradient descent took towards the minimum.

(h) Test your algorithm with different learning rates, number of iterations, and starting points.

---

10. `https://docs.scipy.org/doc/scipy/reference/generated/scipy.integrate.quad.html`

Chapter 3

Introduction to Scikit-Learn

After exploring the fundamental concepts and theories of machine learning, we are now ready to put them into practice by building machine learning models to solve real-world problems.

Scikit-Learn is the primary Python library for constructing machine learning models outside the realm of deep learning. It provides efficient implementations of a wide range of learning algorithms, along with an extensive suite of tools for data preprocessing, model evaluation, and hyperparameter tuning. In this chapter, we explore the core components and utilities of Scikit-Learn and learn how to use them to solve various machine learning tasks.

This chapter is organized as follows. Section 3.1 describes the main features of the Scikit-Learn library. Section 3.2 explains how to install the library. Section 3.3 introduces the Estimator API, the core interface for machine learning algorithms in Scikit-Learn. Section 3.4 outlines the typical workflow for building a machine learning model. Section 3.5 demonstrates this workflow on a classification task using the Iris dataset. Section 3.6 shows how to streamline the workflow using Scikit-Learn pipelines. Section 3.7 discusses the cross-validation technique for model evaluation. Section 3.8 presents various techniques for hyperparameter tuning, including grid search, random search, and Bayesian optimization. Section 3.9 describes the process of preparing a dataset for modeling. Section 3.10 introduces common data preprocessing techniques, including imputation, encoding of categorical variables, and feature scaling. Section 3.11 explains how to create custom machine learning models in Scikit-Learn. Section 3.12 concludes with a summary of the chapter.

Since this chapter is hands-on and implementation-focused, I strongly encourage readers to follow along by coding the examples from scratch as they read, and to experiment with different parameters or options beyond those explicitly discussed. This active approach will reinforce understanding and promote deeper learning. All examples in this chapter are designed to be run in a Jupyter notebook environment and are available for download from the book's GitHub repository[1].

---

1. https://github.com/roiyeho/ml-book/tree/main/Chapter03

3.1   Main Features

Scikit-Learn (also referred to as `sklearn`) is a popular Python library for machine learning model development, widely used in both academia and industry thanks for its simplicity, versatility, and efficiency [473].[2] Its main features are:

- Efficient implementations of a wide range of machine learning algorithms, including supervised, unsupervised, and semi-supervised learning algorithms.

- Utilities for data preprocessing, feature selection and extraction, hyperparameter tuning, model selection, and model evaluation.

- A clean, consistent, and user-friendly API.

- Seamless integration with other Python libraries commonly used in the machine learning pipeline, such as NumPy, Pandas, and Matplotlib.

- High computational efficiency, leveraging NumPy for fast array operations, with core algorithms implemented in Cython (a superset of Python that compiles into C) for additional speed.

- Extensive and detailed documentation available on its official website[3], which features a large number of tutorials and demos for users of all levels.

3.2   Installation

Scikit-Learn can be easily installed using `pip`:

```
pip install scikit-learn
```

At the time of writing this book, the latest version of Scikit-Learn is 1.6.1, which is compatible with Python 3.9 or newer. Scikit-Learn also requires the NumPy and SciPy packages to be installed. Instead of installing each of these packages and managing its version separately, a smoother and more efficient approach is to install Python's **Anaconda distribution**, which comes pre-installed with many essential data science libraries and tools, including NumPy, Pandas, Scikit-Learn, and Jupyter notebook. It can be downloaded from `https://www.anaconda.com/download`.

To verify that Scikit-Learn has been installed successfully, run the following command in your Python interpreter or inside a Jupyter notebook:

```
import sklearn

print(sklearn.__version__)
```

2. Scikit-Learn was originally developed by David Cournapeau as part of a Google Summer of Code project in 2007 and
   was publicly released as an open-source library in 2010. It continues to be actively maintained by a large open-source
   community, with regular updates, improvements, and the addition of new algorithms.

3. `https://scikit-learn.org/stable/`

This command will display the installed version of Scikit-Learn, ensuring that the installation was successful.

3.3   The Estimator API

The estimator API lies at the core of Scikit-Learn, providing a uniform interface for all algorithms implemented in the library. Its design is based on several core principles:

- **Consistency**: All objects share a common interface defined by a small set of core methods.

- **Limited object hierarchy**: Scikit-Learn favors "duck typing" over complex inheritance hierarchies. This means that an object's behavior is determined by the methods it exposes (its API) rather than by its position in the class hierarchy.

- **Sensible defaults**: Each estimator includes reasonable default hyperparameter settings, making it easy to train initial models with minimal configuration.

- **Inspection**: All parameters of the estimator are accessible as public instance variables, promoting transparency and ease of modification.

- **Composition**: Estimators can be easily chained to each other in order to create more complex pipelines, enhancing modularity and flexibility.

The estimator API is centered around three main types of objects: estimators, predictors, and transformers. Each serves a distinct role within the machine learning workflow, as detailed in the following subsections.

3.3.1   Estimators

An **estimator** in Scikit-Learn is any object that learns from data. This includes **classifiers** for classification tasks, **regressors** for regression tasks, **clusterers** for clustering tasks, and **transformers** for data transformations.

Every estimator adheres to the same interface, which includes the following methods:

- `__init__`: The constructor initializes the estimator and sets its hyperparameters. It accepts keyword arguments that define the estimator's behavior, including both hyperparameters that control the learning algorithm (e.g., learning rate) and parameters related to the runtime environment (e.g., the number of CPU cores to use for training). For example, the code below creates a decision tree classifier with specific hyperparameter values:

```
from sklearn.tree import DecisionTreeClassifier

clf = DecisionTreeClassifier(criterion='entropy', max_depth=3)
```

All arguments passed to __init__ are stored as public attributes with the same name, making them accessible to Scikit-Learn's utilities and tools. For example, we can print the hyperparameter values of the classifier as follows:

```
print(clf.criterion)
print(clf.max_depth)
```

```
entropy
3
```

However, it is recommended not to modify these attributes directly after initialization, as this may bypass Scikit-Learn's validation and lead to inconsistent behavior. Instead, use the set_params method (described below) to apply changes safely.

- fit(X, y): This method trains the model on the given dataset. It requires two parameters:
  - X is an array-like object representing the features of the dataset. It should have a shape of (n_samples, n_features), where each row corresponds to a sample and each column to a feature. An array-like object is any object that can be cast into a NumPy array, including lists, tuples, existing NumPy arrays, or pandas DataFrames.
  - y is an array-like object of shape (n_samples,), containing the target values or labels associated with each sample. For unsupervised models, this parameter is optional and defaults to None.

For example, the following code snippet trains the decision tree classifier on a dataset consisting of 5 samples, 4 features, and labels from three classes (0, 1, and 2):

```
X = [[5.1, 3.5, 1.4, 0.2],
     [4.9, 3.0, 1.4, 0.2],
     [7.0, 3.2, 4.7, 1.4],
     [6.4, 3.2, 4.5, 1.5],
     [6.3, 3.3, 6.0, 2.5]]
y = [0, 0, 1, 1, 2]

clf.fit(X, y)
```

After training, the model's learned parameters are stored as attributes with a trailing underscore. For example, in a decision tree classifier, the tree that was built during training is stored in an attribute named tree_. We can print the number of nodes in this tree as follows:

```
clf.tree_.node_count
```

```
5
```

- get_params: This method returns a dictionary with all the parameters of the estimator that were set during initialization and their current values:

```
clf.get_params()
```

```
{'ccp_alpha': 0.0,
 'class_weight': None,
 'criterion': 'entropy',
 'max_depth': 3,
 ...
 'splitter': 'best'}
```

- set_params: This method updates parameters of the estimator that were set during initialization, while performing internal validation. For example, we can change the maximum depth of the decision tree to 5 as follows:

```
clf.set_params(max_depth=5)
```

3.3.2 Predictors

A **predictor** in Scikit-Learn is a type of estimator capable of making predictions, i.e., assigning labels to samples. Every predictor has a predict(X) method, which takes an array-like object X containing a set of samples and returns the predicted labels for these samples. For example, we can use our trained decision tree classifier to assign a label to a new sample as follows:

```
X_test = [[4.7, 3.2, 3.3, 0.2]]

y_pred = clf.predict(X_test)
y_pred
```

```
array([0])
```

The predicted label for the given sample is 0. Note that the argument passed to predict must be a two-dimensional array, even if it contains only one sample.

Additionally, many classifiers in Scikit-Learn provide deeper insight into their predictions through methods such as decision_function(X), which returns a confidence score for each prediction, and predict_proba(X), which returns estimated class probabilities. For example, we can ask the decision tree classifier to provide probability estimates for the three classes using:

```
clf.predict_proba(X_test)
```

```
array([[1., 0., 0.]])
```

Each row in the returned array corresponds to a sample and each column to a class; the values indicate the predicted probability of the sample belonging to each class. In this case, the classifier is fully confident that the sample belongs to the first class (class 0).

Another common feature of predictors is the score(X, y) method, which evaluates the model's performance on a given dataset using its default metric. For example, a decision tree classifier uses accuracy as its default scoring metric:

```
accuracy = clf.score(X, y)
accuracy
```

```
1.0
```

In this example, the classifier achieves 100% accuracy on the training set. While this might seem ideal, such perfect accuracy on a very small and simple training set, is typically a sign of overfitting.

The typical workflow of a predictor in Scikit-Learn, including training and making predictions, is illustrated in Figure 3.1.

3.3.3   Transformers

In Scikit-Learn, a **transformer** is any object that modifies or transforms data, typically as a pre-processing step before modeling. Scikit-Learn provides a wide variety of transformers for tasks such as imputing missing values, encoding categorical variables, feature scaling, and discretization (discussed in Section 3.10).

Similar to other estimators, transformers implement a `fit(X)` method to learn parameters from the data that are needed for the transformation (e.g., the mean and standard deviation for feature scaling). In addition, they provide a `transform(X)` method to apply the transformation using the learned parameters. These two steps are commonly combined using the `fit_transform(X)` method, which simplifies the workflow and is often more efficient than calling `fit` and then `transform` separately.

For example, the `StandardScaler`[4] transformer standardizes each feature by removing the mean and scaling it to unit variance:

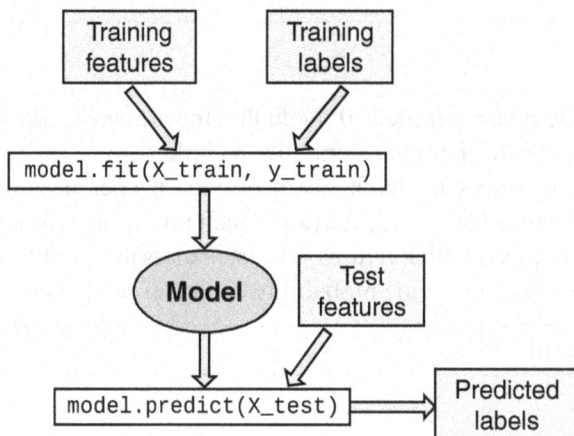

Figure 3.1: A typical workflow of a predictor in Scikit-Learn. The training features and their corresponding labels are provided to the model using the `model.fit(X_train, y_train)` method, which is used to train the model. After training, the `model.predict(X_test)` method applies the trained model to predict labels for new, unseen test features.

---

4. https://scikit-learn.org/stable/modules/generated/sklearn.preprocessing.StandardScaler.html

```
from sklearn.preprocessing import StandardScaler

scaler = StandardScaler()
new_X = scaler.fit_transform(X)
new_X
```

```
array([[-1.04157134,  1.60018938, -1.17729571, -1.0994609 ],
       [-1.28956451, -1.47709789, -1.17729571, -1.0994609 ],
       [ 1.31436383, -0.24618298,  0.58864786,  0.27486523],
       [ 0.5703843 , -0.24618298,  0.48162097,  0.3893924 ],
       [ 0.44638772,  0.36927447,  1.2843226 ,  1.53466417]])
```

It is important to fit the transformer on the training data only and then use the learned parameters to transform both the training and test data. This prevents information from the test set from leaking into the training process. For example, when using StandardScaler, the mean and standard deviation of the features are computed from the training set and then applied to scale the test set. Recomputing these statistics on the test set could distort the transformation and lead to unreliable evaluation results, especially if the test set is small. Therefore, while fit_transform is convenient for preprocessing the training data in a single step, the test set should always be transformed using the transform method alone.

A typical workflow of a transformer in Scikit-Learn, including the fitting and transforming steps, is depicted in Figure 3.2.

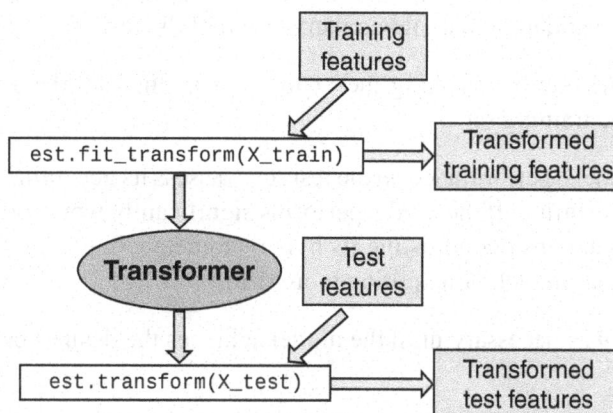

Figure 3.2: A typical workflow of a transformer in Scikit-Learn. The transformer is first fitted to the training features using the est.fit_transform(X_train) method, which both learns the transformation parameters and transforms the training data. The learned parameters are then used to transform the test features using the est.transform(X_test) method. This ensures that both the training and test sets are transformed consistently, without leaking information from the test data.

3.4   Typical Workflow of Building a Model

In Section 2.7, we outlined the main steps involved in constructing a machine learning model. This section demonstrates how to implement these steps using Scikit-Learn. The key steps in building a model with Scikit-Learn are:

1. Load the dataset and organize it into a feature matrix X and a target vector y.

2. Perform exploratory data analysis (EDA) to understand the statistical properties of the data and identify any preprocessing needs.

3. Split the dataset into training and test sets.

4. Prepare the training set by applying a sequence of transformers using their `fit_transform` method. The order of transformations is important; for example, feature scaling should be performed after imputing missing values.

5. Select and instantiate an appropriate estimator, setting its hyperparameters in the constructor.

6. Fit the estimator to the training set by calling its `fit` method.

7. Evaluate the model's performance on the training set. If performance is poor, consider re-visiting the data preprocessing steps, tuning the hyperparameters of the model, or choosing another (typically more complex) model. For hyperparameter tuning, use a separate valida-tion set or cross-validation to avoid contamination of the test set.

8. Transform the test set by invoking the `transform` method on the same transformers that were fitted to the training set.

9. Evaluate the model's performance on the test set to assess its generalization ability and detect any potential overfitting. If the model performs significantly worse on the test set compared to the training set, consider adjusting its hyperparameters (e.g., increasing regularization), choosing a simpler model, or acquiring more data.

10. Repeat steps 4–9 as necessary until the model achieves the desired performance criteria.

3.5   Example: Iris Classification

We now illustrate the workflow outlined in the previous section by applying it to the classic ma-chine learning task of classifying Iris flowers. The Iris dataset, introduced by the statistician Ronald Fisher in 1936 [192], has become a standard benchmark for testing and comparing machine learn-ing algorithms due to its simplicity and well-defined classes.

The dataset contains 150 Iris samples, evenly distributed across three species of Iris: Iris setosa, Iris virginica, and Iris versicolor. Each sample is described by four features—sepal length, sepal width, petal length, and petal width—all measured in centimeters (see Figure 3.3).

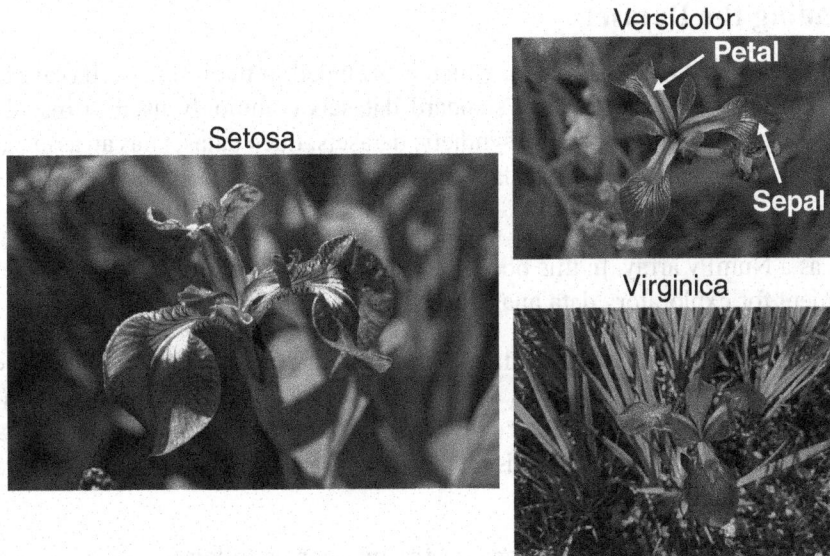

Figure 3.3: Representative images of the three Iris species: Iris setosa, Iris versicolor, and Iris virginica. The upper-right image highlights the distinct petal and sepal structures, which are key features used for classification (Images: left, Walter Erhardt/Shutterstock; top right, Alex Manders/Shutterstock; bottom right, piemags/nature/Alamy Images).

Our goal is to build a model that can classify an Iris flower into one of the three species based on the values of the four features. We begin by importing the libraries needed for this example:

```
import numpy as np
import pandas as pd
import matplotlib.pyplot as plt
import seaborn as sns
```

Next, we fix the random seed to ensure reproducible results. Many machine learning operations involve randomness, such as splitting data into training and test sets or initializing models. Without fixing the seed, you might get different results each time you run the code. By setting a seed, we make sure the same random choices are made every time, making results easier to debug and share. Here is how to set the seed:[5]

```
np.random.seed(42)
```

Note that Scikit-Learn relies on NumPy's random seed internally, but other libraries (such as PyTorch) have their own random number generators that need to be seeded separately in order to ensure full reproducibility.

---

5. The number 42, famously cited as the "Answer to the Ultimate Question of Life, the Universe, and Everything" in Douglas Adams' *The Hitchhiker's Guide to the Galaxy*, is commonly used as a random seed in examples and tutorials. However, this choice is arbitrary and can be replaced with any other number.

3.5.1   Loading the Dataset

Next, we proceed to load the Iris dataset, which is included in the `sklearn.datasets`[6] module. This module provides access to several standard datasets commonly used in machine learning research, as well as functions to generate synthetic datasets. Each dataset has an associated loading function, such as `load_iris` for the Iris dataset. These functions accept the following arguments:

- `as_frame`: If set to `True`, the data is returned as a Pandas DataFrame; otherwise, it is returned as a NumPy array. In this book, we typically set it to `True`, as DataFrames are more convenient for exploratory data analysis (EDA).

- `return_X_y`: If set to `True`, the data is returned as a feature matrix `X` and a label vector `y`. If `False` (the default), it returns a dictionary-like object with the keys: `data` (the feature matrix), `target` (the labels), `feature_names` (feature names), and `target_names` (class names). When `as_frame=True`, this metadata is already included in the DataFrame, so the default is usually sufficient.

To load the Iris dataset, we use the `load_iris`[7] function as follows:

```
from sklearn.datasets import load_iris

X, y = load_iris(as_frame=True, return_X_y=True)
```

This code loads the Iris features into a Pandas DataFrame `X` and the corresponding labels into a Pandas Series `y`. Note that for datasets not included in Scikit-Learn, such as those loaded from CSV files or databases, you typically need to manually separate the features and labels into different variables (see example in Section 3.10.8).

3.5.2   Exploratory Data Analysis (EDA)

We now turn to exploratory data analysis (EDA) of the dataset. EDA is a critical step in the machine learning workflow, aimed at understanding the statistical properties of the data and identifying potential issues such as missing values, non-numerical features, or outliers. This preliminary analysis not only deepens our understanding of the data but also informs the subsequent selection of data preprocessing techniques and machine learning algorithms. For EDA, we typically use the libraries Pandas for data manipulation and statistical analysis, and Matplotlib for visualization.

First, let's examine the first few rows of the dataset to get a sense of its structure. The `head`[8] method from Pandas can be used for this purpose (by default, it returns the top five rows):

```
X.head()
```

Figure 3.4 shows the first five rows of the dataset, with each row displaying the four numerical feature values: sepal length, sepal width, petal length, and petal width.

---

6. `https://scikit-learn.org/stable/datasets.html`
7. `https://scikit-learn.org/stable/modules/generated/sklearn.datasets.load_iris.html`
8. `https://pandas.pydata.org/docs/reference/api/pandas.DataFrame.head.html`

	sepal length (cm)	sepal width (cm)	petal length (cm)	petal width (cm)
0	5.1	3.5	1.4	0.2
1	4.9	3.0	1.4	0.2
2	4.7	3.2	1.3	0.2
3	4.6	3.1	1.5	0.2
4	5.0	3.6	1.4	0.2

Figure 3.4: The first five rows of the Iris dataset

Beyond this initial glance, a deeper exploration of the data typically includes:

1. **Examining the feature data types**: It is important to understand the data type of each feature, as it affects how the data will be processed. This can be done using the `info`[9] method of the DataFrame, which displays the data type of each feature along with the number of non-missing (non-null) values:

```
X.info()
```

```
<class 'pandas.core.frame.DataFrame'>
RangeIndex: 150 entries, 0 to 149
Data columns (total 4 columns):
 #   Column             Non-Null Count   Dtype
---  ------             --------------   -----
 0   sepal length (cm)  150 non-null     float64
 1   sepal width (cm)   150 non-null     float64
 2   petal length (cm)  150 non-null     float64
 3   petal width (cm)   150 non-null     float64
dtypes: float64(4)
memory usage: 4.8 KB
```

Here, all features are numerical (floating-point numbers), and no missing values are present (all features have 150 non-null values).

Feature types can be classified into three main categories:

- **Numerical features**, including:
  - **Continuous features**: Represent measurements that can take any real value within a range (e.g., height, weight, temperature).
  - **Discrete features**: Represent countable quantities that take on integer values (e.g., number of students, movie ratings).

---

9. https://pandas.pydata.org/docs/reference/api/pandas.DataFrame.info.html

- **Categorical features**, including:
  - **Nominal features**: Categories with no inherent order (e.g., colors, country names, occupations).
  - **Ordinal features**: Categories with a meaningful order or ranking (e.g., shirt size: "Small", "Medium", or "Large").
  - **Binary features**: A special case of categorical features with exactly two categories (e.g., Yes/No, True/False).
- **Complex data types**: Data types that consist of multiple values per instance and typically require specialized preprocessing before being used in machine learning models. These include:
  - **Textual features**: Unstructured text data in natural language (e.g., emails, reviews, tweets).
  - **Image features**: Pixel data from images.
  - **Time-series features**: Sequential data indexed by time (e.g., stock prices, sensor readings).
  - **Geospatial features**: Data containing spatial or geographic information (e.g., coordinates, addresses).
  - **Graph/network features**: Data represented by nodes and edges (e.g., social networks, molecule structures).

Identifying the feature types is crucial, as it determines the appropriate preprocessing and analysis techniques. For example, categorical features typically need to be encoded numerically before they can be used in machine learning models, while numerical features may require normalization or standardization to ensure consistent scaling across features (see Section 3.10). It is also important not to rely solely on the data types reported by tools like Pandas, as these may sometimes be misleading. For instance, a feature encoded as integers 1, 2, 3 might actually represent ordinal categories (e.g., "Beginner", "Intermediate", "Expert") rather than true numeric values. Understanding the context and meaning of each feature is essential for selecting the correct preprocessing steps.

2. **Descriptive statistics**: These provide insight into the central tendency and variability of the dataset (see Appendix D.3). Using the DataFrame's describe[10] method, we can obtain summary statistics for each feature, including its mean, standard deviation, minimum and maximum values, and quartiles. This statistical overview helps identify potential anomalies and differences in scale across features. Let's apply this method to the Iris dataset:

```
X.describe()
```

The output, shown in Figure 3.5, reveals useful information about the ranges and distributions of the feature values. For example, sepal length varies between 4.3 and 7.9, whereas

---

10. https://pandas.pydata.org/docs/reference/api/pandas.DataFrame.describe.html

	sepal length (cm)	sepal width (cm)	petal length (cm)	petal width (cm)
count	150.000000	150.000000	150.000000	150.000000
mean	5.843333	3.057333	3.758000	1.199333
std	0.828066	0.435866	1.765298	0.762238
min	4.300000	2.000000	1.000000	0.100000
25%	5.100000	2.800000	1.600000	0.300000
50%	5.800000	3.000000	4.350000	1.300000
75%	6.400000	3.300000	5.100000	1.800000
max	7.900000	4.400000	6.900000	2.500000

Figure 3.5: Summary statistics of the Iris dataset, illustrating central tendencies and variability across features.

sepal width ranges from 2.0 to 4.4. This difference in scale suggests the need for feature scaling, especially for algorithms that are sensitive to feature magnitude. Descriptive statistics can also help flag potential outliers; for example, a maximum value far above the 75th percentile may indicate an anomalous observation.

More advanced statistical analysis of the feature distributions may include assessing their degree of asymmetry (skewness) and tail heaviness (kurtosis) using the Pandas methods `skew`[11] and `kurtosis`[12], respectively.

3. **Visualization of distributions**: Plotting feature distributions reveals their shapes and helps identify any outliers or skewness. This is particularly important for algorithms that assume specific distributional properties. For example, Gaussian naive Bayes assumes that the features within each class are normally distributed. Distributions that are skewed or not aligned with the assumptions of the algorithm may need to be transformed to better fit the model requirements (see Section 3.10.5).

We can use the `pairplot`[13] function from Seaborn to visualize the distributions of the Iris features along with their pairwise relationships. We first combine the features and labels into a single DataFrame so that the target label can be included in the plot:[14]

```
df = pd.concat([X, y], axis=1) # Merge the features and label
sns.pairplot(df, hue='target')
```

---

11. `https://pandas.pydata.org/docs/reference/api/pandas.DataFrame.skew.html`
12. `https://pandas.pydata.org/docs/reference/api/pandas.DataFrame.kurtosis.html`
13. `https://seaborn.pydata.org/generated/seaborn.pairplot.html`
14. If you run this code inside a Jupyter notebook, the plot will be displayed automatically. If you run it from a Python script, you must call `plt.show()` explicitly to display the plot.

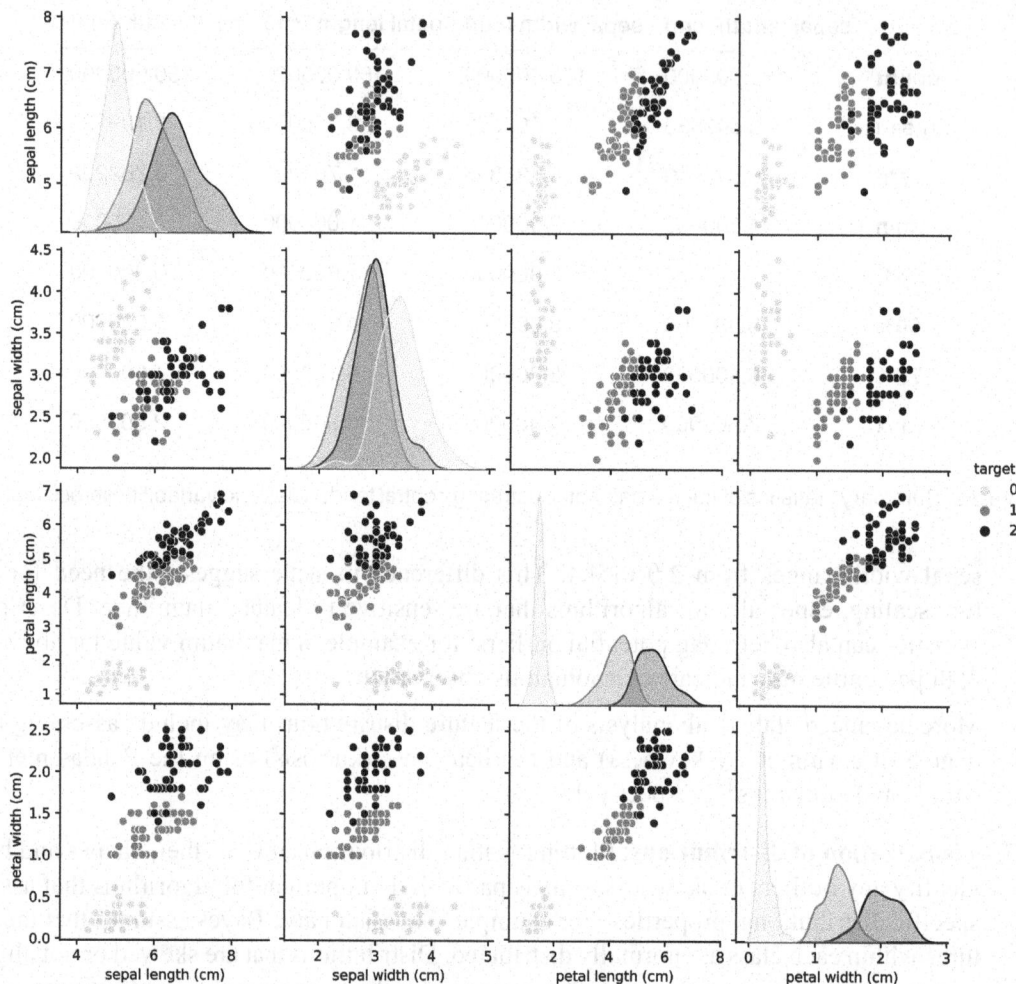

Figure 3.6: Pair plot of the Iris dataset showing feature distributions along the diagonals and pairwise relationships in the off-diagonal scatter plots. Colors indicate the flower species.

Figure 3.6 shows the resulting pair plot, revealing:

- The four features exhibit approximately normal distributions within each class (which is common in many natural datasets).

- Class 0 (Iris setosa) is clearly distinguishable from the other two species.

4. **Correlation analysis**: Investigating the relationships between different features and between features and the target label can provide valuable insights, such as:

  - Features strongly correlated with the target are likely to be good predictors.

- Features that are weakly correlated with the target may be combined or transformed to create more informative ones.

- Strong correlations between features are a common source of multicollinearity (see Section 4.4), which may cause instability in some algorithms and reduce interpretability. Feature selection or dimensionality reduction can help address this by removing redundant features.

To compute correlations, we can use the DataFrame's `corr`[15] method, which returns a matrix of pairwise correlation coefficients between the table's columns. Its `method` parameter specifies the type of correlation to compute: `'pearson'` (the default), `'kendall'`, or `'spearman'` (see Section C.9.7).

Here, we use the **Pearson correlation coefficient**, which measures the strength and direction of the linear relationship between two variables. Its values range from -1 to 1:

- A correlation of $+1$ indicates a perfect positive linear relationship: as one variable increases, the other increases.

- A correlation of -1 indicates a perfect negative linear relationship: as one variable increases, the other decreases.

- A correlation of 0 indicates no linear relationship between the variables, though nonlinear relationships may still exist (which can be captured by other correlation methods).

The following code computes the correlations between the features in the Iris dataset and visualizes them using a heatmap:

```
sns.heatmap(df.corr(), annot=True, cmap='coolwarm')
```

Figure 3.7 shows the resulting heatmap, revealing strong correlations between petal length and petal width, as well as their significant correlation with the target label. Since the Iris dataset contains only four features, we will retain all of them. However, in datasets with many features, it may be beneficial to remove one of the highly correlated features to simplify the model and reduce potential instability caused by multicollinearity.

5. **Class balance check**: In classification tasks, it is essential to check whether the classes are evenly represented in the dataset or whether there is an imbalance. **Class imbalance**, where one or more classes have significantly fewer samples than others, can hinder model training and evaluation by biasing predictions toward the majority class (see Section 5.6).

To check the class distribution in the dataset, we can use the `value_counts` method on the label vector y. This method returns the number of occurrences for each unique class:

---

15. `https://pandas.pydata.org/docs/reference/api/pandas.DataFrame.corr.html`

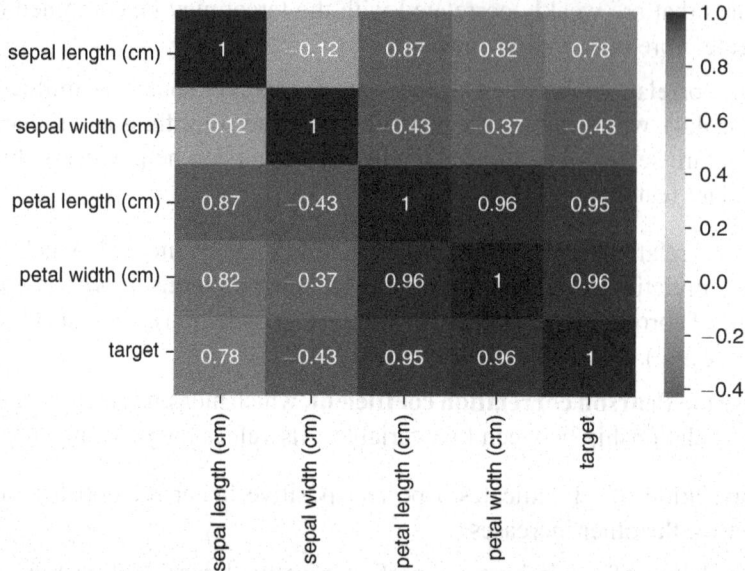

Figure 3.7: Heatmap showing the correlation coefficients between the features in the Iris dataset. Darker shades indicate stronger correlations, with petal length and petal width displaying a particularly strong positive correlation (0.96). The correlation of each feature with the target label (species) is also shown, with petal width having the strongest correlation with the target (0.96).

```
y.value_counts()
```

```
0    50
1    50
2    50
Name: target, dtype: int64
```

In this case, the Iris dataset is perfectly balanced, with each class having exactly 50 samples. Such balance is advantageous for classification tasks, as it ensures that the model is trained on an equal representation of all classes.

3.5.3   Train–Test Split

Before proceeding with any data preprocessing steps, it is crucial to split the dataset into separate training and test sets. Performing this split early ensures that the test set remains completely unseen during model development, providing an unbiased evaluation of the model's performance.[16]

---

16. In general, it is advisable to perform the train–test split even before conducting exploratory data analysis (EDA) to ensure that insights from the test set do not inadvertently influence model development. However, for small datasets, such as Iris, using the entire dataset for EDA may be preferable, as splitting too early may result in unreliable descriptive statistics or visualizations due to limited sample size.

For the train–test split, we can use Scikit-Learn's `train_test_split`[17] helper function:

```
from sklearn.model_selection import train_test_split

X_train, X_test, y_train, y_test = train_test_split(X, y, random_state=42,
                                                    stratify=y)
```

By default, this function splits the dataset into 75% training and 25% test. These proportions can be adjusted using the `train_size` or `test_size` parameters. Both parameters can be specified either as a fraction of the dataset (e.g., `test_size=0.2` for 20% test data) or as an absolute number of samples (e.g., `test_size=50` to allocate exactly 50 samples for testing). If only one parameter is specified, the other is automatically inferred to ensure that the entire dataset is used.

The `random_state` parameter sets the random seed used for shuffling the data before the split, ensuring reproducible results across multiple calls of the function. It is recommended to fix this seed even if a global random seed has already been set in NumPy, as `random_state` guarantees that the data split remains consistent regardless of any changes to the global random state. For example, if additional random operations (e.g., shuffling, random sampling) are performed prior to calling `train_test_split`, using `random_state` ensures that the split remains unaffected by these changes.

In classification problems, especially when working with imbalanced datasets, it is important to maintain the same proportion of classes in both the training and test sets. Setting `stratify=y` in the call to `train_test_split` ensures that the class distribution in the training and test sets mirrors the distribution in the original dataset.

Let's examine the sizes of the training and test sets after the split:

```
X_train.shape, X_test.shape, y_train.shape, y_test.shape
```

```
((112, 4), (38, 4), (112,), (38,))
```

Here, the training set contains 112 samples, and the test set has 38 samples. We can also examine the class distribution after the split:

```
y_train.value_counts()
```

```
0    38
2    37
1    37
Name: target, dtype: int64
```

```
y_test.value_counts()
```

---

17. https://scikit-learn.org/stable/modules/generated/sklearn.model_selection.train_test_split.html

```
1    13
2    13
0    12
Name: target, dtype: int64
```

As shown, the class distribution is preserved across both the training and test sets.

3.5.4   Data Preprocessing

The next step is to clean the training set and prepare it for modeling. Fortunately, the Iris dataset contains only numerical features and has no missing values, so no imputation or type conversions are needed.

Although the Iris features are already on roughly similar scales, it may still be beneficial to standardize them—especially for algorithms that rely on distance metrics or gradient-based optimization—as having standardized variables (with zero mean and unit variance) can improve convergence speed and enhance numerical stability.

To standardize the dataset, we can use the StandardScaler[18] transformer. This transformer scales each feature to have zero mean and unit variance (see Section 3.10.7). We can apply this transformation to the training set as follows:

```
from sklearn.preprocessing import StandardScaler

scaler = StandardScaler()
X_train_scaled = scaler.fit_transform(X_train)
```

Let's inspect the first few entries of the transformed training features:

```
X_train_scaled[:5]
```

The output is:

```
array([[ 1.79213839, -0.60238047,  1.31532306,  0.92095427],
       [ 2.14531053, -0.60238047,  1.65320421,  1.05135487],
       [-0.4446185 , -1.50797259, -0.03620155, -0.25265117],
       [ 0.26172578, -0.60238047,  0.13273902,  0.13855064],
       [-0.4446185 , -1.28157456,  0.13273902,  0.13855064]])
```

As shown, Scikit-Learn transformers typically convert the dataset from a Pandas DataFrame into a NumPy array—the standard format expected by most machine learning models. For a more detailed discussion on data preprocessing techniques, see Section 3.10.

---

18. https://scikit-learn.org/stable/modules/generated/sklearn.preprocessing.StandardScaler.html

3.5.5   Training the Model

The next critical step is selecting an appropriate machine learning algorithm. When uncertain about which model to choose, it is often best to start with a simple, fast-to-train model to establish a baseline. This allows you to quickly obtain initial results and verify that your setup, including the data loading and preprocessing steps, is working properly. A baseline model also serves as a reference point for evaluating the performance of more complex models later. If the simple model already provides satisfactory results, you may choose to retain it rather than introduce unnecessary complexity.

For the Iris dataset, we use logistic regression as our baseline model, since it is simple, efficient to train, supports multi-class classification, and requires minimal hyperparameter tuning. To implement this, we create an instance of the `LogisticRegression`[19] class from `sklearn.linear_model`:

```
from sklearn.linear_model import LogisticRegression

clf = LogisticRegression(random_state=42)
```

Logistic regression usually performs well with its default hyperparameters, so we will use them initially. Additionally, we fix the random seed using the `random_state` parameter to ensure that repeated runs of the model with the same data and parameters produce the same results, making it easier to evaluate and compare the model's performance.

Next, we train the model using the scaled training data:

```
clf.fit(X_train_scaled, y_train)
```

After training, it is often useful to inspect the model's learned parameters. For logistic regression, we can examine the coefficients associated with each feature using the `coef_` attribute:

```
clf.coef_
```

```
array([[-1.049416  ,  1.1534895 , -1.62864463, -1.56781588],
       [ 0.49537647, -0.53075959, -0.26388111, -0.80838681],
       [ 0.55403953, -0.62272991,  1.89252574,  2.37620269]])
```

Each row in this array contains the four learned coefficients (one for each feature) corresponding to a specific Iris class. These coefficients determine the contribution of each feature to the decision boundary for that class, as we discuss further in Chapter 5.

3.5.6   Model Evaluation

To assess the performance of our classifier, we start by evaluating its accuracy on the training set using the `score` method, which returns the proportion of correctly classified samples:

---

19. https://scikit-learn.org/stable/modules/generated/sklearn.linear_model.LogisticRegression.
html

```
train_accuracy = clf.score(X_train_scaled, y_train)
print(f'Train accuracy: {train_accuracy:.4f}')
```

```
Train accuracy: 0.9643
```

An accuracy of 96.43% on the training set is quite strong, though this is a relatively simple classification problem with a small and clean dataset. In addition, accuracy alone does not provide a complete picture of model performance. Additional classification metrics such as precision, recall, and F1 score, which offer deeper insights into model performance, will be discussed in Section 5.5.

Next, we evaluate the model's performance on the test set. Before doing so, we must apply the same preprocessing steps used during training. In this case, that means scaling the test data using the already fitted StandardScaler. Remember to use the transform method, and not fit_transform, so that the scaling is based solely on the statistics learned from the training set:

```
X_test_scaled = scaler.transform(X_test)
```

We can now evaluate the classifier on the test set:

```
test_accuracy = clf.score(X_test_scaled, y_test)
print(f'Test accuracy: {test_accuracy:.4f}')
```

```
Test accuracy: 0.9211
```

The test accuracy is 92.11%, about 4% lower than the training accuracy, but still indicates strong model performance. While this gap might suggest mild overfitting, it is more likely due to sampling variability from the small test set. A more reliable estimate of generalization performance will be obtained in Section 3.7.

3.5.7   Experimenting with Different Classifiers

After evaluating our initial model, it is often beneficial to experiment with alternative classifiers to determine which performs best for the given dataset. Each classifier has its own strengths and weaknesses, and a model that works well for one task may not be as effective for another.

We begin by defining a dictionary of classifiers, where each key is a model name and the value is an instance of the corresponding classifier:

```
from sklearn.neighbors import KNeighborsClassifier
from sklearn.tree import DecisionTreeClassifier
from sklearn.ensemble import RandomForestClassifier
from sklearn.ensemble import GradientBoostingClassifier
from sklearn.svm import SVC
from sklearn.neural_network import MLPClassifier

# Create a dictionary of classifiers
classifiers = {
    'Logistic Regression': LogisticRegression(random_state=42),
```

```
    'KNN': KNeighborsClassifier(),
    'Decision Tree': DecisionTreeClassifier(random_state=42),
    'Random Forest': RandomForestClassifier(random_state=42),
    'Gradient Boosting': GradientBoostingClassifier(random_state=42),
    'SVM': SVC(random_state=42)
    'MLP': MLPClassifier(random_state=42)
}
```

Next, we iterate over the dictionary, fitting each model to the training data and evaluating its performance on both the training and test sets:

```
results = {}

for name, clf in classifiers.items():
    clf.fit(X_train_scaled, y_train)
    results[name] = {}
    results[name]['Training Accuracy'] = clf.score(X_train_scaled, y_train)
    results[name]['Test Accuracy'] = clf.score(X_test_scaled, y_test)
```

Lastly, we convert the `results` dictionary into a DataFrame to make it easier to compare model performance across classifiers:

```
results_df = pd.DataFrame.from_dict(results).T
results_df
```

The DataFrame in Figure 3.8 summarizes the performance of each classifier. By comparing both the training and test accuracies, we can identify models that generalize well and those that may be overfitting. For example, the decision tree classifier achieves a perfect score on the training set (1.0) but only 0.895 on the test set, indicating possible overfitting—a common issue with

	Train Accuracy	Test Accuracy
Logistic Regression	0.964286	0.921053
KNN	0.982143	0.921053
Decision Tree	1.000000	0.894737
Random Forest	1.000000	0.921053
Gradient Boosting	1.000000	0.973684
SVM	0.964286	0.947368
MLP	0.964286	0.868421

Figure 3.8: Comparison of training and test accuracies for various classifiers on the Iris dataset. The Gradient Boosting classifier exhibits the best performance, achieving the highest accuracy on both sets, while the Decision Tree shows signs of overfitting with perfect training accuracy but lower test accuracy.

decision trees that can easily memorize the training data. Conversely, the gradient boosting classifier achieves high accuracy on both sets, indicating a good balance between learning the training patterns and generalizing to unseen data.

It is important to note that all classifiers were used with their default hyperparameters, which may not be optimal for this dataset. Fine-tuning these parameters can lead to significant performance gains. Techniques for hyperparameter tuning are discussed in Section 3.8.

3.5.8 Using the Model for Predictions

Since the gradient boosting classifier achieved the highest test score, we will use it as our final model for making predictions on new, unseen data. In machine learning, the process of applying a trained model to new inputs is known as **inference**.

In Scikit-Learn, predictions are made using the `predict` method of a trained estimator. This method takes a matrix of samples as input and returns a vector with the predicted labels for each sample. For example, let's use the gradient boosting classifier to predict the class of a sample from the test set:

```
clf = classifiers['Gradient Boosting']

test_sample = [X_test_scaled[5]]
y_pred = clf.predict(test_sample)
print(y_pred)
```

```
[1]
```

Note that the `predict` method requires a 2D array as input, even when predicting a single instance. To ensure the test sample is treated as a matrix, we enclose its feature vector in square brackets `[]`. In this case, the model predicts that the sample belongs to class 1 (versicolor). To verify this prediction, we compare it to the true label:

```
true_label = y_test.iloc[5]
print(true_label)
```

```
1
```

The true label matches the predicted class, confirming the model's correct inference for this sample.

3.6 Pipelines

When working with datasets that require multiple preprocessing steps, it is recommended to organize the workflow using a **pipeline**. In Scikit-Learn, a pipeline is created using the `Pipeline`[20] class, which defines a sequence of data transformations ending with an estimator that trains the final machine learning model (see Figure 3.9).

---

20. `https://scikit-learn.org/stable/modules/generated/sklearn.pipeline.Pipeline.html`

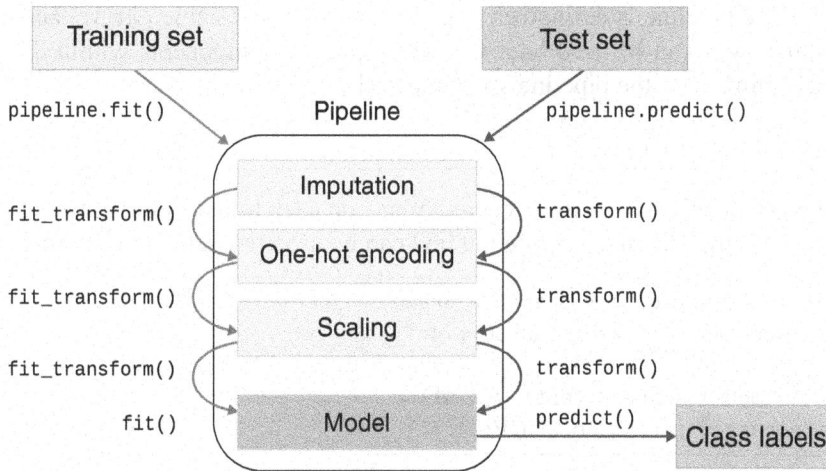

Figure 3.9: A typical pipeline in Scikit-Learn, which encapsulates a sequence of data preprocessing steps followed by a machine learning model. The process begins with the training set undergoing sequential transformations, such as imputation, one-hot encoding, and scaling. After preprocessing, the data is used to train the model. For new, unseen data in the test set, the same transformations are applied without re-fitting, ensuring consistent data handling. The model is then used to make predictions, producing class labels. This systematic approach streamlines the process of model training and testing by ensuring that all data are processed identically.

Using a pipeline offers several benefits:

- The pipeline consolidates all preprocessing steps and the estimator into a single object, making it easier to manage, reuse, and deploy the model.

- It ensures that the correct methods are called automatically at each stage: during training, `fit_transform` is called on each transformer, and during prediction, only `transform` is applied.

- Pipelines integrate seamlessly with tools like cross-validation and grid search, enabling simultaneous tuning of both the preprocessing steps and model hyperparameters in a unified framework (see Section 3.8).

For example, let's define a simple pipeline for the Iris classification task consisting of two steps: feature scaling using `StandardScaler`, followed by classification with `LogisticRegression`:

```
from sklearn.pipeline import Pipeline

model = Pipeline([
    ('scaler', StandardScaler()),
    ('clf', LogisticRegression())
])
```

Each step in the pipeline is defined as a tuple consisting of a name (string) and an estimator. The names of the steps can be used later to access specific components within the pipeline. To train the model, simply call the pipeline's `fit` method:

```
model.fit(X_train, y_train)
```

This method sequentially calls `fit_transform()` on each transformer and `fit()` on the final estimator. Likewise, the pipeline's `score` method can be used to evaluate the model:

```
train_accuracy = model.score(X_train, y_train)
print(f'Train accuracy: {train_accuracy:.4f}')

test_accuracy = model.score(X_test, y_test)
print(f'Test accuracy: {test_accuracy:.4f}')
```

```
Train accuracy: 0.9643
Test accuracy: 0.9211
```

As expected, these results are consistent with those obtained earlier.

To make predictions on new samples, we use the pipeline's `predict` method. This automatically applies all required transformations using each transformer's `transform` method, followed by the final estimator's `predict` method:

```
y_pred = model.predict([X_test.iloc[5]])
print(y_pred)
```

```
[1]
```

Individual steps within the pipeline can be accessed either by their index using the `steps` attribute or by their name using the `named_steps` attribute. For example, to access the logistic regression estimator (which is the second step in our pipeline), either approach can be used:

```
# Accessing by index
model.steps[1]
```

```
('clf', LogisticRegression())
```

```
# Accessing by name
model.named_steps['clf']
```

```
LogisticRegression()
```

To modify the parameters of a specific step in the pipeline, use the pipeline's `set_params` method. The parameter name must be prefixed with the step name, followed by a double underscore. For example, to change the penalty type of the logistic regression classifier from the default '12' to '11':

```
model.set_params(clf__penalty='l1')
```

Printing the pipeline object displays all parameters that have been modified from their default values:

```
print(model)
```

```
Pipeline(steps=[('scaler', StandardScaler()),
                ('clf', LogisticRegression(penalty='l1'))])
```

In addition to creating pipelines using the `Pipeline` class, Scikit-Learn offers a convenient utility function called `make_pipeline`[21]. This function simplifies the pipeline creation by automatically assigning names to each step based on the types of the estimators. For example:

```
from sklearn.pipeline import make_pipeline
```

```
model = make_pipeline(StandardScaler(), LogisticRegression())
model
```

```
Pipeline(steps=[('standardscaler', StandardScaler()),
                ('logisticregression', LogisticRegression())])
```

3.7 Cross-Validation

Splitting a dataset into fixed training and test sets can be problematic, especially when the test set is small. For example, in Section 3.5.6, we evaluated our logistic regression model on a test set with only 12 or 13 samples per Iris species. Such small test sets introduce statistical uncertainty in performance estimates, making it difficult to draw confident conclusions about whether one algorithm outperforms another.

Moreover, repeatedly using the test set for model evaluation and tuning can lead to overfitting to the test data. This issue, where the test data influences the model development process, is a form of **data leakage** that undermines the test set's ability to provide an unbiased evaluation of the model's generalization performance.

Cross-validation (CV) is a widely used technique that addresses these concerns by providing more reliable performance estimates while using all the available data for both training and validation [563, 79].

The most common form of cross-validation is **_k_-fold cross-validation**, in which the training set is divided into k equal-sized subsets (folds). At iteration i ($1 \leq i \leq k$), the i-th subset is used as the validation set, while the remaining $k-1$ subsets are used for training. This process is repeated k times, so that each subset is used as the validation set exactly once. The k evaluation results are then averaged to produce a single estimate of the model's performance. The procedure is summarized in Algorithm 3.1 and illustrated in Figure 3.10.

---

21. https://scikit-learn.org/stable/modules/generated/sklearn.pipeline.make_pipeline.html

---

Algorithm 3.1 K-Fold Cross-Validation

Input:

D: a dataset of samples

A: a learning algorithm that maps a dataset to a learned model

S: a scoring function that maps a model and dataset to a scalar score

k: the number of folds

1: Split D into k equal-sized subsets $D_1, D_2, \ldots, D_k$

2: Initialize an empty list *scores*

3: **for** $i = 1$ **to** k **do**

4:      $D_{\text{train}} \leftarrow D \setminus D_i$ ▷ Use all data except D_i for training

5:      $D_{\text{val}} \leftarrow D_i$ ▷ Use D_i for validation

6:      Train the model: $h \leftarrow A(D_{\text{train}})$

7:      Evaluate the model: $s \leftarrow S(h, D_{\text{val}})$

8:      Append s to *scores*

9: **return** *scores*

All Data				
Training Set				Test set

Split 1	Fold 1	Fold 2	Fold 3	Fold 4	Fold 5
Split 2	Fold 1	Fold 2	Fold 3	Fold 4	Fold 5
Split 3	Fold 1	Fold 2	Fold 3	Fold 4	Fold 5
Split 4	Fold 1	Fold 2	Fold 3	Fold 4	Fold 5
Split 5	Fold 1	Fold 2	Fold 3	Fold 4	Fold 5

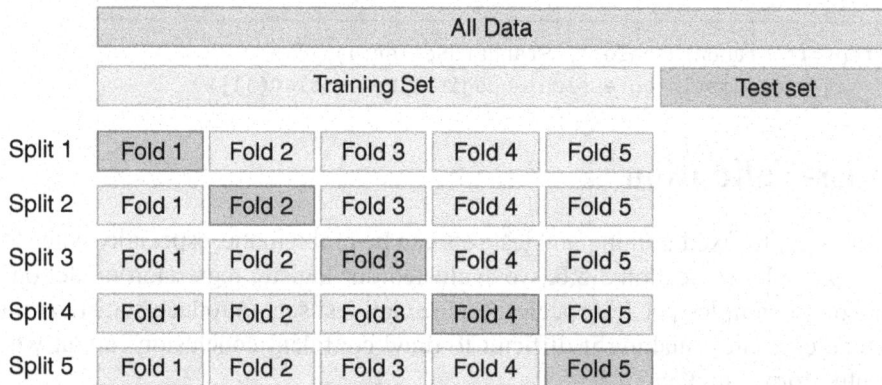

Figure 3.10: Illustration of 5-fold cross-validation process. Each row represents a different split of the dataset into five folds. Light blue folds are used for training, and the light green fold is held out as the validation set in each split.

In the special case of $k = n$, where n is the number of samples in the dataset, this method is known as **Leave-One-Out Cross-Validation (LOOCV)**. In LOOCV, each iteration uses a single sample for validation and the remaining $n - 1$ samples for training. LOOCV is particularly useful when dealing with very small datasets, as it allows nearly all data to be used for training. However, it can be computationally expensive, since the model needs to be trained n times. In addition, the evaluation scores can have high variance, as each score is based on a single observation.

In Scikit-Learn, cross-validation can be performed using the function `cross_val_score`[22]. Its cv argument determines the cross-validation splitting strategy and can take one of the following values:

- `None` (the default): Uses 5-fold cross-validation.

- An integer: Specifies the number of folds.

- An iterable yielding (train, test) splits as arrays of indices.

- A custom splitter object: Provides finer control over the splitting strategy.

The choice of splitting strategy also depends on the type of estimator:

- Classifiers: If cv is an integer or `None`, `StratifiedKFold`[23] is used by default. This ensures that each fold preserves the class distribution of the original dataset.

- Regressors and other estimators: If cv is an integer or `None`, `KFold`[24] is used. This simply divides the dataset into k equal-sized consecutive folds.

In both cases, unless the `shuffle` parameter is explicitly set to `True`, the dataset is not shuffled before splitting, ensuring that the splits remain consistent across multiple calls to `cross_val_score`.

For example, let's use cross-validation to evaluate our logistic regression classifier on the Iris dataset:

```
from sklearn.model_selection import cross_val_score

scores = cross_val_score(model, X_train, y_train, cv=5)
print('CV scores:', np.round(scores, 4))
print(f'Average score: {scores.mean():.4f} ± {scores.std():.4f}')
```

```
CV scores: [1.      0.9565 0.9545 1.      0.9091]
Average score: 0.9640 ± 0.0339
```

As mentioned in Section 3.5.6, the logistic regression model achieved 92.11% accuracy on a test set of 38 samples. In contrast, the average cross-validation score—computed over five folds of the 112-sample training set—is 96.4%. While this score offers a more robust estimate of the model's performance than a single test split, the relatively high standard deviation (3.39%) indicates variability across folds.

By default, `cross_val_score` uses the estimator's `score` method to evaluate the model. This behavior can be modified by passing either a custom scoring function or the name of a predefined scoring function. Scikit-Learn provides a wide range of built-in evaluation metrics in the

---

22. https://scikit-learn.org/stable/modules/generated/sklearn.model_selection.cross_val_score.
    html
23. https://scikit-learn.org/stable/modules/generated/sklearn.model_selection.StratifiedKFold.
    html
24. https://scikit-learn.org/stable/modules/generated/sklearn.model_selection.KFold.html

`sklearn.metrics`[25] module. For example, to use F1 score instead of the default accuracy, we can modify the call to `cross_val_score` as follows:

```
scores = cross_val_score(model, X_train, y_train, cv=5, scoring='f1_macro')
print('CV scores:', np.round(scores, 4))
print(f'Average score: {scores.mean():.4f} ± {scores.std():.4f}')
```

```
CV scores: [1.      0.9556 0.9556 1.      0.9048]
Average score: 0.9632 ± 0.0353
```

In the Iris dataset, which has a balanced distribution of classes, metrics such as accuracy and F1 score typically produce similar values (see Section 5.5 for details).

3.8   Hyperparameter Tuning

Hyperparameters are settings that control various aspects of the learning process, including the model architecture, its capacity, and the optimization technique. Fine-tuning these settings can help achieve a better balance between underfitting and overfitting, leading to improved generalization performance as well as increased training efficiency and faster convergence.

Hyperparameter tuning (also known as **hyperparameter optimization** or **HPO**) refers to the process of searching for the combination of hyperparameter values that yields the best generalization performance [43, 654]. This tuning process can be manual, automated, or a combination of both.

Manual tuning involves adjusting the hyperparameters based on intuition, experience, or educated guesses. In practice, only a small subset of hyperparameters tends to have a significant impact on the model's performance, while others can often remain at their default values. As you deepen your understanding of each learning algorithm in the following chapters and gain practical experience with diverse datasets, your intuition for identifying the most critical hyperparameters will improve. However, manual tuning can be time-consuming and labor-intensive, often requiring multiple iterations and evaluations.

To address these challenges, **automated tuning** methods use algorithms to systematically explore the hyperparameter space, reducing reliance on human intuition. The main techniques for automated hyperparameter tuning include:

- **Grid search**: An exhaustive search over a predefined set of hyperparameter values (see Section 3.8.1).

- **Random search**: Randomly samples the hyperparameter space a specified number of times (see Section 3.8.2).

- **Bayesian optimization**: A probabilistic model-based strategy that balances exploration and exploitation to efficiently search complex spaces (see Section 3.8.3).

---

25. `https://scikit-learn.org/stable/modules/model_evaluation.html`

Hyperparameter optimization differs from the typical optimization of a model's internal parameters (e.g., the weights learned during training) in several ways:

- Hyperparameters are often discrete or categorical variables, which cannot be optimized using gradient-based methods such as gradient descent. Instead, they require discrete or heuristic search methods, which are generally less efficient.

- Evaluating each combination of hyperparameters requires training a new model from scratch, making this process computationally expensive.

- The results from different hyperparameter settings can be noisy or inconsistent, making it difficult to determine whether improvements are due to better hyperparameters or other factors such as random initialization or data splits.

Overall, hyperparameter tuning is both an art and a science. Automated methods can save time and systematically explore large hyperparameter spaces, but they are often computationally intensive, especially when applied to complex models or large datasets. Manual tuning remains valuable for narrowing the search space and focusing automated methods on promising regions. As a result, practitioners often adopt a hybrid approach, using their intuition and experience to guide automated searches toward the most impactful hyperparameters and their effective ranges.

3.8.1   Grid Search

Grid search is a common approach to hyperparameter tuning that exhaustively evaluates all possible combinations of specified hyperparameter values. It consists of the following steps:

1. Define a set of candidate values for each hyperparameter.

2. Create a grid of all possible combinations of these values.

3. Train a separate model on each combination and evaluate its performance using cross-validation.

4. Select the combination that yields the best cross-validation score.

5. Train a final model on the entire training set using the selected hyperparameters.

In Scikit-Learn, this process is implemented via the `GridSearchCV`[26] class from the `model_selection` module. Its key parameters are listed in Table 3.1 (the first two are mandatory).

`GridSearchCV` implements the standard estimator API, including the `fit`, `predict`, and `score` methods:

- `fit` initiates the grid search process and fits the estimator on the training data using all combinations of parameters.

- `predict` uses the best estimator to generate predictions.

- `score` returns the evaluation score of the best estimator on a given dataset.

---

26. https://scikit-learn.org/stable/modules/generated/sklearn.model_selection.GridSearchCV.html

Parameter	Description	Default
`estimator`	The estimator to be tuned.	-
`param_grid`	A dictionary whose keys are the parameter names and values are lists of settings to try.	-
`scoring`	A scoring function used to evaluate the model. The default value `None` means that the `score` method of the estimator will be used.	`None`
`n_jobs`	Number of jobs (threads) to run in parallel for the grid search. If set to `-1`, then all CPUs are used. The default value `None` means that only one CPU is used.	`None`
`refit`	Whether to refit the estimator using the best-found parameters on the entire dataset.	`True`
`cv`	The cross-validation splitting strategy. The default value `None` uses 5-fold cross-validation.	`True`
`verbose`	The verbosity of log messages during the search. Values greater than 0 enable progress messages.	`0`

Table 3.1: Key parameters of `GridSearchCV`

For example, let's tune the hyperparameters of the decision tree classifier on the Iris dataset, since it showed signs of overfitting the training set. Decision tree classifiers have a relatively large number of hyperparameters, as detailed in Chapter 8. However, in practice, it is often unnecessary to tune all of them, since only a few typically have a significant impact on the performance of the model. In our example, we will tune the following hyperparameters:

- `criterion`: The function used to evaluate how good a split in the tree is.

- `max_depth`: The maximum allowed depth of the tree. Limiting the depth can help reduce overfitting.

- `min_samples_leaf`: The minimum number of samples required to form a leaf node. Increasing this value can lead to simpler trees.

First, we import the estimator's class and `GridSearchCV`:

```
from sklearn.tree import DecisionTreeClassifier
from sklearn.model_selection import GridSearchCV
```

Next, we define a grid of values to explore for each hyperparameter:

```
param_grid = {
    'criterion': ['gini', 'entropy'],
    'max_depth': np.arange(1, 11),
    'min_samples_leaf': np.arange(1, 11)
}
```

The `GridSearchCV` object is initialized with the estimator and the parameter grid, along with optional arguments such as `cv` for specifying the number of cross-validation folds:

```
clf = DecisionTreeClassifier(random_state=42)
grid_search = GridSearchCV(clf, param_grid, cv=3, n_jobs=-1)
```

Next, we fit the grid search model to the training data:

```
grid_search.fit(X_train, y_train)
```

After fitting, we can inspect the best hyperparameter combination and the corresponding cross-validation score:

```
grid_search.best_params_
```

```
{'criterion': 'gini', 'max_depth': 2, 'min_samples_leaf': 1}
```

```
print(f'Best score: {grid_search.best_score_:.4f}')
```

```
Best score: 0.9374
```

We can also evaluate the model with the best-found parameters on the test set using the `score` method:

```
test_accuracy = grid_search.score(X_test, y_test)
print(f'Test accuracy: {test_accuracy:.4f}')
```

```
Test accuracy: 0.9211
```

By tuning the model's hyperparameters, we improved its test accuracy from 89.47% to 92.11%. This demonstrates the effectiveness of hyperparameter tuning in enhancing generalization performance.

To obtain a full report on the grid search, we can use its `cv_results_` attribute, which provides detailed information about the performance of each parameter combination tested during the search. This attribute returns a dictionary that includes the hyperparameters for each grid point, the average cross-validation score and standard deviation, and the time taken to fit each model. We can convert this dictionary into a Pandas DataFrame for easier inspection, as follows:

```
df = pd.DataFrame(grid_search.cv_results_)
df = df[['params', 'mean_test_score', 'std_test_score']]
df
```

Figure 3.11 shows the first few rows of the resulting DataFrame. In this example, grid search evaluated a total of $2 \times 10 \times 10 = 200$ hyperparameter combinations (2 options for the `crtierion` parameter and 10 each for `max_depth` and `min_samples_leaf`). Since `cv=3`, each combination was evaluated across 3 folds, resulting in a total of 600 model training iterations.

	params	mean_test_score	std_test_score
0	{'criterion':'gini','max_depth':1,'min_samples_leaf':1}	0.660740	0.011216
1	{'criterion':'gini','max_depth':1,'min_samples_leaf':2}	0.660740	0.011216
2	{'criterion':'gini','max_depth':1,'min_samples_leaf':3}	0.660740	0.011216
3	{'criterion':'gini','max_depth':1,'min_samples_leaf':4}	0.660740	0.011216
4	{'criterion':'gini','max_depth':1,'min_samples_leaf':5}	0.660740	0.011216
...	...	...	...
195	{'criterion':'entropy','max_depth':10,'min_samples_leaf':6}	0.937411	0.013089
196	{'criterion':'entropy','max_depth':10,'min_samples_leaf':7}	0.937411	0.013089
197	{'criterion':'entropy','max_depth':10,'min_samples_leaf':8}	0.937411	0.013089
198	{'criterion':'entropy','max_depth':10,'min_samples_leaf':9}	0.937411	0.013089
199	{'criterion':'entropy','max_depth':10,'min_samples_leaf':10}	0.937411	0.013089

Figure 3.11: The first rows of the grid search results

Overall, grid search is a simple and intuitive method for hyperparameter optimization. Its main drawback is the high computational cost, as the number of combinations grows exponentially with the number of hyperparameter values, requiring numerous models to be trained and evaluated.

3.8.2   Random Search

Random search offers a more efficient approach to hyperparameter tuning, especially when the parameter space is large or computational resources are limited [44]. Unlike grid search, which exhaustively tries all possible combinations, random search selects combinations of hyperparameters at random from a specified distribution. The process consists of the following steps:

1. Define a parameter space by specifying ranges or probability distributions for each hyperparameter.

2. Randomly sample combinations of hyperparameters from this space.

3. Train and evaluate a model for each sampled combination.

4. Select the combination that yields the best performance based on the cross-validation score.

5. Train a final model on the full training set using the selected hyperparameters.

Scikit-Learn implements random search through the `RandomizedSearchCV`[27] class, which has a similar interface to `GridSearchCV`. However, its constructor introduces several parameters to support random sampling:

---

27. https://scikit-learn.org/stable/modules/generated/sklearn.model_selection.
RandomizedSearchCV.html

- param_distributions: This parameter serves the same purpose as param_grid in GridSearchCV, but supports random sampling instead of exhaustive search. It is a dictionary where the keys are parameter names and the values specify how to sample each parameter. The values can be either a list or a NumPy array of discrete options (sampled uniformly), or a distribution object from scipy.stats[28] for sampling continuous values.

- n_iter: The number of hyperparameter combinations to sample. This controls the tradeoff between computational cost and the likelihood of finding a good configuration.

- random_state: An integer seed that ensures reproducibility of the random sampling.

Here is a simple example of how to use RandomizedSearchCV to tune the hyperparameters of a DecisionTreeClassifier on the Iris dataset:

```
from sklearn.model_selection import RandomizedSearchCV

# Define the parameter space
param_dist = {
    'criterion': ['gini', 'entropy'],
    'max_depth': np.arange(1, 11),
    'min_samples_leaf': np.arange(1, 11)
}

# Create a RandomizedSearchCV instance
clf = DecisionTreeClassifier(random_state=42)
random_search = RandomizedSearchCV(clf, param_dist, n_iter=20, cv=3,
                                   random_state=42, n_jobs=-1)

# Fit to the training data
random_search.fit(X_train, y_train)
```

The best parameters found by the search are:

```
random_search.best_params_
```

```
{'min_samples_leaf': 6, 'max_depth': 10, 'criterion': 'gini'}
```

The accuracy of the best model on the test set is:

```
test_accuracy = random_search.score(X_test, y_test)
print(f'Test accuracy: {test_accuracy:.4f}')
```

```
Test accuracy: 0.9211
```

Despite evaluating only 20 random combinations (compared to the 200 tested by grid search), random search achieved comparable performance on the test set. Similar to GridSearchCV, the results of all the search iterations can be accessed via the cv_results_ attribute.

28. https://docs.scipy.org/doc/scipy/reference/stats.html

3.8.3   (*) Bayesian Optimization

Bayesian optimization [429, 216] is a powerful method for optimizing black-box functions—functions that lack a closed-form expression and are expensive to evaluate—such as the generalization performance of a machine learning model. In the context of hyperparameter tuning, it builds a probabilistic model of the objective function and uses it to iteratively select promising hyperparameter configurations based on past evaluations.

The main steps of the process are:

1. **Define the objective function**: This function evaluates the performance of the machine learning model and serves as the target for optimization (e.g., it can be the cross-validation score). It is typically expensive to compute, as it requires training and validating the model for a given hyperparameter configuration.

2. **Choose a surrogate model**: The surrogate model is a probabilistic approximation of the true objective function, constructed from the results of previously evaluated hyperparameter configurations. It predicts the expected performance at new points in the hyperparameter space and also quantifies the uncertainty of these predictions. This allows the optimization process to estimate the potential benefit of evaluating unexplored configurations without retraining the model each time.

3. **Select an acquisition function**: The acquisition function defines a utility over the hyperparameter space, indicating how promising each point is based on the surrogate model's predictions and associated uncertainty. It balances **exploration**, which favors regions with high uncertainty, and **exploitation**, favoring regions known to perform well. This exploration-exploitation tradeoff is a key concept in reinforcement learning as well, and will be discussed in more depth in Volume III of this book.

4. **Iteratively updating the model**: At each iteration, the acquisition function is maximized to select the next hyperparameter configuration to evaluate. The objective function is then computed for this configuration, and the resulting performance is used to update the surrogate model. Through successive iterations, this process refines the model's approximation of the objective function and, gradually converging toward an optimal set of hyperparameters while minimizing the number of costly evaluations.

A complete coverage of Bayesian optimization is beyond the scope of this book. For more detailed and rigorous introduction, see the recent book *Bayesian optimization* by Roman Garnett [216].

While Scikit-Learn does not support Bayesian optimization, several open-source libraries provide efficient implementations, such as `scikit-optimize`[29] and Optuna[30]. For example, `scikit-optimize` offers a user-friendly interface that is compatible with Scikit-Learn's API. You can easily install it using `pip`:

```
pip install scikit-optimize
```

---

29. `https://scikit-optimize.github.io/stable`
30. `https://optuna.org`

This library provides the `BayesSearchCV`[31] class, which functions similarly to `GridSearchCV` and has similar parameters, but employs Bayesian optimization to search the hyperparameter space more efficiently. Below is an example of hyperparameter tuning using `scikit-optimize`:

```python
from skopt import BayesSearchCV
from skopt.space import Categorical, Integer

# Define the search space for hyperparameters
search_space = {
    'criterion': Categorical(['gini', 'entropy']),
    'max_depth': Integer(1, 11),
    'min_samples_leaf': Integer(1, 11)
}

# Create a BayesSearchCV instance
clf = DecisionTreeClassifier(random_state=42)
bayes_search = BayesSearchCV(clf, search_space, n_iter=20, cv=3,
                             random_state=42, n_jobs=-1)

# Perform the Bayesian optimization search
bayes_search.fit(X_train, y_train)
```

The best parameters found by the search are:

```python
bayes_search.best_params_
```

```python
OrderedDict([('criterion', 'entropy'),
             ('max_depth', 8),
             ('min_samples_leaf', 10)])
```

And the accuracy of the best model on the test set is:

```python
test_accuracy = bayes_search.score(X_test, y_test)
print(f'Test accuracy: {test_accuracy:.4f}')
```

```
Test accuracy: 0.9211
```

Compared to grid and random search, Bayesian optimization is more **sample-efficient**, often achieving good results with fewer evaluations of the objective function. However, it is conceptually more complex and its effectiveness heavily depends on the choice of surrogate model and acquisition function.

3.9 Data Preparation

Data preparation is the process of transforming raw data into a structured and clean format suitable for building machine learning models. It aims to improve the quality, integrity, and usability of the data, and address common issues such as missing values, noise, outliers, and incompatible formats.

---

31. https://scikit-optimize.github.io/stable/modules/generated/skopt.BayesSearchCV.html

The well-known phrase "Garbage in, garbage out" captures a central truth in machine learning: the performance of a model is strongly tied to the quality of the data it is trained on. Cleaner, more informative data allows the model to better capture the underlying structure of the problem and generalize effectively to unseen examples.

Data preparation is often the most time-consuming step in the machine learning workflow, as it requires substantial manual effort to collect data from diverse sources, clean and integrate it, and transform it into a usable format.

The data preparation process typically involves the following activities (not necessarily in this order):

1. **Data Preprocessing**: This is usually the first step in data preparation, aimed at cleaning and organizing the data for effective analysis. Data preprocessing techniques are discussed in Section 3.10.

2. **Feature Selection**: Select the most relevant features for model construction while removing irrelevant or redundant ones. Feature selection methods are discussed in the second volume of the book, as they are closely related to dimensionality reduction.

3. **Feature Extraction**: Transform raw input data into a more informative set of features that can represent the data more effectively. For example, in text analysis, using the raw text is often not suitable for machine learning algorithms. Instead, the text is typically converted into numerical representations such as bag-of-words or TF-IDF vectors (see Section 7.6.3).

4. **Feature Engineering**: Use domain knowledge to construct new features or combine existing ones to enhance the predictive power of the model. For example, in a healthcare application, basic features such as weight and height may be combined to derive a more informative attribute like Body Mass Index (BMI). Feature engineering is discussed in Section 4.6.4.

5. **Data Sampling**: Select a representative subset of the dataset, often to address class imbalance or reduce computational cost (see Section 5.6).

6. **Data Augmentation**: Increase the size and diversity of the dataset by generating new examples through transformations. For example, in image processing, this may involve rotations, scaling, or color adjustments to create varied versions of existing images. This technique helps improve model robustness and prevent overfitting by simulating a wider range of potential input scenarios.

Additional data preparation tasks may include **data integration** (combining datasets from different sources to create a unified view), **data anonymization** (masking or removing personally identifiable information to protect user privacy), and **data governance and compliance** (ensuring that the dataset complies with legal and ethical standards).

The main modules in Scikit-Learn that support data preparation tasks are:

- `sklearn.preprocessing`[32] provides transformers for common preprocessing tasks including scaling, normalization, encoding categorical features, and discretization.

- `sklearn.impute`[33] contains tools for handling missing values through various imputation techniques.

- `sklearn.feature_extraction`[34] handles extracting features from unstructured data such as text and image data.

- `sklearn.feature_selection`[35] provides a variety of algorithms and statistical methods for feature selection.

3.10   Data Preprocessing

Data preprocessing is the process of cleaning, transforming, and organizing a dataset to make it suitable for analysis and modeling. The main tasks involved in data preprocessing are:

1. Data cleaning (Section 3.10.1)

2. Handling missing data (Section 3.10.2)

3. Encoding categorical data (Section 3.10.3)

4. Detecting and handling outliers (Section 3.10.4)

5. Handling skewed data (Section 3.10.5)

6. Discretization (Section 3.10.6)

7. Scaling and normalization (Section 3.10.7)

The exact sequence of preprocessing steps can vary depending on the characteristics of the dataset and the chosen modeling approach. Some steps may depend on the completion of others. For example, normalization is typically conducted after addressing issues such as missing values and outliers. Moreover, data preprocessing is often an iterative process; for example, detecting outliers may lead back to data cleaning in order to correct or remove these anomalies.

Importantly, in supervised learning, preprocessing should typically be applied only to the input features and not to the target labels, as modifying the labels can adversely affect the model's predictions on new samples.

Additionally, certain data types such as text, images, or time-series data require specialized preprocessing techniques. These include, for example, tokenization for text, rescaling for images, and windowing or interpolation for time-series data.

---

32. https://scikit-learn.org/stable/modules/preprocessing.html
33. https://scikit-learn.org/stable/modules/impute.html
34. https://scikit-learn.org/stable/modules/feature_extraction.html
35. https://scikit-learn.org/stable/modules/feature_selection.html

3.10.1   Data Cleaning

Data cleaning (or data cleansing) involves correcting or removing incorrect, inaccurate, inconsistent, irrelevant, or duplicate data from a dataset. These issues can arise from various sources, such as:

- Data entry errors (e.g., an invalid postal code, typographical errors).

- Out-of-range values (e.g., a negative product price).

- Corruption during transmission or storage of the data.

- Integration of inconsistent or conflicting data from different sources (e.g., the same customer recorded in two systems with different addresses).

- Inconsistent formatting for dates, phone numbers, names of states, etc.

- Mixed units of measurement (e.g., using both centimeters and feet to measure length).

- Inclusion of features irrelevant to the analysis, such as user ID or timestamps.

Data cleaning is typically carried out using a combination of manual inspection and automated tools. It often requires domain expertise to correctly identify and resolve the issues, especially when the inconsistencies are subtle or context-dependent.

3.10.2   Handling Missing Values

Missing data is one of the most common issues in real-world datasets. It can arise from various factors, such as null values in databases or optional fields in forms that users chose not to complete. In Python, missing values are typically represented as None or np.nan (short for Not a Number).

Since most machine learning algorithms cannot deal with missing values directly, addressing them is a critical step in the data preprocessing pipeline. Common strategies for handling missing data include:

- **Removing samples or features with missing values**: Removing samples is appropriate when only a small fraction of them contain missing values, thus minimizing the risk of losing valuable information. In contrast, features with a large proportion of missing values (e.g., more than 50%) may be discarded as they are unlikely to contribute meaningful predictive power.

- **Imputing missing values**: This involves replacing missing entries with simple summary statistics, such as the mean, median, or mode of the corresponding feature. Imputation enables the use of all available data while minimizing distortion to the overall feature distribution.

- **Predictive imputation**: More advanced techniques involve training machine learning models to predict the missing values based on the other features in the dataset. While this method often results in more accurate imputations, it adds complexity and computational overhead to the preprocessing pipeline.

Scikit-Learn provides several imputers for handling missing values:

- SimpleImputer[36] replaces missing values using simple features statistics (mean, median, most frequent) or a constant value. Its key parameters are:

  - strategy: The statistic used for imputation. The options are 'mean' (default), 'median', 'most_frequent', and 'constant'. For categorical features, only the options 'most_frequent' and 'constant' are supported.

  - fill_value: The constant used to replace missing values when the strategy is 'constant'.

  - missing_values: Defines what is considered a missing value (defaults to np.nan).

Example usage:

```
from sklearn.impute import SimpleImputer

imputer = SimpleImputer(strategy='mean')
X = [[np.nan, 5, np.nan], [2, 4, 10], [3, None, 5]]
imputer.fit_transform(X)
```

Output:
```
array([[ 2.5,  5. ,  7.5],
       [ 2. ,  4. , 10. ],
       [ 3. ,  4.5,  5. ]])
```

Note that both np.nan and None values have been imputed with the mean value of their respective column.

- KNNImputer[37] uses the k-nearest neighbors approach, imputing missing values with the mean of the k nearest complete samples. The parameter n_neighbors controls the number of neighbors (defaults to 5).

Example usage:

```
from sklearn.impute import KNNImputer

imputer = KNNImputer(n_neighbors=2)
X = [[1, 2, np.nan], [3, 2, 3], [6, np.nan, 5], [7, 8, 10]]
imputer.fit_transform(X)
```

Output:
```
array([[ 1.,  2.,  4.],
       [ 3.,  2.,  3.],
       [ 6.,  5.,  5.],
       [ 7.,  8., 10.]])
```

---

36. https://scikit-learn.org/stable/modules/generated/sklearn.impute.SimpleImputer.html
37. https://scikit-learn.org/stable/modules/generated/sklearn.impute.KNNImputer.html

- IterativeImputer[38] implements an advanced imputation technique that models each feature with missing values as a function of the other features and uses regression to estimate the missing entries. At the time of this writing, this imputer is still considered experimental, so its API may change in future versions of Scikit-Learn. In addition, you must explicitly enable it by importing enable_iterative_imputer.

Example usage:

```
from sklearn.experimental import enable_iterative_imputer
from sklearn.impute import IterativeImputer

imputer = IterativeImputer()
X = [[1, 2], [2, 4], [4, 8], [np.nan, 3], [5, np.nan]]
imputer.fit_transform(X)
```

Output:
```
array([[ 1.          ,  2.          ],
       [ 2.          ,  4.          ],
       [ 4.          ,  8.          ],
       [ 1.50000846,  3.          ],
       [ 5.          , 10.00000145]])
```

In this example, the imputer has learned that the second feature is twice the first and uses this relationship to fill in the missing values.

3.10.3   Encoding Categorical Data

Most machine learning models require numerical input, so categorical features must be transformed into a suitable numerical format. The main approaches to encoding categorical data are:

- **Ordinal encoding** assigns a unique integer to each category, typically reflecting a meaningful order among the categories. For example, a feature like EducationLevel with categories HighSchool, BA, MA, and PhD might be encoded as 0, 1, 2, and 3, respectively, to reflect increasing levels of education.

For ordinal encoding, Scikit-Learn provides the class OrdinalEncoder[39]. By default, it assigns integers based on the alphabetical order of the categories, but a custom ordering can be specified using the categories parameter. Example usage:

```
from sklearn.preprocessing import OrdinalEncoder

encoder = OrdinalEncoder()
X = [['LowIncome', 'BA'], ['HighIncome', 'PhD'], ['MediumIncome', 'BA']]
encoder.fit_transform(X)
```

---

38. https://scikit-learn.org/stable/modules/generated/sklearn.impute.IterativeImputer.html
39. https://scikit-learn.org/stable/modules/generated/sklearn.preprocessing.OrdinalEncoder.html

Output:
```
array([[1., 0.],
       [0., 1.],
       [2., 0.]])
```

Advantages of ordinal encoding:

  – Preserves the ordinal relationship between categories, when it exists.

  – Does not increase the dataset's dimensionality.

Disadvantages:

  – May introduce a misleading sense of order when applied to nominal categories.

  – The magnitude of the assigned integers can disproportionately influence the model's predictions—for example, a value of 2 may be treated as being twice as important as a value of 1.

• **One-hot encoding** converts a categorical feature into a set of binary features, each representing a single category (see Figure 3.12). For example, one-hot encoding a `Color` variable with categories `Red`, `Green`, and `Blue` creates three new binary features, each representing one of these colors. A sample with the value `Green` would be encoded as [0, 1, 0], where the 1 indicates membership in the green category and the 0s indicate absence from the others.

For one-hot encoding, Scikit-Learn provides the class `OneHotEncoder`[40]. Example usage:

```
from sklearn.preprocessing import OneHotEncoder

encoder = OneHotEncoder()

X = [['LowIncome', 'BA'], ['HighIncome', 'PhD'], ['MediumIncome', 'BA']]
encoder.fit_transform(X).toarray()
```

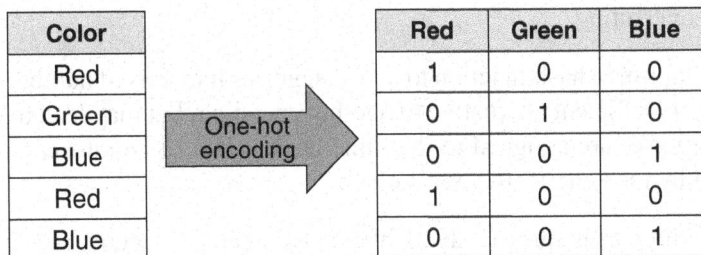

Color
Red
Green
Blue
Red
Blue

One-hot encoding

Red	Green	Blue
1	0	0
0	1	0
0	0	1
1	0	0
0	0	1

Figure 3.12: One-hot encoding of the `Color` variable. The process converts each category (Red, Green, Blue) into a separate binary feature, indicating presence (1) or absence (0) of that category in the sample.

---

40. https://scikit-learn.org/stable/modules/generated/sklearn.preprocessing.OneHotEncoder.html

Output:

```
array([[0., 1., 0., 1., 0.],
       [1., 0., 0., 0., 1.],
       [0., 0., 1., 1., 0.]])
```

The first three columns in the output correspond to the income levels, and the last two to the education levels. By default, OneHotEncoder returns a **sparse matrix**—an efficient format for storing matrices with many zeros (implemented as a SciPy csr_matrix object). To display this matrix in a readable format, you can convert it to a standard NumPy array using the toarray method. Note that most Scikit-Learn estimators can operate directly on sparse matrices, so converting them to a dense format is unnecessary and may be even inefficient for training.

When using ordinal or one-hot encoding, it is important to account for unseen categories that may appear in test samples but were not present in the training data. By default, both OrdinalEncoder and OneHotEncoder raise an error when encountering unknown categories. To avoid this, you can set the handle_unknown parameter to 'ignore', which encodes unknown categories as a vector of zeros. Ideally, the model should be periodically retrained on updated data that includes the new categories in order to maintain accuracy over time.

Advantages of one-hot encoding:

- Does not impose any ordering on the categories.
- Enables the model to learn independent mappings between each category and the target label.

Disadvantages:

- Can significantly increase the dataset's dimensionality, especially when applied to categorical features with high cardinality. For example, one-hot encoding a variable representing U.S. zip codes would create 41,704 binary features (equal to the number of zip codes in the U.S.). Such an expansion increases computational cost and may lead to overfitting.

• **Hash encoding** uses a hash function to map categories into a fixed number of dimensions. It offers a memory-efficient alternative to one-hot encoding, but may lead to collisions, where different categories are assigned to the same hash value. In Scikit-Learn, this encoding is implemented by the FeatureHasher[41] class.

Additional encoding techniques are available in the category_encoders[42] package, which is part of scikit-learn-contrib, a collection of community-contributed extensions to the Scikit-Learn library.

---

41. https://scikit-learn.org/stable/modules/generated/sklearn.feature_extraction.FeatureHasher.html
42. https://contrib.scikit-learn.org/category_encoders

3.10.4 Detecting and Handling Outliers

Outliers are data points that significantly deviate from the rest of the dataset. They may arise from data entry or measurement errors, but they can also represent genuine, rare observations. Effective detection and handling of outliers is crucial, as they can significantly impact the performance of many machine learning models.

Common methods to detect outliers include:

- **Statistical measures**: These quantify how far a data point deviates from the rest of the distribution. A common example is the **z-score**, which measures how many standard deviations a data point is from the mean:

$$z = \frac{x - \mu}{\sigma}, \tag{3.1}$$

where μ is the mean and σ is the standard deviation of the data. Data points with a large absolute z-score (e.g., greater than 3) are often flagged as potential outliers.

- **Box plot**: A visual tool for identifying outliers based on the data's quartile distribution (see Figure 3.13). The box extends from the first quartile (Q1) to the third quartile (Q3), with a line at the median. The "whiskers" outside the box reach the most extreme data points within 1.5 times the interquartile range (IQR = Q3 - Q1) from the box's edges. Data points that lie above or below these whiskers are typically considered outliers.

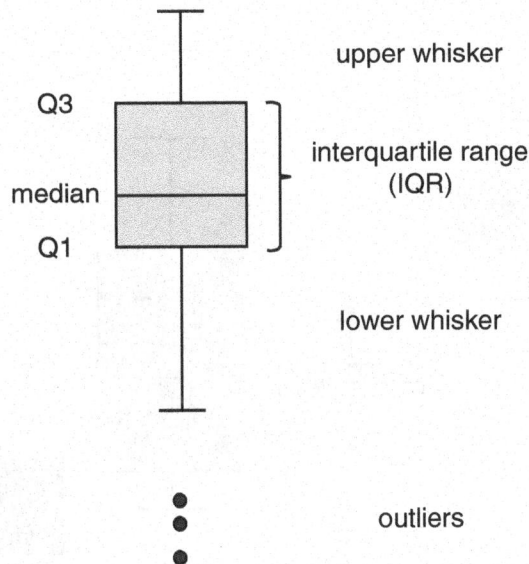

Figure 3.13: A box plot visualizing the distribution of data through its quartiles. The box spans from the first quartile (Q1) to the third quartile (Q3), with a line marking the median. The whiskers extend to the furthest points within 1.5 times the interquartile range (IQR) from the box's edges. Data points beyond this range are considered outliers.

In Python, you can easily generate this plot using the `boxplot`[43] function from the Seaborn library. Here is an example using the Iris dataset:

```
import seaborn as sns
from sklearn.datasets import load_iris

X, y = load_iris(as_frame=True, return_X_y=True)
sns.boxplot(data=X)
```

The resulting figure (Figure 3.14) illustrates the distribution of each feature in the Iris dataset, highlighting several outliers in sepal width. These outliers are likely natural variations within the Iris species, rather than erroneous or anomalous data points, given that this is a well-studied and validated dataset.

- **Anomaly detection algorithms**, such as isolation forest and one-class SVM, which are discussed in Volume II of the book.

Once anomalous outliers are identified, they can be handled in various ways:

- **Removing outliers**: The simplest option, but it should be applied cautiously to avoid discarding valid and potentially informative observations.

- **Imputing outliers**: Treating the outliers as missing values and imputing them using the methods described in Section 3.10.2.

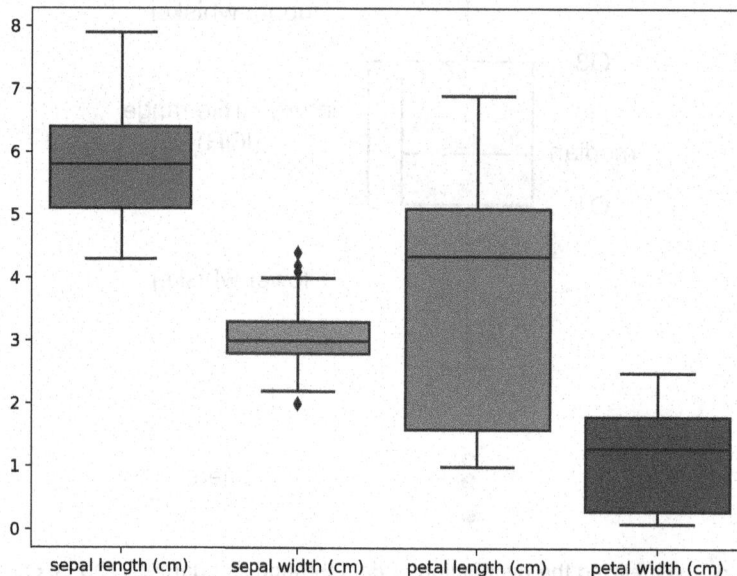

Figure 3.14: Box plots of the features in the Iris dataset

---

43. https://seaborn.pydata.org/generated/seaborn.boxplot.html

- **Capping values**: Defining thresholds for extreme values and replacing values beyond those limits with the threshold itself.

- **Winsorization**: A technique that replaces extreme values with the nearest specified percentile value. For example, a 90% winsorization replaces all values above the 95th percentile with the value at the 95th percentile, and all values below the 5th percentile with the 5th percentile value.

3.10.5   Handling Skewed Data

Skewed data refers to data that is not symmetrically distributed around the mean, typically exhibiting a long tail on one side. Skewness can negatively affect the performance of certain machine learning models, especially those assuming a symmetric or normal distribution of features.

There are several methods to address skewness:

- **Logarithmic transformation** is effective for reducing right skew (positive skew). It compresses larger values more than smaller ones, thereby pulling in the long tail of the distribution.

- **Exponential transformation** applies an exponent to the data, which can help reduce left skew (negative skew) by expanding lower values more than higher ones.

- **Power transformations** involve raising the data to a power selected through maximum likelihood estimation, aiming to make the distribution more symmetric and approximately normal. For power trasformations, Scikit-Learn's `PowerTransformer`[44] class offers two options:

  - **Box–Cox transformation**: Requires all input values to be strictly positive and is defined by:

  $$x' = \begin{cases} \dfrac{x^\lambda - 1}{\lambda} & \text{if } \lambda \neq 0 \\ \ln(x) & \text{if } \lambda = 0 \end{cases} \tag{3.2}$$

  The value of λ is automatically selected to make the data distribution as close to normal as possible.

  - **Yeo–Johnson transformation**: An extension of the Box–Cox method that can handle zero and negative values as well.

  The following example applies the Box–Cox transformation to a dataset drawn from a log-normal distribution in order to make it more Gaussian-like:

---

44. `https://scikit-learn.org/stable/modules/generated/sklearn.preprocessing.PowerTransformer.html`

```
from sklearn.preprocessing import PowerTransformer

# Sample points from a log-normal distribution
x = np.random.RandomState(0).lognormal(size=500)

# Apply a Box-Cox transformation
pt = PowerTransformer('box-cox')
x_new = pt.fit_transform(x.reshape(-1, 1))

# Plot histograms before and after the transformation
plt.figure(figsize=(10, 3.5))
plt.subplot(121)
plt.hist(x, bins=50)
plt.title('Before Transformation')
plt.xlabel('$x$')
plt.ylabel('Frequency')

plt.subplot(122)
plt.hist(x_new, bins=50)
plt.title('After Transformation')
plt.xlabel('$x$')
plt.ylabel('Frequency')
```

The resulting figure (Figure 3.15) shows the distribution of the data before and after the transformation, demonstrating the effectiveness of the Box–Cox method in normalizing skewed distributions.

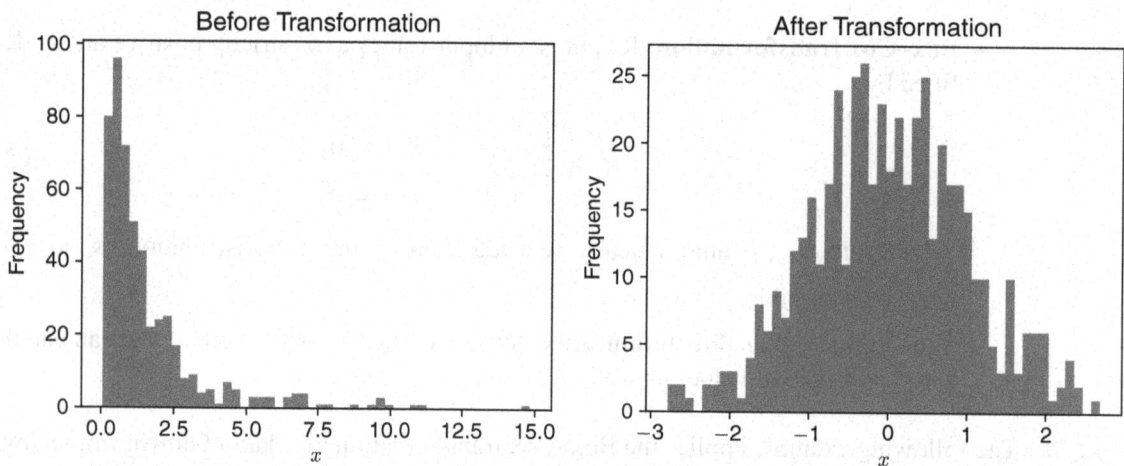

Figure 3.15: Histograms before and after applying a Box–Cox transformation to data drawn from a log-normal distribution. The transformation reduces skewness and makes the distribution more Gaussian-like.

3.10.6   Discretization

Discretization is an operation that converts a continuous-valued feature into a discrete one by dividing its range of values into a set of **intervals** (or **bins**). Formally, it takes a feature whose values lie within the range $[a, b]$ and partitions them into a set of n bins: $[a, x_1], (x_1, x_2], \ldots, (x_n, b]$.

There are two main approaches to discretization:

- **Equal-width binning**: Divides the range $[a, b]$ into bins of equal width. This approach is most effective when the data is approximately uniformly distributed across the range.

- **Equal-frequency (equal-depth) binning**: Creates bins that contain the same number of data points (except possibly the last one). This method is useful for skewed distributions, as it avoids producing bins with very few or no data points.

For example, consider an Age feature with the following values:

$$1, 3, 4, 7, 11, 12, 15, 17, 24, 31, 35, 36, 40, 41, 43, 46, 50, 74, 77, 86.$$

If we discretize it into 5 bins using the two approaches described earlier, the resulting intervals are:

- Equal-width binning: The range $86 - 1 = 85$ is divided by 5, giving bins of width 17. The resulting bins are: $[1, 18], (18, 35], (35, 52], (52, 69], (69, 86]$.

- Equal-frequency binning: With 20 values, each of the 5 bins contains 4 values. The bins are: $[1, 7], (7, 17], (17, 36], (36, 46], (46, 86]$.

Discretization offers several advantages:

- Some machine learning algorithms, such as naive Bayes and association rule learning, cannot directly handle continuous data, making discretization a necessary preprocessing step.

- Discretization can enhance the model expressiveness by enabling the learning of independent mappings between each interval and the target label. This can lead to more accurate predictions as it allows the model to respond differently to distinct ranges within a feature (see example in Section 4.6.5).

- Discretization helps reduce the impact of outliers and extreme values by assigning them to the same bins as typical observations.

On the downside, discretization may lead to information loss and introduce bias, especially if the number of bins is too small or the bin edges are poorly defined.

In Scikit-Learn, the KBinsDiscretizer[45] class is used for discretization. Its key parameters include:

- n_bins: Number of bins to create (default is 5).

---

45. https://scikit-learn.org/stable/modules/generated/sklearn.preprocessing.KBinsDiscretizer.html

- encode: Specifies how to represent the discretized result. The options are:

  - 'onehot' (default): Encodes each bin as a binary feature using a one-hot encoding format. For each sample, the feature corresponding to its bin is set to 1, and all others are set to 0.

  - 'onehot-dense': Same as 'onehot', but returns a dense NumPy array instead of a sparse matrix.

  - 'ordinal': Encodes bins using ordinal integers, with bin indices ranging from 0 to n_bins - 1.

- strategy: Determines how the bins edges are computed. The options are 'uniform' (equal-width binning), 'quantile' (equal-frequency binning), and 'kmeans' (bins defined using k-means clustering). The default is 'quantile'.

Example for discretizing features into three equal-width bins using ordinal encoding:

```
from sklearn.preprocessing import KBinsDiscretizer

discretizer = KBinsDiscretizer(n_bins=3, strategy='uniform', encode='ordinal')
X = [[-0.2, 2.0, -1],
     [-0.1, 2.5, -0.5],
     [0.1, 2.8, 0],
     [0.2, 3.0, 2]]
discretizer.fit_transform(X)
```

Output:

```
array([[0., 0., 0.],
       [0., 1., 0.],
       [2., 2., 1.],
       [2., 2., 2.]])
```

You can inspect the bin edges using the bin_edges_ attribute:

```
discretizer.bin_edges_
```

```
[array([-0.2      , -0.06666667,  0.06666667,  0.2       ])
 array([2.       ,  2.33333333,  2.66666667,  3.       ])
 array([-1.,  0.,  1.,  2.])]
```

3.10.7 Scaling and Normalization

Feature scaling is an essential preprocessing step that ensures all features are on a similar scale or range, preventing any one feature from disproportionately influencing the learning process. It is particularly important for algorithms that are sensitive to feature magnitudes, including:

- Algorithms that involve distance calculations, such as k-nearest neighbors and most clustering algorithms. In this case, scaling ensures that each feature contributes equally to distance computations, which is crucial for the accuracy of these models.

- Gradient-based algorithms, such as the ones used to train logistic regression models and neural networks. When features differ in scale, gradient descent may take uneven steps in different directions, leading to slower convergence or causing the algorithm to get trapped in poor local minima (see Section E.4.1.6).

The main methods for feature scaling are:

- **Standardization (z-score normalization)**: This method rescales each feature by subtracting its mean and dividing by its standard deviation:

$$z = \frac{x - \mu}{\sigma}, \tag{3.3}$$

where x is a feature value, μ is the mean of the feature, and σ is its standard deviation.

In Scikit-Learn, standardization can be performed using the StandardScaler[46] class:

```
from sklearn.preprocessing import StandardScaler

scaler = StandardScaler()
X = [[1, -1, 2],
    [2, 0, 0],
    [0, 1, -1]]
scaler.fit_transform(X)
```

Output:

```
array([[ 0.        , -1.22474487,  1.33630621],
       [ 1.22474487,  0.        , -0.26726124],
       [-1.22474487,  1.22474487, -1.06904497]])
```

Advantages of standardization:

- The scaled features have mean 0 and standard deviation 1, which can benefit algorithms that assume standardized inputs, such as Principal Component Analysis (PCA).

- It preserves the relative spacing between values, meaning the standardized differences reflect the original differences in scale.

Disadvantages of standardization:

- The scaled values may still span different numerical ranges across features, especially when features have outliers or heavy-tailed distributions.

---

46. https://scikit-learn.org/stable/modules/generated/sklearn.preprocessing.StandardScaler.html

  – It is sensitive to outliers, as these can skew the mean and standard deviation used for
    scaling (though generally less so than in min-max scaling).

  – It reduces interpretability of the data by transforming values away from their original
    units and scale (a drawback shared by most scaling methods).

- **Min-max scaling**: This method rescales each feature to a fixed range, typically [0, 1]. The
  transformation is given by:

$$x' = \frac{x - \min x}{\max x - \min x},$$
(3.4)

where x is a feature value, and $\min x$, $\max x$ are the minimum and maximum values of the
feature, respectively.[47]

Min-max scaling may change the relative spacing between the values, especially when outliers are present. For example, consider the dataset [2, 3, 4, 5, 6, 7, 8, 9, 10, 50], where 50
is an outlier. After min-max scaling, the values become approximately [0, 0.0208, 0.0417,
0.0625, ..., 1]. The presence of the outlier stretches the range, causing the majority of the
values to cluster tightly near 0 and making differences between them less noticeable.

Conversely, standardization rescales the data to have mean 0 and standard deviation 1, producing the values [-0.626, -0.551, -0.477, -0.402, ..., 2.950]. This transformation preserves
the natural spacing between values, including the outlier at 2.950.

In Scikit-Learn, min-max scaling can be performed using the `MinMaxScaler`[48] class:

```
from sklearn.preprocessing import MinMaxScaler

scaler = MinMaxScaler()
X = [[1, -1, 2],
     [2, 0, 0],
     [0, 1, -1]]
scaler.fit_transform(X)
```

Output:

```
array([[0.5        , 0.        , 1.        ],
       [1.        , 0.5        , 0.33333333],
       [0.        , 1.        , 0.        ]])
```

---

47. This technique is sometimes called *normalization*, although the term can also refer to scaling vectors to unit norm.
48. https://scikit-learn.org/stable/modules/generated/sklearn.preprocessing.MinMaxScaler.html

Advantages of min-max scaling:

- It scales all features to the same range, which is useful when features must be directly comparable or combined.
- The transformation to a [0, 1] range is beneficial for certain loss or activation functions, where the most significant gradient changes occur within this interval, leading to more stable and efficient training.

Disadvantages of min-max scaling:

- It is highly sensitive to outliers, which can cause the scaling to compress the majority of the data into a narrow interval.
- Unlike standardization, it does not normalize the variance, so features with larger variance may continue to exert greater influence on the learning algorithm, particularly in distance-based methods.
- New values outside the training range can fall outside [0, 1], leading to unexpected behavior unless handled explicitly.

- **Robust scaling**: This method is more robust to outliers than the other scaling methods discussed above. Instead of using the mean and standard deviation, it uses the median and interquartile range (IQR), which are both less affected by extreme values. The transformation formula is:

$$x' = \frac{x - \text{median}(x)}{\text{IQR}(x)}. \tag{3.5}$$

In Scikit-Learn, the RobustScaler[49] class can be used for this type of scaling:

```
from sklearn.preprocessing import RobustScaler

scaler = RobustScaler()
X = [[1, -1, 2],
     [2, 0, 0],
     [0, 1, -1]]
scaler.fit_transform(X)
```

```
array([[ 0.        , -1.        ,  1.33333333],
       [ 1.        ,  0.        ,  0.        ],
       [-1.        ,  1.        , -0.66666667]])
```

---

49. https://scikit-learn.org/stable/modules/generated/sklearn.preprocessing.RobustScaler.html

Advantages of robust scaling:

  – It is less sensitive to outliers than standardization or min-max scaling.

Disadvantages of robust scaling:

  – As with standard scaling, it does not scale the data to a fixed range, which can be a disadvantage for algorithms that assume or benefit from inputs confined to a specific interval.

  – Interpretation of the scaled values can be less intuitive compared to methods that map data to a standard range (e.g., [0, 1]).

3.10.8   Example: The Adult Dataset

We now demonstrate the data preprocessing steps discussed above using the well-known Adult dataset (also called the Census Income dataset), which originates from the 1994 US Census Bureau database [35]. The task is to predict whether an individual's annual income exceeds $50,000, based on various demographic and employment-related attributes.

The dataset contains 48,842 instances and 14 features, which are described in Table 3.2. The target variable has two possible labels: ">50K" and "<=50K". This dataset is more challenging to work with than simpler datasets like Iris, as it includes both continuous and categorical features, and several features have missing values.

Feature	Description
age	Age of the individual in years
workclass	Type of employment (e.g., private, self-employed, government)
fnlwgt	Sampling weight representing how many people this individual represents
education	Highest level of education completed
education-num	Education level in numerical form
marital-status	Marital status of the individual
occupation	Type of occupation
relationship	Role in the household, e.g., "Wife" or "Husband"
race	Race of the individual
sex	Sex of the individual, either "Male" or "Female"
capital-gain	Income from capital gains
capital-loss	Losses from capital investments
hours-per-week	Number of hours of work per week
native-country	Country of origin

Table 3.2: Description of the features in the Adult dataset

3.10.8.1   Loading the Dataset

We first import the required libraries and fix NumPy's random seed:

```
import numpy as np
import pandas as pd
import matplotlib.pyplot as plt
import seaborn as sns


np.random.seed(42)
```

In Scikit-Learn, the Adult dataset can be loaded using the `fetch_openml`[50] function, which retrieves it from OpenML[51], a public repository of machine learning datasets:

```
from sklearn.datasets import fetch_openml

X, y = fetch_openml('adult', version=2, return_X_y=True, as_frame=True)
```

The function `fetch_openml` takes several arguments in addition to the dataset's name:

- `version`: Specifies which version of the dataset to use. The Adult dataset has four versions on OpenML; version 2 corresponds to the original, unprocessed dataset.

- `return_X_y`: If `True`, returns the features `X` and the target `y` as a tuple, instead of a Bunch object that also includes metadata such as feature names.

- `as_frame`: If `True`, returns the data as Pandas DataFrames instead of NumPy arrays, making them easier to inspect and manipulate.

3.10.8.2   Data Exploration

We begin our exploration by examining the first few rows of the dataset:

```
X.head()
```

Figure 3.16 shows the first five rows of the dataset, illustrating the structure and content of the raw records. Next, we inspect the data types and identify which columns contain missing values:

---

50. https://scikit-learn.org/stable/modules/generated/sklearn.datasets.fetch_openml.html
51. https://www.openml.org

	age	workclass	fnlwgt	education	education-num	marital-status	occupation	relationship	race	sex	capital-gain	capital-loss
0	25.0	Private	226802.0	11th	7.0	Never-married	Machine-op-inspct	Own-child	Black	Male	0.0	0.0
1	38.0	Private	89814.0	HS-grad	9.0	Married-civ-spouse	Farming-fishing	Husband	White	Male	0.0	0.0
2	28.0	Local-gov	336951.0	Assoc-acdm	12.0	Married-civ-spouse	Protective-serv	Husband	White	Male	0.0	0.0
3	44.0	Private	160323.0	Some-college	10.0	Married-civ-spouse	Machine-op-inspct	Husband	Black	Male	7688.0	0.0
4	18.0	NaN	103497.0	Some-college	10.0	Never-married	NaN	Own-child	White	Female	0.0	0.0

Figure 3.16: The first five rows of the Adult dataset. Showing the first 12 out of 14 features due to space constraints

```
X.info()
```

```
RangeIndex: 48842 entries, 0 to 48841
Data columns (total 14 columns):
 #   Column          Non-Null Count  Dtype
---  ------          --------------  -----
 0   age             48842 non-null  float64
 1   workclass       46043 non-null  category
 2   fnlwgt          48842 non-null  float64
 3   education       48842 non-null  category
 4   education-num   48842 non-null  float64
 5   marital-status  48842 non-null  category
 6   occupation      46033 non-null  category
 7   relationship    48842 non-null  category
 8   race            48842 non-null  category
 9   sex             48842 non-null  category
 10  capital-gain    48842 non-null  float64
 11  capital-loss    48842 non-null  float64
 12  hours-per-week  48842 non-null  float64
 13  native-country  47985 non-null  category
dtypes: category(8), float64(6)
memory usage: 2.6 MB
```

The dataset includes 14 features: 8 categorical and 6 numerical. Three features have missing values: workclass, occupation, and native-country. Let's also examine the labels:

```
y.head()
```

```
0      <=50K
1      <=50K
2       >50K
3       >50K
4      <=50K
Name: class, dtype: category
Categories (2, object): ['>50K', '<=50K']
```

The labels in this dataset are categorical with two possible outcomes: `'>50K'` and `'<=50K'`. These must be converted into a numerical format before they can be used for training.

To check for class imbalance, we compute the relative frequency of each class:

```
y.value_counts() / y.value_counts().sum()
```

```
<=50K    0.760718
>50K     0.239282
```

The class distribution is somewhat imbalanced but not to a degree that would significantly hinder model training or evaluation.

At this stage, one would typically conduct a more comprehensive exploratory analysis, including inspecting feature distributions, examining correlations, and detecting outliers. However, since our focus here is on data preprocessing, we will limit our exploration to these basic checks.

3.10.8.3 Data Preprocessing

The feature matrix and the label vector must be processed separately because the estimator's `fit` method expects them as separate inputs. In addition, when the model is used to make predictions on new data, only the feature preprocessing pipeline is applied, since the new samples do not include labels.

Let's first encode the labels into a numerical format. To this end, we use the `LabelEncoder`[52] class from Scikit-Learn, which assigns a unique integer to each label. It functions similarly to `OrdinalEncoder`, except that it it is designed for one-dimensional arrays rather than columns in a multi-dimensional array. We apply it to our labels vector as follows:

```
from sklearn.preprocessing import LabelEncoder

label_encoder = LabelEncoder()
y = label_encoder.fit_transform(y)
y
```

```
array([0, 0, 1, ..., 0, 0, 1])
```

---

52. https://scikit-learn.org/stable/modules/generated/sklearn.preprocessing.LabelEncoder.html

The transformed label vector y is now a NumPy array, where 0 represents "<=50K" and 1 represents ">50K".

For the feature matrix, we perform the following preprocessing steps:

1. Impute the missing values in the columns `workclass`, `occupation`, and `native-country`. Since these columns are categorical, we use a `SimpleImputer` with the strategy set to `'most_frequent'`, which replaces missing values with the most common value in each column.

2. Convert the categorical features into a numerical format using one-hot encoding.

3. Scale the numerical features using `StandardScaler` to ensure that they contribute equally to the model's predictions.

Since these steps apply to different subsets of features (categorical vs. numerical), we use the `ColumnTransformer`[53] class. It allows different transformations to be applied to specific columns and automatically combines the results into a single feature matrix, making it easy to integrate into a larger pipeline.

We first define a pipeline for transforming the categorical features:

```
from sklearn.pipeline import Pipeline
from sklearn.impute import SimpleImputer
from sklearn.preprocessing import OneHotEncoder

categorical_transformer = Pipeline([
    ('imputer', SimpleImputer(strategy='most_frequent')),
    ('onehot', OneHotEncoder(handle_unknown='ignore'))
])
```

Next, we define a pipeline for transforming the numerical features:

```
from sklearn.preprocessing import StandardScaler

numerical_transformer = Pipeline([
    ('scaler', StandardScaler())
])
```

To construct the `ColumnTransformer`, we need to specify which features are categorical and which are numerical. Rather than listing them manually, we can utilize the DataFrame's `select_dtypes`[54] method to extract the column names based on their data types:

```
categorical_cols = X.select_dtypes(include='category').columns.to_list()
numerical_cols = X.select_dtypes(exclude='category').columns.to_list()
```

---

53. https://scikit-learn.org/stable/modules/generated/sklearn.compose.ColumnTransformer.html
54. https://pandas.pydata.org/docs/reference/api/pandas.DataFrame.select_dtypes.html

We are now ready to define the `ColumnTransformer`, which applies the appropriate prepro-cessing pipeline to each subset of features:

```
from sklearn.compose import ColumnTransformer

preprocessor = ColumnTransformer([
    ('cat', categorical_transformer, categorical_cols),
    ('num', numerical_transformer, numerical_cols)
])
```

Finally, we combine the column transformer with a classifier in a single pipeline. This ensures that all preprocessing steps are applied automatically during both training and prediction. Here, we use a gradient boosting classifier:

```
from sklearn.ensemble import GradientBoostingClassifier

model = Pipeline([
    ('pre', preprocessor),
    ('clf', GradientBoostingClassifier())
])
```

3.10.8.4   Training the Model

We first split the dataset into 80% training and 20% test:

```
from sklearn.model_selection import train_test_split

X_train, X_test, y_train, y_test = train_test_split(X, y, test_size=0.2, stratify=y,
                                                     random_state=42)
```

Next, we fit the model to the training data:

```
model.fit(X_train, y_train)
```

3.10.8.5   Evaluating the Model

We evaluate the model's performance on both the training and test sets:

```
train_accuracy = model.score(X_train, y_train)
print(f'Train accuracy: {train_accuracy:.4f}')

test_accuracy = model.score(X_test, y_test)
print(f'Test accuracy: {test_accuracy:.4f}')
```

The results are:

```
Train accuracy: 0.8690
Test accuracy: 0.8676
```

The test accuracy is very close to the training accuracy, indicating that the model generalizes well to new data. Further improvements can be achieved by tuning hyperparameters (prior work using extensive hyperparameter tuning and gradient boosting has reached up to 88.16% on this dataset [100]), experimenting with alternative classifiers or preprocessing methods, or by engineering new features (see Exercise 3.14).

3.11   Building Your Own Estimators

In many real-world applications, it is necessary to develop custom machine learning models or implement novel algorithms that are not available in existing libraries. In such cases, you can create a custom estimator. To ensure seamless integration with Scikit-Learn's ecosystem, the estimator should be compatible with the Estimator API. This enables the use of core Scikit-Learn utilities such as pipelines, cross-validation, and grid search with your custom estimator.

Scikit-Learn's API follows the principle of *duck typing*, which means that an object is recognized as an estimator based on the methods it implements, rather than its class inheritance. At a minimum, a valid estimator must implement the `fit`, `get_params`, and `set_params` methods. If the estimator is also a predictor, it should provide a `predict` method; if it is a transformer, it should include `transform` and optionally `fit_transform`.

To reduce the amount of boilerplate code, you can subclass the `BaseEstimator`[55] class in `sklearn.base`, which provides default implementations for `get_params` and `set_params`. Depending on the estimator type, you can also inherit from one of the following mixin classes in `sklearn.base`:

- `ClassifierMixin`[56] for classifiers, which adds a `score` method returning classification accuracy.

- `RegressorMixin`[57] for regressors, which adds a `score` method returning the R^2 score.

- `ClusterMixin`[58] for clustering estimators, which adds a `fit_predict` method.

- `TransformerMixin`[59] for transformers, which adds a `fit_transform` method.

To help you get started, Scikit-Learn provides a project template for building custom estimators.[60]

---

55. https://scikit-learn.org/stable/modules/generated/sklearn.base.BaseEstimator.html
56. https://scikit-learn.org/stable/modules/generated/sklearn.base.ClassifierMixin.html
57. https://scikit-learn.org/stable/modules/generated/sklearn.base.RegressorMixin.html
58. https://scikit-learn.org/stable/modules/generated/sklearn.base.ClusterMixin.html
59. https://scikit-learn.org/stable/modules/generated/sklearn.base.TransformerMixin.html
60. https://github.com/scikit-learn-contrib/project-template/blob/master/skltemplate/_template.py

As an example, let's implement a simple classifier, `NearestNeighborClassifier`, which is a simplified version of k-nearest neighbors (KNN) for the special case of $k = 1$. This classifier assigns to a given input x the label of the training sample closest to it in Euclidean distance. The implementation is shown below:

```python
import numpy as np

from sklearn.base import BaseEstimator, ClassifierMixin
from sklearn.utils.validation import check_X_y, check_is_fitted, check_array
from sklearn.utils.multiclass import unique_labels
from sklearn.metrics import euclidean_distances

class NearestNeighborClassifier(BaseEstimator, ClassifierMixin):
    """A simple 1-nearest neighbor classifier."""
    def __init__(self):
        pass # No hyperparameters

    def fit(self, X, y):
        """Fit the classifier to the training data."""
        X, y = check_X_y(X, y)
        self.classes_ = unique_labels(y)

        self.X_ = X
        self.y_ = y
        return self

    def predict(self, X):
        """Perform classification on an array of test vectors X."""
        check_is_fitted(self, ['X_', 'y_'])
        X = check_array(X)

        closest = np.argmin(euclidean_distances(X, self.X_), axis=1)
        return self.y_[closest]
```

This example highlights several important practices when building a custom estimator:

- The estimator inherits from both `BaseEstimator` and `ClassifierMixin`, which provide default implementations for methods such as `get_params`, `set_params`, and `score`.

- The `__init__` method typically defines the model's hyperparameters as public attributes with default values. Since this classifier has no hyperparameters, the method is left empty.

- The `fit` method validates the input using `check_X_y` and stores the training data in `self.X_` and `self.y_`, following Scikit-Learn's convention of appending an underscore to fitted attributes. The unique class labels are saved in `self.classes_` to support compatibility with Scikit-Learn utilities, such as model evaluation functions.

- This classifier is an example for a **lazy learner**: it does not build an explicit model during training but instead stores the training data and performs all computation at prediction time.

- The `predict` method first checks that the estimator has been fitted using `check_is_fitted` and validates the input with `check_array`. It then computes the Euclidean distances between the test and training samples and assigns each test sample the label of the nearest training sample, using the functions `euclidean_distances` and `np.argmin`.

Let's test our classifier on the Iris dataset. We first load the dataset and split it into training and test sets:

```
from sklearn.datasets import load_iris
from sklearn.model_selection import train_test_split

X, y = load_iris(return_X_y=True)
X_train, X_test, y_train, y_test = train_test_split(X, y, stratify=y,
                                                    random_state=42)
```

We now create an instance of our custom estimator and fit it to the training set:

```
clf = NearestNeighborClassifier()
clf.fit(X_train, y_train)
```

Since our estimator inherits from `ClassifierMixin`, it automatically has a `score` method that computes the mean accuracy on a given dataset. The accuracy of the model on the training and test sets is:

```
train_accuracy = clf.score(X_train, y_train)
print(f'Train accuracy: {train_accuracy:.4f}')

test_accuracy = clf.score(X_test, y_test)
print(f'Test accuracy: {test_accuracy:.4f}')
```

```
Train accuracy: 1.0000
Test accuracy: 0.9474
```

The perfect accuracy on the training set is expected, as each sample's closest neighbor is itself. The high accuracy on the test set is somewhat surprising (it is even higher than our tuned decision tree classifier!), but it demonstrates the effectiveness of simple learning algorithms such as KNN in cases where the data is well-structured and the classes are clearly separated. That said, relying on a single nearest neighbor for prediction can lead to overfitting, as the model becomes highly sensitive to noise and outliers in the training data (we explore KNN in more depth in Chapter 6).

3.11.1   Custom Transformers

Custom transformers allow you to implement specific data cleaning or preprocessing tasks that are not covered by Scikit-Learn's built-in transformers. To create a custom transformer, you need to subclass both `BaseEstimator` and `TransformerMixin`, and then implement the `fit` and `transform` methods.

For simpler, stateless transformations, such as unit conversions or log transformations, you can utilize the `FunctionTransformer`[61] class. This utility wraps any Python function into an object that implements the Scikit-Learn transformer interface. For example, the following transformer converts measurement values from inches to centimeters:

```
from sklearn.preprocessing import FunctionTransformer

inch_to_cm = FunctionTransformer(lambda x: x * 2.54)
```

Since `FunctionTransformer` is stateless by default, its `fit` method performs no action. Thus, you can apply the transformation directly using the `transform` method:

```
X = np.array([[1, 2, 3], [4, 5, 6]])
inch_to_cm.transform(X)
```

This produces:

```
array([[ 2.54,  5.08,  7.62],
       [10.16, 12.7 , 15.24]])
```

3.12   Summary

This chapter provided a comprehensive overview of Scikit-Learn, guiding you through the typical workflow of building a machine learning model: from initial data exploration and preprocessing to model training and evaluation. Along the way, we introduced key tools and techniques such as transformers for data preprocessing, pipelines for chaining operations, cross-validation for robust model evaluation, and grid search for hyperparameter tuning.

By mastering these foundational tools, you are now equipped to tackle a wide range of machine learning tasks using Scikit-Learn's flexible and consistent interface. The practical exercises at the end of this chapter will help you solidify these concepts and gain hands-on experience applying them to real-world problems.

In the chapters ahead, we will delve into specific machine learning algorithms, exploring both their theoretical foundations and practical implementations. We begin with linear regression—one of the earliest predictive models, which forms the basis for many modern machine learning techniques.

---

61. `https://scikit-learn.org/stable/modules/generated/sklearn.preprocessing.FunctionTransformer.html`

3.13   Exercises

3.13.1   Multiple-Choice Questions

3.1. We have a dataset with missing values, categorical features, and numerical features with different scales. Which of the following represents the correct order for preprocessing this dataset?

    (a) feature scaling → imputation → discretization → one-hot encoding

    (b) one-hot encoding → imputation → discretization → feature scaling

    (c) imputation → one-hot encoding → discretization → feature scaling

    (d) imputation → discretization → one-hot encoding → feature scaling

3.2. Which of the following is true about the `fit` method in the Estimator API?

    (a) It modifies the object it is called on.

    (b) It returns the trained model object.

    (c) It computes the evaluation score on the training set.

    (d) It can be applied only to supervised learning models.

3.3. Which of the following statements is true about the `Pipeline` class?

    (a) It sequentially applies a list of transforms and a final estimator.

    (b) It requires all but the last estimator to implement the `fit_transform` method.

    (c) It can be used in conjunction with `GridSearchCV` for hyperparameter tuning.

    (d) It can handle different data types (such as text and numeric data) in the same step.

3.4. Which statement is true about the `SimpleImputer` class?

    (a) It can only be used for imputing missing values in numerical data.

    (b) It can replace missing values using a constant value specified by the user.

    (c) It can only handle missing values represented by `np.nan` or `None`.

    (d) It automatically detects the best imputation strategy for each column based on its data type.

3.5. Consider the following list:

```
data = [['Orange', 'Apple'], ['Banana', 'Apple'], ['Cherry', 'Banana']]
```

We would like to convert the string values in this list into numerical ones using `OrdinalEncoder`. What will be the numerical representation of the data after the following transformation?

```
from sklearn.preprocessing import OrdinalEncoder
OrdinalEncoder().fit_transform(data)
```

(a) [[2, 0], [0, 0], [1, 1]]

(b) [[3, 0], [1, 0], [2, 1]]

(c) [3, 0, 1, 0, 2, 1]

(d) [0, 0, 0, 0, 0, 0]

3.6. Which statement is true about the RobustScaler class?

(a) It changes the probability distribution of the data to be standard normal.

(b) It scales the data using statistics that are robust to outliers.

(c) It confines the data to be within a predefined range.

(d) It preserves the relative spacing between all values in the dataset.

3.7. You apply standard scaling to a numerical feature in the training set using its mean μ_{train} and variance σ^2_{train}. Which statement about standardizing the same feature in the test set is true?

(a) The test set should be standardized using its own mean and variance.

(b) The test set should be standardized using the training set's mean μ_{train} and variance σ^2_{train}.

(c) The test set should be standardized using the overall mean and variance of both the training and test sets combined.

(d) The test set should not be modified in any way.

3.8. What are the advantages of using cross-validation for model evaluation?

(a) It eliminates the need for a separate test set, as the model is tested during the cross-validation process.

(b) It ensures that every observation from the original dataset has the chance of appearing in the training and validation set, thus reducing bias in model evaluation.

(c) It prevents overusing the test set for model tuning and evaluation.

(d) It significantly reduces the time taken for model training as it divides the training set into smaller subsets.

3.9. Which of the following statements about the GridSearchCV class is true?

(a) It can only be applied to supervised learning estimators.

(b) The cv parameter allows specifying the number of cross-validation folds.

(c) It automatically refits the best model on the entire dataset.

(d) It allows parallel processing to speed up the grid search.

3.10. Which of the following methods needs to be implemented by every custom estimator?

    (a) `fit`

    (b) `predict`

    (c) `get_params`

    (d) `score`

3.13.2   Programming Exercises

3.11. The Breast Cancer Wisconsin (Diagnostic) dataset[62] is used to predict whether a breast mass is benign or malignant. It contains 569 samples with 30 numerical features derived from digitized images of fine-needle aspirates (FNA) of breast masses. The features include measurements such as the texture, area, and smoothness of the cell nuclei in the images.

    (a) Load the dataset using the `load_breast_cancer`[63] function from `sklearn.datasets`.

    (b) Display the first few records of the dataset to understand its structure and features.

    (c) Conduct an initial exploratory data analysis (EDA) to examine the statistical properties of the data (e.g., feature distributions, correlations with the target label, class balance).

    (d) Split the dataset into a training set and a test set (e.g., 80% training, 20% testing).

    (e) Choose a simple classification algorithm such as logistic regression, k-nearest neighbors, or a decision tree classifier.

    (f) Train the chosen model on the training set.

    (g) Evaluate the model's performance by computing its accuracy on both the training and test sets. Does the model appear to overfit, underfit, or neither? Justify your answer.

3.12. Implement the k-fold cross-validation algorithm (Algorithm 3.1) from scratch:

    (a) Write a Python function that takes as input a dataset, a Scikit-Learn classifier, and the number of folds k, and returns the mean and standard deviation of the cross-validated accuracy of the classifier.

    (b) Test your function on the Breast Cancer Wisconsin dataset (see Exercise 3.11) using different values of k. Analyze and discuss how the variance in model performance changes as k increases.

    (c) (*) Extend your function to support stratified k-fold cross-validation (similar to Scikit-Learn's `StratifiedKFold`). Compare the results with standard k-fold cross-validation. Discuss the advantages of stratification, especially in imbalanced datasets.

---

62. https://archive.ics.uci.edu/dataset/17/breast+cancer+wisconsin+diagnostic
63. https://scikit-learn.org/stable/modules/generated/sklearn.datasets.load_breast_cancer.html

3.13. The Cleveland Heart Disease dataset[64] is a widely used dataset in machine learning for the healthcare domain, where the goal is to predict the presence of heart disease in patients. It includes attributes such as age, sex, chest pain type, resting blood pressure, cholesterol, fasting blood sugar, and electrocardiographic results. The target variable is a binary indicator of heart disease.

In this exercise, you will build a complete machine learning pipeline, including data exploration, preprocessing, model training, hyperparameter tuning, and evaluation, to predict heart disease based on the available features.

(a) Load the dataset using Scikit-Learn's `fetch_openml` function:

```
X, y = fetch_openml('heart-c', version=2, return_X_y=True, as_frame=True)
```

(b) Data exploration:

   i. Conduct exploratory data analysis (EDA) to examine the structure and statistical properties of the dataset.

   ii. Visualize feature distributions and relationships using scatter plots, histograms, and pair plots. Clearly label all plots and include legends where appropriate.

(c) Data preprocessing: Create a Scikit-Learn pipeline that integrates all necessary preprocessing steps along with the model. Your pipeline should:

   i. Handle missing values appropriately.

   ii. Convert categorical variables to numerical representations.

   iii. Normalize or standardize continuous features.

   iv. Use a `ColumnTransformer` to apply the correct transformations to categorical and numerical features.

(d) Model training:

   i. Split the dataset into training and test sets.

   ii. Choose at least three different machine learning models (e.g., `LogisticRegression`, `DecisionTreeClassifier`, `RandomForestClassifier`) to compare within your pipeline.

   iii. Build your code in a modular way so that you can easily swap models without duplicating the pipeline construction or preprocessing code.

   iv. Train the pipeline on the training set for each model.

   v. Compare the models by evaluating their accuracy on both the training and test sets.

(e) Model tuning:

   i. For each of the three models, perform hyperparameter tuning using `GridSearchCV` or `RandomizedSearchCV`.

---

64. `https://www.openml.org/search?type=data&id=982`

     ii. Evaluate each tuned model on the test set and compare their performance.

  (f) Write a short report summarizing your process and findings, including key data insights, model comparison results, and conclusions.

3.14. Using the Adult dataset (described in Section 3.10.8), perform the following data preprocessing steps and analyze their impact on model performance:

  (a) Discretize the Age attribute into age groups (e.g., Young, Middle-Aged, Senior).

  (b) Discretize the hours-per-week feature into categories like Part-Time, Full-Time, and Over-Time based on the hours worked.

  (c) Simplify the education feature by combining primary and secondary education types into broader categories.

  (d) Group marital status into broader categories such as Married and Single.

  (e) Consolidate countries into larger geographic regions (e.g., Asia, Europe, North America).

3.15. Implement a custom classifier that always predicts the majority class from the training data, regardless of the input features. Test your classifier on the Breast Cancer Wisconsin dataset, described in Exercise 3.11. Compare the results with a standard classifier to demonstrate the limitations of a majority class predictor.

3.16. Implement a custom transformer called Winsorizer that performs winsorization on a dataset by replacing values outside the specified upper and lower percentile thresholds with the corresponding threshold values. Test the transformer on a sample dataset, such as the Iris dataset, and compare the dataset before and after applying the transformation to evaluate its effect.

3.17. Kaggle[65] is a popular platform for machine learning and data science competitions. Participating in competitions can sharpen your problem-solving skills, gain experience with real-world datasets, help you learn from the broader machine learning community, and even offer opportunities to win prize money.

In this exercise, you will participate in a practice Kaggle competition based on the Titanic dataset, which challenges you to predict the survival of passengers aboard the Titanic based on features such as age, fare, class of travel, and gender.

  (a) Register for a Kaggle account at https://www.kaggle.com/account/login.

  (b) Download the Titanic dataset from the Titanic: Machine Learning from Disaster[66] competition page. The dataset consists of two files: train.csv and test.csv. The train.csv file contains both the input features and the survival labels, while test.csv

---

65. https://www.kaggle.com/
66. https://www.kaggle.com/competitions/titanic

contains only the input features without the labels. Since the true outcomes for `test.csv` are hidden, you will use `train.csv` both for training your model and for validation/tuning.

(c) Load the training and test datasets into Pandas DataFrames.

(d) Perform exploratory data analysis (EDA) to understand the structure of the dataset (e.g., check for missing values, explore feature distributions, and identify key variables).

(e) Preprocess the data (e.g., handle missing values, encode categorical variables, scale numerical features).

(f) Split the training data into a training set and a validation set for model evaluation and tuning.

(g) Choose a classification algorithm (e.g., logistic regression, decision tree, random forest) and train it on the training set.

(h) Evaluate your model's performance on the validation set.

(i) Use your model to generate predictions for the provided test dataset.

(j) Format your predictions according to the competition requirements and submit them on Kaggle to see how your model performs on unseen data.

(k) Experiment with different algorithms, hyperparameters, and preprocessing strategies to improve your model's performance. Track how these changes affect your leaderboard score.

Chapter 4

Linear Regression

Linear regression is one of the most fundamental predictive models in machine learning and statistics. Its origins trace back to the early 19th century, when Legendre and Gauss used linear regression to predict the movement of the planets based on astronomical data.

The main objective in regression analysis is to predict the value of a dependent variable (the target) based on one or more independent variables (the input features). Its applications span a wide range of fields, from forecasting stock prices using various economic indicators to estimating crop yields based on climate data and detecting tumors in CT scans.

In linear regression, we assume that the target variable is a linear function of the input features, and the goal is to determine the coefficients that best describe this relationship based on the observed data.

This chapter covers in depth both the theory and practical implementation of linear regression models. It is organized as follows. Section 4.1 formally defines the linear regression problem. Section 4.2 introduces Ordinary Least Squares (OLS), the most common method for solving linear regression problems. Section 4.3 focuses on simple linear regression problems, where the dataset contains only one feature, and shows how to derive a closed-form solution to these problems. Section 4.4 extends this closed-form solution to multiple linear regression problems, where the dataset can contain any number of features. Section 4.5 explores various metrics for evaluating regression models. Section 4.6 applies linear regression to a real-world housing price prediction task. Section 4.7 outlines the key assumptions underlying linear regression models and presents strategies for addressing potential violations of these assumptions. Section 4.8 introduces gradient descent as an alternative approach for solving linear regression problems, particularly useful for large datasets and online learning scenarios. Section 4.9 presents alternative loss functions to least squares that can work better when the dataset contains outliers. Section 4.10 discusses nonlinear regression problems and various approaches for handling them. Section 4.11 explores how regularization techniques can be integrated into linear regression to prevent overfitting. Section 4.12 delves into Bayesian linear regression, demonstrating how linear regression can be integrated into a Bayesian inference framework. Section 4.13 concludes with a summary of the key points discussed in the chapter.

4.1   Formal Definitions and Notations

In regression problems, we are given a set of n labeled samples: $D = \{(\mathbf{x}_1, y_1), \ldots, (\mathbf{x}_n, y_n)\}$. Each $\mathbf{x}_i = (x_{i1}, x_{i2}, \ldots, x_{id})^T$ is a vector that contains the features of the i-th sample, and y_i is a continuous value representing the target for that sample. The features are also referred to as the **independent variables**, **predictors**, or **explanatory variables**, and the target variable is also known as the **dependent variable** or **response**.

In **linear regression**, we assume that there is a linear relationship between the feature vector $\mathbf{x}$ and the target variable y. Thus, the model's hypothesis (i.e., prediction function) is defined as:

$$h(\mathbf{x}) = w_0 + w_1 x_1 + \ldots + w_d x_d. \tag{4.1}$$

Here, $w_0, \ldots, w_d$ are the model's **parameters** or **weights**, representing the coefficients that define the relationship between $\mathbf{x}$ and y. The parameter w_0, known as the **intercept** or **bias**, represents the value of the target y when all the input features $x_1, \ldots, x_d$ are zero. Without an intercept, the model is forced to pass through the origin, which may result in a poor fit.

To simplify the notation, we introduce a constant feature $x_0 = 1$. This allows us to express the model in vectorized form by defining the feature vector as $\mathbf{x} = (x_0, x_1, \ldots, x_d)^T$ and the parameter vector as $\mathbf{w} = (w_0, w_1, \ldots, w_d)^T$. We can then write the prediction function compactly as a dot product of these two vectors:

$$h_{\mathbf{w}}(\mathbf{x}) = \mathbf{w}^T \mathbf{x} = \sum_{j=0}^{d} w_j x_j. \tag{4.2}$$

We use the notation $h_{\mathbf{w}}(\mathbf{x})$ to emphasize the function's dependence on the parameter vector $\mathbf{w}$. When $\mathbf{w}$ is fixed or clear from the context, we may omit the subscript and write $h(\mathbf{x})$ for simplicity.

The central task in linear regression is to find the parameter vector $\mathbf{w}$ that yields predictions $h_{\mathbf{w}}(\mathbf{x})$ as close as possible to the actual values y. In other words, we seek the parameter vector that best *fits* the observed data.

4.2   Ordinary Least Squares (OLS)

The first step in developing a linear regression model is to choose an appropriate loss function, which quantifies the discrepancy between the model's predictions and the observed target values.

The most commonly used loss function in linear regression is the **squared loss**. It is defined as the square of the **residual**, which is the difference between the target value and the model's prediction:

$$L_{\text{squared}}(y, h_{\mathbf{w}}(\mathbf{x})) = (y - h_{\mathbf{w}}(\mathbf{x}))^2. \tag{4.3}$$

To evaluate the overall fit of the model across all training samples, we define the **cost function** as the average of these squared losses:

$$J(\mathbf{w}) = \frac{1}{n} \sum_{i=1}^{n} (y_i - h_{\mathbf{w}}(\mathbf{x}_i))^2 = \frac{1}{n} \sum_{i=1}^{n} (y_i - \mathbf{w}^T \mathbf{x}_i)^2. \tag{4.4}$$

This function is known as the **least squares** criterion when used for model optimization, and as **mean squared error (MSE)** when used to evaluate the model's performance (see Section 4.5). The regression method that minimizes this function is called **ordinary least squares (OLS)**.

It can be shown that the least squares cost function is strictly convex (see Exercise 4.18). This guarantees that any local minimum of the function is also a global minimum, thereby simplifying the optimization process.

Although OLS is the most common approach to fitting linear regression models, other methods—such as **least absolute deviations (LAD)** regression—may be preferable in settings where robustness to outliers is important (see Section 4.9).

4.2.1 OLS and Maximum Likelihood

One of the key reasons for the widespread use of ordinary least squares (OLS) is its interpretation from a maximum likelihood perspective. The following theorem establishes the relationship between OLS and maximum likelihood estimation (MLE).

Theorem 4.1. *The OLS estimator is the maximum likelihood estimator for the parameters of a linear regression model, assuming that the model's error terms (i.e., the unobserved noise) are independent and normally distributed with zero mean and constant variance.*

Proof. Consider the linear regression model:

$$y_i = \mathbf{w}^T \mathbf{x}_i + \epsilon_i, \tag{4.5}$$

where y_i is the target value for the i-th sample, $\mathbf{x}_i \in \mathbb{R}^d$ is the feature vector, $\mathbf{w} \in \mathbb{R}^d$ is the parameter vector, and ϵ_i is the error term representing noise or unmodeled effects.

Assume that the error terms ϵ_i are independent and normally distributed with mean zero and variance σ^2, that is, $\epsilon_i \sim \mathcal{N}(0, \sigma^2)$. Then the target variables y_i are also independent and normally distributed with mean $\mathbf{w}^T \mathbf{x}_i$ and variance σ^2, i.e., $y_i \sim \mathcal{N}(\mathbf{w}^T \mathbf{x}_i, \sigma^2)$.[1]

The likelihood of observing a single target value y_i, given the corresponding input $\mathbf{x}_i$ and the parameter vector $\mathbf{w}$, is:

$$p(y_i | \mathbf{x}_i, \mathbf{w}) = \frac{1}{\sqrt{2\pi}\sigma} \exp\left(-\frac{(y_i - \mathbf{w}^T \mathbf{x}_i)^2}{2\sigma^2}\right). \tag{4.6}$$

---

1. Adding a constant to a normally distributed variable results in a new normal distribution with the mean shifted by that constant.

Since the samples are assumed to be independent, the likelihood of the model parameters $\mathbf{w}$, given the dataset $(X, \mathbf{y})$, is:

$$\mathcal{L}(\mathbf{w}|X, \mathbf{y}) = \prod_{i=1}^{n} p(y_i|\mathbf{x}_i, \mathbf{w}) = \prod_{i=1}^{n} \frac{1}{\sqrt{2\pi}\sigma} \exp\left(-\frac{(y_i - \mathbf{w}^T\mathbf{x}_i)^2}{2\sigma^2}\right). \tag{4.7}$$

Taking the logarithm gives the log-likelihood function:

$$\log \mathcal{L}(\mathbf{w}|X, \mathbf{y}) = \sum_{i=1}^{n} \log\left(\frac{1}{\sqrt{2\pi}\sigma} \exp\left[-\frac{(y_i - \mathbf{w}^T\mathbf{x}_i)^2}{2\sigma^2}\right]\right)$$

$$= -n\log(\sqrt{2\pi}\sigma) - \frac{1}{2\sigma^2} \sum_{i=1}^{n}(y_i - \mathbf{w}^T\mathbf{x}_i)^2. \tag{4.8}$$

The first term is constant with respect to $\mathbf{w}$, so maximizing the log-likelihood is equivalent to minimizing the sum of squared losses, $\sum_{i=1}^{n}(y_i - \mathbf{w}^T\mathbf{x}_i)^2$. Therefore, the MLE for $\mathbf{w}$ coincides with the OLS estimator. $\square$

Although the normality assumption may seem restrictive, it is often reasonable in practice. Many sources of error—such as measurement noise in physical instruments or aggregated random effects—tend to follow a normal distribution due to the central limit theorem (see Section C.14.3).

4.3   Simple Linear Regression

Simple linear regression models the relationship between a single independent variable x and a dependent variable y. The objective is to find a linear function that accurately predicts y based on x. Mathematically, this model is defined as:

$$h(x) = w_0 + w_1 x. \tag{4.9}$$

Here, $h(x)$ represents the equation of a straight line, where w_1 is the slope, describing the rate of change of y with respect to x, and w_0 is the intercept, indicating where the line intersects the y-axis. Geometrically, the task is to find the line that best fits the data points (known as the **regression line**) by minimizing the residuals, as illustrated in Figure 4.1.

To determine the optimal coefficients w_0 and w_1, we use the **least squares method**, which minimizes the sum of squared residuals between the observed values and the predictions of the model. This corresponds to minimizing the following cost function:

$$J(w_0, w_1) = \frac{1}{n} \sum_{i=1}^{n}(y_i - h(x_i))^2 = \frac{1}{n} \sum_{i=1}^{n}(y_i - (w_0 + w_1 x_i))^2. \tag{4.10}$$

To identify the coefficients w_0 and w_1 that minimize $J(w_0, w_1)$, we compute the partial derivatives of J with respect to each parameter and set them to zero. This procedure leads to a system of

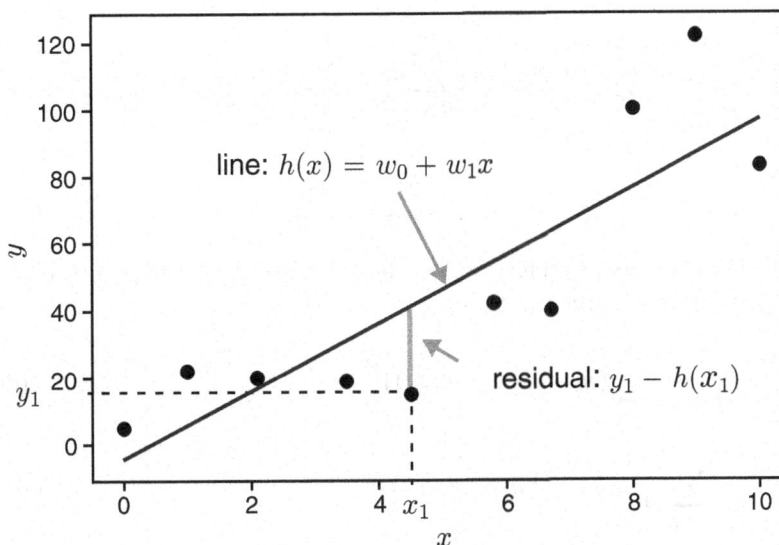

Figure 4.1: In simple linear regression, the goal is to find the best-fitting line, represented as $h(x) = w_0 + w_1x$. The solid fitted line shows the optimal solution. The vertical distances between the black data points and the line are the residuals; one such residual is highlighted in the figure. The optimal line minimizes the sum of squared residuals using the method of least squares.

linear equations (known as the **normal equations**) that can be solved to find the optimal parameter values. We begin with the partial derivative of J with respect to w_0:

$$\frac{\partial}{\partial w_0} J(w_0, w_1) = \frac{\partial}{\partial w_0} \frac{1}{n} \sum_{i=1}^{n} (y_i - (w_0 + w_1 x_i))^2 \qquad \text{(definition of } J\text{)}$$

$$= \frac{1}{n} \sum_{i=1}^{n} \frac{\partial}{\partial w_0} (y_i - (w_0 + w_1 x_i))^2 \qquad \text{(sum of derivatives)}$$

$$= \frac{1}{n} \sum_{i=1}^{n} \left[2 (y_i - (w_0 + w_1 x_i)) \frac{\partial}{\partial w_0} (y_i - (w_0 + w_1 x_i)) \right] \qquad \text{(chain rule)}$$

$$= \frac{1}{n} \sum_{i=1}^{n} 2 (y_i - (w_0 + w_1 x_i)) \cdot (-1) \qquad \text{(partial derivative)}$$

$$= \frac{1}{n} \sum_{i=1}^{n} 2(w_0 + w_1 x_i - y_i). \qquad \text{(rearranging terms)}$$

Setting the derivative to zero gives:

$$\sum_{i=1}^{n} 2(w_0 + w_1 x_i - y_i) = 0$$

$$nw_0 + w_1 \sum_{i=1}^{n} x_i - \sum_{i=1}^{n} y_i = 0$$

$$w_0 = \frac{\sum_{i=1}^{n} y_i - w_1 \sum_{i=1}^{n} x_i}{n}. \tag{4.11}$$

Equation (4.11) expresses w_0 in terms of w_1 and the observed data points. Next, we compute the partial derivative of J with respect to w_1:

$$\frac{\partial}{\partial w_1} J(w_0, w_1) = \frac{\partial}{\partial w_1} \frac{1}{n} \sum_{i=1}^{n} (y_i - (w_0 + w_1 x_i))^2 \qquad \text{(definition of } J\text{)}$$

$$= \frac{1}{n} \sum_{i=1}^{n} \frac{\partial}{\partial w_1} (y_i - (w_0 + w_1 x_i))^2 \qquad \text{(sum of derivatives)}$$

$$= \frac{1}{n} \sum_{i=1}^{n} \left[2 (y_i - (w_0 + w_1 x_i)) \frac{\partial}{\partial w_1} (y_i - (w_0 + w_1 x_i)) \right] \qquad \text{(chain rule)}$$

$$= \frac{1}{n} \sum_{i=1}^{n} 2 (y_i - (w_0 + w_1 x_i)) x_i. \qquad \text{(partial derivative)}$$

Setting this derivative to zero yields:

$$\sum_{i=1}^{n} 2 (y_i - (w_0 + w_1 x_i)) x_i = 0$$

$$\sum_{i=1}^{n} x_i y_i - w_0 \sum_{i=1}^{n} x_i - w_1 \sum_{i=1}^{n} x_i^2 = 0.$$

Substituting the expression for w_0 from Equation (4.11) into this equation gives:

$$\sum_{i=1}^{n} x_i y_i - \left(\frac{\sum_{i=1}^{n} y_i - w_1 \sum_{i=1}^{n} x_i}{n} \right) \sum_{i=1}^{n} x_i - w_1 \sum_{i=1}^{n} x_i^2 = 0$$

$$\sum_{i=1}^{n} x_i y_i - \frac{\sum_{i=1}^{n} x_i \sum_{i=1}^{n} y_i}{n} + \frac{w_1 \left(\sum_{i=1}^{n} x_i \right)^2}{n} - w_1 \sum_{i=1}^{n} x_i^2 = 0$$

$$w_1 \left[\frac{\left(\sum_{i=1}^{n} x_i \right)^2}{n} - \sum_{i=1}^{n} x_i^2 \right] = \frac{\sum_{i=1}^{n} x_i \sum_{i=1}^{n} y_i}{n} - \sum_{i=1}^{n} x_i y_i.$$

Solving for w_1, we obtain:

$$w_1 = \frac{n \sum_{i=1}^{n} x_i y_i - \sum_{i=1}^{n} x_i \sum_{i=1}^{n} y_i}{n \sum_{i=1}^{n} x_i^2 - \left(\sum_{i=1}^{n} x_i \right)^2}. \tag{4.12}$$

Equations (4.11) and (4.12), which determine the coefficients of the best-fitting regression line, are collectively known as the **closed-form solution** to simple linear regression.

4.3.1 Numerical Example

We now apply the closed-form solution to explore the linear relationship between people's height and weight using real-world data. The dataset used in this example consists of the average heights and weights of American women aged 30–39, as reported in *The World Almanac and Book of Facts (1975)* [153]. It contains ten data points, shown in Table 4.1.

Using Equations (4.11) and (4.12), we can compute the coefficients of the regression line that best fits the observed data points. These equations involve terms that are used repeatedly, such as $\sum x_i, \sum y_i, \sum x_i^2$, and $\sum x_i y_i$. These are systematically organized in Table 4.2, which simplifies the process of calculating the coefficients.

Using the totals from the last row of the table, the coefficients of the regression line can be computed as follows:

Height (m)	Weight (kg)
1.55	55.84
1.60	58.57
1.63	59.93
1.68	63.11
1.70	64.47
1.73	66.28
1.75	68.10
1.78	69.92
1.80	72.19
1.83	74.46

Table 4.1: Average heights and weights of American women aged 30–39, sourced from *The World Almanac and Book of Facts, 1975*.

i	x_i	y_i	x_i^2	$x_i y_i$
1	1.55	55.84	2.4025	86.5520
2	1.60	58.57	2.5600	93.7120
3	1.63	59.93	2.6569	97.6859
4	1.68	63.11	2.8224	106.0248
5	1.70	64.47	2.8900	109.5990
6	1.73	66.28	2.9929	114.6644
7	1.75	68.10	3.0625	119.1750
8	1.78	69.92	3.1684	124.4576
9	1.80	72.19	3.2400	129.9420
10	1.83	74.46	3.3489	136.2618
Σ	**17.05**	**652.87**	**29.1445**	**1118.0745**

Table 4.2: Computation of regression coefficients for height and weight of American women aged 30–39. The table includes squared heights (x_i^2) and height-weight products ($x_i y_i$), which are required for evaluating Equations (4.11) and (4.12).

$$w_1 = \frac{10 \cdot 1118.0745 - 17.05 \cdot 652.87}{10 \cdot 29.1445 - 17.05^2} = 66.4127,$$

$$w_0 = \frac{652.87 - 66.4127 \cdot 17.05}{10} = -47.9467.$$

Thus, the equation of the fitted line is:

$$y = -47.9467 + 66.4127x.$$

This equation suggests that for every centimeter increase in height, the average weight of an American woman in this age group increases by approximately 0.664 kg (since the slope is 66.4 kg per meter).

4.3.2   Implementation in Python

Clearly, manual computation of the regression coefficients becomes impractical for larger datasets. In such cases, we can use Python, and particularly the NumPy library, to compute the coefficients efficiently. We begin by defining a function that computes the regression coefficients for any two-dimensional dataset, based on Equations (4.11) and (4.12):

```
import numpy as np

def find_coefficients(x, y):
    n = len(x) # Number of data points
```

```
# Compute the slope
w1 = (n * np.dot(x, y) - np.sum(x) * np.sum(y)) /
        (n * np.sum(x**2) - np.sum(x)**2)

# Compute the intercept
w0 = (np.sum(y) - w1 * np.sum(x)) / n
return w0, w1
```

This function leverages NumPy's vectorized operations (see Section F.1.3) to efficiently compute the slope w_1 and intercept w_0 of the regression line without using explicit loops. Vectorization not only simplifies the code but also significantly improves performance, especially when working with large datasets.

Next, we define the data points and use Matplotlib to visually inspect them:

```
import matplotlib.pyplot as plt

# The data points
heights = np.array([1.55, 1.60, 1.63, 1.68, 1.70, 1.73, 1.75, 1.78, 1.80, 1.83])
weights = np.array([55.84, 58.57, 59.93, 63.11, 64.47, 66.28, 68.10, 69.92, 72.19,
                    74.46])

# Function to plot data points
def plot_data(x, y):
    plt.scatter(x, y)
    plt.xlabel('Height (m)')
    plt.ylabel('Weight (kg)')
    plt.grid()

# Plotting the data
plot_data(heights, weights)
```

The scatter plot in Figure 4.2 illustrates the relationship between height and weight. We now compute the regression coefficients using the previously defined function:

```
w0, w1 = find_coefficients(heights, weights)
print(f'w0 = {w0:.4f}')
print(f'w1 = {w1:.4f}')
```

The resulting coefficients are:

```
w0 = -47.9468
w1 = 66.4128
```

These values closely align with those derived from our manual calculation.

Next, we enhance our visualization by adding the regression line to the scatter plot. The following function plots the line by first determining the minimum and maximum values of x, computing

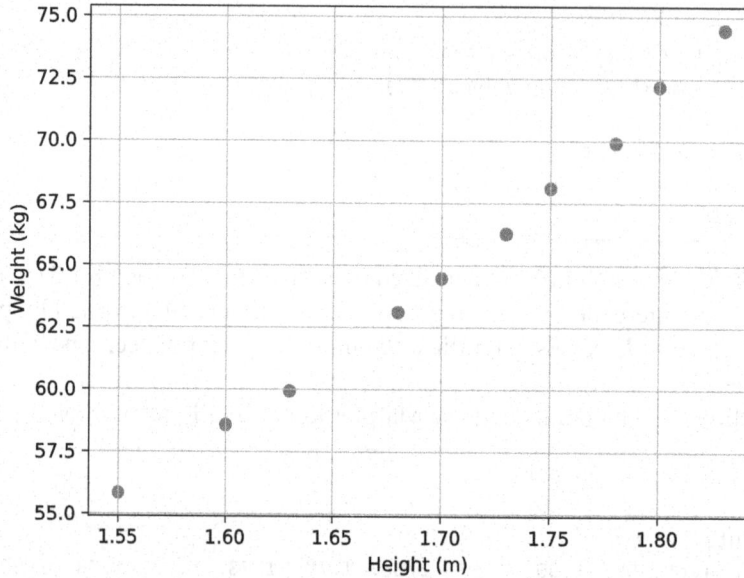

Figure 4.2: Scatter plot of height and weight data, illustrating the potential linear relationship between the two variables.

their corresponding y values using the regression equation $y = w_0 + w_1 x$, and then drawing a straight line that connects these two endpoints:

```
def plot_regression_line(x, y, w0, w1):
    # Determine the start and end points of the regression line
    p_x = np.array([x.min(), x.max()])
    p_y = w0 + w1 * p_x

    # Plot the regression line in red
    plt.plot(p_x, p_y, 'r')

# Plotting the data points with the regression line
plot_data(heights, weights)
plot_regression_line(heights, weights, w0, w1)
```

The resulting plot, shown in Figure 4.3, clearly illustrates how well the linear model fits the observed data, confirming an approximately linear relationship between height and weight.

4.4   Multiple Linear Regression

In this section, we extend the closed-form solution presented in Section 4.3 to handle multiple input variables. To simplify the derivation in the general case, we represent the features using the

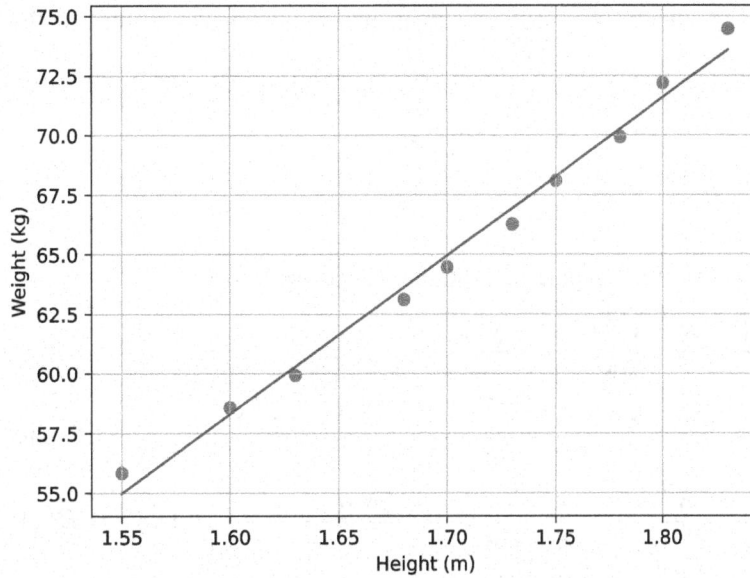

Figure 4.3: Scatter plot of the height and weight data overlaid with the regression line, demonstrating the effectiveness of the simple linear regression model.

design matrix X, which contains all the feature values and an additional column of 1s to account for the intercept term:

$$X = \begin{pmatrix} 1 & x_{11} & x_{12} & \cdots & x_{1d} \\ 1 & x_{21} & x_{22} & \cdots & x_{2d} \\ \vdots & \vdots & \vdots & \ddots & \vdots \\ 1 & x_{n1} & x_{n2} & \cdots & x_{nd} \end{pmatrix} \tag{4.13}$$

The corresponding target values are represented by the vector $\mathbf{y} = (y_1, \ldots, y_n)^T$. With this notation, we can express the least squares cost function in matrix form as follows:

$$J(\mathbf{w}) = \frac{1}{n}(X\mathbf{w} - \mathbf{y})^T(X\mathbf{w} - \mathbf{y}). \tag{4.14}$$

Proof. We first observe that:

$$X\mathbf{w} - \mathbf{y} = \begin{pmatrix} w_0 x_{1,0} + \ldots + w_d x_{1,d} \\ \vdots \\ w_0 x_{n,0} + \ldots + w_d x_{n,d} \end{pmatrix} - \begin{pmatrix} y_1 \\ \vdots \\ y_n \end{pmatrix} = \begin{pmatrix} \mathbf{w}^T \mathbf{x}_1 \\ \vdots \\ \mathbf{w}^T \mathbf{x}_n \end{pmatrix} - \begin{pmatrix} y_1 \\ \vdots \\ y_n \end{pmatrix} = \begin{pmatrix} h_{\mathbf{w}}(\mathbf{x}_1) - y_1 \\ \vdots \\ h_{\mathbf{w}}(\mathbf{x}_n) - y_n \end{pmatrix}.$$

Since the dot product of a vector $\mathbf{u}$ with itself, $\mathbf{u}^T\mathbf{u}$, equals the sum of the squares of its components, we have:

$$(X\mathbf{w} - \mathbf{y})^T(X\mathbf{w} - \mathbf{y}) = \sum_{i=1}^{n}(h_{\mathbf{w}}(\mathbf{x}_i) - y_i)^2.$$

$\square$

To minimize $J(\mathbf{w})$, we compute its gradient with respect to $\mathbf{w}$:

$$\frac{\partial J(\mathbf{w})}{\partial \mathbf{w}} = \frac{1}{n} \cdot \frac{\partial\left((X\mathbf{w} - \mathbf{y})^T(X\mathbf{w} - \mathbf{y})\right)}{\partial \mathbf{w}} \qquad \text{(definition of } J)$$

$$= \frac{1}{n} \cdot \frac{\partial\left((X\mathbf{w})^T X\mathbf{w} - (X\mathbf{w})^T\mathbf{y} - \mathbf{y}^T(X\mathbf{w}) + \mathbf{y}^T\mathbf{y}\right)}{\partial \mathbf{w}} \qquad \text{(expanding brackets)}$$

$$= \frac{1}{n} \cdot \frac{\partial\left(\mathbf{w}^T X^T X\mathbf{w} - \mathbf{y}^T(X\mathbf{w}) - \mathbf{y}^T(X\mathbf{w}) + \mathbf{y}^T\mathbf{y}\right)}{\partial \mathbf{w}} \qquad ((AB)^T = B^T A^T, \mathbf{x}^T\mathbf{y} = \mathbf{y}^T\mathbf{x})$$

$$= \frac{1}{n} \cdot \frac{\partial\left(\mathbf{w}^T X^T X\mathbf{w} - 2\mathbf{y}^T(X\mathbf{w})\right)}{\partial \mathbf{w}} \qquad (\mathbf{y}^T\mathbf{y} \text{ is not a function of } \mathbf{w})$$

$$= \frac{1}{n} \cdot \frac{\partial\left(\mathbf{w}^T(X^T X)\mathbf{w} - 2(X^T\mathbf{y})^T\mathbf{w}\right)}{\partial \mathbf{w}} \qquad \text{(matrix multiplication associativity)}$$

$$= \frac{1}{n}\left(\frac{\partial\left(\mathbf{w}^T(X^T X)\mathbf{w}\right)}{\partial \mathbf{w}} - 2\frac{\partial\left((X^T\mathbf{y})^T\mathbf{w}\right)}{\partial \mathbf{w}}\right) \qquad \text{(derivatives of sum of functions)}$$

$$= \frac{1}{n}\left(2X^T X\mathbf{w} - 2\frac{\partial\left((X^T\mathbf{y})^T\mathbf{w}\right)}{\partial \mathbf{w}}\right) \qquad \left(\text{for a symmetric } A, \frac{\partial \mathbf{x}^T A\mathbf{x}}{\partial \mathbf{x}} = 2A\mathbf{x}\right)$$

$$= \frac{1}{n}\left(2X^T X\mathbf{w} - 2X^T\mathbf{y}\right) \qquad \left(\text{for any vector } \mathbf{u}, \frac{\partial \mathbf{u}^T\mathbf{x}}{\partial \mathbf{x}} = \mathbf{u}\right)$$

In the last two steps, we applied standard identities from matrix calculus to differentiate quadratic and linear forms of multivariable functions (see Section B.9.1). Setting the gradient of $J(\mathbf{w})$ to zero yields the following system of linear equations:

$$X^T X\mathbf{w} = X^T\mathbf{y}. \tag{4.15}$$

These are known as the **normal equations**. The term "normal" originates from the geometric interpretation of these equations: the residual vector $\mathbf{y} - X\mathbf{w}$ is orthogonal (or "normal" in the geometric sense) to the subspace spanned by the columns of the design matrix X (see Figure 4.4). The objective in least squares regression is to find the weight vector $\mathbf{w}$ that minimizes the perpendicular distance from $\mathbf{y}$ to this subspace.

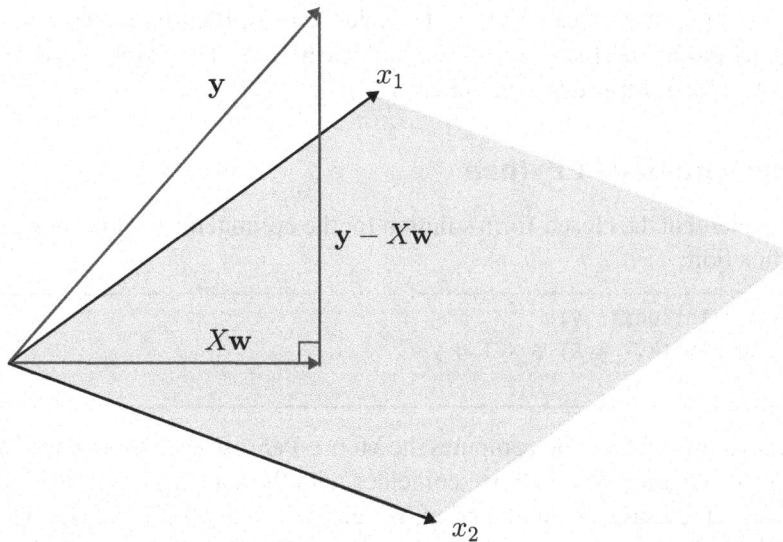

Figure 4.4: Geometric Interpretation of the normal equations in least squares regression. The residuals, represented by $\mathbf{y} - X\mathbf{w}$, are orthogonal to the subspace spanned by the columns of the design matrix X (illustrated here as the axes x_1 and x_2). The least squares solution seeks to minimize these residuals by finding the weight vector $\mathbf{w}$ that yields the shortest perpendicular distance from the vector $\mathbf{y}$ to the column subspace of X.

If the columns of X are linearly independent (i.e., X has full rank), then the matrix $X^T X$ is invertible (see Exercise 4.14). Under this condition, we can express the solution to the normal equations as:

$$\mathbf{w}^* = (X^T X)^{-1} X^T \mathbf{y}. \tag{4.16}$$

Although linear dependence among the columns of X is uncommon, it can arise under certain conditions. For example, it may occur when one variable is a linear transformation of another (e.g., the same feature measured in different units), or when the dataset contains more features than observations. In the latter case, X has more columns than rows and cannot be full rank, making $X^T X$ noninvertible and preventing the normal equations from having a unique solution.

When $X^T X$ is not invertible, the **Moore-Penrose pseudoinverse** can be used to compute the regression coefficients. The pseudoinverse of a matrix A, denoted A^+, generalizes the concept of a matrix inverse to non-invertible or non-square matrices and provides a least-squares solution to the system $A\mathbf{x} = \mathbf{y}$, minimizing the residual norm $\|A\mathbf{x} - \mathbf{y}\|^2$ (see Section A.3.9.3 for details).

Accordingly, the solution to the normal equations can be written more generally as:

$$\mathbf{w}^* = (X^T X)^+ X^T \mathbf{y}, \tag{4.17}$$

where $\mathbf{w}^*$ minimizes the least squares cost function $\|X\mathbf{w} - \mathbf{y}\|^2$, even when the normal equations do not have a unique solution.

A more common issue than exact linear dependence is **multicollinearity,** where two or more features are highly but not perfectly correlated with each other. This issue, along with methods to detect and handle it, is discussed in Section 4.7.1.

4.4.1   Implementation in Python

We can easily implement the closed-form solution for the optimal regression coefficients $\mathbf{w}^*$ using the following function:

```python
def closed_form_solution(X, y):
    w = np.linalg.pinv(X.T @ X) @ X.T @ y
    return w
```

The np.linalg.pinv[2] function computes the Moore-Penrose pseudoinverse of a matrix. When the matrix is invertible, the pseudoinverse coincides with the standard inverse.

To demonstrate the usage of this function, we generate a synthetic dataset with two features and a target variable that is a linear combination of these features plus some Gaussian noise:

```python
def generate_data(n=100):
    # Generate synthetic data with two features and a linearly correlated label
    np.random.seed(42)

    x1 = 2 * np.random.rand(n)
    x2 = 3 * np.random.rand(n)
    y = 5 + 1 * x1 + 2 * x2 + np.random.randn(n)
    X = np.c_[x1, x2] # Concatenate the two features
    return X, y

X, y = generate_data()
```

We would like to find the coefficients of a linear regression model $y = w_0 + w_1 x_1 + w_2 x_2$ that best fits the data. Before computing the regression coefficients, we manually add a column of ones to the feature matrix to include the intercept term in the model:

```python
# Add a column of ones to X for the intercept term
n = len(X)
X_b = np.c_[np.ones((n, 1)), X]

# Compute the optimal coefficients
w = closed_form_solution(X_b, y)
print('Optimal coefficients:', np.round(w, 4))
```

```
Optimal coefficients: [4.9106 0.8291 2.2398]
```

---

2. https://numpy.org/doc/stable/reference/generated/numpy.linalg.pinv.html

The coefficients closely approximate the true parameters [5, 1, 2] that were used to generate the target variable. The small discrepancies between the estimated coefficients and the true values can be attributed to the Gaussian noise added to the data and the limited sample size.

To visualize the results, we can plot the data points and the fitted regression plane using a 3D plot as follows:

```
from mpl_toolkits.mplot3d import Axes3D # For 3D plotting

# Set up the figure for 3D plotting
fig = plt.figure()
ax = fig.add_subplot(111, projection='3d')

# Plot the data points
x1, x2 = X[:, 0], X[:, 1]
ax.scatter(x1, x2, y, color='blue')

# Create a mesh grid for the regression plane
x1_surf, x2_surf = np.meshgrid(np.linspace(x1.min(), x1.max(), 20),
                    np.linspace(x2.min(), x2.max(), 20))

# Calculate corresponding y values for the mesh grid
y_surf = w[0] + w[1] * x1_surf + w[2] * x2_surf

# Plot the regression plane
ax.plot_surface(x1_surf, x2_surf, y_surf, color='red', alpha=0.3)

ax.set_xlabel('$x_1$')
ax.set_ylabel('$x_2$')
ax.set_zlabel('$y$')
```

The resulting 3D plot in Figure 4.5 demonstrates how the regression plane fits the given data points, effectively capturing the underlying linear relationship between the features and the target variable.

4.4.2   The LinearRegression Class

Scikit-Learn's LinearRegression[3] class provides a convenient and efficient implementation of ordinary least squares regression using the closed-form solution. Its fit method computes the regression coefficients for the given dataset, and its predict method generates predictions for new input samples.

Let's apply this class to our synthetically generated dataset. Note that when fit_intercept=True (the default), LinearRegression automatically augments the feature matrix with a column of ones to account for the intercept term, eliminating the need to add it manually.

3. https://scikit-learn.org/stable/modules/generated/sklearn.linear_model.LinearRegression.html

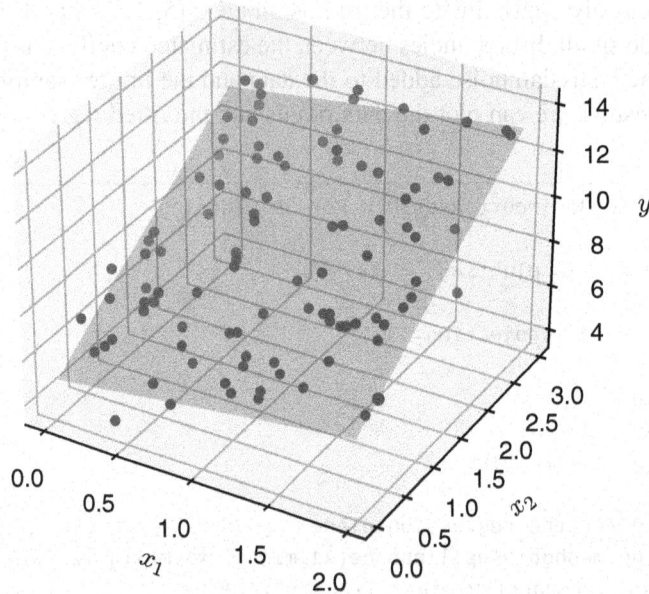

Figure 4.5: 3D plot of the synthetic dataset and the fitted regression plane, showing the relationship between the two independent variables x_1 and x_2 and the dependent variable y as modeled by multiple linear regression.

```
from sklearn.linear_model import LinearRegression

model = LinearRegression()
model.fit(X, y)
```

The model's coefficients are stored in two attributes:

- coef_ contains the coefficients for the input features $(w_1, \ldots, w_d)$.

- intercept_ stores the intercept term (w_0).

We can examine these values as follows:

```
print('Intercept:', np.round(model.intercept_, 4))
print('Coefficients:', np.round(model.coef_, 4))
```

The output is:

```
Intercept: 4.9106
Coefficients: [0.8291 2.2398]
```

These coefficients match those obtained using NumPy's closed-form solution. However, unlike the manual approach, which explicitly inverts $X^T X$ and may be numerically unstable, the

`LinearRegression` class uses a more robust technique based on Singular Value Decomposition (SVD) to avoid direct inversion and better handle ill-conditioned matrices and multicollinearity.

4.5 Regression Evaluation Metrics

Several metrics are commonly used to evaluate the performance of regression models, including RMSE (Root Mean Squared Error), MAE (Mean Absolute Error), and R^2 score [99, 115]. Recall from Section 2.2.6 that an evaluation metric is used to assess the trained model on a holdout dataset (such as a validation or test set), in contrast to a loss or cost function, which is used to guide the model's learning process and is typically computed on the training set.

4.5.1 RMSE

The **Root Mean Squared Error (RMSE)** is the square root of the Mean Squared Error (MSE), defined as:

$$\text{RMSE} = \sqrt{\frac{1}{n} \sum_{i=1}^{n} (y_i - \hat{y}_i)^2}, \tag{4.18}$$

where $\hat{y}_i$ denotes the model's predicted value for the i-th sample. Taking the square root of MSE restores the metric to the same units as the target variable, making it easier to interpret. A lower RMSE indicates a better fit to the data, with an RMSE of 0 corresponding to a perfect model.

To calculate RMSE, we can use the `root_mean_squared_error`[4] function from the `sklearn.metrics`[5] module, which provides a variety of scoring functions for evaluating model performance. These functions typically require two inputs: the true labels (`y_true`) and the model's predictions (`y_pred`).

For example, we can compute the RMSE of our linear regression model from the previous section as follows:

```
from sklearn.metrics import root_mean_squared_error as RMSE

y_pred = model.predict(X)
rmse = RMSE(y, y_pred)
print(f'RMSE: {rmse:.4f}')
```

```
RMSE: 0.9725
```

An RMSE of 0.9725 indicates that the typical size of the prediction error is approximately 0.97. This closely matches the standard deviation of the Gaussian noise (1.0) used to generate the target variable, which is also defined as the square root of the average squared deviations from

---

4. https://scikit-learn.org/stable/modules/generated/sklearn.metrics.root_mean_squared_error.html

5. https://scikit-learn.org/stable/modules/classes.html#module-sklearn.metrics

the mean. However, RMSE should not be interpreted as the average magnitude of the errors—that interpretation is more appropriate for MAE (discussed in the next section).

Advantages of RMSE:

- RMSE is expressed in the same units as the target variable, making the results easier to interpret.

- By squaring the errors, RMSE gives greater weight to larger deviations—useful when large errors are especially undesirable (e.g., in medical dose prediction, where large deviations can have serious consequences).

Disadvantages of RMSE:

- RMSE is scale-dependent, making it unsuitable for comparing models across datasets with different target scales.

- The squaring of errors makes RMSE sensitive to outliers, which can lead to an overestimation of the typical prediction error when extreme values are present.

4.5.2   MAE

Mean Absolute Error (MAE) measures the average magnitude of the errors. It is calculated as the average of the absolute differences between the predicted and observed values:

$$\text{MAE} = \frac{1}{n} \sum_{i=1}^{n} |y_i - \hat{y}_i|. \tag{4.19}$$

We can evaluate the MAE for our regression model using the following code:

```
from sklearn.metrics import mean_absolute_error

mae = mean_absolute_error(y, y_pred)
print(f'MAE: {mae:.4f}')
```

```
MAE: 0.7748
```

An MAE of 0.7748 indicates that, on average, the model's predictions deviate from the actual values by 0.7748 units.

Advantages of MAE:

- MAE is simple and intuitive, providing a direct measure of the average error in the same units as the target variable.

- It is less sensitive to outliers than RMSE, since it does not square the errors.

Disadvantages of MAE:

- Like RMSE, MAE is scale-dependent, which can limit its usefulness when comparing model performance across datasets with different target scales.

- MAE treats all errors equally, which may be suboptimal in applications where large deviations are especially costly.

4.5.3 R^2 Score

The R^2 score, also known as the **coefficient of determination**, measures the goodness-of-fit of a regression model by comparing its prediction errors to those of a simple baseline model that always predicts the mean of the target variable, $\bar{y}$. It is defined as:

$$R^2 = 1 - \frac{\sum_{i=1}^{n}(y_i - \hat{y}_i)^2}{\sum_{i=1}^{n}(y_i - \bar{y})^2}. \tag{4.20}$$

An R^2 score of 1 indicates perfect predictions, a score of 0 implies that the model performs no better than the baseline, and a negative score suggests that the model performs worse than simply predicting the mean.

The R^2 score can also be understood as the proportion of variance in the dependent variable that is explained by the independent variables. This interpretation is based on decomposing the total variance of the target variable into two parts: the variance explained by the model and the residual variance that remains unexplained:

- **Total Variance (TV)** is the overall variance in the target variable y, calculated as the sum of squared deviations of the actual target values from their mean:

$$TV = \sum_{i=1}^{n}(y_i - \bar{y})^2. \tag{4.21}$$

- **Explained Variance (EV)** is the portion of the total variance explained by the model, computed as the sum of squared differences between the model's predictions and the target mean:

$$EV = \sum_{i=1}^{n}(\hat{y}_i - \bar{y})^2. \tag{4.22}$$

- **Residual Variance (RV)** represents the variance that the model fails to explain, computed as the sum of squared residuals:

$$RV = \sum_{i=1}^{n}(y_i - \hat{y}_i)^2. \tag{4.23}$$

The total variance can be expressed as the sum of explained and residual variance:

$$TV = EV + RV. \tag{4.24}$$

Substituting into the definition of R^2, we obtain:

$$R^2 = 1 - \frac{RV}{TV} = 1 - \frac{RV}{EV + RV} = \frac{EV}{TV}. \tag{4.25}$$

In other words, the R^2 score is the ratio of the variance explained by the model to the total variance in the data. A higher R^2 score indicates that the model explains a greater proportion of the variability in the target variable, while a lower score suggests that the independent variables fail to account for much of the observed variation.

To compute the R^2 score, we can use the r2_score[6] function from the sklearn.metrics module. Alternatively, we can simply invoke the score method on the LinearRegression model instance, as R^2 is the default scoring metric for regressors in Scikit-Learn:

```
r2_score = model.score(X, y)
print(f'R2 score: {r2_score:.4f}')
```

```
R2 score: 0.8094
```

An R^2 score of 0.8094 indicates that the model explains a substantial portion of the variance in the target variable using the given predictors.

Advantages of R^2 score:

- R^2 is scale-independent and unaffected by the units of the target variable, making it suitable for comparing models across different datasets.

- It provides a standardized metric (typically between 0 and 1) that facilitates model comparison and interpretation.

- It quantifies the proportion of variance in the target variable that is explained by the predictors, offering insight into the model's explanatory power.

Disadvantages of R^2 score:

- R^2 does not capture the absolute magnitude of prediction errors. A high R^2 score does not guarantee small errors if the target variable has high variance.

- R^2 may increase when irrelevant predictors are added to the model, as they can capture spurious variance in the target variable due to chance correlations, potentially leading to overfitting.

  This issue can be mitigated by using the **adjusted R^2 score**, which penalizes the standard R^2 to account for the number of predictors, providing a more reliable estimate of the model's true explanatory power [419].

---

6. https://scikit-learn.org/stable/modules/generated/sklearn.metrics.r2_score.html

4.6 Example: Predicting Housing Prices

In this section, we build a linear regression model to predict housing prices using the California housing dataset[7] from Scikit-Learn. Derived from the 1990 US Census, this dataset contains aggregated data for each census block group (district) in California, typically encompassing between 600 and 3,000 residents [462]. Each district is described by eight attributes such as median income, median house age, and average number of rooms per household, which are summarized in Table 4.3. The target variable is the median house value in each district, measured in hundreds of thousands of dollars.

Understanding the features that affect housing prices can offer valuable insights not only for real estate valuation but also for informing public policy and economic planning by highlighting key factors that influence housing affordability.

The complete source code for this example, as presented throughout this section, is available in the accompanying Jupyter notebook `CaliforniaHousingPricePrediction.ipynb`[8] on GitHub.

4.6.1 Loading and Exploring the Dataset

We first import the necessary libraries and fix the random seed for reproducibility:

```
import numpy as np
import pandas as pd
import matplotlib.pyplot as plt

np.random.seed(42)
```

Feature	Description
MedInc	Median income in the block group (in tens of thousands of dollars)
HouseAge	Median house age in the block group (in years)
AveRooms	Average number of rooms per household
AveBedrms	Average number of bedrooms per household
Population	Total population in the block group
AveOccup	Average number of people per household
Latitude	Latitude coordinate of the block group
Longitude	Longitude coordinate of the block group

Table 4.3: Description of the features in the California housing dataset

---

7. https://scikit-learn.org/stable/modules/generated/sklearn.datasets.fetch_california_housing.html

8. https://github.com/roiyeho/ml-book/blob/main/Chapter04/CaliforniaHousingPricePrediction.ipynb

Next, we load the California housing dataset from `sklearn.datasets`:

```
from sklearn.datasets import fetch_california_housing

X, y = fetch_california_housing(as_frame=True, return_X_y=True)
```

To facilitate exploration of the dataset, we combine the feature matrix X and the target vector y into a single DataFrame using the `pd.concat`[9] function. We then display the first few rows of the table (see Figure 4.6):

```
housing_df = pd.concat([X, y], axis=1)
housing_df.head()
```

We further examine the dataset using the `info` method to inspect the data types and check for missing values:

```
<class 'pandas.core.frame.DataFrame'>
RangeIndex: 20640 entries, 0 to 20639
Data columns (total 9 columns):
 #   Column       Non-Null Count   Dtype
---  ------       --------------   -----
 0   MedInc       20640 non-null   float64
 1   HouseAge     20640 non-null   float64
 2   AveRooms     20640 non-null   float64
 3   AveBedrms    20640 non-null   float64
 4   Population   20640 non-null   float64
 5   AveOccup     20640 non-null   float64
 6   Latitude     20640 non-null   float64
 7   Longitude    20640 non-null   float64
 8   MedHouseVal  20640 non-null   float64
dtypes: float64(9)
memory usage: 1.4 MB
```

	MedInc	HouseAge	AveRooms	AveBedrms	Population	AveOccup	Latitude	Longitude	MedHouseVal
0	8.3252	41.0	6.984127	1.023810	322.0	2.555556	37.88	−122.23	4.526
1	8.3014	21.0	6.238137	0.971880	2401.0	2.109842	37.86	−122.22	3.585
2	7.2574	52.0	8.288136	1.073446	496.0	2.802260	37.85	−122.24	3.521
3	5.6431	52.0	5.817352	1.073059	558.0	2.547945	37.85	−122.25	3.413
4	3.8462	52.0	6.281853	1.081081	565.0	2.181467	37.85	−122.25	3.422

Figure 4.6: The first five rows of the California housing dataset, displaying eight input features for each district such as median income (`MedInc`), median house age (`HouseAge`), and average number of rooms per household (`AveRooms`). The target variable, median house value (`MedHouseVal`), is shown in the last column.

---

9. https://pandas.pydata.org/docs/reference/api/pandas.concat.html

As shown, all features are numerical and there are no missing values, thus no initial data preprocessing is needed. Moreover, since we will use the closed-form solution for ordinary least squares, feature scaling is not necessary (see Exercise 4.15).

We now split the dataset, using 80% of the data for training and the remaining 20% for testing:

```
from sklearn.model_selection import train_test_split

X_train, X_test, y_train, y_test = train_test_split(X, y, test_size=0.2,
                                                    random_state=42)
```

4.6.2 Building the Model

We are now ready to build and train a linear regression model:

```
from sklearn.linear_model import LinearRegression

reg = LinearRegression()
reg.fit(X_train, y_train)
```

After training, we can inspect the model's learned coefficients (weights). In linear models, such as linear regression and logistic regression, these coefficients have a clear interpretation: they directly represent the contribution of each input feature to the model's predictions (often referred to as **feature importance**). The magnitude of each coefficient indicates how strongly the feature affects the target variable, while the sign indicates the direction of the relationship.

To view the coefficients, we can use the `intercept_` and `coef_` attributes of the trained model:

```
print('Intercept:', np.round(reg.intercept_, 4))
print('Coefficients:', np.round(reg.coef_, 4))
```

```
Intercept: -37.0233
Coefficients: [ 0.4487  0.0097 -0.1233  0.7831 -0. -0.0035 -0.4198 -0.4337]
```

Since the features have different scales, the raw coefficients are not directly comparable. To assess relative importance, we normalize the coefficients by dividing each one by the standard deviation of its corresponding feature:

```
normalized_coef = reg.coef_ / X_train.std(axis=0)
print(np.round(normalized_coef, 4))
```

```
MedInc        0.2356
HouseAge      0.0008
AveRooms     -0.0517
AveBedrms     1.8078
Population   -0.0000
AveOccup     -0.0003
Latitude     -0.1965
Longitude    -0.2162
```

The features with the greatest influence on the model's predictions (holding all other features constant) are the average number of bedrooms (AveBedrms) and median income (MedInc), both positively correlated with house value. Geographic location, captured by latitude and longitude, also plays a significant role, with negative coefficients—reflecting the trend that housing prices tend to decrease as one moves farther from the coast (longitude increases eastward and latitude increases northward within California).

4.6.3   Evaluating the Model

Next, we evaluate the model's performance on both the training and test sets, using the RMSE and R^2 score:

```
from sklearn.metrics import root_mean_squared_error as RMSE


# Evaluation on the training set
train_rmse = RMSE(y_train, reg.predict(X_train))
train_r2 = reg.score(X_train, y_train)
print(f'Train RMSE: {train_rmse:.4f}, R2: {train_r2:.4f}')


# Evaluation on the test set
test_rmse = RMSE(y_test, reg.predict(X_test))
test_r2 = reg.score(X_test, y_test)
print(f'Test RMSE: {test_rmse:.4f}, R2: {test_r2:.4f}')
```

The results are as follows:

```
Train RMSE: 0.7197, R2: 0.6126
Test RMSE: 0.7456, R2: 0.5758
```

The test RMSE value indicates that, on average, the model's predictions deviate by approximately \$74,500 from the actual house prices in the test set. Given that the average house price in the dataset is around \$200,000, this represents a substantial prediction error. Similarly, the test R^2 score of 0.5758 shows that the model explains only 57.58% of the variance in housing prices, leaving a large portion of the variability unaccounted for.

The relatively low R^2 scores on both the training and test sets suggest that the model is underfitting, indicating that a linear model may not be flexible enough to capture the underlying complexity of the data.

4.6.4   Feature Engineering

Feature engineering is a critical step of model development, where new features are derived from the existing dataset to better capture patterns or relationships relevant to the prediction task. This process often draws on domain knowledge and thoughtful reasoning about the problem context.

New features can sometimes be constructed using simple arithmetic operations between existing features, such as addition or multiplication. In other cases, more nuanced domain-specific insights are needed to derive meaningful features that are predictive of the target variable.

In the California housing dataset, consider the AveRooms variable, which represents the average number of rooms per household. On its own, this feature may not be a strong predictor of housing prices: areas with larger, lower-income families, for example, may have more rooms per household but still exhibit lower median house values.

A potentially more informative feature is the ratio of the average number of rooms to the average household size (AveOccup), which approximates the number of rooms per person. This value may better reflect the standard of living and could correlate more strongly with median house prices.

To explore this hypothesis, let's add the new feature to our dataset:

```
X['RoomsPerIndividual'] = X['AveRooms'] / X['AveOccup']
```

We can evaluate the correlation between our newly created feature and the target variable using the DataFrame's corrwith[10] method. This method computes the Pearson correlation coefficients between the columns of the DataFrame and a given Series or DataFrame (in this case, we provide the target variable as the argument):

```
correlations = X.corrwith(y).sort_values(ascending=False)
print(correlations)
```

The correlation coefficients are:

```
MedInc                0.688075
RoomsPerIndividual    0.209482
AveRooms              0.151948
HouseAge              0.105623
AveOccup             -0.023737
Population           -0.024650
Longitude            -0.045967
AveBedrms            -0.046701
Latitude             -0.144160
```

Interestingly, the new feature RoomsPerIndividual has a stronger correlation (0.209) with the median house price than either of its original components (AveRooms and AveOccup), suggesting that it may provide additional predictive value.

Note: The feature RoomsPerIndividual is derived using only row-level information and does not rely on dataset-wide statistics. Therefore, it can be safely computed before splitting the data. In contrast, features that depend on global statistics (such as the mean or variance of a column) should be computed using only the training set to avoid data leakage.

---

10. https://pandas.pydata.org/docs/reference/api/pandas.DataFrame.corrwith.html

To assess whether this new feature improves model performance, we re-split the dataset into training and test sets using the same random seed to ensure consistency:

```
X_train, X_test, y_train, y_test = train_test_split(X, y, test_size=0.2,
                                            random_state=42)
```

We then retrain our model and evaluate its performance using the R^2 score:

```
reg.fit(X_train, y_train)
print(f'R2 score (train): {reg.score(X_train, y_train):.4f}')
print(f'R2 score (test): {reg.score(X_test, y_test):.4f}')
```

The revised model yields the following results:

```
R2 score (train): 0.6489
R2 score (test): 0.6395
```

By introducing just one additional feature, we observe a notable improvement in performance on both the training and test sets. For example, the test R^2 score increased from 0.5758 to 0.6395. This demonstrates the potential impact that thoughtful feature engineering can have on improving a model's predictive ability.

4.6.5   Discretization

As discussed in Section 3.10.6, discretization transforms continuous-valued features into discrete bins. This technique can help capture nonlinear relationships that a standard linear regression model may fail to represent.

In the California housing dataset, location-related features such as Longitude and Latitude can particularly benefit from discretization. By converting these continuous features into categorical bins, the model can more easily distinguish between geographically distinct regions, rather than assuming a smooth, continuous variation in housing prices across the map.

To illustrate this, consider a simplified scenario where house prices are predicted using only longitude. A simple linear regression model for this relationship takes the form

$$h(x) = w_0 + w_1 x,$$

where x denotes the longitude. This model assumes a direct linear relationship between longitude and the house price. For example, if $w_0 = 0$, the model predicts that a house located at longitude $x = 20$ is twice as expensive as one at $x = 10$, regardless of the learned coefficient w_1. This implies a uniform rate of price change across the entire range of longitudes—an unrealistic assumption, given that luxury neighborhoods may lie between areas with lower housing prices.

By discretizing the longitude into k bins, the model can learn distinct correlations between each region and housing prices (see Figure 4.7). This effectively changes the model to:

$$h(x) = w_0 + w_1 x_1 + \ldots + w_k x_k,$$

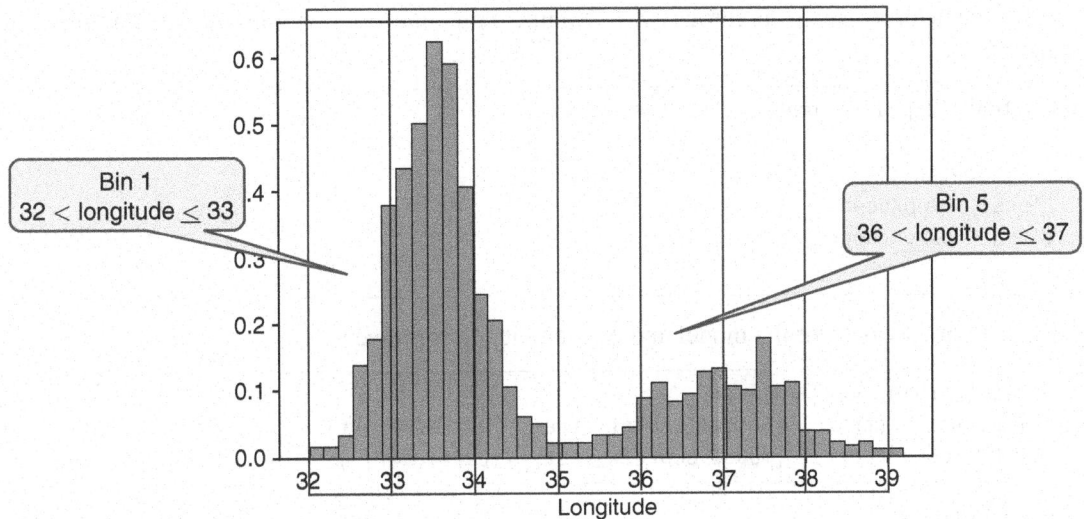

Figure 4.7: Discretization of longitude values into seven bins of equal width (one degree each), allowing the model to learn a separate coefficient for each region.

where $x_1, \ldots, x_k$ are binary variables indicating whether the house falls into a specific longitude bin. Unlike the original continuous formulation, this version allows the model to assign separate coefficients to each region, capturing nonlinear spatial patterns. In particular, it can assign different prices to houses that are numerically close in longitude but belong to different bins.

To demonstrate the benefits of discretizing location-based features, we now discretize the Longitude and Latitude columns of the California housing dataset into 10 intervals. To that end, we first define a ColumnTransformer that applies a KBinsDiscretizer to these two columns:

```
from sklearn.compose import ColumnTransformer
from sklearn.preprocessing import KBinsDiscretizer

columns = ['Longitude', 'Latitude']
preprocessor = ColumnTransformer([
    ('discretizer', KBinsDiscretizer(n_bins=10), columns)
], remainder='passthrough')
```

The argument remainder='passthrough' ensures that all features not explicitly listed in the transformer (i.e., columns other than Longitude and Latitude) are left unchanged and included in the output. Without this setting, any columns not specified would be dropped during the transformation.

Next, we incorporate this preprocessing step into a pipeline together with the linear regression model:

```
from sklearn.pipeline import Pipeline

model = Pipeline([
    ('pre', preprocessor),
    ('reg', LinearRegression())
])
```

We are now ready to fit the model and evaluate its performance:

```
model.fit(X_train, y_train)
print(f'R2 score (train): {model.score(X_train, y_train):.4f}')
print(f'R2 score (test): {model.score(X_test, y_test):.4f}')
```

The results are:

```
R2 score (train): 0.6701
R2 score (test): 0.6679
```

Once again, we observe a noticeable improvement in the model's performance. The test R^2 score increased from 0.6395 to 0.6679, highlighting the added predictive value of discretizing the geographical features. We can take this further by discretizing additional features, such as AveOccup and the engineered feature RoomsPerIndividual. This approach enables the model to capture more localized and nonlinear effects:

```
# Extend the list of columns to discretize
columns = ['Longitude', 'Latitude', 'AveOccup', 'RoomsPerIndividual']
preprocessor = ColumnTransformer([
    ('discretizer', discretizer, columns)
], remainder='passthrough')

# Redefine the model pipeline with the updated preprocessor
model = Pipeline([
    ('pre', preprocessor),
    ('reg', LinearRegression())
])

model.fit(X_train, y_train)
print(f'R2 score (train): {model.score(X_train, y_train):.4f}')
print(f'R2 score (test): {model.score(X_test, y_test):.4f}')
```

The updated results are:

```
R2 score (train): 0.7057
R2 score (test): 0.6912
```

Not bad! By combining feature engineering and discretization, we have improved the test R^2 score from 0.5758 to 0.6912—representing a relative increase of approximately 20% in explained variance. Nonetheless, the results suggest that the model is still underfitting the data. This is likely due to its inherent inability to capture complex, nonlinear relationships between the features and housing prices. In Section 4.10, we explore more flexible, nonlinear regression models that may provide more accurate predictions.

4.6.6 Error Analysis

Beyond evaluating overall performance metrics, examining specific instances where the model's predictions deviate significantly from the true values can provide valuable insights. Such analysis can help determine whether the errors stem from issues in the dataset, such as outliers or other data irregularities, or from the model's inability to capture complex relationships. If the errors are data-related, measures such as data cleaning or adding more samples to the dataset could make the model more robust. Conversely, if the model's simplicity is the underlying issue, switching to more expressive models, such as nonlinear regression, may lead to better performance.

A simple approach for inspecting prediction errors is to compute the residuals $|y - \hat{y}|$ on the test set and examine the samples with the largest residuals:

```
# Compute the residuals on the test samples
y_test_pred = model.predict(X_test)
residuals = np.abs(y_test - y_test_pred)

# Add the residuals to the DataFrame
housing_df.loc[X_test.index, 'Residual'] = residuals

# Sort the samples in a descending order of the residuals
housing_df.sort_values('Residual', ascending=False).head(10)
```

The test samples with the largest residuals are shown in Figure 4.8. Notably, 7 out of the top 10 samples have a median house price of exactly 5, suggesting a hard cap of $500,000 in the dataset. Further investigation confirms that this is the maximum price in the dataset, with 965 samples hitting this ceiling. Such capping can impair the model's performance, particularly near the upper end of the target range, where the model is unable to distinguish among high-value cases.

To mitigate the impact of capped target values, consider one of the following options: removing the capped samples from the dataset if they constitute only a small fraction of the data; estimating their true values using relationships with other features; applying a transformation to the target variable, such as logarithmic scaling, to reduce the influence of extreme values; or using robust loss functions such as Huber loss that are less sensitive to outliers than the squared loss (see Section 4.9).

4.7 Linear Regression Assumptions

Linear regression relies on several key assumptions about the predictors, the target variable, and their relationship. Although these assumptions are often reasonable, real-world data can sometimes

	MedInc	HouseAge	AveRooms	AveBedrms	Population	AveOccup	Latitude	Longitude	MedHouseVal	Residual
6688	0.4999	28.0	7.677419	1.870968	142.0	4.580645	34.15	−118.08	5.00001	4.672149
459	1.1696	52.0	2.436000	0.944000	1349.0	5.396000	37.87	−122.25	5.00001	4.394115
10574	1.9659	6.0	4.795455	1.159091	125.0	2.840909	33.72	−117.70	5.00001	4.144971
12069	4.2386	6.0	7.723077	1.169231	228.0	3.507692	33.83	−117.55	5.00001	3.420554
19542	1.7679	39.0	5.000000	0.888889	22.0	2.444444	37.63	−120.92	4.50000	3.265618
20325	4.5833	21.0	7.278431	1.082353	863.0	3.384314	34.28	−119.04	5.00001	3.236227
17237	3.8456	27.0	5.627171	1.081716	2591.0	2.646578	34.43	−119.66	5.00001	3.128281
17306	2.7275	17.0	5.574286	1.051429	681.0	1.945714	34.38	−119.55	5.00001	2.953196
20349	7.3004	32.0	5.724138	0.758621	63.0	2.172414	34.17	−119.08	1.25000	2.870557
9421	3.7500	38.0	5.770732	0.956098	628.0	3.063415	37.86	−122.53	4.78600	2.867266

Figure 4.8: The ten test samples from the California housing dataset with the largest residuals, highlighting the issue of capped prices.

violate them. Various techniques are available to address such violations, but they often make the modeling process more complex and may require more data to maintain accuracy.

In the following subsections, we outline the key assumptions underlying standard linear regression models, along with common strategies for diagnosing and addressing potential violations. In this section, we assume the prediction function of the model has the form given in (4.5):

$$y_i = \mathbf{w}^T \mathbf{x}_i + \epsilon_i, \quad i = 1, \dots, n,$$

where ϵ_i denotes the random noise term, also known as the irreducible error.

4.7.1 Multicollinearity

As discussed in Section 4.4, standard least squares estimation requires the design matrix X to have full column rank, i.e., the predictor variables must be linearly independent. If the features are linearly dependent, there is no unique solution to the normal equations, and it becomes necessary to use the Moore–Penrose pseudoinverse to obtain a solution.

A more common issue in practice is **multicollinearity**, which occurs when two or more features are highly, but not perfectly, correlated [184]. Multicollinearity can lead to numerical instability during model fitting, as small perturbations in the data can cause large variations in the estimated coefficients. Moreover, it reduces the interpretability of the model, as it becomes difficult to determine the individual contributions of correlated features to the model's predictions.

A popular method for detecting multicollinearity is **variance inflation factor (VIF)**, which quantifies how much the variance of a regression coefficient is inflated due to multicollinearity [36, 451]. The VIF for a given predictor is calculated by regressing that variable against all the other predictors in the model and computing the coefficient of determination R_i^2 (as defined in Section 4.5.3):

$$\text{VIF}_i = \frac{1}{1 - R_i^2}. \tag{4.26}$$

A high R_i^2 value indicates that predictor i can be well approximated by a linear combination of the other predictors, suggesting multicollinearity. As R_i^2 approaches 1, the denominator in the VIF formula approaches zero, causing the VIF to increase sharply. A VIF above 5 (corresponding to $R_i^2 = 0.8$) suggests a moderate level of multicollinearity, while a VIF above 10 ($R_i^2 = 0.9$) is often considered a more serious issue.

Below is an example for detecting multicollinearity using the California housing dataset. The `variance_inflation_factor`[11] function from `statsmodel` is used to compute the variance inflation factor (VIF) for each feature:

```
import pandas as pd
from sklearn.datasets import fetch_california_housing
from sklearn.preprocessing import StandardScaler
from statsmodels.stats.outliers_influence import variance_inflation_factor

# Load the dataset
X, y = fetch_california_housing(as_frame=True, return_X_y=True)
feature_names = X.columns

# Standardize the features
scaler = StandardScaler()
X_scaled = scaler.fit_transform(X)

# Create a DataFrame with standardized features
X_scaled_df = pd.DataFrame(X_scaled, columns=feature_names)

# Calculate VIF for each feature
vif_data = pd.DataFrame()
vif_data['Feature'] = X_scaled_df.columns
vif_data['VIF'] = [variance_inflation_factor(X_scaled_df.values, i)
                   for i in range(X_scaled_df.shape[1])]
print(vif_data)
```

The output is:

```
     Feature        VIF
0     MedInc   2.501295
1   HouseAge   1.241254
2   AveRooms   8.342786
3   AveBedrms  6.994995
4  Population  1.138125
5    AveOccup  1.008324
6    Latitude  9.297624
7   Longitude  8.962263
```

---

11. https://www.statsmodels.org/dev/generated/statsmodels.stats.outliers_influence.variance_ inflation_factor.html

The features `AveRooms`, `Latitude`, and `Longitude` have VIF values greater than 8, suggesting that they are highly correlated with other features in the dataset. This indicates potential multicollinearity issues, which may affect the stability and interpretability of the model.

Strategies for dealing with multicollinearity include:

- Removing highly correlated features: Eliminate one or more of the correlated variables to reduce redundancy (typically using domain knowledge to retain the most relevant predictor).

- Principal Component Regression (PCR): Apply principal component analysis (PCA) to transform the predictors into a smaller set of uncorrelated components, and then fit a linear regression model to these components [303].

- Partial Least Squares (PLS) regression: Projects the feature matrix X and the target y onto a lower-dimensional space that maximizes their covariance [218]. This helps mitigate multicollinearity by replacing the original predictors with uncorrelated components. In Scikit-Learn, it is implemented in the `PLSRegression` class.

- Applying regularization: Use techniques such as ridge regression or elastic net to shrink the coefficients of correlated variables and reduce the impact of multicollinearity (see Section 4.11).

- Collecting additional data: Adding more data can help mitigate multicollinearity by improving the stability and reliability of the estimated coefficients.

4.7.2   Homoscedasticity

Homoscedasticity refers to the assumption that the errors have **constant variance**, i.e., $\mathrm{Var}[\epsilon_i] = \sigma^2$ for some constant σ [128]. In other words, the variability of the errors remains the same across all values of the independent variables. When this assumption is violated and the variance of the error changes depending on the value of the predictors, the model exhibits **heteroscedasticity**.

In many real-world situations, homoscedasticity does not hold. For example, variables with larger predicted values often exhibit greater variability. Consider predicting the price of a house: for a luxury home valued at $1,000,000, the actual price may reasonably range from $900,000 to $1,100,000, implying a standard deviation of about $100,000. In contrast, for a smaller house valued at $100,000, a deviation of $100,000 would be unrealistic, as it would imply a range from $0 to $200,000. In this case, the error variance increases with the magnitude of the predicted value, thereby violating the homoscedasticity assumption.

Heteroscedasticity can cause several issues in linear regression models:

- Less reliable predictions: When the variance of the errors increases with the predictors but the model assumes constant variance, it underestimates the true variability in those regions—leading to overconfident predictions and potentially misleading inference.

- Unreliable estimates of predictor importance: Heteroscedasticity can distort the model's assessment of how strongly each predictor is associated with the target variable. This may result in misleading conclusions about which variables are most influential.

- Misleading evaluation scores: Goodness-of-fit metrics such as R^2 and adjusted R^2 may be distorted, causing the model to appear more or less accurate than it actually is.

A simple method for detecting heteroscedasticity is to use a **residual plot**, which shows the residuals plotted against either the predicted values or a selected predictor variable. In a homoscedastic model, the residuals should appear randomly scattered around zero with no discernible pattern. If the spread of the residuals increases or decreases with the predicted values (or any predictor), this indicates heteroscedasticity.

Below is an example for generating a residual plot for the California housing dataset to assess homoscedasticity:

```
# Load dataset and split into train/test sets
X, y = fetch_california_housing(return_X_y=True)
X_train, X_test, y_train, y_test = train_test_split(X, y, test_size=0.2,
                                                    random_state=42)

# Fit a linear regression model
model = LinearRegression()
model.fit(X_train, y_train)

# Make predictions on the test set
y_pred = model.predict(X_test)

# Calculate residuals
residuals = y_test - y_pred

# Plot residuals vs. predicted values
plt.scatter(y_pred, residuals, edgecolors='k')
plt.axhline(0, color='red', linestyle='--')
plt.xlabel('Predicted Values')
plt.ylabel('Residuals')
```

Figure 4.9 shows the residual plot, which helps visually assess if the residuals are randomly distributed (suggesting homoscedasticity) or exhibit a pattern indicating heteroscedasticity.

There are several strategies for addressing heteroscedasticity:

- Transforming the target variable: Apply a transformation such as the logarithm, square root, or Box-Cox transformation to stabilize the variance. This can help reduce heteroscedasticity and make the relationship between the predictors and the target more suitable for linear modeling.

- Weighted least squares (WLS): Assigns weights to observations based on the variance of their errors [536]. Observations with higher error variance receive smaller weights compared to observations with lower variance. This helps reduce the impact of heteroscedasticity by giving more influence to observations with more reliable (less variable) errors.

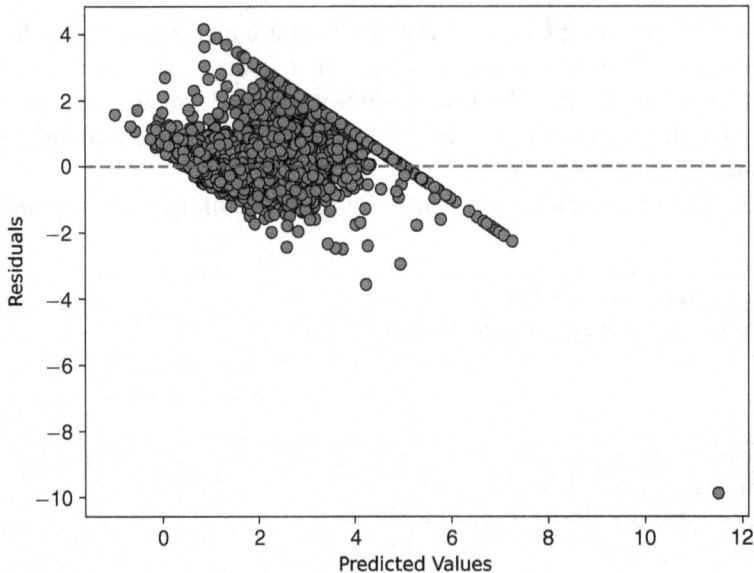

Figure 4.9: Residual plot showing the residuals versus predicted values for the California housing dataset. The horizontal red line indicates where the residuals are zero. A pattern in the spread of residuals, such as an increasing or decreasing spread, would suggest heteroscedasticity. In this case, there appears to be a diagonal band of points stretching from around (1.0, 4.0) to (7.0, -2.0), but it is largely due to the dataset's $500,000 cap on the target values (clipping), rather than true heteroscedasticity.

- Robust regression techniques: Apply regression methods that are less sensitive to heteroscedasticity and outliers. This includes, for example, **Huber regression**, which uses a robust loss function to reduce the influence of extreme values (see Section 4.9), and **ridge regression**, which stabilizes the model by applying a penalty to large coefficients (see Section 4.11.1).

- Robust standard errors: Also known as **heteroscedasticity-consistent standard errors**, this technique adjusts the error estimates after the model has been fitted to account for non-constant variance [619]. It provides more reliable inference, including confidence intervals (see Section D.6), even when the homoscedasticity assumption is violated.

4.7.3   Additional Assumptions

In addition to homoscedasticity and the absence of multicollinearity, several other assumptions are important for the validity of linear regression models:

- **Linearity**: The target variable is assumed to be a linear function of the predictors plus a random noise: $y_i = \mathbf{w}^T \mathbf{x}_i + \epsilon_i$. If this assumption is violated, various techniques can be used to model nonlinear relationships, such as polynomial regression (see Section 4.10.2) or

applying nonlinear transformations to the predictors (e.g., logarithmic or square-root transformations). Alternatively, more flexible models like decision trees or neural networks may
provide better performance in capturing complex, nonlinear patterns.

- **Independence of errors**: The errors ϵ_i are assumed to be uncorrelated, i.e., $\mathbb{E}[\epsilon_i \epsilon_j] = 0$ for
  $i \neq j$. This assumption is often violated in sequential data, such as time series or textual
  data, where observations tend to be correlated.

  When errors are correlated, ordinary least squares (OLS) is no longer efficient, and alternative methods such as **autoregressive (AR) models** [63] or **generalized least squares (GLS)**
  [11] can provide better results by explicitly modeling the correlation structure.

- **Exogeneity**: The irreducible errors should have zero mean, i.e., $\mathbb{E}[\epsilon_i] = 0$. This ensures that
  the errors are due to random noise rather than any systematic relationship with the predictors.

  If this assumption is violated, the model may consistently make predictions that are biased
  in a certain direction. For example, if higher values of a predictor tend to produce positive
  residuals, the model may systematically underestimate the outcomes for large values of that
  predictor. In such cases, advanced techniques like **instrumental variable regression** can
  help eliminate the endogeneity bias [16].

- **Normality of errors**: In some settings, it is further assumed that the irreducible errors are
  normally distributed, i.e., $\epsilon_i \sim \mathcal{N}(0, \sigma^2)$. While this is not necessary for obtaining unbiased coefficient estimates, it is important for constructing valid confidence intervals and
  performing hypothesis tests. In addition, under the normality assumption, the ordinary least
  squares estimator coincides with the maximum likelihood estimator (see Section 4.2.1).

  When the errors deviate significantly from normality, it may indicate the presence of outliers
  or suggest that the target variable or predictors need to be transformed (e.g., via a logarithmic
  transformation). If normality cannot be achieved, non-parametric methods such as **quantile
  regression** [322], which make fewer distributional assumptions, may be a better choice.

While linear regression provides a simple and interpretable modeling framework, its assumptions must be carefully validated in practice. When these assumptions are violated, various techniques and model extensions can be applied to mitigate their impact and produce more reliable
results.

4.8   Gradient Descent for Linear Regression

The normal equations provide an analytical solution for finding the optimal coefficients $\mathbf{w}^*$ in
linear regression. However, this approach has several important limitations:

- Computational cost: Solving the normal equations requires inverting the matrix $X^T X$, which
  has a time complexity of $\mathcal{O}(d^3)$, where d is the number of features. This becomes impractical
  for high-dimensional datasets.

- Memory requirements: Computing $X^T X$ and its inverse requires loading the entire dataset into memory, which may be infeasible for very large or distributed datasets.

- Numerical instability: If $X^T X$ is nearly singular or ill-conditioned, the matrix inversion can lead to significant numerical errors (see Section A.3.18).

- Lack of online learning support: Any change in the dataset requires re-computing the entire inverse of $X^T X$, making this method unsuitable for streaming or dynamically updated data.

A widely used alternative is **gradient descent**, an iterative optimization technique that updates the model parameters in the direction of the negative gradient to minimize the cost function. This technique is used to train a wide range of machine learning models, including logistic regression, neural networks, and other models that do not have a closed-form solution.

For linear regression, gradient descent is especially attractive because:

- The least squares cost function is convex, ensuring convergence to the global minimum.

- It avoids the need for matrix inversion, reducing computational overhead.

- It can be applied to datasets that are too large to fit in memory (when using stochastic or mini-batch variants).

- It naturally supports online and incremental learning.

The two main variants of gradient descent commonly used in machine learning are:

- **Batch gradient descent**: Computes the gradient of the cost function with respect to the parameters w using the entire dataset at each iteration. While this method provides stable and deterministic updates that steadily reduce the cost, it can be computationally expensive and slow for large datasets.

- **Stochastic gradient descent (SGD)**: Updates the parameters w after processing each training example or a small subset of the dataset (a mini-batch). Although SGD introduces noise into the updates, it often converges faster in practice and can help the algorithm escape shallow local minima.

The gradient descent method and its variants are explained thoroughly in Appendix E. In this section, we focus on their application to linear regression.

4.8.1   Batch Gradient Descent

Batch gradient descent (also known as **deterministic gradient descent**) computes the gradient of the loss function over the entire training dataset at each iteration. This approach ensures a stable and consistent progression toward the minimum, making it suitable for problems that require high precision in the final solution.

The general procedure for gradient descent is presented in Algorithm E.1. When applied to machine learning, the objective function $f(\mathbf{x})$ corresponds to the model's cost function (e.g., the least squares cost in linear regression), and the variable $\mathbf{x}$ represents the model parameters (such as the weight vector $\mathbf{w}$).

In order to apply gradient descent to a specific machine learning model, we must provide the algorithm with the gradient of the cost function. This can be derived analytically or computed automatically using tools such as automatic differentiation (discussed in Volume II).

Specifically, in linear regression, we aim to minimize the least squares cost function over the given n training examples:

$$J(\mathbf{w}) = \frac{1}{n} \sum_{i=1}^{n} (y_i - h_{\mathbf{w}}(\mathbf{x}_i))^2,$$

where $h_{\mathbf{w}}(\mathbf{x}_i) = \sum_{j=0}^{d} w_j x_{ij}$ is the predicted value for input $\mathbf{x}_i$.

To find the gradient of $J(\mathbf{w})$, we compute its partial derivative with respect to each weight w_j:

$$\frac{\partial J}{\partial w_j} = \frac{\partial}{\partial w_j} \frac{1}{n} \sum_{i=1}^{n} (y_i - h_{\mathbf{w}}(\mathbf{x}_i))^2 \qquad \text{(definition of } J\text{)}$$

$$= \frac{1}{n} \sum_{i=1}^{n} \frac{\partial}{\partial w_j} (y_i - h_{\mathbf{w}}(\mathbf{x}_i))^2 \qquad \text{(linearity of the derivative)}$$

$$= \frac{1}{n} \sum_{i=1}^{n} 2(y_i - h_{\mathbf{w}}(\mathbf{x}_i)) \frac{\partial}{\partial w_j} (y_i - h_{\mathbf{w}}(\mathbf{x}_i)) \qquad \text{(chain rule)}$$

$$= \frac{1}{n} \sum_{i=1}^{n} 2(y_i - h_{\mathbf{w}}(\mathbf{x}_i))(-x_{ij}) \qquad \text{(since } \partial h_{\mathbf{w}}(\mathbf{x}_i)/\partial w_j = x_{ij}\text{)}$$

$$= -\frac{2}{n} \sum_{i=1}^{n} (y_i - h_{\mathbf{w}}(\mathbf{x}_i)) x_{ij}.$$

Thus, we can write the gradient vector as:

$$\nabla_{\mathbf{w}} J(\mathbf{w}) = -\frac{2}{n} \sum_{i=1}^{n} (y_i - h_{\mathbf{w}}(\mathbf{x}_i)) \mathbf{x}_i.$$

Accordingly, the batch gradient descent update rule becomes:

$$\mathbf{w} \leftarrow \mathbf{w} - \alpha \nabla_{\mathbf{w}} J(\mathbf{w}) = \mathbf{w} - \alpha \frac{2}{n} \sum_{i=1}^{n} (h_{\mathbf{w}}(\mathbf{x}_i) - y_i) \mathbf{x}_i,$$

where we flipped the sign in the residual term to write it as $h_{\mathbf{w}}(\mathbf{x}_i) - y_i$.

In practice, the factor of 2 is typically absorbed into the learning rate α, yielding the simplified update rule:

$$\mathbf{w} \leftarrow \mathbf{w} - \frac{\alpha}{n} \sum_{i=1}^{n} (h_{\mathbf{w}}(\mathbf{x}_i) - y_i) \mathbf{x}_i. \qquad (4.27)$$

4.8.1.1   Implementation in Python

We now implement the batch gradient descent algorithm for linear regression using the following custom estimator:

```python
from sklearn.base import BaseEstimator, RegressorMixin

class LinearRegressionBatchGD(BaseEstimator, RegressorMixin):
    """Linear regression using batch gradient descent"""
    def __init__(self, alpha=0.1, max_iter=1000, tol=0.0001):
        self.alpha = alpha       # Learning rate
        self.max_iter = max_iter # Maximum number of iterations
        self.tol = tol           # Tolerance for stopping criterion

    def fit(self, X, y):
        n = X.shape[0] # Number of samples
        d = X.shape[1] # Number of features

        # Add an intercept term (bias) to X
        X_b = np.c_[np.ones(n), X]

        # Initialize the parameter vector with random values
        self.w_ = np.random.randn(d + 1)

        self.losses_ = [] # Tracks the loss over iterations

        # Training loop
        for i in range(self.max_iter):
            # Compute predictions
            y_pred = X_b @ self.w_

            # Calculate loss (mean squared error)
            loss = np.mean((y_pred - y)**2)
            self.losses_.append(loss)

            # Check for convergence
            if i > 0 and (self.losses_[-2] - loss) < self.tol:
                break

            # Compute gradients
            gradients = 1 / n * X_b.T @ (y_pred - y)

            # Update weights
            self.w_ -= self.alpha * gradients
```

```
def predict(self, X):
    n = X.shape[0]
    X_b = np.c_[np.ones(n), X] # Add intercept term
    y_pred = X_b @ self.w_
    return y_pred
```

The gradient descent updates are implemented using NumPy's efficient vectorized operations, which significantly speed up computation. The key steps in each iteration are:

1. Compute the model's predictions for the entire training set using $\hat{y} = X_b\mathbf{w}$, where X_b is the feature matrix with an added bias term (a column of ones).

2. Compute the gradient of the cost function with a single matrix multiplication: $\mathbf{g} = \dfrac{1}{n}X_b^T(\hat{y} - y).$

3. Update the parameter vector using the gradient descent rule: $\mathbf{w} \leftarrow \mathbf{w} - \alpha\mathbf{g}$.

These steps are repeated until the algorithm converges to a minimum of the cost function, as determined by the specified tolerance (`tol`), or until it reaches the maximum number of iterations (`max_iter`). The algorithm monitors convergence by checking whether the improvement in the loss falls below the tolerance between successive iterations.

Let's test our implementation on the synthetic dataset introduced in Section 4.4:

```
X, y = generate_data()

model = LinearRegressionBatchGD()
model.fit(X, y)
```

It is important to scale the input features when using gradient descent to avoid divergence and ensure stable convergence (see Section E.4.1.6). In this case, the two features x_1 and x_2 have similar scales, so explicit scaling is not necessary. Let's examine the learned coefficients:

```
print('Coefficients:', np.round(model.w_, 4))
```

```
Coefficients: [4.7455 0.9104 2.2863]
```

These coefficients are close to those obtained using the normal equations, indicating that our gradient descent implementation performs as expected. The number of iterations it took for the algorithm to converge is:

```
print('Number of iterations for convergence:', len(model.losses_))
```

```
Number of iterations for convergence: 182
```

Finally, let's evaluate the model's performance using the standard metrics:

```
from sklearn.metrics import root_mean_squared_error as RMSE

y_pred = model.predict(X)
rmse = RMSE(y, y_pred)
print(f'RMSE: {rmse:.4f}')

r2_score = model.score(X, y)
print(f'R2 score: {r2_score:.4f}')
```

```
RMSE: 0.9746
R2 score: 0.8085
```

These results are nearly identical to those obtained using the normal equations (RMSE 0.9725 and R^2 score 0.8094), demonstrating the consistency between the two approaches.

4.8.1.2   Learning Curves

A common way to analyze the behavior of gradient descent algorithms is to plot the **learning curve**, which shows the loss on the training set as a function of the number of iterations. This plot illustrates how the loss evolves over time and provides insight into the algorithm's convergence behavior.

```
# Plot the learning curve
plt.plot(model.losses_)
plt.xlabel('Iteration')
plt.ylabel('Loss')
```

The learning curve in Figure 4.10 shows that most of the loss reduction occurs in the first few iterations, demonstrating the effectiveness of gradient descent in rapidly moving toward the minimum. As the algorithm continues, the loss stabilizes, signaling convergence.

4.8.2   Stochastic Gradient Descent (SGD)

Stochastic gradient descent (SGD) is a widely used variant of gradient descent that updates the model parameters using a single training example or a small random number of examples at each iteration (see Section E.4.2). In the context of linear regression, after observing each example $(\mathbf{x}_i, y_i)$, the weights are updated as:

$$\mathbf{w} \leftarrow \mathbf{w} - \alpha(h_{\mathbf{w}}(\mathbf{x}_i) - y_i)\mathbf{x}_i. \tag{4.28}$$

Unlike batch gradient descent, which follows a smooth trajectory by computing gradients over the entire dataset, SGD introduces randomness into the updates. Since each step is based on a single (or a few) training examples, the update direction may deviate from the true gradient of the cost function. While this noise can help escape shallow local optima or plateaus, it may also cause the algorithm to oscillate around the minimum rather than fully converge.

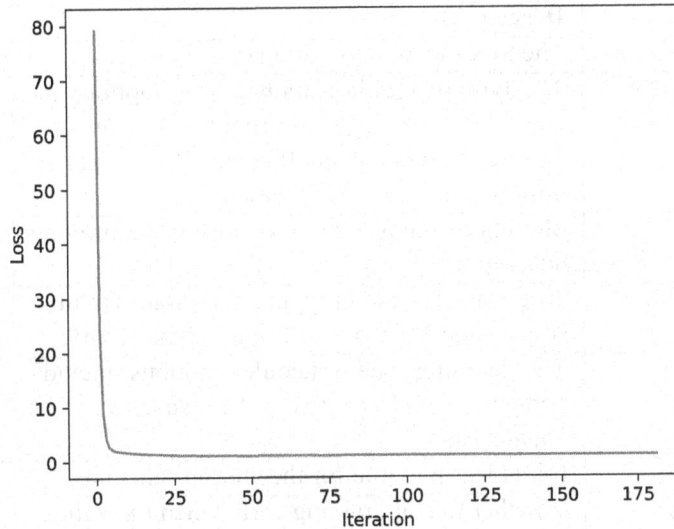

Figure 4.10: Learning curve of batch gradient descent for linear regression applied to a synthetic dataset. The plot illustrates rapid loss reduction in the early iterations, followed by stabilization as the algorithm approaches the minimum.

To improve stability, it is common to gradually reduce the learning rate over time—a technique known as **learning rate annealing**—which allows the algorithm to take smaller, more refined steps as it approaches the minimum. See Section E.4.2.1 for a discussion of practical learning rate schedules.

SGD is one of the most widely used optimization algorithms in machine learning, and we will encounter it frequently throughout this book.

4.8.2.1   The `SGDRegressor` Class

The `SGDRegressor`[12] class in Scikit-Learn implements the SGD algorithm for fitting linear regression models. The key parameters of this class are outlined in Table 4.4. Note that in Scikit-Learn, `alpha` refers to the regularization coefficient (typically denoted by λ in mathematical notation), while the learning rate is controlled by the parameters `eta0` and `learning_rate`.

To demonstrate the use of `SGDRegressor`, we fit a linear regression model to the California housing dataset using stochastic gradient descent. First, we fetch the dataset and split it into training and test sets:

```
from sklearn.datasets import fetch_california_housing
from sklearn.model_selection import train_test_split

X, y = fetch_california_housing(as_frame=True, return_X_y=True)
X_train, X_test, y_train, y_test = train_test_split(X, y, test_size=0.2,
                                                    random_state=42)
```

---

12. https://scikit-learn.org/stable/modules/generated/sklearn.linear_model.SGDRegressor.html

Parameter	Description	Default Value
loss	The loss function to optimize.	squared_error
penalty	The type of regularization to use. Options include 'l1', 'l2', 'elasticnet', or None.	'l2'
alpha	The regularization coefficient. Higher values impose stronger regularization.	0.0001
max_iter	Maximum number of passes over the training data (epochs).	1000
tol	Tolerance for the stopping criterion. Training stops when loss > previous_loss - tol.	0.001
learning_rate	The learning rate schedule. Options include 'constant', 'optimal', 'invscaling', or 'adaptive'.	'invscaling'
eta0	Initial learning rate for the chosen schedule.	0.01
early_stopping	Whether to stop training early when the validation score does not improve.	False
validation_fraction	Fraction of the training data to set aside as validation for early stopping.	0.1
n_iter_no_change	Number of iterations with no improvement before stopping the training. Convergence is checked against the training or validation loss depending on whether early_stopping is False or True, respectively.	5

Table 4.4: Key parameters of the SGDRegressor class

Next, we create an instance of SGDRegressor and fit it to the training set:

```
from sklearn.linear_model import SGDRegressor

model = SGDRegressor()
model.fit(X_train, y_train)
```

The R^2 scores of this model on the training and test sets are:

```
print(f'R2 score (train): {model.score(X_train, y_train):.4f}')
print(f'R2 score (test): {model.score(X_test, y_test):.4f}')
```

```
R2 score (train): -64066325035282430173045063680.0000
R2 score (test): -64065584159543795873711390720.0000
```

These scores are extremely poor! Such results typically indicate that gradient descent has diverged, which often happens when the input features have very different scales, or when the learning rate is too high. To resolve this issue, we standardize the features by defining a pipeline that includes a `StandardScaler` followed by `SGDRegressor`:

```
from sklearn.preprocessing import StandardScaler
from sklearn.linear_model import SGDRegressor
from sklearn.pipeline import Pipeline

model = Pipeline([
    ('scaler', StandardScaler()),
    ('reg', SGDRegressor(random_state=42))
])
```

After fitting this pipeline to the training set:

```
model.fit(X_train, y_train)
```

The R^2 scores improve dramatically:

```
R2 score (train): 0.6047
R2 score (test): 0.5798
```

These results are very close to those obtained using the normal equations (training R^2 score 0.6126 and test R^2 score 0.5758). The slight underperformance on the training set is expected with SGD, which approximates the global minimum rather than computing it exactly. Interestingly, this slight underfitting can sometimes lead to better generalization, as seen in the slightly higher test score.

4.8.2.2 Early Stopping

Early stopping is a common regularization technique used to prevent overfitting when training a model with iterative methods such as gradient descent [484, 647]. During training, the model's performance is monitored on a holdout validation set, and the training is stopped when validation performance begins to deteriorate. This prevents the model from continuing to optimize beyond the point of best generalization, thereby avoiding overfitting and also reducing unnecessary computation time.

To enable early stopping in `SGDRegressor`, you need to set the `early_stopping` parameter to `True`. Three additional parameters control the behavior of early stopping:

- `validation_fraction`: The proportion of training data to reserve for validation. The default is 0.1, meaning that 10% of the training data is used to monitor validation performance.

- `n_iter_no_change`: The number of consecutive iterations (epochs) with no improvement to wait before stopping. If early stopping is enabled, this criterion is evaluated on the validation loss; otherwise, it is based on the training loss. The default value is 5 iterations.

- `tol`: The minimum change in the monitored loss required to qualify as an improvement. Default is `1e-3`.

Let's redefine our pipeline with early stopping enabled and fit it to the training data:

```
model = Pipeline([
    ('scaler', StandardScaler()),
    ('reg', SGDRegressor(early_stopping=True, random_state=42))
])
model.fit(X_train, y_train)
```

The R^2 scores this time are:

```
R2 score (train): 0.5807
R2 score (test): 0.5875
```

The test set score increased from 0.5798 to 0.5875, indicating a slight improvement in generalization due to early stopping. We can check how many iterations were completed before the stopping criterion was triggered by examining the `n_iter_` attribute of the regressor:

```
print('Number of iterations:', model.named_steps['reg'].n_iter_)
```

```
Number of iterations: 9
```

A drawback of early stopping is the need to allocate part of the training data for validation, which effectively reduces the amount of data available for learning.

4.9   Alternative Loss Functions

As mentioned in Section 4.2, in addition to the squared loss function, other loss functions can be utilized in regression problems to address specific challenges. The main drawback of squared loss is its sensitivity to outliers, as squaring the errors amplifies the influence of large deviations, which can adversely affect the fitted model.

Two common alternative loss functions for regression are:

- **Absolute loss** (or L1 loss) is defined as the absolute difference between the predicted value $\hat{y} = h(\mathbf{x})$ and the true target y:

$$L_{\text{abs}}(y, \hat{y}) = |y - \hat{y}|. \tag{4.29}$$

This loss function is less sensitive to outliers than squared loss. However, its non-differentiability at zero can pose challenges for optimization algorithms that rely on gradients, such as gradient descent.

- **Huber loss** [282] combines the squared loss and absolute loss. It employs squared loss for errors smaller than a threshold δ (typically set to 1) and switches to absolute loss for larger errors. It is defined as:

$$L_{\text{huber}}(y, \hat{y}) = \begin{cases} \frac{1}{2}(y - \hat{y})^2 & \text{for } |y - \hat{y}| \leq \delta, \\ \delta|y - \hat{y}| - \frac{1}{2}\delta^2 & \text{otherwise.} \end{cases} \tag{4.30}$$

This loss function is differentiable, making it well-suited for gradient-based optimization, while being more robust against outliers than squared loss. However, it is more computationally intensive than both absolute loss and squared loss, and it lacks the maximum likelihood interpretation associated with the latter.

Figure 4.11 illustrates the three loss functions discussed above.

To demonstrate the practical implications of using different loss functions, consider the following synthetic dataset:

```
x = np.array([0.5, 1.8, 2.4, 3.5, 4.2, 4.8, 5.8, 6.1, 7.2, 8.7, 10])
y = np.array([0.1, 0.2, 0.3, 0.4, 0.7, 1, 0.9, 1.2, 1.4, 1.8, 10])
```

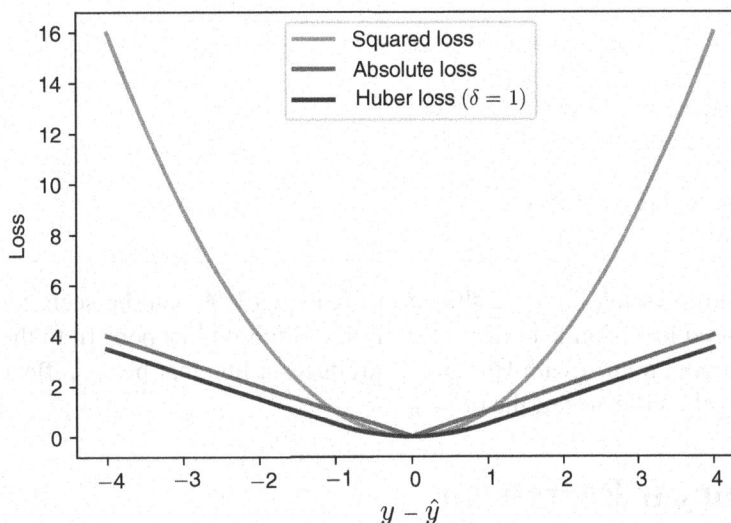

Figure 4.11: Comparison of common loss functions used in regression analysis. Squared loss increases quadratically with error magnitude, making it sensitive to outliers. Absolute loss increases linearly, providing a more robust measure against outliers. Huber loss combines both approaches by acting like squared loss for small errors and like absolute loss for larger errors, thereby mitigating the impact of outliers while maintaining smoothness.

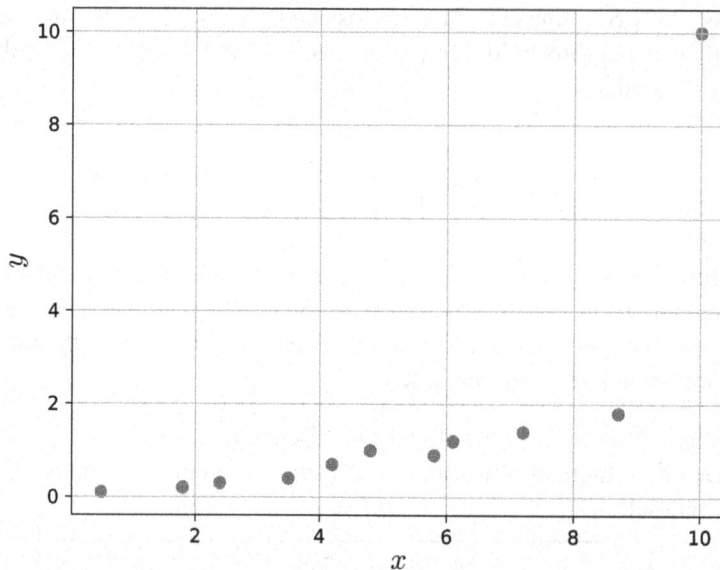

Figure 4.12: A dataset with an outlier at (10, 10)

Figure 4.12 shows the dataset, which contains an outlier at the point (10, 10). To examine the effect of the loss function on model performance, we train two SGDRegressor models on this dataset—one using squared loss and the other using Huber loss:

```
X = x.reshape(-1, 1) # Reshape x to a 2D array

reg1 = SGDRegressor(loss='squared_error')
reg1.fit(X, y)

reg2 = SGDRegressor(loss='huber')
reg2.fit(X, y)
```

The resulting regression lines are shown in Figure 4.13. As can be seen, the regression line trained with squared loss is pulled toward the outlier, resulting in a poor fit to the rest of the data. In contrast, the model trained with Huber loss produces a line that better reflects the underlying trend by reducing the influence of the outlier.

4.10   Nonlinear Regression

In many real-world problems, the relationship between the input features and the target variable is inherently nonlinear, requiring alternative regression techniques. Nonlinear regression problems generally fall into two categories:

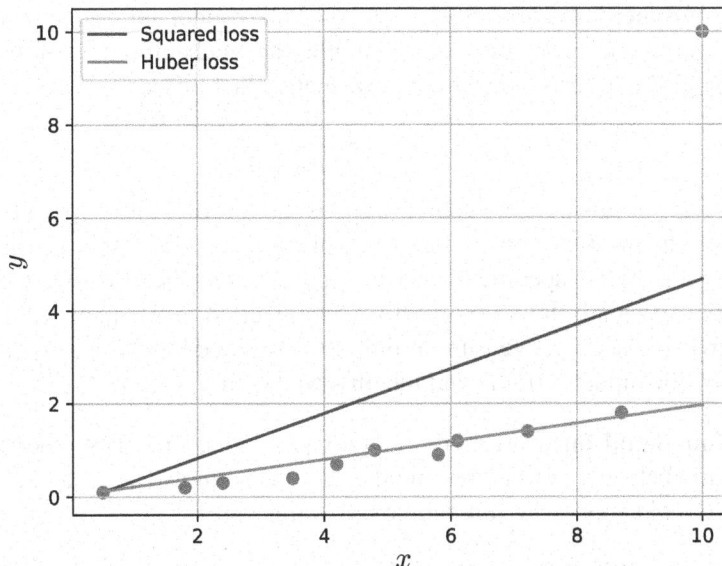

Figure 4.13: Comparison of regression lines obtained using squared loss versus Huber loss. The model trained with squared loss is strongly affected by the outlier, while Huber loss yields a regression line that is more robust to outliers by blending the properties of L1 and L2 losses.

1. **Known functional form**: In this type of problems, the functional form of the relationship between the features and the target is known in advance, and the goal is to estimate the parameters of this function from the observed data. The techniques used depend on the specific structure of the function:

   (a) **Linearizable functions**: Some nonlinear functions can be transformed into a linear form using suitable mathematical transformations. For example, the power function $y = ax^b$ becomes linear after applying logarithms to both sides: $\log y = \log a + b \log x$, which is linear in $\log x$ and thus can be handled using standard linear regression methods (see Section 4.10.1).

   (b) **Basis function expansion**: Other functions can be expressed as linear combinations of known functions of x (called **basis functions**):

   $$f(x) = w_1\phi_1(x) + w_2\phi_2(x) + \ldots + w_k\phi_k(x). \tag{4.31}$$

   A common example is **polynomial regression**, in which the prediction function is represented as a polynomial of degree d:

   $$f(x) = w_0 + w_1 x + w_2 x^2 + \ldots + w_d x^d. \tag{4.32}$$

   By treating $x, x^2, \ldots, x^d$ as the input features, the problem reduces to a multiple linear regression problem, allowing us to estimate the coefficients $w_0, \ldots, w_d$ using standard linear regression techniques (see Section 4.10.2).

(c) **Truly nonlinear models**: Some relationships cannot be easily transformed or decomposed into a linear form. For example, the Michaelis-Menten model for enzyme kinetics [351] describes the rate of enzymatic reactions as:

$$y = \frac{w_1 x}{w_0 + x}.$$ (4.33)

where x is the substrate concentration, y is the reaction rate, w_1 is the maximum rate, and w_0 is the substrate concentration at which the reaction rate is half of w_1. The parameters w_0 and w_1 are specific to each enzyme and must be estimated from experimental data. This typically involves iterative optimization techniques, such as gradient descent, where the objective is to minimize the squared loss between the predicted value given by the model formula and the observed data.

2. **Unknown functional form**: In more complex problems, such as predicting house prices, the relationship between the features and the target is unknown and may not follow a simple formula. Two main approaches are employed in this case:

(a) **Polynomial fitting**: Even without knowing the true function, one can attempt to fit a polynomial to the data. The *Weierstrass approximation theorem* (see Section B.5.4.4) guarantees that any continuous function on a closed interval can be approximated by a polynomial arbitrarily well. Thus, polynomial regression may provide a good fit to the data even when the underlying relationship is not polynomial (see Section 4.10.2.3).

(b) **Nonparametric methods**: Nonparametric regression models do not assume a fixed functional form but instead infer the relationship between the features and the target directly from the data. Examples include k-nearest neighbors regression (Section 6.8), regression trees (Section 8.6), and support vector regression (Section 11.6). These methods are flexible but often require larger datasets, as both the structure and the parameters of the model must be learned from the data.

4.10.1 Transformable Nonlinear Regression

Various nonlinear functions can be transformed into linear forms, enabling the use of linear regression techniques to determine their coefficients. For example, consider the power function $y = ax^b$, where the objective is to estimate the coefficients a and b from the given data. The fitting process consists of the following steps:

1. Linearizing the function: We begin by transforming the nonlinear equation into a linear one. For the power function, this is achieved by taking the logarithm of both sides, resulting in:

$$\log y = \log a + b \log x.$$

2. Redefining variables and coefficients: We introduce new variables: $\mathcal{Y} = \log y$, $\mathcal{X} = \log x$, and define the coefficients as $\alpha = \log a$ and $\beta = b$. This reformulates the equation as a linear relationship:

$$\mathcal{Y} = \alpha + \beta \mathcal{X}.$$

3. Applying linear regression: With the transformed variables, we can apply standard linear regression to estimate the coefficients α and β.

4. Reverting to the original coefficients: Finally, we convert the estimated coefficients back to their original scale:

$$a = e^{\alpha}, b = \beta.$$

A similar process can be applied to other types of nonlinear functions, as described in Table 4.5. It is important to note, however, that while linear regression finds the optimal coefficients for the transformed relationship, the resulting model may not minimize the original (untransformed) error. This is because the loss function is applied in the transformed space. Therefore, this method provides a useful approximation, but it may not always produce the best-fitting model in the original nonlinear domain.

4.10.2 Polynomial Regression

Polynomial regression is a widely used technique for modeling nonlinear relationships between input features and a continuous target variable. To introduce the basic idea, we start with the simple case of a single scalar input variable, where the model's hypothesis is represented as a polynomial of degree d in the input x:

$$h(x) = w_0 + w_1 x + w_2 x^2 + \ldots + w_d x^d. \tag{4.34}$$

The degree d is a hyperparameter of the model, typically selected based on cross-validation performance or prior knowledge of the underlying relationship between x and y.

Although the model is nonlinear in the input variable x, it remains linear with respect to the parameters $w_0, w_1, \ldots, w_d$. By treating each power $x, x^2, \ldots, x^d$ as a separate feature, polynomial regression can be cast as a special case of multiple linear regression. This enables the use of standard linear regression techniques, such as the normal equations or gradient descent, to estimate the optimal parameter vector $\mathbf{w}^*$.

	Function	**Model Transformation**	**Parameters Transformation**
Power	$y = ax^b$	$\mathcal{Y} = \log y, \mathcal{X} = \log x$	$\alpha = \log a, \beta = b$
Exponential	$y = ab^x$	$\mathcal{Y} = \log y, \mathcal{X} = x$	$\alpha = \log a, \beta = \log b$
Logarithmic	$y = \log(ax^b)$	$\mathcal{Y} = y, \mathcal{X} = \log x$	$\alpha = \log a, \beta = b$
Reciprocal	$y = \frac{1}{a+bx}$	$\mathcal{Y} = \frac{1}{y}, \mathcal{X} = x$	$\alpha = a, \beta = b$
Square root	$y = a + b\sqrt{x}$	$\mathcal{Y} = y, \mathcal{X} = \sqrt{x}$	$\alpha = a, \beta = b$

Table 4.5: Transformations of nonlinear functions into linear forms

To apply the closed-form solution for ordinary least squares in polynomial regression, we first construct the design matrix X, which contains the powers of the input data up to degree d:

$$X = \begin{pmatrix} 1 & x_1 & x_1^2 & \cdots & x_1^d \\ 1 & x_2 & x_2^2 & \cdots & x_2^d \\ \vdots & \vdots & \vdots & \ddots & \vdots \\ 1 & x_n & x_n^2 & \cdots & x_n^d \end{pmatrix}. \tag{4.35}$$

Given this design matrix, the optimal coefficients can be found using the normal equations (Equation (4.16)):

$$\mathbf{w}^* = (X^T X)^{-1} X^T \mathbf{y}. \tag{4.36}$$

4.10.2.1 Quadratic Regression Example

We now demonstrate using the closed-form solution to fit a quadratic regression model. Consider the scenario of throwing a ball into the air and measuring its height h_i at various times t_i. Suppose we collect the measurements shown in Table 4.6.

From basic physics, we know that the ball's height can be modeled as a quadratic function of time, considering its initial upward velocity and acceleration due to gravity:

$$h_i = w_1 t_i + w_2 t_i^2 + \epsilon. \tag{4.37}$$

Here, w_1 represents the initial velocity of the ball, w_2 is related to the acceleration due to gravity, and ϵ captures measurement noise and other unmodeled effects.

To estimate the coefficients w_1 and w_2, we first construct a design matrix X that includes a column of ones (for the intercept), a column for t_i, and a column for t_i^2:

```
import numpy as np

t = np.array([0, 1, 2, 3, 4, 5]) # time in seconds
h = np.array([0, 4.16, 7.15, 9.32, 10.41, 10.5]) # height in meters

X = np.c_[np.ones(len(t)), t, t**2]
print(X)
```

t_i (seconds)	h_i (meters)
0	0
1	4.16
2	7.15
3	9.32
4	10.41
5	10.5

Table 4.6: Measurements of the height of a ball as a function of time

The resulting design matrix is:

```
[[ 1.  0.  0.]
 [ 1.  1.  1.]
 [ 1.  2.  4.]
 [ 1.  3.  9.]
 [ 1.  4. 16.]
 [ 1.  5. 25.]]
```

We now apply the closed-form solution (Equation (4.16)) to compute $\mathbf{w}^*$:

```
w = np.linalg.inv(X.T @ X) @ X.T @ h
print(w)
```

The estimated coefficients are:

```
[ 0.01535714  4.59325    -0.49910714]
```

Thus, the fitted quadratic model is: $h = -0.5t^2 + 4.59t + 0.02$. We can now plot the data and the fitted curve:

```
import matplotlib.pyplot as plt

plt.scatter(t, h, c='k')
t_test = np.linspace(0, 5, 100)
h_test = w[0] + w[1] * t_test + w[2] * t_test**2
plt.plot(t_test, h_test, c='r')
plt.xlabel('Time (seconds)')
plt.ylabel('Height (meters)')
```

The resulting plot in Figure 4.14 shows how the quadratic regression model captures the trajectory of the ball.

4.10.2.2 Feature Crosses

So far, we have considered polynomial regression models with a single input feature x. When the dataset contains multiple features, the model can include not only the powers of each individual feature up to a certain degree d, but also interaction terms between different features.

A **feature cross** is formed by multiplying (crossing) two or more input features. For example, the term $x_1 x_2$ is a feature cross derived from the product of x_1 and x_2. Including such interaction terms can improve the model's ability to capture complex relationships that are not evident when features are considered independently.

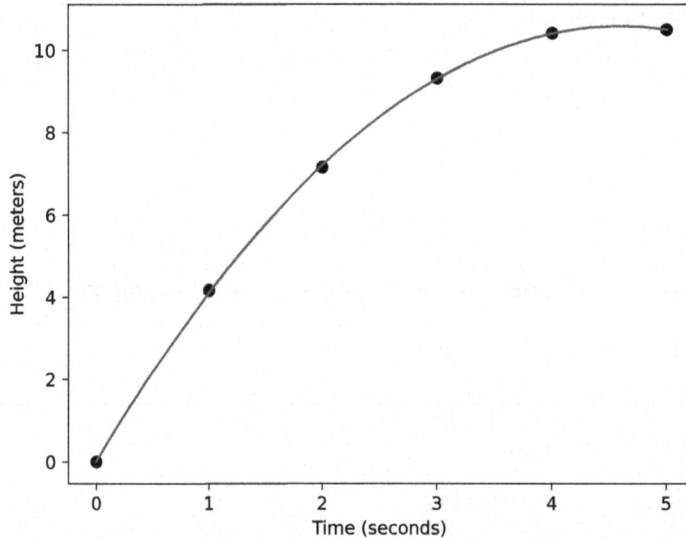

Figure 4.14: Quadratic function fitted to the ball's height measurements over time

In polynomial regression with degree d and multiple features, the model typically includes all powers of individual features up to degree d, along with all possible interaction terms whose total degree does not exceed d. For example, given three features x_1, x_2, x_3 and degree $d = 2$, the expanded set of features would include: $x_1, x_2, x_3, x_1x_2, x_1x_3, x_2x_3, x_1^2, x_2^2$, and x_3^2. The corresponding design matrix would take the form:

$$
X = \begin{pmatrix}
1 & x_{11} & x_{12} & x_{13} & x_{11}x_{12} & x_{11}x_{13} & x_{12}x_{13} & x_{11}^2 & x_{12}^2 & x_{13}^2 \\
1 & x_{21} & x_{22} & x_{23} & x_{21}x_{22} & x_{21}x_{23} & x_{22}x_{23} & x_{21}^2 & x_{22}^2 & x_{23}^2 \\
\vdots & \vdots & \vdots & \vdots & \vdots & \vdots & \vdots & \vdots & \vdots & \vdots \\
1 & x_{n1} & x_{n2} & x_{n3} & x_{n1}x_{n2} & x_{n1}x_{n3} & x_{n2}x_{n3} & x_{n1}^2 & x_{n2}^2 & x_{n3}^2
\end{pmatrix}.
$$

It is important to note that the number of feature crosses grows exponentially with both the number of original variables and the polynomial degree. This exponential increase can lead to overfitting and high computational costs. Therefore, selecting an appropriate degree d is crucial for balancing model complexity and generalization.

Scikit-Learn provides the `PolynomialFeatures`[13] class for generating polynomial and interaction features from an existing design matrix. It automatically adds all polynomial combinations of the input features up to a specified degree, which is passed as a parameter to the constructor. The following code demonstrates how to use this class to transform a matrix containing three samples and two features:

---

13. `https://scikit-learn.org/stable/modules/generated/sklearn.preprocessing.PolynomialFeatures.html`

```
from sklearn.preprocessing import PolynomialFeatures

X = np.array([[0, 1], [2, 3], [4, 5]])
poly_features = PolynomialFeatures(degree=2)
X_new = poly_features.fit_transform(X)
print(X_new)
```

The resulting transformed matrix is:

```
[[ 1.  0.  1.  0.  0.  1.]
 [ 1.  2.  3.  4.  6.  9.]
 [ 1.  4.  5. 16. 20. 25.]]
```

Each row now contains the expanded feature set: the intercept term x_0, the original features x_1 and x_2, and the second-degree polynomial terms x_1^2, $x_1 x_2$, and x_2^2, in that order.

4.10.2.3 Polynomial Regression Example

The following example demonstrates how polynomial regression can be applied to a dataset where the functional form of the relationship between the features and the target is unknown. In this example, we fit polynomial functions of varying degrees to a synthetic dataset generated from a noisy sine wave.

First, we sample 50 data points from the function $\sin x$ over the interval $[0, 10]$, adding Gaussian noise with mean 0 and standard deviation 0.2 to simulate real-world measurement errors:

```
def make_data(n_samples=50, std=0.2):
    x = np.random.rand(n_samples) * 10
    err = np.random.normal(size=n_samples) * std
    y = np.sin(x) + err
    return x, y

x, y = make_data()
```

The scatter plot of these data points is shown in Figure 4.15. To prepare the data for polynomial regression, we reshape the vector x into a matrix with a single column:

```
X = x.reshape(-1, 1)
```

Next, we define a helper function to construct a polynomial regression pipeline, consisting of `PolynomialFeatures` for feature expansion followed by a `LinearRegression` model:

```
from sklearn.pipeline import Pipeline
from sklearn.preprocessing import PolynomialFeatures
from sklearn.linear_model import LinearRegression

def PolynomialRegression(degree=2):
    return Pipeline([('poly', PolynomialFeatures(degree)),
                     ('reg', LinearRegression())])
```

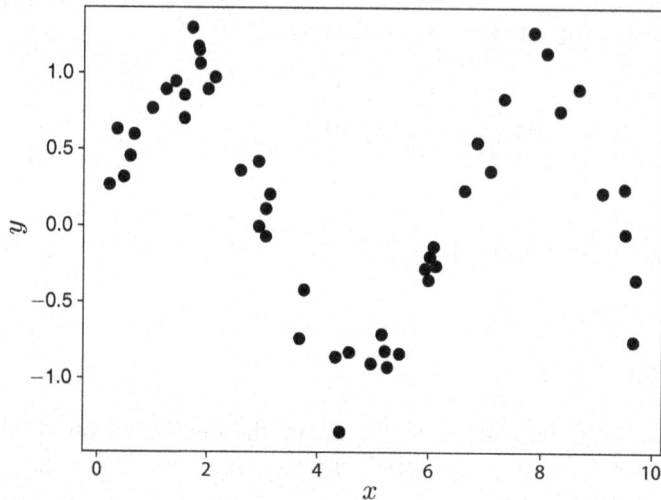

Figure 4.15: Data sampled from a noisy sine function over the interval [0, 10].

We now use this function to fit polynomials of degrees 1 to 10 to the data:

```
# Create a 2x5 subplot grid
fig, axes = plt.subplots(2, 5, figsize=(10, 4), sharex=True)
plt.subplots_adjust(hspace=0.5)

# Generate evenly spaced values from 0 to 10 for testing the polynomial fits
X_test = np.linspace(0, 10, 100).reshape(-1, 1)

# Iterate over the subplots and fit polynomials of degree 1 through 10
for ax, degree in zip(axes.flat, range(1, 11)):
    # Plot the original data
    ax.scatter(X, y, color='k', s=5)

    # Create and fit a polynomial regression model of the current degree
    model = PolynomialRegression(degree)
    model.fit(X, y)

    # Use the fitted model to predict values over the test range
    y_test = model.predict(X_test)

    # Plot the predicted polynomial
    ax.plot(X_test, y_test, color='r')
    ax.set_title(f'degree {degree}')

# Set common labels for the axes
fig.text(0.5, 0.02, '$x$', ha='center', va='center')
fig.text(0.09, 0.5, '$y$', ha='center', va='center', rotation='vertical')
```

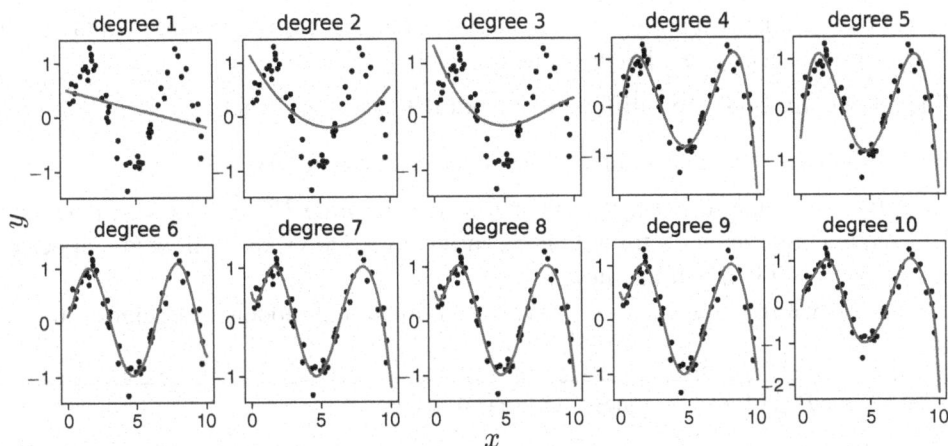

Figure 4.16: Polynomials of degrees 1 to 10 fitted to the data points. Lower-degree models underfit, while higher-degree models overfit. The degree-6 polynomial achieves a reasonable balance between bias and variance.

The resulting plots (see Figure 4.16) illustrate the bias–variance tradeoff: low-degree polynomials (e.g., 1–3) underfit the data, failing to capture the sinusoidal pattern; high-degree polynomials (above 7) overfit the data, capturing noise and producing unnecessarily complex curves; a degree-6 polynomial provides a good balance, closely approximating the underlying sine curve without excessive variance.

From a theoretical standpoint, for any set of n distinct points in the plane, there exists a unique polynomial of degree at most $n - 1$ that passes through all of them (see Exercise 4.23). In this example, the dataset contains of 50 points, so a degree-49 polynomial would perfectly fit the data, including the noise. However, such a model is prone to severe overfitting and is likely to generalize poorly to new inputs.

4.10.2.4 Validation Curves

For more complex, higher-dimensional problems, visual inspection of polynomial fits becomes impractical. A more systematic approach for selecting the optimal polynomial degree is to use a **validation curve**. This curve plots the training and validation scores across different values of a chosen hyperparameter, helping identify the one that offers the best balance between bias and variance.

Scikit-Learn provides the `validation_curve`[14] function in `sklearn.model_selection` for this purpose. It takes as input the model (`estimator`), the feature matrix (`X`), the target vector (`y`), the name of the hyperparameter to evaluate (`param_name`), the range of values to test (`param_range`), and the number of cross-validation folds (`cv`).

---

14. https://scikit-learn.org/stable/modules/generated/sklearn.model_selection.validation_curve.
   html

The function returns two arrays: `train_scores` and `validation_scores`, both of which are NumPy arrays with shape `(len(param_range), cv)`. That is:

- Each row corresponds to a different value of the hyperparameter.

- Each column corresponds to one of the cross-validation folds.

By averaging over the columns, we obtain the mean training R^2 score and mean validation R^2 score for each hyperparameter setting, which can be plotted to visualize how model performance changes with the complexity of the model.

For example, we use this function to evaluate polynomial models of degrees 1 to 15 on our dataset:

```
from sklearn.model_selection import validation_curve

degrees = np.arange(1, 16)
train_scores, val_scores = validation_curve(
                    PolynomialRegression(),
                    X, y,
                    param_name='poly__degree',
                    param_range=degrees,
                    cv=5
                )
plt.plot(degrees, np.mean(train_scores, axis=1), 'b', label='Training score')
plt.plot(degrees, np.mean(val_scores, axis=1), 'r', label='Validation score')
plt.legend()
plt.xlabel('Polynomial degree')
plt.ylabel('$R^2$ score')
```

The resulting validation curve (Figure 4.17) shows that the validation score increases up to degree 6, after which it begins to decline, while the training score continues to rise. This divergence signals the onset of overfitting, where the model starts capturing noise in the training data rather than the true underlying relationship. Based on this curve, a polynomial of degree 6 offers a good tradeoff between underfitting and overfitting, consistent with our earlier conclusion from visually inspecting the fitted polynomials.

Another strategy for selecting the optimal polynomial degree is to perform a grid search over a range of candidate degrees:

```
from sklearn.model_selection import GridSearchCV

param_grid = {'poly__degree': np.arange(1, 16)}
grid = GridSearchCV(PolynomialRegression(), param_grid, cv=5, n_jobs=-1)
grid.fit(X, y)

print('Optimal polynomial degree:', grid.best_params_['poly__degree'])
print('Best R2 score:', grid.best_score_)
```

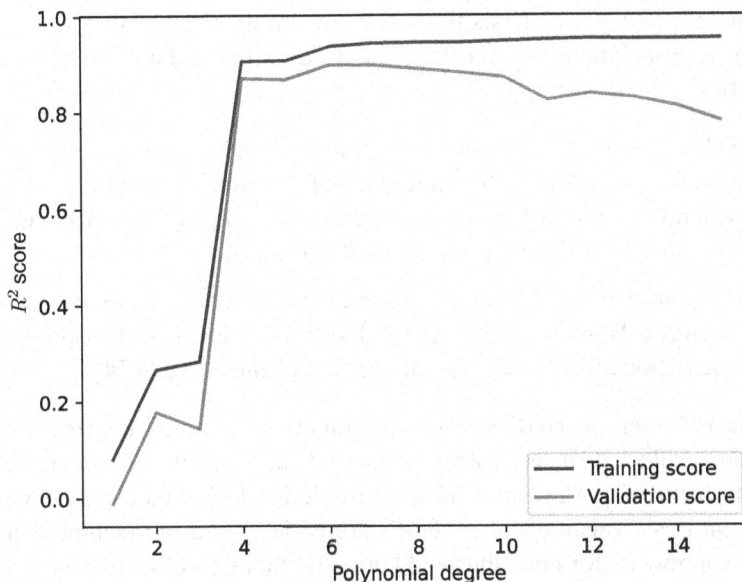

Figure 4.17: Training and validation R^2 scores for polynomial degrees from 1 to 15. The plot illustrates the overfitting effect: while the training score continues to increase, the validation score peaks around degree 6 and then declines.

The output from the grid search is:

```
Optimal polynomial degree: 6
Best R2 score: 0.8996347814330881
```

This result is consistent with both the validation curve and our earlier visual inspection.

4.10.3 Other Basis Functions

While polynomial regression is a versatile method for modeling nonlinear relationships, it represents just one instance within a broader class of models based on **basis functions**. Basis functions transform the input features into a new space where simple models, such as linear regression, can capture more complex patterns. They typically belong to the same function family (e.g., polynomials, splines, or Gaussians).

In basis function regression, the hypothesis is a linear combination of functions applied to the input x:

$$h(x) = w_0 + w_1\phi_1(x) + w_2\phi_2(x) + \ldots + w_d\phi_d(x). \tag{4.38}$$

Here, $\phi_1(x), \ldots, \phi_d(x)$ are basis functions from the chosen family, and d is a hyperparameter that controls the model complexity. As in polynomial regression, the hypothesis remains linear in the model parameters $w_0, \ldots, w_d$, allowing standard linear regression techniques to be used for estimating the optimal coefficients.

In polynomial regression, the basis functions are simply powers of x, i.e., $\phi_i(x) = x^i$. However, other types of basis functions can offer greater flexibility and may be better suited to specific data characteristics:

- **Splines**: Splines are piecewise polynomials that provide flexible modeling by fitting different polynomial segments to different regions of the input space [147]. They are particularly effective when the relationship between variables changes across the range of inputs, providing a smoother fit while adapting to local variations.

  The `SplineTransformer`[15] class in Scikit-Learn generates B-spline basis functions from the input features. B-splines are popular due to their local control properties—modifying the fit in one region affects only a small portion of the curve [178].

- **Radial Basis Functions (RBFs)**: RBFs are functions centered at specific points in the input space, whose values decrease with increasing distance from the center, typically following a Gaussian form [83]. They are useful for modeling localized patterns, where the effect of a feature diminishes with distance. RBFs are widely used in machine learning algorithms, including support vector machines and kernel methods (see Section 11.3.5).

- **Wavelets**: Wavelets are basis functions that vary both in scale and location, enabling them to capture localized features in the data and analyze patterns at different resolutions [393]. They are particularly effective for detecting transient or non-smooth structures, such as sharp changes or discontinuities. Wavelets are widely applied in signal processing due to their ability to compactly represent complex patterns.

Experimenting with different basis functions and evaluating their performance via cross-validation can help identify the most effective model for a given task.

4.11 Regularized Linear Regression

Regularization is a technique used in linear regression to reduce overfitting and improve the model's generalization performance. While simple regression models with only a few features typically have low risk of overfitting, regularization becomes crucial in more complex settings—such as polynomial regression with high degrees or high-dimensional feature spaces—where the model might otherwise fit the noise or irrelevant features in the training data.

As introduced in Section 2.6.2, regularization involves adding a penalty term to the cost function that reflects the complexity of the model:

$$\text{Cost}(h) = \text{TrainingError}(h) + \lambda \cdot \text{Complexity}(h). \tag{4.39}$$

The parameter λ is the **regularization coefficient** (also called **regularization strength**), which controls the tradeoff between fitting the data and keeping the model simple. A higher value of λ

---

15. https://scikit-learn.org/stable/modules/generated/sklearn.preprocessing.SplineTransformer.
   html

penalizes complex models more heavily, leading to solutions with lower variance but potentially higher bias.

In parametric models like linear regression, model complexity is typically measured by the magnitude of the parameter vector $\|\mathbf{w}\|$. Larger weights make the model more sensitive to small changes in the input, increasing the risk of overfitting. This effect is especially pronounced in polynomial regression, where large coefficients can lead to highly oscillatory behavior between data points (see Section B.2.3).

Encouraging smaller weights introduces a bias toward **smoother functions**—functions that vary more gradually with changes in the input—reflecting the common assumption in machine learning that the relationship between inputs and outputs is relatively smooth.

We distinguish between two types of regularization, depending on which norm is applied to the parameter vector:

- **L1 regularization** uses the L1 norm of $\mathbf{w}$, defined as the sum of the absolute values of the weights:

$$\|\mathbf{w}\|_1 = |w_0| + |w_1| + \ldots + |w_d|. \tag{4.40}$$

In L1 regularization, the derivative of $|w_i|$ with respect to w_i is $\text{sign}(w_i)$, which causes the optimization process to subtract a constant (proportional to the regularization strength) from each weight. When a weight becomes small enough, this penalty shrinks it exactly to zero rather than allowing it to change sign, as doing so would increase the L1 norm. This results in a **sparse** weight vector, where some weights are exactly zero, effectively removing the corresponding features from the model.

- **L2 regularization** (or **weight decay**) uses the squared L2 norm of $\mathbf{w}$, defined as the sum of the squares of the weights:

$$\|\mathbf{w}\|_2^2 = w_0^2 + w_1^2 + \ldots + w_d^2. \tag{4.41}$$

In L2 regularization, the derivative of w_i^2 is $2w_i$, thus the penalty applied to each weight is proportional to its current value. This penalizes larger weights more heavily, while smaller weights shrink less, leading to more uniform shrinkage across all features. Unlike L1 regularization, L2 does not produce exact zeros, since the penalty gradually decreases as the weights approach zero. As a result, all features are retained in the model, though with smaller coefficients.

Regularization can be interpreted in two equivalent ways: as adding a penalty to the objective function or as imposing a constraint on the parameters. For example, minimizing the L1 regularized cost function

$$\text{Cost}(h) = \text{TrainingError}(h) + \lambda \|\mathbf{w}\|_1$$

is equivalent to solving the constrained optimization problem

$$\min_{\mathbf{w}} \text{TrainingError}(h) \quad \text{subject to} \quad \|\mathbf{w}\|_1 \leq t,$$

for some constraint bound $t > 0$, where the exact relationship between λ and t depends on the formulation and can be derived using Lagrange multipliers. Similarly, L2 regularization corresponds to the constraint $\|\mathbf{w}\|_2^2 \leq t$.

Based on this constrained view, we can develop a geometric interpretation that highlights the differences between L1 and L2 regularization. As shown in Figure 4.18, the L1 constraint $\|\mathbf{w}\|_1 \leq t$ forms a diamond-shaped region centered at the origin in weight space, while the L2 constraint $\|\mathbf{w}\|_2^2 \leq t$ corresponds to a circular (or spherical, in higher dimensions) region. The elliptical contours of the training error are more likely to touch the corners of the diamond, leading to sparse solutions where some weights are exactly zero. In contrast, the circular constraint of L2 tends to intersect these contours more smoothly, shrinking all weights but typically not forcing any to zero.

The bias term w_0 is typically excluded from regularization because it is not multiplied by the input features and does not affect the model's sensitivity to input changes. Forcing w_0 toward zero would shift the prediction surface (e.g., the regression line or hyperplane) toward the origin, which may be too restrictive and lead to poor fits, especially when the true relationship does not pass through the origin.

In the next sections, we will demonstrate how to incorporate these two types of regularization into linear regression models.

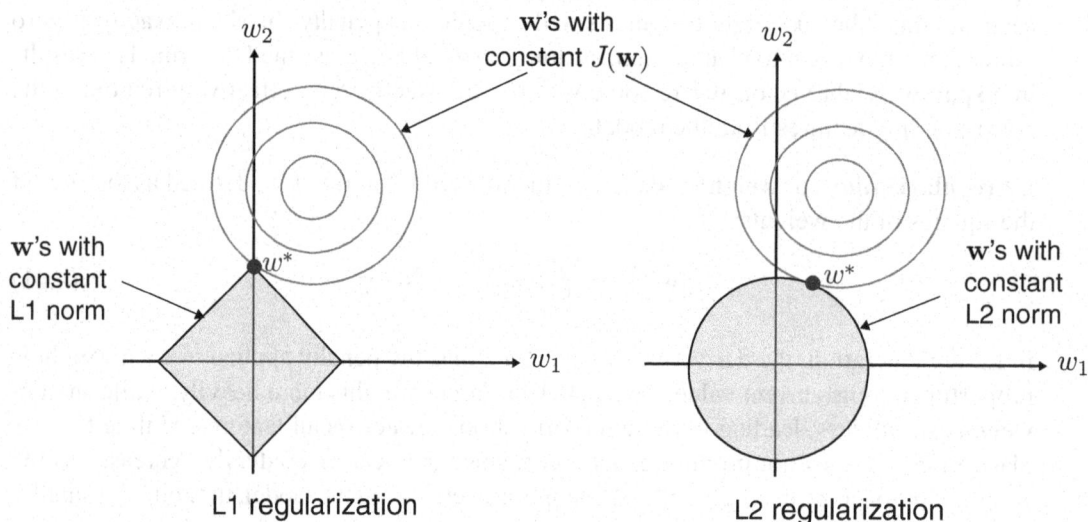

Figure 4.18: Comparison of L1 and L2 regularization techniques. L1 regularization corresponds to a diamond-shaped constraint in weight space, often leading to sparse solutions where some weights are exactly zero. L2 regularization corresponds to a circular constraint, resulting in more uniform shrinkage of all weights without forcing any to zero.

4.11.1 Ridge Regression

Ridge regression extends linear regression by adding an L2 penalty to the least squares cost function [274]. This penalty discourages large weights by adding their squared magnitudes to the objective:

$$J(\mathbf{w}) = \frac{1}{n} \sum_{i=1}^{n} (h_{\mathbf{w}}(\mathbf{x}_i) - y_i)^2 + \lambda \sum_{j=1}^{d} w_j^2. \tag{4.42}$$

Here, λ is the regularization coefficient that controls the strength of the penalty. Similar to standard linear regression, ridge regression can be solved via both a closed-form solution and iterative methods like gradient descent (see Exercise 4.24).

In Scikit-Learn, ridge regression is implemented by the following classes:

- The `Ridge`[16] class supports multiple solvers, including the closed-form solution via Cholesky decomposition. By default, the best solver is chosen automatically based on the shape and properties of the input data. The regularization strength is specified using the `alpha` parameter, with a default value of 1.0.

- The `SGDRegressor`[17] class with `penalty='l2'` for a solution based on stochastic gradient descent (SGD). The regularization strength is also specified using the `alpha` parameter, though its default value is set to 0.0001. Since SGD updates the weights more frequently, a smaller `alpha` is used to prevent over-penalization.

To demonstrate how regularization can help control overfitting in high-degree polynomial models, we apply ridge regression to fit a 10th-degree polynomial to the dataset sampled from $f(x) = \sin x$, introduced in Section 4.10.2.3.

We start by defining a pipeline consisting of the following steps:

1. `StandardScaler` for feature scaling—an important step in regularized models to ensure that all features contribute equally to the penalty term.

2. `PolynomialFeatures` to generate polynomial features up to degree 10.

3. `Ridge` for regularized regression using the L2 penalty.

```
from sklearn.preprocessing import PolynomialFeatures, StandardScaler
from sklearn.linear_model import Ridge
from sklearn.pipeline import Pipeline

def RidgePolynomialRegression(degree, alpha=1):
    return Pipeline([('scaler', StandardScaler()),
                     ('poly', PolynomialFeatures(degree)),
                     ('ridge', Ridge(alpha))])
```

---

16. https://scikit-learn.org/stable/modules/generated/sklearn.linear_model.Ridge.html
17. https://scikit-learn.org/stable/modules/generated/sklearn.linear_model.SGDRegressor.html

Next, we train 10 models with different values of λ, ranging from 0.00001 to 10,000, to observe how regularization strength affects the fitted curve:

```
# Create a 2x5 subplot grid
fig, axes = plt.subplots(2, 5, figsize=(10, 4), sharex=True)
plt.subplots_adjust(hspace=0.5)

# Generate evenly spaced values from 0 to 10 for testing the polynomial fits
X_test = np.linspace(0, 10, 100).reshape(-1, 1)

# Loop over 10 iterations, increasing alpha by a factor of 10 each time
alpha = 0.00001
for ax in axes.flat:
    # Plot the original data
    ax.scatter(X, y, color='k', s=5)

    # Create and fit the ridge polynomial regression model
    model = RidgePolynomialRegression(degree=10, alpha=alpha)
    model.fit(X, y)

    # Use the fitted model to predict values over the test range
    y_test = model.predict(X_test)

    # Plot the predicted polynomial
    ax.plot(X_test, y_test, color='r')
    ax.set_title(f'$\lambda = ${alpha}')

    alpha *= 10

# Set common labels for the axes
fig.text(0.5, 0.02, '$x$', ha='center', va='center')
fig.text(0.09, 0.5, '$y$', ha='center', va='center', rotation='vertical')
```

Figure 4.19 shows the fitted polynomials. For very small λ values, the model fits the noise in the data, resulting in overfitting. As λ increases, the model becomes progressively smoother and less flexible. At very high λ values, the penalty dominates, leading to underfitting, until the polynomial becomes almost linear. An intermediate λ (around 1 in this example) provides a good balance between bias and variance, capturing the shape of the sine function without overfitting.

Let's now examine how the coefficients of the polynomial change as we progressively increase the regularization strength λ:

```
alpha = 0.00001

# Loop over 10 iterations, increasing alpha by a factor of 10 each time
for i in range(10):
    # Create and fit the ridge polynomial regression model
```

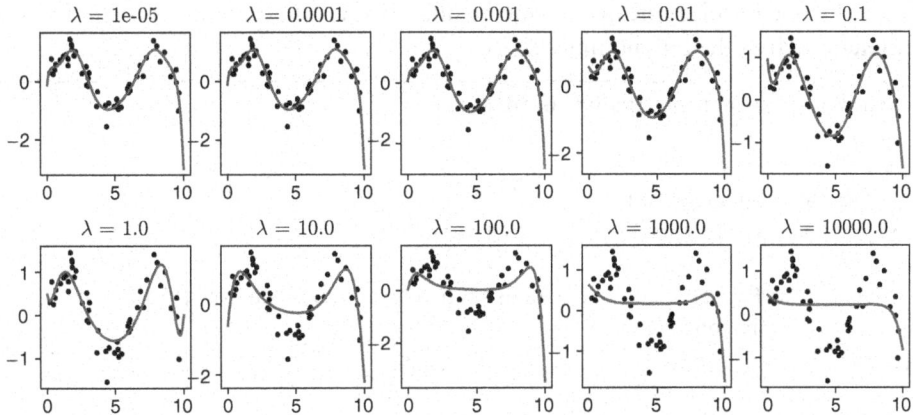

Figure 4.19: Polynomial fits of degree 10 using ridge regression across a range of regularization strengths λ. The plots demonstrate how increasing λ smooths the fitted curve and reduces overfitting, eventually causing underfitting as λ becomes too large.

```
model = RidgePolynomialRegression(degree=10, alpha=alpha)
model.fit(X, y)

# Extract the intercept and coefficients from the fitted model
intercept = model.named_steps['ridge'].intercept_
coef = model.named_steps['ridge'].coef_[1:]
coef = np.hstack((intercept, coef))
print(np.round(coef, 3))


alpha *= 10
```

The output is:

```
[-0.963 -0.053  3.339 -2.75  -0.241  5.017 -2.465 -2.808  1.548  0.506 -0.284]
[-0.963 -0.066  3.346 -2.678 -0.276  4.905 -2.413 -2.744  1.518  0.494 -0.278]
[-0.96  -0.165  3.381 -2.114 -0.515  4.031 -2.026 -2.241  1.287  0.397 -0.232]
[-0.929 -0.446  3.244 -0.506 -0.717  1.527 -1.284 -0.792  0.738  0.116 -0.111]
[-0.818 -0.503  2.53   0.125 -0.125  0.208 -0.997  0.101  0.335 -0.073 -0.013]
[-0.554 -0.405  1.281 -0.046  0.374  0.11  -0.23   0.23  -0.197 -0.096  0.071]
[-0.228 -0.203  0.426 -0.042  0.292  0.023  0.091  0.02  -0.128  0.011  0.009]
[ 0.032 -0.051  0.082 -0.025  0.079 -0.011  0.062 -0.002  0.024  0.014 -0.023]
[ 0.166 -0.006  0.012 -0.002  0.015  0.001  0.018  0.003  0.017 -0.004 -0.007]
[ 0.222 -0.001  0.001 -0.    0.002 -0.    0.003 -0.    0.003 -0.003 -0.001]
```

As λ increases, the magnitudes of the polynomial coefficients shrink progressively. We can see that the coefficients are gradually driven closer to zero, but they do not vanish entirely. This behavior reflects the nature of L2 regularization, which penalizes large weights without eliminating features altogether. The intercept term (appearing as the first number in each row) remains unaffected, as the regularization penalty applies only to the feature coefficients.

The optimal value of λ is typically selected using grid search, often in combination with other hyperparameters such as the polynomial degree:

```python
from sklearn.model_selection import GridSearchCV

param_grid = {
    'poly__degree': np.arange(1, 21),
    'ridge__alpha': np.logspace(-5, 4, num=10)
}
grid = GridSearchCV(RidgePolynomialRegression(degree=10), param_grid, cv=5,
                    n_jobs=-1)
grid.fit(X, y)

print(grid.best_params_)
```

The function `np.logspace`[18] generates values that are evenly spaced on a logarithmic scale. Here, we use it to produce 10 values ranging from 10^{-5} to 10^4, resulting in the sequence $[10^{-5}, 10^{-4}, 10^{-3}, \ldots, 10^3, 10^4]$. This covers a wide range of possible regularization strengths across several orders of magnitude.

The output from the grid search is:

```
{'poly__degree': 4, 'ridge__alpha': 0.1}
```

This indicates that the best-performing model uses a polynomial of degree 4 with a regularization coefficient of $\lambda = 0.1$.

4.11.2 Lasso Regression

Lasso (Least Absolute Shrinkage and Selection Operator) regression extends linear regression by adding an L1 penalty to the least squares cost function [578]:

$$J(\mathbf{w}) = \frac{1}{n} \sum_{i=1}^{n} (h_{\mathbf{w}}(\mathbf{x}_i) - y_i)^2 + \lambda \sum_{j=1}^{d} |w_j|. \tag{4.43}$$

Unlike ridge regression, which shrinks all coefficients toward zero, lasso regression can drive some coefficients exactly to zero. This sparsity-inducing property makes lasso particularly useful for feature selection, especially in high-dimensional settings where many features may be irrelevant.

Because the absolute value function is not differentiable at zero, lasso regression does not have a closed-form solution. Instead, it is solved using iterative optimization techniques such as coordinate descent.

---

18. https://numpy.org/doc/stable/reference/generated/numpy.logspace.html

4.11.2.1   (*) Coordinate Descent

A common optimization technique for solving the lasso problem is **coordinate descent**, which minimizes the cost function with respect to one parameter at a time while keeping all others fixed (see Section E.4.5 for a general discussion of the method). For lasso regression, coordinate descent has been shown to be particularly effective, offering fast convergence to the optimal solution [198, 200].

In this section, we develop the update rule for each coefficient in the coordinate descent algorithm for lasso regression, while handling the non-differentiability of the L1 penalty at zero using subgradients.

We start from the lasso cost function, including a factor of $1/2$ in front of the squared loss to simplify the derivative expressions and align them with standard treatments in the literature [198]:

$$J(\mathbf{w}) = \frac{1}{2n} \sum_{i=1}^{n} (h_{\mathbf{w}}(\mathbf{x}_i) - y_i)^2 + \lambda \sum_{j=1}^{d} |w_j|. \tag{4.44}$$

We assume that the predictors x_{ij} are standardized to have zero mean and unit variance[19], which implies that

$$\frac{1}{n} \sum_{i=1}^{n} x_{ij} = 0, \quad \frac{1}{n} \sum_{i=1}^{n} x_{ij}^2 = 1, \quad \text{for } j = 1, \dots, d.$$

To derive the coordinate update for a single coefficient w_j, we fix all other coefficients $\tilde{w}_k$ (for $k \neq j$) and isolate the objective with respect to w_j. This gives the following coordinate-wise cost function:

$$J(w_j) = \frac{1}{2n} \sum_{i=1}^{n} \left(y_i - \sum_{k \neq j} x_{ik} \tilde{w}_k - x_{ij} w_j \right)^2 + \lambda |w_j|. \tag{4.45}$$

Let us define the **partial residual**:

$$r_i^{(j)} = y_i - \sum_{k \neq j} x_{ik} \tilde{w}_k,$$

which represents the part of the error attributable to predictor x_j. Substituting this into the cost function gives:

$$J(w_j) = \frac{1}{2n} \sum_{i=1}^{n} \left(r_i^{(j)} - x_{ij} w_j \right)^2 + \lambda |w_j|. \tag{4.46}$$

---

19. Standardization (or feature scaling) is essential when using regularization, as it ensures that all features contribute equally to the penalty term.

We now compute the derivative of $J(w_j)$ with respect to w_j, assuming $w_j \neq 0$:

$$\frac{\partial J(w_j)}{\partial w_j} = \frac{1}{2n}\sum_{i=1}^{n} 2\left(r_i^{(j)} - x_{ij}w_j\right)(-x_{ij}) + \lambda\,\text{sign}(w_j)$$

$$= -\frac{1}{n}\sum_{i=1}^{n} x_{ij}r_i^{(j)} + w_j + \lambda\,\text{sign}(w_j).$$

Let us define:

$$z = \frac{1}{n}\sum_{i=1}^{n} x_{ij}r_i^{(j)},$$

so the optimality condition becomes:

$$\frac{\partial J(w_j)}{\partial w_j} = -z + w_j + \lambda\,\text{sign}(w_j) = 0,$$

which yields the solution:

$$w_j^* = z - \lambda\,\text{sign}(w_j^*).$$

Next, we consider the case $w_j = 0$, where the cost function is not differentiable. To handle this, we use the concept of subgradients (see Section B.11.9).

The subdifferential of $|w_j|$ at zero is the interval $[-1, 1]$, meaning:

$$\frac{d}{dw_j}|w_j| = \begin{cases} \text{sign}(w_j) & \text{if } w_j \neq 0, \\ \in [-1, 1] & \text{if } w_j = 0. \end{cases}$$

Substituting $w_j = 0$ into the derivative of the cost function, we obtain:

$$\frac{\partial J(w_j)}{\partial w_j} = -z + \lambda\,[-1, 1].$$

The optimality condition requires that zero lies in the subdifferential:

$$0 \in -z + \lambda[-1, 1] \quad \Leftrightarrow \quad z \in \lambda[-1, 1] \quad \Leftrightarrow \quad |z| \leq \lambda.$$

Therefore, when $|z| \leq \lambda$, the subgradient condition is satisfied, and the optimal solution is $w_j = 0$.

Putting both cases together, the update for w_j is:

$$w_j^* = \begin{cases} 0 & \text{if } |z| \leq \lambda, \\ z - \lambda\,\text{sign}(z) & \text{if } |z| > \lambda. \end{cases}$$

This update can be expressed more compactly using the **soft-thresholding operator**:

$$w_j^* = \text{sign}(z) \cdot (|z| - \lambda)_+, \tag{4.47}$$

where $(\cdot)_+ = \max(0, \cdot)$ denotes the positive part function. We define the soft-thresholding operator as:

$$S(z, \lambda) = \text{sign}(z) \cdot \max\left(|z| - \lambda, 0\right), \tag{4.48}$$

so that:

$$w_j^* = S(z, \lambda). \tag{4.49}$$

The soft-thresholding operator shrinks coefficients toward zero by an amount λ and sets them exactly to zero if the shrinkage is larger than the absolute value. This behavior allows lasso to achieve both regularization and feature selection simultaneously.

The coordinate descent algorithm has several key advantages in the context of lasso regression:

- Each update is computationally inexpensive, as it modifies only one coefficient at a time while moving the solution closer to the optimum. This makes the algorithm highly efficient and scalable for large datasets.

- It is guaranteed to converge to the global optimum of the lasso objective [198].

- It naturally extends to more complex regularization schemes such as elastic net, which combines both L1 and L2 penalties (see Section 4.11.3).

4.11.2.2 Lasso Regression in Scikit-Learn

In Scikit-Learn, lasso regression can be performed using the following classes:

- The `Lasso`[20] class implements the coordinate descent method described above. The regularization strength is specified using the `alpha` parameter whose default value is 1.0.

- The `SGDRegressor`[21] class with `penalty='l1'` uses stochastic gradient descent. While SGD is well-suited for very large datasets or online learning scenarios, it may not converge to a solution as sparse as that obtained by coordinate descent.

For example, we can apply lasso regression to our dataset by simply replacing the `Ridge` class with `Lasso` in the pipeline:

```
from sklearn.linear_model import Lasso

def LassoPolynomialRegression(degree, alpha=1):
    return Pipeline([('scaler', StandardScaler()),
                    ('poly', PolynomialFeatures(degree)),
                    ('lasso', Lasso(alpha))])
```

---

20. https://scikit-learn.org/stable/modules/generated/sklearn.linear_model.Lasso.html
21. https://scikit-learn.org/stable/modules/generated/sklearn.linear_model.SGDRegressor.html

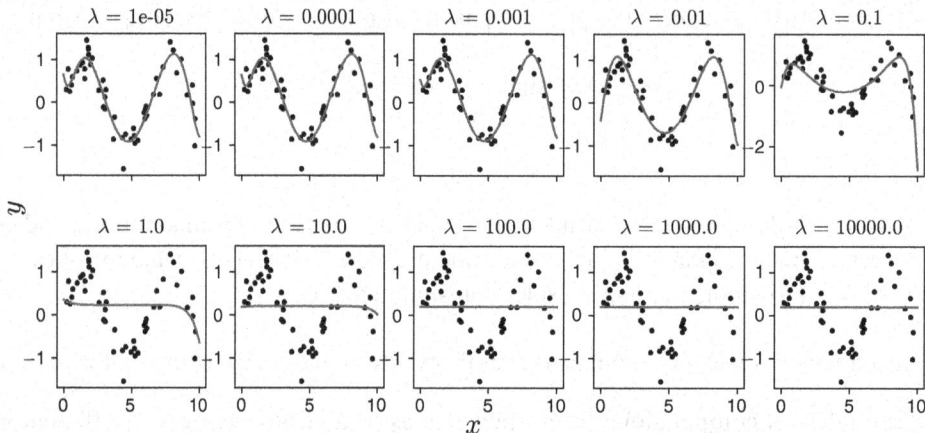

Figure 4.20: Polynomial fits using lasso regression with varying regularization strengths (λ). As λ increases, the model becomes increasingly sparse, with many coefficients reduced to zero, effectively removing the corresponding features from the model. This demonstrates lasso's ability to perform feature selection, especially at higher λ values.

By running lasso regression with various values of λ, we observe the strong impact of L1 regularization on the model coefficients, as illustrated in Figure 4.20. Examining the progression of the coefficients as λ increases further demonstrates lasso's sparsity-inducing property:

```
[-0.886 -0.598  3.128  0.276 -1.33   0.275 -0.042 -0.041  0.036 -0.032  0.014]
[-0.884 -0.595  3.116  0.274 -1.319  0.273 -0.044 -0.04   0.035 -0.031  0.014]
[-0.865 -0.569  2.999  0.258 -1.206  0.248 -0.061 -0.031  0.029 -0.03   0.014]
[-0.683 -0.299  1.882  0.031 -0.108  0.085 -0.279  0.036  0.     -0.013  0.011]
[-0.215 -0.04   0.676 -0.     0.     -0.     0.     0.    -0.      0.01  -0.012]
[ 0.232 -0.     0.    -0.     0.     -0.     0.    -0.     0.     -0.002 -0.   ]
[ 0.205 -0.     0.    -0.     0.     -0.    -0.    -0.    -0.     -0.    -0.   ]
[ 0.196 -0.     0.    -0.     0.     -0.    -0.    -0.    -0.     -0.    -0.   ]
[ 0.196 -0.     0.    -0.     0.     -0.    -0.    -0.    -0.     -0.    -0.   ]
[ 0.196 -0.     0.    -0.     0.     -0.    -0.    -0.    -0.     -0.    -0.   ]
```

Compared to ridge regression, lasso exhibits a much sharper reduction in coefficients, with many driven exactly to zero. This highlights the effectiveness of lasso regression in producing simpler and more interpretable models.

4.11.3   Elastic Net Regression

Elastic net offers a middle ground between ridge and lasso regressions by incorporating both L1 and L2 penalties [671]. This hybrid approach is controlled by a mixing parameter $r \in [0, 1]$, which balances the contributions of the two regularizations. The elastic net cost function is given by:

$$J(\mathbf{w}) = \frac{1}{n} \sum_{i=1}^{n} (h_{\mathbf{w}}(\mathbf{x}_i) - y_i)^2 + r\lambda \sum_{j=1}^{d} |w_j| + \frac{1-r}{2} \lambda \sum_{j=1}^{d} w_j^2. \qquad (4.50)$$

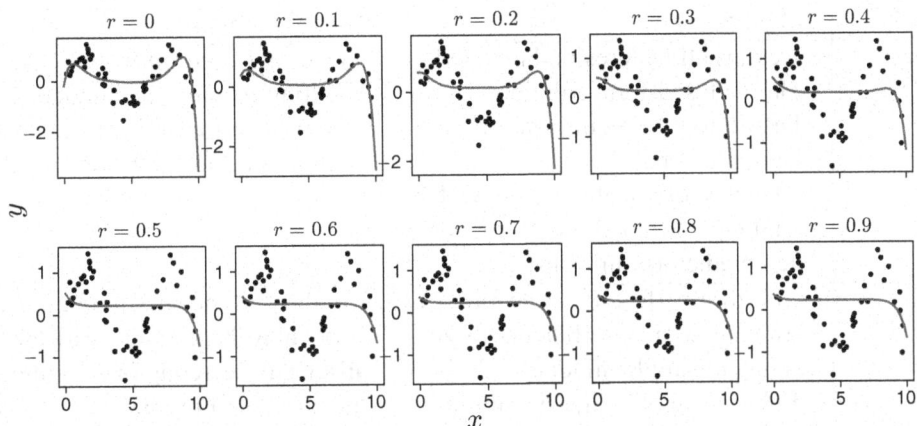

Figure 4.21: Polynomial fits using elastic net regression with $\lambda = 1.0$, illustrating the transition from L2 regularization ($r = 0$) to L1 regularization ($r = 1$). As the mixing parameter r increases, the model becomes sparser, with more coefficients driven to zero.

When $r = 0$, elastic net reduces to ridge regression, and when $r = 1$, it becomes equivalent to lasso regression.

In Scikit-Learn, elastic net regression is supported by the following classes:

- The `ElasticNet`[22] class uses the coordinate descent method. It requires two key parameters during initialization: `alpha`, which represents the overall regularization strength λ (defaults to 1.0), and `l1_ratio`, which specifies the mixing parameter r (defaults to 0.5).

- The `SGDRegressor` class with `penalty='elasticnet'`, which employs stochastic gradient descent (SGD). It also accepts the parameters `alpha` and `l1_ratio`, with default values of 0.0001 and 0.15, respectively.

Figure 4.21 illustrates the effect of varying the mixing parameter r from 0 to 1 in elastic net regression with $\lambda = 1.0$. As r increases, the model favors the L1 penalty more strongly, leading to increased sparsity by shrinking more coefficients toward zero.

Table 4.7 summarizes the key advantages and disadvantages of the three regularized regression models.

4.12   (*) Bayesian Linear Regression

Bayesian linear regression provides a probabilistic framework for regression analysis by incorporating prior beliefs about the model's parameters and updating these beliefs with observed data using Bayes' theorem [219]. This framework allows not only for point estimates of parameters but also for full posterior distributions, enabling uncertainty quantification in predictions.

---

22. https://scikit-learn.org/stable/modules/generated/sklearn.linear_model.ElasticNet.html

Model	Advantages	Disadvantages
Ridge	- Retains all features in the model. - Has a closed-form solution. - Distributes the regularization across all coefficients. - Handles multicollinearity well by shrinking the coefficients of correlated predictors uniformly.	- Does not perform feature selection, resulting in non-sparse models. - May overfit in high-dimensional settings due to inclusion of all features.
Lasso	- Performs feature selection by shrinking some coefficients to zero, leading to simpler models. - Enhances model interpretability by removing irrelevant features.	- In the presence of multicollinearity, lasso may behave unpredictably by arbitrarily selecting one feature from the correlated predictors and shrinking the others to zero. - Does not have a closed-form solution.
Elastic Net	- Combines the strengths of ridge and lasso. - Performs feature selection while maintaining group-wise shrinkage. - Offers more stable feature selection and better generalization in high-dimensional settings.	- More computationally intensive than lasso or ridge alone. - Requires tuning both λ and the mixing ratio r.

Table 4.7: Comparison of advantages and disadvantages of regularized regression models.

A Bayesian regression model is defined by the following components:

- **Likelihood of the data**: We assume that the observed labels follow a multivariate normal distribution centered at the linear model $X\mathbf{w}$, similar to the assumption made in the MLE derivation of ordinary least squares (see Section 4.2.1):

$$p(\mathbf{y}|X, \mathbf{w}) = \mathcal{N}(y|X\mathbf{w}, \alpha^{-1}I), \qquad (4.51)$$

where α is the **precision** (inverse of the variance) of the noise. This parameter is often treated as an unknown and estimated from the data. The assumption of a diagonal covariance matrix reflects the conditional independence of the labels given the model parameters.

- **Prior over the coefficients**: Different choices of prior distributions over the regression coefficients correspond to different regularization schemes. For example, in **Bayesian ridge regression**, we use a zero-mean isotropic Gaussian prior:

$$p(\mathbf{w}|\lambda) = \mathcal{N}(\mathbf{w}|0, \lambda^{-1}I), \qquad (4.52)$$

where λ is the precision of the prior. This prior penalizes large weights and shrinks them toward zero, analogous to L2 regularization in frequentist ridge regression. The Gaussian distribution is a **conjugate prior** to the Gaussian likelihood, which ensures that the posterior distribution remains Gaussian (see Section D.8.4).

- **Prior over the precisions**: To complete the model, we place gamma priors over the precision parameters α and λ:

$$p(\lambda \mid a_\lambda, b_\lambda) = \frac{b_\lambda^{a_\lambda}}{\Gamma(a_\lambda)} \lambda^{a_\lambda - 1} e^{-b_\lambda \lambda}, \qquad (4.53)$$

$$p(\alpha \mid a_\alpha, b_\alpha) = \frac{b_\alpha^{a_\alpha}}{\Gamma(a_\alpha)} \alpha^{a_\alpha - 1} e^{-b_\alpha \alpha}. \qquad (4.54)$$

Here, a_λ, b_λ, and a_α, b_α are hyperparameters representing the shape and rate of the gamma priors (see Section C.6.5.7). The gamma distribution is a conjugate prior to the precision of a Gaussian distribution, which ensures that the posterior distribution over the precisions also belongs to the gamma family.

- **Posterior distribution**: After observing the data, we use Bayes' theorem to update our beliefs about the parameters. For the regression weights, the posterior is proportional to the product of the likelihood and the prior:

$$p(\mathbf{w}|\mathbf{y}, X) \propto p(\mathbf{y}|X, \mathbf{w}) \cdot p(\mathbf{w}). \qquad (4.55)$$

In Bayesian ridge regression, the use of conjugate priors ensures that the posterior distribution over the regression coefficients remains Gaussian and can be computed in closed form. Note that the posterior covariance matrix is generally not diagonal, reflecting correlations between the model coefficients induced by the data.

Bayesian linear regression naturally incorporates regularization through the prior distribution on the parameters $\mathbf{w}$. A stronger prior, i.e., one with higher precision, corresponds to stronger regularization, as it places more weight on values of $\mathbf{w}$ close to the prior mean (typically zero). The strength of this penalty is controlled by the prior precision λ, which plays a role analogous to the regularization coefficient in classical models.

A key advantage of Bayesian regression is that the effective regularization adapts to the data. When the data strongly supports certain parameter values, the influence of the prior diminishes, allowing the model to fit the data more closely. In contrast, when data is scarce or noisy, the model relies more on the prior, helping to prevent overfitting.

Scikit-Learn provides an implementation of Bayesian regression in the `BayesianRidge`[23] class. Here is a simple example of how to use it:

---

23. `https://scikit-learn.org/stable/modules/generated/sklearn.linear_model.BayesianRidge.html`

```
from sklearn.linear_model import BayesianRidge

X = [[0, 0], [1, 1], [2, 2], [3, 3]]
y = [0, 1, 2, 3]

model = BayesianRidge()
model.fit(X, y)
print(model.coef_)
```

Output:

```
[0.49999993 0.49999993]
```

The `BayesianRidge` class has four hyperparameters: `alpha_1`, `alpha_2`, `lambda_1`, and `lambda_2`, corresponding to the shape and rate parameters of the gamma priors over the precision parameters α and λ defined earlier. By default, they are set to small values (10^{-6}), representing non-informative priors that let the data primarily determine the posterior.

The main advantages of Bayesian regression are:

- The ability to incorporate prior knowledge or beliefs about the model parameters, which can improve reliability when data is limited.

- Probabilistic predictions that quantify uncertainty, offering more informative outputs than point estimates.

- Improved robustness to ill-posed problems (e.g., multicollinearity), thanks to the regularizing effect of the prior.

- Automatic regularization that adapts to the data, balancing model complexity and generalization.

Its limitations include:

- Higher computational cost compared to traditional linear regression, especially in high-dimensional settings.

- Sensitivity to the choice of priors, which may require tuning or domain expertise.

- Bayesian inference has a steeper learning curve, particularly for practitioners unfamiliar with Bayesian concepts and inference.

For a more detailed discussion on Bayesian regression, refer to the book *Bayesian Data Analysis* by Gelman et al. [219], which provides a comprehensive introduction to Bayesian modeling and inference.

4.13 Summary

This chapter has explored linear regression and various approaches for solving regression problems. The key takeaways are as follows:

- Linear regression models the relationship between a set of features and a continuous target variable using a linear function of the model parameters.

- Ordinary least squares (OLS) regression estimates the model parameters by minimizing the mean squared error between the model's predictions and the actual targets. OLS can be interpreted as a maximum likelihood estimate when the error terms are independent, normally distributed, and have zero mean.

- Two main approaches for solving linear regression problems are the normal equations, which provide a closed-form solution, and gradient descent, which is preferred for large datasets or online learning. Effective application of gradient descent requires appropriate feature scaling and careful tuning of the learning rate.

- Common evaluation metrics for regression tasks include the R^2 score, which measures the proportion of variance explained by the model, and RMSE, which quantifies the prediction error in the same units as the target variable.

- Feature engineering, guided by domain expertise, is essential for improving model performance by creating new, meaningful input features.

- Validating key assumptions such as linear independence of features, homoscedasticity (constant variance of errors), and normality of the residuals is important for ensuring reliable and accurate predictions.

- Linear regression can be extended to model nonlinear relationships by transforming the input variables into polynomial features. However, such models are more prone to overfitting and require careful tuning and evaluation.

- Regularization methods such as L1 (lasso) and L2 (ridge) help mitigate overfitting by penalizing large coefficients. Elastic net combines both penalties to balance feature selection and shrinkage.

- A key strength of linear regression is its interpretability: the model coefficients directly quantify the impact of each feature on the target, making the model's predictions easier to understand and explain.

4.14 Exercises

4.14.1 Multiple-Choice Questions

4.1. We would like to predict the number of publications of PhD students in their second year based on the number of publications in their first year. Let x represent the first-year publication count, and y the count in the second year. Based on the four training samples shown in Table 4.8, we fit a linear regression model of the form $h(x) = w_0 + w_1 x$ to the data. What is the value of w_1?

x	y
1	2
4	3
0	1
3	2

Table 4.8: Number of publications of PhD students

   (a) 0.4

   (b) 0.8

   (c) 1.2

   (d) 1.6

4.2. You have a dataset with 200 samples and 10,000 features. Which approach is more suitable for fitting the parameters of a linear regression model to this dataset?

   (a) The closed-form solution, since gradient descent might get stuck in a local minimum.

   (b) The closed-form solution, since it can find the parameters faster than gradient descent.

   (c) Gradient descent, since a closed-form solution cannot be computed when the number of features is greater than the number of samples.

   (d) Gradient descent, since it will be more computationally efficient than the closed-form solution.

4.3. We are performing ordinary least-squares linear regression. Which of the following will never increase the training error, as measured by the mean squared error?

   (a) Adding polynomial features

   (b) Using feature selection to remove some of the features

   (c) Adding L1 regularization to encourage sparse weights

   (d) Centering the design matrix (so each feature has mean zero)

4.4. Let $\mathbf{w}^*$ be the solution obtained using the normal equations for ordinary least squares linear regression. If all the input features were scaled by a factor of k (but not the labels y), what would be the resulting solution?

   (a) $\frac{1}{k}\mathbf{w}^*$

   (b) $\frac{1}{k^2}\mathbf{w}^*$

   (c) $k\mathbf{w}^*$

   (d) $k^2\mathbf{w}^*$

4.5. How does the bias–variance decomposition of lasso regression compare with that of ordinary least squares regression?

   (a) Lasso has larger bias and larger variance.

   (b) Lasso has larger bias and smaller variance.

   (c) Lasso has smaller bias and larger variance.

   (d) Lasso has smaller bias and smaller variance.

4.6. The statistical assumptions that justify the least squares loss function are:

   (a) The features are normally distributed.

   (b) The relationship between the features and the target is linear in the parameters.

   (c) The irreducible errors are independently and identically distributed (i.i.d.).

   (d) The mean of the residuals is zero.

4.7. Which of the following statements is true about regression evaluation metrics?

   (a) MAE is more sensitive to outliers than RMSE.

   (b) R^2 score can be negative.

   (c) Multiplying all the residuals by 2 will cause the RMSE to double.

   (d) Adding more features to the model usually leads to an increase in the R^2 score on the training set.

4.8. Which of the following hyperparameters can affect the bias–variance tradeoff?

   (a) λ, the regularization coefficient in ridge regression

   (b) α, the learning rate in gradient descent

   (c) the maximum number of iterations in gradient descent

   (d) d, the polynomial degree in polynomial regression

4.9. Which of the following is an advantage of stochastic gradient descent over batch gradient descent?

  (a) It is guaranteed to reach the global minimum for convex functions.

  (b) It produces more stable and consistent updates.

  (c) It can escape local minima more easily.

  (d) It typically has faster convergence for large datasets.

  (e) It is better suited for incremental learning.

4.10. Which of the following models is more susceptible to multicollinearity?

  (a) A linear regression model with two independent variables

  (b) A polynomial regression model of degree 3 with one variable

  (c) A polynomial regression model of degree 2 with two variables (including their feature crossing)

  (d) A ridge regression model

  (e) A lasso regression model

4.14.2 Theoretical Exercises

4.11. A study group is analyzing the relationship between study time and exam performance. They have collected data representing the number of hours studied and the corresponding exam scores for a group of students, shown in Table 4.9.

Hours Studied	Exam Score
1	52
2	59
4	67
6	81
8	90

Table 4.9: Relationship between hours studied and exam scores for a study group

  (a) Manually fit a linear regression model to the data using the closed-form solution. Show all the steps in your calculation.

  (b) Compute the mean squared error (MSE) of the model.

  (c) Use the derived model to predict the exam score for students who studied for 3 and 5 hours, respectively.

4.12. Prove that the sum of residuals $r_i = y_i - \hat{y}_i$ in ordinary least squares (OLS) regression is always zero.

4.13. Derive the normal equations (Equation (4.15)) without using matrix calculus, i.e., by computing the partial derivatives of the cost function $\frac{\partial J(\mathbf{w})}{\partial w_j}$ for $j = 0, \ldots, d$ and equating them to zero.

4.14. (*) Prove that $X^T X$ is invertible if and only if the columns of X are linearly independent (i.e., X has a full column rank).

Hint:

- For the forward direction: Assume that the columns of X are linearly independent. Consider the quadratic form $\mathbf{v}^T X^T X \mathbf{v}$ and show that it is strictly positive for all nonzero vectors $\mathbf{v}$, implying that $X^T X$ is positive definite and therefore invertible.
- For the reverse direction: Assume that $X^T X$ is invertible. Suppose, for contradiction, that the columns of X are linearly dependent. Use the fact that there exists a nonzero vector $\mathbf{v}$ such that $X\mathbf{v} = 0$ to derive a contradiction.

4.15. Explain why feature scaling is not required when using the closed-form solution of ordinary least squares, whereas it is important when using gradient descent.

4.16. Discuss the challenges of applying linear regression in high-dimensional spaces ($d >> n$, where d is the number of features and n is the number of observations). What are the implications for coefficient stability, model interpretability, and computational efficiency? Consider both the closed-form solution and gradient descent approaches.

4.17. We have a linear regression model that was trained on a dataset D. If we duplicate every sample in D and then retrain the model using the duplicated dataset, what will happen to the learned weights of the model? Explain your reasoning.

4.18. (*) Prove that the least squares cost function (Equation (4.14)) is convex. *Hint*: Recall that a function is convex if and only if its Hessian matrix is positive semidefinite.

4.19. Can the RMSE of a regression model on a given dataset increase while its R^2 score on the same dataset decreases? If yes, provide an example. If no, prove why not.

4.20. Derive a batch gradient descent training algorithm that minimizes the sum of squared errors for a regression model, whose output h depends on the input features x_j as follows:

$$h = w_0 + w_1 x_1 + w_1 x_1^3 + w_2 x_2 + w_2 x_2^3 + \ldots + w_d x_d + w_d x_d^3.$$

Provide the gradient descent update rule in the form $w_j \leftarrow w_j - \ldots$ for $0 \leq j \leq n$.

4.21. You are given the following set of five points: $(-2, 0)$, $(-1, 0)$, $(0, 1)$, $(1, 0)$, and $(2, 0)$, where the first element of each pair is the predictor variable x, and the second element is the target variable y.

(a) Manually fit a parabola (a function of the form $y = ax^2 + bx + c$) to the given data points using the normal equations.

(b) Draw a plot that shows the data points and the best fitting parabola (you can use Python for the plotting).

4.22. (*) How many features will be generated by applying the `PolynomialFeatures` transformer with degree d to a dataset with n features (including all the interaction terms)? Show your computation.

4.23. (*) Prove that for any set of n unique points, there is a polynomial of degree at most $n-1$ that passes through all the points. *Hint*: Use Lagrange interpolation to construct the polynomial, where each term equals 1 at one point and 0 at all the others (see Section B.2.3.1).

4.24. In this exercise, we will derive the closed-form solution and gradient descent update rule for ridge regression. Recall that the cost function in ridge regression is:

$$J(\mathbf{w}) = \frac{1}{n} \sum_{i=1}^{n} (h(\mathbf{x}_i) - y_i)^2 + \lambda \sum_{j=0}^{d} w_j^2,$$

where λ is the regularization coefficient. For simplicity, assume that the intercept w_0 is also regularized.

(a) Prove that the vector $\mathbf{w}^*$ that minimizes $J(\mathbf{w})$ is:

$$\mathbf{w}^* = \left(X^T X + \lambda I\right)^{-1} X^T \mathbf{y},$$

where X is the $n \times (d+1)$ design matrix, whose i-th row is $\mathbf{x}_i$, and $\mathbf{y}$ is the column vector of target values.

(b) What happens to the optimal $\mathbf{w}^*$ when $\lambda = 0$? $\lambda \to +\infty$? $\lambda \to -\infty$? Explain your answer.

(c) Find the partial derivatives $\frac{\partial J}{\partial w_j}$ for an arbitrary w_j, considering all weights $j \in \{0, \ldots, d\}$.

(d) Based on the derived partial derivatives, formulate the gradient descent update rule for ridge regression. Compare it with the update rule for standard linear regression. How does this difference affect gradient descent, assuming $\lambda > 0$? Consider the impact both when w_j is positive and when it is negative.

(e) Discuss the importance of selecting an appropriate regularization coefficient λ for ridge regression. Which strategies or methods could guide this choice?

4.25. Figure 4.22 shows six data points that were sampled from an unknown function $f(x)$ with some noise, such that for every point $y_i = f(x_i) + \epsilon_i$. We decided to model $f(x)$ using a polynomial of degree 5, $h(x) = \sum_{j=0}^{5} w_j x^j$. To avoid overfitting, we use L2 regularization with a regularization strength λ.

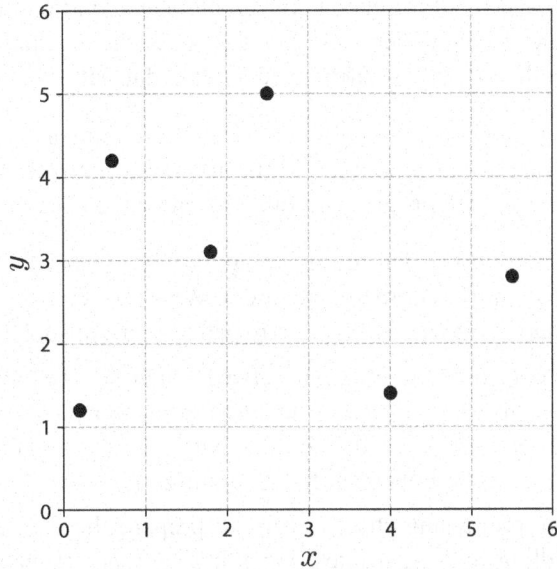

Figure 4.22: Sample data points for polynomial regression analysis

(a) Write the objective function for this optimization problem.

(b) Sketch (qualitatively) the fitted polynomial curve for $\lambda = 0$ on Figure 4.22.

(c) Discuss the behavior of the model as $\lambda \to \infty$, and illustrate this on Figure 4.22.

(d) If w_0 is also subjected to regularization, describe and illustrate the model's behavior as $\lambda \to \infty$ on Figure 4.22.

4.14.3   Programming Exercises

4.26. The Students Marks Dataset[24] is a simple dataset that contains information on students' study time, the number of courses taken, and their marks. Your task is to build a linear regression model to predict a student's mark based on the number of hours they studied and the number of courses they took.

(a) Load the dataset and perform basic exploratory data analysis (e.g., check for missing values, summary statistics).

(b) Split the data into training and test sets using an 80/20 split.

(c) Fit a linear regression model using the training data to predict the students' marks based on their study time and the number of courses taken.

(d) Compute the root mean squared error (RMSE) and R^2 score of the model on both the training and test sets.

---

24. https://www.kaggle.com/datasets/yasserh/student-marks-dataset

(e) Plot the residuals (the difference between the actual and predicted marks) against the predicted values. What patterns do you observe in the residual plot, and what does this tell you about the model's performance and the dataset?

4.27. The diabetes dataset[25] provided by Scikit-Learn contains data on 442 diabetes patients, each with 10 baseline features such as age, BMI, and average blood pressure. The goal is to forecast the patient's disease progression one year after the baseline measurements.

(a) Begin by examining the dataset, using appropriate statistics and visualizations (e.g., histograms, box plots, summary statistics). What can you learn about the distribution of the target and features? Are there any patterns or unusual observations?

(b) Calculate the correlation coefficient between each feature and the target variable and visualize the results (e.g., using a heatmap or scatter plots). Which features show a strong correlation (either positive or negative) with the target variable? Discuss which features might be most important for predicting disease progression.

(c) Discuss the preprocessing steps needed to prepare the dataset for regression analysis (e.g., handling missing values, encoding categorical features, scaling numerical features) and apply them to the dataset.

(d) Split the data into training and test sets.

(e) Build a simple linear regression model using Scikit-Learn's `LinearRegression` class and fit it to the training set.

(f) Evaluate the model's performance by calculating the RMSE and R^2 score both on the training and test sets. Is the model overfitting or underfitting? How well does it generalize to the test set?

(g) Explore the effect of regularization by training `Ridge` and `Lasso` regression models. Perform cross-validation to identify the optimal value of λ that gives the best performance. Compare the regularized models with the simple linear regression model. Did regularization improve the performance? Why or why not?

4.28. The dataset shown in Table 4.10 consists of two variables: x (independent variable) and y (dependent variable). Initial observations suggest that the relationship between x and y is nonlinear. Your task is to determine an appropriate transformation that linearizes the relationship between x and y and fit a linear regression model to the transformed variables.

(a) Plot the data points to visually inspect the relationship. Does it appear linear or nonlinear? Comment on any trends or patterns you observe.

(b) Choose an appropriate transformation for x, y, or both to linearize the relationship. Explain why you chose this transformation.

(c) Apply the transformation to the data. Plot the transformed data to visually assess whether the relationship between the transformed x and y appears more linear.

---

25. `https://scikit-learn.org/stable/modules/generated/sklearn.datasets.load_diabetes.html`

x	y
1	2
2	5
3	6.8
4	8.2
5	9.1

Table 4.10: A sample dataset with a nonlinear relationship between x and y

    (d) Fit a linear regression model to the transformed variables. Provide the equation of the fitted model, expressing it in terms of the original variables. Plot the resulting function together with the original data points.

    (e) Evaluate the performance of your linear regression model using appropriate metrics such as the R^2 score and RMSE. Compare the model's performance before and after the transformation.

4.29. You have been hired as an analyst at a green energy company to improve the efficiency of solar panels. Your current project involves understanding how the efficiency of solar panels is affected by two main factors: the average daily sunlight hours and the average daily temperature. A dataset with 50 samples is provided to you in the file `solar_panels.csv`[26], available on the book's git repository. Preliminary analysis suggests that the relationship between these factors and the efficiency is nonlinear.

    (a) Visualize the dataset by plotting `SunlightHours` and `Temperature` against `Efficiency` to understand the distribution.

    (b) Use `PolynomialFeatures` from `sklearn.preprocessing` to expand your feature set with polynomial features up to the 3rd degree.

    (c) Divide the dataset into training and test sets using an 80%-20% split.

    (d) Fit a linear regression model on the training set using the transformed polynomial features.

    (e) Assess the model's performance on the test set by calculating the RMSE and the R^2 score.

    (f) Plot the model's predictions against the actual `Efficiency` values to visualize the fit.

    (g) Experiment with different degrees for the polynomial features (e.g., 2, 3, 4) and explore how the model's performance varies with each degree. Discuss your observations regarding overfitting and underfitting.

26. https://github.com/roiyeho/ml-book/blob/main/Chapter04/datasets/solar_panels.csv

4.30. The Ames housing dataset, available on Kaggle[27] and also on the book's git repository[28], presents a more challenging task than simpler datasets like the California housing dataset. It contains a rich set of features describing aspects of residential homes in Ames, Iowa, and includes both numerical and categorical data, along with instances with missing values.

Your task is to develop a regression model to predict the sale price of houses in the Ames housing dataset. Your solution should include the following steps:

(a) Exploratory Data Analysis (EDA):

 i. Perform an exploratory data analysis to understand the distribution of key features and the target variable (`SalePrice`). Are there any outliers or anomalies in the data?

 ii. Investigate the relationship between the target variable and potential predictor variables using appropriate statistics and visualizations.

(b) Data Preprocessing:

 i. Identify features with missing values and devise a strategy to handle them. Would you impute the missing values, or would you remove or ignore them? Justify your choice.

 ii. Convert categorical features into a form that could be provided to machine learning algorithms. Discuss the encoding scheme you chose and why.

 iii. Investigate the numerical features and discuss why feature scaling might be necessary. Apply a feature scaling method to the numerical features, such as standard scaling, min-max scaling, or robust scaling. Provide a brief justification for your chosen method.

(c) Feature Engineering: Create new features that might improve your model's performance. Explain the rationale behind each new feature.

(d) Model Selection: Choose at least three different regression models to apply to this problem (e.g., standard linear regression, ridge regression, polynomial regression). Explain your choice of models and any assumptions they make about the data.

(e) Model Training and Tuning:

 i. Train your chosen model on the training data. How do you ensure that you are not overfitting?

 ii. Apply hyperparameter tuning to at least one of your models. Describe the process and how you selected the final model parameters.

---

27. https://www.kaggle.com/competitions/house-prices-advanced-regression-techniques
28. https://github.com/roiyeho/ml-book/tree/main/Chapter04/datasets

(f) Evaluation and Interpretation:

    i. Evaluate the performance of your models on the test set using appropriate metrics such as RMSE, MAE, and R^2 score. Discuss the strengths and weaknesses of each model based on their performance.

    ii. Provide an interpretation of your model results. Which features are most important for predicting house prices, and how do they impact the price?

(g) Conclude with a summary of your findings and any recommendations for further analysis or potential applications of your model.

4.31. The Student Performance Dataset[29] in the UCI machine learning repository provides a wide range of attributes related to the academic achievements of higher education students. This includes their grades, demographics, social life, and school-related features. The data was meticulously collected from school reports and surveys. It is divided into two separate datasets corresponding to student performance in Mathematics (mat) and Portuguese language (por).

Develop a regression model to analyze and predict student performance. Use a similar process to the one described in the previous exercise, including steps like data exploration, preprocessing, feature extraction, model development, evaluation, and result interpretation.

4.32. Implement the stochastic gradient descent (SGD) algorithm (Algorithm E.2) with a linear decay schedule for the learning rate. Follow these steps:

(a) Implement the SGD algorithm with a learning rate that decays linearly over time, according to the following schedule:

$$\alpha_t = \frac{\alpha_0}{1 + \gamma t},$$

where α_0 is the initial learning rate, γ is the decay factor, and t is the iteration number.

(b) Apply your SGD implementation to the California housing dataset.

(c) Evaluate the performance of your model by calculating the RMSE and R^2 score on the training and test sets. Compare the performance with other optimization methods such as the closed-form solution and batch gradient descent.

(d) Experiment with different initial learning rates and decay factors. Discuss the impact of the learning rate schedule on the convergence of the algorithm.

(e) Plot the learning curves, showing how the training error decreases over iterations, for various learning rate schedules. Analyze how well your model converges and whether it reaches the global minimum efficiently.

(f) Reflect on the benefits and drawbacks of using a linear decay schedule for SGD. Under what conditions does this schedule help or hinder convergence?

---

29. https://archive.ics.uci.edu/dataset/320/student+performance

4.33. In this exercise, you will use Scikit-Learn's `SGDRegressor` class to simulate mini-batch gradient descent. You will incrementally update the model by using the `partial_fit` method with subsets of the training data (mini-batches). The goal is to understand how mini-batch size affects model performance and convergence speed.

   (a) Load the California housing dataset using `fetch_california_housing` from `sklearn.datasets`.

   (b) Split the dataset into training and test sets using an 80/20 split.

   (c) Standardize the features using a `StandardScaler`. Ensure that you fit the scaler only on the training data, and apply it to both the training and test data.

   (d) Implement mini-batch gradient descent using the following steps:
      i. Set the batch size n_{batch} (e.g., 128).
      ii. Create an instance of `SGDRegressor`.
      iii. Shuffle the training data at the start of each epoch.
      iv. In each epoch, divide the training data into mini-batches of size n_{batch}. For each mini-batch, update the model using the `partial_fit` method.
      v. Repeat for a fixed number of epochs (e.g., 10).

   (e) After training, evaluate the model using the R^2 score on both the training and test sets.

   (f) Experiment with different mini-batch sizes (e.g., 32, 64, 256) and epochs (e.g., 10, 20, 50). Plot the R^2 score on the test set over multiple epochs for different mini-batch sizes.

   (g) Analyze how the mini-batch size affects the model's convergence speed and final performance. Discuss whether smaller or larger mini-batch sizes lead to faster convergence and if there is a tradeoff in test set performance.

   (h) (Optional) Compare the performance and convergence speed of mini-batch gradient descent with full-batch gradient descent and stochastic gradient descent.

Chapter 5

Logistic Regression

Logistic regression is a foundational algorithm for classification tasks, where the goal is to predict the class or category of a given input, such as determining whether an email is spam or not, or predicting whether a patient has a certain disease based on clinical features. Because of its simplicity, interpretability, and effectiveness, it is widely used as a baseline model against which more complex classifiers are compared.

Originally developed for binary classification, logistic regression models the probability that an input belongs to the "positive" class rather than the "negative" class by applying the logistic (sigmoid) function to a linear combination of the input features. This function maps real-valued inputs to the interval [0, 1], allowing the output to be interpreted as a probability. The term "regression" reflects the fact that the model's output is a continuous value between 0 and 1; however, in machine learning it is typically used for classification by thresholding the predicted probability (typically at 0.5) to produce a binary label.

When extended to multi-class problems, logistic regression is known as multinomial logistic regression or softmax regression. In this case, the softmax function replaces the sigmoid function so that the predicted probabilities across all classes sum to one, allowing the model to predict the probability of the input belonging to one of several mutually exclusive classes.

This chapter provides a comprehensive treatment of logistic regression, covering both its theoretical underpinnings and practical applications. The chapter is organized as follows. Section 5.1 introduces different types of classification problems. Section 5.2 formally defines the logistic regression model and its computational process. Section 5.3 covers optimization techniques for training logistic regression models, including the implementation of gradient-based optimization in Python. Section 5.4 demonstrates how to use Scikit-Learn's built-in classes to efficiently train logistic regression models in practice. Section 5.5 discusses common metrics for evaluating classifiers. Section 5.6 presents methods for handling imbalanced datasets with highly skewed class distributions. Section 5.7 introduces general strategies for extending binary classifiers to multi-class problems. Section 5.8 introduces multinomial logistic regression and demonstrates its application to the well-known MNIST handwritten digits dataset. Section 5.9 broadens the discussion to generalized linear models (GLMs), a flexible framework that extends linear regression and logistic regression to handle a wide range of response distributions. Finally, Section 5.10 concludes with a summary.

5.1   Classification Problems

In classification problems, we are given a set of n labeled samples: $D = \{(\mathbf{x}_1, y_1), \ldots,$ $(\mathbf{x}_n, y_n)\}$, where $\mathbf{x}_i = (x_{i1}, x_{i2}, \ldots, x_{id})^T$ is the feature vector of the i-th sample, and $y_i \in 1, \ldots, k$ is its class label. The goal is to learn a function that maps input vectors to their corresponding classes.

Classification problems can be categorized based on the number and structure of the class labels:

1. **Binary classification**: Each input belongs to one of two classes ($k = 2$), such as spam ($y = 1$) or not spam ($y = 0$). The less frequent or more informative class (e.g., spam) is typically designated as the **positive** class and the other as the **negative** class.

2. **Multi-class classification**: In this setting, there are more than two possible classes ($k > 2$), and each input is assigned to exactly one of them. For example, in digit recognition, each image is classified into one of ten classes, corresponding to the digits 0, 1, ..., 9.

3. **Multi-label classification**: Each input may be associated with multiple classes simultaneously. For example, a news article may be tagged as belonging to both the "Finance" and "Technology" categories.

4. **Multi-output classification**: Each input has multiple outputs, each corresponding to a distinct classification task. For example, an object in an image might be classified by both its shape (e.g., circle, square) and its color (e.g., red, blue).

Some algorithms, such as logistic regression and support vector machines (SVMs), were originally designed for binary classification. However, there are general techniques that can extend any binary classifier to multi-class and multi-label settings (see Section 5.7).

5.2   The Logistic Regression Model

Logistic regression is a binary classification model that estimates the probability that a given input belongs to the positive class, based on one or more predictor variables [137, 277]. Recall that in linear regression, the output is modeled as a linear function of the input: $y = \mathbf{w}^T \mathbf{x}$, which produces continuous values in $(-\infty, \infty)$. However, classification tasks require predicting discrete labels or probabilities that lie within $[0, 1]$. To achieve this, we apply a nonlinear transformation f to the linear predictor, producing a valid probability:

$$p = f(\mathbf{w}^T \mathbf{x}). \tag{5.1}$$

This approach defines a broad family of models known as **generalized linear models (GLMs)** (see Section 5.9), of which logistic regression is a special case. Before introducing the specific form of f used in logistic regression, we first define the concepts of odds and log-odds.

The **odds** (or **odds ratio**) of an event expresses the likelihood that the event occurs relative to it not occurring. If p denotes the probability that an event occurs, then the odds of that event are defined as the ratio of p to $1 - p$:

$$\text{odds}(p) = \frac{p}{1 - p}. \tag{5.2}$$

For example, if the probability of rain tomorrow is 0.75, the odds of rain are $\frac{0.75}{1-0.75} = 3$, meaning rain is three times more likely than no rain.

In binary classification, the odds represent the ratio between the probability that a sample belongs to the positive class and the probability that it belongs to the negative class. Unlike probabilities, which range between 0 and 1, odds can take values from 0 to ∞, providing a more sensitive measure of likelihood, especially when probabilities approach 0 or 1.

The **log-odds**, or **logit**, is the natural logarithm of the odds:

$$\text{logit}(p) = \log\left(\frac{p}{1 - p}\right). \tag{5.3}$$

The logit function, shown in Figure 5.1, transforms probabilities from the interval $[0, 1]$ to the entire real line $(-\infty, +\infty)$.

Logistic regression assumes that the log-odds of the positive class is a linear combination of the input features. This formulation allows us to model classification using the familiar linear form, applied to the log-odds rather than directly to the output probability:

$$z = \text{logit}(p) = w_0 + w_1 x_1 + \cdots + w_d x_d = \mathbf{w}^T \mathbf{x}. \tag{5.4}$$

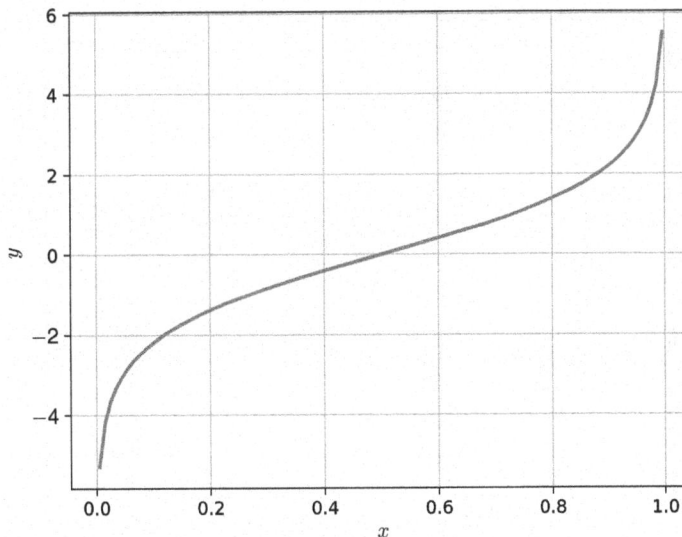

Figure 5.1: The logit function maps probabilities in [0, 1] to the real line, transforming low probabilities into large negative values and high probabilities into large positive values.

Here, $\mathbf{x} = (1, x_1, \ldots, x_d)^T$ is the input vector including the bias term, $\mathbf{w} = (w_0, \ldots, w_d)^T$ is the weight vector, and $p = P(y = 1|\mathbf{x})$ is the predicted probability of the positive class.

To convert the linear prediction z into a probability, we apply the **sigmoid function** (or the **logistic function**), denoted by $\sigma(z)$, which is the inverse of the logit:

$$p = \sigma(z) = \frac{1}{1 + e^{-z}} = \frac{1}{1 + e^{-\mathbf{w}^T\mathbf{x}}}. \tag{5.5}$$

To see that the sigmoid function is the inverse of the logit, we start from the logit equation and solve for p:

$$\log\left(\frac{p}{1-p}\right) = z$$

$$\frac{p}{1-p} = e^z$$

$$p = (1-p)e^z$$

$$p + pe^z = e^z$$

$$p(1 + e^z) = e^z$$

$$p = \frac{e^z}{1 + e^z} = \frac{1}{1 + e^{-z}} = \sigma(z).$$

The sigmoid function maps real numbers to the interval $[0, 1]$, ensuring that the model's output is a valid probability. It has a characteristic "S"-shaped curve (see Figure 5.2).

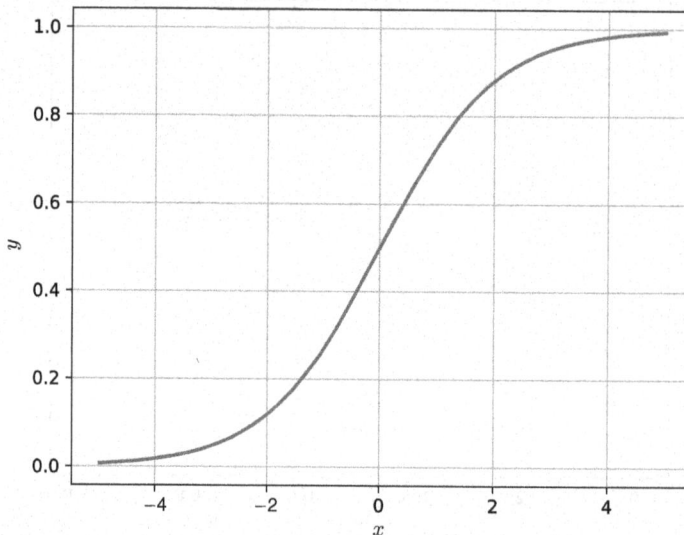

Figure 5.2: The sigmoid function: An "S"-shaped curve that maps real-valued inputs to probabilities in $[0, 1]$. It is used in logistic regression to convert log-odds into probabilities.

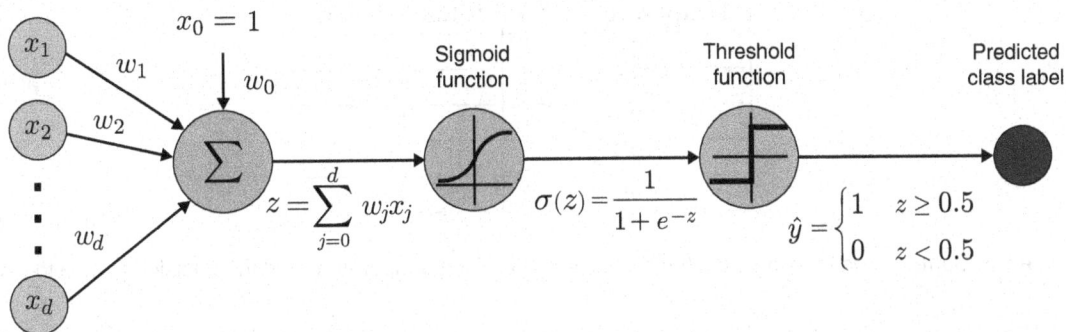

Figure 5.3: The computational process of the logistic regression model. Input features $x_1, x_2, \ldots, x_d$ are combined in a weighted sum, followed by the application of the sigmoid function to produce a probability. A threshold is then applied to assign the input into one of the two classes.

The sigmoid function also satisfies the following useful properties, which simplify the derivation of the gradient during model training (see Exercise 5.13):

$$\sigma(-z) = 1 - \sigma(z), \tag{5.6}$$

$$\sigma'(z) = \sigma(z)(1 - \sigma(z)). \tag{5.7}$$

In summary, given an input vector $\mathbf{x}$, the logistic regression model computes the probability that the target label is 1 using:

$$p = P(y = 1|\mathbf{x}) = \frac{1}{1 + e^{-\mathbf{w}^T \mathbf{x}}}. \tag{5.8}$$

If the predicted probability p exceeds a certain threshold (commonly set at 0.5), the model classifies the sample as belonging to class 1; otherwise, it is classified as class 0. The computational process of logistic regression, from the input features to the final classification, is depicted in Figure 5.3.

5.2.1 Numerical Example

Suppose we are studying the likelihood of individuals choosing to bike to work based on the temperature on a given day. The predictor variable x is the temperature in degrees Celsius, and the binary outcome variable y equals 1 if the individual bikes to work and 0 otherwise. We have collected five data samples, as shown in Table 5.1.

We can use logistic regression to predict the probability that someone will bike to work based on the temperature. The logistic regression model is given by:

$$P(y = 1|x) = \frac{1}{1 + e^{-(w_0 + w_1 x)}},$$

where w_0 is the intercept and w_1 is the coefficient for temperature.

Temperature (°C)	Bikes to work
10	0
15	0
20	1
25	1
30	1

Table 5.1: Sample data for examining the relationship between temperature and the decision to bike to work

Let's assume that through some estimation process (described in Section 5.3), we obtain the parameter values $w_0 = -12.94$ and $w_1 = 0.74$. The resulting model becomes:

$$P(y = 1|x) = \frac{1}{1 + e^{-(-12.94 + 0.74x)}}.$$

Using this model, we can compute the predicted probability of biking to work at various temperatures:

$$P(y = 1|x = 10) = \frac{1}{1 + e^{-(-12.94 + 0.74 \cdot 10)}} = 0.0039,$$

$$P(y = 1|x = 20) = \frac{1}{1 + e^{-(-12.94 + 0.74 \cdot 20)}} = 0.8640,$$

$$P(y = 1|x = 25) = \frac{1}{1 + e^{-(-12.94 + 0.74 \cdot 25)}} = 0.9961.$$

At 10°C, there is only a 0.39% chance of biking to work. At 20°C, the probability increases sharply to 86.4%, and by 25°C, it rises to nearly 100%.

Figure 5.4 shows the logistic regression curve based on this model. The sigmoid shape reflects the smooth transition from low to high probability as temperature increases. The horizontal dashed line at $y = 0.5$ represents the classification threshold used to distinguish between the two outcomes.

5.2.2 Decision Boundaries

In classification problems, **decision boundaries** refer to the set of points in the feature space where a model assigns equal probability (or score) to two or more classes. Understanding these boundaries can provide insight into the model's ability to distinguish between classes and helps identify regions of uncertainty, where the model's confidence is low.

In logistic regression, the decision boundary between the two classes is defined by the set of points where $p = 0.5$, which corresponds to a log-odds value of zero: $\mathbf{w}^T\mathbf{x} = 0$. This equation describes a hyperplane in the feature space that is orthogonal to the weight vector $\mathbf{w}$ (see Figure 5.5). Points on one side of this hyperplane ($\mathbf{w}^T\mathbf{x} > 0$) are classified as positive, while those on the other side ($\mathbf{w}^T\mathbf{x} < 0$) are classified as negative.

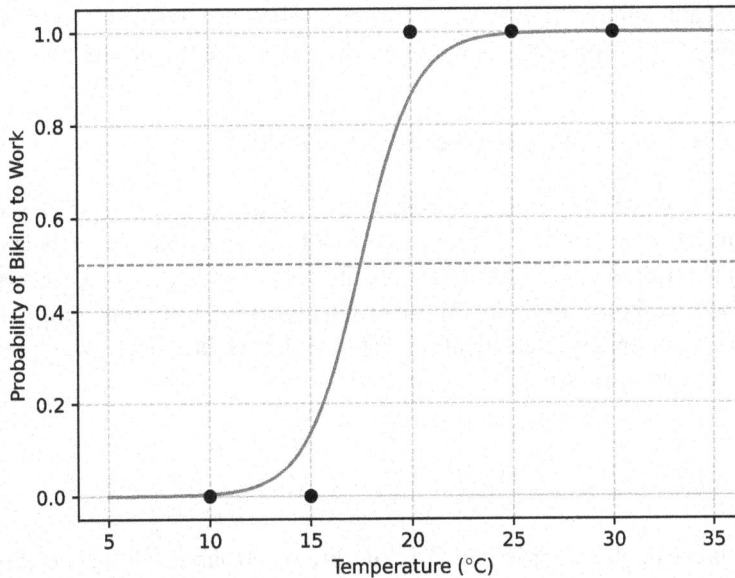

Figure 5.4: The sigmoidal curve of the logistic regression model predicting the probability of biking to work as a function of temperature. The curve transitions smoothly from low to high probability, with the decision boundary indicated by the horizontal line at $y = 0.5$.

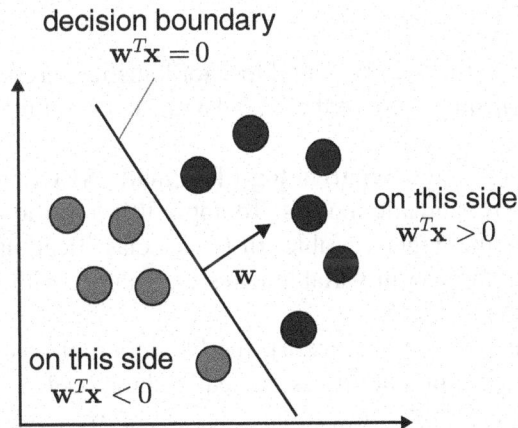

Figure 5.5: The decision boundary in logistic regression is defined by the hyperplane $\mathbf{w}^T\mathbf{x} = 0$, which separates the feature space into two regions. Points for which $\mathbf{w}^T\mathbf{x} > 0$ are classified as positive (red), while those for which $\mathbf{w}^T\mathbf{x} < 0$ are classified as negative (blue). The weight vector $\mathbf{w}$ is orthogonal to the decision boundary.

The linearity of this boundary makes logistic regression a **linear classifier**, meaning it separates the classes using a linear decision surface. Linear models are known for their simplicity and interpretability, making them a popular choice in many practical applications.

5.3   Training a Logistic Regression Model

When training logistic regression models, the objective is to find a parameter vector $\mathbf{w}$ that makes the predicted probabilities $p = \sigma(\mathbf{w}^T\mathbf{x})$ as close as possible to the actual class labels y. To achieve this, we define a suitable loss function that measures the discrepancy between the model's predictions and the true labels, and then apply an optimization algorithm to minimize this function.

A natural candidate for binary classification is the **0–1 loss function**, which simply checks whether a prediction is correct or not:

$$L_{0-1}(y, \hat{y}) = \begin{cases} 1 & \hat{y} \neq y, \\ 0 & \hat{y} = y, \end{cases} \tag{5.9}$$

where y is the true label of the sample and $\hat{y}$ is the predicted label. However, this function is non-differentiable and it ignores the model's predicted probabilities, making it unsuitable for optimizing logistic regression models.

Another common loss function—the squared loss, which we used in linear regression—is also inappropriate for logistic regression, for several reasons: it assumes a continuous target and normally distributed errors; it leads to a non-convex objective when combined with the sigmoid function; and it lacks a meaningful probabilistic interpretation for classification.

5.3.1   Log Loss

Given the limitations of the 0–1 loss and squared loss for logistic regression, we need a loss function that reflects the probabilistic nature of the model and can be optimized using gradient-based methods.

As discussed in Section 2.5, the **negative log-likelihood (NLL)** provides a principled way to define loss functions in probabilistic models. To apply it in logistic regression, we first need to specify a distribution for the target variable. In binary classification, a natural choice is the Bernoulli distribution, where a random variable takes the value 1 with probability p and 0 with probability $1 - p$ (see Section C.5.6.1).

Under this model, for a given sample $(\mathbf{x}, y)$, the likelihood of observing a positive label is $P(y = 1|\mathbf{x}) = p$, where p is the probability estimated by the model. Similarly, the likelihood of observing a negative sample is $P(y = 0|\mathbf{x}) = 1 - p$. These two cases can be combined into a single expression:

$$P(y|\mathbf{x}) = p^y(1 - p)^{1-y}. \tag{5.10}$$

This formula compactly represents both possibilities: when $y = 1$, it simplifies to $P(y|\mathbf{x}) = p$; and when $y = 0$, it yields $P(y|\mathbf{x}) = 1 - p$.

Thus, the log-likelihood of observing the true label under the model is:

$$\log P(y|\mathbf{x}) = y \log p + (1 - y) \log(1 - p). \tag{5.11}$$

Negating this log-likelihood gives us the **log loss**, also known as the **logistic loss** or **binary cross-entropy loss**, defined as:

$$L_{\log}(y, p) = -y \log p - (1 - y) \log(1 - p). \tag{5.12}$$

Figure 5.6 shows the log loss as a function of p when $y = 1$. For $y = 0$, the curve is mirrored, exhibiting the same behavior from the perspective of the opposite class. As shown, the log loss reaches its minimum value of 0 for perfect predictions ($p = y$) and approaches infinity as the model becomes increasingly confident in the wrong class (i.e., $p \to 0$ when $y = 1$, and vice versa).

To evaluate the model's performance on the entire training set, we define a cost function that averages the log loss across all the training samples:

$$J(\mathbf{w}) = -\frac{1}{n} \sum_{i=1}^{n} [y_i \log p_i + (1 - y_i) \log(1 - p_i)]. \tag{5.13}$$

For computational efficiency, this function can be written in vectorized form as:

$$J(\mathbf{w}) = -\frac{1}{n} \left(\mathbf{y}^T \log \mathbf{p} + (1 - \mathbf{y}^T) \log(1 - \mathbf{p}) \right). \tag{5.14}$$

Here, $\mathbf{y} = (y_1, \ldots, y_n)$ and $\mathbf{p} = (p_1, \ldots, p_n)$ are vectors of the true labels and the predicted probabilities for all training samples, respectively, and $\mathbf{1}$ is a vector of ones of size n. The $\log(\mathbf{x})$ operation is applied element-wise on the vector $\mathbf{x}$.

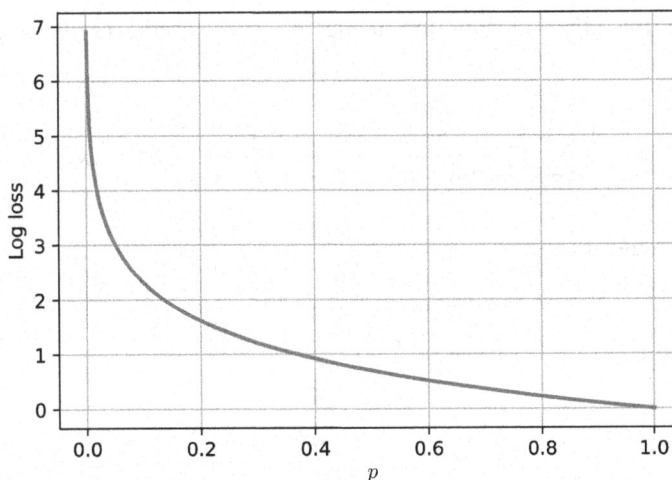

Figure 5.6: The log loss as a function of the predicted probability p for when the true label is $y = 1$. The loss increases sharply as p approaches 0, penalizing incorrect predictions more heavily when the model is confident in them.

This cost function is convex, meaning that any local minimum is also a global minimum. However, due to the nonlinearities introduced by the sigmoid and logarithm functions, there is no closed-form solution for the optimal parameters $\mathbf{w}^*$. As a result, we must use iterative optimization techniques, such as gradient descent or Newton's method, to minimize the cost. These methods are explored in the following subsections.

5.3.2 Gradient Descent

To minimize the cost function $J(\mathbf{w})$ using gradient descent, we compute its partial derivatives with respect to each weight w_j as follows:

1. Start with the definitions of the cost function and the predicted probabilities $p_i = \sigma(\mathbf{w}^T x_i)$:

$$\frac{\partial}{\partial w_j} J(\mathbf{w}) = \frac{\partial}{\partial w_j} \left[-\frac{1}{n} \sum_{i=1}^{n} \left[y_i \log(\sigma(\mathbf{w}^T \mathbf{x}_i)) + (1 - y_i) \log(1 - \sigma(\mathbf{w}^T \mathbf{x}_i)) \right] \right]$$

2. Move the derivative inside the summation:

$$\frac{\partial}{\partial w_j} J(\mathbf{w}) = -\frac{1}{n} \sum_{i=1}^{n} \left[y_i \frac{\partial}{\partial w_j} \log(\sigma(\mathbf{w}^T \mathbf{x}_i)) + (1 - y_i) \frac{\partial}{\partial w_j} \log(1 - \sigma(\mathbf{w}^T \mathbf{x}_i)) \right]$$

3. Apply the chain rule to differentiate the logarithmic terms:

$$\frac{\partial}{\partial w_j} J(\mathbf{w}) = -\frac{1}{n} \sum_{i=1}^{n} \left[\left(\frac{y_i}{\sigma(\mathbf{w}^T \mathbf{x}_i)} - \frac{1 - y_i}{1 - \sigma(\mathbf{w}^T \mathbf{x}_i)} \right) \frac{\partial}{\partial w_j} \sigma(\mathbf{w}^T \mathbf{x}_i) \right]$$

4. Differentiate the sigmoid function using $\sigma'(z) = \sigma(z)(1 - \sigma(z))$, and note that $\frac{\partial}{\partial w_j} \mathbf{w}^T x_i = x_{ij}$:

$$\frac{\partial}{\partial w_j} J(\mathbf{w}) = -\frac{1}{n} \sum_{i=1}^{n} \left[\left(\frac{y_i}{\sigma(\mathbf{w}^T \mathbf{x}_i)} - \frac{1 - y_i}{1 - \sigma(\mathbf{w}^T \mathbf{x}_i)} \right) \sigma(\mathbf{w}^T \mathbf{x}_i) \left(1 - \sigma(\mathbf{w}^T \mathbf{x}_i) \right) x_{ij} \right]$$

5. Simplify the expression:

$$\frac{\partial}{\partial w_j} J(\mathbf{w}) = -\frac{1}{n} \sum_{i=1}^{n} \left[\left(y_i \left(1 - \sigma(\mathbf{w}^T \mathbf{x}_i) \right) - (1 - y_i) \sigma(\mathbf{w}^T \mathbf{x}_i) \right) x_{ij} \right]$$

$$= -\frac{1}{n} \sum_{i=1}^{n} \left[\left(y_i - \sigma(\mathbf{w}^T \mathbf{x}_i) \right) x_{ij} \right]$$

$$= \frac{1}{n} \sum_{i=1}^{n} \left[(p_i - y_i) x_{ij} \right]. \tag{5.15}$$

That is, the partial derivative of the cost function with respect to w_j is the average over the training samples of the product of the prediction error $(p_i - y_i)$ and the corresponding feature value x_{ij}.

For computational efficiency, the full gradient of the cost function can be written in vectorized form as follows:

$$\nabla_{\mathbf{w}} J(\mathbf{w}) = \frac{1}{n} X^T (\mathbf{p} - \mathbf{y}), \tag{5.16}$$

where X^T is the transpose of the feature matrix X, $\mathbf{p}$ contains the model's predicted probabilities for all samples, and $\mathbf{y}$ contains the corresponding true labels. The difference $\mathbf{p} - \mathbf{y}$ represents the prediction errors for all the training examples.

In batch gradient descent, the weights are updated iteratively according to the following update rule:

$$\mathbf{w} \leftarrow \mathbf{w} - \alpha \frac{1}{n} X^T (\mathbf{p} - \mathbf{y}), \tag{5.17}$$

where α is a learning rate that controls the step size of each update.

In stochastic gradient descent (SGD), the weights are updated after each individual training sample. The update rule for SGD is:

$$\mathbf{w} \leftarrow \mathbf{w} - \alpha(p - y)\mathbf{x}, \tag{5.18}$$

where p is the predicted probability, y is the true label, and $\mathbf{x}$ is the feature vector of the current sample.

5.3.3 Implementation in Python

In this section, we implement the logistic regression model in Python from scratch. This includes computing the cost function and its gradient, optimizing the model using gradient descent, evaluating the model's performance, and visualizing the resulting decision boundaries.[1]

For this demonstration, we use the Iris dataset introduced in Section 3.5. We simplify the original three-class problem by considering only setosa and versicolor flowers, reducing it to a binary classification task. In addition, we use only the first two features: sepal width and sepal length, to allow for easier visualization of the decision boundary in a two-dimensional space.

We start by importing the required libraries and fixing the random seed for reproducibility:

```
import numpy as np
import matplotlib.pyplot as plt
import seaborn as sns

np.random.seed(42)
```

---

1. Implementing machine learning algorithms from scratch is a highly valuable exercise that can deepen your understanding of how they work and may spark ideas for algorithmic improvements or even entirely new methods. Throughout this book, you will find several opportunities to do so.

5.3.3.1   Data Loading and Visualization

We proceed by loading the Iris dataset, selecting only the first two features (sepal length and sepal width), and filtering the samples to include only setosa and versicolor flowers (class 0 and class 1):

```
from sklearn.datasets import load_iris

iris = load_iris()
X = iris.data[:, :2] # Use only the first two features
y = iris.target
class_labels = iris.target_names

# Filter for setosa and versicolor flowers
X = X[(y == 0) | (y == 1)]
y = y[(y == 0) | (y == 1)]
```

To gain an initial understanding of the data distribution, we visualize the dataset using the following function:

```
def plot_data(X, y):
    sns.scatterplot(x=X[:, 0], y=X[:, 1],
                    hue=class_labels[y], style=class_labels[y],
                    palette=['r','b'], markers=('s','o'), edgecolor='k')
    plt.xlabel(iris.feature_names[0])
    plt.ylabel(iris.feature_names[1])
    plt.legend()

plot_data(X, y)
```

The function sns.scatterplot[2] from Seaborn creates a scatter plot of the samples, with color and marker style determined by their class label. (Reproducing the same styling in Matplotlib would require significantly more code.) As illustrated in Figure 5.7, the two classes are linearly separable, making this dataset well-suited for a linear classification model such as logistic regression.

5.3.3.2   Data Preparation

Although both features are numeric, they have different ranges: sepal length ranges from 4.3 to 7.0, while sepal width ranges from 2.0 to 4.4. Although the feature ranges are relatively similar, standardizing them can still improve the convergence of gradient descent.

Additionally, we need to add a bias term to the model by appending a column of ones to the feature matrix X. This step should be performed after feature scaling, as the bias term must remain a column of ones (standardizing it would incorrectly convert it into a column of zeros).

---

2. https://seaborn.pydata.org/generated/seaborn.scatterplot.html

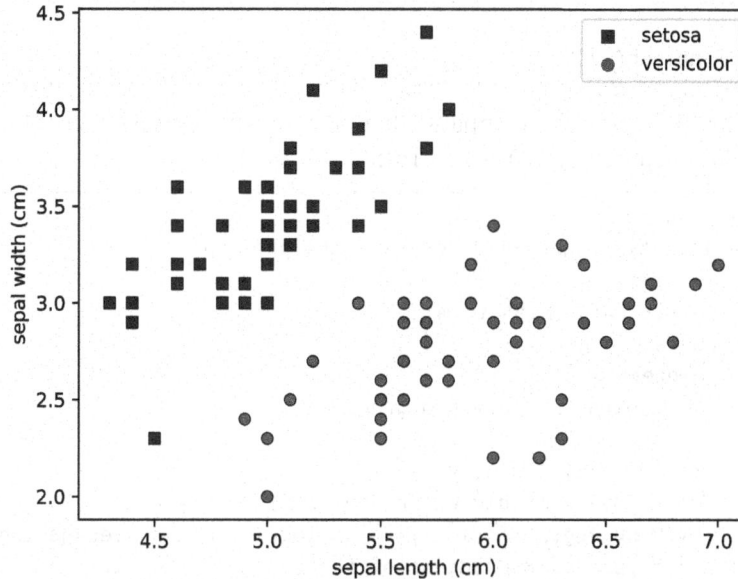

Figure 5.7: Scatter plot of the Iris dataset showing sepal width and sepal length for two species: setosa (squares) and versicolor (circles). Since the data is linearly separable, it is well-suited for linear classifiers such as logistic regression.

The complete data preparation process is shown below:

```
from sklearn.model_selection import train_test_split
from sklearn.preprocessing import StandardScaler

# Split the dataset into training and test sets
X_train, X_test, y_train, y_test = train_test_split(X, y, random_state=42)

# Standardize the features
scaler = StandardScaler()
X_train_scaled = scaler.fit_transform(X_train)
X_test_scaled = scaler.transform(X_test)

# Add a column of ones for the bias term
n_train = X_train_scaled.shape[0]
n_test = X_test_scaled.shape[0]
X_train_b = np.hstack((np.ones((n_train, 1)), X_train_scaled))
X_test_b = np.hstack((np.ones((n_test, 1)), X_test_scaled))
```

5.3.3.3   Model Implementation

We are now ready to implement the logistic regression model. First, we define a utility function for computing the sigmoid function:

```python
def sigmoid(z):
    return 1 / (1 + np.exp(-z))
```

Next, we introduce a function for computing both the logistic regression cost function and its gradient, as defined in Equations (5.14) and (5.16):

```python
def cost_function(X, y, w):
    """Compute the logistic regression cost and its gradient.
    Args:
        X: Feature matrix (with bias term)
        y: Target labels
        w: Model parameters
    Returns: Tuple containing the cost and gradient
    """
    n = len(y) # Number of training samples
    p = sigmoid(np.dot(X, w)) # Predicted probabilities for y = 1
    cost = -(1/n) * (y @ np.log(p) + (1 - y) @ np.log(1 - p)) # Average log loss
    grad = (1/n) * X.T @ (p - y) # Gradient of the cost

    return cost, grad
```

We now implement batch gradient descent to optimize the model parameters (see Algorithm E.1):

```python
def optimize_model(X, y, alpha=0.1, max_iter=1000, tol=0.0001):
    """Optimize the model parameters using batch gradient descent.
    Args:
        X: Feature matrix (with bias term)
        y: Target labels
        alpha: Learning rate
        max_iter: Maximum number of iterations
        tol: Tolerance for the stopping criterion
    Returns:
        w: The optimized parameters
        cost_history: List of cost values at each iteration
    """
    w = np.random.rand(X.shape[1]) # Random parameter initialization
    cost_history = [] # Track cost at each iteration

    for i in range(max_iter):
        cost, grad = cost_function(X, y, w) # Compute cost and gradient
        w = w - alpha * grad # Update parameters
        cost_history.append(cost)

        # Check for convergence
        if i > 0 and (cost_history[-2] - cost) < tol:
            print(f'Convergence reached after {i} iterations.')
            return w, cost_history
```

```
print('Reached maximum iterations without convergence.')
return w, cost_history
```

This function initializes the model's parameters randomly and iteratively updates them in the direction of the negative gradient. This process continues until either the maximum number of iterations is reached or the cost improvement falls below the specified tolerance. The function returns both the optimized parameters and the history of the cost values, which can be used later to analyze the learning process.

We now apply this function to find the optimal parameters for our logistic regression model:

```
w_opt, cost_history = optimize_model(X_train_b, y_train)
print('Optimized weights:', w_opt)
```

The output is:

```
Convergence reached after 395 iterations.
Optimized weights: [ 0.42026863  2.88499483 -2.2992438 ]
```

We now plot the learning curve using the cost history:

```
plt.plot(cost_history)
plt.xlabel('Iteration')
plt.ylabel('Cost')
```

The learning curve shown in Figure 5.8 demonstrates a rapid decrease in cost during the early iterations, followed by a gradual leveling off as the model converges to the optimal parameter values.

5.3.3.4   Making Predictions

Now that we have optimized the model's parameters, we can use them to make predictions on new data. Since the model was trained on standardized features, any new input must be scaled using the same transformation applied during training. Additionally, we need to add a bias term (a column of ones) to the scaled feature matrix before computing the predicted probabilities.

The following function computes the probability that a given sample (or group of samples) belongs to the positive class, after scaling the input features and adding the bias term:

```
def predict_prob(X_new, w_opt, scaler):
    """Compute the probability of the positive class for samples in X_new."""
    X_new_scaled = scaler.transform(X_new)
    X_new_b = np.hstack((np.ones((X_new_scaled.shape[0], 1)), X_new_scaled))
    p = sigmoid(X_new_b @ w_opt)
    return p
```

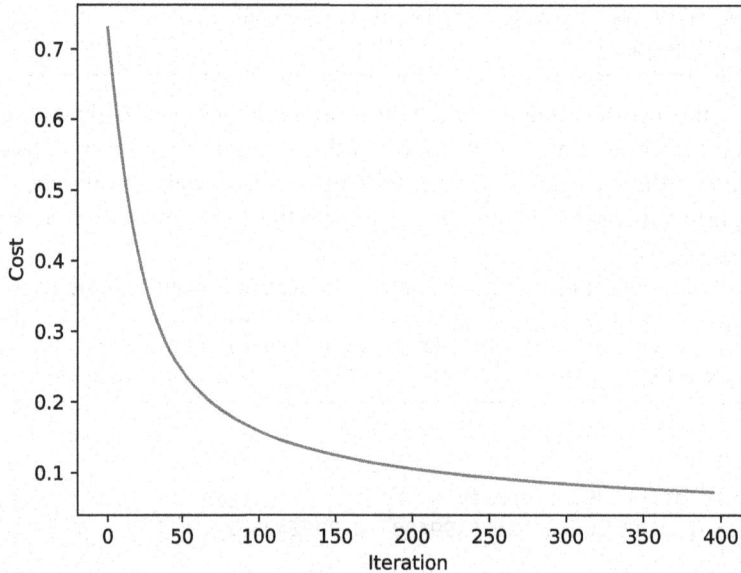

Figure 5.8: Learning curve of logistic regression on the simplified Iris dataset. The cost steadily decreases throughout the iterations, with a sharper drop at the beginning, and gradually levels off as the model approaches convergence.

For example, we can use this function to estimate the probability that a new flower with sepal length of 6 cm and sepal width of 2 cm is a versicolor (the positive class):

```
prob = predict_prob([[6, 2]], w_opt, scaler)
print(prob)
```

```
[0.9996311]
```

The output indicates a 99.96% chance that the flower is versicolor, demonstrating the model's strong confidence in this prediction, as the sample is located well within the versicolor region. Conversely, for a sample with sepal length of 5.5 cm and sepal width of 3.1 cm, which lies closer to the decision boundary, we have:

```
prob = predict_prob([[5.5, 3.1]], w_opt, scaler)
print(prob)
```

```
[0.59593864]
```

This produces a lower probability (59.59%), reflecting the model's greater uncertainty near the decision boundary.

To classify samples based on these probabilities, we apply a threshold (by default 0.5) to determine the class assignment. The following function implements this thresholding:

```
def predict(X_new, w_opt, scaler, threshold=0.5):
    """Classify samples as 0 or 1 using a probability threshold."""
    p = predict_prob(X_new, w_opt, scaler)
    y_pred = (p >= threshold).astype(int)
    return y_pred
```

Applying this function to our earlier examples:

```
y_pred = predict([[6, 2], [5.5, 3]], w_opt, scaler)
y_pred
```

The output is:

```
array([1, 1])
```

This result indicates that both samples are classified as versicolor.

5.3.3.5 Model Evaluation

We now evaluate the performance of our trained model. A key evaluation metric for classification tasks is **accuracy**, which measures the proportion of correctly predicted instances:

$$\text{accuracy} = \frac{1}{n} \sum_{i=1}^{n} \mathbb{1}(y_i = \hat{y}_i), \tag{5.19}$$

where $\mathbb{1}$ is the indicator function that returns 1 if the condition inside is true and 0 otherwise. A related metric is the **error rate**, which represents the proportion of misclassified instances. It is simply the complement of accuracy:

$$\text{error rate} = 1 - \text{accuracy}. \tag{5.20}$$

The following function computes the model's accuracy on a given dataset:

```
def evaluate_model(X, y, w_opt, scaler):
    """Calculate the model's accuracy on the given dataset."""
    y_pred = predict(X, w_opt, scaler) # Predict class labels
    accuracy = np.mean(y == y_pred) # Proportion of correct predictions
    return accuracy
```

Using this function, we now assess the model's accuracy on the training and test sets:

```
train_accuracy = evaluate_model(X_train, y_train, w_opt, scaler)
print(f'Train accuracy: {train_accuracy:.4f}')
```

```
test_accuracy = evaluate_model(X_test, y_test, w_opt, scaler)
print(f'Test accuracy: {test_accuracy:.4f}')
```

The output is:

```
Train accuracy: 1.0000
Test accuracy: 1.0000
```

These scores indicate that the model perfectly separates the two classes on both the training and test sets.

5.3.3.6   Plotting the Decision Boundary

Since our dataset is two-dimensional, we can visualize the decision boundary that separates the two classes. This boundary corresponds to the region where the model assigns equal probabilities to both classes, i.e., where $\sigma(\mathbf{w}^T\mathbf{x}) = 0.5$, which implies $\mathbf{w}^T\mathbf{x} = 0$. For a two-dimensional feature space, this is a line defined by:

$$w_0 + w_1 x_1 + w_2 x_2 = 0.$$

Rearranging this equation gives an explicit form for plotting:

$$x_2 = -\frac{w_1}{w_2}x_1 - \frac{w_0}{w_2},$$

where $-\frac{w_1}{w_2}$ is the slope and $-\frac{w_0}{w_2}$ is the y-intercept. The following function plots this decision boundary:

```
def plot_decision_boundary(X, y, w_opt):
    """Plot the decision boundary between the classes."""
    # Extract the min and max values of the first feature (x1)
    x1_min, x1_max = X[:, 0].min(), X[:, 0].max()

    # Create a range of values for x1
    line_x = np.array([x1_min, x1_max])

    # Compute the corresponding y values (x2) using the decision boundary equation
    line_y = -1 / w_opt[2] * (w_opt[1] * line_x + w_opt[0])

    # Plot the decision boundary as a dashed line
    plt.plot(line_x, line_y, c='k', ls='--')
```

We can now plot the decision boundary over the scaled feature space:

```
X_scaled = scaler.transform(X)
plot_data(X_scaled, y)
plot_decision_boundary(X_scaled, y, w_opt)
```

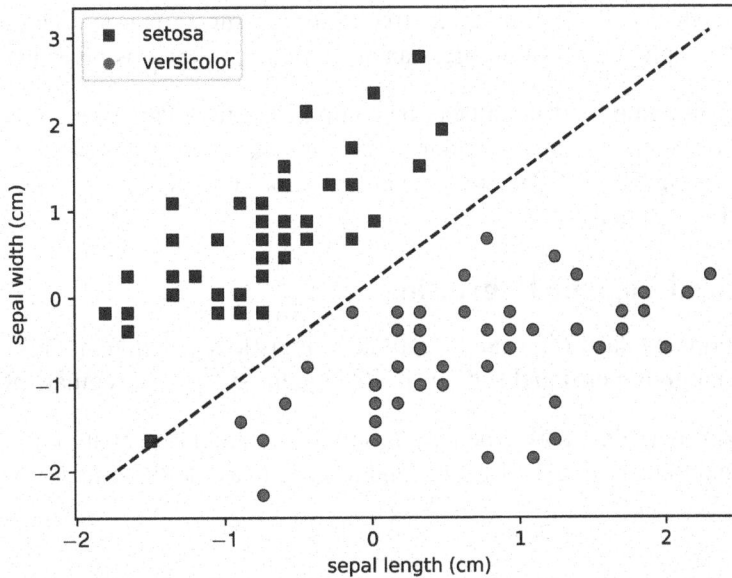

Figure 5.9: The decision boundary (dashed line) produced by the logistic regression model, perfectly separating the two flower species: setosa (squares) and versicolor (circles), based on sepal length and sepal width. The boundary represents the threshold where the model assigns equal probabilities to both classes.

Figure 5.9 illustrates the decision boundary. As shown, the logistic regression model perfectly separates the two classes.

5.3.4 Newton's Method

An alternative and often more efficient optimization technique for logistic regression is **Newton's method**. Unlike gradient descent, which uses only first-order information (the gradient), Newton's method also incorporates second-order information via the Hessian matrix. This enables it to adjust both the search direction and the step size at each iteration based on the local curvature of the cost function. As a result, Newton's method often converges much faster—with a quadratic convergence rate, compared to the linear rate of gradient descent—particularly near the minimum. For a detailed discussion of Newton's method, see Section E.5.1.

When applied to logistic regression, Newton's method updates the weight vector using the following rule:

$$\mathbf{w} \leftarrow \mathbf{w} - H^{-1}(\mathbf{w}) \nabla_{\mathbf{w}} J(\mathbf{w}), \tag{5.21}$$

where:

- $\nabla_{\mathbf{w}} J(\mathbf{w})$ is the gradient of the cost function at $\mathbf{w}$, as given in Equation 5.16.

- $H^{-1}(\mathbf{w})$ is the inverse of the Hessian matrix of the cost function at $\mathbf{w}$. In Exercise 5.15, you will derive the explicit form of the Hessian and examine when it is invertible.

Computing and inverting the Hessian can be computationally expensive, especially for large datasets or high-dimensional models. To address this, **quasi-Newton methods** such as L-BFGS and Newton-CG (see Section E.5.2), offer scalable alternatives by approximating the Hessian rather than computing it directly.

5.3.5 Regularized Logistic Regression

As in linear regression, regularization can be applied to logistic regression models to reduce overfitting, especially in high-dimensional settings [516]. Common types of regularization include:

- **L2 regularization (ridge)** adds a penalty equal to the sum of the squared weights to the cost function, discouraging large coefficients and leading to a smoother decision boundary. The cost function becomes:

$$J(\mathbf{w}) = \left[-\sum_{i=1}^{n} y_i \log \sigma(\mathbf{w}^T \mathbf{x}_i) + (1 - y_i) \log(1 - \sigma(\mathbf{w}^T \mathbf{x}_i)) \right] + \lambda \|\mathbf{w}\|_2^2, \qquad (5.22)$$

  where λ is the regularization coefficient controlling the strength of the penalty.

- **L1 regularization (lasso)** adds a penalty equal to the sum of absolute values of the weights to the cost function, encouraging sparsity by driving some coefficients exactly to zero. This allows the model to automatically select a relevant subset of features for the classification task. The cost function becomes:

$$J(\mathbf{w}) = \left[-\sum_{i=1}^{n} y_i \log \sigma(\mathbf{w}^T \mathbf{x}_i) + (1 - y_i) \log(1 - \sigma(\mathbf{w}^T \mathbf{x}_i)) \right] + \lambda \|\mathbf{w}\|_1. \qquad (5.23)$$

- **Elastic net regularization** combines the L1 and L2 penalties, balancing sparsity and coefficient shrinkage. This is especially useful when there is multicollinearity or when both regularization and feature selection are desired:

$$J(\mathbf{w}) = \left[-\sum_{i=1}^{n} y_i \log \sigma(\mathbf{w}^T \mathbf{x}_i) + (1 - y_i) \log(1 - \sigma(\mathbf{w}^T \mathbf{x}_i)) \right] + \lambda_1 \|\mathbf{w}\|_1 + \lambda_2 \|\mathbf{w}\|_2^2,$$

$$(5.24)$$

  where λ_1 and λ_2 control the relative weights of the two penalties.

Optimization techniques such as gradient descent and quasi-Newton methods can also be applied to minimize these regularized cost functions.

5.4 Logistic Regression in Scikit-Learn

Scikit-Learn provides the following classes for training logistic regression models:

- `LogisticRegression`[3] offers a highly optimized implementation that supports several solvers, including L-BFGS, Newton-CG, and SAG (Stochastic Average Gradient). These solvers provide fast and reliable convergence for a wide range of problem sizes.

- `SGDClassifier`[4] fits linear classifiers using stochastic gradient descent (SGD), making it particularly suitable for very large datasets and online learning. While more scalable, it typically converges more slowly than `LogisticRegression` and requires careful tuning of hyperparameters such as the learning rate.

In this section, we explore both classes and demonstrate how to use them on the Iris dataset.

5.4.1 The `LogisticRegression` Class

Scikit-learn provides the `LogisticRegression` class for fitting logistic regression models. This class offers several efficient solvers, including L-BFGS (the default), Newton-CG, and SAG, which are generally more effective than gradient descent for this task. See Appendix E for more details on these algorithms.

Additionally, `LogisticRegression` supports various regularization techniques, including L1, L2, and elastic net, as well as multinomial logistic regression for multi-class problems (see Section 5.8). Table 5.2 summarizes the key parameters of the class.

For example, let's apply the `LogisticRegression` class to the simplified Iris dataset from Section 5.3.2. First, we load the dataset and split it into training and test sets, using the same random seed to allow comparison with our previous results:

```
from sklearn.datasets import load_iris
from sklearn.model_selection import train_test_split

iris = load_iris()
X = iris.data[:, :2] # Use only the first two features
y = iris.target
class_labels = iris.target_names

# Filter for setosa and versicolor flowers
X = X[(y == 0) | (y == 1)]
y = y[(y == 0) | (y == 1)]

X_train, X_test, y_train, y_test = train_test_split(X, y, random_state=42)
```

3. https://scikit-learn.org/stable/modules/generated/sklearn.linear_model.LogisticRegression. html
4. https://scikit-learn.org/stable/modules/generated/sklearn.linear_model.SGDClassifier.html

Parameter	Description	Default
solver	Optimization algorithm to use. Options include: `'lbfgs'`, `'liblinear'`, `'newton-cg'`, `'newton-cholesky'`, `'sag'`, or `'saga'`.	`'lbfgs'`
penalty	Type of regularization to apply. Options are: `'l1'`, `'l2'`, `'elasticnet'`, or `None`.	`'l2'`
C	Inverse of the regularization coefficient $(1/\lambda)$; smaller values specify stronger regularization.	`1.0`
l1_ratio	Elastic net mixing parameter that controls the balance between L1 and L2 penalties. Used only when penalty=`'elasticnet'`.	`None`
max_iter	Maximum number of iterations for the solver to converge.	`100`
tol	Tolerance for the stopping criterion.	`0.0001`
class_weight	Weights associated with classes, given as {class: weight}, useful for handling imbalanced datasets.	`None`

Table 5.2: Key parameters of the `LogisticRegression` class

Note that `LogisticRegression` automatically handles the addition of the bias term to the feature matrix. We now build a pipeline consisting of a `StandardScaler` and a `LogisticRegression` classifier:

```
from sklearn.pipeline import Pipeline
from sklearn.preprocessing import StandardScaler
from sklearn.linear_model import LogisticRegression

model = Pipeline([
    ('scaler', StandardScaler()),
    ('clf', LogisticRegression(random_state=42))
])
model.fit(X_train, y_train)
```

The accuracy of the model on the training and test sets is:

```
train_accuracy = model.score(X_train, y_train)
print(f'Train accuracy: {train_accuracy:.4f}')

test_accuracy = model.score(X_test, y_test)
print(f'Test accuracy: {test_accuracy:.4f}')
```

```
Train accuracy: 1.0000
Test accuracy: 1.0000
```

The model achieves perfect accuracy on both sets. Let's also check how many iterations were required for convergence:

```
print('Number of iterations:', model['clf'].n_iter_[0])
```

```
Number of iterations: 8
```

The L-BFGS solver converged in just 8 iterations, highlighting its efficiency compared to the basic gradient descent implementation from Section 5.3.2, which required about 400 iterations to converge.

5.4.2 The `SGDClassifier` Class

Another way to perform logistic regression in Scikit-Learn is by using the `SGDClassifier` class, which solves classification tasks using stochastic gradient descent (SGD).

This class operates similarly to `SGDRegressor` that solves regression tasks using SGD (see Section 4.8.2.1) and shares many of the same hyperparameters. By default, `SGDClassifier` uses the `'hinge'` loss, which corresponds to a linear SVM. To perform logistic regression, the `loss` parameter must be set to `'log_loss'`, as shown below:

```
from sklearn.linear_model import SGDClassifier

model = Pipeline([
    ('scaler', StandardScaler()),
    ('clf', SGDClassifier(loss='log_loss', random_state=42))
])
model.fit(X_train, y_train)
```

The number of iterations needed for this classifier to converge is:

```
print('Number of iterations:', model['clf'].n_iter_)
```

```
Number of iterations: 12
```

In this case, convergence using SGD took slightly longer than the quasi-Newton method used by `LogisticRegression`.

5.5 Classification Evaluation Metrics

Classification tasks often involve **imbalanced datasets**, where the classes are not equally represented in the data [260, 331]. These datasets are typically dominated by a large number of "normal" (negative) examples with only a small fraction of "interesting" (positive) ones. For example, medical imaging datasets for cancer detection—such as chest X-rays or mammograms—often exhibit severe class imbalance, with most images labeled as normal and only a small fraction (e.g., less than 1%) containing cancerous findings.

Class imbalance is also common in domains such as fraud detection, network intrusion detection, rare disease diagnosis, and natural disaster prediction. In all of these cases, the minority class is typically the one of greatest interest, despite its rarity.

Imbalanced datasets pose two main challenges to classification algorithms:

- **Standard metrics can be misleading.** Accuracy, in particular, often fails to reflect the true model performance in imbalanced settings. For example, in a fraud detection task with only 1% fraudulent transactions, a naive model that always predicts "legitimate" achieves 99% accuracy—giving a false impression of strong performance, even though it fails to detect any fraud. In such cases, identifying the minority class (e.g., fraudulent transactions) is far more important than maximizing overall accuracy. This highlights the need for evaluation metrics that place greater emphasis on minority class performance.

- **Algorithms tend to favor the majority class.** Most classification algorithms are designed to minimize the overall error rate, which inherently biases them toward the majority class. The limited number of minority class examples makes it difficult for the model to learn their patterns, often resulting in poor performance—sometimes with minority class accuracy as low as 0–10%.

In high-stakes domains such as healthcare, this imbalance can have serious consequences. A model that fails to detect rare conditions, despite correctly classifying the majority of healthy cases, may lead to missed diagnoses, delayed treatments, and adverse patient outcomes.

Section 5.6 explores strategies for improving model performance on imbalanced data, including resampling techniques and cost-sensitive learning algorithms.

5.5.1   The Credit Card Fraud Detection Dataset

To illustrate the challenges posed by imbalanced datasets, we will use the Credit Card Fraud Detection[5] dataset hosted on Kaggle. This dataset contains anonymized credit card transactions made by European cardholders over a span of two days in September 2013. It exhibits a severe class imbalance, with only 492 fraudulent transactions among 284,807 in total.

The dataset consists of 30 numerical features, with 28 of them (V1 to V28) derived from applying Principal Component Analysis (PCA) to the original features (used both for anonymization and dimensionality reduction). The remaining features are Time, indicating the elapsed time from the first transaction, and Amount, representing the transaction value. The target variable Class is binary, with 1 indicating fraud and 0 indicating a legitimate transaction.

We begin by loading the dataset from its CSV file and examining the first and last few rows. For clarity, we display only a selected subset of the columns (see Figure 5.10):

```
import pandas as pd

df = pd.read_csv('data/creditcard.csv')
df = df[['Time', 'Amount', 'V1', 'V2', 'V3', 'V4', 'V5', 'Class']]
df
```

---

5. https://www.kaggle.com/datasets/mlg-ulb/creditcardfraud

	Time	Amount	V1	V2	V3	V4	V5	Class
0	0.0	149.62	−1.359807	−0.072781	2.536347	1.378155	−0.338321	0
1	0.0	2.69	1.191857	0.266151	0.166480	0.448154	0.060018	0
2	1.0	378.66	−1.358354	−1.340163	1.773209	0.379780	−0.503198	0
3	1.0	123.50	−0.966272	−0.185226	1.792993	−0.863291	−0.010309	0
4	2.0	69.99	−1.158233	0.877737	1.548718	0.403034	−0.407193	0
...	...	...	...	...	...	...	...	...
284802	172786.0	0.77	−11.881118	10.071785	−9.834783	−2.066656	−5.364473	0
284803	172787.0	24.79	−0.732789	−0.055080	2.035030	−0.738589	0.868229	0
284804	172788.0	67.88	1.919565	−0.301254	−3.249640	−0.557828	2.630515	0
284805	172788.0	10.00	−0.240440	0.530483	0.702510	0.689799	−0.377961	0
284806	172792.0	217.00	−0.533413	−0.189733	0.703337	−0.506271	−0.012546	0

Figure 5.10: A preview of the credit card fraud detection dataset, showing the first and last five rows for selected columns: Time, Amount, PCA-transformed features V1 through V5, and the target label Class.

Let's examine the class distribution:

```
df['Class'].value_counts(normalize=True)
```

```
Class
0    0.998273
1    0.001727
```

As expected, the dataset is highly imbalanced: class 0 (legitimate transactions) makes up 99.82% of the data, while class 1 (fraudulent transactions) constitutes only 0.17%. This imbalance poses a major challenge—models can easily achieve high accuracy by predicting only the majority class while failing to detect any fraud.

As a baseline, we train a logistic regression model on the dataset. First, we need to separate the features and labels:

```
X = df.drop('Class', axis=1)
y = df['Class']
```

Next, we split the dataset into training and test sets, ensuring they maintain the same class proportions using the stratify=y parameter:

```
from sklearn.model_selection import train_test_split

X_train, X_test, y_train, y_test = train_test_split(X, y, random_state=42,
                                   stratify=y)
```

We then define a pipeline with StandardScaler and LogisticRegression and fit it to the training data:

```
from sklearn.pipeline import Pipeline
from sklearn.preprocessing import StandardScaler
from sklearn.linear_model import LogisticRegression

model = Pipeline([
    ('scaler', StandardScaler()),
    ('clf', LogisticRegression(random_state=42))
])
model.fit(X_train, y_train)
```

The model's accuracy on the training and test sets is:

```
train_accuracy = model.score(X_train, y_train)
print(f'Train accuracy: {train_accuracy:.4f}')

test_accuracy = model.score(X_test, y_test)
print(f'Test accuracy: {test_accuracy:.4f}')
```

```
Train accuracy: 0.9992
Test accuracy: 0.9992
```

While these accuracy values appear excellent, they are misleading in the context of such a heavily imbalanced dataset. A model can achieve high accuracy by simply predicting all transactions as legitimate. To better assess the model's performance on the minority class, we explore alternative evaluation metrics in the following subsections.

5.5.2   Confusion Matrix

A **confusion matrix** (also known as a **contingency table**) is a pivotal tool for evaluating classification models and forms the basis for many commonly used performance metrics. The rows of the matrix represent the actual classes, while the columns represent the predicted classes.[6] Each cell (i, j) indicates the number of samples that belong to class i but were predicted as class j. The values along the diagonal represent correct classifications, whereas the off-diagonal values correspond to errors—hence the term "confusion" between classes.

In binary classification, the confusion matrix is a 2×2 table (see Table 5.3), summarizing the model's performance in terms of four components:

- **True Positives (TP)**: Positive samples correctly classified as positive.

- **True Negatives (TN)**: Negative samples correctly classified as negative.

---

6. Some sources use the opposite convention, where rows represent predicted classes and columns represent actual classes. Always check the labeling when interpreting a confusion matrix.

		Predicted Class	
		+	−
Actual Class	+	True Positives (TP)	False Negatives (FN)
	−	False Positives (FP)	True Negatives (TN)

Table 5.3: Confusion matrix for binary classification, illustrating the relationship between the actual and predicted class labels.

- **False Positives (FP)**: Negative samples incorrectly classified as positive (also known as Type I error).

- **False Negatives (FN)**: Positive samples incorrectly classified as negative (also known as Type II error).

A useful way to remember these components is to note that the second letter in the component's name (P or N) refers to the model's prediction (positive or negative), while the first letter (T or F) indicates whether the prediction was correct (true) or incorrect (false). For example, FP refers to cases where the model predicted positive, but the prediction was incorrect (i.e., the actual label was negative).

In Scikit-Learn, the confusion matrix for a trained model can be computed using the `confusion_matrix`[7] function, which takes the true labels and the model's predicted labels as input. For example, we can compute the confusion matrix for our logistic regression model on the test set as follows:

```
from sklearn.metrics import confusion_matrix

y_test_pred = model.predict(X_test)
conf_mat = confusion_matrix(y_test, y_test_pred)
print(conf_mat)
```

The output is:

```
[[71065    14]
 [   46    77]]
```

In Scikit-Learn's confusion matrix, the first row corresponds to the negative class (true negatives and false positives), while the second row corresponds to the positive class (false negatives and true positives). In this case, the matrix shows: 71,065 true negatives (TN), 14 false positives (FP), 46 false negatives (FN), and 77 true positives (TP).

The overall accuracy of the model can be computed from the confusion matrix as:

$$\text{accuracy} = \frac{\text{TP} + \text{TN}}{\text{TP} + \text{TN} + \text{FP} + \text{FN}} = \frac{77 + 71{,}065}{77 + 71{,}065 + 14 + 46} = 99.92\%, \tag{5.25}$$

which confirms the result obtained earlier using Scikit-Learn's `score` method. Despite the high overall accuracy, the confusion matrix also shows that the model correctly identifies only

---

7. https://scikit-learn.org/stable/modules/generated/sklearn.metrics.confusion_matrix.html

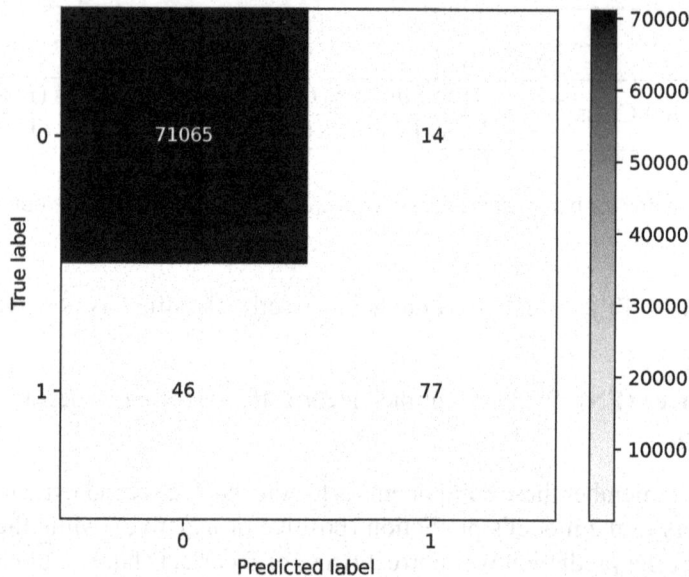

Figure 5.11: Confusion matrix for the logistic regression model on the credit card fraud detection test set.

$77/(46 + 77) = 62.6\%$ of the fraudulent transactions in the test set. This value, known as **recall** (see Section 5.5.3), highlights a significant shortcoming in the model's ability to detect the minority class.

For a better visualization of the confusion matrix (especially in multi-class settings), we can use the `ConfusionMatrixDisplay`[8] class:

```
from sklearn.metrics import import ConfusionMatrixDisplay

disp = ConfusionMatrixDisplay(confusion_matrix=conf_mat)
disp.plot(cmap='Blues')
```

Figure 5.11 provides a graphical representation of the confusion matrix, where color intensity reflects the number of samples in each cell.

5.5.3   Precision and Recall

When working with imbalanced datasets, precision and recall are key evaluation metrics, as they provide a more meaningful assessment than accuracy alone.

Precision measures how many of the instances predicted as positive are actually positive. It is defined as the ratio of true positives to all predicted positives (i.e., true positives plus false positives):

$$\text{Precision} = \frac{\text{TP}}{\text{TP} + \text{FP}}. \tag{5.26}$$

---

8. https://scikit-learn.org/stable/modules/generated/sklearn.metrics.ConfusionMatrixDisplay.html

Recall (also known as **sensitivity** or **true positive rate**) measures how many of the actual positive instances were correctly identified by the model. It is defined as the ratio of true positives to all actual positives (i.e., true positives plus false negatives):

$$\text{Recall} = \frac{\text{TP}}{\text{TP} + \text{FN}}. \tag{5.27}$$

In many classification tasks, there is an inherent tradeoff between precision and recall. A model that favors precision tries to avoid false positives by being cautious and only predicting positive when it is very confident. In contrast, a model that favors recall tries to avoid false negatives, often by predicting positive more aggressively to ensure that most actual positives are captured.

At the extremes of the tradeoff, a model that classifies every instance as positive would achieve perfect recall but very low precision, since most of its positive predictions would be incorrect. Conversely, a model that classifies every instance as negative would have perfect precision (since there are no false positives) but zero recall.

The relative importance of precision versus recall depends on the application. For example, in spam detection, precision is typically more important, since false positives (legitimate emails flagged as spam) are less desirable than false negatives (spam emails that remain in the inbox). On the other hand, in medical diagnostics, recall is often prioritized, as failing to detect a disease (false negative) can be far more harmful than mistakenly flagging a healthy patient (false positive).

Precision and recall can be computed in Scikit-Learn using the functions `precision_score`[9] and `recall_score`[10], respectively:

```
from sklearn.metrics import precision_score, recall_score

precision = precision_score(y_test, y_test_pred)
print(f'Precision: {precision:.4f}')

recall = recall_score(y_test, y_test_pred)
print(f'Recall: {recall:.4f}')
```

```
Precision: 0.8462
Recall: 0.6260
```

These results indicate that when the model predicts a transaction as fraudulent, it is correct 84.62% of the time (precision). However, it identifies only 62.6% of the actual fraudulent transactions (recall), highlighting the model's difficulty in detecting all positive cases.

---

9. https://scikit-learn.org/stable/modules/generated/sklearn.metrics.precision_score.html
10. https://scikit-learn.org/stable/modules/generated/sklearn.metrics.recall_score.html

5.5.4 F-Scores

Precision and recall can be combined into a single metric known as the **F1 score**, which is defined as their harmonic mean:

$$F_1 = \frac{2}{\dfrac{1}{\text{Precision}} + \dfrac{1}{\text{Recall}}} = 2 \cdot \frac{\text{Precision} \cdot \text{Recall}}{\text{Precision} + \text{Recall}}. \tag{5.28}$$

The harmonic mean penalizes large discrepancies between precision and recall, ensuring that both metrics must be high for the F1 score to be high. This makes the F1 score particularly useful when precision and recall are equally important. In Scikit-Learn, the F1 score can be computed using the `f1_score`[11] function:

```
from sklearn.metrics import f1_score

f1 = f1_score(y_test, y_test_pred)
print(f'F1 score: {f1:.4f}')
```

```
F1 score: 0.7196
```

When precision and recall are not equally important, the more general F_β score introduces a weighting factor β to control the relative importance of recall with respect to precision:

$$F_\beta = (1 + \beta^2) \cdot \frac{\text{Precision} \cdot \text{Recall}}{\beta^2 \cdot \text{Precision} + \text{Recall}}. \tag{5.29}$$

Here, $\beta > 1$ gives more weight to recall while $\beta < 1$ gives more weight to precision. To compute the F_β score in Scikit-Learn, you can use the `fbeta_score`[12] function.

Although these metrics are typically reported on the test set, computing them on the training set as well can provide insight into potential overfitting.

5.5.5 Thresholding

In classification models that produce a continuous output (such as a probability or score), the tradeoff between precision and recall can be adjusted by modifying the **decision threshold**. This threshold determines the value above which a sample is classified as belonging to the positive class.

For example, the `LogisticRegression` class provides a `predict_proba` method that returns the predicted probabilities for each class. By default, a threshold of 0.5 is applied to these probabilities to classify a sample as either positive or negative. Adjusting this threshold allows us to balance precision and recall according to the needs of the application.

In fraud detection, for instance, recall is often prioritized because missing a positive instance (a fraudulent transaction) can have severe consequences. To improve the recall of our model, we can lower the threshold to 0.3:

---

11. `https://scikit-learn.org/stable/modules/generated/sklearn.metrics.f1_score.html`
12. `https://scikit-learn.org/stable/modules/generated/sklearn.metrics.fbeta_score.html`

```
threshold = 0.3 # Lower the threshold to increase recall
probs = model.predict_proba(X_test)[:, 1] # Probabilities for the positive class
y_test_pred = (probs > threshold).astype(int)

precision = precision_score(y_test, y_test_pred)
print(f'Precision: {precision:.4f}')

recall = recall_score(y_test, y_test_pred)
print(f'Recall: {recall:.4f}')
```

```
Precision: 0.7636
Recall: 0.6829
```

Lowering the threshold increases recall from 62.6% to 68.3%, but this comes at the cost of reducing precision from 84.6% to 76.4%.

5.5.6   Precision–Recall Curve

A **precision–recall (PR) curve** is a useful tool for visualizing the tradeoff between precision and recall [81]. It can also be used to evaluate a classifier's overall performance and to compare different classifiers across all possible decision thresholds.

In Scikit-Learn, the `precision_recall_curve`[13] function computes precision and recall values for every possible threshold and returns them along with the corresponding thresholds. These values can then be used to plot the precision–recall curve:

```
from sklearn.metrics import precision_recall_curve

precisions, recalls, thresholds = precision_recall_curve(y_train, probs)
plt.plot(recalls, precisions)
plt.xlabel('Recall')
plt.ylabel('Precision')
plt.legend()
```

Figure 5.12 shows the precision–recall curve for the logistic regression classifier. The plot demonstrates the inherent tradeoff between precision and recall: as recall increases, precision tends to decrease. This occurs because achieving higher recall requires lowering the classification threshold, which leads to more positive predictions, including more false positives. Notably, there is a sharp drop in precision around a recall of 0.8, indicating that any further gains in recall beyond this point result in a significant loss in precision. This highlights the difficulty in maintaining high precision while maximizing recall.

When comparing two classifiers, the one whose PR curve consistently dominates (i.e., lies above and to the right of the other) is generally considered superior. This means that, for the same

---

13. https://scikit-learn.org/stable/modules/generated/sklearn.metrics.precision_recall_curve.
    html

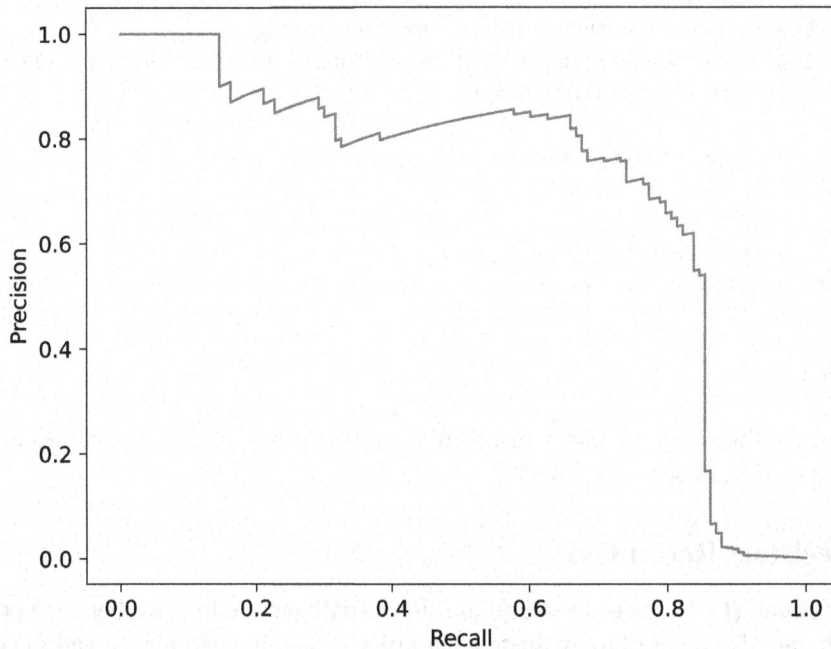

Figure 5.12: Precision–recall curve for the logistic regression classifier on the credit card fraud detection dataset. As recall increases, precision generally decreases, reflecting the challenge of maintaining high precision while achieving high recall.

recall, the superior classifier achieves higher precision—or equivalently for the same precision, it achieves higher recall.

A related plot shows how precision and recall change as a function of the decision threshold. Such a plot provides insight into how adjusting the threshold affects performance and assists in selecting an appropriate threshold based on the application's priorities. The following code generates this plot:

```
plt.plot(thresholds, precisions[:-1], label='Precision')
plt.plot(thresholds, recalls[:-1], label='Recall')
plt.xlabel('Threshold')
plt.ylabel('Metric')
plt.legend()
```

The slicing [:-1] is used because precision_recall_curve returns one more precision–recall pair than there are thresholds. The final pair corresponds to a theoretical threshold of infinity, which has no associated threshold value.

Figure 5.13 shows how both precision and recall vary with the decision threshold. As the threshold increases, recall decreases because the classifier becomes more selective, leading to fewer positive predictions. Conversely, precision tends to increase with a higher threshold, although

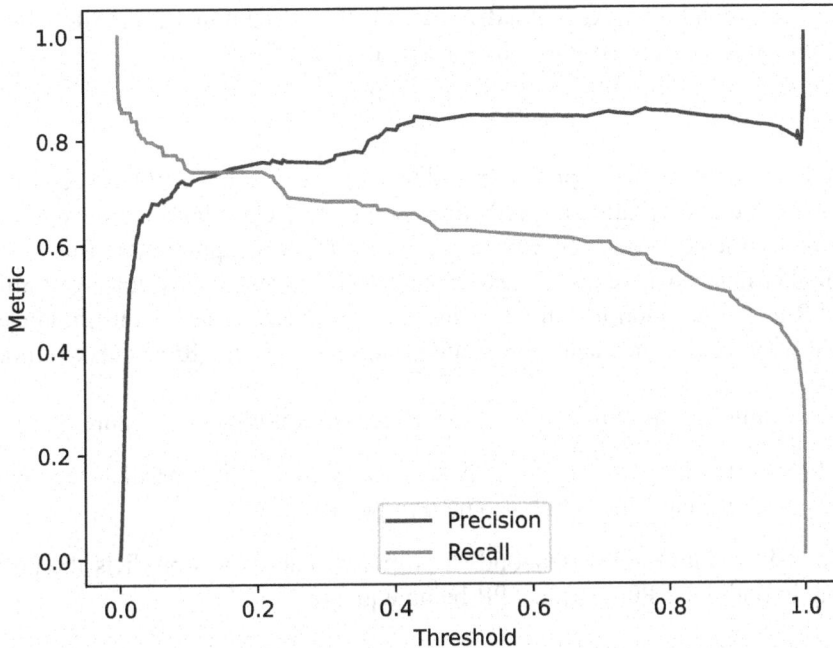

Figure 5.13: Precision and recall as functions of the decision threshold for the logistic regression classifier. As the threshold increases, recall decreases while precision tends to increase. The optimal threshold depends on the specific application and whether higher precision or higher recall is prioritized.

it may fluctuate depending on the balance between true positives and false positives at specific thresholds.

By examining both the PR curve and the precision/recall-vs.-threshold plot, we gain a more complete understanding of how the classifier behaves and can adjust the threshold to achieve the desired balance between precision and recall for a given application.

5.5.7 ROC Curve

The **receiver operating characteristic (ROC)** curve is another valuable tool for evaluating a classifier's performance across different decision thresholds and for comparing multiple classifiers [185].

The x-axis of an ROC curve corresponds to the **false positive rate (FPR)**, which measures the proportion of negative samples incorrectly classified as positive:

$$\text{FPR} = \frac{\text{FP}}{\text{FP} + \text{TN}}. \tag{5.30}$$

The y-axis corresponds to the **true positive rate (TPR)** (also known as **recall**), which measures the proportion of positive samples correctly classified as positive:

$$\text{TPR} = \frac{\text{TP}}{\text{TP} + \text{FN}}. \tag{5.31}$$

Similar to the tradeoff between precision and recall, there is a tradeoff between FPR and TPR. Models that are more conservative in predicting the positive class produce fewer false positives but may miss more true positives, while more aggressive models capture more true positives but at the cost of a higher false positive rate. The ROC curve visualizes this tradeoff by plotting the TPR against the FPR as the decision threshold varies. Because increasing the threshold can never increase the TPR without also increasing (or maintaining) the FPR, the ROC curve is monotonically increasing.

Several key points and lines in the ROC space are worth noting (see Figure 5.14):

- The bottom-left point (0, 0) corresponds to a model that always predicts the negative class, resulting in no false positives but also no true positives.

- The top-right point (1, 1) corresponds to a model that always predicts the positive class, resulting in both the FPR and the TPR being equal to 1.

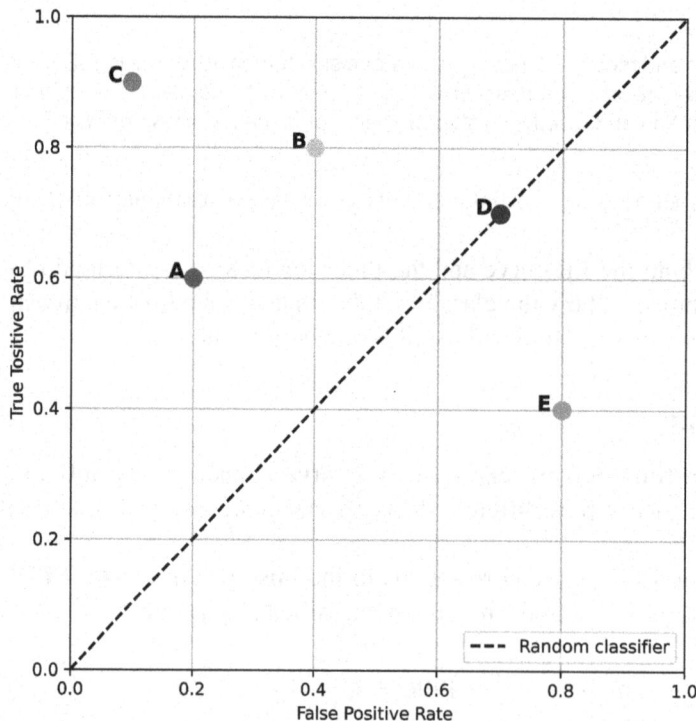

Figure 5.14: ROC curve illustrating five classifiers (A, B, C, D, E). Classifier C outperforms A and B by having both lower FPR and higher TPR. Classifier D demonstrates performance akin to random guessing. Classifier E, which is in the lower-right triangle, performs worse than random but can be negated to achieve a point like B.

- The top-left point (0, 1) corresponds to a perfect classifier, with no false positives and all true positives correctly identified.

- The diagonal line $y = x$ represents a random guesser. For example, a model that guesses the positive class 50% of the time will lie at the point (0.5, 0.5). As the positive-guess rate increases, both TPR and FPR rise together along the diagonal.

- In general, one point in ROC space represents a better classifier than another if it lies further to the northwest (i.e., has a higher TPR and a lower FPR).

Figure 5.14 shows an example of an ROC curve with five classifiers (A, B, C, D, E) plotted according to their true positive rates and false positive rates. The classifiers in the figure exhibit different performance characteristics:

- Classifier A is more conservative than B, prioritizing a lower false positive rate at the expense of missing more true positives.

- Classifier C outperforms both A and B, achieving a lower false positive rate and a higher true positive rate.

- Classifier D behaves like a random classifier that predicts the positive class 70% of the time, resulting in the point (0.7, 0.7).

- Classifier E is located at the point (0.8, 0.4) in the lower-right triangle of the ROC curve, indicating performance worse than random guessing. However, inverting its predictions on every instance would reflect this point across the diagonal, moving it to (0.8, 0.4) and yielding performance identical to that of Classifier B.

An efficient algorithm for generating the ROC curve is shown in Algorithm 5.1. This algorithm exploits the monotonicity of thresholded classifications: any example classified as positive at a given threshold remains positive for all lower thresholds. Therefore, we can sort the examples by their predicted probabilities in descending order and iterate through this sorted list, updating the true positive (TP) and false positive (FP) counts as we go. For each positive example, TP is incremented; for each negative example, FP is incremented. After processing each example, the corresponding point (FPR, TPR) is added to the list of ROC points. These points can then be used to plot the ROC curve.

In Scikit-Learn, the ROC curve can be generated using the roc_curve[14] function:

```
from sklearn.metrics import roc_curve

fpr, tpr, thresholds = roc_curve(y_test, probs)

plt.plot(fpr, tpr, linewidth=2)
plt.plot([0, 1], [0, 1], 'k--') # Diagonal reference line
```

14. https://scikit-learn.org/stable/modules/generated/sklearn.metrics.roc_curve.html

---

Algorithm 5.1 Build ROC Curve

Input:
   L: set of labeled examples
   $f(i)$: classifier's predicted score for example i
   P: number of positive examples
   N: number of negative examples
Output:
   R: a list of ROC points sorted by false positive rate

1: $L_{\text{sorted}} \leftarrow L$ sorted by decreasing f scores
2: $FP \leftarrow 0, TP \leftarrow 0$
3: $R \leftarrow []$
4: **for** $i = 1$ **to** $|L_{\text{sorted}}|$ **do**
5:     Add $\left(\dfrac{FP}{N}, \dfrac{TP}{P} \right)$ to R
6:     **if** $L_{\text{sorted}}[i]$ is a positive example **then**
7:         $TP \leftarrow TP + 1$
8:     **else**
9:         $FP \leftarrow FP + 1$
10: Add $\left(\dfrac{FP}{N}, \dfrac{TP}{P} \right)$ to R ▷ Final point $(1, 1)$
11: **return** R

```
plt.axis([0, 1, 0, 1])
plt.xlabel('False Positive Rate')
plt.ylabel('True Positive Rate')
```

Figure 5.15 shows the ROC curve of the logistic regression classifier on the credit card fraud dataset. The curve starts at $(0, 0)$ and ends at $(1, 1)$, illustrating how the true positive rate and false positive rate vary as the decision threshold changes.

The fact that the ROC curve lies well above the diagonal indicates that the logistic regression model performs significantly better than random guessing. The steep initial rise shows that the classifier is able to identify many true positives while maintaining a low false positive rate—a particularly desirable property in imbalanced settings where correctly identifying the minority class is critical.

However, a low FPR does not necessarily imply high precision. For example, consider a case in which the model is very conservative, predicting the positive class only rarely. In this case, there will be few false positives overall (leading to a low FPR), but those few positive predictions may still be mostly incorrect. As a result, the precision remains low even though the FPR is low. This highlights a limitation of ROC curves: on highly imbalanced datasets, they can present an overly optimistic view of a model's performance.

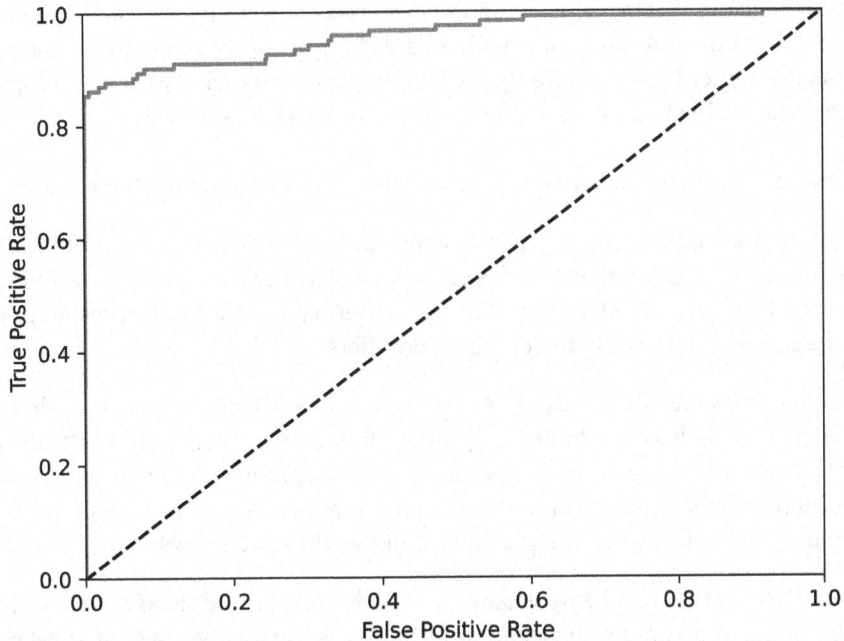

Figure 5.15: ROC curve for the logistic regression classifier on the credit card fraud detection dataset. The curve shows how the true positive rate (TPR) varies with the false positive rate (FPR) across different thresholds. The steep rise at the beginning suggests that the model captures many true positives while generating relatively few false positives.

The **area under the ROC curve (AUC)** provides an overall measure of a classifier's performance across all decision thresholds by calculating the area under the ROC curve [254, 65]. It enables performance comparison between classifiers using a single scalar value. Since the ROC curve lies within a unit square, the AUC ranges from 0 to 1: an AUC of 1 represents a perfect classifier, while an AUC of 0.5 corresponds to random guessing.

Statistically, the AUC represents the probability that the classifier assigns a higher score to a randomly chosen positive instance than to a randomly chosen negative instance. Thus, a classifier with a higher AUC is more likely, on average, to rank positive instances above negative ones.

In Scikit-Learn, the AUC can be computed using the roc_auc_score[15] function:

```
from sklearn.metrics import roc_auc_score

auc = roc_auc_score(y_test, probs)
print(f'AUC: {auc:.4f}')
```

```
AUC: 0.9587
```

15. https://scikit-learn.org/stable/modules/generated/sklearn.metrics.roc_auc_score.html

This result indicates that the logistic regression classifier performs well at distinguishing fraudulent from non-fraudulent transactions, with a 95.87% probability of ranking a randomly chosen positive instance higher than a randomly chosen negative instance. However, a high AUC does not necessarily imply high recall (or high precision) at a particular threshold.

To summarize, the main advantages of ROC curves for classifier evaluation are:

- ROC curves visualize classifier performance across all decision thresholds, allowing for a more holistic evaluation than metrics calculated at a single threshold. Additionally, the area under the ROC curve (AUC) summarizes performance across all thresholds into a single scalar value, making it easy to compare classifiers.

- Unlike precision–recall curves, ROC curves are less affected by changes in the class distribution. This is because both TPR and FPR are calculated independently of the class distribution: TPR is the proportion of true positives among all actual positives, while FPR is the proportion of false positives among all actual negatives. As a result, ROC curves tend to remain stable even when the prevalence of the classes changes.

However, ROC curves can be misleading in highly imbalanced datasets due to how the FPR is computed. When the number of negative instances is very large, even a substantial number of false positives may produce a small FPR. In contrast, precision—defined as the proportion of true positives among all positive predictions—is more sensitive to false positives. As a result, precision–recall (PR) curves are often more informative than ROC curves on highly imbalanced datasets [146].

Overall, there is no single perfect metric for evaluating classification models, as each metric reduces the confusion matrix to a single value and inevitably loses information. A more comprehensive assessment is achieved by considering multiple metrics—such as accuracy, precision, recall, F1 score, and AUC—which together capture different aspects of model performance, including its behavior across decision thresholds and under class imbalance.

5.6   Learning from Imbalanced Data

Imbalanced datasets, in which one class (the minority class) is significantly underrepresented, pose a major challenge for machine learning algorithms [294, 615, 260]. Models trained on such data often become biased toward the majority class, as they have far fewer examples from which to learn the characteristics of the minority class. This imbalance can severely hinder the model's ability to correctly identify minority class instances.

Several strategies have been developed to address class imbalance:

- **Sampling techniques**: These techniques modify the training data in order to balance the class distribution:

- **Oversampling the minority class**: The representation of the minority class is increased by duplicating existing instances or generating synthetic ones. While simple random oversampling may cause overfitting [410], a more effective approach is SMOTE [106], which synthesizes new samples by interpolating between a minority instance and its k nearest neighbors (see Section 5.6.1).

- **Undersampling the majority class**: The number of majority class instances is reduced to achieve a balanced dataset [337]. While this can improve performance on the minority class, it risks losing useful information about the majority class, potentially degrading the overall model performance.

- **Hybrid approaches**: Combining oversampling and undersampling can mitigate the drawbacks of each method, improving the minority class representation without significantly reducing the data available from the majority class [32].

- **Cost-sensitive learning**: Instead of altering the dataset, cost-sensitive methods modify the loss function to penalize errors on minority class instances more heavily (see Section 5.6.2). This approach is especially useful when resampling is impractical or undesirable due to risks of information loss or overfitting, as it directly encourages the model to focus on the minority class.

- **Ensemble methods**: Ensemble techniques combine multiple models to improve performance (see Chapter 9) and are often very effective for imbalanced datasets [209]. By combining predictions from models trained on different data subsets or with different class weights, ensembles mitigate the bias toward the majority class and improve generalization.

- **Anomaly detection techniques**: When the minority class is extremely rare, the classification task can be reframed as an anomaly detection problem, where the goal is to identify instances that deviate significantly from the majority class (this topic is covered in Volume II).

5.6.1   Synthetic Minority Oversampling (SMOTE)

SMOTE (Synthetic Minority Oversampling Technique) [106] is a widely used method for addressing class imbalance by generating synthetic examples of the minority class rather than simply duplicating existing ones. By creating new samples through interpolation, SMOTE increases the diversity of the minority class and reduces the risk of overfitting typically associated with naive oversampling.

The algorithm proceeds as follows:

1. Randomly select a minority class instance x_i.

2. Identify the k nearest neighbors of x_i within the minority class (typically $k = 5$).

3. Randomly select one of these neighbors, denoted x_p.

4. Generate a synthetic sample x_s at a random point along the line segment between x_i and x_p (see Figure 5.16). For each feature j, compute the synthetic feature value as follows:

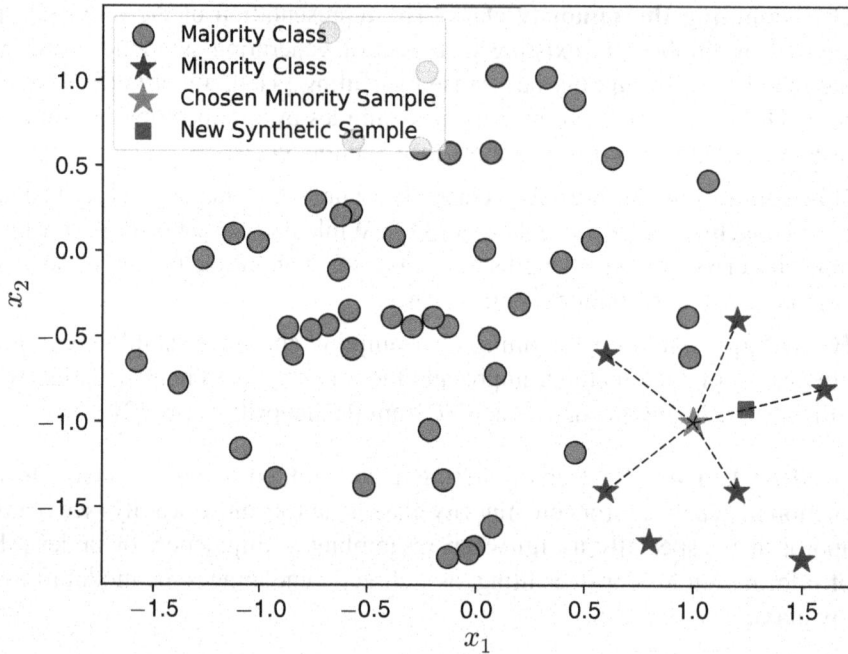

Figure 5.16: Illustration of the SMOTE (Synthetic Minority Oversampling Technique) algorithm. Majority class instances are represented by circles, and minority class instances by stars. The chosen minority instance is highlighted using a lighter star, and its nearest neighbors are connected by dashed lines. A new synthetic sample (represented by a square) is generated at a random position between the selected instance and one of its neighbors.

(a) $d \leftarrow x_{pj} - x_{ij}$

(b) $r \leftarrow$ random number between 0 and 1

(c) $x_{sj} \leftarrow x_{ij} + r \cdot d$

This procedure linearly interpolates between the original instance and its neighbor, generating each feature of the synthetic sample at a random position along the corresponding dimension. This ensures diversity among synthetic samples while preserving the local structure of the minority class.

5. Repeat this process until the desired number of minority samples is reached.

The Python library `imbalanced-learn`[16] provides an implementation of SMOTE, along with many other algorithms and tools for handling imbalanced datasets. It can be easily installed using `pip install imbalanced-learn`.

Let's use the SMOTE[17] class from this library to oversample the fraudulent class in our fraud detection dataset. The key parameters of this class include:

---

16. https://imbalanced-learn.org
17. https://imbalanced-learn.org/stable/references/generated/imblearn.over_sampling.SMOTE.html

- `sampling_strategy`: Controls the resampling ratio, defined as the desired ratio of the number of minority-class samples after resampling to the number of majority-class samples. For example, a value of 0.1 means that the minority class will be resampled to 10% of the size of the majority class. The default value `'auto'` balances the classes so they have the same number of samples. This parameter can strongly affect the balance between recall and precision, so it should be tuned according to the application's objectives.

- `k_neighbors`: Specifies how many nearest neighbors are considered as reference points when creating synthetic samples. The default is 5.

For example, the following code increases the proportion of fraudulent transactions to 1% of the legitimate transactions (up from about 0.17% in the original dataset), improving minority representation without creating an unrealistically balanced dataset, which could distort the true class distribution and lead the model to assume that fraud is much more common than it actually is:

```
from imblearn.over_sampling import SMOTE

smote = SMOTE(random_state=42, sampling_strategy=0.01)
X_train_res, y_train_res = smote.fit_resample(X_train, y_train)
```

It is crucial to apply SMOTE only to the training set to ensure that model evaluation on the test set remains valid. Applying it to the test set could introduce synthetic data, biasing performance metrics and undermining the assessment of generalization to truly unseen examples.

After applying SMOTE, we can inspect the size of the training set:

```
print(f'Before SMOTE: {X_train.shape}')
print(f'After SMOTE: {X_train_res.shape}')
```

```
Before SMOTE: (213605, 30)
After SMOTE: (215368, 30)
```

SMOTE added 1,763 synthetic samples to the minority class. The new class distribution is:

```
y_res.value_counts(normalize=True)
```

```
Class
0    0.990101
1    0.009899
```

As expected, the minority class now makes up about 1% of the majority class. We can now retrain our logistic regression model on the resampled training set:

```
model.fit(X_train_res, y_train_res)
```

The performance metrics of the model on the test set are:

```
y_test_pred = model.predict(X_test)

print(f'Precision: {precision_score(y_test, y_test_pred):.4f}')
print(f'Recall: {recall_score(y_test, y_test_pred):.4f}')
print(f'F1 score: {f1_score(y_test, y_test_pred):.4f}')
```

```
Precision: 0.7500
Recall: 0.8049
F1 score: 0.7765
```

Recall has improved significantly, from 62.6% to 80.49%, while precision decreased from 84.62% to 75%. Overall, the F1 score increased from 71.96% to 77.65%, indicating a better balance between precision and recall.

For comparison, we also evaluate a simple random oversampling approach using the `Random OverSampler`[18] class from the `imbalanced-learn` library:

```
from imblearn.over_sampling import RandomOverSampler

ros = RandomOverSampler(random_state=42, sampling_strategy=0.01)
X_train_res, y_train_res = ros.fit_resample(X_train, y_train)

model.fit(X_train_res, y_train_res)

y_test_pred = model.predict(X_test)
print(f'Precision: {precision_score(y_test, y_test_pred):.4f}')
print(f'Recall: {recall_score(y_test, y_test_pred):.4f}')
print(f'F1 score: {f1_score(y_test, y_test_pred):.4f}')
```

The results are:

```
Precision: 0.7481
Recall: 0.7967
F1 score: 0.7717
```

In this case, random oversampling yields slightly worse results than SMOTE. The difference is small, partly because logistic regression is a linear model and thus cannot fully exploit the diversity introduced by SMOTE's synthetic samples. Since it can only learn linear decision boundaries, the additional synthetic points do not lead to a more expressive class separation.

While SMOTE can be a powerful tool for addressing class imbalance, its effectiveness depends heavily on the specific dataset and the problem context. The synthetic samples it generates may not accurately reflect the true underlying distribution of the minority class, potentially leading to overlap with the majority class or introducing noise.

18. https://imbalanced-learn.org/stable/references/generated/imblearn.over_sampling.
    RandomOverSampler.html

To address these issues, several extensions of SMOTE have been proposed, many of which are implemented in the `imbalanced-learn` library:

- **Borderline SMOTE**: Focuses on minority samples near the decision boundary (the borderline) [252]. It generates synthetic samples in directions where the nearest neighbors belong to the majority class, reinforcing the minority presence in ambiguous areas and helping the model learn a more discriminative boundary. Implemented by the `BorderlineSMOTE` class.

- **SMOTE-ENN (SMOTE+ Edited Nearest Neighbors)**: This hybrid method combines SMOTE with the Edited Nearest Neighbor (ENN) cleaning rule [32]. After generating the synthetic samples, ENN removes instances that differ from the majority of their neighbors, thereby reducing noise and improving the decision boundary. Implemented by the `SMOTEENN` class.

- **SMOTE-Tomek**: Combines SMOTE with the removal of Tomek links [32]. Tomek links are pairs of samples from opposite classes that are each other's nearest neighbors, often indicating borderline cases or noise. Removing these pairs sharpens the decision boundary and improves the effectiveness of SMOTE. Implemented by the `SMOTETomek` class.

- **K-Means SMOTE**: Incorporates k-means clustering into the oversampling process [171]. Synthetic samples are generated within minority-class clusters, making the oversampling process more adaptive to complex and heterogeneous class distributions. Implemented by the `KMeansSMOTE` class.

- **ADASYN (Adaptive Synthetic Sampling)**: Generates more synthetic samples in regions where the minority class is sparse [259]. By adapting the number of synthetic samples to local data density, ADASYN focuses oversampling on harder-to-learn areas of the feature space. Implemented by the `ADASYN` class.

SMOTE remains an active area of research, with ongoing work aimed at improving its effectiveness and scalability [55, 30], integrating it with deep learning models [142], and developing adaptive sampling techniques that respond to real-time model performance [165]. For a comprehensive review of recent progress and open challenges, see Fernández et al. [187].

5.6.2   Cost-Sensitive Learning

Cost-sensitive learning enables models to assign different penalties to different types of errors, allowing mistakes on minority-class instances to be weighted more heavily than those on majority-class instances [180].

Central to this approach is the **cost matrix**, which specifies the cost incurred for each combination of true and predicted classes. Its structure resembles a confusion matrix: rows correspond to actual classes and columns to predicted classes. The entry $C(i, j)$ represents the cost of predicting class j when the true class is i.

Table 5.4 illustrates a cost matrix for a binary classification problem. Typically, correct classifications incur no cost, (i.e., $C(0, 0) = C(1, 1) = 0$), and the cost of misclassifying a minority-class

		Predicted Class	
		$-$	$+$
Actual Class	$-$	$C(0,0)$	$C(0,1)$
	$+$	$C(1,0)$	$C(1,1)$

Table 5.4: Cost matrix for a binary classification problem

	Legitimate	Fraudulent
Approve	$-0.01x$	x
Refuse	$\$10$	0

Table 5.5: Example of a cost matrix for credit card transactions

instance (false negative) is higher than misclassifying a majority-class instance (false positive), i.e., $C(1,0) > C(0,1)$.

In some applications, the entries of the cost matrix are not fixed but depend on the specific instance. For example, in credit card fraud detection, the cost of approving a fraudulent transaction depends on the size of the transaction, as the bank must cover the fraudulent charges. Table 5.5 shows a cost matrix for this scenario, where x denotes the transaction amount in dollars. In this example, approving a fraudulent transaction costs the bank x, while refusing a legitimate transaction incurs a fixed customer dissatisfaction cost. The entry $-0.01x$ in the "Approve/Legitimate" cell represents a small benefit (1% of the transaction value) from approving a legitimate transaction, corresponding to the bank's profit or long-term customer satisfaction.

In cost-sensitive learning, the optimal classification for an instance $\mathbf{x}$ is the one that minimizes the expected misclassification cost, also known as the **Bayes conditional risk**. Specifically, the expected cost of classifying $\mathbf{x}$ as belonging to class j is given by

$$R(j|\mathbf{x}) = \sum_i P(i|\mathbf{x})C(i,j), \tag{5.32}$$

where $P(i|\mathbf{x})$ is the probability that $\mathbf{x}$ belongs to class i, and $C(i,j)$ is the cost of predicting class j when the true class is i.

There are several ways to incorporate cost-sensitive learning into machine learning algorithms:

- **Modifying the objective function**: Many algorithms can incorporate misclassification costs directly into their objective function [658, 338, 12]. For example, in logistic regression, the log loss can be weighted according to the cost matrix, so that errors on minority-class instances receive higher penalties.

- **Adjusting class weights**: Some algorithms allow assigning different weights to classes, which can affect various aspects of the learning process such as split decisions in decision trees [368] or sample selection in random forests [107]. Assigning a higher weight to the minority class encourages the model to focus more on correctly classifying these instances.

- **Adapting learning rates**: In gradient-based optimization, the learning rate can be adapted based on misclassification costs [338]. A higher learning rate for minority-class instances encourages the model to update its parameters more aggressively on these instances.

- **Post-processing decision thresholds**: After training, decision thresholds can be shifted to reflect misclassification costs. For instance, in binary classification, the threshold for predicting the positive class can be lowered when the cost of misclassifying a minority-class instance is higher.

In Scikit-Learn, many algorithms support class weighting through the `class_weight` parameter, which can influence the objective function or other parts of the learning process, depending on the implementation. This parameter accepts either a dictionary mapping class labels to weights, or the string `'balanced'`, which automatically sets weights inversely proportional to the class frequencies so that each class is equally represented. The default value `None` means that no class weighting is applied, so all samples are treated equally.

For example, in our logistic regression model, we can assign a higher weight to the minority class (e.g., 0.8) as follows:

```
model = Pipeline([
    ('scaler', StandardScaler()),
    ('clf', LogisticRegression(class_weight={0: 0.2, 1: 0.8}, random_state=42))
])
model.fit(X_train, y_train)
```

The performance of the model is:

```
y_test_pred = model.predict(X_test)

print(f'Precision: {precision_score(y_test, y_test_pred):.4f}')
print(f'Recall: {recall_score(y_test, y_test_pred):.4f}')
print(f'F1 score: {f1_score(y_test, y_test_pred):.4f}')
```

```
Precision: 0.7520
Recall: 0.7642
F1 score: 0.7581
```

The F1 score of 75.81% is higher than that of the baseline model with equal class weights (71.96%), but slightly lower than the score achieved with SMOTE (77.65%).

Additionally, many algorithms in Scikit-Learn support assigning weights to individual samples using the `sample_weight` argument in the `fit` method:

```
sample_weights = [1, 1, 5, 1, 3, 2] # Example of individual weights
model.fit(X_train, y_train, sample_weight=sample_weights)
```

This can be useful when the cost depends on specific instances, allowing you to give more influence to costly or difficult examples.

SMOTE and class-weight adjustment can also be combined: SMOTE increases the representation of the minority class, while class weighting emphasizes these instances during training. Together, they can leverage the diversity of synthetic samples and the cost-awareness of the learning algorithm to potentially achieve better results.

5.7 Multi-Class Extensions for Binary Classifiers

Multi-class classification involves assigning instances to one of several classes, rather than just two. While some machine learning algorithms, such as decision trees and neural networks, natively support multi-class classification, others like logistic regression and support vector machines (SVMs) are designed for binary classification and must be adapted to handle multiple classes. Two general strategies for extending binary classifiers to multi-class problems are:

- **One-vs-Rest (OvR)** (also known as **One-vs-All (OvA)**): This method trains a separate binary classifier for each class treating that class as the positive class and all other classes combined as the negative class (see Figure 5.17). At prediction time, all classifiers are evaluated and the class with the highest score (e.g., predicted probability) is chosen. If the algorithm only outputs hard labels, we choose one of the classes whose OvR classifier predicts positive, breaking ties with a simple rule (e.g., choosing the class with the smallest index).

- **One-vs-One (OvO)**: In this strategy, a separate binary classifier is trained for every pair of classes (see Figure 5.18). For n classes, this results in $\frac{n(n-1)}{2}$ classifiers. During prediction, each classifier votes for one of its two classes, and the class with the most votes overall is selected. If there is a tie, the decision scores (when available) are aggregated across classifiers to break the tie.

Both OvR and OvO have their strengths and limitations. OvR is computationally more efficient since it trains only n classifiers, and it can make use of prediction scores to select the class with the highest confidence. However, it may suffer from class imbalance: each binary classifier must separate one class from all the others, leading to a large imbalance between positive and negative examples.

Conversely, OvO requires a quadratic number of classifiers, which can be costly to train and evaluate when there are many classes. On the other hand, each classifier only needs to distinguish between two classes, making the subproblems simpler and the individual classifiers faster to train. In practice, OvO often achieves better performance, but at the cost of increased training and prediction time.

Scikit-Learn provides two classes that implement these strategies:

- `OneVsRestClassifier`[19] for the one-vs-rest strategy.

- `OneVsOneClassifier`[20] for the one-vs-one strategy.

---

19. https://scikit-learn.org/stable/modules/generated/sklearn.multiclass.OneVsRestClassifier.html
20. https://scikit-learn.org/stable/modules/generated/sklearn.multiclass.OneVsOneClassifier.html

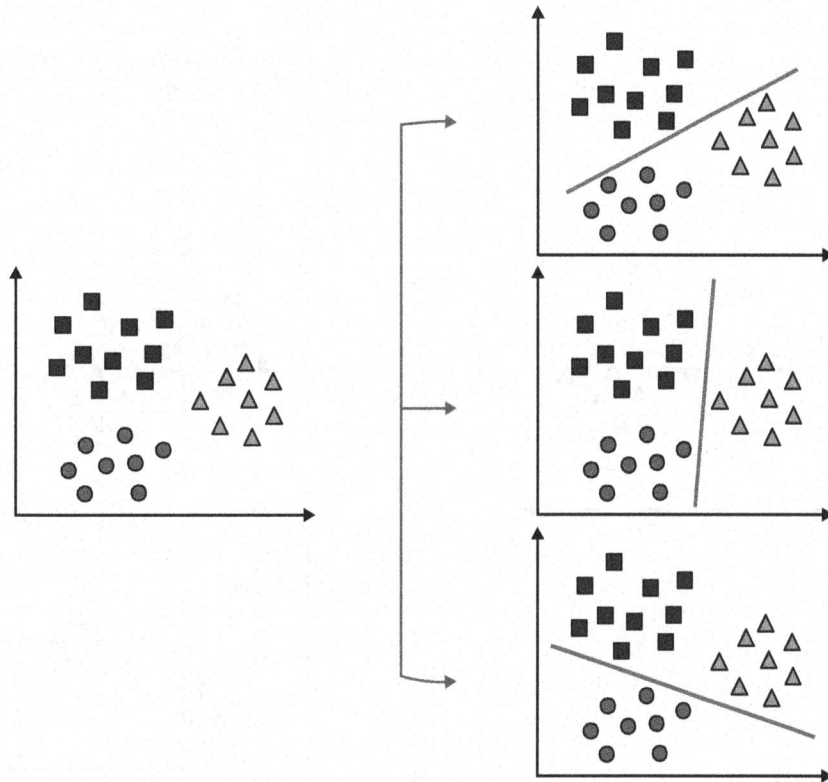

Figure 5.17: Illustration of the one-vs-rest (OvR) strategy for multi-class classification. The left panel shows a dataset with three classes, represented by squares, triangles, and circles. In the right panels, a separate classifier is trained for each class to distinguish it from all others. The final prediction is made by selecting the class with the highest score among all classifiers.

These classes can wrap any binary classifier to enable multi-class classification. For example, you can use logistic regression with the one-vs-rest strategy as follows:

```
from sklearn.linear_model import LogisticRegression
from sklearn.multiclass import OneVsRestClassifier

ovr_classifier = OneVsRestClassifier(LogisticRegression())
```

In addition, some estimators (such as SVMs) automatically select an appropriate multi-class strategy when their `fit` method is called on data with more than two classes.

5.8 Multinomial Logistic Regression

Multinomial logistic regression (also known as **softmax regression**) is an extension of logistic regression for multi-class classification problems [407, 277]. It models the probability of each

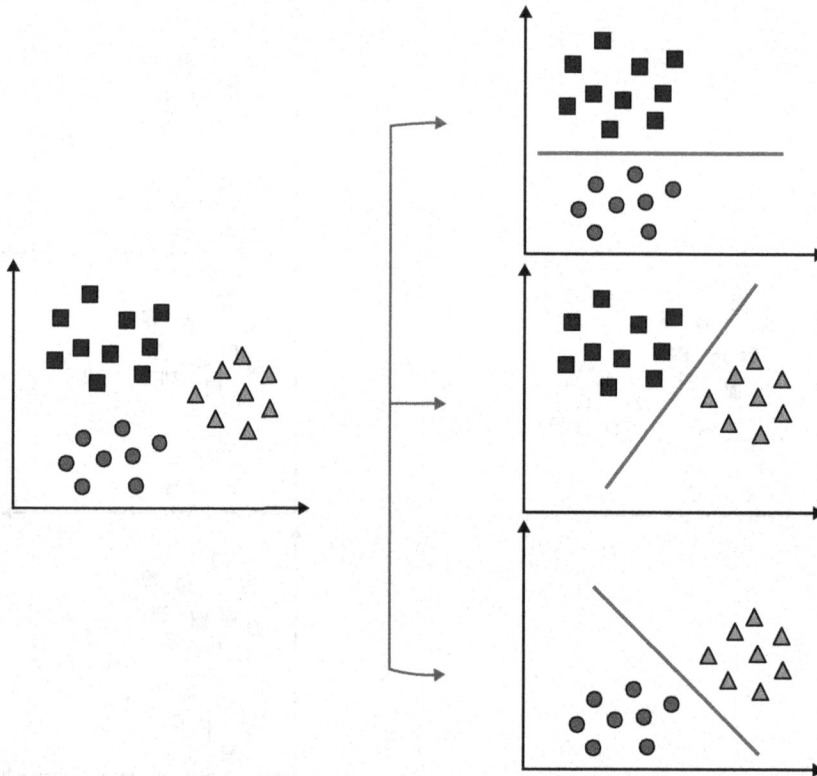

Figure 5.18: Illustration of the one-vs-one (OvO) strategy for multi-class classification. The left panel shows a dataset with three classes: squares, triangles, and circles. The right panels illustrate how a separate classifier is trained for each pair of classes. The final prediction is based on the total number of votes each class receives.

class as a function of the input features, subject to the constraint that all predicted probabilities are nonnegative and sum to one. For example, in an image classification task a multinomial logistic regression model can predict the probabilities that an image contains a cat, a dog, or a car, based on features extracted from the image.

This joint modeling approach is preferred over fitting multiple binary logistic regression models when the class labels are *mutually exclusive*. For example, in the one-vs-rest strategy, a separate binary classifier is trained for each class, making independent predictions. This can lead to probabilities that do not sum to one, even though only one class should be chosen. Multinomial logistic regression addresses this by modeling all classes jointly, ensuring that the predicted probabilities form a valid distribution and capturing shared patterns across classes—for example, how the same image features affect the likelihood of different object categories.

However, when samples can belong to multiple classes simultaneously (for example, a movie labeled as both a comedy and a romance), the softmax assumption of mutually exclusive outcomes no longer applies. In such multi-label classification settings, it is more appropriate to build a separate binary classifier for each class, enabling independent predictions for each label.

5.8.1 Formal Definition

Given an input sample $(\mathbf{x}, y)$, multinomial logistic regression outputs a probability vector $\mathbf{p} = (p_1, \ldots, p_k)^T$, where each component $p_i = P(y = i | \mathbf{x})$ represents the predicted probability that the sample belongs to class i. These probabilities sum to one, i.e., $\sum_{i=1}^{k} p_i = 1$.

As discussed, binary logistic regression models the log-odds of the positive class as a linear function of the input features. Multinomial logistic regression generalizes this idea by modeling the log-odds of each class relative to a **reference class** (typically the last class, k) as a linear function of the input features. For each class $1 \le i < k$, the log-odds of class i versus the reference class k are expressed as:

$$\log \left(\frac{p_i}{p_k} \right) = \mathbf{w}_i^T \mathbf{x}, \tag{5.33}$$

where $\mathbf{w}_i$ is the parameter vector associated with class i.

As a result, $k - 1$ parameter vectors must be estimated from the data: $\mathbf{w}_1, \ldots, \mathbf{w}_{k-1}$. To enable efficient computation of class scores via matrix multiplication, these vectors are typically stacked as the rows of a parameter matrix $W \in \mathbb{R}^{(k-1) \times (d+1)}$:

$$W = \begin{pmatrix} - & \mathbf{w}_1^T & - \\ - & \mathbf{w}_2^T & - \\ & \vdots & \\ - & \mathbf{w}_{k-1}^T & - \end{pmatrix} = \begin{pmatrix} w_{10} & w_{11} & w_{12} & \cdots & w_{1d} \\ w_{20} & w_{21} & w_{22} & \cdots & w_{2d} \\ \vdots & \vdots & \ddots & \vdots & \vdots \\ w_{k-1,0} & w_{k-1,1} & w_{k-1,2} & \cdots & w_{k-1,d} \end{pmatrix}. \tag{5.34}$$

To derive an expression for the predicted probability p_i of each class, we begin by exponentiating both sides of the log-odds equation:

$$\frac{p_i}{p_k} = e^{\mathbf{w}_i^T \mathbf{x}}$$

$$p_i = p_k e^{\mathbf{w}_i^T \mathbf{x}}$$

Since the class probabilities sum to 1, we can express p_k as:

$$p_k = 1 - \sum_{i=1}^{k-1} p_i = 1 - \sum_{i=1}^{k-1} \left(p_k e^{\mathbf{w}_i^T \mathbf{x}} \right)$$

$$p_k + p_k \left(\sum_{i=1}^{k-1} e^{\mathbf{w}_i^T \mathbf{x}} \right) = 1$$

$$p_k \left(1 + \sum_{i=1}^{k-1} e^{\mathbf{w}_i^T \mathbf{x}} \right) = 1$$

$$p_k = \frac{1}{1 + \sum_{i=1}^{k-1} e^{\mathbf{w}_i^T \mathbf{x}}}$$

Substituting this back into the expression for p_i, we obtain for $1 \leq i < k$:

$$p_i = p_k e^{\mathbf{w}_i^T \mathbf{x}} = \frac{e^{\mathbf{w}_i^T \mathbf{x}}}{1 + \sum_{j=1}^{k-1} e^{\mathbf{w}_j^T \mathbf{x}}}. \tag{5.35}$$

To simplify notation, we set $\mathbf{w}_k = 0$ for the reference class. This has no effect on the model because only the log-odds relative to the reference class are used in computing the probabilities. With this convention, $e^{\mathbf{w}_k^T \mathbf{x}} = e^0 = 1$, which allows us to rewrite the class probabilities uniformly as:

$$p_i = \frac{e^{\mathbf{w}_i^T \mathbf{x}}}{\sum_{j=1}^{k} e^{\mathbf{w}_j^T \mathbf{x}}}. \tag{5.36}$$

The expression on the right-hand side corresponds to the **softmax function** applied to the class logits $\mathbf{w}_i^T \mathbf{x}$. The softmax function $\sigma(\mathbf{z})$ maps a vector of real values $\mathbf{z} = (z_1, \ldots, z_k)^T$ to a probability distribution over k classes, defined as:

$$\sigma(\mathbf{z})_i = \frac{e^{z_i}}{\sum_{j=1}^{k} e^{z_j}}. \tag{5.37}$$

It can be easily verified that the components of $\sigma(\mathbf{z})$ lie in the range (0,1) and sum to 1, which confirms that they form a valid probability distribution. The name "softmax" reflects the fact that the function acts as a smooth, differentiable approximation of the argmax function. For example, for the vector $\mathbf{z} = (1, 2, 6)$, the softmax output is $\sigma(\mathbf{z}) = (0.007, 0.018, 0.976)$, indicating a strong preference for the largest input value.

A common issue when computing the softmax function is numerical instability caused by the exponentiation of large logits. This can be mitigated by subtracting the maximum logit $M = \max_{1 \leq i \leq k} z_i$ from all components of the input vector before exponentiation:

$$\sigma(\mathbf{z})_i = \frac{e^{z_i - M}}{\sum_{j=1}^{k} e^{z_j - M}}. \tag{5.38}$$

This transformation leaves the resulting probabilities unchanged while ensuring that all exponents are ≤ 0, which prevents overflow. Most machine learning libraries implement softmax with this shift internally.

Using the softmax function, the output of the multinomial logistic regression model can be written as:

$$\mathbf{p} = \begin{pmatrix} P(y = 1 | \mathbf{x}) \\ \vdots \\ P(y = k | \mathbf{x}) \end{pmatrix} = \begin{pmatrix} \dfrac{e^{\mathbf{w}_1^T \mathbf{x}}}{\sum_{j=1}^{k} e^{\mathbf{w}_j^T \mathbf{x}}} \\ \vdots \\ \dfrac{e^{\mathbf{w}_k^T \mathbf{x}}}{\sum_{j=1}^{k} e^{\mathbf{w}_j^T \mathbf{x}}} \end{pmatrix} = \sigma(W\mathbf{x}), \tag{5.39}$$

where W is the matrix of coefficients (with a row of zeros corresponding to the reference class). Figure 5.19 illustrates the computational process of the multinomial logistic regression model.

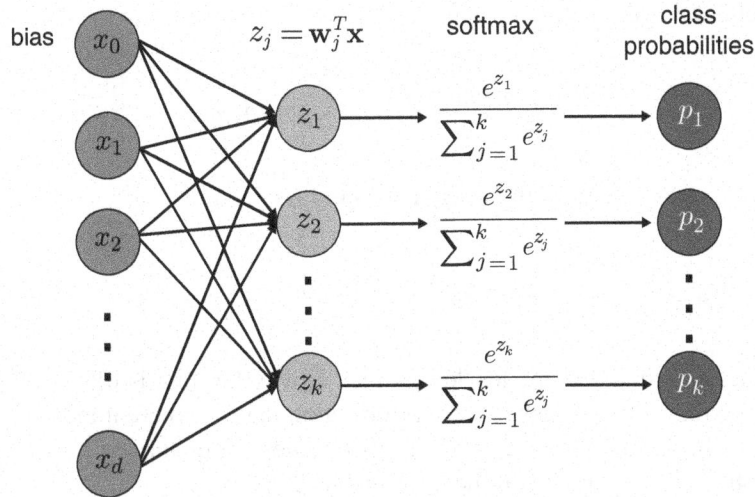

Figure 5.19: The computational process of multinomial logistic regression. The input vector $\mathbf{x} = (x_0, x_1, \ldots, x_d)$ is linearly combined with the weight vectors $\mathbf{w}_1, \mathbf{w}_2, \ldots, \mathbf{w}_k$ to produce the logits $z_1, z_2, \ldots, z_k$. These logits are passed through the softmax function, which transforms them into class probabilities $p_1, p_2, \ldots, p_k$ that sum to 1.

5.8.2 Training the Model

Similar to binary logistic regression, we first define a suitable loss function based on the negative log-likelihood and then use iterative optimization methods such as gradient descent to minimize this function.

5.8.2.1 The Cross-Entropy Loss

In multinomial logistic regression, the model outputs a probability vector $\mathbf{p} = (p_1, \ldots, p_k)$, where p_i represents the predicted probability of class i. However, the true label y for each example is typically stored as an integer index $y \in \{1, \ldots, k\}$. To align the predicted probabilities with the true label, we one-hot encode the label into a binary vector $\mathbf{y} = (y_1, \ldots, y_k)$, where $y_i = 1$ if i is the true class and 0 otherwise.

Our goal is to learn the parameters W that maximize the likelihood of the true labels under the model. We assume that the target variable y follows a **categorical distribution** (see Section C.5.6.7), which generalizes the Bernoulli distribution to $k > 2$ outcomes. In this setting, the model assigns a probability $P(y = i|\mathbf{x}) = p_i$ to each class i, and these probabilities satisfy $\sum_{i=1}^{k} p_i = 1$.

For a given sample $(\mathbf{x}, \mathbf{y})$, where $\mathbf{y} = (y_1, \ldots, y_k)$ is the one-hot representation of the true label, the likelihood of observing the true label under the model (parameterized by W) is:

$$P(\mathbf{y}|\mathbf{x}, W) = p_1^{y_1} \cdot p_2^{y_2} \cdots p_k^{y_k} = \prod_{i=1}^{k} p_i^{y_i}. \tag{5.40}$$

Since only one component $y_j = 1$ (for the true class j) and all others are zero, the likelihood reduces $P(\mathbf{y}|\mathbf{x}, W) = p_j$, the predicted probability of the correct class.

The log-likelihood is therefore

$$\log P(\mathbf{y}|\mathbf{x}, W) = \sum_{i=1}^{k} y_i \log p_i. \tag{5.41}$$

Negating this expression gives the **cross-entropy loss**:

$$L_{\text{CE}}(\mathbf{y}, \mathbf{p}) = - \sum_{i=1}^{k} y_i \log p_i. \tag{5.42}$$

When $k = 2$, this reduces to the log loss, which is why log loss is often called binary cross-entropy. The term *cross-entropy* comes from information theory, where it measures the difference between two probability distributions [134]. In this context, it quantifies the difference between the true label distribution $\mathbf{y}$ and the predicted distribution $\mathbf{p}$.

For example, consider a classification problem with three classes ($k = 3$). Suppose the true class is 2, represented as $\mathbf{y} = (0, 1, 0)$, and the model's predicted probabilities are $\mathbf{p} = (0.3, 0.6, 0.1)$. The cross-entropy loss for this instance is:

$$L_{\text{CE}} = -(0 \cdot \log 0.3 + 1 \cdot \log 0.6 + 0 \cdot \log 0.1) = 0.5108.$$

5.8.2.2 Gradient Descent

Our goal is to minimize the cross-entropy loss in order to find the optimal parameters of the softmax regression model. As in binary logistic regression, this minimization problem does not have a closed-form solution, thus we rely on iterative optimization methods such as gradient descent.

We now derive the gradient of the cross-entropy loss with respect to the model parameters. For class j ($1 \le j \le k$), the gradient with respect to the weight vector $\mathbf{w}_j$ is:

$$\frac{\partial L}{\partial \mathbf{w}_j} = (p_j - y_j)\mathbf{x}, \tag{5.43}$$

where p_j is the predicted probability of class j for the input $\mathbf{x}$, and y_j is the j-th element of the one-hot encoded true label vector $\mathbf{y}$.

To see why this formula holds, we start from the cross-entropy loss:

$$L = - \sum_{i=1}^{k} y_i \log p_i = - \sum_{i=1}^{k} y_i \log \left(\frac{e^{z_i}}{\sum_{d=1}^{k} e^{z_d}} \right) = - \sum_{i=1}^{k} y_i \log \left(\frac{e^{\mathbf{w}_i^T \mathbf{x}}}{\sum_{d=1}^{k} e^{\mathbf{w}_d^T \mathbf{x}}} \right), \tag{5.44}$$

where $z_i = \mathbf{w}_i^T \mathbf{x}$ is the logit for class i.

Using the chain rule, the gradient of L with respect to $\mathbf{w}_j$ is:

$$\frac{\partial L}{\partial \mathbf{w}_j} = \frac{\partial L}{\partial z_j} \frac{\partial z_j}{\partial \mathbf{w}_j}. \tag{5.45}$$

Since for any vector $\mathbf{u}$, we have $\partial(\mathbf{u}^T\mathbf{x})/\partial\mathbf{u} = \mathbf{x}$ (see Section B.9.1.1), it follows that

$$\frac{\partial z_j}{\partial \mathbf{w}_j} = \frac{\partial \mathbf{w}_j^T \mathbf{x}}{\partial \mathbf{w}_j} = \mathbf{x}. \tag{5.46}$$

It remains to compute $\partial L/\partial z_j$. Again applying the chain rule, we differentiate with respect to z_j:

$$\frac{\partial L}{\partial z_j} = -\frac{\partial}{\partial z_j} \sum_{i=1}^{k} y_i \log p_i = -\sum_{i=1}^{k} \frac{y_i}{p_i} \cdot \frac{\partial p_i}{\partial z_j}. \tag{5.47}$$

The partial derivatives of the softmax outputs p_i with respect to the logits z_j are:

1. For $i = j$:

$$\frac{\partial p_i}{\partial z_i} = \frac{\partial}{\partial z_i} \frac{e^{z_i}}{\sum_{d=1}^{k} e^{z_d}} = \frac{\sum_{d=1}^{k} e^{z_d} e^{z_i} - e^{z_i} e^{z_i}}{\left(\sum_{d=1}^{k} e^{z_d}\right)^2} = \frac{e^{z_i}}{\sum_{d=1}^{k} e^{z_d}} \left(\frac{\sum_{d=1}^{k} e^{z_d} - e^{z_i}}{\sum_{d=1}^{k} e^{z_d}}\right)$$

$$= p_i(1 - p_i).$$

2. For $i \neq j$:

$$\frac{\partial p_i}{\partial z_j} = \frac{\partial}{\partial z_j} \frac{e^{z_i}}{\sum_{d=1}^{k} e^{z_d}} = \frac{\sum_{d=1}^{k} e^{z_d} \cdot 0 - e^{z_i} e^{z_j}}{\left(\sum_{d=1}^{k} e^{z_d}\right)^2} = -\frac{e^{z_i}}{\sum_{d=1}^{k} e^{z_d}} \cdot \frac{e^{z_j}}{\sum_{d=1}^{k} e^{z_d}} = -p_i p_j.$$

Substituting into the expression for $\partial L/\partial z_j$, we obtain:

$$\frac{\partial L}{\partial z_j} = -\sum_{i=1}^{k} \frac{y_i}{p_i} \frac{\partial p_i}{\partial z_j} = \sum_{i=1}^{k} \begin{cases} y_i(p_i - 1) & i = j \\ y_i p_j & i \neq j \end{cases}.$$

Let us analyze the sum on the right-hand side. Because the label vector $\mathbf{y}$ is one-hot encoded, there are only two possibilities:

- If j is the true class, $y_j = 1$ and all other components of the vector are zero. In this case, the only nonzero term in the sum corresponds to $i = j$, and the result simplifies to $p_j - 1$, which is equal to $p_j - y_j$.

- Otherwise, $y_j = 0$ and the only nonzero term in the sum comes from the true class $i \neq j$, for which $y_i = 1$. In this case, the sum simplifies to p_j, which also equals $p_j - y_j$ (since $y_j = 0$).

Therefore,

$$\frac{\partial L}{\partial z_j} = p_j - y_j. \tag{5.48}$$

Finally, substituting Equations (5.46) and (5.48) into (5.45) yields:

$$\frac{\partial L}{\partial \mathbf{w}_j} = (p_j - y_j)\mathbf{x},$$

which matches the expression for the gradient given in Equation (5.43).

With the gradient of the loss function in hand, we can now use (stochastic) gradient descent to iteratively update the weights and minimize the loss. The process proceeds as follows:

1. Randomly initialize the weight matrix W.

2. For each training sample:

   (a) Compute the predicted class probabilities $\mathbf{p}$ using Equation (5.39).

   (b) Calculate the gradient of the cross-entropy loss with respect to each weight vector $\mathbf{w}_j$ using Equation (5.43).

   (c) Optionally, compute the cross-entropy loss (Equation (5.42)) to monitor convergence.

   (d) Update the weights $\mathbf{w}_j$ by moving in the opposite direction of the gradient, scaled by the learning rate α:

   $$\mathbf{w}_j \leftarrow \mathbf{w}_j - \alpha(p_j - y_j)\mathbf{x}. \tag{5.49}$$

3. Repeat until a fixed number of iterations is reached, or until the change in the cross-entropy loss falls below a predefined threshold.

You will implement this algorithm in Python in Exercise 5.28.

5.8.3   Example: Classifying Handwritten Digits

The MNIST dataset [155] is a widely used benchmark in image classification, often regarded as the "Hello World" of machine learning due to its simplicity and accessibility. It has been used over the years to showcase the progress of machine learning—ranging from early linear models to deep convolutional neural networks.

The dataset contains 60,000 training images and 10,000 test images of handwritten digits. Each image is a 28×28 grayscale image, with pixel intensities ranging from 0 (black) to 255 (white). To make these images compatible with standard machine learning models, they are typically flattened into 784-dimensional vectors ($28 \times 28 = 784$). In this flattened form, each component x_j of the feature vector $\mathbf{x}$ corresponds to a single pixel.

The goal is to classify each image into one of 10 classes, representing the digits 0 to 9. This is a multi-class classification problem with mutually exclusive classes, making multinomial logistic regression a natural choice since it produces class probabilities that sum to 1.

Scikit-Learn's `LogisticRegression` class supports multi-class classification tasks through its `multi_class` parameter, which defaults to `'auto'`. In this mode, Scikit-Learn automatically selects the multi-class strategy: it uses multinomial logistic regression (`'multinomial'`) if the dataset has more than two classes and the chosen solver supports multinomial loss (all solvers except `'liblinear'`); otherwise, it falls back to the one-vs-rest strategy (`'ovr'`).

5.8.3.1 Loading and Exploring the Dataset

We begin by fetching the MNIST dataset using the `fetch_openml`[21] function:

```
from sklearn.datasets import fetch_openml

X, y = fetch_openml('mnist_784', return_X_y=True, as_frame=False)
```

The parameter `as_frame=False` ensures that the features and labels are returned as NumPy arrays rather than as Pandas objects.

Let's inspect the shape of the feature matrix:

```
print(X.shape)

(70000, 784)
```

The dataset contains 70,000 samples, each represented by a 784-dimensional feature vector corresponding to the 28×28 pixel grid of the images. Next, let's examine the distribution of the digit classes:

```
np.unique(y, return_counts=True)
```

The output shows that the classes are relatively balanced:

```
(array(['0', '1', '2', '3', '4', '5', '6', '7', '8', '9'], dtype=object),
 array([6903, 7877, 6990, 7141, 6824, 6313, 6876, 7293, 6825, 6958],
       dtype=int64))
```

To get a sense of what the digits look like, we can plot the first 50 images:

```
fig, axes = plt.subplots(5, 10, figsize=(10, 5))
for i, ax in enumerate(axes.flat):
    ax.imshow(X[i].reshape(28, 28), cmap='binary')
    ax.axis('off')
```

The resulting visualization is shown in Figure 5.20.

5.8.3.2 Data Preprocessing

Although all pixel values are in the range [0, 255], it is common practice to scale the pixel intensities to the range [0,1] when using gradient-based optimization methods such as gradient descent:

```
X = X / 255.0 # Scale features to [0, 1]
```

---

21. https://scikit-learn.org/stable/modules/generated/sklearn.datasets.fetch_openml.html

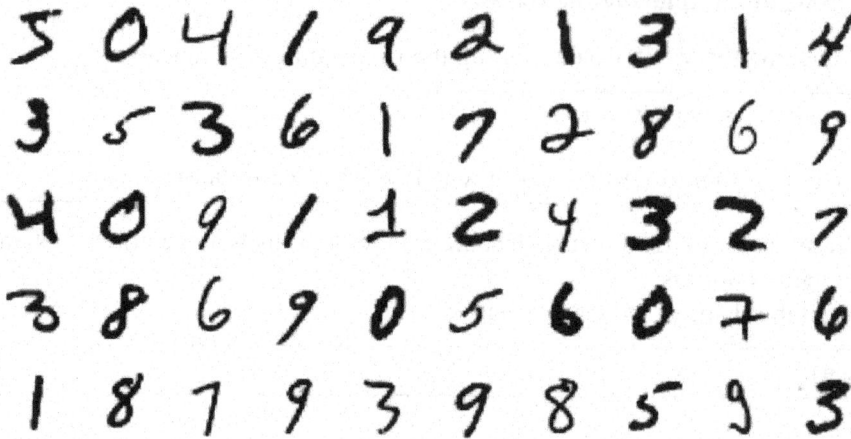

Figure 5.20: The first 50 handwritten digits from the MNIST dataset, arranged in a grid. Each digit is a 28×28 pixel image with pixel intensities ranging from 0 (black) to 255 (white). (Image: MNIST Dataset)

This scaling keeps the input values within a smaller range, which improves the numerical stability of the optimization and prevents the gradients of the softmax function from becoming extremely small (similar to the sigmoid, the softmax function saturates quickly as the input grows), leading to more effective learning.

Since the MNIST dataset consists of 60,000 training images followed by 10,000 test images, we can simply use array slicing to create the training and test sets:

```
train_size = 60000
X_train, y_train = X[:train_size], y[:train_size]
X_test, y_test = X[train_size:], y[train_size:]
```

5.8.3.3 Building the Model

We now instantiate a `LogisticRegression` classifier with default settings and fit it to the training set:

```
from sklearn.linear_model import LogisticRegression

clf = LogisticRegression(random_state=42)
clf.fit(X_train, y_train)
```

During training, you may see a warning indicating that the model did not converge within the default limit of 100 iterations:

```
ConvergenceWarning: lbfgs failed to converge (status=1):
STOP: TOTAL NO. of ITERATIONS REACHED LIMIT.
```

To resolve this, we can increase the maximum number of iterations to 1000:

```
clf = LogisticRegression(max_iter=1000, random_state=42)
clf.fit(X_train, y_train)
```

After increasing the iteration limit, the model converges successfully. To check how many iterations were actually used, we can inspect the n_iter_ attribute:

```
print(clf.n_iter_)
```

```
[265]
```

The output shows that it took 265 iterations for the solver to converge.

5.8.3.4   Evaluating the Model

Since the MNIST dataset is relatively balanced across classes, accuracy can provide a useful first assessment of model performance. We can compute it on both the training and test sets:

```
print(f'Train accuracy: {clf.score(X_train, y_train):.4f}')
print(f'Test accuracy: {clf.score(X_test, y_test):.4f}')
```

```
Train accuracy: 0.9388
Test accuracy: 0.9259
```

These results show that the model generalizes well, achieving good accuracy on both sets. However, more advanced models—particularly deep convolutional neural networks (CNNs)—perform significantly better on MNIST, achieving up to 99.8% accuracy on the test set [125, 269]. This performance gap is expected, as multinomial logistic regression is equivalent to a very shallow neural network with a single linear layer followed by a softmax output.

Although the MNIST class distribution is relatively balanced, additional evaluation metrics can provide deeper insights into the model's behavior and help identify where its errors occur.

A **classification report** summarizes key evaluation metrics for each class, including precision, recall, and F1 score, as well as macro- and weighted-average statistics across all classes. You can generate this report using Scikit-Learn's classification_report[22] function:

```
from sklearn.metrics import import classification_report

y_test_pred = clf.predict(X_test)
report = classification_report(y_test, y_test_pred, digits=4)
print(report)
```

---

22. https://scikit-learn.org/stable/modules/generated/sklearn.metrics.classification_report.html

This produces the following output:

```
          precision    recall  f1-score   support

       0     0.9532    0.9765    0.9647       980
       1     0.9619    0.9789    0.9703      1135
       2     0.9291    0.9012    0.9149      1032
       3     0.9038    0.9119    0.9078      1010
       4     0.9360    0.9389    0.9375       982
       5     0.8954    0.8733    0.8842       892
       6     0.9421    0.9509    0.9465       958
       7     0.9331    0.9232    0.9281      1028
       8     0.8850    0.8768    0.8809       974
       9     0.9095    0.9167    0.9131      1009

accuracy                         0.9259     10000
macro avg     0.9249    0.9248    0.9248     10000
weighted avg  0.9257    0.9259    0.9257     10000
```

The report shows for each class:

- **Precision**: The proportion of predictions for the class that are correct.

- **Recall**: The proportion of actual instances of the class that are correctly classified.

- **F1 score**: The harmonic mean of precision and recall.

- **Support**: The number of instances of the class in the dataset (in this case, the test set).

For example, the slightly lower precision and recall for digits 5 and 8 suggest that the model has more difficulty classifying these digits correctly.

In addition, the report includes two averaged metrics:

- **Macro average**: The unweighted average of the metric across all classes. This is useful for imbalanced datasets, as each class contributes equally to the average, ensuring that minority classes are not dominated by the majority classes.

- **Weighted average**: The average of the metric weighted by the number of instances in each class (its support). This reflects overall performance on the dataset but can obscure poor performance on minority classes.

Another useful metric for imbalanced datasets is the **micro average**, which aggregates the true positives, false positives, and false negatives across all classes and then computes the metric globally. For example, the micro-averaged precision is given by

$$\frac{\sum \text{TPs over all classes}}{\sum \text{TPs over all classes} + \sum \text{FPs over all classes}}.$$

Micro averaging reflects overall performance at the instance level, treating every prediction equally regardless of class. Like weighted averaging, it is influenced by the majority classes, as those classes naturally contribute more instances to the total count.

In Scikit-Learn, the averaging method can be specified in the `precision_score`, `recall_score`, and `f1_score` functions using the `average` parameter (for example, `average='micro'`):

```
from sklearn.metrics import precision_score, recall_score, f1_score

micro_precision = precision_score(y_test, y_test_pred, average='micro')
micro_recall = recall_score(y_test, y_test_pred, average='micro')
micro_f1 = f1_score(y_test, y_test_pred, average='micro')

print(f'Micro Precision: {micro_precision:.4f}')
print(f'Micro Recall: {micro_recall:.4f}')
print(f'Micro F1 Score: {micro_f1:.4f}')
```

```
Micro Precision: 0.9259
Micro Recall: 0.9259
Micro F1 Score: 0.9259
```

For single-label multi-class problems, both micro-precision and micro-recall are equal to the overall accuracy. This is because when aggregating over all classes, every false positive for one class is also a false negative for another, making $\sum \text{FP} = \sum \text{FN}$. In this example, the micro scores are very close to the macro and weighted averages shown in the classification report, as MNIST is fairly balanced and the model performs similarly across classes.

5.8.3.5 Error Analysis

To better understand where the model makes mistakes, we can examine the confusion matrix for the test set predictions:

```
from sklearn.metrics import confusion_matrix, ConfusionMatrixDisplay

cm = confusion_matrix(y_test, y_test_pred)
disp = ConfusionMatrixDisplay(confusion_matrix=cm)
disp.plot(cmap='Blues')
```

Figure 5.21 shows that most errors occur between digits with similar shapes, such as 5 vs. 3 and 2 vs. 8.

To explore specific errors, we can extract cases where the model predicted 3 instead of 5:

```
X_5conf3 = X_test[(y_test == '5') & (y_test_pred == '3')]

# Display these misclassified images in a grid
num_images = len(X_5conf3)
```

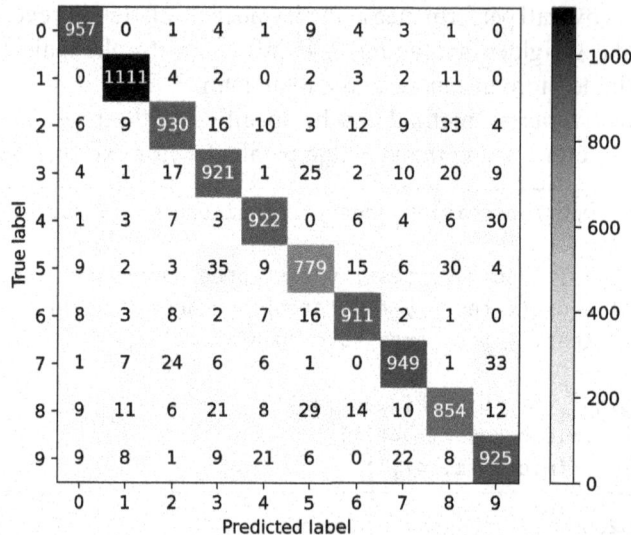

Figure 5.21: Confusion matrix for the MNIST test set predictions. Each entry shows how many instances of a given digit (true label) were predicted as another digit (predicted label). Most errors occur between visually similar digits, such as 3 vs. 5, and 5 vs. 8.

```
rows = 3
cols = (num_images + rows - 1) // rows

fig, axes = plt.subplots(rows, cols, figsize=(cols, rows))
axes = axes.flatten()
for i in range(num_images):
    axes[i].imshow(X_5conf3[i].reshape(28, 28), cmap='binary')
    axes[i].axis('off')

# Hide any unused subplots
for i in range(num_images, len(axes)):
    axes[i].axis('off')
```

Figure 5.22 presents the 35 examples of digit 5 that were misclassified as 3. It is evident that some of these handwritten 5s closely resemble a 3, explaining why the model struggled to distinguish them.

To improve the model's ability to distinguish between similar-looking digits, several strategies can be employed:

- **Data augmentation**: Expand the training set with additional examples of frequently confused digits, either by collecting new samples or by generating synthetic variations of existing images using operations such as rotation, scaling, or adding noise. Such augmentation helps the model learn subtle differences between similar digits, such as 5 and 3.

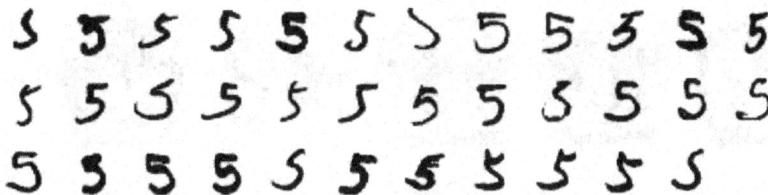

Figure 5.22: Examples of digit 5 from the MNIST test set that were misclassified as 3. Several of these errors appear to result from handwriting styles where the shape of 5 resembles that of a 3. (Image: MNIST Dataset)

- **Feature engineering**: Extract higher-level features from the raw pixel values, such as the number of loops in a digit or the presence of specific curves, to enhance the model's ability to distinguish challenging cases.

5.8.3.6 Model Interpretation

A key advantage of logistic regression over other classification models is its high interpretability: the weight assigned to each feature indicates its contribution to the classification decision.

For the MNIST dataset, we can visualize the learned weights assigned for each pixel in each digit class. This can help us identify which regions of the image contribute most to recognizing each digit.

The weight matrix of the trained model is stored in the `coef_` attribute, whose shape is (10, 784). Each row i corresponds to the weight vector $\mathbf{w}_i$ for class i. By reshaping each row into a 28×28 grid, we can visualize these weights as images:

```
fig, axes = plt.subplots(2, 5, figsize=(15, 5))

for i, ax in enumerate(axes.flat):
    # Reshape the i-th row of the weight matrix and plot it
    img = ax.imshow(clf.coef_[i].reshape(28, 28), cmap='gray', vmin=-0.5, vmax=0.5)
    ax.axis('off')
    ax.set_title(f'Digit {i}')

# Add a colorbar to show the weight scale
fig.colorbar(img, ax=axes.flat)
```

Figure 5.23 visualizes the weight patterns learned by the model. Lighter areas (positive weights) correspond to pixels that support the prediction of that digit, while darker areas (negative weights) correspond to pixels that inhibit the prediction. Pixels shaded in neutral gray (weights close to 0) have little influence on the prediction, often corresponding to background regions near the image borders.

These visualizations provide insight into how the model distinguishes between digits by highlighting the most informative areas of each image. Such understanding can guide future improvements, for example, by augmenting images in those regions or by extracting features from those specific areas.

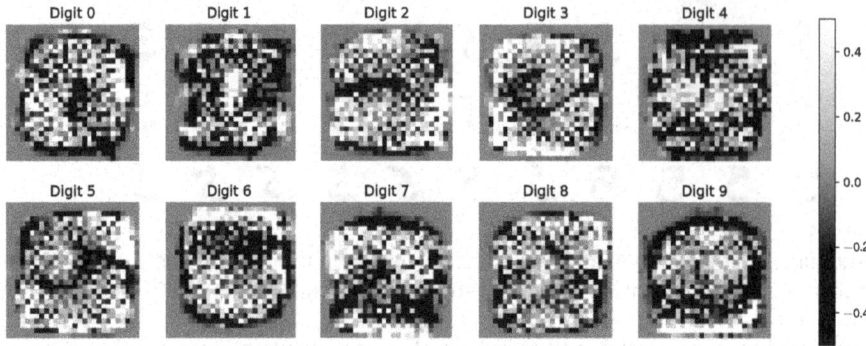

Figure 5.23: Visualization of the weight vectors for each digit class in the multinomial logistic regression model trained on MNIST. Lighter regions represent positive weights that support the prediction of that digit, darker regions represent negative weights that suppress it, and neutral gray regions indicate weights close to zero with minimal impact on the prediction. Notably, the pattern of white pixels in each image roughly outlines the central shape of the digit. (Image: MNIST Dataset)

5.9   (*) Generalized Linear Models

Up to this point, we have studied two important models: linear regression, where the target variable is assumed to follow a normal distribution with a mean equal to a linear combination of the input features; and logistic regression, where the target variable is assumed to follow a Bernoulli distribution whose mean is given by applying the sigmoid function to a linear combination of the features. These models, while seemingly different, share the same underlying structure and are, in fact, special cases of a broader family of models known as **generalized linear models (GLMs)** [440, 167].

Generalized linear models extend the familiar structure of linear models to handle a wide variety of response variable types within a unified framework. They preserve the idea of combining the input features linearly but generalize how the mean of the response variable relates to this linear predictor and allow the response to follow various probability distributions. This allows GLMs to handle binary, count, categorical, and other types of data, while retaining the advantages of linear models, such as computational efficiency and interpretability.

A generalized linear model consists of two main components:

1. **Link function**: This function connects the linear predictor (a linear combination of the input features) to the mean of the response variable y. Formally, a link function g maps the expected value of y, denoted by $\mu = \mathbb{E}[y]$, to the linear predictor η:

$$\eta = g(\mu) = \mathbf{w}^T \mathbf{x}. \qquad (5.50)$$

For example, in logistic regression, the link function is the *logit function*, which maps the probability of the positive class $p = P(y = 1)$ (the mean of the Bernoulli-distributed response variable) to the log-odds, expressed as a linear combination of the features:

$$g(p) = \log\left(\frac{p}{1-p}\right) = \mathbf{w}^T\mathbf{x} = \eta.$$

The **inverse link function** $h = g^{-1}$ maps the linear predictor back to the mean response: $\mu = h(\eta)$. In logistic regression, the inverse link is the *sigmoid function*, which maps η to a probability:

$$h(\eta) = \frac{1}{1 + e^{-\eta}}.$$

2. **Exponential family distributions**: In a generalized linear model, the response variable is assumed to follow a distribution from the **exponential family** (not to be confused with the exponential distribution). This family includes many common distributions such as Bernoulli, Poisson, Gaussian, Gamma, and others, allowing GLMs to model a wide range of data types.

The general form of a probability distribution in the exponential family is

$$p(y|\theta, \phi) = \exp\left(\frac{y\theta - b(\theta)}{a(\phi)} + c(y, \phi)\right), \tag{5.51}$$

where θ is the natural parameter of the distribution (which in general is not the same as the mean), ϕ is the dispersion (or scale) parameter (e.g., the standard deviation in a normal distribution), and $a(\phi)$, $b(\theta)$, and $c(y, \phi)$ are known functions that define the specific distribution.

For example, consider the Bernoulli distribution used in logistic regression. Its probability mass function is:

$$p(y|\eta) = p^y(1-p)^{1-y},$$

where p is the probability of $y = 1$. In logistic regression, this probability is modeled using the sigmoid function:

$$p = \frac{1}{1 + e^{-\eta}} = \frac{e^\eta}{1 + e^\eta}, \quad 1 - p = \frac{1}{1 + e^\eta},$$

where $\eta = \mathbf{w}^T\mathbf{x}$ is the linear predictor. Substituting these expressions into the PMF gives

$$p(y|\eta) = \left(\frac{e^\eta}{1 + e^\eta}\right)^y \left(\frac{1}{1 + e^\eta}\right)^{1-y} = \frac{e^{y\eta}}{1 + e^\eta}.$$

This can be written in exponential-family form as

$$p(y|\eta) = \exp\left(y\eta - \log(1 + e^\eta)\right).$$

Here, $\theta = \eta$, $b(\theta) = \log(1 + e^\eta)$, $a(\phi) = 1$, and $c(y, \phi) = 0$.

This derivation shows that the Bernoulli distribution belongs to the exponential family when parameterized by the log-odds (the natural parameter).

An important consequence of this formulation is that the maximum likelihood estimation (MLE) procedure for GLMs has a unified structure. Given a dataset $\{(\mathbf{x}_i, y_i)\}_{i=1}^{n}$, the log-likelihood under a GLM is

$$\ell(\mathbf{w}) = \sum_{i=1}^{n} \left[\frac{y_i\theta_i - b(\theta_i)}{a(\phi)} + c(y_i, \phi) \right]. \tag{5.52}$$

When the link function is chosen such that the linear predictor equals the natural parameter, $\theta = \eta$, it is called the **canonical link**. This is the default choice in most GLMs, as it leads to simpler expressions. For example, the logit link is canonical for a Bernoulli response, and the identity link is canonical for a normal response.

With a canonical link, the log-likelihood (5.52) simplifies to

$$\ell(\mathbf{w}) = \sum_{i=1}^{n} [y_i\eta_i - b(\eta_i)], \tag{5.53}$$

and its gradient with respect to $\mathbf{w}$ takes the particularly simple form:

$$\frac{\partial \ell}{\partial \mathbf{w}} = \sum_{i=1}^{n} (y_i - \mu_i)\, \mathbf{x}_i, \tag{5.54}$$

where $\mu_i = h(\eta_i)$ is the predicted mean response. Comparing this result with Equations (4.27) and (5.16) shows that the gradients for both linear and logistic regression are special cases of this general GLM gradient.

In Scikit-Learn, a subset of generalized linear models known as Tweedie distributions [589] is implemented by the `TweedieRegressor`[23] class. Key parameters of the class include:

- **power**: Specifies the distribution of the response variable. For example, `power=0` corresponds to a normal distribution, `power=1` to a Poisson distribution, and `power=2` to a gamma distribution.

- **link**: Specifies the link function of the GLM. By default, it is set to `'auto'`, which selects the canonical link corresponding to the chosen `power` parameter (for example, `'identity'` for the normal distribution, and `'log'` for Poisson).

The following example demonstrates how to use `TweedieRegressor` to model sample data that follow a Poisson distribution, such as the number of bike rentals occurring in a fixed time interval given the average temperature:

```
from sklearn.linear_model import TweedieRegressor

X = [[5], [10], [15], [18], [20], [25]] # Daily average temperature (Celsius)
y = [50, 80, 130, 180, 220, 300] # Number of bike rentals
```

23. https://scikit-learn.org/stable/modules/generated/sklearn.linear_model.TweedieRegressor.html

```
reg = TweedieRegressor(power=1, link='log') # power=1 for Poisson
reg.fit(X, y)
print(f'R2 score: {reg.score(X, y):.4f}')
```

R2 score: 0.9884

Here, X contains the predictor values (daily average temperatures) and y is the response (the number of bike rentals for each day). Since we are modeling count data, we assume that each y_i follows a Poisson distribution with rate parameter λ_i, which represents the expected number of rentals on day i. The model relates this rate parameter to the input features via the log link function: $\log \lambda_i = \mathbf{w}^T \mathbf{x}_i$, which implies that $\mathbb{E}[y_i] = \lambda_i = \exp(\mathbf{w}^T \mathbf{x}_i)$. This formulation ensures that the predicted rate λ_i is always positive, while preserving the interpretability of a linear model on the log scale.

5.10 Summary

In this chapter, we explored logistic regression, a foundational method for modeling binary outcomes from a set of input features. By applying the logistic (sigmoid) function to a linear combination of the features, the model produces probabilistic predictions that are easy to interpret. Its simplicity and computational efficiency make logistic regression a strong baseline for many classification problems, particularly when the decision boundary is approximately linear.

We have also discussed extensions of logistic regression to multi-class problems and various strategies for handling imbalanced datasets, including sampling techniques and cost-sensitive learning.

Advantages of logistic regression compared to other classification models:

- It efficiently finds a separating hyperplane when the classes are (approximately) linearly separable.

- It scales well to large datasets, as the number of parameters grows linearly with the number of features.

- It has a convex optimization objective, allowing gradient-based methods to converge efficiently to the global optimum.

- It is typically resistant to overfitting, especially when regularization techniques like L1 or L2 are applied.

- It produces probability estimates rather than only class labels.

- It is highly interpretable, with feature coefficients indicating the influence of each feature on the prediction.

- It requires only a few hyperparameters, making it relatively easy to tune.

Disadvantages of logistic regression:

- It can only represent linear decision boundaries, which may lead to underfitting when the relationship between the features and the target is nonlinear.

- It relies on the assumption of a linear relationship between the predictors and the log-odds of the positive class, which may not hold in real-world data.

- It is often outperformed by more flexible models (e.g., decision trees, neural networks) on data with nonlinear patterns or complex interactions.

- It is sensitive to outliers, which can disproportionately affect the decision boundary.

- High multicollinearity among predictors can hurt the model's effectiveness and interpretability.

- It requires feature scaling for efficient convergence of gradient-based optimization.

- It does not inherently handle missing data; imputation or exclusion of incomplete samples is necessary.

5.11   Exercises

5.11.1   Multiple-Choice Questions

5.1. Which of the following statements is true about logistic regression?

   (a) Logistic regression models the odds ratio as a linear combination of the input features.
   (b) Logistic regression minimizes the cross-entropy loss function.
   (c) Logistic regression has a closed-form analytical solution.
   (d) Logistic regression assumes that the class labels are sampled from a binomial distribution.
   (e) Logistic regression is highly susceptible to multicollinearity among features.

5.2. If a logistic regression classifier predicts a probability of 0.75 for the positive class, what is the corresponding logit value?

   (a) 0.75

   (b) $\dfrac{0.75}{0.25}$

   (c) $\log\left(\dfrac{0.75}{0.25}\right)$

   (d) $\dfrac{1}{1 + e^{-0.75}}$

5.3. You have built a logistic regression model to predict whether a financial transaction is fraudulent ($y = 1$) or legitimate ($y = 0$). The model includes two features: the amount of the transaction (x_1) and the number of transactions made by the user in the last 24 hours (x_2). The coefficients of the logistic regression model are: $w_0 = -3$ (bias), $w_1 = 0.01$, and $w_2 = 0.5$. Which of the following transactions has the highest predicted probability of being fraudulent?

   (a) A transaction of $100 with 2 transactions in the last 24 hours

   (b) A transaction of $200 with 1 transaction in the last 24 hours

   (c) A transaction of $80 with 3 transactions in the last 24 hours

   (d) A transaction of $50 with 4 transactions in the last 24 hours

5.4. You are developing a logistic regression model to classify data into two categories. The training set consists of three one-dimensional points:

   - $x_1 = 3$ with label $y_1 = 1$
   - $x_2 = 1$ with label $y_2 = 1$
   - $x_3 = -1$ with label $y_3 = 0$

   Which of the following are possible values for b (bias) and w (coefficient of x) in the logistic regression model?

   (a) $w = 1, b = 2$
   (b) $w = 0, b = 1$
   (c) $w = -1, b = -2$
   (d) $w = 2, b = 1$

5.5. Which of the following are advantages of Newton's method over gradient descent?

   (a) It converges faster on non-convex functions.

   (b) It has a lower computational cost per iteration.

   (c) It has a faster convergence rate near the optimal solution.

   (d) It is more stable when working with high-dimensional data.

   (e) It automatically adjusts the learning rate at each iteration based on the curvature of the function.

5.6. You have trained a logistic regression model but observed very low accuracy on the training set. Which of the following could be possible reasons for this?

   (a) The number of iterations in gradient descent was too small.

   (b) The number of iterations in gradient descent was too large.

(c) The learning rate in gradient descent was too high.

(d) The learning rate in gradient descent was too low.

(e) The regularization parameter λ was too high.

(f) The features were not scaled properly.

5.7. You are evaluating a spam filter designed to classify emails as either spam ($y = 1$) or ham ($y = 0$). After testing your model on a dataset, you obtain the following confusion matrix values:

- True Positives (TP): 85
- False Positives (FP): 45
- True Negatives (TN): 100
- False Negatives (FN): 15

What is the F1 score of the model?

(a) 0.68

(b) 0.71

(c) 0.74

(d) 0.77

5.8. Which of the following statements about the ROC curve is true?

(a) The ROC curve is a monotonically non-decreasing function.

(b) The ROC curve illustrates the tradeoff between recall and false positive rate at various thresholds.

(c) If the ROC curve passes through the point (1, 1), the model correctly classifies all the positives.

(d) An area under the ROC curve (AUC) of 0.5 suggests that the model's predictions are random.

(e) The ROC curve is sensitive to changes in the class distribution.

5.9. What are the drawbacks of using SMOTE for imbalanced datasets?

(a) The synthetic samples generated by SMOTE might overlap with the majority class, leading to increased misclassification.

(b) SMOTE assumes that synthetic instances created between two minority class instances are always representative of the minority class.

(c) SMOTE can introduce noise into the majority class data.

(d) SMOTE can cause overfitting by making the decision regions for the minority class become overly specific.

(e) SMOTE can cause the model to rely too much on interpolated data, which might affect the generalization ability.

5.10. After training a multinomial logistic regression model on a dataset with four classes, you obtain the following class scores (logits) for a test sample: $[2, 1, -1, 0]$. What is the probability that this sample belongs to the second class?

    (a) 0.2447

    (b) 0.2369

    (c) 0.5761

    (d) 0.1223

5.11.2 Theoretical Exercises

5.11. Consider a logistic regression model developed to predict the likelihood of patients having diabetes based on two health indicators: body mass index (BMI) and age. The model's estimated coefficients are as follows:

- Intercept (w_0): -1.0
- Coefficient for BMI (w_1): 0.05
- Coefficient for age (w_2): 0.03

Calculate the probability that a patient with BMI 35 and age 50 has diabetes according to this model. Show your calculations.

5.12. Consider the dataset shown in Table 5.6, where x is a predictor variable and y is a binary outcome variable.

x	y
1	0
2	0
10	1

Table 5.6: Sample dataset used for logistic regression analysis

    (a) Write the log-likelihood function for the logistic regression model based on the given dataset.

    (b) Provide an expression for the gradient of the log-likelihood function with respect to the coefficients w_0 and w_1.

(c) Perform three iterations of batch gradient descent by hand with a learning rate of $\alpha = 0.5$ to estimate the coefficients w_0 and w_1. Begin with $w_0 = 0$ and $w_1 = 0$, and show all intermediate calculations for each step.

(d) Based on the final estimated coefficients, what are the predicted probabilities for each sample in the dataset?

5.13. Prove the following properties of the sigmoid function $\sigma(z) = \dfrac{1}{1 + e^{-z}}$:

(a) $\sigma(-z) = 1 - \sigma(z)$.

(b) $\sigma'(z) = \sigma(z)(1 - \sigma(z))$.

5.14. The goal of this exercise is to analyze the gradient-based optimization process of logistic regression and interpret the influence of each model component on the update steps and the resulting decision boundary.

(a) Show how the binary logistic regression model can be written in terms of the conditional probability distribution as follows:

$$p(y|\mathbf{x}; \mathbf{w}) = \sigma\left((-1)^{y+1} f(\mathbf{x}; \mathbf{w})\right),$$

where σ is the sigmoid function and $f(\mathbf{x}; \mathbf{w}) = \mathbf{w}^T \mathbf{x}$ is the linear predictor.

(b) Consider the gradient descent algorithm, which seeks to find the maximum likelihood estimation (MLE) solution for logistic regression. Show how to write the update step of the algorithm in the following form:

$$\mathbf{w}^{(t+1)} = \mathbf{w}^{(t)} - \alpha \sum_{i=1}^{n} \left(1 - p(y_i|\mathbf{x}_i; \mathbf{w}^{(t)})\right)(-1)^{y_i} \nabla_{\mathbf{w}} f(\mathbf{x}_i; \mathbf{w}^{(t)}).$$

(c) Try to give an intuitive interpretation of the role of the different variables in the previous update step. Start by ignoring the term $(1 - p(y_i|\mathbf{x}_i; \mathbf{w}^{(t)}))$, and obtain the following simplified update step:

$$\mathbf{w}^{(t+1)} = \mathbf{w}^{(t)} - \alpha \sum_{i=1}^{n} (-1)^{y_i} \nabla_{\mathbf{w}} f(\mathbf{x}_i; \mathbf{w}^{(t)}).$$

Explain how each update step affects the function $f(\mathbf{x}; \mathbf{w})$. Specifically, explain how the value of the function is updated at points $\mathbf{x}_i$, and how it changes depending on whether $y_i = 1$ or $y_i = 0$.

(d) Consider the term $\left(1 - p(y_i|\mathbf{x}_i; \mathbf{w}^{(t)})\right)$ once again. What does this term represent when the model assigns a high probability versus a low probability to a specific sample $(\mathbf{x}_i, y_i)$?

Now, treat this term as a weighting factor that assigns different weights to each example. How does this weighting scheme affect the updates in each step of the gradient descent?

5.15. In this exercise, you will derive the Hessian of the logistic regression cost function, analyze its properties, and formulate the Newton update step.

(a) Starting from the gradient of the logistic regression cost function (Equation (5.16)), derive the Hessian of the cost function with respect to $\mathbf{w}$. Show that the Hessian matrix has the form:

$$H(\mathbf{w}) = \frac{1}{n} X^T R X,$$

where $X \in \mathbb{R}^{n \times d}$ is the design matrix, and $R \in \mathbb{R}^{n \times n}$ is a diagonal matrix with entries $r_i = \sigma(\mathbf{w}^T \mathbf{x}_i)(1 - \sigma(\mathbf{w}^T \mathbf{x}_i))$.

(b) Prove that the logistic regression cost function is convex by showing that the Hessian matrix is positive semidefinite.

(c) Discuss the conditions under which the Hessian $H(\mathbf{w}) = X^T R X$ is invertible. What properties of the data matrix X and the predicted probabilities $\mathbf{p}$ ensure invertibility?

(d) Use your result to derive the Newton update step:

$$\mathbf{w} \leftarrow \mathbf{w} - (X^T R X)^{-1} X^T (\mathbf{p} - \mathbf{y}).$$

5.16. In this exercise we will explore the impact of different regularization strategies on the training error of a logistic regression model. Figure 5.24 shows a two-dimensional training set, where '+' corresponds to class $y = 1$ and 'x' to class $y = 0$. The dataset is linearly separable.

The logistic regression model used for this classification task is:

$$P(y = 1 | \mathbf{x}; \mathbf{w}) = \sigma(w_0 + w_1 x_1 + w_2 x_2) = \frac{1}{1 + \exp(-w_0 - w_1 x_1 - w_2 x_2)}.$$

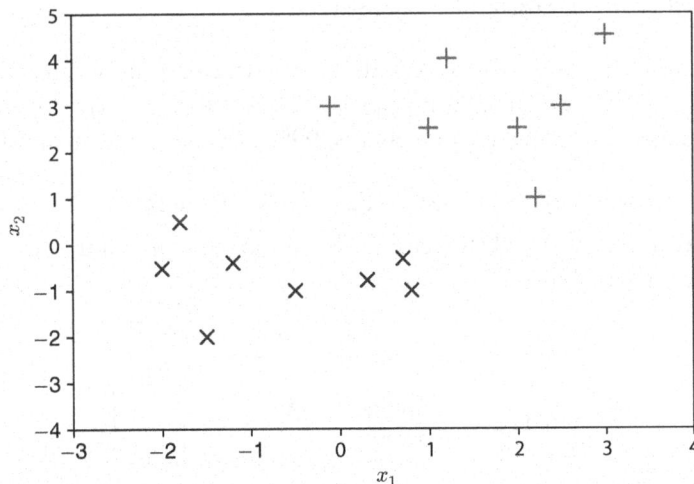

Figure 5.24: Two-dimensional labeled training set, where '+' corresponds to class $y = 1$ and 'x' corresponds to class $y = 0$.

(a) Consider a regularized logistic regression model that maximizes the following penalized log-likelihood:

$$\sum_{i=1}^{n} \log(P(y_i|\mathbf{x}_i; w_0, w_1, w_2)) - \lambda w_j^2,$$

where λ is very large and regularization is applied separately to one parameter w_j at a time (for $j = 0, 1, 2$). For each of the following cases, analyze how the training error is affected. Would you expect the error to increase, decrease, or stay the same? Justify your answer.

   i. Regularizing w_2

   ii. Regularizing w_1

   iii. Regularizing w_0 (the bias term)

(b) Now consider an L1-norm penalty applied to w_1 and w_2 (but not w_0). The penalized log-likelihood is given by:

$$\sum_{i=1}^{n} \log(P(y_i|\mathbf{x}_i; w_0, w_1, w_2)) - \lambda(|w_1| + |w_2|).$$

   i. As λ increases, which coefficient will reach zero first: w_1, w_2, or will they reach zero at the same time?

   ii. For very large λ, what value might you expect w_0 to take? (Note that both classes have the same number of data points.)

   iii. For very large λ, what range of values might you expect w_0 to take if the class labels become unbalanced (e.g., more '+' instances)? Explain how the class imbalance might affect this outcome.

5.17. Suppose that you are working on a spam detection system. You formulated the problem as a classification task where "Spam" is the positive class and "Ham" (non-spam) is the negative class. Your training set contains 1000 emails, 99% of these are Ham and 1% are Spam.

(a) What is the accuracy of a classifier that always predicts Ham?

(b) Suppose you trained a classifier on this training set, and you obtained the confusion matrix shown in Table 5.7.

		Predicted class	
		Spam	Ham
Actual class	Spam	8	2
	Ham	16	974

Table 5.7: Confusion matrix for a spam detection system

What are the accuracy, precision, recall, and F1 score of the classifier?

5.18. Consider a binary classification problem where the positive class constitutes $\alpha\%$ of the dataset, and a classifier that predicts randomly with probability β that a sample belongs to the positive class. What is the expected precision and recall of such a classifier?

5.19. Does increasing recall always lead to a decrease in precision? If true, provide a mathematical proof. If not, provide a counterexample.

5.20. Consider a binary classification problem with an imbalanced dataset, where the positive class is the minority. Suppose you apply the Synthetic Minority Over-sampling Technique (SMOTE) to balance the dataset.

   (a) Prove that SMOTE does not change the decision boundary of a classifier whose predictions depend only on a linear combination of the features and are invariant to linear transformations (e.g., logistic regression). For simplicity, assume that SMOTE generates synthetic points using a single interpolation factor $\lambda \in [0, 1]$ across all dimensions.

   (b) Compare this to cost-sensitive learning, where the classifier's loss function is modified using a cost matrix. Derive the new decision boundary for a linear classifier when under cost-sensitive learning, assuming different misclassification costs for the minority and majority classes. Show that the decision boundary in cost-sensitive learning is not invariant to linear scaling of the input data.

5.21. Prove that the softmax function used in multinomial logistic regression reduces to the sigmoid function when there are only two classes. In addition, show that the cross-entropy loss in this case reduces to the log loss used in binary logistic regression.

5.22. You are given a dataset of images and you need to classify them along two dimensions: dogs vs. cats and indoor vs. outdoor. Should you implement two separate logistic regression classifiers or a single multinomial logistic regression classifier? Justify your answer.

5.23. (*) Show that ordinary least squares (OLS) linear regression is a special case of a generalized linear model (GLM) with a normal distribution and the identity link function.

5.11.3 Programming Exercises

5.24. In this exercise, you will use the Pima Indians Diabetes dataset[24] to train and evaluate a logistic regression model. This dataset includes diagnostic measurements from a large sample of individuals of Pima Indian heritage. The goal is to predict whether the patient shows signs of diabetes based on several predictor variables such as the number of pregnancies the patient has had, BMI, age, insulin level, and other clinical features.

---

24. https://www.openml.org/search?type=data&sort=runs&id=37&status=active

(a) Load the dataset using the `fetch_openml` function:

```
from sklearn.datasets import fetch_openml
X, y = fetch_openml('diabetes', version=1, return_X_y=True, as_frame=True)
```

(b) Exploratory data analysis (EDA):
  i. Conduct an initial analysis to understand the structure of the data (e.g., examine the types of features, check for missing values, etc.).
  ii. Visualize the feature distributions and correlations.
  iii. What is the class distribution of the target variable?

(c) Data preprocessing:
  i. Scale the continuous features appropriately (e.g., using standard scaling) to prepare the data for logistic regression.
  ii. Split the dataset into training and test sets (e.g., 80–20 split).

(d) Model training:
  i. Train a logistic regression model with default settings on the training data.
  ii. How many iterations were needed for the optimization algorithm to converge?

(e) Model evaluation:
  i. Evaluate the model using several metrics: accuracy, precision, recall, F1 score, and the area under the ROC curve (AUC).
  ii. Plot the ROC curve for the model.

(f) Hyperparameter tuning:
  i. Use grid search with cross-validation to find the optimal settings for the hyperparameters, such as the regularization coefficient C and the solver used.
  ii. Evaluate the performance of the model with the optimized parameters on the test set and compare it to the performance of the initial model.

(g) Write a short report summarizing your findings.

5.25. Implement Newton's method for unconstrained optimization and apply it to logistic regression.

(a) Write a Python function that implements Newton's method for minimizing a scalar-valued function $f: \mathbb{R}^n \to \mathbb{R}$ that is twice-differentiable. Your function should take the following inputs:
  - A function $f(\mathbf{x})$ that returns the value of the objective function at a given point $\mathbf{x}$.
  - A function $\nabla f(\mathbf{x})$ that returns the gradient vector at a given point $\mathbf{x}$.
  - A function $H(\mathbf{x})$ that returns the Hessian matrix at a given point $\mathbf{x}$.
  - An initial guess $\mathbf{x}_0$.
  - A tolerance value for convergence.
  - A maximum number of iterations.

(b) Use the following Newton update rule:

$$\mathbf{x}_{n+1} = \mathbf{x}_n - H(\mathbf{x}_n)^{-1} \nabla f(\mathbf{x}_n).$$

Terminate the iterations when either the change in $\mathbf{x}$ or the norm of the gradient is smaller than the given tolerance.

(c) Test your implementation by minimizing a simple convex function such as:

$$f(\mathbf{x}) = (x_1 - 1)^2 + 2(x_2 + 2)^2.$$

Verify that your implementation converges to the global minimum.

(d) Now, apply your Newton optimizer to train a logistic regression model on a binary classification dataset (e.g., the Iris dataset with two classes or a synthetic dataset). Use the log loss as the objective function and compute its gradient and Hessian analytically (see Exercise 5.15).

(e) Compare your implementation with Scikit-Learn's `LogisticRegression(solver='newton-cg')`. Report differences in convergence speed, objective value, and classification accuracy.

(f) Discuss the advantages and limitations of using Newton's method for logistic regression. In which situations might gradient descent or quasi-Newton methods be preferable?

5.26. Implement the algorithm for building an ROC curve for a binary classifier (Algorithm 5.1). Use the following steps:

(a) Write a function that takes the true labels (`y_true`) and predicted probabilities (`y_scores`) from a binary classifier and returns the true positive rates (TPR) and false positive rates (FPR) at all possible classification thresholds.

(b) Write another function that uses these rates to plot the ROC curve using Matplotlib.

(c) Write a function that calculates the Area Under the Curve (AUC) by approximating the integral using the trapezoidal rule. Specifically, if (x_i, y_i) and (x_{i+1}, y_{i+1}) are two consecutive points on the ROC curve, the area of the trapezoid between these points is given by:

$$\text{Area} = \frac{1}{2}(y_{i+1} + y_i) \cdot (x_{i+1} - x_i)$$

Summing the areas of all trapezoids yields the AUC.

(d) Train a binary logistic regression model using the Pima Indians Diabetes dataset (or another binary dataset of your choice).

(e) Use your functions to plot the ROC curve and calculate the AUC score.

(f) Compare the AUC score obtained from your implementation with Scikit-learn's built-in `roc_auc_score` function to ensure correctness.

5.27. In this exercise, you will explore the effectiveness of various imbalanced learning techniques on the Bank Marketing Dataset[25], which contains data from phone calls made by a Portuguese banking institution. The goal is to predict whether clients will subscribe to a term deposit.

    (a) Dataset preparation:

        i. Download the `bank.zip` file from the UCI Machine Learning Repository at this link[26].

        ii. Extract the file `bank.csv` from the downloaded zip file.

        iii. Load it into your notebook using the `pd.read_csv` function as follows:

```
import pandas as pd
df = pd.read_csv('bank.csv', delimiter=';')
```

        iv. Conduct a preliminary data analysis to explore the dataset and assess the degree of class imbalance.

        v. Preprocess the data (e.g., handle missing values, scale continuous features, and encode categorical variables as necessary).

    (b) Initial model training:

        i. Train a logistic regression model using the original, imbalanced dataset.

        ii. Evaluate the model on the test set using metrics such as accuracy, precision, recall, F1 score, and AUC. Additionally, plot both the precision–recall curve and the ROC curve for the test set.

        iii. Optionally, evaluate the model on the training set to check for potential overfitting.

    (c) Class balancing with SMOTE:

        i. Apply SMOTE (Synthetic Minority Over-sampling Technique) to generate synthetic samples and balance the class distribution.

        ii. Visualize the class distribution before and after applying SMOTE (e.g., using a bar plot of class counts).

        iii. Retrain the logistic regression model on the balanced dataset.

        iv. Evaluate the new model on the test set using the same metrics (accuracy, precision, recall, F1 score, and AUC) and compare the results with the original imbalanced model.

        v. Optionally, evaluate the new model on the training set to monitor for overfitting after SMOTE.

    (d) Cost-sensitive learning:

        i. Modify the logistic regression model to handle the imbalance using cost-sensitive learning by adjusting the `class_weight` parameter in Scikit-Learn.

---

25. https://archive.ics.uci.edu/dataset/222/bank+marketing
26. https://archive.ics.uci.edu/ml/machine-learning-databases/00222/bank.zip

    ii. Train the cost-sensitive logistic regression model on the original imbalanced dataset.

    iii. Evaluate this model on the test set using the same metrics and compare the results with both the SMOTE-enhanced model and the baseline.

    iv. Optionally, evaluate the model on the training set to detect potential overfitting or underfitting.

(e) Bonus (other sampling techniques):

- Experiment with other oversampling techniques, such as Borderline SMOTE or ADASYN, using the `imbalanced-learn` package.
- Experiment with under-sampling techniques or combinations of over-sampling and under-sampling.
- Compare the results with SMOTE and cost-sensitive learning to determine the most effective technique for this dataset.

(f) Write a short report summarizing your findings. Your report should include:

    i. A brief description of each class-balancing technique you applied.

    ii. A comparison of model performance across techniques using evaluation metrics (e.g., accuracy, precision, recall, F1 score, and AUC).

    iii. Plots of the ROC and precision–recall curves, with commentary on what they reveal about model behavior.

    iv. A discussion of which technique(s) performed best and under what conditions.

    v. A discussion of how each technique affected the precision–recall tradeoff, and the implications for model selection.

5.28. Implement multinomial logistic regression in Python from scratch using the following steps:

(a) Define the softmax function, which converts raw logits (class scores) into probabilities.

(b) Implement the cross-entropy loss function to measure the difference between the predicted probabilities and the true labels.

(c) Compute the gradient of the loss function with respect to the model parameters.

(d) Implement gradient descent (either batch or stochastic) to optimize the model parameters.

(e) Train the model on the MNIST dataset and plot both the cross-entropy loss and accuracy on the validation set during the learning process.

(f) Evaluate the model's performance on the test set.

(g) Compare the performance of your implementation with Scikit-Learn's multinomial logistic regression implementation (using `LogisticRegression` with `multi_class='multinomial'`).

5.29. Compare three different strategies for multi-class classification using logistic regression: one-vs-rest, one-vs-one, and multinomial logistic regression using the Wine Quality dataset[27]. The target variable in the dataset represents wine quality on a scale from 3 to 8. Use the following steps:

(a) Load the dataset using the `fetch_openml` function:

```
from sklearn.datasets import fetch_openml
X, y = fetch_openml('wine-quality-red', return_X_y=True, as_frame=True)
```

(b) Conduct exploratory data analysis (EDA) to understand the distribution of features and classes.

(c) Split the dataset into training and test sets (e.g., 80–20 split).

(d) Standardize the continuous features for better performance in logistic regression.

(e) Train three different logistic regression models:

- One-vs-rest (OvR) logistic regression.
- One-vs-one (OvO) logistic regression.
- Multinomial logistic regression.

Record the training time for each model.

(f) Evaluate each model's performance on the test set using accuracy. Record the prediction times for each model.

(g) Use Matplotlib to create comparative charts showing:

  i. Training times for the three models.
  ii. Prediction times for the three models.
  iii. Accuracies of the three models on the test set.

(h) Analyze the results:

  i. Which model had the fastest training and prediction times?
  ii. Which model achieved the highest test accuracy?
  iii. Discuss the tradeoffs between model complexity, speed, and predictive performance.

5.30. In this exercise, you will explore different techniques for handling class imbalance in a multi-class setting using the Wine Quality dataset.

(a) Load the dataset using the `fetch_openml` function (see previous exercise).

(b) Conduct exploratory data analysis (EDA) to visualize the class distribution. What do you observe about the class imbalance?

(c) Baseline model:

27. https://www.openml.org/search?type=data&sort=runs&id=287&status=active

      i. Train a multinomial logistic regression model using the original imbalanced dataset.

      ii. Evaluate the performance using precision, recall, F1 score, and AUC. Pay particular attention to the precision and recall for the minority classes.

(d) SMOTE (Synthetic Minority Over-sampling Technique):

      i. Apply SMOTE to the training data to generate synthetic samples for the minority classes. Experiment with different resampling ratios.

      ii. Train a multinomial logistic regression model on the balanced dataset.

      iii. Evaluate the model using the same metrics as before. Compare the performance of the SMOTE-enhanced model with the baseline.

(e) Cost-sensitive learning:

      i. Implement a cost-sensitive logistic regression model by adjusting the class weights (using the `class_weight` parameter).

      ii. Train the cost-sensitive model on the original imbalanced dataset.

      iii. Evaluate the model using the same metrics as before. Compare the performance of the cost-sensitive model with the baseline and SMOTE-enhanced models.

(f) Bonus (other SMOTE variations):

- Experiment with other variations of SMOTE, such as Borderline SMOTE or SMOTE-ENN, using the `imbalanced-learn` package.
- Try under-sampling techniques or combining over-sampling and under-sampling.
- Compare the results with SMOTE and cost-sensitive learning.

(g) Analysis:

- Analyze how each technique affected the performance of the model on the minority classes.
- Which technique gave the best tradeoff between precision and recall for the minority classes?
- Discuss the overall impact of handling class imbalance on the model's generalization and usefulness in a real-world scenario.

5.31. In this exercise, you will explore how variations in the parameters of softmax regression affect the decision boundaries between the classes in a multi-class setting. Consider a softmax regression model used for classifying data points into three classes (0, 1, 2). The class scores (logits) are computed as:

$$z_0 = w_{0,0} + w_{0,1}x_1 + w_{0,2}x_2,$$
$$z_1 = w_{1,0} + w_{1,1}x_1 + w_{1,2}x_2,$$
$$z_2 = w_{2,0} + w_{2,1}x_1 + w_{2,2}x_2.$$

The softmax function is then applied to (z_0, z_1, z_2) to obtain the predicted class probabilities. Assume a fixed initial weight matrix $w_{i,j}$ (e.g., small random values), and use this initialization consistently throughout the exercise.

(a) Single parameter variation:

    i. Choose one parameter from each score function (e.g., $w_{0,1}$, $w_{1,2}$, $w_{2,0}$). Systematically increase and decrease its value while keeping the other parameters constant.

    ii. For each variation, plot the decision boundaries using a grid over the input space $x_1, x_2 \in [-5, 5]$ with a step size of 0.1.

    iii. Describe how the decision boundary changes as a result of the parameter variation. Specifically, note any shifts, rotations, or changes in the shape of the boundary lines.

(b) Simultaneous parameter variation:

    i. Select a pair of parameters from different score functions (e.g., $w_{0,1}$ and $w_{2,1}$). Vary them simultaneously, considering cases where both parameters increase together, decrease together, or change in opposite directions.

    ii. Plot the resulting decision boundaries as above, and analyze how these combined changes affect the shape, orientation, or location of the boundaries.

    iii. Explain how these parameter interactions might affect overall accuracy, precision, and recall, especially in regions near the boundaries.

(c) Geometric interpretation:

    i. Based on your observations from the above experiments, provide a geometric interpretation of the softmax decision boundaries. Explain how the parameters $w_{i,j}$ influence the orientation, slope, and position of these boundaries in the feature space.

    ii. Discuss how changing these parameters affects the relative spacing between boundaries and what this implies for the model's classification behavior.

(d) Practical recommendations:

    i. Based on your findings, provide practical recommendations for adjusting the model parameters to achieve specific classification goals (e.g., maximizing separation between two specific classes).

    ii. Discuss when manual parameter tuning may lead to overfitting or underfitting and how techniques such as regularization can mitigate these risks.

Chapter 6

K-Nearest Neighbors

The k-nearest neighbors algorithm (KNN) is a simple yet powerful machine learning technique. It classifies a new instance by assigning it the most frequent label among its k closest neighbors in the training set. Unlike many algorithms that build an explicit model during training, KNN is a *lazy learner*: it stores the training data and defers most computation until prediction time. It is also a non-parametric, instance-based algorithm, meaning it makes no assumptions about the underlying data distribution and relies directly on the stored training instances for predictions.

Despite its simplicity, KNN can perform remarkably well and sometimes even outperform more sophisticated models in domains where local structure is important. By relying on local neighborhoods for prediction, KNN can create flexible decision boundaries that adapt to the underlying data distribution. This property makes it especially effective for tasks such as recommendation systems and text retrieval, where proximity in feature space often corresponds to semantic similarity (e.g., documents with similar word-frequency profiles are likely to cover similar topics).

However, KNN also faces several challenges. Choosing an appropriate value for k, the number of neighbors to consider, is critical and can significantly affect the model's accuracy. In addition, KNN can be computationally expensive at prediction time, since it must search the entire training set to find the nearest neighbors.

This chapter explores the KNN algorithm in detail and presents strategies to address its limitations. It is organized as follows. Section 6.1 introduces the KNN algorithm for classification, including a Python implementation from scratch. Section 6.2 discusses strategies for selecting the optimal number of neighbors k. Section 6.3 examines different distance metrics used in KNN. Section 6.4 reviews theoretical error bounds on KNN performance. Section 6.5 describes efficient data structures for nearest neighbor searches. Section 6.6 discusses the impact of high-dimensional feature spaces on KNN. Section 6.7 presents a variant of KNN that uses a fixed radius instead of a fixed number of neighbors. Section 6.8 shows how KNN can be applied to regression problems. Section 6.9 discusses extensions of KNN that speed up neighbor searches, improve robustness to noise and outliers, and adapt dynamically to varying data distributions. Section 6.10 explores a range of applications that utilize KNN across various fields. Finally, section 6.11 concludes with a summary.

6.1   K-Nearest Neighbors Classification

The k-nearest neighbor (KNN) classification algorithm, originally introduced by Fix and Hodges in 1951 [194], is based on a simple yet powerful idea: the label of a new sample is likely to match the majority label among its nearest neighbors (see Figure 6.1).

Formally, given a test sample $\mathbf{x}$ (also called a **query point**), its predicted class is:

$$\hat{y} = \underset{c \in C}{\operatorname{argmax}} \sum_{(\mathbf{x}_i, y_i) \in N} \mathbb{1}(y_i = c), \tag{6.1}$$

where C is the set of possible classes, N is the set of the k nearest neighbors of $\mathbf{x}$, and $\mathbb{1}(y_i = c)$ is the indicator function, which equals 1 if $y_i = c$ and 0 otherwise.

The KNN algorithm consists of two main phases:

- **Training Phase:** In this phase, the training data are simply stored (typically in memory) for later use during prediction. To enable faster neighbor searches, data structures such as KD-trees or ball trees may be built at this stage (see Section 6.5).

- **Prediction Phase:** To classify a new instance $\mathbf{x}$, KNN computes the distance between $\mathbf{x}$ and all stored samples using the chosen distance metric. It then identifies the k closest neighbors and assigns $\mathbf{x}$ to the most frequent class among them (see Algorithm 6.1). In the case of a tie, the label is chosen at random from among the tied classes (in binary classification, it is common to choose an odd k to avoid ties).

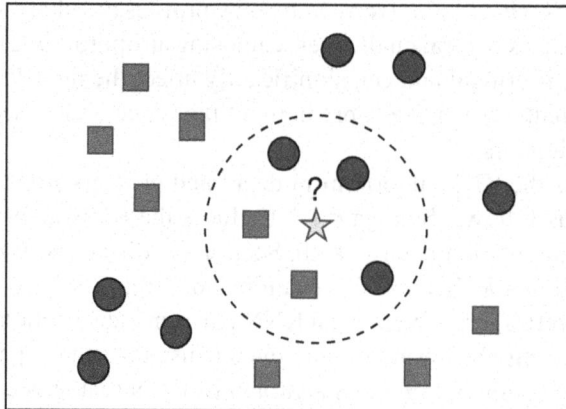

Figure 6.1: K-nearest neighbors (KNN) classification example. The star labeled with "?" represents a new sample to classify. The dashed circle encloses its $k = 5$ nearest neighbors, most of which belong to the circle class. Consequently, the algorithm assigns the new sample to this class.

Algorithm 6.1 K-Nearest Neighbors Classification

Input:
  D: a set of training samples $\{(\mathbf{x}_1, y_1), \ldots, (\mathbf{x}_n, y_n)\}$
  k: the number of nearest neighbors
  $d(\mathbf{x}, \mathbf{x}')$: a distance metric
  $\mathbf{x}$: a test sample

1: **for each** training sample $(\mathbf{x}_i, y_i) \in D$ **do**
2:     Compute the distance $d(\mathbf{x}, \mathbf{x}_i)$ between $\mathbf{x}$ and $\mathbf{x}_i$
3: Let $N \subseteq D$ be the k training samples with the smallest distances to $\mathbf{x}$
4: Predict the label as:
$$\hat{y} = \underset{c}{\operatorname{argmax}} \sum_{(\mathbf{x}_i, y_i) \in N} \mathbb{1}(y_i = c)$$

5: **return** $\hat{y}$

6.1.1   Numerical Example

To illustrate the KNN algorithm, consider the training samples in Table 6.1, each consisting of three features and a binary label. We aim to classify the query point $(1, 0, 1)$ using KNN with $k = 3$ and the Euclidean distance metric.

The Euclidean distance between two vectors $\mathbf{x} = (x_1, x_2, \ldots, x_n)$ and $\mathbf{y} = (y_1, y_2, \ldots, y_n)$ is defined as:

$$d(\mathbf{x}, \mathbf{y}) = \|\mathbf{x} - \mathbf{y}\|_2 = \sqrt{\sum_{i=1}^{n}(x_i - y_i)^2}. \tag{6.2}$$

To simplify the calculations, we compute the squared Euclidean distances. Since squaring is a monotonically increasing function on nonnegative values, it preserves the ordering of distances

i	x_1	x_2	x_3	y
1	1	4	1	1
2	1	0	-2	0
3	0	0	1	0
4	-1	4	0	1
5	-1	-1	1	1
6	1	2	3	1
7	0	-4	0	0
8	1	0	-3	0

Table 6.1: Training samples for the KNN classification example. Each sample includes three features (x_1, x_2, x_3) and a class label (y).

i	x_1	x_2	x_3	y	Squared Distance from $(1, 0, 1)$
1	1	4	1	1	$(1-1)^2 + (4-0)^2 + (1-1)^2 = 16$
2	1	0	-2	0	$(1-1)^2 + (0-0)^2 + (-2-1)^2 = 9$
3	0	0	1	0	$(0-1)^2 + (0-0)^2 + (1-1)^2 = 1$
4	-1	4	0	1	$(-1-1)^2 + (4-0)^2 + (0-1)^2 = 19$
5	-1	-1	1	1	$(-1-1)^2 + (-1-0)^2 + (1-1)^2 = 5$
6	1	2	3	1	$(1-1)^2 + (2-0)^2 + (3-1)^2 = 8$
7	0	-4	0	0	$(0-1)^2 + (-4-0)^2 + (0-1)^2 = 18$
8	1	0	-3	0	$(1-1)^2 + (0-0)^2 + (-3-1)^2 = 16$

Table 6.2: Squared Euclidean distances between the query point (1, 0, 1) and each training sample. Highlighted rows indicate the three nearest neighbors used for classification.

and thus the choice of nearest neighbors. Table 6.2 shows the squared distances from the query point to each training sample.

The three closest samples are 3, 5, and 6, with squared distances of 1, 5, and 8, respectively. The majority label among these neighbors is 1, as two of them (samples 5 and 6) have label 1. Thus, the query vector (1, 0, 1) is classified as belonging to class 1.

6.1.2   Implementation in Python

We now implement a k-nearest neighbors classifier in Python from scratch. The code listing below defines a custom KNNClassifier class, followed by a detailed explanation:

```python
import numpy as np
from sklearn.base import BaseEstimator
from scipy.stats import mode

class KNNClassifier(BaseEstimator):
    def __init__(self, k=5):
        self.k = k # Number of nearest neighbors

    def fit(self, X, y):
        # Store the training examples and their labels
        self.X_train = X
        self.y_train = y

    def predict(self, x):
        # Compute squared Euclidean distances
        distances = np.sum((self.X_train - x)**2, axis=1)
```

```
# Find indices of the k nearest neighbors
neighbors_idx = distances.argsort()[:self.k]

# Get the labels of the nearest neighbors
neighbors_labels = self.y_train[neighbors_idx]

# Return the most frequent label among the neighbors
return mode(neighbors_labels).mode
```

The class defines three methods:

- The `__init__` method initializes the classifier with the number of nearest neighbors k (default is 5).

- The `fit` method stores the training samples and their labels in `self.X_train` and `self.y_train`, respectively.

- The `predict` method classifies a new sample x using the following steps:

  1. Compute squared Euclidean distances: Using NumPy broadcasting (see Section F.1), `self.X_train - x` computes element-wise differences between the test point and each training sample. Squaring and summing the distances across features with `np.sum(..., axis=1)` yields a vector of squared distances between the query point and the training samples.[1]

  2. Select the k nearest neighbors: Apply `argsort()` to the `distances` array and take the first k indices.

  3. Retrieve neighbor labels: Use these indices to extract the corresponding labels from `self.y_train`.

  4. Determine the predicted label: Use `scipy.stats.mode`[2] to find the most frequent label (mode) in the neighbor labels array. This function returns a `ModeResult` object, whose `mode` attribute contains the most common label.

Let's test the implementation on the dataset from Table 6.1. We first define the training set:

```
X_train = np.array([[1, 4, 1], [1, 0, -2], [0, 0, 1], [-1, 4, 0],
                    [-1, -1, 1], [1, 2, 3], [0, -4, 0], [1, 0, -3]])
y_train = np.array([1, 0, 0, 1, 1, 1, 0, 0])
```

Next, we create an instance of `KNNClassifier` with $k = 3$ and fit it to the training data:

```
knn = KNNClassifier(k=3)
knn.fit(X_train, y_train)
```

---

1. This assumes that x is a one-dimensional array representing a single test point. Extending the method to handle multiple test points (as a matrix input) is left as an exercise.

2. `https://docs.scipy.org/doc/scipy/reference/generated/scipy.stats.mode.html`

Finally, we use the classifier to predict the label of a new sample $(1, 0, 1)$:

```
X_new = np.array([1, 0, 1])
label = knn.predict(X_new)
print(f'Label: {label}')
```

```
Label: 1
```

The output is 1, matching the result obtained from the manual computation of the nearest neighbors in the previous section.

6.1.3   Weighted K-Nearest Neighbors

In many cases, neighbors that are closer to the query point are more indicative of its class than those farther away. **Weighted *k*-nearest neighbors (W-KNN)** incorporates this intuition by assigning larger weights to closer neighbors and smaller weights to more distant ones. The choice of weighting function can have a significant impact on the algorithm, as it determines the influence of each neighbor on the prediction.

A popular weighting scheme uses **inverse distance weighting**, where each neighbor's vote is inversely proportional to its distance from the query point [176]. Mathematically, if d_i is the distance from the i-th nearest neighbor to the test point, its corresponding weight w_i is given by:

$$w_i = \frac{1}{d_i}.$$

The predicted label for the test point is then determined by the class whose neighbors have the largest total weight:

$$y = \underset{c \in C}{\operatorname{argmax}} \sum_{(\mathbf{x}_i, y_i) \in N} w_i \cdot \mathbb{1}(y_i = c), \tag{6.3}$$

where N is the set of the k nearest neighbors.

For example, using the dataset in Table 6.1, let's classify the point $(1, 0, 1)$ using KNN with $k = 3$, Euclidean distance, and distance-weighted voting. Table 6.3 shows the distances and corresponding weights of the three nearest neighbors of $(1, 0, 1)$.

i	x_1	x_2	x_3	y	Squared Distance from $(1, 0, 1)$	Weight
3	0	0	1	0	$(0-1)^2 + (0-0)^2 + (1-1)^2 = 1$	$1/1 = 1$
5	-1	-1	1	1	$(-1-1)^2 + (-1-0)^2 + (1-1)^2 = 5$	$1/5 = 0.2$
6	1	2	3	1	$(1-1)^2 + (2-0)^2 + (3-1)^2 = 8$	$1/8 = 0.125$

Table 6.3: Distances and weights of the three nearest neighbors of the query point (1, 0, 1) used for distance-weighted KNN.

The sum of weights for class 0 is 1, while the sum for class 1 is $0.2 + 0.125 = 0.325$. Since class 0 has the higher total weight, the query point is classified as belonging to class 0. This example illustrates how distance-weighted voting can change the classification outcome by giving greater influence to closer neighbors.

6.1.4 The `KNeighborsClassifier` Class

Scikit-Learn provides the `KNeighborsClassifier`[3] class for k-nearest neighbors classification. Its key parameters are summarized in Table 6.4.

To demonstrate the use of this class, we train a `KNeighborsClassifier` on the Iris dataset. As in Section 5.3.3, we restrict the input features to the first two (sepal length and sepal width) to enable visualization of the decision boundaries. This time, however we include all three flower species, as KNN naturally supports multi-class classification.

First, we import the necessary libraries and fix the random seed to ensure reproducibility:

```
import numpy as np
import matplotlib.pyplot as plt
import seaborn as sns

np.random.seed(42)
```

Parameter	Description	Default
n_neighbors	Number of nearest neighbors used for prediction.	5
weights	Weighting scheme applied to the nearest neighbors. Options are `'uniform'` (equal weights), `'distance'` (weight inversely proportional to distance), or a user-defined function.	`'uniform'`
algorithm	Algorithm used to compute the nearest neighbors. Options are `'ball_tree'`, `'kd_tree'`, `'brute'`, or `'auto'`, which selects the most appropriate algorithm based on the dataset (see Section 6.5).	`'auto'`
metric	Metric used for distance computations. Supports any metric from `sklearn.metrics.pairwise.distance_metrics`[4].	`'minkowski'`
p	Power parameter for the Minkowski metric (see Section 6.3.1).	2

Table 6.4: Key parameters of the `KNeighborsClassifier` class

---

3. https://scikit-learn.org/stable/modules/generated/sklearn.neighbors.KNeighborsClassifier.html

4. https://scikit-learn.org/stable/modules/generated/sklearn.metrics.pairwise.distance_metrics.html

Next, we load the Iris dataset and extract the first two features:

```
from sklearn.datasets import load_iris

iris = load_iris()
X = iris.data[:, :2] # Take only the first two features
y = iris.target
```

We then split the dataset into training and test sets:

```
from sklearn.model_selection import train_test_split

X_train, X_test, y_train, y_test = train_test_split(X, y, random_state=42)
```

In general, numerical features should be scaled before building a KNN classifier to ensure that each feature contributes equally to the distance computations. However, in this case, the two selected features have very similar ranges (sepal length: [3.5,5.1], sepal width: [3.0,4.9]), so scaling is not necessary.

Next, we create an instance of `KNeighborsClassifier` with default settings ($k = 5$) and fit it to the training data:

```
from sklearn.neighbors import KNeighborsClassifier

clf = KNeighborsClassifier(n_neighbors=5)
clf.fit(X_train, y_train)
```

Note that `KNeighborsClassifier` is one of the few estimators in Scikit-Learn that does not have a `random_state` parameter, as the algorithm is entirely deterministic.

We now evaluate the model's performance on the training and test sets:

```
print(f'Training accuracy: {clf.score(X_train, y_train):.4f}')
print(f'Test accuracy: {clf.score(X_test, y_test):.4f}')
```

```
Training accuracy: 0.8393
Test accuracy: 0.8158
```

The test accuracy is slightly lower than the training accuracy, indicating that the model generalizes well and does not exhibit severe overfitting. In this case, using $k = 5$ neighbors strikes a good balance between fitting the training data and generalizing to new, unseen data. Section 6.2 discusses strategies for selecting an appropriate value of k in more detail.

Since the dataset is two-dimensional, we can visualize the decision boundaries generated by KNN using the helper function `plot_decision_boundaries`. The implementation of this function

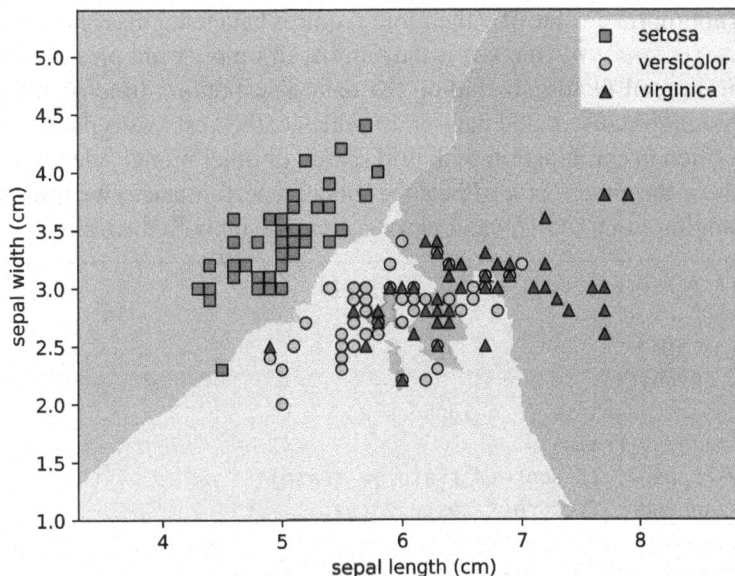

Figure 6.2: Decision boundaries generated by the k-nearest neighbors classifier on the Iris dataset. Each colored region corresponds to a predicted class, and the points represent the actual data samples. The irregular, nonlinear boundaries reflect KNN's sensitivity to local variations in the feature space.

is available in the accompanying notebook `KNeighborsClassifier.ipynb`[5] on Github. We call this function as follows:

```
plot_decision_boundaries(clf, X, y, iris.feature_names[:2], iris.target_names)
```

Figure 6.2 shows that the decision boundaries produced by KNN are highly adaptive, forming irregular and sometimes fragmented shapes that closely follow local variations in the data. This flexibility allows KNN to capture complex class boundaries that linear models and other simple classifiers may fail to detect.

6.2   Choosing the Number of Neighbors

The choice of the number of nearest neighbors k is critical, as it directly impacts the performance of the KNN algorithm. A small k makes the model highly sensitive to noise in the data (e.g., mislabeled samples), leading to high variance and potential overfitting. Conversely, a large k increases the risk of including points from other classes in the neighborhood of the query point, which can dilute the influence of the closest neighbors and result in high bias. In the extreme case where $k = n$ (the size of the training set), the model always predicts the most frequent label in the training data, ignoring the input features entirely.

---

5. https://github.com/roiyeho/ml-book/blob/main/Chapter06/KNeighborsClassifier.ipynb

Choosing an appropriate value of k therefore requires balancing bias and variance. A common rule of thumb is to set $k \approx \sqrt{n}$, where n is the number of training samples. However, the optimal value depends on several factors, including the data distribution, dimensionality of the feature space, and the amount of noise in the dataset. In practice, the best k is typically determined using cross-validation, often in combination with grid search or other model selection techniques.

To examine how the choice of k affects the model's performance, we train a KNN classifier for values of k ranging from 1 to 100 and plot its accuracy on both the training and test sets:

```
n_neighbors, train_scores, test_scores = [], [], []

for k in range(1, 101):
    n_neighbors.append(k)
    clf = KNeighborsClassifier(n_neighbors=k)
    clf.fit(X_train, y_train)
    train_scores.append(clf.score(X_train, y_train))
    test_scores.append(clf.score(X_test, y_test))

plt.plot(n_neighbors, train_scores, label='Training set')
plt.plot(n_neighbors, test_scores, label='Test set')

plt.xlabel('$k$')
plt.ylabel('Accuracy')
plt.xticks(range(0, 101, 5))
plt.legend()
```

As shown in Figure 6.3, the training accuracy decreases as k increases. With $k = 1$, each training sample is classified by itself, yielding almost 100% training accuracy (except for duplicate points with conflicting labels). As k increases, neighbors from other classes are more likely to be included, reducing the model's ability to fit the training data. On the test set, accuracy initially improves as increasing k smooths the decision boundaries and reduces overfitting, peaking around $k = 30$; beyond that, the model begins to underfit and test performance declines.

We can also use grid search with cross-validation to find the optimal k for this dataset (searching over the range 1 to 50):

```
from sklearn.model_selection import GridSearchCV

param_grid = {
    'n_neighbors': np.arange(1, 51)
}
grid = GridSearchCV(KNeighborsClassifier(), param_grid, cv=3, n_jobs=-1)
grid.fit(X_train, y_train)

print(grid.best_params_)
```

```
{'n_neighbors': 29}
```

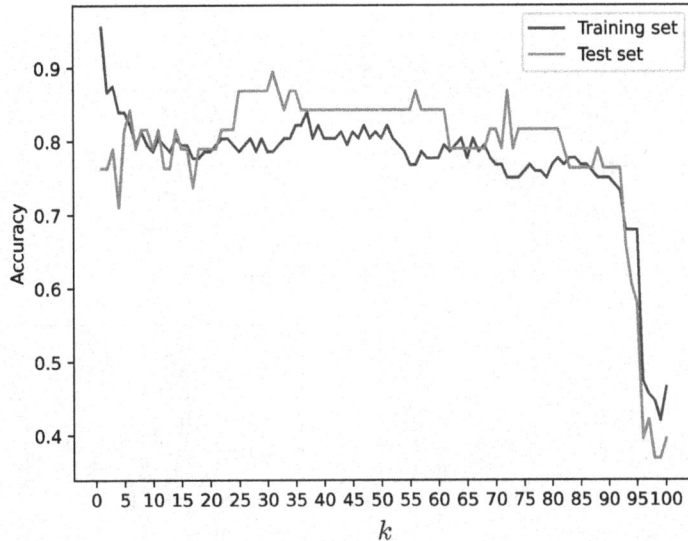

Figure 6.3: Accuracy of the k-nearest neighbors classifier on the Iris dataset for different values of k (from 1 to 100). The plot demonstrates the tradeoff between overfitting and underfitting: small k values achieve higher training accuracy but tend to overfit, whereas larger values reduce overfitting until they become too large and the model begins to underfit. The best performance on the test set occurs around $k = 30$, where the classifier strikes a good balance between bias and variance.

The grid search identifies $k = 29$ as the optimal number of neighbors, consistent with our previous analysis. Using this value, the performance of the model is:

```
print(f'Training accuracy: {grid.score(X_train, y_train):.4f}')
print(f'Test accuracy: {grid.score(X_test, y_test):.4f}')
```

```
Training accuracy: 0.8036
Test accuracy: 0.8684
```

The test accuracy improves significantly from 81.58% (using the default $k = 5$) to 86.84% with $k = 29$, highlighting the importance of tuning the number of neighbors in KNN classification.

Finally, let's examine how the decision boundaries change as we vary k:

```
fig, axes = plt.subplots(1, 4, sharey=True, figsize=(18, 3))
k_values = [1, 5, 30, 50]

for ax, k in zip(axes, k_values):
    clf = KNeighborsClassifier(n_neighbors=k)
    clf.fit(X_train, y_train)
    test_score = clf.score(X_test, y_test)
    plot_decision_boundaries(clf, X, y, iris.feature_names[:2], iris.target_names,
                             ax, legend=None)
    ax.set_title(f'$k = {k}$, test = {test_score:.4f}')
```

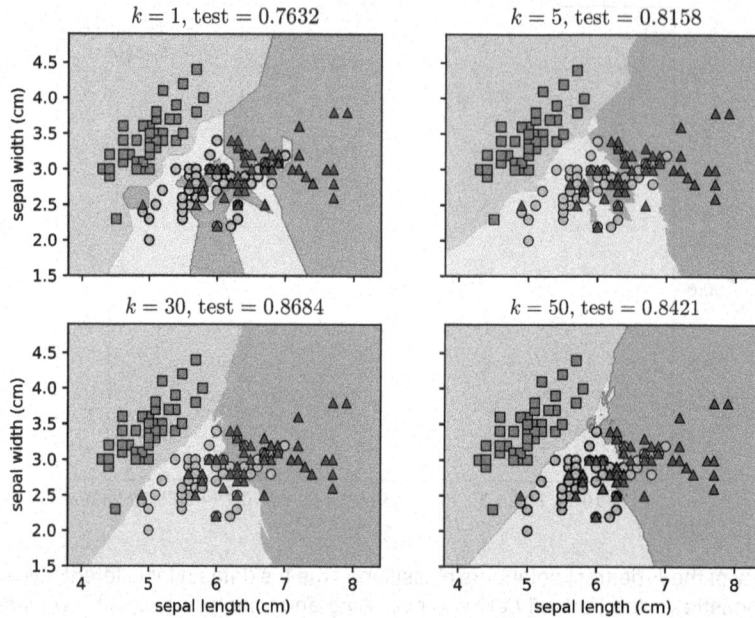

Figure 6.4: Decision boundaries of the KNN classifier on the Iris dataset for different values of k (1, 5, 30, and 50), along with the corresponding test accuracies. As k increases, the boundaries become smoother and more regular, while the model transitions from overfitting to underfitting.

Figure 6.4 illustrates that as k increases, the classifier becomes less sensitive to local variations, producing smoother and more regular decision boundaries.[6]

6.3 Distance Metrics and Similarity Measures

Distance metrics play a central role in many machine learning algorithms, including clustering and nearest neighbor methods, where they are used to quantify the similarity or dissimilarity between data points. The choice of distance metric often depends on the nature of the data, the feature types involved, and the specific goals of the task [7].

Formally, a **distance metric** is a function $d(x, y)$ that measures the dissimilarity between two objects x and y, with larger values indicating greater dissimilarity. The objects may be numbers, vectors, strings, or other structured data types. A valid distance metric must satisfy the following properties for all x, y, z:

- **Non-negativity:** $d(x, y) \geq 0$.

- **Identity of indiscernibles:** $d(x, y) = 0$ if and only if $x = y$.

---

6. While the test accuracy is computed on the held-out test set, the decision boundaries are plotted using the entire dataset (training and test points) to provide a clearer view of how the classifier partitions the feature space.

- **Symmetry:** $d(x, y) = d(y, x)$.

- **Triangle inequality:** $d(x, z) \leq d(x, y) + d(y, z)$. This property ensures that the direct distance between x and z is never greater than any indirect route through a third point y.

In contrast, a **similarity measure** $s(x, y)$ quantifies the similarity between two objects, with larger values indicating greater similarity. Similarity measures are often bounded between 0 (no similarity) and 1 (identical objects).

Several transformations can be used to convert a distance metric into a similarity measure:

- **Inverse distance:**

$$s(x, y) = \frac{1}{1 + d(x, y)} \tag{6.4}$$

This transformation decreases similarity nonlinearly from 1 toward 0 as the distance increases.

- **Linear transformation:**

$$s(x, y) = 1 - \frac{d(x, y)}{\max(d)}, \tag{6.5}$$

where $\max(d)$ is the maximum observed distance in the dataset. Here, similarity decreases linearly from 1 to 0 as the distance increases.

- **Exponential decay:**

$$s(x, y) = e^{-\lambda d(x, y)} \tag{6.6}$$

This transformation decreases similarity exponentially from 1 toward 0 as the distance increases, with the parameter λ controlling the decay rate.

In the following subsections, we examine some of the most commonly used distance metrics in machine learning.

6.3.1 Minkowski Distance

Minkowski distance is a generalization of the Euclidean distance, commonly used to measure the distance between two real-valued vectors. It is defined as:

$$d_p(\mathbf{x}, \mathbf{y}) = \left(\sum_{i=1}^{n} |x_i - y_i|^p \right)^{1/p} . \tag{6.7}$$

Here, n is the number of components in each vector and p is a parameter that determines the type of distance. By adjusting p, the Minkowski distance can adapt to different data characteristics and application needs.

Common choices of p include:

- **Manhattan distance** (also known as **city-block distance** or **taxicab distance**): For $p = 1$, the distance is the sum of absolute differences between the corresponding vector components. It can be visualized as the distance one would travel between two points when restricted to moving along grid lines, similar to navigating the streets of Manhattan.

- **Euclidean distance**: For $p = 2$, the distance reduces to the Euclidean distance, which measures the straight-line distance between two points. It is one of the most commonly used distance metrics in machine learning due to its simplicity and intuitive geometric interpretation.

- **Chebyshev distance** (or **maximum distance**): For $p = \infty$, the distance becomes

$$d_\infty(\mathbf{x}, \mathbf{y}) = \max_i |x_i - y_i|. \tag{6.8}$$

This metric corresponds to the largest absolute difference along any single dimension.

Figure 6.5 illustrates how different Minkowski distances are computed between two points in $\mathbb{R}^2$, and Table 6.5 summarizes typical use cases for each metric.

6.3.2 Mahalanobis Distance

Standard distance metrics, such as Euclidean distance, can be strongly affected by correlations between the input features. When features are correlated, they convey overlapping information, causing their combined effect to be overrepresented in the distance computation. This can lead to

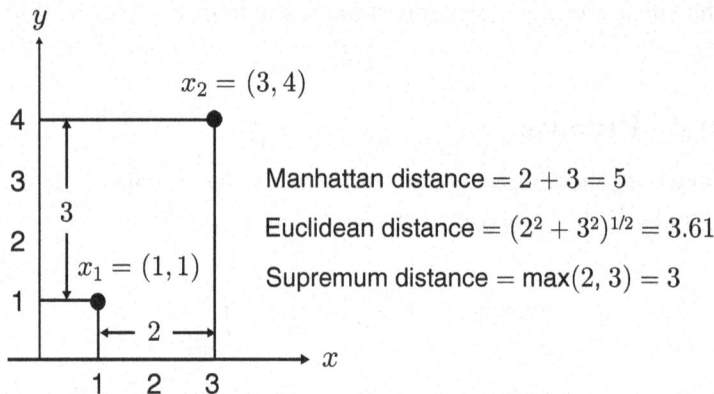

Figure 6.5: Illustration of three distance metrics derived from the Minkowski distance formula. The points $\mathbf{x}_1 = (1, 1)$ and $\mathbf{x}_2 = (3, 4)$ are used to demonstrate: (1) Manhattan distance ($p = 1$) as the sum of absolute differences along each axis; (2) Euclidean distance ($p = 2$) as the straight-line distance between the two points; and (3) Chebyshev (or maximum) distance ($p = \infty$) as the largest absolute difference in any single dimension.

Name	Formula	Typical Use Cases
Manhattan (ℓ_1)	$\sum_{i=1}^{n} |x_i - y_i|$	Commonly used for high-dimensional sparse data. It is more robust to outliers and better suited to high-dimensional spaces than Euclidean distance because it aggregates absolute feature differences linearly rather than squaring them [10].
Euclidean (ℓ_2)	$\left(\sum_{i=1}^{n} |x_i - y_i|^2\right)^{1/2}$	General-purpose distance metric. Squaring emphasizes large differences, which can be useful in tasks such as anomaly detection. It is also differentiable everywhere, making it well-suited for gradient-based optimization.
Chebyshev (ℓ_∞)	$\max_i |x_i - y_i|$	Used in quality control or critical systems where worst-case deviations are more important than average behavior.
Minkowski (ℓ_p)	$\left(\sum_{i=1}^{n} |x_i - y_i|^p\right)^{1/p}$	Flexible distance metric with a tunable parameter p, which can be chosen based on domain knowledge or via cross-validation.

Table 6.5: Common Minkowski distances and their typical use cases

distorted distance measurements that do not accurately reflect the true differences between data points.

The **Mahalanobis distance** generalizes Euclidean distance by taking into account the correlations between features and scaling the feature space according to the data's covariance structure [389]. This adjustment ensures that features with high variance or strong correlations do not dominate the distance computation, resulting in a more balanced measure. Mahalanobis distance is particularly useful in tasks such as classification, clustering, and outlier detection, where accounting for correlations and different feature scales leads to more meaningful distance measurements.

Mathematically, the Mahalanobis distance between vectors $\mathbf{x}$ and $\mathbf{y}$ is defined as:

$$d_{\text{Mahalanobis}}(\mathbf{x}, \mathbf{y}) = \sqrt{(\mathbf{x} - \mathbf{y})^T \Sigma^{-1} (\mathbf{x} - \mathbf{y})}, \tag{6.9}$$

where Σ^{-1} is the inverse of the covariance matrix of the data. For a dataset with n observations $\mathbf{x}_1, \mathbf{x}_2, \ldots, \mathbf{x}_n$, the sample covariance matrix is given by

$$\Sigma = \frac{1}{n-1} \sum_{i=1}^{n} (\mathbf{x}_i - \boldsymbol{\mu})(\mathbf{x}_i - \boldsymbol{\mu})^T, \tag{6.10}$$

where $\boldsymbol{\mu}$ is the sample mean vector. Each entry (i, j) of Σ represents the covariance between the i-th and j-th features (see Section C.11.3). Multiplying by Σ^{-1} rescales the feature space so that correlated features do not artificially inflate the distance.

Figure 6.6 compares Euclidean and Mahalanobis distances on a two-dimensional dataset with correlated features. The dataset contains 300 data points sampled from a multivariate Gaussian distribution with nonzero off-diagonal covariances. The distance between the two large points at

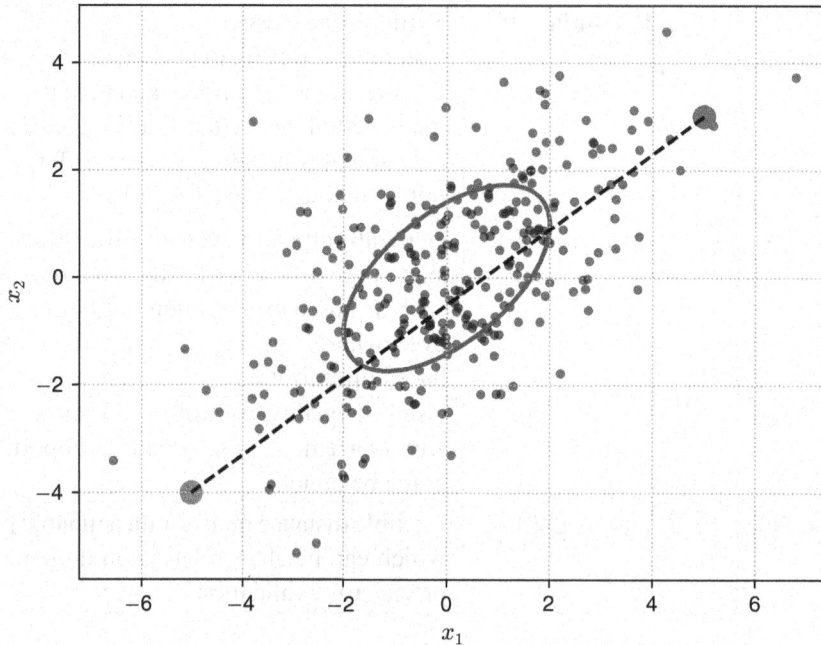

Figure 6.6: Euclidean vs. Mahalanobis distances. The dashed line shows the Euclidean distance between the two highlighted points, treating all directions equally. The blue ellipse shows contours of equal Mahalanobis distance, which account for feature correlations and result in a shorter effective distance along the direction of highest variance (the principal axis of the ellipse).

$(-5, -4)$ and $(5, 3)$ is 12.21 using Euclidean distance but only 5.2 with Mahalanobis distance. The latter accounts for the covariance structure, reducing the influence of directions with high variance in the feature space (in this case, the direction along the principal axis of the elliptical distribution).

6.3.3 Hamming Distance

The **Hamming distance** between two vectors or strings is the number of positions at which the corresponding values (or symbols) are different [251]. It is primarily used for categorical and binary data. For example, the Hamming distance between the binary vectors $\mathbf{x} = (1, 0, 1, 1, 0)$ and $\mathbf{y} = (1, 1, 0, 1, 0)$ is 2, as they differ at the second and third positions.

Hamming distance plays a crucial role in information theory and coding theory, where it enables error detection and correction during data transmission over noisy channels. By quantifying the minimum number of substitutions required to transform one string or binary sequence into another, it provides a direct measure of transmission errors, making it essential for ensuring reliable communication and data integrity.

Beyond coding theory, Hamming distance is also widely used in fields such as genetics, where it measures genetic distance between species by comparing their DNA sequences [479], and in machine learning, where it is quantifies dissimilarities between binary-encoded data.

For sequences of unequal length, or when insertions and deletions must be considered, the **edit distance** (or **Levenshtein distance**) is more appropriate [353]. It measures the minimum number of insertions, deletions, and substitutions needed to transform one sequence into another. Edit distance is widely used in applications such as spelling correction, plagiarism detection, and DNA sequence alignment.

6.3.4 Jaccard Similarity

Jaccard similarity (also known as **Jaccard index**) measures the similarity between two *asymmetric binary vectors*, where agreement on shared positive elements (1s) is more significant than agreement on shared negatives (0s) [289]. It is particularly useful for sparse datasets that contain many zeros and relatively few ones, as the presence of a feature (1) is more informative than its absence (0). Such data structures commonly arise in applications such as text mining and recommendation systems.

For example, in a recommendation system, users are often represented by binary vectors, where a 1 indicates that a product was purchased and a 0 indicates no purchase. These vectors are typically sparse, as users purchase only a small subset of the available products. Unlike Euclidean distance, which can consider two users similar simply because they share many zeros, Jaccard similarity focuses only on positions where at least one user has a 1 (i.e., purchased a product). As a result, the similarity between the vectors (1, 1, 1, 0) and (1, 1, 1, 1) will be much larger than between (0, 0, 0, 1) and (0, 0, 0, 0), although the Euclidean distance is the same.

Formally, the Jaccard similarity between two binary vectors $\mathbf{x}$ and $\mathbf{y}$ is defined as

$$J(\mathbf{x}, \mathbf{y}) = \frac{C_{11}}{C_{01} + C_{10} + C_{11}}, \tag{6.11}$$

where:

- C_{11} is the number of positions where both $\mathbf{x}$ and $\mathbf{y}$ are 1.

- C_{01} is the number of positions where $\mathbf{x}$ is 0 and $\mathbf{y}$ is 1.

- C_{10} is the number of positions where $\mathbf{x}$ is 1 and $\mathbf{y}$ is 0.

For example, for $\mathbf{x} = (1, 0, 0, 1, 0)$ and $\mathbf{y} = (1, 1, 0, 1, 0)$, the Jaccard similarity is:

$$J(\mathbf{x}, \mathbf{y}) = \frac{2}{1 + 0 + 2} = \frac{2}{3}.$$

The corresponding **Jaccard distance** is

$$d_J(\mathbf{x}, \mathbf{y}) = 1 - J(\mathbf{x}, \mathbf{y}) = \frac{C_{01} + C_{10}}{C_{01} + C_{10} + C_{11}}, \tag{6.12}$$

so that for the same example

$$d_J(\mathbf{x}, \mathbf{y}) = 1 - \frac{2}{3} = \frac{1}{3}.$$

6.3.5   Cosine Similarity

Cosine similarity measures the cosine of the angle between two vectors and is particularly useful when vector magnitudes are irrelevant to their similarity [517]. It is commonly used in information retrieval and recommendation systems, where data is often represented as high-dimensional, sparse vectors and the direction of the vector (reflecting the relative feature weights) is more informative than its length.

For example, text documents are often represented by term frequency vectors, where each component indicates the number of occurrences of a particular word (also known as bag-of-words representation). When comparing two documents, we want the similarity to reflect their content rather than their length. For instance, if a document X is concatenated with itself to form a longer document $Y = [X, X]$, its similarity to another document Z should remain unchanged.

Formally, the **cosine similarity** between two vectors $\mathbf{x}$ and $\mathbf{y}$ is defined as:

$$\cos(\theta) = \frac{\mathbf{x}^T \mathbf{y}}{\|\mathbf{x}\| \|\mathbf{y}\|}, \tag{6.13}$$

where θ is the angle between the vectors, $\mathbf{x}^T \mathbf{y}$ is their dot product, and $\|\mathbf{x}\|$ and $\|\mathbf{y}\|$ are their Euclidean norms. When both vectors are normalized to unit length, cosine similarity is simply their dot product.

The cosine similarity score ranges from -1 to 1:

- A value of 1 indicates that the vectors point in the same direction (perfect similarity).

- A value of 0 indicates that the vectors are orthogonal (no similarity).

- A value of -1 indicates that the vectors point in opposite directions (complete dissimilarity).

These cases are illustrated in Figure 6.7.

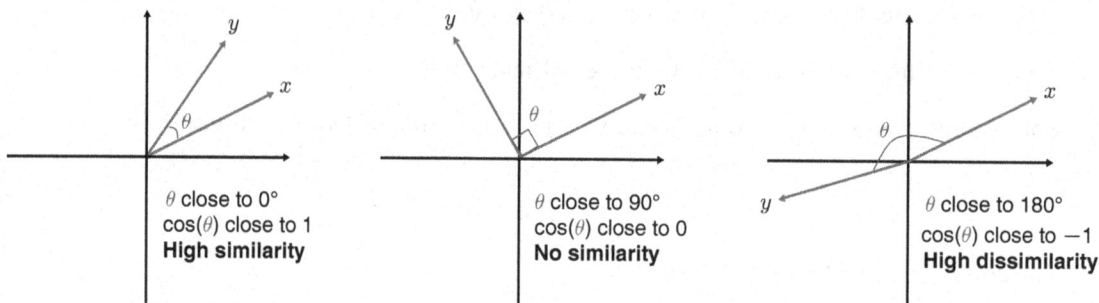

θ close to 0°
cos(θ) close to 1
High similarity

θ close to 90°
cos(θ) close to 0
No similarity

θ close to 180°
cos(θ) close to -1
High dissimilarity

Figure 6.7: Geometric illustration of cosine similarity. The cosine of the angle θ between vectors x and y determines their similarity: smaller angles correspond to higher similarity.

For example, consider the vectors $\mathbf{x} = (1, 2, 3)$ and $\mathbf{y} = (2, 4, 6)$. Their cosine similarity is:

$$\cos(\mathbf{x}, \mathbf{y}) = \frac{1 \cdot 2 + 2 \cdot 4 + 3 \cdot 6}{\sqrt{1^2 + 2^2 + 3^2} \cdot \sqrt{2^2 + 4^2 + 6^2}} = \frac{28}{\sqrt{14} \cdot \sqrt{56}} = 1,$$

showing that despite their different magnitudes, the two vectors point in the same direction and are therefore considered perfectly similar.

The corresponding **cosine distance** is defined as:[7]

$$d(\mathbf{x}, \mathbf{y}) = 1 - \cos(\mathbf{x}, \mathbf{y}). \tag{6.14}$$

In this example,

$$d(\mathbf{x}, \mathbf{y}) = 1 - 1 = 0.$$

6.3.6   Distance Metrics in Scikit-Learn

Scikit-Learn provides a variety of distance metrics in the module `sklearn.metrics.pairwise`[8], which can be used to compute the similarity or dissimilarity between sets of samples.

For example, to compute the Manhattan distance between two vectors, you can use the `manhattan_distances` function:

```
from sklearn.metrics.pairwise import manhattan_distances

X = np.array([[2, 5, 8]])
Y = np.array([[3, 5, 1]])
print(manhattan_distances(X, Y))
```

```
[[8.]]
```

Note that both inputs to the function must be two-dimensional arrays, where each row corresponds to a sample (in this case, both X and Y contain a single sample).

If the desired metric does not have a dedicated function, you can use the general `pairwise_distances` function and specify the metric name via the `metric` parameter. For example, to compute the Hamming distances between two sets of vectors:

```
from sklearn.metrics import pairwise_distances

X = [[1, 0, 1], [0, 1, 1]]
Y = [[1, 1, 0], [0, 1, 0]]
print(pairwise_distances(X, Y, metric='hamming'))
```

```
[[0.66666667 1.         ]
 [0.66666667 0.33333333]]
```

---

7. Although commonly referred to as a "distance," cosine distance is not a true metric as it can violate the triangle inequality and therefore does not satisfy all the properties of a metric space.

8. `https://scikit-learn.org/stable/api/sklearn.metrics.html#module-sklearn.metrics.pairwise`

Each element of the resulting matrix represents the Hamming distance between a row from X and a row from Y.

Many Scikit-Learn estimators also allow specifying a distance metric via the `metric` parameter, either by passing a metric name or by providing a custom function. For example, to use Manhattan distance instead of the default Euclidean distance in `KNeighborsClassifier`:

```
clf = KNeighborsClassifier(metric='manhattan')
```

The choice of distance metric can significantly affect the performance of algorithms such as k-nearest neighbors and should be tuned alongside other hyperparameters (e.g., the value of k).

6.4   (*) KNN Classification Error Bounds

The k-nearest neighbors algorithm enjoys strong theoretical guarantees regarding its classification error. Cover and Hart (1967) proved that, as the number of training samples approaches infinity, the error rate of a 1-NN classifier ($k = 1$) is bounded above by twice the Bayes error rate [133]. The Bayes error rate represents the minimum achievable error rate by any classifier (see Section 2.3.2). Thus, the 1-NN classifier is guaranteed, in the limit of inifinite data, to perform within a constant factor of the best possible classifier.

More specifically, they established the following bound on the expected error E of a 1-NN classifier:

$$E \leq E^* \left(2 - \frac{K}{K-1} E^* \right), \tag{6.15}$$

where K is the number of classes and E^* is the Bayes error rate.

The main steps of the proof are outlined below. While reading the proof is not essential for understanding the algorithm, it illustrates the type of theoretical analysis commonly encountered in machine learning.

Proof. (Sketch) Let $\{x_1, x_2, \ldots, x_n\}$ be the training points, and let x be the query point. Denote by x_k the nearest neighbor of x among the training points. Suppose the classification task involves K classes with prior probabilities $p_1, \ldots, p_K$, and class-conditional densities $f_1(x), \ldots, f_K(x)$, where $f_i(x) = p(x|y = i)$.

By Bayes' theorem, the posterior probability that x belongs to class i, denoted by $\hat{p}_i(x)$, is

$$\hat{p}_i(x) = \frac{p_i f_i(x)}{\sum_{j=1}^{K} p_j f_j(x)}, \quad i = 1, \ldots, K.$$

The probability of misclassifying x is

$$r(x) = \sum_{i \neq j}^{K} \hat{p}_i(x) \hat{p}_j(x_k),$$

which accounts for all cases where the true class i and the neighbor's class j differ.

As $n \to \infty$, the nearest neighbor x_k converges to x, so that $\hat{p}_i(x_k) \to \hat{p}_i(x)$. Substituting this limit into the previous expression gives

$$r(x) = 1 - \sum_{j=1}^{K} \hat{p}_j^2(x). \tag{6.16}$$

The Bayes error at x, denoted by $r^*(x)$, is achieved by predicting the most probable class m with posterior probability $\hat{p}_m(x) = \max_j \hat{p}_j(x)$:

$$r^*(x) = 1 - \hat{p}_m(x).$$

By the Cauchy–Schwarz inequality (see Section A.1.6):

$$\left[\sum_{j \neq m}^{K} \hat{p}_j(x) \right]^2 \leq (K-1) \sum_{j \neq m}^{K} \hat{p}_j^2(x).$$

This follows by applying the inequality to the two vectors $(1, 1, \ldots, 1)$ (of length $K-1$) and $(\hat{p}_j(x))_{j \neq m}$. In other words, the square of the sum of $K-1$ numbers is at most $(K-1)$ times the sum of their squares.

Noting that $\sum_{j \neq m}^{K} \hat{p}_j(x) = 1 - \hat{p}_m(x) = r^*(x)$, this inequality becomes

$$(r^*(x))^2 \leq (K-1) \sum_{j \neq m}^{K} \hat{p}_j^2(x).$$

Adding $(K-1)\hat{p}_m^2(x)$ to both sides and substituting $\hat{p}_m(x) = 1 - r^*(x)$ gives

$$(K-1) \sum_{j=1}^{K} \hat{p}_j^2(x) \geq (r^*(x))^2 + (K-1)(1 - r^*(x))^2.$$

Dividing both sides by $K-1$ yields

$$\sum_{j=1}^{K} \hat{p}_j^2(x) \geq \frac{(r^*(x))^2}{K-1} + (1 - r^*(x))^2.$$

Substituting this into Equation (6.16) gives

$$r(x) \leq 2r^*(x) - \frac{K}{K-1}(r^*(x))^2.$$

Finally, taking expectations on both sides leads to the desired error bound:

$$E \leq E^* \left(2 - \frac{K}{K-1} E^* \right).$$

$\square$

For general KNN classifiers (with $k \geq 1$), Cover and Hart showed that the upper bounds on the error rate are monotonically non-increasing as k increases. In particular, the error rate remains bounded by twice the Bayes error rate for any $k \geq 1$.

Later, Stone (1977) extended this result by showing that KNN's error rate not only decreases with larger k, but actually converges to the Bayes optimal error rate as $k \to \infty$ and $k/n \to 0$ [9] [562]. In other words, KNN is a **consistent** algorithm: with sufficiently large training data, its error rate approaches that of the theoretically optimal classifier that assigns labels based on the true underlying class probabilities.

6.5 (*) Efficient Data Structures for KNN

Computing distances from a query point to all training samples quickly becomes computationally expensive as the dataset grows. The prediction time scales linearly with both the number of samples n and the number of dimensions d, resulting in a complexity of $\mathcal{O}(dn)$. This makes KNN prediction slower than many other algorithms, whose prediction times are typically sublinear in n.

To mitigate these computational challenges, various tree-based data structures have been developed to speed up nearest neighbor search. Examples include KD-trees [41], ball trees [453], VP-trees (Vantage-Point trees) [648], Δ-trees [140], and cover trees [48]. These structures partition the data space so that only a subset of points must be examined during search, offering significant speedups over brute-force search. Beyond KNN, these data structures are also commonly used in clustering, similarity search, and anomaly detection.

In this section, we focus on two widely used structures, KD-trees and ball trees, both of which are supported by Scikit-Learn's KNeighborsClassifier class.

6.5.1   KD-Tree

A **KD-tree** (short for k-dimensional tree) is a binary tree data structure that enables efficient nearest neighbor searches [41, 558]. It recursively partitions the data space into half-spaces along selected dimensions, grouping nearby points into the same or adjacent nodes. This structure significantly reduces the number of distance computations required during a nearest neighbor query.

KD-Tree Construction

A KD-tree is built recursively as follows:

1. **Initialize:** Begin with all data points at the root node.

2. **Select a split dimension:** At each node, choose a dimension to split on. This can be done in a round-robin fashion (cycling through the available dimensions) or by selecting the dimension with the highest variance among the points at that node.

---

9. The condition $k/n \to 0$ ensures that, while the number of neighbors increases, it still represents a vanishing fraction of the total training set, ensuring that predictions are still based on local neighborhoods.

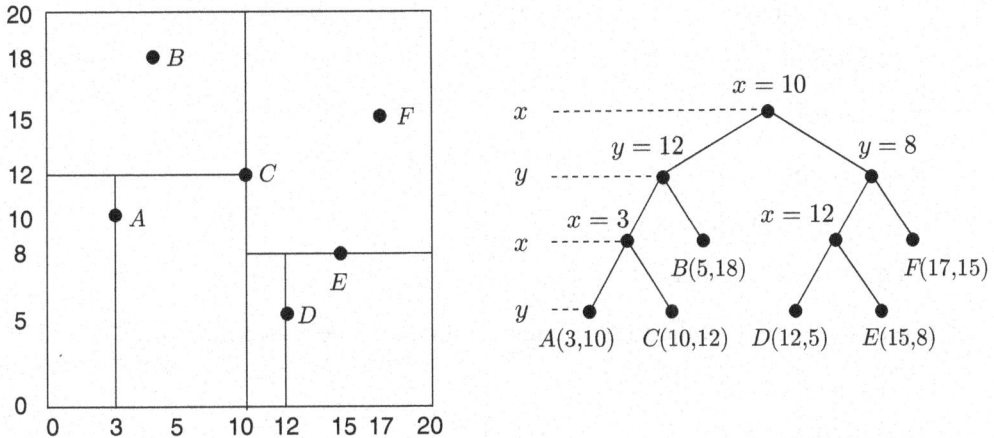

Figure 6.8: A KD-tree built for six data points in two-dimensional space. The left panel shows the corresponding partitioning of the 2D plane: vertical and horizontal lines alternate to split the space into non-overlapping regions, each containing one point. The right panel shows the KD-tree structure, where each internal node stores the splitting dimension and value, and the leaves correspond to individual data points.

3. **Choose a splitting point:** Sort the points along the chosen dimension and select the median value as the splitting point. Using the median helps keep the tree balanced.

4. **Partition the points:** Assign points with values less than or equal to the median to the left child, and those with greater values to the right child.

5. **Recurse and terminate:** Repeat steps 2–4 recursively for each child node until a termination condition is met, such as when the number of points in a node falls below a specified threshold or a maximum tree depth is reached.

For example, consider the KD-tree depicted in Figure 6.8, constructed for the following two-dimensional points: $A(3, 10)$, $B(5, 18)$, $C(10, 12)$, $D(12, 5)$, $E(15, 8)$, and $F(17, 15)$. At each level of the tree, the splitting dimension alternates between the x- and y-axes.

The tree is built as follows:

1. First split (root): Split along the x-axis at $x = 10$ (the lower median of the x-coordinates), dividing the dataset into two groups:

   - Left subtree: $A(3, 10)$, $B(5, 18)$, $C(10, 12)$
   - Right subtree: $D(12, 5)$, $E(15, 8)$, $F(17, 15)$

2. Second split (left subtree): Split along the y-axis at $y = 12$:

   - Left subtree: $A(3, 10)$, $C(10, 12)$
   - Right subtree: $B(5, 18)$

3. Third split (left subtree of the left subtree): Split along the x-axis at $x = 3$:

   - Left subtree: $A(3, 10)$
   - Right subtree: $C(10, 12)$

4. Fourth split (right subtree): Split along the y-axis at $y = 8$:

   - Left subtree: $D(12, 5)$, $E(15, 8)$
   - Right subtree: $F(17, 15)$

5. Final split (left subtree of the right subtree): Split along the x-axis at $x = 12$:

   - Left subtree: $D(12, 5)$
   - Right subtree: $E(15, 8)$

The time complexity of building a KD-tree can be analyzed as follows:

- At each recursive step, we choose a splitting dimension and find the median along that dimension. Using a linear-time median selection algorithm (such as the Median of Medians), the cost of finding the median and partitioning the points at each node is $\mathcal{O}(n)$.

- Since the KD-tree is constructed by recursively splitting on the median, it remains balanced, and its height is at most $\mathcal{O}(\log n)$. Each point is processed once per level, so the total cost across all levels is:

$$\mathcal{O}(n) + \mathcal{O}\left(\frac{n}{2}\right) + \mathcal{O}\left(\frac{n}{4}\right) + \cdots = \mathcal{O}(n \log n).$$

Thus, the overall time complexity for constructing a KD-tree is $\mathcal{O}(n \log n)$. In practice, tree construction is often stopped once a node contains fewer than a predefined number of points (i.e., a maximum leaf size), to limit the tree's depth and improve query efficiency.

Querying the KD-Tree

We begin by describing how to find a single nearest neighbor using a KD-tree, and then extend the method to retrieve the k closest neighbors.

To find the nearest neighbor, the algorithm proceeds as follows:

1. **Start at the root:** Recursively traverse the tree, beginning from the root node.

2. **Follow the closer branch:** At each internal node, compare the query point's coordinate in the current splitting dimension with the node's splitting value. Recurse into the subtree on the side of the split that contains the query point.

3. **Update the current best:** When a leaf node is reached, compute the distance from the query point to the point stored in that leaf. If this distance is smaller than the shortest distance found so far (initially set to infinity), update both the shortest distance and the nearest neighbor.

4. **Backtrack if necessary:** After exploring one branch, determine whether the other branch might contain a closer neighbor by checking whether the query point is closer to the splitting hyperplane than the current best distance. Since the splits are axis-aligned, this reduces to comparing the absolute difference between the query point's coordinate in the splitting dimension and the node's splitting value. If this difference is smaller than the current best distance, recursively search the other branch as well.

5. **Return the result:** After all necessary branches have been explored, return the point associated with the smallest recorded distance as the nearest neighbor.

For example, consider the KD-tree in Figure 6.8, and assume we would like to find the nearest neighbor to the query point $Q(13, 6)$:

1. Root node check: The root node splits at $x = 10$. Since the x-coordinate of Q is 13 (greater than 10), we move to the right subtree.

2. Right subtree split: The right subtree splits at $y = 8$. Because Q has $y = 6$ (less than 8), we move to its left child.

3. Left subtree split: The left subtree splits at $x = 12$. Since $13 > 12$, we proceed to the right child.

4. Leaf node comparison: This node contains the point $E(15, 8)$. We compute the Euclidean distance between Q and E:

$$\sqrt{(13 - 15)^2 + (6 - 8)^2} = \sqrt{8} \approx 2.828.$$

Since this is the first point we have checked, we record E as the current nearest neighbor.

5. Backtracking: After checking E, we backtrack to examine the opposite branches in case they might contain a closer neighbor:

(a) At the $x = 12$ split: The distance between Q to the splitting plane is $|13 - 12| = 1$, which is less than 2.828. Therefore, we check the left child, which contains $D(12, 5)$. The distance between Q and D is:

$$\sqrt{(13 - 12)^2 + (6 - 5)^2} = \sqrt{2} \approx 1.414.$$

Since this is smaller than 2.828, D becomes the current closest neighbor.

(b) At the $y = 8$ split: The distance to the splitting plane is $|6 - 8| = 2$, which is greater than 1.414. Thus, we skip the unexplored right branch.

(c) At the root $x = 10$ split: The distance to the splitting plane is $|13 - 10| = 3$, which is also greater than 1.414. Thus, we do not explore the left branch of the root.

Therefore, the nearest neighbor to $Q(13, 6)$ is $D(12, 5)$, with a distance of approximately 1.414. This example demonstrates how a KD-tree can efficiently find the nearest neighbor with minimal backtracking.

The search algorithm can be extended to find the k nearest neighbors by maintaining a priority queue containing the k closest points found so far. As the tree is traversed, this queue is updated whenever a point closer than the current k-th nearest neighbor is encountered. The decision to explore both child nodes depends on whether the splitting plane intersects the current search region:

- The child node whose region contains the query point is explored first.

- After exploring this subtree, the algorithm checks if the hypersphere centered at the query point, with radius equal to the distance to the current k-th nearest neighbor, intersects the splitting hyperplane.

- If there is an intersection, the other subtree is also explored, as it may contain points closer than those found so far.

The query time complexity of a KD-tree depends strongly on the dimensionality of the data. For low dimensions (typically $d \leq 20$), the tree remains relatively balanced by splitting at the median along each axis, and nearest neighbor queries have an average complexity of $\mathcal{O}(d \log n)$. In high dimensions, however, most points become roughly equidistant from one another (see Section 6.6), so the splitting becomes less effective, leading to more backtracking and overlapping regions. As a result, the query time can approach $\mathcal{O}(dn)$, offering little advantage over a brute-force search.

6.5.2   Ball Tree

A **ball tree** is a binary tree in which each node represents a hypersphere (or "ball") that encloses a subset of the data points [453]. This structure is particularly useful for nearest neighbor search in low- to moderate-dimensional spaces and can sometimes outperform KD-trees when the data are not well aligned with the coordinate axes.

Ball Tree Construction

The construction of a ball tree follows these steps:

1. **Initialize:** Start with all points at the root node.

2. **Select pivots:** Identify the two points that are farthest apart among the points at the current node. These points serve as *pivots*.

3. **Partition points:** Assign each point at the current node to the closer of the two pivots, forming the left and right child nodes.

4. **Define hyperspheres:** For each child node, create a hypersphere that encloses all its points with its center at the mean of the points and the radius equal to the distance from the center to the farthest point.

5. **Recurse and terminate:** Repeat steps 2–4 recursively for each child until a termination condition is met, such as when the number of points falls below a specified threshold or a maximum tree depth is reached.

The time complexity of building a ball tree is typically $\mathcal{O}(dn \log n)$, assuming a balanced tree and that an efficient approximation is used to find the two farthest points (pivots) at each split. However, if the data are unevenly distributed, the tree can become imbalanced, resulting in deeper branches and degraded performance.

Querying the Ball Tree

To find the nearest neighbor using a ball tree:

1. Start at the root and recursively move to the child node whose hypersphere is closer to the query point.

2. If the distance from the query point to the boundary of the other child's hypersphere is less than the distance to the current best neighbor, backtrack and explore that node as well to ensure no closer points are missed.

Similar to KD-trees, nearest neighbor search in ball trees typically costs $\mathcal{O}(d \log n)$, but in high-dimensional spaces the query time can degrade toward $\mathcal{O}(dn)$ as the hyperspheres become less effective at partitioning the points.

Comparing the two data structures, KD-trees are simpler to implement, and perform well on evenly distributed, axis-aligned data. On the other hand, ball trees can sometimes outperform KD-trees on datasets with irregular distributions or varying densities, because they partition the space using hyperspheres rather than axis-aligned splits.

For small datasets, the overhead of building and traversing a tree can outweigh its benefits, since $\log n$ provides limited computational savings relative to n. In such cases, the brute-force method with time complexity $\mathcal{O}(dn)$ may be faster. In addition, the complexity of the brute-force method is largely independent of k, since after computing all distances from the query point, selecting the k smallest distances adds only an $\mathcal{O}(n)$ term. In contrast, the search time in tree-based methods can increase substantially as k grows, because larger values of k typically require more backtracking to explore additional branches.

In Scikit-Learn, the data structure used for the nearest neighbor search is controlled by the `algorithm` parameter of the `KNeighborsClassifier` class. By default, it is set to `'auto'`, which lets Scikit-Learn choose the most suitable algorithm based on the dataset: for small or high-dimensional datasets, `'brute'` is selected; for larger datasets with a moderate number of dimensions (typically fewer than 20) `'kd_tree'` is used, while `'ball_tree'` may be chosen instead if a KD-tree is less effective for the data (e.g., when the data contain many duplicate points).

6.6 The Curse of Dimensionality

The **curse of dimensionality** refers to a range of challenges that arise when working with high-dimensional data [328, 475]. As the number of dimensions increases, the volume of the space grows exponentially and data points become nearly equidistant from one another. As a result, geometric concepts such as "distance" and "neighborhood" lose their discriminative power, undermining the effectiveness of algorithms that depend on them, such as k-nearest neighbors and clustering.

Our geometric intuitions, shaped by a lifetime of experience in three-dimensional space, often break down in higher dimensions. For example, consider a unit square (a square with side length 1) and a randomly chosen point inside it. Define the *border region* as the area within 0.01 units of any edge of the square. The remaining *inner square*, obtained by removing a margin of 0.01 from all sides, has side length 0.99 and area $0.99 \times 0.99 = 0.9801$. Therefore, the probability that the sampled point falls within the border region is

$$1 - 0.9801 = 0.0199,$$

or roughly 2%.

Now consider the same setup with a 1,000-dimensional unit hypercube. The total volume of the hypercube remains 1 (since $1^{1000} = 1$), but the volume of the corresponding inner hypercube with side length 0.99 shrinks exponentially:

$$0.99^{1000} \approx 0.00004317.$$

Thus, the probability that a random point lies in the border region—the space between the inner and outer hypercubes—is

$$1 - 0.00004317 \approx 0.99995683,$$

meaning that over 99.99% of the volume lies near the boundary!

This example illustrates how, in high-dimensional spaces, most of the volume is concentrated near the boundary, resulting in very sparse data and a counterintuitive geometrical structure. In such spaces, distances between points become almost indistinguishable, making all points appear uniformly distant and hindering neighborhood-based methods from capturing meaningful local structure.

To illustrate this, consider a k-nearest neighbors search in a dataset of n points uniformly distributed within a d-dimensional unit hypercube. Define the *k-neighborhood* of a point as the smallest hypercube that contains its k-nearest neighbors, and let l denote the average side length of such a neighborhood. The volume of the neighborhood is l^d and it contains k points by definition, while the entire unit hypercube has volume 1 and contains n points. Therefore, on average, we have:

$$l^d = \frac{k}{n} \quad \Rightarrow \quad l = \left(\frac{k}{n}\right)^{1/d}.$$

This relationship shows that as the number of dimensions d increases, the side length l approaches 1 (e.g., with $k/n = 0.01$, $l \approx 0.63$ when $d = 5$, $l \approx 0.79$ when $d = 10$, and $l \approx 0.95$ when $d = 50$). Consequently, the k-neighborhood occupies an increasingly large fraction of the entire space, making it difficult for neighborhood-based methods to remain truly local in high-dimensional spaces (see also Figure 6.9).

Specifically, in machine learning, the curse of dimensionality implies that algorithms require an increasingly large number of examples as dimensionality grows, in order to adequately cover the feature space. In general, the amount of data needed for a model to generalize effectively grows

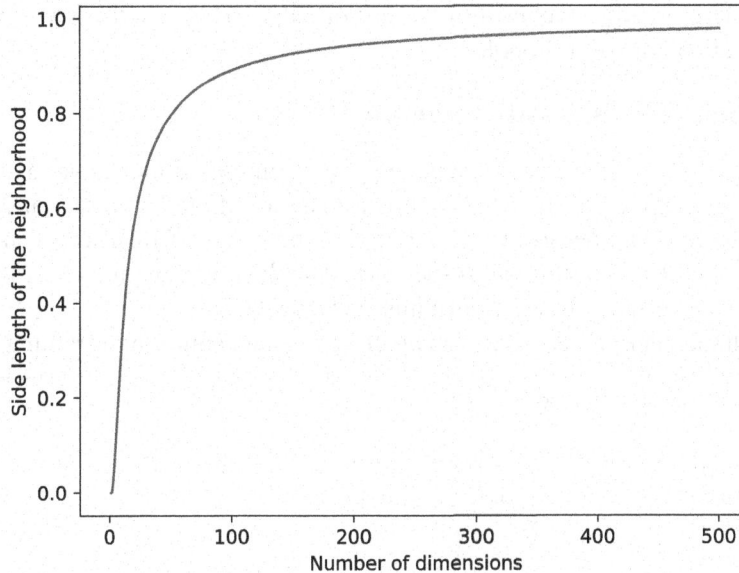

Figure 6.9: Average side length of a neighborhood containing the 10 nearest neighbors in a dataset of 1,000,000 points uniformly distributed within a unit hypercube, plotted as a function of the number of dimensions. As dimensionality increases, the neighborhood size approaches 1 (the side length of the entire hypercube), meaning that neighborhoods cover most of the space. As a result, distance metrics such as Euclidean distance become less informative, and neighborhood-based algorithms like k-nearest neighbors lose their ability to exploit local structure.

exponentially with the number of dimensions. For example, a classifier with n binary features may require up to 2^n examples to cover all possible combinations of feature values. Moreover, when the number of features is large compared to the number of training examples, models become more prone to overfitting, as they have enough capacity to memorize the training data rather than learning generalizable patterns.

Beyond the inefficiency of distance metrics and the risk of overfitting, high-dimensional data introduces several additional challenges:

- Increased computational cost for training and inference

- Greater storage requirements for both the dataset and the model

- Difficulty in visualizing and analyzing the data

- Reduced interpretability of model predictions

Common approaches to mitigate the curse of dimensionality include **feature selection** techniques, which retain only the most informative features, and **dimensionality reduction** techniques, such as Principal Component Analysis (PCA). PCA transforms the original features into a smaller set of uncorrelated variables, called **principal components**, that capture the maximum variance in the data (and therefore preserve most of the information). These methods will be discussed in detail in the second volume of this book.

6.6.1 Example: KNN Classification on MNIST

To illustrate the challenges faced by k-nearest neighbors on high-dimensional datasets, we apply it to the MNIST dataset (see Section 5.8.3). Each image in MNIST consists of 28×28 pixels, resulting in 784 dimensions per example. While this number of dimensions can be considered moderate compared to datasets in domains such as text analysis or genomics, it is still high enough to pose challenges for distance-based algorithms such as KNN.

First, we fetch the dataset, normalize the pixel values, and split it into training and test sets:

```
from sklearn.datasets import fetch_openml

X, y = fetch_openml('mnist_784', return_X_y=True, as_frame=False)
X = X / 255 # normalize pixel values to [0, 1]

train_size = 60000
X_train, y_train = X[:train_size], y[:train_size]
X_test, y_test = X[train_size:], y[train_size:]
```

We now create a KNeighborsClassifier with default settings ($k = 5$) and fit it to the training set:

```
from sklearn.neighbors import KNeighborsClassifier

clf = KNeighborsClassifier()
clf.fit(X_train, y_train)
```

The accuracy of the model on the training and test sets is:

```
print(f'Training accuracy: {clf.score(X_train, y_train):.4f}')
print(f'Test accuracy: {clf.score(X_test, y_test):.4f}')

Training accuracy: 0.9819
Test accuracy: 0.9688
```

We also measure the time it takes to make predictions on the test set:

```
import time

start = time.time()
clf.predict(X_test)
print(f'Prediction time: {time.time() - start:.4f} seconds')

Prediction time: 6.0548 seconds
```

The test accuracy is higher than that of multinomial logistic regression, which achieved 92.59%. However, prediction is slow due to the large number of features.

Next, we explore whether dimensionality reduction can improve these results. To that end, we apply PCA[10] to reduce the number of dimensions from 784 to 50:

```
from sklearn.decomposition import PCA

pca = PCA(n_components=50, random_state=42)
X_train_reduced = pca.fit_transform(X_train)
X_test_reduced = pca.transform(X_test)
clf.fit(X_train_reduced, y_train)
```

The accuracy of the model after dimensionality reduction is:

```
print(f'Training accuracy: {clf.score(X_train_reduced, y_train):.4f}')
print(f'Test accuracy: {clf.score(X_test_reduced, y_test):.4f}')
```

```
Training accuracy: 0.9859
Test accuracy: 0.9748
```

We again measure the prediction time (including the time to apply PCA to the test set):

```
start = time.time()

X_test_reduced = pca.transform(X_test)
clf.predict(X_test_reduced)
print(f'Prediction time (with PCA): {time.time() - start:.4f} seconds')
```

```
Prediction time (with PCA): 1.0917 seconds
```

Dimensionality reduction increases the test accuracy from 96.88% to 97.48%, while also reducing the prediction time by a factor of six.

Finally, we examine how the test accuracy varies with the number of dimensions:

```
n_components_range = range(10, 785, 10)
test_accuracies = []

for n_components in n_components_range:
    pca = PCA(n_components=n_components)
    X_train_reduced = pca.fit_transform(X_train)
    X_test_reduced = pca.transform(X_test)
    clf.fit(X_train_reduced, y_train)
    accuracy = clf.score(X_test_reduced, y_test)
    test_accuracies.append(accuracy)
```

---

10. https://scikit-learn.org/stable/modules/generated/sklearn.decomposition.PCA.html

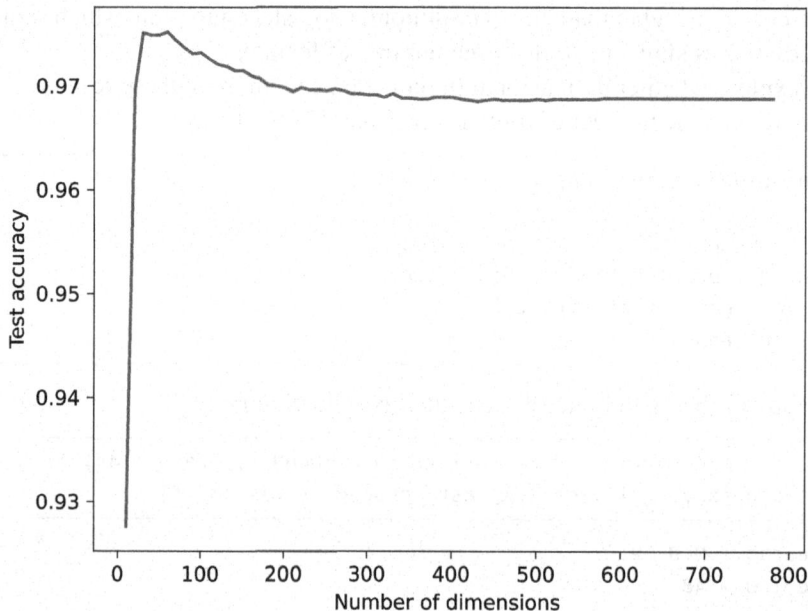

Figure 6.10: Test accuracy of k-nearest neighbors on the MNIST dataset as a function of the number of dimensions, showing optimal performance around 50 dimensions and a gradual decline beyond that.

```
plt.plot(n_components_range, test_accuracies)
plt.xlabel('Number of dimensions')
plt.ylabel('Test accuracy')
```

Figure 6.10 shows the results. The highest accuracy is achieved at around 50 dimensions, beyond which performance gradually declines as more dimensions are added, illustrating the adverse effects of the curse of dimensionality.

This example highlights how dimensionality reduction techniques such as PCA can both improve predictive performance and significantly reduce computation time by mitigating some of the challenges posed by high-dimensional data.

6.7 Radius-based Nearest Neighbors

The radius-based nearest neighbors (RNN) algorithm is a variant of k-nearest neighbors that uses a fixed radius r instead of a fixed number of neighbors k. A prediction is made based on all training points that fall within radius r of the query point. This approach can be advantageous when the data distribution is non-uniform, with regions of varying density. In sparse regions, restricting the search to a fixed radius ensures that only nearby points affect the prediction. In contrast, the standard KNN algorithm may include distant neighbors when few points are nearby, leading to less reliable predictions.

In Scikit-Learn, the `RadiusNeighborsClassifier`[11] class implements this algorithm. We illustrate its use with the Iris dataset from Section 6.1.4.

First, we load the dataset and split it into training and test sets:

```
from sklearn.datasets import load_iris
from sklearn.model_selection import train_test_split

iris = load_iris()
X = iris.data[:, :2] # Use only the first two features
y = iris.target
X_train, X_test, y_train, y_test = train_test_split(X, y, random_state=42)
```

Choosing an appropriate radius is crucial. If r is too small, some points may not have any neighbors within the specified radius, leading to undefined predictions. Conversely, an excessively large radius may include many distant and irrelevant points, similar to the effect of a large k in standard KNN. The optimal value is typically selected through experimentation and cross-validation.

As a starting point, one practical choice for the radius is the median distance between the training samples. To compute these distances, we use the `pdist`[12] function from SciPy.[13]

```
from scipy.spatial.distance import pdist

# Compute pairwise distances on the training data
distances = pdist(X_train)
median_distance = np.median(distances)
print(f'Median distance: {median_distance:.2f}')
```

```
Median distance: 1.08
```

If a test point has no neighbors within the specified radius, the classifier will, by default, raise an error during prediction. To avoid this, we can use the `outlier_label` parameter to assign a default label (e.g., -1) to such points:

```
from sklearn.neighbors import RadiusNeighborsClassifier

clf = RadiusNeighborsClassifier(radius=median_distance, outlier_label=-1)
clf.fit(X_train, y_train)
```

Next, we evaluate the performance of this classifier:

```
print(f'Training accuracy: {clf.score(X_train, y_train):.4f}')
print(f'Test accuracy: {clf.score(X_test, y_test):.4f}')
```

11. https://scikit-learn.org/stable/modules/generated/sklearn.neighbors.
    RadiusNeighborsClassifier.html
12. https://docs.scipy.org/doc/scipy/reference/generated/scipy.spatial.distance.pdist.html
13. Unlike Scikit-Learn's `pairwise_distances`, which returns the full symmetric distance matrix, pdist only computes the upper triangular part and returns it as a 1D array, saving both time and memory.

```
Training accuracy: 0.7946
Test accuracy: 0.7895
```

In this case, the RNN classifier performs slightly worse than KNN, which achieved a test accuracy of 81.58%. To improve performance, we can search for a better value of the radius using grid search:

```
from sklearn.model_selection import GridSearchCV

param_grid = {'radius': [0.5, 0.75, 1.0, 1.25, 1.5]}
grid_search = GridSearchCV(
    RadiusNeighborsClassifier(outlier_label=-1),
    param_grid, cv=3
)
grid_search.fit(X_train, y_train)
print(f'Best radius: {grid_search.best_params_["radius"]}')
```

```
Best radius: 0.75
```

The performance of the model with the best radius is:

```
print(f'Training accuracy: {grid_search.score(X_train, y_train):.4f}')
print(f'Test accuracy: {grid_search.score(X_test, y_test):.4f}')
```

```
Training accuracy: 0.8036
Test accuracy: 0.8421
```

With a smaller radius of 0.75, the test accuracy improved significantly from 78.95% to 84.21%, highlighting the importance of selecting an appropriate radius.

Note that radius-based nearest neighbors generally require more computation time and memory than k-nearest neighbors, since the algorithm must consider all points within the specified radius, which in dense regions can be far more than k.

6.8   K-Nearest Neighbors Regression

The k-nearest neighbors algorithm can also be applied to regression problems, where the target variable is continuous rather than categorical. In this case, the prediction for a query point is computed as the average of the target values of its k nearest neighbors. Formally, the predicted value for a given sample $\mathbf{x}$ is:

$$\hat{y} = \frac{1}{k} \sum_{\mathbf{x}_i \in N} y_i, \tag{6.17}$$

where N denotes the set of k nearest neighbors of $\mathbf{x}$.

Scikit-Learn provides the KNeighborsRegressor[14] class for k-nearest neighbors regression. It has the same hyperparameters as KNeighborsClassifier, including the number of nearest

---

14. https://scikit-learn.org/stable/modules/generated/sklearn.neighbors.KNeighborsRegressor.html

neighbors (n_neighbors), uniform or distance-based weighting (weights), and distance metric (metric). A radius-based variant is also available via the RadiusNeighborsRegressor[15] class, which selects neighbors within a fixed radius.

6.8.1   Example: California Housing Price Prediction

We now use the KNeighborsRegressor class to predict median house values in the California Housing dataset (see Section 4.6 for a detailed description of the dataset).

First, we load the dataset and split it into training and test sets:

```
from sklearn.datasets import fetch_california_housing
from sklearn.model_selection import train_test_split

X, y = fetch_california_housing(as_frame=True, return_X_y=True)
X_train, X_test, y_train, y_test = train_test_split(X, y, test_size=0.2,
                                                    random_state=42)
```

Since the features in this dataset have different scales, we standardize them to prevent any one feature from dominating the distance computations. To that end, we define a pipeline with a standard scaler followed by a KNN regressor:

```
from sklearn.pipeline import Pipeline
from sklearn.preprocessing import StandardScaler
from sklearn.neighbors import KNeighborsRegressor

model = Pipeline([
    ('scaler', StandardScaler()),
    ('reg', KNeighborsRegressor())
])
model.fit(X_train, y_train)
```

The performance of the model on the training and test sets is:

```
print(f'R2 score (train): {model.score(X_train, y_train):.4f}')
print(f'R2 score (test): {model.score(X_test, y_test):.4f}')
```

```
R2 score (train): 0.7969
R2 score (test): 0.6700
```

These results are significantly better than those obtained with linear regression in Section 4.6 (test $R^2 = 0.576$). To further improve the results, we perform a grid search over the key hyperparameters of the model: the number of nearest neighbors, the weighting scheme, and the power parameter p of the Minkowski distance:

---

15. https://scikit-learn.org/stable/modules/generated/sklearn.neighbors.
    RadiusNeighborsRegressor.html

```
from sklearn.model_selection import GridSearchCV

param_grid = {
    'reg__n_neighbors': np.arange(5, 51, 10),
    'reg__weights': ['uniform', 'distance'],
    'reg__p': np.arange(1, 5)
}
grid_search = GridSearchCV(model, param_grid, cv=3, n_jobs=-1)
grid_search.fit(X_train, y_train)
print(grid_search.best_params_)
```

The best parameters found are:

```
{'reg__n_neighbors': 15, 'reg__p': 1, 'reg__weights': 'distance'}
```

This shows that the default settings of Euclidean distance and uniform weighting are not always optimal. The model's performance after tuning is:

```
print(f'R2 score (train): {grid_search.score(X_train, y_train):.4f}')
print(f'R2 score (test): {grid_search.score(X_test, y_test):.4f}')
```

```
R2 score (train): 1.0000
R2 score (test): 0.7205
```

The test R^2 score has significantly improved from 0.67 to 0.7205, highlighting the importance of selecting appropriate values for the number of neighbors, weighting scheme, and the distance metric.

Notice that the training R^2 score reaches 1.0, meaning the tuned model fits the training data perfectly. This occurs because, on the training set, each query coincides with a training point, and with distance-based weighting that self-neighbor dominates the prediction.

6.9 Variants of KNN

Since its introduction in 1951, the k-nearest neighbors algorithm has inspired numerous variants designed to address its key challenges. These include speeding up neighbor searches, improving robustness to noise, and dynamically adjusting the value of k and the distance metric to local data characteristics. In this section, we review several important and commonly used KNN variants (see also a recent survey by Halder et al. [248]).

6.9.1 More Efficient KNN Algorithms

This section focuses on methods that enhance the computational efficiency and scalability of KNN. Some approaches accelerate the exact nearest neighbor search, while others rely on approximate methods that return neighbors that are close but not necessarily the true nearest, trading a small amount of accuracy for speed.

6.9.1.1 Exact Search Methods

The following methods guarantee retrieval of the true nearest neighbors while aiming to reduce the search time:

- **Metric Trees**: Metric trees, such as M-Trees [123], Vantage-Point (VP) trees [648], and cover trees [48], make use of the triangle inequality to prune portions of the search space that cannot possibly contain points closer than the current best candidate.[16]

- **iDistance Indexing** [651]: Partitions the dataset into clusters and encodes high-dimensional points into a one-dimensional index based on their distance from the cluster centers. The resulting index significantly reduces the number of distance computations needed during query processing.

- **GPU-Accelerated KNN** [215, 302]: Graphics Processing Units (GPUs) can parallelize distance computations, achieving substantial speedups on large-scale datasets. Libraries such as Facebook's FAISS[17] (Facebook AI Similarity Search) provide optimized implementations for large-scale nearest neighbor search using GPU acceleration. FAISS has recently become a key component in large language model (LLM) applications, particularly in retrieval-augmented generation (RAG) systems that require fast vector similarity search.

6.9.1.2 Approximate Search Methods

Approximate nearest neighbor (ANN) algorithms speed up search by relaxing the requirement for finding the exact nearest neighbors, making them suitable for very large or high-dimensional datasets [372, 608]. These methods return points that are close to the query point but not necessarily the closest. The intuition is that nearby points tend to belong to the same class, even if they are not the exact nearest neighbors. For example, in recommendation systems returning "similar enough" items is often sufficient and can even help users discover unexpected items.

Popular approximate methods include:

- **Locality-Sensitive Hashing (LSH)** [15]: Projects high-dimensional data into a lower-dimensional space using hash functions that increase the likelihood of similar points mapped to the same bucket. This limits the search to a small number of buckets and reduces distance computations. Beyond nearest neighbor search, LSH is also widely used in tasks such as near-duplicate detection, scalable similarity search, and information retrieval.

- **Product Quantization (PQ)** [295]: Splits the feature space into smaller subspaces and quantizes each one by replacing subvectors with representative codewords from a fixed codebook. PQ is widely used in large-scale retrieval systems such as FAISS.

- **Local Clustered KNN (LC-KNN)** [156]: Combines k-means clustering with KNN to restrict the search to a subset of relevant clusters, avoiding full-dataset searches while maintaining good accuracy.

---

16. Research on metric-tree data structures gained momentum in the late 1990s, including a notable study conducted by Sergey Brin, co-founder of Google [76].

17. https://github.com/facebookresearch/faiss

6.9.2   Handling Noisy Data and Outliers

The following KNN variants are designed to make the algorithm more robust in the presence of noise, mislabeled data, or outliers.

- **Fuzzy KNN** [314]: Assigns class membership probabilities instead of hard labels, allowing a point to belong to multiple classes with different degrees of membership. This reduces the impact of ambiguous or noisy data, and provides a measure of prediction uncertainty.

- **Edited Nearest Neighbors (ENN)** [625]: Improves the training set quality by removing points whose labels disagree with the majority of their k-nearest neighbors, thereby reducing sensitivity to noise and mislabeled data.

- **Tomek Links** [?]: Identifies nearest-neighbor pairs from opposite classes that are each other's closest neighbor (borderline or overlapping cases). Removing the majority-class instance in each pair helps clean class overlap and label noise, sharpening decision boundaries.

6.9.3   Adaptive KNN Algorithms

The following algorithms adapt the value of k or the distance metric dynamically based on the characteristics of the data or local conditions.

- **Adaptive KNN (AdaNN)** [568]: Adjusts the value of k for each query point based on local data density. Smaller k values are used in dense regions to preserve local detail, while large k values are chosen in sparse areas to include more points and reduce sensitivity to noise. This strategy balances overfitting and underfitting, improving generalization across datasets with varying densities.

- **Distance Metric Learning** [644]: Learns a distance function from labeled pairs of similar and dissimilar data points to better capture meaningful relationships in the input space. This can significantly improve KNN performance by making distance calculations more adaptive to the data.

- **Large Margin Nearest Neighbor (LMNN)** [614]: Learns a linear transformation of the input space that pulls points from the same class closer together while pushing points from different classes farther apart.

6.10   Applications of KNN

The k-nearest neighbors algorithm is widely applied in domains where proximity in feature space corresponds to real-world similarity. Notable examples include:

- Recommendation Systems: KNN is widely used in collaborative filtering to recommend products or content based on user similarity or item similarity [522, 639]. For example, it can suggest movies to a user by finding users with similar viewing histories.

- Medical Diagnosis: In healthcare, KNN is used to predict medical outcomes based on patient similarity. For example, it has been applied to detect diabetes, heart disease, and cancer by matching a patient's record to similar cases [108, 538, 28].

- Anomaly Detection: KNN is often used to detect outliers by identifying instances that lie far away from their nearest neighbors. This approach is applied in fraud detection and intrusion detection systems, where unusual patterns can signal malicious activities [358, 371].

- Large Language Models: KNN supports Retrieval-Augmented Generation (RAG) frameworks by retrieving semantically relevant documents for a given query, enabling large language models to incorporate external knowledge into their responses [354].

- Robotics: KNN is used in robotics for proximity-based tasks such as localization and navigation. For example, it supports indoor localization by matching real-time sensor readings to stored data [636], and aids in trajectory planning and obstacle avoidance by comparing the robot's current state to past experiences [245].

6.11 Summary

k-nearest neighbor (KNN) is a simple algorithm that predicts outcomes based on the closest training samples and can be applied to both classification and regression. This chapter covered its main concepts, including the effect of k, distance metrics, the curse of dimensionality, and extensions such as weighted voting and radius-based neighbors. We also introduced techniques to improve the efficiency, robustness, and adaptability of the algorithm.

Advantages of KNN compared to other supervised learning models:

- KNN makes no assumptions about the underlying data distribution and can capture complex, nonlinear patterns in the data, resulting in highly flexible decision boundaries.

- It performs well on many real-world datasets, especially when local neighborhoods in the feature space are predictive of the target.

- The choice of k provides a simple way to control the tradeoff between overfitting and underfitting.

- It supports both classification and regression tasks, and naturally handles multiclass classification without requiring special modifications.

- It requires no explicit training or model building, making it simple to set up aside from optional preprocessing (e.g., KD-trees) to accelerate queries.

- Aggregating multiple neighbors helps reduce the impact of noisy data.

- It requires tuning only a few hyperparameters, primarily the number of neighbors k and the choice of distance metric.

- KNN can incorporate new data points without retraining, making it suitable for dynamic or streaming data.

Disadvantages of KNN:

- It requires computing distances to all training samples at inference, which can be slow for large datasets. Although data structures like KD-trees or ball trees can accelerate neighbor searches, their efficiency deteriorates in high-dimensional spaces.

- Storing the entire training set leads to high memory usage and may require distributed storage when the data cannot fit on a single machine.

- Performance deteriorates in high-dimensional spaces because distances become less meaningful (due to the curse of dimensionality).

- All features contribute equally to distance computations, so irrelevant or noisy features can degrade performance unless feature selection or weighting is applied.

- Outliers can distort distances and lead to incorrect predictions, especially when k is small.

- Performance depends heavily on the choice of k, which must be tuned for each problem to balance overfitting and underfitting.

- KNN is sensitive to class imbalance, as the majority class can dominate local neighborhoods and bias the model's predictions.

- It does not produce an explicit model or provide feature importance scores, which makes its predictions harder to interpret and explain.

6.12   Exercises

6.12.1   Multiple-Choice Questions

6.1. Consider the training set shown in Table 6.6, where each row represents a labeled data point and its distance from a query point x. We want to classify x using the k-nearest neighbors algorithm with $k = 5$ in two different ways:

- Unweighted KNN: All neighbors are given equal weight.
- Weighted KNN: Weights are calculated as $w = 1/d$, where d is the distance from x.

How will the query point x be classified using each method?

  (a) Unweighted KNN: classified as 1, Weighted KNN: classified as 1.

  (b) Unweighted KNN: classified as 1, Weighted KNN: classified as 2.

Point i	Distance from x	Label
1	1	1
2	1	1
3	4	1
4	1.5	2
5	2.5	2
6	2	2
7	3	1
8	1.5	2
9	2.5	1
10	4	1

Table 6.6: A set of training samples and their distances from the query point x

   (c) Unweighted KNN: classified as 2, Weighted KNN: classified as 1.

   (d) Unweighted KNN: classified as 2, Weighted KNN: classified as 2.

6.2. Compared to a 5-nearest neighbor classifier, a 3-nearest neighbor classifier has:

   (a) Lower variance

   (b) Higher variance

   (c) Lower bias

   (d) Higher bias

6.3. What is the number of nearest neighbors k used to generate the decision boundaries shown in Figure 6.11?

   (a) $k = 1$

   (b) $k = 3$

   (c) $k = 5$

   (d) $k = 10$

6.4. What is the cosine similarity between the vectors $(1, 2, 3)$ and $(4, 5, 6)$?

   (a) 0.333

   (b) 0.975

   (c) 5.196

   (d) 32

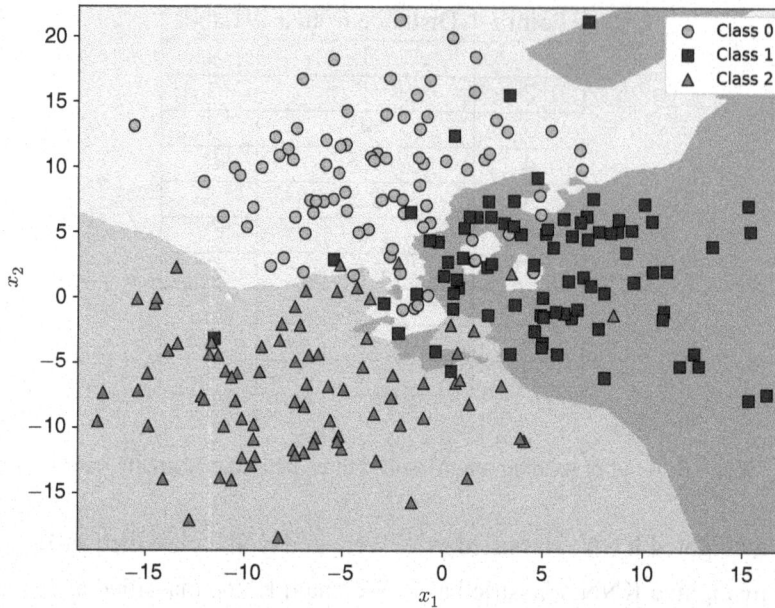

Figure 6.11: Decision boundary produced by KNN

6.5. Which of the following statements about KD-trees is true?

   (a) The runtime complexity of a nearest neighbor search is $\mathcal{O}(d \log n)$.

   (b) The construction of the tree does not depend on the order of the data points.

   (c) KD-trees provide a significant speedup for nearest neighbor searches compared to the brute-force approach in low-dimensional spaces.

   (d) KD-trees are less efficient than ball trees in high-dimensional spaces.

   (e) The runtime complexity increases with the number of neighbors k.

6.6. How is KNN affected by the curse of dimensionality?

   (a) The nearest neighbors become far from each other.

   (b) The nearest neighbors become equidistant from the query point.

   (c) There is a greater risk of underfitting in high-dimensional spaces.

   (d) There is a greater risk of overfitting in high-dimensional spaces.

6.7. Which of the following statements is true about radius-based nearest neighbors (RNN)?

   (a) RNN performs better than KNN in high-dimensional spaces.

   (b) Increasing the radius r lowers the bias and increases the variance.

   (c) RNN may fail to return predictions for some query points.

   (d) RNN can utilize KD-trees for more efficient queries.

6.8. Which of the following strategies can help KNN deal with varying densities in the feature space?

    (a) Use weighted KNN, where closer neighbors have higher influence.

    (b) Use radius-based nearest neighbors to adapt the neighborhood size.

    (c) Perform local scaling of distances based on the density around each point.

    (d) Reduce the number of neighbors k to avoid bias towards the majority classes.

6.9. Which KNN variant accelerates neighbor searches by reducing the number of distance computations?

    (a) Locality-Sensitive Hashing (LSH)

    (b) Edited Nearest Neighbors (ENN)

    (c) Adaptive KNN (AdaNN)

    (d) Cover Trees

    (e) Fuzzy KNN

6.10. Which KNN variant improves its robustness to noisy data?

    (a) Local Clustered KNN (LC-KNN)

    (b) Adaptive KNN (AdaNN)

    (c) Edited Nearest Neighbors (ENN)

    (d) Radius-based Nearest Neighbors (RNN)

    (e) Fuzzy KNN

6.12.2 Theoretical Exercises

6.11. Consider the dataset in Table 6.7, which consists of three numerical features x_1, x_2, and x_3, and a binary output variable y.

    (a) Based on this dataset, classify a new vector $\mathbf{x} = (0, 1, 2)$ using KNN with $k = 3$ and Euclidean distance. Show your computations.

    (b) Classify the same vector using inverse-distance weighting. Do you get the same label as in unweighted KNN?

6.12. In k-nearest neighbors with distance-weighted voting, each neighbor's vote is weighted by the inverse of its distance to the query point:

$$w_i = \frac{1}{d_i},$$

where d_i is the distance between the query point and the i-th neighbor.

Prove that if all k nearest neighbors are equidistant from the query point (i.e., $d_1 = d_2 = \cdots = d_k$), then distance-weighted voting yields the same prediction as unweighted voting.

i	x_1	x_2	x_3	y
1	2	3	2	0
2	3	-1	4	1
3	-2	1	0	0
4	0	3	-2	1
5	3	-2	2	0
6	-1	1	3	1
7	2	-3	0	0
8	-2	1	-1	1
9	1	-2	2	0
10	0	2	-1	1

Table 6.7: A sample dataset for KNN

6.13. Recall from Section 2.6 that the bias–variance decomposition for the expected error of a predictive model can be expressed as:

$$\mathbb{E}\left[(\hat{f}(x) - f(x))^2\right] = \text{Bias}^2(\hat{f}(x)) + \text{Var}(\hat{f}(x)) + \sigma^2,$$

where $\hat{f}(x)$ is the model's prediction, $f(x)$ is the true function, and σ^2 is the irreducible noise.

Use this theorem to analyze how varying k affects both bias and variance in the k-nearest neighbors algorithm. Specifically, explain why a very small k leads to low bias but high variance, and a large k leads to high bias but low variance.

6.14. Prove that the Euclidean distance satisfies the triangle inequality in n-dimensional space by showing that, for any three points $A(x_1, x_2, \ldots, x_n)$, $B(y_1, y_2, \ldots, y_n)$, and $C(z_1, z_2, \ldots, z_n)$, the inequality $d(A, C) \leq d(A, B) + d(B, C)$ holds.

Hint: Represent the distances using vectors, apply vector addition for the sum $\overrightarrow{AC} = \overrightarrow{AB} + \overrightarrow{BC}$, and square both sides to apply the dot product. Then use the Cauchy-Schwarz inequality (see Section A.1.6) to bound the cross-term.

6.15. Provide a detailed example where using Manhattan distance in the k-nearest neighbors algorithm results in an accurate classification of a query point, while using Euclidean distance leads to a misclassification (you can choose any k in your example).

6.16. Prove that as $p \to \infty$, the Minkowski distance between any two points in n-dimensional space converges to the Chebyshev distance. Specifically, show that:

$$\lim_{p \to \infty} d_p(A, B) = \max_{1 \leq i \leq n} |x_i - y_i|,$$

where $A = (x_1, x_2, \ldots, x_n)$ and $B = (y_1, y_2, \ldots, y_n)$ are two points in an n-dimensional space.

Hint: Let $M = \max_{1 \le i \le n} |x_i - y_i|$. Show that $d_p(A, B)$ is bounded below by M and above by $M \cdot n^{1/p}$, and use the squeeze theorem to conclude the limit.

6.17. (*) Let $X_1, \ldots, X_n$ be i.i.d. random variables uniformly distributed on $[0, 1]$. Consider the fixed query point at $x = 0.5$. Let $r_k(x)$ denote the distance from x to its k-th nearest neighbor among $X_1, \ldots, X_n$.

    (a) For a fixed k and large n, explain intuitively why $r_k(x)$ tends to 0 as $n \to \infty$.

    (b) Suppose now that $k = k(n)$ increases with n. What conditions on $k(n)$ ensure that $r_k(x) \to 0$ while also satisfying $k/n \to 0$? Provide at least one concrete example of a function $k(n)$ that meets these conditions.

    (c) Explain why such a choice of $k(n)$ helps the KNN classifier make accurate predictions. *Hint*: Think about the bias–variance tradeoff.

6.18. Build and visualize a KD-tree for the following data points in two-dimensional space: $(2, 3)$, $(5, 4)$, $(9, 6)$, $(4, 7)$, $(8, 1)$, $(7, 2)$. Construct the tree by alternating splits between the x and y coordinates. Illustrate how each split divides the space, and label each node with its corresponding point, similar to Figure 6.8. After constructing the KD-tree, simulate the nearest neighbor search for the query point $Q(6, 5)$.

6.19. Investigate alternative tree-based data structures for nearest neighbor search, such as VP-trees [648], cover trees [48], and Δ-trees [140]:

    (a) For each structure, provide:

- A brief description of how the tree is constructed.
- The query algorithm used for nearest neighbor search.
- Analysis of the time complexity for both construction and querying.

    (b) Compare the advantages and disadvantages of these structures against KD-trees and ball trees. Address the following factors:

- Performance in low vs. high-dimensional spaces.
- Handling of uneven or dense data distributions.
- Scalability and memory usage.
- Ease of implementation and practical use cases.

    (c) (Bonus) Implement one of these tree structures (e.g., VP-tree, cover tree, or Δ-tree) in Python from scratch. Compare its performance to KD-trees or ball trees on a dataset of your choice.

6.20. Read the paper by Andoni and Indyk (2008) titled "Near-optimal hashing algorithms for approximate nearest neighbor in high dimensions" [15]. After reading the paper, answer the following questions:

   (a) Summarize the core idea behind Locality-Sensitive Hashing (LSH) as described in the paper. How does LSH enable efficient approximate nearest neighbor search in high-dimensional spaces?

   (b) Explain the concept of approximation guarantees in ANN algorithms. What is the tradeoff between accuracy and efficiency in these algorithms?

   (c) How does the time complexity of LSH compare to that of an exact nearest neighbor search? Use the notation from the paper to support your explanation.

   (d) Discuss how ANN methods mitigate the impact of the curse of dimensionality on nearest neighbor search.

6.12.3 Programming Exercises

6.21. Apply the KNN algorithm to the Breast Cancer Wisconsin (Diagnostic) dataset[18], where the goal is to classify tumors as benign or malignant. Follow these steps to analyze and optimize the algorithm's performance:

   (a) Data preparation:

      i. Load the dataset using the `load_breast_cancer`[19] function from `sklearn.datasets`.

      ii. Split the dataset into training and test sets using an 80/20 split.

      iii. Apply feature scaling to standardize the dataset.

   (b) Tuning the hyperparameters:

      i. Using 5-fold cross-validation, evaluate a range of values for k (the number of neighbors), for example $k = 1$ to $k = 20$. Plot the cross-validation accuracy as a function of k.

      ii. Compare the performance of KNN using different distance metrics, specifically the Euclidean and Manhattan distances. Use the optimal k found in the previous step.

      iii. Compare unweighted KNN (where all neighbors have equal weight) with weighted KNN (where closer neighbors have more influence). Use the optimal value of k and the best distance metric from the previous steps.

      iv. Perform a grid search over k, the distance metric, and weighting scheme. Report the combination of hyperparameters that yields the best cross-validation score.

---

18. https://archive.ics.uci.edu/dataset/17/breast+cancer+wisconsin+diagnostic
19. https://scikit-learn.org/stable/modules/generated/sklearn.datasets.load_breast_cancer.html

    (c) Final model evaluation:

       i. Using the best combination of hyperparameters, fit the KNN model to the training data.

      ii. Evaluate the performance of the final model on the test set using the accuracy score, confusion matrix, and classification report (precision, recall, F1-score).

    (d) Write a short report summarizing your findings. Discuss how the choice of hyperparameters affected the model's performance, and compare the results of the final model on the test set with the best cross-validation scores.

6.22. (*) Implement the KD-tree data structure discussed in Section 6.5.1, using the following steps:

    (a) Implement the KD-tree construction algorithm. The KD-tree should alternate between splitting on different dimensions (e.g., x_1, x_2, etc.) at each level of the tree. Include an optional parameter `leaf_size` to specify the number of points at which the tree stops splitting and stores data points in leaf nodes. If not provided, set `leaf_size` to 1.

    (b) Implement an efficient neighbor search using the KD-tree to find the k-nearest neighbors to a given query point.

    (c) Demonstrate the usage of your tree on a small synthetic dataset to verify its construction and query efficiency.

    (d) Integrate your KD-tree with the custom KNN estimator shown in Section 6.1.2. Compare the runtime of your KNN implementation with and without the KD-tree for various values of k on the California Housing Dataset. Experiment with different values of `leaf_size` to analyze its impact on runtime.

6.23. Implement the radius-based nearest neighbors (RNN) algorithm from scratch. Follow these steps:

    (a) Create a custom estimator that implements the RNN algorithm for classification. For each query point, find all neighbors within a given radius r, and predict the target class based on the majority vote of the neighbors' classes. Use Euclidean distance as the distance metric. If there is a tie in the majority vote, use a clear tie-breaking rule, e.g., choose the class of the closest neighbor.

    (b) Add a mechanism to handle cases where no neighbors are found within the given radius (e.g., use a default class prediction or assign the class of the nearest neighbor).

    (c) Compare the performance of your RNN implementation to Scikit-Learn's `Radius NeighborsClassifier` on a suitable classification dataset (e.g., the Breast Cancer Wisconsin dataset).

    (d) Experiment with different values of r and plot the classification accuracy and runtime as functions of the radius. Explain how varying the radius impacts the model's performance and computational efficiency.

6.24. Implement the k-nearest neighbors regression algorithm from scratch. Follow these steps:

   (a) Create a custom estimator that implements the k-nearest neighbors regression algorithm. For a given query point, find the k-nearest neighbors and predict the target value as the average of their target values. Use Euclidean distance as the distance metric.

   (b) Test your implementation on the California Housing Dataset. Remember to standardize the features using StandardScaler before fitting the model.

   (c) Compare your implementation to Scikit-Learn's KNeighborsRegressor using the same dataset. Plot the MSE of both implementations as a function of k. Analyze how changing the number of neighbors impacts model performance.

6.25. (*) Implement the approximate nearest neighbors algorithm using Locality-Sensitive Hashing (LSH), based on the paper by Andoni and Indyk [15]. Follow these steps:

   (a) Implement Locality-Sensitive Hashing (LSH) to reduce the dimensionality of the data. Design hash functions that maximize the probability of similar points being hashed to the same bucket.

   (b) Implement an approximate nearest neighbors search using LSH. For each query point, search within the relevant hash buckets to find approximate neighbors.

   (c) Load the MNIST dataset (or another high-dimensional dataset) using the fetch_openml function from sklearn.datasets. Normalize the pixel values to a [0, 1] range.

   (d) Compare the runtime and accuracy of your LSH-based nearest neighbor search to the exact KNN algorithm on the MNIST dataset. Analyze the tradeoff between approximation quality and search speed.

   (e) Plot the accuracy and runtime as functions of the number of hash functions used in LSH. Explain how increasing or decreasing the number of hash functions affects both the accuracy and computational efficiency.

Chapter 7

Naive Bayes

Naive Bayes classifiers are a family of probabilistic models based on Bayes' theorem. They estimate the probability of each class given a set of observed features, under the simplifying (or "naive") assumption that all features are conditionally independent given the class. Although this assumption rarely holds exactly in practice, it leads to models that are highly efficient, scalable, and interpretable.

Different naive Bayes models make different assumptions about the type and distribution of the features. The most common include the Bernoulli model for binary features, the categorical model for discrete categories, the multinomial model for word counts or frequencies, and the Gaussian model for continuous features.

Despite their simplicity, naive Bayes models often perform remarkably well on real-world tasks—particularly in domains such as text classification, sentiment analysis, and medical diagnosis—where the conditional independence assumption is often a reasonable approximation.

In addition to their practical utility, naive Bayes classifiers offer a valuable conceptual foundation for understanding probabilistic reasoning in classification. They provide a clear example of how prior knowledge (in the form of class priors) and evidence from features combine to inform predictions. This makes them a natural starting point for exploring the broader class of probabilistic models in machine learning.

This chapter is organized as follows. Section 7.1 introduces the naive Bayes model, its assumptions and theoretical underpinnings. Section 7.2 presents various variants of the model, including Bernoulli, categorical, multinomial, and Gaussian naive Bayes classifiers. Section 7.3 demonstrates the usage of naive Bayes classifiers in Scikit-Learn. Section 7.4 discusses linear and quadratic discriminant analysis (LDA and QDA), as extensions of Gaussian naive Bayes that allow correlated features and class-specific covariance structures. Section 7.5 provides a primer on natural language processing (NLP) and introduces the main Python libraries used for text analysis. Section 7.6 demonstrates how to use a multinomial naive Bayes classifier to tackle a document classification task. Section 7.7 introduces Bayesian networks, a powerful extension of the naive Bayes model that uses directed acyclic graphs to explicitly model conditional dependencies between variables. Section 7.8 offers an overview of probabilistic graphical models (PGMs), which represent complex joint distributions using graph-based structures. Section 7.9 concludes with a summary.

7.1 The Naive Bayes Model

The naive Bayes model is a foundational probabilistic method for classification, with one of its earliest formal descriptions found in the work of Duda and Hart (1973) [175].

Suppose we have a classification problem with C classes labeled $1, 2, \ldots, C$. For a given sample $\mathbf{x} = (x_1, \ldots, x_d)^T$, the naive Bayes classifier uses Bayes' theorem to compute the posterior probability that the sample belongs to class c:

$$P(y = c | \mathbf{x}) = \frac{P(y = c) P(\mathbf{x} | y = c)}{P(\mathbf{x})}, \tag{7.1}$$

where:

- $P(y = c)$ is the prior probability of class c.

- $P(\mathbf{x} | y = c)$ is the likelihood of observing the features $\mathbf{x}$ given that the sample belongs to class c.

- $P(\mathbf{x})$ is the marginal probability of the features, acting as a normalization factor.

During model training, these probabilities are estimated from the data. The class prior $P(y = c)$ is approximated by the relative frequency of class c in the training set:

$$P(y = c) \approx \frac{n_c}{n}, \tag{7.2}$$

where n_c is the number of training samples in class c and n is the total number of training samples.

Estimating the conditional likelihood $P(\mathbf{x} | y = c)$ presents a significant challenge due to the vast number of possible feature combinations. For example, if $\mathbf{x}$ consists of d binary features, then modeling $P(\mathbf{x} | y)$ directly would require estimating 2^d conditional probabilities for each class, corresponding to every possible combination of the feature values. This approach is not only computationally prohibitive but also impractical, as it requires a vast amount of training data to obtain reliable estimates of all these probabilities.

The **naive Bayes assumption** addresses this issue by assuming that the features are conditionally independent given the class label. That is, once the class y is known, the value of any feature x_i provides no additional information about any other feature x_j. Formally, the likelihood of the feature vector $\mathbf{x} = (x_1, x_2, \ldots, x_d)$ given the class c factorizes into the product of the conditional probabilities of the individual features:

$$P(\mathbf{x} | y = c) = P(x_1 | y = c) \cdot P(x_2 | y = c) \cdots P(x_d | y = c) = \prod_{j=1}^{d} P(x_j | y = c). \tag{7.3}$$

For example, in spam filtering, the model treats the presence of words such as "rich" and "prince" as independent evidence of spam, even if these words tend to appear together. Although this assumption is a simplification of the true data-generating process, it often works surprisingly well in practice, particularly in domains where dependencies among features may be weak or irrelevant to the prediction task, such as text classification and recommendation systems.

Substituting the factorized likelihood from Equation (7.3) into Bayes' theorem gives:

$$P(y = c|\mathbf{x}) = \frac{P(y = c) \prod_{j=1}^{d} P(x_j|y = c)}{P(\mathbf{x})}. \tag{7.4}$$

This factorization drastically reduces the number of parameters that must be estimated from the data. For example, when $\mathbf{x}$ consists of d binary features, the number of parameters decreases from 2^d per class to just d per class. This reduction not only makes the model computationally feasible but also helps mitigate the risk of overfitting, since models with fewer parameters tend to generalize better.

At this stage, we have two options, depending on whether we are interested in the exact class probabilities or simply predicting the most likely class label:

- To compute the exact posterior probabilities, we need to calculate the marginal probability $P(\mathbf{x})$. This can be done by summing over the joint probabilities of $\mathbf{x}$ and each class c:

$$P(\mathbf{x}) = \sum_{c=1}^{C} P(y = c)P(\mathbf{x}|y = c). \tag{7.5}$$

- If we are only concerned with predicting the class label, we can skip computing $P(\mathbf{x})$, since it is the same for all classes. Instead, we directly select the class that maximizes the posterior:

$$\hat{y} = \underset{c \in C}{\operatorname{argmax}}\, P(y = c)P(\mathbf{x}|y = c). \tag{7.6}$$

This classification rule is known as **Maximum A Posteriori (MAP),** as it selects the class with the highest posterior probability given the input. Although this MAP rule is applied here to select among class labels, it is conceptually similar to MAP estimation in Bayesian statistics, where we choose a parameter value θ that maximizes the posterior distribution $p(\theta|D)$ given a dataset D (see Section D.8.2). In both cases, the goal is to make an optimal decision by maximizing posterior belief under uncertainty.

A key advantage of the MAP decision rule is its robustness: the model can still predict the correct class even when the probability estimates are inaccurate, as long as the correct class has the highest estimated posterior. This makes the classifier more tolerant of errors introduced by simplifying assumptions such as conditional independence.

In fact, research has shown that naive Bayes classifiers can still classify accurately even when the conditional independence assumption is strongly violated [170, 253, 659]. The key insight is that classification and probability estimation are fundamentally different tasks: accurate classification may still be possible even when the probability estimates themselves are poor. This distinction helps explain why naive Bayes often performs well in real-world applications.

7.2   Event Models in Naive Bayes

Estimating the conditional probabilities of the features, $P(x_j|y = c)$, is a crucial step in building a naive Bayes classifier. The approach to this estimation depends on the type of features (e.g., discrete or continuous) and the probability distribution assumed for the feature likelihoods.

The probabilistic modeling of these likelihoods is often referred to as an **event model** (or **data model**). Each event model defines a specific form for the class-conditional distribution $P(x_j|y = c)$ and leads to a different variant of the naive Bayes classifier.

In the following subsections, we explore the most common event models and describe how their parameters are estimated from data.

7.2.1   Bernoulli Naive Bayes

In the Bernoulli event model, each feature is treated as an independent binary variable that follows a Bernoulli distribution. In this setting, feature j has a probability p_j of being present in a sample ($x_j = 1$) and a probability of $1 - p_j$ of being absent ($x_j = 0$). For example, in text classification, x_j could indicate whether the j-th word from the vocabulary appears in a given document.

In this model, the conditional probability of x_j given class c is estimated from the frequency of feature j among samples of class c:

$$P(x_j = 1 \mid y = c) \approx \frac{n_{cj}}{n_c}, \tag{7.7}$$

where n_{cj} is the number of samples in class c where feature j is present ($x_j = 1$), and n_c is the total number of samples in class c.

7.2.1.1   Example: Text Classification

Consider a text classification task in which the goal is to classify each document into one of C predefined categories. Given a vocabulary of size $|V|$, each document can be represented as a binary vector $\mathbf{x} = (x_1, x_2, \ldots, x_{|V|})^T$, where x_j corresponds to word w_j from the vocabulary. Each x_j takes the value 1 if w_j appears at least once in the document and 0 otherwise.

Under the naive Bayes assumption, the likelihood of the document given its class factorizes as:

$$P(\mathbf{x}|y = c) = \prod_{j=1}^{|V|} P(w_j|c)^{x_j} (1 - P(w_j|c))^{1-x_j}, \tag{7.8}$$

where $P(w_j|c)$ is the probability that word w_j appears in a document from category c, and $1 - P(w_j|c)$ is the probability that it does not appear. In this model, a document is treated as a collection of independent Bernoulli variables—one for each word in the vocabulary. In the context of text classification, this approach is often referred to as the **multivariate Bernoulli naive Bayes model** to distinguish it from models that incorporate word frequencies or continuous features.

In practice, however, it is common not to explicitly model the absence of words. This is because, in many text classification tasks, the presence of certain words is much more informative than their absence, and explicitly modeling the absence of words would multiply many small probabilities together, resulting in extremely small likelihood values. In this case, the likelihood of a document given its class can be simplified to:

$$P(\mathbf{x}|y = c) = \prod_{j=1}^{|V|} P(w_j|c)^{x_j}, \tag{7.9}$$

where only the words that actually appear in the document contribute to the likelihood.

The parameters of this model are the class-conditional probabilities $\theta_{cj} = P(w_j|c)$ and the class prior probabilities $\theta_c = P(y = c)$. Estimating these parameters from the training data involves computing the relative frequencies of word occurrences and class labels. Specifically, given a labeled training set $D = \{(\mathbf{x}_1, y_1), \ldots, (\mathbf{x}_n, y_n)\}$, the class-conditional probabilities are estimated as:

$$\theta_{cj} = P(w_j|c) \approx \frac{\sum_{i=1}^{|D|} x_{ij} \mathbb{1}(y_i = c)}{\sum_{i=1}^{|D|} \mathbb{1}(y_i = c)}. \tag{7.10}$$

Here, x_{ij} indicates whether word w_j appears in document i, and $\mathbb{1}(y_i = c)$ is an indicator function that equals 1 if the class label of document i is c, and 0 otherwise. These estimates correspond to the maximum likelihood estimates (MLE) of the Bernoulli distribution parameters governing the feature likelihoods (see Exercise 7.14).

The class prior probabilities can be estimated from the relative frequencies of the classes:

$$\theta_c = P(y = c) \approx \frac{\sum_{i=1}^{|D|} \mathbb{1}(y_i = c)}{|D|}. \tag{7.11}$$

Note that the Bernoulli model does not account for how many times a word appears in a document; it only considers whether a word is present or absent. In Section 7.2.3, we will introduce a naive Bayes model that extends this approach by incorporating word frequencies.

7.2.1.2 Decision Boundaries

The decision boundaries formed by the Bernoulli naive Bayes classifier are linear, making it a linear classification model, similar to logistic regression. We now present a proof for the binary classification case; the same reasoning naturally extends to multiclass classification.

Proof. Let $\mathbf{x} = (x_1, x_2, \ldots, x_d)^T$ be a binary feature vector, where each $x_j \in \{0, 1\}$. Our goal is to classify $\mathbf{x}$ into one of two classes, $y = 0$ or $y = 1$.

In the Bernoulli naive Bayes model, each feature x_j follows a Bernoulli distribution parameterized by $\theta_{cj} = P(x_j = 1 \mid y = c)$, which is the probability that feature j is present given class c. Accordingly, $1 - \theta_{cj}$ is the probability that feature j is absent given class c.

The naive Bayes classifier assigns the label $\hat{y}$ according to the maximum a posteriori (MAP) rule:

$$\hat{y} = \underset{c \in \{0,1\}}{\operatorname{argmax}} P(y = c|\mathbf{x}) = \underset{c \in \{0,1\}}{\operatorname{argmax}} P(\mathbf{x}|y = c)P(y = c),$$

where $P(y = c)$ is the class prior and $P(\mathbf{x}|y = c)$ is the class-conditional likelihood.

Under the conditional independence assumption, the class-conditional likelihood can be written as

$$P(\mathbf{x}|y = c) = \prod_{j=1}^{d} P(x_j|y = c)$$

$$= \prod_{j=1}^{d} \theta_{cj}^{x_j} (1 - \theta_{cj})^{1-x_j}.$$

The decision boundary is defined as the set of points where the posterior probabilities for $y = 0$ and $y = 1$ are equal:

$$P(y = 1|\mathbf{x}) = P(y = 0|\mathbf{x}) \Rightarrow \log \left(\frac{P(\mathbf{x}|y = 1)P(y = 1)}{P(\mathbf{x}|y = 0)P(y = 0)} \right) = 0.$$

Taking logarithms and expanding the likelihood terms gives:

$$\log P(\mathbf{x}|y = 1) = \sum_{j=1}^{d} [x_j \log \theta_{1j} + (1 - x_j) \log(1 - \theta_{1j})],$$

$$\log P(\mathbf{x}|y = 0) = \sum_{j=1}^{d} [x_j \log \theta_{0j} + (1 - x_j) \log(1 - \theta_{0j})].$$

Substituting these expressions into the log-ratio equation yields:

$$\sum_{j=1}^{d} \left[x_j \log \frac{\theta_{1j}}{\theta_{0j}} + (1 - x_j) \log \frac{1 - \theta_{1j}}{1 - \theta_{0j}} \right] + \log \frac{P(y = 1)}{P(y = 0)} = 0,$$

$$\sum_{j=1}^{d} \left[x_j \log \frac{\theta_{1j}}{\theta_{0j}} \right] + \sum_{j=1}^{d} \log \frac{1 - \theta_{1j}}{1 - \theta_{0j}} + \log \frac{P(y = 1)}{P(y = 0)} = 0.$$

Define the weights:

$$w_j = \log \frac{\theta_{1j}}{\theta_{0j}}, \quad w_0 = \sum_{j=1}^{d} \log \frac{1 - \theta_{1j}}{1 - \theta_{0j}} + \log \frac{P(y = 1)}{P(y = 0)},$$

Then the decision boundary becomes:

$$\sum_{j=1}^{d} w_j x_j + w_0 = 0,$$

which represents a hyperplane in the feature space. This confirms that the decision boundary of the Bernoulli naive Bayes classifier is linear. $\square$

This result naturally extends to multiclass classification by applying the same reasoning to each pair of classes, yielding linear decision boundaries between them.

7.2.2 Categorical Naive Bayes

The categorical event model generalizes the Bernoulli event model to cases where each feature can take more than two discrete values. In this model, each feature j is assumed to follow a categorical distribution with K_j possible categories (see Section C.5.6.7). For each class c, the probability of feature j taking category k is given by

$$\theta_{cjk} = P(x_j = k \mid y = c), \tag{7.12}$$

and these probabilities must sum to 1:

$$\sum_{k=1}^{K_j} \theta_{cjk} = 1. \tag{7.13}$$

The parameters θ_{cjk} can be estimated from the training data by counting how often j takes the value k among samples of class c:

$$\theta_{cjk} = P(x_j = k \mid y = c) \approx \frac{n_{cjk}}{n_c}, \tag{7.14}$$

where n_{cjk} is the number of samples in class c where $x_j = k$, and n_c is the total number of samples in class c.

7.2.2.1 Example: Customer Purchase Prediction

Table 7.1 presents data on past purchases of customers at a fictitious store. Each row contains information about the customer's age, student status, income level, credit rating, and whether they purchased the target product.

Consider a new customer with the following attributes:

$$[\text{Age} = \text{Young}, \text{Student} = \text{Yes}, \text{Income} = \text{Low}, \text{Credit} = \text{Excellent}].$$

We would like to predict whether this customer will buy the product. Since all features are categorical, we can use the cateogrical naive Bayes model for this task.

	Age	Student	Income	Credit	Buys
1	Young	Yes	High	Fair	No
2	Senior	No	High	Excellent	Yes
3	Middle	Yes	Medium	Fair	Yes
4	Young	Yes	Low	Fair	No
5	Middle	Yes	Low	Excellent	Yes
6	Senior	No	Medium	Excellent	No
7	Young	No	Medium	Excellent	Yes
8	Young	Yes	Medium	Fair	Yes
9	Middle	Yes	High	Excellent	Yes
10	Senior	No	Low	Fair	No

Table 7.1: Data on past purchases of customers

The prior probabilities of the two classes are estimated from the frequency of past purchases:

$$P(\text{Buys = Yes}) = \frac{6}{10} = 0.6, \quad P(\text{Buys = No}) = \frac{4}{10} = 0.4.$$

The likelihood of each feature given the class label is estimated using empirical frequencies:

$$P(\text{Age = Young} \mid \text{Yes}) = \frac{2}{6} = 0.333, \qquad P(\text{Age = Young} \mid \text{No}) = \frac{2}{4} = 0.5,$$

$$P(\text{Student = Yes} \mid \text{Yes}) = \frac{4}{6} = 0.667, \qquad P(\text{Student = Yes} \mid \text{No}) = \frac{2}{4} = 0.5,$$

$$P(\text{Income = Low} \mid \text{Yes}) = \frac{1}{6} = 0.167, \qquad P(\text{Income = Low} \mid \text{No}) = \frac{2}{4} = 0.5,$$

$$P(\text{Credit = Excellent} \mid \text{Yes}) = \frac{4}{6} = 0.667, \qquad P(\text{Credit = Excellent} \mid \text{No}) = \frac{1}{4} = 0.25.$$

Therefore, the posterior probability for Buys = Yes is:

$$P(\text{Yes} \mid \mathbf{x}) = \alpha P(\text{Yes}) \cdot P(\text{Young} \mid \text{Yes}) \cdot P(\text{Student} \mid \text{Yes}) \cdot P(\text{Low} \mid \text{Yes}) \cdot P(\text{Excellent} \mid \text{Yes})$$

$$= \alpha \cdot 0.6 \cdot 0.333 \cdot 0.667 \cdot 0.167 \cdot 0.667$$

$$= 0.0148 \, \alpha,$$

where $\alpha = \frac{1}{P(\mathbf{x})}$ is a normalization factor ensuring that the posterior probabilities sum to 1.
Similarly, for Buys = No:

$$P(\text{No} \mid \mathbf{x}) = \alpha P(\text{No}) \cdot P(\text{Young} \mid \text{No}) \cdot P(\text{Student} \mid \text{No}) \cdot P(\text{Low} \mid \text{No}) \cdot P(\text{Excellent} \mid \text{No})$$

$$= \alpha \cdot 0.4 \cdot 0.5 \cdot 0.5 \cdot 0.5 \cdot 0.25$$

$$= 0.0125 \, \alpha.$$

Since $P(\text{Yes} \mid \mathbf{x}) > P(\text{No} \mid \mathbf{x})$, the model predicts that the customer will buy the product.

To obtain the actual posterior probabilities, we compute the normalization factor α using the fact that the posteriors must sum to 1:

$$0.0148\,\alpha + 0.0125\,\alpha = 1 \;\Rightarrow\; \alpha = \frac{1}{0.0148 + 0.0125} = 36.63.$$

Therefore, the posterior probability that the customer will buy the product is:

$$P(\text{Yes} \mid \mathbf{x}) = 0.0148 \cdot 36.63 = 0.5421.$$

According to the model, the probability that this customer will purchase the product is 54.21%.

7.2.3 Multinomial Naive Bayes

In the **multinomial naive Bayes (MNB)** model, each sample consists of counts of outcomes from a single categorical variable X with K possible values. If we denote these counts by $\mathbf{x} = (x_1, \ldots, x_K)^T$, then x_j represents how many times outcome j appears in the sample.

A common application of this model is text classification using the **bag-of-words (BoW)** representation, where each document is encoded as a vector of word counts over a fixed vocabulary. In this representation, each feature x_j indicates how many times the j-th word from the vocabulary appears in the document (see Table 7.2).

In MNB, the class-conditional probability of $\mathbf{x}$ given a class c follows the multinomial distribution (see Section C.11.6.2):

$$P(\mathbf{x}|y = c) = \frac{N!}{x_1! x_2! \cdots x_K!} \prod_{j=1}^{K} \theta_{cj}^{x_j}, \tag{7.15}$$

where:

- $N = \sum_{j=1}^{K} x_j$ is the total number of feature occurrences (e.g., words) in the sample.

- $\theta_{cj} = P(X = j \mid y = c)$ is the probability of feature j occurring in class c, satisfying $\sum_{j=1}^{K} \theta_{cj} = 1$ (e.g., the probability of the j-th word in documents of class c).

- The multinomial coefficient $\frac{N!}{x_1! x_2! \cdots x_K!}$ counts the number of distinct feature sequences that correspond to the same count vector $\mathbf{x}$. For example, for $\mathbf{x} = (2, 1)$ there are $\frac{3!}{2!1!} = 3$ possible sequences: AAB, ABA, and BAA.

the	cat	sat	on	mat	looked	at	dog	jumped	off
5	2	1	1	2	1	1	1	1	1

Table 7.2: Bag-of-words representation for the sentence: "The cat sat on the mat and looked at the dog. Then the cat jumped off the mat."

To estimate the parameters θ_{cj} from the training data, we use the relative frequency of each feature across all samples of class c:

$$\theta_{cj} = P(X = j \mid y = c) \approx \frac{\sum_{i=1}^{|D|} x_{ij} \mathbb{1}(y_i = c)}{\sum_{i=1}^{|D|} N_i \mathbb{1}(y_i = c)}, \tag{7.16}$$

where x_{ij} denotes the number of times feature j occurs in sample i, and $N_i = \sum_{j=1}^{K} x_{ij}$ is the total number of feature occurrences in sample i.

Similar to the Bernoulli naive Bayes model, the decision boundaries formed by multinomial naive Bayes are linear (see Exercise 7.16). However, for text classification tasks, the multinomial model usually performs better because it accounts for word frequencies rather than just their presence or absence [402].

7.2.3.1 Example: Spam Filter

Consider building a spam filter using the multinomial naive Bayes model, trained on 100 emails, of which 80 are non-spam (ham) and 20 are spam. Table 7.3 shows the counts of words in each type of email.

Suppose we receive a new email containing the text "rich rich friend need money." We want to determine whether this email is more likely to be ham or spam.

First, we compute the class priors from the proportion of emails in each class:

$$P(\text{Ham}) = \frac{80}{100} = 0.8, \quad P(\text{Spam}) = \frac{20}{100} = 0.2.$$

The total number of words in ham emails is 200, and in spam emails is 120. The likelihood of each word in the email given each class is therefore:

$$P(\text{rich} \mid \text{Ham}) = \frac{5}{200} = 0.025, \qquad P(\text{rich} \mid \text{Spam}) = \frac{30}{120} = 0.25,$$

$$P(\text{friend} \mid \text{Ham}) = \frac{80}{200} = 0.4, \qquad P(\text{friend} \mid \text{Spam}) = \frac{20}{120} = 0.167,$$

Word	Count
friend	80
prince	5
rich	5
money	20
need	50
movie	40

(a) Ham emails

Word	Count
friend	20
prince	20
rich	30
money	25
need	25
movie	0

(b) Spam emails

Table 7.3: Word counts for different terms in ham and spam emails

$$P(\text{need} \mid \text{Ham}) = \frac{50}{200} = 0.25, \qquad P(\text{need} \mid \text{Spam}) = \frac{25}{120} = 0.208,$$

$$P(\text{money} \mid \text{Ham}) = \frac{20}{200} = 0.1, \qquad P(\text{money} \mid \text{Spam}) = \frac{25}{120} = 0.208.$$

The word counts in this email are: "rich" = 2, "friend" = 1, "need" = 1, and "money" = 1. Thus, the posterior probability for ham is:

$$P(\text{Ham} \mid \mathbf{x}) = \alpha P(\text{Ham}) \cdot P(\text{rich} \mid \text{Ham})^2 \cdot P(\text{friend} \mid \text{Ham}) \cdot P(\text{need} \mid \text{Ham})$$
$$\cdot P(\text{money} \mid \text{Ham})$$
$$= \alpha \cdot 0.8 \cdot 0.025^2 \cdot 0.4 \cdot 0.25 \cdot 0.1$$
$$= 0.000005\,\alpha,$$

where α is a normalization factor ensuring that the posteriors sum to 1. Similarly, for spam:

$$P(\text{Spam} \mid \mathbf{x}) = \alpha P(\text{Spam}) \cdot P(\text{rich} \mid \text{Spam})^2 \cdot P(\text{friend} \mid \text{Spam})$$
$$\cdot P(\text{need} \mid \text{Spam}) \cdot P(\text{money} \mid \text{Spam})$$
$$= \alpha \cdot 0.2 \cdot 0.25^2 \cdot 0.167 \cdot 0.208 \cdot 0.208$$
$$= 0.0000903\,\alpha.$$

Since $P(\text{Spam} \mid \mathbf{x}) > P(\text{Ham} \mid \mathbf{x})$, the model predicts that the email is spam. Note that the multinomial coefficient in this case $\frac{5!}{2!\,1!\,1!\,1!}$ is the same for both classes. Thus, it cancels out when comparing the two posteriors, although it must be included when computing the exact probabilities.

7.2.4 Laplace Smoothing

When a feature (e.g., a word) does not appear in any training samples from a given class, its estimated likelihood for that class becomes zero. Since the naive Bayes classifier computes the class-conditional likelihood $P(\mathbf{x}|y)$ as a product of the conditional probabilities of the individual features, a single zero value will cause the entire product to become zero. This issue, known as the **zero frequency problem**, can lead to misleading results by completely ignoring the contribution of all other features.

For example, suppose the word "movie" never appears in any spam emails in the training set. In this case, any email containing the word "movie" would automatically be classified as ham, regardless of the presence of other words strongly indicative of spam, such as "rich" and "prince."

To illustrate this effect, consider an email with the text "movie rich rich prince." The posterior for ham is:

$$P(\text{Ham} \mid \mathbf{x}) = \alpha P(\text{Ham}) \cdot P(\text{movie} \mid \text{Ham}) \cdot P(\text{rich} \mid \text{Ham})^2 \cdot P(\text{prince} \mid \text{Ham})$$
$$= \alpha \cdot 0.8 \cdot \frac{40}{200} \cdot \left(\frac{5}{200}\right)^2 \cdot \frac{5}{200}$$
$$= 0.0000025\,\alpha.$$

and for spam:

$$P(\text{Spam} \mid \mathbf{x}) = \alpha P(\text{Spam}) \cdot P(\text{movie} \mid \text{Spam}) \cdot P(\text{rich} \mid \text{Spam})^2 \cdot P(\text{prince} \mid \text{Spam})$$

$$= \alpha \cdot 0.2 \cdot \frac{0}{120} \cdot \left(\frac{30}{120}\right)^2 \cdot \frac{20}{120}$$

$$= 0.$$

Here, $P(\text{Spam} \mid \mathbf{x})$ becomes zero because $P(\text{movie} \mid \text{Spam}) = 0$, and the entire product collapses, ignoring the evidence from the other words.

To address this issue, **Laplace smoothing** adds a **pseudocount** $\alpha > 0$, typically set to 1, to all probability estimates so that no estimated probability becomes exactly zero.[1] This correction is applied to the different naive Bayes models as follows:

- **Bernoulli naive Bayes:** The smoothed estimate of the probability that a binary feature x_j is present in class c is

$$P(x_j = 1 \mid y = c) \approx \frac{n_{cj} + \alpha}{n_c + 2\alpha}, \tag{7.17}$$

where n_{cj} is the number of samples in class c where feature j is present, and n_c is the total number of samples in class c. The denominator includes 2α because the feature can take two values (0 or 1).

- **Categorical naive Bayes:** For a categorical feature x_j with K_j possible values, the smoothed estimate is

$$P(x_j = k \mid y = c) \approx \frac{n_{cjk} + \alpha}{n_c + \alpha K_j}, \tag{7.18}$$

where n_{cjk} is the number of samples in class c where feature j takes value k.

- **Multinomial naive Bayes:** For features counted according to a multinomial model (e.g., word frequencies), the smoothed estimate of the probability of feature j occurring in class c is

$$P(X = j \mid y = c) \approx \frac{n_{cj} + \alpha}{n_c + \alpha K}, \tag{7.19}$$

where n_{cj} is the total count of feature j in class c, $n_c = \sum_{j=1}^{K} n_{cj}$ is the total number of feature occurrences in class c, and K is the total number of distinct features (e.g., the vocabulary size in text classification).

---

1. This smoothing is equivalent to assuming a symmetric Dirichlet prior, with all parameters equal to α, over the feature probabilities for each class (see Section C.11.6.3). In this Bayesian view, the MAP estimate of the multinomial parameters combines the observed counts with the prior belief that all features (e.g., words) are equally likely.

Word	New Count
friend	$80 + 1 = 81$
prince	$5 + 1 = 6$
rich	$5 + 1 = 6$
money	$20 + 1 = 21$
need	$50 + 1 = 51$
movie	$40 + 1 = 41$

(a) Ham emails

Word	New Count
friend	$20 + 1 = 21$
prince	$20 + 1 = 21$
rich	$30 + 1 = 31$
money	$25 + 1 = 26$
need	$25 + 1 = 26$
movie	$0 + 1 = 1$

(b) Spam emails

Table 7.4: Word counts in ham and spam emails after applying Laplace smoothing

Applying Laplace smoothing with $\alpha = 1$ to our spam filter example adds one to each word count, as shown in Table 7.4. The updated totals are $200 + 6 = 206$ for ham and $120 + 6 = 126$ for spam. The posterior probabilities for the email "movie rich rich prince" become:

$$P(\text{Ham} \mid \mathbf{x}) = \alpha \cdot 0.8 \cdot \frac{41}{206} \cdot \left(\frac{6}{206}\right)^2 \cdot \frac{6}{206} = 0.0000039\,\alpha,$$

$$P(\text{Spam} \mid \mathbf{x}) = \alpha \cdot 0.2 \cdot \frac{1}{126} \cdot \left(\frac{31}{126}\right)^2 \cdot \frac{21}{126} = 0.0000160\,\alpha.$$

After smoothing, the email is correctly classified as spam. This example illustrates how Laplace smoothing prevents zero probabilities and allows the model to make better use of all the available evidence.

7.2.5 Gaussian Naive Bayes

So far, we have focused on modeling discrete features. Handling continuous features in naive Bayes classifiers is more challenging, as they do not naturally fit into the framework used for binary or categorical data. Two common strategies for incorporating continuous features are:

- **Discretization**: Partition each continuous feature into intervals (bins), allowing it to be treated as a categorical feature.

- **Probabilistic modeling**: Assume that each feature follows a specific probability distribution and estimate its parameters (e.g., mean and variance) from the training data.

Gaussian Naive Bayes (GNB) adopts the second approach by assuming that the conditional distribution of each continuous feature is Gaussian (normal). Under this model, the conditional density of feature x_j given class c is:

$$p(x_j|y = c) = \frac{1}{\sigma_{cj}\sqrt{2\pi}} \exp\left(-\frac{(x_j - \mu_{cj})^2}{2\sigma_{cj}^2}\right), \tag{7.20}$$

where μ_{cj} and σ_{cj} are the mean and standard deviation of feature j among the samples of class c.

Taking the logarithm of the class-conditional likelihood shows that the log-posterior is a quadratic function of $\mathbf{x}$, leading to quadratic decision boundaries. However, if all classes share the same feature variances (i.e., $\sigma_{cj} = \sigma_j$ for all c), the quadratic terms cancel out and the decision boundaries become linear (see Exercise 7.20).

For example, suppose we wish to predict an individual's gender based on their height, assuming that height in each gender follows a Gaussian distribution with the following parameters:

- Males: $\mu = 175$ cm, $\sigma = 10$ cm

- Females: $\mu = 165$ cm, $\sigma = 8$ cm

If the training set consists of 40% males and 60% females, what is the probability that a person with a height of 172 cm is male or female?

The class prior probabilities are $P(\text{Male}) = 0.4$ and $P(\text{Female}) = 0.6$. The conditional densities for each gender are:

$$p(\text{height} = 172 \mid \text{Male}) = \frac{1}{10\sqrt{2\pi}} \exp\left(-\frac{(172 - 175)^2}{2 \cdot 10^2}\right) = 0.0381,$$

$$p(\text{height} = 172 \mid \text{Female}) = \frac{1}{8\sqrt{2\pi}} \exp\left(-\frac{(172 - 165)^2}{2 \cdot 8^2}\right) = 0.034.$$

The marginal probability of observing a height of 172 cm is:

$$p(\text{height} = 172) = p(\text{height} = 172 \mid \text{Male}) \cdot P(\text{Male}) + p(\text{height} = 172 \mid \text{Female}) \cdot P(\text{Female})$$

$$= 0.0381 \cdot 0.4 + 0.034 \cdot 0.6 = 0.0357.$$

Applying Bayes' theorem gives the posterior probabilities:

$$P(\text{Male} \mid \text{height} = 172) = \frac{p(\text{height} = 172 \mid \text{Male})P(\text{Male})}{p(\text{height} = 172)} = \frac{0.0381 \cdot 0.4}{0.0357} = 0.427,$$

$$P(\text{Female} \mid \text{height} = 172) = \frac{p(\text{height} = 172 \mid \text{Female})P(\text{Female})}{p(\text{height} = 172)} = \frac{0.0340 \cdot 0.6}{0.0357} = 0.571.$$

Thus, a person with a height of 172 cm is more likely to be female (57.1%) than male (42.7%).

7.2.6 Heterogeneous Naive Bayes

When working with datasets that contain both categorical and continuous features, a naive Bayes model can combine different event models to account for the distinct nature of each feature type.

For example, consider a company that wants to predict whether customers will purchase a subscription service based on their age and income level. The dataset includes the following features:

Class	Customers	Age (Mean ± Std)	Low	Medium	High
Purchase = Yes	60	45 ± 8	10	30	20
Purchase = No	40	35 ± 10	25	10	5

Table 7.5: Customer data summary for each class. "Customers" indicates the number of customers in each class; "Age" reports the mean and standard deviation of customer ages; and "Low", "Medium", and "High" indicate the number of customers in each income level.

- Age (continuous): Modeled with a Gaussian distribution.

- Income level (categorical): Takes one of three categories: Low, Medium, and High.

The company has collected data from 100 customers, which is summarized in Table 7.5. We want to predict whether a new customer, who is 40 years old and has a Medium income level, is likely to purchase the subscription.

The posterior probabilities are computed as follows:

1. Class prior probabilities:

$$P(\text{Purchase} = \text{Yes}) = 0.6, \quad P(\text{Purchase} = \text{No}) = 0.4.$$

2. Likelihood for age (Gaussian model):

$$P(\text{Age} = 40 \mid \text{Purchase} = \text{Yes}) = \frac{1}{8\sqrt{2\pi}} \exp\left(-\frac{(40-45)^2}{2\cdot 8^2}\right) = 0.041,$$

$$P(\text{Age} = 40 \mid \text{Purchase} = \text{No}) = \frac{1}{10\sqrt{2\pi}} \exp\left(-\frac{(40-35)^2}{2\cdot 10^2}\right) = 0.0352.$$

3. Likelihood for income level (categorical model):

$$P(\text{Income} = \text{Medium} \mid \text{Purchase} = \text{Yes}) = \frac{30}{60} = 0.5,$$

$$P(\text{Income} = \text{Medium} \mid \text{Purchase} = \text{No}) = \frac{10}{40} = 0.25.$$

4. Unnormalized posteriors:

$$P(\text{Purchase} = \text{Yes} \mid \mathbf{x}) = \alpha P(\text{Purchase} = \text{Yes}) P(\text{Age} = 40 \mid \text{Yes}) P(\text{Income} = \text{Medium} \mid \text{Yes})$$

$$= \alpha \cdot 0.6 \cdot 0.0410 \cdot 0.5$$

$$= 0.0123\,\alpha,$$

$$P(\text{Purchase} = \text{No} \mid \mathbf{x}) = \alpha P(\text{Purchase} = \text{No}) P(\text{Age} = 40 \mid \text{No}) P(\text{Income} = \text{Medium} \mid \text{No})$$

$$= \alpha \cdot 0.4 \cdot 0.0352 \cdot 0.25$$

$$= 0.00352\,\alpha.$$

5. Normalized posteriors:

$$(0.0123 + 0.00352)\alpha = 1 \;\Rightarrow\; \alpha = \frac{1}{0.01582},$$

$$P(\text{Purchase = Yes} \mid \mathbf{x}) = \frac{0.0123}{0.01582} = 0.777,$$

$$P(\text{Purchase = No} \mid \mathbf{x}) = \frac{0.00352}{0.01582} = 0.223.$$

The model predicts that there is approximately a 77.7% chance that the customer will purchase the subscription. This example illustrates how Gaussian and categorical models can be effectively combined within a heterogeneous naive Bayes framework to handle mixed data types.

7.3   Naive Bayes Classifiers in Scikit-Learn

Scikit-Learn's `sklearn.naive_bayes` module provides implementations of all the naive Bayes classifiers discussed in this chapter:

- `BernoulliNB`[2] implements the Bernoulli naive Bayes model.

- `CategoricalNB`[3] implements the categorical naive Bayes model.

- `MultinomialNB`[4] implements the multinomial naive Bayes model.

- `GaussianNB`[5] implements the Gaussian naive Bayes model.

The `BernoulliNB`, `CategoricalNB`, and `MultinomialNB` classifiers include a smoothing parameter `alpha`. Although the default value of 1.0 usually works well, tuning this parameter can yield modest improvements, especially when the training set is small or imbalanced.

The following example demonstrates how to fit a `GaussianNB` model to the two-dimensional Iris dataset introduced in Section 6.1.4, which includes only the sepal length and sepal width features. Since these features are approximately normally distributed within each class (as shown in Figure 3.6), the Gaussian assumption of this model is appropriate.

First, we load the dataset and split it into training and test sets:

```
from sklearn.datasets import load_iris
from sklearn.model_selection import train_test_split

iris = load_iris()
X = iris.data[:, :2]
y = iris.target
X_train, X_test, y_train, y_test = train_test_split(X, y, random_state=42)
```

---

2. https://scikit-learn.org/stable/modules/generated/sklearn.naive_bayes.BernoulliNB.html

3. https://scikit-learn.org/stable/modules/generated/sklearn.naive_bayes.CategoricalNB.html

4. https://scikit-learn.org/stable/modules/generated/sklearn.naive_bayes.MultinomialNB.html

5. https://scikit-learn.org/stable/modules/generated/sklearn.naive_bayes.GaussianNB.html

Next, we create an instance of `GaussianNB` and fit it to the training data:

```
from sklearn.naive_bayes import GaussianNB

clf = GaussianNB()
clf.fit(X_train, y_train)
```

The estimated means and variances of each feature for each class are stored in the `theta_` and `var_` attributes:

```
print('Means:', np.round(clf.theta_, 4))
print('Variances:', np.round(clf.var_, 4))
```

```
Means: [[4.9971 3.4286]
 [5.8872 2.7513]
 [6.5395 2.9789]]
Variances: [[0.1106 0.1455]
 [0.2791 0.0974]
 [0.4261 0.0959]]
```

For example, the first row of the first array contains the means of the two features for the first class. These values are used by the classifier to compute the likelihood of each class.

Let's evaluate the model's performance on the training and test sets:

```
print(f'Training accuracy: {clf.score(X_train, y_train):.4f}')
print(f'Test accuracy: {clf.score(X_test, y_test):.4f}')
```

```
Training accuracy: 0.7768
Test accuracy: 0.8421
```

Notably, the training accuracy of GNB is lower than its test accuracy, suggesting that the model may be underfitting. This underfitting arises because GNB makes strong assumptions about the data—specifically, that each feature is normally distributed and conditionally independent—which may not fully capture the complexity of the dataset.

To gain more insight into the model's behavior, we can plot its decision boundaries:

```
plot_decision_boundaries(clf, X, y, iris.feature_names[:2], iris.target_names)
```

Figure 7.1 shows that the decision boundaries of the GNB classifier are quadratic as expected. This lack of flexibility likely causes the underfitting, as the boundaries fail to clearly separate the versicolor and virginica classes (compare to the more flexible KNN decision boundaries in Figure 6.2).

7.4   (*) Linear and Quadratic Discriminant Analysis

Gaussian naive Bayes assumes that the features $x_1, \ldots, x_d$ are normally distributed and conditionally independent given the class label. If we consider the entire feature vector $\mathbf{x}$ as a random vector,

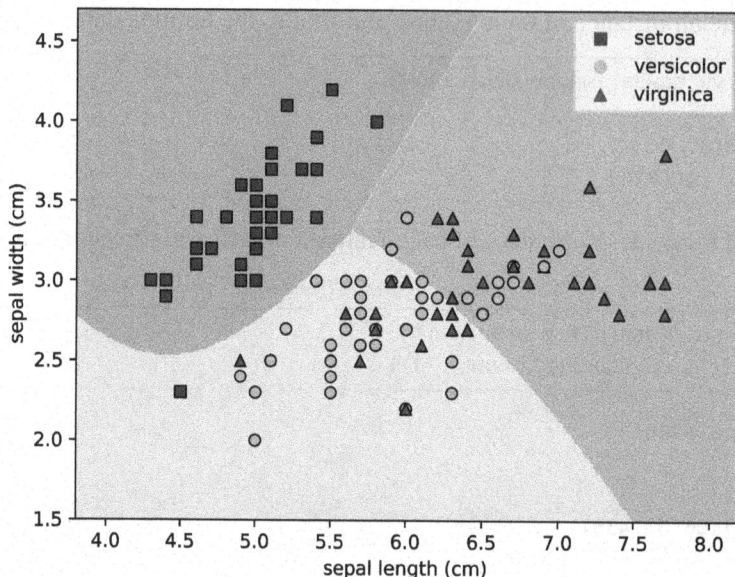

Figure 7.1: Decision boundaries of the Gaussian naive Bayes classifier on the reduced Iris dataset. The quadratic decision boundaries result from assuming that, within each class, the features follow a multivariate normal distribution.

this is equivalent to assuming that the conditional density of $\mathbf{x}$ given class c follows a multivariate Gaussian distribution with a diagonal covariance matrix (see Section C.11.6.1):

$$p(\mathbf{x}|c) \sim \mathcal{N}(\boldsymbol{\mu}_c, \Sigma_c). \tag{7.21}$$

This diagonal structure greatly simplifies the model, but it can be too restrictive in practice because it ignores correlations among features.

Linear Discriminant Analysis (LDA) and **Quadratic Discriminant Analysis (QDA)** relax this independence assumption, allowing for correlated features [175, 258]. Both methods assume that the feature vector follows a class-conditional multivariate Gaussian distribution, but they differ in how they model the covariance structure: QDA estimates a separate covariance matrix for each class, whereas LDA assumes a common covariance matrix for all classes.[6]

Under these models, the class-conditional density of a feature vector $\mathbf{x}$ given class c is:

$$p(\mathbf{x}|y = c) = \frac{1}{(2\pi)^{d/2}|\Sigma_c|^{1/2}} \exp\left(-\frac{1}{2}(\mathbf{x} - \boldsymbol{\mu}_c)^T \Sigma_c^{-1}(\mathbf{x} - \boldsymbol{\mu}_c)\right), \tag{7.22}$$

---

6. The origins of LDA date back to Ronald Fisher's work in the 1930s, where he introduced **Fisher's Discriminant Analysis** to find linear combinations of features that best separate two or more classes [192]. Unlike LDA, Fisher's method does not assume Gaussian feature distributions. Instead, it seeks a projection of the data that maximizes the ratio of between-class to within-class variance, achieving maximal class separation in a lower-dimensional space. Fisher famously applied this method to the Iris dataset to distinguish between the three flower species.

where d is the number of features, $\boldsymbol{\mu}_c = (\mu_{c1}, \ldots, \mu_{cd})^T$ is the mean vector for class c, and Σ_c is the class-specific covariance matrix.

To classify a new observation, we use Bayes' theorem to compute the posterior for each class c:

$$P(y = c|\mathbf{x}) = \frac{p(\mathbf{x}|y = c)P(y = c)}{p(\mathbf{x})}.$$

Taking the logarithm gives the log-posterior:

$$\log P(y = c|\mathbf{x}) = \log p(\mathbf{x}|y = c) + \log P(y = c) + \text{const}$$
$$= -\frac{1}{2} \log |\Sigma_c| - \frac{1}{2}(\mathbf{x} - \boldsymbol{\mu}_c)^T \Sigma_c^{-1}(\mathbf{x} - \boldsymbol{\mu}_c) + \log P(y = c) + \text{const},$$

(7.23)

where the constant term absorbs $p(\mathbf{x})$ and other factors independent of the class. The predicted class is the one that maximizes this log-posterior.

In QDA, the covariance matrix Σ_c is allowed to vary across classes, enabling the model to capture different feature correlations within each class. As a result, the decision boundaries are quadratic, since the log-posterior includes the quadratic term $(\mathbf{x} - \boldsymbol{\mu}_c)^T \Sigma_c^{-1}(\mathbf{x} - \boldsymbol{\mu}_c)$—hence the name *quadratic* discriminant analysis. When the covariance matrices are diagonal, QDA reduces to the Gaussian naive Bayes model.

LDA simplifies QDA by assuming a common covariance matrix for all classes, $\Sigma_c = \Sigma$. Under this assumption, the log-posterior becomes

$$\log P(y = c|\mathbf{x}) = -\frac{1}{2}(\mathbf{x} - \boldsymbol{\mu}_c)^T \Sigma^{-1}(\mathbf{x} - \boldsymbol{\mu}_c) + \log P(y = c) + \text{const}. \quad (7.24)$$

The term $(\mathbf{x} - \boldsymbol{\mu}_c)^T \Sigma^{-1}(\mathbf{x} - \boldsymbol{\mu}_c)$ is the squared Mahalanobis distance between $\mathbf{x}$ and the class mean $\boldsymbol{\mu}_c$, which accounts for correlations between features (see Section 6.3.2).

Expanding the quadratic term shows that the log-posterior can be written as

$$\log P(y = c|\mathbf{x}) = \mathbf{w}_c^T \mathbf{x} + w_{0c} + \text{const}, \quad (7.25)$$

where $\mathbf{w}_c = \Sigma^{-1}\boldsymbol{\mu}_c$ and $w_{0c} = -\frac{1}{2}\boldsymbol{\mu}_c^T \Sigma^{-1}\boldsymbol{\mu}_c + \log P(y = c)$. This expression makes it clear that LDA defines linear decision boundaries because the log-posterior for each class is a linear function of the features.

Using LDA and QDA requires estimating the class priors $P(y = c)$, class means $\boldsymbol{\mu}_c$, and class-specific covariance matrices from the training data. Computing the inverse of Σ can be expensive, especially in high-dimensional settings, so many implementations rely on numerical techniques such as Singular Value Decomposition (SVD) (see Section A.3.21) to evaluate the log-posterior without explicitly inverting Σ.

7.4.1   Example in Scikit-Learn

Scikit-Learn provides implementations of both LDA and QDA in the classes `LinearDiscriminant Analysis`[7] and `QuadraticDiscriminantAnalysis`[8], respectively.

The following example applies LDA to the reduced Iris dataset from the previous section:

```
from sklearn.discriminant_analysis import LinearDiscriminantAnalysis

clf = LinearDiscriminantAnalysis()
clf.fit(X_train, y_train)
```

The training and test accuracies are:

```
print(f'Training accuracy: {clf.score(X_train, y_train):.4f}')
print(f'Test accuracy: {clf.score(X_test, y_test):.4f}')
```

```
Training accuracy: 0.7946
Test accuracy: 0.8684
```

These results show a clear improvement over the Gaussian naive Bayes classifier, which achieved 84.21% accuracy on the test set. LDA's ability to model correlations between features leads to better performance in this case.

Figure 7.2 shows the decision boundaries of the LDA classifier. As expected, the boundaries are linear, reflecting the assumption of a shared covariance matrix.

Key advantages of the LDA and QDA classifiers include:

- Closed-form expressions for the parameter estimates, simplifying the training procedure.

- Strong performance when the assumptions of normally distributed features and, for LDA, a shared covariance matrix hold approximately [661, 653].

- Built-in support for multi-class classification.

- No hyperparameters to tune.

- LDA can also serve as a supervised dimensionality reduction method, projecting data onto a subspace that maximizes class separability [401].

However, these methods also have important limitations:

- Both methods assume multivariate Gaussian features, and substantial deviations from this assumption can significantly degrade their performance.

---

7. https://scikit-learn.org/stable/modules/generated/sklearn.discriminant_analysis.
   LinearDiscriminantAnalysis.html
8. https://scikit-learn.org/stable/modules/generated/sklearn.discriminant_analysis.
   QuadraticDiscriminantAnalysis.html

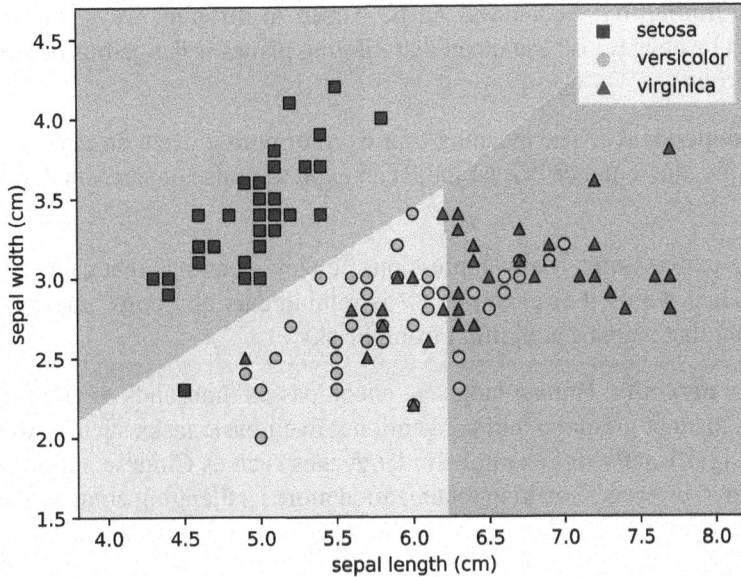

Figure 7.2: Decision boundaries of the LDA classifier on the Iris dataset

- Sensitivity to outliers, since extreme values can distort the estimated means and covariance matrices.

- When the sample size is small, the estimated covariance matrices may be singular or ill-conditioned, making them difficult or impossible to invert.

- In high-dimensional settings, computing the inverse of the covariance matrix becomes computationally expensive, with a time complexity $\mathcal{O}(d^3)$, where d is the number of features.

7.5 Introduction to Natural Language Processing

Natural Language Processing (NLP) is an interdisciplinary field that draws on concepts from computer science, machine learning, and linguistics to enable computers to understand and generate human language [395, 306, 270]. It encompasses a wide range of techniques and tools designed to address the complexity of natural language and to build systems that can work with text and other language data.

Developing systems that can understand human language is challenging due to the inherent richness and ambiguity of natural language [627, 439]. Examples of these challenges include:

- **Polysemy and homonymy**: Words can have multiple meanings depending on context. For example, in "I took the money to the bank," the word "bank" may refer to a financial institution or the land alongside a river.

- **Syntactic ambiguity**: Sentences can be parsed in different ways. For example, "Flying planes can be dangerous" can mean that piloting planes is dangerous or that planes in flight are dangerous.

- **Context dependence**: The meaning of a word or phrase often on the surrounding context. For example, the sentence "Great job!" can express praise or sarcasm depending on tone or context.

- **Idiomatic expressions**: Many expressions convey meanings that cannot be deduced from the individual words. For example, "It is raining cats and dogs" means that it is raining heavily, not that animals are falling from the sky.

- **Linguistic diversity**: Human language encompasses thousands of languages and dialects, each with distinct grammar and conventions. Even basic tasks such as word segmentation can vary significantly; for example, in languages such as Chinese and Japanese, words are not separated by spaces, making tokenization more challenging compared to languages like English.

Despite these challenges, recent NLP systems have shown remarkable success across a wide variety of domains, including:

- **Text classification**: Assigning text documents to predefined categories, such as classifying news articles by topic or detecting spam emails [535, 420].

- **Sentiment analysis**: Determining the emotional tone or attitude expressed in a text, typically classified as "positive," "neutral," or "negative." For example, businesses use this technique to analyze customer feedback from product reviews, social media, and other sources [411, 665].

- **Named entity recognition (NER)**: Identifying and classifying named entities in text—such as people, organizations, and locations—into predefined categories [435, 356]. NER is commonly used in applications such as information extraction and question answering, where it helps understand the context and relationships between entities.

- **Information retrieval (IR)**: Retrieving relevant documents or passages from large text collections in response to a user query. Modern search engines and question-answering systems rely heavily on NLP techniques to improve ranking and relevance [394, 427].

- **Machine translation**: Converting text or speech from one language to another, as popularized by systems like Google Translate [23, 632, 606].

- **Text summarization**: Producing concise summaries of long documents to facilitate efficient information retrieval and rapid understanding of large volumes of text [179, 664].

- **Question answering**: Building systems that retrieve or generate answers to questions posed in natural language, often leveraging structured knowledge bases or search engines [498, 311].

- **Conversational agents**: Developing chatbots and virtual assistants that interact naturally with users. These systems, often powered by large language models (LLMs) such as ChatGPT, integrate multiple NLP capabilities—including question answering, dialogue management, and knowledge retrieval—with more general abilities such as reasoning, planning, and task execution [549, 454].

NLP tasks are often grouped into two broad categories:

- **Natural Language Understanding (NLU)**: Tasks that focus on understanding and analyzing text, such as text classification, sentiment analysis, and named entity recognition.

- **Natural Language Generation (NLG)**: Tasks aimed at producing coherent natural language text, such as answering questions and generating open-ended text, stories, or dialogues.

Some tasks, such as machine translation and text summarization, require both NLU and NLG capabilities, as they involve understanding the input text and generating fluent, semantically appropriate output.

Recent advances in NLP have been driven by powerful language models such as GPT, Claude, LLaMA, and Gemini [667, 455, 581, 222]. Built on the Transformer architecture and trained on massive amounts of text, these models have dramatically improved performance across both NLU and NLG tasks. Beyond setting new standards in NLP, they have also demonstrated broader capabilities such as complex reasoning, code generation, and problem solving. These models will be discussed in detail in Volume III of this book.

7.5.1 The NLP Pipeline

Solving an NLP task generally follows a workflow similar to standard machine learning pipelines, with specific adaptations for handling text data. The main stages in a typical NLP pipeline include:

1. **Data collection**: Collect a relevant set of documents or text samples for the specific task (e.g., customer reviews from Amazon for sentiment analysis). Depending on the problem, data can come from web scraping, public datasets, or user-generated content. Both the quality and quantity of the collected data can significantly impact the model performance.

2. **Text preprocessing**: Clean and transform the raw text, preparing it for downstream analysis or modeling [98]. This typically involves the following steps:

   (a) **Cleaning**: Remove irrelevant or noisy elements from the raw text. This may include stripping out special symbols and HTML tags, standardizing or replacing non-textual elements such as number and dates, and deciding whether to retain or remove punctuation.

   (b) **Normalization**: Standardize the text to a consistent format to reduce variations that are irrelevant to the task. Examples include expanding contractions (e.g., "don't" → "do not"), removing accents or diacritics (e.g., "café" → "cafe"), and applying Unicode normalization to ensure consistent character encoding.

(c) **Lowercasing**: Convert all characters to lowercase to reduce case-related variability. This ensures that "Apple" and "apple" are treated as the same token, which is helpful for tasks such as text classification. However, lowercasing is not recommended for tasks where case carries important information, such as named entity recognition or language modeling.

(d) **Tokenization**: Split the text into smaller units called **tokens**, which can be words, subwords, or characters. A simple approach is word-level tokenization, which breaks the text into words using whitespace and punctuation as boundaries. Modern language models such as GPT use subword-level tokenization, which provides greater flexibility and handles rare or unseen words more effectively [540].

(e) **Removing stop words**: Filter out common words such as articles, pronouns, and prepositions (e.g., "and," "is," and "the"), which carry little semantic meaning and may introduce noise in text analysis tasks. However, removing these words is not recommended for tasks where they play a critical role, such as language modeling and machine translation.

(f) **Stemming and lemmatization**: Reduce words to their base or root form to consolidate variations of the same word. This helps reduce vocabulary size and improve generalization:

  • **Stemming**: Uses simple heuristic rules to strip suffixes, often producing non-dictionary forms (e.g., "better" → "bet").
  • **Lemmatization**: Uses lexical resources and morphological analysis to return the dictionary form (lemma) of a word (e.g., "running" → "run", "better" → "good").

Lemmatization is generally more accurate than stemming, but also more computationally expensive.

Figure 7.3 illustrates the preprocessing pipeline using a simple sentence, showing how the text is progressively transformed at each step.

3. **Text vectorization**: After preprocessing, the text data must be converted into a numerical format suitable for machine learning algorithms. Common approaches for encoding text into numerical vectors include:

  • **Bag-of-Words (BoW)**: Represents each document as a vector of word counts, ignoring word order and context.

  • **Term Frequency-Inverse Document Frequency (TF-IDF)**: Extends the BoW model by downweighting frequently occurring words in the corpus and assigning more weight to terms that are distinctive across documents (see Section 7.6.3).

  • **Word embeddings**: Represent words as dense, continuous-valued vectors that capture both syntactic and semantic relationships between words. This technique is widely used in deep learning architectures for NLP and will be discussed in Volume II of the book.

"Roi wasn't teaching at the University today."

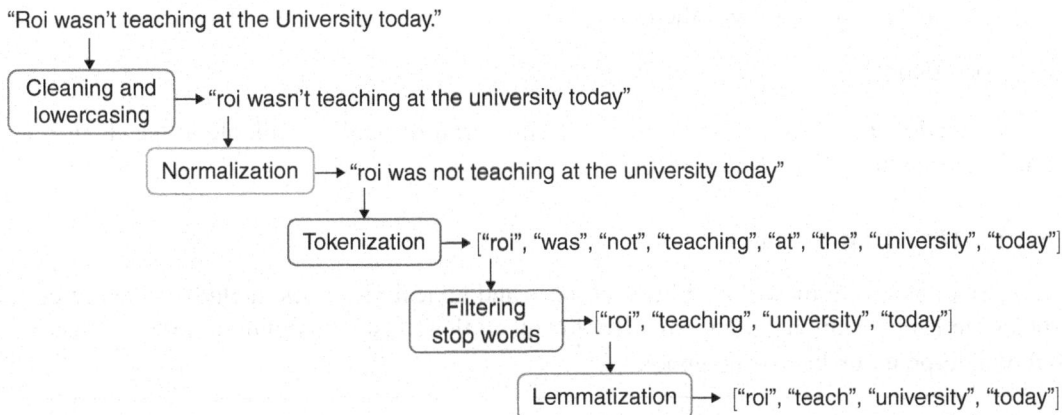

Figure 7.3: Illustration of the text preprocessing pipeline applied to the sentence "Roi wasn't teaching at the University today."

4. **Model training**: Once the text is represented numerically, various machine learning algorithms can be applied depending on the task complexity and the amount of available data [330]. For relatively simple tasks (e.g., text classification) and datasets of small to moderate size, classical algorithms such as naive Bayes, logistic regression, and support vector machines are commonly used due to their efficiency and effectiveness in high-dimensional feature spaces [402, 299]. In contrast, more complex tasks—such as machine translation or question answering—require larger datasets and benefit from deep learning models [599, 650].

5. **Model evaluation**: After training, the model is evaluated on a separate test set to assess how well it generalizes to new, unseen data. For prediction-based tasks such as text classification, general-purpose metrics like accuracy and F1-score are commonly used. For text generation tasks, specialized metrics are typically required; for example, BLEU is widely used in machine translation [466], while ROUGE is commonly applied in text summarization [365].

The following subsections introduce two popular Python libraries for NLP, namely NLTK and spaCy, and explain how they support various stages of the NLP pipeline.

7.5.2 The NLTK Library

NLTK (Natural Language Toolkit)[9] is a widely used open-source Python library for processing human language data [52]. It supports both symbolic and statistical natural language processing, and provides tools for tasks such as tokenization, stemming, tagging, parsing, and semantic reasoning. It also includes a wide range of text collections, such as books, news articles, and conversational transcripts, which can be used for experimentation and research.

---

9. https://www.nltk.org

The library can be easily installed via `pip`:

```
pip install nltk
```

This section introduces some of the key utilities and resources available in NLTK. For more details, refer to the official NLTK website

7.5.2.1   The NLTK Corpora

NLTK gives access to more than 50 text corpora and lexical resources, including literature, news articles, and conversational transcripts. To download these resources, run the following code in a Python interpreter or Jupyter notebook:

```
import nltk
nltk.download()
```

This will launch a graphical user interface (GUI) here you can choose which datasets to download. The selected files will be stored in the `nltk_data` directory in your home folder. After downloading, you can access the corpora using the nltk.corpus[10] module, which provides convenient methods for loading and working with the text data, including:

- **Retrieving raw text**: The `raw` method returns the complete raw text of a corpus. For example, to preview the beginning of the Gutenberg corpus—a collection of literary works sourced from the Gutenberg Project[11]—run:

  ```
  from nltk.corpus import gutenberg

  print(gutenberg.raw()[:200])
  ```

  ```
  [Emma by Jane Austen 1816]

  VOLUME I

  CHAPTER I


  Emma Woodhouse, handsome, clever, and rich, with a comfortable home
  and happy disposition, seemed to unite some of the best blessings
  of existence; an
  ```

- **Listing files in the corpus**: The Gutenberg corpus, like many others in NLTK, consists of multiple files, each corresponding to a different literary work (e.g., books or articles). You can list its file identifiers using the `fileids` method:

---

10. https://www.nltk.org/api/nltk.corpus.html
11. https://www.gutenberg.org

```
gutenberg.fileids()
```

```
['austen-emma.txt',
 'austen-persuasion.txt',
 'austen-sense.txt',
 'bible-kjv.txt',
 'blake-poems.txt',
 ...]
```

- **Retrieving the text of a specific file**: To access the raw content of a specific file, pass its file identifier to the raw method:

```
print(gutenberg.raw('carroll-alice.txt'))
```

```
[Alice's Adventures in Wonderland by Lewis Carroll 1865]

CHAPTER I. Down the Rabbit-Hole

Alice was beginning to get very tired of sitting by her sister on the
bank, and of having nothing to do: once or twice she had peeped into the
book her sister was reading, but it had no pictures or conversations in
it, 'and what is the use of a book,' thought Alice 'without pictures or
conversation?'
...
```

- **Accessing individual words**: The words method returns a list of tokens (words and punctuation) from the text:

```
gutenberg.words('carroll-alice.txt')
```

```
['[', 'Alice', "'", 's', 'Adventures', 'in', ...]
```

- **Calculating word frequencies**: The FreqDist[12] class computes the frequency distribution of words in a corpus. The following example shows how to print the 10 most common words in *Alice's Adventures in Wonderland* and their corresponding counts:

```
from nltk.probability import FreqDist

words = gutenberg.words('carroll-alice.txt')
fd = FreqDist(words)

# Print the 10 most common words
most_common_words = fd.most_common(10)
print(most_common_words)
```

12. https://www.nltk.org/api/nltk.probability.FreqDist.html

```
[(',', 1993), ("'", 1731), ('the', 1527), ('and', 802), ('.', 764),
('to', 725), ('a', 615), ('I', 543), ('it', 527), ('she', 509)]
```

The `nltk.corpus` module also provides access to various dictionaries and lexicons. For example, you can retrieve a list of all English words using the `words` corpus:

```
from nltk.corpus import words
```

```
words.words('en')
```

```
['A',
 'a',
 'aa',
 'aal',
 'aalii',
 'aam',
 'Aani',
 'aardvark',
 'aardwolf',
 ...
]
```

Additionally, NLTK includes lists of stop words in multiple languages. For example, to get a list of stop words in Spanish:

```
from nltk.corpus import stopwords
```

```
print(stopwords.words('spanish'))
```

```
['de', 'la', 'que', 'el', 'en', 'y', 'a', 'los', 'del', 'se', 'las', 'por',
'un', 'para', 'con', 'no', 'una', 'su', 'al', 'lo', 'como', 'más', 'pero',
'sus', 'le', 'ya', 'o', 'este', ...]
```

7.5.2.2   Text Preprocessing and Analysis

The NLTK library provides a wide range of utilities for text preprocessing and linguistic analysis, including:

- **Tokenization**: The `word_tokenize`[13] function performs word-level tokenization, splitting text based on spaces and punctuation:

  ```
  import nltk
  ```

  ```
  text = "Apple is looking at buying a U.K. startup for $1 billion"
  ```

---

13. https://www.nltk.org/api/nltk.tokenize.word_tokenize.html

```
tokens = nltk.word_tokenize(text)
print(tokens)
```

```
['Apple', 'is', 'looking', 'at', 'buying', 'a', 'U.K.', 'startup',
'for', '$', '1', 'billion']
```

NLTK also provides other tokenizers in the `nltk.tokenize`[14] module, which can handle more specific requirements. For example, the `RegexpTokenizer`[15] class allows for tokenization based on user-defined regular expressions. For example, we can use it to remove punctuation and extract only alphanumeric tokens:

```
from nltk.tokenize import RegexpTokenizer

tokenizer = RegexpTokenizer(r'\w+')
tokens = tokenizer.tokenize(text)
print(tokens)
```

```
['Apple', 'is', 'looking', 'at', 'buying', 'a', 'U', 'K', 'startup',
'for', '1', 'billion']
```

This example shows that simple regular expressions like `'\w+'` can sometimes lead to undesirable results, such as splitting "U.K." into "U" and "K." It underscores the importance of choosing a tokenizer that aligns with the specific characteristics of your text and the desired level of granularity.

- **Removing stop words**: Stop words can be removed by filtering out tokens that appear in NLTK's predefined list of stop words. Here is an example:

```
from nltk.corpus import stopwords

tokens = nltk.word_tokenize(text)
stop_words = stopwords.words('english')
filtered_tokens = [token for token in tokens if token.lower() not in stop_words]
print(filtered_tokens)
```

```
['Apple', 'looking', 'buying', 'U.K.', 'startup', '$', '1', 'billion']
```

- **Stemming**: Stemming reduces words to their root form by stripping suffixes, such as "s" in plurals or "ed" for verbs in past tense. NLTK provides several stemmers, with the Porter-Stemmer[16] being one of the most commonly used.[17]

---

14. https://www.nltk.org/api/nltk.tokenize.html
15. https://www.nltk.org/api/nltk.tokenize.RegexpTokenizer.html
16. https://www.nltk.org/_modules/nltk/stem/porter.html
17. The Porter stemming algorithm, introduced by Martin Porter in [483], is a rule-based algorithm that applies a series of suffix-stripping rules in multiple phases.

Here is an example of how to use the Porter stemmer:

```
from nltk.stem import PorterStemmer

ps = PorterStemmer()
tokens = nltk.word_tokenize(text)
stems = [ps.stem(token) for token in tokens]
print(stems)
```

```
['appl', 'is', 'look', 'at', 'buy', 'a', 'u.k.', 'startup', 'for',
'$', '1', 'billion']
```

Note that stemming may produce non-standard forms such as "appl" from "apple." The goal is to bring related words to a common root, not necessarily to valid dictionary entries.

- Lemmatization reduces words to base or dictionary form, while taking into account how the word is used in the sentence (i.e., its part of speech). For instance, the word "running" is lemmatized to "run" when used as a verb, but remains "running" when used as a noun. The output is always a valid English word. In NLTK, the WordNetLemmatizer[18] class performs a lemmatization using WordNet, a large lexical database of English. Here is an example:

```
from nltk.stem import WordNetLemmatizer

wnl = WordNetLemmatizer()
tokens = nltk.word_tokenize("The mice are eating the apple")
lemmas = [wnl.lemmatize(token) for token in tokens]
print(lemmas)
```

```
['The', 'mouse', 'are', 'eating', 'the', 'apple']
```

As shown, "mice" is correctly lemmatized to "mouse," while other words remain unchanged. Lemmatization is more accurate than stemming but typically more computationally expensive, making it preferable in tasks where linguistic precision is important.

- **Computing *n*-grams**: An *n*-gram is a sequence of n contiguous tokens from a text. Such sequences can help NLP models better understand the meaning of words based on their surrounding context. The nltk.util[19] module provides functions for generating n-grams of various lengths, including bigrams ($n = 2$), trigrams ($n = 3$), and ngrams for any n. Here is an example that generates all trigrams from a given text:

```
from nltk.util import trigrams

tokens = nltk.word_tokenize(text)
list(trigrams(tokens))
```

---

18. https://www.nltk.org/api/nltk.stem.WordNetLemmatizer.html
19. https://www.nltk.org/api/nltk.util.html

```
[('Apple', 'is', 'looking'),
 ('is', 'looking', 'at'),
 ('looking', 'at', 'buying'),
 ('at', 'buying', 'a'),
 ('buying', 'a', 'U.K.'),
 ('a', 'U.K.', 'startup'),
 ('U.K.', 'startup', 'for'),
 ('startup', 'for', '$'),
 ('for', '$', '1'),
 ('$', '1', 'billion')]
```

- **Part-of-speech (POS) tagging**: Parts-of-speech are grammatical categories that describe the syntactic role of words in a sentence. Common categories include nouns, verbs, adjectives, adverbs, pronouns, determiners, prepositions, conjunctions, and interjections. Identifying POS tags is crucial for many NLP tasks, including parsing, lemmatization, named entity recognition, and sentiment analysis.

  NLTK provides the function `nltk.pos_tag`[20], which tags a given list of tokens with their corresponding parts of speech. For example:

```
tokens = nltk.word_tokenize(text)
tagged = nltk.pos_tag(tokens)
print(tagged)
```

```
[('Apple', 'NNP'), ('is', 'VBZ'), ('looking', 'VBG'), ('at', 'IN'),
('buying', 'VBG'), ('a', 'DT'), ('U.K.', 'NNP'), ('startup', 'NN'),
('for', 'IN'), ('$', '$'), ('1', 'CD'), ('billion', 'CD')]
```

  In this output, `'NNP'` represents a proper noun (singular), `'VBG'` indicates a verb in the present participle form, and `'DT'` stands for a determiner. These tags follow the Penn Treebank POS tagset[21], a widely used standard in the NLP community [397].

- **Named Entity Recognition (NER)**: NER is an important subtask in many NLP applciations. It identifies and categorizes named entities in text into predefined types.

  Common categories include:

    - **Person**: Names of individuals.
    - **Organization**: Names of companies, institutions, agencies, and other groups.
    - **Location**: Names of geographical entities, such as cities, countries, or regions.

  Depending on the library or model, additional categories may also be included, such as dates and times, monetary values, events, and languages.

  In NLTK, the `nltk.chunk.ne_chunk`[22] function performs named entity recognition on a list of POS-tagged tokens. For example:

---

20. https://www.nltk.org/api/nltk.tag.pos_tag.html
21. https://www.ling.upenn.edu/courses/Fall_2003/ling001/penn_treebank_pos.html
22. https://www.nltk.org/api/nltk.chunk.ne_chunk.html

```
text = "Former US president Donald Trump holds rally in Indianola, Iowa"
tokens = nltk.word_tokenize(text)
tagged = nltk.pos_tag(tokens)
entities = nltk.chunk.ne_chunk(tagged)
print(entities)
```

```
(S
  Former/JJ
  (GPE US/NNP)
  president/NN
  (PERSON Donald/NNP Trump/NNP)
  holds/VBZ
  rally/RB
  in/IN
  (GPE Indianola/NNP)
  ,/,
  (GPE Iowa/NNP))
```

In this example, several named entities are detected:

- GPE (Geo-Political Entity): "US," "Indianola," and "Iowa" are recognized as geographical locations.
- PERSON: "Donald Trump" is identified as a person.

- **Parsing**: NLTK provides advanced parsing algorithms for syntactic analysis, including context-free grammar parsers and dependency parsers, available in the `nltk.parse`[23] module. These tools are useful for applications that require a detailed understanding of sentence structure, such as information extraction and machine translation.

We covered here the main utilities provided by NLTK, but the library includes many more, including text classification, n-gram language modeling, text entailment, and tree visualization. For a more in-depth exploration of NLTK, refer to the official documentation or the free online book, Natural Language Processing with Python[24] by the creators of NLTK—Steven Bird, Ewan Klein, and Edward Loper [53].

7.5.3   The spaCy Library

spaCy is a powerful and efficient library designed for production-grade natural language processing. It emphasizes performance, scalability, and ease of integration into real-world applications. Key features of spaCy include:

---

23. https://www.nltk.org/api/nltk.parse.html
24. https://www.nltk.org/book

- **Production-focused design**: While NLTK is primarily geared toward educational purposes and prototyping, spaCy is optimized for high-performance and large-scale NLP tasks.

- **Fast execution**: Much of spaCy is implemented in Cython rather than pure Python, enabling significantly faster execution of core components such as tokenization and syntactic parsing.

- **Comprehensive NLP functionality**: Similar to NLTK, spaCy supports a wide range of tasks, including tokenization, lemmatization, part-of-speech tagging, and named entity recognition.

- **Modular and customizable pipeline**: spaCy offers a flexible pipeline architecture in which components (e.g., tagger, parser, NER) can be easily added, removed, or customized.

- **Integration with deep learning**: spaCy integrates seamlessly with deep learning frameworks such as PyTorch and Tensorflow, enabling users to incorporate neural models into their NLP workflows.

- **Multilingual support**: spaCy includes native support for multiple languages, making it a good choice for multilingual NLP projects.

spaCy can be easily installed via pip:

```
pip install spacy
```

After installing spaCy, you need to download a language model, which typically includes a tokenizer, part-of-speech tagger, syntactic parser, lemmatizer, and named entity recognizer. spaCy offers various models for different languages and model sizes[25]. For example, to download a small English model, run the following command:

```
python -m spacy download en_core_web_sm
```

This section provides an overview of spaCy's main features. For more detailed information and documentation, visit the official spaCy website[26].

7.5.3.1   Core Components of spaCy

The core components of spaCy revolve around a few main classes that enable efficient text processing and analysis. Below are some of the key classes:

---

25. spaCy models are available in four sizes: sm (small), md (medium), lg (large), and trf (transformer-based). Small models are the fastest and lightest but offer lower accuracy. Medium and large models include word vectors and provide better performance, while transformer models offer the highest accuracy using state-of-the-art deep learning architectures at the cost of speed and resource usage.

26. https://spacy.io

- Language[27]: This is the central class for processing text. It contains the shared vocabulary, tokenization rules, and processing pipeline. A Language object is created by loading a spaCy model with the spacy.load[28] function:

```
import spacy

nlp = spacy.load('en_core_web_sm') # Load the small English model
```

- Doc[29]: The Doc object represents a processed text—a sequence of tokens with all their annotations. It is produced by applying the pipeline to a string of text:

```
doc = nlp("Apple is looking at buying a U.K. startup for $1 billion")
```

- Token[30]: Each token in a Doc is represented as a Token object. You can iterate over the Doc to access individual tokens:

```
print([token.text for token in doc])
```

```
['Apple', 'is', 'looking', 'at', 'buying', 'a', 'U.K.', 'startup', 'for',
'$', '1', 'billion']
```

Note that "$1" is split into two tokens: "$" and "1," while "U.K." is treated as a single token. spaCy's tokenizer uses language-specific rules to preserve common abbreviations and multi-character symbols as single units.

Each token also has various linguistic attributes, such as its lemma and part of speech:

```
for token in doc:
    print(token.text, token.lemma_, token.pos_)
```

```
Apple Apple PROPN
is be AUX
looking look VERB
at at ADP
buying buy VERB
a a DET
U.K. U.K. PROPN
startup startup NOUN
for for ADP
```

27. https://spacy.io/api/language
28. https://spacy.io/api/top-level#spacy.load
29. https://spacy.io/api/doc
30. https://spacy.io/api/token

```
$ $ SYM
1 1 NUM
billion billion NUM
```

- **Named entities**: Named entities in the document can be accessed using the `doc.ents` attribute:

```
for entity in doc.ents:
    print(entity.text, entity.label_)
```

```
Apple ORG
U.K. GPE
$1 billion MONEY
```

7.5.3.2 Language Processing Pipelines

The `Language` object in spaCy includes an associated language processing pipeline[31], which is a sequence of components applied in order to each `Doc` object created by the model. By default, the pipeline includes a tokenizer, POS tagger, syntactic parser, lemmatizer, and NER component. Custom components, such as statistical models or additional processing functions, can also be added to the pipeline to enrich the `Doc` object with extra annotations.

To view the components in the current pipeline and their execution order, use:

```
print(nlp.pipe_names)
```

```
['tok2vec', 'tagger', 'parser', 'attribute_ruler', 'lemmatizer', 'ner']
```

To add a custom component, define a function and register it using the `@Language.component` decorator, then add it to the pipeline using `nlp.add_pipe`[32]. The following example adds a component that prints the number of tokens in the processed document:

```
from spacy.language import Language

# Define a custom component function
@Language.component('custom_component')
def custom_component(doc):
    print("Processing document length:", len(doc))
    return doc

# Add the component to the pipeline
nlp.add_pipe('custom_component', last=True)

# Process text to see the effect of the component
doc = nlp("Apple is looking at buying a U.K. startup for $1 billion")
```

---

31. https://spacy.io/usage/processing-pipelines
32. https://spacy.io/api/language#add_pipe

The output is:

```
Processing document length: 12
```

The field of natural language processing is broad and rapidly evolving, and this section has only scratched the surface. One of the most influential NLP libraries in recent years is the Hugging Face[33] library, which offers cutting-edge models and extensive support for large language models. We will explore Hugging Face and its ecosystem in Volume III, where modern neural architectures and generative models are discussed in depth. For now, we return to our main thread and apply a naive Bayes model to a document classification task using the NLP tools introduced in this section.

7.6 Document Classification Example

In the following example, we demonstrate how to build a simple NLP pipeline to tackle a document classification task using a multinomial naive Bayes classifier (see Section 7.2.3).

We use the 20 Newsgroups dataset[34], a widely used benchmark in text classification research [342]. It contains 18,846 newsgroup posts, nearly evenly distributed across 20 different topics. These posts were collected from various Usenet newsgroups in the early 1990s and cover a wide range of subjects, including sports, finance, politics, religion, and computer hardware—providing a diverse and realistic corpus of online discussions from that era.

We begin by importing the required libraries and fixing the random seed:

```
import numpy as np
import matplotlib.pyplot as plt
import pandas as pd

np.random.seed(42)
```

7.6.1 Loading the Dataset

The fetch_20newsgroups[35] function from Scikit-Learn allows us to download the text documents from the 20 Newsgroups dataset. The documents can be retrieved either as a combined set or as separate training and test sets using the subset parameter. The division between the training and test sets is based on the posting dates of the messages, with a specific cutoff date separating the two.

By default, the text documents include metadata such as headers (e.g., the post date), footers (e.g., signatures), and quoted text from earlier messages. Since this metadata is largely irrelevant to our classification task (though it may be useful in applications like spam filtering), we exclude it from the dataset using the remove parameter.

---

33. https://huggingface.co
34. http://qwone.com/~jason/20Newsgroups
35. https://scikit-learn.org/stable/modules/generated/sklearn.datasets.fetch_20newsgroups.html

The following code downloads the predefined training and test sets excluding headers, footers, and quotes:

```
from sklearn.datasets import fetch_20newsgroups

train_set = fetch_20newsgroups(subset='train', remove=('headers', 'footers',
                                                       'quotes'))
test_set = fetch_20newsgroups(subset='test', remove=('headers', 'footers', 'quotes'))
```

The initial download of the documents may take a few minutes. However, once downloaded, the files are cached locally in the `scikit_learn_data` folder under your home directory, allowing for faster loading in future runs.

The `fetch_20newsgroups` function returns a dictionary-like object with the following attributes:

- `data`: the raw text of the documents.

- `target`: the numeric target labels for each document.

- `target_names`: the names of the corresponding categories.

Let's assign the documents and their labels to appropriate variables:

```
X_train, y_train = train_set.data, train_set.target
X_test, y_test = test_set.data, test_set.target
```

7.6.2 Data Exploration

To better understand the structure and distribution of the dataset, we start with some basic data exploration steps. First, we check the number of documents in the training and test sets:

```
print('Number of training documents:', len(X_train))
print('Number of test documents:', len(X_test))
```

```
Number of training documents: 11314
Number of test documents: 7532
```

The output shows that approximately 60% of the documents are in the training set and 40% in the test set. Next, we examine the dataset's categories to get a sense of the topics it covers:

```
categories = train_set.target_names
print(categories)
```

```
['alt.atheism', 'comp.graphics', 'comp.os.ms-windows.misc',
 'comp.sys.ibm.pc.hardware', 'comp.sys.mac.hardware', 'comp.windows.x',
 'misc.forsale', 'rec.autos', 'rec.motorcycles', 'rec.sport.baseball',
 'rec.sport.hockey', 'sci.crypt', 'sci.electronics', 'sci.med', 'sci.space',
 'soc.religion.christian', 'talk.politics.guns', 'talk.politics.mideast',
 'talk.politics.misc', 'talk.religion.misc']
```

As shown above, the dataset covers a broad range of topics, including technology, sports, science, religion, and politics. Some categories are closely related, such as comp.sys.mac.hardware and comp.sys.ibm.pc.hardware, which may pose challenges for the classifier due to overlapping vocabulary.

To examine the distribution of class labels in the training set, we use the following code:

```
np.unique(y_train, return_counts=True)
```

```
(array([ 0,  1,  2,  3,  4,  5,  6,  7,  8,  9, 10, 11, 12, 13, 14, 15, 16,
        17, 18, 19]),
 array([480, 584, 591, 590, 578, 593, 585, 594, 598, 597, 600, 595, 591,
        594, 593, 599, 546, 564, 465, 377], dtype=int64))
```

The output confirms that the dataset is relatively balanced across the 20 categories.

Finally, we inspect a sample document to get a sense of the type of content we are working with:

```
print(X_train[0])
```

```
I was wondering if anyone out there could enlighten me on this car I saw
the other day. It was a 2-door sports car, looked to be from the late 60s/
early 70s. It was called a Bricklin. The doors were really small. In addition,
the front bumper was separate from the rest of the body. This is
all I know. If anyone can tellme a model name, engine specs, years
of production, where this car is made, history, or whatever info you
have on this funky looking car, please e-mail.
```

The label of this document in the dataset is:

```
print('Document label:', categories[y_train[0]])
```

```
Document label: rec.autos
```

The document clearly discusses a car and is appropriately labeled under rec.autos.

7.6.3 Text Vectorization

To apply machine learning algorithms to text documents, they must first be preprocessed and converted into numerical vectors—a process known as **vectorization**.

One simple and widely used method for text vectorization is the **bag-of-words (BOW)** model. This approach constructs a vocabulary of all unique words in the training corpus and represents each document as a vector indicating the presence or frequency of these words in that document. While easy to implement, the BOW model has several limitations:

- It treats all words equally, without distinguishing between frequently occurring and rare terms, potentially diminishing the importance of more informative words.

- Longer documents tend to have higher word counts, which can skew the feature values unless normalization is applied.

- The resulting vectors are typically high-dimensional and very sparse, with the number of dimensions equal to the vocabulary size, which can lead to issues related to the curse of dimensionality (see Section 6.6).

- It ignores word order and context, losing important semantic and syntactic information.

An improved text representation that addresses some of these limitations is **TF-IDF (Term Frequency-Inverse Document Frequency)**, originally developed for information retrieval systems [518]. TF-IDF combines two measures: the frequency of a term within a document (term frequency) and its rarity across the entire corpus (inverse document frequency). This approach downweights common but uninformative words (e.g., articles and prepositions) and upweight terms that are more distinctive, making the representation more reflective of each document's content.

Formally, let D be a collection of documents, $d \in D$ a specific document, and t a term appearing in d. The TF-IDF score of t in d is computed as the product of two components:

- **Term Frequency (TF)**: Measures how frequently the term t appears in document d, normalized by the total numbers of terms in d:

$$\text{tf}(t, d) = \frac{\text{freq}(t, d)}{|d|}, \tag{7.26}$$

where $\text{freq}(t, d)$ is the number of times t appears in d, and $|d|$ is the total number of terms in the document.

- **Inverse Document Frequency (IDF)**: Quantifies how rare the term is across the corpus:

$$\text{idf}(t, D) = \log\left(\frac{|D|}{\text{df}(t)}\right), \tag{7.27}$$

where $|D|$ is the total number of documents in the corpus, and $\text{df}(t)$ is the number of documents in which t appears at least once. The logarithm causes very common words like "the" to have an IDF near zero, so they receive almost no weight in the final representation.

The TF-IDF score is then given by:

$$\text{tfidf}(t, d, D) = \text{tf}(t, d) \cdot \text{idf}(t, D) = \frac{\text{freq}(t, d)}{|d|} \log\left(\frac{|D|}{\text{df}(t, D)}\right). \tag{7.28}$$

Common words that appear in many documents receive low TF-IDF scores due to their low inverse document frequency. In contrast, rare terms, which are often more informative for distinguishing between documents, receive higher scores and thus contribute more to the document's vector representation.

As a simple example, assume that we have three documents in the corpus:

1. "The cat sat on the mat"

2. "A dog barked at the moon"

3. "The cat and the dog played together"

To compute the TF-IDF score for the word "cat" in the first document, we follow these steps:

1. Term frequency: The word "cat" appears once in a six-word document, so

$$\text{tf}(t, d) = \frac{1}{6}.$$

2. Inverse document frequency: "Cat" appears in two of the three documents in the corpus, so

$$\text{idf}(t, D) = \log\left(\frac{3}{2}\right) = 0.176.$$

3. TF-IDF score: The final score is the product of the two:

$$\text{tfidf}(t, d, D) = \text{tf}(t, d) \cdot \text{idf}(t, D) = \frac{1}{6} \cdot 0.176 = 0.029.$$

Scikit-Learn provides the following classes for text preprocessing and vectorization:

- `CountVectorizer`[36]: Implements the bag-of-words model by converting text documents into vectors of token counts.

- `TfidfVectorizer`[37]: Applies the TF-IDF transformation, weighting terms according to their rarity in the corpus.

Table 7.6 summarizes the key parameters available in both transformers. Note that these transformers support many of the text preprocessing techniques discussed earlier, including tokenization, lowercasing, and stop word removal. However, they do not support more advanced techniques such as stemming, lemmatization, or POS tagging. For these tasks, you can use other NLP-focused Python libraries, such as NLTK or spaCy, as discussed in Section 7.5. For the purposes of this demonstration, though, the preprocessing features provided by Scikit-Learn are sufficient.

36. https://scikit-learn.org/stable/modules/generated/sklearn.feature_extraction.text.
    CountVectorizer.html
37. https://scikit-learn.org/stable/modules/generated/sklearn.feature_extraction.text.
    TfidfVectorizer.html

Parameter	Description	Default
lowercase	Converts all characters to lowercase before tokenization.	True
token_pattern	Regular expression that defines what counts as a token. The default pattern matches tokens with two or more alphanumeric characters.	'\b\w\w+\b'
stop_words	Removes stop words. If set to 'english', a built-in English stop word list is used. If None, no stop words are removed. A custom list can also be provided.	None
ngram_range	Specifies the range of n-gram sizes to extract. For example, (1, 2) extracts unigrams and bigrams.	(1, 1)
max_features	Limits the number of terms to the top max_features terms, ranked by term frequency across the corpus. If None, all terms are included.	None
max_df	Excludes terms that appear in more than the specified proportion or number of documents, thereby removing common and less informative terms. A float in [0.0, 1.0] indicates a proportion; an integer indicates an absolute count.	1.0
min_df	Excludes terms that appear in fewer than the specified proportion or number of documents, thereby reducing noise by ignoring very rare terms.	1
preprocessor	A custom preprocessing function applied before tokenization.	None
tokenizer	A custom tokenization function. Overrides the default regex-based tokenization.	None

Table 7.6: Key parameters of CountVectorizer and TfidfVectorizer

For example, let's apply the TfidfVectorizer to the training set:

```
from sklearn.feature_extraction.text import TfidfVectorizer

vectorizer = TfidfVectorizer()
X_train_vec = vectorizer.fit_transform(X_train)
```

The TfidfVectorizer transforms the training documents into a matrix where each row represents a document and each column corresponds to a unique token from the corpus. The dimensions of the resulting matrix are:

```
print(X_train_vec.shape)
```

```
(11314, 101631)
```

This output indicates that the training set contains 11,314 documents and 101,631 unique tokens. We can inspect the first few tokens in the vocabulary using the vectorizer's get_features_names_out method:

```
vocab = vectorizer.get_feature_names_out()
print(vocab[:10])
```

```
['00' '000' '0000' '00000' '000000' '00000000' '0000000004' '00000000b'
 '00000001' '00000001b']
```

The first tokens are numeric, appearing before alphabetic tokens because of the ASCII character ordering.

The TfidfVectorizer returns the data matrix as a SciPy sparse matrix, where only nonzero elements are stored to save memory. This is necessary because the TF-IDF vectors representing the documents are very sparse—most entries are zero, as each document contains only a small subset of the vocabulary. To illustrate the level of sparsity, we can compute the average number of nonzero elements per document (nnz stands for the total number of nonzero entries in the matrix):

```
print(X_train_vec.nnz / X_train_vec.shape[0])
```

```
97.54525366802191
```

This indicates that, on average, only about 98 out of the 101,631 possible features are nonzero in each document vector, representing about 0.1% of the total features. Such extreme sparsity is typical in text data.

To inspect the actual content of the feature matrix, we can convert a small portion of the sparse matrix to a dense NumPy array using the toarray method:

```
import pandas as pd

df = pd.DataFrame(X_train_vec[:5].toarray(), columns=vocab)
df
```

Figure 7.4 shows the **document-term matrix** for the first five documents. The cell values indicate the TF-IDF score assigned to each term within each document. This matrix serves as the input to the text classification model.

	00	000	0000	00000	000000	00000000	0000000004	00000000b	00000001	00000001b	...	zznkzz	zznp	zzrk	zzy_3w	zzz	zzzoh
0	0.0	0.0	0.0	0.0	0.0	0.0	0.0	0.0	0.0	0.0	...	0.0	0.0	0.0	0.0	0.0	0.0
1	0.0	0.0	0.0	0.0	0.0	0.0	0.0	0.0	0.0	0.0	...	0.0	0.0	0.0	0.0	0.0	0.0
2	0.0	0.0	0.0	0.0	0.0	0.0	0.0	0.0	0.0	0.0	...	0.0	0.0	0.0	0.0	0.0	0.0
3	0.0	0.0	0.0	0.0	0.0	0.0	0.0	0.0	0.0	0.0	...	0.0	0.0	0.0	0.0	0.0	0.0
4	0.0	0.0	0.0	0.0	0.0	0.0	0.0	0.0	0.0	0.0	...	0.0	0.0	0.0	0.0	0.0	0.0

5 rows × 101631 columns

Figure 7.4: Document-term matrix displaying the TF-IDF scores for the first five documents in the training set. Each row corresponds to a document and each column to a unique token from the corpus. The matrix is highly sparse, with most entries equal to zero.

7.6.4 Building the Model

For this task, we use the multinomial naive Bayes classifier, which usually performs better than the multivariate Bernoulli classifier in text classification tasks. Although the MNB classifier is traditionally used with raw word counts, it can also be applied to continuous features such as TF-IDF values. In this case, the TF-IDF score for each term acts as a weighted frequency of that term. During prediction, the classifier computes the log-likelihood of each class using the formula:

$$\log P(y = c|\mathbf{x}) \propto \log P(c) + \sum_{t \in V} x_t \log P(t|c), \tag{7.29}$$

where $x_t = \text{tfidf}(t, d)$ is the TF-IDF score of term t in document d (instead of the raw count of t), and $P(t|c)$ is the estimated conditional probability of term t given class c, computed from word counts with additive smoothing. Although this use of TF-IDF is not fully probabilistically justified under the multinomial model, it often performs well in practice and is widely adopted.

To implement this model, we create a pipeline that combines TF-IDF vectorization with a multinomial naive Bayes classifier and fit it to the training set:

```
from sklearn.pipeline import Pipeline
from sklearn.feature_extraction.text import TfidfVectorizer
from sklearn.naive_bayes import MultinomialNB

model = Pipeline([
    ('vect', TfidfVectorizer()),
    ('clf', MultinomialNB(alpha=0.01))
])
model.fit(X_train, y_train)
```

Note that we set the smoothing parameter α to a small value (0.01) because TF-IDF values are typically normalized between 0 and 1. Using the default setting of $\alpha = 1$ may apply excessive smoothing, unintentionally boosting the influence of terms that are rare or missing in certain classes.

7.6.5 Evaluating the Model

Next, we evaluate the performance of the model on both the training and test sets. Since the dataset is relatively balanced across categories, accuracy is a suitable metric for evaluation:

```
print(f'Accuracy (train): {model.score(X_train, y_train):.4f}')
print(f'Accuracy (test): {model.score(X_test, y_test):.4f}')
```

The output is:

```
Accuracy (train): 0.9589
Accuracy (test): 0.7002
```

The model achieves high accuracy on the training set but performs significantly worse on the test set, indicating potential overfitting. While overfitting is more commonly associated with complex models, it can also occur in simpler models like naive Bayes—especially when the input space is high-dimensional, as is often the case in text classification with sparse representations like TF-IDF.

Another explanation for this discrepancy is that the test documents were posted at a later time than the training documents. As a result, shifts in writing style or vocabulary over time may hinder the model's ability to classify them accurately. To test this hypothesis, we can combine the training and test sets and then perform a random split (keeping a 60% train/40% test ratio) to assess whether the temporal distribution affects the model's performance:

```
from sklearn.model_selection import train_test_split

# Combine the original training and test data
X_combined = X_train + X_test
y_combined = np.concatenate([y_train, y_test])

# Perform a random split into new training and test sets
X_new_train, X_new_test, y_new_train, y_new_test = train_test_split(
    X_combined, y_combined, test_size=0.4, random_state=42
)

# Fit the model on the new training data
model.fit(X_new_train, y_new_train)

# Evaluate the model on the new data sets
train_accuracy = model.score(X_new_train, y_new_train)
test_accuracy = model.score(X_new_test, y_new_test)

print(f'Accuracy (new train): {train_accuracy:.4f}')
print(f'Accuracy (new test): {test_accuracy:.4f}')
```

The output is:

```
Accuracy (new train): 0.9563
Accuracy (new test): 0.7506
```

The improvement in test accuracy (from 70.02% to 75.06%) confirms that the temporal distribution of the documents impacts model performance, though it is likely not the only factor.

To gain deeper insight into the model's performance, let's examine the confusion matrix on the test set:

```
from sklearn.metrics import confusion_matrix, ConfusionMatrixDisplay

model.fit(X_train, y_train) # Refit the model on the original training set
y_test_pred = model.predict(X_test)
```

```
conf_mat = confusion_matrix(y_test, y_test_pred)
disp = ConfusionMatrixDisplay(confusion_matrix=conf_mat)
fig, ax = plt.subplots(figsize=(10, 8))
disp.plot(ax=ax, cmap='Blues')
```

As shown in Figure 7.5, many misclassifications occur between closely related topics, such as:

- 79 misclassifications between `alt.atheism` (topic 0) and `soc.religion.christian` (topic 15).

- 91 misclassifications between `talk.politics.misc` (topic 18) and `talk.politics.guns` (topic 16).

- 96 misclassifications between `talk.religion.misc` (topic 19) and `soc.religion.christian` (topic 15).

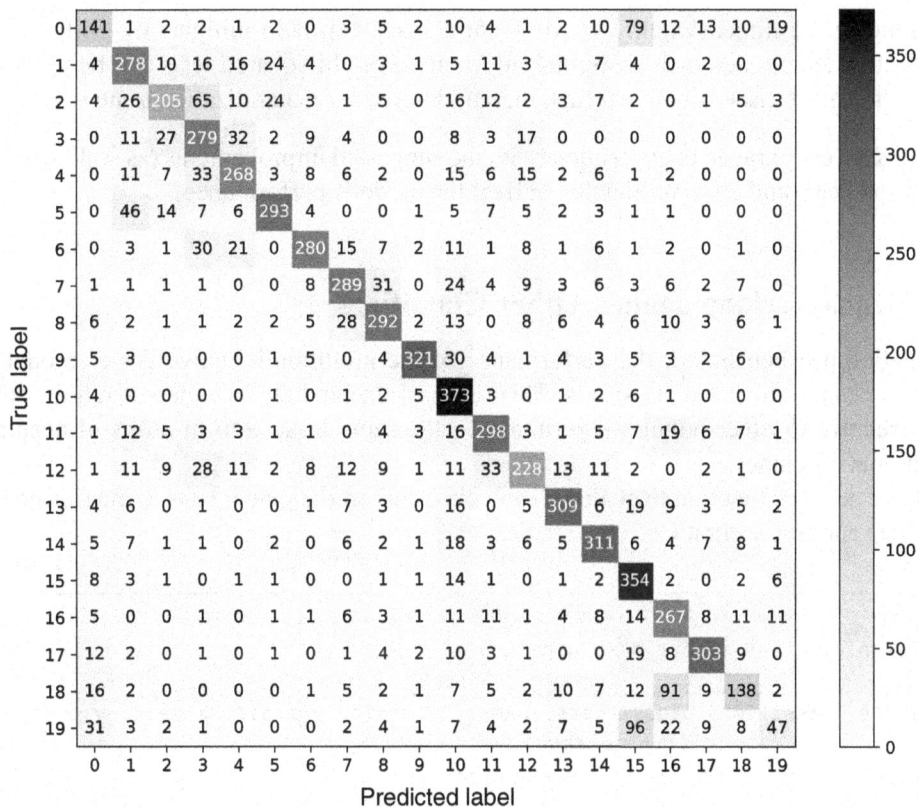

True \ Pred	0	1	2	3	4	5	6	7	8	9	10	11	12	13	14	15	16	17	18	19
0	141	1	2	2	1	2	0	3	5	2	10	4	1	2	10	79	12	13	10	19
1	4	278	10	16	16	24	4	0	3	1	5	11	3	1	7	4	0	2	0	0
2	4	26	205	65	10	24	3	1	5	0	16	12	2	3	7	2	0	1	5	3
3	0	11	27	279	32	2	9	4	0	0	8	3	17	0	0	0	0	0	0	0
4	0	11	7	33	268	3	8	6	2	0	15	6	15	2	6	1	2	0	0	0
5	0	46	14	7	6	293	4	0	0	1	5	7	5	2	3	1	1	0	0	0
6	0	3	1	30	21	0	280	15	7	2	11	1	8	1	6	1	2	0	1	0
7	1	1	1	1	0	0	8	289	31	0	24	4	9	3	6	3	6	2	7	0
8	6	2	1	1	2	2	5	28	292	2	13	0	8	6	4	6	10	3	6	1
9	5	3	0	0	0	1	5	0	4	321	30	4	1	4	3	5	3	2	6	0
10	4	0	0	0	0	1	0	1	2	5	373	3	0	1	2	6	1	0	0	0
11	1	12	5	3	3	1	1	0	4	3	16	298	3	1	5	7	19	6	7	1
12	1	11	9	28	11	2	8	12	9	1	11	33	228	13	11	2	0	2	1	0
13	4	6	0	1	0	0	1	7	3	0	16	0	5	309	6	19	9	3	5	2
14	5	7	1	1	0	2	0	6	2	1	18	3	6	5	311	6	4	7	8	1
15	8	3	1	0	1	1	0	0	1	1	14	1	0	1	2	354	2	0	2	6
16	5	0	0	1	0	1	1	6	3	1	11	11	1	4	8	14	267	8	11	11
17	12	2	0	1	0	1	0	1	4	2	10	3	1	0	0	19	8	303	9	0
18	16	2	0	0	0	0	1	5	2	1	7	5	2	10	7	12	91	9	138	2
19	31	3	2	1	0	0	0	2	4	1	7	4	2	7	5	96	22	9	8	47

Figure 7.5: Confusion matrix of the multinomial naive Bayes model for the 20 newsgroups classification task. Darker cells along the diagonal indicate correct classifications, while off-diagonal cells show misclassifications. The classifier struggles the most with topics that have overlapping vocabulary or closely related content, such as `talk.politics.misc` vs. `talk.politics.guns`.

To enhance classification accuracy, several improvements can be considered:

- Some classes are inherently difficult to separate due to shared vocabulary and overlapping themes. Increasing the number of training examples from these categories, or merging them into a broader category, could help the model learn better distinctions.

- The default vectorizer settings, such as using only unigrams (single words) and including all terms regardless of frequency, may not yield the most informative features. Tuning hyperparameters like `min_df`, `max_df`, and `ngram_range` can help capture more meaningful patterns while filtering out noise.

- While TF-IDF improves upon raw frequency counts, it still ignores word meaning and context. More advanced representations, such as word embeddings (e.g., Word2Vec, GloVe), can capture semantic relationships between words—though they require switching to models that support dense, continuous inputs.

- Reducing the dimensionality of the feature space can help mitigate overfitting. Features selection techniques such as mutual information or chi-squared tests can be used to retain only the most discriminative terms, thereby improving generalization to new data.

Readers are encouraged to experiment with the suggested improvements (as well as other ideas not discussed here) and observe how they affect the model's performance.

7.6.6   Benchmarking against Other Classifiers

In this section, we benchmark the performance of the multinomial naive Bayes model against several other commonly used classifiers. This comparison can help us understand how well MNB performs relative to other popular algorithms on the same task, both in terms of accuracy and computational efficiency.

First, we define a function to evaluate each classifier on the given dataset, measuring both the training time and test accuracy:

```
import time
from sklearn.pipeline import make_pipeline

def evaluate_classifiers(classifiers, names, X_train, y_train, X_test, y_test,
                         verbose=True):
    evaluations = [] # Stores the evaluation results

    # Iterate over all classifiers
    for clf, name in zip(classifiers, names):
        start_time = time.time()

        # Define a pipline with TF-IDF vectorizer and the given classifier
```

```
        model = make_pipeline(TfidfVectorizer(), clf)
        model.fit(X_train, y_train)

        # Calculate the training time and accuracy on the test set
        training_time = time.time() - start_time
        test_accuracy = model.score(X_test, y_test)

        # Store the results in a dictionary
        evaluation = {
            'classifier': name,
            'training_time': training_time,
            'test_accuracy': test_accuracy
        }
        if verbose:
            print(evaluation)
        evaluations.append(evaluation)
    return evaluations
```

We now apply it to a set of six different classifiers, including MNB:

```
from sklearn.naive_bayes import BernoulliNB
from sklearn.linear_model import LogisticRegression
from sklearn.neighbors import KNeighborsClassifier
from sklearn.ensemble import RandomForestClassifier
from sklearn.svm import LinearSVC

classifiers = [
    MultinomialNB(alpha=0.01),
    BernoulliNB(alpha=0.01),
    LogisticRegression(random_state=42),
    KNeighborsClassifier(n_neighbors=10),
    RandomForestClassifier(random_state=42),
    LinearSVC(random_state=42)
]
names = ['Multinomial NB', 'Bernoulli NB', 'Logistic Regression', 'KNN',
         'Random Forests', 'LinearSVC']

evaluations = evaluate_classifiers(classifiers, names, X_train, y_train, X_test,
                                   y_test)
```

Next, we plot the test set accuracy for each classifier:

```
df = pd.DataFrame(evaluations).set_index('classifier')

df['test_accuracy'].plot.barh(color='cyan')
plt.xlabel('Accuracy on Test Set')
```

```
plt.ylabel('')
for index, value in enumerate(df['test_accuracy']):
    plt.text(value, index, f'{value * 100:.2f}%', va='center', ha='right')
```

Figure 7.6 shows the results. The multinomial naive Bayes classifier achieves the highest accuracy, confirming its suitability for this task. Its superior performance over Bernoulli naive Bayes is expected, as it leverages term frequency information, which tends to be more informative than simple binary indicators in text classification tasks. The KNN classifier performs significantly worse than the others, likely due to the curse of dimensionality associated with the high-dimensional sparse TF-IDF features.

We also compare the training times:

```
df['training_time'].plot.barh(color='red')
plt.xlabel('Training Time (sec)')
plt.ylabel('')
for index, value in enumerate(df['training_time']):
    plt.text(value, index, f'{value:.2f}')
```

As shown in Figure 7.7, the MNB classifier has the shortest training time. Although KNN also trains quickly, its prediction time is much slower as it must compute distances to all training samples at inference time.

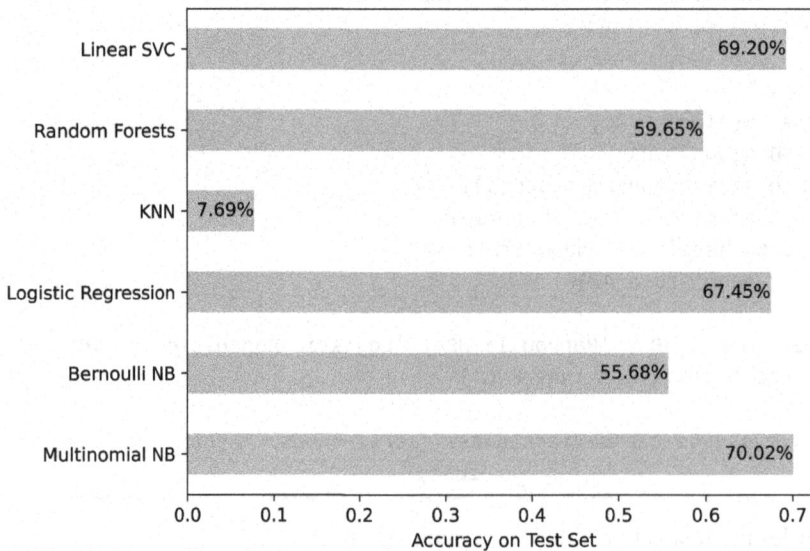

Figure 7.6: Comparison of test set accuracy among various classifiers on the document classification task. Multinomial naive Bayes achieves the highest accuracy, followed closely by the linear support vector classifier (SVC). KNN performs significantly worse due to the high-dimensionality and sparsity of the feature space.

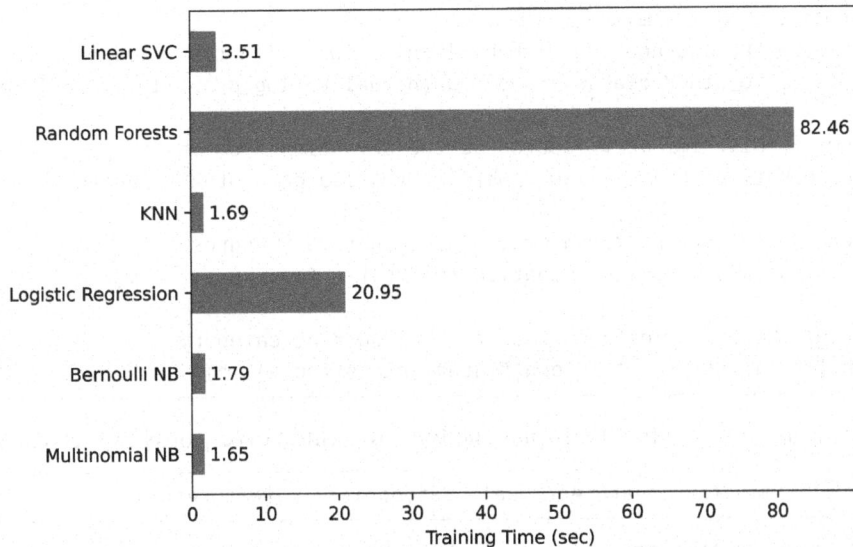

Figure 7.7: Comparison of training time among various classifiers on the document classification task. Multinomial naive Bayes trains the fastest, demonstrating its efficiency.

7.6.7 Identifying the Most Discriminative Features

Naive Bayes models allow us to easily identify the most discriminative features of each class—those terms that are much more likely to appear in one class than in others. This is especially valuable in text classification, where such features correspond to highly indicative words for each category.

In Scikit-Learn's `MultinomialNB` class, the `feature_log_prob_` attribute stores the log-probabilities $\log P(x_j|y = c)$ of each feature x_j given class c, organized as a matrix of shape (C, d), where C is the number of classes and d is the number of features.

To identify the most discriminative features for each category, we compute how much the log-probability of each word in that class deviates from its average log-probability across all other classes. Words with the highest positive deviation are considered the most discriminative.

The following function extracts and displays the top n discriminative words for each class:

```
def show_top_n_discriminative_features(model, categories, n_features):
    # Get the feature names from the vectorizer
    feature_names = model.named_steps['vect'].get_feature_names_out()

    # Retrieve the trained classifier from the pipeline
    clf = model.named_steps['clf']

    # Get the log-probabilities of features given each class
    log_prob = clf.feature_log_prob_
```

```
for i, category in enumerate(categories):
    # Compute the average log-probabilities across all other classes
    avg_log_prob_other_classes = np.mean(np.delete(log_prob, i, axis=0), axis=0)

    # Compute discriminative scores as the deviation from the average
    discriminative_scores = log_prob[i] - avg_log_prob_other_classes

    # Get indices of the top-n most discriminative features
    top_n = np.argsort(discriminative_scores)[-n_features:][::-1]

    # Print the top-n feature names for the current category
    print(f"{category}: {' '.join(feature_names[top_n])}")
```

We can now use this function to display the top 5 discriminative words in each category:

```
show_top_n_discriminative_features(model, categories, n_features=5)
```

```
alt.atheism: atheism atheists islam bobbe beauchaine
comp.graphics: cview pov tiff polygon 3d
comp.os.ms-windows.misc: ax cica ini win3 w4wg
comp.sys.ibm.pc.hardware: ide scsi vlb irq controller
comp.sys.mac.hardware: quadra centris lciii c650 duo
comp.windows.x: widget motif x11r5 xterm xlib
misc.forsale: obo forsale shipping sega lens
rec.autos: toyota autos honda convertible wagon
rec.motorcycles: bike bikes motorcycle helmet harley
rec.sport.baseball: pitching braves alomar phillies sox
rec.sport.hockey: nhl hockey leafs playoffs espn
sci.crypt: encryption nsa clipper escrow crypto
sci.electronics: amp circuit 8051 voltage transformer
sci.med: geb chastity n3jxp dsl cadre
sci.space: orbit lunar spacecraft shuttle moon
soc.religion.christian: jesus christians christianity christ scripture
talk.politics.guns: firearms firearm feustel jmd batf
talk.politics.mideast: armenians armenian israeli israel arab
talk.politics.misc: stephanopoulos deane libertarians garrett homosexual
talk.religion.misc: jesus rosicrucian christians amorc morality
```

These terms offer valuable insight into how the model distinguishes between categories. For instance, technical terms like quadra, scsi, and motif reflect specific hardware and software domains, while religious or political categories often include group or geopolitical names.

7.7 Bayesian Networks

A **Bayesian network (BN)** (also known as a **Bayesian belief network**) is a probabilistic graphical model that represents a set of random variables and their conditional dependencies using a directed acyclic graph (DAG) [469, 204, 264]. This structure enables a compact factorization of the joint probability distribution of the variables, substantially reducing the number of parameters in the model compared to specifying the full joint distribution explicitly.

Unlike the naive Bayes model, Bayesian networks can capture dependencies among features, offering greater flexibility in representing real-world distributions. In addition to classification, they are widely used for probabilistic inference, causal reasoning, and decision-making under uncertainty.

7.7.1 Formal Definition

Formally, let $\mathcal{X} = \{X_1, \ldots, X_n\}$ be a set of discrete random variables. A Bayesian network over $\mathcal{X}$ is a pair (G, Θ), where:

- G is a directed acyclic graph whose nodes correspond to the variables $X_1, \ldots, X_n$. An edge from X_i to X_j ($X_i \to X_j$) indicates that X_j is directly dependent on X_i in the joint distribution represented by the network.

- Θ is a set of parameters that define the conditional probability distributions of the variables. Each variable X_i is associated with a conditional distribution $P(X_i \mid \text{Pa}(X_i))$, where $\text{Pa}(X_i)$ denotes the set of its parent nodes in the graph.

  For each possible value x_i of X_i and each configuration π_i of its parents (i.e., a particular assignment of values to the variables in $\text{Pa}(X_i)$), Θ includes a parameter $\theta_{x_i|\pi_i} = P(x_i|\pi_i)$.

The graph G encodes the following independence assumptions: each variable X_i is conditionally independent of its non-descendants given its parents:

$$X_i \perp\!\!\!\perp \text{NonDescendants}(X_i) \mid \text{Pa}(X_i). \tag{7.30}$$

Based on these assumptions, the joint probability distribution of the variables in $\mathcal{X}$ can be factorized as:

$$P(X_1, \ldots, X_n) = \prod_{i=1}^{n} P(X_i \mid \text{Pa}(X_i)). \tag{7.31}$$

This result follows directly from the chain rule of probability together with the conditional independence assumptions encoded in the graph (see Exercise 7.22).

This factorization of the joint distribution shows that the global behavior of the network can be captured through local dependencies: each variable depends only on its parents. As a result, the joint probability can be computed efficiently, greatly simplifying inference and probabilistic reasoning, as illustrated in the following example.

7.7.2   Bayesian Network Example

Consider the Bayesian network depicted in Figure 7.8, which models the likelihood of a patient having heart disease based on their lifestyle, cholesterol level, and blood pressure.

This network consists of the following binary random variables:

- Lifestyle (L): active (1) or sedentary (0)

- Cholesterol (C): high (1) or normal (0), influenced by lifestyle

- Blood pressure (B): high (1) or normal (0), influenced by lifestyle and cholesterol

- Heart disease (H): present (1) or absent (0), influenced by cholesterol and blood pressure

The joint distribution over these four variables factorizes as:

$$P(L, C, B, H) = P(H|B, C)P(B|L, C)P(C|L)P(L).$$

Suppose we want to compute the probability that a patient has heart disease given that they have high blood pressure, i.e., $P(H = 1|B = 1)$. Using the definition of conditional probability:

$$P(H = 1 \mid B = 1) = \frac{P(H = 1, B = 1)}{P(B = 1)}.$$

$P(L=1)$
0.3

L	$P(C = 1|L)$
0	0.3
1	0.2

L	C	$P(B = 1|L, C)$
0	0	0.05
0	1	0.1
1	0	0.03
1	1	0.07

B	C	$P(H = 1|B, C)$
0	0	0.05
0	1	0.2
1	0	0.3
1	1	0.5

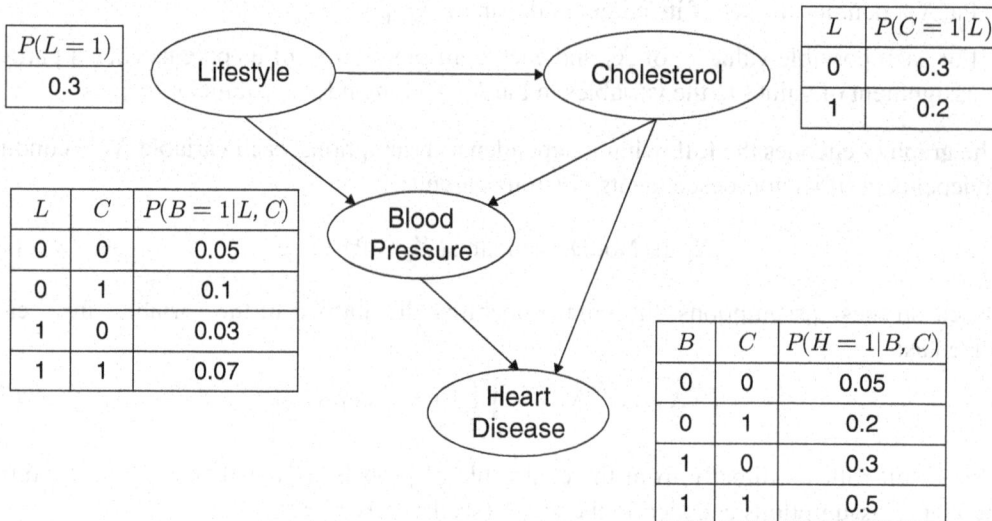

Figure 7.8: A Bayesian network illustrating the dependencies among lifestyle (L), cholesterol level (C), blood pressure (B), and heart disease (H). Each node is associated with a conditional probability table (CPT) specifying the probability that the variable takes the value 1, given different combinations of its parent values. To save space, each table lists only the probabilities for the value 1; the probabilities for 0 can be inferred as the complement to 1.

First, we compute $P(H = 1, B = 1)$ by marginalizing over the other two variables, L and C:

$$P(H = 1, B = 1) = \sum_{l,c} P(H = 1, B = 1, L = l, C = c)$$

$$= \sum_{l,c} P(H = 1 \mid B = 1, C = c)P(B = 1 \mid L = l, C = c)P(C = c \mid L = l)P(L = l)$$

$$= [P(H = 1 \mid B = 1, C = 0)P(B = 1 \mid L = 0, C = 0)P(C = 0 \mid L = 0)P(L = 0)$$
$$+ P(H = 1 \mid B = 1, C = 1)P(B = 1 \mid L = 0, C = 1)P(C = 1 \mid L = 0)P(L = 0)$$
$$+ P(H = 1 \mid B = 1, C = 0)P(B = 1 \mid L = 1, C = 0)P(C = 0 \mid L = 1)P(L = 1)$$
$$+ P(H = 1 \mid B = 1, C = 1)P(B = 1 \mid L = 1, C = 1)P(C = 1 \mid L = 1)P(L = 1)]$$

$$= 0.3 \cdot 0.05 \cdot 0.7 \cdot 0.7 + 0.5 \cdot 0.1 \cdot 0.3 \cdot 0.7 + 0.3 \cdot 0.03 \cdot 0.8 \cdot 0.3 + 0.5 \cdot 0.07 \cdot 0.2 \cdot 0.3$$

$$= 0.00735 + 0.0105 + 0.00216 + 0.0021$$

$$= 0.02211.$$

We now compute $P(B = 1)$ by marginalizing over its parent variables, L and C:

$$P(B = 1) = \sum_{l,c} P(B = 1, L = l, C = c)$$

$$= \sum_{l,c} P(B = 1 \mid L = l, C = c)P(C = c \mid L = l)P(L = l)$$

$$= [P(B = 1 \mid L = 0, C = 0)P(C = 0 \mid L = 0)P(L = 0)$$
$$+ P(B = 1 \mid L = 0, C = 1)P(C = 1 \mid L = 0)P(L = 0)$$
$$+ P(B = 1 \mid L = 1, C = 0)P(C = 0 \mid L = 1)P(L = 1)$$
$$+ P(B = 1 \mid L = 1, C = 1)P(C = 1 \mid L = 1)P(L = 1)]$$

$$= 0.05 \cdot 0.7 \cdot 0.7 + 0.1 \cdot 0.3 \cdot 0.7 + 0.03 \cdot 0.8 \cdot 0.3 + 0.07 \cdot 0.2 \cdot 0.3$$

$$= 0.0245 + 0.021 + 0.0072 + 0.0042$$

$$= 0.0569.$$

Finally, the conditional probability is:

$$P(H = 1 \mid B = 1) = \frac{P(H = 1, B = 1)}{P(B = 1)} = \frac{0.02211}{0.0569} = 0.3887.$$

This result indicates that a patient with high blood pressure has approximately a 38.87% probability of having heart disease, according to the Bayesian network model.

7.7.3   Inference in Bayesian Networks

In the previous example, we computed probabilities manually by summing over all possible configurations of the hidden variables. While this is manageable for small networks, such manual computation becomes quickly intractable as the number of variables and dependencies increases.

Inference in Bayesian networks refers to the process of computing marginal or conditional probabilities from the joint distribution defined by the network. It is typically categorized into two types: **exact inference**, which computes precise probability distributions, and **approximate inference**, which estimates these distributions when exact computation becomes infeasible due to the network's complexity.

The most straightforward approach to exact inference is **enumeration**, which involves summing over the full joint distribution to compute marginal or conditional probabilities. While this method is conceptually simple, it becomes computationally infeasible as the number of variables increases.

A more efficient technique for exact inference is **variable elimination**, which simplifies the computation of marginal or conditional probabilities by systematically summing out irrelevant variables [662, 149]. The main steps of the algorithm are:

1. Select an elimination order for the variables that are not involved in the query (i.e., variables that are neither observed nor part of the target distribution). The elimination order can significantly affect the efficiency of the algorithm.

2. Iteratively eliminate each variable by summing it out. At each step, update the intermediate factors—temporary functions over subsets of variables that result from summing out a variable.

3. Return the final factor representing the distribution over the remaining variables (typically the query and evidence variables).

However, exact inference in general Bayesian networks is known to be NP-hard [129], and becomes computationally intractable in large or densely connected networks due to the exponential growth in the number of possible configurations of the variables. To address this challenge, various **approximate inference** techniques have been developed. These methods trade off exactness for scalability, providing estimates of marginal or conditional probabilities when exact computation is too costly.

A major class of approximate methods is based on **sampling**, which generates random samples from the distribution defined by the Bayesian network. These samples are then used to estimate the desired probabilities by computing empirical frequencies. The accuracy of these estimates improves with the number of samples and, under mild conditions, they converge to the true probabilities.

Common sampling-based methods include:

- **Likelihood weighting** [208]: Samples are generated by fixing the observed variables to their evidence values and sampling the remaining variables according to their conditional distributions. Each sample is weighted by the likelihood of the evidence under that sample.

- **Rejection sampling** [266]: Samples are drawn from the prior distribution, and any sample inconsistent with the evidence is discarded. While conceptually simple, this method can be highly inefficient when the evidence is unlikely under the prior.

- **Gibbs sampling** [221]: A method that repeatedly samples each variable conditioned on the current values of all the others. This process gradually produces samples that approximate the true posterior distribution.

These sampling techniques are also widely used in reinforcement learning, and we will revisit them in Volume III when we discuss Monte Carlo methods for decision-making under uncertainty.

7.7.4 (*) Learning Bayesian Networks from Data

Building a Bayesian network from a given dataset involves two main tasks: learning the structure of the network (i.e., the dependencies among variables) and estimating the conditional probability distributions for each node. Various approaches have been developed for both tasks:

1. **Structure Learning**: This task involves identifying the network structure that best captures the dependencies in the data. Several approaches are commonly used:

   - **Score-based methods**: These methods define a score function, such as the minimum description length (MDL)[38], to evaluate how well a given network structure fits the data while penalizing network complexity to prevent overfitting. A search algorithm such as greedy hill-climbing or a genetic algorithm is then used to find the structure that maximizes the score [341, 116].

   - **Constraint-based methods**: These methods use statistical tests, such as conditional independence tests, to discover (in)dependencies among variables. A structure learning algorithm then constructs a graph that reflects the detected conditional independencies [556].

   - **Hybrid methods**: These combine constraint-based and score-based techniques. For example, a constraint-based method may be used to propose an initial structure, which is then refined via score-based optimization [205, 584].

---

38. The **Minimum Description Length (MDL)** principle is a formalization of Occam's razor in information theory and machine learning. It states that the best model for a dataset is the one that leads to the shortest total description—combining the length of the model itself and the length of the data when encoded using that model. In the context of Bayesian networks, MDL balances model complexity (number of parameters or edges) with data fit, helping to prevent overfitting.

- **Expert knowledge**: In some domains, prior knowledge can guide or constrain the structure learning process. Experts may manually specify the network or restrict the search space by forbidding or enforcing certain edges.

2. **Parameter Estimation**: Once the network structure is established, we need to estimate the conditional probability distributions for each node. Common approaches include:

   - **Maximum likelihood estimation (MLE)**: Estimate the probabilities directly from observed frequencies in the dataset, similar to parameter estimation in naive Bayes models [136]. This method relies on having enough data to ensure reliable estimates.

   - **Bayesian estimation**: Assumes prior distributions over the parameters and updates them using the data to obtain posterior distributions [264]. This approach is particularly useful for small datasets or when incorporating prior knowledge.

7.8   (*) Probabilistic Graphical Models

Probabilistic graphical models (PGMs) are a broad class of models that represent complex joint probability distributions using graph-based structures [326, 343, 305]. These graphs encode conditional independence assumptions by modeling local interactions among random variables. They decompose complex problems into smaller, structured subproblems, facilitating scalable learning and inference, enhancing interpretability, and supporting the incorporation of expert knowledge.

PGMs are widely used in areas such as information extraction, speech recognition, gene discovery, and disease diagnosis, where they support inference from incomplete or noisy data. In modern machine learning, they complement deep learning by adding structure and interpretability to neural networks in hybrid models such as Bayesian neural networks and variational autoencoders (VAEs).

In addition to Bayesian networks, PGMs include several other model families:

- **Markov Chains** [399, 449]: Sequential models in which each state depends only on the previous state—a property known as the **Markov assumption**. Markov chains are common in time series analysis, natural language processing, and other domains with temporal dynamics.

- **Hidden Markov Models (HMMs)** [493]: Extensions of Markov chains that introduce hidden (latent) states and observable outputs. Each hidden state depends only on the previous one, and observations are generated conditionally on the current state. HMMs are widely used in speech recognition, bioinformatics, time series modeling, and other sequence labeling tasks.

- **Dynamic Bayesian Networks (DBNs)** [143]: Generalize HMMs by allowing multiple interacting variables at each time step and supporting more expressive temporal and intra-slice dependencies. DBNs are used to model complex dynamic systems, such as human activity recognition and financial processes.

- **Markov Networks** (or **Markov Random Fields (MRFs)**) [250, 530]: Undirected graphical models where edges represent symmetric relationships between variables. The joint distribution is factorized over cliques (fully connected subsets of nodes), with each clique associated with a potential function that captures local interactions. Markov networks are commonly used in image processing, spatial statistics, and information extraction.

- **Conditional Random Fields (CRFs)** [339]: Undirected graphical models that directly model the conditional distribution of target variables given observed inputs $P(\mathbf{y}|\mathbf{x})$, instead of the full joint distribution $P(\mathbf{x}, \mathbf{y})$. This allows CRFs to focus on the prediction task while avoiding unnecessary assumptions about the input distribution.

- **Factor Graphs** [336]: Bipartite graphs with variable and factor nodes that explicitly represent the factorization of a joint distribution, supporting efficient inference through message-passing algorithms such as belief propagation.

- **Chain Graphs** [344]: Graphical models that combine directed and undirected edges, generalizing both Bayesian and Markov networks to allow more flexible dependency structures.

The open-source library pgmpy[39] (Probabilistic Graphical Models using Python) provides implementations of many PGM variants, including Bayesian networks, Markov networks, and DBNs [17]. It supports structure learning, parameter estimation, and both exact and approximate inference.

For a deeper treatment of probabilistic graphical models, refer to the classical textbook by Koller and Friedman, *Probabilistic Graphical Models: Principles and Techniques* [326].

7.9 Summary

This chapter explored the family of naive Bayes classifiers, highlighting their practical strengths and theoretical limitations. It also introduced key concepts and tools from natural language processing, and demonstrated how naive Bayes classifiers can be applied effectively to tasks such as text classification. The chapter concluded with an overview of Bayesian networks and other probabilistic graphical models that can model complex dependencies among variables.

Advantages of naive Bayes compared to other classification models:

- Naive Bayes is extremely fast to train and make predictions, with linear time complexity in the number of features and samples, making it well-suited for large-scale datasets and online learning.

- Despite its strong independence assumptions, naive Bayes often performs well in practice, especially when feature dependencies are weak or have limited impact.

- The conditional independence assumption reduces the number of parameters, lowering model complexity and helping to prevent overfitting.

---

39. https://pgmpy.org

- It can make accurate predictions even when probability estimates are poor, as long as only the class label is needed.

- It naturally supports multi-class classification and handles class imbalance without modification.

- It is robust to irrelevant or noisy features, which tend to be averaged out during prediction.

- It can ignore missing features during likelihood computation, avoiding the need for imputation.

- It requires minimal hyperparameter tuning (only the smoothing parameter).

- It is highly interpretable due to its direct probabilistic formulation.

Disadvantages of naive Bayes:

- It assumes that features are conditionally independent given the class—a simplification that rarely holds in practice and can degrade performance when strong correlations exist.

- It produces linear (or quadratic) decision boundaries, limiting its ability to capture complex, non-linear relationships.

- It assumes all features contribute equally to the prediction, which may be inaccurate when certain features are significantly more informative.

- It generally underperforms compared to more flexible models, particularly when feature interactions are important.

- It assigns zero probability to features unseen during training (e.g., out-of-vocabulary words), which can lead to incorrect predictions. Smoothing helps but does not fully solve this issue.

- It cannot natively handle continuous variables without assuming a specific distribution (e.g., Gaussian) or discretizing them, which may degrade performance.

- It is only applicable to classification problems.

7.10 Exercises

7.10.1 Multiple-Choice Questions

7.1. Consider a Bernoulli naive Bayes classifier trained on a dataset where 60% of the examples belong to class A and 40% belong to class B. The probability of observing feature X given class A is 0.5, and the probability of observing feature X given class B is 0.2. What is the posterior probability that a new instance belongs to class A given that it has feature X?

(a) 0.71

(b) 0.75

(c) 0.79

(d) 0.85

7.2. Given the dataset shown in Table 7.7, we would like to classify the vector $\mathbf{x} = (x_1 = A, x_2 = B, x_3 = B)$ using categorical naive Bayes. Which of the following statements is true?

x_1	x_2	x_3	y
A	B	C	1
B	A	B	1
C	B	A	-1
A	C	B	-1

Table 7.7: Training data for categorical naive Bayes

(a) $P(y = 1|\mathbf{x}) = 0.5 \cdot P(y = -1|\mathbf{x})$

(b) $P(y = 1|\mathbf{x}) = 0.75 \cdot P(y = -1|\mathbf{x})$

(c) $P(y = 1|\mathbf{x}) = P(y = -1|\mathbf{x})$

(d) $P(y = 1|\mathbf{x}) = 2P(y = -1|\mathbf{x})$

7.3. Increasing the Laplace smoothing parameter α will likely increase:

(a) bias

(b) variance

(c) overfitting

(d) underfitting

7.4. Consider a multinomial naive Bayes classifier trained on a text corpus with two classes: spam and non-spam. The vocabulary size is $|V| = 6$, and the word counts observed in the training data are shown in Table 7.8. Assuming a Laplace smoothing with $\alpha = 1$, what is the probability of the word "offer" appearing in a spam message?

(a) 0.290

(b) 0.322

(c) 0.355

(d) 0.387

Word	Spam Count	Non-Spam Count
offer	10	2
free	7	1
money	5	0
hello	0	8
meeting	2	10
schedule	1	9

Table 7.8: Word counts in the training data for spam and non-spam classes

7.5. Which of the following statements are true about Gaussian naive Bayes (GNB)?

   (a) The decision boundary of Gaussian naive Bayes is always quadratic.

   (b) Gaussian naive Bayes assumes that the covariance matrix of the features for each class is diagonal.

   (c) The parameters of Gaussian naive Bayes are estimated using the method of maximum likelihood.

   (d) Gaussian naive Bayes is robust to outliers due to the Gaussian assumption.

7.6. Which of the following steps is commonly involved in text preprocessing for NLP tasks?

   (a) Tokenization

   (b) Text normalization

   (c) Feature scaling

   (d) Named entity recognition

7.7. Which of the following are advantages of the spaCy library over NLTK?

   (a) It has built-in support for deep learning integration.

   (b) Its tokenization methods are more efficient and faster than NLTK's.

   (c) It provides built-in algorithms for text classification tasks.

   (d) It includes pretrained pipelines for multiple languages.

   (e) Its NLP pipelines are more customizable than NLTK's.

7.8. What are the advantages of TF-IDF for representing text documents?

   (a) It reduces the impact of frequently occurring words in the document.

   (b) It normalizes the length of documents, making them comparable.

   (c) It takes into account the context of the words.

   (d) It assigns higher weights to terms that appear in fewer documents.

   (e) It generates less sparse vectors than the bag-of-words representation.

7.9. Which of the following statements is true about Bayesian networks?

    (a) A Bayesian network represents a joint probability distribution over a set of random variables.

    (b) The structure of a Bayesian network can be learned from data.

    (c) Bayesian networks cannot handle missing data during inference.

    (d) A Bayesian network with n nodes, where each node has at most k parents, requires at most $\mathcal{O}(kn)$ parameters to specify all conditional probability distributions.

    (e) A naive Bayes classifier can be modeled as a Bayesian network with only one level of child nodes.

7.10. Which of the following is an advantage of naive Bayes over other classifiers?

    (a) It has a fast training time, even on large datasets.

    (b) It performs well with high-dimensional data.

    (c) It is less prone to overfitting with small datasets.

    (d) It can naturally handle both continuous and categorical features without preprocessing.

    (e) It requires no feature scaling or normalization.

7.10.2 Theoretical Exercises

7.11. Table 7.9 shows patient recovery data for predicting whether a new patient will recover within a week, based on treatment type, symptom severity, and age group. What is the probability that the following patient will recover within a week: [Treatment = Surgery, Symptoms = Moderate, Age = Young]. Assume no smoothing is applied. Show your computations.

	Treatment	Symptoms	Age	Recovery
1	Medication	Mild	Young	Yes
2	Surgery	Severe	Senior	No
3	Therapy	Moderate	Adult	Yes
4	Surgery	Severe	Senior	No
5	Medication	Mild	Young	Yes
6	Therapy	Moderate	Senior	No
7	Medication	Moderate	Adult	Yes
8	Therapy	Moderate	Young	No
9	Medication	Severe	Senior	No
10	Surgery	Severe	Young	Yes

Table 7.9: Patient recovery data

7.12. Given a set of features $x_1, x_2, \ldots, x_d$ and a class label y, assume that the features are pair-wise conditionally independent given the class label, i.e., for any pair of features x_i and x_j:

$$P(x_i, x_j|y) = P(x_i|y)P(x_j|y).$$

(a) Show that this pairwise conditional independence assumption does not imply that the features are mutually conditionally independent, i.e., that the joint distribution necessarily factorizes as:

$$P(\mathbf{x}|y) = \prod_{j=1}^{d} P(x_j|y).$$

(b) (*) Conversely, show that if the joint distribution of the features given the class can be expressed as:

$$P(\mathbf{x}|y) = \prod_{j=1}^{d} P(x_j|y),$$

then the features are pairwise conditionally independent given the class label, i.e., for any pair of features x_i and x_j, it follows that:

$$P(x_i, x_j|y) = P(x_i|y)P(x_j|y).$$

7.13. Prove that the maximum a posteriori (MAP) estimate is equivalent to the maximum likelihood estimate (MLE) when the class priors are equal. Specifically, show that when all class priors $P(y = c)$ are equal, the MAP estimation rule

$$\hat{y}_{\text{MAP}} = \underset{c}{\text{argmax}}\ P(y = c|\mathbf{x})$$

simplifies to the MLE rule

$$\hat{y}_{\text{MLE}} = \underset{c}{\text{argmax}}\ P(\mathbf{x}|y = c).$$

7.14. Derive the maximum likelihood estimate (MLE) for the parameters $\theta_{cj} = P(x_j = 1 \mid y = c)$ in a Bernoulli naive Bayes model. Prove that the MLE for θ_{cj} is given by:

$$\theta_{cj} = \frac{\sum_{i=1}^{n} x_{ij}\mathbb{1}(y_i = c)}{\sum_{i=1}^{n} \mathbb{1}(y_i = c)},$$

where $x_{ij} \in \{0, 1\}$ indicates whether feature j is present in the i-th instance, and $\mathbb{1}(y_i = c)$ is the indicator function for class c. Use the following steps:

(a) Define the likelihood function of the model parameters given the training data, under the naive Bayes assumption.

(b) Write down the log-likelihood function.

(c) Differentiate the log-likelihood with respect to θ_{cj} and solve for the MLE.

7.15. (*) In a multinomial naive Bayes model for text classification, derive the maximum likelihood estimate (MLE) for the parameters $\theta_{cj} = P(w_j|y = c)$. Show that the MLE is given by:

$$\theta_{cj} = \frac{\sum_{i=1}^{n} x_{ij} \mathbb{1}(y_i = c)}{\sum_{i=1}^{n} N_i \mathbb{1}(y_i = c)},$$

where x_{ij} represents the count of word w_j in the i-th document, $N_i = \sum_{j=1}^{|V|} x_{ij}$ is the total word count for the i-th document, and $\mathbb{1}(y_i = c)$ is an indicator function for class c.

Note that in this exercise, you will need to use the Lagrange multiplier to enforce the normalization constraint:

$$\sum_{j=1}^{|V|} \theta_{cj} = 1,$$

which ensures that the probabilities for all words in the vocabulary sum to 1.

(a) Define the likelihood function of the model parameters, considering the multinomial distribution for word counts.

(b) Write down the log-likelihood function and include the Lagrange term to account for the normalization constraint.

(c) Differentiate the log-likelihood with respect to θ_{cj} and solve for the MLE.

7.16. Prove that the decision boundaries formed by multinomial naive Bayes are linear.

7.17. The multinomial naive Bayes algorithm is a popular method for email spam filtering, utilizing the bag-of-words representation to model the frequency of word occurrences in emails.

(a) A spam classifier has been trained on a large email corpus, and Table 7.10 lists several estimated word probabilities $P(w|c)$ for the spam and ham classes. Given a new email containing the words send money, determine for which values of $P(y = \text{spam})$ the classifier would predict the email as spam. Show your calculations.

Word	Spam Probability	Ham Probability
send	1/8	1/12
your	1/4	1/4
money	1/6	1/8
to	1/3	1/3
account	1/4	1/6

Table 7.10: Estimated word probabilities for the spam and ham classes

(b) Now consider a different training corpus consisting of the following emails:

(Spam) `urgent, contact me to claim your prize`

(Ham) `let's meet for coffee tomorrow`

(Ham) `please send the report by Friday`

(Spam) `you have won a gift card, claim it now to claim your reward`

(Spam) `urgent! your account requires immediate verification`

Estimate the following probabilities, assuming no smoothing is applied (ignore punctuation):

   i. $P(\text{claim} \mid \text{spam})$

   ii. $P(\text{account} \mid \text{ham})$

(c) Now re-estimate the same word probabilities using Laplace smoothing with $\alpha > 0$ and vocabulary size V.

(d) We now relax the naive Bayes assumption by taking into account the relationship between consecutive words. Instead of assuming that each word is independent given the label, the new approach models the probability of a word based on both the label and its preceding word, i.e., $P(w_i|y, w_{i-1})$.

   i. With a vocabulary size of V, calculate the total number of conditional probabilities that need to be estimated in this new model.

   ii. Discuss the potential advantages and disadvantages of this approach compared to the original naive Bayes model.

7.18. In this exercise, you will explore various theoretical aspects of Laplace smoothing and its impact on probability estimation in the multinomial naive Bayes model.

(a) Explain how Laplace smoothing affects the classification of test instances that contain rare or previously unseen words. Why might it improve generalization, and what are its potential drawbacks?

(b) Consider a binary classification problem using the multinomial naive Bayes model with Laplace smoothing. Show how increasing the smoothing parameter α affects the posterior probabilities. Discuss how this, in turn, impacts the decision boundary of the classifier.

(c) Explain why Laplace smoothing is not applicable to continuous features in naive Bayes models.

(d) (*) Derive the maximum likelihood estimate (MLE) for the parameters of a multinomial naive Bayes model with Laplace smoothing. Show that the smoothed estimate is given by:

$$\theta_{cj} = \frac{\sum_{i=1}^{n} x_{ij} \mathbb{1}(y_i = c) + \alpha}{\sum_{i=1}^{n} N_i \mathbb{1}(y_i = c) + \alpha K},$$

where x_{ij} is the count of feature j in instance i, N_i is the total count of all features in instance i, $\mathbb{1}(y_i = c)$ is an indicator function for class c, and K is the number of possible features.

(e) (*) Show that Laplace smoothing can be interpreted as a form of Bayesian estimation using a symmetric Dirichlet prior (see Section C.11.6.3), the conjugate prior for the multinomial distribution. Explain the connection between the smoothing parameter α and the hyperparameters of the Dirichlet prior.

7.19. Table 7.11 represents training data for predicting whether a student will pass or fail a final exam based on their study time (in hours), class participation, and previous test score.

	Study Time	Participation	Previous Test	Final Exam
1	10.2	Active	85	Pass
2	3.5	Low	40	Fail
3	7.8	Moderate	60	Pass
4	2.0	Low	35	Fail
5	9.0	Active	70	Pass
6	4.5	Low	55	Fail
7	12.3	Active	90	Pass
8	5.5	Moderate	45	Fail
9	8.2	Moderate	80	Pass
10	1.5	Active	50	Fail

Table 7.11: Training data for student performance prediction

Using a naive Bayes classifier, predict whether a new student with the following characteristics will pass the final exam: [Study Time = 6.0, Participation = Moderate, Previous Test = 70].

- Assume that the continuous features (Study Time and Previous Test) follow a normal distribution.
- For the categorical feature (Participation), use a frequency-based probability estimation.

Show your computations, including the calculation of the priors, likelihoods, and posterior probabilities.

7.20. In Gaussian naive Bayes, the conditional likelihood of a feature vector $\mathbf{x} = (x_1, \ldots, x_d)$ given class $y = c$ is modeled as:

$$p(\mathbf{x}|y = c) = \prod_{j=1}^{d} \frac{1}{\sqrt{2\pi}\sigma_{cj}} \exp\left(-\frac{(x_j - \mu_{cj})^2}{2\sigma_{cj}^2}\right),$$

where μ_{cj} and σ_{cj} are the mean and standard deviation of feature j for class c, respectively.

(a) Show that if all features share the same variance across classes, i.e., $\sigma_{cj} = \sigma_j$ for all c, the decision boundaries between any two classes are linear in $\mathbf{x}$.

(b) Show that if at least one feature has class-dependent variance (i.e., σ_{cj} differs across classes), then the decision boundaries become quadratic in $\mathbf{x}$.

7.21. Given the following small corpus of documents, calculate the TF-IDF scores for the words highlighted in **bold**. Show the detailed computations of the term frequency (TF), inverse document frequency (IDF), and the resulting TF-IDF score for each highlighted word in each document.

(a) "The **quick** brown fox jumps over the lazy dog."

(b) "The athlete was very **fast** on the track."

(c) "A **quick** brown fox is faster than a **quick** black dog."

(d) "The **quick** runner finished the race ahead of everyone."

7.22. Let $\mathcal{X} = \{X_1, \ldots, X_n\}$ be a set of discrete random variables, and let G be a directed acyclic graph (DAG) defining a Bayesian network structure over these variables. Assume the variables are ordered according to a topological ordering of G. That is, for every directed edge $X_i \rightarrow X_j$ in the graph, X_i appears before X_j in the ordering.

Prove that under the conditional independence assumptions encoded by G, the joint probability distribution can be factorized as:

$$P(X_1, \ldots, X_n) = \prod_{i=1}^{n} P(X_i \mid \mathrm{Pa}(X_i)),$$

where $\mathrm{Pa}(X_i)$ denotes the set of parent variables of X_i in the graph.

7.23. Consider the Bayesian network depicted in Figure 7.9, which models the likelihood of a vehicle requiring major maintenance based on its age, mileage, and maintenance history.

The network includes the following variables:

- Age (A): A binary variable representing the vehicle's age, where 1 indicates over 5 years, and 0 indicates 5 years or less.

- Mileage (M): A categorical variable representing the vehicle's mileage, which can take values of low (0), medium (1), or high (2). The mileage also depends on the vehicle's age.

- Maintenance History (MH): A categorical variable representing the regularity of past maintenance, which can take values of poor (0), occasional (1), or good (2). The maintenance history also depends on the vehicle's age.

- Major Maintenance (MM): A binary variable indicating whether major maintenance is needed (1) or not needed (0). This depends on both the mileage and the maintenance history.

Calculate the probability that a vehicle needs major maintenance given that its age is less than 5 years ($A = 0$) and its mileage is categorized as medium ($M = 1$).

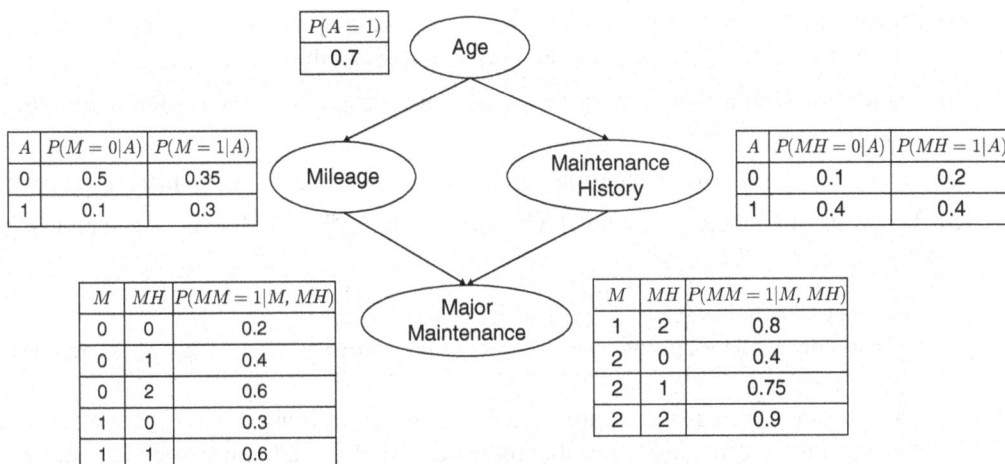

Figure 7.9: A Bayesian network representing the factors influencing the likelihood of a vehicle requiring major maintenance. The network includes nodes for Age, Mileage, Maintenance History, and Major Maintenance, with conditional probability tables for each variable. The table for Major Maintenance (MM) is split into two parts due to space constraints, displaying the probabilities of Major Maintenance given various combinations of Mileage (M) and Maintenance History (MH).

7.24. (*) Consider Corollary 1 from the paper "Beyond Independence Conditions for the Optimality of the Simple Bayes Classifier" by Domingos and Pazzani [169], which states:

> The SBC (Simple Bayesian Classifier, which is another name for the naive Bayes classifier) is locally optimal in half the volume of the space of possible values of (p, r, s).

(a) Define the parameters p, r, and s as they are used in the paper.

(b) Explain what it means for the naive Bayes classifier to be *locally optimal* in this context.

(c) Prove Corollary 1 by showing that the volume of the parameter space where the naive Bayes classifier is locally optimal equals half the total volume.

(d) Discuss the implications of this result. What does it suggest about the practical effectiveness and robustness of the naive Bayes classifier, especially when the conditional independence assumption is violated?

7.10.3 Programming Exercises

7.25. In this exercise you will implement a categorical naive Bayes classifier from scratch. The classifier should support datasets with binary or categorical features. Follow the steps below to complete the task:

(a) Implement the necessary calculations for the likelihoods, priors, and posterior probabilities, taking into account the categorical nature of the features.

(b) Implement Laplace smoothing to handle zero-frequency issues when computing the conditional probabilities.

(c) Ensure that your implementation handles missing values in the dataset appropriately.

(d) Test your implementation on the Mushroom dataset[40], which can be loaded using the `fetch_openml` function:

```
from sklearn.datasets import fetch_openml
X, y = fetch_openml('mushroom', version=1, return_X_y=True, as_frame=True)
```

The dataset consists of 22 categorical features describing various characteristics of mushrooms, and the target variable indicates whether each mushroom is poisonous or edible.

(e) Compare the accuracy of your implementation with that of Scikit-Learn's `CategoricalNB` classifier.

(f) Discuss any differences in accuracy or computational performance between your implementation and Scikit-Learn's implementation. Suggest possible reasons for these differences.

7.26. The Reuters corpus in the NLTK library consists of news documents categorized into various topics such as economics, trade, commodities, and politics. Each document is assigned one or more categories based on its content, making it a multi-label dataset. In this exercise, you will focus on analyzing the structure and content of the corpus rather than building a classifier.

(a) Display the total number of documents in the corpus.

(b) List all the categories available in the corpus along with the number of documents in each category.

(c) Randomly select a document from the corpus.

(d) Tokenize the document into words, print the total word count, and provide a sample of the text by displaying 20 randomly selected words.

(e) Find the 10 most common words using a frequency distribution.

(f) Use `nltk.sent_tokenize` to split the document into sentences. Print the total number of sentences and the first three sentences.

(g) Apply POS tagging to the first 10 tokens and display their parts of speech.

(h) Filter out stop words and print the new word count.

(i) Perform named entity recognition (NER) and list all the identified entities and their types.

---

40. https://archive.ics.uci.edu/dataset/73/mushroom

(j) Compute the bag-of-words representation for the first 10 documents in the "coffee" category. Construct a document-term matrix for these documents and display it.

(k) Create a TF-IDF matrix for these documents using Scikit-Learn's `TfidfVectorizer` and display the top five words with the highest TF-IDF scores in each document.

7.27. In this exercise you will build a multinomial naive Bayes classifier to automatically assign category labels to documents from the Reuters corpus in the NLTK library. This is a multi-label classification task, as each document in the Reuters corpus can belong to multiple categories. Follow these steps:

(a) Load the corpus and convert it into a document-term matrix using a text vectorizer.

(b) Convert the list of category labels for each document into a binary vector using a multi-label binarization approach (e.g., Scikit-Learn's `MultiLabelBinarizer`).

(c) Implement a one-vs-rest approach using Scikit-Learn's `OneVsRestClassifier` with a `MultinomialNB` base classifier. This will train one binary classifier per category to predict whether a document belongs to that category.

(d) Use a suitable evaluation metric (e.g., micro/macro-averaged F1 score) to assess the performance of your classifier. Note that Scikit-Learn's `OneVsRestClassifier` outputs a binary matrix indicating predicted class memberships, which can be evaluated directly using functions such as `f1_score` or `classification_report`.

(e) Experiment with different text preprocessing techniques, such as TF-IDF weighting, stemming, removing stop words, or using n-grams. Evaluate how these choices affect classifier performance.

7.28. A spam filter is a program that classifies email messages as either spam or ham (non-spam). The filter distinguishes between ham and spam by analyzing the email features such as the presence of certain words in the email's body, patterns in the email's header, or the frequency of internet domains mentioned. In this exercise, you will train a spam filter using the Apache SpamAssassin[41] public mail corpus, which is a widely recognized benchmark for building and evaluating spam filters [418, 508, 398].

(a) Download the following files from the SpamAssassin public corpus[42], which are also mirrored on the book's GitHub repository[43]:

- `20030228_easy_ham.tar.bz2`: Contains 2,500 easily classifiable ham emails.
- `20030228_hard_ham.tar.bz2`: Includes 250 more challenging ham emails, which are useful for testing the robustness of the filter.
- `20030228_spam.tar.bz2`: Contains 500 typical spam emails.
- `20030228_spam_2.tar.bz2`: Provides an additional set of 1,400 spam emails.

---

41. https://spamassassin.apache.org
42. https://spamassassin.apache.org/old/publiccorpus
43. https://github.com/roiyeho/ml-book/tree/main/Chapter07/datasets

(b) Extract the files and familiarize yourself with the data format. Note that each email is stored as a separate file in the standard RFC 5322 format, which is commonly used for email messages. This format consists of a headers section containing metadata fields (e.g., From, Subject, Date) followed by the body section of the email. The zipped files may also contain an additional cmds file, which can be ignored.

(c) Merge the spam emails and ham emails into two separate lists.

(d) Parse the email messages using Python's email[44] and BeautifulSoup[45] libraries to extract their subjects and bodies. Handle multipart messages by retrieving all their text parts. Example for parsing an email message:

```python
import email
from bs4 import BeautifulSoup

def parse_email(file_path):
    with open(file_path, 'rb') as f:
        msg = email.message_from_bytes(f.read())

    subject = msg.get('Subject')
    body_parts = []

    if msg.is_multipart():
        for part in msg.walk():
            ctype = part.get_content_type()
            cdisp = part.get('Content-Disposition')

            if ctype == 'text/plain' and 'attachment' not in cdisp:
                body_parts.append(part.get_payload(decode=True))
    else:
        body_parts.append(msg.get_payload(decode=True))

    body = ''.join(map(str, body_parts))
    body = BeautifulSoup(body, 'html.parser').get_text()

    return subject, body
```

(e) Convert each email into a numerical vector, using tokenization, removal of stop words, and TF-IDF vectorization. Optionally, extract additional features, such as the number of capitalized words or domain name occurrences.

(f) Split the dataset into training and test sets using a 80–20 split.

(g) Train different classifiers (e.g., multinomial naive Bayes, k-nearest neighbors, logistic regression) and evaluate them using metrics like accuracy, F1-score, precision,

---

44. https://docs.python.org/3/library/email.html
45. https://www.crummy.com/software/BeautifulSoup/bs4/doc

and recall. Generate precision-recall or ROC curves to better understand classifier performance.

(h) Display the confusion matrix and the classification report for the best model on both the training and test sets.

(i) Analyze how training set size affects classifier performance by training the model increasing fractions of the training data. Plot a curve showing test set accuracy as a function of the training set size.

(j) Identify the ten most indicative tokens of spam by calculating:

$$\log\left(\frac{P(\text{token } i \mid \text{email is spam})}{P(\text{token } i \mid \text{email is ham})}\right).$$

Estimate the token probabilities using a trained naive Bayes model with Laplace smoothing. Display the top tokens with the highest log-ratio values.

7.29. In this exercise, you will build a basic information retrieval (IR) system that ranks and returns documents based on a user's query. The system will use TF-IDF scores to measure the relevance of each document to the query. Follow these steps:

(a) Document collection: Store a collection of documents in a suitable format (e.g., a list of strings or external text files).

(b) Preprocessing: Use Scikit-Learn's `TfidfVectorizer` to tokenize the documents, remove stop words, and compute the TF-IDF scores for each term. Store the resulting values in a document-term matrix.

(c) Query handling:

    i. Prompt the user to input a search query.

    ii. Preprocess and transform the query using the same `TfidfVectorizer` fitted on the documents to obtain its TF-IDF vector representation.

(d) Ranking and retrieval:

    i. Compute the cosine similarity between the query's TF-IDF vector and the document vectors.

    ii. Rank the documents by similarity score and return the top N most relevant documents.

(e) Evaluation: Test your system with different queries and analyze how effectively it returns relevant documents.

7.30. In this exercise, you will perform sentiment analysis using the IMDb Movie Reviews Dataset[46]. This dataset contains 50,000 reviews evenly split into 25,000 training and 25,000 testing sets, with equal numbers of positive and negative reviews. It is already preprocessed and encoded as sequences of word indices corresponding to a built-in word dictionary. You can download and load the dataset using TensorFlow's Keras API (make sure TensorFlow is installed by running `pip install tensorflow`):

---

46. https://ai.stanford.edu/~amaas/data/sentiment

```
from tensorflow.keras.datasets import imdb

(X_train, y_train), (X_test, y_test) = imdb.load_data()
```

Here, X_train is a list of sequences, where each sequence represents a movie review as a series of integers. These integers correspond to word indices in a dictionary that was built from the words in the dataset. To map indices to words and vice versa, use the following code:

```
# Get the word-to-index mapping
word_index = imdb.get_word_index()

# Reverse the mapping to get index-to-word
index_to_word = {index + 3: word for word, index in word_index.items()}
index_to_word[0] = '<PAD>'
index_to_word[1] = '<START>'
index_to_word[2] = '<UNK>'
index_to_word[3] = '<UNUSED>'

# Example: decoding the first review
decoded_review = ' '.join([index_to_word[i] for i in X_train[0]])
print(decoded_review)
```

(a) Download and load the IMDb Movie Reviews Dataset.

(b) Use the index_to_word mapping to decode each list of indices into a string of words (i.e., the original review text).

(c) Experiment with three different classifiers:

  i. Bernoulli naive Bayes: Convert the text data into binary feature vectors that indicate the presence or absence of each word (e.g., using CountVectorizer with binary=True).

  ii. Multinomial naive Bayes (Bag-of-Words): Use the bag-of-words representation to transform the text into count-based feature vectors.

  iii. Multinomial naive Bayes (TF-IDF): Use TF-IDF vectors instead of raw counts to represent the reviews.

(d) Train each classifier on the training set and evaluate them on the test set using accuracy, precision, recall, and F1 score.

(e) Analyze differences in performance among the classifiers and the impact of using bag-of-words versus TF-IDF.

(f) Identify a few misclassified reviews and discuss potential reasons for the errors.

(g) Suggest possible improvements to the model or preprocessing techniques.

7.31. In this exercise, you will implement a Gaussian naive Bayes classifier from scratch. The classifier should be able to handle continuous features. Follow these steps:

(a) Implement the Gaussian naive Bayes algorithm, including:

  i. Calculating the mean and variance for each feature in each class using the training data.

  ii. Computing the likelihood for a given feature value using the Gaussian probability density function:

  $$p(x \mid \mu, \sigma^2) = \frac{1}{\sqrt{2\pi\sigma^2}} \exp\left(-\frac{(x - \mu)^2}{2\sigma^2}\right).$$

  iii. Calculating the prior probabilities for each class.

  iv. Using Bayes' theorem to compute the posterior probabilities and predict the most probable class. Consider using the logarithm of the likelihoods to avoid underflow.

(b) Test your implementation on a dataset with continuous features, such as the Wine Quality Dataset[47].

(c) Compare the performance of your implementation with Scikit-Learn's `GaussianNB` and discuss any differences in accuracy and runtime.

(d) Analyze how well the assumptions of Gaussian naive Bayes (i.e., the assumptions of normally distributed features and conditional independence of features) hold for this dataset. Use visualizations such as histograms or Q-Q plots[48] for each feature, grouped by class, to support your analysis.

7.32. (*) In this exercise, you will implement the variable elimination algorithm for inference in a Bayesian network and test it on a simple medical diagnosis scenario. Follow these steps:

(a) Design a data structure to represent a Bayesian network, where each node corresponds to a discrete random variable and directed edges encode conditional dependencies between them. Include support for specifying conditional probability tables (CPTs) for each node.

(b) Implement the variable elimination algorithm [326, Chapter 9.4] to perform probabilistic inference. Given a query variable and a set of observed variables (evidence), compute the posterior distribution over the query by successively summing out hidden variables.

---

47. https://archive.ics.uci.edu/dataset/109/wine
48. A Q-Q (quantile-quantile) plot is a graphical tool used to assess whether a dataset follows a specific theoretical distribution, typically a normal distribution. It plots the quantiles of the dataset against the quantiles of the theoretical distribution. For generating this plot, you can use the `scipy.stats.probplot` function from SciPy.

(c) Test your implementation on a small medical diagnosis network:

- Define a simple Bayesian network with disease variables such as `flu` and `cold`, and symptom variables such as `fever`, `cough`, and `sore throat`.
- Specify reasonable conditional probability tables (CPTs) based on common medical knowledge or synthetic values.

(d) Allow the system to take evidence in the form of observed symptoms (e.g., `fever = True`, `cough = False`) and output the posterior probabilities of each disease.

(e) Implement the same network in `pgmpy` and use its built-in inference engine (e.g., `VariableElimination`) to perform the same queries. Discuss any observed differences in the results.

Chapter 8

Decision Trees

Decision trees are powerful and versatile machine learning models that make predictions by applying a sequence of simple decision rules organized in a tree-like structure. Decision trees are flexible, non-parametric models that make no assumptions about the underlying data distribution, making them suitable for a wide range of applications.

A major advantage of decision trees is their transparency: the tree structure can be visualized, making the model's decision-making process easy to understand, even for non-experts. This interpretability is especially important in high-stakes fields such as medicine and finance, where the predictions of the model must be justified and clearly communicated to stakeholders, regulators, or patients.

However, the flexibility of decision trees also makes them prone to overfitting, especially when they are grown to full depth. This risk can be mitigated through pruning, which removes branches of the tree that do not contribute to better generalization, or by using ensemble methods such as random forests, which combine multiple trees to enhance predictive accuracy and robustness (discussed in the next chapter).

This chapter is organized as follows. Section 8.1 formally defines decision trees and explains how they are used for making predictions. Section 8.2 presents the tree construction algorithm, including the impurity measures used for splitting nodes. Section 8.3 discusses pruning techniques—both pre-pruning and post-pruning—that help prevent overfitting and improve generalization. Section 8.4 reviews notable decision tree algorithms developed over the years. Section 8.5 demonstrates the usage of decision trees in Scikit-Learn. Section 8.6 describes how decision trees can be adapted for regression tasks. Section 8.7 demonstrates how decision trees can be applied to multi-output problems. Section 8.8 introduces oblique decision trees, which use linear combinations of features for splits instead of a single feature at each node. Section 8.9 concludes with a summary.

8.1 Decision Tree Definition

A **decision tree** is a predictive model that maps input features to target values using a tree-like structure [489, 73, 377]. The model recursively partitions the input space into subregions using

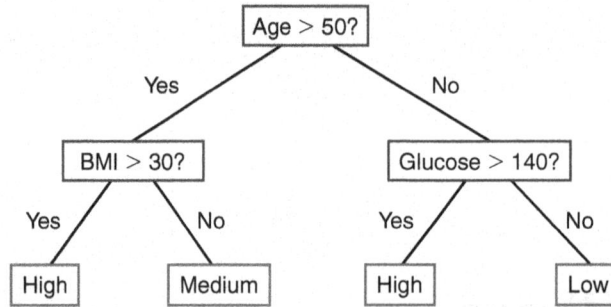

Figure 8.1: A simple decision tree for predicting diabetes risk based on three attributes: age, BMI, and glucose level. Internal nodes represent decision rules that split the data, while leaf nodes indicate the predicted risk level (High, Medium, or Low). For example, a patient older than 50 years with a BMI less than 30 is classified as having Medium risk.

simple, feature-based decision rules, selected to optimize a specific criterion such as information gain.

Each **internal node** in the tree represents a test on a feature, with branches corresponding to the possible outcomes of the test. The **leaves** represent the final predictions: a class label in classification tasks or a continuous value in regression tasks. When applied to classification problems, these models are often called **classification trees**; when used for regression, they are referred to as **regression trees**.

For example, consider the decision tree depicted in Figure 8.1, which predicts whether a patient is at risk for diabetes based on their age, body mass index (BMI), and glucose level.

To classify a new instance, the process starts at the root node. The decision rule at that node is evaluated, and the branch corresponding to the result of that evaluation is followed. This procedure is repeated at each subsequent node until a leaf node is reached, at which point the instance is assigned the label associated with that leaf.

For example, to classify a patient who is 55 years old, has a BMI of 28, and a glucose level of 160, we follow these steps:

1. Start at the root node: "Is Age > 50?" → Yes.

2. Move to the left child: "Is BMI > 30?" → No.

3. Proceed to the right child, which is a leaf node that predicts a risk level of Medium.

This patient is therefore classified as having a medium risk for diabetes.

8.2   Decision Tree Construction

A decision tree is constructed in a top-down fashion by recursively partitioning the dataset into increasingly homogeneous subsets. The process begins with the root node, which contains all the samples in the training set. At each node, the data is split into two or more subsets based on a test of a feature (e.g., $A > 10$ for a numerical feature, or $A =$ "Some value" for a categorical one). The feature used for splitting is selected according to a criterion that measures node impurity or homogeneity (see Section 8.2.1).

This recursive splitting continues until a stopping condition is met—typically, when all samples at a node belong to the same class or when no remaining features are available for splitting. The pseudocode for the decision tree construction algorithm is presented in Algorithm 8.1.

Algorithm 8.1 BuildDecisionTree(D, A, f)

Input:
    D: a set of training samples $\{(\mathbf{x}_i, y_i)\}_{i=1}^n$
    A: a set of attributes (features)
    f: a function used to select the best splitting feature at each node

1: Create a root node r
2: **if** all samples in D have the same class label c **then**
3:     Label r with class c
4:     **return** r
5: **else if** A is empty **then**
6:     Label r with the most common class label in D
7:     **return** r
8: **else**
9:     $a \leftarrow$ feature in A that best splits D according to f
10:     Assign feature a to r
11:     **for each** possible value v_i of a **do**
12:         Add a new branch B below r, labeled $a = v_i$
13:         $D_i \leftarrow$ the subset of D where $a = v_i$
14:         **if** D_i is empty **then**
15:             Add a leaf node to B, labeled with the majority class in D
16:         **else**
17:             $T \leftarrow$ BuildDecisionTree(D_i, $A - \{a\}$, f)
18:             Attach subtree T to B
19:     **return** r

The algorithm begins by checking whether all samples at the current node belong to the same class. If so, the recursion terminates and the node becomes a leaf labeled with that class. If no features remain for further partitioning, the node is also made a leaf and labeled with the most common class among the samples.

Otherwise, the algorithm selects the best feature for splitting according to the specified impurity criterion and partitions the data into subsets corresponding to each possible value of that feature. If a subset is empty—meaning that no training instances follow the specific combination of feature values along the path from the root to the current node—the algorithm creates a leaf node for that branch labeled with the majority class in the parent node. This ensures that the tree provides a complete prediction path for any input, even when certain combinations of feature values are not present in the training data.

The construction process is recursive, as indicated by the call $T \leftarrow$ BuildDecisionTree(D_i, $A - \{a\}$, f), which builds a subtree for each subset until a stopping condition is reached. In this recursive call, the selected feature a is removed from the list of available features A to prevent it from being used again along the same path.

The algorithm shown in Algorithm 8.1 supports **multi-way splits**, meaning that a separate branch is created for each possible value of the selected feature. Other variants of tree construction, such as CART (see Section 8.4), allow only **binary splits**, where each node divides the data into exactly two subsets. In these cases, the algorithm selects a subset S of values that best splits the data, resulting in two branches: one for samples with values in S and another for the remaining values. This approach permits the same feature to be reused along the same path down the tree, allowing for more flexible partitioning of the data (at the expense of increased computation time).

It is important to note that the decision tree construction algorithm follows a **greedy approach**: at each node, it selects the split that yields the greatest immediate reduction in impurity, without considering the long-term effect on the overall tree structure. Consequently, the algorithm is not guaranteed to produce the optimal decision tree—that is, the smallest tree that correctly classifies all training samples. In fact, Hyafil and Rivest (1976) proved that finding such an optimal tree is an NP-complete problem [286].

8.2.1   Node Impurity Criteria

Selecting the most effective feature for splitting the data at each node is crucial for building an accurate and efficient decision tree. Ideally, the chosen feature should partition the dataset into subsets that are more homogeneous in their class labels than the parent node, thereby guiding the tree toward pure nodes that contain samples from a single class.

For example, consider the two decision trees shown in Figure 8.2. The root node of each tree starts with an equal mix of 10 examples: 5 positive and 5 negative. In the first tree, feature A is used to split the data, resulting in two subsets: one with 6 examples (4 positive, 2 negative) and another with 4 examples (1 positive, 3 negative). In contrast, the second tree splits on feature B, producing two completely mixed subsets: one with 6 examples (3 positive, 3 negative) and another with 4 examples (2 positive, 2 negative). The resulting child nodes in this case are no more informative than the root, offering no gain in class separation. Clearly, feature A is preferred in this case, as it moves the tree closer to pure nodes and improves its ability to distinguish between classes.

The ideal feature is one that splits the data into completely pure subsets, each containing examples from only one class. However, such perfect separation is rarely achievable in practice. When no feature produces pure splits, **node impurity measures** are used to evaluate how effectively each candidate feature reduces class heterogeneity. The two most commonly used impurity measures are information gain and Gini index, which are described in the following subsections.

8.2.1.1   Information Gain

Information gain is based on the concept of **entropy** from information theory, which quantifies the uncertainty associated with the outcomes of a random variable. This concept was first introduced by Claude Shannon in his seminal work on communication theory (1948) [545].

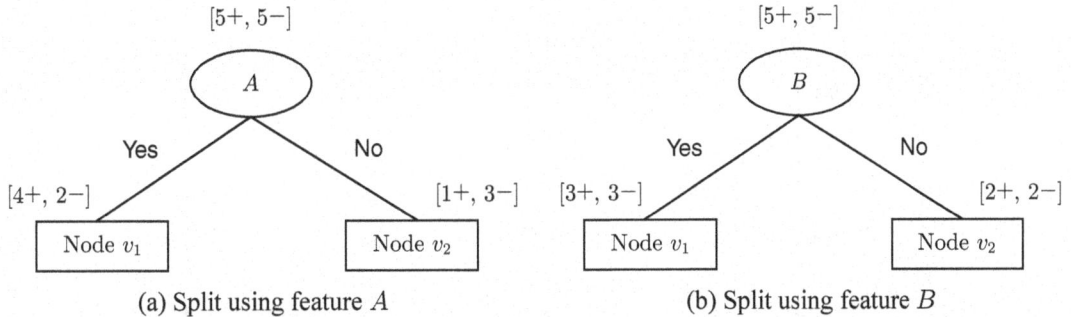

(a) Split using feature A (b) Split using feature B

Figure 8.2: Comparison of two feature splits in a decision tree. The root node in both cases starts with 10 examples: 5 positive (+) and 5 negative (-). (a) Splitting by feature A results in more homogeneous subsets: node v_1 contains 4 positive and 2 negative examples, while node v_2 contains 1 positive and 3 negative examples. (b) Splitting by feature B leads to completely mixed subsets: node v_1 contains 3 positive and 3 negative examples, and node v_2 contains 2 positive and 2 negative examples. Feature A provides a more effective split, producing subsets with greater class separation.

8.2.1.1.1 Entropy Definition

Let X be a discrete random variable with possible values $x_1, x_2, \ldots, x_n$, and let $p(x_i)$ denote the probability that $X = x_i$. The entropy of X, denoted by $H(X)$, is defined as:[1]

$$H(X) = -\sum_{i=1}^{n} p(x_i) \log_2 p(x_i), \tag{8.1}$$

where we define $0 \log 0 = 0$ by convention (justified by the limit $\lim_{p \to 0+} p \log p = 0$). The base-2 logarithm is used because entropy is usually measured in bits—the standard unit in information theory.[2]

For example, consider a fair coin toss, where the outcome X follows a Bernoulli distribution with $p = 0.5$ for heads. The entropy of X is:

$$H(X) = -0.5 \log_2 0.5 - 0.5 \log_2 0.5 = 1.$$

If the coin is biased, with heads occurring with probability $p = 0.8$, the entropy decreases:

$$H(X) = -0.8 \log_2 0.8 - 0.2 \log_2 0.2 \approx 0.721.$$

This lower entropy reflects the reduced uncertainty in the outcome: since one result is more likely than the other, the toss becomes more predictable. In general, the more predictable a variable is, the lower its entropy.

---

1. Shannon originally derived this formula by requiring that any reasonable measure of uncertainty satisfy a few basic properties: (1) continuity with respect to the probabilities, (2) maximality when all outcomes are equally likely, and (3) an additivity property stating that the total uncertainty of a compound event should equal the sum of the uncertainties of its parts. These conditions uniquely determine the entropy function up to a positive multiplicative constant. See [545].
2. In other contexts, such as continuous probability distributions, entropy is sometimes measured in *nats* by using the natural logarithm (ln) instead of $\log_2$. The choice of base changes the unit but not the underlying concept.

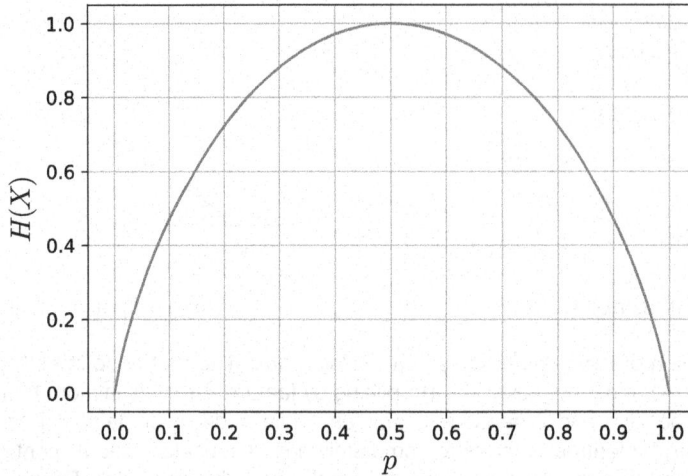

Figure 8.3: Entropy of a random variable $X \sim$ Bernoulli(p) as a function of the probability p. The entropy is highest at $p = 0.5$, where the outcome is most uncertain. As p approaches 0 or 1, the entropy decreases as the outcome becomes more predictable.

Figure 8.3 illustrates how the entropy of a Bernoulli random variable varies with the success probability p. The entropy reaches its maximum value of 1 at $p = 0.5$, representing maximum uncertainty about the outcome. As p approaches 0 or 1, the entropy decreases, reflecting increased predictability. At the extremes, where the outcome is completely predictable ($p = 0$ or $p = 1$), the entropy is 0, indicating no uncertainty.

Entropy can also be viewed as the minimum average number of bits required to encode the outcomes of a random variable.

For example, suppose we wish to transmit the result of rolling a 4-face die. If the die is fair, each of the four outcomes is equally likely, and the entropy of the distribution is:

$$H(X) = -4 \cdot \frac{1}{4} \log_2 \frac{1}{4} = 2 \text{ bits.}$$

In this case, exactly 2 bits are needed to represent each outcome (e.g., 00, 01, 10, 11), since all outcomes are equally likely.

Now consider a biased die where outcome 1 occurs with probability 0.5, and the remaining outcomes $\{2, 3, 4\}$ each occur with probability $1/6$. The entropy of this distribution is:

$$H(X) = -0.5 \log_2 0.5 - 3 \cdot \frac{1}{6} \log_2 \frac{1}{6} \approx 1.792 \text{ bits.}$$

The lower entropy reflects that fewer bits are needed on average to encode this more predictable distribution.

Indeed, in this case we can apply Huffman coding to assign shorter codes to more probable outcomes [283]. For example, outcome 1 may be encoded as 0, outcome 2 as 10, outcome 3 as 110, and outcome 4 as 111.

The expected number of bits per outcome with this code is:

$$L = 0.5 \cdot 1 + \frac{1}{6} \cdot (2 + 3 + 3) \approx 1.833 \text{ bits.}$$

This shows that Huffman coding can achieve near-optimal efficiency, approaching the theoretical limit given by the entropy.

8.2.1.1.2 Entropy of a Tree Node

We now apply the concept of entropy to decision trees by defining the entropy of a node v. Suppose we have a classification problem with k classes, and let $P(y = i \mid v)$ denote the fraction of training samples at node v that belong to class i. The entropy of node v, denoted as $H(v)$, is defined as:

$$H(v) = -\sum_{i=1}^{k} P(y = i \mid v) \log_2 P(y = i \mid v). \tag{8.2}$$

Here, $H(v)$ quantifies the uncertainty in the class labels of the samples at node v. A higher entropy indicates a more mixed distribution of classes (greater impurity), while lower entropy suggests a more skewed distribution, where one or a few classes dominate.

For example, consider the left child of the root node in the decision tree shown in Figure 8.2a. This node contains 4 positive examples and 2 negative examples, so its entropy is:

$$H(v_1) = -\frac{4}{6} \log_2 \frac{4}{6} - \frac{2}{6} \log_2 \frac{2}{6} \approx 0.918.$$

When all the samples at a node belong to the same class, the entropy is $H(v) = 0$, indicating complete certainty about the class label. Conversely, when the samples are evenly distributed across all k classes, the entropy reaches its maximum value:

$$H(v) = -\sum_{i=1}^{k} \frac{1}{k} \log_2 \frac{1}{k} = k \cdot \frac{1}{k} \log_2 k = \log_2 k. \tag{8.3}$$

For example, with $k = 2$ classes, the maximum entropy is $\log_2(2) = 1$, which matches the entropy of a Bernoulli variable with $p = 0.5$.

8.2.1.1.3 Information Gain from a Split

Information gain measures the reduction in entropy achieved by splitting a node v based on a feature A. It is defined as the difference between the entropy of node v and the weighted average of the entropies of its child nodes $v_1, \ldots, v_k$ after the split, where the weights correspond to the proportion of samples assigned to each child node:

$$\text{IG}(A) = H(v) - \sum_{i=1}^{k} \frac{n_i}{n} H(v_i). \tag{8.4}$$

Here, n is the number of samples at the parent node v, and n_i is the number of samples at child node v_i.

For example, consider the decision tree in Figure 8.2a. The entropy of the root node is:

$$H(v) = -\frac{5}{10} \log_2 \frac{5}{10} - \frac{5}{10} \log_2 \frac{5}{10} = 1.$$

The entropy of the left child is $H(v_1) = 0.918$, as calculated earlier, and the entropy of the right child is:

$$H(v_2) = -\frac{1}{4} \log_2 \frac{1}{4} - \frac{3}{4} \log_2 \frac{3}{4} \approx 0.811.$$

Thus, the information gain from splitting the root node using feature A is:

$$\text{IG}(A) = 1 - \left(\frac{6}{10} \cdot 0.918 + \frac{4}{10} \cdot 0.811 \right) = 0.125.$$

When building a decision tree using information gain, the objective at each node is to select the attribute that maximizes the information gain, thereby achieving the greatest reduction in entropy. This is done by evaluating all available features at the node and computing the information gain for each one. Since the entropy of the parent node remains constant during this evaluation, it is sufficient to compare the weighted average entropies of the child nodes resulting from each potential split (see example in Section 8.2.2).

8.2.1.2   Gain Ratio

The information gain criterion tends to favor attributes with many distinct values. For example, splitting customer records based on customer ID would result in zero entropy (since each child node would contain exactly one record), leading to maximum information gain. However, such an attribute would be a poor choice, as customer ID typically carries no meaningful information for predicting the class label.

To address this bias, **gain ratio** adjusts the information gain by penalizing splits that produce a large number of subsets [491]. It does so by first computing the entropy of the split itself, known as the **split information**:

$$\text{SplitInfo}(A) = - \sum_{i=1}^{k} \frac{n_i}{n} \log_2 \frac{n_i}{n}, \tag{8.5}$$

where k is the number of child nodes, n is the number of samples at node v, and n_i is the number of samples at child node v_i. Splits that result in a larger number of subsets will generally have higher split information. For example, when all subsets are of equal size, the split information is $\log_2 k$ (see Equation (8.3)), which increases monotonically with the number of subsets.

The gain ratio is then defined as the ratio between the information gain and the split information:

$$\text{GainRatio}(A) = \frac{\text{IG}(A)}{\text{SplitInfo}(A)}. \tag{8.6}$$

This criterion has an information-theoretic justification: it evaluates how efficiently the information provided by feature A (measured by $\mathrm{SplitInfo}(A)$) is used to reduce uncertainty about the class label (measured by $\mathrm{IG}(A)$). A high gain ratio indicates that the split not only provides a large reduction in entropy but also does so using a relatively small amount of information, making it both informative and efficient.

For example, consider the decision tree in Figure 8.2a. The split information for feature A is:

$$\mathrm{SplitInfo}(A) = -\frac{6}{10} \log_2 \frac{6}{10} - \frac{4}{10} \log_2 \frac{4}{10} = 0.971.$$

Thus, the gain ratio for feature A is:

$$\mathrm{GainRatio}(A) = \frac{0.125}{0.971} = 0.129.$$

An alternative approach, used by algorithms such as CART, is to allow only binary splits in the tree. When all splits are binary, the bias toward features with a large number of distinct values is eliminated. However, binary splitting can significantly increase computational complexity: an attribute with k distinct values has $2^{k-1} - 1$ possible non-trivial binary partitions. It can also lead to deeper and less interpretable trees, as unrelated feature values may be grouped together, and multiple tests on the same feature may be needed.

8.2.1.3   Gini Index

Gini index (or **Gini impurity**)[3] is a popular criterion for measuring node impurity in decision trees, often used as an alternative to entropy. It quantifies the likelihood of a sample being misclassified if it were randomly labeled according to the class distribution at a given node. The more mixed the class distribution, the higher the Gini index.

Formally, let $p_1, p_2, \ldots, p_k$ denote the class probabilities at a node v. The probability that a sample from class i is misclassified is $1 - p_i$. The Gini index is computed as the expected misclassification rate:

$$\mathrm{Gini}(v) = \sum_{i=1}^{k} p_i(1 - p_i) = \sum_{i=1}^{k} p_i - \sum_{i=1}^{k} p_i^2 = 1 - \sum_{i=1}^{k} p_i^2. \tag{8.7}$$

Thus, the Gini index is equal to one minus the sum of the squared class probabilities.

For example, consider the left child of the root node in the decision tree shown in Figure 8.2a, which contains 4 positive examples and 2 negative ones. Its Gini index is

$$\mathrm{Gini}(v) = 1 - \left(\frac{4}{6}\right)^2 - \left(\frac{2}{6}\right)^2 = 0.444.$$

---

3. Named after the Italian statistician and demographer Corrado Gini (1884–1965), who introduced the Gini coefficient to measure income inequality.

The Gini index attains its minimum value of 0 when all samples belong to the same class, and its maximum value of $1 - 1/k$ when the samples are evenly distributed across the classes (see Exercise 8.12).

To evaluate the quality of a split using the Gini index, we calculate the reduction in Gini impurity:

$$\Delta_{\text{Gini}}(A) = \text{Gini}(v) - \sum_{i=1}^{k} \frac{n_i}{n} \text{Gini}(v_i), \tag{8.8}$$

where n is the number of samples at the parent node v, and n_i is the number of samples at child node v_i. The feature that yields the highest reduction in Gini impurity is selected for splitting.

For example, the reduction in Gini impurity for feature A in Figure 8.2a is:

$$\Delta_{\text{Gini}}(A) = 0.5 - \frac{6}{10} \cdot 0.444 - \frac{4}{10} \cdot 0.375 = 0.0836.$$

Figure 8.4 compares the Gini index and entropy (scaled by a factor of 1/2) for a Bernoulli random variable as the parameter p varies from 0 to 1. As shown, the two curves differ only slightly. Entropy assigns slightly higher impurity values than Gini for the same class distribution. As a result, Gini is more likely to accept splits that create one pure node while the other remains mixed, often resulting in slightly more imbalanced trees. Overall, empirical studies have found no significant difference in performance between the two measures [433, 576].

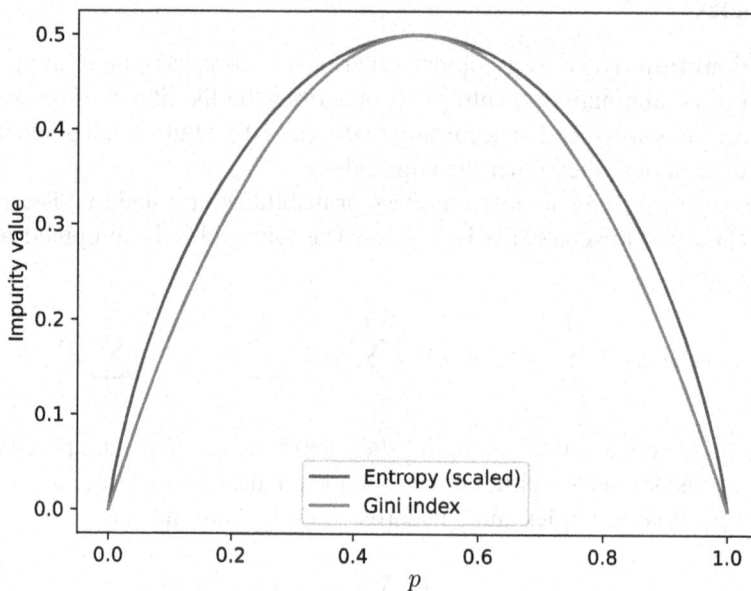

Figure 8.4: Comparison of scaled entropy and Gini index for a Bernoulli random variable, with probability p ranging from 0 to 1. Both measures behave similarly: they their maximum at $p = 0.5$, indicating the highest uncertainty, and approach zero as p approaches 0 or 1, where uncertainty is minimized.

Nevertheless, the Gini index is often preferred for its computational efficiency, as it avoids logarithmic calculations. For example, Scikit-Learn's decision tree classifier uses the Gini index as the default impurity measure (see Section 8.5).

8.2.2 Diabetes Prediction Example

We now demonstrate the construction of a complete decision tree from top to bottom, using information gain as the splitting criterion. Table 8.1 presents a small fictitious training dataset used to predict the likelihood of diabetes based on four categorical features: Age, BMI, History (family history of diabetes), and Exercise (frequency of physical activity). The target variable is Risk, indicating whether the individual is at Low or High risk of developing diabetes.

To simplify notation, we denote the entropy of a node with p positive and n negative examples as:

$$I(p, n) = -\frac{p}{p+n} \log_2 \left(\frac{p}{p+n}\right) - \frac{n}{p+n} \log_2 \left(\frac{n}{p+n}\right). \tag{8.9}$$

We begin by computing the entropy of the root node, which contains all 15 samples in the dataset:

$$H(\text{Risk}) = I(7, 8) = -\frac{7}{15} \log_2 \frac{7}{15} - \frac{8}{15} \log_2 \frac{8}{15} = 0.997.$$

	Age	BMI	History	Exercise	Risk
1	Young	Normal	None	High	Low
2	Adult	Obese	Severe	Medium	High
3	Young	Normal	Severe	Medium	Low
4	Senior	Obese	None	Low	High
5	Young	Obese	None	High	Low
6	Adult	Normal	Severe	High	High
7	Young	Overweight	Mild	Low	High
8	Senior	Overweight	None	High	Low
9	Adult	Obese	None	High	Low
10	Senior	Overweight	Mild	Medium	High
11	Adult	Overweight	None	High	Low
12	Senior	Normal	Severe	Medium	Low
13	Young	Overweight	Mild	Medium	Low
14	Adult	Normal	Mild	Low	High
15	Senior	Overweight	Severe	Medium	High

Table 8.1: Fictitious training dataset for predicting diabetes risk. The dataset consists of 15 samples, each described by four categorical features: Age (Young, Adult, Senior), BMI (Normal, Overweight, Obese), History (None, Mild, Severe), and Exercise (Low, Medium, High). The target label, Risk, shown in the last column, indicates whether the individual is at Low or High risk of developing diabetes.

Next, we compute the information gain for each attribute to determine the best initial split:

$$IG(\text{Age}) = 0.997 - \frac{5}{15}I(1,4) - \frac{5}{15}I(3,2) - \frac{5}{15}I(3,2) = 0.109,$$

$$IG(\text{BMI}) = 0.997 - \frac{5}{15}I(2,3) - \frac{6}{15}I(3,3) - \frac{4}{15}I(2,2) = 0.00668,$$

$$IG(\text{History}) = 0.997 - \frac{6}{15}I(1,5) - \frac{4}{15}I(3,1) - \frac{5}{15}I(3,2) = 0.197,$$

$$IG(\text{Exercise}) = 0.997 - \frac{3}{15}I(3,0) - \frac{6}{15}I(3,3) - \frac{6}{15}I(1,5) = 0.337.$$

Among all features, Exercise yields the highest information gain (0.337) and is therefore selected for the root split. This results in three branches based on exercise frequency:

1. Exercise = Low (samples 4, 7, 14): All samples in this subset have Risk = High, so this becomes a leaf node labeled "High".

2. Exercise = Medium (samples 2, 3, 10, 12, 13, 15): This subset contains a mix of 3 Low and 3 High labels, so further splitting is required.

3. Exercise = High (samples 1, 5, 6, 8, 9, 11): This subset also has mixed labels (5 Low, 1 High) and requires further splitting.

The structure of the decision tree after the first split is depicted in Figure 8.5.

Let's now examine the second child node of the root, corresponding to Exercise = Medium. The samples in this subset are listed in Table 8.2. The entropy at this node is:

$$H(\text{Risk}) = I(3,3) = 1.$$

We now compute the information gain for each of the remaining attributes:

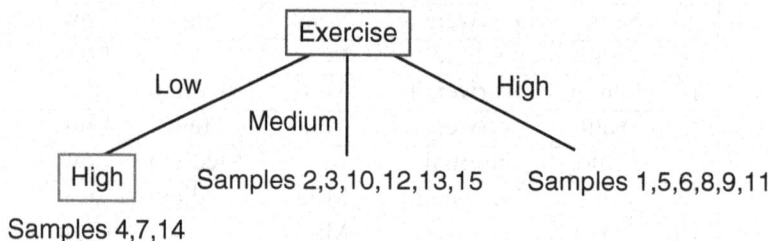

Figure 8.5: First split of the decision tree using the Exercise attribute. The root node is divided into three branches: Low, Medium, and High. The Low branch contains a pure subset of high-risk samples and is marked as a leaf node labeled "High". The Medium and High branches contain mixed labels and require additional splits.

	Age	BMI	History	Exercise	Risk
2	Adult	Obese	Severe	Medium	High
3	Young	Normal	Severe	Medium	Low
10	Senior	Overweight	Mild	Medium	High
12	Senior	Normal	Severe	Medium	Low
13	Young	Overweight	Mild	Medium	Low
15	Senior	Overweight	Severe	Medium	High

Table 8.2: Samples with Exercise = Medium

$$IG(\text{Age}) = 1 - \frac{2}{6}I(0,2) - \frac{1}{6}I(1,0) - \frac{3}{6}I(2,1) = 0.541,$$

$$IG(\text{BMI}) = 1 - \frac{2}{6}I(0,2) - \frac{3}{6}I(2,1) - \frac{1}{6}I(1,0) = 0.541,$$

$$IG(\text{History}) = 1 - \frac{2}{6}I(1,1) - \frac{4}{6}I(2,2) = 0.$$

Both Age and BMI yield the highest information gain (0.541), so either can be chosen. Suppose we select Age. This results in the following subsets:

1. Age = Young (samples 3, 13): Both have Risk = Low, so this becomes a leaf node labeled "Low."

2. Age = Adult (sample 2): A single instance with Risk = High; forms a leaf node labeled "High."

3. Age = Senior (samples 10, 12, 15): This subset has mixed labels and can be further split by BMI: Normal → Low risk, Overweight → High risk. Since no samples have BMI = Obese, that branch is assigned the majority class of the parent node, "High."

Figure 8.6 shows the decision tree after handling the splits in the Exercise = Medium branch.

Lastly, we handle the third child node of the root, where Exercise = High. The samples in this node are shown in Table 8.3. In this subset, all samples except sample 6 are labeled as Low risk. Sample 6 is unique in that it has History = Severe, while all other samples have History = None. Therefore, we use History as the splitting criterion for this node. As there are no samples with History = Mild in this subset, the leaf node for this option is labeled with the majority class from the parent node, "Low".

The final decision tree is shown in Figure 8.7. This tree perfectly classifies all the training samples. In general, growing a decision tree to its full depth—where each leaf node is pure—can achieve 100% accuracy on the training set, unless samples with identical attributes have conflicting class labels. However, fully grown trees are prone to overfitting, as they become overly tailored to the training data and often generalize poorly to unseen data. For example, the classification of samples with Exercise = Medium and Age = Adult as High risk is based on a single training example. To mitigate overfitting, tree pruning techniques are commonly applied (see Section 8.3).

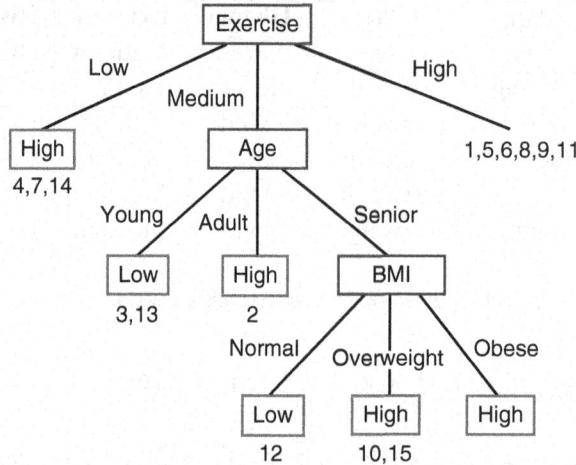

Figure 8.6: The decision tree after splitting the Exercise = Medium branch. The Age attribute divides samples into Young, Adult, and Senior groups, with Young and Adult groups assigned Low and High risk labels, respectively. The Senior group is further split by BMI, with Normal BMI leading to Low risk and Overweight BMI to High risk. The Obese node is assigned High risk based on its parent node's majority label. The numbers below each node are the row indices of the training samples that reach that node.

	Age	BMI	History	Exercise	Risk
1	Young	Normal	None	High	Low
5	Young	Obese	None	High	Low
6	Adult	Normal	Severe	High	High
8	Senior	Overweight	None	High	Low
9	Adult	Obese	None	High	Low
11	Adult	Overweight	None	High	Low

Table 8.3: Samples with Exercise = High

8.2.3   Handling Continuous Features

Up to this point, we have considered only categorical features. Numerical features with continuous values require a different approach for determining split points. To handle such features, we treat each observed value in the training data as a potential split point, and use the chosen node impurity measure to determine the optimal split. This procedure is as follows:

1. Sort the training samples by the continuous feature under consideration, obtaining values $v_1 < v_2 < \ldots < v_n$.

2. Identify candidate split points: For each consecutive pair of values (v_i, v_{i+1}), compute the midpoint $\dfrac{v_i + v_{i+1}}{2}$ as a potential split point. As an optimization, only consider midpoints where the class label changes between v_i and v_{i+1}, since the maximum impurity reduction can only occur at one of these points (see Exercise 8.17).

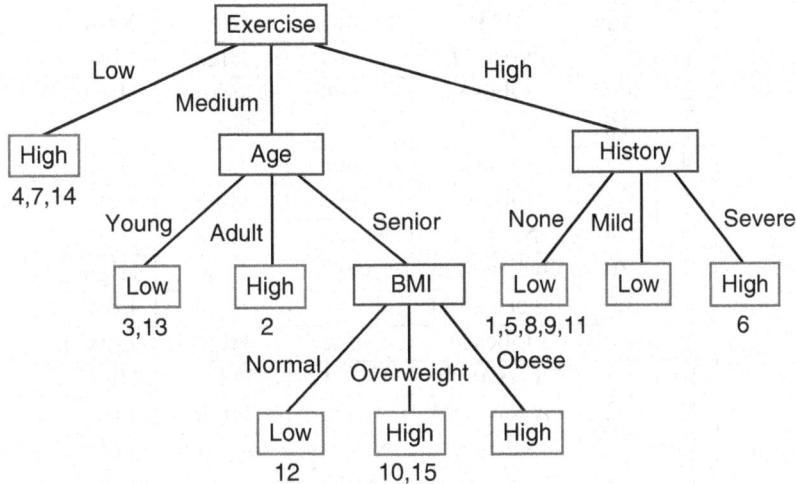

Figure 8.7: Final decision tree for predicting diabetes risk from four features: Exercise, Age, BMI, and History. This tree is grown to full depth, producing pure leaf nodes and achieving 100% training accuracy. While this ensures perfect classification of the training set, it may lead to overfitting.

3. Calculate impurity reduction:

   (a) Scan through each candidate split point, updating the class label counts for the subsets below and above the threshold.

   (b) For each split, compute the impurity (entropy or Gini index) of the resulting subsets and their weighted average, where the weights correspond to the proportion of samples in each subset.

4. Select the split that minimizes the weighted average impurity.

To illustrate this process, suppose the Age feature in the previous example is numerical rather than categorical (see Table 8.4). Figure 8.8 shows the evaluation of all potential split points for the Age feature, along with their corresponding weighted average entropy. The optimal split occurs at Age = 27.5, where the left subset contains 4 Low risk samples and the right subset contains 7 High and 4 Low risk samples.

8.2.4 Runtime Complexity

We now analyze the time complexity of decision tree construction and prediction. Let n be the number of samples in the training set and d the number of features. Constructing a decision tree involves several computational steps:

- At each internal node, evaluating a continuous feature requires sorting the samples by that feature's values, which takes $\mathcal{O}(n \log n)$ time in the worst case. After sorting, a linear scan to identify the optimal split point incurs an additional $\mathcal{O}(n)$ cost. Consequently, for d continuous features, finding the best split at a single node requires $\mathcal{O}(dn \log n)$ time.

	Age	BMI	History	Exercise	Risk
1	25	Normal	None	High	Low
2	44	Obese	Severe	Medium	High
3	18	Normal	Severe	Medium	Low
4	65	Obese	None	Low	High
5	22	Obese	None	High	Low
6	48	Normal	Severe	High	High
7	30	Overweight	Mild	Low	High
8	60	Overweight	None	High	Low
9	53	Obese	None	High	Low
10	67	Overweight	Mild	Medium	High
11	42	Overweight	None	High	Low
12	62	Normal	Severe	Medium	Low
13	25	Overweight	Mild	Medium	Low
14	40	Normal	Mild	Low	High
15	70	Overweight	Severe	Medium	High

Table 8.4: Training data for diabetes risk prediction with a numerical Age feature

Age

Sorted values	18	22	25	30	40	42	44	48	53	60	62	65	67	70
Class	Low	Low	Low	High	High	Low	High	High	Low	Low	Low	High	High	High

Split points			20		23.5		27.5		35		41		43		46		50.5		56.5		61		63.5		66		68.5			
	≤	>	≤	>	≤	>	≤	>	≤	>	≤	>	≤	>	≤	>	≤	>	≤	>	≤	>	≤	>	≤	>	≤	>	≤	>
Risk = High	0	7	0	7	0	7	0	7	1	6	2	5	2	5	3	4	4	3	4	3	4	3	4	3	5	2	6	1	7	0
Risk = Low	0	8	1	7	2	6	4	4	4	4	4	4	5	3	5	3	5	3	6	2	7	1	8	0	8	0	8	0	8	0
Entropy	0.997		0.933		0.863		__0.693__		0.888		0.961		0.912		0.969		0.995		0.971		0.910		0.735		0.833		0.920		0.997	

Figure 8.8: Evaluation of potential split points for the Age feature. Each candidate split point is the midpoint between two consecutive sorted Age values, dividing the data into High and Low risk subsets. The table shows the class distributions and weighted average entropy for each split. The optimal split, at Age = 27.5, yields the lowest weighted average entropy of 0.693.

- The total runtime complexity depends on how balanced the splits are:

  - In the worst case, where each split isolates a single sample, the tree becomes a linear chain of depth n, and the overall complexity is $\mathcal{O}(dn^2 \log n)$.

  - In the average case, where splits are relatively balanced, the tree has depth $\mathcal{O}(\log n)$. At depth ℓ, there are at most 2^ℓ nodes, each processing about $n/2^\ell$ samples, yielding $\mathcal{O}(dn \log n)$. Summing over all $\mathcal{O}(\log n)$ levels gives a total complexity of $\mathcal{O}(dn \log^2 n)$.

Sorting the continuous feature values at each node is the most computationally intensive step in the construction. To reduce this cost, several optimization techniques have been proposed.

One notable example is the SPRINT algorithm [541], which improves efficiency by pre-sorting the continuous features at the beginning of the process. It maintains the sorted values of each feature in an **attribute list,** where each entry contains the feature value, class label, and sample index. When a node is split, the attribute lists are partitioned according to the split, preserving the original order of values within each subset. This eliminates the need to re-sort the values at each node, significantly reducing the computational overhead.

The time complexity of making predictions with a decision tree is $\mathcal{O}(h)$, where h is the height of the tree. The height depends on several factors including the balance of the tree, whether splits are binary or multi-way, and whether pruning has been applied. For multi-way splits, h is at most d, since each feature can be used at most once along any path from the root to a leaf.

8.3 Tree Pruning

Decision trees are among the few machine learning models capable of achieving perfect accuracy on their training data. While such a perfect fit underscores the model's flexibility, it also reveals one of its main limitation—the tendency to overfit by capturing noise and spurious patterns that do not generalize well to unseen data.

A common strategy to mitigate overfitting in decision trees is **tree pruning** [73, 490, 181]. Pruning removes tree branches that contribute little to predictive accuracy, thereby improving its generalization performance and making the model easier to interpret. The two main pruning approaches, pre-pruning and post-pruning, are discussed below.

8.3.1 Pre-pruning

Pre-pruning stops the tree from growing to its full depth, preventing it from perfectly fitting the training data. This is achieved by applying one of the following stopping criteria during the tree construction process:

- **Maximum depth**: Restricts the tree to a fixed number of levels, directly limiting its size.

- **Minimum samples to split**: A node is split only if it contains at least a specified number of samples, ensuring that splits are supported by sufficient data.

- **Minimum samples per leaf**: Ensures that each leaf contains at least a specified number of samples, reducing the risk of statistically unreliable leaves.

- **Maximum leaf nodes**: Grows the tree in a best-first manner—prioritizing splits that yield the largest impurity reduction—until the specified number of leaves is reached.

- **Minimum impurity decrease**: Allows a split only if it reduces impurity (e.g., entropy or Gini index) by at least the specified threshold.

In practice, multiple criteria are often combined. For example, limiting the maximum depth constrains the overall size of the tree, while enforcing a minimum number of samples per leaf ensures that each splitting decision is based on enough data.

8.3.2 Post-pruning

Post-pruning involves first growing the decision tree to its maximum depth (or a large initial size) and then removing nodes that do not contribute significantly to generalization in a bottom-up fashion [490, 423, 181]. Each pruned subtree is replaced by a leaf labeled with the majority class of the samples it previously covered. Pruning continues as long as it improves a predefined criterion reflecting the model's ability to generalize.

Several post-pruning strategies exist, differing in how they prioritize and select subtrees for pruning. This section focuses on two of the most widely used methods.

8.3.2.1 Reduced Error Pruning

Reduced Error Pruning (REP) is a simple yet effective post-pruning technique that removes nodes from the tree if their elimination does not degrade performance on a separate validation set [490]. It consists of the following steps:

1. Split the dataset into training and validation sets.

2. Grow the decision tree to full depth on the training set.

3. Traverse the tree from the leaves upward, pruning any node whose removal does not increase the validation error. Each pruned node is replaced by a leaf labeled with the majority class of its former subtree.

4. Repeat until no further pruning improves (or maintains) validation performance.

REP is easy to implement and has time complexity that is linear in the number of nodes. However, because it follows a greedy approach, it may produce suboptimal trees by failing to consider alternative pruning sequences.

8.3.2.2 Cost-Complexity Pruning

A more advanced pruning technique, known as **cost-complexity pruning** (or **weakest link pruning**), often produces more efficient and better-generalizing trees. This method was introduced as part of the CART algorithm [73].

Cost-complexity pruning balances training accuracy against model complexity using a cost-complexity measure. For a tree T, the **cost-complexity** is defined as:

$$R_\alpha(T) = R(T) + \alpha|\tilde{T}|, \tag{8.10}$$

where:

- $R(T)$ is the total misclassification error of T on the training data, calculated as the sum of errors across all leaves of T:

$$R(T) = \sum_{t \in \tilde{T}} R(t) = \sum_{t \in \tilde{T}} r(t)p(t). \tag{8.11}$$

Here, $\tilde{T}$ denotes the set of leaves in T, and $R(t)$ is the misclassification error at leaf t, computed as $r(t)p(t)$, where $r(t)$ is the error rate at t (the proportion of misclassified samples reaching t) and $p(t)$ is the fraction of training samples reaching t.

- $|\tilde{T}|$ is the number of leaves in T, representing the tree complexity.

- $\alpha \geq 0$ is a regularization parameter that controls the tradeoff between the tree size and training accuracy. Higher values of α penalize larger trees more heavily, leading to more aggressive pruning.

Since the optimal value of α is initially unknown, the algorithm generates a sequence of progressively smaller trees $T_0, T_1, \ldots, T_k = \{t_1\}$, where T_0 is the fully grown tree and T_k contains only the root node t_1. Each tree T_i minimizes $R_\alpha(T)$ for some α_i, with $\alpha_0 = 0 < \alpha_1 < \ldots < \alpha_k$.

Although α can take any positive real value, the original tree T has only a finite number of distinct subtrees. As a result, the subtree that minimizes the cost-complexity for a given α, denoted $T(\alpha)$, remains optimal as α increases—until a critical threshold α' is reached, at which point a smaller subtree $T(\alpha')$ becomes preferable.

At each pruning round i, the goal is to determine the next critical value of α and identify the subtree within T_i that minimizes $R_\alpha(T_i)$. To that end, for each internal node t in T_i, we compute the cost-complexity of the subtree rooted at t and compare it with the cost-complexity that would result if that subtree were replaced by the single node t.

The cost-complexity of the subtree rooted at t, denoted T_t, is:

$$R_\alpha(T_t) = R(T_t) + \alpha|\tilde{T}_t|,$$

whereas the cost-complexity of t as a single-node tree is:

$$R_\alpha(t) = R(t) + \alpha.$$

As long as $R_\alpha(T_t) < R_\alpha(\{t\})$, pruning T_t would increase the cost-complexity, so T_t is preferred over replacing it with the single node $\{t\}$. However, as α increases, there will eventually be a critical value at which $R_\alpha(T_t) = R_\alpha(\{t\})$. At this point, pruning T_t becomes preferable, as it yields the same cost-complexity but with a simpler, single-node structure. This critical value α can be found by solving:

$$R_\alpha(T_t) = R_\alpha(\{t\}) \Rightarrow R(T_t) + \alpha|\tilde{T}_t| = R(t) + \alpha,$$

which simplifies to:

$$\alpha = \frac{R(t) - R(T_t)}{|\tilde{T}_t| - 1}. \tag{8.12}$$

This expression gives the smallest value of α for which replacing the subtree T_t with a single leaf t becomes cost-effective.

Our objective is to identify the first node in the tree for which $R_\alpha(\{t\}) = R_\alpha(T_t)$ as α increases. This node, denoted $\bar{t}$ and referred to as the **weakest link**, is the one that minimizes the function

$$g(t) = \frac{R(t) - R(T_t)}{|\tilde{T}_t| - 1}. \tag{8.13}$$

The node $\bar{t}$ is the best candidate for the current pruning step, as removing its subtree results in the smallest increase in cost-complexity across the entire tree (i.e., $R_\alpha(\{t\}) - R_\alpha(T_t)$ is minimal).

Once $\bar{t}$ is identified, we prune its subtree $T_{\bar{t}}$, yielding a new tree T_{i+1}, and set $\alpha_{i+1} = g(\bar{t})$ as the next critical value in the cost-complexity sequence. This process is then repeated with T_{i+1}: we identify the next weakest link $\bar{t}_{i+1}$, prune its subtree to obtain T_{i+2}, and set $\alpha_{i+2} = g(\bar{t}_{i+1})$, and so on.

This iterative procedure generates a sequence of progressively smaller subtrees:

$$T_0 > T_1 > T_2 > \ldots > T_k,$$

along with a corresponding sequence of increasing α values:

$$\alpha_0 < \alpha_1 < \alpha_2 < \ldots < \alpha_k,$$

where T_0 is the fully grown tree with $\alpha_0 = 0$.

Finally, the optimal tree is selected by evaluating each subtree T_i (for $i = 0, 1, \ldots, k$) on an independent validation set or via cross-validation. Cross-validation generally provides a more reliable estimate of generalization performance, but at a higher computational cost than using a single validation set.

Cost-Complexity Pruning Example

Consider the decision tree shown in Figure 8.9, which classifies a dataset of 20 data points: 9 positive and 11 negative. The right side of the figure shows the distribution of these points in the feature space.

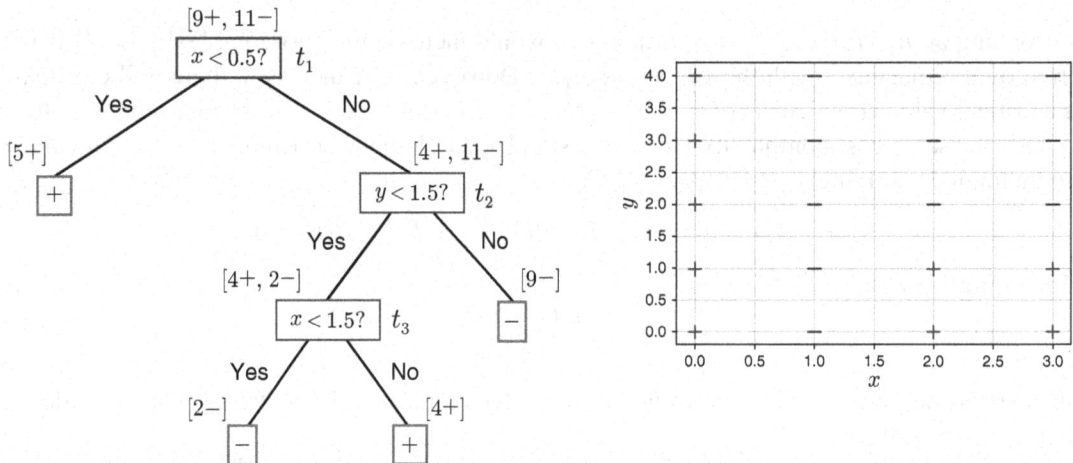

Figure 8.9: The initial decision tree before cost-complexity pruning. The tree on the left perfectly classifies all 20 data points, which are visualized on the right. Each internal node displays the splitting feature and the counts of positive and negative examples reaching it, while leaf nodes indicate the final class label (+ for positive, − for negative).

We apply cost-complexity pruning to the tree, starting with $\alpha_0 = 0$. In the first pruning iteration, three internal nodes are candidates for pruning: t_1 (the root), t_2, and t_3. The values of the pruning criterion $g(t)$ for these nodes are shown in Table 8.5.

The minimum value of $g(t)$ is 0.1, which occurs for both t_2 and t_3. In the case of a tie, we prune the subtree with fewer nodes, which in this case is t_3. The next critical value is set to $\alpha_1 = 0.1$. The resulting tree is shown in Figure 8.10.

In the second iteration, we re-evaluate the remaining candidates t_1 and t_2. Their $g(t)$ values are shown in Table 8.6.

Since $g(t_2)$ is the minimum, we prune the subtree rooted at t_2 and set $\alpha_2 = 0.1$. The updated tree is shown in Figure 8.11.

t	$R(t)$	$R(T_t)$	$g(t)$
t_1	$\dfrac{9}{20} \cdot \dfrac{20}{20} = 0.45$	0	$\dfrac{0.45 - 0}{4 - 1} = 0.15$
t_2	$\dfrac{4}{15} \cdot \dfrac{15}{20} = 0.2$	0	$\dfrac{0.2 - 0}{3 - 1} = 0.1$
t_3	$\dfrac{2}{6} \cdot \dfrac{6}{20} = 0.1$	0	$\dfrac{0.1 - 0}{2 - 1} = 0.1$

Table 8.5: Cost-complexity calculations for the first pruning iteration

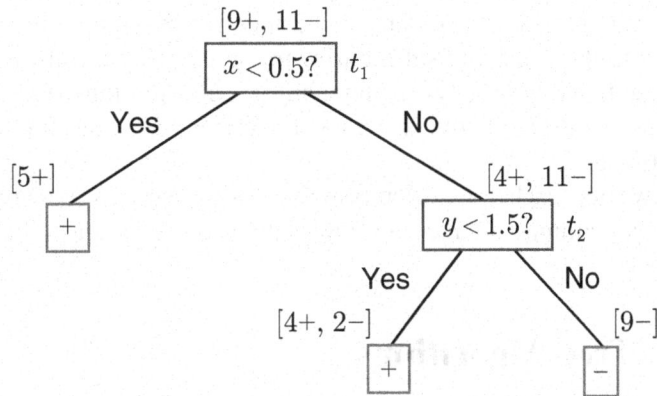

Figure 8.10: After the first pruning iteration: the subtree rooted at node t_3 has been pruned.

t	$R(t)$	$R(T_t)$	$g(t)$
t_1	$\dfrac{9}{20} \cdot \dfrac{20}{20} = 0.45$	$\dfrac{2}{20} = 0.1$	$\dfrac{0.45 - 0.1}{3 - 1} = 0.175$
t_2	$\dfrac{4}{15} \cdot \dfrac{15}{20} = 0.2$	$\dfrac{2}{20} = 0.1$	$\dfrac{0.2 - 0.1}{2 - 1} = 0.1$

Table 8.6: Cost-complexity calculations for the second pruning iteration

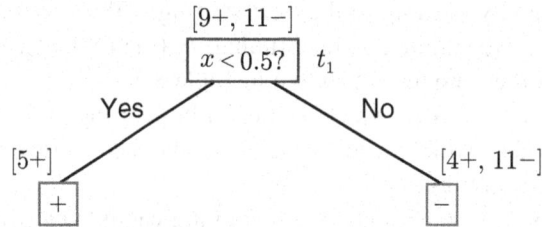

Figure 8.11: After the second pruning iteration: node t_2 has been pruned, leaving a simplified tree with the root t_1 and two leaves.

In the third and final iteration, the only remaining candidate for pruning is the root node t_1. The next critical value is:

$$\alpha_3 = g(t_1) = \frac{9/20 - 4/20}{2 - 1} = 0.25.$$

The sequence of critical α values is therefore:

$$\alpha_0 = 0, \quad \alpha_1 = 0.1, \quad \alpha_2 = 0.1, \quad \alpha_3 = 0.25.$$

The optimal α is selected based on the model's performance on a validation set or via cross-validation (see Section 8.5.3).

Comparing pre-pruning and post-pruning, pre-pruning is generally more efficient in terms of runtime because it limits the number of splits during tree construction, while post-pruning requires building the entire tree first and then evaluating many possible prunings. On the other hand, post-pruning often achieves better predictive accuracy, as pruning decisions are made with access to the complete tree structure.

In practice, the two approaches are often combined: a large tree is first grown until a stopping criterion is met (e.g., a minimum number of samples per leaf), and post-pruning is then applied to further simplify the tree.

8.4   Decision Tree Algorithms

Over the years, a variety of decision tree algorithms have been developed, each offering distinct approaches to tree construction and pruning. These differences include the choice of node impurity criterion, binary versus multi-way splits, handling of continuous features, and the use of pre-pruning or post-pruning. Three foundational algorithms are:

- **ID3 (Iterative Dichotomiser 3)** [489]: Developed by Ross Quinlan in the late 1970s, ID3 is one of the earliest and most influential decision tree algorithms. It uses information gain as the splitting criterion and supports multi-way splits (similar to Algorithm 8.1). ID3 can handle only categorical features, so continuous features must be discretized before training. It does not include a pruning mechanism, which makes the model prone to overfitting.

- **C4.5** [491]: Introduced by Quinlan in 1993 as a successor to ID3, C4.5 extends the algorithm by supporting both continuous and categorical features. It also incorporates a post-pruning method based on estimated error rates from the training data (similar in spirit to reduced error pruning but without requiring a separate validation set).

- **CART (Classification and Regression Trees)** [73]: Introduced by Breiman et al. in 1984, CART supports both classification and regression tasks. Unlike ID3 and C4.5, it uses only binary splits and selects the splitting feature using the Gini index rather than information gain (in classification tasks). It also introduced the cost-complexity pruning method described in Section 8.3.2.2. CART remains one of the most widely used decision tree algorithms, with an optimized implementation available in Scikit-Learn (see Section 8.5).

In addition to these foundational algorithms, numerous variants of decision tree algorithms have been developed over the years to address specific challenges, including:

- using alternative impurity criteria [424, 313, 547, 102];

- introducing new post-pruning methods [446, 422, 414];

- supporting multivariate splits (see Section 8.8);

- improving the efficiency of tree construction [413, 541, 510];

- enhancing scalability to large and high-dimensional datasets [359, 281];

- enabling parallel and distributed tree construction [91, 461, 537];

- handling imbalanced datasets [124, 374];

- incorporating cost-sensitive learning [368, 195];

- processing streaming data and adapting to concept drift [298, 284, 211];

- learning Bayesian decision trees for improved uncertainty quantification [117, 118];

- developing soft decision trees with probabilistic splits [288, 207];

- developing fairness-aware decision trees that reduce predictive bias [307, 495];

- facilitating causal inference [355, 663].

For an overview of recent developments in decision tree learning, see [131].

8.5   Decision Trees in Scikit-Learn

Scikit-Learn's `DecisionTreeClassifier`[4] class provides an efficient implementation of classification trees based on the CART algorithm. It includes parameters for controlling various aspects of the tree construction, such as the splitting criterion, pre- and post-pruning settings, and class imbalance handling. Table 8.7 outlines the key parameters of this class.

While the CART algorithm supports both categorical and numerical features, Scikit-Learn currently requires all features to be numerical. Therefore, categorical features must be encoded before training (e.g., with `OneHotEncoder`).

To demonstrate the use of `DecisionTreeClassifier`, we train it on the reduced Iris dataset used in previous chapters (see Section 6.1.4), which contains only the first two features: sepal length and sepal width. We begin by loading the dataset and splitting it into training and test sets:

Parameter	Description	Default
`criterion`	Impurity measure used for splits. Options: `'gini'` (Gini index), `'entropy'` (information gain), and `'log_loss'`.	`'gini'`
`splitter`	Split selection strategy: `'best'` (best split among all features) or `'random'` (best among a random subset of features, size set by `max_features`).	`'best'`
`max_depth`	Maximum depth of the tree. If `None`, nodes are expanded until all leaves are pure or contain fewer than `min_samples_split` samples.	`None`
`min_samples_split`	Minimum number of samples required to split a node.	`2`
`min_samples_leaf`	Minimum number of samples required at a leaf node.	`1`
`max_features`	Number of features to consider when searching for the best split. If `None`, all features are considered.	`None`
`max_leaf_nodes`	Maximum number of leaf nodes. If `None`, it is unlimited.	`None`
`min_impurity_decrease`	Minimum impurity decrease required to split a node.	`0.0`
`class_weight`	Class weights for handling imbalanced data. If `None`, all classes are weighted equally.	`None`
`ccp_alpha`	Complexity parameter for cost-complexity pruning. Higher values lead to more aggressive pruning.	`0.0`

Table 8.7: Key parameters of the `DecisionTreeClassifier` class

---

4. `https://scikit-learn.org/stable/modules/generated/sklearn.tree.DecisionTreeClassifier.html`

```
from sklearn.datasets import load_iris
from sklearn.model_selection import train_test_split

iris = load_iris()
X = iris.data[:, :2]
y = iris.target

X_train, X_test, y_train, y_test = train_test_split(X, y, random_state=42)
```

Since all features are numerical, no additional preprocessing is needed (decision trees do not require feature scaling).

Next, we create an instance of `DecisionTreeClassifier` with default settings and fit it to the training data:

```
from sklearn.tree import DecisionTreeClassifier

clf = DecisionTreeClassifier(random_state=42)
clf.fit(X_train, y_train)
```

In Scikit-Learn, if multiple splits yield the same impurity improvement, the tie is resolved randomly. Setting the `random_state` parameter ensures that the same choice is made in each run, making the results reproducible.

We then evaluate the model's performance on the training and test sets:

```
print(f'Training accuracy: {clf.score(X_train, y_train):.4f}')
print(f'Test accuracy: {clf.score(X_test, y_test):.4f}')
```

```
Training accuracy: 0.9554
Test accuracy: 0.6579
```

The large gap between training and test accuracy indicates overfitting. To visualize the learned decision boundaries, we can use the helper function from Section 6.1.4:

```
plot_decision_boundaries(clf, X, y, iris.feature_names, iris.target_names)
```

Figure 8.12 displays the decision boundaries generated by the decision tree. The boundaries are **rectilinear**, composed of straight lines and right angles. This is a consequence of the tree splitting on a single feature at each node, which produces axis-aligned boundaries. In addition, the figure illustrates the model's tendency to overfit, as it tries to closely match each individual training sample.

8.5.1   Pre-Pruning the Tree

To address the overfitting issue, we can limit the growth of the decision tree by applying one of the pre-pruning techniques. For example, we can set the maximum depth of the tree to three levels:

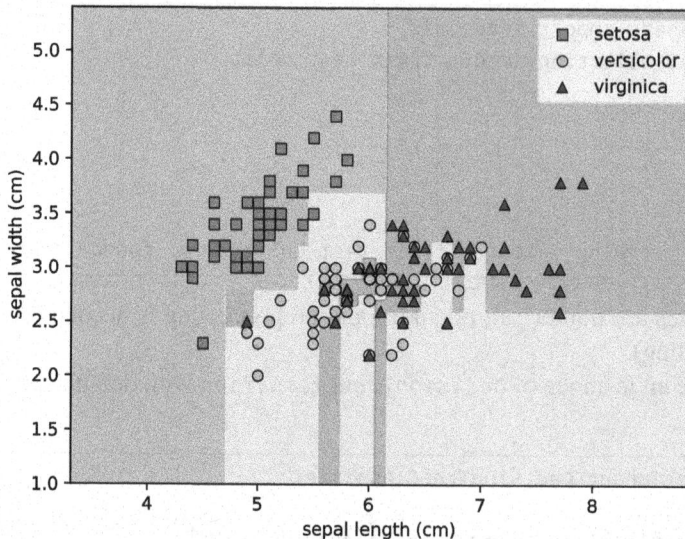

Figure 8.12: Decision boundaries of a decision tree classifier on the Iris dataset, illustrating rectilinear, axis-aligned boundaries and clear signs of overfitting.

```
clf_pruned = DecisionTreeClassifier(max_depth=3, random_state=42)
clf_pruned.fit(X_train, y_train)
```

The accuracy of the pruned tree is:

```
print(f'Training accuracy: {clf_pruned.score(X_train, y_train):.4f}')
print(f'Test accuracy: {clf_pruned.score(X_test, y_test):.4f}')
```

```
Training accuracy: 0.8214
Test accuracy: 0.7632
```

The test accuracy improved significantly from 65.79% to 76.32%, indicating that the pruned tree generalizes better to unseen data. At the same time, the decrease in training accuracy confirms that the model is no longer overfitting the training set. To visualize the effect of pruning on the decision boundaries, we can plot them again:

```
plot_decision_boundaries(clf_pruned, X, y, iris.feature_names[:2], iris.target_names)
```

Figure 8.13 shows the decision boundaries of the pruned tree. Compared to the unpruned tree, the boundaries are noticeably smoother and less fragmented, reflecting a better capture of the overall structure of the data.

Rather than manually selecting the pre-pruning criteria, we can perform a grid search to find the optimal combination of parameters:

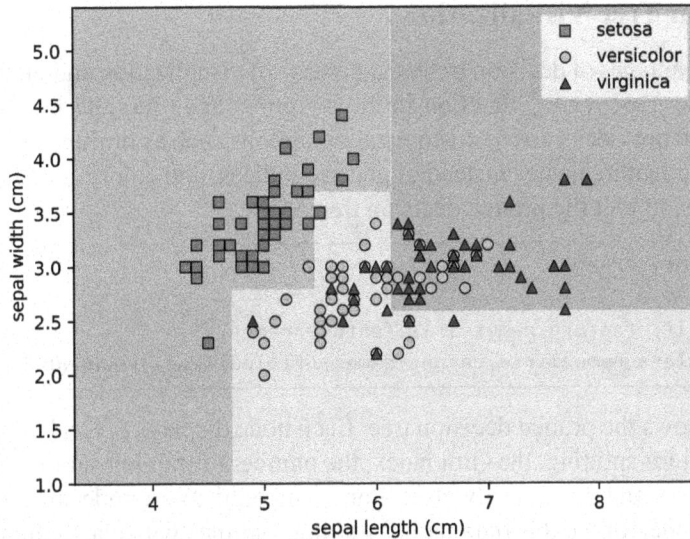

Figure 8.13: Decision boundaries of the pruned decision tree on the Iris dataset, showing smoother, more generalized regions compared to the unpruned tree.

```
from sklearn.model_selection import GridSearchCV

param_grid = {
    'criterion': ['gini', 'entropy'],
    'max_depth': np.arange(1, 11),
    'min_samples_split': np.arange(2, 11),
    'min_impurity_decrease': np.arange(0.0, 0.5, 0.05)
}
clf = DecisionTreeClassifier(random_state=42)
grid_search = GridSearchCV(clf, param_grid, cv=3, n_jobs=-1)
grid_search.fit(X_train, y_train)
```

The best parameters found by the grid search are:

```
grid_search.best_params_
```

```
{'criterion': 'gini',
 'max_depth': 3,
 'min_impurity_decrease': 0.0,
 'min_samples_split': 2}
```

In this case, the optimal parameters match those of our earlier pruned classifier: a maximum depth of 3, with the other parameters at their default values.

8.5.2 Decision Tree Visualization

One of the key advantages of decision trees is their ease of visualization and interpretability. Scikit-Learn provides the `plot_tree`[5] function in the `sklearn.tree` module for visualizing decision trees. This function provides various customization options such as limiting the displayed depth of the tree, displaying feature names instead of generic indices, and coloring nodes by their majority class. For example, to plot the pruned decision tree:

```
from sklearn import tree

tree.plot_tree(clf, feature_names=iris.feature_names,
               class_names=iris.target_names, filled=True, rounded=True)
```

Figure 8.14 shows the pruned decision tree. Each node displays several properties: the feature and threshold used for splitting, the Gini index, the number of training samples reaching the node, the class distribution, and the majority class. For example, the root node splits on "sepal length $\leq$ 5.45", has a Gini index of 0.666, contains 112 training samples with class counts [35, 39, 38], and has versicolor as the majority class.

8.5.3 Post-Pruning the Tree

Scikit-Learn implements the cost-complexity pruning algorithm discussed in Section 8.3.2. This pruning is controlled by the `ccp_alpha` parameter, which corresponds to the α parameter in the algorithm used to determine the optimal subtree size. Higher `ccp_alpha` values lead to more extensive pruning. By default, `ccp_alpha` is set to 0.0, meaning no post-pruning is applied.

Determining the optimal `ccp_alpha` value typically involves evaluating the model's performance across the sequence of α values found during pruning, using either a validation set or cross-validation. To facilitate this process, the `DecisionTreeClassifier` class provides the `cost_complexity_pruning_path`[6] method, which returns the sequence of α values along with the corresponding total leaf impurities of the pruned trees. The following code obtains and plots these values:

```
clf = DecisionTreeClassifier(random_state=42)
path = clf.cost_complexity_pruning_path(X_train, y_train)
ccp_alphas, impurities = path.ccp_alphas, path.impurities

plt.plot(ccp_alphas[:-1], impurities[:-1], marker='o', drawstyle='steps-post')
plt.xlabel('$\alpha$')
plt.ylabel('Total Impurity of Leaves')
plt.plot()
```

---

5. https://scikit-learn.org/stable/modules/generated/sklearn.tree.plot_tree.html
6. https://scikit-learn.org/stable/modules/generated/sklearn.tree.DecisionTreeClassifier.html#
   sklearn.tree.DecisionTreeClassifier.cost_complexity_pruning_path

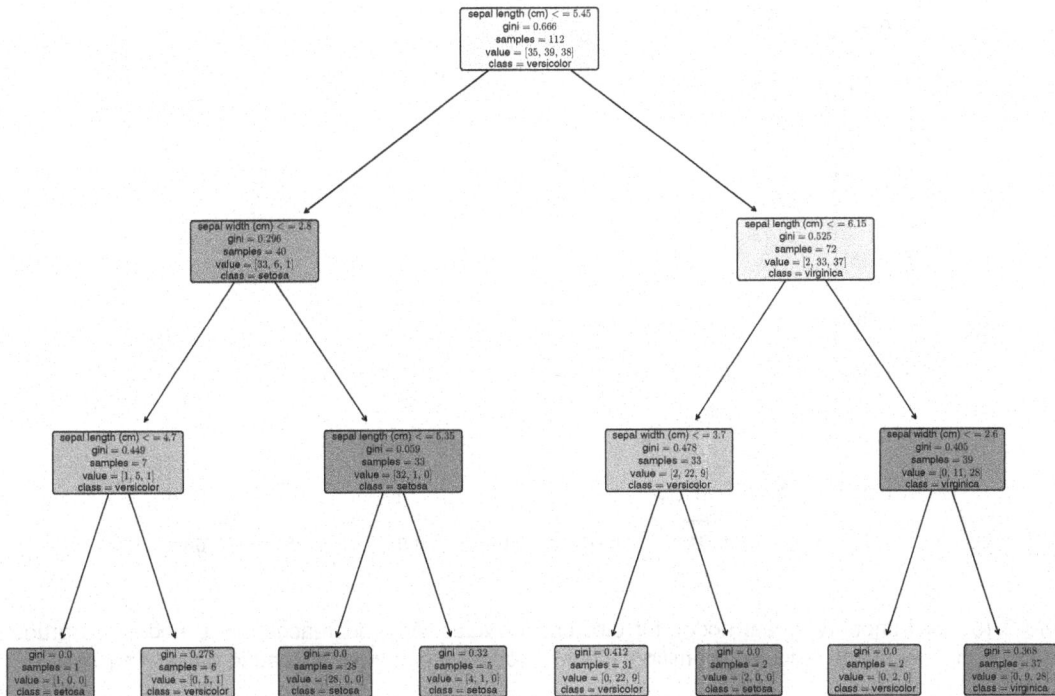

Figure 8.14: Visualization of the pruned decision tree for the Iris dataset. Each node displays the feature and threshold for the split, Gini impurity, sample count, class distribution, and the majority class. The color of each node reflects the majority class, with more saturated colors indicating purer nodes.

We exclude the last α value in `ccp_alphas` from the plot because it corresponds to pruning the tree down to a single node, resulting in a trivial model. Figure 8.15 shows how the total leaf impurity changes as a function of α. For small α values, the impurity increases sharply as highly specific, overfitting splits are removed. At $\alpha \approx 0.02$, the curve enters a flat region where no further pruning occurs until a much larger penalty is imposed on the tree size. Increasing α beyond this point may cut branches that are still useful for prediction, raising the risk of underfitting.

To evaluate the impact of each α on the model's performance, we train and evaluate a decision tree for each value:

```
ccp_alphas = ccp_alphas[:-1]
train_scores, test_scores = [], []


for ccp_alpha in ccp_alphas:
    clf = DecisionTreeClassifier(random_state=42, ccp_alpha=ccp_alpha)
    clf.fit(X_train, y_train)
    train_scores.append(clf.score(X_train, y_train))
    test_scores.append(clf.score(X_test, y_test))
```

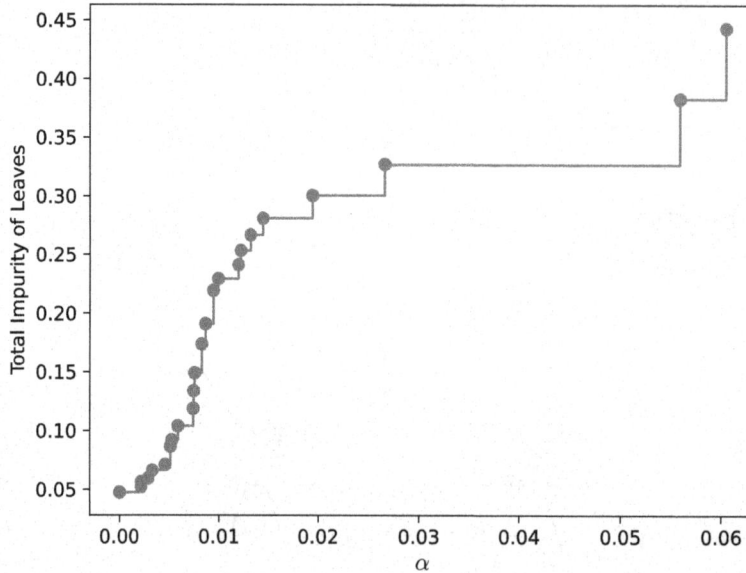

Figure 8.15: Total impurity in leaf nodes for different α values. As α increases, more nodes are pruned, simplifying the model and reducing overfitting, though excessive pruning may lead to underfitting.

```
plt.xlabel('$\alpha$')
plt.ylabel('Accuracy')
plt.plot(ccp_alphas, train_scores, marker='o', label='Training set',
         drawstyle='steps-post')
plt.plot(ccp_alphas, test_scores, marker='o', label='Test set',
         drawstyle='steps-post')
plt.legend()
```

Figure 8.16 shows the training and test accuracies for different values of α. Initially, pruning improves the test accuracy by reducing overfitting, but beyond $\alpha = 0.02$, excessive pruning causes it to decline, indicating underfitting. In this example, ccp_alpha = 0.02 offers the best balance between model complexity and generalization.

Although this example uses the test set to choose α, it is better to determine the optimal value using a separate validation set or cross-validation to avoid contaminating the test set.

8.5.4 Handling Missing Values

Handling missing values is an important aspect of decision tree construction, as missing data can affect both the quality of the splits and the interpretability of the model. Several approaches have been proposed in the literature for dealing with missing values in decision trees:

- Exclude features with missing values from consideration during split selection, and choose among the remaining features. This strategy is used by CART [73].

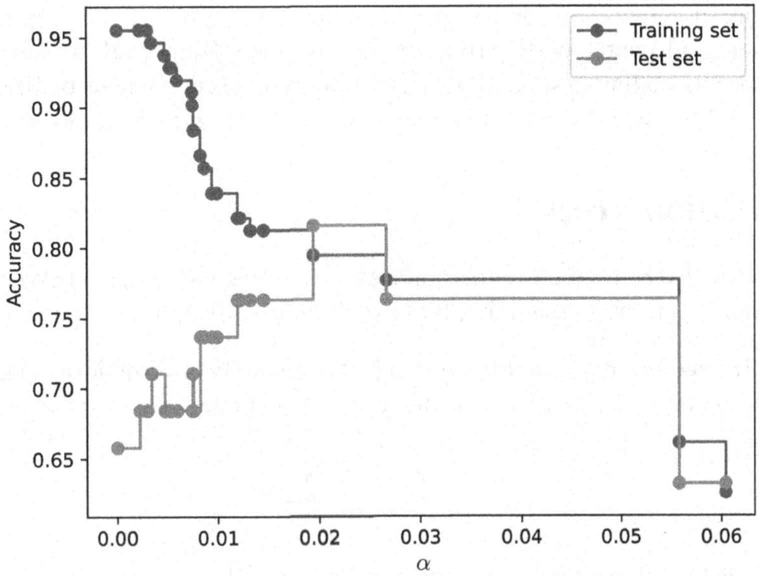

Figure 8.16: Plot of training and test set accuracies for different α values, illustrating the tradeoff between model complexity and generalization. $\alpha = 0.02$ represents the optimal setting in this case.

- For each candidate splitting feature, if a sample has a missing value for that feature, temporarily assign it to all child nodes created by the split. The sample is weighted in each branch according to the fraction of training samples with known values for that feature that follow that branch. The chosen split is the one that minimizes the weighted impurity (Gini index or entropy) across all samples, including those with missing values. This strategy is utilized by C4.5 [491].

- Impute missing values locally within each node, using only the samples that reach that node [378]. This local imputation avoids making global assumptions about the data distribution (unlike imputation performed before tree construction).

- Treat missing values as a separate category within the feature, creating a dedicated branch in the tree for them [376]. This allows the model to learn from missingness patterns in the data, which may carry predictive information.

The `DecisionTreeClassifier` class in Scikit-Learn handles missing values in a slightly different manner:

- During training: When evaluating a feature with missing values, the algorithm considers directing all samples with missing values to either the left or right child node and chooses the direction that yields the greatest impurity reduction.

- During prediction: If a feature had no missing values during training but is missing in a new sample, the sample is sent to the child node that received the most training samples—representing the most likely path based on the training data distribution.

Although decision trees can handle missing values internally, pre-training imputation is recommended when a substantial portion of a feature is missing. High levels of missingness can bias the splitting process, leading to suboptimal trees. Imputing missing values beforehand results in a more complete dataset, which can improve the reliability of splits and overall model performance.

8.6   Regression Trees

Decision trees can also be used for regression tasks. Adapting the decision tree construction algorithm (Algorithm 8.1) for regression involves two main modifications:

- **Leaf node prediction**: In classification, a leaf node predicts the majority class of its samples. In regression trees, the prediction is the mean of the target values in the leaf:

$$\bar{y}_v = \frac{1}{n_v} \sum_{i \in S_v} y_i, \tag{8.14}$$

where S_v is the set of samples in node v and $n_v = |S_v|$.

- **Impurity measure**: Instead of classification measures such as Gini index or entropy, regression trees typically use the mean squared error (MSE) to evaluate split quality. The MSE at node v is given by

$$\text{MSE}(v) = \frac{1}{n_v} \sum_{i \in S_v} (y_i - \bar{y}_v)^2, \tag{8.15}$$

where $\bar{y}_v$ is the mean target value at node v. This quantity corresponds to the variance of the target values in the node. A smaller MSE indicates more homogeneous targets, which typically leads to more accurate predictions. At each node, we choose the split that yields the largest reduction in MSE.

8.6.1   Numerical Example

To illustrate how regression trees work, consider the toy dataset in Table 8.8, where the task is to predict house prices given their size.

Size (100 sq ft)	Price (1000s of USD)
1.1	150
1.3	200
1.5	240
1.7	280
2.0	310

Table 8.8: Sample dataset for predicting house prices based on their size

To find the best split at the root node, we first sort the sizes and examine the midpoints between consecutive values: 1.2, 1.4, 1.6, and 1.85. For each candidate split, we compute the MSE for the left and right child nodes, and then calculate the weighted average across both nodes. The optimal split is the one with the lowest weighted average, thereby maximizing the reduction in impurity. The calculations for each potential split are shown in Table 8.9.

For example, the weighted average MSE for the split at 1.4 is calculated as follows:

- Left node:

  - Sizes $= (1.1, 1.3)$, Prices $= (150, 200)$
  - Mean price $= \dfrac{150 + 200}{2} = 175$
  - MSE $= \dfrac{(150 - 175)^2 + (200 - 175)^2}{2} = 625$

- Right node:

  - Sizes $= (1.5, 1.7, 2.0)$, Prices $= (240, 280, 310)$
  - Mean price $= \dfrac{240 + 280 + 310}{3} = 276.67$
  - MSE $= \dfrac{(240 - 276.67)^2 + (280 - 276.67)^2 + (310 - 276.67)^2}{3} = 822.22$

- Weighted average MSE $= \dfrac{2}{5} \cdot 625 + \dfrac{3}{5} \cdot 822.22 = 743.33$.

The split at 1.4 gives the lowest weighted MSE (743.33), and is therefore chosen for the root node. The predictions for the resulting leaf nodes are:

- Left node prediction: $\dfrac{150 + 200}{2} = 175$

- Right node prediction: $\dfrac{240 + 280 + 310}{3} = 276.67$

Split	Left Node Prices	Right Node Prices	Left MSE	Right MSE	Avg MSE
1.2	150	200, 240, 280, 310	0	1718.75	1375
1.4	150, 200	240, 280, 310	625	822.22	743.33
1.6	150, 200, 240	280, 310	1355.56	225	903.33
1.85	150, 200, 240, 280	310	2318.75	0	1855

Table 8.9: Mean squared error for each potential split in the regression tree example. The last column shows the average MSE across the child nodes, weighted by the proportion of samples in each node.

8.6.2 The `DecisionTreeRegressor` Class

Scikit-Learn provides an implementation of regression trees in the `DecisionTreeRegressor`[7] class. This class shares many parameters with `DecisionTreeClassifier`, but uses `'squared_error'` (MSE) as the criterion for node impurity, instead of `'gini'` or `'entropy'`.

To demonstrate this class, we apply it to the California housing dataset, which we previously analyzed with linear regression (Section 4.6) and k-nearest neighbors regression (Section 6.8). First, we fetch the dataset:

```
from sklearn.datasets import fetch_california_housing

data = fetch_california_housing()
X, y = data.data, data.target
feature_names = data.feature_names
```

Since the dataset has only numerical features and no missing values, no preprocessing is needed. Next, we split the dataset into training and test sets:

```
from sklearn.model_selection import train_test_split

X_train, X_test, y_train, y_test = train_test_split(X, y, test_size=0.2,
                                                    random_state=42)
```

We then train a `DecisionTreeRegressor` with default settings to establish a baseline performance:

```
from sklearn.tree import DecisionTreeRegressor

reg = DecisionTreeRegressor(random_state=42)
reg.fit(X_train, y_train)
```

The model's performance on the training and test sets is:

```
print(f'R2 score (train): {reg.score(X_train, y_train):.4f}')
print(f'R2 score (test): {reg.score(X_test, y_test):.4f}')
```

```
R2 score (train): 1.0000
R2 score (test): 0.6221
```

The large gap between the training and test scores indicates overfitting, which is common for unpruned trees. To address this, we can constrain the tree's size. Let's perform a grid search to find the optimal maximum depth and minimum number of samples per leaf:

---

7. https://scikit-learn.org/stable/modules/generated/sklearn.tree.DecisionTreeRegressor.html

```
from sklearn.model_selection import GridSearchCV

param_grid = {
    'max_depth': np.arange(5, 16),
    'min_samples_leaf': np.arange(2, 11),
}
reg = DecisionTreeRegressor(random_state=42)
grid_search = GridSearchCV(reg, param_grid, cv=3, n_jobs=-1)
grid_search.fit(X_train, y_train)
print(grid_search.best_params_)
```

```
{'max_depth': 13, 'min_samples_leaf': 10}
```

The performance of the optimized tree is:

```
print(f'R2 score (train): {grid_search.score(X_train, y_train):.4f}')
print(f'R2 score (test): {grid_search.score(X_test, y_test):.4f}')
```

```
R2 score (train): 0.8474
R2 score (test): 0.7227
```

The optimized tree achieves a significantly better score on the test set, outperforming both linear regression (test $R^2 = 0.5758$) and the KNN regressor (test $R^2 = 0.7168$) on this dataset.

Similar to classification trees, we can visualize the learned decision tree. However, the optimized tree has 13 levels, making it impractical to display in full. Thus, we limit the visualization to the first three levels:

```
from sklearn import tree

model = grid_search.best_estimator_
tree.plot_tree(model, max_depth=3, feature_names=feature_names,
               filled=True, rounded=True, fontsize=4)
```

Figure 8.17 shows the resulting regression tree.

8.6.2.1   Feature Importances

Decision trees can also provide insights into how much each input feature contributes to the model's predictions. This can be useful for both model interpretation and feature selection. Both `DecisionTreeClassifier` and `DecisionTreeRegressor` include a `feature_importances_` attribute, which quantifies how much each feature contributes to reducing the impurity. For each feature, these contributions are summed over all splits where it is used and weighted by the number of samples involved in each split. Lastly, the importances are normalized so that they sum to 1 across all features.

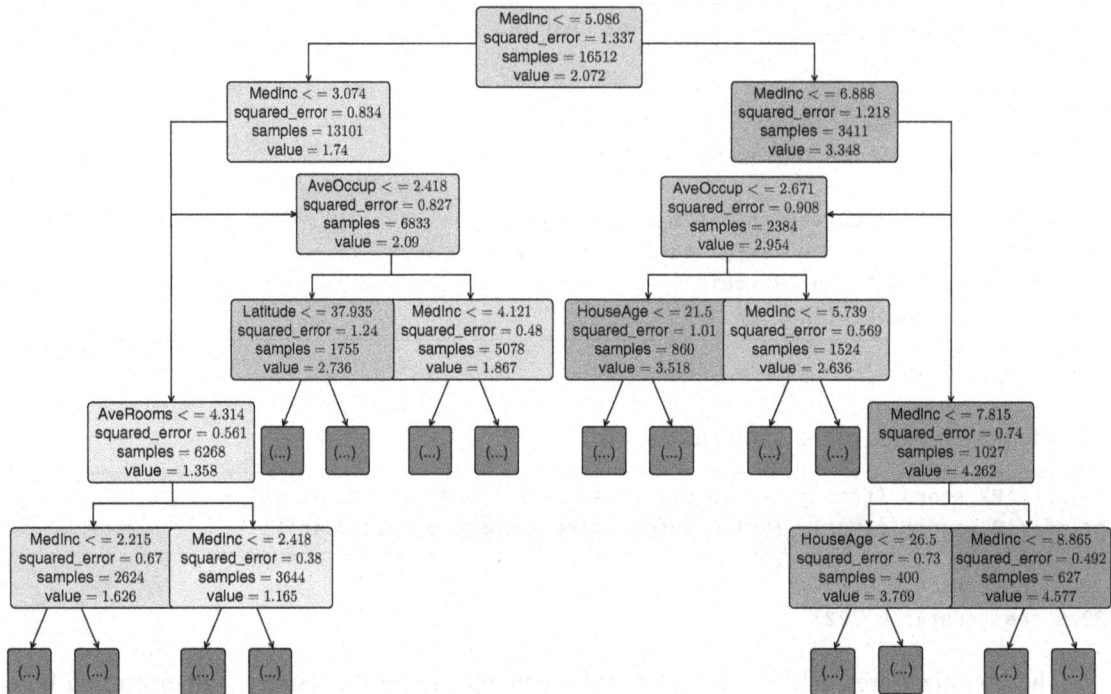

Figure 8.17: The first three levels of the optimized regression tree built on the California housing dataset. Each node displays the splitting feature and threshold, the sum of squared errors (number of samples × MSE), the number of samples, and the average target value. Color intensity represents the node's prediction, with darker shades indicating higher predicted values.

For the California housing dataset, we can identify the most important features as follows:

```
# Sort the features by their importance in descending order
sorted_idx = np.argsort(model.feature_importances_)[::-1]

for idx in sorted_idx:
    print(f'{feature_names[idx]}: {model.feature_importances_[idx]:.4f}')
```

```
MedInc: 0.6022
AveOccup: 0.1323
Latitude: 0.0849
Longitude: 0.0719
HouseAge: 0.0470
AveRooms: 0.0392
AveBedrms: 0.0118
Population: 0.0106
```

According to this measure, the most important features for predicting median house value are MedInc (median income), AveOccup (average occupancy per household), Latitude, and Longitude.

8.7 Multi-Output Problems

A **multi-output problem** is a supervised learning task where the objective is to predict multiple outputs simultaneously for a given input [638]. If the output variables are binary, it is referred to as **multi-label classification** [585]; if they are discrete with more than two categories, it is called **multi-output classification** [49]; and if they are continuous, it is known as **multi-output regression** (or **multivariate regression**) [74, 60].

In multi-output problems, each sample has a target vector of length m, and the targets for all samples form a two-dimensional matrix Y of size (n, m), where n is the number of samples and m is the number of outputs.

When the outputs are independent, a simple approach is to train a separate model for each output dimension. However, when the outputs are correlated, using a single model that predicts all m outputs jointly can be more effective. This joint modeling approach reduces training time (since only one model needs to be built) and can improve predictive accuracy by leveraging the relationships between the outputs. Several algorithms support this approach, including k-nearest neighbors, decision trees, and neural networks.

Multi-output problems arise in various domains, including image recognition (e.g., detecting multiple objects in an image), financial forecasting (e.g., predicting several related economic indicators), and medical diagnosis (e.g., predicting the presence of multiple related conditions).

Decision trees can naturally handle multi-output problems, with a few adaptations:

- Storing m output values at each leaf node instead of a single value.

- When evaluating splits, the impurity (e.g., Gini index, entropy, MSE) is computed separately for each output, and the impurity reductions are averaged across all m outputs.

The `DecisionTreeClassifier` class in Scikit-Learn automatically applies these adaptations when the parameter y passed to the `fit` method is a matrix of shape (n_samples, n_outputs).

8.7.1 Face Reconstruction Example

In this example, we use a multi-output regression tree to reconstruct images of face. The inputs x consist of the pixels from the upper half of each face, while the outputs y are the pixels from the lower half.

For this task, we use the Olivetti faces dataset[8] from Scikit-Learn. This dataset contains 400 grayscale images of 40 individuals (10 images per person) captured under varying conditions, including changes in lighting, facial expressions, and accessories such as glasses. Each image is 64×64 pixels, with pixel values normalized to the range [0, 1].

We first fetch the dataset:

```
from sklearn.datasets import fetch_olivetti_faces

X, y = fetch_olivetti_faces(return_X_y=True)
```

8. https://scikit-learn.org/stable/datasets/real_world.html#olivetti-faces-dataset

The shape of the feature matrix is:

```
X.shape
```

```
(400, 4096)
```

This indicates that X contains 400 images, each represented as a flat vector of 4096 pixel values. Let's plot the first 10 images:

```
n_faces = 10
fig, axes = plt.subplots(1, n_faces, figsize=(10, 10))
image_shape = (64, 64)

for ax, image in zip(axes, X[:n_faces]):
    ax.imshow(image.reshape(image_shape), cmap='gray')
    ax.axis('off')
```

As shown in Figure 8.18, these images depict variations of the same individual, taken from different angles and under varying lighting conditions.

Next, we create the training and test sets for the image reconstruction task. To ensure an objective evaluation, we test our model on images of individuals who are not part of the training set. Since the label vector y contains person indices from 0 to 39, we can use it to designate the images of the last 5 individuals as the test set:

```
# Separate images of individuals not seen during training
train = X[y < 35] # Training set: individuals 0 to 34
test = X[y >= 35] # Test set: individuals 35 to 39
```

We now define the inputs and outputs for the reconstruction task. The inputs are the pixels from the upper half of each face, and the outputs are the corresponding pixels from the lower half:

```
n_pixels = X.shape[1]
n_half = n_pixels // 2
# Upper half of the faces used as input
X_train = train[:, :n_half]
X_test = test[:, :n_half]

# Lower half of the faces used as output
Y_train = train[:, n_half:]
Y_test = test[:, n_half:]
```

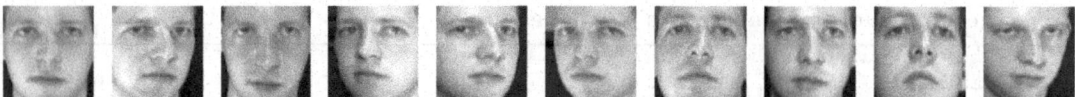

Figure 8.18: The first 10 images from the Olivetti faces dataset, showing variations in orientation and lighting for the same individual. (Images: AT&T Laboratories Cambridge)

Next, we fit a regression tree to the training set:

```
from sklearn.tree import DecisionTreeRegressor

model = DecisionTreeRegressor(random_state=42)
model.fit(X_train, Y_train)
```

To evaluate the model's performance, we use the mean absolute error (MAE), which is well-suited for this task because it directly measures the average deviation in pixel intensity between the predicted and true images. In image reconstruction, this provides an intuitive sense of how far, on average, the predictions are from the actual pixel values.[9]

```
from sklearn.metrics import mean_absolute_error as MAE

Y_train_pred = model.predict(X_train)
print(f'MAE (train): {MAE(Y_train, Y_train_pred):.4f}')
Y_test_pred = model.predict(X_test)
print(f'MAE (test): {MAE(Y_test, Y_test_pred):.4f}')
```

```
MAE (train): 0.0000
MAE (test): 0.1335
```

The model achieves a perfect score on the training set. Test performance is also strong, with a mean absolute error of 0.1335 per pixel. Since pixel intensities are scaled between 0 and 1, this represents a relatively small reconstruction error.

To visually inspect the reconstruction results, we display 10 random test images alongside their reconstructions:

```
# Choose 10 random test images
n_test_faces = 10
face_ids = np.random.RandomState(42).choice(len(X_test), size=n_test_faces,
                                            replace=False)

# Plot the original and reconstructed faces
fig, axes = plt.subplots(2, n_test_faces, figsize=(10, 2))
for i, face_id in enumerate(face_ids):
    original_face = test[face_id]

    # Combine the original upper half with the predicted lower half
    reconstructed_face = np.hstack((X_test[face_id], Y_test_pred[face_id]))
```

---

9. Although R^2 is a common regression metric, it can be misleading in multi-output tasks such as image reconstruction. This is because R^2 compares the prediction error to the variance of the true values for each output. If the variance of some pixel values is very low (e.g., in background regions), even small prediction errors can result in negative R^2 scores, suggesting poor performance despite low absolute error.

```
axes[0, i].imshow(original_face.reshape(image_shape), cmap='gray')
axes[1, i].imshow(reconstructed_face.reshape(image_shape), cmap='gray')

if i == 0:
    # Label the first column and hide ticks
    axes[0, i].set_ylabel('Original', size=8)
    axes[1, i].set_ylabel('Reconstructed', size=8)
    for row in range(2):
        axes[row, i].set_xticks([])
        axes[row, i].set_yticks([])
else:
    # Hide axes for the other columns
    axes[0, i].axis('off')
    axes[1, i].axis('off')
```

Figure 8.19 displays the reconstructed faces, showing a mix of well-reconstructed images and others with noticeable inaccuracies. Despite the limited training data, the model captures the general facial structure reasonably well.

8.8   Oblique Decision Trees

All the decision trees discussed so far fall under the category of **univariate decision trees (UDTs)**, where each node split is based on a single feature (e.g., $x < 10$). In contrast, **multivariate decision trees (MDTs)** allow splits that involve multiple features, such as $2x_1 + 5x_2 < 20$ [77, 89].

A common type of multivariate split is a **linear split**, which compares a linear combination of the input features to a threshold:

$$\sum_{j=1}^{d} w_j x_j < v, \tag{8.16}$$

where w_j is the coefficient for feature j and v is the threshold.

Figure 8.19: Original (top row) and reconstructed (bottom row) faces from the Olivetti dataset, with the lower half of each face predicted by the regression tree model. (Images: AT&T Laboratories Cambridge)

This inequality defines a hyperplane in the feature space. While axis-parallel splits in UDTs produce decision boundaries aligned with the coordinate axes, linear splits in MDTs form **oblique hyperplanes**—boundaries that can be oriented at arbitrary angles. This flexibility allows MDTs to capture more complex interactions between features and increases the representational capacity of the model.

Decision trees that use multivariate linear splits are known as **oblique decision trees (ODTs)** [434]. ODTs generalize axis-parallel trees: if each split uses only a single nonzero weight, the tree reduces to the standard univariate form.

ODTs often produce more compact trees, requiring fewer nodes and shallower depth to match or exceed the accuracy of UDTs, especially when the data exhibit complex, nonlinear relationships among features.

For example, consider a dataset with two features, x and y, where the optimal decision boundary is diagonal, such as $x + y = v$ for some constant v (see Figure 8.20). A univariate decision tree would need many axis-aligned splits to approximate this boundary, resulting in a deep and complex tree structure. Conversely, an oblique decision tree can separate the classes with a single split of the form $x + y < v$.

While oblique trees are more expressive, they also have several drawbacks:

- Higher computational cost: Finding the optimal split in each node requires solving a high-dimensional optimization problem, making ODT construction significantly more expensive than that of standard trees.

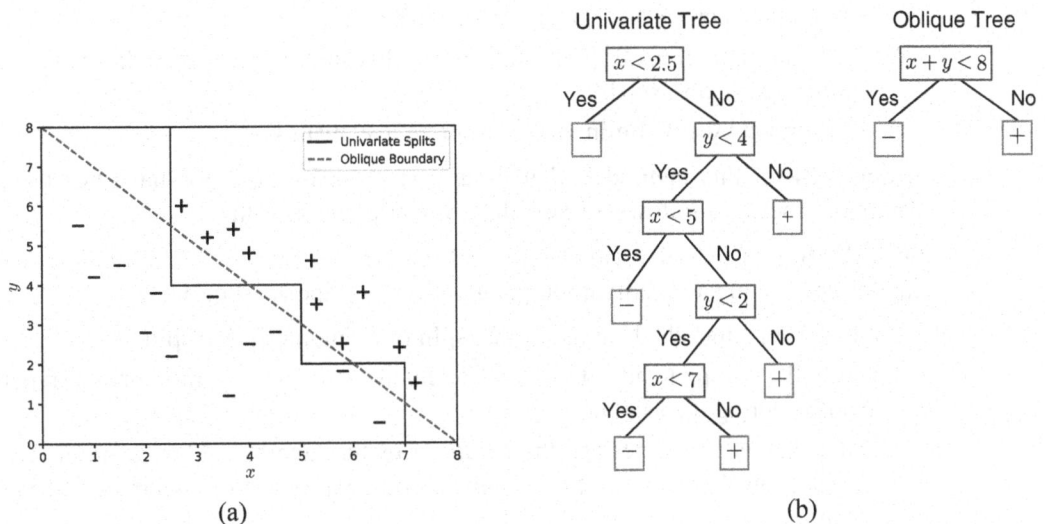

Figure 8.20: Comparison of univariate and oblique decision trees on a two-class dataset separated by a diagonal boundary. (a) Multiple axis-aligned splits (solid lines) are needed to approximate the boundary while a single oblique split (dashed line) suffices. (b) The resulting tree structures: the oblique tree achieves perfect separation in one split, whereas the univariate tree requires multiple levels.

- Risk of overfitting: Their greater flexibility can lead to overfitting to the training data, producing overly complex boundaries that generalize poorly.

- Reduced interpretability: Since each oblique split involves multiple features, the resulting decisions are less intuitive and harder to explain.

8.8.1   (*) Inducing Oblique Trees

Constructing an oblique decision tree involves determining the coefficients $\mathbf{w} = (w_1, \ldots, w_d)$ and the threshold v that define each multivariate split. Since exhaustively searching over all possible coefficient values is computationally infeasible[10], numerous algorithms have been developed to efficiently approximate high-quality splits. These algorithms can be broadly grouped into the following families:

- **Local search methods**: These methods iteratively refine an initial split, typically chosen at random or based on a univariate split, by optimizing the coefficients until a stopping criterion is met. Two prominent algorithms in this family include:

  - **CART-LC (Classification and Regression Trees with Linear Combination)** [73] is an extension to CART that supports linear combinations of features at each split:
    * Begin with the best univariate split.
    * Use hill climbing to iteratively adjust the split coefficients one at a time, testing small adjustments (± 0.25) for each coefficient w_j.
    * Cycle through all coefficients until no further improvement in split quality (e.g., Gini index) is observed.
    * Perform backward elimination to remove irrelevant features.

    A drawback of this method is that it can get stuck in local optima, since the hill-climbing procedure follows a fixed, deterministic search path.

  - **OC1 (Oblique Classifier 1)** [434] extends CART-LC by introducing random perturbations and conjugate gradient jumps in order to escape local optima:
    * Start from either the best univariate split or a random initial split.
    * Use hill climbing to adjust one coefficient at a time, incorporating random perturbations during the search.
    * After convergence, perturb the resulting hyperplane by adding a small random vector to its direction vector $\mathbf{w}$, encouraging exploration of nearby directions in feature space.
    * Perform multiple random restarts to explore different regions of the search space.

    OC1 often achieves higher accuracy and more stable solutions than CART-LC.

---

10. The problem of finding the optimal multivariate split at a given node is NP-hard [263].

- **Statistical methods** [378, 278, 376]: These methods generate candidate linear combinations of features (e.g., using linear discriminant analysis) and evaluate their association with the target using statistical tests (e.g., ANOVA for continuous targets or chi-square for categorical targets). The optimal split point along each projection is then computed analytically, often under distributional assumptions such as multivariate normality. These methods are highly efficient as they rely on closed-form solutions rather than iterative optimization.

- **Global search methods**: These methods explore large regions of the parameter space using global optimization techniques such as simulated annealing or genetic algorithms. A notable example is **GATree** [465, 340], which uses genetic programming to evolve both the tree structure and the split parameters, optimizing a fitness function that balances predictive accuracy and model complexity.

- **Geometrical approaches**: These approaches exploit the geometric structure of the data to define splits based on class-specific spatial patterns. A representative example is the **Geometric Decision Tree** algorithm [396], which constructs one hyperplane per class by minimizing the average Euclidean distance of class members to their respective hyperplane. The final split is then chosen based on either the midpoint (for parallel hyperplanes) or the angle bisector that minimizes impurity.

- **Linear programming methods**: These methods formulate tree induction as a mixed-integer optimization (MIO) problem, with continuous variables for split coefficients and integer variables for binary routing decisions. A prominent example is **OCT (Optimal Classification Trees)** [47], which jointly optimizes the tree structure and the split parameters within a compact MIO formulation. When solved to completion, OCT yields globally optimal trees for the specified objective and constraints (e.g., maximum depth or minimum leaf size).

- **Neural approaches**: These methods extend oblique decision trees by replacing linear split functions with nonlinear splits modeled by neural networks. In **Neural Trees** [244], each internal node contains a small neural network that transforms the input features before applying a threshold, enabling the model to learn complex, nonlinear decision boundaries while preserving the tree's hierarchical structure. More recent variants, such as **Deep Neural Decision Trees (DNDT)** [645], combine deep neural architectures with decision trees to further enhance expressive power.

8.9   Summary

This chapter provided a comprehensive exploration of decision trees, from their basic definition and construction algorithm to advanced variants such as oblique trees. We examined how trees recursively partition the feature space using simple decision rules derived from impurity measures such as information gain and the Gini index, and demonstrated their application in both classification and regression tasks. Practical aspects such as handling continuous features, missing values, and multi-output problems were also addressed, along with pruning strategies to control overfitting. Decision trees serve not only as powerful standalone models but also as the foundation for ensemble methods such as random forests and gradient boosting, which will be covered in the next chapter.

Advantages of decision trees compared to other supervised learning models:

- They are easy to understand and interpret, making them transparent "white-box" models.

- They are highly flexible, capable of modeling complex, nonlinear relationships in the data and achieving perfect separation between classes on the training set.

- They make no assumptions about feature types or the underlying data distribution.

- They require minimal data preparation: they can natively handle categorical features, tolerate missing values during training and prediction, and do not require feature scaling.

- They automatically capture feature interactions (i.e., feature crosses), reducing the need for manual feature engineering.

- They support both classification (including multi-label and multi-output) and regression tasks.

- They provide fast prediction times, proportional to the tree depth (typically logarithmic in the number of training samples).

- They offer feature importance scores that can aid in model interpretation and feature selection.

- They are robust to irrelevant and redundant features, as these are unlikely to be selected for splits.

Disadvantages of decision trees:

- They are prone to overfitting, especially when fully grown; pruning or ensemble methods can help mitigate this.

- They are built greedily, selecting locally optimal splits without guaranteeing a globally optimal or minimal tree.

- They produce axis-aligned (rectilinear) decision boundaries, which may struggle with complex geometric patterns. Oblique decision trees can mitigate this limitation.

- They are sensitive to small changes in the data, which can lead to significantly different tree structures.

- They can be computationally and memory intensive on large or high-dimensional datasets, as the trees may become deep and complex.

- They tend to perform poorly on imbalanced datasets, often favoring the majority class. This can be mitigated with resampling techniques (e.g., SMOTE) or by adjusting class weights.

- While small trees are easy to interpret, large or deep trees can become difficult to understand due to the many branches and conditions.

- Regression trees produce piecewise-constant predictions and may struggle to extrapolate beyond the range of the training data.

8.10 Exercises

8.10.1 Multiple-Choice Questions

8.1. Which of the following statements about decision trees is true?

 (a) Increasing the depth of a decision tree leads to a decrease in test accuracy.

 (b) Information gain is always strictly positive at every split.

 (c) Decision trees are invariant to monotonic transformations of features, such as taking the logarithm or squaring a feature.

 (d) Pruning a decision tree always leads to a decrease in training accuracy.

8.2. Consider a node in a decision tree containing samples from four classes, with the following number of samples from each class: [10, 20, 30, 40]. What is the entropy at this node?

 (a) 1.5

 (b) 1.85

 (c) 2.1

 (d) 2.25

8.3. For the dataset in Table 8.10, which feature gives the highest information gain when used as the root split?

 (a) A

 (b) B

 (c) C

 (d) D

A	B	C	D	Y
1	Low	High	Even	Positive
0	Medium	High	Odd	Negative
0	High	Low	Odd	Positive
0	Low	Medium	Even	Negative
1	Medium	Low	Odd	Positive

Table 8.10: Sample dataset with four categorical features and a target variable Y

8.4. A decision tree classifier, using the Gini index as the splitting criterion, splits a node into two child nodes with the following class distributions:

- Left child: 5 samples of class 0, 15 samples of class 1.
- Right child: 8 samples of class 0, 2 samples of class 1.

What is the reduction in the Gini index after the split?

(a) 0.134

(b) 0.257

(c) 0.368

(d) 0.491

8.5. Which strategies can help mitigate the risk of overfitting in decision trees?

(a) Ensuring that each leaf node contains samples from only one class.

(b) Using multivariate splits instead of univariate splits.

(c) Limiting the number of nodes in the tree.

(d) Using L2 regularization.

(e) Applying post-pruning to remove branches that do not improve the model's performance.

8.6. We have a dataset with a single feature and the following values along with their corresponding class labels:

- Feature values: 1, 2, 4, 5, 7, 8, 10, 11, 12, 14
- Class labels: A, A, B, B, A, B, A, A, A, B

Which of the following values would be the optimal threshold for splitting on this feature in order to minimize the Gini index? (ties are possible)

(a) 3

(b) 6

(c) 9

(d) 13

8.7. Which of the following statements about cost-complexity pruning is true?

(a) As α increases, branches that contribute least to reducing the training error are pruned first.

(b) Higher values of α tend to prune deeper branches first.

(c) For any subtree T_t and $\alpha > 0$, $R_\alpha(T_t) \geq R_\alpha(t)$.

(d) There may be two subtrees t_1 and t_2 of T, where t_1 is contained within t_2, and both have the same $g(t)$ value.

8.8. In which of the following scenarios would a decision tree most likely underperform compared to a linear model?

(a) The dataset contains categorical features with high cardinality and no natural ordering.

(b) The dataset contains a high number of features, most of which are noisy or irrelevant.

(c) The dataset consists of mostly linear relationships between the features and the target variable, with minimal interactions.

(d) The dataset is imbalanced, with one class being significantly underrepresented.

8.9. How does `DecisionTreeClassifier` handle missing values during training?

(a) It ignores any instance that contains missing values.

(b) It imputes the missing values before making a split.

(c) It applies a probability weighting scheme to distribute samples with missing values across all branches.

(d) It directs all samples with missing values to the child node that maximizes impurity reduction.

8.10. Consider the data points shown in Figure 8.21. Which of the following decision tree classifiers can perfectly classify all these points with four or fewer splits?

(a) A standard decision tree with axis-aligned splits

(b) Adding a new feature $|x_1| + |x_2|$ to each data point and then applying a standard decision tree

(c) A standard decision tree with polynomial features of degree 2

(d) An oblique decision tree with multivariate linear splits

8.10.2 Theoretical Exercises

8.11. Suppose you and your friends are stranded on a tropical island with a variety of unfamiliar fruits. To survive, you must figure out which fruits are safe to eat. Four people try fruits A, B, D, and E and find them edible, while five others try different fruits C, F, G, H, and I, and experience stomach aches.

Based on this, you have collected training data for these nine fruits, summarized in Table 8.11. Each fruit is described by four binary attributes: shape (IsRound), appearance (IsColorful), texture (HasSpikes), and taste (IsSweet). Your task is to use this information to predict the edibility of three new fruits (J, K, and L) based on their features.

(a) Calculate the entropy for the IsEdible attribute.

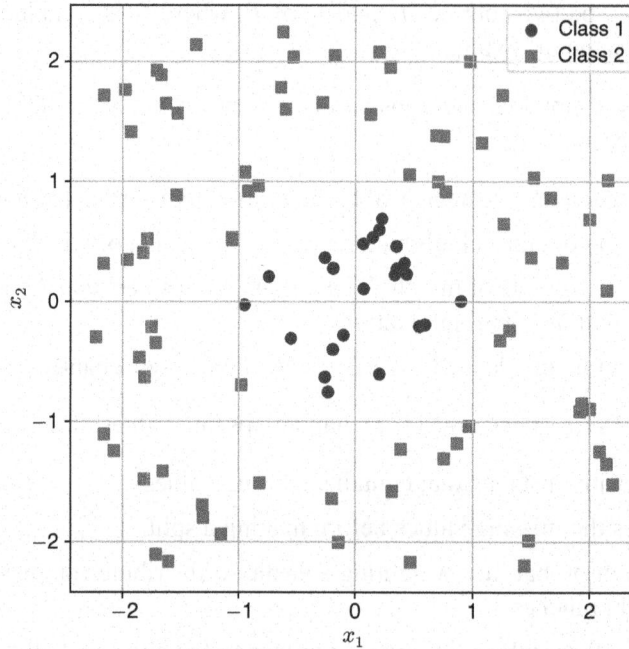

Figure 8.21: Scatter plot of a dataset with two classes. Blue points (Class 1) are clustered in a diamond-shaped region near the center, while purple squares (Class 2) are distributed outside this region.

Sample	IsRound	IsColorful	HasSpikes	IsSweet	IsEdible
A	1	1	0	1	Yes
B	1	1	0	0	Yes
C	0	1	1	1	No
D	1	0	1	0	Yes
E	0	1	0	1	Yes
F	0	0	1	1	No
G	1	0	0	0	No
H	1	0	1	1	No
I	0	1	1	1	No
J	1	1	0	0	?
K	0	0	1	1	?
L	1	1	1	0	?

Table 8.11: Sample dataset of fruits from a tropical island, where the goal is to predict edibility based on four attributes.

(b) Determine which attribute should be at the root of the decision tree using information gain as the splitting criterion. Show your calculations.

(c) Construct the full decision tree by inspecting the data directly. No need to compute information gain at every level.

(d) Using your decision tree, classify the new fruits J, K, and L.

8.12. In this exercise, you will explore several fundamental properties of entropy. Let X be a discrete random variable with k possible outcomes and probability distribution $\mathbf{p} = (p_1, p_2, \ldots, p_k)$. The entropy of X is defined as:

$$H(X) = -\sum_{i=1}^{k} p_i \log_2 p_i.$$

(a) Prove that $H(X) \geq 0$ for any probability distribution $\mathbf{p}$.

(b) Show that the entropy $H(X)$ is maximized when the distribution $\mathbf{p}$ is uniform, i.e., $p_i = 1/k$ for all i. Express the maximum entropy in terms of k.

(c) Prove that entropy is a concave function of the probability distribution $\mathbf{p}$. *Hint*: Use Jensen's inequality (see Section B.11.8) and the fact that $\log(x)$ is concave.

(d) Let X and Y be two independent random variables with entropies $H(X)$ and $H(Y)$, respectively. Prove that their **joint entropy** $H(X, Y)$, which is the entropy of their joint distribution, is equal to the sum of their individual entropies:

$$H(X, Y) = H(X) + H(Y).$$

(e) For any two random variables X and Y, prove that the joint entropy satisfies:

$$H(X, Y) \leq H(X) + H(Y).$$

(f) The **conditional entropy** of X given Y is defined as:

$$H(X|Y) = H(X, Y) - H(Y).$$

Prove that $H(X|Y) \leq H(X)$, showing that conditioning on Y does not increase the uncertainty about X. *Hint*: Equality holds if and only if X and Y are independent.

(g) The **mutual information** between X and Y is defined as the reduction in uncertainty about X due to knowledge of Y:

$$I(X; Y) = H(X) - H(X|Y).$$

Using the result from the previous part, prove that $I(X; Y) \geq 0$, and conclude that mutual information is zero if and only if X and Y are independent.

8.13. Prove that any split in a decision tree yields a non-negative information gain, i.e., the entropy of a parent node is always greater than or equal to the weighted average of the entropies of its child nodes. Follow these steps:

   (a) Express the entropy of the parent node in terms of the overall class probabilities q_j and the entropy of each child node in terms of its class probabilities p_{ij}.

   (b) Define w_i as the fraction of samples that go to child node i. Express the weighted average entropy of the child nodes in terms of w_i and p_{ij}.

   (c) Write the information gain as the difference between the entropy of the parent node and the weighted average entropy of the child nodes.

   (d) Substitute $q_j = \sum_{i=1}^{m} w_i p_{ij}$ (the total probability of class j across all child nodes) into the information gain expression.

   (e) Show that the resulting expression can be written as a sum of terms involving $\log\left(\frac{p_{ij}}{q_j}\right)$.

   (f) Use Jensen's inequality and the convexity of $-\log(x)$ to conclude that this expression is always non-negative.

8.14. In this exercise, you will explore several properties of the Gini index. Let X be a discrete random variable with k possible classes and a probability distribution $\mathbf{p} = (p_1, p_2, \ldots, p_k)$. The Gini index of X is defined as:

$$G(X) = 1 - \sum_{i=1}^{k} p_i^2.$$

   (a) Prove that $G(X) \geq 0$ for any probability distribution $\mathbf{p}$.

   (b) Show that the Gini index $G(X)$ is maximized when $\mathbf{p}$ is a uniform distribution, i.e., when $p_i = \frac{1}{k}$ for all i. Express the maximum value in terms of k.

   (c) Show that the Gini index is minimized (i.e., $G(X) = 0$) when X has a degenerate distribution, meaning that all probability mass is concentrated on a single class.

   (d) (*) Prove that the Gini index of the parent node is always greater than or equal to the weighted average of the Gini indices of the child nodes, i.e.,

$$G(\text{Parent}) \geq \sum_{i=1}^{m} w_i G(C_i),$$

   where w_i is the fraction of samples that go to child node C_i and $G(C_i)$ denotes the Gini index of child node C_i.

8.15. The **misclassification rate** is sometimes suggested as a simpler alternative to impurity measures such as entropy or the Gini index for evaluating splits in decision trees. Let X be a discrete random variable with k possible classes and a probability distribution

$\mathbf{p} = (p_1, p_2, \ldots, p_k)$. The misclassification rate of X is defined as the proportion of samples that do not belong to the majority class:

$$M(X) = 1 - \max_{1 \le i \le k} p_i.$$

(a) Explain why using misclassification rate as the splitting criterion may lead to suboptimal splits compared to entropy or Gini index.

(b) Provide a numerical example for a binary split that produces purer child nodes (as measured by the Gini index) but leaves the misclassification rate unchanged.

8.16. Consider the majority function on n binary variables $x_1, x_2, \ldots, x_n$, which outputs 1 if more than half of the variables are 1, and 0 otherwise.

(a) Show that any decision tree that computes the majority function for n variables requires at least $2^{\frac{n}{2}}$ nodes.

(b) Explain why a simple linear model, such as logistic regression, can represent the majority function using only n coefficients.

(c) What are the implications of this result for the efficiency of decision trees when representing Boolean or other discrete functions?

8.17. Let X be a continuous feature with sorted values $x_1 < x_2 < \cdots < x_n$, and let $y_i \in \{0, 1\}$ denote the binary class label corresponding to x_i. Consider potential split points that lie between each pair of adjacent feature values, that is, in the interval (x_i, x_{i+1}) for $i = 1, \ldots, n-1$.

Prove that the split point that achieves the highest information gain must lie between two adjacent values x_i and x_{i+1} whose class labels differ (i.e., $y_i \ne y_{i+1}$).

8.18. You are provided with a dataset from an online retail store, which includes data about past purchases of customers, such as the time spent on the website (in minutes), number of page views, their membership status, and whether or not they made a purchase (see Table 8.12). Your goal is to construct a decision tree that uses these features to determine the likelihood of a purchase.

(a) Build a complete decision tree for this dataset using the Gini index as the impurity criterion. You may treat both TimeOnSite and PageViews as continuous features.

(b) Predict the outcome for new customers with the following attributes:
- <TimeOnSite = 50, PageViews = 10, Membership = Yes>
- <TimeOnSite = 25, PageViews = 22, Membership = No>

8.19. Consider the decision tree shown in Figure 8.22, which is used to classify a dataset of 30 data points: 12 positive and 18 negative examples. Prune the tree using the cost-complexity pruning method, removing one subtree at a time in order of weakest link (smallest α) until only the root node remains. Show the sequence of α values generated during the pruning process.

	TimeOnSite	PageViews	Membership	Purchase
1	5	8	No	No
2	45	15	Yes	Yes
3	20	25	No	Yes
4	35	18	Yes	No
5	15	5	Yes	No
6	60	30	Yes	Yes
7	10	9	No	No
8	40	20	No	Yes

Table 8.12: Sample dataset from an online retail store

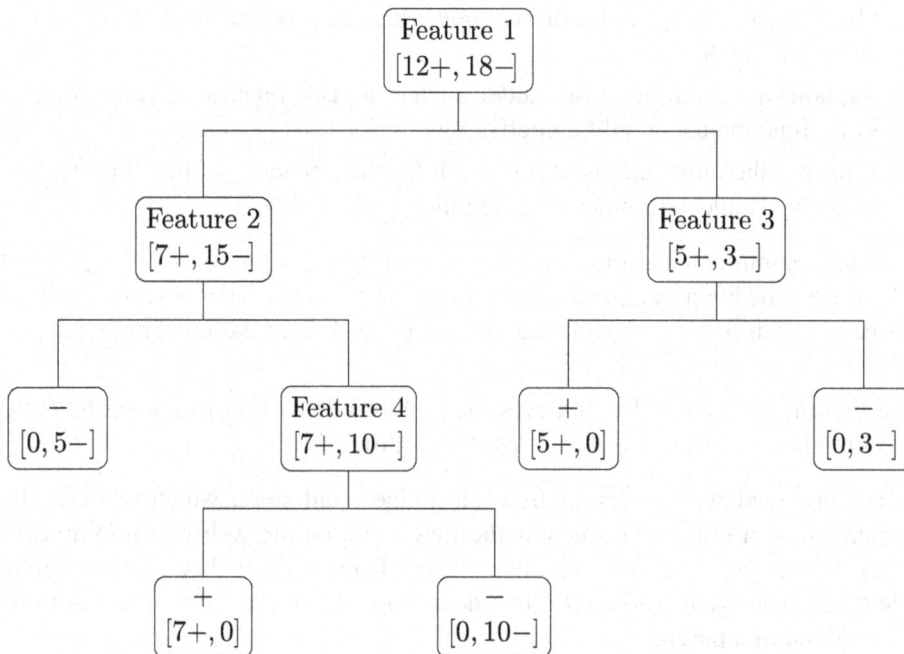

Figure 8.22: Decision tree used to demonstrate cost-complexity pruning

8.20. Prove the following properties of cost-complexity pruning:

(a) Show that the first subtree to be pruned (i.e., the one corresponding to the smallest value of α) is the one that minimizes the ratio $\frac{\Delta R(T_t)}{\Delta |\tilde{T}_t|}$, where $\Delta R(T_t)$ is the increase in training error when the subtree T_t is replaced by a leaf, and $\Delta |\tilde{T}_t|$ is the corresponding reduction in the number of leaves.

(b) Prove that the sequence of pruned trees $T(\alpha)$ forms a nested sequence, i.e., if $\alpha_1 < \alpha_2$, then $T(\alpha_2)$ is a subtree of $T(\alpha_1)$. In other words, any node pruned at a particular α remains pruned for all higher values of α.

(c) Prove that the training error of the pruned tree $T(\alpha)$ is monotonically non-decreasing as α increases. That is, show that if $\alpha_1 < \alpha_2$, then $R(T(\alpha_1)) \leq R(T(\alpha_2))$.

8.21. A **piecewise constant function** is a function that takes on constant values within specific, non-overlapping regions of the input space, with changes in value occurring only at boundaries between regions. Formally, suppose the input space $\mathbb{R}^d$ is divided into N disjoint regions $R_1, R_2, \ldots, R_N$. Then a piecewise constant function $f \colon \mathbb{R}^d \to \mathbb{R}$ can be written as:

$$f(\mathbf{x}) = c_i, \quad \text{for } \mathbf{x} \in R_i,$$

where c_i is a constant for each region R_i.

(a) Show that a regression tree generates a piecewise constant function for the target variable.

(b) Explain why this piecewise constant structure may be less effective for modeling functions that are continuous and smooth.

(c) Describe a scenario where a simple linear model such as linear regression may perform better than a regression tree when approximating a continuous function.

8.22. Investigate methods for constructing oblique decision trees, including OC1 [434], QUEST [378], OCT [47], and two other methods of your choice.

(a) For each method, provide:
- a brief description of how the tree is constructed, including the key algorithms or optimization techniques used.
- an analysis of the time complexity for both training and prediction.

(b) Compare the advantages and disadvantages of these methods. Address the following factors:
- Optimality of the splits
- Susceptibility to local minima
- Risk of overfitting
- Computational complexity and scalability
- Ease of implementation and practical use cases

8.10.3 Programming Exercises

8.23. Build a decision tree classifier for income prediction using the Adult Income dataset[11] (see Section 3.10.8). The dataset includes features such as age, education, occupation, and hours worked per week, with a binary target variable indicating whether income is greater than $50,000 or not. Follow these steps:

---

11. https://archive.ics.uci.edu/ml/datasets/adult

(a) Load the dataset using the following code:

```
from sklearn.datasets import fetch_openml

X, y = fetch_openml('adult', version=2, return_X_y=True, as_frame=True)
```

(b) Encode the categorical variables using one-hot encoding.

(c) Train a `DecisionTreeClassifier` with default parameters to establish a baseline model.

(d) Evaluate the model using metrics such as accuracy, precision, recall, F1 score, and ROC-AUC score.

(e) Use grid search to optimize the hyperparameters, including the impurity criterion, maximum depth, minimum samples per leaf, and cost-complexity pruning parameter (`ccp_alpha`).

(f) Compare your optimized model to the baseline.

(g) Address class imbalance using techniques such as resampling or class weighting, and compare the results to the previous models.

(h) Analyze the confusion matrix to understand the model's performance in terms of false positives and false negatives.

(i) Visualize the decision tree (limit `max_depth` for readability).

(j) Identify the most important features for predicting income using feature importances.

8.24. Implement the decision tree construction algorithm and cost-complexity pruning in Python from scratch. Use the following steps:

(a) Basic decision tree implementation:

  i. Implement the tree construction algorithm as described in Algorithm 8.1, using information gain as the splitting criterion. You can assume that all features are continuous, except for the discrete target variable. Restrict the tree to binary splits only.

  ii. Include an optional parameter to control the maximum depth of the tree. If no maximum depth is specified, build the entire tree until all leaves are pure or no further splitting is possible. Otherwise, stop building the tree once the specified depth has been reached.

  iii. Implement a simple text-based visualization of the decision tree using ASCII characters. For example:

```
|-- [Feature1 <= 2.5]
|   |-- [Feature2 <= 1.5]: Class A
|   |-- [Feature2 > 1.5]: Class B
|-- [Feature1 > 2.5]: Class C
```

iv. Test your implementation on the Iris dataset and display the resulting decision tree. Compare your tree to the one produced by `DecisionTreeClassifier` in Scikit-Learn. Analyze and discuss any differences in structure and performance between the two trees.

(b) Handling missing values:

   i. Extend your decision tree implementation to handle datasets with missing values using at least three of the following approaches:

     A. Ignore features with missing values when considering candidate splits.

     B. Handle samples with missing values by sending them down all possible branches of the split and aggregating the predictions using weighted probabilities.

     C. Impute the missing values using the mean or median of the feature values within the current node.

     D. Evaluate the impurity reduction for directing samples with missing values to the left or right child node, and choose the direction that results in greater impurity reduction.

   ii. Compare the performance of your chosen approaches on datasets with varying levels of missing data. Use an existing dataset (e.g., Iris or Wine from Scikit-Learn), and randomly replace a specified percentage (e.g., 10%, 30%, 50%) of entries with `NaN` values. Ensure that the missing values are distributed across different features. Run multiple simulations to obtain robust comparisons.

(c) Cost-complexity pruning:

   i. Implement the cost-complexity pruning algorithm as described in Section 8.3.2.

   ii. Allow users to specify the complexity parameter α to control the extent of pruning.

   iii. Test your pruning algorithm on the Iris dataset. Visualize the decision tree before and after pruning for different values of α.

   iv. Generate plots that show the impact of various α values on the size of the tree and the model's cross-validated accuracy.

8.25. Build a regression tree to predict hourly bike rentals using the Bike Sharing dataset[12] from the UCI machine learning repository. The dataset contains hourly data from a bike rental system in Washington D.C., with features such as time of day, weather conditions, temperature, and windspeed. The target variable is the number of bikes rented per hour. Use the following steps:

(a) Download and extract the dataset from the UCI machine learning repository. Load the `hour.csv` file into a DataFrame.

(b) Perform exploratory data analysis (EDA) to explore the features, identify patterns, and understand relationships within the data.

(c) Drop the `dteday` column, as its information is already captured by other features such as `yr`, `mnth`, `hr`, and `weekday`.

---

12. `https://archive.ics.uci.edu/dataset/275/bike+sharing+dataset`

(d) Encode integer categorical variables such as `mnth`, `hr`, and `holiday` using one-hot encoding. This can improve performance by allowing the model to treat them as discrete categories.

(e) Split the dataset into training and test sets.

(f) Train a `DecisionTreeRegressor` with default parameters to establish a baseline and evaluate it using metrics such as RMSE and R^2 score.

(g) Use grid search to optimize hyperparameters such as `max_depth` and `min_samples_leaf`.

(h) Engineer new features that might improve the model's performance, such as a binary `is_peak_hour` indicator for common rush hours.

(i) Evaluate the performance of the optimized model and compare it to the baseline.

(j) Analyze the residuals to identify any patterns that the model fails to capture.

(k) Visualize the decision tree to understand how the model partitions the feature space.

(l) Identify the features that have the greatest impact on bike rental volumes.

8.26. Build a multi-output decision tree model to predict students' scores in mathematics, reading, and writing based on demographic and school-related attributes. Use the Student Performance in Exams[13] dataset from Kaggle. Follow these steps:

(a) Load the dataset into a DataFrame.

(b) Preprocess the features:

    i. Apply one-hot encoding to categorical variables.

    ii. Define the target as a vector of the three continuous scores: `math score`, `reading score`, and `writing score`.

(c) Split the data into training and test sets.

(d) Train a multi-output `DecisionTreeRegressor` (with default parameters) on the training set.

(e) Evaluate the model's performance:

    i. Report RMSE and R^2 score for each target variable on the test set, and the macro-average (mean across the three outputs).

    ii. Create a residual plot for each target to inspect systematic errors.

(f) Hyperparameter tuning:

    i. Use grid search over `max_depth`, `min_samples_leaf`, and `ccp_alpha`.

    ii. Compare the tuned model's performance to the baseline.

---

13. https://www.kaggle.com/datasets/spscientist/students-performance-in-exams

    (g) Compare models:

        i. Train three separate single-output trees (one per subject) and compare them to the multi-output tree in terms of RMSE/R^2 score, depth, and number of leaves.

        ii. Train a linear regression model and compare its performance to the tree-based models.

    (h) Interpretability:

        i. Visualize the decision tree (limit `max_depth` for readability).

        ii. Compute and discuss feature importances; identify the top factors influencing each score.

8.27. (*) In this exercise, you will implement the OC1 (Oblique Classifier 1) algorithm from scratch and compare its performance to a standard univariate decision tree.

    (a) Thoroughly read and understand the paper "A System for Induction of Oblique Decision Trees" by Murthy et al., which introduced the OC1 algorithm [434].

    (b) Implement the OC1 algorithm:

        i. Initialize the split at each node using a univariate threshold on one feature.

        ii. Use hill-climbing to adjust the coefficients of a linear combination of features, improving the impurity reduction at the node. Introduce small random perturbations to the coefficients to escape local optima.

        iii. After the hill-climbing converges, perturb the hyperplane coefficients by adding a small random vector to explore alternative directions and escape local optima.

        iv. Use multiple random restarts to increase the likelihood of finding a good split.

        v. Recursively apply this process at each child node to construct the full tree.

    (c) Model comparison and analysis:

        i. Select a classification dataset for comparison. You can use a built-in dataset from Scikit-Learn, such as Wine, Breast Cancer, or Digits.

        ii. Split it into training and testing sets (e.g., an 80–20 split).

        iii. Standardize the features to ensure fair comparison, as oblique trees are sensitive to feature scales.

        iv. Train both your OC1-based oblique decision tree and a univariate decision tree using Scikit-Learn's `DecisionTreeClassifier`.

        v. Compare the two models in terms of classification accuracy, training time, and tree complexity (depth and size).

        vi. (Optional) Visualize the decision boundaries for each model on two-dimensional projections of the feature space. Compare how the models differ in splitting the feature space.

        vii. Discuss situations where oblique trees (such as OC1) are expected to outperform standard axis-aligned trees.

    (d) Write a short report summarizing your implementation, experimental results, and key insights from the comparison between oblique and univariate decision trees.

Chapter 9

Ensemble Methods

Ensemble methods are a powerful and widely used class of machine learning techniques that combine multiple base models to form a more accurate and robust predictor than any individual model alone.

The core idea behind ensemble learning is that aggregating the predictions of diverse models—each of which may capture different patterns or make different errors—can lead to better generalization. Ensembles also tend to reduce variance by averaging the predictions of multiple simpler models, rather than relying on a single, complex model that might overfit the training data. Furthermore, ensembles can effectively expand the hypothesis space, enabling them to model more complex patterns than any individual model could represent on its own.

As a result, ensemble methods are among the most effective algorithms for supervised learning, consistently delivering state-of-the-art performance across a wide range of tasks. Their success is particularly evident in machine learning competitions, where they play a central role in many winning solutions.

This chapter introduces the key principles of ensemble learning, beginning with simple aggregation techniques such as voting and averaging, and progressing to more advanced strategies including bagging, boosting, and stacking. For each method, we explain how it works, examine its strengths and limitations, and demonstrate how to apply it effectively in practice.

The chapter is organized as follows. Section 9.1 introduces the concept of ensembles and explains why they often outperform individual models. Section 9.2 provides an overview of different types of ensemble methods. Section 9.3 describes ensembles that combine model predictions using simple techniques such as majority voting or averaging. Section 9.4 explores bagging ensembles, which train the same base model on randomly sampled subsets of the training data to reduce variance. Section 9.5 introduces random forests, a popular bagging-based ensemble of decision trees that increases model diversity by selecting a random subset of features at each split. Section 9.6 examines boosting ensembles, which sequentially train models to correct the errors made by their predecessors. Section 9.7 discusses AdaBoost, a foundational boosting algorithm that transforms weak learners into a strong ensemble by focusing on hard-to-classify examples. Section 9.8 explores gradient boosting, which minimizes prediction errors by fitting new models to the residuals of the current ensemble. Section 9.9 introduces stacking, which uses a meta-model to learn how to best combine the predictions of several base models. Section 9.10 concludes with a summary of the chapter and an overview of open challenges and research directions.

9.1   Introduction and Motivation

An **ensemble** is a machine learning model that combines the predictions of multiple **base models** (also called **base learners**) to produce a more robust overall prediction [67, 161, 457, 669, 515]. We denote the base models by h_k, for $k = 1, \ldots, K$, where K is the total number of models in the ensemble.

Given an input sample $\mathbf{x}$, the ensemble's prediction $h(\mathbf{x})$ is obtained by aggregating the outputs of the individual base models (see Figure 9.1):

- In classification, the ensemble predicts the most frequent class label among the base classifiers using majority voting:

$$h(\mathbf{x}) = \underset{y}{\mathrm{argmax}} \sum_{k=1}^{K} \mathbb{1}(h_k(\mathbf{x}) = y), \tag{9.1}$$

   where $\mathbb{1}(\cdot)$ is the indicator function, equal to 1 if the k-th classifier predicts y and 0 otherwise.

- In regression, the ensemble prediction is the average of the outputs of the base regressors:

$$h(\mathbf{x}) = \frac{1}{K} \sum_{k=1}^{K} h_k(\mathbf{x}). \tag{9.2}$$

The strength of ensemble methods lies in their ability to combine diverse models in a way that individual errors tend to offset one another. As a result, the ensemble often achieves better predictive performance than any single base model. This naturally raises the question: *How does aggregating the predictions of multiple models usually lead to improved accuracy?*

One way to build intuition is through a real-world analogy. Suppose a patient's X-ray is reviewed by five independent radiologists, each with an 85% accuracy rate. While any one radiologist can make a mistake, it is unlikely that most will make the same mistake on the same case if their errors are independent. By taking a majority vote, the combined diagnosis is more accurate than any individual opinion (in this case, about 97.3%). This is a classical example of the *wisdom of the crowd*: combining multiple independent but imperfect judgments can lead to a remarkably accurate overall decision.

Formally, suppose we have an ensemble of n classifiers, each with an individual error rate ϵ (the probability of misclassifying a given input). If the classifiers' errors are independent, the number of incorrect predictions, denoted by k, follows a Binomial distribution:

$$k \sim \mathrm{Binomial}(n, \epsilon),$$

since each prediction is an independent Bernoulli trial with error probability ϵ.

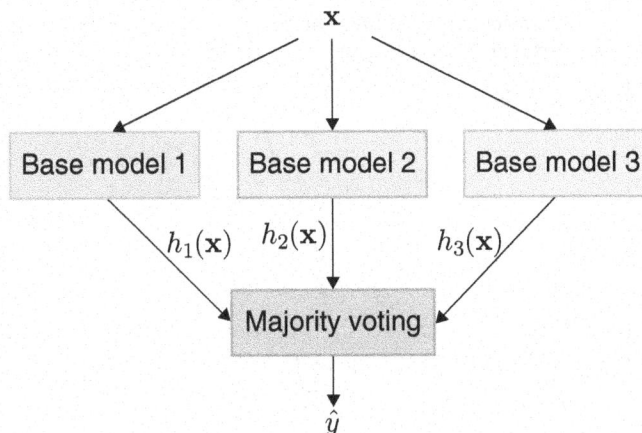

Figure 9.1: Illustration of an ensemble model comprising three base models. For classification tasks, the ensemble combines the base predictions $h_1(\mathbf{x})$, $h_2(\mathbf{x})$, and $h_3(\mathbf{x})$ using majority voting to obtain the final prediction $\hat{y}$. In regression tasks, the predictions are averaged instead.

With majority voting, the ensemble misclassifies an input only if more than half of the base classifiers are wrong. Therefore, its error rate is given by:

$$\epsilon_{\text{ensemble}} = P\left(k \geq \lceil n/2 \rceil\right) = \sum_{k=\lceil n/2 \rceil}^{n} \binom{n}{k} \epsilon^k (1-\epsilon)^{n-k}. \tag{9.3}$$

For example, with $n = 25$ base classifiers, each having an error rate of $\epsilon = 0.2$, the ensemble's error rate is:

$$\epsilon_{\text{ensemble}} = \sum_{k=13}^{25} \binom{25}{k} 0.2^k\, 0.8^{25-k} \approx 0.000369.$$

This is substantially lower than the individual error rate of 0.2, illustrating the potential benefit of combining multiple models whose errors are uncorrelated.

More generally, we can examine how the ensemble error rate varies with the base error rate ϵ. As shown in Figure 9.2, the critical threshold occurs at $\epsilon = 0.5$. When the individual classifiers perform better than random guessing (i.e., $\epsilon < 0.5$), the ensemble achieves a much lower error rate than the base classifiers. However, when $\epsilon > 0.5$, the ensemble performs worse than any single classifier, since majority voting amplifies systematic errors when most base models are likely to be wrong.

The effect of the number of classifiers n can be seen by fixing $\epsilon < 0.5$ and increasing n. Under the assumption of independent errors, the ensemble error then decreases exponentially with n, bounded by $\epsilon_{\text{ensemble}} \leq \exp(-2\gamma^2 n)$, where $\gamma = 0.5 - \epsilon > 0$ is the margin above random guessing.[1] This implies that even classifiers that are only slightly better than random guessing can, when combined in sufficient numbers, yield an ensemble with very high accuracy.

---

1. This bound follows from Hoeffding's inequality applied to the binomial tail probability $P(k \geq \lceil n/2 \rceil)$; see Section C.13.5.3.

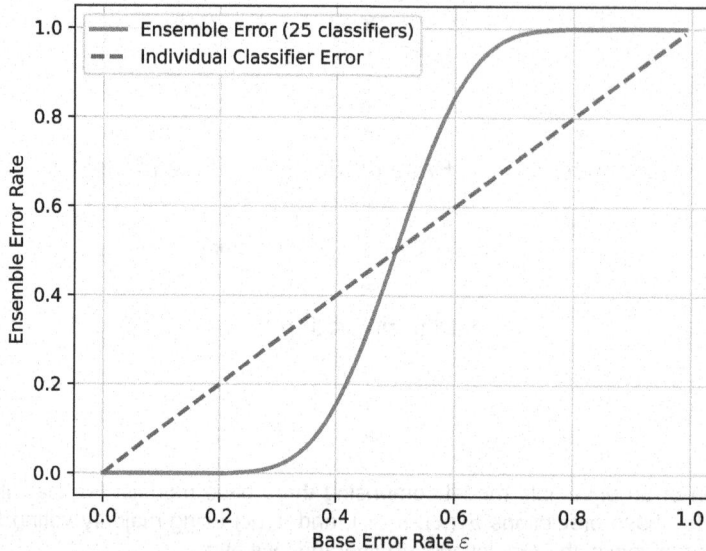

Figure 9.2: Ensemble error rate as a function of the base error rate ϵ for an ensemble of 25 independent classifiers. When $\epsilon < 0.5$, the ensemble achieves a significantly lower error rate than the base models, illustrating the benefit of combining multiple classifiers that each perform better than random guessing.

This analysis reveals two essential conditions for an ensemble to be effective:

- **Independence of errors**: The errors of the base classifiers should be uncorrelated. While perfect independence is rarely achievable in practice, empirical evidence shows that even modest diversity among classifiers can greatly improve the ensemble's performance.

- **Base accuracy above chance**: Each base classifier should perform better than random guessing. Classifiers that are only slightly better than random guessers (i.e., $\epsilon = 0.5 - \gamma$ for small $\gamma > 0$) are called **weak learners**. Combining many weak learners can produce a **strong learner** with substantially higher accuracy—a principle exploited by ensemble methods to reduce both bias and variance.

These two conditions are supported by a theoretical analysis of ensemble learning known as the **ambiguity decomposition** [335]. This decomposition shows that the generalization error of an ensemble equals the average generalization error of its individual base models minus a term that quantifies their diversity—that is, the extent to which their predictions differ. Thus, an effective ensemble must consist of base models that are both accurate and diverse.

However, striking the right balance between these two properties is difficult. Highly accurate models often share similar biases and tend to make correlated errors, which reduces diversity. Consequently, ensemble methods must carefully navigate the tradeoff between individual model accuracy and diversity to achieve the best overall performance.

Another motivation for using ensemble methods is their ability to enhance the model's expressive power and expand its effective hypothesis space. For example, combining multiple linear

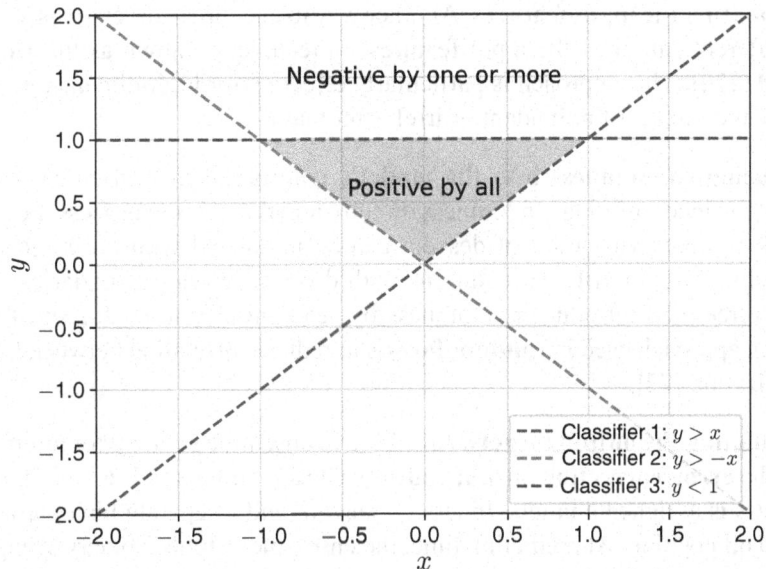

Figure 9.3: An ensemble model composed of three linear classifiers with distinct decision boundaries: $y > x$, $y > -x$, and $y < 1$. A point is classified as positive only if all three classifiers agree, resulting in the triangular region labeled "Positive by all." This gray region represents a more expressive decision boundary than any individual linear classifier can achieve on its own.

classifiers can yield complex, nonlinear decision boundaries that are unattainable by any single model, as illustrated in Figure 9.3.

9.2   Types of Ensemble Methods

There are various approaches to constructing ensembles, each employing a different strategy to encourage diversity among the base models. The main types of ensemble methods include:

- **Using different learning algorithms**. This approach constructs a **heterogeneous ensemble** by combining base models trained with different learning algorithms or the same algorithm with varying hyperparameter settings (e.g., k-nearest neighbors with different values of k) [618]. Such ensembles leverage the complementary strengths of the individual models, improving the ensemble's overall robustness and performance.

- **Manipulating the training examples**. A common strategy is to train each base model on a different subset of the training data. This includes methods such as **bagging**, which trains each model on a dataset created by sampling instances from the original training set with replacement [67], and **boosting**, where each subsequent model is trained on a reweighted dataset that focuses on hard-to-predict examples [197, 201].

- **Manipulating the input features**. Another way to encourage diversity is to train each model on a different subset of the input features—a technique known as the **random subspace method** [272]. This approach is particularly effective for high-dimensional data, as it helps mitigate the impact of redundant or irrelevant features.

- **Introducing randomness into the model's training**. Some ensemble methods promote diversity by incorporating randomness directly into the training process. For example, neural networks trained with gradient descent can be initialized with different random weights, often converging to different solutions with diverse decision boundaries [255]. Similarly, decision trees can introduce randomness by selecting a random subset of features at each split—an approach used in **random forests** to reduce correlation between trees and improve generalization [72].

- **Manipulating the output targets**. An effective ensemble strategy for multi-class classification is the **error-correcting output codes (ECOC)** framework [163, 525]. In this approach, each class is assigned a unique binary *codeword*, and a separate binary classifier is trained for each bit position. At prediction time, the ensemble outputs a binary string, which is compared to the predefined class codewords, and the closest match is chosen as the predicted class. This scheme improves robustness by allowing the ensemble to tolerate errors made by individual classifiers.

Hybrid ensemble methods combine multiple ensemble strategies to take advantage of their complementary strengths. For example, we can build an ensemble of neural networks, each trained on a different subset of the training data, initialized with different random weights, and configured with different hyperparameters. The predictions from these diverse networks can then be aggregated using a meta-model trained to combine their outputs effectively (a technique known as **stacking**).

In the following sections, we discuss these strategies in more detail.

9.3 Using Different Learning Algorithms

A straightforward way to build an ensemble is by combining models trained with different learning algorithms [168, 20]. Since each algorithm tends to capture different aspects of the data, their combination often leads to improved generalization and robustness.

For classification tasks, a simple strategy for aggregating the predictions of multiple classifiers is to use voting. Two commonly used voting strategies are:

- **Hard voting**: Each base classifier votes for a single class label, and the ensemble predicts the label that receives the majority of votes.

- **Soft voting**: Each base classifier outputs a probability distribution over the classes, and the ensemble predicts the label with the highest cumulative probability.

Classifier	Class 1	Class 2	Class 3
1	0.2	0.5	0.3
2	0.6	0.1	0.3
3	0.3	0.4	0.3
Σ	**1.1**	**1.0**	**0.9**

Table 9.1: Example illustrating soft voting. The ensemble predicts class 1 because it has the highest cumulative probability, obtained by summing the predicted probabilities from each classifier.

For example, consider an ensemble of three classifiers that output probability distributions over three classes, as shown in Table 9.1. Using soft voting, the ensemble predicts class 1, which has the highest cumulative probability (1.1). However, if only hard labels are available, the ensemble would instead predict class 2. This is because classifiers 1 and 3 vote for class 2, while classifier 2 votes for class 1, giving class 2 a two-to-one majority.

Soft voting often performs better than hard voting because it takes into account the confidence of each classifier's prediction, giving more weight to highly confident predictions. However, it requires that all base classifiers provide probability estimates rather than just the final class labels.

In regression tasks, the ensemble typically produces the final output by averaging the predictions of the base regressors. In some cases, a weighted average can be used to give greater influence to models that are known to be more accurate or reliable.

9.3.1 Voting Ensembles in Scikit-Learn

Scikit-Learn provides the following classes for building **voting ensembles**, which combine a given set of estimators using a simple voting strategy:

- `VotingClassifier`[2] is used for classification. Its key parameters include:
  - `estimators`: A list of (`str`, `estimator`) tuples specifying the names and corresponding objects of the base classifiers. These base estimators are trained when you call the `fit` method of the `VotingClassifier`, and the fitted models are stored in its `estimators_` attribute.
  - `voting`: The voting strategy to use, either `'hard'` (default) or `'soft'`.
  - `weights`: A list of weights to assign to the base classifiers, affecting their contribution to the final prediction. The default is `None`, which means equal weights.

- `VotingRegressor`[3] is used for regression tasks. It generates the final prediction by averaging the outputs of the base estimators. Like `VotingClassifier`, it supports the `estimators` and `weights` parameters, but it does not have a `voting` parameter.

2. https://scikit-learn.org/stable/modules/generated/sklearn.ensemble.VotingClassifier.html
3. https://scikit-learn.org/stable/modules/generated/sklearn.ensemble.VotingRegressor.html

The following example applies the `VotingClassifier` estimator to a synthetic classification dataset generated using Scikit-Learn's `make_classification`[4] function. This function offers fine-grained control over the structure and complexity of the classification task through a wide range of configurable parameters. It creates normally distributed clusters centered at the vertices of an n-dimensional hypercube, with each class assigned one or more clusters. Key parameters of the function include the number of informative and redundant features, number of clusters per class, and the degree of class separation (see Table 9.2).

Let's use the `make_classification` function to generate a dataset with 500 samples, two informative features, and three classes:

```
from sklearn.datasets import make_classification

X, y = make_classification(
    n_samples=500, n_classes=3, n_clusters_per_class=1, n_features=2,
    n_informative=2, n_redundant=0, class_sep=0.8, random_state=42
)
```

Parameter	Description	Default
n_samples	Number of samples to generate.	100
n_features	Total number of features, including informative, redundant, and repeated features.	20
n_informative	Number of informative features that contribute to class separability and define the dimensionality of the hypercube used to generate the class labels.	2
n_redundant	Number of redundant features, generated as random linear combinations of the informative features.	2
n_repeated	Number of repeated features, which are duplicate copies of randomly selected informative or redundant features.	0
n_classes	Number of target classes.	2
n_clusters_per_class	Number of clusters assigned to each class.	2
class_sep	Controls the separation between classes by scaling the hypercube size; larger values increase the distance between clusters, making classification easier.	1.0

Table 9.2: Key parameters of the `make_classification` function

4. https://scikit-learn.org/stable/modules/generated/sklearn.datasets.make_classification.html

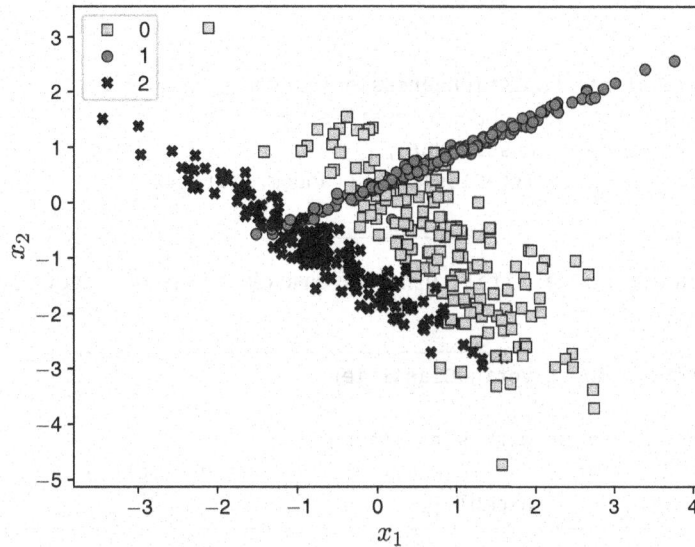

Figure 9.4: A synthetic dataset with three classes generated using the `make_classification` function from Scikit-Learn. The plot illustrates significant overlap among the three classes. Class 1 (circles) tends to align along a diagonal direction, while class 0 (squares) and class 2 (crosses) are more broadly scattered.

We can visualize the dataset using a scatter plot:

```
import seaborn as sns

sns.scatterplot(x=X[:, 0], y=X[:, 1], hue=y, style=y, markers=('s', 'o', 'X'),
                edgecolor='black')
plt.xlabel('$x_1$')
plt.ylabel('$x_2$')
```

Figure 9.4 shows the generated data points. We then split the dataset into training and test sets:

```
from sklearn.model_selection import train_test_split

X_train, X_test, y_train, y_test = train_test_split(X, y, random_state=42)
```

Next, we define our base classifiers. In this example, we use four classifiers with their default settings: logistic regression, k-nearest neighbors, Gaussian naive Bayes, and a decision tree:

```
from sklearn.linear_model import LogisticRegression
from sklearn.neighbors import KNeighborsClassifier
from sklearn.naive_bayes import GaussianNB
from sklearn.tree import DecisionTreeClassifier
```

```
# Create the base classifiers
models = {
    'Logistic Regression': LogisticRegression(random_state=42),
    'K-Nearest Neighbors': KNeighborsClassifier(),
    'Gaussian Naive Bayes': GaussianNB(),
    'Decision Tree': DecisionTreeClassifier(random_state=42)
}
```

We then create a `VotingClassifier` using the base classifiers and specify soft voting to combine their predictions:

```
from sklearn.ensemble import VotingClassifier

# Create the voting ensemble with soft voting
ensemble = VotingClassifier(list(models.items()), voting='soft')
models['Voting Ensemble'] = ensemble
```

We now train each of the base classifiers, along with the voting ensemble, and evaluate their performance:

```
results = {}

for name, model in models.items():
    model.fit(X_train, y_train)
    results[name] = {
        'Train Accuracy': np.round(model.score(X_train, y_train), 4),
        'Test Accuracy': np.round(model.score(X_test, y_test), 4)
    }

results_df = pd.DataFrame.from_dict(results).T
results_df
```

The results are shown in Figure 9.5. As depicted, the voting ensemble achieves the highest test accuracy among all models, demonstrating the benefit of combining multiple diverse classifiers.

To gain deeper insight into the behavior of the voting ensemble, we plot the decision boundaries of the base classifiers alongside the ensemble, using only the test set to avoid overcrowding the visualization:

```
feature_names = ['$x_1$', '$x_2$']
class_labels = np.array(['0', '1', '2'])
fig, axes = plt.subplots(2, 3, figsize=(10, 6), sharey=True)

for name, model, ax in zip(models.keys(), models.values(), axes.flat):
    plot_decision_boundaries(model, X_test, y_test, feature_names, class_labels,
                             ax=ax, legend=False)
```

	Train Accuracy	Test Accuracy
Logistic Regression	0.8453	0.840
K-Nearest Neighbors	0.9280	0.920
Gaussian Naive Bayes	0.7653	0.792
Decision Tree	1.0000	0.904
Voting Ensemble	0.9520	0.944

Figure 9.5: Comparison of training and test accuracy for the individual base classifiers and the voting ensemble on the synthetic classification dataset. The voting ensemble achieves the highest test accuracy (0.944), surpassing the performance of all individual models. Note the overfitting behavior of the decision tree, which achieves perfect training accuracy but lower test accuracy compared to the ensemble.

```
    ax.set_title(name)

axes[1][2].axis('off') # Hide the empty subplot
fig.subplots_adjust(hspace=0.4) # Adjust the vertical spacing
```

Figure 9.6 show the decision boundaries of the four base classifiers and the voting ensemble. By combining diverse classifiers, the ensemble produces a more robust decision surface that mitigates the weaknesses of individual models, such as overfitting or limited capacity.

9.4 Bagging Ensembles

Bagging (short for **B**ootstrap **Agg**regat**ing**) is an ensemble technique that builds multiple instances of the same learning algorithm, each trained on a different random subset of the training data [67].[5] These subsets are generated using **bootstrap sampling**, where each training subset is created by sampling with replacement from the original dataset.[6]

Formally, bagging proceeds as follows:

1. **Input**: A training set of n examples, $D = \{(\mathbf{x}_i, y_i)\}_{i=1}^{n}$; a specified number of base models K; and a learning algorithm A.

2. **Bootstrap sampling and training**: For each $k = 1, \ldots, K$:

   - Draw a bootstrap sample D_k by sampling n examples with replacement from D.
   - Train a base model h_k on D_k using algorithm A.

---

5. The idea was introduced in 1996 by Leo Breiman (1928–2005), who made significant contributions to statistical machine learning, including the development of bagging, random forests, and additive models.
6. This process is closely related to the bootstrap method introduced in Section D.6.5, which uses resampling to approximate the sampling distribution of a statistic. In bagging, the same idea is used to generate diverse training sets, each approximating an independent sample drawn from the underlying data-generating distribution.

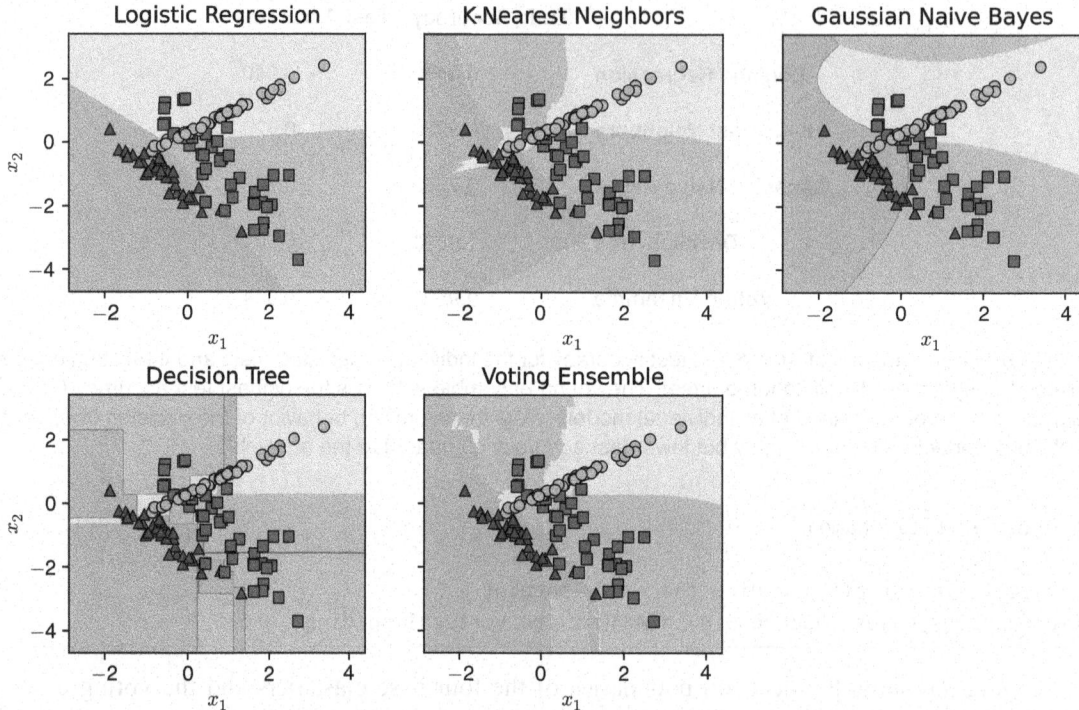

Figure 9.6: Decision boundaries of the four base classifiers (logistic regression, k-nearest neighbors, Gaussian naive Bayes, and decision tree) and their voting ensemble, shown on the test subset of a synthetic dataset generated with `make_classification`. The ensemble yields smoother, more generalized decision regions by integrating the complementary strengths of its base models.

3. **Prediction aggregation**:

   - For a new input $\mathbf{x}$, obtain predictions $h_1(\mathbf{x}), \ldots, h_K(\mathbf{x})$.

   - Aggregate the predictions using majority voting (for classification) or averaging (for regression).

Compared to simple voting ensembles, a key advantage of bagging lies in its scalability: it enables the construction of large ensembles—often consisting of hundreds or even thousands of models—by repeatedly applying the same base learner to different bootstrap samples. In addition, bagging enjoys appealing theoretical properties: under the assumption that the base learners are independent, bagging reduces variance without increasing bias, thereby improving generalization (see Exercise 9.14).

Bagging is particularly effective for **unstable learning algorithms**, such as decision trees or neural networks, that are highly sensitive to small changes in the training data. For these models, bootstrap sampling introduces meaningful diversity, helping reduce variance and improve predictive accuracy. In contrast, for more stable algorithms like linear regression or k-nearest neighbors, which are less affected by fluctuations in the data, the benefits of bagging are usually limited [67].

Sample	x	y
1	0.1	0
2	0.4	0
3	0.5	1
4	0.6	1
5	0.8	1
6	1.0	0

Table 9.3: Training set used to illustrate the construction of a bagging ensemble

9.4.1 Numerical Example

To illustrate how bagging works, consider the dataset shown in Table 9.3. It contains six examples, each with a single feature x and a binary class label y.

We construct a bagging ensemble of $K = 3$ simple decision trees, each consisting of a single split, commonly referred to as **decision stumps**. We first generate three bootstrap samples from the training set by sampling with replacement. For illustration, suppose the generated bootstrap samples are:

D_1: Examples 1, 1, 2, 3, 5, 6 ($x = [0.1, 0.1, 0.4, 0.5, 0.8, 1.0]$)

D_2: Examples 3, 3, 4, 5, 5, 6 ($x = [0.5, 0.5, 0.6, 0.8, 0.8, 1.0]$)

D_3: Examples 1, 1, 2, 2, 6, 6 ($x = [0.1, 0.1, 0.4, 0.4, 1.0, 1.0]$)

Training each decision stump on its respective bootstrap sample yields:

1. **Stump 1**: Optimal split at $x > 0.45$

   - Predicts $y = 0$ for $x \leq 0.45$, $y = 1$ otherwise.
   - Correctly classifies all but example 6 (true label 0).

2. **Stump 2**: Optimal split at $x > 0.9$

   - Predicts $y = 1$ for $x \leq 0.9$, $y = 0$ otherwise.
   - Perfect on D_2 but misclassifies examples 1 and 2 in the original dataset.

3. **Stump 3**: The model makes no split, as all examples in D_3 belong to class 0.

   - Predicts $y = 0$ for all examples.
   - Perfect on D_3 but misclassifies examples 3, 4, and 5 in the original dataset.

Table 9.4 shows the predictions of the individual stumps as well as the combined prediction of the ensemble using majority voting. In this case, the ensemble correctly classifies all training examples despite errors made by the individual models.

Round	$x = 0.1$	$x = 0.4$	$x = 0.5$	$x = 0.6$	$x = 0.8$	$x = 1.0$
1	0	0	1	1	1	1
2	1	1	1	1	1	0
3	0	0	0	0	0	0
Majority Vote	0	0	1	1	1	0
Actual Class	0	0	1	1	1	0

Table 9.4: Predictions of the individual models and the bagging ensemble on the training set, demonstrating how majority voting corrects individual errors.

9.4.2   Variations of Bagging

Several variations of bagging have been proposed, each modifying the way subsets of the training data are selected for each base model:

- **Pasting** [71]: Similar to bagging but samples *without* replacement. While bagging typically uses bootstrap samples of the same size as the original training set, pasting must use smaller subsets—otherwise, all base models would be trained on the same dataset. The advantage of pasting is that it reduces redundancy within each training set, which can increase model diversity. However, because each subset is smaller than the full training set, this can lead to higher bias, especially on small datasets.

- **Random subspaces** (also called **feature bagging**) [272]: Selects a random subset of features for each base model while using all the training samples. This method is particularly effective for high-dimensional datasets, where reducing the number of features can lower variance and help prevent overfitting to noisy or irrelevant attributes.

- **Random patches** [381]: Combines bagging and random subspaces by selecting a random subset of both training instances and features for each base model. This approach increases model diversity, reduces variance, and lowers computational cost, but it can also increase bias, particularly on small or low-dimensional datasets.

9.4.3   Bagging Ensembles in Scikit-Learn

Scikit-Learn provides the following classes for implementing bagging ensembles:

- `BaggingClassifier`[7] for classification tasks.

- `BaggingRegressor`[8] for regression tasks.

Both classes share the same set of parameters, which are summarized in Table 9.5.

For example, let's train a bagging ensemble of 100 unpruned decision trees on the synthetic classification dataset from Section 9.3.1:

---

7. https://scikit-learn.org/stable/modules/generated/sklearn.ensemble.BaggingClassifier.html
8. https://scikit-learn.org/stable/modules/generated/sklearn.ensemble.BaggingRegressor.html

Parameter	Description	Default
estimator	The base estimator used to build the ensemble. If None, a decision tree is used (DecisionTreeClassifier for classification or DecisionTreeRegressor for regression).	None
n_estimators	The number of base estimators in the ensemble.	10
max_samples	The number of samples to draw from the training set for each base estimator. If specified as a float, it represents the fraction of the training set size.	1.0
max_features	The number of features to draw from the training set for each base estimator. If specified as a float, it represents the fraction of the total number of features.	1.0
bootstrap	Whether samples are drawn with replacement (bagging) or without replacement (pasting).	True
bootstrap_features	Whether features are drawn with replacement.	False
oob_score	Whether to use out-of-bag samples to estimate the generalization error.	False
n_jobs	The number of parallel jobs for training and prediction. None means 1, and -1 uses all available processors.	None

Table 9.5: Key parameters of the BaggingClassifier and BaggingRegressor classes

```
from sklearn.ensemble import BaggingClassifier
from sklearn.tree import DecisionTreeClassifier

clf = BaggingClassifier(DecisionTreeClassifier(), n_estimators=100, random_state=42,
                        n_jobs=-1)
clf.fit(X_train, y_train)
```

Here, we set n_jobs=-1 to utilize all available CPU cores, enabling parallel training of the decision trees in the ensemble. This can significantly speed up the training process, especially when using a large number of estimators.

The performance of the ensemble is:

```
print(f'Train accuracy: {clf.score(X_train, y_train):.4f}')
print(f'Test accuracy: {clf.score(X_test, y_test):.4f}')
```

```
Train accuracy: 1.0000
Test accuracy: 0.9360
```

The test accuracy of the ensemble is higher than that of a single decision tree (0.904), illustrating how bagging can reduce model variance and improve generalization.[9]

---

9. While the ensemble achieves perfect training accuracy, this is not necessarily indicative of overfitting. Bagging methods can maintain low generalization error by reducing variance, even when they fit the training set perfectly.

Let's examine how the number of base estimators affects the performance of the bagging ensemble. The following code snippet trains ensembles with different numbers of base estimators, ranging from 1 to 100 in steps of 5, and then plots the training and test accuracy for each setting:

```python
train_accuracies = []
test_accuracies = []
n_estimators_range = [1] + list(range(5, 101, 5))

# Train bagging ensembles with varying number of base estimators
for n_estimators in n_estimators_range:
    clf = BaggingClassifier(DecisionTreeClassifier(), n_estimators=n_estimators,
                            random_state=42, n_jobs=-1)
    clf.fit(X_train, y_train)
    train_accuracies.append(clf.score(X_train, y_train))
    test_accuracies.append(clf.score(X_test, y_test))

# Plot the training and test accuracy
plt.plot(n_estimators_range, train_accuracies, label='Train Accuracy', marker='o')
plt.plot(n_estimators_range, test_accuracies, label='Test Accuracy', marker='o')
plt.xlabel('Number of Base Estimators')
plt.ylabel('Accuracy')
plt.legend()
plt.grid(alpha=0.5)
```

Figure 9.7 shows that training accuracy increases steadily and reaches 100% after about 40 estimators, reflecting the ensemble's ability to fit the training data better as more trees are added. The test accuracy initially increases, peaking around 15–20 estimators, then fluctuates slightly and stabilizes near 93.6%. This shows a typical behavior of bagging ensembles, where adding more estimators does not cause overfitting, even though the model becomes more complex, thanks to the variance-reducing effect of bagging.

Figure 9.8 compares the decision boundaries of the best-performing bagging ensemble (15 trees) with those of a single decision tree. The single tree produces axis-aligned boundaries that closely follow the training points, including small, isolated regions—signs of fitting to noise. In contrast, the bagging ensemble produces smoother and more contiguous regions, with fewer abrupt changes, indicating a more stable decision surface that generalizes better.

9.4.4   Out-of-Bag Evaluation

In bagging, each bootstrap sample contains, on average, approximately 63.2% of the original training examples (see Exercise 9.13), leaving the remaining 36.8% unused. These unused examples, known as **out-of-bag (OOB) samples**, can be used to estimate the ensemble's generalization error without requiring a separate validation set.

To compute the **OOB estimate** of the generalization error, each training example is evaluated using only the models that did not include it in their bootstrap sample. Their predictions are then aggregated by majority voting (classification) or averaging (regression). Because OOB estimates are based only on a subset of the models in the ensemble, they tend to slightly overestimate the true error; however, they have been shown to closely match the test set performance in practice [68].

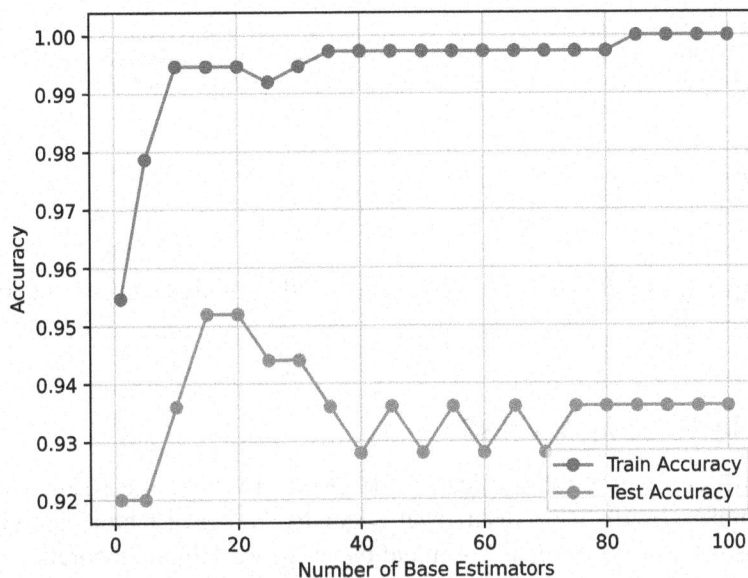

Figure 9.7: Training and test accuracy of a bagging ensemble as a function of the number of base estimators. Training accuracy reaches 100% at around 40 estimators, while test accuracy peaks between 15 and 20 estimators and then stabilizes.

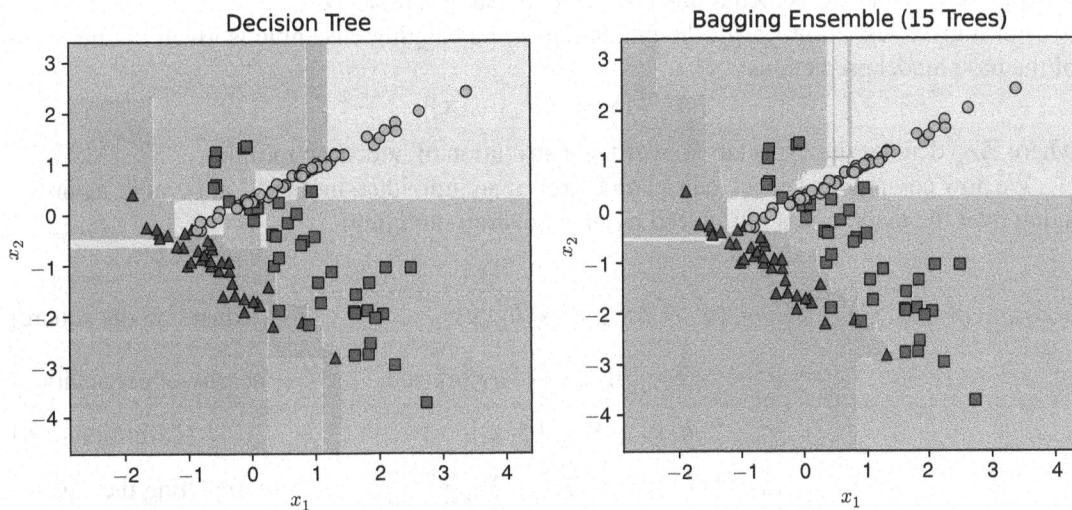

Figure 9.8: Decision boundaries created by a single decision tree (left) and a bagging ensemble of 15 trees (right) on the synthetic classification dataset. The single tree forms axis-aligned boundaries that closely fit the training data, whereas the bagging ensemble smooths out irregularities by averaging predictions across trees, resulting in more coherent regions that generalize better.

In Scikit-Learn, OOB evaluation can be enabled by setting `oob_score=True` in the constructor of the ensemble:

```
clf = BaggingClassifier(DecisionTreeClassifier(), n_estimators=15,
                        random_state=42, n_jobs=-1, oob_score=True)
clf.fit(X_train, y_train)
print('OOB score:', clf.oob_score_)
```

```
OOB score: 0.88
```

In this example, the OOB accuracy is 88%, which indeed underestimates the true test accuracy of 95.2%.

9.4.5   (*) Why Bagging Works?

This section provides a theoretical justification for the effectiveness of bagging—specifically, why a bagging ensemble typically achieves a lower generalization error than its individual base models. The analysis is based on Breiman's seminal paper, which laid the theoretical foundations for bagging ensembles [67]. We focus here on regression problems; for an extension of the analysis to classification, see the original paper.

Let $D = \{(\mathbf{x}_i, y_i)\}_{i=1}^n$ be a set of training examples drawn independently from some probability distribution P, where y is a continuous target variable. In bagging, we generate K bootstrap samples $\{D_k\}_{k=1}^K$, each consisting of n independent samples drawn with replacement from D. A separate base model h_k is then trained on each bootstrap sample D_k.

For a given test point $(\mathbf{x}, y)$, the prediction of the bagging ensemble is given by the average of the base model predictions:

$$h(\mathbf{x}) = \mathbb{E}_{D_k}[h_k(\mathbf{x})], \tag{9.4}$$

where $\mathbb{E}_{D_k}$ denotes the expectation over the distribution of bootstrap samples.

We now compute the expected squared error of an individual model h_k at point $\mathbf{x}$, again averaging over the randomness introduced by the bootstrap sampling:

$$
\begin{aligned}
\mathbb{E}_{D_k}\left[(y - h_k(\mathbf{x}))^2\right] &= \mathbb{E}_{D_k}\left[y^2 - 2yh_k(\mathbf{x}) + h_k^2(\mathbf{x})\right] && \text{(expanding the square)} \\
&= y^2 - 2y\,\mathbb{E}_{D_k}[h_k(\mathbf{x})] + \mathbb{E}_{D_k}[h_k^2(\mathbf{x})] && \text{(linearity of expectation)} \\
&= y^2 - 2yh(\mathbf{x}) + \mathbb{E}_{D_k}[h_k^2(\mathbf{x})] && \text{(definition of } h) \\
&= (y - h(\mathbf{x}))^2 - h^2(\mathbf{x}) + \mathbb{E}_{D_k}[h_k^2(\mathbf{x})] && \text{(completing the square)} \\
&= (y - h(\mathbf{x}))^2 - (\mathbb{E}_{D_k}[h_k(\mathbf{x})])^2 \\
&\quad + \mathbb{E}_{D_k}[h_k^2(\mathbf{x})] && \text{(definition of } h)
\end{aligned}
$$

$$= (y - h(\mathbf{x}))^2 + \mathrm{Var}_{D_k}(h_k(\mathbf{x})) \qquad\qquad \text{(definition of variance)}$$

$$\geq (y - h(\mathbf{x}))^2. \qquad\qquad\qquad\quad \text{(variance is nonnegative)}$$

Thus, we have shown that the squared error of the ensemble is bounded above by the expected squared error of a single base model:

$$(y - h(\mathbf{x}))^2 \leq \mathbb{E}_{D_k}\left[(y - h_k(\mathbf{x}))^2 \right]. \qquad\qquad (9.5)$$

From the derivation of the bound, we see that the gap between the two errors is exactly the variance of the base models, $\mathrm{Var}_{D_k}(h_k(\mathbf{x}))$, illustrating the variance-reducing effect of bagging. When this variance is small—that is, when the predictions $h_k(\mathbf{x})$ are stable across bootstrap samples—the benefit of bagging is limited. In contrast, for high-variance base models, bagging can substantially reduce the variance component of the error, thereby lowering the generalization error. As a result, bagging is particularly effective for unstable learners that are sensitive to fluctuations in the training data, such as decision trees.

9.5   Random Forests

Random forests (RF), introduced by Breiman in 2001, are ensembles of decision trees that combine two sources of randomness: bagging and random feature selection [72] (see Figure 9.9). As in standard bagging, each tree is trained on a a bootstrap sample of the training data (i.e., a random subset drawn with replacement). In addition, only a randomly selected subset of features is considered at each split, rather than all features.

Randomizing the feature selection at each split reduces the correlation between the trees. For example, when a few features are strongly predictive of the target, they may dominate the splits in many trees, leading to high inter-tree correlation. By limiting the candidate features considered at each split, random forests mitigate this correlation, achieving a greater reduction in variance than standard bagging. Empirical studies have consistently shown that random forests outperform standard bagging on a wide range of benchmark datasets [72, 96, 188].

Unlike individual decision trees, random forests typically do not use pruning. Bootstrap sampling and random feature selection reduce overfitting by preventing individual trees from focusing too narrowly on dominant patterns. Moreover, allowing trees to grow to their full depth enhances their expressive power and thus helps reduce bias.

More than two decades after their introduction, random forests remain among the most effective and widely used supervised learning algorithms [600]. They have been widely adopted in various application domains, including bioinformatics [159, 228], fraud detection [620, 370], customer churn prediction [132, 635], fault detection [642, 643], and medical diagnosis [317, 345, 624].

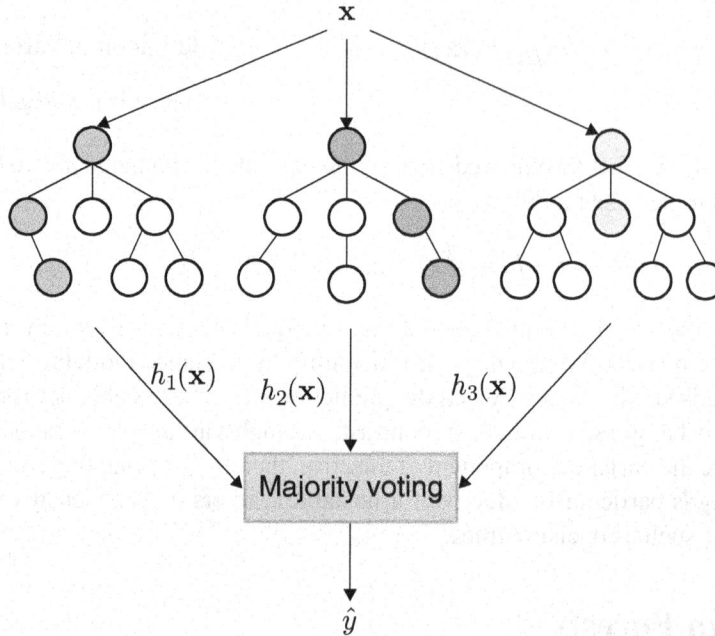

Figure 9.9: Illustration of a random forest model. The input sample x is evaluated by an ensemble of decision trees, each trained on a different bootstrap sample and using a randomly selected subset of features at each split. The final prediction $\hat{y}$ is obtained by aggregating the individual predictions $h_1(\mathbf{x})$, $h_2(\mathbf{x})$, and $h_3(\mathbf{x})$ through majority voting (for classification) or averaging (for regression).

9.5.1 Random Forests in Scikit-Learn

Scikit-Learn provides the following classes for working with random forests:

- `RandomForestClassifier`[10] for classification tasks.

- `RandomForestRegressor`[11] for regression tasks.

These classes share many hyperparameters with the decision tree estimators, such as `criterion`, `max_depth`, and `min_samples_leaf`, which control how each individual tree in the ensemble is grown. They also include several hyperparameters that configure the ensemble itself, including:

- `n_estimators`: Number of trees in the forest (defaults to 100).

- `max_features`: Number of features to consider at each split. It can be an integer, a float (fraction of the total number of features), `'sqrt'` (square root of the total features), `'log2'`

---

10. https://scikit-learn.org/stable/modules/generated/sklearn.ensemble.RandomForestClassifier.html

11. https://scikit-learn.org/stable/modules/generated/sklearn.ensemble.RandomForestRegressor.html

(base-2 logarithm of the total features), or None (use all features). The default is `'sqrt'` for a `RandomForestClassifier` and `1.0` (all features) for `RandomForestRegressor`.

- `max_samples`: Number of samples to draw from the training set for each tree (i.e., the bootstrap sample size). It can be an integer, a float (fraction of the total number of samples), or None (uses all training samples; this is the default).

9.5.1.1 Classification Example

We now train a `RandomForestClassifier` on the synthetic classification dataset from Section 9.3.1 using its default settings: an ensemble of 100 fully-grown trees, each trained on a bootstrap sample of the same size as the training set, with $\sqrt{d}$ features (where d is the total number of features) considered at each split:

```
from sklearn.ensemble import RandomForestClassifier

clf = RandomForestClassifier(random_state=42, n_jobs=-1)
clf.fit(X_train, y_train)
```

As in bagging, `n_jobs` controls the level of parallelism across CPU cores; here we set `n_jobs=-1` to use all available cores for training. The model's performance is:

```
print(f'Train accuracy: {clf.score(X_train, y_train):.4f}')
print(f'Test accuracy: {clf.score(X_test, y_test):.4f}')
```

```
Train accuracy: 1.0000
Test accuracy: 0.9440
```

The random forest achieves a test accuracy of 94.4%, slightly higher than the bagging ensemble's 93.6% with the same number of estimators.

Figure 9.10 shows how training and test accuracy evolve as the number of estimators increases. Unlike the bagging ensemble, where test accuracy peaked early and then declined, in the random forest it remains stable around the peak, reflecting a more effective variance reduction due to the lower correlation among the trees.

Empirical studies have shown that, in random forests, increasing the number of estimators decreases prediction error monotonically without causing overfitting. However, beyond a certain point, the performance gains become negligible [72, 460]. Consequently, the number of estimators is typically chosen based on the computational resources available. In practice, a few hundred to several thousand trees are commonly used, depending on the size and complexity of the dataset.

Other hyperparameters, such as the number of features considered at each split and the maximum tree depth, can also significantly influence performance and are typically tuned using grid search or randomized search.

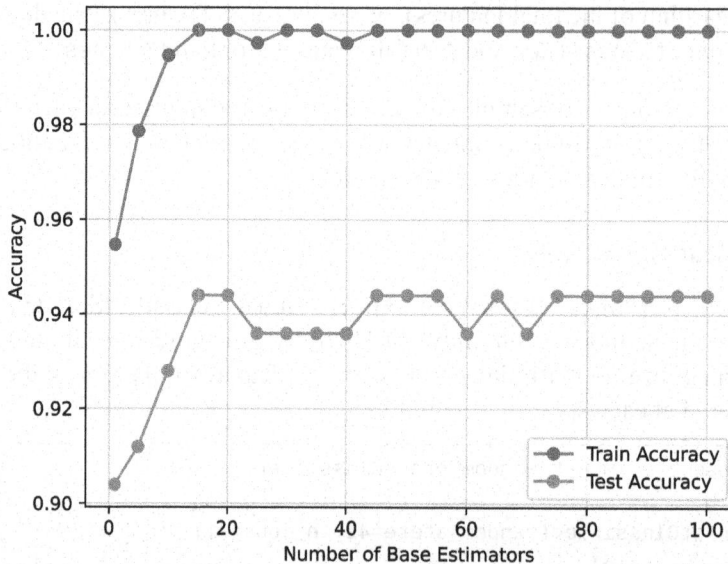

Figure 9.10: Training and test accuracy of a random forest classifier as a function of the number of base estimators. Both metrics converge and remain stable as more estimators are added, showing no signs of overfitting.

9.5.1.2 Regression Example

We now demonstrate how to use random forests to solve a regression task by applying the RandomForestRegressor to the California housing dataset (see Section 4.6). We first fetch the dataset and split it into training and test sets:

```
from sklearn.datasets import fetch_california_housing
from sklearn.model_selection import train_test_split

X, y = fetch_california_housing(return_X_y=True)
X_train, X_test, y_train, y_test = train_test_split(X, y, test_size=0.2,
                                                    random_state=42)
```

We then train a RandomForestRegressor using the default hyperparameters:

```
from sklearn.ensemble import RandomForestRegressor

reg = RandomForestRegressor(random_state=42, n_jobs=-1)
reg.fit(X_train, y_train)
```

Evaluating the model:

```
print(f'R2 score (train): {reg.score(X_train, y_train):.4f}')
print(f'R2 score (test): {reg.score(X_test, y_test):.4f}')
```

```
R2 score (train): 0.9736
R2 score (test): 0.8051
```

These results are significantly better than those achieved by a single regression tree after tuning (test R^2 score of 0.7227), as well as by other models we previously applied to this problem, including k-nearest neighbors (0.7205) and linear regression (0.5758). This demonstrates the effectiveness of random forests in reducing variance and improving generalization.

Next, we explore whether the performance can be further improved by tuning the ensemble's hyperparameters. We conduct a randomized search over the number of estimators, bootstrap sample size, number of features to consider at each split, and the minimum number of samples at a leaf node:

```
from sklearn.model_selection import RandomizedSearchCV

params = {
    'n_estimators': np.arange(50, 501, 50),
    'max_samples': np.arange(0.5, 1.01, 0.1),
    'max_features': ['sqrt', 'log2', None],
    'min_samples_leaf': np.arange(1, 11)
}

reg = RandomForestRegressor(random_state=42)
random_search = RandomizedSearchCV(reg, params, n_iter=50, cv=3, random_state=42,
                                   n_jobs=-1)
random_search.fit(X_train, y_train)
print(random_search.best_params_)
```

The best hyperparameters found are:

```
{'n_estimators': 500, 'min_samples_leaf': 1,
 'max_samples': 0.7999999999999999, 'max_features': 'log2'}
```

Evaluating the tuned model:

```
print(f'R2 score (train): {random_search.score(X_train, y_train):.4f}')
print(f'R2 score (test): {random_search.score(X_test, y_test):.4f}')
```

```
R2 score (train): 0.9640
R2 score (test): 0.8157
```

The R^2 score on the test set improved from 0.8051 to 0.8157, illustrating how hyperparameter tuning can improve the generalization performance of random forest models.

9.5.1.3 Feature Importances

Random forests can provide a more reliable estimate of feature importances than single decision trees. As discussed in Section 8.6.2.1, the importance of a feature in a single decision tree is based on its contribution to reducing node impurity. In a random forest, these impurity reductions are averaged across all the trees in the ensemble, resulting in a more stable and robust measure of feature importance.

We can access the feature importances of a random forest model using the `feature_importances_` attribute:

```
# Sort the features by their importance in a descending order
best_reg = random_search.best_estimator_
sorted_idx = np.argsort(best_reg.feature_importances_)[::-1]

# Retrieve the feature names
data = fetch_california_housing()
feature_names = data.feature_names

for idx in sorted_idx:
    print(f'{data.feature_names[idx]}: {best_reg.feature_importances_[idx]:.4f}')
```

```
MedInc: 0.3963
AveOccup: 0.1275
Latitude: 0.1248
Longitude: 0.1196
AveRooms: 0.1059
HouseAge: 0.0546
AveBedrms: 0.0399
Population: 0.0312
```

Compared to the single decision tree, the random forest distributes feature importance more evenly across the features, reducing the dominance of any single predictor. For example, the feature importance of `MedInc` decreased from 0.6022 in the single tree to 0.3963 in the ensemble.

9.5.2   (*) Analyzing the Generalization Error

As noted in Section 9.1, a foundational result in ensemble learning theory states that the generalization error of an ensemble depends on two main factors: the accuracy of its base learners and the correlation between their predictions.

Breiman (2001) provided a more refined analysis of these factors in the context of random forests [72]. Before presenting his result, we introduce a few key definitions.

Consider a random forest trained for a classification task with C classes. Let $D = \{(\mathbf{x}_i, y_i)\}_{i=1}^n$ be a training set drawn i.i.d. from a joint distribution $P(\mathbf{x}, y)$, where $y_i \in \{1, \ldots, C\}$. Let $\{D_k\}_{k=1}^K$ denote K bootstrap samples of size n, drawn with replacement from D, and let h_k be the decision tree trained on D_k.

Breiman's analysis is based on the following key quantities:

- **Margin**: The margin of the ensemble at a data point $(\mathbf{x}, y)$ represents the gap between the fraction of trees in the ensemble that vote for the correct class and the fraction that vote for the highest-voted incorrect class:

$$mg(\mathbf{x}, y) = \frac{1}{K} \sum_{k=1}^{K} \mathbb{1}(h_k(\mathbf{x}) = y) - \max_{j \neq y} \frac{1}{K} \sum_{k=1}^{K} \mathbb{1}(h_k(\mathbf{x}) = j), \qquad (9.6)$$

where $\mathbb{1}(\cdot)$ is the indicator function, equal to 1 if its argument is true and 0 otherwise.

- **Strength**: The strength of the ensemble is the expected margin over the data-generating distribution:

$$s = \mathbb{E}_{(\mathbf{x},y) \sim P}[mg(\mathbf{x}, y)]. \qquad (9.7)$$

It measures, on average, how confidently the ensemble separates the correct class from the others.

- **Average correlation**: The average correlation of the ensemble quantifies how similar the predictions of different trees are: the more frequently the trees make the same predictions, the higher the correlation. It is defined as:

$$\bar{\rho} = \mathbb{E}_{i \neq j}[\rho(h_i(\mathbf{x}), h_j(\mathbf{x}))], \qquad (9.8)$$

where ρ denotes the Pearson correlation coefficient between the outputs of trees h_i and h_j, treated as random variables over the input space:

$$\rho(h_i, h_j) = \frac{1}{\sigma_i \sigma_j} \mathbb{E}_{\mathbf{x}} \left[(h_i(\mathbf{x}) - \mu_i)(h_j(\mathbf{x}) - \mu_j) \right], \qquad (9.9)$$

with $\mu_i = \mathbb{E}_{\mathbf{x}}[h_i(\mathbf{x})]$ and $\sigma_i^2 = \mathbb{E}_{\mathbf{x}}[(h_i(\mathbf{x}) - \mu_i)^2]$.

Using these definitions, Breiman derived the following upper bound on the prediction error (PE) of the ensemble, i.e., the probability that the ensemble misclassifies a new instance:

$$PE \leq \frac{\bar{\rho}(1 - s^2)}{s^2}. \qquad (9.10)$$

This inequality shows that the generalization error decreases as the strength of the ensemble s increases and/or the average correlation $\bar{\rho}$ decreases. However, there is often a tradeoff between these two factors, which is closely related to the classical bias–variance tradeoff. Increasing the strength of each tree—for example, by allowing it to grow deep, using all available features at each split, or training on a large bootstrap sample—typically reduces bias but also increases the correlation between trees, thereby limiting the variance reduction benefit of averaging. Conversely, decreasing the correlation between trees—for instance, by restricting the feature set at each split or reducing the bootstrap sample size—can lower the ensemble's variance but may weaken the strength of individual trees, thereby increasing bias.

In his concluding remarks, Breiman noted that the theoretical analysis does not fully account for the strong empirical performance of random forests compared to standard bagging. He suggested that random forests may reduce not only variance but also bias, although the exact underlying mechanism remains unclear. This intriguing observation has been further investigated in recent studies (e.g., [416, 369]).

9.5.3 Extra Trees

Extra Trees (short for **Ext**remely **Ra**ndomized Trees) introduce an additional level of randomization beyond that used in random forests [224]. In addition to randomly selecting a subset of features to consider at each node, extra trees also choose the split point at random for each candidate continuous feature.

Specifically, for a feature x with minimum and maximum values $x_{\min}$ and $x_{\max}$ among the samples reaching the node, a candidate split point x_c is drawn uniformly from the interval $[x_{\min}, x_{\max}]$. This process is repeated for each candidate feature and the feature–split pair that yields the greatest reduction in node impurity is selected for the actual split.

Extra trees reduce variance more aggressively than random forests by producing more diverse trees. However, they may also increase bias, since split points are no longer chosen to optimally separate the data. To mitigate this, it is common to use the entire original training set to build each tree rather than bootstrap samples.

Another advantage of extra trees is their computational efficiency. Since split points are chosen randomly, extra trees avoid the costly sorting of feature values at each node. As a result, the time complexity of building a tree decreases from $\mathcal{O}(dn^2 \log n)$ to $\mathcal{O}(kn)$, where $k < d$ is the number of features considered at each split.

In their original study, Geurts et al. [224] reported that extra trees performed slightly better than random forests on 22 out of 24 datasets, which included 12 classification and 12 regression tasks. At the same time, both methods significantly outperformed a single pruned decision tree and standard bagging.

Scikit-Learn provides implementations of extra trees in the `ExtraTreesClassifier`[12] and `ExtraTreesRegressor`[13] classes. These classes share the same hyperparameters as their random forest counterparts, with one key difference: the default value of the `bootstrap` parameter is `False`, meaning that each tree is trained on the entire original training set rather than a bootstrap sample.

For example, let's train an `ExtraTreesRegressor` on the California housing dataset:

```
from sklearn.ensemble import ExtraTreesRegressor

reg = ExtraTreesRegressor(random_state=42)
reg.fit(X_train, y_train)

print(f'R2 score (train): {reg.score(X_train, y_train):.4f}')
print(f'R2 score (test): {reg.score(X_test, y_test):.4f}')
```

The evaluation results are:

```
R2 score (train): 1.0000
R2 score (test): 0.8060
```

---

12. https://scikit-learn.org/stable/modules/generated/sklearn.ensemble.ExtraTreesClassifier.html
13. https://scikit-learn.org/stable/modules/generated/sklearn.ensemble.ExtraTreesRegressor.html

In this case, the extra trees regressor achieves a test R^2 score that is nearly identical to that of the random forest before tuning (0.8051).

9.5.4 Variants of Random Forests

Over the years, several extensions of random forests have been proposed to increase diversity, support oblique splits, handle class imbalance, and enable online learning. Notable variants include:

- **Forest-RC (Random Combination)** [72]: Breiman proposed this variant of random forests to support oblique splits (see Section 8.8) by forming linear combinations of randomly selected features with randomly drawn coefficients. Multiple such combinations are evaluated at each node, and the one that yields the greatest impurity reduction is used for the split. By enabling oblique splits, Forest-RC can capture more complex feature interactions and increase diversity among trees, potentially improving predictive performance.

- **Balanced Random Forests (BRF)** [107]: Addresses imbalanced datasets by training each tree on a balanced bootstrap sample, created by randomly undersampling each class to match the size of the smallest one, thereby improving performance on minority classes. An implementation is available in the `BalancedRandomForestClassifier`[14] class from the `imbalanced-learn` library.

- **Rotation Forests** [504]: Promotes diversity by applying Principal Component Analysis (PCA) to random subsets of features before training each tree. PCA transforms the original features into uncorrelated principal components that capture directions of maximum variance. This effectively "rotates" the feature space, reducing correlation between trees and potentially improving the enesemble's generalization performance.

- **Sparse Projection Oblique Randomer Forests (SPORF)** [579]: A more recent variant that uses sparse random projections—linear combinations of a small subset of features—to form oblique splits at each node. SPORF has demonstrated improved accuracy and robustness compared to standard random forests and other ensemble methods on various benchmark classification tasks. An open-source implementation is available at `neurodata.io/forests`[15].

- **Online Random Forests** [514, 157]: Designed for streaming data, this variant incrementally updates the ensemble as new data arrives, eliminating the need for retraining from scratch. Each tree is updated independently by maintaining candidate splits at the leaves and collecting statistics over time. When enough data accumulates and a split meets a predefined quality threshold, the leaf is split into two child nodes. Online random forests are well-suited for real-time applications such as sensor networks, fraud detection, and adaptive analytics.

---

14. `https://imbalanced-learn.org/stable/references/generated/imblearn.ensemble.BalancedRandomForestClassifier.html`
15. `https://neurodata.io/forests`

9.5.5 Summary

Random forests are powerful ensemble models that aggregate the predictions of many decision trees trained on random subsets of the data and features. Their continued success across diverse applications, despite the rise of more complex models, underscores their enduring relevance as both a practical tool and a benchmark for supervised learning.

Advantages of random forests compared to other supervised learning models:

- They are less prone to overfitting than individual decision trees due to bootstrap sampling and random feature selection at each split.

- They can capture complex interactions between features and nonlinear relationships by aggregating the predictions of multiple diverse trees.

- They are known for high predictive accuracy across a wide range of real-world tasks, making them a reliable choice for practical applications.

- They are effective with high-dimensional data, as the random selection of features at each split reduces overfitting and mitigates the curse of dimensionality.

- They are robust to noise and outliers, since ensemble averaging reduces the impact of individual noisy or extreme data points.

- They inherit many benefits of decision trees, such as support for mixed data types, handling of missing values without imputation, and multi-class and multi-output learning capabilities.

- They are highly parallelizable, as the trees can be trained independently, enabling efficient use of multi-core and distributed environments.

- They provide meaningful feature importance scores that improve model interpretability and aid in feature selection.

- Unlike many other supervised learning models, random forests provide a theoretical bound on generalization error, expressed as a function of the strength and correlation of the base learners.

Disadvantages of random forests:

- Training can be computationally intensive, especially on large datasets or when using a large number of trees.

- They typically require high memory usage, as all individual trees must be stored in memory during both training and prediction.

- Predictions are slower compared to simpler models due to the need to aggregate outputs across all trees in the ensemble.

- They require careful tuning of several hyperparameters—such as the number of trees, the number of features considered at each split, and the maximum tree depth—to achieve a good balance between model complexity and diversity.

- They are less interpretable than simpler models such as single decision trees or linear models, since predictions are based on averaging outputs from many decision paths.

- They can struggle with imbalanced datasets, as trees tend to become biased toward the majority class, leading to poor performance on underrepresented classes.

- They are less effective on datasets with a small number of features, as the benefit of feature subsampling diminishes when there are few features to choose from.

9.6 Boosting Ensembles

Boosting is a powerful ensemble technique that builds a sequence of base models, where each model is trained to correct the errors made by its predecessors [197, 201, 527]. Unlike bagging, which trains base learners independently on different bootstrap samples, boosting constructs the ensemble sequentially, with each new model focusing more on the instances that previous models misclassified—often referred to as **hard-to-classify examples**.

The base models used in boosting are typically **weak learners,** i.e., models that perform only slightly better than random guessing. Despite their simplicity, weak learners offer several advantages: they are fast to train and tend to have low variance, making them less susceptible to overfitting. When combined appropriately, boosting can transform these simple models into a highly accurate predictor that generalizes well to unseen data.

A common choice for the base learner in boosting is a **decision stump**—a shallow decision tree with only one split, producing two leaf nodes (see Figure 9.11).

Numerous empirical studies have demonstrated the superior performance of boosting over bagging across a wide range of benchmark datasets [492, 33, 162, 96, 438].

The two most prominent boosting methods are AdaBoost and gradient boosting, which are discussed in the following sections.

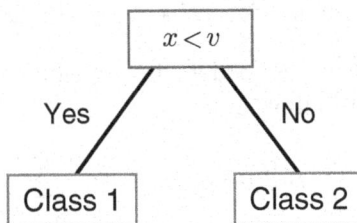

Figure 9.11: An example of a decision stump with a single decision rule. The rule $x < v$, where x is the feature and v the split point, partitions the data into two classes: class 1 if the condition is satisfied, and class 2 otherwise.

9.7   AdaBoost

AdaBoost (short for **Ada**ptive **Boost**ing), introduced by Freund and Schapire in 1995,[16] is one of the earliest and most influential boosting algorithms, known for both its solid theoretical foundations and strong empirical performance [196, 197, 526].

AdaBoost maintains a distribution of weights over the training examples and updates it iteratively: in each boosting round, the weights of misclassified examples are increased, while those of correctly classified ones are decreased. This reweighting strategy encourages subsequent weak learners to focus more on the harder examples that previous models misclassified.

With enough boosting iterations, the ensemble can drive the training error arbitrarily close to zero. Remarkably, the reduction in training error occurs very quickly: in just $\mathcal{O}(\log n)$ boosting rounds (where n is the number of training examples), the ensemble can perfectly fit the training set. In practice, however, it is often desirable to stop training before reaching zero training error in order to prevent overfitting.

In this section, we first introduce the original AdaBoost algorithm for binary classification, along with its theoretical guarantees, and then describe its extensions to multi-class classification and regression.

9.7.1   The AdaBoost Algorithm

AdaBoost was originally developed for binary classification tasks, where the training set consists of labeled examples $\{(\mathbf{x}_1, y_1), \ldots, (\mathbf{x}_n, y_n)\}$ with $y_i \in \{-1, 1\}$.[17]

AdaBoost maintains a distribution of weights over the training examples, denoted by D. The weight of example i in boosting round t ($t = 1, \ldots, T$) is denoted by $D_t(i)$. Initially, all examples have equal weights:

$$D_1(i) = \frac{1}{n}, \quad \text{for } i = 1, \ldots, n. \tag{9.11}$$

The algorithm performs T boosting rounds, with each round consisting of the following steps:

1. Train a weak learner h_t using the current weights D_t. Depending on the implementation, the learner may incorporate D_t directly (e.g., by weighting samples in node impurity computations according to D_t), or randomly sample training examples according to D_t (e.g., an example with twice the weight is twice as likely to be selected).

2. Compute the error rate ϵ_t of h_t, defined as the probability of misclassifying a training example under the current distribution D_t:

$$\epsilon_t = P_{i \sim D_t}[h_t(\mathbf{x}_i) \neq y_i] = \sum_{i:\ h_t(\mathbf{x}_i) \neq y_i} D_t(i). \tag{9.12}$$

---

16. Freund and Schapire were awarded the prestigious Gödel Prize in 2003 for their work on boosting. The prize, named after the renowned logician Kurt Gödel, is awarded annually for outstanding papers in theoretical computer science.
17. Representing the class labels as -1 and 1, rather than 0 and 1, simplifies the mathematical formulation, without otherwise affecting the algorithm.

3. Compute the weight α_t of the weak learner, which determines its contribution to the final ensemble:

$$\alpha_t = \eta \log \left(\frac{1 - \epsilon_t}{\epsilon_t} \right),$$

(9.13)

where $\eta \in (0, 1]$ is a learning rate that controls how aggressively the algorithm adapts the weights in each round.

α_t has several important properties:

- It represents the log-odds of correct versus incorrect classification and is inversely related to the error rate ϵ_t: a lower ϵ_t yields a higher α_t.
- Since h_t is a weak learner with $\epsilon_t < 0.5$, α_t is guaranteed to be positive.
- α_t controls both the magnitude of the weight updates applied to the training examples (see next step) and the contribution of h_t to the final prediction—more accurate classifiers are assigned greater weights (see Equation (9.17)).

4. Update the weight distribution to assign more importance to misclassified examples:

$$D_{t+1}(i) = \frac{D_t(i) \exp(-\alpha_t y_i h_t(\mathbf{x}_i))}{Z_t},$$

(9.14)

where Z_t is a normalization factor that ensures D_{t+1} remains a valid probability distribution (i.e., the weights sum to 1):

$$Z_t = \sum_{i=1}^{n} D_t(i) \exp(-\alpha_t y_i h_t(\mathbf{x}_i)).$$

(9.15)

This update rule increases the weights of misclassified examples while decreasing the weights of correctly classified ones:

- **Misclassified example**: When $y_i \neq h_t(\mathbf{x}_i)$, we have $y_i h_t(\mathbf{x}_i) = -1$ (since either $y_1 = 1$ and $h_t(\mathbf{x}_i) = -1$, or vice versa). In this case, the update becomes:

$$D_{t+1}(i) = \frac{D_t(i) \exp(\alpha_t)}{Z_t}.$$

Since $\alpha_t > 0$, we have $\exp(\alpha_t) > 1$, so the weight increases: $D_{t+1}(i) > D_t(i)$

- **Correctly classified example**: When $y_i = h_t(\mathbf{x}_i)$, we have $y_i h_t(\mathbf{x}_i) = 1$. In this case, the update becomes:

$$D_{t+1}(i) = \frac{D_t(i) \exp(-\alpha_t)}{Z_t}.$$

Since $\alpha_t > 0$, we have $\exp(-\alpha_t) < 1$, so the weight decreases: $D_{t+1}(i) < D_t(i)$.

The exponential function in AdaBoost's update rule serves two key purposes. First, it amplifies the difference in weight between correctly and incorrectly classified examples, causing the algorithm to rapidly shift focus toward harder examples. Second, it allows AdaBoost to be interpreted as an iterative procedure for minimizing the **exponential loss function**, defined as

$$L_{\exp}(y, h(\mathbf{x})) = \exp(-yh(\mathbf{x})), \tag{9.16}$$

which provides a theoretical foundation for its effectiveness and convergence properties [201, 526].

The final hypothesis $H(\mathbf{x})$ is defined as a weighted majority vote over the T weak learners, where each h_t is weighted by its corresponding coefficient α_t:

$$H(\mathbf{x}) = \text{sign}\left(\sum_{t=1}^{T} \alpha_t h_t(\mathbf{x})\right), \tag{9.17}$$

where $\text{sign}(z)$ returns 1 if $z \geq 0$, and -1 otherwise.

The complete AdaBoost algorithm is summarized in the pseudocode shown in Algorithm 9.1.

9.7.2   Numerical Example on a Toy Dataset

We now demonstrate the AdaBoost algorithm on a toy dataset. Consider the training set shown in Table 9.6, which consists of 10 two-dimensional examples with binary labels. We will run three rounds of boosting on this training set using decision stumps as the weak learners and a learning rate of $\eta = 0.5$.

	x_1	x_2	y
1	1	4	1
2	1.5	2	1
3	2	1	-1
4	2.5	4.5	-1
5	3	6	1
6	3.5	4	-1
7	4	3	-1
8	4.5	7	1
9	5	5.5	1
10	5.5	1.5	-1

Table 9.6: The training set for the AdaBoost toy example

Algorithm 9.1 AdaBoost

Input:

    Training set $\{(\mathbf{x}_1, y_1), \ldots, (\mathbf{x}_n, y_n)\}$, where $y_i \in \{-1, +1\}$

    Weak learner algorithm

    Number of boosting rounds T

    Learning rate $\eta \in (0, 1]$

1: Initialize weights: $D_1(i) = 1/n$ for $i = 1, \ldots, n$

2: **for** $t = 1$ **to** T **do**

3:    Train a weak learner using distribution D_t to obtain hypothesis h_t

4:    Calculate the error rate of h_t:

$$\epsilon_t = \sum_{i:\, h_t(\mathbf{x}_i) \neq y_i} D_t(i)$$

5:    Compute the learner weight

$$\alpha_t = \eta \log \left(\frac{1 - \epsilon_t}{\epsilon_t} \right)$$

6:    Update the weights for $i = 1, \ldots, n$:

$$D_{t+1}(i) = \frac{D_t(i) \exp(-\alpha_t y_i h_t(\mathbf{x}_i))}{Z_t}$$

    where Z_t is a normalization factor ensuring that $\sum_{i=1}^{n} D_{t+1}(i) = 1$.

7: Output the final hypothesis:

$$H(\mathbf{x}) = \text{sign} \left(\sum_{t=1}^{T} \alpha_t h_t(\mathbf{x}) \right)$$

First Boosting Round

Initially, all examples have equal weights: $D_1(i) = 0.1$ for all $i = 1, \ldots, 10$. The best decision stump in the first round uses the split $x_2 \leq 5$, assigning -1 to the left node and 1 to the right node (see Figure 9.12).

This decision stump incorrectly classifies examples 1 and 2, each with weight 0.1. Therefore, its error rate is:

$$\epsilon_1 = 2 \cdot 0.1 = 0.2.$$

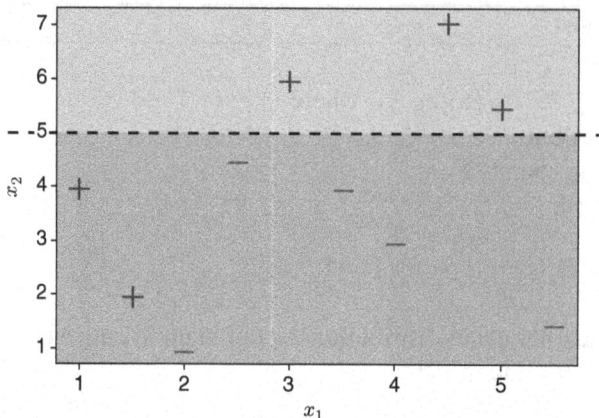

Figure 9.12: The decision stump used in the first boosting round, defined by the split $x_2 \leq 5$. The region below the dashed line is labeled -1, and the region above is labeled 1. This stump misclassifies two examples, (1, 4) and (1.5, 2), which lie in the negative region but have a true label of 1.

The weight α_1 is calculated as:

$$\alpha_1 = 0.5 \log \left(\frac{1 - 0.2}{0.2} \right) = 0.693.$$

For the misclassified examples, the new unnormalized weight is:

$$w_{\text{incorrect}} = 0.1 \cdot e^{0.693} = 0.2,$$

whereas for the correctly classified examples, the new unnormalized weight is:

$$w_{\text{correct}} = 0.1 \cdot e^{-0.693} = 0.05.$$

The normalization constant is:

$$Z_1 = 2 \cdot 0.2 + 8 \cdot 0.05 = 0.8.$$

Thus, the normalized weights are:

$$w_{\text{incorrect}} = \frac{0.2}{0.8} = 0.25, \quad w_{\text{correct}} = \frac{0.05}{0.8} = 0.0625.$$

After the first boosting round, the weights of the misclassified examples increase from 0.1 to 0.25, while the weights of the correctly classified examples decrease to 0.0625. Table 9.7 shows the updated weight distribution D_2 after the first boosting round.

	x_1	x_2	y	$D_2(i)$
1	1	4	1	0.25
2	1.5	2	1	0.25
3	2	1	-1	0.0625
4	2.5	4.5	-1	0.0625
5	3	6	1	0.0625
6	3.5	4	-1	0.0625
7	4	3	-1	0.0625
8	4.5	7	1	0.0625
9	5	5.5	1	0.0625
10	5.5	1.5	-1	0.0625

Table 9.7: The weight distribution D_2 after the first boosting round

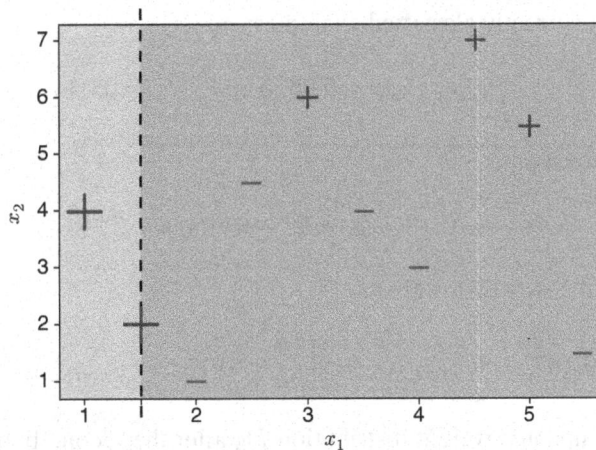

Figure 9.13: Decision stump for the second boosting round, defined by the split $x_1 \leq 1.5$. The region to the left of the dashed line is labeled 1, while the region to the right is labeled -1. The size of the symbols represents the weights of the examples, with larger symbols indicating higher weights. This stump misclassifies three positive examples: (3, 6), (4.5, 7), and (5, 5.5), which fall in the negative region but have true label 1.

Second Boosting Round

Since examples 1 and 2 have higher weights due to their previous misclassification, the second decision stump prioritizes classifying them correctly. A decision stump that achieves this while minimizing the total number of errors uses the split $x_1 \leq 1.5$, assigning 1 to the left node and -1 to the right node (see Figure 9.13).

This decision stump misclassifies examples 5, 8, and 9, each with a weight of 0.0625. Thus, its error rate is:

$$\epsilon_2 = 3 \cdot 0.0625 = 0.1875.$$

The learner weight is:

$$\alpha_2 = 0.5 \log \left(\frac{1 - 0.1875}{0.1875} \right) = 0.733.$$

The weights are updated as follows before normalization:

- For the misclassified examples (5, 8, 9):

$$w_{\text{incorrect}} = 0.0625 \cdot e^{0.733} = 0.13.$$

- For the correctly classified examples 1 and 2, which had higher weights:

$$w_{\text{correct\_high}} = 0.25 \cdot e^{-0.733} = 0.12.$$

- For the remaining correctly classified examples:

$$w_{\text{correct\_low}} = 0.0625 \cdot e^{-0.733} = 0.03.$$

The normalization constant is:

$$Z_2 = 3 \cdot 0.13 + 2 \cdot 0.12 + 6 \cdot 0.03 = 0.78.$$

Thus, the normalized new weights are:

$$w_{\text{incorrect}} = \frac{0.12}{0.78} = 0.167, \quad w_{\text{correct\_high}} = \frac{0.12}{0.78} = 0.154, \quad w_{\text{correct\_low}} = \frac{0.03}{0.78} = 0.038.$$

Table 9.8 shows the updated weight distribution D_3 after the second boosting round.

	x_1	x_2	y	$D_3(i)$
1	1	4	1	0.154
2	1.5	2	1	0.154
3	2	1	-1	0.038
4	2.5	4.5	-1	0.038
5	3	6	1	0.167
6	3.5	4	-1	0.038
7	4	3	-1	0.038
8	4.5	7	1	0.167
9	5	5.5	1	0.167
10	5.5	1.5	-1	0.038

Table 9.8: The weight distribution D_3 after the second boosting round

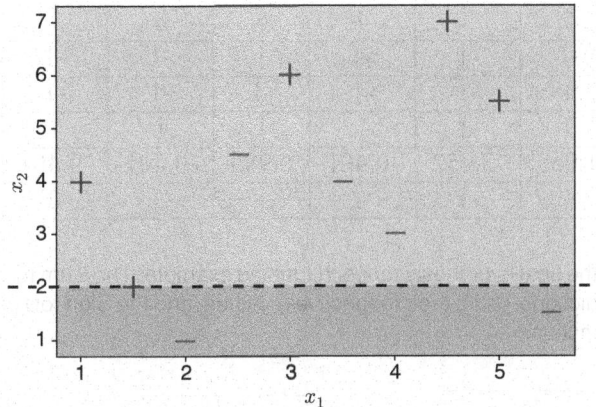

Figure 9.14: Decision stump for the third boosting round, defined by the split $x_2 \geq 2$. The region below the dashed line is labeled −1, and the region above is labeled 1. This stump misclassifies three negative examples in the positive region that should be labeled -1.

Third Boosting Round

The third decision stump prioritizes classifying correctly examples 1, 2, 5, 8, and 9, which now have higher weights. A decision stump that best separates these samples uses the split $x_2 \geq 2$, assigning 1 to the left node and -1 to the right node (see Figure 9.14).

This decision stump misclassifies examples 4, 6, and 7, each with a weight of 0.038. Therefore, its error rate is:

$$\epsilon_3 = 3 \cdot 0.038 = 0.114.$$

The weight of this model is:

$$\alpha_3 = 0.5 \log \left(\frac{1 - 0.114}{0.114} \right) = 1.025.$$

Since this is the last boosting round, no further weight updates are required.

The Final Hypothesis

The final hypothesis of the ensemble combines the predictions of the three decision stumps using a weighted majority vote, where each stump's vote is weighted by its corresponding model weight:

$$H(\mathbf{x}) = \text{sign}(0.693h_1(\mathbf{x}) + 0.733h_2(\mathbf{x}) + 1.025h_3(\mathbf{x})).$$

Table 9.9 shows the predictions of the final ensemble for all training examples. The rows labeled Round 1, Round 2, and Round 3 correspond to the predictions of h_1, h_2, and h_3, respectively. The Sum row shows the weighted sum of these predictions, where each prediction is multiplied by the corresponding model weight α_i. The Sign row displays the final classification of each example

Example	1	2	3	4	5	6	7	8	9	10
Round 1	-1	-1	-1	-1	1	-1	-1	1	1	-1
Round 2	1	1	-1	-1	-1	-1	-1	-1	-1	-1
Round 3	1	1	-1	1	1	1	1	1	1	-1
Sum	1.065	1.065	-2.452	-0.401	0.985	-0.401	-0.401	0.985	0.985	-2.452
Sign	1	1	-1	-1	1	-1	-1	1	1	-1

Table 9.9: Predictions of the final hypothesis for each training example. The Sum row shows the weighted sum of the weak learners' predictions, using their respective α values, and the Sign row gives the final classification after applying the sign function.

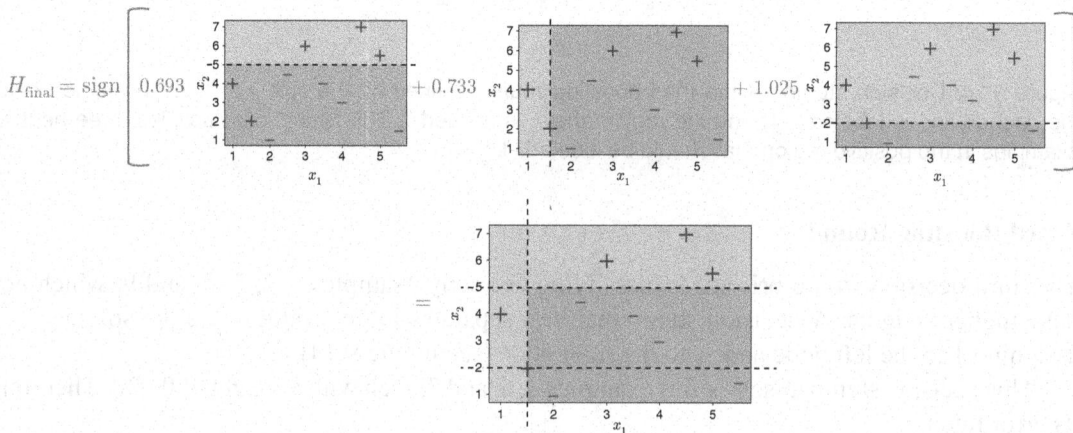

Figure 9.15: Visualization of the final hypothesis formed by AdaBoost. The top row shows the three individual decision stumps along with their corresponding weights ($\alpha_1 = 0.693$, $\alpha_2 = 0.733$, and $\alpha_3 = 1.025$), which determine the contribution of each weak learner to the final hypothesis. The bottom row illustrates the decision boundaries resulting from their weighted combination. As shown, the final ensemble correctly classifies all training examples.

after applying the sign function. As shown, the ensemble correctly classifies all training examples, illustrating how AdaBoost can combine weak learners into a highly accurate classifier.

Figure 9.15 presents a visual summary of the final AdaBoost ensemble. The top row shows how each decision stump partitions the feature space, while the bottom row displays the ensemble's overall prediction surface. The figure illustrates how boosting iteratively refines the model by focusing on previously misclassified points, resulting in a highly accurate classifier.

9.7.3   Analyzing the Prediction Error

A key theoretical property of AdaBoost is that its training error decreases exponentially with the number of boosting rounds [197]. This result highlights the algorithm's ability to effectively transform a collection of weak learners into a strong ensemble.

Formally, let ϵ_t denote the training error of the weak learner h_t at round t. Define the **edge** of the weak learner as $\gamma_t = 0.5 - \epsilon_t$, which quantifies how much h_t outperforms random guessing. Then, the training error of the final ensemble is bounded by (see Exercise 9.16):

$$\epsilon_{\text{ensemble}} \leq \prod_{t=1}^{T} 2\sqrt{\epsilon_t(1-\epsilon_t)} = \prod_{t=1}^{T} \sqrt{1-4\gamma_t^2} \leq \exp\left(-2\sum_{t=1}^{T}\gamma_t^2\right). \qquad (9.18)$$

Let $\gamma > 0$ denote the minimum edge achieved by the weak learners across all boosting rounds, i.e., $\gamma = \min_t \gamma_t$. Then $\gamma_t \geq \gamma$ for all $t = 1, \ldots, T$, and the bound becomes:

$$\epsilon_{\text{ensemble}} \leq \exp(-2T\gamma^2). \qquad (9.19)$$

This result indicates that the training error of the ensemble decreases exponentially with the number of boosting rounds T, provided that each weak learner performs at least slightly better than random guessing. It highlights AdaBoost's ability to transform weak learners into a highly accurate classifier by repeatedly focusing on the hardest-to-classify examples.

Surprisingly, AdaBoost often resists overfitting even when trained for many rounds, despite the increasing complexity of the ensemble. This behavior—seemingly at odds with statistical learning theory—is a well-documented characteristic of boosting and one of the main reasons for its strong empirical success.

A notable explanation for this phenomenon is the **margins theory** proposed by Schapire et al. [528]. According to this theory, even after the training error reaches zero, continued boosting can still improve the model's **margins**—defined as the difference between the weighted vote for the correct label and the most confident incorrect label (similar to the margin defined in Section 9.5.2 for random forests). Larger margins reflect greater confidence in predictions and are associated with better generalization. Consequently, AdaBoost can continue training and still improve test performance without overfitting, as long as the weak learners are not overly complex relative to the size of the training set.

In practice, overfitting is typically monitored on an independent validation set. If the validation performance begins to deteriorate, the boosting process can be stopped early—similar to the early stopping technique used in gradient-based optimization (see Section 4.8.2.2).

9.7.4 Extending AdaBoost to Multi-Class Classification

AdaBoost was originally developed for binary classification. Extending it to multi-class problems involves nontrivial complexities that have led to the development of several specialized variants.

A key difficulty stems from AdaBoost's requirement that each weak learner achieves an error rate $\epsilon_t < 0.5$ under the current weight distribution D_t. In the binary case, this condition is equivalent to requiring the weak learner to perform better than random guessing. However, in the multi-class setting with K classes, a random guesser has an error rate of $\frac{K-1}{K}$, making the $\epsilon_t < 0.5$ condition overly restrictive. For example, when $K = 10$, a random guesser has an expected error of 0.9, so a weak learner with an error of 0.5 is already substantially better than random guessing.

Despite this, AdaBoost enforces the strict threshold $\epsilon_t < 0.5$, and violating it can severely disrupt the algorithm. If a weak learner's error exceeds 0.5, it receives a negative weight $\alpha_t < 0$, effectively reversing its vote in the ensemble. This can destabilize the boosting process and degrade overall performance.

SAMME (**S**tagewise **A**dditive **M**odeling using a **M**ulticlass **E**xponential loss) [670] addresses this challenge by adjusting the computation of α_t to account for the number of classes K. Specifically, it modifies the original AdaBoost formula by adding a correction term $\log(K - 1)$:

$$\alpha_t = \log\left(\frac{1 - \epsilon_t}{\epsilon_t}\right) + \log(K - 1). \tag{9.20}$$

This adjustment ensures that α_t remains positive as long as the classifier performs better than random guessing—that is, its accuracy exceeds $1/K$, rather than having to exceed 0.5 (see Exercise 9.18). The addition of the $\log(K - 1)$ term can also be interpreted as a natural extension of the exponential loss function to the multi-class case [670]. Notably, when $K = 2$, SAMME reduces to the original AdaBoost algorithm.

SAMME.R (R for Real) is a variant of SAMME that uses the class probabilities estimates produced by the weak learners, rather than just the predicted class labels. By incorporating this additional information, SAMME.R often converges more quickly and achieves better performance, particularly when the weak learners can provide well-calibrated probability estimates.

Both SAMME and SAMME.R are implemented in Scikit-Learn via the AdaBoost `Classifier` class (see Section 9.7.6).

9.7.5 (*) Extending AdaBoost to Regression Tasks

AdaBoost.R, introduced by Freund and Schapire in the original AdaBoost paper [197], extends AdaBoost to regression by reducing the regression task into a series of binary classification problems. Although it preserves AdaBoost's theoretical guarantees, it is rarely used in practice due to its complexity and sensitivity to noise.

AdaBoost.R2, proposed by Drucker [172], offers an alternative approach that directly tackles the regression problem. It is supports a range of loss functions and often performs well in practice, although it lacks the theoretical guarantee of achieving zero training error in a finite number of boosting iterations.

Similar to the original AdaBoost, AdaBoost.R2 builds an ensemble of weak learners, where each regressor is trained on a weighted dataset that emphasizes the errors of its predecessors. However, it measures prediction errors using a normalized loss function rather than binary misclassification, and combines the base predictions using a weighted median instead of a majority vote. The pseudocode of the algorithm is provided in Algorithm 9.2.

We now examine key steps of the algorithm in more detail.

In step 6, the loss for each training example is computed using a normalized absolute error, ensuring that loss values lie within the interval $[0, 1]$. This normalization allows for a consistent weighting scheme across rounds. Other loss functions that are similarly bounded can also be employed—for example, a normalized squared loss:

$$L_i^t = \frac{|h_t(\mathbf{x}_i) - y_i|^2}{\left(\max_{j=1}^n |h_t(\mathbf{x}_j) - y_j|\right)^2}. \tag{9.21}$$

Algorithm 9.2 AdaBoost.R2

Input:

> Training set $\{(\mathbf{x}_1, y_1), \ldots, (\mathbf{x}_n, y_n)\}$, where $y_i \in [0, 1]$
> Weak regression learner
> Number of boosting rounds T

1: Initialize all weights: $w_i^1 = 1$, for $i = 1, \ldots, n$
2: **for** $t = 1$ **to** T **do**
3:     Normalize the weights to form a probability distribution:

$$p_i^t = \frac{w_i^t}{\sum_{j=1}^n w_j^t}$$

4:     Sample n training examples with replacement according to p_i^t
5:     Train a weak regression model h_t on the sampled dataset
6:     Compute normalized absolute loss for each example:

$$L_i^t = \frac{|h_t(\mathbf{x}_i) - y_i|}{\max_{j=1}^n |h_t(\mathbf{x}_j) - y_j|}$$

7:     Compute the average weighted loss:

$$\epsilon_t = \sum_{i=1}^n p_i^t L_i^t$$

8:     Compute model weight:

$$\beta_t = \frac{\epsilon_t}{1 - \epsilon_t}$$

9:     Update the sample weights:

$$w_i^{t+1} = w_i^t \cdot \beta_t^{1-L_i^t}$$

10: Output the final hypothesis:

$$H(\mathbf{x}) = \inf \left\{ y \in [0, 1] \;\middle|\; \sum_{t:\, h_t(\mathbf{x}) \leq y} \log\left(\frac{1}{\beta_t}\right) \geq \frac{1}{2} \sum_{t=1}^T \log\left(\frac{1}{\beta_t}\right) \right\}$$

In step **8**, a confidence measure β_t (analogous to α_t in the original AdaBoost) is computed based on the model's average loss ϵ_t. A lower value of β_t indicates greater confidence in the model's predictions.

In step 9, the sample weights are updated by multiplying each weight by $\beta_t^{1-L_i^t}$. If a training example incurs a high loss $L_i^t \approx 1$, then $1 - L_i^t \approx 0$, making $\beta_t^{1-L_i^t} \approx 1$, and the weight remains nearly unchanged. Conversely, if the loss L_i^t is small ($L_i^t \approx 0$) then $1 - L_i^t \approx 1$, and the weight is scaled down by approximately β_t. Thus, the weights are reduced more aggressively for well-predicted examples, shifting the model's focus toward harder-to-predict cases.

In step 10, the final hypothesis aggregates the predictions of all base regressors using a weighted median, which operates as follows:

1. For each possible outcome y, compute a cumulative score by summing $\log(1/\beta_t)$ over all base models h_t such that $h_t(\mathbf{x}) \leq y$. Models with lower error (and thus smaller β_t) are assigned greater weight through the factor $1/\beta_t$. The logarithmic transformation smooths these weights and prevents any single model from having excessive influence.

2. The final prediction is the smallest value of y for which the cumulative score reaches at least half of the total sum of all model scores. This ensures that the prediction reflects a majority consensus among the base learners. Unlike simple averaging, this median-based aggregation offers robustness to outliers and extreme predictions from individual models.

The AdaBoost.R2 algorithm is implemented in Scikit-Learn via the `AdaBoostRegressor` class (see the next section).

9.7.6   AdaBoost in Scikit-Learn

Scikit-Learn provides the following classes for implementing AdaBoost:

- `AdaBoostClassifier`[18]: Supports both binary and multi-class classification using the SAMME algorithm (see Section 9.7.4).

- `AdaBoostRegressor`[19]: Implements the AdaBoost.R2 algorithm for regression tasks (see Section 9.7.5).

Key parameters of these classes include:

- `estimator`: Specifies the base learner used in the ensemble. By default, it is a `DecisionTreeClassifier` with `max_depth=1` (i.e., a decision stump) for classification and a `DecisionTreeRegressor` with `max_depth=3` for regression.

- `n_estimators`: The number of base estimators to use (default is 50).

- `learning_rate`: Shrinks the contribution of each base learner by the given factor, corresponding to the parameter η in Algorithm 9.1. Lower values can reduce the risk of overfitting but may require more estimators to maintain performance (the default is 1.0).

---

18. https://scikit-learn.org/stable/modules/generated/sklearn.ensemble.AdaBoostClassifier.html
19. https://scikit-learn.org/stable/modules/generated/sklearn.ensemble.AdaBoostRegressor.html

For example, let's train an AdaBoost classifier on the synthetic classification dataset introduced in Section 9.3.1. We first instantiate an `AdaBoostClassifier` object with its default settings, which use 50 decision stumps and a learning rate of 1.0. The classifier is then fit to the training set:

```
from sklearn.ensemble import AdaBoostClassifier

clf = AdaBoostClassifier(random_state=42)
clf.fit(X_train, y_train)
```

Next, we evaluate the model's performance on the training and test sets:

```
print(f'Train accuracy: {clf.score(X_train, y_train):.4f}')
print(f'Test accuracy: {clf.score(X_test, y_test):.4f}')
```

```
Train accuracy: 0.5867
Test accuracy: 0.5520
```

The low accuracy on both sets suggests that the model is underfitting the data. This underperformance may stem from the limited capacity of decision stumps to model complex patterns or from the relatively small number of boosting rounds. Consequently, tuning the model's hyperparameters is crucial for achieving better performance.

The key hyperparameters in AdaBoost include the number of estimators, the learning rate, and the complexity of the base estimators (e.g., maximum depth of the decision tree). These hyperparameters are interdependent and must be carefully balanced to achieve optimal performance. For example, reducing the learning rate slows the updates to the weight distributions $D(i)$, which can help prevent overfitting to noisy samples. However, this typically requires more boosting rounds to correct the errors of earlier models, potentially resulting in a larger ensemble and an increased risk of overfitting.

To optimize the hyperparameters of our AdaBoost classifier, we perform a randomized search over these key parameters:

```
from sklearn.tree import DecisionTreeClassifier
from sklearn.model_selection import RandomizedSearchCV

params = {
    'n_estimators': np.arange(50, 501, 50),
    'learning_rate': np.arange(0.1, 1.0, 0.1),
    'estimator__min_samples_leaf': np.arange(1, 11)
}
clf = AdaBoostClassifier(estimator=DecisionTreeClassifier(), random_state=42)
random_search = RandomizedSearchCV(clf, params, n_iter=50, cv=3, random_state=42,
                                   n_jobs=-1)
random_search.fit(X_train, y_train)
print(random_search.best_params_)
```

Note that to tune the hyperparameters of the decision tree base estimator, you must explicitly pass it to the constructor of `AdaBoostClassifier` and use the prefix `estimator__` in the parameter grid to reference its internal parameters.

The best hyperparameter combination found is:

```
{'n_estimators': 300, 'learning_rate': 0.4, 'estimator__max_depth': 3}
```

The performance of the tuned model is:

```
print(f'Train accuracy: {random_search.score(X_train, y_train):.4f}')
print(f'Test accuracy: {random_search.score(X_test, y_test):.4f}')
```

```
Train accuracy: 1.0000
Test accuracy: 0.9520
```

The training and test accuracies have improved significantly, primarily due to the larger number of estimators and the increased depth of the decision trees.

9.7.7 Summary

AdaBoost is a powerful ensemble method that combines multiple weak learners, typically shallow decision trees, into a single strong predictor. It builds the ensemble iteratively by increasing the weights of training examples misclassified by previous learners, thereby emphasizing harder-to-classify instances. Although the original algorithm was designed for binary classification, it has been extended to support multi-class classification (e.g., using the SAMME algorithm) and regression tasks (e.g., AdaBoost.R2).

Advantages of AdaBoost compared to other supervised learning methods:

- It builds a strong ensemble by combining weak learners that individually underfit the data, often resulting in better generalization and reduced risk of overfitting.

- It often achieves high predictive accuracy, particularly on low-noise datasets.

- It provides strong theoretical guarantees, such as exponential decay of the training error with increasing boosting rounds.

- Training is efficient due to the use of simple base learners that are fast to train.

- It supports early stopping based on validation performance, enabled by its sequential training process—a feature not typically available in bagging-based methods.

- Unlike bagging methods and random forests, AdaBoost uses the full dataset in each round without subsampling either examples or features.

- It provides reliable feature importance estimates by aggregating contributions across weighted base learners.

Disadvantages of AdaBoost:

- It is highly sensitive to outliers and mislabeled examples, which can be assigned exponentially increasing weights if repeatedly misclassified.

- Its performance strongly depends on the quality and capacity of the base learners: overly complex models can lead to overfitting, while extremely weak learners may require many boosting rounds and generalize poorly.

- It requires careful tuning of several hyperparameters—including the number of boosting rounds, the learning rate, and base learner complexity—to achieve optimal performance.

- Training can be computationally intensive, especially on large datasets or with many boosting rounds, as AdaBoost's sequential nature limits parallelization (unlike bagging methods).

- It does not support incremental learning; adding new data requires retraining the entire ensemble from scratch.

- It is generally less interpretable than simpler models due to the layered combination of many weak learners.

9.8   Gradient Boosting

Gradient boosting is an ensemble learning method that combines the principles of boosting with gradient-based optimization [201, 199, 438]. It constructs a sequence of predictive models, typically shallow regression trees (see Section 8.6), where each model is trained to correct the errors of the current ensemble by minimizing a suitable loss function.

Unlike AdaBoost, which adjusts instance weights to prioritize misclassified examples, gradient boosting fits each base model directly to the residual errors of the current ensemble. More precisely, at each iteration, a base learner is trained to approximate the negative gradient of the loss function with respect to the current ensemble's predictions. By adding the output of this learner to the ensemble, the method effectively performs gradient descent in function space. That is, rather than updating the parameters of a single model, gradient boosting incrementally improves the prediction function itself—a process known as **functional gradient descent**.

Gradient boosting is more flexible than AdaBoost, as it naturally supports a wide range of loss functions and learning tasks, including binary classification, multi-class classification, and regression, without requiring changes to the core algorithm.

When decision trees are used as the base learners, gradient boosting is commonly referred to as **gradient-boosted decision trees (GBDT)** or **gradient boosting machines (GBM)**.

The gradient boosting algorithm, introduced by Jerome Friedman in 2001 [201], has since evolved into a family of powerful algorithms—including XGBoost, LightGBM, and CatBoost—that significantly enhance the predictive performance and scalability of the original method. These algorithms are explored in depth in the next chapter.

Gradient boosting and its modern variants have consistently demonstrated outstanding performance on structured (tabular) data, often achieving state-of-the-art results across a wide range of supervised learning tasks—and in many cases, even outperforming deep learning methods [240, 550, 406].

9.8.1   Intuitive Introduction

In this section, we illustrate how gradient boosting works in the context of a simple regression problem. Consider a training set $\{(\mathbf{x}_i, y_i)\}_{i=1}^n$, where y is a continuous target variable. Gradient boosting constructs a sequence of weak models, typically regression trees with 3–5 levels, where each model is trained to predict the residuals of the current ensemble—that is, the differences between the actual targets and the ensemble's current predictions. By iteratively adding these regression trees to the ensemble, the overall prediction error gradually decreases over time. The procedure unfolds as follows:

1. Fit a base model $h_1(\mathbf{x})$ to the target values y.

2. Set the initial ensemble: $F_1(\mathbf{x}) = h_1(\mathbf{x})$.

3. Compute the residuals: $r_1 = y - F_1(\mathbf{x})$.

4. Fit a new base model $h_2(\mathbf{x})$ to the residuals r_1.

5. Update the ensemble: $F_2(\mathbf{x}) = F_1(\mathbf{x}) + h_2(\mathbf{x})$. This improves the predictions by bringing them closer to the actual targets.

6. Compute the new residuals: $r_2 = y - F_2(\mathbf{x})$.

7. Fit another base model $h_3(\mathbf{x})$ to the residuals r_2.

8. Update the ensemble: $F_3(\mathbf{x}) = F_2(\mathbf{x}) + h_3(\mathbf{x})$, further improving the ensemble's predictions.

9. Repeat this process for M iterations: at each step, fit a new model to the current residuals and update the ensemble.

10. Return the final ensemble $F_M(\mathbf{x})$.

We demonstrate this process in Python by building a sequence of regression trees, where each tree is trained to predict the residuals left by the previous models. First, we create a synthetic dataset with a single input feature x, uniformly sampled from the interval $[-0.5, 0.5]$, and a target variable defined as a quadratic function of x with added Gaussian noise:

```
n_samples = 100

X = np.random.rand(n_samples, 1) - 0.5
y = 5 * X[:, 0] ** 2 + 0.1 * np.random.randn(n_samples)
```

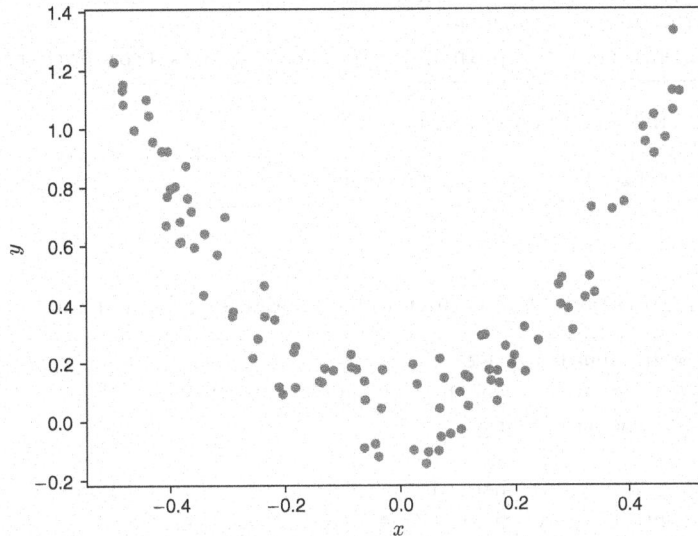

Figure 9.16: Synthetic dataset sampled from a quadratic function with added Gaussian noise

The resulting data points are shown in Figure 9.16.

We now build an ensemble of three regression trees, each with a maximum depth of 2, to predict the target value y from x. The first regression tree h_1 is fitted to the original target values:

```
h1 = DecisionTreeRegressor(max_depth=2, random_state=42)
h1.fit(X, y) # Fit the first tree
```

The first ensemble F_1 consists of this single tree:

```
F1 = [h1] # The first ensemble
F1_pred = h1.predict(X) # Predictions of F1
```

The R^2 score of the first ensemble is:

```
print(f'R2 score of F1: {r2_score(y, F1_pred):.4f}')
```

```
R2 score of F1: 0.7819
```

Next, we fit a second regression tree h_2 to the residuals of F_1:

```
y2 = y - F1_pred # Residuals of F1
h2 = DecisionTreeRegressor(max_depth=2, random_state=42)
h2.fit(X, y2) # Fit the second tree
```

We then add h_2 to the ensemble to form F_2, and update its predictions by summing the outputs of both trees:

```
F2 = [h1, h2] # The second ensemble
F2_pred = sum(h.predict(X) for h in F2) # Sum predictions from both trees
```

The R^2 score of the second ensemble is:

```
print(f'R2 score of F2: {r2_score(y, F2_pred):.4f}')
```

```
R2 score of F2: 0.8802
```

Lastly, a third regression tree h_3 is fitted to the residuals of F_2, and added to the ensemble:

```
y3 = y - F2_pred # Residuals of F2
h3 = DecisionTreeRegressor(max_depth=2, random_state=42)
h3.fit(X, y3) # Fit the third tree

F3 = [h1, h2, h3] # The third ensemble
F3_pred = sum(h.predict(X) for h in F3) # Final predictions
```

The R^2 score of the final ensemble is:

```
print(f'R2 score of F3: {r2_score(y, F3_pred):.4f}')
```

```
R2 score of F3: 0.9124
```

Notice how the R^2 score gradually increases as each tree is added to the ensemble, illustrating the effectiveness of gradient boosting in improving predictive performance. Figure 9.17 shows the residuals and the ensemble's predictions after each boosting iteration, clearly demonstrating how the model's fit to the target values improves over time. The code used to generate this plot is available in the Jupyter notebook `IntuitiveIntroduction.ipynb`[20] on the book's GitHub repository.

9.8.2   The Gradient Boosting Algorithm

The approach described in the previous section can be generalized to a wide range of learning tasks (e.g., classification) and loss functions. Instead of fitting the residuals (which are typically defined only in regression problems), each weak learner $h_m(\mathbf{x})$ is trained to approximate the **negative gradient** of the loss function with respect to the current ensemble's predictions $F_{m-1}(\mathbf{x})$. This negative gradient points in the direction of steepest descent of the loss function, indicating how the ensemble's predictions should be adjusted to minimize the loss.

In the special case of least squares regression, the negative gradient is proportional to the residuals $y - F_{m-1}(\mathbf{x})$, so fitting the negative gradient is equivalent to fitting the residuals:

---

20. https://github.com/roiyeho/ml-book/blob/main/Chapter09/Gradient%20Boosting/
       IntuitiveIntroduction.ipynb

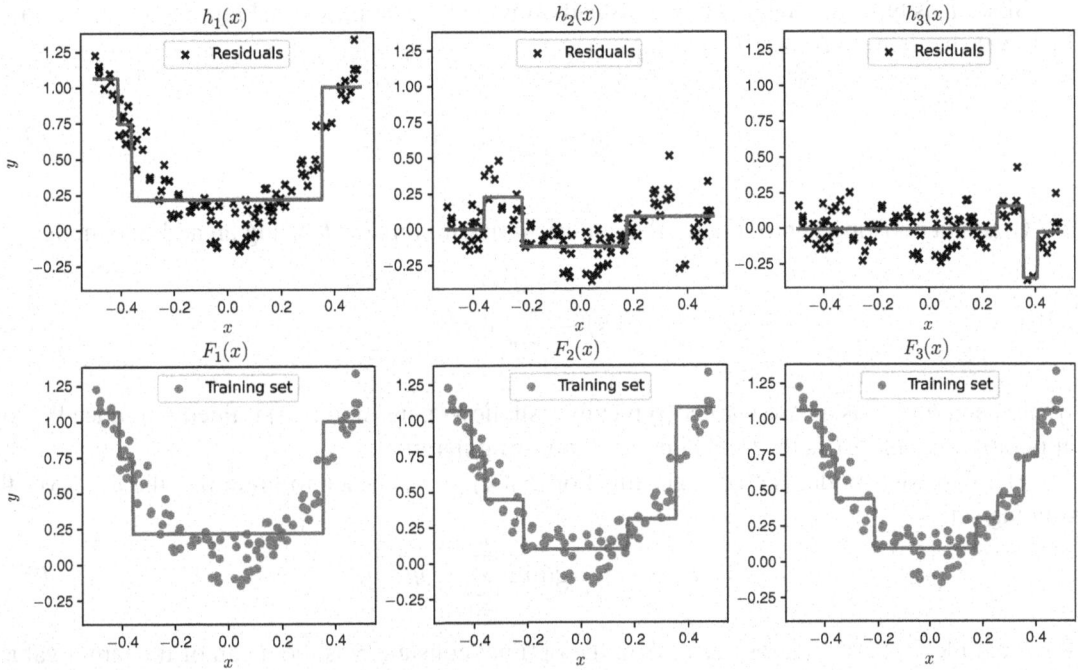

Figure 9.17: Visualization of model improvement using gradient boosting on a synthetic quadratic dataset. The top row shows the residuals that each successive regression tree—$h_1(x)$, $h_2(x)$, and $h_3(x)$—is trained to predict, along with their corresponding predictions. The bottom row displays the cumulative predictions of the ensembles, $F_1(x)$, $F_2(x)$, and $F_3(x)$. As additional trees are incorporated into the ensemble, its predictions become increasingly accurate, demonstrating how gradient boosting progressively improves the model's fit.

$$L_{\text{squared}}(y, F_{m-1}(\mathbf{x})) = (y - F_{m-1}(\mathbf{x}))^2, \tag{9.22}$$

$$-\frac{\partial L_{\text{squared}}(y, F_{m-1}(\mathbf{x}))}{\partial F_{m-1}(\mathbf{x})} = 2(y - F_{m-1}(\mathbf{x})). \tag{9.23}$$

Note that, unlike standard gradient descent, the derivative is taken with respect to the model's predictions $F_{m-1}(\mathbf{x})$ and not its parameters, since we are optimizing the prediction function itself.

Based on this key insight, we now derive a general gradient boosting algorithm applicable to any differentiable loss function. Recall that in supervised learning, the goal is to find a prediction function from input vectors $\mathbf{x}$ to labels y that minimizes the expected loss over the data-generating distribution P:

$$F^* = \underset{F}{\arg\min}\, \mathbb{E}_{(\mathbf{x}, y) \sim P}[L(y, F(\mathbf{x}))]. \tag{9.24}$$

Since P is typically unknown, we instead minimize the empirical risk, defined as the average loss over the training dataset $D = \{(\mathbf{x}_i, y_i)\}_{i=1}^{n}$:

$$\hat{F} = \underset{F}{\text{argmin}} \sum_{i=1}^{n} L(y_i, F(\mathbf{x}_i)). \tag{9.25}$$

Gradient boosting approximates the empirical risk minimizer $\hat{F}$ using an additive model:

$$\hat{F}(\mathbf{x}) = \sum_{m=0}^{M} h_m(\mathbf{x}), \tag{9.26}$$

where each $h_m(\mathbf{x})$ is a base learner (typically a shallow regression tree) trained to reduce the loss at iteration m, and M is the total number of boosting iterations.

The first base model is a constant function $F_0(\mathbf{x}) = \gamma$, chosen to minimize the loss over the training set:

$$F_0(\mathbf{x}) = \underset{\gamma}{\text{argmin}} \sum_{i=1}^{n} L(y_i, \gamma). \tag{9.27}$$

For example, in least-squares regression, the optimal constant γ is the mean of the target values, as this minimizes the mean squared loss. Other learning tasks lead to different choices of γ, as we will see later.

Then, for $m = 1, 2, \ldots, M$, the model is incrementally updated in a greedy, stage-wise fashion:

$$F_m(\mathbf{x}) = F_{m-1}(\mathbf{x}) + h_m(\mathbf{x}), \tag{9.28}$$

where each base learner h_m is selected to minimize the loss of the updated ensemble on the training data:

$$h_m = \underset{h \in H}{\text{argmin}} \sum_{i=1}^{n} L(y_i, F_{m-1}(\mathbf{x}_i) + h(\mathbf{x}_i)). \tag{9.29}$$

This optimization problem is defined over functions h, rather than parameter vectors in Euclidean space, and thus cannot be solved using standard optimization techniques like gradient descent. Instead, gradient boosting employs a **functional gradient descent** approach: it seeks a function h_m whose values at the training inputs $\mathbf{x}_i$ align with the steepest descent directions of the loss. These directions are given by the negative gradient of the loss function with respect to the current ensemble's predictions F_{m-1}.

Formally, the negative gradient vector at iteration m is defined as

$$\mathbf{r}_m = (r_{m1}, \ldots, r_{mn})^T,$$

where each component is given by

$$r_{mi} = -\frac{\partial L(y_i, F_{m-1}(\mathbf{x}_i))}{\partial F_{m-1}(\mathbf{x}_i)}. \tag{9.30}$$

The components r_{mi} are called **pseudo-residuals** because they play a similar role to residuals in regression: they indicate how the model's predictions should be adjusted to reduce the loss.

The base model h_m is chosen to approximate the negative gradient by fitting to the pseudo-residuals using a least-squares criterion:

$$h_m = \underset{h \in H}{\mathrm{argmin}} \sum_{i=1}^{n} [r_{mi} - h(\mathbf{x}_i)]^2. \tag{9.31}$$

In other words, each boosting iteration fits a base model h_m to the negative gradient of the loss with respect to the current ensemble's predictions. Geometrically, this amounts to finding a function in the hypothesis space H whose vector of predictions at the training points best aligns with the negative gradient vector $\mathbf{r}_m$—that is, a function whose output vector is "most parallel" to $\mathbf{r}_m$. Adding h_m to the ensemble then reduces the loss in the steepest descent direction, gradually improving the model. This approach transforms the complex functional optimization problem in Equation (9.29) into the simpler least-squares problem in Equation (9.31).

Overall, gradient boosting operates like gradient descent in function space rather than parameter space. At each iteration, it selects a new function from the hypothesis space H, rather than adjusting the parameters of a fixed hypothesis h. This allows the use of flexible, non-parametric base learners such as decision trees, which do not depend on a fixed number of parameters.

The optimal step size for updating the ensemble at each iteration is typically determined using a **line search** (see Section E.4.1.4). This involves finding the scalar coefficient β_m that minimizes the loss function along the current update direction:

$$\beta_m = \underset{\beta}{\mathrm{argmin}} \sum_{i=1}^{n} L\left(y_i, F_{m-1}(\mathbf{x}_i) + \beta h_m(\mathbf{x}_i)\right). \tag{9.32}$$

This one-dimensional optimization problem is relatively easy to solve, either analytically (in simple cases such as least squares) or via efficient numerical methods, since it involves minimizing a scalar function with respect to a single variable β.

To improve generalization, Friedman introduced a **shrinkage factor** (or learning rate) that scales the step size at each iteration [202]:

$$F_m(\mathbf{x}) = F_{m-1}(\mathbf{x}) + \nu \beta_m h_m(\mathbf{x}), \tag{9.33}$$

where $0 < \nu \leq 1$ is the shrinkage factor (typically $\nu \leq 0.1$).

Shrinkage reduces the influence of each base model, allowing the ensemble to improve more gradually. This often leads to better generalization but requires more boosting iterations. Like AdaBoost, gradient boosting is generally resistant to overfitting—performance tends to plateau rather than degrade, even after many iterations (see Section 9.8.6).

The complete gradient boosting algorithm is summarized in Algorithm 9.3. The specific implementations of steps 3 and 4 in the algorithm depend on the choice of loss function and base learner. Detailed derivations for regression trees and common loss functions, such as squared loss and log loss, are provided in Section 9.8.4.

Algorithm 9.3 Gradient Boosting

Input:

 Training set $\{(\mathbf{x}_i, y_i)\}_{i=1}^{n}$
 Differentiable loss function $L(y, \hat{y})$
 Weak learning algorithm
 Number of boosting iterations M
 Learning rate ν

1: Initialize the ensemble with a constant model:

$$F_0(\mathbf{x}) = \operatorname*{argmin}_{\gamma} \sum_{i=1}^{n} L(y_i, \gamma)$$

2: **for** $m = 1$ **to** M **do**
3:   Compute the pseudo-residuals:

$$r_{im} = -\frac{\partial L(y_i, F_{m-1}(\mathbf{x}_i))}{\partial F_{m-1}(\mathbf{x}_i)}, \quad i = 1, \ldots, n$$

4:   Fit a base model $h_m(\mathbf{x})$ to predict the pseudo-residuals r_{im} from the features $\mathbf{x}_i$
5:   Perform a line search to find the optimal step size:

$$\beta_m = \operatorname*{argmin}_{\beta} \sum_{i=1}^{n} L\left(y_i, F_{m-1}(\mathbf{x}_i) + \beta h_m(\mathbf{x}_i)\right)$$

6:   Update the ensemble:

$$F_m(\mathbf{x}) = F_{m-1}(\mathbf{x}) + \nu \beta_m h_m(\mathbf{x})$$

7: **return** the final ensemble $F_M(\mathbf{x})$

9.8.3 Stochastic Gradient Boosting

In a follow-up paper, Friedman introduced **stochastic gradient boosting**, a simple yet effective extension of gradient boosting that incorporates random subsampling of the training data, similar to bagging [202]. In this method, each boosting iteration fits a base learner to a randomly selected subset of the training data (sampled *without* replacement).

 This strategy increases the diversity among the base learners, helping to mitigate overfitting and improve generalization. It also enables the use of out-of-bag (OOB) samples—those not included in the current subset—for estimating the model's generalization error without requiring a separate validation set (see Section 9.4.4).

Empirical results from Friedman's study show that stochastic gradient boosting often outperforms traditional gradient boosting, even when using the same number of base models. The gains are especially pronounced on small datasets or when using complex, overfitting-prone learners. Additionally, training is typically faster since each base model is fit to a smaller dataset.

Choosing the subsample size involves balancing predictive performance and computational efficiency. Smaller subsamples tend to increase diversity among base learners and reduce overfitting, but may also introduce bias and require more boosting iterations to achieve competitive performance. Friedman's experiments suggest that using 50% of the training data per iteration often works well in practice, though the optimal subsample size can vary depending on the characteristics of the dataset.

9.8.4 Gradient-Boosted Decision Trees

Gradient-boosted decision trees (GBDT), also known as gradient-boosted trees (GBT) or gradient boosting machines (GBM), implement the gradient boosting framework using regression trees as base learners.

At each boosting iteration m, a regression tree h_m is trained to fit the pseudo-residuals r_{im}, which are components of the negative gradient of the loss function with respect to the current ensemble's predictions F_{m-1}. These trees are typically grown using mean squared error (MSE) as the splitting criterion, resulting in regions where the pseudo-residuals are more homogeneous and have lower variance. Although called "regression trees," these models are not restricted to regression problems—they are used here to approximate gradients, which can be derived from any differentiable loss function, including those used in classification.

Unlike AdaBoost, which commonly employs decision stumps, GBDT uses shallow trees with greater depth (typically between three and five levels). Decision stumps are often too simplistic to provide meaningful gradient corrections, while fully grown trees that perfectly fit the residuals would overfit and leave no signal for subsequent learners. Shallow trees strike a good balance: they are expressive enough to capture important feature interactions, yet constrained enough to avoid overfitting and to preserve residual information for future updates.

Since the regression trees are not fully grown, the leaf nodes typically contain samples with varying pseudo-residuals. For least-squares regression, the optimal prediction for each leaf is simply the average of the pseudo-residuals in that leaf. However, this does not extend naturally to other loss functions, such as those used in classification. A more general approach is to determine the output value for each leaf by minimizing the total loss incurred by the ensemble after adding the new regression tree.

Formally, let J_m denote the number of leaves in the regression tree h_m. The tree partitions the input space into J_m disjoint regions, $R_{1m}, \ldots, R_{J_m,m}$, with each region corresponding to a leaf node. Each leaf outputs a constant value γ_{jm}, computed based on the training samples in region R_{jm}. The function represented by the tree can thus be written as:

$$h_m(\mathbf{x}) = \sum_{j=1}^{J_m} \gamma_{jm} \mathbb{1}\{\mathbf{x} \in R_{jm}\}. \tag{9.34}$$

This expression indicates that the tree output $h_m(\mathbf{x})$ is equal to the constant γ_{jm} assigned to the region R_{jm} containing the input $\mathbf{x}$.

To determine the optimal output value γ_{jm} for each leaf, we minimize the loss over all training examples assigned to that leaf:

$$\gamma_{jm} = \underset{\gamma}{\operatorname{argmin}} \sum_{\mathbf{x}_i \in R_{jm}} L(y_i, F_{m-1}(\mathbf{x}_i) + \gamma). \tag{9.35}$$

This optimization finds the best constant increment to add to the current ensemble prediction $F_{m-1}(\mathbf{x}_i)$ for all examples in region R_{jm}. Conceptually, this step corresponds to performing a one-dimensional line search in function space to determine the optimal update along the direction defined by the new tree.

Typically, the values γ_{jm} can be computed analytically in closed form, with the exact expression depending on the chosen loss function. Once all the coefficients γ_{jm} have been determined, the ensemble is updated as follows:

$$F_m(\mathbf{x}) = F_{m-1}(\mathbf{x}) + \nu \sum_{j=1}^{J_m} \gamma_{jm} \mathbb{1}\{\mathbf{x} \in R_{jm}\}. \tag{9.36}$$

where ν is the learning rate. This update adds the contribution of the new tree to the ensemble prediction, scaled by ν, with each input $\mathbf{x}$ receiving the output value of the leaf it falls into.

Algorithm 9.4 outlines the general pseudocode for constructing gradient-boosted decision trees. The implementation details of the initial model (line 1), the computation of pseudo-residuals (line 3), and the calculation of the optimal γ_{jm} coefficients (line 6) depend on the specific loss function. The following subsections describe how these steps are carried out for regression, binary classification, and multi-class classification. In Exercise 9.26, you will implement this algorithm in Python from scratch.

9.8.4.1 Regression Problems

This subsection describes how gradient-boosted decision trees are applied to regression tasks, focusing specifically on least-squares regression.

Initial Model

In least-squares regression, the objective is simply to minimize the squared loss:

$$L_{\text{squared}}(y, F(\mathbf{x})) = (y - F(\mathbf{x}))^2. \tag{9.37}$$

The constant prediction that minimizes the total squared loss over the training set is the mean of the target values:

$$F_0(\mathbf{x}) = \frac{1}{n} \sum_{i=1}^{n} y_i. \tag{9.38}$$

This result can be easily derived by differentiating the loss and solving for the minimizer (left as an exercise).

Algorithm 9.4 Gradient-Boosted Decision Trees

Input:

Training set $\{(\mathbf{x}_i, y_i)\}_{i=1}^n$
Differentiable loss function $L(y, \hat{y})$
Number of boosting iterations M
Learning rate ν

1: Initialize the ensemble with a constant model:

$$F_0(\mathbf{x}) = \underset{\gamma}{\arg\min} \sum_{i=1}^n L(y_i, \gamma)$$

2: **for** $m = 1$ to M **do**
3:     Compute the pseudo-residuals:

$$r_{im} = -\frac{\partial L(y_i, F_{m-1}(\mathbf{x}_i))}{\partial F_{m-1}(\mathbf{x}_i)}, \quad i = 1, \ldots, n$$

4:     Fit a regression tree to the pseudo-residuals r_{im}
5:     Let the leaf regions be $R_{1m}, \ldots, R_{J_m,m}$
6:     **for** $j = 1$ **to** J_m **do**
7:         Compute the optimal leaf value:

$$\gamma_{jm} = \underset{\gamma}{\arg\min} \sum_{\mathbf{x}_i \in R_{jm}} L(y_i, F_{m-1}(\mathbf{x}_i) + \gamma)$$

8:     Update the ensemble:

$$F_m(\mathbf{x}) = F_{m-1}(\mathbf{x}) + \nu \sum_{j=1}^{J_m} \gamma_{jm} \mathbb{1}\{\mathbf{x} \in R_{jm}\}$$

9: **return** the final ensemble $F_M(\mathbf{x})$

Pseudo-Residuals Computation

At each boosting iteration, $m = 1, \ldots, M$, a regression tree is fit to the pseudo-residuals. These are given by the negative partial derivatives of the squared loss with respect to the predictions of the current ensemble $F_{m-1}(\mathbf{x}_i)$:

$$r_{im} = -\frac{\partial L_{\text{squared}}(y_i, F_{m-1}(\mathbf{x}_i))}{\partial F_{m-1}(\mathbf{x}_i)} = 2(y_i - F_{m-1}(\mathbf{x}_i)). \tag{9.39}$$

Thus, in this case, the pseudo-residuals are simply twice the standard regression residuals.

Output Values for Leaf Nodes

After constructing the regression tree, the next step is to determine the optimal output value for each leaf node. For each region R_{jm} defined by the tree, we find the value γ_{jm} that minimizes the squared loss over the training samples in that region:

$$L = \sum_{\mathbf{x}_i \in R_{jm}} [y_i - (F_{m-1}(\mathbf{x}_i) + \gamma_{jm})]^2 . \tag{9.40}$$

To find the optimal γ_{jm}, we differentiate the loss function with respect to γ_{jm} and set the derivative to zero:

$$\frac{\partial L}{\partial \gamma_{jm}} = -2 \sum_{\mathbf{x}_i \in R_{jm}} (y_i - F_{m-1}(\mathbf{x}_i) - \gamma_{jm}) = 0,$$

$$\sum_{\mathbf{x}_i \in R_{jm}} \gamma_{jm} = \sum_{\mathbf{x}_i \in R_{jm}} (y_i - F_{m-1}(\mathbf{x}_i)),$$

$$\gamma_{jm} = \frac{\sum_{\mathbf{x}_i \in R_{jm}} (y_i - F_{m-1}(\mathbf{x}_i))}{|R_{jm}|}, \tag{9.41}$$

where $|R_{jm}|$ denotes the number of training examples in region R_{jm}. Thus, the optimal output value for each leaf is the average of the residuals in its corresponding region.

9.8.4.2   Binary Classification

Gradient boosting can be adapted for binary classification by mapping the continuous output of the ensemble $F(\mathbf{x})$ to a probability in the range $[0, 1]$. Similar to logistic regression (see Section 5.2), this is achieved by applying the sigmoid (logistic) function $\sigma(x)$, which transforms $F(\mathbf{x})$ into the estimated probability that the sample $\mathbf{x}$ belongs to the positive class:

$$p = P(y = 1|\mathbf{x}) = \sigma(F(\mathbf{x})) = \frac{1}{1 + e^{-F(\mathbf{x})}}. \tag{9.42}$$

In this formulation, $F(\mathbf{x})$ represents the log-odds, that is, the logarithm of the odds ratio:

$$F(\mathbf{x}) = \log \frac{p}{1 - p}. \tag{9.43}$$

To train the model, we minimize the log loss over the training examples $(\mathbf{x}_i, y_i)$, defined as (see Section 5.3.1):

$$L_{\log}(y_i, F(\mathbf{x}_i)) = -y_i \log p_i - (1 - y_i) \log(1 - p_i), \tag{9.44}$$

where $p_i = \sigma(F(\mathbf{x}_i))$.

Initial Model

The initial model $F_0(\mathbf{x})$ is set to a constant equal to the log-odds of the positive class in the training set:

$$F_0(\mathbf{x}) = \log \frac{n_+}{n_-}, \tag{9.45}$$

where n_+ and n_- denote the number of positive and negative samples, respectively. This initial value represents the prior log-odds before any trees are added to the ensemble.

Pseudo-Residuals Computation

The pseudo-residuals r_{im} are defined as the negative partial derivatives of the log loss with respect to the current ensemble's predictions $F_{m-1}(\mathbf{x}_i)$. Let $p_{im} = \sigma(F_{m-1}(\mathbf{x}_i))$ denote the predicted probability at iteration $m - 1$. Using the chain rule and the derivative of the sigmoid function $\sigma'(x) = \sigma(x)(1 - \sigma(x))$, we obtain:

$$
\begin{aligned}
r_{im} &= -\frac{\partial L_{\log}(y_i, F_{m-1}(\mathbf{x}_i))}{\partial F_{m-1}(\mathbf{x}_i)} \\[2mm]
&= -\frac{\partial\left(-y_i \log p_{im} - (1 - y_i)\log(1 - p_{im})\right)}{\partial p_{im}} \cdot \frac{\partial p_{im}}{\partial F_{m-1}(\mathbf{x}_i)} \\[2mm]
&= \frac{\partial\left(y_i \log p_{im} + (1 - y_i)\log(1 - p_{im})\right)}{\partial p_{im}} \cdot \frac{\partial p_{im}}{\partial F_{m-1}(\mathbf{x}_i)} \\[2mm]
&= \left(\frac{y_i}{p_{im}} - \frac{1 - y_i}{1 - p_{im}}\right) \cdot p_{im}(1 - p_{im}) \\[2mm]
&= y_i(1 - p_{im}) - (1 - y_i)p_{im} \\[2mm]
&= y_i - p_{im}.
\end{aligned}
\tag{9.46}
$$

The pseudo-residuals are simply the differences between the true labels y_i and the predicted probabilities p_{im}. When constructing the regression trees, splits are selected to increase the homogeneity of the pseudo-residuals within each region, encouraging samples with similar prediction errors to be grouped into the same leaf.

Output Values for Leaf Nodes

The optimal coefficient γ_{jm} adjusts the model's predictions in region R_{jm} to minimize the total log loss over the samples in that region. It is obtained by solving:

$$\gamma_{jm} = \underset{\gamma}{\arg\min} \sum_{\mathbf{x}_i \in R_{jm}} L(y_i, F_{m-1}(\mathbf{x}_i) + \gamma)$$

$$= \underset{\gamma}{\arg\min} \sum_{\mathbf{x}_i \in R_{jm}} [-y_i \log(\sigma(F_{m-1}(\mathbf{x}_i) + \gamma)) - (1 - y_i) \log(1 - \sigma(F_{m-1}(\mathbf{x}_i) + \gamma))]$$

$$(9.47)$$

Due to the nonlinearity of the sigmoid and logarithmic functions, this optimization problem has no closed-form solution. To address this, we use Newton's method, which iteratively approximates the minimum of the loss function using second-order information (see Section E.5.1). However, rather than running Newton's method to convergence for each leaf, we take only a single Newton step as an efficient approximation. This greatly reduces computation time per boosting round and helps mitigate overfitting, as the ensemble is updated incrementally and refined over successive iterations.

To determine the optimal Newton step, we first approximate the loss function using a second-order Taylor expansion around the current ensemble prediction $F_{m-1}(\mathbf{x}_i)$:

$$L(y_i, F_{m-1}(\mathbf{x}_i) + \gamma) \approx L(y_i, F_{m-1}(\mathbf{x}_i)) + \frac{\partial L(y_i, F_{m-1}(\mathbf{x}_i))}{\partial F_{m-1}(\mathbf{x}_i)}\gamma + \frac{1}{2}\frac{\partial^2 L(y_i, F_{m-1}(\mathbf{x}_i))}{\partial F_{m-1}(\mathbf{x}_i)^2}\gamma^2.$$

$$(9.48)$$

This provides a local quadratic approximation of the objective. To minimize the approximated loss, we differentiate with respect to γ and set the derivative to zero:

$$\frac{\partial L(y_i, F_{m-1}(\mathbf{x}_i) + \gamma)}{\partial \gamma} \approx \frac{\partial L(y_i, F_{m-1}(\mathbf{x}_i))}{\partial F_{m-1}(\mathbf{x}_i)} + \frac{\partial^2 L(y_i, F_{m-1}(\mathbf{x}_i))}{\partial F_{m-1}(\mathbf{x}_i)^2}\gamma = 0. \qquad (9.49)$$

Solving for γ gives:

$$\gamma = -\frac{\dfrac{\partial L(y_i, F_{m-1}(\mathbf{x}_i))}{\partial F_{m-1}(\mathbf{x}_i)}}{\dfrac{\partial^2 L(y_i, F_{m-1}(\mathbf{x}_i))}{\partial F_{m-1}(\mathbf{x}_i)^2}}. \qquad (9.50)$$

Thus, the optimal value of γ is given by the ratio of the negative first derivative of the loss function with respect to the current ensemble prediction (i.e., the pseudo-residual) to its second derivative. Extending this result to all samples in region R_{jm}, we obtain the optimal adjustment γ_{jm} for that region:

$$\gamma_{jm} = -\frac{\sum_{\mathbf{x}_i \in R_{jm}} \dfrac{\partial L(y_i, F_{m-1}(\mathbf{x}_i))}{\partial F_{m-1}(\mathbf{x}_i)}}{\sum_{\mathbf{x}_i \in R_{jm}} \dfrac{\partial^2 L(y_i, F_{m-1}(\mathbf{x}_i))}{\partial F_{m-1}(\mathbf{x}_i)^2}}. \qquad (9.51)$$

Note that this formula is applicable to any twice-differentiable loss function, not just the log loss.

To apply this result to the log loss, we first compute its first and second derivatives. The first derivative with respect to the ensemble prediction is (as previously shown in Equation (9.46)):

$$\frac{\partial L_{\log}(y_i, F_{m-1}(\mathbf{x}_i))}{\partial F_{m-1}(\mathbf{x}_i)} = p_{im} - y_i, \tag{9.52}$$

where $p_{im} = \sigma(F_{m-1}(\mathbf{x}_i))$.

The second derivative is obtained by differentiating the first:

$$\frac{\partial^2 L_{\log}(y_i, F_{m-1}(\mathbf{x}_i))}{\partial F_{m-1}(\mathbf{x}_i)^2} = \frac{\partial[\sigma(F_{m-1}(\mathbf{x}_i)) - y_i]}{\partial F_{m-1}(\mathbf{x}_i)} = \sigma(F_{m-1}(\mathbf{x}_i))(1 - \sigma(F_{m-1}(\mathbf{x}_i)))$$

$$= p_{im}(1 - p_{im}). \tag{9.53}$$

Substituting into the Newton update formula, we obtain the optimal step:

$$\gamma = \frac{y_i - p_{im}}{p_{im}(1 - p_{im})}. \tag{9.54}$$

This expression can be interpreted as follows. The numerator, $y_i - p_{im}$, measures the discrepancy between the predicted probability p_{im} and the true label y_i, indicating both the direction and magnitude of the needed correction. The denominator, $p_{im}(1 - p_{im})$, acts as a scaling factor that reflects the model's confidence in its prediction. When p_{im} is close to 0 or 1 (i.e., the model is confident), the denominator is small, resulting in a larger adjustment γ. Conversely, when p_{im} is closer to 0.5 (i.e., the model is uncertain), the denominator is larger, leading to a more conservative update. Thus, the update is scaled to apply larger corrections to confidently incorrect predictions and smaller ones to uncertain cases, using the second derivative to adjust the step size based on the local curvature of the loss.

Extending this result to all samples in region R_{jm}, we obtain the optimal adjustment γ_{jm} for that region:

$$\gamma_{jm} = \frac{\sum_{\mathbf{x}_i \in R_{jm}} (y_i - p_{im})}{\sum_{\mathbf{x}_i \in R_{jm}} p_{im}(1 - p_{im})}. \tag{9.55}$$

9.8.4.3   Multi-Class Classification

In a multi-class classification problem with K classes, gradient boosting constructs K regression trees at each of the M boosting rounds—one for each class. Let h_{mk} denote the tree built for class k in round m.

Let p_{imk} be the predicted probability that sample $\mathbf{x}_i$ belongs to class k at boosting round m. Similar to multinomial logistic regression (see Section 5.8), this probability is modeled using the softmax function applied to the current ensemble scores for all classes:

$$p_{imk} = \frac{e^{F_{mk}(\mathbf{x}_i)}}{\sum_{j=1}^{K} e^{F_{mj}(\mathbf{x}_i)}}, \tag{9.56}$$

where $F_{mk}(\mathbf{x}_i)$ is the cumulative score for class k up to boosting round m:

$$F_{mk}(\mathbf{x}_i) = F_{0k}(\mathbf{x}_i) + \sum_{j=1}^{m} h_{jk}(\mathbf{x}_i). \tag{9.57}$$

Here, F_{0k} is the initial model for class k, and h_{jk} is the regression tree for class k in round j.

The optimization objective in multi-class classification is to minimize the cross-entropy loss, which quantifies the discrepancy between the predicted probabilities and the true class labels (see Section 5.8.2.1):

$$L_{\text{CE}}(\mathbf{y}_i, \mathbf{F}_m(\mathbf{x}_i)) = -\sum_{k=1}^{K} y_{ik} \log p_{imk}, \tag{9.58}$$

where $\mathbf{y}_i$ is the one-hot encoded vector representing the true label of $\mathbf{x}_i$, $\mathbf{F}_m(\mathbf{x}_i) = (F_{m1}(\mathbf{x}_i),$ $F_{m2}(\mathbf{x}_i), \ldots, F_{mK}(\mathbf{x}_i))$ is the vector of ensemble scores for all classes at boosting round m, and p_{imk} is the predicted probability for class k, as defined in Equation (9.56).

Initial Model

The initial model for each class is defined as the logarithm of the class's prior probability, computed from the class distribution in the training set:

$$F_{0k}(\mathbf{x}) = \log\left(\frac{n_k}{n}\right), \tag{9.59}$$

where n_k is the number of training samples in class k, and n is the total number of training samples. Note that F_{0k} is a constant and does not depend on the input $\mathbf{x}$.

Pseudo-Residuals Computation

At each boosting round m, K regression trees are fit to the pseudo-residuals for each class k. These pseudo-residuals are the negative partial derivatives of the cross-entropy loss with respect to the class-specific outputs $F_{mk}(\mathbf{x}_i)$ (see Exercise 9.21):

$$r_{imk} = -\frac{\partial L_{\text{CE}}(\mathbf{y}_i, \mathbf{F}_m(\mathbf{x}_i))}{\partial F_{mk}(\mathbf{x}_i)} = y_{ik} - p_{imk}. \tag{9.60}$$

This expression is identical to the one derived for binary classification (Equation (9.46)) when applied to class k, since the log loss is a special case of the cross-entropy loss with two classes.

Output Values for Leaf Nodes

To find the optimal values γ_{jmk} used to update the model's predictions in each region R_{jmk} of the tree for class k, we first compute the second derivative of the cross-entropy loss with respect to the predictions of the current ensemble (see Exercise 9.21):

$$\frac{\partial^2 L_{\text{CE}}(\mathbf{y}_i, \mathbf{F}_m(\mathbf{x}_i))}{\partial F_{mk}(\mathbf{x}_i)^2} = p_{imk}(1 - p_{imk}). \tag{9.61}$$

This yields the following expression for the optimal leaf value γ_{jmk}:

$$\gamma_{jmk} = \frac{\sum_{\mathbf{x}_i \in R_{jmk}} (y_{ik} - p_{imk})}{\sum_{\mathbf{x}_i \in R_{jmk}} p_{imk}(1 - p_{imk})}. \tag{9.62}$$

	Age	Income	Education	Buys
1	25	Low	High School	1
2	30	Low	College	1
3	22	Medium	College	1
4	35	Low	High School	0
5	28	Medium	College	0
6	40	High	College	1

Table 9.10: Toy training dataset for illustrating the gradient boosting process

9.8.5 Numerical Example on a Toy Dataset

To better understand the gradient boosting process, we illustrate it using a small binary classification problem. Table 9.10 shows a toy dataset containing information about six customers. The objective is to predict whether a customer will buy a product based on three input features: the customer's age, income level (Low, Medium, or High), and education level (High School or College).

We will manually build a gradient boosting classifier using shallow regression trees with a maximum depth of 2. To emphasize the effect of each boosting iteration, we use a relatively large learning rate of $\nu = 0.5$. Each decision tree is built using binary splits, following the CART algorithm.

9.8.5.1 Model Initialization

The model is initialized with a constant prediction equal to the log-odds of the positive class in the training data:

$$F_0(\mathbf{x}) = \log\left(\frac{\text{Count of } y_i = 1}{\text{Count of } y_i = 0}\right) = \log\left(\frac{4}{2}\right) \approx 0.693.$$

After model initialization, the predicted probability for all the samples is:

$$p_{i0} = \sigma(F_0(\mathbf{x})) = \frac{1}{1 + e^{-0.693}} \approx 0.667.$$

The initial pseudo-residuals, computed as $y_i - p_{i0}$, are shown in Table 9.11.

9.8.5.2 First Boosting Round

In the first boosting round, we construct a regression tree to fit the initial pseudo-residuals. At each node, the tree-growing algorithm selects the split that yields the greatest reduction in the mean squared error (MSE) of the pseudo-residuals. The goal is to create partitions where the residuals are as homogeneous as possible, thereby improving prediction accuracy.

	Log-odds $F_0(\mathbf{x}_i)$	Probability $p_{i0} = \sigma(F_0(\mathbf{x}_i))$	Label y_i	Pseudo-residual $y_i - p_{i0}$
1	0.693	0.667	1	$1 - 0.667 = 0.333$
2	0.693	0.667	1	$1 - 0.667 = 0.333$
3	0.693	0.667	1	$1 - 0.667 = 0.333$
4	0.693	0.667	0	$0 - 0.667 = -0.667$
5	0.693	0.667	0	$0 - 0.667 = -0.667$
6	0.693	0.667	1	$1 - 0.667 = 0.333$

Table 9.11: Predicted probabilities and pseudo-residuals after model initialization

Regression Tree Fitting

We begin by determining the best split for the root node. The mean of the pseudo-residuals for all six training samples is:
$$\frac{4 \cdot 0.333 + 2 \cdot (-0.667)}{6} = 0.$$

The MSE at the root node (i.e., the variance of the pseudo-residuals) is then:

$$\frac{4 \cdot (0.333 - 0)^2 + 2 \cdot (-0.667 - 0)^2}{6} = 0.222.$$

Next, we evaluate the reduction in MSE achieved by each possible split. For example, consider the split on Education = High School:

- Left group (Education = High School): samples 1, 4

- Right group (Education = College): samples 2, 3, 5, 6

Left group MSE:

- Pseudo-residuals: $[0.333, -0.667]$

- Mean: $\frac{0.333 + (-0.667)}{2} = -0.167$

- MSE: $\frac{(0.333 - (-0.167))^2 + (-0.667 - (-0.167))^2}{2} = 0.25$

Split	Left Node	Left MSE	Right Node	Right MSE	ΔMSE
Income = Low	[1, 2, 4]	0.222	[3, 5, 6]	0.222	0
Income = Medium	[3, 5]	0.25	[1, 2, 4, 6]	0.1875	0.0137
Income = High	[6]	0	[1, 2, 3, 4, 5]	0.24	0.022
Education = HS	[1, 4]	0.25	[2, 3, 5, 6]	0.1875	0.0137
Age < 23.5	[3]	0	[1, 2, 4, 5, 6]	0.24	0.022
Age < 26.5	[1, 3]	0	[2, 4, 5, 6]	0.25	0.0553
Age < 29	[1, 3, 5]	0.222	[2, 4, 6]	0.222	0
Age < 32.5	[1, 2, 3, 5]	0.1875	[4, 6]	0.25	0.0137
Age < 37.5	[1, 2, 3, 4, 5]	0.24	[6]	0	0.022

Table 9.12: Candidate root node splits and their corresponding MSE reductions. The Left Node and Right Node columns list the sample indices in each child; Left MSE and Right MSE report the MSE of the pseudo-residuals within each group; ΔMSE denotes the reduction in MSE from the split. HS = High School.

Right group MSE:

- Pseudo-residuals: $[0.333, 0.333, -0.667, 0.333]$

- Mean: $\dfrac{0.333 + 0.333 + (-0.667) + 0.333}{4} = 0.083$

- MSE: $\dfrac{3 \cdot (0.333 - 0.083)^2 + (-0.667 - 0.083)^2}{4} = 0.1875$

Overall reduction in MSE:

- Weighted average of the MSEs after the split:

$$\frac{2}{6} \cdot 0.25 + \frac{4}{6} \cdot 0.1875 = 0.2083$$

- Reduction in MSE: $0.222 - 0.2083 = 0.0137$

Table 9.12 shows the reductions in MSE for all candidate splits at the root. For the continuous feature Age, we sort the values and consider the midpoints between consecutive ages as potential split thresholds.

The best split is Age < 26.5, achieving the greatest reduction in MSE (0.0553). The left child node resulting from this split contains samples with identical pseudo-residuals, leading to an MSE of 0. Therefore, no further splits are needed in that branch.

We now examine the right child node, which contains samples 2, 4, 5, and 6. The MSE of their pseudo-residuals is 0.25. Table 9.13 lists all possible splits for these four samples and the corresponding MSE reductions.

In this case, four splits achieve the maximum reduction in MSE (0.0835). We arbitrarily choose Income = Medium for the split. Since the tree is limited to a maximum depth of two, no further splitting is performed. The final regression tree from the first boosting round is shown in Figure 9.18.

Split	Left Node	Left MSE	Right Node	Right MSE	ΔMSE
Income = Low	[2, 4]	0.25	[5, 6]	0.25	0
Income = Medium	[5]	0	[2, 4, 6]	0.222	0.0835
Income = High	[6]	0	[2, 4, 5]	0.222	0.0835
Education = HS	[4]	0	[2, 5, 6]	0.222	0.0835
Age < 29	[5]	0	[2, 4, 6]	0.222	0.0835
Age < 32.5	[2, 5]	0.25	[4, 6]	0.25	0
Age < 37.5	[2, 4, 5]	0.222	[6]	0	0.0835

Table 9.13: Candidate splits at the right child node and their corresponding MSE reductions

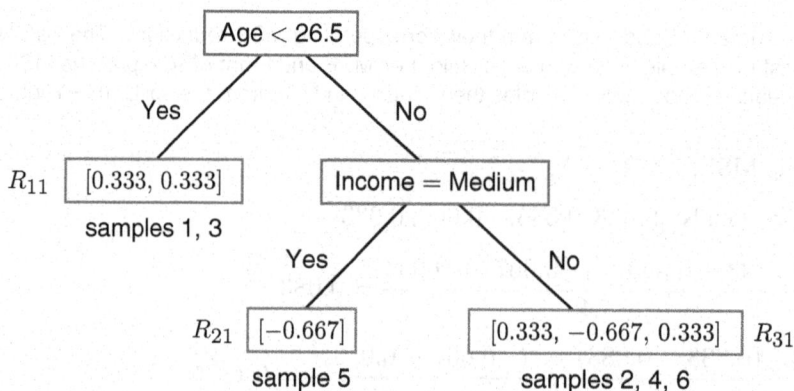

Figure 9.18: The regression tree constructed in the first boosting round. Each leaf node shows the pseudo-residuals, its region label R_{j1}, and the sample indices assigned to that region.

Computing Output Values for the Leaf Nodes

We now compute the output values γ_{j1} for each leaf node using Equation (9.55):

$$\gamma_{j1} = \frac{\sum_{\mathbf{x}_i \in R_{j1}}(y_i - p_{i0})}{\sum_{\mathbf{x}_i \in R_{j1}} p_{i0}(1 - p_{i0})}.$$

Since all initial predicted probabilities are $p_{i0} = 0.667$, we obtain:

$$\gamma_{11} = \frac{0.333 + 0.333}{0.667(1 - 0.667) + 0.667(1 - 0.667)} = 1.5,$$

$$\gamma_{21} = \frac{-0.667}{0.667(1 - 0.667)} = -3,$$

$$\gamma_{31} = \frac{2 \cdot 0.333 + (-0.667)}{3 \cdot 0.667(1 - 0.667)} = 0.$$

	Log-odds $F_1(\mathbf{x}_i) = F_0(\mathbf{x}_i) + \nu h_1(\mathbf{x}_i)$	Probability $p_{i1} = \sigma(F_1(\mathbf{x}_i))$	Label y_i	Pseudo-residual $y_i - p_{i1}$
1	$0.693 + 0.5 \cdot 1.5 = 1.443$	0.809	1	$1 - 0.809 = 0.191$
2	$0.693 + 0.5 \cdot 0 = 0.693$	0.667	1	$1 - 0.667 = 0.333$
3	$0.693 + 0.5 \cdot 1.5 = 1.443$	0.809	1	$1 - 0.809 = 0.191$
4	$0.693 + 0.5 \cdot 0 = 0.693$	0.667	0	$0 - 0.667 = -0.667$
5	$0.693 + 0.5 \cdot (-3) = -0.807$	0.309	0	$0 - 0.309 = -0.309$
6	$0.693 + 0.5 \cdot 0 = 0.693$	0.667	1	$1 - 0.667 = 0.333$

Table 9.14: Updated probabilities and pseudo-residuals after the first boosting round. The term $h_1(\mathbf{x}_i)$ denotes the output of the first regression tree.

Updating the Ensemble

Finally, we update the ensemble predictions using Equation 9.36:

$$F_1(\mathbf{x}) = F_0(\mathbf{x}) + \nu \sum_{j=1}^{J_1} \gamma_{j1} \mathbb{1}\{\mathbf{x} \in R_{j1}\}.$$

Each sample's predicted log-odds is adjusted based on the output value γ_{j1} of the leaf it falls into. Table 9.14 shows the updated log-odds, predicted probabilities, and pseudo-residuals after the first boosting round. The updated probabilities are now closer to the true labels, resulting in correct classification for 5 out of 6 samples (all except sample 4), assuming a classification threshold of $p > 0.5$.

9.8.5.3 Second Boosting Round

The second boosting round fits a new regression tree to the updated pseudo-residuals from the first round.

Regression Tree Fitting

We begin by determining the best split for the root node. Table 9.15 shows the MSE reductions for all candidate splits at the root.

The best split is Education = High School, which yields the greatest reduction in MSE (0.0312). This split assigns samples 1 and 4 to the left child, and samples 2, 3, 5, and 6 to the right child.

In the left child node, both samples share the same values for Income and Education, so the only feature we can use for further splitting is Age. We choose the threshold Age < 30, which is the midpoint between their ages (25 and 35).

The right child node (samples 2, 3, 5, and 6) has an initial MSE of 0.0697. Table 9.16 shows the possible splits for this node and their corresponding MSE reductions.

The highest MSE reduction (0.0385) is achieved by both Income = Medium and Age < 29. We arbitrarily choose Income = Medium for the split. As the tree has now reached the maximum depth of 2, no further splits are made. Figure 9.19 shows the resulting regression tree from this boosting round.

Split	Left Node	Left MSE	Right Node	Right MSE	ΔMSE
Income = Low	[1, 2, 4]	0.195	[3, 5, 6]	0.0758	0.0036
Income = Medium	[3, 5]	0.0625	[1, 2, 4, 6]	0.174	0.00217
Income = High	[6]	0	[1, 2, 3, 4, 5]	0.142	0.0207
Education = HS	[1, 4]	0.184	[2, 3, 5, 6]	0.0697	0.0312
Age < 23.5	[3]	0	[1, 2, 4, 5, 6]	0.159	0.0065
Age < 26.5	[1, 3]	0	[2, 4, 5, 6]	0.185	0.0157
Age < 29	[1, 3, 5]	0.0555	[2, 4, 6]	0.222	0.00025
Age < 32.5	[1, 2, 3, 5]	0.0595	[4, 6]	0.25	0.016
Age < 37.5	[1, 2, 3, 4, 5]	0.142	[6]	0	0.0207

Table 9.15: Candidate root node splits in the second regression tree and their corresponding MSE reductions.

Split	Left Node	Left MSE	Right Node	Right MSE	ΔMSE
Income = Low	[2]	0	[3, 5, 6]	0.0758	0.0128
Income = Medium	[3, 5]	0.0625	[2, 6]	0	0.0385
Income = High	[6]	0	[2, 3, 5]	0.0758	0.0128
Age < 25	[3]	0	[2, 5, 6]	0.0916	0.001
Age < 29	[3, 5]	0.0625	[2, 6]	0	0.0385
Age < 35	[2, 3, 5]	0.0758	[6]	0	0.0128

Table 9.16: Candidate splits at the right child node in the second regression tree and their corresponding MSE reductions.

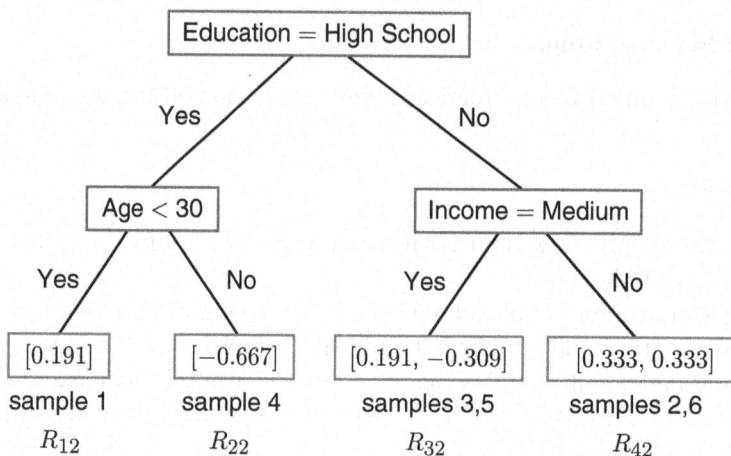

Figure 9.19: The regression tree constructed in the second boosting round

Computing Output Values for the Leaf Nodes

We now compute the output values γ_{j2} for the leaf nodes using the updated probabilities and pseudo-residuals from Table 9.14:

$$\gamma_{12} = \frac{0.191}{0.809 \cdot (1 - 0.809)} = 1.236,$$

$$\gamma_{22} = \frac{-0.667}{0.667 \cdot (1 - 0.667)} = -3,$$

$$\gamma_{32} = \frac{0.191 + (-0.309)}{0.809 \cdot (1 - 0.809) + 0.309 \cdot (1 - 0.309)} = -0.321,$$

$$\gamma_{42} = \frac{2 \cdot 0.333}{2 \cdot 0.667 \cdot (1 - 0.667)} = 1.5.$$

Updating the Ensemble

Finally, we update the ensemble prediction function using:

$$F_2(\mathbf{x}) = F_1(\mathbf{x}) + \nu \sum_{j=1}^{J_2} \gamma_{j2} \mathbb{1}\{\mathbf{x} \in R_{j2}\}.$$

Table 9.17 shows the updated log-odds, probabilities, and predicted labels after the second boosting round. The ensemble now correctly classifies all training examples, demonstrating the effectiveness of gradient boosting.

9.8.5.4   Making Predictions on New Samples

Let's now use the trained ensemble to make a prediction for a new customer with the following attributes:

[Age = 33, Income = Medium, Education = High School]

	Log-odds $F_2(\mathbf{x}_i) = F_1(\mathbf{x}_i) + \nu h_2(\mathbf{x}_i)$	Probability $p_{i2} = \sigma(F_2(\mathbf{x}_i))$	Predicted Label $\mathbb{1}\{p_{i2} > 0.5\}$	True Label y_i
1	$1.443 + 0.5 \cdot 1.236 = 2.061$	0.887	1	1
2	$0.693 + 0.5 \cdot 1.5 = 1.443$	0.809	1	1
3	$1.443 + 0.5 \cdot (-0.321) = 1.283$	0.783	1	1
4	$0.693 + 0.5 \cdot (-3) = -0.807$	0.309	0	0
5	$-0.807 + 0.5 \cdot (-0.321) = -0.968$	0.275	0	0
6	$0.693 + 0.5 \cdot 1.5 = 1.443$	0.809	1	1

Table 9.17: Updated probabilities and predicted class labels after the second boosting round, using a classification threshold of 0.5. The term $h_2(\mathbf{x}_i)$ denotes the output of the second regression tree.

First, we determine which terminal region the sample falls into in each regression tree:

- In the first tree, the sample goes right at the root since Age < 26.5 is false, and then left because Income = Medium is true. Thus, the sample belongs to region R_{21}.

- In the second tree, the sample goes left at the root since Education = High School is true, and then right because Age < 30 is false. Therefore, the sample belongs to region R_{22}.

As a result, the estimated log-odds that this customer will buy the product are:

$$F_2(\mathbf{x}) = F_0(\mathbf{x}) + \nu(\gamma_{21} + \gamma_{22}) = 0.693 + 0.5 \cdot (-3 + (-3)) = -2.307.$$

The predicted probability is:

$$p = \sigma(F_2(\mathbf{x})) = \frac{1}{1 + e^{-(-2.307)}} = 0.0905.$$

Since $p < 0.5$, the model predicts that this customer will not buy the product.

9.8.6   Gradient Boosting in Scikit-Learn

Scikit-Learn provides the following classes for gradient-boosted decision trees:

- `GradientBoostingClassifier`[21] for classification tasks

- `GradientBoostingRegressor`[22] for regression tasks

By default, these classes use regression trees with a maximum depth of 3 as base learners. They provide a range of hyperparameters for configuring both the decision trees (e.g., `max_depth`, `min_samples_leaf`) and the boosting process itself (e.g., `learning_rate`, `n_estimators`). Table 9.18 summarizes the key hyperparameters.

In addition, the gradient boosting classes expose several useful attributes:

- `n_estimators_`: The actual number of trees fitted. This may be less than the `n_estimators` parameter if early stopping was triggered.

- `estimators_`: An array containing the fitted regression trees.

- `train_score_`: An array containing the training loss after each boosting iteration.

- `oob_scores_`: The loss values computed on the out-of-bag samples at each boosting iteration (available only if `subsample < 1.0`).

- `feature_importances_`: The importance of each feature, computed as the normalized total reduction in MSE attributed to that feature across all trees.

21. https://scikit-learn.org/stable/modules/generated/sklearn.ensemble.
    GradientBoostingClassifier.html
22. https://scikit-learn.org/stable/modules/generated/sklearn.ensemble.
    GradientBoostingRegressor.html

Parameter	Description	Default
`loss`	The loss function to minimize. For classification: `'log_loss'` or `'exponential'` (similar to AdaBoost). For regression: `'squared_error'`, `'absolute_error'`, `'huber'`, or `'quantile'`.	`'log_loss'` or `'squared_error'`
`n_estimators`	Number of boosting iterations.	`100`
`learning_rate`	Shrinks the contribution of each tree to the ensemble's prediction.	`0.1`
`subsample`	Fraction of samples used to fit each tree.	`1.0`
`max_features`	Number of features considered at each node split. Can be an integer, a float, or `'sqrt'`, `'log2'`, or `'None'` (use all features).	`None`
`init`	Initial model to start boosting from. `None` uses prior class probabilities (for classification) or mean target value (for regression). `'zero'` initializes predictions to zero. Custom estimators can also be provided.	`None`
`validation_fraction`	Fraction of the training set used as a validation set for early stopping.	`0.1`
`n_iter_no_change`	Number of consecutive iterations without improvement on the validation loss before stopping training. If `None`, early stopping is disabled.	`None`
`tol`	Minimum improvement in validation loss required to continue training when early stopping is enabled.	`0.0001`

Table 9.18: Key parameters of the gradient boosting classes in Scikit-Learn

9.8.6.1 Classification Example

As an example, we train a gradient boosting classifier on the synthetic classification dataset from Section 9.3.1. After creating the dataset and splitting it into training and test sets, we instantiate a `GradientBoostingClassifier` with default settings: an ensemble of 100 regression trees, each with a maximum depth of 3, a learning rate of 0.1, and no subsampling. We then fit the model to the training set:

```
from sklearn.ensemble import GradientBoostingClassifier

clf = GradientBoostingClassifier(random_state=42)
clf.fit(X_train, y_train)
```

Next, we evaluate the model's performance on both the training and test sets:

```
print(f'Train accuracy: {clf.score(X_train, y_train):.4f}')
print(f'Test accuracy: {clf.score(X_test, y_test):.4f}')
```

```
Train accuracy: 1.0000
Test accuracy: 0.9120
```

The model achieves 91.2% accuracy on the test set. The gap between the training and test accuracies suggests potential overfitting. To address this, we can tune the model's hyperparameters to improve generalization. Common adjusted hyperparameters in gradient boosting include the number of estimators, learning rate, maximum tree depth, subsample fraction, and the number of features considered at each split. We now use a randomized search with 50 iterations to explore different combinations of these parameters:

```
from sklearn.model_selection import RandomizedSearchCV

params = {
    'n_estimators': np.arange(50, 501, 50),
    'learning_rate': np.arange(0.1, 1.01, 0.1),
    'max_depth': np.arange(3, 11),
    'subsample': np.arange(0.5, 1.01, 0.1),
    'max_features': ['sqrt', 'log2', None]
}

clf = GradientBoostingClassifier(random_state=42)
random_search = RandomizedSearchCV(clf, params, n_iter=50, cv=3, random_state=42,
                                   n_jobs=-1)
random_search.fit(X_train, y_train)
print(random_search.best_params_)
```

The best hyperparameters found are:

```
{'subsample': 0.6, 'n_estimators': 450, 'max_features': 'sqrt',
'max_depth': 7, 'learning_rate': 0.1}
```

The tuned model consists of 450 trees, each with a maximum depth of 7, trained on a random 60% subsample of the training data, with a random subset of $\sqrt{d}$ features considered at each split and a learning rate of 0.1. The performance of the optimized model is:

```
print(f'Train accuracy: {random_search.score(X_train, y_train):.4f}')
print(f'Test accuracy: {random_search.score(X_test, y_test):.4f}')
```

```
Train accuracy: 1.0000
Test accuracy: 0.9440
```

The test accuracy improves significantly after tuning, and the optimized model performs comparably to both random forests and AdaBoost on this dataset.

9.8.6.2   Regression Example

To illustrate gradient boosting for regression, let's train a gradient boosting regressor on the California housing dataset. After loading the dataset and splitting it into training and test sets, we instantiate a `GradientBoostingRegressor` with default settings and fit it to the training data:

```
from sklearn.ensemble import GradientBoostingRegressor

reg = GradientBoostingRegressor(random_state=42)
reg.fit(X_train, y_train)
```

We then evaluate the model's performance:

```
print(f'R2 score (train): {reg.score(X_train, y_train):.4f}')
print(f'R2 score (test): {reg.score(X_test, y_test):.4f}')
```

```
R2 score (train): 0.8049
R2 score (test): 0.7756
```

This initial result is slightly lower than that of the random forests before tuning (test R^2 score 0.8051). One reason for this difference is that `RandomForestRegressor` uses fully grown trees by default, while `GradientBoostingRegressor` defaults to shallow trees with a maximum depth of 3. Both models use the same number of trees (100), but the deeper trees in random forest are better able to capture higher-order feature interactions. Moreover, the small gap between the training and test scores, along with the relatively modest training accuracy, suggests that the gradient boosting model is underfitting—likely due to the limited capacity of the shallow trees.

To improve the model's performance, we perform a randomized search to tune its hyperparameters:

```
from sklearn.model_selection import RandomizedSearchCV

params = {
    'n_estimators': np.arange(50, 501, 50),
    'learning_rate': np.arange(0.1, 1.01, 0.1),
    'max_depth': np.arange(3, 11),
    'subsample': np.arange(0.5, 1.01, 0.1),
    'max_features': ['sqrt', 'log2', None]
}
reg = GradientBoostingRegressor(random_state=42)
random_search = RandomizedSearchCV(reg, params, n_iter=50, cv=3, random_state=42,
                                   n_jobs=-1)
random_search.fit(X_train, y_train)
print(random_search.best_params_)
```

The best hyperparameters found are:

```
{'subsample': 0.8999999999999999, 'n_estimators': 400, 'max_features': 'log2',
'max_depth': 5, 'learning_rate': 0.1}
```

This optimized model consists of 400 trees with a maximum depth of 5, each trained on a random 90% subsample of the data. At each split, a number of features equal to $\log_2 d$ is randomly selected, and the learning rate is 0.1. The performance of the tuned model is:

```
print(f'R2 score (train): {random_search.score(X_train, y_train):.4f}')
print(f'R2 score (test): {random_search.score(X_test, y_test):.4f}')
```

```
R2 score (train): 0.9297
R2 score (test): 0.8447
```

This result clearly demonstrates the strength of gradient boosting on this task. After tuning, the model outperforms all previously tested models on this dataset. For comparison, the second-best model—the tuned random forest regressor—achieved a test R^2 score of 0.8124.

9.8.6.3   Learning Curves and Early Stopping

To track the model's performance and detect potential signs of overfitting, we can plot the training and test errors across boosting iterations. The `staged_predict` method generates predictions using the sequence of partial ensembles formed after each boosting iteration. This allows us to evaluate the model's performance on the validation or test set at each stage of the training:

```
from sklearn.metrics import mean_squared_error as MSE

# Compute the test MSE at each boosting iteration using staged predictions
best_reg = random_search.best_estimator_
test_score = np.zeros(best_reg.n_estimators_)
for i, y_test_pred in enumerate(best_reg.staged_predict(X_test)):
    test_score[i] = MSE(y_test, y_test_pred)

# Plot the training and test MSE over boosting iterations
plt.plot(np.arange(best_reg.n_estimators), best_reg.train_score_,
         label='Training loss')
plt.plot(np.arange(best_reg.n_estimators), test_score, 'r', label='Test loss')
plt.xlabel('Boosting iterations')
plt.ylabel('MSE')
plt.legend()
```

The learning curve in Figure 9.20 shows that the minimum test error is reached after approximately 100 iterations, after which the test curve flattens and decreases only slightly. This illustrates the robustness of gradient boosting models to overfitting: as more trees are added, the model's performance does not degrade—a behavior that has been confirmed in empirical studies [199].

Instead of performing an exhaustive search to find the optimal number of trees, a more efficient alternative is to use early stopping. This approach involves setting a high value for n_estimators

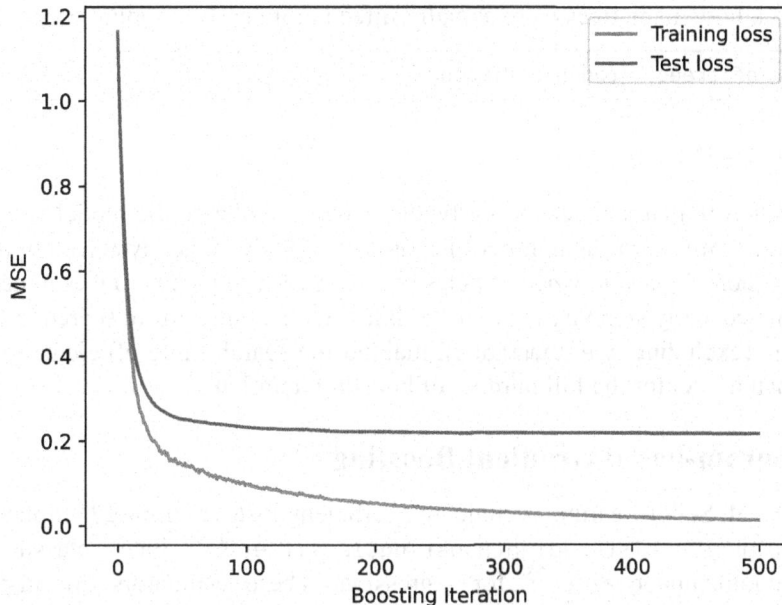

Figure 9.20: Learning curve for the gradient boosting regressor on the California housing dataset, showing the MSE on both the training and test sets over boosting iterations. The minimum test error occurs around 100 iterations, after which the error stabilizes, illustrating the model's resistance to overfitting even as the number of trees increases.

(e.g., 1000) and terminating training when the validation score fails to improve for a specified number of consecutive iterations. In Scikit-Learn's gradient boosting estimators, early stopping is enabled by setting n_iter_no_change to an integer (by default, it is None, meaning early stopping is disabled).

The following code trains a gradient boosting regressor with early stopping enabled, using the optimized settings found by the randomized search and 1000 boosting iterations:

```
reg = GradientBoostingRegressor(
    n_estimators=1000, max_depth=5, subsample=0.9, max_features='log2',
    n_iter_no_change=20, random_state=42
)
reg.fit(X_train, y_train)

print(f'R2 score (train): {reg.score(X_train, y_train):.4f}')
print(f'R2 score (test): {reg.score(X_test, y_test):.4f}')
```

```
R2 score (train): 0.9201
R2 score (test): 0.8370
```

The performance is slightly worse than that of the tuned model from the randomized search, primarily because 10% of the training data is held out as a validation set for early stopping. This reduces the effective training set size, which can impact model accuracy.

We can check how many trees were actually fitted before early stopping was triggered:

```
print(f'Number of trees: {reg.n_estimators_}')
```

```
Number of trees: 384
```

Early stopping offers a practical and efficient way to regularize the model without performing an exhaustive search over the number of estimators. By dynamically selecting the number of trees based on validation performance, it helps prevent overfitting and reduces unnecessary computation. In practice, early stopping is often combined with a randomized search to tune the other hyperparameters (excluding `n_estimators`), making the search more efficient by avoiding the need to train each model for the full number of boosting iterations.

9.8.7   Histogram-based Gradient Boosting

Recent versions of Scikit-Learn[23] include two efficient histogram-based implementations of gradient boosting: `HistGradientBoostingClassifier`[24] for classification and `HistGradientBoostingRegressor`[25] for regression. These estimators are inspired by the histogram-based algorithm used in LightGBM (see Section 10.2), which speeds up training by discretizing continuous features into bins, thereby reducing the number of candidate split points.

The training process for these estimators involves the following steps:

1. **Discretization**: Continuous features are discretized into a fixed number of bins, each corresponding to a range of values and identified by an integer index.

2. **Histogram construction**: At each tree node, a histogram is built for every feature, where each bin accumulates the sum of gradient statistics (e.g., pseudo-residuals) from samples that fall into that bin.

3. **Split finding**: The optimal split is selected by scanning the histograms, eliminating the need to sort continuous feature values at each node.

In addition to improved runtime efficiency, these estimators offer two key advantages over the standard gradient boosting estimators:

- Parallelization: Many operations during the training process are parallelized, such as computing gradients across samples and evaluating split points across features.

- Native support for categorical features: Categorical variables can be passed directly without manual encoding. Each category is mapped to an integer index and treated as a bin in the histogram, where gradient statistics (e.g., sum of pseudo-residuals) are accumulated. To avoid

---

23. Since version 0.21, released in May 2019
24. https://scikit-learn.org/stable/modules/generated/sklearn.ensemble.
    HistGradientBoostingClassifier.html
25. https://scikit-learn.org/stable/modules/generated/sklearn.ensemble.
    HistGradientBoostingRegressor.html

evaluating all $2^{k-1} - 1$ possible binary splits, the categories are sorted by these aggregated statistics, and only the $k - 1$ adjacent splits in the resulting order are considered.

On the downside, discretizing continuous features into bins may lead to a slight loss of accuracy. However, the resulting speedup often allows for more boosting iterations within the same computational budget, which can offset this loss and improve overall model performance.

The histogram-based estimators share many parameters with the standard gradient boosting ones, but there are several key differences:

- The number of boosting iterations is controlled by `max_iter` instead of `n_estimators`.

- The default tree settings differ: `max_depth=None`, `max_leaf_nodes=31`, and `min_samples_leaf=20`.

- Early stopping is controlled by the `early_stopping` parameter, which defaults to `'auto'`. In this mode, early stopping is enabled when the dataset contains more than 10,000 samples.

In addition, these estimators introduce several new parameters:

- `max_bins`: Specifies the maximum number of bins used for feature discretization (up to 255), with an extra bin reserved for missing values.

- `categorical_features`: Specifies the categorical features (via a boolean mask or a list of column indices); each must have no more than `max_bins` unique categories.

- `l2_regularization`: Adds an L2 penalty to the loss function to discourage large leaf outputs, similar in concept to ridge regression.

For example, let's fit a `HistGradientBoostingRegressor` to the California housing dataset:

```
from sklearn.ensemble import HistGradientBoostingRegressor

reg = HistGradientBoostingRegressor(random_state=42)
reg.fit(X_train, y_train)
```

The model's performance on the training and test sets is:

```
print(f'R2 score (train): {reg.score(X_train, y_train):.4f}')
print(f'R2 score (test): {reg.score(X_test, y_test):.4f}')
```

```
R2 score (train): 0.8805
R2 score (test): 0.8355
```

These results surpass those of the untuned gradient boosting regressor (test R^2 score 0.7756), primarily due to the default hyperparameter settings of the histogram-based estimator, which allow for deeper and more expressive trees.

To further improve performance, we can fine-tune the model using a randomized search over key hyperparameters:

```
from sklearn.model_selection import RandomizedSearchCV

params = {
    'max_iter': np.arange(50, 501, 50),
    'max_bins': np.arange(50, 251, 50),
    'learning_rate': np.arange(0.1, 1.01, 0.1),
    'max_leaf_nodes': np.arange(10, 101, 5),
    'max_features': np.arange(0.1, 1.01, 0.1)
}
reg = HistGradientBoostingRegressor(random_state=42)
random_search = RandomizedSearchCV(reg, params, n_iter=50, cv=3, random_state=42,
                                   n_jobs=-1)
random_search.fit(X_train, y_train)
print(random_search.best_params_)
```

The best hyperparameters found are:

```
{'max_leaf_nodes': 80, 'max_iter': 500, 'max_features': 0.30000000000000004,
'max_bins': 200, 'learning_rate': 0.1}
```

The performance of the tuned model is:

```
print(f'R2 score (train): {random_search.score(X_train, y_train):.4f}')
print(f'R2 score (test): {random_search.score(X_test, y_test):.4f}')
```

```
R2 score (train): 0.9279
R2 score (test): 0.8440
```

This result is comparable to the tuned standard gradient boosting regressor (test R^2 score of 0.8447), despite using only 90% of the training data due to early stopping, which is automatically enabled for this dataset since it has more than 10,000 samples.

Moreover, the histogram-based estimator offers significantly faster training. Consider the following timing comparison:

```
%%timeit
reg = HistGradientBoostingRegressor(random_state=42)
reg.fit(X_train, y_train)
```

```
319 ms ± 61 ms per loop (mean ± std. dev. of 7 runs, 1 loop each)
```

```
%%timeit
from sklearn.ensemble import GradientBoostingRegressor
reg = GradientBoostingRegressor(random_state=42)
reg.fit(X_train, y_train)
```

```
3.55 s ± 55.3 ms per loop (mean ± std. dev. of 7 runs, 1 loop each)
```

On average, the histogram-based estimator is over 10 times faster than the standard gradient boosting regressor. These results highlight the computational advantages of histogram-based gradient boosting, particularly for large datasets.

9.8.8 Summary

Gradient boosting is a flexible and powerful ensemble method that extends gradient descent to function space. At each iteration, it fits a base learner to the pseudo-residuals (i.e., the negative gradients of the loss) of the current ensemble, progressively improving the model. This iterative refinement reduces both bias and variance, leading to strong predictive performance.

Advantages of gradient boosting compared to other supervised learning algorithms:

- It produces highly accurate models and consistently ranks among the top-performing algorithms for structured data.

- It effectively models complex, nonlinear relationships in the data.

- It is generally resistant to overfitting: test accuracy remains stable even with many trees.

- It supports a wide range of loss functions, making it suitable for diverse tasks such as classification, regression, ranking, and imbalanced learning problems.

- It performs well even with limited data, unlike other complex models (such as neural networks), which usually require large amounts of data.

- It is less sensitive to outliers than AdaBoost, which can exponentially amplify the weights of misclassified examples. In contrast, gradient boosting fits to the residuals, whose magnitudes are bounded by the loss function.

- Recent implementations, such as histogram-based gradient boosting, offer substantial speedups and better scalability on large datasets.

- It supports incremental learning by adding new trees to the existing ensemble without retraining from scratch.

- It inherits the strengths of decision trees, including support for heterogeneous feature types and native handling of missing values.

- It provides reliable estimates of feature importance, similar to those produced by random forests and AdaBoost.

Disadvantages of gradient boosting:

- Training can be computationally intensive, especially on large datasets or with many boosting rounds. However, modern implementations (such as XGBoost) support parallelization and GPU-based training, which significantly accelerate the process.

- It requires careful tuning of multiple hyperparameters, such as the number of trees, learning rate, and maximum tree depth, in order to achieve optimal performance.

- Inference can be slower compared to simpler models, as predictions require aggregating outputs from many trees. However, unlike training, tree evaluations during inference can be parallelized, helping to mitigate the slowdown.

- It is generally harder to interpret than simpler models due to the cumulative effect of many updates across numerous trees.

9.9   Stacking Ensembles

Stacking ensembles (also known as **stacked generalization**) combine the outputs of multiple base models by training a separate **meta-learner** to aggregate their predictions [629, 69]. Unlike simple aggregation methods such as majority voting or averaging, stacking learns to optimally weigh and combine the base model predictions to make more accurate final predictions.

Stacking is particularly effective when the base models are diverse (e.g., based on different learning algorithms), enabling the meta-learner to leverage their complementary strengths.

A typical stacking ensembles consists of two levels of models (see Figure 9.21):

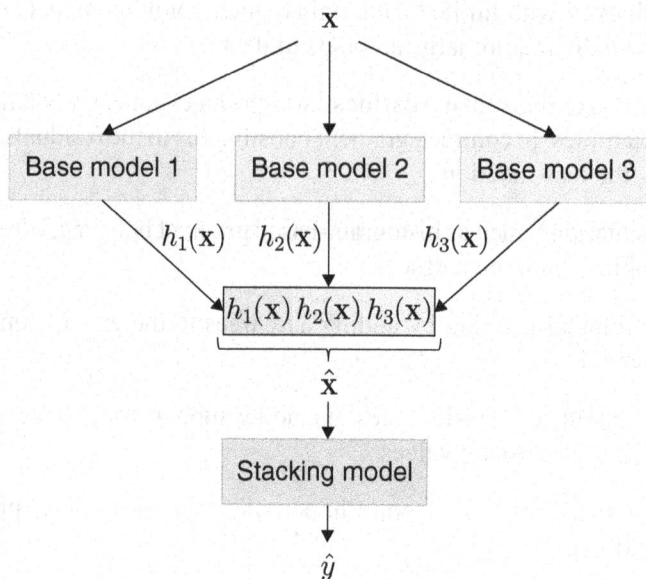

Figure 9.21: Illustration of a stacking ensemble with two levels. The level-0 models (base models) include a diverse set of algorithms trained on the same input features $\mathbf{x}$. Their predictions, $h_1(\mathbf{x})$, $h_2(\mathbf{x})$, and $h_3(\mathbf{x})$, are combined to form a new feature vector $\hat{\mathbf{x}}$, which serves as input to the level-1 meta-model. The meta-model then learns to optimally combine these predictions to generate the final output $\hat{y}$.

- **Level-0 models (base models)**: These models are trained independently, usually on the same training data. Unlike bagging and boosting, stacking typically uses base models built with different algorithms (which may themselves be ensembles), in order to maximize diversity.

- **Level-1 model** (also called a **meta-model** or **blender**): This model learns to combine the predictions of the base models in a way that minimizes the overall prediction error.

In more advanced setups, stacking can be extended beyond two levels by introducing additional layers of meta-models, creating a hierarchical structure that further refines the final predictions (see Section 9.9.2).

The training process of a stacking ensemble involves the following steps:

1. **Train the base models**: Split the original training data into a base-training set and a validation set. Train each base model independently on the base-training set.

2. **Generate meta-model training data**: Use the trained base models to make predictions on the validation set. These predictions, along with the true labels, form a new dataset used to train the meta-model.

3. **Train the meta-model**: The meta-model learns to map the base models' predictions to the target values. It can be trained using any supervised learning algorithm, such as linear regression, a neural network, or another ensemble method.

4. **Retrain the base models (optional)**: To utilize all available data, the base models are often retrained on the entire training set before making predictions on new data.

To train a more accurate meta-model, its training data can be generated using k-fold cross-validation of the base models instead of relying on a single validation set. This approach proceeds as follows:

1. Split the original training set into k equally sized folds.

2. For each fold, designate it as the validation fold. Train the base models on the remaining $k - 1$ folds and generate predictions on the held-out fold.

3. Repeat this process until every fold has served once as the validation set.

4. Collect the out-of-fold predictions from all base models. These predictions, along with the corresponding true labels, form the training set for the meta-model.

A key advantage of this approach is that the meta-model is trained on a dataset of the same size as the original training set, since every instance is used exactly once for validation. This typically results in a more robust and accurate meta-model, as it is trained on a more representative dataset. However, this benefit comes at the cost of increased training time, as each base model must be trained k times.

Stacked generalization can be viewed as a generalization of the standard cross-validation used for model selection. In traditional k-fold cross-validation, k models are trained and the one with the lowest validation error is chosen, which is equivalent to using a meta-model that applies a simple winner-takes-all rule. In contrast, stacking learns to combine the predictions of all base models by training a dedicated meta-model on their predictions, and is therefore expected to perform at least as well as the best single model selected via cross-validation.

9.9.1   Example of Stacking

To demonstrate the stacking process using the cross-validation approach, consider a binary classification problem with a dataset of 100 samples. Suppose we construct an ensemble composed of three base models: logistic regression, a decision tree, and a neural network. To generate training data for the meta-model, we use five-fold cross-validation on the original dataset. The training process of the ensemble consists of the following steps:

1. Split the training set into five folds. For each fold:

    (a) Train each base model on the remaining four folds (80 samples)
    (b) Use the trained models to make predictions on the held-out fold (20 samples)

    Repeat this process across all five folds to obtain out-of-fold predictions for every training sample. For illustration, assume that we obtain the following predictions:

    - Logistic regression predictions: [1, 0, 1, 1, . . ., 0] (100 predictions)
    - Decision tree predictions: [0, 1, 0, 1, . . ., 1] (100 predictions)
    - Neural network predictions: [0, 1, 1, 0, . . ., 1] (100 predictions)

2. Combine the out-of-fold predictions from the three base models to form a new dataset for training the meta-model. The resulting dataset contains, for each instance, the predictions from the three base models as input features and the true label as the target (see Table 9.19).

	Logistic Regression	Decision Tree	Neural Network	True Label
1	1	0	0	0
2	0	1	1	1
3	1	0	1	0
4	1	1	0	1
⋮	⋮	⋮	⋮	⋮
100	0	1	1	1

Table 9.19: Training dataset for the meta-model, consisting of the base model predictions and the corresponding true labels.

3. Train a meta-model on the dataset from the previous step. The meta-model learns to combine the base model predictions to minimize the overall prediction error. For example, if the meta-model is linear, the final prediction can be expressed as:

$$f(\mathbf{x}) = w_1 h_1(\mathbf{x}) + w_2 h_2(\mathbf{x}) + w_3 h_3(\mathbf{x}),$$

where $h_1(\mathbf{x})$, $h_2(\mathbf{x})$, and $h_3(\mathbf{x})$ are the predictions of the three base models, and w_1, w_2, and w_3 are the weights learned by the meta-model.

9.9.2 Stacking Hierarchies

Since the meta-model is itself a predictor, it can also be stacked to create higher-level ensembles. For example, a *level-2 meta-model* can combine the outputs of multiple level-1 meta-models, creating a deeper stacking hierarchy.

A notable example of such a hierarchy appeared in the winning solution to the Netflix Prize. The Netflix Prize was a competition held by Netflix from 2006 to 2009 to improve its movie recommendation system [39]. The goal was to predict user ratings for movies based on historical user preferences. A grand prize of $1,000,000 was offered to the team that could achieve at least a 10% improvement over Netflix's existing algorithm.

The winning team, "BellKor's Pragmatic Chaos," used a sophisticated stacking ensemble with three hierarchical levels [580]:

1. **Level-0 models (base models)**: These consisted of a diverse set of over 100 recommendation algorithms, including neighborhood-based models and matrix factorization techniques. Each model was trained independently on the same dataset to generate rating predictions.

2. **Level-1 meta-models**: The predictions from the base models served as input features to various level-1 meta-models. These meta-models were trained using different subsets of base predictions and employed a variety of blending techniques such as polynomial regression, neural networks, and gradient-boosted decision trees.

3. **Level-2 meta-model (final blender)**: At the top level, predictions from both the base models and the level-1 meta-models were combined using a level-2 blender—a linear model that produced the final rating predictions.

The success of this approach highlights the power of stacking ensembles. By incorporating multiple layers of learners, stacking hierarchies can capture complex interactions and yield substantial gains in predictive accuracy.

9.9.3   Stacking Classes in Scikit-Learn

Scikit-Learn provides two classes for implementing stacking ensembles: StackingClassifier[26] for classification tasks and StackingRegressor[27] for regression tasks.

Key parameters of these classes include:

- estimators: A list of base estimators to be stacked. Each element in the list is a tuple consisting of a string (the estimator's name) and an estimator instance.

- final_estimator: The meta-model used to combine the predictions of the base estimators. By default, LogisticRegression is used for classification and RidgeCV (ridge regression with built-in cross-validation) for regression. Multiple stacking layers can be created by setting final_estimator to another StackingClassifier or StackingRegressor instance.

- cv: Defines the cross-validation strategy for generating training data for the meta-model. The default is None, which corresponds to a 5-fold cross-validation.

For example, we apply a StackingRegressor to the California housing dataset, using four base models and a linear regression meta-model:

```python
from sklearn.linear_model import LinearRegression
from sklearn.neighbors import KNeighborsRegressor
from sklearn.tree import DecisionTreeRegressor
from sklearn.ensemble import HistGradientBoostingRegressor
from sklearn.ensemble import StackingRegressor

estimators = [
    ('linear', LinearRegression()),
    ('knn', KNeighborsRegressor()),
    ('dt', DecisionTreeRegressor(random_state=42)),
    ('hist', HistGradientBoostingRegressor(random_state=42))
]
final_estimator = LinearRegression()
reg = StackingRegressor(estimators, final_estimator, n_jobs=-1)
reg.fit(X_train, y_train)
```

The performance of the stacking ensemble is:

```python
print(f'R2 score (train): {reg.score(X_train, y_train):.4f}')
print(f'R2 score (test): {reg.score(X_test, y_test):.4f}')
```

```
R2 score (train): 0.8902
R2 score (test): 0.8371
```

26. https://scikit-learn.org/stable/modules/generated/sklearn.ensemble.StackingClassifier.html
27. https://scikit-learn.org/stable/modules/generated/sklearn.ensemble.StackingRegressor.html

This result shows a slight improvement over the best individual model in the ensemble, the histogram-based gradient boosting regressor, which achieved a test R^2 score of 0.8355 before tuning. For comparison, a `VotingRegressor`, which simply averages the predictions of the same base models, achieves the following results:

```
from sklearn.ensemble import VotingRegressor

reg = VotingRegressor(estimators)
reg.fit(X_train, y_train)

print(f'R2 score (train): {reg.score(X_train, y_train):.4f}')
print(f'R2 score (test): {reg.score(X_test, y_test):.4f}')
```

```
R2 score (train): 0.8651
R2 score (test): 0.7302
```

As shown, stacking yields a substantial performance gain over simple averaging, illustrating the benefit of training a meta-model to combine predictions in a data-driven way.

9.10   Summary

This chapter provided a comprehensive overview of ensemble methods—powerful techniques that improve the accuracy and robustness of machine learning models by combining the outputs of multiple individual learners. The main types of ensemble methods include:

- **Bagging**: Builds multiple models on different bootstrap samples to reduce variance and mitigate overfitting. Random forests extend bagging by selecting random subsets of features to consider at each split, further increasing model diversity and reducing correlation among trees.

- **Boosting**: A sequential technique in which each model is trained to correct the errors of its predecessors. In AdaBoost, instance weights are adjusted to focus on hard-to-classify examples, while gradient boosting fits new models to the residuals of previous predictions to progressively reduce the overall prediction error.

- **Stacking**: A hierarchical approach where one or more meta-models learn to combine the predictions of diverse base models. By leveraging the complementary strengths of the base models, stacking often leads to improved predictive performance.

In general, bagging ensembles consistently outperform individual models by reducing variance. Boosting methods can offer even greater improvements, but their sequential nature limits parallelization and increases computational cost. AdaBoost is particularly sensitive to noisy data, while gradient boosting is more robust and flexible but can be slower to train. Recent variants such as histogram-based gradient boosting enable faster training and better scalability by using efficient approximations and parallel computations. Stacking provides a flexible framework that can integrate both individual models and ensembles, often yielding strong performance through learned model combination.

Ensemble methods continue to be an active area of research, with ongoing work focused on:

- enhancing scalability through efficient implementations and parallelism [617, 360, 388],

- improving interpretability of ensemble predictions [646, 361, 31],

- strengthening robustness against noise and adversarial inputs [582, 310, 385],

- ensuring fairness in ensemble-based decision-making [227, 186],

- integrating ensemble methods with deep learning architectures [212, 90],

- adapting ensembles to evolving data streams and non-stationary environments [332, 242, 463],

- and developing ensemble techniques for large language models (LLMs), including strategies for combining outputs before, during, or after inference [112].

9.11   Exercises

9.11.1   Multiple-Choice Questions

9.1. Which of the following are common advantages of using bagging ensembles, assuming all base models are trained with the same learning algorithm?

   (a) Bagging tends to reduce the bias of the model.

   (b) Bagging tends to reduce the variance of the model.

   (c) Bagging can help mitigate overfitting.

   (d) Bagging can help mitigate underfitting.

9.2. Which of the following statements about bagging are true?

   (a) Bagging without replacement (pasting) is more likely to overfit compared to bagging with replacement.

   (b) Bagging is not effective with logistic regression, because all the base learners learn exactly the same decision boundary.

   (c) Bagging works better with unstable algorithms like decision trees.

   (d) Out-of-bag errors tend to underestimate the generalization error of bagging ensembles.

   (e) Bagging is highly parallelizable, making it well suited for large-scale machine learning problems.

9.3. In random forests, which of the following algorithmic choices is expected to reduce the variance of the model?

   (a) Increase the number of trees.

   (b) Increase the maximum depth of each tree.

   (c) Increase the minimum number of samples required for a split.

   (d) Reduce the number of features considered in each split.

   (e) Standardize the features.

9.4. Which of the following statements about AdaBoost are true?

   (a) At boosting round t, AdaBoost increases the weight of samples that were misclassified by the majority of the first $t - 1$ base models.

   (b) If each weak learner achieves an accuracy greater than 50% on the training set, AdaBoost can always achieve 100% training accuracy given enough iterations.

   (c) Increasing the number of weak learners reduces the risk of overfitting.

   (d) The effectiveness of AdaBoost can degrade if the weak learners are too complex.

   (e) Adaboost can still benefit from weak learners that achieve only 10% accuracy on the training set.

9.5. Consider a single iteration of AdaBoost applied to four data points, starting with uniform weights and using a learning rate of $\eta = 1$. Each data point has a true label and a predicted label, both of which can be either +1 or −1. Table 9.20 shows some of the initial and updated weights, with certain values omitted. Based on the provided information, which of the following statements can be determined with certainty?

	True Label	Predicted Label	Initial Weight	Updated Weight
x_1	+1	+1	1/4	?
x_2	?	?	1/4	0.0833
x_3	?	?	1/4	?
x_4	−1	−1	1/4	?

Table 9.20: Results of the first AdaBoost iteration

   (a) The classifier prediction for x_2 is +1.

   (b) The data point x_3 is misclassified.

   (c) The updated weight of x_3 is 0.75.

   (d) The updated weight of x_4 is 0.25.

	True Label	Initial Probability	Pseudo-residual	Updated Probability
x_1	1	0.333	?	0.691
x_2	?	?	?	?
x_3	0	?	?	?

Table 9.21: Results of the first gradient boosting iteration. "Initial Probability" represents the model's probability estimate for the positive class before any trees are added. "Pseudo-residual" is the negative gradient of the loss with respect to the predicted log-odds. "Updated Probability" indicates the updated probability estimate for the positive class after the first boosting iteration.

9.6. Assume a gradient boosting model is trained on a binary classification task with a learning rate of 0.5. Table 9.21 describes the first boosting iteration on three data points using pseudo-residuals computed from the negative gradient of the log loss. Based on the given information, which of the following statements can be determined with certainty?

(a) The pseudo-residual for x_1 is 0.667.

(b) The true label of x_2 is 1.

(c) The initial probability assigned to x_3 is 0.333.

(d) The updated probability for x_3 is greater than 0.15.

9.7. What are the advantages of histogram-based gradient boosting compared to traditional gradient boosting methods?

(a) It supports continuous features directly without discretization.

(b) It typically achieves higher accuracy than traditional gradient boosting.

(c) It significantly reduces training time.

(d) It reduces memory usage.

(e) It can effectively handle high-cardinality categorical features.

9.8. Which of the following models can achieve perfect classification accuracy on the dataset shown in Figure 9.22? Assume that the decision trees use only axis-aligned splits.

(a) Random forests with decision stumps

(b) AdaBoost with decision stumps

(c) AdaBoost with depth-two decision trees

(d) Gradient boosting with decision stumps

9.9. Which of the following statements about stacking ensembles are true?

(a) Stacking combines multiple base models using a weighted average, where the weights are learned by a meta-model.

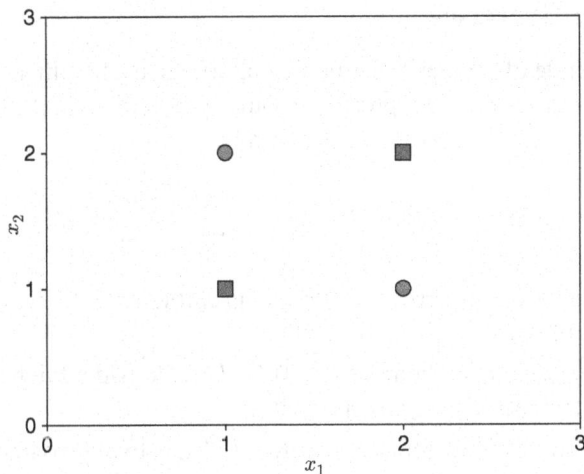

Figure 9.22: An XOR-like dataset for binary classification

(b) The meta-model in a stacking ensemble is trained using the original input features and the predictions of the base models.

(c) A stacking ensemble performs at least as well as the best individual base model in the ensemble.

(d) Cross-validation is often used in stacking to generate predictions from the base models for training the meta-model.

(e) Stacking is more effective when the base models are more diverse.

9.10. Which of the following statements about ensemble methods in Scikit-Learn are true?

(a) `VotingClassifier` requires that all base estimators are trained on the same dataset.

(b) `RandomForestClassifier` requires all categorical features to be encoded as numerical values.

(c) `ExtraTreesClassifier` uses fully-grown decision trees as the base estimators by default.

(d) `AdaBoostClassifier` can only use decision trees as the base estimators.

(e) `HistGradientBoostingClassifier` has early stopping enabled by default.

9.11.2   Theoretical Exercises

9.11. Consider an ensemble of n independent base classifiers, each with an individual error rate ϵ. The ensemble makes an incorrect prediction only if more than half of its base classifiers are wrong. Thus, the ensemble's error rate is given by:

$$\epsilon_{ensemble} = P\left(k \geq \lceil n/2 \rceil\right) = \sum_{k=\lceil n/2 \rceil}^{n} \binom{n}{k} \epsilon^k (1-\epsilon)^{n-k}.$$

(a) Calculate the ensemble error rate for an ensemble with 15 base classifiers, each with an error rate of 0.3.

(b) Prove that $\epsilon_{ensemble} < \epsilon$ whenever $\epsilon < 0.5$. *Hint*: Consider tail behavior of the binomial distribution Binomial(n, ϵ) when $\epsilon < 0.5$.

(c) Use the central limit theorem (see Section C.14.3) to approximate $\epsilon_{ensemble}$ for large n using the normal distribution.

(d) Use the result from the previous part to show that when $\epsilon < 0.5$, the ensemble error $\epsilon_{ensemble}$ decreases monotonically with n and approaches 0 as $n \to \infty$.

9.12. Consider an ensemble composed of k regression models. Assume that the prediction error of each model i $(1 \leq i \leq k)$ for an input sample $(\mathbf{x}, y)$ is given by

$$\epsilon_i = y - \hat{y}_i,$$

where y is the true target value of the sample, and $\hat{y}_i$ is the prediction made by the i-th model. Assume that the errors follow a multivariate normal distribution with zero mean, i.e., $\mathbb{E}[\epsilon_i] = 0$.

The variance and covariance of the errors are given by:

$$\text{Var}(\epsilon_i) = \mathbb{E}[\epsilon_i^2] = v,$$

$$(\epsilon_i, \epsilon_j) = \mathbb{E}[\epsilon_i \epsilon_j] = c \quad \text{for } i \neq j.$$

The ensemble's output is the average of the k base model predictions.

(a) Show that the expected squared error of the ensemble is given by:

$$\frac{1}{k}v + \frac{k-1}{k}c.$$

Hint: First, express the ensemble prediction error as the average of the base model errors. Then, use the identity

$$\left(\sum_{i=1}^{k} \epsilon_i\right)^2 = \sum_{i=1}^{k}\sum_{j=1}^{k} \epsilon_i \epsilon_j$$

to compute the expected squared error.

(b) Under what conditions does the ensemble perform better than the base models?

9.13. Show that in bagging, each bootstrap sample contains approximately 63.2% of the unique examples from the original training set. *Hint*: Use the fact that $\left(1 - \frac{1}{n}\right)^n \approx e^{-1}$ for large n.

9.14. Prove that bagging reduces the variance of the predictor without increasing its bias when the base learners are independent and have the same bias, leading to a lower expected generalization error. Specifically, consider a regression problem and use the bias–variance decomposition of the expected squared error:

$$\mathbb{E}[(f(x) - \hat{f}(x))^2] = \text{Bias}^2(\hat{f}(x)) + \text{Var}(\hat{f}(x)) + \sigma^2,$$

where $f(x)$ is the true function, $\hat{f}(x)$ is the prediction of the model, $\text{Bias}(\hat{f}(x)) = f(x) - \mathbb{E}[\hat{f}(x)]$ is the bias, $\text{Var}(\hat{f}(x))$ is the variance of the model's prediction due to the randomness of the training set, and σ^2 is the irreducible error.

9.15. Consider the dataset shown in Figure 9.23, where each two-dimensional point $\mathbf{x}_i$ is labeled with a class $y_i \in \{+1, -1\}$. The data points are as follows:

- Class -1: $(1, 1), (2, 3.5), (2, 5), (3, 6), (5, 1.5)$
- Class $+1$: $(4, 5), (4, 6), (6, 4), (6, 5), (6, 6)$

We apply the AdaBoost algorithm to this dataset using decision stumps as the weak learners and a learning rate of $\eta = 0.5$.

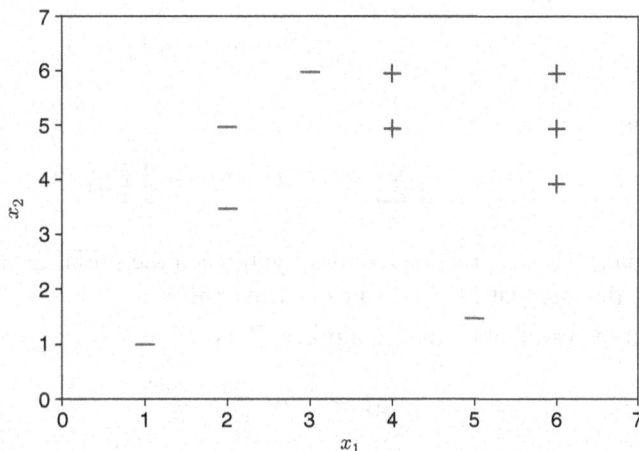

Figure 9.23: Two-dimensional dataset used for running AdaBoost. The red points represent class -1 and the blue points represent class +1.

(a) Run three iterations of the algorithm, detailing the selection of each decision stump and the corresponding updates to the sample weights. If multiple stumps have the same minimum error, you may choose any of them.

(b) Combine the three decision stumps and provide the equation for the final ensemble classifier.

(c) Determine how many training examples are correctly classified by the ensemble after the third iteration.

9.16. In this exercise you will analyze the training error of AdaBoost. Consider a set of n examples (x_i, y_i), where $y_i \in \{-1, 1\}$ is the class label of x_i. Let $h_t(x)$ denote the weak classifier obtained at boosting iteration t, and let α_t be its weight. The final ensemble prediction is given by:

$$H(x) = \text{sign}(f(x)), \quad \text{where } f(x) = \sum_{t=1}^{T} \alpha_t h_t(x).$$

(a) Show that the training error of the ensemble can be bounded from above by the average exponential loss:

$$\epsilon_{\text{ensemble}} = \frac{1}{n} \sum_{i=1}^{n} \mathbb{1}(H(x_i) \neq y_i) \leq \frac{1}{n} \sum_{i=1}^{n} \exp(-f(x_i)y_i).$$

Hint: Use the inequality $e^{-x} \geq 1$ when $x \leq 0$.

(b) Recall the Adaboost weight update formula:

$$D_{t+1}(i) = \frac{D_t(i) \exp(-\alpha_t y_i h_t(x_i))}{Z_t},$$

where Z_t is a normalization factor:

$$Z_t = \sum_{i=1}^{n} D_t(i) \exp(-\alpha_t y_i h_t(x_i)).$$

Prove that:

$$\frac{1}{n} \sum_{i=1}^{n} \exp(-f(x_i)y_i) = \prod_{t=1}^{T} Z_t.$$

Hint: Expand $D_{t+1}(i)$ recursively until you reach the initial distribution $D_1(i) = \frac{1}{n}$. Then, use the fact that $D_{t+1}(i)$ sums to 1 over all i.

(c) Prove that the value of α_t that minimizes Z_t is:

$$\alpha_t^* = \frac{1}{2} \log \left(\frac{1 - \epsilon_t}{\epsilon_t} \right),$$

where ϵ_t is the error rate of classifier h_t:

$$\epsilon_t = \sum_{i=1}^{n} D_t(i) \mathbb{1}(h_t(x_i) \neq y_i).$$

Hint: Express Z_t as:

$$Z_t = (1 - \epsilon_t) \exp(-\alpha_t) + \epsilon_t \exp(\alpha_t),$$

by separating the sums over correctly classified and misclassified examples.

(d) Prove that for α_t^* (i.e., the value used in AdaBoost when the learning rate is 0.5), we have:
$$Z_t = 2\sqrt{\epsilon_t(1-\epsilon_t)}.$$

(e) Suppose each weak classifier is slightly better than random, so that $\epsilon_t = \frac{1}{2} - \gamma_t$ for some $\gamma_t > 0$. Prove that $Z_t \leq \exp(-2\gamma_t^2)$. *Hint*: Use the inequality $\log(1-x) \leq -x$ for $0 < x \leq 1$.

(f) Let $\gamma > 0$ be a constant such that $\gamma_t \geq \gamma$ for all t. Show that the training error of the ensemble decreases exponentially with the number of rounds T:
$$\epsilon_{\text{ensemble}} \leq \exp(-2T\gamma^2).$$

(g) Using the result from the previous part, derive an upper bound on the number of boosting iterations T needed to achieve zero error on the training set.

(h) Discuss what happens if the weak learner returns a classifier with error rate $\epsilon_t > 0.5$ in a given boosting round. Is it still possible to use this classifier in AdaBoost? If so, how?

9.17. Show that in AdaBoost, if the same weak learner is used twice in two consecutive boosting rounds, its error rate in the second round will be exactly $\epsilon_{t+1} = 0.5$, assuming a learning rate of $\eta = 0.5$. Conclude why it is not beneficial for AdaBoost to select the same weak learner in successive rounds. *Hint*: Use the result from the previous question that the normalization factor is given by $Z_t = 2\sqrt{\epsilon_t(1-\epsilon_t)}$.

9.18. In multi-class settings, the SAMME algorithm extends the traditional AdaBoost method to handle multiple classes. The weight α_t assigned to each weak classifier is given by (see Equation (9.20)):
$$\alpha_t = \log\left(\frac{1-\epsilon_t}{\epsilon_t}\right) + \log(K-1),$$

where ϵ_t is the error rate of the classifier at iteration t and K is the number of classes.

Prove that $\alpha_t > 0$ if and only if the classifier performs better than random guessing.

9.19. Consider Arcing-4x, a variant of AdaBoost suggested by Breiman in 1998 [70]. This algorithm differs from AdaBoost in the following key aspects:

- The weak classifiers are combined using unweighted voting, rather than assigning weights based on performance.

- The training distribution is updated by considering misclassifications made by **all** previous models, not just the most recent one. Specifically, for the i-th example in the training set, let m_i denote the number of times it was misclassified by the first k classifiers. The probability p_i for selecting example i for training classifier $k+1$ is defined as:
$$p_i = \frac{1+m_i^4}{\sum_{i=1}^{n}(1+m_i^4)}.$$

Analyze how Arcing-4x differs from AdaBoost with respect to error reduction and model robustness. Specifically:

(a) Discuss the impact of using unweighted voting in the Arcing-4x algorithm compared to the weighted voting scheme in AdaBoost.

(b) Explain how considering the cumulative misclassification history affects the distribution updates and the algorithm's ability to focus on difficult examples.

(c) Compare the theoretical implications for convergence speed and robustness to noisy data between Arcing-4x and AdaBoost.

9.20. In this exercise, we will apply gradient boosting to a regression problem using the small dataset shown in Table 9.22. The goal is to predict the price of a house (in thousands of USD) based on four attributes: size (in square feet), number of bedrooms, age of the house (in years), and location quality (rated from 1 to 3).

	Size (sq ft)	Bedrooms	Age	Location	Price ($1000)
1	1500	3	10	2	250
2	1800	4	20	1	300
3	2400	3	30	3	450
4	1400	2	5	2	200
5	1200	2	15	1	190
6	2200	4	10	3	400

Table 9.22: Example training data for house price prediction

We will build an ensemble of three gradient-boosted trees with a maximum depth of 2 and a learning rate of $\nu = 0.5$.

(a) Start with an initial model that predicts a constant value equal to the average house price in the training data.

(b) Fit a regression tree to the residuals from the initial model. Show the resulting tree (e.g., the splits and the predicted values in each leaf). Note: You do not need to show all MSE calculations for every possible split. However, you should show the MSE calculation for the split you selected at each level of the tree and briefly justify your choice.

(c) Update the ensemble by adding the predictions from this tree, scaled by the learning rate ν.

(d) Repeat the process for two more boosting rounds. In each round, compute the new residuals, fit a regression tree of maximum depth 2 to the residuals, and add the scaled predictions of the new tree to the ensemble. Show the structure of each resulting tree.

(e) Show the final predictions of the ensemble on the training examples. Calculate the mean squared error (MSE) of these final predictions.

9.21. In this question, you will explore gradient-boosted trees for multi-class classification and derive the equations for updating the model. Follow these steps to complete the derivation:

(a) Consider a multi-class classification problem with K classes. Using the softmax function, express the predicted probability p_{imk} that sample $\mathbf{x}_i$ belongs to class k at the m-th boosting round in terms of the cumulative output $F_{m,k}(\mathbf{x}_i)$ of the trees trained for class k up to round m.

(b) Formulate the cross-entropy loss function for sample $\mathbf{x}_i$ at the m-th boosting round, assuming the true label is encoded as a one-hot vector $\mathbf{y}_i$. Express the loss in terms of the predicted probabilities p_{imk}.

(c) Compute the first derivative of the cross-entropy loss with respect to $F_{m,k}(\mathbf{x}_i)$. Use this derivative to define the pseudo-residuals r_{imk} for class k and explain how they are used to fit the next regression tree.

Hint: Recall that the gradient of the cross-entropy loss with respect to the logit z_j (i.e., the model's raw output for class j) is (see Section 5.8.2.2):

$$\frac{\partial L}{\partial z_j} = p_j - y_j,$$

where p_j is the predicted probability for class j, and y_j is the corresponding component of the one-hot encoded true label vector.

(d) Compute the second derivative of the cross-entropy loss with respect to $F_{m,k}(\mathbf{x}_i)$.

(e) Using the results from parts (c) and (d), derive the formula for the leaf output values γ_{jmk} that minimize the cross-entropy loss for the samples in region R_{jmk} of the regression tree for class k, based on Equation (9.51).

9.22. (*) NGBoost (Natural Gradient Boosting) generalizes gradient boosting to produce probabilistic predictions. Instead of returning a single point estimate for each prediction, NGBoost models the entire conditional distribution of the target variable given the features, allowing for meaningful uncertainty estimates. For example, consider a weather forecasting application that predicts tomorrow's temperature based on various atmospheric variables. While a standard regression model might only provide a single "best guess" estimate (e.g., 15°C), NGBoost can answer probabilistic queries such as, "What is the probability the temperature will be between 16°C and 18°C?"

NGBoost achieves this by estimating the parameters θ of a specified conditional probability distribution $P_\theta(y|\mathbf{x})$. For example, if P is a normal distribution, θ represents the mean μ and standard deviation σ. To train this multi-parameter model, NGBoost uses natural gradients, which take into account the geometry of the parameter space to produce more efficient and stable updates.

(a) Read the paper "NGBoost: Natural Gradient Boosting for Probabilistic Prediction" by Duan et al. (2020) [174], and answer the following questions:

    i. What is probabilistic regression, and how is it different from standard regression?

    ii. What is a scoring rule, and why is it important in training probabilistic models?

    iii. What are natural gradients, and how do they differ from ordinary gradients?

    iv. How do natural gradients improve the efficiency and stability of parameter updates in NGBoost?

(b) Summarize the main steps of the NGBoost algorithm in your own words, including:

    i. how NGBoost estimates the parameters of a conditional probability distribution.

    ii. how NGBoost iteratively fits base learners to the gradients and updates the parameters of the distribution using natural gradients.

    iii. why the same scaling factor $\rho^{(m)}$ must be used to update all distribution parameters.

    iv. how the final ensemble can be used for making predictions.

(c) The NGBoost algorithm is described in the paper in general terms for any choice of a base learner f, probability distribution P, and a scoring rule. Derive the specific equations and training steps for the following common case:

    • Regression trees as base learners.

    • A normal distribution for P.

    • Maximum likelihood as the scoring rule.

Write the log-likelihood loss function for the normal distribution, derive the gradients with respect to the parameters μ and σ, and explain how regression trees fit these gradients during boosting.

(d) Discuss how probabilistic predictions from NGBoost can improve decision-making in domains such as finance, healthcare, or meteorology.

(e) Survey other methods for probabilistic regression, such as Quantile Regression [322], Gaussian Processes [499], Quantile Regression Forests [415], Bayesian Additive Regression Trees (BART) [118], and Distributional Regression Forests [529]. Compare at least three of these methods to NGBoost in terms of:

    i. how each method models uncertainty in predictions.

    ii. computational efficiency and scalability.

    iii. applicability to different types of problems.

    iv. interpretability and ease of use.

9.11.3 Programming Exercises

9.23. The goal of this exercise is to demonstrate how bagging can reduce the variance of model predictions. You will implement a bagging ensemble of 100 polynomial regression models, each trained on noisy samples of the $\sin(x)$ function, and analyze how bagging improves predictive accuracy compared to individual models under various conditions. Follow these steps:

(a) Create 100 datasets, each containing 50 random samples from the $\sin(x)$ function over the range $[0, 10]$. For each data point x_i, add a small amount of Gaussian noise $\mathcal{N}(0, \sigma^2)$ (e.g., $\sigma = 0.1$) to simulate realistic measurement variability.

(b) For each dataset, fit a polynomial regression model using a fixed degree (e.g., 3 or 4).

(c) Generate a separate test set of 200 evenly spaced points over the range $[0, 10]$, without added noise. This set will be used to evaluate how closely the models approximate the true $\sin(x)$ function.

(d) Compute the ensemble prediction on the test set by averaging the outputs of the 100 polynomial models. Compute the RMSE of the ensemble predictions compared to the true sine values. Also compute the average RMSE of the individual models. Compare the two to assess the variance reduction achieved by bagging.

(e) Analyze the effect of ensemble size. Starting with the first 10 models and increasing in increments of 10 up to all 100, compute the ensemble RMSE at each step. Plot the RMSE as a function of the number of models, and analyze the trend.

(f) Analyze the effect of noise level. Repeat the full experiment (data generation, model training, and ensemble prediction) for different noise levels (e.g., $\sigma = 0.05, 0.1, 0.2, 0.5$). For each noise level, compute both the ensemble RMSE and the average RMSE of the individual models. Plot these results as a function of σ, and discuss how increasing noise affects the performance of both.

(g) Analyze the effect of model complexity. Repeat the experiment for different polynomial degrees (e.g., 2, 3, 4, 5, and 6). For each degree, compute the ensemble RMSE and the average RMSE of the individual models. Plot both as a function of polynomial degree, and discuss how bagging affects performance as model complexity increases.

9.24. In this exercise, you will compare the performance of several ensemble methods on a synthetic classification dataset and analyze their behavior under various conditions.

(a) Generate and prepare the data:

i. Use the `make_moons`[28] function from Scikit-Learn to generate a moons dataset with 100 samples and 20% noise:

```
from sklearn.datasets import make_moons

X, y = make_moons(n_samples=100, noise=0.2, random_state=42)
```

ii. Visualize the dataset using a scatter plot, coloring points by class label.

iii. Split the dataset into 80% training and 20% testing.

---

28. https://scikit-learn.org/stable/modules/generated/sklearn.datasets.make_moons.html

   (b) Train and evaluate ensemble classifiers:

   i. Train the following ensemble classifiers: `RandomForestClassifier`, `ExtraTreesClassifier`, `AdaBoostClassifier`, `GradientBoostingClassifier`, and `HistGradientBoostingClassifier`.

   ii. Report the training and test accuracy for each classifier.

   iii. Plot the decision boundary of each classifier on the training data, and compare how their shapes differ.

   (c) Analyze the impact of noise:

   i. Vary the noise level in the `make_moons` function (e.g., 0.1, 0.2, 0.3, 0.4, 0.5) and analyze how the test accuracy of each classifier changes. Additionally, visualize and compare how the decision boundaries evolve with increasing noise.

   ii. Introduce artificial label noise by flipping a random fraction (e.g., 10%) of the class labels. Compare the robustness of the ensemble classifiers to this noise by evaluating their performance on the original test set. Discuss which method is more resilient and explain why.

   (d) Analyze the impact of training set size:

   i. Generate datasets with increasing sample sizes (e.g., 50, 100, 200, 500, 1000), keeping the noise level fixed (e.g., 0.2). For each size, train and evaluate the classifiers.

   ii. Plot test accuracy as a function of training set size. Discuss how data size affects generalization performance.

   (e) Write a short report summarizing your findings.

9.25. In this exercise, you will implement the AdaBoost algorithm for binary classification from scratch, following the steps outlined in Algorithm 9.1. Proceed with the following steps:

   (a) Implement AdaBoost:

   i. Implement the AdaBoost algorithm using decision stumps (i.e., `DecisionTreeClassifier` with `max_depth=1`) as weak learners.

   ii. Simulate the effect of adjusting the example weights using two techniques:

   A. Sample weighting: Use the `sample_weight` parameter when fitting `DecisionTreeClassifier` to adjust the influence of each training example based on its current weight.

   B. Resampling: At each boosting iteration, perform sampling with replacement. The probability of selecting each sample should be proportional to its current weight.

   (b) Choose a standard binary classification dataset from Scikit-Learn, such as the Breast Cancer dataset, and split it into 80% training and 20% testing.

(c) Model Evaluation:

  i. Train your AdaBoost implementation on the training set and evaluate its performance on the test set using metrics like accuracy and AUC.

  ii. Compare the performance of the AdaBoost ensemble to a single decision tree trained on the same dataset.

  iii. Compare the performance (accuracy, AUC) and training time of your custom implementation with Scikit-Learn's `AdaBoostClassifier`. Discuss any differences in predictive performance or computational efficiency.

  iv. Compare the use of class weighting vs. resampling. Report and discuss differences in accuracy, AUC, and training dynamics.

(d) Visualize how the sample weights evolve over the boosting iterations by plotting their distributions at selected rounds (e.g., iterations 1, 5, 10, and final).

(e) Write a short summary describing the behavior of your AdaBoost implementation, its performance compared to Scikit-Learn's built-in classifier, and the impact of different weighting strategies on learning dynamics and model accuracy.

9.26. In this exercise, you will implement the gradient-boosted decision trees (GBDT) algorithm (Algorithm 9.4). Your implementation should follow a modular object-oriented design using the following classes:

- `GBDTNode`: Represents a node in the regression tree. This class should include the following attributes:

  - `is_leaf`: A boolean indicating whether the node is a leaf.
  - `left_child`: A reference to the left child node.
  - `right_child`: A reference to the right child node.
  - `split_feature_idx`: Index of the feature used to split this node.
  - `split_threshold`: The threshold value used to split the data.
  - `gamma`: Output value for the node if it is a leaf.

  In addition, it should include the following methods:

  - `__init__()`: Initializes the node with default values, such as setting `is_leaf` to `False` and initializing `left_child` and `right_child` to `None`.
  - `build(X, gradients, hessians, curr_depth, max_depth)`: Recursively builds the regression tree by determining the best split based on the pseudo-residuals (negative gradients). If a stopping criterion is met (e.g., reaching `max_depth` or only one sample is left in the node), the node becomes a leaf and calculates its output values using the `calc_leaf_weight` method.
  - `find_best_split(X, gradients)`: Finds the feature and split point that achieve the greatest reduction in the variance of the pseudo-residuals.
  - `calc_leaf_weight(gradients, hessians)`: Computes the output value for a leaf node using Equation (9.51).

- predict(x): Predicts the outcome for a given sample x by recursively traversing the tree. If the node is not a leaf, it moves to the left or right child based on the split_threshold. If the node is a leaf, it returns the output value gamma.

- **GBDTTree**: Represents a regression tree in the ensemble. It defines an attribute root which is a reference to the root node. In addition, it includes the following methods:

  - __init__(): Initializes the tree with root set to None.
  - build(X, gradients, hessians, max_depth): Instantiates the root node and calls its build method with the provided parameters.
  - predict(x): Delegates the prediction task to the root node of the tree.

- **GBDTBaseModel**: Base class for GBDT estimators, compatible with the Scikit-Learn API. This class includes the following attributes:

  - n_estimators: The number of trees in the ensemble.
  - max_depth: The maximum depth of each regression tree.
  - learning_rate: Shrinkage factor for tree outputs.
  - estimators_: A list of fitted GBDTTree instances.

In addition, it includes the following methods:

  - __init__(): Initializes the model parameters: n_estimators, max_depth, and learning_rate.
  - fit(X, y): Trains the model by building an ensemble of decision trees. In each iteration, computes the gradients and Hessians of the loss function, builds a new tree, and adds it to the ensemble.
  - get_output_values(X): Returns the raw predictions of the ensemble by summing the outputs of all trees, each scaled by the learning_rate.
  - get_base_prediction(y): An abstract method for computing the initial prediction, to be implemented in subclasses.
  - calc_gradients(y, outputs): An abstract method for computing the first-order derivatives of the loss function.
  - calc_hessians(y, outputs): An abstract method for computing the second-order derivatives (Hessians) of the loss function.
  - predict(X): An abstract method for making final predictions.

- **GBDTRegressor**: A subclass of GBDTBaseModel for handling regression tasks. This class should override the following methods:

  - get_base_prediction(y): Returns the mean of the target variable y.

- `calc_gradients(y, output)`: Returns the first derivatives of the squared loss function.
- `calc_hessians(y, output)`: Returns the second derivatives of squared loss.
- `predict(X)`: Returns the raw ensemble output as the final prediction.

- `GBDTClassifier`: A subclass of `GBDTBaseModel` for handling binary classification tasks. This class should override the following methods:

  - `get_base_prediction(y)`: Computes the log-odds of the positive class.
  - `calc_gradients(y, output)`: Returns the first derivatives of the log loss function.
  - `calc_hessians(y, output)`: Returns the second derivatives of log loss.
  - `predict_proba(X)`: Applies the sigmoid function to the ensemble outputs to produce probabilities.
  - `predict(X)`: Returns class label predictions (0 or 1) based on whether the predicted probabilities exceed 0.5.

Test your implementation using the following steps:

(a) Choose a regression task (e.g., the California Housing dataset) and a binary classification task (e.g., the Breast Cancer dataset).

(b) Evaluate the performance of your `GBDTRegressor` and `GBDTClassifier` on both the training and test sets using appropriate evaluation metrics.

(c) Compare the performance of your custom GBDT implementation with Scikit-Learn's `GradientBoostingRegressor` and `GradientBoostingClassifier`. Discuss any differences in results, efficiency, or behavior.

(d) Reflect on your implementation and consider potential areas for improvement or optimization.

9.27. Conduct a comparative analysis of the various ensemble methods discussed in this chapter using standard classification datasets. Follow these steps:

(a) Choose five classification datasets from the UCI Machine Learning Repository[29] that vary in the number of samples, features, and classes. For your convenience, Table 9.23 provides a selection of commonly used datasets for evaluating classification methods.

(b) Load each dataset into your environment.

---

29. `https://archive.ics.uci.edu/`

Dataset	Samples	Features	Classes	Description
Banknote Authentication[30]	1,371	5	2	Features extracted from images of banknotes, used to determine whether a banknote is genuine or counterfeit.
Breast Cancer[31]	569	30	2	Diagnostic data for breast cancer detection, extracted from images of cell nuclei to classify tumors as benign or malignant.
Chess (King-Rook vs. King-Pawn)[32]	3,196	36	2	Endgame positions in chess, used to classify whether the first player can force a win given a specific board configuration.
Glass Identification[33]	214	9	7	Chemical analysis data used to classify types of glass, often used in forensic analysis.
Bank Marketing[34]	45,211	17	2	Marketing data from a Portuguese bank, used to predict whether a client will subscribe to a term deposit.
Segment[35]	2,310	19	7	Image segmentation data, classifying pixels into seven categories based on low-level visual features.
Wine Quality (Red)[36]	1,599	11	10	Quality ratings of red wine samples from the Vinho Verde region, based on physico-chemical measurements.
Magic Gamma Telescope[37]	19,020	10	2	Data from a gamma-ray telescope used to classify whether an event is a high-energy gamma ray or background noise.
Soybean (Large)[38]	683	35	19	Data on various soybean diseases, used to classify plant conditions.
Default of Credit Card Clients[39]	30,000	24	2	Credit card data used to predict whether a client will default on their next payment.

Table 9.23: Examples of UCI classification datasets with diverse properties

(c) Apply necessary preprocessing steps such as encoding categorical variables or handling missing values.

(d) Split each dataset into 80% training and 20% testing.

---

30. https://archive.ics.uci.edu/ml/datasets/banknote+authentication
31. https://archive.ics.uci.edu/ml/datasets/Breast+Cancer+Wisconsin+(Diagnostic)
32. https://archive.ics.uci.edu/dataset/22/chess%2Bking%2Brook%2Bvs%2Bking%2Bpawn
33. https://archive.ics.uci.edu/ml/datasets/Glass+Identification
34. https://archive.ics.uci.edu/ml/datasets/Bank+Marketing
35. https://archive.ics.uci.edu/ml/datasets/Image+Segmentation
36. https://archive.ics.uci.edu/ml/datasets/Wine+Quality
37. https://archive.ics.uci.edu/ml/datasets/MAGIC+Gamma+Telescope
38. https://archive.ics.uci.edu/ml/datasets/Soybean+(Large)
39. https://archive.ics.uci.edu/ml/datasets/default+of+credit+card+clients

(e) For each dataset, train the following ensemble classifiers from Scikit-Learn using their default settings:

- `RandomForestClassifier`
- `ExtraTreesClassifier`
- `AdaBoostClassifier`
- `GradientBoostingClassifier`
- `HistGradientBoostingClassifier`

Record the training time of each method.

(f) Evaluate the performance of each ensemble method on the training and test sets using accuracy and AUC as the primary metrics. Display the results in a summary table for each dataset, showing the training time, training accuracy, test accuracy, training AUC, and test AUC for each ensemble method.

(g) Include an additional table that summarizes the average test accuracy and AUC across all datasets to compare overall performance.

(h) Perform hyperparameter tuning using grid search or random search. To keep runtime reasonable, restrict the search space to 2–3 values per parameter. Examples:

- `RandomForestClassifier` and `ExtraTreesClassifier`: n_estimators, max_depth, min_samples_split, min_samples_leaf.
- `AdaBoostClassifier`: n_estimators, learning_rate, base_estimator.
- `GradientBoostingClassifier`: n_estimators, learning_rate, max_depth.
- `HistGradientBoostingClassifier`: max_iter, learning_rate, max_depth.

(i) Compare the performance of each algorithm before and after hyperparameter tuning. Add the tuned results to the same summary table as the default results. Discuss any gains in performance along with changes in model training time.

(j) If time permits, repeat each experiment with 5 different random seeds. Report the mean and standard deviation of accuracy and AUC across runs. Comment on the stability and robustness of each ensemble method.

(k) Write a short report summarizing your findings, including when and why certain methods (e.g., bagging vs. boosting) perform better, the impact of hyperparameter tuning on performance, and any insights or recommendations for selecting and tuning ensemble methods for different types of datasets.

9.28. In this exercise, you will compare the performance of stacking ensembles using Scikit-Learn's `StackingClassifier`, experiment with different meta-models and evaluate how they perform relative to the individual models and a simple voting ensemble. Follow these steps:

(a) Choose a classification dataset from Scikit-Learn (e.g., Breast Cancer). Split it into 80% training and 20% testing.

(b) Train and evaluate base models:

    i. Train `LogisticRegression`, `KNeighborsClassifier`, `RandomForest Classifier`, and `GradientBoostingClassifier` on the training set.

    ii. Evaluate each model on the training and test sets using accuracy and AUC.

(c) Create a stacking ensemble:

    i. Create a `StackingClassifier` using the models above as base learners and `LogisticRegression` as the meta-model.

    ii. Train and evaluate the stacking ensemble using accuracy and AUC.

(d) Experiment with different meta-models:

    i. Replace `LogisticRegression` with other meta-models, such as `SVC`, `DecisionTreeClassifier`, or `MLPClassifier`.

    ii. Train and evaluate each stacking ensemble and compare their performance with each other.

(e) Implement a voting ensemble:

    i. Create a `VotingClassifier` with the same base models, and test both hard and soft voting strategies.

    ii. Compare the performance of the voting ensemble with the stacking ensembles and the individual models.

(f) Organize all evaluation results (accuracy, AUC) in a comparison table. Include rows for individual models, each stacking variant, and the voting ensemble.

(g) Bonus: Construct a two-level stacking ensemble:

    i. Train multiple first-level stacking ensembles using different meta-models, e.g., `LogisticRegression`, `SVC`, or `DecisionTreeClassifier`.

    ii. Use the predictions from these first-level stacking ensembles as features for a second-level meta-model (e.g., `RandomForestClassifier` or `MLPClassifier`).

    iii. Train and evaluate the two-level stacking ensemble, and compare its performance with the individual base models, one-level stacking ensembles, and the voting ensemble.

    iv. Analyze the impact of using different first-level and second-level meta-models on the overall performance.

(h) Write a short report summarizing your findings, including how stacking compares to individual models and voting ensembles, which meta-models performed best and why, and practical recommendations for applying stacking in real-world scenarios.

Chapter 10

Gradient Boosting Libraries

This chapter explores three popular gradient boosting algorithms: XGBoost, LightGBM, and CatBoost, which introduce innovative techniques to enhance the performance, scalability, and robustness of gradient boosting. Each algorithm is supported by a dedicated Python library that provides highly optimized implementations and advanced features such as parallel or GPU-based training. These libraries have set new standards for efficiency and accuracy in supervised learning and are capable of handling massive datasets with millions of samples.

XGBoost is widely recognized for its predictive performance and scalability, making it a popular choice in data science competitions and real-world applications. LightGBM achieves fast training times through techniques such as histogram-based learning and selective sampling of high-gradient instances. CatBoost addresses the issues of target leakage and prediction shift by using ordered boosting and specialized handling of categorical features.

The chapter is organized as follows. Section 10.1 explores XGBoost in detail, including its underlying algorithm, a step-by-step implementation in Python from scratch, and key features of the XGBoost library. Section 10.2 introduces LightGBM, highlighting innovations such as gradient-based one-side sampling (GOSS) and exclusive feature bundling. Section 10.3 examines CatBoost and its advanced techniques for preventing prediction shifts, including target encoding and ordered boosting. Section 10.4 presents a large-scale evaluation of these frameworks on the Higgs Boson dataset, which contains over 10 million examples. Finally, Section 10.5 concludes with a summary of the chapter.

10.1 XGBoost

XGBoost (eXtreme Gradient Boosting) is a highly efficient and scalable open-source library for gradient boosting. Developed by Tianqi Chen in 2016 as part of his PhD research [109], it quickly gained prominence within the machine learning community due to its superior performance, flexibility, and speed. XGBoost has powered numerous winning solutions in Kaggle competitions [166], especially in tasks involving structured (tabular) data, solidifying its status as a foundational tool in modern machine learning practice.

XGBoost introduces several key innovations compared to traditional gradient boosting:

- **Regularization:** Adds L1 and L2 regularization to the objective function to control model complexity and reduce overfitting.

- **Second-order optimization:** Utilizes second-order gradient information (Hessians) to perform more accurate and efficient updates, a technique often called **Newton boosting**.

- **Efficient split finding:** Implements a weighted quantile sketch algorithm to quickly identify optimal split points during tree construction.

- **Sparse-aware learning:** Efficiently handles missing values and high-dimensional sparse data using a sparsity-aware split-finding algorithm.

- **Parallel and distributed training:** Supports parallel and distributed computation, enabling faster training on multi-core and cluster environments.

- **Cache-aware data structure:** Uses a block-based layout to store gradient statistics, improving memory access and enabling efficient out-of-core computation for large datasets.

Some of these innovations, such as regularization and second-order optimization, are integral to the XGBoost algorithm itself, while others—such as parallel training and cache-aware data structures—are engineering enhancements at the library level that improve scalability and efficiency in practical applications.

You can easily install the XGBoost library using `pip`:[1]

```
pip install xgboost
```

At the time of this writing, the latest version is 3.0.1. For detailed documentation including API references, tutorials, and usage examples, visit the official XGBoost documentation page[2].

10.1.1   The XGBoost Algorithm

The XGBoost algorithm [109] builds upon the gradient boosting framework introduced in Section 9.8, while incorporating several enhancements to improve both predictive accuracy and computational efficiency. These include the incorporation of regularization terms into the objective function and the use of second-order (Newton-like) optimization in function space instead of functional gradient descent. In this section, we present the main steps of the algorithm, following the structure of the original XGBoost paper while expanding on each step to provide a more detailed explanation.

---

1. On Windows, XGBoost requires DLLs from the Visual C++ Redistributable. These are typically included with Visual Studio, but can also be downloaded separately from https://learn.microsoft.com/en-us/cpp/windows/latest-supported-vc-redist.
2. https://xgboost.readthedocs.io

As in standard gradient-boosted decision trees (GDBT), XGBoost builds an ensemble of regression trees, where the overall prediction is expressed as a sum of K additive functions:

$$F(\mathbf{x}) = \sum_{k=1}^{K} f_k(\mathbf{x}), \quad f_k \in \mathcal{F}, \tag{10.1}$$

where K denotes the number of trees, f_k is the prediction function of the k-th base model, F is the final ensemble prediction, and $\mathcal{F}$ is the space of all possible functions represented by regression trees.[3]

Given a loss function $L(y, F(\mathbf{x}))$ that quantifies the discrepancy between the true label y and the ensemble's prediction $F(\mathbf{x})$, XGBoost aims to minimize this loss over the training data while avoiding overfitting. To that end, it introduces a **regularized objective function** that combines the empirical loss with a penalty term on the complexity of the individual trees:

$$J = \sum_{i=1}^{n} L(y_i, F(\mathbf{x}_i)) + \sum_{k=1}^{K} \omega(f_k). \tag{10.2}$$

Here, $\omega(f_k)$ quantifies the complexity of the tree f_k, which will be defined more precisely in Section 10.1.1.2. XGBoost differs from traditional tree-based models by incorporating regularization directly into the objective function, rather than relying on external constraints such as limiting the tree depth.

Since the objective function J includes functions as parameters (the f_k's), it cannot be optimized using traditional parameter-based methods like gradient descent. Instead, XGBoost trains the model incrementally, adding one tree at a time in a greedy, stepwise manner—similar to the original gradient boosting approach:

$$F_k(\mathbf{x}) = F_{k-1}(\mathbf{x}) + f_k(\mathbf{x}), \tag{10.3}$$

where F_k represents the ensemble after the k-th iteration. The newly added tree f_k is chosen to minimize the regularized objective at step k:

$$
\begin{aligned}
J_k &= \sum_{i=1}^{n} L(y_i, F_k(\mathbf{x}_i)) + \omega(f_k) \\
&= \sum_{i=1}^{n} L(y_i, F_{k-1}(\mathbf{x}_i) + f_k(\mathbf{x}_i)) + \omega(f_k).
\end{aligned}
\tag{10.4}
$$

In other words, the goal is to find a tree f_k that reduces the overall training loss without becoming overly complex. However, finding the optimal tree within the space of all possible trees is computationally intractable. Instead, XGBoost constructs each tree to take a single step toward minimizing the regularized objective, effectively moving the model closer to the optimum at each iteration.

---

3. We avoid using our usual notation $h(\mathbf{x})$ for base models, as h will later refer to the Hessian of the loss function.

10.1.1.1   Newton Boosting

While traditional gradient boosting updates the model in the direction of the negative gradient of the loss function—effectively performing gradient descent in function space—XGBoost performs a second-order optimization based on Newton's method in function space, a technique known as **Newton boosting**. Newton's method incorporates curvature information via the second derivative of the loss, which often leads to faster convergence (see Section E.5.1). It is particularly efficient when the second derivative of the objective function is easy to compute and well-behaved (i.e., smooth, bounded, and numerically stable), as is the case for common loss functions in supervised learning such as squared loss or log loss.

To implement Newton boosting, we begin with a second-order Taylor expansion of the loss function at a given training point $\mathbf{x}_i$, centered at the current ensemble prediction $F_{k-1}(\mathbf{x}_i)$:

$$L(y_i, F_{k-1}(\mathbf{x}_i) + f_k(\mathbf{x}_i)) \approx L(y_i, F_{k-1}(\mathbf{x}_i)) + g_i f_k(\mathbf{x}_i) + \frac{1}{2} h_i f_k^2(\mathbf{x}_i), \qquad (10.5)$$

where g_i and h_i are the first- and second-order partial derivatives of the loss function with respect to the current prediction (referred to as the gradients and Hessians in the XGBoost paper):

$$g_i = \frac{\partial L(y_i, F_{k-1}(\mathbf{x}_i))}{\partial F_{k-1}(\mathbf{x}_i)}, \qquad (10.6)$$

$$h_i = \frac{\partial^2 L(y_i, F_{k-1}(\mathbf{x}_i))}{\partial F_{k-1}(\mathbf{x}_i)^2}. \qquad (10.7)$$

Incorporating the second-order approximation into the objective function at iteration k yields:

$$J_k = \sum_{i=1}^{n} \left[L(y_i, F_{k-1}(\mathbf{x}_i)) + g_i f_k(\mathbf{x}_i) + \frac{1}{2} h_i f_k^2(\mathbf{x}_i) \right] + \omega(f_k). \qquad (10.8)$$

Since the term $L(y_i, F_{k-1}(\mathbf{x}_i))$ is independent of f_k, it does not affect the optimization and can be omitted. This leads to the simplified objective:

$$J_k = \sum_{i=1}^{n} \left[g_i f_k(\mathbf{x}_i) + \frac{1}{2} h_i f_k^2(\mathbf{x}_i) \right] + \omega(f_k). \qquad (10.9)$$

The goal is now to construct a regression tree f_k that minimizes this regularized objective, but we must first define how the complexity of a tree is measured.

10.1.1.2   Definition of Tree Complexity

To define the complexity of a regression tree, we first write a more explicit expression for the function $f(\mathbf{x})$ computed by the tree.

Let T be the number of leaves in the tree, and let $\mathbf{w} = (w_1, \ldots, w_T)$ denote the vector of weights (or scores) assigned to the leaf nodes. Define a function $q(\mathbf{x}) : \mathbb{R}^d \to \{1, \ldots, T\}$ that maps each input $\mathbf{x} \in \mathbb{R}^d$ to the index of the leaf it falls into, based on the tree's decision rules. The prediction function of the tree can then be written as:

$$f(\mathbf{x}) = w_{q(\mathbf{x})}. \tag{10.10}$$

In other words, f assigns to each input $\mathbf{x}$ the weight of the leaf node it reaches in the tree.

The complexity of the tree is defined as:

$$\omega(f) = \gamma T + \frac{1}{2} \lambda \sum_{j=1}^{T} w_j^2. \tag{10.11}$$

The first term γT penalizes the number of leaves in the tree, where γ is a hyperparameter that controls model complexity. The second term, $\frac{1}{2} \lambda \sum_{j=1}^{T} w_j^2$, penalizes large leaf weights, with λ serving as an ℓ_2-regularization parameter. Increasing γ results in shallower trees, while increasing λ encourages smaller leaf weights, thereby reducing the tree's contribution to the overall ensemble prediction—an effect analogous to shrinkage in traditional gradient boosting.

With this definition of tree complexity, we can now reformulate the objective function at boosting iteration k as follows:

$$\begin{aligned} J_k &= \sum_{i=1}^{n} \left[g_i w_{q(\mathbf{x}_i)} + \frac{1}{2} h_i w_{q(\mathbf{x}_i)}^2 \right] + \gamma T + \frac{1}{2} \lambda \sum_{j=1}^{T} w_j^2 \\ &= \sum_{j=1}^{T} \left[\left(\sum_{i \in I_j} g_i \right) w_j + \frac{1}{2} \left(\sum_{i \in I_j} h_i + \lambda \right) w_j^2 \right] + \gamma T, \end{aligned} \tag{10.12}$$

where $I_j = \{i | q(\mathbf{x}_i) = j\}$ is the set of indices of the training samples assigned to the j-th leaf. This reformulation groups terms by leaf, leveraging the fact that all samples in the same leaf share the same weight w_j.

To simplify the objective function, we define:

$$G_j = \sum_{i \in I_j} g_i, \quad H_j = \sum_{i \in I_j} h_i, \tag{10.13}$$

where G_j and H_j denote the sums of gradients and Hessians for the samples assigned to leaf j, respectively. Substituting these into the objective yields:

$$J_k = \sum_{j=1}^{T} \left[G_j w_j + \frac{1}{2} (H_j + \lambda) w_j^2 \right] + \gamma T. \tag{10.14}$$

Our goal is to determine the leaf weights w_j that minimize this function. Taking the derivative of J_k with respect to each w_j gives:

$$\frac{\partial J_k}{\partial w_j} = G_j + (H_j + \lambda) w_j. \tag{10.15}$$

Setting this derivative to zero yields the optimal weight for each leaf:

$$w_j^* = -\frac{G_j}{H_j + \lambda}. \tag{10.16}$$

Substituting these optimal weights back into the objective function gives the minimum value of the regularized objective at iteration k:

$$
\begin{aligned}
J^* &= \sum_{j=1}^{T} \left[G_j \left(-\frac{G_j}{H_j + \lambda} \right) + \frac{1}{2}(H_j + \lambda) \left(-\frac{G_j}{H_j + \lambda} \right)^2 \right] + \gamma T \\
&= \sum_{j=1}^{T} \left[-\frac{G_j^2}{H_j + \lambda} + \frac{1}{2}\frac{G_j^2}{H_j + \lambda} \right] + \gamma T \\
&= -\frac{1}{2} \sum_{j=1}^{T} \frac{G_j^2}{H_j + \lambda} + \gamma T.
\end{aligned}
\tag{10.17}
$$

By selecting leaf weights that minimize the regularized objective, XGBoost builds decision trees that balance reduction in training loss with model complexity, thereby helping to prevent overfitting and improve generalization.

10.1.1.3   Building the Regression Tree

At each boosting iteration, XGBoost builds a regression tree to minimize the cost function J_k using a greedy, top-down approach. At each node of the tree, it evaluates all possible splits by computing the reduction in the cost function resulting from each candidate split.

Formally, let I_l and I_r denote the sets of samples that would be assigned to the left and right child nodes after a split, and let $I = I_l \cup I_r$ be the set of samples at the parent node. The sums of gradients and Hessians at the child nodes are given by:

$$
\begin{aligned}
G_L &= \sum_{i \in I_L} g_i, \quad H_L = \sum_{i \in I_L} h_i, \\
G_R &= \sum_{i \in I_R} g_i, \quad H_R = \sum_{i \in I_R} h_i.
\end{aligned}
\tag{10.18}
$$

The corresponding sums at the parent node are:

$$
\begin{aligned}
G &= \sum_{i \in I} g_i = G_L + G_R, \\
H &= \sum_{i \in I} h_i = H_L + H_R.
\end{aligned}
\tag{10.19}
$$

To evaluate a potential split, XGBoost compares the optimal cost before and after the split using the expression in Equation (10.17).

Before the split, the contribution of the parent node to the objective is:

$$J_{\text{before}}^* = -\frac{1}{2} \cdot \frac{G^2}{H + \lambda} + \gamma.$$

After the split, this is replaced by the contributions of the child nodes:

$$J_{\text{after}}^* = -\frac{1}{2} \left(\frac{G_L^2}{H_L + \lambda} + \frac{G_R^2}{H_R + \lambda} \right) + 2\gamma.$$

The gain from the split is the difference between these two quantities:

$$\Delta = J_{\text{before}}^* - J_{\text{after}}^* = \frac{1}{2} \left(\frac{G_L^2}{H_L + \lambda} + \frac{G_R^2}{H_R + \lambda} - \frac{G^2}{H + \lambda} \right) - \gamma. \tag{10.20}$$

This equation is used to evaluate all candidate splits, and the one with the highest gain (i.e., the greatest reduction in cost) is selected. If the best gain is less than 0—that is, the cost reduction is less than γ—the parent node is not split and instead becomes a leaf.

Once the tree is fully constructed, the optimal weight of each leaf node is assigned using Equation (10.16). The ensemble prediction is then updated as follows:

$$F_k(\mathbf{x}) = F_{k-1}(\mathbf{x}) + \eta \sum_{j=1}^{T} w_j \mathbb{1}\{\mathbf{x} \in R_j\}, \tag{10.21}$$

where $\eta \in (0, 1)$ is the learning rate, and R_j denotes the set of samples assigned to leaf j.

10.1.1.4   The Complete Algorithm

Algorithm 10.1 presents the pseudocode for the complete XGBoost algorithm. It uses a helper function, BuildTree (Algorithm 10.2), which constructs the next regression tree in the ensemble. The BuildTree function, in turn, calls another helper function, FindBestSplit (Algorithm 10.3), which evaluates all candidate splits at a given node and returns the one with the highest gain. The result is returned as a tuple containing the subsets of samples assigned to the left and right child nodes, along with their corresponding sums of gradients and Hessians.

In the following subsections, we derive explicit formulas for the gradient and Hessian of the loss function for several common learning problems.

10.1.1.5   Regression Problems

In regression tasks, the squared loss function is commonly used:

$$L(y_i, F_{k-1}(\mathbf{x}_i)) = (y_i - F_{k-1}(\mathbf{x}_i))^2. \tag{10.22}$$

Algorithm 10.1 XGBoost

Input:

I: Training set $\{(\mathbf{x}_i, y_i)\}_{i=1}^n$, where $\mathbf{x}_i \in \mathbb{R}^d$

$L(y, \hat{y})$: Twice-differentiable loss function

K: Number of boosting iterations

η: Learning rate

λ: Regularization coefficient

γ: Minimum gain required to perform a split

1: Initialize the model with a constant prediction:

$$F_0(\mathbf{x}) = \underset{c}{\operatorname{argmin}} \sum_{i=1}^n L(y_i, c)$$

2: **for** $k = 1$ **to** K **do**:

3:     Sum the gradients and Hessians over all training samples:

$$G \leftarrow \sum_{i \in I} \frac{\partial L(y_i, F_{k-1}(\mathbf{x}_i))}{\partial F_{k-1}(\mathbf{x}_i)}$$

$$H \leftarrow \sum_{i \in I} \frac{\partial^2 L(y_i, F_{k-1}(\mathbf{x}_i))}{\partial F_{k-1}(\mathbf{x}_i)^2}$$

4:     $\mathcal{T} \leftarrow \texttt{BuildTree}(I, G, H, F_{k-1}, \gamma)$

5:     Let $R_1, \ldots, R_T$ be the terminal regions of $\mathcal{T}$

6:     **for** $j = 1$ **to** T **do**:

7:         Compute the output value for each leaf node:

$$w_j \leftarrow -\frac{G_j}{H_j + \lambda}$$

        where G_j and H_j are the sums of gradients and Hessians at leaf node j.

8:     Update the model:

$$F_k(\mathbf{x}) \leftarrow F_{k-1}(\mathbf{x}) + \eta \sum_{j=1}^T w_j \mathbb{1}\{\mathbf{x} \in R_j\}$$

9: **return** the final ensemble $F_K(\mathbf{x})$

The first derivative of the squared loss with respect to the current ensemble prediction is:

$$g_i = \frac{\partial L(y_i, F_{k-1}(\mathbf{x}_i))}{\partial F_{k-1}(\mathbf{x}_i)} = 2(F_{k-1}(\mathbf{x}_i) - y_i). \tag{10.23}$$

Algorithm 10.2 `BuildTree`$(I, G, H, F_{k-1}, \gamma)$

Input:

    I: Indices of samples at the current node
    G: Sum of gradients for the samples in I
    H: Sum of Hessians for the samples in I
    F_{k-1}: The ensemble from the previous iteration
    γ: Minimum gain required to perform a split

1: Create a root node r and store the tuple (I, G, H) in it
2: $(\Delta, I_L, G_L, H_L, I_R, G_R, H_R) \leftarrow$ `FindBestSplit`$(I, G, H, F_{k-1}, \gamma)$
3: **if** $\Delta < 0$ **then**   ▷ Gain from the best split is less than γ
4:     **return** r
5: **else**
6:     $\mathcal{T}_L \leftarrow$ `BuildTree`$(I_L, G_L, H_L, F_{k-1}, \gamma)$
7:     Attach $\mathcal{T}_L$ as the left child of r
8:     $\mathcal{T}_R \leftarrow$ `BuildTree`$(I_R, G_R, H_R, F_{k-1}, \gamma)$
9:     Attach $\mathcal{T}_R$ as the right child of r
10:    **return** r

The second derivative, or Hessian, is constant:

$$h_i = \frac{\partial^2 L(y_i, F_{k-1}(\mathbf{x}_i))}{\partial F_{k-1}(\mathbf{x}_i)^2} = \frac{\partial [2(F_{k-1}(\mathbf{x}_i) - y_i)]}{\partial F_{k-1}(\mathbf{x}_i)} = 2. \tag{10.24}$$

Substituting these expressions into the formula for the optimal leaf weight yields:

$$w_j^* = -\frac{G_j}{H_j + \lambda} = -\frac{\sum_{i \in I_j} 2(F_{k-1}(\mathbf{x}_i) - y_i)}{2|I_j| + \lambda}, \tag{10.25}$$

where I_j denotes the set of indices of the samples assigned to leaf j.

10.1.1.6   Binary Classification

In binary classification, the log loss function is commonly used:

$$L(y_i, F_{k-1}(\mathbf{x}_i)) = -y_i \log p_i - (1 - y_i) \log(1 - p_i), \tag{10.26}$$

where $p_i = \sigma(F_{k-1}(\mathbf{x}_i))$ is the probability predicted by the current ensemble (via the sigmoid function) that the sample belongs to the positive class.

    The first and second derivatives of the log loss with respect to the prediction of the current ensemble are given by (see Section 9.8.4.2):

$$\frac{\partial L(y_i, F_{k-1}(\mathbf{x}_i))}{\partial F_{k-1}(\mathbf{x}_i)} = p_i - y_i, \tag{10.27}$$

Algorithm 10.3 FindBestSplit(I, G, H, F_{k-1}, γ)

Input:

    I: Indices of samples at the current node
    G: Sum of gradients for the samples in I
    H: Sum of Hessians for the samples in I
    F_{k-1}: The ensemble from the previous iteration
    γ: Minimum gain required to perform a split

1: $\Delta_{\max} \leftarrow 0$ $\triangleright$ Initialize the maximum gain
2: $\mathcal{S} \leftarrow$ nil $\triangleright$ Initialize the best split as nil
3: **for** $j = 1$ **to** d **do** $\triangleright$ Iterate over all the features
4:     $I_L \leftarrow \emptyset,\ G_L \leftarrow 0,\ H_L \leftarrow 0$
5:     $I_{\text{sorted}} \leftarrow I$ sorted by the j-th feature values x_{ij}
6:     **for** $i \in I_{\text{sorted}}$ **do** $\triangleright$ Compute the gain from each split point
7:         $g_i \leftarrow \dfrac{\partial L(y_i, F_{k-1}(\mathbf{x}_i))}{\partial F_{k-1}(\mathbf{x}_i)}$
8:         $h_i \leftarrow \dfrac{\partial^2 L(y_i, F_{k-1}(\mathbf{x}_i))}{\partial F_{k-1}(\mathbf{x}_i)^2}$
9:         $I_L \leftarrow I_L \cup \{i\},\ G_L \leftarrow G_L + g_i,\ H_L \leftarrow H_L + h_i$ $\triangleright$ Add i to the left child
10:       $I_R \leftarrow I - I_L,\ G_R \leftarrow G - G_L,\ H_R \leftarrow H - H_L$
11:       $\Delta \leftarrow \dfrac{1}{2}\left(\dfrac{G_L^2}{H_L + \lambda} + \dfrac{G_R^2}{H_R + \lambda} - \dfrac{G^2}{H + \lambda} \right) - \gamma$ $\triangleright$ Eq. (10.20)
12:       **if** $\Delta > \Delta_{\max}$ **then** $\triangleright$ Update the best split
13:           $\Delta_{\max} \leftarrow \Delta$
14:           $\mathcal{S} \leftarrow (I_L, G_L, H_L, I_R, G_R, H_R)$
15: **return** $\Delta_{\max}, \mathcal{S}$

$$\frac{\partial^2 L(y_i, F_{k-1}(\mathbf{x}_i))}{\partial F_{k-1}(\mathbf{x}_i)^2} = p_i(1 - p_i). \tag{10.28}$$

Therefore, the optimal output value for leaf j is:

$$w_j^* = -\frac{G_j}{H_j + \lambda} = \frac{\sum_{i \in I_j}(y_i - p_i)}{\sum_{i \in I_j}[p_i(1 - p_i)] + \lambda}, \tag{10.29}$$

where I_j denotes the set of indices of the samples assigned to leaf j.

This formula closely resembles the one used in standard gradient boosting for binary classification (see Equation (9.55)), with the addition of the regularization term λ, which penalizes large leaf weights.

10.1.1.7 Multi-Class Classification

In multi-class classification, XGBoost constructs C trees in each boosting iteration, one for each class, following an approach similar to standard gradient boosting (see Section 9.8.4.3).

The cross-entropy loss is commonly used in this setting:

$$L(y_i, F_{k-1}(\mathbf{x}_i)) = -\sum_{c=1}^{C} y_{ic} \log p_{ic}, \qquad (10.30)$$

where $F_{k-1}(\mathbf{x}_i)$ is the vector of class scores predicted by the current ensemble, y_{ic} is a binary indicator that equals 1 if sample $\mathbf{x}_i$ belongs to class c, and p_{ic} is the predicted probability that $\mathbf{x}_i$ belongs to class c, computed using the softmax function:

$$p_{ic} = \frac{\exp(F_{k-1,c}(\mathbf{x}_i))}{\sum_{c'=1}^{C} \exp(F_{k-1,c'}(\mathbf{x}_i))}. \qquad (10.31)$$

The gradients and Hessians of the cross-entropy loss with respect to the predicted score for each class are given by:

$$g_{ic} = \frac{\partial L(y_i, F_{k-1}(\mathbf{x}_i))}{\partial F_{k-1,c}(\mathbf{x}_i)} = p_{ic} - y_{ic}, \qquad (10.32)$$

$$h_{ic} = \frac{\partial^2 L(y_i, F_{k-1}(\mathbf{x}_i))}{\partial F_{k-1,c}(\mathbf{x}_i)^2} = p_{ic}(1 - p_{ic}). \qquad (10.33)$$

Therefore, for each leaf j and class c, the optimal output value is:

$$w_{jc}^* = -\frac{G_{jc}}{H_{jc} + \lambda} = \frac{\sum_{i \in I_j} (y_{ic} - p_{ic})}{\sum_{i \in I_j} p_{ic}(1 - p_{ic}) + \lambda}, \qquad (10.34)$$

where I_j denotes the set of indices of the samples assigned to leaf j.

10.1.2 Numerical Example on a Toy Dataset

We now demonstrate the XGBoost algorithm using the same toy dataset introduced in Section 9.8.5 (see Table 9.10). To solve this binary classification task, we construct an ensemble of regression trees using XGBoost with the following settings:

- Maximum tree depth: 2

- Learning rate: $\eta = 0.5$

- Minimum split gain: $\gamma = 0$ (no minimum, suitable for shallow trees)

- Regularization on leaf weights: $\lambda = 0.1$

- Number of boosting iterations: 2 (i.e., we build two trees)

	Log-odds $F_0(\mathbf{x}_i)$	Probability $p_i = \sigma(F_0(\mathbf{x}_i))$	Label y_i	Gradient $g_i = p_i - y_i$	Hessian $h_i = p_i(1 - p_i)$
1	0.693	0.667	1	$0.667 - 1 = -0.333$	$0.667(1 - 0.667) = 0.222$
2	0.693	0.667	1	$0.667 - 1 = -0.333$	$0.667(1 - 0.667) = 0.222$
3	0.693	0.667	1	$0.667 - 1 = -0.333$	$0.667(1 - 0.667) = 0.222$
4	0.693	0.667	0	$0.667 - 0 = 0.667$	$0.667(1 - 0.667) = 0.222$
5	0.693	0.667	0	$0.667 - 0 = 0.667$	$0.667(1 - 0.667) = 0.222$
6	0.693	0.667	1	$0.667 - 1 = -0.333$	$0.667(1 - 0.667) = 0.222$

Table 10.1: Initial log-odds, predicted probabilities, gradients, and Hessians for the training samples

10.1.2.1 Model Initialization

Since this is a binary classification problem, we initialize the ensemble with a constant value equal to the log-odds of the positive class in the training data:

$$F_0(\mathbf{x}) = \log\left(\frac{4}{2}\right) = 0.693.$$

Using this initial prediction, we compute the gradients and Hessians of the log loss function for each training sample, as shown in Table 10.1.

10.1.2.2 First Boosting Round

In the first boosting round, we fit a regression tree to the initial gradients and Hessians. At each node, we evaluate candidate splits and select the one that yields the highest gain, computed according to Equation 10.20.

Regression Tree Fitting

We begin by determining the optimal split at the root node. The sums of the gradients and Hessians at the root are:[4]

$$G = 4 \cdot (-0.333) + 2 \cdot 0.667 = 0.002,$$

$$H = 6 \cdot 0.222 = 1.332.$$

Next, we compute the gain for each potential split at the root. For example, consider a split based on the Education feature:

- Left group (Education = High School): Samples 1, 4

- Right group (Education = College): Samples 2, 3, 5, 6

---

4. Due to rounding the values to three decimal places, some results in this example may appear slightly off (e.g., $4 \cdot (-0.333) + 2 \cdot 0.667 \approx 0.002$ instead of exactly zero).

The gradient and Hessian sums for each group are:

- Education = High School:

$$G_L = -0.333 + 0.667 = 0.334$$

$$H_L = 2 \cdot 0.222 = 0.444$$

- Education = College:

$$G_R = -0.333 + (-0.333) + 0.667 + (-0.333) = -0.332$$

$$H_R = 4 \cdot 0.222 = 0.888$$

The gain from this split is computed as follows:

$$\Delta = \frac{1}{2} \left(\frac{G_L^2}{H_L + \lambda} + \frac{G_R^2}{H_R + \lambda} - \frac{G^2}{H + \lambda} \right) - \gamma$$

$$= \frac{1}{2} \left(\frac{0.334^2}{0.444 + 0.1} + \frac{(-0.332)^2}{0.888 + 0.1} - \frac{0.002^2}{1.332 + 0.1} \right) - 0 = 0.158.$$

Table 10.2 shows the gain values for all candidate splits. The split with the highest gain is Age < 26.5. The left child node resulting from this split contains samples 1 and 3, both of which have the same gradients and Hessians. This indicates perfect homogeneity, so no further splits are needed for that node.

Next, we determine the optimal split for the right child node, which contains samples 2, 4, 5, and 6. The sums of gradients and Hessians at this node are:

$$G = -0.333 + 0.667 + 0.667 + (-0.333) = 0.668,$$

$$H = 4 \cdot 0.222 = 0.888.$$

Split	G_L	H_L	G_R	H_R	Δ
Income = Low	0.001	0.666	0.001	0.666	0
Income = Medium	0.334	0.444	−0.332	0.888	0.158
Income = High	−0.333	0.222	0.335	1.110	0.219
Education = HS	0.334	0.444	−0.332	0.888	0.158
Age < 23.5	−0.333	0.222	0.335	1.110	0.219
Age < 26.5	−0.666	0.444	0.668	0.888	0.634
Age < 29	0.001	0.666	0.001	0.666	0
Age < 32.5	−0.332	0.888	0.334	0.444	0.158
Age < 37.5	0.335	1.110	−0.333	0.222	0.219

Table 10.2: Candidate splits at the root node and their corresponding gain. G_L and H_L represent the sum of gradients and Hessians for the left child, while G_R and H_R refer to the right child. The column Δ indicates the reduction in the cost function achieved by each split. HS stands for High School.

Table 10.3 shows all possible splits for these four samples and the gain achieved by each one. In this case, two splits: Income = High and Age < 37.5, achieve the highest gain of 0.6. We arbitrarily select Income = High as the split. Since the maximum tree depth is limited to two, no further splits are made beyond this point. The resulting regression tree is shown in Figure 10.1.

Computing Output Values for the Leaf Nodes

Next, we compute the optimal weights for the leaf nodes using Equation 10.16:

$$w_j = -\frac{G_j}{H_j + \lambda},$$

where G_j and H_j are the sums of gradients and Hessians for all samples assigned to leaf j. The computed weights for the three leaf nodes are:

$$w_1 = -\frac{-0.666}{0.444 + 0.1} = 1.224,$$

Split	G_L	H_L	G_R	H_R	Δ
Income = Low	0.334	0.444	0.334	0.444	−0.021
Income = Medium	0.667	0.222	0.001	0.666	0.465
Income = High	−0.333	0.222	1.001	0.666	0.600
Education = HS	0.667	0.222	0.001	0.666	0.465
Age < 29	0.667	0.222	0.001	0.666	0.465
Age < 32.5	0.334	0.444	0.334	0.444	−0.021
Age < 37.5	1.001	0.666	−0.333	0.222	0.600

Table 10.3: Candidate splits at the right child node and their corresponding gain.

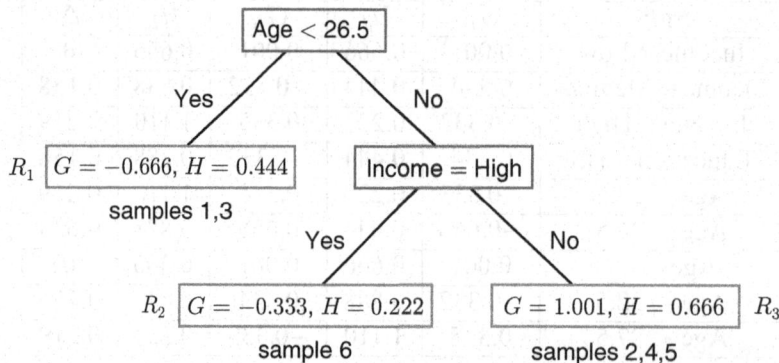

Figure 10.1: The regression tree constructed in the first boosting round. Each leaf node is annotated with the sum of gradients, the sum of Hessians, the region label R_j, and the indices of the samples that fall into that region.

	Log-odds $F_1(\mathbf{x}_i) = F_0(\mathbf{x}_i) + \eta h_1(\mathbf{x}_i)$	Probability $p_i = \sigma(F_1(\mathbf{x}_i))$	Label y_i	Gradient $g_i = p_i - y_i$	Hessian $h_i = p_i(1 - p_i)$
1	$0.693 + 0.5 \cdot 1.224 = 1.305$	0.787	1	−0.213	0.168
2	$0.693 + 0.5 \cdot (-1.307) = 0.039$	0.510	1	−0.490	0.250
3	$0.693 + 0.5 \cdot 1.224 = 1.305$	0.787	1	−0.213	0.168
4	$0.693 + 0.5 \cdot (-1.307) = 0.039$	0.510	0	0.510	0.250
5	$0.693 + 0.5 \cdot (-1.307) = 0.039$	0.510	0	0.510	0.250
6	$0.693 + 0.5 \cdot 1.034 = 1.210$	0.770	1	−0.230	0.177

Table 10.4: Updated log-odds, predicted probabilities, gradients, and Hessians for the training samples after the first boosting round. The term $h_1(\mathbf{x}_i)$ denotes the output of the first regression tree for sample $\mathbf{x}_i$, which corresponds to the weight w_j of the leaf node j that the sample falls into.

$$w_2 = -\frac{-0.333}{0.222 + 0.1} = 1.034,$$

$$w_3 = -\frac{1.001}{0.666 + 0.1} = -1.307.$$

Updating the Ensemble

Finally, the ensemble's predictions are updated using Equation 10.21:

$$F_1(\mathbf{x}) = F_0(\mathbf{x}) + \eta \sum_{j=1}^{T} w_j \mathbb{1}\{\mathbf{x} \in R_j\}.$$

That is, each sample's prediction is incremented by the output of the regression tree, scaled by the learning rate η. Table 10.4 shows the updated log-odds, predicted probabilities, and the new gradients and Hessians after the first boosting round. The results demonstrate how the model's predictions move closer to the true labels. Based on a threshold of $p > 0.5$, the updated ensemble correctly classifies 4 out of the 6 training samples.

10.1.2.3 Second Boosting Round

In the second boosting round, we fit another regression tree to the updated gradients and Hessians obtained from the first round.

Regression Tree Fitting

We begin by identifying the best split for the root node. The gradients and Hessians at the root sum to $G = -0.126$ and $H = 1.264$. Table 10.5 shows the gain computations for all candidate splits at the root.

The split Age < 26.5 achieves the highest gain. This split divides the samples into a left child node containing samples 1 and 3, and a right child node containing samples 2, 4, 5, and 6.

Split	G_L	H_L	G_R	H_R	Δ
Income = Low	−0.193	0.668	0.067	0.595	0.022
Income = Medium	0.297	0.418	−0.423	0.845	0.174
Income = High	−0.230	0.177	0.104	1.086	0.094
Education = HS	0.297	0.418	−0.423	0.845	0.174
Age < 23.5	−0.213	0.168	0.087	1.095	0.082
Age < 26.5	−0.426	0.336	0.300	0.927	0.246
Age < 29	0.084	0.586	−0.210	0.677	0.028
Age < 32.5	−0.406	0.836	0.280	0.427	0.157
Age < 37.5	0.104	1.086	−0.230	0.177	0.094

Table 10.5: Candidate splits at the root node of the second regression tree and their corresponding gain

Split	G_L	H_L	G_R	H_R	Δ
Income = Low	0.020	0.500	0.280	0.427	0.031
Income = Medium	0.510	0.250	−0.210	0.677	0.356
Income = High	−0.230	0.177	0.530	0.750	0.217
Education = HS	0.510	0.250	−0.210	0.677	0.356
Age < 29	0.510	0.250	−0.210	0.677	0.356
Age < 32.5	0.020	0.500	0.280	0.427	0.031
Age < 37.5	0.530	0.750	−0.230	0.177	0.217

Table 10.6: Candidate splits at the right child node in the second regression tree and their corresponding gain.

The two samples in the left child node have identical gradients and Hessians, so no further splits are needed for this node.

For the right child node, the sums of the gradients and Hessians are:

$$G = -0.49 + 0.51 + 0.51 + (-0.23) = 0.3,$$

$$H = 0.25 + 0.25 + 0.25 + 0.177 = 0.927.$$

Table 10.6 shows all possible splits for these four samples and the gain achieved by each one. Here, three splits achieve the highest gain of 0.356. We arbitrarily choose Education = High School as the splitting condition. Since the maximum tree depth has been reached, no further splits are made. The resulting regression tree for this round is shown in Figure 10.2.

Computing Output Values for the Leaf Nodes

We now compute the optimal weights for the leaf nodes using Equation 10.16, as described in the previous boosting round:

$$w_1 = -\frac{-0.568}{0.406 + 0.1} = 1.123,$$

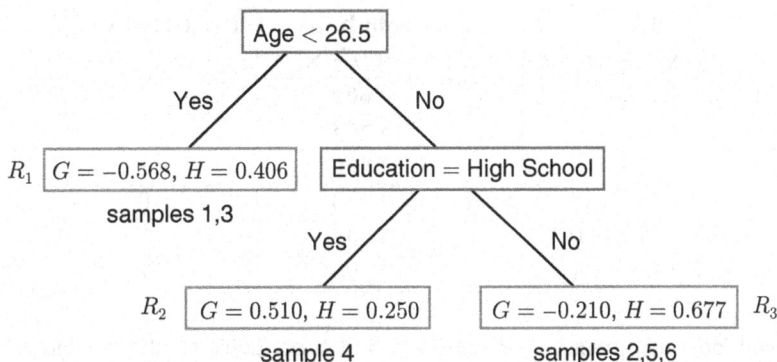

Figure 10.2: The regression tree constructed in the second boosting round. Each leaf node is annotated with the sum of gradients, the sum of Hessians, the region label R_j, and the sample indices that fall into that region.

$$w_2 = -\frac{0.51}{0.25 + 0.1} = -1.457,$$

$$w_3 = -\frac{-0.21}{0.677 + 0.1} = 0.27.$$

Updating the Ensemble

Finally, we update the ensemble's predictions using the outputs of the second regression tree:

$$F_2(\mathbf{x}) = F_1(\mathbf{x}) + \eta \sum_{j=1}^{T} w_j \mathbb{1}\{\mathbf{x} \in R_j\}.$$

Table 10.7 shows the updated log-odds, predicted probabilities, predicted labels (based on a threshold of $p > 0.5$), and the true labels. The ensemble now correctly classifies 5 out of the 6 samples in the training set. Sample 5 is still misclassified as positive, but its predicted probability (0.543) is close to the decision threshold and is likely to be corrected in subsequent boosting rounds.

10.1.3 Implementation in Python from Scratch

This section presents a simplified implementation of XGBoost in Python, consisting of approximately 250 lines of code. The goal is to illuminate the core principles behind the algorithm through a hands-on example that favors clarity over performance. I hope this implementation not only reinforces your understanding of how XGBoost works, but also inspires you to experiment with your own modifications.

Unlike the official XGBoost library, which is implemented in highly optimized C++ code and designed for industrial-scale applications, our version makes several simplifying assumptions for instructional purposes:

	Log-odds $F_2(\mathbf{x}_i) = F_1(\mathbf{x}_i) + \eta h_2(\mathbf{x}_i)$	Probability $p_i = \sigma(F_2(\mathbf{x}_i))$	Predicted Label $\mathbb{1}\{p_i > 0.5\}$	True Label y_i
1	$1.305 + 0.5 \cdot 1.123 = 1.867$	0.866	1	1
2	$0.039 + 0.5 \cdot 0.270 = 0.174$	0.543	1	1
3	$1.305 + 0.5 \cdot 1.123 = 1.867$	0.866	1	1
4	$0.039 + 0.5 \cdot (-1.457) = -0.689$	0.334	0	0
5	$0.039 + 0.5 \cdot 0.270 = 0.174$	0.543	1	0
6	$1.210 + 0.5 \cdot 0.270 = 1.345$	0.793	1	1

Table 10.7: Updated log-odds, predicted probabilities, and class labels for the training samples after the second boosting round

- The entire codebase is written in Python. In contrast, the official XGBoost library is implemented primarily in C++ to maximize performance, with a Python interface that serves as a thin wrapper over the C++ core.

- It does not include advanced optimizations for handling large datasets, such as weighted quantile sketching, out-of-core training, or distributed computation (see Section 10.1.4).

- It supports only regression and binary classification tasks, whereas the XGBoost library also handles multi-class classification, ranking, survival analysis, and other specialized use cases. In Exercise 10.11, you will extend the implementation to support multi-class classification.

- It includes a limited set of hyperparameters: n_estimators, max_depth, learning_rate, reg_lambda[5], and gamma. You will extend this set in Exercise 10.11.

Despite its simplicity, this implementation achieves competitive predictive performance on several benchmark datasets, as demonstrated in Sections 10.1.3.7 and 10.1.3.8.

10.1.3.1   Code Structure

The source code is organized into five classes, each defined in its own module (.py file):

- XGBNode: Represents a single node in a regression tree. This class is responsible for determining the optimal split based on the gradients and Hessians of the loss function.

- XGBTree: Represents a single regression tree within the ensemble, providing methods for constructing the tree and applying it to input samples.

- XGBBaseModel: A base class for all XGBoost models, designed to be compatible with the Scikit-Learn API. It implements shared functionality such as model training and prediction.

- XGBRegressor: A subclass of XGBBaseModel for regression tasks.

- XGBClassifier: A subclass of XGBBaseModel for binary classification tasks.

---

5. Since lambda is a reserved keyword in Python, we use reg_lambda to represent the regularization parameter λ, following the convention in the XGBoost library.

The complete source code is available in the `xgboost_from_scratch`[6] directory on the book's GitHub repository. In the following sections, we walk through each component of the implementation in detail.

10.1.3.2   The `XGBNode` Class

This class represents a single node in an XGBoost regression tree. It implements key components of the XGBoost algorithm, including finding the optimal split at the current node and computing the output value for leaf nodes.

The constructor initializes the node as an internal node with its child nodes set to `None`:

```python
import numpy as np

class XGBNode:
    """A node in an XGBoost regression tree"""
    def __init__(self):
        self.is_leaf: bool = False
        self.left_child: XGBNode = None
        self.right_child: XGBNode = None
```

The `build` method recursively constructs the tree. It stops when any of the following criteria are met:

- The node contains only one training sample.

- The maximum tree depth has been reached.

- No split yields a positive gain in the regularized objective.

```python
def build(self, X, grads, hessians, curr_depth, max_depth, reg_lambda, gamma):
    """Recursively build the subtree rooted at this node."""
    # Stop if only one sample remains or the maximum tree depth is reached
    if len(X) == 1 or curr_depth >= max_depth:
        self.is_leaf = True
        self.weight = self.calc_leaf_weight(grads, hessians, reg_lambda)
        return

    # Find the best split at this node
    best_gain, best_split = self.find_best_split(X, grads, hessians, reg_lambda,
                                                 gamma)
```

---

6. https://github.com/roiyeho/ml-book/tree/main/Chapter10/XGBoost/xgboost_from_scratch

```
    # If no split yields a positive gain, make this node a leaf
    if best_gain < 0:
        self.is_leaf = True
        self.weight = self.calc_leaf_weight(grads, hessians, reg_lambda)
        return
    else:
        # Store the split information in the node
        feature_idx, threshold, left_samples_idx, right_samples_idx = best_split
        self.split_feature_idx = feature_idx
        self.split_threshold = threshold

        # Recursively build the left and right subtrees
        self.left_child = XGBNode()
        self.left_child.build(X[left_samples_idx], grads[left_samples_idx],
                              hessians[left_samples_idx], curr_depth + 1,
                              max_depth, reg_lambda, gamma)
        self.right_child = XGBNode()
        self.right_child.build(X[right_samples_idx], grads[right_samples_idx],
                               hessians[right_samples_idx], curr_depth + 1,
                               max_depth, reg_lambda, gamma)
```

When a stopping criterion is met, the node becomes a leaf and its weight is computed using the following method, which implements Equation (10.16):

```
def calc_leaf_weight(self, grads, hessians, reg_lambda):
    """Calculate the optimal weight for a leaf node."""
    denominator = np.sum(hessians) + reg_lambda
    if denominator == 0:
        return 0.0 # Degenerate case (zero curvature and no regularization)
    return -np.sum(grads) / denominator
```

If the node is eligible for further splitting, the find_best_split method evaluates all possible split points across all features and returns the one that yields the highest gain in the objective function:

```
def find_best_split(self, X, grads, hessians, reg_lambda, gamma):
    """Find the optimal split point by evaluating all possible splits."""
    G = np.sum(grads) # Total gradient
    H = np.sum(hessians) # Total Hessian
    best_gain = float('-inf')
    best_split = None

    # Iterate over all features
    for j in range(X.shape[1]):
        G_left, H_left = 0, 0

        # Sort the samples by the j-th feature
        sorted_samples_idx = np.argsort(X[:, j])
```

```
    # Evaluate each potential split point
    for i in range(0, X.shape[0] - 1):
        G_left += grads[sorted_samples_idx[i]]
        H_left += hessians[sorted_samples_idx[i]]
        G_right = G - G_left
        H_right = H - H_left

        # Calculate the gain of the current split
        curr_gain = self.calc_split_gain(G, H, G_left, H_left, G_right, H_right,
                                         reg_lambda, gamma)

        # Update the best split if the current gain is higher
        if curr_gain > best_gain:
            best_gain = curr_gain
            threshold = (X[sorted_samples_idx[i], j] +
                            X[sorted_samples_idx[i + 1], j]) / 2
            left_samples_idx = sorted_samples_idx[:i + 1]
            right_samples_idx = sorted_samples_idx[i + 1:]
            best_split = (j, threshold, left_samples_idx, right_samples_idx)

return best_gain, best_split
```

The `calc_split_gain` method implements the gain calculation described in Equation (10.20):

```
def calc_split_gain(self, G, H, G_left, H_left, G_right, H_right, reg_lambda, gamma):
    """Calculate the gain resulting from a candidate split."""
    def calc_term(g, h):
        return g**2 / (h + reg_lambda)

    gain = 0.5 * (calc_term(G_left, H_left) + calc_term(G_right, H_right) -
                  calc_term(G, H)) - gamma
    return gain
```

Finally, the `predict` method computes the output of the tree for a given input sample. It recursively traverses the tree by comparing the feature values to the split thresholds, continuing until a leaf node is reached. The prediction is then given by the weight stored in that leaf:

```
def predict(self, x):
    """Traverse the tree and return the prediction for a given sample."""
    if self.is_leaf:
        return self.weight
    else:
        if x[self.split_feature_idx] <= self.split_threshold:
            return self.left_child.predict(x)
        else:
            return self.right_child.predict(x)
```

10.1.3.3 The `XGBTree` Class

This class represents a single regression tree within the XGBoost ensemble. The constructor initializes the root node to `None`:

```
from xgb_node import XGBNode

class XGBTree:
    """Represents a regression tree in the XGBoost ensemble."""
    def __init__(self):
        self.root: XGBNode = None
```

The `build` method creates the root node and initiates the recursive tree construction by calling its `build` method with the dataset and hyperparameters:

```
def build(self, X, grads, hessians, max_depth, reg_lambda, gamma):
    """Initiate the recursive construction of the tree starting from the root."""
    self.root = XGBNode()
    curr_depth = 0
    self.root.build(X, grads, hessians, curr_depth, max_depth, reg_lambda, gamma)
```

Once the tree has been constructed, it can be used to make predictions. The `predict` method simply delegates this task to the root node:

```
def predict(self, x):
    """Predict the output for a given sample by traversing the tree."""
    if self.root is not None:
        return self.root.predict(x)
    else:
        raise Exception("The tree has not been built yet.")
```

10.1.3.4 The `XGBBaseModel` Class

This abstract class serves as the base class for XGBoost estimators. It inherits from `BaseEstimator` to ensure compatibility with the Scikit-Learn API and implements the `fit` and `predict` methods.

The constructor defines the hyperparameters that control various aspects of the boosting process. To ensure consistency, their names and default values follow those defined in the XGBoost library:

- `n_estimators`: Number of trees in the ensemble (default: 100).

- `max_depth`: Maximum depth of each tree (default: 6).

- `learning_rate`: Shrinkage factor applied to each tree's prediction (default: 0.3).

- `reg_lambda`: L2 regularization term on leaf weights (default: 1).

- `gamma`: Minimum loss reduction required to split a node (default: 0).

```python
import numpy as np
from abc import ABC, abstractmethod
from sklearn.base import BaseEstimator
from typing import List
from xgb_tree import XGBTree

class XGBBaseModel(ABC, BaseEstimator):
    """Base class for XGBoost estimators, compatible with the Scikit-Learn API."""
    def __init__(self, n_estimators=100, max_depth=6, learning_rate=0.3,
                 reg_lambda=1, gamma=0, verbose=0):
        self.n_estimators = n_estimators    # Number of trees
        self.max_depth = max_depth          # Maximum tree depth
        self.learning_rate = learning_rate  # Shrinkage factor
        self.reg_lambda = reg_lambda        # L2 regularization term
        self.gamma = gamma                  # Minimum loss reduction to split
        self.verbose = verbose              # Verbosity level for logging
```

The `fit` method manages the construction of the ensemble. It iteratively builds regression trees that minimize the loss function and adds them to the ensemble:

```python
def fit(self, X, y):
    """Build an ensemble of decision trees from the input data."""
    # Initialize predictions with a constant base value
    self.base_pred = self.get_base_prediction(y)

    self.estimators: List[XGBTree] = []
    for i in range(self.n_estimators):
        # Get predictions of the current ensemble
        output = self.get_output_values(X)

        # Compute gradients and Hessians of the loss function
        grads = self.calc_gradients(y, output)
        hessians = self.calc_hessians(y, output)

        # Build a new tree and add it to the ensemble
        tree = XGBTree()
        tree.build(X, grads, hessians, self.max_depth, self.reg_lambda, self.gamma)
        self.estimators.append(tree)

        if self.verbose and i % 10 == 0:
            print(f'Boosting iteration {i}')
    return self
```

The `get_output_values` method computes the ensemble's predictions for a given dataset. It starts with the base prediction and incrementally adds the contributions of each tree in the ensemble, scaled by the learning rate:

```
def get_output_values(self, X):
    """Compute the ensemble predictions for the given dataset."""
    # Initialize the output with the base prediction
    output = np.full(X.shape[0], self.base_pred)

    # Add the predictions from each tree, scaled by the learning rate
    for estimator in self.estimators:
        output += self.learning_rate * np.array([estimator.predict(x) for x in X])

    return output
```

Finally, a set of abstract methods is defined to ensure that all subclasses implement the computations required for their specific task (e.g., regression or classification). These include methods for computing the base prediction, as well as the first- and second-order derivatives of the loss function:

```
@abstractmethod
def get_base_prediction(self, y):
    """Return the initial prediction value for the model."""
    pass

@abstractmethod
def calc_gradients(self, y, output):
    """Compute the first-order derivatives (gradients) of the loss function."""
    pass

@abstractmethod
def calc_hessians(self, y, output):
    """Compute the second-order derivatives (Hessians) of the loss function."""
    pass

@abstractmethod
def predict(self, X):
    """Return the final predictions for the input samples."""
    pass
```

10.1.3.5 The `XGBRegressor` Class

The `XGBRegressor` class is a subclass of `XGBBaseModel`, designed for regression tasks. It also inherits from `RegressorMixin` to gain access to Scikit-Learn's regression utilities, such as the score method for computing R^2 scores.

The constructor calls the base class initializer to set the hyperparameters:

```python
import numpy as np
from xgb_base_model import XGBBaseModel
from sklearn.base import RegressorMixin

class XGBRegressor(XGBBaseModel, RegressorMixin):
    """An XGBoost estimator for regression tasks."""
    def __init__(self, n_estimators=100, max_depth=6, learning_rate=0.3,
                 reg_lambda=1, gamma=0, verbose=0):
        super().__init__(n_estimators, max_depth, learning_rate, reg_lambda, gamma,
                         verbose)
```

The base prediction of the ensemble is set to the mean of the target values:

```python
def get_base_prediction(self, y):
    """Return the mean of the target variable as the initial prediction."""
    return np.mean(y)
```

The gradients and Hessians of the squared loss function are computed using Equations (10.23) and (10.24):

```python
def calc_gradients(self, y, output):
    """Compute the gradients of the squared loss function."""
    grads = 2 * (output - y)
    return grads

def calc_hessians(self, y, output):
    """Return the constant Hessian of the squared loss function."""
    hessians = np.full(len(y), 2)
    return hessians
```

Predictions for new samples are obtained directly from the ensemble's output:

```python
def predict(self, X):
    """Return the ensemble's output values as the final predictions."""
    y_pred = self.get_output_values(X)
    return y_pred
```

10.1.3.6 The XGBClassifier Class

This XGBClassifier class is a subclass of XGBBaseModel, designed for classification tasks (currently limited to binary classification). It also inherits from ClassifierMixin to access Scikit-Learn's classification utilities, such as the score method for computing accuracy scores.

The constructor calls the base class initializer to set the hyperparameters:

```python
import numpy as np
from xgb_base_model import XGBBaseModel
from sklearn.base import ClassifierMixin

class XGBClassifier(XGBBaseModel, ClassifierMixin):
    """An XGBoost estimator for binary classification tasks."""
    def __init__(self, n_estimators=100, max_depth=6, learning_rate=0.3,
                 reg_lambda=1, gamma=0, verbose=0):
        super().__init__(n_estimators, max_depth, learning_rate, reg_lambda, gamma,
                         verbose)
```

The base prediction is set to the log-odds of the positive class in the dataset:

```python
def get_base_prediction(self, y):
    """Return the log-odds of the positive class as the initial prediction."""
    prob = np.sum(y == 1) / len(y)
    return np.log(prob / (1 - prob))
```

The gradients and Hessians of the log loss function are computed using Equations (10.27) and (10.28):

```python
def sigmoid(self, x):
    """Apply the sigmoid function."""
    return 1 / (1 + np.exp(-x))

def calc_gradients(self, y, output):
    """Compute the gradients of the log loss function."""
    prob = self.sigmoid(output)
    grads = prob - y
    return grads

def calc_hessians(self, y, output):
    """Compute the Hessians of the log loss function."""
    prob = self.sigmoid(output)
    hessians = prob * (1 - prob)
    return hessians
```

The `predict_proba` method applies the sigmoid function to the ensemble's output to obtain the probability of the positive class:

```python
def predict_proba(self, X):
    """Return the predicted probabilities of the positive class."""
    log_odds = self.get_output_values(X)
    prob = self.sigmoid(log_odds)
    return prob
```

The `predict` method returns binary class labels by thresholding the predicted probabilities at 0.5:

```python
def predict(self, X):
    """Return binary class labels based on the predicted probabilities."""
    prob = self.predict_proba(X)
    y_pred = np.where(prob > 0.5, 1, 0)
    return y_pred
```

We have now successfully implemented XGBoost from scratch in fewer than 250 lines of code (including comments and blank lines)! We now proceed to evaluate its performance and compare it to the XGBoost library and other gradient boosting models.

10.1.3.7 Regression Example

In this section, we evaluate our custom XGBoost regressor and compare its performance with the official XGBoost implementation and Scikit-Learn's gradient boosting models.

We begin by importing the required libraries and modules:

```python
import time

from sklearn.datasets import fetch_california_housing
from sklearn.model_selection import train_test_split
from xgb_regressor import XGBRegressor as CustomXGBRegressor
from xgboost import XGBRegressor
from sklearn.ensemble import GradientBoostingRegressor, HistGradientBoostingRegressor
```

Next, we load the California housing dataset and split it into training and test sets:

```python
X, y = fetch_california_housing(return_X_y=True)
X_train, X_test, y_train, y_test = train_test_split(X, y, test_size=0.2,
                                                    random_state=42)
```

We now define a utility function to train a regression model, record its training time, and evaluate its performance on both the training and test sets:

```python
def evaluate_model(name, model, X_train, y_train, X_test, y_test):
    """Train a regressor, measure training time, and evaluate performance."""
    print(name)
    print('-' * 30)

    # Measure training time
    train_start_time = time.time()
    model.fit(X_train, y_train)
    elapsed = time.time() - train_start_time
    print(f'Training time: {elapsed:.3f} sec')
```

```
# Evaluate performance
train_score = model.score(X_train, y_train)
print(f'R2 score (train): {train_score:.4f}')
test_score = model.score(X_test, y_test)
print(f'R2 score (test): {test_score:.4f}\n')
```

We then instantiate four regression models for comparison: our custom XGBoost regressor, the official XGBoost implementation, and two gradient boosting regressors from Scikit-Learn (GradientBoostingRegressor and HistGradientBoostingRegressor). Each model is initialized with default settings and evaluated using our utility function:

```
# Define models in a dictionary
models = {
    'CustomXGBRegressor': CustomXGBRegressor(),
    'XGBRegressor': XGBRegressor(random_state=42),
    'GradientBoostingRegressor': GradientBoostingRegressor(random_state=42),
    'HistGradientBoostingRegressor': HistGradientBoostingRegressor(random_state=42)
}

# Evaluate each model and print the results
for name, model in models.items():
    evaluate_model(name, model, X_train, y_train, X_test, y_test)
```

We obtain the following results:

```
CustomXGBRegressor
-----------------------------------
Training time: 385.685 sec
R2 score (train): 0.8902
R2 score (test): 0.8162


XGBRegressor
-----------------------------------
Training time: 1.246 sec
R2 score (train): 0.9446
R2 score (test): 0.8301


GradientBoostingRegressor
-----------------------------------
Training time: 3.569 sec
R2 score (train): 0.8049
R2 score (test): 0.7756
```

```
HistGradientBoostingRegressor
-----------------------------------
Training time: 0.434 sec
R2 score (train): 0.8805
R2 score (test): 0.8355
```

The performance of our custom XGBoost is competitive, achieving a test R^2 score of 0.8162—slightly below that of the XGBoost library (0.8301), but significantly better than Scikit-Learn's `GradientBoostingRegressor` (0.7756). Interestingly, `HistGradientBoosting Regressor` achieves the highest test score of 0.8355 while also having the shortest training time.

The notably long training time of our custom implementation, exceeding 6 minutes, is expected. This is due to the lack of low-level optimizations and the inherent performance limitations of pure Python, especially when compared to the highly optimized C++ backends used in the XGBoost and Scikit-Learn libraries.

10.1.3.8 Classification Example

To evaluate our XGBoost classifier, we use the Breast Cancer Dataset[7] from Scikit-Learn—a widely used benchmark for binary classification tasks. The objective is to predict whether a breast mass is benign or malignant. The dataset contains 569 samples, each with 30 numerical features extracted from digitized images of fine needle aspirates (FNA) of breast masses. These features include measurements such as texture, area, and smoothness of the cell nuclei.

We begin by importing the necessary libraries and modules:

```
import time

from sklearn.datasets import load_breast_cancer
from sklearn.model_selection import train_test_split
from xgb_classifier import XGBClassifier as CustomXGBClassifier
from xgboost import XGBClassifier
from sklearn.ensemble import GradientBoostingClassifier,
    HistGradientBoostingClassifier
```

Next, we load the dataset and split it into training and test sets:

```
X, y = load_breast_cancer(return_X_y=True)
X_train, X_test, y_train, y_test = train_test_split(X, y, random_state=42)
```

Similar to the regression example, we define a utility function that trains a classifier, measures its training time, and evaluates its performance:

---

7. https://scikit-learn.org/stable/datasets/toy_dataset.html#breast-cancer-dataset

```
def evaluate_model(name, model, X_train, y_train, X_test, y_test):
    """Train a classifier, measure training time, and evaluate performance."""
    print(name)
    print('-' * 35)

    # Measure training time
    train_start_time = time.time()
    model.fit(X_train, y_train)
    elapsed = time.time() - train_start_time
    print(f'Training time: {elapsed:.3f} sec')

    # Evaluate performance
    train_score = model.score(X_train, y_train)
    print(f'Accuracy (train): {train_score:.4f}')
    test_score = model.score(X_test, y_test)
    print(f'Accuracy (test): {test_score:.4f}\n')
```

We then instantiate four classifiers for comparison: our custom XGBoost classifier, the official XGBoost implementation, and two gradient boosting classifiers from Scikit-Learn (GradientBoostingClassifier and HistGradientBoostingClassifier). Each model is initialized with default settings and evaluated using our utility function:

```
# Define models in a dictionary
models = {
    'CustomXGBClassifier': CustomXGBClassifier(),
    'XGBClassifier': XGBClassifier(random_state=42),
    'GradientBoostingClassifier': GradientBoostingClassifier(random_state=42),
    'HistGradientBoostingClassifier': HistGradientBoostingClassifier(random_state=42)
}

# Evaluate each model and print the results
for name, model in models.items():
    evaluate_model(name, model, X_train, y_train, X_test, y_test)
```

The results we obtain are as follows:

```
CustomXGBClassifier
-----------------------------------
Training time: 19.253 sec
Accuracy (train): 1.0000
Accuracy (test): 0.9720


XGBClassifier
-----------------------------------
Training time: 1.105 sec
Accuracy (train): 1.0000
Accuracy (test): 0.9650
```

```
GradientBoostingClassifier
-----------------------------------
Training time: 0.460 sec
Accuracy (train): 1.0000
Accuracy (test): 0.9580

HistGradientBoostingClassifier
-----------------------------------
Training time: 0.261 sec
Accuracy (train): 1.0000
Accuracy (test): 0.9510
```

Surprisingly, our custom model achieves the highest test accuracy, slightly outperforming all other models. However, its training time is significantly longer compared to the highly optimized implementations in the XGBoost and Scikit-Learn libraries.

10.1.4 XGBoost Optimizations

Beyond the core algorithm, the XGBoost library incorporates a range of algorithmic and system-level optimizations that improve efficiency, scalability, and predictive performance. This section explores several key techniques that contribute to XGBoost's strong performance in real-world applications.

10.1.4.1 Approximate Split Finding Algorithm

The **exact greedy algorithm** for split finding, described in Algorithm 10.3, involves sorting the feature values at every tree node and evaluating all possible split points. While this approach ensures highly accurate splits, it is computationally intensive and requires the entire dataset to reside in memory, limiting its scalability.

To address these limitations, XGBoost introduces an **approximate split finding algorithm**, designed to handle large-scale and distributed datasets. Similar to the histogram-based gradient boosting approach (see Section 9.8.7), this algorithm discretizes continuous feature values into a fixed number of bins. At each node, gradient statistics (i.e., the sums of gradients and Hessians) are aggregated within these bins and used to evaluate a small set of candidate split points.

XGBoost offers two variants of the approximate algorithm:

- **Global variant**: Candidate split points are selected once at the beginning of tree construction and reused across all nodes.

- **Local variant**: Candidate split points are recalculated after each split, adapting to local feature distributions and enabling more precise splits.

The global variant is more efficient due to reduced overhead in updating the candidate splits, but generally requires a larger initial set of candidates to maintain split quality throughout the tree.

Empirical results show that both variants can achieve accuracy comparable to the exact algorithm while significantly reducing training time [109].

10.1.4.2   Weighted Quantile Sketch

XGBoost implements a novel technique called **weighted quantile sketch** to efficiently handle datasets with instances of varying importance. Instance weighting is commonly used in cost-sensitive learning to give more influence to certain data points—such as those from minority classes or with higher associated costs (see Section 5.6.2). When user-defined weights are not provided, XGBoost automatically assigns instance weights based on the second derivative of the loss function with respect to the model's prediction (Hessian) at each data point.

The Hessian measures the curvature of the loss function and reflects how sensitive the loss is to changes in the model's predictions. In the context of gradient boosting, a higher Hessian value that improving the prediction at that point would lead to a larger reduction in the loss. To emphasize these critical areas, XGBoost assigns greater weights to instances with larger Hessians and adjusts the feature binning process to balance the total weight across bins. As a result, a bin may contain either many low-weight samples or a few high-weight ones, depending on the distribution of instance importance.

By reallocating bin boundaries to equalize total weight rather than sample count, the algorithm achieves finer granularity in regions with high curvature, leading to more accurate split decisions and improved model performance.

Traditional quantile sketch algorithms, such as the Greenwald-Khanna algorithm [238], efficiently approximate quantiles but do not account for instance weights. XGBoost extends these methods by introducing a specialized data structure that adapts to the distribution and magnitude of instance weights, enabling accurate weighted quantile estimation without explicitly sorting the data.

10.1.4.3   Sparsity-Aware Split Finding

XGBoost includes a sparsity-aware split finding algorithm designed to efficiently handle missing feature values. At each tree node, the algorithm evaluates the potential gain from assigning samples with missing values to either the left or right child node and selects the direction that yields the greatest gain.[8]

In addition, XGBoost treats zero entries in sparse input matrices as missing and learns their optimal direction (left or right) during split finding. This contrasts with standard decision tree implementations, which typically treat zero as a valid feature value. By treating zero as missing, XGBoost can skip unnecessary computations and focus split evaluation only on nonzero entries.

10.1.4.4   System-Level Optimizations

Beyond algorithmic improvements, XGBoost incorporates several system- and hardware-level optimizations to further enhance its scalability and training efficiency:

---

8. This strategy is similar to how Scikit-Learn handles missing values in decision trees; see Section 8.5.4.

- **Distributed computation**: XGBoost supports distributed execution through frameworks such as Apache Hadoop, Apache Spark, and Dask. By leveraging multiple machines in a cluster, it can efficiently process large-scale datasets in parallel.

- **GPU acceleration**: XGBoost includes built-in support for GPU-based training, which significantly speeds up computation by parallelizing operations across thousands of GPU cores. This is particularly beneficial for large datasets, where GPU acceleration can dramatically reduce training time.

- **Out-of-core computation**: For datasets that do not fit into memory, XGBoost employs out-of-core techniques that divide the data into blocks and stream them from disk, one block at a time. This enables efficient training even on memory-constrained machines.

- **Column blocks for parallel learning**: XGBoost stores the dataset in column blocks using the compressed sparse column (CSC) format. This layout improves memory locality and enables parallel processing of multiple tree nodes during training, as individual features can be accessed independently.

- **Cache-aware access**: During tree construction, XGBoost uses cache-aware data access strategies to align memory usage with CPU cache behavior. This reduces cache misses and memory latency, improving training speed.

10.1.5 The XGBoost Library

This section introduces the main interfaces and classes provided by the XGBoost library, along with their key hyperparameters and configuration settings. The Python implementation of the library supports three primary interfaces to accommodate different user needs:

- **Native XGBoost API**: Offers fine-grained control over model training and configuration, suitable for advanced users who require flexibility and access to low-level settings.

- **Scikit-Learn API**: Provides a user-friendly interface compatible with the Scikit-Learn ecosystem, enabling easy integration with tools for preprocessing, hyperparameter tuning, and evaluation.

- **Dask Interface**: Enables distributed training on large-scale datasets across multiple CPUs or GPUs using the Dask parallel computing framework.

In the following subsections, we describe the first two interfaces in detail. For information on using XGBoost with Dask, please refer to the official XGBoost documentation.[9]

10.1.5.1 The Native API

The native API of XGBoost is designed for advanced users who require fine-grained control over the training process and direct access to the library's core functionality. This interface is particularly useful for implementing custom workflows, optimizing memory usage, and experimenting

---

9. `https://xgboost.readthedocs.io/en/stable/tutorials/dask.html`

with specialized configurations not available in higher-level APIs. It provides several highly optimized core objects, including:

- `DMatrix`[10]: An internal data structure for storing the input dataset. It can be constructed from various data sources, including NumPy arrays, Pandas DataFrames, and CSV files. The `DMatrix` object precomputes key statistics, such as feature histograms and quantile sketches, enabling faster and more efficient model training.

- `Booster`[11]: Represents a trained XGBoost model, which is created from a `DMatrix` object using the `xgboost.train`[12] function. It provides several methods for interacting with the model, such as:

  - `predict(data)`: Generates predictions for the specified `DMatrix`.
  - `eval(data)`: Evaluates the model on a given `DMatrix` and returns metrics such as the average loss.
  - `get_score()`: Returns feature importance scores computed from the trained model.

The following example demonstrates how to train a binary classification model on the Breast Cancer dataset using XGBoost's native API. We first import the `xgboost` module:

```
import xgboost as xgb
```

Next, we load the dataset and split it into training and test sets:

```
from sklearn.datasets import load_breast_cancer
from sklearn.model_selection import train_test_split

X, y = load_breast_cancer(return_X_y=True)
X_train, X_test, y_train, y_test = train_test_split(X, y, random_state=42)
```

We then create a `DMatrix` object from the training set:

```
d_train = xgb.DMatrix(X_train, y_train)
```

Next, we define the model parameters in a dictionary:

```
params = {'objective': 'binary:logistic',
          'eval_metric': ['error'],
          'seed': 42}
```

These parameters include:

- `objective`: Defines the learning task and its associated loss function. Here, `'binary:logistic'` specifies a binary classification task using log loss. The default objective is `'reg:squarederror'`, which is used for least-squares regression.

---

10. https://xgboost.readthedocs.io/en/latest/python/python_api.html#xgboost.DMatrix
11. https://xgboost.readthedocs.io/en/latest/python/python_api.html#xgboost.Booster
12. https://xgboost.readthedocs.io/en/latest/python/python_api.html#xgboost.train

- eval_metric: Specifies the evaluation metric used to assess model performance. Here, the 'error' metric computes the classification error rate. The default metric depends on the learning task—for example, 'rmse' for regression and 'logloss' for binary classification.

- seed: Sets the random seed for reproducibility.

Other configurable parameters of XGboost are discussed in Section 10.1.5.3.

We now train the model using the xgboost.train function:

```
clf = xgb.train(params, d_train, num_boost_round=10)
```

Here, num_boost_round specifies the number of boosting rounds, which defaults to 10 if not explicitly set.

To evaluate the model, we use the eval method, which returns the chosen evaluation metric for a given dataset:

```
print(clf.eval(d_train))
```

The output is:

```
[0] eval-error:0.00469483568075117
```

This indicates a classification error of approximately 0.47%, which corresponds to a training accuracy of 99.53%.

To evaluate the model on the test set, we wrap the test data in a DMatrix and call the same method:

```
d_test = xgb.DMatrix(X_test, y_test)
print(clf.eval(d_test))
```

The output is:

```
[0] eval-error:0.03496503496503497
```

This indicates a test classification error of approximately 3.5%, or a test accuracy of 96.5%.

To make predictions on new data, we use the predict method, which returns class probabilities. For example, to obtain the estimated probability of the positive class for the first five test samples:

```
test_samples = xgb.DMatrix(X_test[:5])
y_pred = clf.predict(test_samples)
print(y_pred)
```

Output:

```
[0.9661875  0.03187571 0.04126738 0.97855264 0.9803145]
```

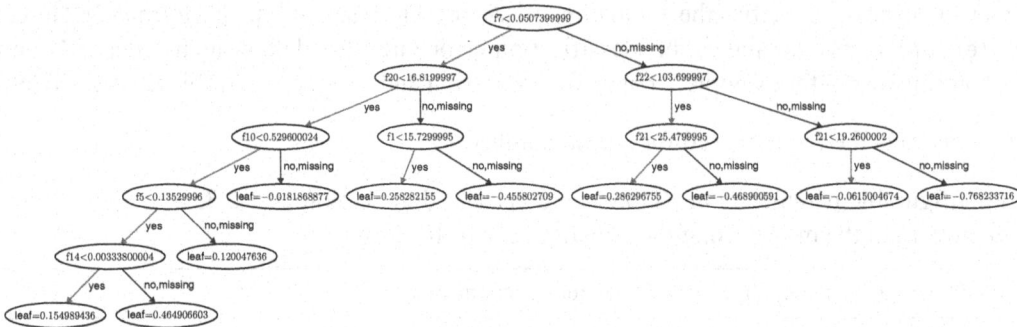

Figure 10.3: Visualization of the first decision tree in the XGBoost ensemble. Internal nodes display the split conditions, while leaf nodes show the output values for samples reaching that node. Red edges indicate the "yes" branch (condition satisfied), and blue edges indicate the "no" branch. Missing values are directed according to the default direction learned during training, with edge labels such as "yes_missing" or "no_missing" indicating the the selected branch.

To convert these probabilities into binary labels, we apply a threshold of 0.5:

```
labels = (y_pred > 0.5).astype(int)
print(labels)
```

```
[1 0 0 1 1]
```

Additionally, the decision trees in the ensemble can be visualized using the xgboost.plot_tree function.[13] For example, to plot the first tree in the ensemble:

```
xgb.plot_tree(clf, tree_idx=0)
fig = plt.gcf()
fig.set_size_inches(150, 100) # Increase figure size to improve readability
plt.show()
```

Figure 10.3 displays the resulting decision tree, including the split conditions at internal nodes and the predicted values at the leaf nodes.[14]

10.1.5.2   Scikit-Learn API

In addition to its native interface, XGBoost provides a Scikit-Learn-compatible API that simplifies usage and integrates seamlessly with Scikit-Learn utilities such as pipelines and grid search. This API consists of thin wrapper classes around XGBoost's core functionality, enabling access to most features while adhering to Scikit-Learn conventions. However, certain advanced capabilities, such as defining custom objective functions, are only available via the native API.

---

13. This function requires the graphviz package, which can be installed via: pip install graphviz.
14. The exact numbers shown in the figure may vary across different versions of XGBoost.

The Scikit-Learn API includes the following estimator classes:

- `XGBRegressor`[15]: For regression tasks.

- `XGBClassifier`[16]: For binary and multiclass classification tasks.

- `XGBRanker`[17]: For learning-to-rank tasks.[18]

For example, we can train an `XGBClassifier` on the Breast Cancer dataset as follows:

```
from xgboost import XGBClassifier

clf = XGBClassifier(random_state=42)
clf.fit(X_train, y_train)
```

We can evaluate the model's accuracy using the standard `score` method:

```
print(f'Train accuracy: {clf.score(X_train, y_train):.4f}')
print(f'Test accuracy: {clf.score(X_test, y_test):.4f}')
```

```
Train accuracy: 1.0000
Test accuracy: 0.9650
```

These results match those obtained using the native API. However, in general, results may differ between the two APIs due to differences in default parameter settings. For instance, `XGBClassifier` uses 100 estimators by default, whereas the native API used only 10 boosting rounds.

Instead of relying on a fixed number of boosting rounds, a more effective strategy is to use **early stopping**. In XGBoost, this is enabled by setting the `early_stopping_rounds` parameter, which specifies the number of consecutive rounds without improvement on a validation set before training is halted (the default is `None`, meaning early stopping is disabled). In addition, a validation set must be provided to the `fit` method via the `eval_set` parameter. The following example demonstrates how to apply early stopping:

```
# Split the training data into 90% training and 10% validation
X_train, X_val, y_train, y_val = train_test_split(
    X_train, y_train, test_size=0.1, random_state=42
)
```

---

15. https://xgboost.readthedocs.io/en/stable/python/python_api.html#xgboost.XGBRegressor

16. https://xgboost.readthedocs.io/en/stable/python/python_api.html#xgboost.XGBClassifier

17. https://xgboost.readthedocs.io/en/stable/python/python_api.html#xgboost.XGBRanker

18. Learning to rank is a supervised learning task where the goal is to order items by relevance or preference. Ranking models are commonly used in information retrieval systems (to rank retrieved documents), recommendation systems (to prioritize suggestions), and large language models (to rank retrieved passages from external sources). See [373] for a detailed overview of learning to rank.

```
# Initialize the classifier with early stopping
clf = XGBClassifier(early_stopping_rounds=5, random_state=42)

# Train the model with a validation set
clf.fit(X_train, y_train, eval_set=[(X_val, y_val)])
```

The resulting model performance is:

```
print(f'Train accuracy: {clf.score(X_train, y_train):.4f}')
print(f'Test accuracy: {clf.score(X_test, y_test):.4f}')
```

```
Train accuracy: 1.0000
Test accuracy: 0.9650
```

You can retrieve the iteration with the best validation performance using the best_iteration attribute:

```
print('Best iteration:', clf.best_iteration)
```

```
Best iteration: 26
```

We can see that the same test accuracy was achieved with only 26 boosting rounds instead of 100. Note that early stopping requires holding out part of the training data for validation, which can be a drawback for small datasets. In such cases, a common strategy is to use early stopping to identify the optimal number of rounds, and then retrain the model on the full training set using that number.

10.1.5.3 XGBoost Parameters

The XGBoost library provides a rich set of parameters for customizing and fine-tuning the boosting process. Understanding these parameters is essential for optimizing model performance, as XGBoost can be sensitive to their values, especially on complex or imbalanced datasets.

This section reviews the most important parameters available in the Scikit-Learn estimators, organized by category. These parameters are also supported in the native API, although some may have different names or default values. For example, the learning rate parameter is called learning_rate in the Scikit-Learn API and eta in the native API. For a complete and up-to-date list of parameters, consult the official XGBoost documentation[19].

Learning Task and Objective

Table 10.8 summarizes the parameters related to defining the learning task and its associated objective function.

---

19. https://xgboost.readthedocs.io/en/latest/parameter.html

Parameter	Description	Default
objective	Specifies the learning task and associated loss function, written as a string in the format 'task:objective'. The default value depends on the estimator type, for example 'binary:logistic' for XGBClassifier and 'reg:squarederror' for XGBRegressor.	-
base_score	Sets the initial prediction score before any boosting rounds. By default, this value is automatically inferred from the training data, e.g., the mean of the target in regression or the log-odds of the positive class in binary classification.	-
scale_pos_weight	Controls the balance between positive and negative classes by scaling the weight of positive examples. Useful for imbalanced classification problems.	1

Table 10.8: Parameters for defining the learning task and objective in XGBoost

Tree Construction Algorithm

XGBoost supports several tree construction algorithms, controlled by the tree_method parameter:

- 'exact': Uses an exact algorithm that evaluates all possible split points to find the optimal one. While precise, it is computationally expensive and suitable only for small datasets that fit in memory.

- 'approx': Employs a weighted quantile sketch to precompute candidate split points before building each tree, using the Hessians as weights (see Section 10.1.4.2). This method strikes a good balance between speed and accuracy.

- 'hist': Constructs feature histograms using a one-time global quantile sketch with uniform weights. It avoids repeated sketching and is generally faster than 'approx', especially on large datasets.

- 'auto' (default): Automatically selects the most appropriate method. Since version 1.3, it defaults to 'hist', which provides strong performance across a wide range of scenarios.

When tree_method is set to 'hist' or 'approx', the max_bin parameter specifies the maximum number of bins used to discretize the continuous features. The default value is 256. Increasing max_bin allows for finer-grained splits, which can improve accuracy, especially for high-cardinality features, but also increases memory usage and computational cost.

Note that only the 'hist' method is supported on GPU. When using device='gpu', XGBoost automatically sets tree_method='gpu_hist' internally.

In addition to choosing the tree construction method, XGBoost also allows users to specify the tree growth policy. In traditional decision tree construction algorithms, such as CART, a depth-first approach is commonly used. This method recursively splits nodes along each branch as deeply as possible until a stopping criterion is met. In contrast, XGBoost supports two distinct tree growth strategies, specified by the `grow_policy` parameter:

- **Depth-wise (level-wise) growth** (`'depthwise'`): Splits all nodes at the current depth before proceeding to the next level. This uniform expansion produces balanced trees, which are generally less prone to overfitting, since no single branch can grow disproportionately. It also results in trees that are easier to interpret. This is the default growth policy.

- **Leaf-wise (best-first) growth** (`'lossguide'`): At each step, this policy selects the leaf node whose split yields the greatest reduction in the loss function. This strategy often achieves higher accuracy with fewer splits, but may lead to unbalanced trees that are more susceptible to overfitting if not properly regularized.

Controlling Overfitting

XGBoost provides several mechanisms to mitigate overfitting:

- **Model complexity control**: Constrains the complexity of individual trees and the entire ensemble using parameters such as the number of boosting rounds (`n_estimators`), learning rate (`learning_rate`), maximum tree depth (`max_depth`), minimum child weight (`min_child_weight`), and regularization terms (`reg_lambda` and `reg_alpha`).

- **Randomization**: Introduces stochasticity by subsampling training instances (`subsample`) and randomly selecting a subset of features at each node (`colsample_bynode`), level (`colsample_bylevel`), or tree (`colsample_bytree`).

Table 10.9 summarizes the key parameters for controlling overfitting in XGBoost.

System and Environment Parameters

Table 10.10 lists key parameters for configuring the runtime behavior and environment of XGBoost.

10.1.5.4   Hyperparameter Tuning

Careful hyperparameter tuning can significantly enhance the performance of XGBoost models. Scikit-Learn's utilities, such as `GridSearchCV` and `RandomizedSearchCV`, can automate this process. The example below demonstrates how to tune an `XGBRegressor` using randomized search on the California housing dataset.

We begin by training a baseline model with default hyperparameters:

```
from xgboost import XGBRegressor

reg = XGBRegressor(random_state=42)
reg.fit(X_train, y_train)
```

Parameter	Description	Default
n_estimators	Number of boosting rounds (trees).	100
learning_rate	Shrinkage factor applied to each tree's prediction. Smaller values make learning more conservative and reduce overfitting.	0.3
gamma	Minimum loss reduction required to split a node. Higher values lead to shallower trees, reducing the risk of overfitting.	0
reg_lambda	L2 regularization term on leaf weights. Penalizes large weights to improve generalization.	1
reg_alpha	L1 regularization term on leaf weights. Encourages sparsity by pushing weights toward zero.	0
max_depth	Maximum tree depth. A value of 0 indicates no limit.	6
min_child_weight	Minimum sum of instance weights (Hessians) required in a child node. Higher values prevent learning overly specific patterns.	1
max_leaves	Maximum number of leaves allowed in a tree. A value of 0 means no limit.	0
early_stopping_rounds	Stops training if the validation score does not improve for the specified number of rounds. The default value None disables early stopping.	None
subsample	Fraction of training instances used for each boosting round. Lower values reduce overfitting but may increase bias.	1
colsample_bytree	Fraction of features randomly selected for each tree.	1
colsample_bylevel	Fraction of features randomly selected for each tree level.	1
colsample_bynode	Fraction of features randomly selected for each node.	1

Table 10.9: Key parameters for controlling overfitting in XGBoost

The performance of the baseline model is:

```
print(f'R2 score (train): {reg.score(X_train, y_train):.4f}')
print(f'R2 score (test): {reg.score(X_test, y_test):.4f}')
```

```
R2 score (train): 0.9446
R2 score (test): 0.8301
```

Next, we perform a randomized search over several key hyperparameters:

```
from sklearn.model_selection import RandomizedSearchCV

params = {
    'n_estimators': [10, 50, 100, 200, 500, 1000],
    'learning_rate': np.arange(0.1, 1.01, 0.1),
```

Parameter	Description	Default
device	Specifies the hardware device used for training. Set to `'gpu'` to enable GPU acceleration.	`'cpu'`
nthread	Number of parallel threads used for training. If not set, all available threads are used.	-
random_state	Sets the random number generator seed. Affects subsampling, feature sampling, and tree construction.	None
verbosity	Controls the amount of logging output: 0 = silent, 1 = warning, 2 = info, 3 = debug.	1

Table 10.10: Parameters for configuring the runtime environment of XGBoost

```
'gamma': np.logspace(-5, 0, 6), # [1e-5, 1e-4, ..., 0.1, 1]
'reg_lambda': np.logspace(-5, 0, 6),
'max_depth': np.arange(3, 11),
'subsample': np.arange(0.5, 1.01, 0.1),
'colsample_bynode': np.arange(0.5, 1.01, 0.1)
}

reg = XGBRegressor(random_state=42)
random_search = RandomizedSearchCV(reg, params, n_iter=50, cv=3,
                                   random_state=42, n_jobs=-1)
random_search.fit(X_train, y_train)
print(random_search.best_params_)
```

The best hyperparameters found are:

```
{'subsample': 0.7999999999999999, 'reg_lambda': 0.001, 'n_estimators': 1000,
'max_depth': 5, 'learning_rate': 0.1, 'gamma': 0.0001,
'colsample_bynode': 0.7999999999999999}
```

The performance of the tuned model is:

```
print(f'R2 score (train): {random_search.score(X_train, y_train):.4f}')
print(f'R2 score (test): {random_search.score(X_test, y_test):.4f}')
```

```
R2 score (train): 0.9724
R2 score (test): 0.8483
```

After just 50 iterations of randomized search, the tuned model shows a notable improvement over the baseline. The test R^2 score increases from 0.8301 to 0.8483, highlighting the importance of hyperparameter tuning in unlocking the full predictive power of XGBoost.

10.1.5.5 Handling Categorical Features

XGBoost natively supports categorical features, eliminating the need for manual preprocessing such as one-hot or ordinal encoding prior to training.

Traditional decision trees handle categorical variables by evaluating all possible binary partitions of the k categories, resulting in $2^{k-1} - 1$ potential splits. This exhaustive enumeration quickly becomes computationally infeasible as k increases. XGBoost avoids this exhaustive search by exploiting a key property of its splitting criterion: it aims to maximize homogeneity of gradient statistics within the resulting groups after the split.

XGBoost's approach is based on a classic result by Walter D. Fisher (1958) [193]. Fisher showed that to split k categories into two maximally homogeneous groups based on a score assigned to each category, we can sort the categories by their scores and consider only the $k - 1$ splits between adjacent categories in this ordering—the optimal binary split is guaranteed to be among these.

For example, consider a categorical feature representing colors:

$$A = \{\text{Red}, \text{Blue}, \text{Green}, \text{Yellow}\}.$$

Suppose each color is assigned its corresponding wavelength (in nanometers):

$$f(\text{Red}) = 700, \quad f(\text{Yellow}) = 580, \quad f(\text{Green}) = 530, \quad f(\text{Blue}) = 470.$$

To partition A into two subsets that minimize the variation in wavelength within each subset, we first sort the categories by their assigned values:

$$A_{\text{sorted}} = [\text{Blue}, \text{Green}, \text{Yellow}, \text{Red}].$$

Instead of evaluating all $2^{k-1} - 1 = 7$ binary partitions of A, we consider only the $k - 1 = 3$ adjacent splits in the sorted list:

- Partition 1: $\{\text{Blue}\}, \{\text{Green}, \text{Yellow}, \text{Red}\}$

- Partition 2: $\{\text{Blue}, \text{Green}\}, \{\text{Yellow}, \text{Red}\}$

- Partition 3: $\{\text{Blue}, \text{Green}, \text{Yellow}\}, \{\text{Red}\}$

The gaps between the subsets are computed as the score differences between adjacent categories:

- Partition 1: $f(\text{Green}) - f(\text{Blue}) = 60$

- Partition 2: $f(\text{Yellow}) - f(\text{Green}) = 50$

- Partition 3: $f(\text{Red}) - f(\text{Yellow}) = 120$

The optimal split is the one with the largest gap, as it best separates dissimilar categories while keeping similar ones together. In this case, this is Partition 3:

$$A_1 = \{\text{Blue}, \text{Green}, \text{Yellow}\}, \quad A_2 = \{\text{Red}\}.$$

Implementation in XGBoost

XGBoost applies this idea to gradient boosting by using the following procedure:

1. Group the training samples by category and compute the sum of gradients G_c and sum of Hessians H_c for each category c.

2. Compute an output value for each category using the formula

$$w_c = -\frac{G_c}{H_c + \lambda},$$

   which corresponds to the optimal weight the model would assign to a leaf containing only that category.

3. Sort the categories by their output values w_c.

4. Evaluate the $k - 1$ possible binary splits between adjacent categories in this sorted list to find the one that maximizes the gain.

This approach significantly reduces the computational complexity of finding the optimal split from $\mathcal{O}(2^k)$ to $\mathcal{O}(k \log k)$, where the latter accounts for sorting the categories by their output values.

To enable XGBoost's native support for categorical data:

- Load your data into a Pandas DataFrame and ensure that all categorical columns have the data type `'category'`. By default, non-numeric columns in Pandas are represented as `'object'`, so you must explicitly convert them using `.astype('category')`.

- When creating the XGBoost estimator, set `enable_categorical=True` in the constructor to activate native categorical handling.

- Optionally, use the `max_cat_to_onehot` parameter to configure the encoding strategy. By default, XGBoost uses one-hot encoding for categorical features with at most 4 unique values, and applies partition-based splitting (as described above) for features with higher cardinality.

Example using the Adults Dataset

For example, consider training an `XGBClassifier` on the Adults dataset, which contains 8 categorical and 6 numerical features (see Section 3.10.8). First, we load the dataset as a DataFrame and inspect the data types of the columns:

```
from sklearn.datasets import fetch_openml

X, y = fetch_openml('adult', version=2, return_X_y=True, as_frame=True)
X.info()
```

```
<class 'pandas.core.frame.DataFrame'>
RangeIndex: 48842 entries, 0 to 48841
Data columns (total 14 columns):
 #   Column          Non-Null Count  Dtype
---  ------          --------------  -----
 0   age             48842 non-null  int64
 1   workclass       46043 non-null  category
 2   fnlwgt          48842 non-null  int64
 3   education       48842 non-null  category
 4   education-num   48842 non-null  int64
 5   marital-status  48842 non-null  category
 6   occupation      46033 non-null  category
 7   relationship    48842 non-null  category
 8   race            48842 non-null  category
 9   sex             48842 non-null  category
 10  capital-gain    48842 non-null  int64
 11  capital-loss    48842 non-null  int64
 12  hours-per-week  48842 non-null  int64
 13  native-country  47985 non-null  category
dtypes: category(8), int64(6)
memory usage: 2.6 MB
```

In this case, all categorical columns are already defined with the `'category'` data type, so no additional conversion is needed. However, we still need to convert the target labels `'>50K'` and `'<=50K'` into binary values (1 and 0):

```
from sklearn.preprocessing import LabelEncoder

label_encoder = LabelEncoder()
y = label_encoder.fit_transform(y)
```

Next, we split the data into training and test sets:

```
X_train, X_test, y_train, y_test = train_test_split(
    X, y, test_size=0.2, stratify=y, random_state=42
)
```

We now instantiate an `XGBClassifier` with `enable_categorical=True` and fit it to the training data:

```
from xgboost import XGBClassifier

clf = XGBClassifier(enable_categorical=True, random_state=42)
clf.fit(X_train, y_train)
```

Finally, we evaluate the model's accuracy:

```
print(f'Train accuracy: {clf.score(X_train, y_train):.4f}')
print(f'Test accuracy: {clf.score(X_test, y_test):.4f}')
```

```
Train accuracy: 0.9034
Test accuracy: 0.8751
```

This result outperforms the one obtained with `GradientBoostingClassifier` in Section 3.10.8 (86.76% test accuracy), and with proper hyperparameter tuning, the performance of `XGBClassifier` can be improved even further.

In summary, XGBoost is a powerful and flexible gradient boosting framework that consistently delivers strong results across a wide range of datasets and tasks. Achieving optimal results often requires careful data preparation and hyperparameter tuning. While XGBoost remains one of the most widely used and effective boosting tools, newer libraries such as LightGBM and Cat-Boost introduce additional innovations and optimizations. The following sections explore these alternatives and highlight their distinctive features.

10.2   LightGBM

LightGBM (short for **Light Gradient Boosting Machine**) is a high-performance gradient boosting framework developed by Microsoft Research in 2017 [312]. It is known for its exceptional training speed, low memory footprint, and scalability to large datasets.

To install LightGBM, use:

```
pip install lightgbm
```

Comprehensive guides and usage examples can be found in the official LightGBM documentation[20].

10.2.1   Main Features

LightGBM introduced several innovations that contributed to its success, including histogram-based training and leaf-wise tree growth. Although similar techniques have since been adopted by other libraries such as XGBoost and Scikit-Learn, LightGBM retains a number of distinctive features—most notably its support for gradient-based one-side sampling (GOSS) and exclusive feature bundling (EFB). This section describes these unique features.

10.2.1.1   Gradient-based One-Side Sampling (GOSS)

Gradient-based One-Side Sampling (GOSS) is a key optimization in LightGBM that improves training efficiency by reducing the number of data points used to grow each tree. Inspired by the idea in AdaBoost of focusing on harder examples, GOSS prioritizes instances with large gradients,

20. https://lightgbm.readthedocs.io/en/stable/index.html

i.e., examples where the model's current prediction is still poor and the loss can be significantly reduced.

To understand why the gradient serves as an indicator of prediction difficulty, recall that in gradient boosting, we compute the gradient of the loss function with respect to the current model's prediction $F(\mathbf{x}_i)$. This gradient quantifies how sensitive the loss is to small changes in the prediction:

$$\frac{\partial L(y_i, F(\mathbf{x}_i))}{\partial F(\mathbf{x}_i)} \approx \frac{L(y_i, F(\mathbf{x}_i) + \epsilon) - L(y_i, F(\mathbf{x}_i))}{\epsilon},$$

for a small $\epsilon > 0$. A large gradient means that a small adjustment to the prediction leads to a large change in the loss, indicating that the model has room for improvement on that instance. Conversely, a gradient close to zero suggests that the loss is near a local minimum, and thus the model already fits that training example well.[21] This insight motivates the GOSS strategy: by focusing on instances with large gradients, LightGBM concentrates learning on the most informative samples, accelerating convergence while maintaining predictive performance.

When GOSS is applied, the training set for each tree is constructed from two subsets:

- A fixed top fraction a of the training instances with the largest gradient magnitudes.

- A random fraction b of the remaining instances with smaller gradients.

This ensures that the model focuses on the most informative (hard) examples while still retaining a representative subset of the easier ones.

To correct for the bias introduced by this selective sampling, the low-gradient instances are upweighted by a factor of $(1-a)/b$ when computing split gains. This adjustment allows LightGBM to approximate the split gains more accurately, as if they were computed using the full dataset.

10.2.1.2 Exclusive Feature Bundling (EFB)

Exclusive Feature Bundling (EFB) is a feature reduction technique in LightGBM that improves training efficiency by combining sparse features that are (almost) mutually exclusive—that is, features that rarely take nonzero values at the same time.

For example, consider four binary features representing mutually exclusive colors: Red, Blue, Green, and Yellow. Since only one of these features is active (nonzero) per instance, they can be bundled into a single feature (e.g., `Color`) where Red = 0, Blue = 1, Green = 2, and Yellow = 3. This representation is similar in form to ordinal encoding, though the numerical values do not imply any order.

During histogram construction, the bundled feature is treated as a standard categorical feature, with each unique value corresponding to one of the original categories. Gradient statistics are computed for each value, and splits are evaluated using the aggregated statistics. This allows LightGBM to reduce the number of features without affecting split quality.

Rather than requiring strict mutual exclusivity, LightGBM allows a limited number of overlaps (conflicts) within each bundle, where two features have nonzero values at the same instance.

---

21. For many common loss functions, the gradient is directly related to the prediction error. For example, for squared loss, it is $y_i - \hat{y}_i$; for cross-entropy loss, it is $y_i - p_i$.

The maximum allowed number of conflicts per bundle is controlled by a user-defined threshold K. To form the bundles, the algorithm first computes the number of pairwise conflicts between features and sorts them in descending order of conflict count. Each feature is then greedily assigned to the first bundle where the total number of conflicts remains below K; if no such bundle exists, a new one is created.

EFB is particularly effective for high-dimensional datasets with many sparse features, such as those resulting from one-hot encoding or bag-of-words representations, where mutual exclusivity among features is common.

10.2.1.3 Additional Optimizations

LightGBM supports many of the optimizations and customizations available in XGBoost, including:

- An extensive set of hyperparameters for controlling the boosting process, including learning rate, maximum tree depth, bootstrap subsampling, column sampling, and regularization.

- Leaf-wise tree growth, which splits the leaf that yields the greatest reduction in loss, similar to XGBoost's `'lossguide'` growth policy.

- GPU acceleration, which speeds up training by leveraging massively parallel computation.

- Native support for categorical features, eliminating the need for manual encoding.

- Distributed training, which enables model training to scale across multiple machines.

- Sparsity-aware split finding, which selects optimal default directions for missing values and zero entries in sparse data during tree construction.

10.2.2 Scikit-Learn API

Similar to XGBoost, the LightGBM Python package provides multiple interfaces: a native API, a Scikit-Learn API, and a Dask API for distributed computing. The Scikit-Learn API includes the following classes:

- `LGBMRegressor`[22] for regression tasks.

- `LGBMClassifier`[23] for classification tasks.

- `LGBMRanker`[24] for learning-to-rank tasks.

The key parameters of these classes are summarized in Table 10.11. Some parameter have aliases (e.g., `learning_rate` and `eta`), and while many are shared with XGBoost, their default values may differ. For example, unlike XGBoost, LightGBM imposes no depth limit on trees by

---

22. https://lightgbm.readthedocs.io/en/stable/pythonapi/lightgbm.LGBMRegressor.html
23. https://lightgbm.readthedocs.io/en/stable/pythonapi/lightgbm.LGBMClassifier.html
24. https://lightgbm.readthedocs.io/en/stable/pythonapi/lightgbm.LGBMRanker.html

Parameter	Description	Default
objective	Specifies the learning objective. The default depends on the estimator type, such as 'regression' for LGBMRegressor and 'binary' or 'multiclass' for LGBMClassifier.	-
n_estimators	Number of boosting iterations.	100
learning_rate	Shrinkage factor applied to each tree's output.	0.1
min_split_gain	Minimum loss reduction required to split a node.	0
reg_lambda	L2 regularization term on leaf weights.	0
reg_alpha	L1 regularization term on leaf weights.	0
max_depth	Maximum tree depth. A value ≤ 0 means no limit.	-1
min_child_weight	Minimum sum of instance weights (Hessians) needed in a child node.	0.001
min_child_samples	Minimum number of samples required in a child node.	20
max_leaves	Maximum number of leaves in a tree.	31
early_stopping_rounds	Stops training if the validation score does not improve for the specified number of iterations.	0
subsample	Fraction of data used per iteration (only active when data_sample_strategy='bagging').	1
colsample_bytree	Fraction of features randomly selected for each tree.	1
colsample_bynode	Fraction of features randomly selected at each node.	1
categorical_features	A list of categorical features, specified by index or name.	""
class_weight	Class weights in the form {class label: weight}, used to address class imbalance.	None
data_sample_strategy	Sampling strategy for data points used in tree construction: 'bagging' or 'goss'.	'bagging'
top_rate	Fraction of large-gradient data retained during GOSS.	0.2
other_rate	Fraction of small-gradient data retained during GOSS.	0.1

Table 10.11: Key parameters of LightGBM

default (max_depth=-1), but it limits the number of leaves to 31 by default and requires a minimum of 20 samples per leaf node—similar to the histogram-based gradient boosting estimators in Scikit-Learn.

10.2.3 Regression Example

We now demonstrate how to use LightGBM for regression on the California housing dataset. After loading and splitting the dataset (not shown), we create an instance of LGBMRegressor and fit it to the training data:

```
from lightgbm import LGBMRegressor

reg = LGBMRegressor(random_state=42)
reg.fit(X_train, y_train)
```

Evaluating the model:

```
print(f'R2 score (train): {reg.score(X_train, y_train):.4f}')
print(f'R2 score (test): {reg.score(X_test, y_test):.4f}')
```

```
R2 score (train): 0.8831
R2 score (test): 0.8360
```

The test R^2 score is slightly higher than the one achieved by the baseline XGBoost model with default parameters (0.8301).

By default, LightGBM uses the `bagging` sampling strategy, which randomly selects data points for constructing each tree. An alternative approach is GOSS, which focuses on the most informative examples by retaining those with the largest gradients.

To activate GOSS, set the `data_sample_strategy` parameter to `'goss'`. The sampling ratios for large- and small-gradient instances are controlled by the `top_rate` and `other_rate` parameters, respectively. Their default values are 0.2 and 0.1.

Let's now apply GOSS to the same dataset:

```
reg = LGBMRegressor(random_state=42, data_sample_strategy='goss')
reg.fit(X_train, y_train)
```

Re-evaluating the model:

```
print(f'R2 score (train): {reg.score(X_train, y_train):.4f}')
print(f'R2 score (test): {reg.score(X_test, y_test):.4f}')
```

```
R2 score (train): 0.8823
R2 score (test): 0.8392
```

Using GOSS resulted in a slightly higher test score compared to the default bagging strategy (0.8360). While GOSS can speed up training, it is most beneficial on large datasets, where the computational savings from selective sampling outweigh the overhead of ranking and selecting gradients. On smaller datasets, the default bagging strategy is typically more efficient.

10.3   CatBoost

CatBoost (short for **Cat**egorical **Boost**ing) is a gradient boosting library developed by researchers at Yandex[25] [485]. It introduces innovative techniques to address two common sources of bias in standard gradient boosting methods:

---

25. Yandex is a Russian multinational technology company known for its internet-related services, including Russia's largest search engine. CatBoost was released as open source in 2018.

- **Target leakage**: When encoding categorical features using target statistics (such as the mean target value per category), there is a risk of leaking information from the target variable into the input features. This leakage can cause the model to overfit to the training set, reducing its ability to generalize (see Section 10.3.1).

- **Prediction shift**: In standard gradient boosting, the pseudo-residuals (negative gradients) used to train each base learner are computed on the same dataset that is used to fit the learner. This creates a feedback loop in which the model learns from its own predictions, introducing a systematic bias. Over successive iterations, this bias accumulates and causes the estimated gradients to drift away from the true gradients under the data-generating distribution, ultimately degrading generalization performance (see Section 10.3.2).

To address these issues, CatBoost introduces two key innovations. First, it uses an **ordered target encoding** strategy for categorical features, in which the encoding of each example is based only on previously seen data points, thereby avoiding target leakage. Second, it implements **ordered boosting**, where the gradient for each instance is computed using base models that were trained without that instance, thus preventing prediction shift. Together, these techniques reduce overfitting and improve the model's ability to generalize to unseen data.

Empirical studies have shown that CatBoost often outperforms other gradient boosting frameworks such as XGBoost and LightGBM, although this typically comes at the cost of longer training times [40, 406, 519].

10.3.1 Target Encoding

We begin by examining CatBoost's unique approach to handling categorical features.

As discussed previously, a common method for handling categorical features in machine learning is one-hot encoding, which represents each category as a separate binary feature. While effective in some settings, one-hot encoding poses several challenges for tree-based models:

- It significantly increases the dimensionality of the input space, especially for high-cardinality variables. This can lead to higher memory usage and potential performance degradation due to the curse of dimensionality.

- Since gradient-boosted trees use binary splits, each binary feature resulting from one-hot encoding typically results in a separate node. This may produce excessively deep trees and increase the risk of overfitting.

An alternative approach is to use the original categorical features directly by evaluating all possible subsets of categories when searching for the best split. However, this quickly becomes computationally intractable as the number of categories increases. XGBoost improves the efficiency of this search by using gradient statistics to approximate the best split, but this approximation can become unreliable when data is limited—such as for rare categories or in deeper nodes of the tree where only a few samples remain.

To address these limitations, another approach known as **target encoding** replaces each categorical value with the average target value for that category, thereby capturing the statistical relationship between the category and the target variable.

Formally, consider a dataset of n examples $\{\mathbf{x}_i, y_i\}_{i=1}^{n}$, where $y_i \in \mathbb{R}$, and suppose the k-th feature is categorical. For a given sample $\mathbf{x}_i$, the value x_{ik} is replaced by:

$$\frac{\sum_{j=1}^{n} \mathbb{1}(x_{jk} = x_{ik}) \cdot y_j}{\sum_{j=1}^{n} \mathbb{1}(x_{jk} = x_{ik})}, \tag{10.35}$$

where $\mathbb{1}$ is the indicator function, equal to 1 when its argument is true and 0 otherwise. This expression computes the mean of the target variable over all training samples that share the same category value as x_{ik}.

As an example, consider the toy dataset shown in Table 10.12, which is used to predict whether an item will be purchased based on its color.

The target encoding for the color Blue is calculated as follows:

$$\frac{\sum_{i:\,\text{Color}_i\,=\,\text{Blue}} y_i}{\sum_{i:\,\text{Color}_i}} = \frac{1+0+1+1}{4} = \frac{3}{4} = 0.75.$$

This value indicates that, on average, 75% of the items with the color Blue were purchased, suggesting a strong association between that category and the likelihood of purchase.

Target encoding addresses the high-dimensionality and sparsity issues of one-hot encoding, and it can help decision tree learning by grouping samples with similar target values into the same branch. However, a major drawback of target encoding is its susceptibility to overfitting due to **target leakage**. This occurs because the encoding uses the target value y_i of sample $\mathbf{x}_i$ to compute its own feature representation, thereby leaking information about the label into the input features. In the extreme case where a category appears only once in the dataset, the encoded value will exactly equal y_i, causing the model to memorize the label. As a result, the model gains an unfair advantage during training, which harms its ability to generalize to unseen data.

One way to mitigate this problem is to split the dataset into two parts: one for computing the target statistics and the other for training the model. However, this solution reduces the amount

	Color	Purchased
1	Blue	1
2	Blue	0
3	Red	1
4	Green	1
5	Blue	1
6	Green	0
7	Blue	1
8	Red	0

Table 10.12: A toy dataset for demonstrating target encoding

of data available for both tasks, potentially degrading the reliability of the estimated statistics and the performance of the learned model.

10.3.1.1 Ordered Target Encoding

CatBoost introduces a more sophisticated approach to target encoding that avoids target leakage while still utilizing the entire dataset for training. For each instance i, the categorical feature value is encoded using information only from instances with indices less than i. To accomplish this, CatBoost first applies a random permutation to the dataset to eliminate any sequential structure that might introduce spurious correlations (e.g., temporal dependencies), and then computes the average target value for each instance using only the preceding examples in the permutation.

Formally, let $\sigma = (\sigma_1, \ldots, \sigma_n)$ be a permutation of the dataset indices such that σ_i is the index of the i-th sample in the permuted dataset. For example, if $\sigma = (3, 1, 4, 2)$, the first sample in the permutation corresponds to the original third sample, the second corresponds to the original first sample, and so on.

Using this permutation, the k-th feature of the i-th sample, $x_{\sigma_i, k}$, is encoded as:

$$\frac{\left(\sum_{j=1}^{i-1} \mathbb{1}(x_{\sigma_j, k} = x_{\sigma_i, k}) \cdot y_{\sigma_j}\right) + a \cdot P}{\left(\sum_{j=1}^{i-1} \mathbb{1}(x_{\sigma_j, k} = x_{\sigma_i, k})\right) + a}. \tag{10.36}$$

This formula computes a smoothed estimate of the average target value for the category $x_{\sigma_i, k}$, using only the preceding examples in the permutation that share the same category. The smoothing parameter $a > 0$ and the prior target value P help stabilize the estimate, especially when the number of matching preceding samples is small. The prior also ensures that the encoding is well-defined for the first few elements in the permutation, where no previous samples may share the same category. For regression, P is typically set to the overall mean of the target values; for binary classification, it is the proportion of positive samples in the training set.

For example, consider the encoding of the color Blue for sample 7 in Table 10.12, assuming the identity permutation ($\sigma = (1, 2, \ldots, n)$) and a smoothing parameter $a = 0.1$. The prior, representing the proportion of positive samples, is $P = 5/8 = 0.625$. Using this prior, the encoding is computed as:

$$\frac{\left(\sum_{\substack{1 \le i \le 6 \\ \text{Color}_i = \text{Blue}}} y_i\right) + aP}{\left(\sum_{\substack{1 \le i \le 6 \\ \text{Color}_i = \text{Blue}}} 1\right) + a} = \frac{1 + 0 + 1 + 0.1 \cdot 0.625}{3 + 0.1} \approx 0.665.$$

To improve the robustness of target statistics during boosting, especially for samples appearing earlier in the sequence, CatBoost generates a new random permutation in each boosting iteration to compute the encodings. This strategy prevents any single permutation from dominating the target statistics and helps reduce overfitting.

10.3.2   Gradient Estimation Bias

A similar prediction shift issue arises during the computation of gradients in the gradient boosting process.

In traditional gradient boosting, we construct a sequence of base models h_t, where each model is trained to predict the negative gradients (or pseudo-residuals) of the loss function with respect to the current ensemble predictions:

$$- g_t(\mathbf{x}, y) = \frac{\partial L(y, F_{t-1}(\mathbf{x}))}{\partial F_{t-1}(\mathbf{x})}, \tag{10.37}$$

where $F_{t-1}(\mathbf{x})$ denotes the current ensemble prediction, and $L(y, F_{t-1}(\mathbf{x}))$ is the loss function.

Ideally, we want h_t to approximate the true gradient of the loss function over the entire input distribution—not just the gradient computed on the training data—as our ultimate goal is to minimize the generalization error. Specifically, we would like the base learner to minimize the expected squared difference between its predictions and the true negative gradient of the loss function:

$$h_t = \underset{h \in H}{\operatorname{argmin}} \, \mathbb{E}_{\mathbf{x}, y} \left[(-g_t(\mathbf{x}, y) - h(\mathbf{x}))^2 \right], \tag{10.38}$$

where H denotes the space of allowable base models (e.g., decision trees).

In practice, however, the gradient can only be estimated on the training samples. Consequently, the base model h_t is fitted to the pseudo-residuals of the training points by minimizing the squared error over the training set:

$$\hat{h}_t = \underset{h \in H}{\operatorname{argmin}} \, \frac{1}{n} \sum_{i=1}^{n} (-g_t(\mathbf{x}_i, y_i) - h(\mathbf{x}_i))^2. \tag{10.39}$$

This approximation introduces a **prediction bias**, since the gradients (pseudo-residuals) are estimated from the same data used to train the model that minimizes them. This overlap between gradient computation and model fitting creates a feedback loop in which errors in one iteration propagate and amplify in subsequent iterations. As a result, a cycle of compounding bias can arise:

1. The distribution of the training-set gradients $g_t(\mathbf{x}_i, y_i)$ deviates from the true gradient distribution $g_t(\mathbf{x}, y)$ over the entire input space.

2. The fitted model $\hat{h}_t$, trained on the approximated gradients $g_t(\mathbf{x}_i, y_i)$, becomes a biased estimate of the ideal base model h_t.

3. The updated ensemble $F_t = F_{t-1} + \hat{h}_t$ inherits this bias, further propagating the error.

4. The gradients in the next iteration, $g_{t+1}(\mathbf{x}_i, y_i)$, are computed using the predictions of the biased ensemble F_t, further amplifying the bias in subsequent iterations.

10.3.3 Ordered Boosting

CatBoost addresses the problem of gradient estimation bias by introducing **ordered boosting**, a technique that imposes an ordering on the gradient computations and estimates the gradient for each instance using only models that were trained without that instance.

Algorithm 10.4 shows the pseudocode for a basic version of the ordered boosting procedure. At the beginning of the training, a random permutation σ of the n training indices is sampled. We interpret $\sigma(i)$ as the position of sample i in the permuted order. For example, if the permutation is $(3, 1, 4, 2)$, then $\sigma(3) = 1$, $\sigma(1) = 2$, $\sigma(4) = 3$, and $\sigma(2) = 4$.

The boosting process maintains n ensembles, denoted $M_1, \ldots, M_n$, where each ensemble M_k is trained on the first k samples in the permuted order. In each boosting iteration, the gradient for training sample i is computed using model $M_{\sigma(i)-1}$, which was trained without sample i (see Figure 10.4). For example, the gradient for sample 4 is computed using $M_{\sigma(4)-1} = M_2$, which was trained on the first two permuted samples $\{3, 1\}$.

Then, n base models $h_1, \ldots, h_n$ (typically regression trees) are constructed. Each h_i is trained using only the first i permuted samples and added to its corresponding ensemble M_i. For example, if $\sigma = (3, 1, 4, 2)$, then h_3 is trained on the samples $\{3, 1, 4\}$.

The final ensemble returned by the algorithm is M_n, which was built using all the training samples $\mathbf{x}_1, \ldots, \mathbf{x}_n$.

Algorithm 10.4 Ordered Boosting

Input:
    D: Training set $\{(\mathbf{x}_i, y_i)\}_{i=1}^n$
    T: Number of boosting iterations
    `BuildBaseModel`: A procedure that trains a base learner on a given dataset

1: $\sigma \leftarrow$ a random permutation of $\{1, \ldots, n\}$ $\triangleright\ \sigma(i)$ = position of sample i in the permutation
2: **for** $i = 1$ **to** n **do** $\triangleright$ Initialize the ensembles
3:     $M_i \leftarrow 0$
4: **for** $t = 1$ **to** T **do** $\triangleright$ Run T boosting iterations
5:     **for** $i = 1$ **to** n **do** $\triangleright$ Compute the pseudo-residuals
6:
$$r_i \leftarrow -\frac{\partial L(y_i, M_{\sigma(i)-1}(\mathbf{x}_i))}{\partial M_{\sigma(i)-1}(\mathbf{x}_i)}$$

7:     **for** $i = 1$ **to** n **do**
8:         $h_i \leftarrow$ `BuildBaseModel`$(\{(\mathbf{x}_j, r_j) \mid \sigma(j) \leq i\})$ $\triangleright$ Train on the first i permuted samples
9:         $M_i \leftarrow M_i + h_i$ $\triangleright$ Update the ensemble
10: **return** the final ensemble M_n

$$M_4$$

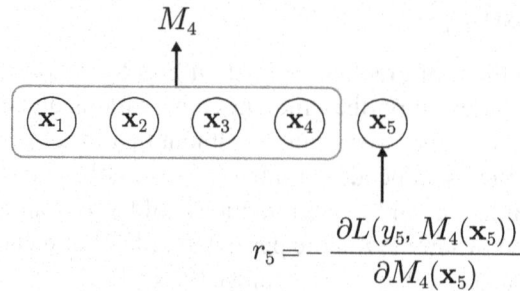

$$r_5 = -\frac{\partial L(y_5, M_4(\mathbf{x}_5))}{\partial M_4(\mathbf{x}_5)}$$

Figure 10.4: Illustration of the ordered boosting technique in CatBoost. The training samples are ordered according to the selected permutation σ. The pseudo-residual r_5 for sample $\mathbf{x}_5$ is computed using the ensemble M_4, which was trained only on the preceding examples $\mathbf{x}_1, \ldots, \mathbf{x}_4$. This ensures that the pseudo-residual of $\mathbf{x}_5$ is estimated using a model that did not include it during training, thereby preventing prediction shift.

10.3.4   (*) Enhanced Ordered Boosting

While effective in mitigating gradient bias, the basic ordered boosting algorithm described in the previous section has several practical limitations:

- Training n separate ensembles, one for each training sample, is computationally expensive and becomes prohibitive for large datasets.

- Early models in the permutation are trained on very few examples, leading to unreliable gradient estimates for the corresponding samples.

- For datasets with categorical variables, it is crucial to use consistent permutations for both target statistics computation and gradient estimation in order to avoid target leakage.

CatBoost addresses these issues by:

- Repeating the boosting process with s different random permutations to improve the reliability of gradient estimates, especially for early samples in each sequence.

- Building a single tree structure per boosting iteration that is shared across all permutations and ensembles, while computing separate leaf values for each ensemble. This significantly reduces computational cost.

- Using the same set of permutations for both target statistics and gradient computations to ensure consistency and prevent target leakage.

At the start of the process, CatBoost generates $s + 1$ independent random permutations of the training set. The permutations $\sigma_1, \ldots, \sigma_s$ are used for constructing the regression trees, while σ_0 is reserved for finalizing their leaf values.

During boosting, the algorithm maintains sn **supporting models**, with one model for each (permutation, sample) pair. Model M_{rj} (for $1 \leq r \leq s, 1 \leq j \leq n$) is trained using the first j samples in permutation σ_r. The prediction of M_{rj} on sample $\mathbf{x}_i$ is denoted by $M_{rj}(i)$.

At each boosting iteration t, the algorithm constructs a shared tree structure T_t, which is used to update all sn ensembles. The leaf values of the tree are then adjusted individually for each model M_{rj}, ensuring that updates respect the ordering constraints of the corresponding (r, j) pair.

Each iteration t consists of the following steps:

1. Draw a random permutation σ_r from $\{\sigma_1, \ldots, \sigma_s\}$.

2. Compute target statistics for all categorical features using the ordering defined by σ_r.

3. Compute gradient estimates using the ordered model. For each training sample i ($1 \leq i \leq n$), compute the gradient using the model $M_{r,\sigma_r(i)-1}$, which was trained only on the samples preceding i in the permutation:

$$g_{r,i} = \frac{\partial L(y_i, M_{r,\sigma_r(i)-1}(\mathbf{x}_i))}{\partial M_{r,\sigma_r(i)-1}(\mathbf{x}_i)}. \tag{10.40}$$

4. Store all the gradient estimates in a vector $\mathbf{g}$.

5. Construct a shared regression tree T_t using all the training samples $\mathbf{x}_1, \ldots, \mathbf{x}_n$. The tree structure is determined based on aggregated gradient statistics from the ensemble models $M_{r1}, \ldots, M_{rn}$ corresponding to permutation σ_r.

For each candidate split, we compute the contribution of sample i to the resulting leaf node using the average gradient of preceding samples in the permutation that fall into the same leaf:

$$\Delta_i \leftarrow \text{avg}\left(g_{r,\sigma_r(p)-1} \mid \text{leaf}_r(p) = \text{leaf}_r(i), \, \sigma_r(p) < \sigma_r(i)\right). \tag{10.41}$$

This aggregation ensures that earlier samples, whose gradients are used in more models, have a greater influence on the structure of the shared tree, while preserving the causal ordering that avoids target leakage.

To illustrate, consider the permutation $\sigma = (3, 1, 4, 2)$ over the training samples $\{\mathbf{x}_1, \mathbf{x}_2, \mathbf{x}_3, \mathbf{x}_4\}$. Now, suppose a candidate split assigns $\{\mathbf{x}_3, \mathbf{x}_1, \mathbf{x}_4\}$ to the left child and $\mathbf{x}_2$ to the right.

When computing the contribution Δ_i for each sample $\mathbf{x}_i$ in the left child, only the gradients of samples that both fall into the same leaf and appear earlier in the permutation are included in the averaging process. In this case, Δ_2 (the average gradient for $\mathbf{x}_1$, which is the second sample in the permutation) is computed using the gradient of $\mathbf{x}_3$, since it appears earlier in the permutation and belongs to the same leaf. Similarly, Δ_3 (for $\mathbf{x}_4$) is computed using the gradients of both $\mathbf{x}_3$ and $\mathbf{x}_1$, which precede it and share the same leaf assignment.

Returning to the general procedure, after computing the Δ_i values for all samples, the quality of the split is evaluated by measuring the cosine similarity between the vector of aggregated contributions $\mathbf{\Delta}$ and the original gradient vector $\mathbf{g}$, i.e., $\cos(\mathbf{\Delta}, \mathbf{g})$. This criterion favors splits in which the aggregated leaf contributions are well aligned with the original gradients, resulting in child nodes with more homogeneous pseudo-residuals.

6. The tree structure T_t is used to update all the sn supporting models. Each ensemble M_{kj} shares the same tree structure T_t but assigns different leaf values based on its specific permutation σ_k and training set $(\sigma_k(1), \ldots, \sigma_k(j))$.

   Specifically, for each training sample i in the prefix $(\sigma_k(1), \ldots, \sigma_k(j))$, the prediction in model M_{kj} is updated by averaging the gradients of all earlier samples in the permutation that belong to the same leaf:

   $$M_{kj}(i) \leftarrow M_{kj}(i) - \alpha \cdot \text{avg}\left(g_{k,\sigma_k(p)-1} \mid \text{leaf}_k(p) = \text{leaf}_k(i),\ \sigma_k(p) < \sigma_k(i)\right), \quad (10.42)$$

   where α is the learning rate.

   This update rule implicitly assigns higher weight to earlier samples in the permutation, as their gradients contribute to the updates of many subsequent samples that fall into the same leaf. As a result, samples with broader influence across the ensemble have a proportionally larger impact on the final predictions.

Although the tree structures are shared across permutations, the target statistics used for categorical splits vary with the permutation. As a result, the same sample may be routed to different leaves in different models. To ensure consistency in the final predictions, a separate held-out permutation σ_0, not used during training, is employed to finalize the leaf values.

Each sample is routed through every tree T_t using its fixed structure, and the target statistics are computed based on the samples that precede it in σ_0. The final value of each leaf is then set to the average pseudo-residual of the samples assigned to it. The overall prediction for a sample is obtained by summing the outputs from all trees.

10.3.5 Additional Features

Beyond its innovative boosting methodology, CatBoost incorporates several additional techniques and optimizations designed to improve its predictive performance, computational efficiency, and scalability.

10.3.5.1 Oblivious Trees

Instead of standard decision trees, CatBoost uses **oblivious decision trees**, also known as **symmetric trees**, where the same split condition is applied at all nodes at the same depth [324]. This results in a balanced and highly regular tree structure, as illustrated in Figure 10.5. This symmetric structure offers several advantages:

- **Fast prediction**: Tree traversal time is logarithmic in the number of leaves, ensuring efficient inference.

- **Built-in regularization**: The constrained structure reduces model complexity, helping prevent overfitting.

- **Simplified training**: Since the same split is used across a level, computations can be reused, accelerating the search for optimal splits.

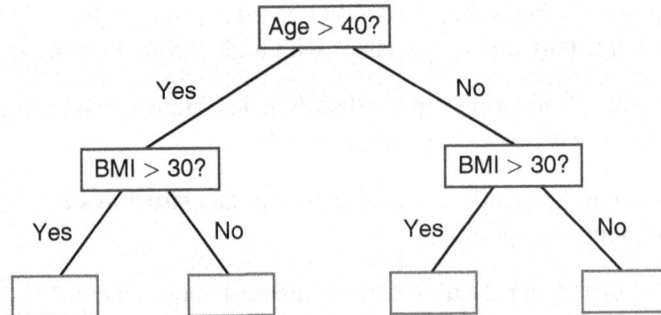

Figure 10.5: Illustration of an oblivious decision tree. Each level applies the same feature and threshold for splitting (e.g., Age > 40 at the root and BMI > 30 at the second level), yielding a symmetric and balanced tree structure.

10.3.5.2 Feature Combinations

Standard target encoding treats categorical features independently and may fail to capture important interactions between them. In particular, different combinations of categories can be mapped to the same numerical values if their individual components share the same target statistics.

For example, let A and B be binary categorical features, and define the target as $y = 1$ if exactly one of them is 1, and $y = 0$ otherwise, i.e., $y = \mathbb{1}(A \oplus B)$, where $\oplus$ denotes the XOR operation. Assume that all four binary combinations of (A, B) occur equally often in the dataset.

With standard target encoding applied independently to each feature, we obtain:

$$\mathbb{E}[y|A = 0] = \mathbb{E}[y|A = 1] = \mathbb{E}[y|B = 0] = \mathbb{E}[y|B = 1] = 0.5.$$

As a result, all input combinations are encoded as $(0.5, 0.5)$, even though their original categories and corresponding target values differ. For instance, the inputs $(A, B) = (1, 0)$ and $(1, 1)$ receive the same encoding, despite having different target values.

To address this limitation, CatBoost dynamically constructs combinations of categorical features during training, allowing the model to capture interaction effects more effectively:

- At each tree node, CatBoost evaluates combinations of previously used categorical features (or combinations thereof) with all other categorical features in the dataset.

- Target statistics for these new feature combinations are computed on the fly, allowing the model to identify informative splits without requiring an exhaustive search.

This greedy strategy balances expressiveness and computational efficiency, enabling CatBoost to model complex patterns in high-cardinality categorical data.

10.3.5.3 System-Level Optimizations

CatBoost incorporates several system-level optimizations to improve training efficiency, scalability, and resource utilization, making it competitive with other gradient boosting libraries such as XGBoost and LightGBM:

- GPU acceleration: CatBoost supports GPU-based training, which significantly speeds up computations, especially on large datasets with high-cardinality categorical features.

- Distributed training: CatBoost supports distributed training across multiple GPUs and across multiple machines in a cluster via Apache Spark.

- Efficient memory usage: CatBoost uses compact data structures and optimized algorithms to reduce its memory footprint.

- Optimized binning for numerical features: CatBoost applies a highly efficient binning strategy tailored to its oblivious tree architecture and GPU-based computations, reducing preprocessing time and improving training speed.

10.3.6   Library Installation

CatBoost can be easily installed via `pip`:

```
pip install catboost
```

Visit the official CatBoost documentation[26] for comprehensive guidance on API usage, parameter tuning, and advanced features.

10.3.7   CatBoost API

CatBoost's Python package provides a user-friendly interface that is fully compatible with Scikit-Learn, allowing seamless integration into existing machine learning workflows. The main classes provided by the API are:

- `CatBoostRegressor`[27] for regression tasks.

- `CatBoostClassifier`[28] for classification tasks.

- `CatBoostRanker`[29] for learning-to-rank tasks.

Key parameters of the CatBoost estimators are listed in Table 10.13. Many of these parameters are similar to those in XGBoost and LightGBM, although they may have different names or default values. Additionally, some parameters in CatBoost have aliases, e.g., `n_estimators` can also be specified as `iterations`, making it easier for users transitioning from other libraries.

One of CatBoost's strengths is its ability to automatically select suitable values for key hyperparameters based on the characteristics of the dataset, the learning task, and the values of other hyperparameters. If a default value is not explicitly specified in the last column of Table 10.13, it means the default is determined dynamically under such conditions. For example, the default

---

26. `https://catboost.ai`
27. `https://catboost.ai/docs/en/concepts/python-reference_catboostregressor`
28. `https://catboost.ai/docs/en/concepts/python-reference_catboostclassifier`
29. `https://catboost.ai/docs/en/concepts/python-reference_catboostranker`

Parameter	Description	Default
`loss_function` `objective`	Loss function used for training. Defaults are `'Logloss'` for binary classification, `'Multiclass'` for multi-class classification, and `'RMSE'` for regression.	-
`iterations` `n_estimators`	Number of boosting iterations (trees).	1000
`learning_rate` `eta`	Shrinkage factor applied to each tree's prediction. The default depends on the loss function and number of iterations.	-
`l2_leaf_reg` `reg_lambda`	L2 regularization term applied to leaf weights.	3.0
`depth` `max_depth`	Maximum depth of each tree. The default depends on the `grow_policy`.	-
`min_data_in_leaf` `min_child_samples`	Minimum number of samples required in a leaf.	1
`max_leaves`	Maximum number of leaves in a tree. Relevant only for non-symmetric grow policies.	31
`early_stopping_rounds`	Stops training if validation score does not improve for the given number of iterations.	False
`subsample`	Fraction of samples used for fitting each tree (bagging). The default depends on the dataset size and `bootstrap_type`.	-
`bootstrap_type`	Sampling method for bagging: `'Bayesian'`, `'Bernoulli'`, `'MVS'`, `'Poisson'`, or `'No'`.	`'Bayesian'`
`rsm` `colsample_bylevel`	Fraction of features sampled at each level of the tree.	1
`cat_features`	List of categorical features (by index or name). Automatically inferred for columns in Pandas with the `category` data type.	None
`one_hot_max_size`	Maximum number of categories to one-hot encode (larger sets use target encoding).	-
`class_weights`	Class weights used for handling class imbalance.	None
`grow_policy`	Tree growing policy: `'SymmetricTree'`, `'Depthwise'`, or `'LossGuide'`.	`'SymmetricTree'`
`task_type`	Computing device: `'CPU'` or `'GPU'`.	`'CPU'`

Table 10.13: Key parameters of CatBoost. The Parameter column includes common aliases used in the Python API. Parameters with a dash in the Default column have dynamic defaults determined by factors such as dataset size, loss function, and grow policy.

value of `max_depth` (maximum tree depth) is 6, unless `grow_policy` is set to `'Lossguide'`, in which case the default increases to 16.

This intelligent default behavior allows CatBoost to perform well out of the box, often requiring less manual tuning compared to XGBoost and LightGBM [40].

10.3.8   Regression Example

The following example demonstrates the application of CatBoost to the California housing dataset. After loading the dataset and splitting it into training and test sets, we create an instance of `CatBoostRegressor` with default settings and fit it to the training data:

```
from catboost import CatBoostRegressor

reg = CatBoostRegressor(random_state=42)
reg.fit(X_train, y_train)
```

Next, we evaluate the model's performance on both the training and test sets:

```
print(f'R2 score (train): {reg.score(X_train, y_train):.4f}')
print(f'R2 score (test): {reg.score(X_test, y_test):.4f}')
```

```
R2 score (train): 0.9126
R2 score (test): 0.8482
```

The test R^2 score of CatBoost (0.8482) outperforms the baseline (untuned) models of XGBoost (0.8301) and LightGBM (0.8360). However, this comparison should be interpreted with care:

- CatBoost trains with more boosting iterations by default (`iterations=1000`), compared to XGBoost and LightGBM (`n_estimators=100`).

- Many of CatBoost's hyperparameters are dynamically selected based on dataset characteristics, often leading to stronger out-of-the-box performance.

Up to this point, the datasets explored in this book have been small to medium in size, containing up to tens of thousands of examples (e.g., the California housing dataset includes 20,640 examples). While sufficient for illustrative purposes, this scale is modest compared to modern big data applications, which often involve millions of records. In the next section, we evaluate the gradient boosting libraries on a much larger and more complex dataset, and compare their efficiency and predictive performance against other supervised learning algorithms.

10.4   The Higgs Boson Machine Learning Challenge

The 2012 discovery of the Higgs Boson, often called the "God particle," was a landmark achievement in physics [2]. It confirmed the final missing piece of the Standard Model of particle physics by explaining how elementary particles acquire mass, a breakthrough that earned François Englert and Peter Higgs the 2013 Nobel Prize in Physics.

The discovery was made at CERN's Large Hadron Collider (LHC), the world's most powerful particle accelerator. At the LHC, high-energy protons are accelerated in opposite directions along a circular path and collide at near-light speeds, producing hundreds of particles per second. These collision events are classified as either *background* or *signal* events. Background events arise from known particle decays, while signal events—such as the decay of a Higgs Boson into two tau particles—indicate potentially new phenomena. Detecting signal events is highly challenging due to the overwhelming amount of background noise, requiring the use of advanced analytical and machine learning techniques.

To tackle this challenge, the Higgs Boson Machine Learning Challenge was launched on Kaggle in 2014 [8]. It quickly became one of Kaggle's most popular competitions, attracting 1,785 teams and generating a total of 35,772 submissions.

Participants were given simulated data consisting of 250,000 training examples and 550,000 test examples, each described by 30 features capturing various kinematic properties of the detected particles, such as energy, momentum, and angular measurements relative to the collision axis. The task was to classify each event as a signal (i.e., a possible Higgs boson decay) or a background event.

The competition dataset was derived from a larger dataset used by researchers in high-energy physics, consisting of 11 million examples and 28 features. Of these, 21 represent raw measurements from particle detectors, while the remaining 7 are high-level features engineered by physicists to aid in signal-background discrimination.[30]

In our experiments, we use the full 11-million-example dataset. In the following sections, we benchmark the gradient boosting libraries on this dataset and compare their performance both to each other and to the results reported in an earlier work by Baldi et al. (2014) [25], which predates the development of the modern libraries covered in this chapter.

The code for this benchmarking experiment is available in the HiggsBenchmarking.ipynb notebook on the book's GitHub repository.

10.4.1   Data Loading and Exploration

The full Higgs dataset[31] is available from the UCI Machine Learning Repository. To use the dataset, download the `higgs.zip` archive and extract the `higgs.csv` file. Note that the corresponding `fetch_openml` function in Scikit-Learn provides only a smaller version of the dataset, containing approximately 100,000 examples.

We begin by importing the required libraries and setting the random seed for reproducibility:

```
import numpy as np
import matplotlib.pyplot as plt
```

---

30. The competition dataset included two additional metadata columns: `EventId`, a unique identifier for each event, and `Weight`, which indicates the statistical importance of the event for evaluation purposes.

31. https://archive.ics.uci.edu/dataset/280/higgs

	0	1	2	3	4	5	6	7	8	9 ...	19	20
0	1.0	0.869293	−0.635082	0.225690	0.327470	−0.689993	0.754202	−0.248573	−1.092064	0.000000 ...	−0.010455	−0.045767
1	1.0	0.907542	0.329147	0.359412	1.497970	−0.313010	1.095531	−0.557525	−1.588230	2.173076 ...	−1.138930	−0.000819
2	1.0	0.798835	1.470639	−1.635975	0.453773	0.425629	1.104875	1.282322	1.381664	0.000000 ...	1.128848	0.900461
3	0.0	1.344385	−0.876626	0.935913	1.992050	0.882454	1.786066	−1.646778	−0.942383	0.000000 ...	−0.678379	−1.360356
4	1.0	1.105009	0.321356	1.522401	0.882808	−1.205349	0.681466	−1.070464	−0.921871	0.000000 ...	−0.373566	0.113041

Figure 10.6: A snapshot of the Higgs dataset showing the first five rows and a subset of its 29 columns. Each row represents a single collision event, and the columns correspond to kinematic features derived from particle physics simulations. The first column specifies the class label, with 1 indicating a signal event and 0 indicating a background event.

```
import pandas as pd
import time
from sklearn.metrics import roc_auc_score

np.random.seed(42)
```

We then load the dataset from the extracted CSV file using Pandas:

```
df = pd.read_csv('data/higgs.csv', header=None)
df.head()
```

Because the dataset contains over 11 million examples, the loading process may take several minutes. Once loaded, the first five rows of the dataset are displayed, as shown in Figure 10.6.

Next, we perform some basic data exploration. While the df.info method confirms that all columns are of type float64, it does not show the number of non-null entries due to the dataset's size. To count the total number of missing values across the entire DataFrame, we use:

```
missing_values = df.isnull().sum().sum()
print(missing_values)
```

```
0
```

The first sum() computes the number of missing values in each column, returning a Series. The second sum() aggregates this Series to give the total number of missing entries. The result indicates that there are no missing values in the dataset.

We also examine the class distribution of the labels:

```
df[0].value_counts()
```

```
1.0     5829123
0.0     5170877
Name: count, dtype: int64
```

The dataset is relatively balanced, with approximately 53% of the events labeled as signal (1.0) and 47% as background (0.0).

10.4.2 Dataset Preparation

The label y is stored in the first column of the table, so we need to separate it from the feature columns and convert its type from floating point to integer:

```
X = df.drop([0], axis=1)
y = df[0].astype(int)
```

Next, we split the dataset into training and test sets. Following the approach used by Baldi et al. [25], we allocate the last 500,000 examples to the test set:

```
test_size = 500000
X_train, y_train = X[:-test_size], y[:-test_size]
X_test, y_test = X[-test_size:], y[-test_size:]

print('Training set size:', len(X_train))
print('Test set size:', len(X_test))
```

```
Training set size: 10500000
Test set size: 500000
```

After partitioning, the training set contains 10.5 million examples and the test set contains 500,000 examples. Since all features in this dataset are numerical, there are no missing values, and the features are already on comparable scales, no additional preprocessing is required.

10.4.3 Benchmarking Gradient Boosting Algorithms

We now evaluate the performance of five algorithms on the Higgs dataset: logistic regression, Scikit-Learn's histogram-based gradient boosting, XGBoost, LightGBM, and CatBoost. All classifiers are evaluated using their default settings. GPU acceleration is enabled for LightGBM and CatBoost, while both CPU and GPU variants of XGBoost are included to compare training times.

The primary evaluation metric used by Baldi et al. was the Area Under the Curve (AUC), which evaluates model performance across all possible classification thresholds (see Section 5.5.7). In addition to AUC, we also record the test accuracy and training time for each model. The function below trains and evaluates each classifier, storing the results in a dictionary for easy comparison:

```
def evaluate_classifiers(classifiers, X_train, y_train, X_test, y_test,
                         verbose=True):
    results = {}
```

```
for name, clf in classifiers.items():
    # Train the classifier and measure the training time
    start_time = time.time()
    clf.fit(X_train, y_train)
    training_time = time.time() - start_time

    # Compute accuracy and AUC on the test set
    test_accuracy = clf.score(X_test, y_test)
    test_auc = roc_auc_score(y_test, clf.predict_proba(X_test)[:, 1])

    # Store the evaluation metrics in a dictionary
    results[name] = {
        'Training Time (s)': np.round(training_time, 3),
        'Test Accuracy (%)': test_accuracy * 100,
        'Test AUC': test_auc
    }
    if verbose:
        print(results[name])

return results
```

We now instantiate the classifiers for the experiment:

```
from sklearn.linear_model import LogisticRegression
from sklearn.ensemble import HistGradientBoostingClassifier
from xgboost import XGBClassifier
from lightgbm import LGBMClassifier
from catboost import CatBoostClassifier

classifiers = {
    'LogisticRegression': LogisticRegression(random_state=42),
    'HistGradientBoosting': HistGradientBoostingClassifier(random_state=42),
    'XGBoost (CPU)': XGBClassifier(random_state=42, verbosity=0),
    'XGBoost (GPU)': XGBClassifier(device='gpu', random_state=42, verbosity=0),
    'LightGBM': LGBMClassifier(device='gpu', random_state=42, verbose=0),
    'CatBoost': CatBoostClassifier(task_type='GPU', random_state=42, verbose=0)
}

results = evaluate_classifiers(classifiers, X_train, y_train, X_test, y_test)
```

Finally, we display the results in tabular form for easy comparison:

```
results_df = pd.DataFrame.from_dict(results).T
results_df
```

The results, presented in Figure 10.7, show that XGBoost (GPU) achieved the best test performance in terms of both accuracy (74.15%) and AUC (0.823), while also having the shortest

	Test Accuracy (%)	Test AUC	Training Time (s)
LogisticRegression	64.1376	0.684415	35.118
HistGradientBoosting	73.1720	0.812152	175.034
XGBoost (CPU)	74.1528	0.823515	82.585
XGBoost (GPU)	74.1496	0.823470	27.661
LightGBM	73.1520	0.812210	73.560
CatBoost	73.0466	0.810493	253.875

Figure 10.7: Comparative performance of gradient boosting libraries on the Higgs dataset. The table shows the test accuracy, AUC, and training time for each model. XGBoost (GPU) achieved both the highest test performance and shortest training time. All gradient boosting models significantly outperformed logistic regression, which served as the baseline.

training time (27.66 seconds). This highlights the exceptional efficiency of XGBoost when applied to large-scale datasets like the Higgs dataset.

The other gradient boosting models—LightGBM, CatBoost, and HistGradientBoosting—achieved similar levels of accuracy (73.15%, 73.05%, and 73.17%, respectively) and AUC. CatBoost had the longest training time at 253.87 seconds, despite using the GPU. This reflects the algorithm's additional computational overhead, particularly due to ordered boosting and the use of multiple permutations during training. HistGradientBoosting, which does not support GPU acceleration, also required a substantial training time (175.03 seconds).

As expected, all gradient boosting models substantially outperformed the baseline logistic regression model, which achieved only 64.14% accuracy and took 35.11 seconds to train. While logistic regression is relatively efficient, its linear nature makes it ill-suited for modeling the complex decision boundaries present in this dataset.

For comparison, Baldi et al. reported a test AUC of 0.810 for gradient boosting, 0.816 for a shallow neural network with a single hidden layer, and 0.885 for a deep neural network with five hidden layers on the same dataset (see Table 1 in [25]). Relative to these results, our gradient boosting models—particularly XGBoost that achieved a test AUC of 0.823—demonstrate notable improvements, highlighting the progress made in gradient boosting algorithms and implementations over the past decade.

For a more robust statistical evaluation, each algorithm should be run multiple times with different random seeds, reporting the average and standard deviation of the results. Nonetheless, gradient boosting algorithms typically produce consistent outcomes across different runs, particularly when using their default settings. A more principled approach to experimental evaluation of machine learning algorithms, including the use of statistical significance testing, is presented in Section 12.3.

10.5   Summary

In this chapter, we explored the design and performance of three popular gradient boosting libraries: XGBoost, LightGBM, and CatBoost. We introduced their key algorithmic innovations, system-level optimizations, and APIs, illustrating their usage with code examples on both small-scale datasets and large-scale datasets (e.g., the Higgs dataset).

Overall, the three libraries exhibit comparable predictive performance, with XGBoost standing out for its exceptional training speed—but also showing sensitivity to hyperparameter settings.

A more extensive comparative study by Bentéjac et al. (2021) supports several of our findings [40]. Their analysis evaluated both default and tuned versions of XGBoost, LightGBM, CatBoost, standard gradient boosting, and random forests across 28 classification datasets from the UCI Machine Learning Repository. The main conclusions from their study are:

- No single algorithm consistently outperforms the others across all datasets.

- The best-performing methods, based on their average rank across all datasets, are tuned CatBoost and tuned XGBoost. However, their performance is not statistically different from that of tuned LightGBM, tuned gradient boosting, and both tuned and default random forests.

- XGBoost and LightGBM, when used with default hyperparameters, are among the least successful methods, performing statistically worse than their tuned counterparts. In contrast, the CatBoost and random forests perform well even with default settings, avoiding the computational burden of hyperparameter tuning.

- LightGBM is the fastest algorithm overall, with XGBoost demonstrating similar training speed. In contrast, CatBoost is significantly slower than both.

- Some hyperparameters, such as the subsampling rate and the number of features considered at each split, tend to have minimal impact on performance. By fixing their values, the hyperparameter search space becomes smaller, allowing more effective tuning of critical parameters—leading to shorter tuning time and potentially better results.

Ultimately, choosing the right gradient boosting library depends on the characteristics of the dataset, the performance requirements, and the available computational resources.

10.6   Exercises

10.6.1   Multiple-Choice Questions

10.1. What are the differences between the XGBoost algorithm and traditional gradient boosting?

    (a) XGBoost incorporates regularization terms into the objective function.

    (b) XGBoost supports a histogram-based approach to approximate split finding.

      (c) XGBoost incorporates both gradient and Hessian (second-derivative) information during optimization, while traditional gradient boosting relies only on gradients.

      (d) XGBoost grows the decision trees leaf-wise while traditional gradient boosting grows them depth-wise.

      (e) Unlike traditional gradient boosting, XGBoost introduces parallelization into the training process.

10.2. Which of the following statements about XGBoost are true?

      (a) The weight of a leaf node is determined by the ratio of the sum of gradients to the sum of Hessians for the samples that belong to that leaf.

      (b) Tree construction stops when the gain from a potential split becomes negative.

      (c) The native API of XGBoost is more efficient than its Scikit-Learn API.

      (d) XGBoost handles missing values by learning the optimal direction for missing data during tree construction.

10.3. What is the purpose of the weighted quantile sketch algorithm in XGBoost?

      (a) To efficiently calculate the Hessians of the loss function for each potential split point.

      (b) To efficiently find optimal split points in the presence of weighted data.

      (c) To ensure a uniform distribution of the Hessians across all data points.

      (d) To generate more candidate split thresholds in regions of the feature space where the cumulative Hessian weight is higher.

10.4. In XGBoost, which of the following settings is likely to increase bias and reduce variance of the model?

      (a) increasing `n_estimators`

      (b) decreasing `learning_rate`

      (c) increasing `subsample`

      (d) decreasing `gamma`

      (e) increasing `reg_lambda`

      (f) increasing `min_child_weight`

      (g) changing `tree_method` to `'exact'`

      (h) changing `grow_policy` to `'lossguide'`

10.5. A dataset contains a categorical feature representing five cities:

$$A = \{\text{Boston, Chicago, Denver, Atlanta, Seattle}\}.$$

Suppose each city is assigned a numeric score based on average response time (in seconds) from a model:

$$f(\text{Boston}) = 105, f(\text{Chicago}) = 140, f(\text{Denver}) = 90, f(\text{Atlanta}) = 125, f(\text{Seattle}) = 150.$$

We want to partition the categories into two groups to minimize variation within each group.

What is the optimal split according to Fisher's theorem?

(a) {Boston, Chicago, Seattle}, {Denver, Atlanta}

(b) {Denver, Boston}, {Atlanta, Chicago, Seattle}

(c) {Chicago, Denver}, {Boston, Atlanta, Seattle}

(d) {Denver, Boston, Atlanta}, {Chicago, Seattle}

(e) {Denver}, {Boston, Atlanta, Chicago, Seattle}

10.6. In LightGBM, when gradient-based one-side sampling (GOSS) is enabled, and the parameters `top_rate` and `other_rate` are set to 0.5 and 0.2, respectively, how many samples will be used to build each tree if the training set contains 10,000 instances?

(a) 2,000

(b) 5,000

(c) 6,000

(d) 7,000

10.7. Which of the following statements about the Exclusive Feature Bundling (EFB) technique in LightGBM are true?

(a) EFB reduces the dimensionality of the dataset by bundling sparse features into a single feature.

(b) EFB requires that features in a bundle must not have nonzero values in the same location.

(c) EFB treats the bundled feature as a continuous feature during histogram binning.

(d) EFB may increase the bias of the model.

10.8. In standard gradient boosting, prediction bias occurs because:

(a) Gradient boosting assumes that the weak learners are independent, whereas each learner is actually trained on the residuals of the previous ones.

(b) Gradients are computed on the same training samples used to train the base models.

(c) The gradient distribution on the training set deviates from the true gradient distribution over the entire input space.

(d) Errors from biased gradient estimates can accumulate as the ensemble is updated iteratively.

10.9. Which of the following statements about CatBoost is true?

    (a) It uses the same feature and split threshold for all nodes at the same level of the tree.

    (b) It can construct splits that are based on combinations of multiple features.

    (c) It applies one-hot encoding to categorical features with a small number of categories.

    (d) It employs an ordered boosting algorithm where each model is trained only on samples that were not used in previous boosting iterations.

10.10. (*) In CatBoost, what is the purpose of using multiple random permutations of the training set?

    (a) To reduce overfitting by introducing randomness into the computation of target encodings.

    (b) To improve the robustness of target statistics by averaging over different data orderings.

    (c) To ensure that each boosting iteration uses a different subset of the training samples.

    (d) To address the unreliability of gradient estimations for samples that appear early in the sequence.

    (e) To allow parallelization of computations across different permutations.

10.6.2 Programming Exercises

10.11. Extend the basic implementation of XGBoost introduced in Section 10.1.3 by adding the following features:

    (a) Add support for multi-class classification.

    (b) Implement an early stopping mechanism that halts the training process if the validation score does not improve for a specified number of iterations.

    (c) Add a bootstrap subsampling option such that each tree in the ensemble is trained on a random subset of the training data.

    (d) Implement the histogram-based variant of XGBoost (`'hist'`), where feature bins are created globally at the beginning of the training and used for collecting gradient statistics throughout the training process.

    (e) Add native support for handling categorical features based on Fisher's theorem similar to the approach used in XGBoost (see Section 10.1.5.5).

    (f) Incorporate a mechanism to handle missing values by learning the optimal direction (left or right) for missing data at each split during training.

    (g) Add support for additional hyperparameters from the XGBoost library, such as `scale_pos_weight` for handling class imbalance and `grow_policy` for determining the tree growth policy.

10.12. In this exercise, you will explore how different hyperparameters affect the performance of an XGBoost model. You will analyze both individual parameters and their combinations to gain a comprehensive understanding of their impact.

(a) Choose five classification datasets from the UCI Machine Learning Repository with varying properties such as number of samples, features, and classes (see Table 9.23 for a list of commonly used datasets).

(b) Train a baseline XGBoost model with default hyperparameters on these datasets. Document performance metrics such as accuracy, F1 score, and AUC as a reference for subsequent experiments.

(c) Systematically vary each of the following key parameters individually to observe their impact on performance:

- n_estimators: Number of boosting rounds, e.g., 50, 100, 300, 500, 1000.
- max_depth: Maximum tree depth, e.g., 2, 3, 5, 7, 10, 100.
- learning_rate: Step size shrinkage, e.g., 0.025, 0.05, 0.1, 0.2, 0.3.
- subsample: Fraction of samples used in each tree, e.g., 0.15, 0.5, 0.75, 1.0.
- colsample_bylevel: Features per level, e.g., 'log2', 'sqrt', 0.25, 1.0.
- gamma: Minimum loss reduction for a split, e.g., 0, 0.1, 0.2, 0.5, 1.0, 1.5, 2.0.
- reg_lambda: L2 regularization strength, e.g., 0.01, 0.1, 0.5, 1.0, 10.

(d) Explore the interaction between parameters by tuning combinations of two or more parameters simultaneously. Use grid search to identify how these combinations affect performance compared to individual parameter tuning.

(e) Perform a random search across all hyperparameters to find the best combination for each dataset. Compare the results with those obtained from grid search.

(f) (Optional) Apply Bayesian optimization techniques using libraries such as scikit-optimize or Optuna to refine the search for the best hyperparameters. Compare the efficiency and effectiveness of Bayesian optimization with random search.

(g) For each experiment, record model performance and analyze how each hyperparameter (or combination) influences the results. Create visualizations such as heatmaps or line charts to illustrate performance differences across parameter settings.

(h) Write a detailed report summarizing your findings:

- Highlight the most critical hyperparameters for optimizing XGBoost models.
- Compare the efficiency and effectiveness of grid search, random search, and Bayesian optimization.
- Provide practical guidelines for tuning XGBoost on similar tasks.

10.13. In this exercise, you will implement and compare different versions of target encoding and evaluate their effectiveness against one-hot encoding on multiple datasets with categorical features. Follow these steps:

   (a) Basic target encoding: Implement a basic version of target encoding that computes the mean of the target variable for each category, using all the samples in the dataset.

   (b) Ordered target encoding: Modify the target encoding implementation so that each category's encoding is computed only using samples that appear earlier in the sequence. This approach avoids overfitting by preventing the current sample's target value from influencing its own encoding.

   (c) Permutation-based target encoding: Extend the implementation to use multiple random permutations of the dataset, averaging the target encodings across permutations to improve robustness and reduce overfitting, as done in CatBoost.

   (d) Compare the effectiveness of these three target encoding strategies and one-hot encoding on several datasets with categorical features from the UCI Machine Learning Repository. For example, you could use the Adult dataset[32], Bank Marketing dataset[33], and Mushroom dataset[34].

   (e) Train several classification models (e.g., logistic regression or random forests) using each encoding strategy. Evaluate their performance using metrics such as accuracy, AUC, and F1 score, and measure their training time.

   (f) Write a short report summarizing your findings.

10.14. Implement the basic version of ordered boosting described in Section 10.3.3 using the following steps:

   (a) Implement Algorithm 10.4 for binary classification tasks. Use `DecisionTreeRegressor` from Scikit-Learn as the base model for your implementation.

   (b) Test your ordered boosting implementation on a binary classification dataset, such as the Breast Cancer dataset from Scikit-Learn.

   (c) Compare the performance of ordered boosting to that of standard gradient boosting, using `GradientBoostingClassifier` from Scikit-Learn. Use metrics such as accuracy, AUC, F1 score, and training time for the comparison.

   (d) Summarize your results in a short report. Highlight the performance differences between ordered boosting and standard gradient boosting, and discuss possible reasons for these variations.

10.15. In this exercise, you will compare the performance of the three gradient boosting libraries (XGBoost, LightGBM, and CatBoost) alongside standard gradient boosting, random forests, and logistic regression on five datasets from the UCI Machine Learning Repository. You will analyze both default and tuned versions of each model.

---

32. https://archive.ics.uci.edu/dataset/2/adult
33. https://archive.ics.uci.edu/dataset/222/bank+marketing
34. https://archive.ics.uci.edu/dataset/73/mushroom

(a) Choose five classification datasets from the UCI Machine Learning Repository, ensuring diversity in the number of samples, features, and classes. Document key characteristics of each dataset (e.g., number of samples, number of features, class distribution) in a table.

(b) Train the following models on all five datasets using their default hyperparameters:

- XGBoost
- LightGBM
- CatBoost
- Standard gradient boosting (`GradientBoostingClassifier` from Scikit-Learn)
- Histogram-based gradient boosting (`HistGradientBoostingClassifier` from Scikit-Learn)
- Random forests
- Logistic regression

Evaluate their performance using metrics such as accuracy, F1 score, and AUC. Record the training time and prediction time for each model.

(c) Perform hyperparameter tuning for each model using grid search or random search. Suggested hyperparameters to tune include:

- Gradient boosting models: `n_estimators`, `max_depth`, `learning_rate`, `subsample`, `colsample_bytree`
- XGBoost: `gamma`, `reg_lambda`
- LightGBM: `boosting_type`, `top_rate`, `other_rate`, `feature_fraction_bynode`
- CatBoost: `leaf_estimation_iterations`, `l2_leaf_reg`
- Random forests: `n_estimators`, `max_depth`, `max_features`, `min_samples_split`
- Logistic regression: `C` (inverse of regularization strength), `solver`

Compare the performance of the tuned models to their default versions.

(d) Comparison and analysis:

 i. Compare the default and tuned versions of all models across datasets. Use aggregated performance metrics (e.g., mean and standard deviation of accuracy across datasets) and visualizations (e.g., bar charts, line plots) to present the results.

 ii. Analyze the relative strengths and weaknesses of each algorithm for different types of datasets. Discuss scenarios where gradient boosting outperforms other models and situations where simpler models like logistic regression or random forests are more effective.

(e) Read the paper *A Comparative Analysis of Gradient Boosting Algorithms* by Candice Bentéjac et al. [40]. Compare the findings of the paper to your experimental results. Address the following:

- How do your conclusions align or differ from those presented in the paper?
- Are there datasets or scenarios where your observations diverge from the paper's conclusions? If so, explain why this might be the case.
- What insights from the paper complement or enhance your analysis?

10.16. In this exercise, you will evaluate the performance of the different gradient boosting libraries on a large-scale dataset. The goal is to understand how these libraries handle massive datasets and compare their effectiveness in terms of accuracy, speed, and resource utilization.

(a) Download the Microsoft Malware Prediction Dataset[35] from Kaggle. This dataset is used to predict the probability that a Windows machine will get infected by malware, based on various properties of that machine. The training set contains approximately 9 million records with 82 features, comprising both categorical and numerical data. Your task is to predict the HasDetections column, which indicates whether malware was detected on the machine.

(b) Compare the performance of the three gradient boosting libraries: XGBoost, LightGBM, and CatBoost on this dataset. Enable GPU acceleration to enhance training efficiency. If you do not have access to a local GPU, consider using platforms such as Google Colab[36] or Kaggle Notebooks[37], which offer free access to GPU resources.

(c) Evaluate each model based on the following metrics: training accuracy, test accuracy, training speed, prediction speed, and memory usage. Conduct each experiment at least three times with different random seeds to ensure the results are reliable.

(d) Write a report summarizing your findings. Include details about each library's performance and discuss any notable differences observed.

(e) (Optional) Submit your best model to Kaggle as a late submission to the Microsoft Malware Prediction[38] competition. Compare your results with those on the leaderboard to assess how your model stacks up against others.

---

35. https://www.kaggle.com/competitions/microsoft-malware-prediction/data
36. https://colab.research.google.com
37. https://www.kaggle.com/docs/notebooks
38. https://www.kaggle.com/competitions/microsoft-malware-prediction/overview

Chapter 11

Support Vector Machines

Support vector machines (SVMs) are a foundational method in machine learning, introduced in the 1960s by Vladimir Vapnik and colleagues as part of statistical learning theory.

The primary objective of SVMs is to find a hyperplane that separates data points from two different classes. Unlike logistic regression, which also learns a linear boundary, SVMs seek the *optimal* hyperplane—the one that maximizes the margin, or the minimum distance between the hyperplane and the closest data points from each class. A larger margin typically leads to better generalization and greater robustness to noise.

SVMs rose to prominence in the 1990s as one of the most effective supervised learning algorithms, particularly in high-dimensional settings. While their popularity has declined with the advent of deep learning, the core principles behind SVMs—such as margin-based classification, convex optimization, and kernel methods—remain central to modern machine learning. Indeed, many advanced algorithms draw upon the same theoretical foundations.

SVMs offer a rich opportunity to deepen your understanding of the theory behind machine learning. Studying them provides insight into geometric decision boundaries, dual optimization, the bias–variance tradeoff, and the role of regularization—all of which are essential to mastering the field.

The chapter is organized as follows. Section 11.1 introduces the foundational SVM optimization problem for linear classification and presents various approaches for solving it. Section 11.2 extends the formulation to soft-margin SVM, which allows margin violations to accommodate non-linearly separable datasets. Section 11.3 delves into kernel methods—a powerful technique that enables linear models to address nonlinear problems by implicitly mapping data into higher-dimensional feature spaces. Section 11.4 applies the kernel trick to extend SVMs to nonlinear classification tasks. Section 11.5 introduces ν-SVM, an alternative formulation that provides more intuitive control over the model complexity and the number of support vectors. Section 11.6 explores support vector regression (SVR), which adapts SVMs to regression tasks. Section 11.7 covers efficient algorithms for training SVMs on large-scale datasets. Section 11.8 addresses model calibration, which deals with aligning predicted probabilities with true outcomes. Finally, Section 11.9 concludes with a summary of the key concepts and techniques discussed throughout the chapter.

11.1 Hard-Margin SVM

Support vector machines (SVMs) are a foundational class of supervised learning algorithms, deeply rooted in statistical learning theory. Their theoretical principles and practical applications have been extensively studied in numerous texts and research papers [61, 130, 596, 262, 597, 139, 534, 533].

We begin our study of SVMs with the simplest scenario: binary classification with linearly separable data. As in logistic regression, the goal is to find a hyperplane that separates the two classes. However, when the data is linearly separable, there are infinitely many such hyperplanes, leading to a natural question: *which hyperplane should we choose?*

Figure 11.1 illustrates two such hyperplanes. The one on the left has a narrow margin, while the one on the right achieves a wider separation. A narrow-margin hyperplane tends to be more sensitive to noise—small perturbations in training samples near the boundary can significantly shift its position, potentially leading to overfitting. In contrast, a wider margin offers greater robustness to noise and often generalizes better to new, unseen data.

In SVM, the objective is to choose the hyperplane that maximizes the **margin**—the distance to the nearest data point from either class. For this reason, it is often referred to as a **maximum-margin classifier**. When no violations of this margin are permitted (i.e., all training points lie on the correct side of the margin), the resulting model is known as a **hard-margin SVM**.

11.1.1 Problem Formulation

Given a training set of n samples $D = \{(\mathbf{x}_i, y_i)\}_{i=1}^{n}$, where each sample consists of a feature vector $\mathbf{x}_i \in \mathbb{R}^d$ and a corresponding label $y_i \in \{-1, 1\}$, the objective of a hard-margin SVM is to find a hyperplane of the form $\mathbf{w}^T\mathbf{x} + b = 0$ that separates the positive samples ($y_i = 1$) from the negative ones ($y_i = -1$), while maximizing the margin between them.

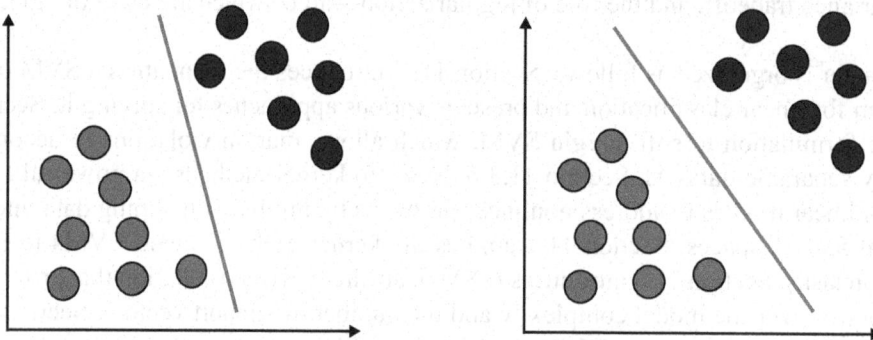

Figure 11.1: Two possible separating hyperplanes for a linearly separable dataset. The hyperplane on the left has a narrow margin and is more sensitive to variations in the data. The one on the right maximizes the margin and is more likely to generalize well. SVM selects the latter by explicitly optimizing for the maximum margin.

There are several differences between the formal definitions of SVM and logistic regression:

- SVM uses class labels 1 and -1, rather than 1 and 0. This convention simplifies the formulation of the optimization problem and leads to a more compact expression for the decision boundary conditions.

- SVM predicts the class label directly (as 1 or -1), without estimating class probabilities such as $P(y = 1)$, thereby eliminating the need for a logistic (sigmoid) function.

- In SVM, the bias term b is treated separately from the weight vector $\mathbf{w}$. In contrast, logistic regression typically incorporates the bias by appending a constant feature $x_0 = 1$ to the input vector, allowing the bias to be absorbed into $\mathbf{w}$.

The **margin** (also known as the **street width**) of the separating hyperplane, denoted by γ, is defined as the perpendicular distance between the hyperplane and the closest data points from each class (see Figure 11.2). These closest points, called **support vectors**, lie on the boundaries of the margin and play a crucial role in determining the position and orientation of the hyperplane. Any change to a support vector, such as its removal or perturbation, can alter the decision boundary.

Before formulating the maximum-margin objective function, we first express the margin in terms of the model parameters $(\mathbf{w}, b)$ and the training examples. To do so, we use a fundamental result from geometry: the distance from a point $\mathbf{x}_0$ to a hyperplane defined by $\mathbf{w}^T\mathbf{x} + b = 0$ is given by

$$d = \frac{|\mathbf{w}^T\mathbf{x}_0 + b|}{\|\mathbf{w}\|}. \tag{11.1}$$

For the sake of completeness, the proof is provided below.

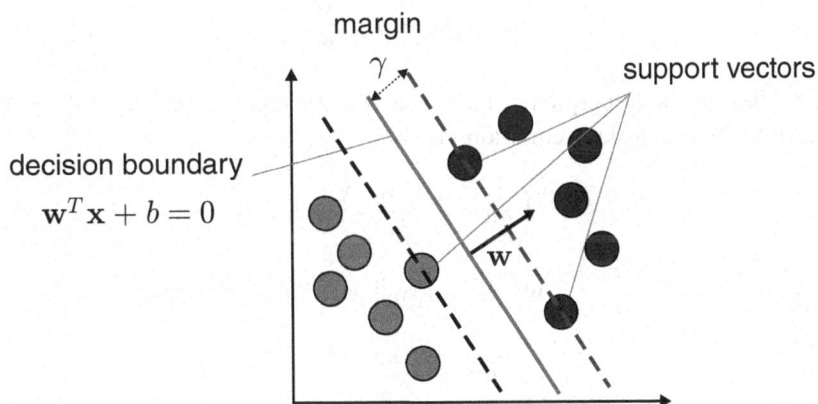

Figure 11.2: Illustration of the optimal hyperplane in a hard-margin SVM. The decision boundary, represented by $\mathbf{w}^T\mathbf{x} + b = 0$, separates the two classes. The margin γ is the perpendicular distance between the decision boundary and the nearest data points from each class, known as the support vectors. The vector $\mathbf{w}$ determines the orientation of the hyperplane and is orthogonal to the decision boundary. The dashed lines indicate the boundaries of the margin on either side of the hyperplane.

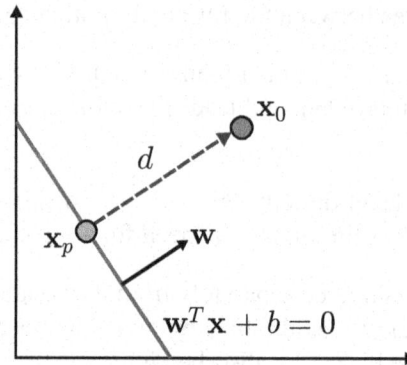

Figure 11.3: The distance d from a point $\mathbf{x}_0$ to the hyperplane $\mathbf{w}^T \mathbf{x} + b = 0$. The point $\mathbf{x}_p$ represents the projection of $\mathbf{x}_0$ onto the hyperplane. The distance is measured along the line perpendicular to the hyperplane, aligned with the direction of the vector $\mathbf{w}$.

Proof. Consider a point $\mathbf{x}_0$ that lies above the hyperplane, i.e., $\mathbf{w}^T \mathbf{x}_0 + b > 0$. We aim to find the distance d from $\mathbf{x}_0$ to the hyperplane (see Figure 11.3). The shortest distance occurs along the direction orthogonal to the hyperplane, defined by the normal vector $\mathbf{w}$. Let $\mathbf{x}_p$ denote the projection of $\mathbf{x}_0$ onto the hyperplane. Then, the vector connecting $\mathbf{x}_p$ to $\mathbf{x}_0$ must be parallel to $\mathbf{w}$.

Since $\mathbf{x}_0$ lies on a line perpendicular to the hyperplane, it can be written as:

$$\mathbf{x}_0 = \mathbf{x}_p + d \cdot \frac{\mathbf{w}}{\|\mathbf{w}\|}, \tag{11.2}$$

where $\frac{\mathbf{w}}{\|\mathbf{w}\|}$ is a unit vector in the direction of $\mathbf{w}$. Rearranging this expression gives:

$$\mathbf{x}_p = \mathbf{x}_0 - d \cdot \frac{\mathbf{w}}{\|\mathbf{w}\|}. \tag{11.3}$$

Because $\mathbf{x}_p$ lies on the hyperplane, it must satisfy the equation $\mathbf{w}^T \mathbf{x}_p + b = 0$. Substituting Equation 11.3 into the hyperplane equation yields:

$$\mathbf{w}^T \left(\mathbf{x}_0 - d \cdot \frac{\mathbf{w}}{\|\mathbf{w}\|} \right) + b = 0,$$

$$\mathbf{w}^T \mathbf{x}_0 - d\|\mathbf{w}\| + b = 0,$$

$$d = \frac{\mathbf{w}^T \mathbf{x}_0 + b}{\|\mathbf{w}\|}.$$

Since distance must be nonnegative, we take the absolute value of $\mathbf{w}^T \mathbf{x}_0 + b$ to account for the fact that the point $\mathbf{x}_0$ may lie on either side of the hyperplane. Thus, the distance is

$$d = \frac{|\mathbf{w}^T \mathbf{x}_0 + b|}{\|\mathbf{w}\|}. \tag{11.4}$$

$\square$

Since the margin is defined as the distance from the hyperplane to the closest data point from either class, it can be expressed as

$$\gamma = \min_{i=1,\ldots,n} \frac{|\mathbf{w}^T\mathbf{x}_i + b|}{\|\mathbf{w}\|}. \tag{11.5}$$

In the optimal solution, the closest points from both classes lie at equal distance from the hyperplane. Therefore, it suffices to compute the margin using only the positive examples ($y_i = 1$):

$$\gamma = \min_{i:\, y_i=1} \frac{\mathbf{w}^T\mathbf{x}_i + b}{\|\mathbf{w}\|}. \tag{11.6}$$

11.1.2 Maximum-Margin Optimization

In hard-margin SVMs, we require that no training sample violates the margin—that is, the distance of every point from the hyperplane must be at least γ. Since the distance from a point $\mathbf{x}_i$ to the hyperplane $\mathbf{w}^T\mathbf{x} + b = 0$ is given by $\frac{|\mathbf{w}^T\mathbf{x}_i+b|}{\|\mathbf{w}\|}$, we enforce the following constraints:

$$\mathbf{w}^T\mathbf{x}_i + b \geq \gamma\|\mathbf{w}\| \quad \text{if } y_i = 1,$$
$$\mathbf{w}^T\mathbf{x}_i + b \leq -\gamma\|\mathbf{w}\| \quad \text{if } y_i = -1.$$

Multiplying both sides of each constraint by $y_i \in \{-1, 1\}$ yields a single condition:

$$y_i(\mathbf{w}^T\mathbf{x}_i + b) \geq \gamma\|\mathbf{w}\|, \quad i = 1,\ldots,n. \tag{11.7}$$

The quantity $y_i(\mathbf{w}^T\mathbf{x}_i + b)$ is known as the **functional margin** of the classifier with respect to the sample $(\mathbf{x}_i, y_i)$. It reflects the model's confidence in the classification: larger positive values indicate that the point lies farther on the correct side of the hyperplane, while negative values indicate misclassification. Dividing the functional margin by $\|\mathbf{w}\|$ gives the **geometric margin**, which corresponds to the signed Euclidean distance from the point to the hyperplane.

We can now formulate the **maximum-margin optimization** problem as follows:

$$\max_{\mathbf{w},b} \quad \gamma,$$
$$\text{subject to} \quad y_i(\mathbf{w}^T\mathbf{x}_i + b) \geq \gamma\|\mathbf{w}\|, \quad i = 1,\ldots,n. \tag{11.8}$$

This problem is difficult to solve directly, as it involves maximizing a quantity γ that is itself defined as the minimum distance over all training samples, resulting in a nested max–min structure. However, we can simplify the problem using an important observation: rescaling both $\mathbf{w}$ and b by a positive constant scales the functional margin and the norm of $\mathbf{w}$ by the same factor, leaving

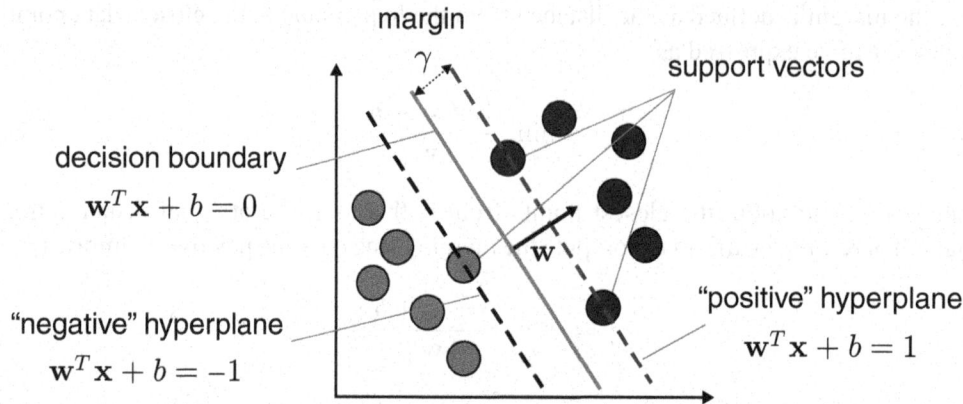

Figure 11.4: The key components of a hard-margin SVM classifier. The decision boundary $\mathbf{w}^T\mathbf{x} + b = 0$ lies midway between the "positive" hyperplane $\mathbf{w}^T\mathbf{x} + b = 1$ and the "negative" hyperplane $\mathbf{w}^T\mathbf{x} + b = -1$. The support vectors lie exactly on these two hyperplanes. The margin γ is defined as the distance from the decision boundary to either margin hyperplane.

the geometric margin unchanged.[1] This scaling freedom allows us to fix the scale by choosing $\gamma\|\mathbf{w}\| = 1$, under which the margin simplifies to:

$$\gamma = \frac{1}{\|\mathbf{w}\|}. \tag{11.9}$$

With this normalization, maximizing the margin γ is equivalent to minimizing $\|\mathbf{w}\|$. The constraints on the data points then simplify to:

$$y_i(\mathbf{w}^T\mathbf{x}_i + b) \geq 1, \quad i = 1,\dots,n. \tag{11.10}$$

These inequalities are tight for the **support vectors**—the data points that lie exactly on the margin. Geometrically, they define the two hyperplanes that bound the margin on either side of the separating hyperplane (see Figure 11.4). For support vectors, the following equalities hold:

$$\mathbf{w}^T\mathbf{x}_i + b = 1 \quad \text{if } y_i = 1, \tag{11.11}$$

$$\mathbf{w}^T\mathbf{x}_i + b = -1 \quad \text{if } y_i = -1. \tag{11.12}$$

Instead of directly minimizing $\|\mathbf{w}\|$, we typically minimize $\frac{1}{2}\|\mathbf{w}\|^2$. This simplifies the optimization process by making the objective function quadratic, while yielding the same optimal solution. Consequently, the problem of finding the maximum-margin separating hyperplane reduces to the following quadratic optimization problem:

$$\min_{\mathbf{w},b} \quad \frac{1}{2}\|\mathbf{w}\|^2,$$
$$\text{subject to} \quad y_i(\mathbf{w}^T\mathbf{x}_i + b) \geq 1, \quad i = 1,\dots,n. \tag{11.13}$$

1. For example, replacing $\mathbf{w}$ with $c\mathbf{w}$ and b with cb for some constant $c > 0$ results in the same separating hyperplane, since the equation $(c\mathbf{w})^T\mathbf{x} + cb = 0$ can be divided by c without affecting the decision boundary.

This formulation is known as the **primal form** of the SVM, as it directly optimizes the parameters $\mathbf{w}$ and b of the separating hyperplane.[2] Because this formulation involves a convex quadratic objective with linear constraints, the resulting optimization problem is convex and has a unique global solution. It can be solved using standard **quadratic programming (QP)** solvers, such as the CVXOPT library in Python (see Section 11.1.5).

11.1.3 Generalization Error

A well-known theoretical result shows that, under certain conditions, the expected generalization error of a hard-margin SVM is bounded by the ratio of the expected number of support vectors to the number of training samples [130]:

$$\mathbb{E}[P(\text{error})] \leq \frac{\mathbb{E}[|\mathcal{S}|]}{n}, \tag{11.14}$$

where the expectation is taken over all possible training sets of size n drawn i.i.d. from the data-generating distribution, and $|\mathcal{S}|$ is number of support vectors.

This result implies that the generalization ability of an SVM is closely tied to the fraction of training samples that become support vectors. When the optimal hyperplane is defined by a relatively small number of support vectors, the model is more likely to perform well on unseen data.

This bound also helps explain why SVMs often perform well in high-dimensional settings, where many other machine learning algorithms tend to overfit. Since the decision boundary is determined solely by the support vectors—whose number typically remains small and relatively stable regardless of the dimensionality of the feature space—SVMs can generalize effectively in high-dimensional spaces, even when the number of features exceeds the number of training samples.

11.1.4 The Dual Problem

The dual formulation of the SVM problem leverages **Lagrange duality**, a powerful tool in constrained optimization (see Section E.6.7). It transforms the constrained (primal) problem into a corresponding **dual problem** by introducing **Lagrange multipliers** that incorporate the constraints into the objective function. Solving the dual problem can offer both computational and theoretical advantages, as will be demonstrated later in this section. For convex problems satisfying mild regularity conditions such as Slater's condition (which the SVM optimization problem satisfies), **strong duality** holds: the optimal values of the primal and dual problems are equal.

In general, the dual problem is derived through the following procedure:

1. Construct the **Lagrangian** $\mathcal{L}$ by introducing a nonnegative Lagrange multiplier α_i for each inequality constraint. The goal is to find a saddle point of the Lagrangian: a point that minimizes $\mathcal{L}$ with respect to the **primal variables** and maximizes it with respect to the **dual variables** α. This saddle-point condition is equivalent to satisfying the **Karush-Kuhn-Tucker (KKT) conditions**, which characterize the optimality of solutions in constrained optimization problems (see Section E.6.6).

---

2. This objective is reminiscent of logistic regression with L2 regularization, where the goal is to find a separating hyperplane while minimizing $\|\mathbf{w}\|^2$. This shows how SVM's margin maximization can be interpreted as a form of regularization: minimizing $\|\mathbf{w}\|^2$ not only increases the margin but also controls the model's complexity.

2. Minimize the Lagrangian with respect to the primal variables, treating the dual variables α as fixed.

3. Substitute the resulting expressions back into the Lagrangian to obtain the **dual function**, which depends only on the dual variables.

4. Maximize this dual function with respect to α, subject to the nonnegativity constraints $\alpha_i \geq 0$.

We now apply this procedure to the hard-margin SVM optimization problem. Recall that the primal form of SVM involves minimizing $\frac{1}{2}\|\mathbf{w}\|^2$ subject to the constraints $y_i(\mathbf{w}^T\mathbf{x}_i + b) \geq 1$. To incorporate these constraints into the objective, we introduce a nonnegative Lagrange multiplier $\alpha_i \geq 0$ for each constraint and define the Lagrangian as:

$$\mathcal{L}(\mathbf{w}, b, \boldsymbol{\alpha}) = \frac{1}{2}\|\mathbf{w}\|^2 - \sum_{i=1}^{n} \alpha_i \left[y_i(\mathbf{w}^T\mathbf{x}_i + b) - 1 \right]. \tag{11.15}$$

We begin by minimizing $\mathcal{L}$ with respect to the primal variables $\mathbf{w}$ and b. Taking the partial derivative of $\mathcal{L}$ with respect to $\mathbf{w}$ and setting it to zero gives:

$$\frac{\partial \mathcal{L}(\mathbf{w}, b, \boldsymbol{\alpha})}{\partial \mathbf{w}} = \mathbf{w} - \sum_{i=1}^{n} \alpha_i y_i \mathbf{x}_i = 0. \tag{11.16}$$

This yields the following expression for $\mathbf{w}$:

$$\mathbf{w} = \sum_{i=1}^{n} \alpha_i y_i \mathbf{x}_i. \tag{11.17}$$

Substituting this expression back into the Lagrangian yields:

$$\mathcal{L}(\mathbf{w}, b, \boldsymbol{\alpha}) = \frac{1}{2}\left(\sum_{i=1}^{n} \alpha_i y_i \mathbf{x}_i\right)^T \left(\sum_{j=1}^{n} \alpha_j y_j \mathbf{x}_j\right) - \sum_{i=1}^{n} \alpha_i \left[y_i \left(\sum_{j=1}^{n} (\alpha_j y_j \mathbf{x}_j)^T \mathbf{x}_i + b \right) - 1 \right]$$

$$= \frac{1}{2}\sum_{i=1}^{n}\sum_{j=1}^{n} \alpha_i \alpha_j y_i y_j \mathbf{x}_i^T \mathbf{x}_j - \sum_{i=1}^{n} \alpha_i \left[\sum_{j=1}^{n} y_i \alpha_j y_j \mathbf{x}_j^T \mathbf{x}_i + y_i b - 1 \right]$$

$$= \frac{1}{2}\sum_{i=1}^{n}\sum_{j=1}^{n} \alpha_i \alpha_j y_i y_j \mathbf{x}_i^T \mathbf{x}_j - \sum_{i=1}^{n}\sum_{j=1}^{n} \alpha_i \alpha_j y_i y_j \mathbf{x}_i^T \mathbf{x}_j - b\sum_{i=1}^{n} \alpha_i y_i + \sum_{i=1}^{n} \alpha_i$$

$$= -\frac{1}{2}\sum_{i=1}^{n}\sum_{j=1}^{n} \alpha_i \alpha_j y_i y_j \mathbf{x}_i^T \mathbf{x}_j + \sum_{i=1}^{n} \alpha_i - b\sum_{i=1}^{n} \alpha_i y_i. \tag{11.18}$$

Next, we compute the partial derivative of $\mathcal{L}$ with respect to b and set it to zero:

$$\frac{\partial \mathcal{L}(\mathbf{w}, b, \boldsymbol{\alpha})}{\partial b} = \sum_{i=1}^{n} \alpha_i y_i = 0, \tag{11.19}$$

which introduces the equality constraint:

$$\sum_{i=1}^{n} \alpha_i y_i = 0. \tag{11.20}$$

Substituting this result back into the Lagrangian eliminates the term involving b. This leads to the following optimization problem, known as the **hard-margin SVM dual problem**:

$$\max_{\boldsymbol{\alpha}} \quad \sum_{i=1}^{n} \alpha_i - \frac{1}{2} \sum_{i=1}^{n} \sum_{j=1}^{n} \alpha_i \alpha_j y_i y_j \mathbf{x}_i^T \mathbf{x}_j,$$

$$\text{subject to} \quad \alpha_i \geq 0, \quad i = 1, \ldots, n, \tag{11.21}$$

$$\sum_{i=1}^{n} \alpha_i y_i = 0.$$

The dual problem is also a convex optimization problem with inequality constraints. However, it differs from the primal formulation in two important ways. First, the dual problem has n optimization variables (one per training sample), whereas the primal problem has d variables, corresponding to the number of features. Solving the dual can therefore be more efficient in high-dimensional settings where $d > n$, such as in gene expression analysis, where we often have thousands of genes as features but only a small number of samples per condition.

Second, the training data enter the dual problem only through dot products of the form $\mathbf{x}_i^T \mathbf{x}_j$. This property will become crucial when we introduce the kernel trick, which enables nonlinear classification by replacing these dot products with kernel functions that implicitly map the data into high-dimensional feature spaces (see Section 11.4).

11.1.4.1 The Optimal Hyperplane

The solution to the dual problem provides the optimal values of the Lagrange multipliers $\boldsymbol{\alpha}$. From these multipliers, we need to recover the optimal weight vector $\mathbf{w}$ and bias b that define the separating hyperplane.

The weight vector $\mathbf{w}$ can be obtained directly from Equation (11.17):

$$\mathbf{w} = \sum_{i=1}^{n} \alpha_i y_i \mathbf{x}_i.$$

Recovering the bias b is less straightforward, since it was eliminated during the derivation of the dual problem.

The **Karush-Kuhn-Tucker (KKT) conditions**, which are necessary conditions for optimality in constrained optimization problems, allow us to recover the bias. Specifically, the **complementary slackness** condition states that for each inequality constraint, the product of the corresponding Lagrange multiplier and the constraint expression must be zero. Therefore, for each training sample x_i, the following condition must hold:

$$\alpha_i[y_i(\mathbf{w}^T\mathbf{x}_i + b) - 1] = 0. \tag{11.22}$$

This implies the following two cases:

1. If $\alpha_i > 0$, then $y_i(\mathbf{w}^T\mathbf{x}_i + b) = 1$. These points lie exactly on the margin and are known as support vectors.

2. If $\alpha_i = 0$, then $y_i(\mathbf{w}^T\mathbf{x}_i + b) - 1 \geq 0$, which implies that:

   - The point lies strictly outside the margin:

     $$y_i(\mathbf{w}^T\mathbf{x}_i + b) > 1.$$

   - or it lies exactly on the margin but does not affect the decision boundary, since its corresponding multiplier is $\alpha_i = 0$.[3]

Therefore, only the support vectors have nonzero Lagrange multipliers $\alpha_i > 0$, while all other training points have $\alpha_i = 0$ and do not contribute to the model. Consequently, we can express the weight vector $\mathbf{w}$ as a linear combination of the support vectors alone:

$$\mathbf{w} = \sum_{i \in \mathcal{S}} \alpha_i y_i \mathbf{x}_i, \tag{11.23}$$

where $\mathcal{S}$ denotes the set of support vectors. From this expression, we see that support vectors with larger α_i contribute more significantly to $\mathbf{w}$, and therefore play a greater role in shaping the decision boundary.

To compute the bias b, we use any support vector $\mathbf{x}_i$, which satisfies:

$$y_i(\mathbf{w}^T\mathbf{x}_i + b) = 1.$$

Since $y_i \neq 0$, we can divide both sides by y_i:

$$\mathbf{w}^T\mathbf{x}_i + b = \frac{1}{y_i}$$

$$b = \frac{1}{y_i} - \mathbf{w}^T\mathbf{x}_i.$$

---

3. For example, if two identical points $\mathbf{x}_1 = \mathbf{x}_2$ both lie on the margin, the decision boundary remains unchanged if one of them is removed. In this case, only one acts as a support vector with $\alpha > 0$, while the other has $\alpha = 0$.

Since $y_i = \pm 1$, it follows that $\frac{1}{y_i} = y_i$, so the formula simplifies to:

$$b = y_i - \mathbf{w}^T \mathbf{x}_i. \tag{11.24}$$

To improve numerical stability, the bias is typically computed by averaging this quantity over all the support vectors:

$$b = \frac{1}{|\mathcal{S}|} \sum_{i \in \mathcal{S}} \left(y_i - \mathbf{w}^T \mathbf{x}_i \right), \tag{11.25}$$

where $|\mathcal{S}|$ is the number of support vectors.

To classify a new data point $\mathbf{x}$, we evaluate the decision function at that point:

$$\mathbf{w}^T \mathbf{x} + b = \left(\sum_{i \in \mathcal{S}} \alpha_i y_i \mathbf{x}_i \right)^T \mathbf{x} + b = \sum_{i \in \mathcal{S}} \alpha_i y_i \mathbf{x}_i^T \mathbf{x} + b. \tag{11.26}$$

The sign of this value determines the predicted class: a positive value corresponds to the positive class ($y = 1$), while a negative value corresponds to the negative class ($y = -1$).

This formulation highlights a key property of SVMs: predictions depend only on the support vectors. Since the number of support vectors is typically much smaller than the total number of training samples, this significantly reduces both the storage and computational cost at prediction time. Moreover, the model becomes more interpretable, as only the support vectors define the decision boundary.

11.1.4.2 Matrix Formulation

The dual SVM problem is also a quadratic optimization problem that can be solved efficiently using standard quadratic programming (QP) solvers. These solvers typically require the problem to be expressed in matrix form (see Section 11.1.5). In this section, we show how to rewrite the dual problem in that format.

We begin by rewriting the quadratic term in the objective as

$$\sum_{i=1}^{n} \sum_{j=1}^{n} \alpha_i \alpha_j y_i y_j \mathbf{x}_i^T \mathbf{x}_j = \boldsymbol{\alpha}^T H \boldsymbol{\alpha}, \tag{11.27}$$

where $H \in \mathbb{R}^{n \times n}$ is a symmetric matrix with entries $H_{ij} = y_i y_j \mathbf{x}_i^T \mathbf{x}_j$. This expression follows from the general identity for quadratic forms (see Section A.3.19):

$$\mathbf{v}^T A \mathbf{v} = \sum_{i=1}^{n} \sum_{j=1}^{n} v_i A_{ij} v_j. \tag{11.28}$$

The matrix H can be computed efficiently using:

$$H = \mathbf{y} \mathbf{y}^T \odot X X^T, \tag{11.29}$$

where $\mathbf{y}\mathbf{y}^T$ is the outer product of the target vector, XX^T is the matrix of dot products between all pairs of training points (also known as the **Gram matrix**), and the operator $\odot$ denotes element-wise (Hadamard) product.

The linear term in the objective can be written as a dot product:

$$\sum_{i=1}^{n} \alpha_i = \mathbf{1}^T \boldsymbol{\alpha}, \tag{11.30}$$

where $\mathbf{1} \in \mathbb{R}^n$ is a vector of ones.

The equality constraint $\sum_{i=1}^{n} \alpha_i y_i = 0$ becomes:

$$\mathbf{y}^T \boldsymbol{\alpha} = 0. \tag{11.31}$$

Putting everything together, we can express the dual SVM problem in matrix form as:

$$
\begin{aligned}
\max_{\boldsymbol{\alpha}} \quad & \mathbf{1}^T \boldsymbol{\alpha} - \frac{1}{2}\boldsymbol{\alpha}^T H \boldsymbol{\alpha}, \\
\text{subject to} \quad & \boldsymbol{\alpha} \succeq \mathbf{0}, \\
& \mathbf{y}^T \boldsymbol{\alpha} = 0.
\end{aligned}
\tag{11.32}
$$

Here, $\boldsymbol{\alpha} \succeq \mathbf{0}$ means that each component satisfies $\alpha_i \geq 0$ for $i = 1, \dots, n$.

11.1.5   Implementation in Python

In this section, we implement a hard-margin SVM from scratch, using the CVXOPT optimization library to solve the underlying quadratic programming problem. The complete code example can be found in the SVMFromScratch.ipynb[4] notebook on GitHub.

CVXOPT[5] (Python Software for Convex Optimization) is an efficient open-source library designed for solving convex optimization problems. It supports a variety of problem types, including linear programming (LP), quadratic programming (QP), and semidefinite programming (SDP), as long as the problem satisfies the required convexity conditions.

The library can be easily installed via pip:

```
pip install cvxopt
```

To solve a quadratic program, CVXOPT expects the problem to be formulated in the following standard form:

$$
\begin{aligned}
\min_{\mathbf{x}} \quad & \frac{1}{2}\mathbf{x}^T P \mathbf{x} + \mathbf{q}^T \mathbf{x}, \\
\text{subject to} \quad & G\mathbf{x} \preceq \mathbf{h}, \\
& A\mathbf{x} = \mathbf{b},
\end{aligned}
\tag{11.33}
$$

---

4. https://github.com/roiyeho/ml-book/blob/main/Chapter11/SVMFromScratch.ipynb
5. https://cvxopt.org

where:

- $\mathbf{x}$ is the variable vector to be optimized.

- P is a symmetric, positive semidefinite matrix representing the quadratic part of the objective function. Its semidefiniteness ensures convexity and guarantees a unique global minimum value (provided a feasible solution exists).

- $\mathbf{q}$ is a vector defining the linear component of the objective.

- G is a matrix whose rows contain the coefficients of the inequality constraints. The solution must satisfy the element-wise condition $G\mathbf{x} \preceq \mathbf{h}$.

- $\mathbf{h}$ is a vector defining the upper bounds for the inequality constraints.

- A is a matrix whose rows contain the coefficients of the equality constraints. The solution must satisfy $A\mathbf{x} = \mathbf{b}$.

- $\mathbf{b}$ is a vector specifying the target values for the equality constraints.

Note that the dual SVM problem in Equation (11.32) is a maximization problem, while CVXOPT requires the problem to be expressed in minimization form. To accommodate this, we negate the objective function to obtain an equivalent minimization problem:

$$\min_{\boldsymbol{\alpha}} \quad \frac{1}{2}\boldsymbol{\alpha}^T H \boldsymbol{\alpha} - \mathbf{1}^T \boldsymbol{\alpha},$$
$$\text{subject to} \quad \alpha_i \geq 0, \quad i = 1, \ldots, n, \tag{11.34}$$
$$\mathbf{y}^T \boldsymbol{\alpha} = 0.$$

We now express the SVM dual problem in CVXOPT's standard form by establishing the following equivalences:

- $\mathbf{x} = \boldsymbol{\alpha}$: the vector of optimization variables.

- $P = H$, where $H = \mathbf{y}\mathbf{y}^T \odot X X^T$ defines the quadratic part of the objective function. This matrix is positive semidefinite because both $\mathbf{y}\mathbf{y}^T$ and $X X^T$ are positive semidefinite with nonnegative entries, and the element-wise product of two such matrices is also positive semidefinite by the Schur product theorem (see [276, Theorem 7.5.3]).

- $\mathbf{q} = -\mathbf{1}$: the linear term of the negated objective.

- $G = -I$: enforces $\alpha_i \geq 0$ by expressing it as $-\alpha_i \leq 0$ for all $i = 1, \ldots, n$.

- $\mathbf{h} = \mathbf{0}$: the upper bounds for the inequality constraints.

- $A = \mathbf{y}^T$: a single-row matrix representing the equality constraint $\mathbf{y}^T \boldsymbol{\alpha} = 0$.

- $\mathbf{b} = (0)$: a vector enforcing the (single) equality constraint.

We are now ready to implement a hard-margin SVM classifier in Python. We start by importing the required libraries and defining the model as a custom Scikit-Learn classifier:

```python
import numpy as np
import matplotlib.pyplot as plt
from cvxopt import matrix, solvers
from sklearn.base import BaseEstimator, ClassifierMixin

class HardMarginSVM(BaseEstimator, ClassifierMixin):
    def fit(self, X, y):
```

The `fit` method consists of several parts, which we explain and implement step by step:

1. First, we determine the number of samples and reshape the label vector y into a column vector to ensure correct broadcasting in subsequent matrix operations:

```python
n_samples = X.shape[0]
y_vec = y.reshape(-1, 1) # Reshape y into a column vector
```

2. Next, we define the matrices required to express the dual problem in the standard quadratic programming form expected by CVXOPT:

```python
# Quadratic programming problem formulation
P = matrix((y_vec @ y_vec.T)*(X @ X.T))   # Quadratic term of the objective
q = matrix(-np.ones(n_samples))           # Linear term of the objective
G = matrix(-np.eye(n_samples))            # Inequality constraints: -alpha <= 0
h = matrix(np.zeros(n_samples))           # Bounds for the inequality constraints
A = matrix(y_vec.T, (1, n_samples), 'd') # Equality constraint
b = matrix(0.0)                           # Value of the equality constraint
```

The CVXOPT solver requires all parameters, including scalars and vectors, to be expressed as matrix objects. The `matrix` function from CVXOPT converts NumPy arrays or lists into solver-compatible matrices. Setting the data type to `'d'` (double-precision float) in the matrix A converts the integer label values (-1 or 1) to floats, as CVXOPT requires all input matrices to have the same data type.

3. We now solve the quadratic programming problem using the `cvxopt.solvers.qp` function, which takes as input the matrices defining the objective and constraints:

```python
# Solve the quadratic programming problem
solution = solvers.qp(P, q, G, h, A, b)
```

4. After solving the optimization problem, we extract the Lagrange multipliers and identify the support vectors. To account for numerical precision errors, we consider as nonzero only those multipliers greater than a small threshold (e.g., 10^{-5}):

```
# Extract the Lagrange multipliers from the solution
alphas = np.array(solution['x']).flatten()

# Identify the support vectors (nonzero Lagrange multipliers)
support_vector_indices = alphas > 1e-5

# Save the nonzero multipliers, support vectors, and their labels
self.alphas_ = alphas[support_vector_indices]
self.support_vectors_ = X[support_vector_indices]
self.support_vector_labels_ = y[support_vector_indices]
```

5. Finally, we compute the weight vector $\mathbf{w}$ and the bias b of the separating hyperplane using Equations (11.23) and (11.25). The weight vector is computed as a linear combination of the support vectors, with each coefficient given by the product of the corresponding Lagrange multiplier and class label, $\alpha_i y_i$. The bias is computed by averaging, over all support vectors, the difference between the true label y_i and the dot product $\mathbf{w}^T \mathbf{x}$.

```
# Compute the weight vector and bias of the separating hyperplane
self.coef_ = (self.alphas_ * self.support_vector_labels_) @ \
                self.support_vectors_
self.intercept_ = np.mean(
    self.support_vector_labels_ - self.support_vectors_ @ self.coef_
)
```

We also define the methods used for making predictions. The decision_function method computes the functional margin of each input sample (proportional to its signed distance from the decision boundary), and the predict method assigns class labels based on the sign of these margins:

```
def decision_function(self, X):
    """Compute the functional margins (raw decision scores)"""
    return X @ self.coef_ + self.intercept_

def predict(self, X):
    """Classify data points based on the sign of the decision function"""
    return np.sign(self.decision_function(X))
```

Note that SVMs do not naturally produce probability estimates, unlike logistic regression. However, the raw decision scores can be converted into calibrated probabilities using techniques such as Platt scaling (see Section 11.8).

11.1.5.1 Testing the Implementation

Let's test our custom SVM classifier on a simplified version of the Iris dataset, which includes only the first two features of each flower (sepal length and sepal width) and two flower types: setosa and versicolor. As discussed in Section 5.3.3, this dataset is linearly separable and thus well-suited for training a hard-margin SVM.

We first load the dataset and convert the labels from {0, 1} to {-1, 1}, as required by the SVM formulation:

```
from sklearn.datasets import load_iris

iris = load_iris()
X = iris.data[:, :2] # Use only the first two features
y = iris.target
class_labels = iris.target_names

# Filter for setosa and versicolor flowers (labels 0 and 1)
X = X[(y == 0) | (y == 1)]
y = y[(y == 0) | (y == 1)]

# Convert labels from {0, 1} to {-1, 1}
y = 2 * y - 1
```

Next, we split the dataset into training and test sets:

```
from sklearn.model_selection import train_test_split

X_train, X_test, y_train, y_test = train_test_split(X, y, random_state=42)
```

SVMs are sensitive to feature scales because they maximize the margin between classes—that is, the distance between the decision boundary and the closest training points from each class. When features have very different ranges, one may dominate the computation of distances, potentially skewing the decision boundary. In this case, however, the selected Iris features already have similar scales, so we can safely skip feature scaling.

We now create an instance of our HardMarginSVM class and fit it to the training set:

```
model = HardMarginSVM()
model.fit(X_train, y_train)
```

The CVXOPT solver prints the following progress information during the optimization:

```
    pcost       dcost       gap    pres   dres
 0: -1.4047e+01 -3.0811e+01  2e+02  1e+01  2e+00
 1: -2.6255e+01 -3.1831e+01  9e+01  5e+00  7e-01
 2: -4.8755e+01 -4.6481e+01  8e+01  4e+00  5e-01
 3: -4.3936e+01 -4.5169e+01  7e+01  2e+00  3e-01
 4: -3.6054e+01 -3.5550e+01  7e+00  2e-01  3e-02
 5: -3.3810e+01 -3.3813e+01  7e-02  2e-03  3e-04
 6: -3.3795e+01 -3.3795e+01  7e-04  2e-05  3e-06
 7: -3.3795e+01 -3.3795e+01  7e-06  2e-07  3e-08
 8: -3.3795e+01 -3.3795e+01  7e-08  2e-09  3e-10
Optimal solution found.
```

An optimal solution was found after just eight iterations. Let's evaluate the model's accuracy on the training and test sets:

```
print(f'Training accuracy: {model.score(X_train, y_train):.4f}')
print(f'Test accuracy: {model.score(X_test, y_test):.4f}')
```

```
Training accuracy: 1.0000
Test accuracy: 1.0000
```

As expected, the SVM classifier perfectly separates the two classes. Since the dataset is two-dimensional, we can visualize the model's decision boundary, margins, and support vectors to better understand the model's behavior. The following helper function plots these elements:

```
def plot_svm_decision_boundary(model, X, y, feature_names=None,
                               class_labels=None, ax=None, legend=True):
    if feature_names is None:
        feature_names = ['$x_1$', '$x_2$']
    if class_labels is None:
        class_labels = ['Class 0', 'Class 1']
    ax = ax or plt.gca()

    # Plot the training points
    ax.scatter(X[y == 0][:, 0], X[y == 0][:, 1], c='red', s=50,
               edgecolors='k', label=class_labels[0])
    ax.scatter(X[y == 1][:, 0], X[y == 1][:, 1], c='blue', s=50,
               edgecolors='k', label=class_labels[1])

    # Create a grid of points to evaluate the model
    x0, x1 = np.meshgrid(
        np.linspace(X[:, 0].min() - 0.1, X[:, 0].max() + 0.1, 250),
        np.linspace(X[:, 1].min() - 0.1, X[:, 1].max() + 0.1, 250)
    )
    grid = np.c_[x0.ravel(), x1.ravel()]

    # Plot the decision boundary and margins
    y_decision = model.decision_function(grid).reshape(x0.shape)
    ax.contour(x0, x1, y_decision, levels=[-1, 0, 1], linestyles=['--', '-', '--'],
               colors='k')

    # Fill class regions
    y_pred = model.predict(grid).reshape(x0.shape)
    custom_cmap = plt.cm.colors.ListedColormap(['red', 'blue'])
    ax.contourf(x0, x1, y_pred, alpha=0.3, cmap=custom_cmap)
```

```
# Highlight the support vectors
if hasattr(model, 'support_vectors_'):
    ax.scatter(model.support_vectors_[:, 0], model.support_vectors_[:, 1], s=150,
               facecolors='none', edgecolors='black', label='support vectors')

ax.set_xlabel(feature_names[0])
ax.set_ylabel(feature_names[1])
if legend:
    ax.legend()
```

Note that this function assumes the labels are 0/1, as it is also intended to be used with Scikit-Learn's SVM classifiers, which use 0/1 labels by default rather than -1/1. To visualize our custom classifier, we first convert the training labels:

```
y_train_bin = np.where(y_train == -1, 0, y_train) # Convert labels from -1/1 to 0/1
plot_svm_decision_boundary(model, X_train, y_train_bin, iris.feature_names[:2],
                           class_labels)
```

Figure 11.5 shows the results of the hard-margin SVM classifier on the Iris dataset. The decision boundary perfectly separates the two classes, with only two support vectors from each class. This demonstrates SVM's ability to achieve optimal class separation using only a minimal subset of critical data points, ensuring both efficiency and simplicity.

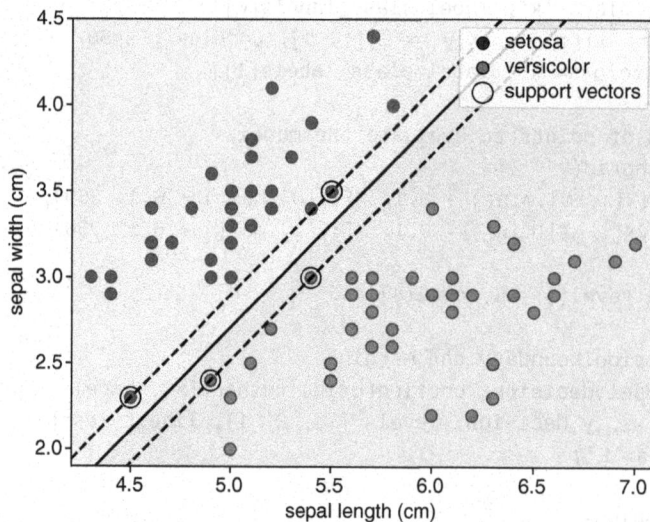

Figure 11.5: Results of the hard-margin SVM classifier on the Iris dataset. The decision boundary (solid line) separates the two classes, with the margins shown as dashed lines. The support vectors, which determine the position and orientation of the decision boundary, are indicated by a circular outline around the points. The shaded regions represent the predicted class areas.

11.1.6 Scikit-Learn SVM Classes

Scikit-Learn provides several classes for implementing support vector machines, each offering different algorithmic tradeoffs in terms of optimization strategy, kernel support, and scalability. The SVM-based classification classes include:

- LinearSVC[6]: Implements an efficient linear support vector classifier based on the LIBLINEAR library [183], which uses a coordinate descent algorithm to solve the optimization problem. It can handle both the primal and dual formulations, depending on the data and the setting of the dual parameter. In practice, it scales nearly linearly with the number of samples, making it well-suited for large datasets. However, it does not support kernel-based (nonlinear) classification.

- SVC[7]: A flexible support vector classifier that supports both linear and nonlinear classification through kernel functions (see Section 11.3). It solves the dual optimization problem using the LIBSVM library [103]. While powerful, its training time typically scales at least quadratically with the number of samples, making it less suitable for very large datasets.

- NuSVC[8]: Similar to SVC, but uses an alternative formulation that replaces the regularization parameter C with ν. This parameter provides a more intuitive way to control the tradeoff between model complexity and training accuracy (see Section 11.5).

- SGDClassifier[9]: Uses stochastic gradient descent (SGD) to optimize linear classification models, and can be used to train a linear SVM by setting loss='hinge' (see Section 11.2.3). It is especially useful for large-scale and online learning tasks, as it supports incremental updates and does not require the entire dataset to reside in memory.

The equivalent support vector regression classes will be introduced in Section 11.6.

11.1.7 The LinearSVC Class

The LinearSVC class provides an efficient implementation of linear support vector classification. Its key parameters are listed in Table 11.1. In addition, it exposes several attributes that are useful for inspecting the trained model:

- coef_: Array of shape (n_classes, n_features) containing the coefficients of the separating hyperplane(s).

- intercept_: Array of shape (n_classes,) containing the bias term(s).

- n_iter_: Number of iterations run by the solver before convergence.

Note that, unlike other SVM classes such as SVC, LinearSVC does not expose the support vectors used in the model.

---

6. https://scikit-learn.org/stable/modules/generated/sklearn.svm.LinearSVC.html
7. https://scikit-learn.org/stable/modules/generated/sklearn.svm.SVC.html
8. https://scikit-learn.org/stable/modules/generated/sklearn.svm.NuSVC.html
9. https://scikit-learn.org/stable/modules/generated/sklearn.linear_model.SGDClassifier.html

Parameter	Description	Default
penalty	Type of regularization to apply. Options are `'l1'` and `'l2'`.	`'l2'`
loss	Loss function to optimize. Options are `'hinge'` or `'squared_hinge'`.	`'squared_hinge'`
dual	Whether to solve the dual or primal optimization problem. The default setting `'auto'` chooses the dual when the number of features exceeds the number of samples.	`'auto'`
tol	Tolerance for the stopping criteria.	`0.0001`
C	Regularization parameter controlling the tradeoff between margin size and classification error.	`1.0`
multi_class	Strategy for multi-class classification: `'ovr'` (one-vs-rest) or `'crammer_singer'` (directly optimizes a multi-class objective).	`'ovr'`
class_weight	Class weights for handling imbalanced data. Can be `'balanced'` or a dictionary mapping class labels to weights.	`None`
max_iter	Maximum number of iterations for the solver to converge.	`1000`

Table 11.1: Key parameters of the `LinearSVC` class

Let's demonstrate the use of `LinearSVC` on the same reduced Iris dataset from Section 11.1.5.1. We follow the same steps for loading the dataset as described earlier. However, unlike our custom implementation, Scikit-Learn's SVM classes accept class labels in $\{0, 1\}$ directly and do not require conversion to $\{-1, 1\}$.

After loading the dataset, we create an instance of `LinearSVC` and fit it to the training set:

```
from sklearn.svm import LinearSVC

model = LinearSVC(random_state=42)
model.fit(X_train, y_train)
```

Next, we evaluate the model's accuracy on the training and test sets:

```
print(f'Training accuracy: {model.score(X_train, y_train):.4f}')
print(f'Test accuracy: {model.score(X_test, y_test):.4f}')
```

```
Training accuracy: 0.9867
Test accuracy: 1.0000
```

The training accuracy is not perfect, indicating that the algorithm did not find a hyperplane that completely separates all training samples. This is expected, as `LinearSVC` uses a soft-margin approach by default, which allows some margin violations to improve generalization (discussed in the next section). To approximate the behavior of a hard-margin SVM, we can set the regularization parameter C to a very large value (note: using C=np.inf will raise an error, as it is not supported):

```
model = LinearSVC(C=1e10, random_state=42)
model.fit(X_train, y_train)
```

After adjusting C, the model achieves perfect accuracy on the training set:

```
print(f'Training accuracy: {model.score(X_train, y_train):.4f}')
print(f'Test accuracy: {model.score(X_test, y_test):.4f}')
```

```
Training accuracy: 1.0000
Test accuracy: 1.0000
```

11.2 Soft-Margin SVM

In many real-world datasets, the data is not linearly separable, meaning that no hyperplane can perfectly divide the data points into distinct classes without misclassifications. To handle such cases, **soft-margin SVM**, introduced by Cortes and Vapnik in 1995 [130], extends the standard SVM framework by relaxing the hard-margin constraint $y_i(\mathbf{w}^T\mathbf{x}_i+b) \geq 1$. This relaxation allows some data points to violate the margin, enabling the model to deal effectively with overlapping class distributions.

Margin violations fall into two categories:

- Points inside the margin: These points satisfy $0 < y_i(\mathbf{w}^T\mathbf{x}_i + b) < 1$. They are correctly classified but lie closer to the decision boundary than the margin allows.

- Misclassified points: These points satisfy $y_i(\mathbf{w}^T\mathbf{x}_i+b) \leq 0$, meaning they fall on the wrong side of the decision boundary and are misclassified.

To allow such violations, soft-margin SVM introduces a set of nonnegative **slack variables** $\xi_i \geq 0$ for $i = 1, \ldots, n$, which quantify the extent to which each training sample violates the margin constraints. These slack variables enable a more flexible margin by relaxing the strict inequalities of the hard-margin formulation. The modified constraints are:

$$\mathbf{w}^T\mathbf{x}_i + b \geq 1 - \xi_i \quad \text{if } y_i = 1, \tag{11.35}$$

$$\mathbf{w}^T\mathbf{x}_i + b \leq -1 + \xi_i \quad \text{if } y_i = -1. \tag{11.36}$$

Equivalently, both constraints can be written compactly as:

$$y_i(\mathbf{w}^T\mathbf{x}_i + b) \geq 1 - \xi_i, \quad \text{for all } i \in 1, \ldots, n. \tag{11.37}$$

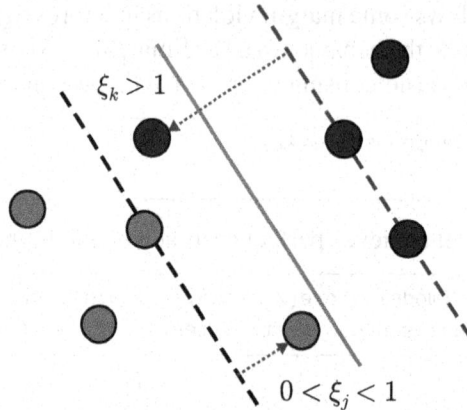

Figure 11.6: Illustration of slack variables in soft-margin SVM. The blue point with $0 < \xi_j < 1$ lies within the margin but remains correctly classified, while the red point with $\xi_k > 1$ is misclassified, lying on the wrong side of the decision boundary. The slack variables ξ_j and ξ_k quantify the degree of violation relative to the margin constraints.

The magnitude of each slack variable ξ_i indicates the degree to which the corresponding data point violates the margin constraint (see Figure 11.6):

- $0 \leq \xi_i < 1$: The data point lies inside the margin but is still correctly classified.

- $\xi_i \geq 1$: The data point is misclassified, lying on the wrong side of the decision boundary.

Soft-margin SVM seeks to balance two competing objectives: maximizing the margin and minimizing the number and severity of margin violations. A wider margin can improve generalization but may lead to misclassifications, while reducing violations typically results in a narrower margin and greater risk of overfitting. This tradeoff reflects the classic bias–variance dilemma.

To control this tradeoff, the soft-margin formulation introduces a **regularization parameter** $C > 0$, which governs the balance between maximizing the margin and penalizing violations.

This leads to the **primal optimization problem** for soft-margin SVM:

$$
\min_{\mathbf{w}, b, \boldsymbol{\xi}} \quad \frac{1}{2}\|\mathbf{w}\|^2 + C\sum_{i=1}^{n}\xi_i,
$$

$$
\text{subject to} \quad y_i(\mathbf{w}^T\mathbf{x}_i + b) \geq 1 - \xi_i, \quad i = 1, \ldots, n, \tag{11.38}
$$

$$
\xi_i \geq 0, \quad i = 1, \ldots, n.
$$

In this formulation:

- The first term, $\frac{1}{2}\|\mathbf{w}\|^2$, promotes a wider margin by minimizing the squared norm of the weight vector $\mathbf{w}$.

- The second term, $C\sum_{i=1}^{n}\xi_i$, penalizes margin violations in proportion to their severity, as quantified by the slack variables ξ_i.

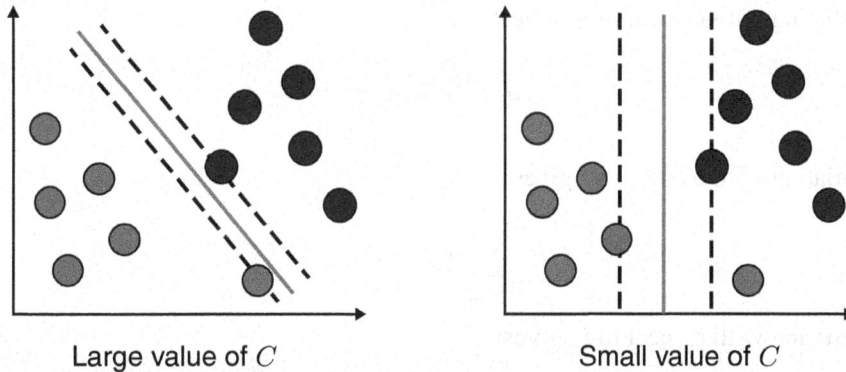

Large value of C Small value of C

Figure 11.7: Effect of the regularization parameter C on the SVM decision boundary. A large C (left) penalizes margin violations more heavily, resulting in a tighter fit with a narrower margin. A small C (right) allows more margin violations, resulting in a wider margin that may generalize better.

The regularization parameter C determines the relative importance of these two objectives: a larger C prioritizes minimizing violations, typically resulting in a narrower margin and a tighter fit to the training data (Figure 11.7, left), whereas a smaller C allows more violations, encouraging a wider margin that may generalize better to unseen data (Figure 11.7, right).

11.2.1   The Dual Problem

As in the hard-margin case, we can derive the dual form of the soft-margin optimization problem using Lagrange duality. The Lagrangian is given by:

$$\mathcal{L}(\mathbf{w}, b, \boldsymbol{\xi}, \boldsymbol{\alpha}, \boldsymbol{\mu}) = \frac{1}{2}\|\mathbf{w}\|^2 + C\sum_{i=1}^{n}\xi_i - \sum_{i=1}^{n}\alpha_i\left[y_i(\mathbf{w}^T\mathbf{x}_i + b) - 1 + \xi_i\right] - \sum_{i=1}^{n}\mu_i\xi_i, \quad (11.39)$$

where:

- $\boldsymbol{\alpha} = (\alpha_1, \ldots, \alpha_n)$ are the Lagrange multipliers for the constraints $y_i(\mathbf{w}^T\mathbf{x}_i + b) \geq 1 - \xi_i$, with $\alpha_i \geq 0$.

- $\boldsymbol{\mu} = (\mu_1, \ldots, \mu_n)$ are the Lagrange multipliers for the constraints $\xi_i \geq 0$, with $\mu_i \geq 0$.

To find the saddle point of the Lagrangian, we minimize $\mathcal{L}$ with respect to the primal variables $\mathbf{w}$, b, and ξ_i, and maximize it with respect to the dual variables α_i and μ_i. Since the derivation proceeds similarly to the hard-margin case, we omit the intermediate steps and leave the full derivation as an exercise (see Exercise 11.13).

We start by differentiating $\mathcal{L}$ with respect to the primal variables $\mathbf{w}$, b, and ξ_i, and setting the derivatives to zero.

Differentiating with respect to $\mathbf{w}$ gives:

$$\mathbf{w} = \sum_{i=1}^{n} \alpha_i y_i \mathbf{x}_i. \tag{11.40}$$

Differentiating with respect to b gives:

$$\sum_{i=1}^{n} \alpha_i y_i = 0. \tag{11.41}$$

Differentiating with respect to ξ_i gives:

$$\alpha_i + \mu_i = C. \tag{11.42}$$

Since $\mu_i \geq 0$, it follows that $\alpha_i \leq C$. This introduces an upper bound on each dual variable α_i.

Substituting Equation (11.40) into the Lagrangian and applying the optimality conditions for b and ξ_i yields the dual objective function:

$$\mathcal{L} = \sum_{i=1}^{n} \alpha_i - \frac{1}{2} \sum_{i=1}^{n} \sum_{j=1}^{n} \alpha_i \alpha_j y_i y_j \mathbf{x}_i^T \mathbf{x}_j. \tag{11.43}$$

Thus, the dual problem becomes:

$$\max_{\boldsymbol{\alpha}} \quad \sum_{i=1}^{n} \alpha_i - \frac{1}{2} \sum_{i=1}^{n} \sum_{j=1}^{n} \alpha_i \alpha_j y_i y_j \mathbf{x}_i^T \mathbf{x}_j,$$

$$\text{subject to} \quad 0 \leq \alpha_i \leq C, \quad i = 1, \ldots, n, \tag{11.44}$$

$$\sum_{i=1}^{n} \alpha_i y_i = 0.$$

Note that the only difference between the soft-margin and hard-margin dual problems (Equation (11.21)) is the additional constraint $\alpha_i \leq C$. When $C = \infty$, this constraint becomes inactive, and the soft-margin dual reduces to the hard-margin dual form.

After solving the dual problem and obtaining the optimal values of the dual variables $\boldsymbol{\alpha}$, we need to recover the parameters of the separating hyperplane. The optimal weight vector $\mathbf{w}$ is computed using Equation (11.40). To compute the bias term b, we apply the KKT complementarity slackness conditions, which state that for each inequality constraint, the product of the Lagrange multiplier and the constraint value must be zero. In our case, this yields the following two conditions:

$$\alpha_i \left[y_i (\mathbf{w}^T \mathbf{x}_i + b) - 1 + \xi_i \right] = 0, \tag{11.45}$$

$$\mu_i \xi_i = 0. \tag{11.46}$$

Together with the equality $\alpha_i + \mu_i = C$, these conditions allow us to characterize the role of each data point in defining the decision boundary:

1. $\alpha_i = 0$: Outside the margin (not a support vector)
   If $\alpha_i = 0$, then $\mu_i = C > 0$, and complementarity slackness implies $\xi_i = 0$. Substituting into the margin constraint gives $y_i(\mathbf{w}^T\mathbf{x}_i + b) \geq 1$. These points lie outside the margin (or exactly on it without being support vectors) and have no effect on the decision boundary.

2. $0 < \alpha_i < C$: On the margin (support vector)
   If $0 < \alpha_i < C$, then $\mu_i = C - \alpha_i > 0$, which implies $\xi_i = 0$. Complementary slackness then gives $y_i(\mathbf{w}^T\mathbf{x}_i + b) = 1$. These points lie exactly on the margin and are support vectors, as they influence the decision boundary (since $\alpha_i > 0$).

3. $\alpha_i = C$: Inside the margin or misclassified (support vector)
   In this case, $\mu_i = 0$, so $\xi_i > 0$, and complementarity slackness implies $y_i(\mathbf{w}^T\mathbf{x}_i + b) = 1 - \xi_i \leq 1$. These points either lie inside the margin or on the wrong side of the decision boundary. They are also support vectors as they influence the decision boundary.

Therefore, the support vectors are precisely those data points for which $0 < \alpha_i \leq C$. These points either lie exactly on the margin or violate it, i.e., they satisfy $y_i(\mathbf{w}^T\mathbf{x}_i + b) \leq 1$.

To determine the bias term b, we select one of the support vectors that lies exactly on the margin (i.e., with $\xi_i = 0$), and thus satisfies:

$$y_i(\mathbf{w}^T\mathbf{x}_i + b) - 1 = 0. \tag{11.47}$$

Solving for b gives:

$$b = y_i - \mathbf{w}^T\mathbf{x}_i. \tag{11.48}$$

To improve numerical stability, b is typically computed by averaging over all the support vectors that lie on the margin. Let $\mathcal{S}_m$ denote the set of such support vectors. Then:

$$b = \frac{1}{|\mathcal{S}_m|} \sum_{i \in \mathcal{S}_m} \left(y_i - \mathbf{w}^T\mathbf{x}_i\right). \tag{11.49}$$

11.2.2 Soft-Margin SVM in Scikit-Learn

The following example demonstrates the application of soft-margin SVM to a dataset with overlapping decision areas. We first generate a synthetic dataset using the make_classification[10] function, configured to create two clusters of 200 points with considerable class overlap:

```
from sklearn.datasets import make_classification

X, y = make_classification(
    n_samples=200, n_features=2, n_informative=2, n_redundant=0,
    n_clusters_per_class=1, class_sep=1.5, random_state=42
)
```

10. https://scikit-learn.org/stable/modules/generated/sklearn.datasets.make_classification.html

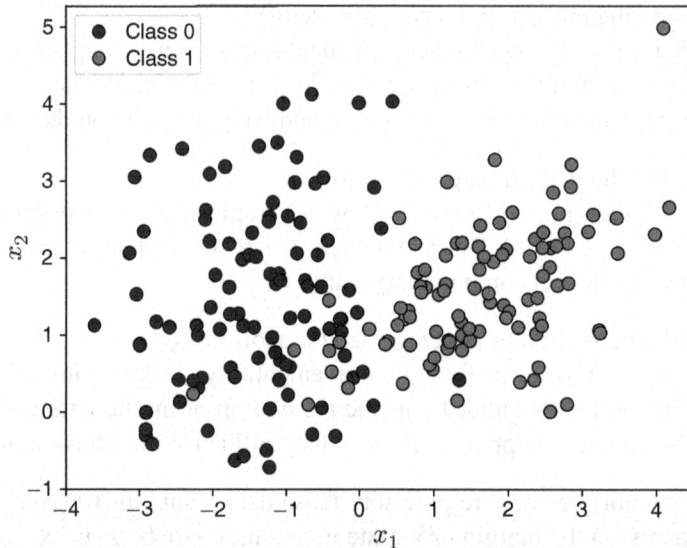

Figure 11.8: Synthetic dataset generated with `make_classification`, showing two classes with overlapping decision areas.

Figure 11.8 shows the generated dataset. As can be seen, there is significant overlap between the two classes, making this dataset a good example for illustrating how soft-margin SVM handles data that is not linearly separable.

Next, we split the dataset into training and test sets:

```
from sklearn.model_selection import train_test_split

X_train, X_test, y_train, y_test = train_test_split(X, y, random_state=42)
```

To explore the impact of the regularization parameter C on the model's performance, we train multiple `LinearSVC` models with varying C values. For each model, we plot the resulting decision boundaries and report its accuracy on both the training and test sets:

```
from sklearn.svm import LinearSVC

# Train LinearSVC models with various C values
fig, axes = plt.subplots(2, 2, figsize=(8, 6), sharex=True, sharey=True)

for ax, C in zip(axes.flat, [0.01, 0.1, 1, 10]):
    model = LinearSVC(C=C, random_state=42)
    model.fit(X_train, y_train)
    train_score = model.score(X_train, y_train)
    test_score = model.score(X_test, y_test)
```

```
# Plot the decision boundaries and scores
plot_svm_decision_boundary(model, X_train, y_train, ax=ax, legend=False)
ax.set_title(f'$C$ = {C}, train = {train_score:.4}, test = {test_score:.4}',
             fontsize=11)
```

The results, shown in Figure 11.9, illustrate how increasing C affects the soft-margin SVM. As C increases, the model places more emphasis on minimizing margin violations, leading to narrower margins and higher training accuracy. However, this can result in overfitting, as indicated by the drop in test accuracy.

Proper tuning of C is essential for achieving the right balance between margin maximization and error minimization, which directly impacts the bias–variance tradeoff. This is typically done by performing a grid search over candidate C values to identify the optimal regularization strength.

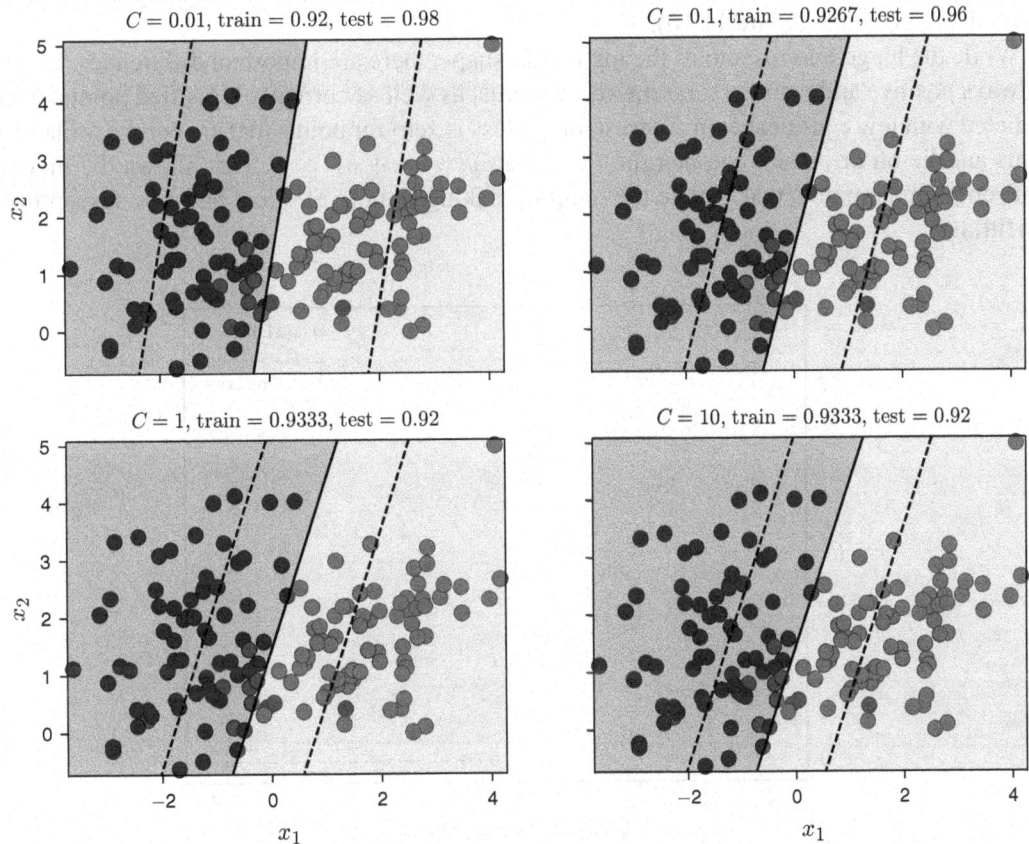

Figure 11.9: Effect of varying the regularization parameter C on the decision boundaries and classification accuracy of soft-margin SVM. Each subplot shows the decision boundary along with the corresponding training and test accuracies for the selected C value. Lower C values result in wider margins with greater tolerance for misclassifications, promoting better generalization, while higher C values produce narrower margins that fit the training data more closely, increasing the risk of overfitting.

11.2.3   Hinge Loss

Instead of explicitly introducing slack variables to handle margin violations, an alternative approach is to incorporate these penalties directly into the objective function using a suitable loss function. This reformulation leads to an unconstrained optimization problem, which can be efficiently solved using methods such as gradient descent.

The loss function used to penalize margin violations is called the **hinge loss**, defined as:

$$L_{\text{hinge}}(y_i, \hat{y}_i) = \max(0, 1 - y_i\hat{y}_i) = \max(0, 1 - y_i(\mathbf{w}^T\mathbf{x}_i + b)).   \quad (11.50)$$

The hinge loss is zero when the sample $\mathbf{x}_i$ lies on the correct side of the margin, i.e., $y_i(\mathbf{w}^T\mathbf{x}_i + b) \geq 1$. Otherwise, the loss increases linearly with the degree of margin violation. The name "hinge" reflects the shape of the function, which has a sharp transition from a flat region (zero loss) to a linear region where violations are penalized proportionally, resembling a mechanical hinge (see Figure 11.10).

While the hinge loss resembles the log loss in shape, there are important differences. Log loss is always positive and penalizes misclassified points, as well as correctly classified points that are predicted with low confidence. In contrast, hinge loss is zero for points that are correctly classified points and lie on or outside the margin, i.e., when $y(\mathbf{w}^T\mathbf{x} + b) \geq 1$. This allows the model to focus only on the points that violate the margin, making it more efficient and less susceptible to overfitting.

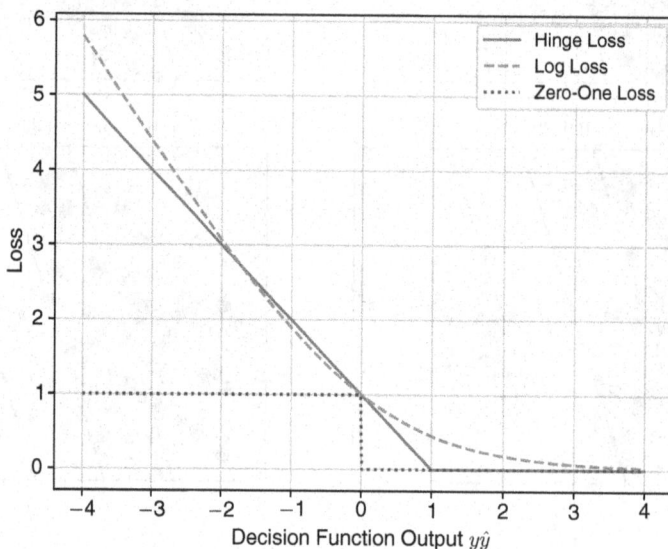

Figure 11.10: Comparison of hinge loss, zero–one loss, and log loss. Hinge loss is piecewise linear, assigning zero loss for correctly classified points that lie outside the margin. Zero–one loss is binary and non-convex, assigning zero loss to any correctly classified point. Log loss is smooth and strictly positive, assigning nonzero loss even to confidently correct predictions, though the penalty decreases as the confidence increases.

Integrating the hinge loss into the primal SVM objective (Equation (11.38)) yields the following unconstrained optimization problem:

$$\min_{\mathbf{w},b} \lambda \frac{\|\mathbf{w}\|^2}{2} + \sum_{i=1}^{n} \max(0, 1 - y_i(\mathbf{w}^T \mathbf{x}_i + b)). \tag{11.51}$$

This objective function consists of two terms:

- A regularization term, $\frac{1}{2}\|\mathbf{w}\|^2$, which penalizes large weights and promotes a wider margin.

- An empirical loss term, $\sum_{i=1}^{n} \max(0, 1 - y_i(\mathbf{w}^T \mathbf{x}_i + b))$, which penalizes margin violations by summing the hinge loss over all training samples.

The regularization coefficient λ controls the tradeoff between maximizing the margin and minimizing margin violations, analogous to the parameter C in the constrained soft-margin SVM formulation. A larger value of λ corresponds to stronger regularization (i.e., smaller C), encouraging a wider margin at the cost of allowing more margin violations.

The resulting objective function is strictly convex, ensuring the existence of a unique global minimum and allowing for efficient optimization using standard techniques such as gradient descent.

In Scikit-Learn, the hinge loss can be optimized using stochastic gradient descent via the SGDClassifier class by setting its loss parameter to 'hinge' (the default setting). The alpha parameter specifies the regularization strength λ; its default value of 0.0001 corresponds to $C = 10,000$ in LinearSVC. See Section 5.4.2 for further details.

Gradient descent offers several advantages for SVM training. It scales well to large datasets, as it avoids the need to compute or store the $n \times n$ matrices required by quadratic programming. It also supports incremental learning, making it suitable for streaming data and distributed computing. On the other hand, it is limited to linear SVMs and cannot directly handle nonlinear classification problems, which require kernel methods and quadratic programming (see Section 11.4). Moreover, convergence depends on careful tuning of the learning rate and can be slow when the problem is ill-conditioned. Lastly, since the hinge loss is not differentiable at the margin, optimization must rely on subgradient methods rather than standard gradient descent.

11.3   Kernel Methods

Kernel methods are a powerful class of techniques in machine learning that enable linear models, such as support vector machines, to handle complex, nonlinear problems [533, 546]. The key idea is to implicitly map the input data into a high-dimensional feature space, where a linear decision boundary can separate data that is not linearly separable in the original input space.

Formally, a **feature mapping** is a function $\phi \colon \mathbb{R}^d \to \mathcal{H}$ that transforms input vectors from the original d-dimensional space into a feature space $\mathcal{H}$, which is typically much higher-dimensional (or even infinite-dimensional).

In the context of nonlinear SVMs, the goal is to find a mapping ϕ such that the transformed data in $\mathcal{H}$ becomes linearly separable, even if it is not linearly separable in $\mathbb{R}^d$. Crucially, this mapping is not computed explicitly, since working directly in the high-dimensional feature space is often computationally expensive or infeasible (e.g., when $\mathcal{H}$ has infinite dimensions). Instead, the **kernel trick** allows us to compute inner products in $\mathcal{H}$ directly from the original input space using a kernel function (see Section 11.3.2), enabling efficient learning in high-dimensional spaces.[11]

11.3.1   Intuition and Motivation

To build intuition for kernel methods, we consider how a simple transformation can enable a linear model to handle data that is not linearly separable in its original input space.

Figure 11.11 shows a synthetic two-dimensional dataset consisting of two concentric circles, generated using the `make_circles`[12] function from Scikit-Learn.

In the original two-dimensional space, the classes are clearly not linearly separable. However, by applying the following mapping to a three-dimensional space, we can make them linearly separable:

$$\phi(x_1, x_2) = (z_1, z_2, z_3) = (x_1, x_2, x_1^2 + x_2^2). \tag{11.52}$$

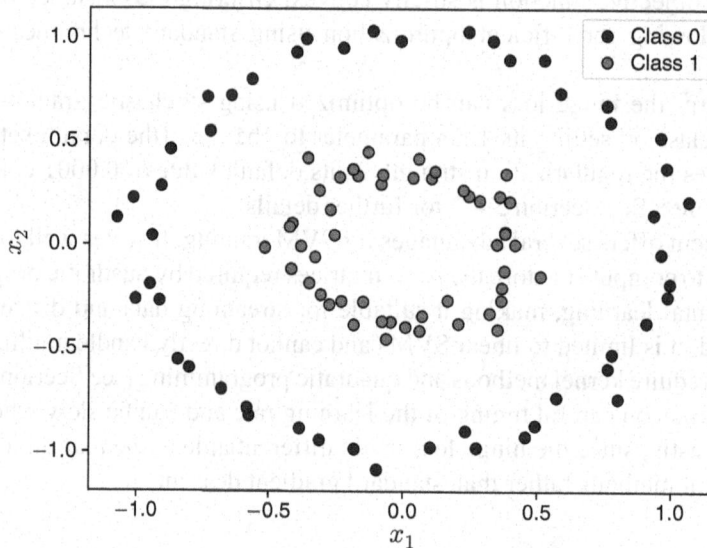

Figure 11.11: A synthetic dataset generated using `make_circles`, illustrating two concentric classes that are not linearly separable in the original input space.

---

11. When $\mathcal{H}$ is finite-dimensional, it is typically a Euclidean space $\mathbb{R}^m$, where the inner product is the standard dot product. In more general cases, $\mathcal{H}$ may be infinite-dimensional—commonly a **Hilbert space**—equipped with a more general inner product. Hilbert spaces generalize Euclidean spaces to infinite dimensions while preserving the structure induced by inner products. For simplicity, we continue to use the dot product notation $\phi(\mathbf{x})^T \phi(\mathbf{z})$ instead of the more general Hilbert space notation $\langle \phi(\mathbf{x}), \phi(\mathbf{z}) \rangle$ for inner products.

12. https://scikit-learn.org/stable/modules/generated/sklearn.datasets.make_circles.html

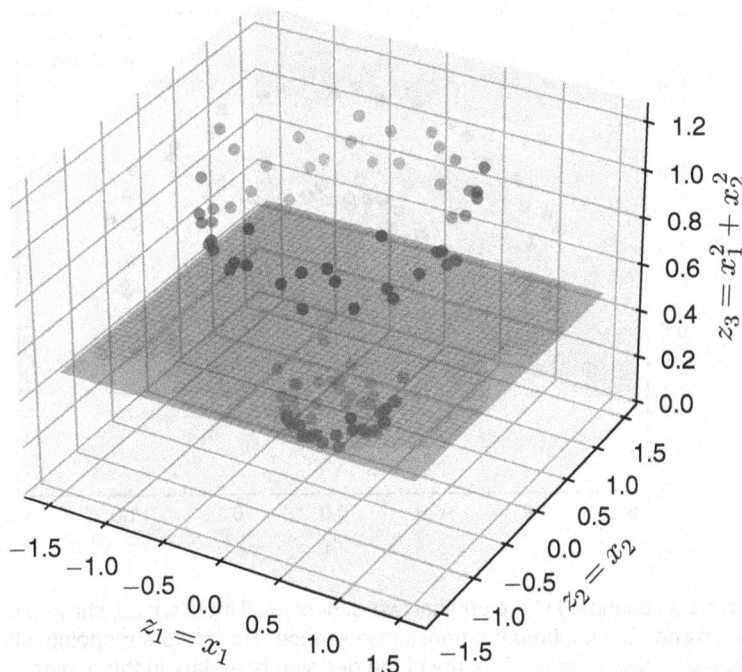

Figure 11.12: The dataset transformed into a three-dimensional space using the mapping $\phi(x_1, x_2) = (x_1, x_2, x_1^2 + x_2^2)$. The plane $z_3 = 0.5$ separates the two classes, illustrating the benefit of lifting the data into a higher-dimensional space.

This transformation introduces a new feature, $z_3 = x_1^2 + x_2^2$, which represents the squared distance of the point (x_1, x_2) from the origin. Since the two classes lie on rings of different radii, they become separable based on their z_3-values. As shown in Figure 11.12, the classes can now be separated by the plane $z_3 = 0.5$ in the transformed space.

When projected back into the original two-dimensional input space, the separating plane $z_3 = 0.5$ represents the equation $x_1^2 + x_2^2 = 0.5$, which defines a circle of radius $\sqrt{0.5} \approx 0.707$. This is illustrated in Figure 11.13, where the decision boundary appears as a dashed circle.

While the previous example used a manually constructed and easily visualizable transformation, identifying a suitable mapping ϕ for real-world datasets is often far more challenging. Moreover, explicitly computing the transformation can be computationally prohibitive, especially when the feature space has very high or even infinite dimensionality.

This is where kernel methods shine: they enable linear algorithms to operate in high-dimensional spaces without explicitly performing the transformation. This technique, known as the kernel trick, is described in the next section.

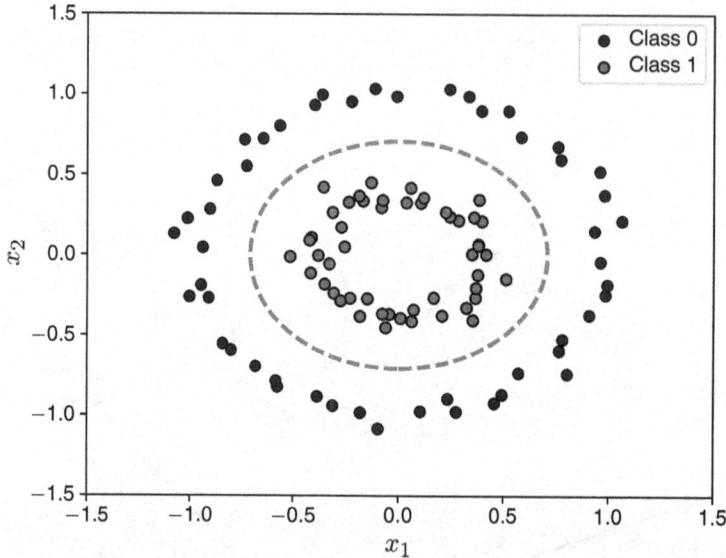

Figure 11.13: The decision boundary in the original two-dimensional input space, shown as a dashed circle, is the projection of the plane $z_3 = 0.5$ from the transformed space. This feature mapping allows a linear model to separate the classes, despite the nonlinearity of the decision boundary in the original space.

11.3.2   The Kernel Trick

Some machine learning algorithms, such as support vector machines (SVMs) and principal component analysis (PCA), rely only on dot products between input vectors, i.e., expressions of the form $\mathbf{x}_i^T \mathbf{x}_j$. In such cases, the **kernel trick** provides a powerful technique to implicitly perform computations in a high-dimensional feature space $\mathcal{H}$, without explicitly computing the mapping $\phi(\mathbf{x})$ or even knowing what ϕ is.

The core idea is to use a **kernel function** $k(\mathbf{x}, \mathbf{z})$ that computes the dot product between the images of two input vectors in the feature space:

$$k(\mathbf{x}, \mathbf{z}) = \phi(\mathbf{x})^T \phi(\mathbf{z}). \qquad (11.53)$$

This kernel function operates directly on the original input vectors $\mathbf{x}$ and $\mathbf{z}$, bypassing the need to compute or represent the feature vectors $\phi(\mathbf{x})$ and $\phi(\mathbf{z})$ explicitly. As a result, the computational cost of evaluating $k(\mathbf{x}, \mathbf{z})$ depends only on the dimensionality of the input space, rather than on the potentially much higher (or even infinite) dimensionality of the feature space.

For example, consider an input vector $\mathbf{x} \in \mathbb{R}^d$, and let $\phi(\mathbf{x})$ denote the feature vector containing all monomials of $\mathbf{x}$ up to degree 3:

$$\phi(\mathbf{x}) = \big(1, \underbrace{x_1, \ldots, x_d}_{\text{degree 1}}, \underbrace{x_1^2, x_1 x_2, \ldots, x_d^2}_{\text{degree 2}}, \underbrace{x_1^3, x_1^2 x_2, \ldots, x_d^3}_{\text{degree 3}}\big)^T.$$

The dimensionality of $\phi(\mathbf{x})$ scales as $\binom{d+3}{3} = \mathcal{O}(d^3)$, which quickly becomes computationally expensive as d grows.

Despite the high dimensionality of the feature space, the dot product $\phi(\mathbf{x})^T \phi(\mathbf{z})$ can be computed efficiently without explicitly constructing the feature vectors. Specifically:

$$
\begin{aligned}
\phi(\mathbf{x})^T \phi(\mathbf{z}) &= 1 + \sum_{i=1}^{d} x_i z_i + \sum_{i,j \in \{1,\ldots,d\}} x_i x_j z_i z_j + \sum_{i,j,k \in \{1,\ldots,d\}} x_i x_j x_k z_i z_j z_k \\
&= 1 + \sum_{i=1}^{d} x_i z_i + \left(\sum_{i=1}^{d} x_i z_i \right)^2 + \left(\sum_{i=1}^{d} x_i z_i \right)^3 \\
&= 1 + \mathbf{x}^T \mathbf{z} + (\mathbf{x}^T \mathbf{z})^2 + (\mathbf{x}^T \mathbf{z})^3.
\end{aligned} \tag{11.54}
$$

This shows that the dot product in the feature space can be expressed entirely in terms of the dot product $\mathbf{x}^T \mathbf{z}$ in the original input space. The corresponding kernel function is known as a **polynomial kernel** of degree 3, defined as:

$$
k(\mathbf{x}, \mathbf{z}) = (1 + \mathbf{x}^T \mathbf{z})^3. \tag{11.55}
$$

Expanding this kernel using the binomial theorem gives:[13]

$$
k(\mathbf{x}, \mathbf{z}) = 1 + 3(\mathbf{x}^T \mathbf{z}) + 3(\mathbf{x}^T \mathbf{z})^2 + (\mathbf{x}^T \mathbf{z})^3. \tag{11.56}
$$

This kernel implicitly computes the dot products between all monomials of degree up to 3 of $\mathbf{x}$ and $\mathbf{z}$, without explicitly constructing the feature vectors.

The computation of $k(\mathbf{x}, \mathbf{z})$ requires only $\mathcal{O}(d)$ operations, in contrast to the $\mathcal{O}(d^3)$ operations needed to compute $\phi(\mathbf{x})^T \phi(\mathbf{z})$ directly. This efficiency illustrates the main benefit of the kernel trick: it enables algorithms to work in high-dimensional feature spaces without incurring the associated computational cost.

11.3.3 Constructing Valid Kernels

To leverage the kernel trick, we must use **valid kernels**—that is, functions that correspond to a dot product in some feature space.

One way to verify that a function is a valid kernel is to explicitly show that it can be expressed as a dot product between two feature-mapped vectors. For example, consider the quadratic kernel:

$$
k(\mathbf{x}, \mathbf{z}) = (\mathbf{x}^T \mathbf{z})^2,
$$

---

13. The coefficients in this expansion differ from those in Equation (11.54), but this does not affect the behavior of the learning algorithm, since the model can learn appropriate weights for the features in the transformed space.

where $\mathbf{x}, \mathbf{z} \in \mathbb{R}^d$. We can expand this function as follows:

$$k(\mathbf{x}, \mathbf{z}) = \left(\sum_{i=1}^{d} x_i z_i \right) \left(\sum_{j=1}^{d} x_j z_j \right)$$

$$= \sum_{i=1}^{d} \sum_{j=1}^{d} x_i x_j z_i z_j$$

$$= \sum_{i=1}^{d} \sum_{j=1}^{d} (x_i x_j)(z_i z_j).$$

This expansion suggests the following feature mapping, which includes all pairwise products of the input features:

$$\phi(\mathbf{x}) = (x_1 x_1, x_1 x_2, \ldots, x_1 x_d, x_2 x_1, \ldots, x_d x_d)^T.$$

Thus, the quadratic kernel can be expressed as the dot product in the feature space:

$$k(\mathbf{x}, \mathbf{z}) = \phi(\mathbf{x})^T \phi(\mathbf{z}),$$

confirming that it is a valid kernel function.

While verifying kernel validity through explicit feature mappings is possible for simple examples, it quickly becomes impractical for more complex kernels or high-dimensional feature spaces. Fortunately, there are general principles that allow us to construct new valid kernels from existing ones, without needing to derive the underlying feature map explicitly.

Specifically, the following operations are guaranteed to preserve kernel validity (see Exercise 11.16):[14]

- **Sum**: If k_1 and k_2 are valid kernels, then their sum $k_1 + k_2$ is also a valid kernel.

- **Product**: If k_1 and k_2 are valid kernels, then their product $k_1 \cdot k_2$ is also a valid kernel.

- **Nonnegative scaling**: If $c > 0$ and k is a valid kernel, then $c \cdot k$ is also a valid kernel.

- **Function of a kernel**: If f is a function whose Taylor expansion has nonnegative coefficients, and k is a valid kernel, then $f(k)$ is also a valid kernel. For example, $\exp(k)$ is valid whenever k is valid.

11.3.4   Mercer's Theorem

Mercer's theorem provides a necessary and sufficient condition for a function to be a valid kernel [417]. It allows us to verify kernel validity using matrix properties—specifically, positive

---

14. For a more comprehensive list of operations that preserve kernel validity, see [533, Chapter 3].

semidefiniteness—without requiring an explicit feature mapping. Before stating the theorem, we first define the concept of a kernel matrix.

Let $k(\mathbf{x}, \mathbf{z})$ be a kernel function, and consider any finite set of points $\{\mathbf{x}_1, \mathbf{x}_2, \ldots, \mathbf{x}_n\} \subset \mathbb{R}^d$. The corresponding **kernel matrix** (also known as the **Gram matrix**) is the $n \times n$ matrix K defined by:

$$K_{ij} = k(\mathbf{x}_i, \mathbf{x}_j) = \phi(\mathbf{x}_i)^T \phi(\mathbf{x}_j).$$

This matrix contains all pairwise dot products in the feature space.

Mercer's theorem can now be stated as follows:

Theorem 11.1 (Mercer). *Let $k \colon \mathbb{R}^d \times \mathbb{R}^d \to \mathbb{R}$ be a symmetric function. Then k is a valid kernel if and only if, for every finite set of points $\{\mathbf{x}_1, \mathbf{x}_2, \ldots, \mathbf{x}_n\} \subset \mathbb{R}^d$, the corresponding kernel matrix $K \in \mathbb{R}^{n \times n}$, defined by $K_{ij} = k(\mathbf{x}_i, \mathbf{x}_j)$, is positive semidefinite.*[15]

Proof. We first prove the "only if" direction of the theorem: if k is a valid kernel, then the corresponding kernel matrix K is positive semidefinite.

Since k is a valid kernel, there exists a mapping ϕ from the input space into a feature space $\mathcal{H}$ such that

$$k(\mathbf{x}, \mathbf{z}) = \phi(\mathbf{x})^T \phi(\mathbf{z}).$$

Then, for any vector $\mathbf{z} \in \mathbb{R}^n$, we have:

$$\mathbf{z}^T K \mathbf{z} = \sum_{i=1}^{n} \sum_{j=1}^{n} z_i z_j \, k(\mathbf{x}_i, \mathbf{x}_j)$$

$$= \sum_{i=1}^{n} \sum_{j=1}^{n} z_i z_j \, \phi(\mathbf{x}_i)^T \phi(\mathbf{x}_j)$$

$$= \left(\sum_{i=1}^{n} z_i \phi(\mathbf{x}_i) \right)^T \left(\sum_{j=1}^{n} z_j \phi(\mathbf{x}_j) \right)$$

$$= \left\| \sum_{i=1}^{n} z_i \phi(\mathbf{x}_i) \right\|^2 \geq 0.$$

Since $\mathbf{z} \in \mathbb{R}^n$ was arbitrary, this shows that K is positive semidefinite.

We now prove the converse: if the kernel matrix K is positive semidefinite, then it can be expressed as a Gram matrix of dot products in some feature space.

---

15. A symmetric matrix $K \in \mathbb{R}^{n \times n}$ is positive semidefinite if $\mathbf{v}^T K \mathbf{v} \geq 0$ for all $\mathbf{v} \in \mathbb{R}^n$.

Since K is symmetric, by the spectral theorem (see Section A.3.15.5) it has an eigendecomposition:

$$K = Q\Lambda Q^T,$$

where $Q \in \mathbb{R}^{n \times n}$ is an orthonormal matrix whose columns are the eigenvectors of K, and Λ is a diagonal matrix with its eigenvalues. Because K is positive semidefinite, all entries of Λ are nonnegative.

We define a feature vector $\phi(\mathbf{x}_i) \in \mathbb{R}^n$ for each point $\mathbf{x}_i$ as follows:

$$\phi(\mathbf{x}_i) = \Lambda^{1/2} Q^T \mathbf{e}_i,$$

where $\mathbf{e}_i \in \mathbb{R}^n$ is the i-th standard basis vector (i.e., a vector with 1 in position i and 0 elsewhere). This defines a mapping from the sample $\{\mathbf{x}_1, \ldots, \mathbf{x}_n\}$ into the Euclidean space $\mathbb{R}^n$, which serves as our feature space for this proof.

Then, the dot product between two feature vectors becomes:

$$\phi(\mathbf{x}_i)^T \phi(\mathbf{x}_j) = \mathbf{e}_i^T Q\Lambda Q^T \mathbf{e}_j = K_{ij}.$$

Thus, K is the Gram matrix of dot products in the feature space $\mathbb{R}^n$. Since this construction applies to any finite set $\{\mathbf{x}_1, \ldots, \mathbf{x}_n\} \subset \mathbb{R}^d$, it follows that k is a valid kernel function. $\qquad \square$

Mercer's theorem allows us to verify the validity of kernels using the properties of positive semidefinite matrices. For example, consider the function

$$k(x, y) = xy + 1,$$

where $x, y \in \mathbb{R}$. To demonstrate that k is a valid kernel, consider a finite set of points $\{x_1, x_2, \ldots, x_n\} \subset \mathbb{R}$. The corresponding kernel matrix K has entries

$$K_{ij} = k(x_i, x_j) = x_i x_j + 1.$$

This matrix can be expressed as the sum of two outer products:

$$K = \mathbf{x}\mathbf{x}^T + \mathbf{1}\mathbf{1}^T,$$

where $\mathbf{x} = (x_1, x_2, \ldots, x_n)^T$ and $\mathbf{1} \in \mathbb{R}^n$ is the all-ones vector.

Every outer product of a vector with itself is positive semidefinite. For example, the outer product $\mathbf{x}\mathbf{x}^T$ satisfies, for any $\mathbf{v} \in \mathbb{R}^n$:

$$\mathbf{v}^T (\mathbf{x}\mathbf{x}^T)\mathbf{v} = (\mathbf{v}^T\mathbf{x})(\mathbf{x}^T\mathbf{v}) = (\mathbf{v}^T\mathbf{x})^2 \geq 0.$$

The same holds for $\mathbf{1}\mathbf{1}^T$. Since the sum of two positive semidefinite matrices is also positive semidefinite, it follows that K is positive semidefinite. This can be verified directly:

$$\mathbf{v}^T K \mathbf{v} = \mathbf{v}^T (\mathbf{x}\mathbf{x}^T + \mathbf{1}\mathbf{1}^T)\mathbf{v} = (\mathbf{v}^T\mathbf{x})^2 + (\mathbf{v}^T\mathbf{1})^2 \geq 0.$$

Thus, $k(x, y) = xy + 1$ is a valid kernel by Mercer's theorem.

On the other hand, the function $k(x, y) = x - y$ is not a valid kernel, because the resulting kernel matrix is not symmetric (since $x - y \neq y - x$ in general). Symmetry is a necessary condition for a matrix to be positive semidefinite, and thus for a function to be a valid kernel.

11.3.5 Common Kernels

Several kernel functions are commonly used in machine learning to allow linear models to capture nonlinear relationships by implicitly mapping the input data into higher-dimensional spaces:

- **Polynomial kernels**: Polynomial kernels enable models to learn decision boundaries that are polynomial functions of the input features. They are defined as:

$$k(\mathbf{x}, \mathbf{z}) = (\gamma \mathbf{x}^T \mathbf{z} + c)^d, \tag{11.57}$$

  where:

  - d specifies the degree of the polynomial.
  - $\gamma > 0$ is a scaling factor that adjusts the magnitude of the input features before the polynomial expansion. A larger γ magnifies the contribution of the nonlinear terms in the transformed feature space, allowing the model to capture finer distinctions between inputs. Conversely, a smaller γ suppresses these terms, resulting in a transformation that behaves more linearly.

    For example, in a degree-2 polynomial kernel,

$$k(\mathbf{x}, \mathbf{z}) = (\gamma \mathbf{x}^T \mathbf{z})^2,$$

    setting $\gamma = 10$ amplifies the second-order terms by a factor of 100 (due to the square), increasing model complexity. In contrast, $\gamma = 0.1$ suppresses these terms by a factor of 0.01.
  - $c \geq 0$ is a constant that allows the inclusion of lower-degree terms. When $c = 0$, the kernel includes only terms of exact degree d. Setting $c > 0$ introduces additional lower-degree components into the expansion, which enable the model to capture both high-order and low-order interactions.

    For example, with $d = 2$, the kernel expands as:

$$k(\mathbf{x}, \mathbf{z}) = (\gamma \mathbf{x}^T \mathbf{z} + c)^2 = \gamma^2 (\mathbf{x}^T \mathbf{z})^2 + 2\gamma c (\mathbf{x}^T \mathbf{z}) + c^2,$$

    which includes quadratic, linear, and constant terms.

  The **linear kernel** is a special case of the polynomial kernel with $d = 1$, $\gamma = 1$, and $c = 0$. In this case, the kernel reduces to the standard dot product:

$$k(\mathbf{x}, \mathbf{z}) = \mathbf{x}^T \mathbf{z}.$$

- **Radial basis function (RBF) kernels**: Also known as **Gaussian kernels**, RBF kernels are among the most widely used kernels in machine learning due to their flexibility and strong empirical performance across a wide range of tasks. They are defined as:

$$k(\mathbf{x}, \mathbf{z}) = \exp(-\gamma \|\mathbf{x} - \mathbf{z}\|^2), \tag{11.58}$$

where $\|\mathbf{x} - \mathbf{z}\|$ is the Euclidean distance between the input vectors, and $\gamma > 0$ is a parameter that controls the width (or spread) of the kernel.

The RBF kernel has several important properties:

- Nonparametric behavior: Unlike polynomial kernels, which impose a fixed algebraic structure on feature interactions, the RBF kernel is nonparameteric—it does not assume any specific functional form. Instead, it is defined entirely by distances between inputs, allowing it to flexibly adapt to a wide range of patterns in the data.

- Locality: Each data point primarily influences its surrounding region, making the RBF kernel well-suited for capturing smooth, localized structures.

- Smoothness control: The parameter γ determines how rapidly the kernel value decays with distance. A larger γ results in a narrower kernel, emphasizing local interactions and making the model more sensitive to nearby data points. Conversely, a smaller γ produces a wider kernel, allowing each data point to influence a broader region. Figure 11.14 shows how the kernel value varies with Euclidean distance for different γ values.

- Infinite-dimensional feature mapping: The RBF kernel implicitly maps input vectors to an infinite-dimensional feature space. This allows models to construct highly flexible, nonlinear decision boundaries without explicitly computing the transformed features.

- Distance-based similarity: The RBF kernel assigns higher values to inputs that are close together in the original space, and lower values to those that are far apart. This aligns well with the intuition that similar inputs should produce similar predictions.

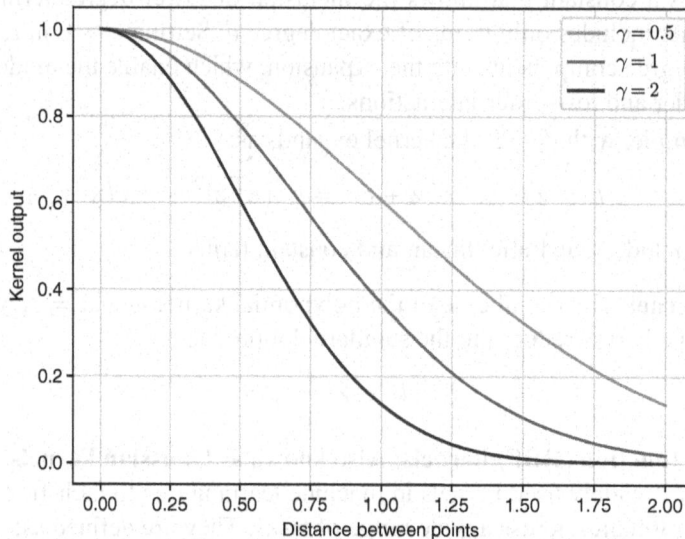

Figure 11.14: Effects of varying γ on the RBF kernel. Higher γ values cause the kernel value to decay more sharply with distance, focusing the kernel's influence on nearby points. Conversely, lower γ values lead to a more gradual decay, allowing each point to influence a broader region.

- Universal approximator: The RBF kernel is universal, meaning that with appropriate parameters, it can approximate any continuous function on a compact domain arbitrarily well. This property gives it strong theoretical expressive power.

- **Sigmoid kernels**: Inspired by neural networks, these kernels produce S-shaped, bounded outputs that resemble the activation used in the output of a two-layer perceptron. The sigmoid kernel is defined as:

$$k(\mathbf{x}, \mathbf{z}) = \tanh(\gamma \mathbf{x}^T \mathbf{z} + c), \tag{11.59}$$

where γ controls the slope of the function and c acts as a bias term, shifting the function and influencing the position of the decision boundary.

Unlike polynomial and RBF kernels, the sigmoid kernel is not always valid: certain values of γ and c can produce a kernel matrix that is not positive semidefinite. This can violate the assumptions of kernel-based methods like SVMs, potentially leading to instability or suboptimal results.

In addition to these commonly used kernels, more specialized or domain-specific kernels have been developed. For example, string kernels measure similarity based on common substrings and are useful for text data [375], while graph kernels are designed for learning tasks involving structured graph data [602].

11.4 Nonlinear SVM

Nonlinear SVMs, also known as **kernel SVMs**, extend linear SVMs to handle datasets that are not linearly separable in the original input space. They achieve this by implicitly mapping the input vectors into a higher-dimensional feature space, where a linear (or approximately linear) decision boundary may exist, and then solving the linear SVM optimization problem in that space. This is made efficient through the kernel trick, which allows the algorithm to compute dot products in the feature space without explicitly constructing the mapped vectors.

Formally, let $\phi \colon \mathbb{R}^d \to \mathcal{H}$ denote a mapping from the input space into a feature space $\mathcal{H}$. In that space, a separating hyperplane takes the form

$$\mathbf{w}^T \phi(\mathbf{x}) + b = 0. \tag{11.60}$$

To find the optimal soft-margin hyperplane in the feature space, we solve the the dual optimization problem (cf. Equation (11.44)):

$$\max_{\boldsymbol{\alpha}} \quad \sum_{i=1}^{n} \alpha_i - \frac{1}{2} \sum_{i=1}^{n} \sum_{j=1}^{n} \alpha_i \alpha_j y_i y_j \phi(\mathbf{x}_i)^T \phi(\mathbf{x}_j),$$

$$\text{subject to} \quad 0 \le \alpha_i \le C, \quad i = 1, \ldots, n, \tag{11.61}$$

$$\sum_{i=1}^{n} \alpha_i y_i = 0.$$

This dual formulation depends only on dot products of the form $\phi(\mathbf{x}_i)^T\phi(\mathbf{x}_j)$, which can be computed efficiently using a suitable kernel function. Let $k(\mathbf{x}, \mathbf{z})$ denote such a function. By substituting the kernel in place of the dot product, the dual optimization problem becomes:

$$\max_{\boldsymbol{\alpha}} \quad \sum_{i=1}^{n}\alpha_i - \frac{1}{2}\sum_{i=1}^{n}\sum_{j=1}^{n}\alpha_i\alpha_j y_i y_j k(\mathbf{x}_i, \mathbf{x}_j),$$

$$\text{subject to} \quad 0 \le \alpha_i \le C, \quad i = 1, \ldots, n, \tag{11.62}$$

$$\sum_{i=1}^{n}\alpha_i y_i = 0.$$

In matrix notation, the dual problem can be written more compactly as:

$$\max_{\boldsymbol{\alpha}} \quad \mathbf{1}^T\boldsymbol{\alpha} - \frac{1}{2}\boldsymbol{\alpha}^T Y K Y \boldsymbol{\alpha},$$

$$\text{subject to} \quad 0 \le \alpha_i \le C, \quad i = 1, \ldots, n, \tag{11.63}$$

$$\mathbf{y}^T\boldsymbol{\alpha} = 0,$$

where K is the kernel matrix with entries $K_{ij} = k(\mathbf{x}_i, \mathbf{x}_j)$, and Y is a diagonal matrix with the class labels y_i along the diagonal. This optimization problem can be efficiently solved using standard quadratic programming (QP) solvers.

After determining the optimal Lagrange multipliers $\boldsymbol{\alpha}$, we can recover the weight vector $\mathbf{w}$ of the separating hyperplane in the feature space as a linear combination of the support vectors (cf. Equation (11.40)):

$$\mathbf{w} = \sum_{i\in\mathcal{S}}\alpha_i y_i \phi(\mathbf{x}_i), \tag{11.64}$$

where $\mathcal{S}$ denotes the set of support vectors.

The bias term b is computed by averaging over the support vectors that lie exactly on the margin (i.e., those with $0 < \alpha_i < C$; cf. Equation (11.49)):

$$b = \frac{1}{|\mathcal{S}_m|}\sum_{i\in\mathcal{S}_m}\left(y_i - \mathbf{w}^T\phi(\mathbf{x}_i)\right). \tag{11.65}$$

Substituting the expression for $\mathbf{w}$ into the equation above yields:

$$b = \frac{1}{|\mathcal{S}_m|}\sum_{i\in\mathcal{S}_m}\left(y_i - \sum_{j=1}^{n}\alpha_j y_j \phi(\mathbf{x}_j)^T\phi(\mathbf{x}_i)\right). \tag{11.66}$$

This shows that b can be computed using only dot products between feature-mapped vectors.

To classify a new input $\mathbf{x}$, we evaluate the sign of the decision function in the feature space:

$$h(\mathbf{x}) = \text{sign}(\mathbf{w}^T\phi(\mathbf{x}) + b) = \text{sign}\left(\sum_{i=1}^{n}\alpha_i y_i \phi(\mathbf{x}_i)^T\phi(\mathbf{x}) + b\right). \tag{11.67}$$

Since the prediction depends only on dot products between the test point $\mathbf{x}$ and the support vectors, all of which can be computed using the kernel function $k(\mathbf{x}_i, \mathbf{x})$, there is no need to explicitly compute the mapping $\phi(\mathbf{x})$. This is the essence of the *kernel trick*: both training and prediction are carried out entirely through kernel evaluations.

11.4.1 The svc Class

In Scikit-Learn, kernel-based support vector machines are implemented using the svc class. This class supports both standard kernels (see Section 11.3.5) and custom user-defined kernels. The key parameters of this class are listed in Table 11.2.

In addition, the svc class provides several attributes for inspecting the fitted model:

- dual_coef_: Dual coefficients of the support vectors, equal to $\alpha_i y_i$ for each support vector.

- intercept_: The bias term b in the decision function.

- n_iter_: Number of iterations the solver ran before converging.

- support_: Indices of the support vectors in the training set.

- support_vectors_: An array of shape (n_{SV}, d) containing the support vectors, where n_{SV} is the number of support vectors and d is the number of features.

Parameter	Description	Default
c	Regularization parameter controlling the tradeoff between maximizing the margin and minimizing classification error.	1.0
kernel	Specifies the kernel type. Options: 'linear', 'poly', 'rbf', 'sigmoid', 'precomputed' (for a user-supplied kernel matrix), or a callable function.	'rbf'
degree	Degree of the polynomial kernel function (used only if kernel='poly').	3
gamma	Kernel coefficient γ for the polynomial, RBF, or sigmoid kernels. Options: 'scale' ($\gamma = 1/(d \cdot \mathrm{Var}(X))$), 'auto' ($\gamma = 1/d$), or a float.	'scale'
coef0	The independent term c used in polynomial and sigmoid kernels.	0.0
max_iter	Maximum number of iterations for the solver to converge (-1 indicates no limit).	-1
probability	Whether to enable probability estimates via Platt scaling, fitted using an internal 5-fold cross-validation.	False
class_weight	Class weights for handling imbalanced datasets. Options: 'balanced' or a dictionary mapping class labels to weights.	None

Table 11.2: Key parameters of the svc class

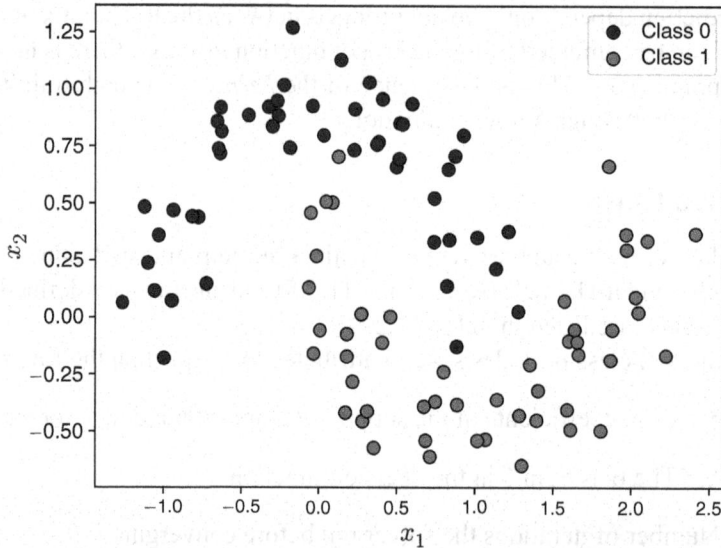

Figure 11.15: Synthetic dataset generated using make_moons, consisting of two interleaving classes in a crescent moon shape. This nonlinear dataset highlights the limitations of linear classifiers and demonstrates the effectiveness of kernel-based methods.

For example, let's apply the SVC class with different kernels to the moons dataset, which consists of two interleaving half moons. We begin by generating the dataset using the make_moons[16] function from Scikit-Learn:

```
from sklearn.datasets import make_moons

X, y = make_moons(n_samples=100, noise=0.15, random_state=42)
```

Figure 11.15 shows the resulting dataset. Next, we split the dataset into training and test sets:

```
from sklearn.model_selection import train_test_split

X_train, X_test, y_train, y_test = train_test_split(X, y, test_size=0.3,
                                                    random_state=42)
```

Although the features in this dataset are on a similar scale, applying feature scaling can improve both numerical stability and model performance, especially since input scaling affects the geometry of the feature space and the similarity computed by the kernel. We use StandardScaler to standardize the features:

```
from sklearn.preprocessing import StandardScaler
scaler = StandardScaler()
```

16. https://scikit-learn.org/stable/modules/generated/sklearn.datasets.make_moons.html

```
X_train_scaled = scaler.fit_transform(X_train)
X_test_scaled = scaler.transform(X_test)
```

We then configure and train four SVM classifiers, each using a different kernel: `linear`, `poly`, `rbf`, and `sigmoid`. All other parameters are left at their default values:

```
from sklearn.svm import SVC

# Create SVM models with different kernels
kernels = ['linear', 'poly', 'rbf', 'sigmoid']
models = []
for kernel in kernels:
    model = SVC(kernel=kernel)
    model.fit(X_train_scaled, y_train)
    models.append((kernel, model))
```

Note that the `SVC` class does not require a random seed, as the underlying `LIBSVM` implementation is deterministic. The `random_state` parameter is ignored unless `probability=True` is specified to enable probability estimates.

Let's plot the decision boundaries found by each SVM model along with their test accuracy:

```
# Plot decision boundaries
fig, axes = plt.subplots(2, 2, figsize=(10, 10))
for (kernel, model), ax in zip(models, axes.flat):
    ax.set_title(f'{kernel} kernel')
    plot_svm_decision_boundary(model, X_train_scaled, y_train, ax=ax, legend=False)

    # Calculate and display test accuracy
    test_accuracy = model.score(X_test_scaled, y_test)
    ax.text(0.05, 0.95, f'Test Accuracy: {test_accuracy:.3f}', transform=ax.transAxes,
            verticalalignment='top', bbox=dict(boxstyle='round', facecolor='white',
            alpha=0.5))
```

Figure 11.16 shows the decision boundaries produced by each kernel. The RBF kernel achieves the best results on this dataset, reaching 96.7% accuracy on the test set. Its flexibility and ability to adapt to local patterns enable it to capture the intricate, nonlinear structure of the two interleaving half-moons.

The polynomial kernel performs similarly to the linear kernel. While it can model some curvature, its fixed degree limits its expressiveness, making it less suitable for complex decision boundaries. The sigmoid kernel performs worst, producing decision boundaries that are overly steep or poorly aligned with the data's structure.

This example highlights the importance of selecting an appropriate kernel when using nonlinear SVMs. Each kernel imposes a different structure on the feature space and induces a distinct type of decision boundaries, which can significantly affect the model's ability to generalize to unseen data.

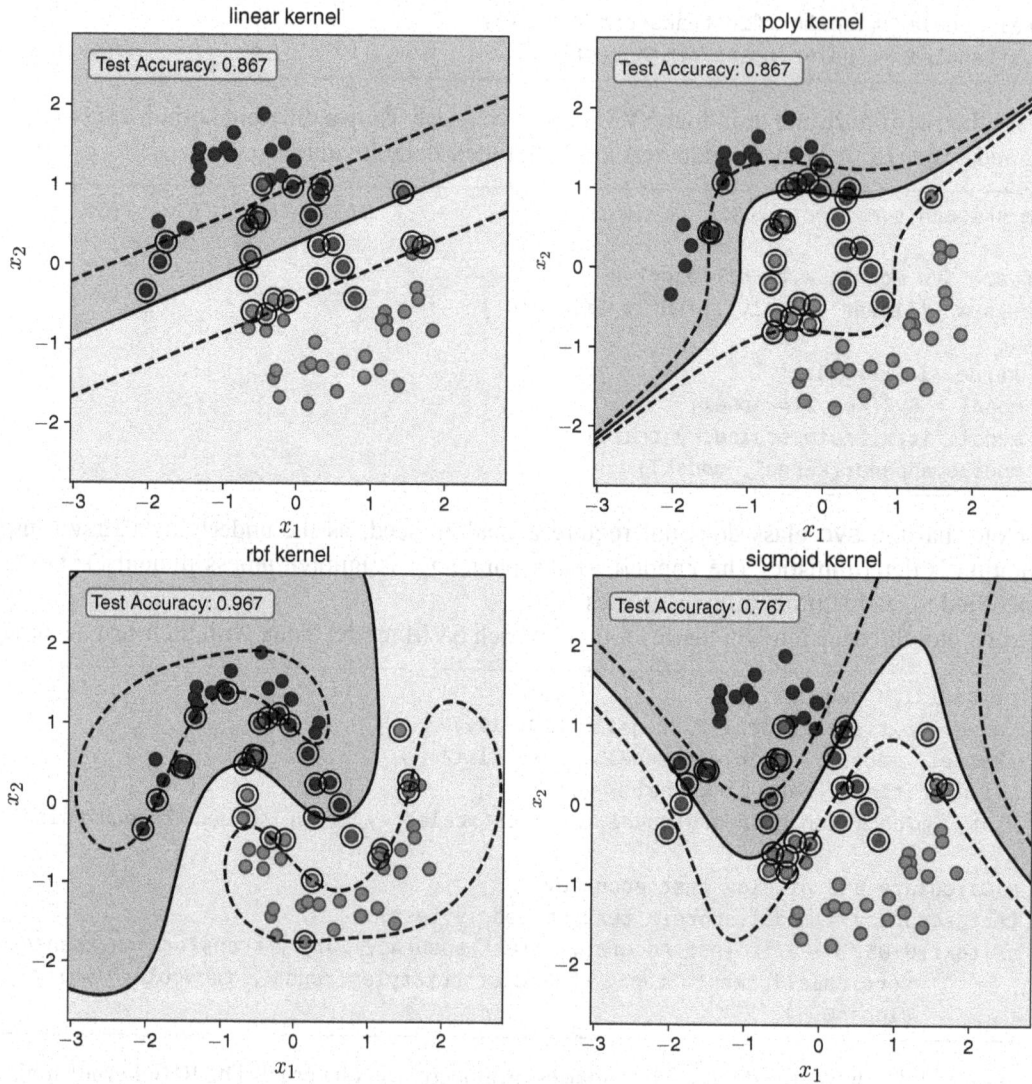

Figure 11.16: Comparison of decision boundaries for SVM models with different kernels on the moons dataset. Each subplot shows the decision boundary (solid lines), margins (dashed lines), classified regions (shaded areas), and support vectors (indicated by circles). The RBF kernel achieves the highest test accuracy (96.7%), demonstrating its ability to adapt to complex, nonlinear patterns. The polynomial and linear kernels perform similarly (86.7%), with the polynomial kernel capturing some curvature but still lacking the flexibility of the RBF kernel. The sigmoid kernel performs the worst (76.7%), producing decision boundaries that are poorly aligned with the data distribution.

11.4.2 Hyperparameter Tuning

Support vector machines are highly sensitive to the choice of hyperparameters, particularly the regularization parameter C, the kernel type, and kernel-specific parameters such as the polynomial degree (for polynomial kernels) and γ (for RBF and other kernels).

These parameters play a crucial role in controlling the bias–variance tradeoff. For example, γ controls the locality of the kernel function: higher values make the decision boundary more sensitive to nearby points, potentially resulting in complex boundaries that closely fit the training data. Conversely, lower values spread each point's influence more broadly, producing smoother boundaries that may generalize better but risk underfitting by overlooking important local patterns.

Let's examine how varying the value of γ affects the model's behavior for $\gamma = 0.01, 0.1, 1, 10$. The following code trains multiple SVM models with the RBF kernel, each using a different γ value, and visualizes their decision boundaries along with test accuracy:

```
fig, axes = plt.subplots(2, 2, figsize=(10, 10))

gamma_values = [0.01, 0.1, 1, 10]
for gamma, ax in zip(gamma_values, axes.flat):
    ax.set_title(f'$\gamma = {gamma}$')

    # Train SVM with the specified gamma value
    model = SVC(kernel='rbf', gamma=gamma)
    model.fit(X_train_scaled, y_train)

    # Plot the decision boundaries
    plot_svm_decision_boundary(model, X_train_scaled, y_train, ax=ax, legend=False)

    # Calculate and display test accuracy
    test_accuracy = model.score(X_test_scaled, y_test)
    n_support_vectors = len(model.support_vectors_)
    ax.text(0.05, 0.95, f'Test Accuracy: {test_accuracy:.3f}', transform=ax.transAxes,
            verticalalignment='top', bbox=dict(boxstyle='round', facecolor='white',
            alpha=0.5))
```

Figure 11.17 shows the resulting decision boundaries. As γ increases, the margin in the high-dimensional feature space becomes narrower, which is reflected in the reduced spacing between the dashed lines, representing the "positive" and "negative" hyperplanes defined by $\mathbf{w}^T \phi(\mathbf{x}) + b = \pm 1$. This narrowing causes the model to fit more tightly to individual data points, leading to increasingly complex decision boundaries in the input space and a higher risk of overfitting.

Conversely, when γ is low, the decision boundary becomes overly smooth and nearly linear, making it too simplistic to capture the data's nonlinear structure. At $\gamma = 1$ (the default value in Scikit-Learn), the model achieves a good balance, producing a decision boundary that effectively captures the underlying structure of the data without overfitting or underfitting.

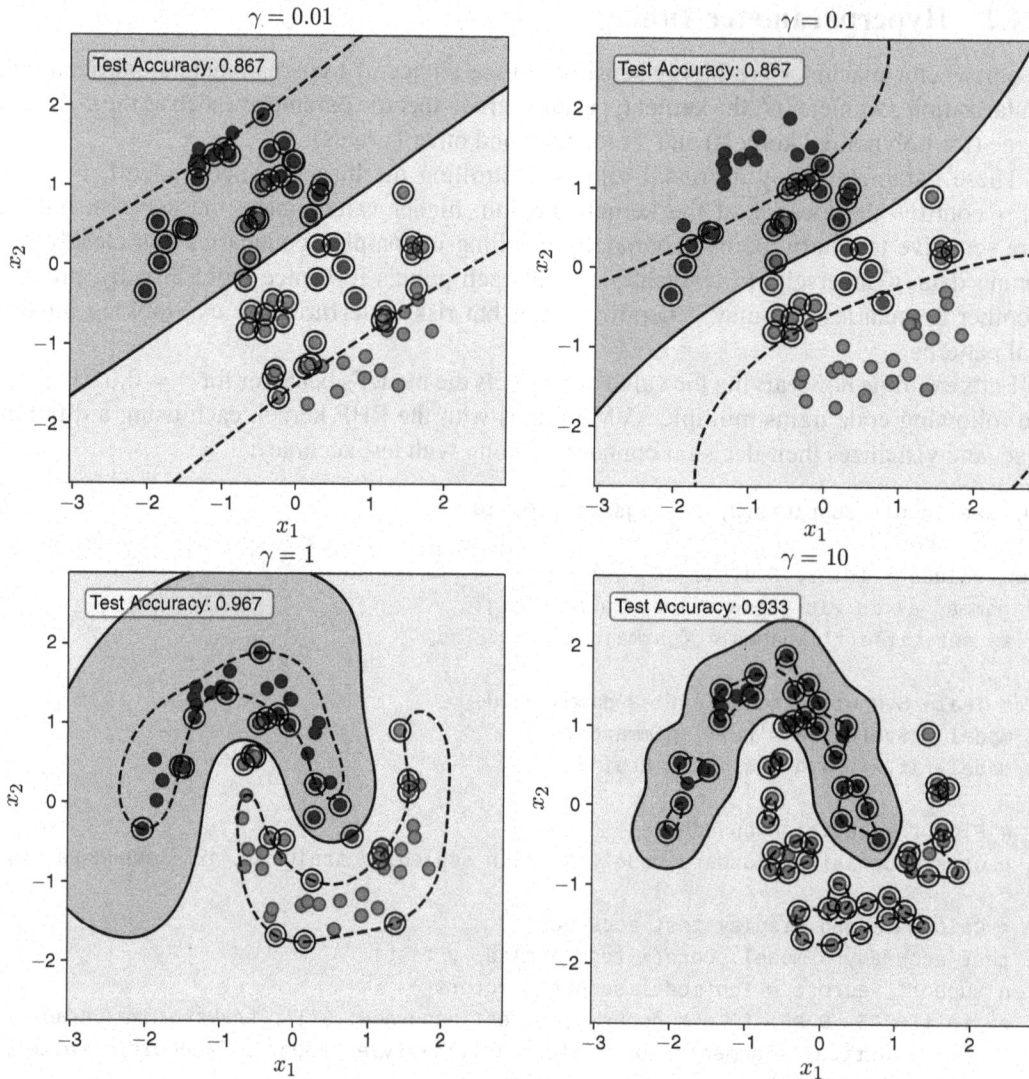

Figure 11.17: Decision boundaries of SVM with an RBF kernel for varying γ values on the moons dataset. As γ increases, the decision boundary becomes tighter around individual data points, increasing sensitivity to noise and the risk of overfitting. Conversely, lower γ values lead to smoother, more generalized boundaries that may underfit the data. In this experiment, the best generalization occurs at $\gamma = 1$, which achieves the highest test accuracy (96.7%).

Typically, SVM hyperparameters are tuned using automated search methods such as grid search or randomized search in order to achieve a good balance between bias and variance. For regularization parameters such as C and γ, it is common to use logarithmically spaced values (e.g., [0.01, 0.1, 1, 10]), as they span several orders of magnitude and efficiently explore both low and high regularization regimes.

In the following example, we use a randomized search to tune key hyperparameters, including the kernel type, regularization parameter (C), and kernel-specific parameters:

```python
from sklearn.model_selection import RandomizedSearchCV

params = {
    'kernel': ['linear', 'poly', 'rbf', 'sigmoid'],
    'C': [0.1, 1, 10, 100],
    'gamma': ['scale', 'auto', 0.01, 0.1, 1, 10, 100],
    'coef0': [0, 0.5, 1, 10],
    'degree': [2, 3, 4, 5]
}
random_search = RandomizedSearchCV(SVC(), params, n_iter=50, cv=3,
                                   random_state=42, n_jobs=-1)
random_search.fit(X_train, y_train)
print(random_search.best_params_)
```

The best hyperparameters found are:

```python
{'kernel': 'rbf', 'gamma': 10, 'degree': 3, 'coef0': 1, 'C': 1}
```

The performance of the model with these settings is:

```python
print(f'Training accuracy: {random_search.score(X_train, y_train):.4f}')
print(f'Test accuracy: {random_search.score(X_test, y_test):.4f}')
```

```
Training accuracy: 1.0000
Test accuracy: 0.9667
```

Interestingly, the best model found by randomized search achieves the same test accuracy as the earlier RBF model with default parameters (C=1 and gamma='scale'). This shows that SVC's default settings often perform well—especially on low-dimensional datasets with relatively simple structure and limited noise.

11.5 ν-SVM

ν-SVM, proposed by Schölkopf et al. (2000) [534], is an alternative formulation of the soft-margin SVM in which the regularization parameter C is replaced with a new parameter $\nu \in (0, 1]$. This formulation provides a more direct and interpretable way to control the tradeoff between margin violations and model complexity.

The parameter ν has a dual interpretation:

- It specifies an upper bound on the fraction of margin violations.

- It specifies a lower bound on the fraction of support vectors.

This dual role makes ν more interpretable than C, as it enables practitioners to directly express the desired tolerance for misclassification and the sparsity of the decision function. A larger value of ν permits more margin violations, allowing for greater flexibility but potentially resulting in more support vectors (and hence a more complex model). Conversely, a smaller ν limits the number of support vectors, which may improve interpretability and reduce prediction time, but increases the risk of underfitting complex datasets.

The dual optimization problem for ν-SVM is given by:

$$
\max_{\boldsymbol{\alpha}} \quad -\frac{1}{2} \sum_{i=1}^{n} \sum_{j=1}^{n} \alpha_i \alpha_j y_i y_j \phi(\mathbf{x}_i)^T \phi(\mathbf{x}_j),
$$

$$
\text{subject to} \quad 0 \leq \alpha_i \leq \frac{1}{n}, \quad i = 1, \ldots, n,
$$

$$
\sum_{i=1}^{n} \alpha_i y_i = 0, \tag{11.68}
$$

$$
\sum_{i=1}^{n} \alpha_i \geq \nu.
$$

Compared with the dual form of the standard C-SVM (Equation (11.61)), the ν-SVM formulation introduces two key differences:

- The linear term $\sum_{i=1}^{n} \alpha_i$ is absent from the objective function, resulting in a purely quadratic form. This typically leads to a more uniform optimization landscape and improved numerical stability.

- The additional constraint $\sum_{i=1}^{n} \alpha_i \geq \nu$ enforces that at least a fraction ν of the training points become support vectors. In this formulation, support vectors satisfy $0 < \alpha_i \leq 1/n$: points with $\alpha_i = 1/n$ lie exactly on the margin, while those with $0 < \alpha_i < 1/n$ correspond to margin violations.

In Scikit-Learn, the ν-SVC algorithm is implemented by the NuSVC class. This class supports the same kernel types as the SVC class and shares many of its parameters. The primary distinction lies in the regularization scheme: NuSVC uses the parameter nu (default: 0.5) instead of C to control the tradeoff between margin width and classification errors.

To explore the effect of different ν values, we train multiple NuSVC models on the moons dataset using $\nu \in \{0.1, 0.3, 0.5, 0.7\}$. The code below plots the resulting decision boundaries and annotates each subplot with the corresponding test accuracy and number of support vectors:

```
from sklearn.svm import NuSVC

fig, axes = plt.subplots(2, 2, figsize=(10, 10))

nu_values = [0.1, 0.3, 0.5, 0.7]
for nu, ax in zip(nu_values, axes.flat):
    ax.set_title(f'$\\nu = {nu}$')
```

```
# Train NuSVC with the current nu value
model = NuSVC(nu=nu, kernel='rbf')
model.fit(X_train_scaled, y_train)

# Plot the decision boundary
plot_svm_decision_boundary(model, X_train_scaled, y_train, ax=ax, legend=False)

# Calculate test accuracy and number of support vectors
test_accuracy = model.score(X_test_scaled, y_test)
n_support_vectors = len(model.support_vectors_)

ax.text(0.5, 0.01, f'Test Acc: {test_accuracy:.3f}\n#SV: {n_support_vectors}',
        ha='center', va='bottom', transform=ax.transAxes, fontsize=9,
        bbox=dict(boxstyle='round', facecolor='white', alpha=0.5))
```

Figure 11.18 shows the results. As illustrated, increasing ν leads to wider margins in feature space, allowing more margin violations and resulting in a larger number of support vectors. This produces smoother, less complex decision boundaries in input space. This behavior is analogous to decreasing C in standard C-SVM, which also increases the model's tolerance for margin violations and promotes better generalization.

The highest test accuracy is achieved at intermediate values of ν (0.3 or 0.5). Notably, the model with $\nu = 0.3$ uses fewer support vectors (26 vs. 38), leading to a more compact representation and faster prediction times.

11.6   Support Vector Regression (SVR)

Support vector regression (SVR) extends the support vector machine framework to regression tasks [173, 554].

Like linear regression, SVR seeks a linear function $h(\mathbf{x}) = \mathbf{w}^T\mathbf{x} + b$ that approximates the target values. However, instead of minimizing the squared error, SVR introduces a **tolerance parameter** ϵ that defines a margin of acceptable error around the predicted values.

Specifically, SVR aims to find a function that fits the data such that deviations from the true values are no greater than ϵ for as many training points as possible. This defines a margin of width 2ϵ, centered around the regression function $h(\mathbf{x})$, known as the **ϵ-tube** or **ϵ-insensitive region** (see Figure 11.19). Errors that fall within this tube are considered negligible and do not contribute to the loss. Only predictions that deviate from the true values by more than ϵ are penalized.

In the **soft-margin** formulation of SVR, violations of the ϵ-tube are allowed but penalized, enabling the model to tolerate noise or outliers. In contrast, the **hard-margin** formulation strictly prohibits any such violations.

SVR is especially useful in applications where large prediction errors are costly or potentially dangerous, such as in safety-critical systems. In such applications, avoiding large deviations beyond a specified error tolerance is often more important than minimizing the average prediction error.

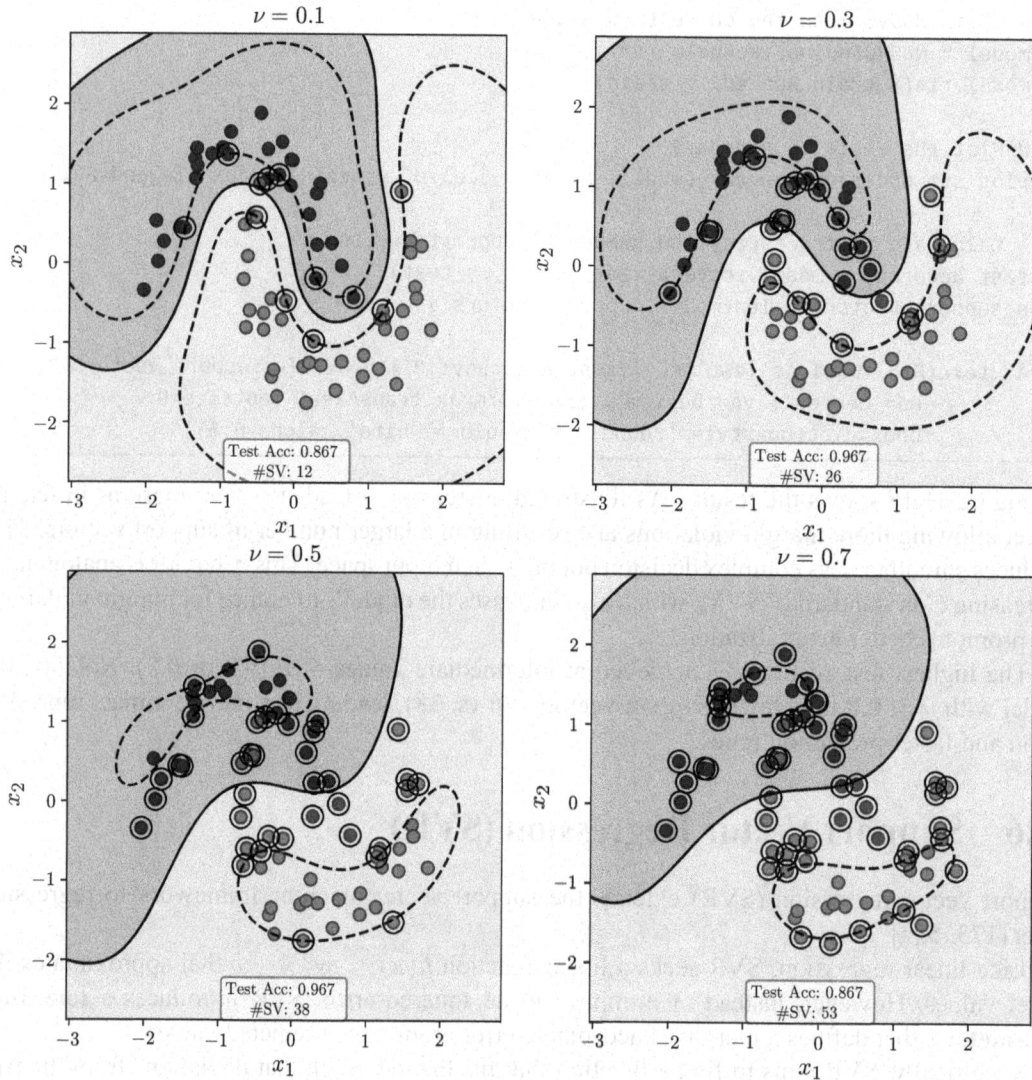

Figure 11.18: Decision boundaries of ν-SVM with an RBF kernel on the moons dataset for different ν values. Increasing ν leads to wider margins, more margin violations, and a larger number of support vectors (denoted by #SV). Intermediate values ($\nu = 0.3$ or $\nu = 0.5$) achieve the highest test accuracy, with $\nu = 0.3$ yielding fewer support vectors and a more efficient solution.

The **hard-margin SVR** optimization problem can be formulated as follows:

$$\min_{\mathbf{w}, b} \quad \frac{1}{2} \|\mathbf{w}\|^2,$$

$$\text{subject to} \quad y_i - \mathbf{w}^T \mathbf{x}_i - b \leq \epsilon, \quad i = 1, \ldots, n,$$

$$\mathbf{w}^T \mathbf{x}_i + b - y_i \leq \epsilon, \quad i = 1, \ldots, n. \tag{11.69}$$

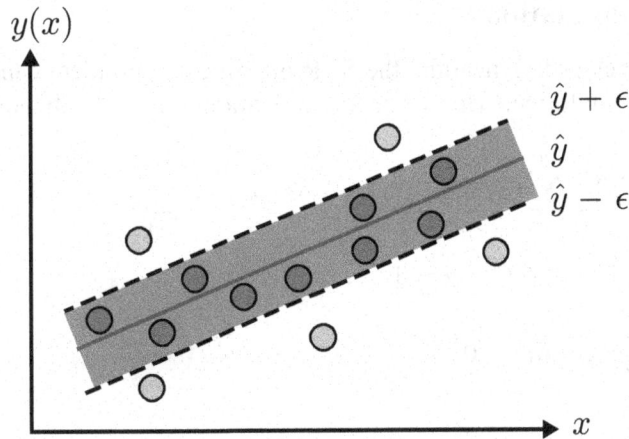

Figure 11.19: Illustration of the ϵ-tube in support vector regression. The solid line represents the predicted values $\hat{y} = h(\mathbf{x})$, while the dashed lines $\hat{y} + \epsilon$ and $\hat{y} - \epsilon$ define the bounds of the ϵ-tube. Points inside the tube fall within the acceptable error margin and incur no penalty. Points outside the tube violate the margin and are penalized in the soft-margin formulation or disallowed in the hard-margin formulation.

The objective has two components: minimizing $\|\mathbf{w}\|^2$ and ensuring that all predictions fall within the ϵ-tube. Minimizing $\|\mathbf{w}\|^2$ encourages the regression function $h(\mathbf{x}) = \mathbf{w}^T\mathbf{x}$ to change more gradually with respect to the input, as $\|\mathbf{w}\|$ controls the steepness of the function (in one-dimensional space, it corresponds to the absolute value of the slope; in higher dimensions, it represents the magnitude of the gradient vector). This promotes flatter functions that are less sensitive to noise and generalize better to unseen data.

The hard-margin formulation assumes that all training samples can be fit within the ϵ-tube. However, this is often unrealistic in practice due to noise, outliers, or model limitations. To allow violations of the tube, the **soft-margin SVR** introduces slack variables ξ_i and $\hat{\xi}_i$, which quantify the extent to which predictions fall below or above the ϵ-tube, respectively.

The resulting optimization problem is:

$$\min_{\mathbf{w}, b, \boldsymbol{\xi}, \hat{\boldsymbol{\xi}}} \quad \frac{1}{2}\|\mathbf{w}\|^2 + C\sum_{i=1}^{n}(\xi_i + \hat{\xi}_i),$$

$$\text{subject to} \quad y_i - \mathbf{w}^T\mathbf{x}_i - b \leq \epsilon + \xi_i, \quad i = 1, \dots, n, \tag{11.70}$$

$$\mathbf{w}^T\mathbf{x}_i + b - y_i \leq \epsilon + \hat{\xi}_i, \quad i = 1, \dots, n,$$

$$\xi_i, \hat{\xi}_i \geq 0, \quad i = 1, \dots, n.$$

The regularization parameter C controls the tradeoff between flatness and tolerance for violations: larger values penalize deviations from the ϵ-tube more heavily, while smaller values favor flatter functions that allow more violations in exchange for better generalization.

11.6.1   Dual Formulation

Similar to support vector classification, the SVR optimization problem can be expressed in dual form using Lagrange multipliers (for a detailed derivation, see [533, Chapter 1.3]):

$$\max_{\alpha,\hat{\alpha}} \quad -\frac{1}{2}\sum_{i=1}^{n}\sum_{j=1}^{n}(\alpha_i - \hat{\alpha}_i)(\alpha_j - \hat{\alpha}_j)\mathbf{x}_i^T\mathbf{x}_j - \epsilon\sum_{i=1}^{n}(\alpha_i + \hat{\alpha}_i) + \sum_{i=1}^{n}y_i(\alpha_i - \hat{\alpha}_i),$$

$$\text{subject to} \quad 0 \leq \alpha_i, \hat{\alpha}_i \leq C, \quad i = 1,\ldots,n,$$

$$\sum_{i=1}^{n}(\alpha_i - \hat{\alpha}_i) = 0.$$

$$\text{(11.71)}$$

The dual variables α_i and $\hat{\alpha}_i$ correspond to the constraints that define the ϵ-tube. Only data points for which $\alpha_i > 0$ or $\hat{\alpha}_i > 0$ contribute to the model. These points, known as **support vectors**, either lie outside the ϵ-tube or exactly on its boundary.

After solving the dual problem, the weight vector can be recovered as:

$$\mathbf{w} = \sum_{i=1}^{n}(\alpha_i - \hat{\alpha}_i)\mathbf{x}_i. \qquad (11.72)$$

The bias term b is computed by applying the KKT conditions and analyzing the complementary slackness relationships involving the slack variables (see [533]).

Predictions for new data points are then given by:

$$h(\mathbf{x}) = \mathbf{w}^T\mathbf{x} + b = \sum_{i=1}^{n}(\alpha_i - \hat{\alpha}_i)\mathbf{x}_i^T\mathbf{x} + b. \qquad (11.73)$$

Since both training and prediction in SVR rely solely on dot products between data points, the method can be extended to nonlinear regression by replacing the dot product $\mathbf{x}_i^T\mathbf{x}_j$ with a suitable kernel function $k(\mathbf{x}_i, \mathbf{x}_j)$. This allows SVR to model complex, nonlinear relationships without explicitly computing the transformation to the high-dimensional feature space.

11.6.2   Epsilon-Insensitive Loss Function

To simplify optimization and enable the use of gradient-based methods, the constrained SVR problem can be reformulated as an unconstrained optimization problem by introducing a suitable loss function—analogous to how hinge loss is used in support vector classification.

The loss function used in SVR, known as the **ϵ-insensitive loss function**, is defined as:

$$L_\epsilon(y, \hat{y}) = \begin{cases} 0 & \text{if } |y - \hat{y}| \leq \epsilon, \\ |y - \hat{y}| - \epsilon & \text{otherwise.} \end{cases} \qquad (11.74)$$

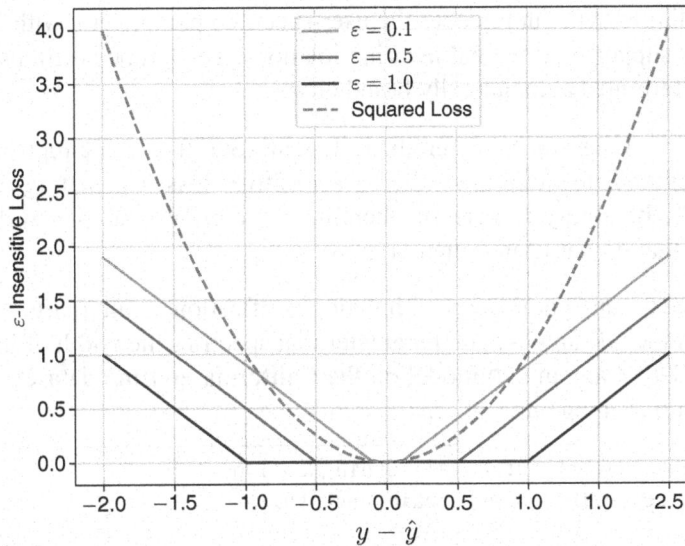

Figure 11.20: Comparison of the ϵ-insensitive loss function (for various values of ϵ) with the squared loss. The ϵ-insensitive loss ignores errors within the margin $|y-\hat{y}| \leq \epsilon$, resulting in flat regions around zero. Outside this margin, the penalty increases linearly with the magnitude of the error. In contrast, the squared loss penalizes all deviations quadratically, regardless of their size.

This loss defines an insensitive region of width ϵ around the target value y (see Figure 11.20). Prediction errors within this region are ignored, while those exceeding ϵ are penalized linearly in proportion to their magnitude. As a result, ϵ-insensitive loss is robust to small fluctuations in the data while remaining responsive to larger deviations.

11.6.3 SVR in Scikit-Learn

Scikit-Learn provides four classes for support vector regression, analogous to those available for classification tasks:

- LinearSVR[17]: Designed for linear regression problems, this class solves the SVR optimization problem using a coordinate descent algorithm. It is computationally efficient and scales well to large datasets, but does not support nonlinear kernels.

- SVR[18]: Supports both linear and nonlinear regression using kernel functions. However, it can be computationally expensive for large datasets, since computing the kernel matrix requires at least quadratic time and memory in the number of samples.

---

17. https://scikit-learn.org/stable/modules/generated/sklearn.svm.LinearSVR.html
18. https://scikit-learn.org/stable/modules/generated/sklearn.svm.SVR.html

- NuSVR[19]: Similar to SVR, but replaces the user-specified parameter ϵ with ν, which controls the fraction of support vectors and margin violations. The ϵ-tube is still used internally, but its width is determined automatically based on ν.

- SGDRegressor[20]: Uses stochastic gradient descent (SGD) to solve regression problems. It can be configured to minimize the ϵ-insensitive loss by setting `loss='epsilon_insensitive'`. Its ability to perform incremental learning makes it well-suited for very large datasets that do not fit into memory.

These classes share many parameters with their classification counterparts. However, most of them (except NuSVR) include an epsilon parameter that specifies the width of the ϵ-tube.

As an example, let's train an SVR model on the California housing dataset. We first load the dataset and split it into training and test sets:

```
from sklearn.datasets import fetch_california_housing
from sklearn.model_selection import train_test_split

X, y = fetch_california_housing(return_X_y=True)
X_train, X_test, y_train, y_test = train_test_split(X, y, test_size=0.2,
                                                    random_state=42)
```

SVR models are sensitive to the scale of input features because the algorithm relies on distances and dot products when constructing the regression function. Therefore, it is essential to standardize the data. We use a pipeline that combines StandardScaler with an SVR estimator and fit it to the training set:

```
from sklearn.pipeline import make_pipeline
from sklearn.preprocessing import StandardScaler
from sklearn.svm import SVR

model = make_pipeline(StandardScaler(), SVR())
model.fit(X_train, y_train)
```

We then evaluate the model's performance:

```
print(f'R2 score (train): {model.score(X_train, y_train):.4f}')
print(f'R2 score (test): {model.score(X_test, y_test):.4f}')
```

```
R2 score (train): 0.7486
R2 score (test): 0.7276
```

The test R^2 score outperforms simpler models such as linear regression (0.5758) and k-nearest neighbors (0.7205), but falls short of more advanced methods like gradient boosting with LightGBM (0.8556). Further performance gains may be possible through hyperparameter tuning.

19. https://scikit-learn.org/stable/modules/generated/sklearn.svm.NuSVR.html
20. https://scikit-learn.org/stable/modules/generated/sklearn.linear_model.SGDRegressor.html

11.7 (*) Efficient Methods for Training SVMs

Training a kernel SVM using a generic quadratic programming (QP) solver is often computationally infeasible for large datasets due to the need to store and compute the full kernel matrix $K \in \mathbb{R}^{n \times n}$, which contains all pairwise dot products between training examples. A naive implementation typically requires solving a system of equations derived from the KKT conditions, incurring a computational cost of $\mathcal{O}(n^3)$ due to matrix inversion or similarly costly operations.

Beyond computational cost, memory usage can also become a major bottleneck. For example, a dataset with 100,000 samples results in a kernel matrix that consumes approximately 40 GB of memory[21], far exceeding the RAM available on most personal computers.

11.7.1 Chunking

One of the earliest methods developed to address the computational challenges of training SVMs is **chunking**, introduced by Vapnik in 1982 for hard-margin SVMs [595]. The key idea is to reduce the size of each optimization problem by solving the dual formulation on smaller subsets of the data, incrementally incorporating only the most informative examples. The algorithm proceeds as follows:

1. Subset division: Partition the training set into smaller subsets, each containing a limited number of examples.

2. Initial optimization: Solve the QP problem on the first subset. If it is not linearly separable, the entire dataset is deemed inseparable. Otherwise, compute the optimal hyperplane for this subset.

3. Support vector extension: Identify the support vectors from the current solution (those with nonzero Lagrange multipliers α_i). Construct a new working set by combining these support vectors with any examples from the next subset that violate the current margin condition, i.e., those not satisfying $y_i(\mathbf{w}^T \mathbf{x}_i + b) \geq 1$, where $\mathbf{w}$ and b are defined by the current support vectors.

4. Iterative optimization: Repeat the process by solving the QP on the new working set and expanding it with newly violating examples. The algorithm terminates after all subsets have been processed, either finding a separating hyperplane or determining that the dataset is non-separable.

Chunking reduces computational cost by solving smaller optimization problems in each iteration that involve only the support vectors and margin violators. However, it can still be inefficient due to the overhead of solving multiple subproblems with overlapping examples—namely, the support vectors that persist across iterations.

---

21. Assuming 32-bit floating-point precision (4 bytes per entry), the total memory required is $100,000^2 \times 4 = 40 \times 10^9$ bytes.

11.7.2 Sequential Minimal Optimization (SMO)

A widely adopted method for efficiently training SVMs is **Sequential Minimal Optimization (SMO)**, proposed by John Platt in 1998 [480]. SMO simplifies the SVM quadratic programming problem by decomposing it into a sequence of two-variable sub-problems, each of which can be solved analytically. This approach eliminates the need for general-purpose numerical QP solvers and significantly reduces computational complexity.

The main steps of the algorithm are:

1. Initialize parameters: Set all Lagrange multipliers to $\alpha_i = 0$, initialize the bias b, and define a convergence threshold based on the KKT conditions.

2. Select the first Lagrange multiplier: Choose α_i that most strongly violates the KKT conditions, i.e., the one with the largest deviation from optimality.

3. Select the second Lagrange multiplier: Choose α_j to maximize the expected improvement in the objective when paired with α_i. Common heuristics include maximizing the absolute error difference between α_i and α_j, or selecting α_j based on cached error values.

4. Solve the two-variable sub-problem: Jointly optimize α_i and α_j subject to the constraints $0 \leq \alpha_i, \alpha_j \leq C$ and $\alpha_i y_i + \alpha_j y_j = $ const. Since this is effectively a one-dimensional quadratic problem, it has a closed-form solution.

5. Update the bias term: Adjust the bias b to reflect the changes in α_i and α_j, ensuring consistency with the KKT conditions.

6. Check convergence: Repeat steps 2–5 until all α_i satisfy the KKT conditions within the specified tolerance.

In terms of computational complexity, each iteration of SMO involves selecting two Lagrange multipliers, which requires $\mathcal{O}(n)$ time, and solving the resulting two-variable sub-problem, which takes $\mathcal{O}(1)$ time. Although the worst-case number of iterations is $\mathcal{O}(n^2)$—particularly in the presence of noisy data or many borderline points—empirical studies show that SMO often converges much faster in practice, with total runtime scaling approximately linearly with n [480, 4].

In Scikit-Learn, kernel-based SVM estimators—including the classes SVC, NuSVC, SVR, and NuSVR—are implemented using the LIBSVM library, which employs the SMO algorithm to solve the underlying quadratic programming problem.

11.7.3 Kernel Approximation Methods

While the approaches discussed in the previous section significantly reduce the computational time required to solve the SVM optimization problem, they still require constructing and storing the full kernel matrix, which imposes a memory complexity of $\mathcal{O}(n^2)$. This becomes a limiting factor for large datasets, where the kernel matrix may no longer fit in memory.

To address this issue, **kernel approximation methods** have been developed to reduce both memory usage and computational cost, allowing kernel methods to scale more effectively. Two widely used approaches are:

- **Nyström Method** [623]: Approximates the kernel matrix using a smaller, representative subset of the data. It selects $m \ll n$ landmark points and constructs a low-rank approximation of the full $n \times n$ kernel matrix using only kernel evaluations between these landmark points and the full dataset. The approximation is given by:

$$K \approx CW^{\dagger}C^{T}, \tag{11.75}$$

where $C \in \mathbb{R}^{n \times m}$ contains the kernel values between all n data points and the m landmark points, $W \in \mathbb{R}^{m \times m}$ is the kernel matrix between the landmark points themselves, and $W^{\dagger}$ denotes the Moore–Penrose pseudoinverse of W.

In Scikit-Learn, this method is implemented in the `Nystroem`[22] class.

- **Random Fourier Features** [496]: Maps the data into a lower-dimensional feature space to linearly approximate the kernel function by leveraging **Bochner's theorem**, which states that any continuous, shift-invariant kernel (such as the RBF kernel) can be represented as the Fourier transform of a probability distribution [58]. Specifically, the RBF kernel

$$k(\mathbf{x}, \mathbf{z}) = \exp\left(-\frac{\|\mathbf{x} - \mathbf{z}\|^2}{2\sigma^2}\right)$$

can be approximated by computing random Fourier features of the form

$$\phi(\mathbf{x}) = \sqrt{\frac{2}{D}}\cos(W\mathbf{x} + \mathbf{b}), \tag{11.76}$$

where $W \in \mathbb{R}^{D \times d}$ consists of D i.i.d. samples drawn from the multivariate normal distribution $\mathcal{N}(\mathbf{0}, \sigma^{-2}I)$, and $\mathbf{b} \in \mathbb{R}^D$ contains D i.i.d. samples drawn uniformly from the interval $[0, 2\pi]$. The dot product $\phi(\mathbf{x})^T\phi(\mathbf{z})$ then provides an approximation to $k(\mathbf{x}, \mathbf{z})$.

In Scikit-Learn, this method is implemented in the `RBFSampler`[23] class.

11.7.4 Fast Solvers for Linear SVMs

Over the years, several efficient algorithms for training linear SVMs have been developed, enabling them to scale to much larger datasets than kernel SVMs [300, 544, 104, 280, 364].

These algorithms are commonly implemented in two main variants, depending on the loss function used:

- **L1-SVM**, which minimizes the **hinge loss**:

$$L(\mathbf{w}) = \sum_{i=1}^{n}\max(0, 1 - y_i\mathbf{w}^T\mathbf{x}_i), \tag{11.77}$$

---

22. https://scikit-learn.org/stable/modules/generated/sklearn.kernel_approximation.Nystroem.html
23. https://scikit-learn.org/stable/modules/generated/sklearn.kernel_approximation.RBFSampler.html

leads to an optimization problem that includes box constraints on the dual variables, $0 \leq \alpha_i \leq C$. The hinge loss encourages sparse solutions (i.e., fewer support vectors), but its non-differentiability necessitates specialized optimization techniques.

- **L2-SVM**, which minimizes the **squared hinge loss**:

$$L(\mathbf{w}) = \sum_{i=1}^{n} \max(0, 1 - y_i \mathbf{w}^T \mathbf{x}_i)^2, \qquad (11.78)$$

yields a differentiable objective function and typically leads to more stable optimization process. Unlike L1-SVM, it does not impose upper bounds on the dual variables, as the dual constraints reduce to $\alpha_i \geq 0$, allowing for faster convergence in practice.

A widely used and highly efficient solver for linear SVMs is **Dual Coordinate Descent (DCD)**, a coordinate descent method that operates in the dual space and supports both L1-SVM and L2-SVM formulations [280]. The method updates one dual variable at a time while enforcing the constraints using projected gradients. It is particularly effective for large-scale and sparse datasets, offering an excellent balance between convergence speed, memory efficiency, and scalability. Due to its effectiveness, DCD is implemented in the LIBLINEAR library, which serves as the underlying solver for the LinearSVC class in Scikit-Learn. Exercise 11.22 explores this method in more detail.

11.8   Model Calibration

Support vector machines do not inherently provide posterior probability estimates. Instead, they output real-valued decision scores in the range $[-\infty, \infty]$, corresponding to the functional margin $f(\mathbf{x}) = \mathbf{w}^T \mathbf{x} + b$. The sign of this score determines the predicted class, and its magnitude reflects the confidence of the prediction, i.e., how far the input lies from the decision boundary. While these scores are useful for classification, they lack a direct probabilistic interpretation.

In many applications, however, probability estimates $P(y|\mathbf{x})$ are more useful than raw decision scores, as they support uncertainty quantification and risk-aware decision-making. For example, in medical diagnosis, probability estimates can help prioritize further testing or treatment options based on the predicted likelihood of a disease. In natural language processing, language models rely on well-formed probability distributions to sample or rank likely continuations of a given text sequence.

Even when classifiers do provide probability estimates, these estimates are often *not calibrated*—that is, they do not accurately reflect the true posterior probabilities. For example, decision trees tend to produce poorly calibrated probabilities, as they base their estimates on the class distribution in the leaf node reached by the input. When the leaf contains only a few training samples, these estimates can be unreliable and overly confident, e.g., predicting a probability of 1.0 for a class simply because all three samples in the leaf belong to it. Such overconfidence can be problematic in high-stake domains such as medical diagnosis, where decisions based on misleading probabilities may lead to adverse outcomes.

Model calibration refers to the process of adjusting a model's output scores or predicted probabilities so that they more accurately reflect the true likelihood of each class [481, 656, 657, 447, 243].

Formally, a binary classifier is said to be **well-calibrated** if, for all predicted probability values $s \in [0, 1]$, the following holds:

$$\lim_{n \to \infty} P(y = 1 \mid \hat{p}(\mathbf{x}) = s) = s, \tag{11.79}$$

that is, among all samples for which the classifier predicts a probability of s, the proportion that actually belong to the positive class converges to s as the number of such samples n increases.

For example, if a well-calibrated classifier assigns a probability of 0.8 to a group of samples, then approximately 80% of those samples should actually belong to the positive class.

11.8.1 Calibration Plots

The calibration of a classifier can be visually inspected using a **calibration plot**, also known as a **reliability diagram**. This plot compares the model's predicted probabilities with the observed empirical frequencies of the positive class. Specifically, for each predicted probability value s, it plots the empirical probability $P(y = 1 \mid \hat{p}(\mathbf{x}) = s)$, calculated as the proportion of samples assigned the probability s that actually belong to the positive class (see Figure 11.21).

For a perfectly calibrated classifier, all points on the calibration plot lie along the diagonal line $y = x$, indicating perfect agreement between the predicted probabilities and observed outcomes. Deviations from this line indicate miscalibration: points above the diagonal correspond to **under-confident** predictions (the classifier underestimates the true probability), while points below it reflect **overconfident** predictions (the classifier overestimates the probability).

Calibration plots are typically constructed using a separate test set to evaluate the model's ability to produce well-calibrated probabilities on unseen data. In practice, the number of unique predicted probabilities can be much larger than the number of test samples, making it infeasible to compute reliable empirical probabilities for each individual value. To address this, the predicted probabilities are grouped into bins (e.g., ten equally spaced intervals), and for each bin, the average predicted probability is plotted against the observed proportion of positive samples within that bin.

In the following example, we compare the calibration performance of five classifiers: logistic regression, Gaussian naive Bayes, decision trees, gradient boosting, and a linear SVM with naively scaled outputs. We begin by generating a synthetic binary classification dataset with 10 features and split it into training and test sets:

```
from sklearn.datasets import make_classification
from sklearn.model_selection import train_test_split

X, y = make_classification(
    n_samples=100000, n_features=10, n_informative=2, n_redundant=2, random_state=42
)
X_train, X_test, y_train, y_test = train_test_split(X, y, random_state=42)
```

To demonstrate that the raw decision scores produced by a linear SVM are not well-calibrated, we apply a simple min–max scaling to convert these scores into probabilities. To that end, we define a custom subclass of LinearSVC that overrides the predict_proba method to use min–max scaling instead of the default Platt scaling (described in Section 11.8.2):

```
from sklearn.svm import LinearSVC

class NaivelyCalibratedLinearSVC(LinearSVC):
    """LinearSVC with naively scaled decision scores."""
    def fit(self, X, y):
        super().fit(X, y)
        df = self.decision_function(X)
        self.df_min_ = df.min()
        self.df_max_ = df.max()

    def predict_proba(self, X):
        df = self.decision_function(X)

        # Min-max scale the decision scores to [0, 1]
        calibrated_df = (df - self.df_min_) / (self.df_max_ - self.df_min_)

        # Clip values to [0, 1] to handle potential rounding errors
        proba_pos_class = np.clip(calibrated_df, 0, 1)
        proba_neg_class = 1 - proba_pos_class
        proba = np.c_[proba_neg_class, proba_pos_class]
        return proba
```

Next, we define a list of classifiers to evaluate:

```
from sklearn.linear_model import LogisticRegression
from sklearn.naive_bayes import GaussianNB
from sklearn.tree import DecisionTreeClassifier
from sklearn.ensemble import GradientBoostingClassifier

# Define a list of classifiers to evaluate their calibration performance
classifiers = [
    ('Logistic Regression', LogisticRegression(random_state=42)),
    ('Naive Bayes', GaussianNB()),
    ('SVC (MinMax Calibrated)', MinMaxCalibratedSVC(random_state=42)),
    ('Decision Tree', DecisionTreeClassifier(min_samples_leaf=5, random_state=42)),
    ('Gradient Boosting', GradientBoostingClassifier(random_state=42))
]
```

For the decision tree classifier, we set min_samples_leaf=5 to reduce overfitting and avoid extreme probability estimates based on very small sample sizes.

Finally, we define a function to generate calibration plots for these classifiers, utilizing Scikit-Learn's CalibrationDisplay[24] class. The CalibrationDisplay.from_estimator method plots the mean predicted probability (x-axis) against the observed fraction of positive labels (y-axis),

24. https://scikit-learn.org/stable/modules/generated/sklearn.calibration.CalibrationDisplay.
    html

grouping predictions into bins (5 by default). Since each call to `from_estimator` creates a new figure by default, we create a single subplot and pass it explicitly to ensure that all calibration curves appear on the same plot:

```
from sklearn.calibration import CalibrationDisplay

def generate_calibration_plots(classifiers, X_train, y_train, X_test, y_test):
    # Define the figure and add a single subplot
    fig = plt.figure()
    ax_calibration_curve = fig.add_subplot()
    colors = plt.get_cmap('Dark2')
    markers = ['^', 'v', 's', 'o', 'p']

    for i, (name, clf) in enumerate(classifiers):
        # Fit classifier and generate calibration plot
        clf.fit(X_train, y_train)
        display = CalibrationDisplay.from_estimator(
            clf, X_test, y_test, n_bins=10, name=name, ax=ax_calibration_curve,
            color=colors(i), marker=markers[i]
        )
    plt.grid(alpha=0.5)

generate_calibration_plots(classifiers, X_train, y_train, X_test, y_test)
```

Figure 11.21 shows the calibration plots for the five classifiers. Key insights from the plots:

- Logistic regression: The predictions are well-calibrated, with the curve closely following the diagonal line. This is expected, as logistic regression minimizes the log loss, which directly penalizes discrepancies between the predicted probabilities and the true labels.

- Naive Bayes: The calibration curve has an inverted sigmoid shape, with most predictions concentrated near the extremes. This is due to the model's strong assumption that features are conditionally independent given the class label. When this assumption is violated, the model treats correlated features as if they are independent, causing it to count the same evidence multiple times. This leads to overconfident predictions, often pushing the probabilities too close to 0 or 1.

- SVM (min–max scaled): The calibration curve has a sigmoidal shape, reflecting SVM's tendency to avoid extreme scores near 0 and 1. This occurs because the raw decision scores are not linearly related to the true class probabilities. As a result, even confident predictions that lie far from the margin may yield scores that are not close to 0 or 1 after min–max scaling.

- Decision tree: The calibration curve is irregular and non-monotonic, indicating poor calibration. This arises from the tree's coarse probability estimates, which are based on the class

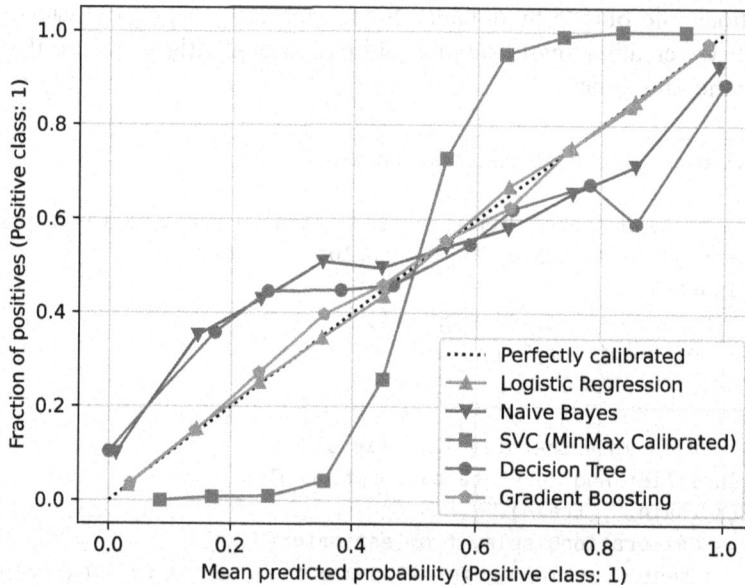

Figure 11.21: Calibration plots for various classifiers, illustrating how well the predicted probabilities of each classifier align with the empirical class proportions. See the main text for detailed discussion.

proportions within each leaf. With `min_samples_leaf=5`, the model can only output a limited set of discrete probability values $(0.0, 0.2, 0.4, \ldots, 1.0)$, which may poorly reflect the true posterior probabilities.

- Gradient boosting: The calibration curve lies close to the diagonal, indicating better-calibrated predictions. Unlike a single decision tree, gradient-boosted trees average the outputs of many trees, smoothing the predicted probabilities and improving calibration.

In addition to calibration plots, model calibration can be evaluated quantitatively using the **Brier score**, which measures the mean squared difference between the predicted probabilities and the true binary labels [75]:

$$\text{Brier Score} = \frac{1}{n} \sum_{i=1}^{n} \left(p_i - y_i \right)^2, \tag{11.80}$$

where n is the number of samples, p_i is the predicted probability of the positive class for the i-th sample, and $y_i \in \{0, 1\}$ is the corresponding true label.

Like log loss, the Brier score penalizes discrepancies between predicted probabilities and true labels. However, it uses a quadratic penalty rather than a logarithmic one, making it less sensitive to confidently incorrect predictions. In Scikit-Learn, the Brier score can be computed using the `brier_score_loss`[25] function from `sklearn.metrics`.

In the following sections, we explore two popular methods for model calibration.

---

25. `https://scikit-learn.org/stable/modules/generated/sklearn.metrics.brier_score_loss.html`

11.8.2   Platt Scaling

Platt proposed a method for transforming SVM decision scores into calibrated probabilities by passing them through a sigmoid function [481]. This approach involves fitting a sigmoid to the model's decision scores using an independent **calibration set**.

Formally, let $s(\mathbf{x})$ denote the decision score output by the SVM. To obtain calibrated probabilities, the scores are passed through a sigmoid of the form:

$$P(y = 1|s) = \frac{1}{1 + \exp(As + B)}, \tag{11.81}$$

where the parameters A and B are learned using maximum likelihood estimation on a separate set of score–label pairs (s_i, y_i). Specifically, they are found by minimizing the log loss:

$$\underset{A,B}{\text{argmin}} \ -\sum_i \left[y_i \log(p_i) + (1 - y_i) \log(1 - p_i) \right], \tag{11.82}$$

where

$$p_i = \frac{1}{1 + \exp(As_i + B)}. \tag{11.83}$$

Interestingly, Platt showed that a calibrated SVM, i.e., an SVM followed by sigmoid calibration, can sometimes achieve higher classification accuracy (in terms of 0/1 loss) than an uncalibrated SVM. This suggests that the standard SVM decision threshold of zero is not always Bayes-optimal.

To apply Platt scaling in Scikit-Learn, there are two main options:

- SVM-based estimators: When using `SVC` or `NuSVC` with `probability=True`, Platt scaling is automatically applied when calling the `predict_proba` method. The learned sigmoid parameters can be accessed via the `probA_` and `probB_` attributes. Note that `LinearSVC` does not support `predict_proba` and only provides decision scores.

- General calibration: For other estimators, Scikit-Learn provides the `CalibratedClassifierCV`[26] class, which supports both Platt scaling and isotonic regression (described in the next section). This class uses cross-validation to fit and calibrate the model. For each cross-validation fold:

  - The base estimator is trained on the training subset.
  - The trained model is calibrated on the validation subset using the chosen calibration method.

During inference, the predicted probabilities are averaged across the calibrated models from each fold. This approach helps stabilize the calibration process, particularly on small or noisy datasets where using a single held-out calibration set may lead to overfitting or unreliable estimates.

---

26. https://scikit-learn.org/stable/modules/generated/sklearn.calibration.
    CalibratedClassifierCV.html

The key parameters of `CalibratedClassifierCV` are:

- `estimator`: The base classifier whose outputs are to be calibrated. If not specified, the default is `LinearSVC`.
- `method`: The calibration method: `'sigmoid'` for Platt scaling (the default), or `'isotonic'` for isotonic regression.
- `cv`: The cross-validation strategy. By default, 5-fold cross-validation is used.

The code below applies Platt scaling to the previously defined classifiers using `CalibratedClassifierCV` and replacing `MinMaxCalibratedSVC` with a standard `LinearSVC`:

```
from sklearn.calibration import CalibratedClassifierCV
from sklearn.svm import LinearSVC

# Define base estimators
base_classifiers = [
    ('Logistic Regression', LogisticRegression(random_state=42)),
    ('Naive Bayes', GaussianNB()),
    ('SVC', LinearSVC(random_state=42)),
    ('Decision Tree', DecisionTreeClassifier(min_samples_leaf=5, random_state=42)),
    ('Gradient Boosting', GradientBoostingClassifier(random_state=42))
]

# Apply Platt scaling to each classifier
classifiers = [(name, CalibratedClassifierCV(estimator, cv=3))
               for name, estimator in base_classifiers]

# Generate calibration plots
generate_calibration_plots(classifiers, X_train, y_train, X_test, y_test)
```

Figure 11.22 shows the calibration plots after applying Platt scaling. As expected, Platt scaling effectively transforms the SVM decision scores into well-calibrated probabilities, correcting the sigmoidal distortion in the raw scores. It also improves the overly confident predictions of naive Bayes and decision trees, although these models remain imperfectly calibrated.

Advantages of Platt scaling for model calibration include:

- It performs well when the model's decision scores have a roughly sigmoid-shaped relationship with the true probabilities, as is often the case with SVMs.

- It requires relatively little calibration data to estimate the sigmoid parameters accurately.

However, Platt scaling also has several limitations:

- It may yield poor calibration when the relationship between model scores and true probabilities is not well approximated by a sigmoid function, as is common with naive Bayes and decision tree models.

- It is sensitive to outliers in the decision scores or labels, which can distort the fitted sigmoid and reduce calibration quality.

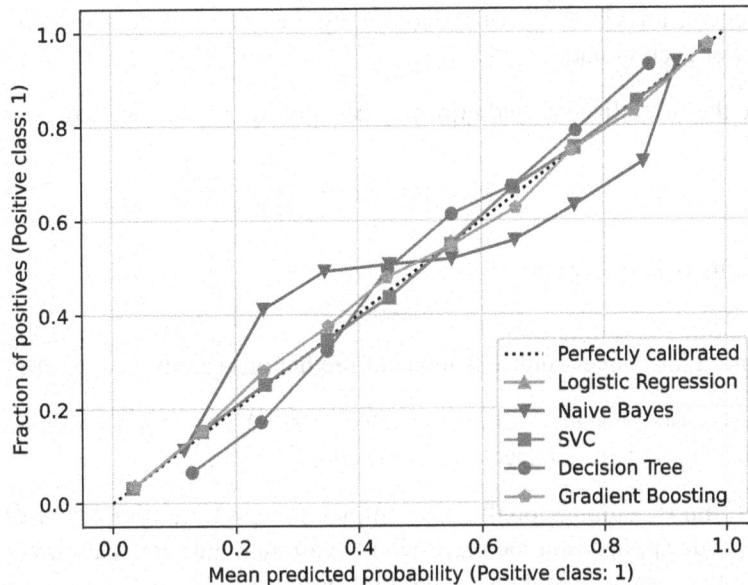

Figure 11.22: Calibration plots for various classifiers after applying Platt scaling. Models such as SVC, naive Bayes, and decision trees show significant improvements in calibration, while already well-calibrated models like logistic regression and gradient boosting remain closely aligned with the diagonal.

11.8.3 Isotonic Regression

Isotonic regression is a more flexible calibration method that can correct any monotonic distortion in the predicted probabilities [656, 657].

Unlike Platt scaling, which assumes a sigmoid-shaped relationship between decision scores and probabilities, isotonic regression makes a much weaker assumption: namely, that the true relationship is monotonic. That is, higher scores should correspond to higher probabilities of belonging to the positive class.

Under this assumption, the goal is to learn a monotonically increasing (isotonic) function h that maps decision scores to calibrated probabilities. This function is fitted by minimizing the squared error on a calibration set $\{(s_i, y_i)\}$:

$$\operatorname*{argmin}_{h} \sum_{i} (y_i - h(s_i))^2. \tag{11.84}$$

A widely used algorithm for solving this problem is the **pair-adjacent violators (PAV)** algorithm, which produces a stepwise constant isotonic function [22]. The PAV algorithm works as follows:

1. Sort the calibration set $\{(s_i, y_i)\}$ in ascending order of the scores s_i.

2. For each data point, assign an initial prediction equal to its true label: $h_i = y_i$, where $y_i \in \{0, 1\}$, and set the initial weight $w_i = 1$.

3. Iteratively check for violations of monotonicity, i.e., pairs of adjacent predictions where $h_{i-1} > h_i$. For each violation:

   (a) Merge the two adjacent predictions by computing the weighted average:

   $$h_{\text{merged}} = \frac{w_{i-1}h_{i-1} + w_i h_i}{w_{i-1} + w_i}.$$

   (b) Set the merged weight to:

   $$w_{\text{merged}} = w_{i-1} + w_i.$$

4. Repeat the merging process until all adjacent predictions satisfy $h_{i-1} \leq h_i$.

5. Return a piecewise-constant function f such that $f(s_i) = h_i$ for all training points, and f remains constant between adjacent decision scores.

The PAV algorithm is computationally efficient, with linear time complexity $\mathcal{O}(n)$.

The following code applies isotonic regression to calibrate the same classifiers as before (the code for recreating the base estimators is omitted for brevity):

```
# Apply isotonic regression to each classifier
classifiers = [(name, CalibratedClassifierCV(estimator, method='isotonic', cv=3))
                for name, estimator in base_classifiers]

# Generate calibration plots
generate_calibration_plots(classifiers, X_train, y_train, X_test, y_test)
```

Figure 11.23 shows the resulting calibration plots. As illustrated, isotonic regression substantially improves the calibration of naive Bayes and decision tree models, bringing their predicted probabilities closer to the diagonal. For the other classifiers, isotonic regression produces results similar to those obtained by Platt scaling.

Advantages of isotonic regression for model calibration:

- It can effectively capture complex monotonic distortions between decision scores and true probabilities.

- Unlike Platt scaling, it does not assume a specific functional form (e.g., a sigmoid), allowing it to flexibly adapt to various calibration curve shapes.

Disadvantages of isotonic regression:

- It is prone to overfitting when calibration data are limited and generally requires more samples than Platt scaling to achieve reliable calibration.[27]

- It assumes a monotonic relationship between scores and probabilities, which may not hold in all cases.

---

27. According to Scikit-Learn's documentation, isotonic regression may not perform well with fewer than 1000 calibration samples.

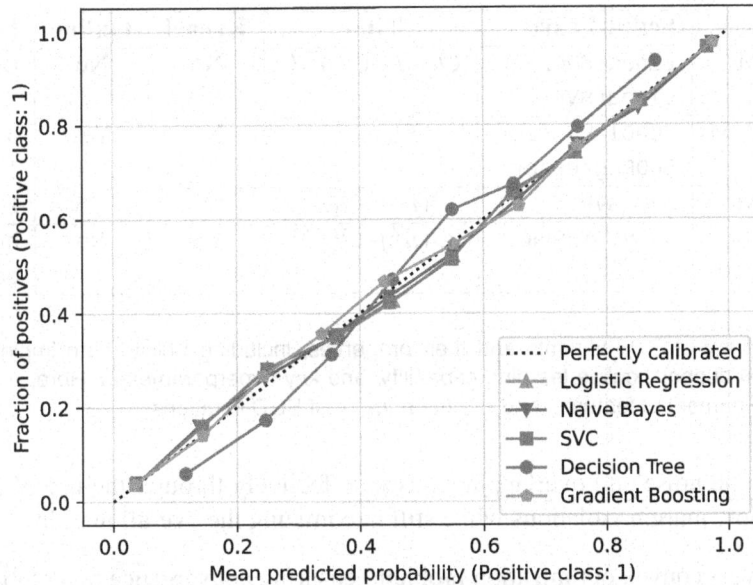

Figure 11.23: Calibration plots for various classifiers after applying isotonic regression. Significant improvements are observed for models such as naive Bayes and decision trees.

Both Platt scaling and isotonic regression are primarily designed for binary classification, and extending them to multiclass settings is nontrivial. A common workaround is to decompose the multiclass problem into one-vs-all binary tasks, calibrate each binary classifier separately, and then recombine the calibrated outputs into a multiclass probability distribution [657].

11.9 Summary

Support vector machines (SVMs) are versatile supervised learning models with strong theoretical foundations. They perform well across a wide range of tasks, especially in high-dimensional settings. With the use of kernel methods, SVMs can model nonlinear decision boundaries by implicitly mapping the data into higher-dimensional feature spaces.

Table 11.3 summarizes the different SVM variants discussed in this chapter, along with their key properties.

Advantages of SVMs compared to other supervised learning models:

- They often perform well on small- to medium-sized datasets, as maximizing the margin encourages good generalization and robustness to noise.

- They are among the most effective algorithms for high-dimensional datasets, as the decision function depends only on the support vectors, making the model's complexity largely independent of the number of features.

	Scikit-Learn	Time	Kernel	Online	Hyperparameters
Linear SVM	LinearSVC, LinearSVR	$\mathcal{O}(nd)\text{–}\mathcal{O}(n^2d)$	No	No	c
SGD-based SVM	SGDClassifier, SGDRegressor	$\mathcal{O}(Ind)$	No	Yes	alpha, eta0, learning_rate
Kernel SVM	SVC, SVR	$\mathcal{O}(n^2)\text{–}\mathcal{O}(n^3)$	Yes	No	C, kernel, gamma
ν-SVM	NuSVC, NuSVR	$\mathcal{O}(n^2)\text{–}\mathcal{O}(n^3)$	Yes	No	nu, kernel, gamma

Table 11.3: Summary of SVM variants and their properties, including Scikit-Learn implementations, time complexity, kernel support, online learning capability, and key hyperparameters. Here, n is the number of samples, d is the number of features, and I is the number of SGD iterations.

- They handle noise and overlapping classes effectively through the use of slack variables, which allow margin violations while still maximizing the overall margin.

- They solve a convex optimization problem, ensuring convergence to a global optimum.

- The kernel trick enables SVMs to model a wide range of nonlinear decision boundaries and adapt to diverse data distributions.

- They are grounded in statistical learning theory, which provides generalization guarantees based on factors such as margin size and the number of support vectors.

- Regularization parameters such as C and ν provide explicit control over the bias–variance tradeoff.

- They produce sparse solutions, relying only on the support vectors for predictions, which reduces memory usage and enables fast inference.

- SVM variants support a wide range of learning tasks, including classification, regression, clustering, and anomaly detection.

- Linear SVMs are interpretable, as the learned coefficients directly reflect the contribution of each feature to the decision function.

Disadvantages of SVMs:

- Training can be computationally expensive for large datasets, especially for kernel SVMs, whose time complexity can reach $\mathcal{O}(n^3)$ in the worst case.

- Performance depends heavily on the choice of kernel function and hyperparameters, such as the regularization strength C and kernel-specific parameters like γ.

- SVMs natively support only binary classification; handling multi-class problems requires OvR or OvO strategies, which can substantially increase computational complexity.

- They require data preprocessing, including handling missing values, encoding categorical features, and applying feature scaling.

- Kernel-based SVMs are generally difficult to interpret, as their decision boundaries arise from complex nonlinear transformations in high-dimensional feature spaces.

- They do not provide probability estimates by default and require post-hoc calibration (e.g., Platt scaling) to produce reliable probability outputs.

11.10   Exercises

11.10.1   Multiple-Choice Questions

11.1. We trained a linear SVM on a binary classification problem and obtained $\mathbf{w} = (2, 5, 1)$. We also know that $\mathbf{x} = (3, -1, 1)$ is a support vector and is classified by the SVM as -1. What is the value of the bias b in the separating hyperplane?

  (a) -1

  (b) -3

  (c) 1

  (d) 3

11.2. We trained a linear SVM on a binary classification problem and obtained the support vectors shown in Table 11.4.

	x_1	x_2	y
1	0	6	1
2	5	4	1
3	2	0	-1

Table 11.4: Support vectors from a hard-margin SVM classification problem

What is the decision score $h(\mathbf{x})$ for a test data point $\mathbf{x} = (3, 3)$?

  (a) $-1/13$

  (b) $1/13$

  (c) $4/13$

  (d) $7/13$

11.3. In a soft-margin SVM, which of the following changes would likely cause the margin to shrink?

  (a) Increasing the value of C

  (b) Decreasing the value of C

(c) Adding a data point that violates the margin

(d) Adding an uninformative feature to the dataset

11.4. Which of the following statements is true about the dual form of soft-margin SVM?

(a) The dual form only depends on the inner products of the data points, enabling the use of kernel methods.

(b) The dual form can be solved using gradient descent.

(c) The number of dual variables optimized is equal to the number of training samples.

(d) Solving the dual form with quadratic programming scales at least quadratically with the number of training samples.

(e) The support vectors are the data points for which $\alpha_i \geq 0$.

11.5. While training a linear SVM model for a Kaggle competition, you observe that its training accuracy is 83% and validation accuracy is 58%. Which of the following is likely to improve the validation accuracy to 80% or higher?

(a) Standardizing the features

(b) Decreasing the value of C

(c) Using a kernel-based SVM with an RBF kernel instead of a linear SVM

(d) Training the model on more data

(e) Removing irrelevant or redundant features

11.6. Which of the following statements about the hinge loss function is correct?

(a) It increases linearly for predictions on the wrong side of the margin.

(b) It equals zero when the predicted value and the actual label have the same sign.

(c) Minimizing the hinge loss will provide an optimal solution to the soft-margin SVM optimization problem.

(d) It is a convex function.

11.7. Which of the following statements about kernels is true?

(a) For $x, y \in \mathbb{R}$, $k(x, y) = x^2 y$ is a valid kernel.

(b) For $x, y \in \mathbb{R}$, $k(x, y) = e^{x+y}$ is a valid kernel.

(c) For any mapping $\phi(\mathbf{x})$, there is a kernel function $k(\mathbf{x}, \mathbf{y})$ that can efficiently evaluate $\phi(\mathbf{x})^T \phi(\mathbf{y})$ without explicitly computing $\phi(\mathbf{x})$ and $\phi(\mathbf{y})$.

(d) For every valid kernel $k(\mathbf{x}, \mathbf{y})$, there exists a finite-dimensional feature map $\phi(\mathbf{x})$, such that $k(\mathbf{x}, \mathbf{y}) = \phi(\mathbf{x})^T \phi(\mathbf{y})$.

11.8. Which of the following statements about the performance of SVM models is true?

    (a) For linearly separable data, a hard-margin SVM always achieves higher training accuracy than a logistic regression.

    (b) For nonlinearly separable data, logistic regression always achieves higher training accuracy than a hard-margin SVM.

    (c) For linearly separable data, a hard-margin SVM typically yields higher test accuracy than a soft-margin SVM.

    (d) For nonlinearly separable data, a kernel-based SVM typically yields higher training accuracy than a linear soft-margin SVM.

    (e) For nonlinearly separable data, a kernel-based SVM typically achieves higher test accuracy than a linear soft-margin SVM.

11.9. Which of the following statements about support vector regression (SVR) is correct?

    (a) The goal of SVR is to maximize the margin between the support vectors and the decision boundary.

    (b) The support vectors in SVR are the data points that lie outside the ϵ-tube or on its borders.

    (c) The ϵ-insensitive loss function is smaller or equal to the squared loss.

    (d) SVR cannot use kernel functions as its optimization function involves operations that are not dot products.

11.10. Which of the following statements about model calibration are true?

    (a) Model calibration aims to improve the accuracy of a model's predictions.

    (b) A well-calibrated binary classifier would generate a score of 0.8 for approximately 80% of the examples actually belonging to the positive class.

    (c) A model with exponential distortions in its predicted probabilities has a tendency to be overconfident.

    (d) Platt scaling uses a logistic regression model to map uncalibrated predictions to calibrated probabilities.

    (e) Isotonic regression is more likely to produce well-calibrated probabilities than Platt scaling for models that tend to overfit.

11.10.2 Theoretical Exercises

11.11. We trained a linear SVM on the two-dimensional dataset shown in Table 11.5. After solving the dual optimization problem using a quadratic programming (QP) solver, we obtained the Lagrange multipliers shown in the last column of the table.

	$\mathbf{x}_i$	y_i	α_i
1	(1, 3)	+1	0
2	(2, 2)	+1	0.312
3	(4, 4)	−1	0.187
4	(5, 1)	−1	0.125
5	(6, 3)	−1	0

Table 11.5: Training dataset for linear SVM. The columns indicate the index of each data point, the feature vector $\mathbf{x}_i$, the class label y_i, and the Lagrange multiplier α_i obtained from solving the dual problem.

(a) What are the support vectors?

(b) Compute the weight vector $\mathbf{w}$ and bias b of the optimal separating hyperplane.

(c) Write the equation of the separating hyperplane, and sketch it together with the data points. Include the margin boundaries in your figure.

(d) What is the margin width γ of the hyperplane?

(e) For the test point $\mathbf{x} = (3, 2)$, compute the decision score (i.e., the signed distance to the hyperplane) and predicted label. Does this point lie inside or outside the margin?

11.12. Prove that for a dataset containing two points, $\mathbf{x}_1$ and $\mathbf{x}_2$, each from a different class, the optimal solution to the hard-margin SVM problem is a separating hyperplane that is orthogonal to the line segment connecting the two points and passes through their midpoint (see a two-dimensional illustration in Figure 11.24).

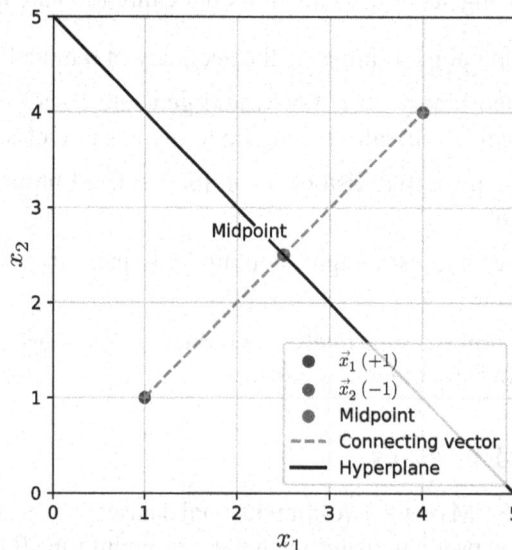

Figure 11.24: The optimal separating hyperplane for two data points in a hard-margin SVM

Furthermore, prove that the parameters of the optimal hyperplane are given by:

$$\mathbf{w} = \frac{2}{\|\mathbf{x}_1 - \mathbf{x}_2\|^2}(\mathbf{x}_1 - \mathbf{x}_2), \quad b = -\frac{1}{2}(\mathbf{x}_1 + \mathbf{x}_2)^T \mathbf{w}.$$

(a) Derive the expressions for $\mathbf{w}$ and b by solving the primal optimization problem.

(b) Derive the same expressions by solving the dual optimization problem.

11.13. In this exercise, you will derive the dual form of the soft-margin SVM optimization problem, as given in Equation (11.44). Follow these steps:

(a) Write the primal form of the soft-margin SVM optimization problem, including both the objective function and the constraints.

(b) Construct the Lagrangian $\mathcal{L}$ by introducing Lagrange multipliers for each constraint.

(c) Compute the partial derivatives of $\mathcal{L}$ with respect to the primal variables $(\mathbf{w}, b, \xi)$ and set them equal to zero. Use the resulting conditions to express the primal variables in terms of the Lagrange multipliers.

(d) Substitute these expressions back into the Lagrangian to eliminate the primal variables. Simplify the resulting expression to derive the dual optimization problem, and show that it can be written as:

$$\max_{\alpha} \quad \sum_{i=1}^{n} \alpha_i - \frac{1}{2} \sum_{i=1}^{n} \sum_{j=1}^{n} \alpha_i \alpha_j y_i y_j \mathbf{x}_i^T \mathbf{x}_j,$$

$$\text{subject to} \quad 0 \leq \alpha_i \leq C, \quad i = 1, \ldots, n,$$

$$\sum_{i=1}^{n} \alpha_i y_i = 0.$$

11.14. Prove the following properties of the hinge loss function, defined as

$$L_{\text{hinge}}(y_i, \hat{y}_i) = \max(0, 1 - y_i \hat{y}_i).$$

(a) Show that the hinge loss is strictly positive only for data points that violate the margin.

(b) Prove that the hinge loss function is convex. *Hint*: Use the fact that the pointwise maximum of two convex functions is also convex (see Exercise B.85).

(c) Show that the hinge loss bounds from above the zero–one loss:

$$L_{\text{hinge}}(y_i, \hat{y}_i) \geq L_{0-1}(y_i, \hat{y}_i),$$

where the zero–one loss is defined as:

$$L_{0-1}(y_i, \hat{y}_i) = \begin{cases} 1 & \text{if } y_i \hat{y}_i \leq 0, \\ 0 & \text{otherwise.} \end{cases}$$

(d) Compute the subgradient of the hinge loss with respect to $\hat{y}_i$, including the case when the function is not differentiable.

11.15. Explore the effects of varying the regularization parameter C in a soft-margin SVM with a quadratic kernel (i.e., a polynomial kernel of degree 2). The dataset used for this exercise is shown in Figure 11.25. Provide qualitative answers to the questions below, and use the figure to sketch how the decision boundary would change in each case.

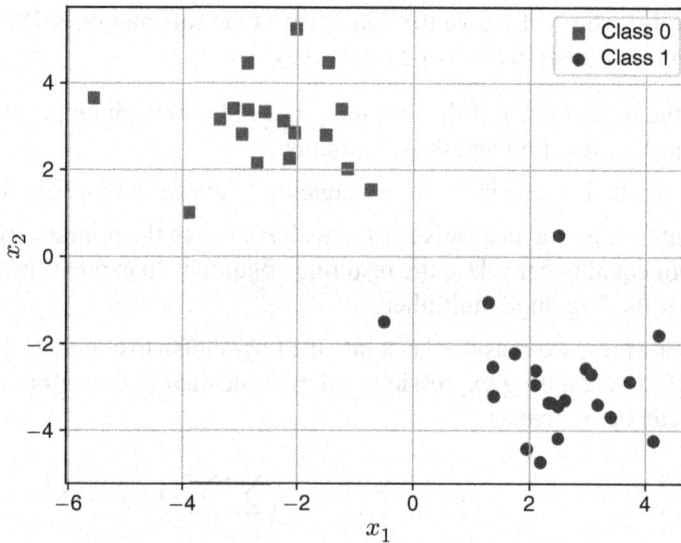

Figure 11.25: A sample dataset for exploring the effects of varying the regularization parameter C in an SVM with a quadratic kernel. Draw your answers on this figure.

(a) What is the likely position of the decision boundary when C is very large? Explain your reasoning.

(b) Where would you expect the decision boundary to lie when $C \approx 0$?

(c) Which value of C is likely to be more effective for this dataset, and why?

(d) Suggest a position for a new data point that would not alter the decision boundary when C is large.

(e) Suggest a position for a new data point that would significantly alter the decision boundary when C is large.

11.16. In this exercise, you will prove the validity of several commonly used kernels, including the polynomial and RBF kernels.

As discussed in the chapter, there are two main approaches to establish the validity of a kernel function:

- **Mercer's theorem**: A kernel is valid if the corresponding kernel matrix is positive semidefinite (PSD) for any finite dataset. This approach typically involves algebraic or matrix-theoretic arguments to demonstrate the PSD property.

- **Feature maps**: A kernel is valid if it can be expressed as a dot product in some feature space, i.e., there exists a mapping ϕ such that $k(\mathbf{x}, \mathbf{z}) = \phi(\mathbf{x})^T \phi(\mathbf{z})$. This approach involves either explicitly constructing ϕ or demonstrating that the kernel corresponds to such a dot product.

For each of the following cases, prove that k is a valid kernel, assuming that the given k_1 and k_2 are valid kernels. Whenever possible, provide proofs using both approaches. Note that some proofs build upon results from earlier parts of the exercise.

(a) $k(\mathbf{x}, \mathbf{z}) = ck_1(\mathbf{x}, \mathbf{z})$, where $c > 0$.

(b) $k(\mathbf{x}, \mathbf{z}) = k_1(\mathbf{x}, \mathbf{z}) + k_2(\mathbf{x}, \mathbf{z})$. *Hint*: For the feature map approach, construct a new feature map by concatenating those of k_1 and k_2.

(c) $k(\mathbf{x}, \mathbf{z}) = k_1(\mathbf{x}, \mathbf{z}) \cdot k_2(\mathbf{x}, \mathbf{z})$.

    i. Mercer's theorem: Use Schur product theorem [276], which states that the element-wise (Hadamard) product of two PSD matrices is also PSD.

    ii. (*) Feature map: Construct a combined feature map using the Kronecker product of the feature maps of k_1 and k_2. For two vectors $\mathbf{u} \in \mathbb{R}^m$ and $\mathbf{v} \in \mathbb{R}^n$, their Kronecker product is defined as:

$$\mathbf{u} \otimes \mathbf{v} = \begin{bmatrix} u_1 v_1 \\ u_1 v_2 \\ \vdots \\ u_1 v_n \\ u_2 v_1 \\ u_2 v_2 \\ \vdots \\ u_m v_n \end{bmatrix}.$$

    That is, the Kronecker product generates all pairwise products between elements of the two vectors.

(d) The polynomial kernel: $k(\mathbf{x}, \mathbf{z}) = (\mathbf{x}^T \mathbf{z} + 1)^d$, where $d > 0$ is an integer.

    i. Mercer's theorem: Use the fact that an integer power of a PSD matrix is also PSD. This follows from the Schur product theorem.

    ii. (*) Feature map: Use the identity

$$(x + 1)^d = \sum_{k=0}^{d} \binom{d}{k} x^k$$

to write the kernel as

$$k(\mathbf{x}, \mathbf{z}) = \sum_{k=0}^{d} \binom{d}{k} (\mathbf{x}^T \mathbf{z})^k.$$

Then, expand each term $(\mathbf{x}^T \mathbf{z})^k$ using the multinomial theorem:

$$(\mathbf{x}^T \mathbf{z})^k = \left(\sum_{i=1}^{n} x_i z_i \right)^k = \sum_{|\boldsymbol{\alpha}|=k} \frac{k!}{\alpha_1! \cdots \alpha_n!} \prod_{i=1}^{n} x_i^{\alpha_i} z_i^{\alpha_i}.$$

Show that this expression corresponds to a dot product in a higher-dimensional space and construct the explicit feature map $\phi(\mathbf{x})$ accordingly.

(e) $k(\mathbf{x}, \mathbf{z}) = \exp(k_1(\mathbf{x}, \mathbf{z}))$.

  i. Mercer's theorem: Use the Taylor expansion of the exponential function:

$$\exp(x) = \sum_{n=0}^{\infty} \frac{x^n}{n!}.$$

  Apply this expansion to the kernel matrix K_1 and analyze the properties of the resulting matrix.

  ii. (**) Feature map: Use the Taylor expansion above to show that the feature space consists of all degree-n Kronecker products of the feature vectors induced by $k_1(\mathbf{x}, \mathbf{z}) = \mathbf{x}^T \mathbf{z}$, each weighted by $\frac{1}{\sqrt{n!}}$. Show that this defines a valid dot product in an (infinite-dimensional) feature space.

(f) The RBF kernel: $k(\mathbf{x}, \mathbf{z}) = \exp(-\gamma \|\mathbf{x} - \mathbf{z}\|^2)$, where $\gamma > 0$. *Hint*: Expand the squared norm and use the results from previous parts.

11.17. In this question, you will develop a kernelized version of the 1-nearest-neighbors (1-NN) classifier by applying the kernel trick to operate in an implicit feature space.

Recall that the 1-NN classifier assigns a new input vector $\mathbf{x}$ to the class of its closest training sample $\mathbf{x}'$, using the squared Euclidean distance $\|\mathbf{x} - \mathbf{x}'\|^2$.

(a) Show that the squared Euclidean distance can be expressed using only dot products between input vectors, and derive the corresponding 1-NN classification rule.

(b) Apply the kernel trick to obtain a kernelized version of the 1-NN classifier. Write down the resulting classification rule in terms of the kernel function $k(\mathbf{x}, \mathbf{x}')$.

(c) Explain the advantages of using the kernelized version of the 1-NN classifier compared to the standard version.

11.18. In this question, you will derive a kernelized version of linear regression by extending the ordinary least squares (OLS) algorithm to operate in a high-dimensional feature space using the kernel trick.

Recall that the gradient descent update rule for standard linear regression with weight vector $\mathbf{w} \in \mathbb{R}^d$ is given by:

$$\mathbf{w} \leftarrow \mathbf{w} + \alpha \sum_{i=1}^{n} \left(y_i - \mathbf{w}^T \mathbf{x}_i \right) \mathbf{x}_i,$$

where α is the learning rate, and $(\mathbf{x}_i, y_i)$ is the i-th training sample.

Now, let $\phi \colon \mathbb{R}^d \to \mathbb{R}^p$ be a feature map that transforms each input $\mathbf{x}$ into a high-dimensional feature vector $\phi(\mathbf{x})$, and let $k(\mathbf{x}, \mathbf{z}) = \phi(\mathbf{x})^T \phi(\mathbf{z})$ be the kernel function corresponding to ϕ.

(a) Write the gradient descent update rule for the weight vector $\mathbf{w}$ in the high-dimensional feature space $\mathbb{R}^p$, using $\phi(\mathbf{x})$ instead of $\mathbf{x}$. Why does this become computationally expensive when p is very large?

(b) Prove that at every step of gradient descent, the weight vector $\mathbf{w}$ can be written as a linear combination of the mapped training examples:

$$\mathbf{w} = \sum_{j=1}^{n} \alpha_j \phi(\mathbf{x}_j),$$

where α_j are scalar coefficients. Assume that $\mathbf{w}$ is initialized to $\mathbf{0}$, and show by induction that this form is preserved after each gradient descent update.

(c) Derive the update rule for the coefficients α_j by substituting the expression for $\mathbf{w}$ into the gradient descent update. Express the result using only kernel values $k(\mathbf{x}_i, \mathbf{x}_j)$.

(d) Write the prediction rule for a new input $\mathbf{x}$ using the learned coefficients α_j and kernel function evaluations $k(\mathbf{x}, \mathbf{x}_j)$.

(e) Summarize the complete kernelized linear regression algorithm using gradient descent.

11.19. (*) In this exercise, you will explore the kernelized version of ridge regression using the representer theorem. Ridge regression in its standard form solves the following optimization problem:

$$\min_{\mathbf{w} \in \mathbb{R}^d, b \in \mathbb{R}} \|\mathbf{w}\|^2 + \lambda \sum_{i=1}^{n} \left(y_i - \mathbf{w}^T \mathbf{x}_i - b \right)^2,$$

where $\mathbf{w} \in \mathbb{R}^d$ is the weight vector, $b \in \mathbb{R}$ is the bias term, and $\lambda > 0$ is the regularization parameter.

Let $\phi \colon \mathbb{R}^d \to \mathbb{R}^p$ be a feature map that transforms input vectors into a high-dimensional feature space. According to the **representer theorem** [532], the solution to a regularized empirical risk minimization problem, such as ridge regression, lies in the span of the mapped training examples and can therefore be expressed as:

$$\mathbf{w} = \sum_{i=1}^{n} \alpha_i \phi(\mathbf{x}_i),$$

where $\alpha = [\alpha_1, \alpha_2, \ldots, \alpha_n]^T$ are coefficients that depend on the training data.

This allows ridge regression to be generalized to a high-dimensional feature space using a kernel using a kernel function $k(\mathbf{x}, \mathbf{z}) = \phi(\mathbf{x})^T \phi(\mathbf{z})$, without explicitly computing the feature map.

(a) Reformulate the ridge regression objective for the high-dimensional feature space $\mathbb{R}^p$ by replacing each $\mathbf{x}_i$ with its mapped feature vector $\phi(\mathbf{x}_i)$.

(b) Based on the representer theorem, substitute $\mathbf{w} = \sum_{i=1}^{n} \alpha_i \phi(\mathbf{x}_i)$ into the ridge regression objective, and express the resulting optimization problem entirely in terms of the coefficient vector α and the kernel matrix $K \in \mathbb{R}^{n \times n}$. Show that the optimal α satisfies:

$$(K + \lambda I)\alpha = \mathbf{y},$$

where $\mathbf{y} = [y_1, y_2, \ldots, y_n]^T$ is the vector of training targets.

(c) Write the prediction rule for a new input $\mathbf{x}$ in terms of α and the kernel function.

(d) Discuss how the choice of kernel function (e.g., linear, polynomial, RBF) and the regularization parameter λ influence the model's capacity and generalization ability. Provide examples of underfitting and overfitting scenarios based on these choices.

(e) Compare kernel ridge regression (KRR) and support vector regression (SVR) in terms of their loss function, robustness to outliers, sparsity of the coefficient vector α, and computational efficiency.

11.20. You are given a binary classification dataset with a single real-valued feature $x \in \mathbb{R}$ and labels $y \in \{-1, 1\}$. The dataset includes three positive examples ($y = 1$) at $x = \{-3, 2, 3\}$ and three negative examples ($y = -1$) at $x = \{-1, 0, 1\}$.

(a) Is it possible to perfectly separate the positive and negative examples using a linear boundary in the original 1D space? Justify your answer.

(b) Define the feature mapping $\phi(x) = (x, x^2)$, which maps each input from $\mathbb{R}$ into $\mathbb{R}^2$. Apply this mapping to all data points and list their transformed coordinates. Plot the transformed points in the new 2D feature space.

(c) In the transformed $\mathbb{R}^2$ space, is a linear separator capable of perfectly classifying the data? Provide a brief explanation.

(d) Derive the kernel function $k(x, z)$ corresponding to the mapping $\phi(x)$, and express it explicitly in terms of x and z.

(e) Using geometric reasoning in the feature space, find the equation of the maximum-margin hyperplane in the form $w_1 z_1 + w_2 z_2 + b = 0$, where $(z_1, z_2) = \phi(x)$. Determine the values of w_1, w_2, and b, and compute the margin.

(f) Plot the separating hyperplane along with the margin boundaries in the 2D feature space. Highlight the support vectors in your plot.

(g) Map the separating hyperplane back to the original input space. Plot the resulting decision boundary and describe its shape.

(h) Calculate the Lagrange multipliers α_i and the bias term b for the SVM decision function:

$$h(x) = \text{sign}\left(\sum_{i \in S} \alpha_i y_i k(x, x_i) + b\right),$$

where S is the set of support vectors. *Hint*: Use the dual form of the SVM and the constraints on the α_i values.

11.21. Discuss how each of the following changes affects: (1) the margin width of the SVM (referring to the margin in the high-dimensional feature space for kernel methods), (2) the number of support vectors, (3) the shape and complexity of the decision boundary in the original input space, and (4) the bias–variance tradeoff:

(a) Increasing the value of C in a soft-margin SVM

(b) Increasing the polynomial degree in an SVM with a polynomial kernel

(c) Increasing the value of γ in an SVM with an RBF kernel

(d) Switching from a linear kernel to an RBF kernel

(e) Increasing the value of ν in a ν-SVM

(f) Increasing the value of ϵ in support vector regression (SVR)

(g) Increasing the class weight of the minority class in an imbalanced dataset

11.22. (*) LIBLINEAR is a popular library for solving large-scale linear SVM problems. Its algorithm is based on a dual coordinate descent method, as described in the paper *A Dual Coordinate Descent Method for Large-scale Linear SVM* by Hsieh et al. (2008) [280]. Read the paper carefully and answer the following questions:

(a) Describe the main steps of the dual coordinate descent algorithm as outlined in the paper.

(b) Explain the differences between the L1-SVM and L2-SVM formulations. How does the algorithm handle these differences in terms of the objective function and the optimization process?

(c) The algorithm relies on the projected gradient method to enforce box constraints on the dual variables. Describe how the projected gradient is computed and why it is necessary.

(d) Explain why the algorithm is guaranteed to converge to the optimal solution.

(e) What is the computational complexity of a single iteration of the algorithm in terms of n (number of instances) and d (number of features)? How does the algorithm exploit sparsity to improve efficiency?

(f) The authors state that the algorithm achieves an ϵ-optimal solution in $\mathcal{O}(\log(1/\epsilon))$ iterations. Derive this result from the linear convergence rate established in Theorem 1. What does this imply about the overall runtime complexity of the algorithm?

(g) Describe the shrinking technique and how it reduces the number of computations while preserving convergence guarantees.

(h) The paper compares dual coordinate descent with other solvers such as Pegasos, TRON, SVM^{perf}, and PCD (Primal Coordinate Descent). Compare these methods in terms of their applicability to L1-SVM vs. L2-SVM, computational efficiency, memory usage, and convergence behavior.

(i) Although the method is designed for linear SVMs, how might it be extended to kernelized SVMs? What challenges would this adaptation present?

(j) Suggest potential improvements to the algorithm or its implementation. How might it be further optimized or generalized to other problem settings?

(k) (Optional) Implement a simplified version of the dual coordinate descent algorithm for L1-SVM and test it on a small dataset.

11.10.3 Programming Exercises

11.23. Support vector machines (SVMs) are well-suited for high-dimensional datasets, where the number of features far exceeds the number of samples. This property makes them effective for tasks such as biomedical classification, where each sample may be represented by thousands of measured attributes.

The Arcene dataset[28], originally created for the NIPS 2003 feature selection challenge, involves distinguishing between cancerous and normal tissue samples based on mass-spectrometric data. Each sample includes 10,000 features: 7,000 derived from real measurements and 3,000 synthetic features, which were artificially generated to test the ability of the algorithms to ignore irrelevant attributes.

(a) Download and load the dataset:

　　 i. Download the Arcene dataset from the UCI Machine Learning Repository.

　　 ii. Extract the following files into a local directory:

- `arcene_train.data`: Contains 100 training samples, each with 10,000 features (whitespace-separated).
- `arcene_train.labels`: Binary labels for the training samples (1 = cancer, -1 = normal).
- `arcene_valid.data`: Contains 100 validation samples.
- `arcene_valid.labels`: Binary labels for the validation samples.

　　 Note: The file `arcene_test.data` contains 700 unlabeled test samples that will not be used in this exercise.

---

28. https://archive.ics.uci.edu/dataset/167/arcene

iii. Load the dataset into Pandas DataFrames using the following code:

```
import pandas as pd

data_path = 'datasets'

# Load training data
X_train = pd.read_csv(f'{data_path}/arcene_train.data', sep='\s+',
                      header=None)
y_train = pd.read_csv(f'{data_path}/arcene_train.labels',
                      header=None).squeeze()


# Load test data
X_test = pd.read_csv(f'{data_path}/arcene_valid.data', sep='\s+',
                     header=None)
y_test = pd.read_csv(f'{data_path}/arcene_valid.labels',
                     header=None).squeeze()
```

(b) Data exploration:

    i. Examine the distribution of the class labels. Is the dataset balanced?

    ii. Plot histograms or boxplots for a random subset of features. What do you observe?

    iii. Compute the pairwise correlation between features (or a subset). Do you notice any strong correlations or redundancies?

(c) Data preprocessing:

    i. Identify and remove any features with zero or near-zero variance. Why might these features be uninformative?

    ii. Standardize the features to have zero mean and unit variance. Why is this step important when using SVMs?

(d) Train a linear SVM:

    i. Use the LinearSVC class to train a linear SVM classifier on the training data using the default regularization parameter ($C = 1$).

    ii. Evaluate the model's performance on the training and test sets using metrics such as accuracy and AUC.

    iii. Test different values of C (e.g., $10^{-6}, 10^{-5}, \ldots, 10^{-1}$). How does regularization affect the performance?

    iv. (Optional) Use PCA or t-SNE to project the data to 2D and visualize the decision boundary.

(e) Experiment with nonlinear kernels:

    i. Use the SVC class with nonlinear kernels such as RBF or polynomial. Start with the default configuration and then tune kernel-specific hyperparameters like gamma (RBF) and degree (polynomial).

ii. Compare the performance with linear SVM. Which kernel works best and why?

iii. (Optional) Visualize the decision boundaries in the reduced 2D space.

(f) Train at least three other classifiers (e.g., logistic regression, random forest, and gradient boosting) on the same dataset. Evaluate their performance using appropriate metrics and compare the results with those of the SVM models.

(g) Write a short report summarizing your findings, including your data exploration, preprocessing steps, implementation details, experimental results, and key observations.

11.24. In this exercise, you will analyze the behavior of different SVM kernels on a synthetic nonlinear dataset.

(a) Generate a synthetic XOR dataset using the following code:

```
import numpy as np

X = np.random.randn(200, 2)
y = np.logical_xor(X[:, 0] > 0, X[:, 1] > 0)
y = y.astype(int) # Convert boolean to integer labels
```

This creates 200 two-dimensional data points labeled according to the XOR logic, where each point is labeled 1 when the coordinates have opposite signs, and 0 otherwise.

(b) Create a scatter plot of the data using different colors or markers for the two classes.

(c) Split the dataset into 80% training set and 20% test set.

(d) Train four SVM classifiers using Scikit-Learn's SVC class with the following kernels: linear, polynomial, RBF, and sigmoid. Use default parameters for each kernel.

(e) Evaluate each model on the training and test sets using accuracy and AUC.

(f) Create a 2×2 grid of subplots, each displaying the decision boundary for one kernel. Annotate each subplot with training/test accuracy and the number of support vectors.

(g) Explore parameter tuning for the polynomial and RBF kernels:

- Vary the degree of the polynomial kernel (e.g., 2, 3, 4, 5).
- Vary the γ parameter for the RBF kernel (e.g., 0.01, 0.1, 1, 10).

Visualize how these changes affect the decision boundary and performance.

(h) Compare ν-SVM with standard C-SVM:

i. Train NuSVC models with the same four kernels and evaluate them on the XOR dataset.

ii. Visualize the decision boundaries for each kernel and annotate each subplot with training/test accuracy and the number of support vectors.

    iii. Experiment with different ν values (e.g., 0.1, 0.3, 0.5, 0.7, 0.9) and analyze their impact on model accuracy, boundary shape, and number of support vectors.

    iv. Discuss the differences between SVC and NuSVC in terms of performance, decision boundaries, generalization ability, and computational efficiency.

(i) Summarize your findings: which model and kernel performed best on the XOR dataset, and why?

11.25. In this exercise, you will implement an SVM with an RBF kernel from scratch using the CVXOPT library. Follow these steps:

(a) Recall the dual formulation of kernel SVM, expressed in matrix form (Equation (11.63)):

$$\max_{\alpha} \quad \mathbf{1}^T \alpha - \frac{1}{2} \alpha^T Y K Y \alpha,$$

$$\text{subject to} \quad 0 \leq \alpha_i \leq C, \quad i = 1, \ldots, n,$$

$$\mathbf{y}^T \alpha = 0,$$

where α is the vector of Lagrange multipliers, K is the kernel matrix, Y is a diagonal matrix with the training labels y_i on the diagonal, and C is the regularization parameter.

(b) Design a custom estimator KernelSVC with the following components:

- Hyperparameters: regularization parameter C and kernel width γ
- Methods: fit for training and predict for prediction

(c) Implement the RBF kernel function:

$$K(\mathbf{x}_i, \mathbf{x}_j) = \exp(-\gamma \|\mathbf{x}_i - \mathbf{x}_j\|^2).$$

(d) Prepare the inputs for the CVXOPT solver:

- Y: Diagonal matrix with $Y_{ii} = y_i$
- K: Kernel matrix with entries $K_{ij} = K(\mathbf{x}_i, \mathbf{x}_j)$
- $P = YKY$: Matrix with entries $P_{ij} = y_i y_j K_{ij}$
- q: A vector of -1s
- G: Matrix enforcing the constraints $0 \leq \alpha_i \leq C$
- h: Right-hand side vector for the inequality constraints $G\alpha \leq h$
- $A = \mathbf{y}^T$: Row vector for the equality constraint
- $b = 0$: Scalar for the equality constraint

(e) Solve the QP problem to obtain the Lagrange multipliers α, and identify the support vectors.

(f) Compute the bias term b using any support vector k:

$$b = y_k - \sum_{i=1}^{n} \alpha_i y_i K(\mathbf{x}_i, \mathbf{x}_k).$$

(g) Implement the decision function:

$$f(\mathbf{x}) = \sum_{i=1}^{n} \alpha_i y_i K(\mathbf{x}_i, \mathbf{x}) + b$$

and use it to classify new data points.

(h) Test your implementation on a synthetic dataset:

   i. Generate a nonlinear dataset using the `make_moons` function:

```
from sklearn.datasets import make_moons

X, y = make_moons(n_samples=100, noise=0.2, random_state=42)
y = 2*y - 1 # Convert labels from {0, 1} to {-1, +1}
```

   ii. Split the dataset into training and test sets.

   iii. Train your `KernelSVC` model on the training set.

   iv. Evaluate the accuracy of the model on both the training and test sets.

   v. Visualize the decision boundary and highlight the support vectors.

11.26. Implement a face recognition system using SVM on the Labeled Faces in the Wild (LFW) dataset from Scikit-Learn.

(a) Load the LFW dataset using `fetch_lfw_people`[29], selecting only individuals with at least 50 images each.

(b) Display several images from the dataset along with their corresponding labels.

(c) Split the data into 80% training and 20% test sets.

(d) Build a pipeline with feature scaling (`StandardScaler`) and an RBF-kernel SVM classifier (`SVC`).

(e) Use `RandomizedSearchCV` to tune the hyperparameters C and γ over a suitable range.

(f) Evaluate the best model on the test set and display a classification report with precision, recall, and F1 score.

(g) Plot the confusion matrix to examine how well the model is performing across different classes.

(h) Analyze the most confident misclassifications:

   i. Sort the misclassified test images by their predicted probability in decreasing order (using `predict_proba`).

   ii. Display the top 10 images along with their true label, predicted label (highlighted in red), and predicted probability.

29. `https://scikit-learn.org/stable/modules/generated/sklearn.datasets.fetch_lfw_people.html`

iii. Discuss possible reasons for these errors (e.g., strong visual similarity between individuals, variations in pose or lighting, or low image quality).

(i) Compare the performance and runtime efficiency of different multi-class strategies:

- One-vs-Rest (OvR): Use `SVC` with `decision_function_shape= 'ovr'`.
- One-vs-One (OvO): Use `SVC` with `decision_function_shape= 'ovo'`.
- Crammer–Singer method: Use `LinearSVC` with `multi_class= 'crammer_singer'`.

(j) Write a short report summarizing your findings, challenges faced, and potential improvements.

11.27. In this exercise, you will explore the effect of the ϵ parameter in support vector regression (SVR) under varying noise levels.

(a) Create a synthetic 1D dataset based on the sinc[30] function, defined as:

$$\text{sinc}(x) = \frac{\sin(\pi x)}{\pi x},$$

which is commonly used in signal processing.

Generate three datasets corresponding to low, medium, and high noise levels ($\sigma = 0.05, 0.1, 0.2$) using the following code:

```
import numpy as np

x = np.linspace(-1, 1, 100)
noise_levels = [0.05, 0.1, 0.2]
datasets = [(x, np.sinc(x) + np.random.normal(scale=noise, size=x.shape))
            for noise in noise_levels]
```

(b) For each noise level, train a `LinearSVR` model using the following ϵ values: $\{0.01, 0.1, 0.2, 0.5\}$.

i. Plot the predicted regression line together with the data points for each (σ, ϵ) combination.

ii. Visualize the ϵ-tube by shading the region between $\hat{y} \pm \epsilon$ using `plt.fill_between`[31].

(c) Repeat the analysis using `SVR` with an RBF kernel:

i. Train an `SVR` model with the same set of ϵ values for each noise level.

ii. Plot the predicted curve and the ϵ-tube for each (σ, ϵ) combination.

iii. Compare the results of `SVR` with `LinearSVR` in terms of prediction accuracy, the flexibility of the ϵ-tube, and the number of support vectors.

---

30. https://en.wikipedia.org/wiki/Sinc_function
31. https://matplotlib.org/stable/api/_as_gen/matplotlib.pyplot.fill_between.html

11.28. (*) Implement the chunking method for training a hard-margin SVM, as described in Section 11.7. This method partitions the dataset into smaller subsets and iteratively solves the SVM optimization problem on these subsets. By focusing on only a fraction of the data at a time, it enables more efficient training on large datasets.

(a) Split the input dataset into multiple smaller subsets (chunks). Let the number of chunks be a configurable parameter.

(b) Iteratively train a hard-margin SVM using these steps:

  i. Start with the first chunk and solve the SVM optimization problem (e.g., using the CVXOPT library) to identify the initial support vectors (i.e., data points with to nonzero Lagrange multipliers).

  ii. For each subsequent chunk:

    A. Combine the current support vectors with the examples from the new chunk that violate the margin constraints of the current solution.

    B. Re-solve the SVM optimization problem on this combined set to obtain an updated set of support vectors.

  iii. Repeat until all chunks have been processed. The final solution corresponds to the separating hyperplane obtained after the last iteration (if the data is linearly separable).

(c) Evaluate your implementation:

  i. Test the chunking method on a linearly separable dataset (e.g., using make_classification with class_sep=2).

  ii. Compare the chunking method with training a standard SVM on the full dataset. Analyze differences in model accuracy, training time, and memory usage.

11.29. Compare the calibration of different classifiers using Platt scaling and isotonic regression. Follow these steps:

(a) Select a binary classification dataset from the UCI machine learning repository (e.g, the Adult Income dataset).

(b) Split the data into 70% training and 30% test sets.

(c) Train five different classifiers on the training set, including logistic regression, Gaussian naive Bayes, random forest, linear SVM, and SVM with an RBF kernel. For LinearSVC and SVC, create custom subclasses that override predict_proba to return normalized decision scores within the [0, 1] range, as demonstrated in Section 11.8.

(d) Plot the calibration curves for all classifiers using Scikit-Learn's CalibrationDisplay class.

(e) Compute the Brier score for each classifier using the uncalibrated predictions to establish a baseline.

(f) Calibrate each classifier using Scikit-Learn's `CalibratedClassifierCV` class with the following methods:

   i. Platt scaling (`method='sigmoid'`).

   ii. Isotonic regression (`method='isotonic'`).

(g) Plot the calibration curves for all calibrated models and include the corresponding Brier scores in the legend.

(h) Analyze the results by comparing calibration quality across classifiers and methods, and discuss when each calibration approach is more appropriate.

Chapter 12

Summary and Additional Resources

As we bring this first volume to a close, it is worth reflecting on the substantial ground we have covered. We began with core concepts and principles that form the foundation of machine learning, such as model capacity, the bias–variance tradeoff, regularization, and optimization. Building on this foundation, we explored a wide range of learning algorithms, including linear regression, naive Bayes, decision trees, and support vector machines. We demonstrated how to apply these methods across diverse data types—including tabular data, images, and text—as well as how to handle practical challenges such as missing values, varying feature scales, and class imbalance. Along the way, we introduced essential Python libraries like Scikit-Learn, NLTK, and XGBoost, which provide practical tools for applying these techniques in real-world settings.

This concluding chapter offers a high-level recap of the key ideas covered in this volume, along with best practices and resources to support both practical applications and academic research in machine learning. The chapter is organized as follows. Section 12.1 summarizes the key concepts introduced in the book. Section 12.2 reviews the strengths and limitations of the supervised learning algorithms discussed, and includes a runtime complexity table to help assess their scalability. Section 12.3 outlines best practices for designing and executing machine learning experiments—from experimental setup to statistical analysis of results—illustrated with a detailed Python example. Section 12.4 offers guidance for pursuing research in machine learning, including tips on writing academic papers, an overview of key conferences and journals, and open research questions that are being actively explored by the research community. Section 12.5 discusses machine learning competitions as a valuable opportunity to engage with real-world problems and apply your skills in a practical setting. Section 12.6 recommends resources for further learning to deepen your knowledge and explore more advanced topics beyond the scope of this book. Section 12.7 offers a glimpse into the second volume of the book. Finally, Section 12.8 includes a set of integrative exercises designed to reinforce and synthesize the knowledge you have gained throughout this book.

12.1 Supervised Learning Summary

Machine learning enables systems to automatically learn patterns from data, making it especially useful for tasks that are too complex, dynamic, or poorly defined for traditional rule-based programming. Among the various branches of machine learning, **supervised learning** is the most widely studied and applied. It relies on **labeled data**, consisting of input–output pairs $(\mathbf{x}, y)$, where $\mathbf{x}$ represents the input features and y the corresponding target. Inputs can range from simple numerical vectors to complex data types such as text, images, or sequences, often requiring **feature engineering** to transform them into a suitable numerical format.

The primary goal in supervised learning is to learn a function $f(\mathbf{x})$ that accurately maps inputs to outputs, based on the observed data. In **classification**, f predicts a class label or a probability distribution over classes, while in **regression**, it outputs a continuous value.

Models can be broadly divided into parametric and nonparametric types. **Parametric models**, such as linear and logistic regression, assume a fixed functional form defined by a set of parameters $\mathbf{w}$. These models are computationally efficient and interpretable but limited in flexibility. In contrast, **nonparametric models**, such as k-nearest neighbors and decision trees, do not have a fixed number of parameters, allowing them to adapt their complexity to the data.

Many supervised learning algorithms aim to model the **data-generating process** by associating inputs and outputs through suitable probability distributions. For example, naive Bayes classifiers model the class-conditional distributions of the inputs and apply **Bayes' theorem** to infer the most probable label, whereas logistic regression treats the output as a Bernoulli random variable whose parameter p is given by applying the **logistic (sigmoid) function** to a linear combination of the input features.

The **no free lunch theorem** states that no single learning algorithm is universally optimal across all possible problems. Fortunately, real-world problems are not uniformly distributed over the space of all functions. Instead, they often exhibit useful structure—such as **smoothness** (nearby inputs tend to have similar outputs) and **limited complexity** (they can be approximated by models with relatively few parameters)—which machine learning algorithms can exploit to generalize effectively.

Learning involves optimizing an **objective function**, such as minimizing prediction error or maximizing likelihood, by searching the **hypothesis space**—the set of functions expressible by the chosen model class. For parametric models, this is typically achieved using optimization algorithms like **gradient descent** or **Newton's method**. Conversely, nonparametric models often rely on heuristic or greedy algorithms, such as the recursive partitioning algorithm used to build decision trees.

Some natural objective functions, such as the 0–1 loss in classification, are non-differentiable or difficult to optimize directly. As a result, models are often trained using **surrogate loss functions**, such as log loss, which are typically derived from **maximum likelihood estimation**. These surrogates enable optimization via gradient-based methods, though they may not perfectly align with the task-specific objective. As such, model performance is typically assessed using **evaluation metrics** such as accuracy, precision, recall, or AUC—metrics that better reflect the practical goals of the task and account for **class imbalance**, where one class dominates the dataset and standard accuracy may be misleading.

Ultimately, the success of a machine learning model depends on its **generalization ability**, i.e., how well it performs on new, unseen data. Models that perform well on the training data but poorly on unseen examples are said to **overfit**, while those that perform poorly on both are said to **underfit**. Comparing the model's performance on the training and test sets can help diagnose these issues: a large gap typically indicates overfitting, whereas consistently low performance suggests underfitting.

Achieving good generalization performance requires striking a balance between between **bias** and **variance**. High-bias models are overly simplistic and may fail to capture the underlying patterns in the data, while high-variance models are too sensitive to the training set, fitting noise or idiosyncrasies that do not generalize well to new examples. Techniques like **regularization** (penalizing model complexity) and **early stopping** (halting training based on validation performance) help manage the **bias–variance tradeoff** and improve generalization.

Hyperparameters, such as regularization strength or learning rate, control model complexity and influence the training dynamics. **Hyperparameter tuning** methods, including grid search, random search, and Bayesian optimization, combined with **cross-validation** for reliable model evaluation, are crucial for achieving strong performance while avoiding overfitting.

Ensemble methods further improve generalization by combining the strengths of multiple models. Common approaches include **bagging** (training models on different subsets of the data to reduce variance), **boosting** (building models sequentially, where each one focuses on the errors of its predecessors), and **stacking** (using a meta-learner to combine the predictions of diverse models). Ensembles typically outperform single models on complex tasks and are widely used in practice due to their consistently strong performance across diverse domains.

High-dimensional data introduces additional challenges, collectively known as the **curse of dimensionality**, where distances become less meaningful and data sparsity impedes learning. Techniques such as **feature selection** and **dimensionality reduction** can help mitigate these issues by identifying the most informative features or projecting the data into a lower-dimensional space that preserves its essential structure.

While much of machine learning research focuses on designing better models and algorithms, empirical evidence suggests that increasing the amount of **high-quality data** is often the most effective way to improve performance. In many cases, simple models trained on large datasets can outperform more complex models trained on limited data. However, acquiring high-quality labeled data can be costly and time-consuming. To address this, recent advances have focused on leveraging large amounts of unlabeled data using models such as **semi-supervised learning** and **self-supervised learning**, which combine elements of supervised learning with other learning paradigms. These models will be explored in depth in future volumes of this series.

Despite rapid advancements in the field—especially in areas like deep learning, large language models (LLMs), and agentic AI systems—progress in the core foundations of machine learning remains essential. Research on topics such as generalization, optimization, model capacity, and training dynamics, as explored in this book, continues to steer the development of more reliable, efficient, and theoretically grounded algorithms. At the same time, growing concerns around explainability, fairness, and robustness are reshaping how machine learning systems are designed and deployed, emphasizing the need for models that are not only accurate but also transparent, trustworthy, and scalable.

12.2 Choosing a Learning Algorithm

With the abundance of machine learning algorithms available today, choosing the most appropriate one can be daunting. Fortunately, many real-world problems can be effectively addressed using a small set of well-established models. The choice of algorithm typically depends on several key

Algorithm	Pros	Cons
Linear Regression	Simple and interpretable; has a closed-form solution	Assumes linearity; sensitive to outliers and multicollinearity
Logistic Regression	Fast and interpretable; effective on high-dimensional, linearly separable data	Cannot capture complex non-linear patterns; sensitive to outliers
K-Nearest Neighbors (KNN)	Non-parametric and flexible; no training phase; effective when similar instances have similar labels	Slow inference; sensitive to noise; affected by the curse of dimensionality
Naive Bayes	Extremely fast; effective on high-dimensional, sparse data (e.g., text)	Strong independence assumption; may underperform if this is violated
Decision Tree	Easy to interpret; flexible and non-parametric; can fit the training data perfectly	Prone to overfitting; sensitive to small data perturbations
Random Forest	High predictive accuracy; robust to overfitting; provides feature importance scores	Less interpretable than single trees; slower to train
Gradient Boosting	Strong predictive performance; effectively handles complex patterns; supports custom loss functions	Sensitive to hyperparameters; slower to train; limited parallelism
Support Vector Machine (SVM)	Effective in high-dimensional spaces; robust to overfitting	Computationally expensive on large datasets; sensitive to kernel and parameter settings

Table 12.1: Summary of common supervised learning algorithms

factors: the type of learning task (e.g., classification or regression), the characteristics of the data (such as dataset size, feature types, and dimensionality), and practical considerations including training and prediction time, scalability, robustness to noise, and interpretability.

Table 12.1 summarizes the main supervised learning algorithms covered in this book, outlining their key strengths and limitations to help guide model selection.

12.2.1   Runtime Complexity

Another important consideration when comparing algorithms is their computational complexity, both during training and inference. Table 12.2 summarizes the asymptotic runtime complexities of the same set of algorithms. These values serve as general guidelines; actual runtimes may depend on additional factors such as the specific implementation, data characteristics, hardware used (e.g., CPU vs. GPU), and degree of parallelism.

Algorithm	Training	Inference	Comments
Linear Regression	$\mathcal{O}(nd^2 + d^3)$	$\mathcal{O}(d)$	Assumes closed-form solution; training with SGD takes $\mathcal{O}(Id)$.
Logistic Regression	$\mathcal{O}(I(nd + d^2))$	$\mathcal{O}(d)$	Shown for quasi-Newton methods (e.g., `lbfgs`); other solvers may vary.
KNN	$\mathcal{O}(1)$	$\mathcal{O}(nd)$	No training phase; inference can be accelerated using tree-based structures.
Naive Bayes	$\mathcal{O}(nd)$	$\mathcal{O}(d)$	
Decision Tree	$\mathcal{O}(dn \log n)$	$\mathcal{O}(h)$	Tree height h ranges from $\log n$ (balanced) to n (worst case).
Random Forest	$\mathcal{O}(Tdn \log n)$	$\mathcal{O}(Th)$	Training and prediction are parallelizable across individual trees.
Gradient Boosting	$\mathcal{O}(Tdn \log n)$	$\mathcal{O}(Th)$	Traditionally sequential; modern libraries such as XGBoost exploit parallelism.
SVM	$\mathcal{O}(n^2 d + n^3)$	$\mathcal{O}(d)$	Linear SVMs reduce training time to $\mathcal{O}(nd)$.

Table 12.2: Runtime complexities of common supervised learning algorithms. Notation: n is the number of training samples, d the number of features, I the number of iterations in gradient-based methods, T the number of trees in ensemble models, and h the height of a decision tree.

12.3 Conducting Machine Learning Experiments

Systematic experimentation lies at the heart of machine learning research and development. Whether evaluating a new model, comparing algorithms, or tuning hyperparameters, a structured workflow is essential for obtaining reliable and reproducible results. This section outlines best practices for rigorous experimental design and execution.

12.3.1 Designing Experiments

Effective experimentation goes beyond simply running models: it involves formulating well-defined questions, designing fair comparisons, and drawing valid conclusions. A rigorous methodology helps ensure that your findings are reliable, reproducible, and scientifically sound. The following guidelines outline key principles to consider when designing machine learning experiments:

- Set clear objectives: Start by defining the goals of your experiment. Are you proposing a new algorithm, adapting an existing method to a new domain, or aiming to improve its performance in terms of accuracy, robustness, or computational efficiency?

  Clearly articulate both the null hypothesis (e.g., "The proposed method performs no better than the baseline") and the alternative hypothesis (e.g., "The proposed method achieves at least a 2% absolute improvement in accuracy over the baseline"). See Section D.7 for a detailed discussion on hypothesis testing.

- Choose appropriate evaluation metrics: Select metrics that are aligned with the objectives of the task and the priorities of the application domain. For example, in medical diagnosis, recall may be more important than precision.

- Select appropriate datasets: Use datasets that support the objectives of your experiment. For standard tasks like image classification or sentiment analysis, benchmark datasets such as MNIST, CIFAR-10, or IMDb facilitate direct comparisons with prior work. When proposing a new algorithm, evaluate it on multiple datasets that vary in characteristics such as size, dimensionality, feature types, number of classes, degree of class imbalance, and domain. This helps demonstrate the robustness and generalizability of your method across diverse settings.[1]

- Establish performance benchmarks: Identify reference points for evaluating your model, such as simple baselines (e.g., predicting the majority class in a classification task), state-of-the-art methods from the literature, or public leaderboard scores. Establishing these baselines early makes your results easier to interpret and compare.

- Consider ethical implications: Ethical considerations should be integrated throughout the project lifecycle—from data collection to model deployment. Key aspects include:

  – Detecting and mitigating bias: Examine datasets and model outputs for potential biases, such as underrepresentation of certain demographic groups. For example, facial recognition models trained on datasets that lack sufficient representation of certain ethnic groups may produce systematically biased predictions.

  – Privacy protection: Ensure that sensitive data is anoynmized and handled in compliance with data protection laws and ethical guidelines, such as the General Data Protection Regulation (GDPR)[2].

  – Fairness and transparency: Promote fairness, accountability, and transparency in your models using established guidelines such as IBM's AI Fairness 360[3] and the EU Ethics Guidelines for Trustworthy AI[4].

In some domains, these practices are not merely recommended—they are legally mandated. For instance, the EU AI Act[5] defines rules that must be followed by a broad range of AI systems deployed in the EU, while the HIPAA[6] governs the protection of healthcare data in the United States.

---

1. As a reviewer of academic papers, I often encounter submissions that propose new methods but evaluate them on only one or two datasets or environments. Such limited scope makes it difficult to assess the true contribution of the work and raises concerns about potential "cherry-picking" of favorable results.
2. https://commission.europa.eu/law/law-topic/data-protection_en
3. https://aif360.readthedocs.io
4. https://digital-strategy.ec.europa.eu/en/library/ethics-guidelines-trustworthy-ai
5. https://artificialintelligenceact.eu
6. https://www.hhs.gov/programs/hipaa

- Plan for scalability: As experiments grow in scale, local computational resources may become insufficient. Estimate memory, runtime, and storage requirements in advance. If needed, leverage cloud platforms such as AWS[7], Google Cloud[8], or Microsoft Azure[9] to conduct large-scale experiments efficiently and cost-effectively.

- Ensure reproducibility: Reproducibility relies on meticulous documentation and version control. Use tools such as Git to track changes in code, configurations, and experimental setups. Record all details necessary to rerun the experiment under the same conditions, including hyperparameters, random seeds, and dataset splits. Tools like MLflow[10] and Weights & Biases[11] facilitate experiment tracking and result comparison across runs, while containerization tools such as Docker[12] can capture the full runtime environment, including libraries, dependencies, and system configurations.

12.3.2   Running Experiments

Once your experimental design is in place, conducting experiments in a structured and disciplined manner is essential for drawing reliable and reproducible conclusions. The following best practices help ensure the integrity, transparency, and utility of your experimental results:

- Account for randomness with multiple runs: When stochastic elements are involved, such as random initialization or data shuffling, run each experiment multiple times with different random seeds. Report the mean and standard deviation of the results to reflect performance variability and support robust conclusions. Record the random seeds used in each run to support reproducibility.

- Preprocess data consistently: Apply the same preprocessing steps (e.g., feature scaling, imputation of missing values) across all experiments. Inconsistent preprocessing can introduce confounding factors and undermine the validity of your comparisons.

- Use cross-validation when feasible: Rather than relying on a single train/validation/test split, use cross-validation to obtain more reliable performance estimates, especially when working with limited data.

- Establish a baseline: Start with a simple model (e.g., logistic regression or a shallow decision tree) to establish a reference point for comparison. Unless a more complex model provides clear, measurable gains, simpler alternatives are often preferable due to their interpretability and ease of deployment (Occam's razor).

- Tune hyperparameters efficiently: Rather than exhaustively searching the entire hyperparameter space, use informed strategies such as coarse-to-fine search to balance performance

7. https://aws.amazon.com
8. https://cloud.google.com
9. https://azure.microsoft.com
10. https://mlflow.org
11. https://wandb.ai/site
12. https://www.docker.com

gains with computational cost. Be mindful of overfitting to the validation set, especially when tuning on small datasets.

- Reserve the test set for final evaluation: Do not use the test set during training, model selection, or hyperparameter tuning. Use it only once, at the end of the process, to obtain an unbiased estimate of the model's generalization performance.

- Perform qualitative evaluation: In addition to quantitative metrics, inspect individual cases of misclassification or poor predictions. This can help uncover systematic errors in the data, feature engineering, model design, or code implementation.

- Test model robustness: Evaluate your model under varied conditions, such as noisy inputs, missing data, or distribution shifts, to assess its reliability in real-world scenarios.

12.3.3   Reporting and Documenting Results

Clear reporting and visualization are essential for communicating the results of your machine learning experiments. The following best practices help ensure that your findings are interpretable, reproducible, and meaningful:

- Report standard metrics and variability: Use widely accepted performance metrics appropriate for the task. For classification, include metrics such as accuracy, precision, recall, F1 score, and AUC-ROC. For regression, use metrics such as RMSE, MAE, and R^2. Report both the mean and standard deviation (or confidence intervals, when appropriate) across multiple random seeds or cross-validation folds to reflect variability and ensure robust conclusions.

- Use visualizations to evaluate performance: Supplement numerical metrics with diagnostic visualizations such as confusion matrices, ROC curves, precision–recall curves, and classification reports. Learning curves are especially useful for identifying underfitting or overfitting during training.

- Design clear and accessible visualizations: Ensure that all plots have clearly labeled axes, descriptive titles, and appropriate legends. Use readable font sizes and color schemes with sufficient contrast to maintain legibility across devices and when printed in grayscale.

- Log raw results: In addition to summary statistics (e.g., means and standard deviations), record raw outputs such as per-fold scores or individual run metrics. These detailed results are essential for in-depth analysis and for conducting statistical significance tests.

- Document experimental configurations: Record all relevant settings that influence the experiment, including hyperparameters, preprocessing steps, system specifications, and library versions. Thorough documentation is critical for ensuring reproducibility and facilitating future comparisons.

- Assess model calibration: Evaluate how well predicted probabilities align with true outcomes using reliability diagrams and metrics like the Brier score (see Section 11.8).

- Test for statistical significance: Use appropriate statistical tests to determine whether observed performance differences between models are statistically significant (see Section 12.3.4.8).

- Interpret results in context: Go beyond reporting metrics—explain what the results mean for the specific problem. Discuss whether the task objectives were met, acknowledge any limitations or unexpected findings, and relate the results to real-world or business impact (e.g., cost savings, improved decision-making, or enhanced user experience).

12.3.4 End-to-End Example

This section presents a complete machine learning experiment that compares the performance of several classifiers on the digits dataset[13] from Scikit-Learn. The workflow demonstrates some of the best practices discussed earlier, including repeated runs with different random seeds, performance visualization, result logging, and statistical testing.

The complete code is available in the notebook `ConductingMLExperiments.ipynb`[14] on the book's GitHub repository.

12.3.4.1 Initial Setup

We begin by importing standard libraries for numerical computation, data handling, visualization, timing, and logging:

```
import numpy as np
import pandas as pd
import matplotlib.pyplot as plt
import time
import os
import csv
```

In earlier examples, we initialized the random seed globally using `np.random.seed(42)` to ensure consistent results. Here, we instead set a distinct random seed before each evaluation round, for example, once per model and per cross-validation iteration. This allows specific results to be reproduced without rerunning the entire set of experiments and helps maintain reproducibility even if additional sources of randomness are introduced or the execution order changes.

12.3.4.2 Data Preparation

Next, we load the digits dataset, split it into training and test sets, and standardize the features:

```
from sklearn.datasets import load_digits
from sklearn.model_selection import train_test_split
from sklearn.preprocessing import StandardScaler
```

---

13. This dataset is a smaller version of MNIST, containing 1,797 grayscale images of handwritten digits (0–9), each of size 8 × 8 pixels. https://scikit-learn.org/stable/datasets/toy_dataset.html#digits-dataset
14. https://github.com/roiyeho/ml-book/blob/main/Chapter12/ConductingMLExperiments.ipynb

```
X, y = load_digits(return_X_y=True)
X_train, X_test, y_train, y_test = train_test_split(X, y, test_size=0.2,
                                                    random_state=42)


scaler = StandardScaler()
X_train = scaler.fit_transform(X_train)
X_test = scaler.transform(X_test)
```

12.3.4.3 Training and Evaluation

We now define a set of models to evaluate on the digits dataset, covering a diverse range of algorithmic families: linear models, tree-based methods, instance-based learning, and neural networks[15].
Each model is initialized with its default hyperparameters to establish a fair baseline for comparison. The only exception is LogisticRegression, where the maximum number of iterations is
increased to 1,000 to ensure convergence:

```
from sklearn.linear_model import LogisticRegression
from sklearn.neighbors import KNeighborsClassifier
from sklearn.ensemble import RandomForestClassifier, HistGradientBoostingClassifier
from sklearn.svm import SVC
from sklearn.neural_network import MLPClassifier

models = {
    'Logistic Regression': LogisticRegression(max_iter=1000),
    'KNN': KNeighborsClassifier(),
    'Random Forest': RandomForestClassifier(),
    'Gradient Boosting': HistGradientBoostingClassifier(),
    'SVM': SVC(),
    'MLP': MLPClassifier()
}
```

Each model is evaluated on the digits dataset using five-fold cross-validation, repeated with
three different random seeds, resulting in $3 \times 5 = 15$ evaluation rounds per model. For each model,
we report the mean accuracy, standard deviation, and average training time across these 15 rounds.

To enable finer control over the evaluation process, we use Scikit-Learn's KFold[16] class instead
of the cross_val_score utility. This allows us to iterate explicitly over each fold, measure the
training time, and log detailed metrics. The KFold class partitions the dataset into k consecutive
folds and provides the train/test indices for each split. By instantiating KFold with a different
random seed for each run, we ensure varied training/validation splits across evaluation rounds.

Note that some estimators, such as KNeighborsClassifier, do not accept a random_state
parameter. In such cases, variability in the results arises solely from the shuffled splits rather than
internal stochasticity.

---

15. Although neural networks have not yet been discussed in detail, we include them here for completeness. Note that
    Scikit-Learn does not support deep learning; the MLPClassifier used here is a classical multi-layer perceptron
    (MLP) with a relatively small number of hidden units.

16. https://scikit-learn.org/stable/modules/generated/sklearn.model_selection.KFold.html

The function below performs the full evaluation procedure:

```python
from sklearn.model_selection import KFold

def run_experiments(models, X_train, y_train, n_seeds=3):
    """
    Train and evaluate each model using multiple random seeds and cross-validation.
    Returns a dictionary mapping model names to evaluation metrics.
    """
    results = {}

    for name, model in models.items():
        accuracy_scores = []
        training_times = []

        for seed in range(42, 42 + n_seeds):
            # Set random seed if applicable
            if 'random_state' in model.get_params():
                model.set_params(random_state=seed)

            # Cross-validation with shuffled splits
            cv = KFold(n_splits=5, shuffle=True, random_state=seed)
            for train_index, test_index in cv.split(X_train):
                X_cv_train, X_cv_test = X_train[train_index], X_train[test_index]
                y_cv_train, y_cv_test = y_train[train_index], y_train[test_index]

                # Fit model and record training time
                start_time = time.time()
                model.fit(X_cv_train, y_cv_train)
                end_time = time.time()
                training_time = end_time - start_time
                training_times.append(training_time)

                # Evaluate the model on the test fold
                score = model.score(X_cv_test, y_cv_test)
                accuracy_scores.append(score)

        results[name] = {
            'raw_accuracy_scores': accuracy_scores,
            'accuracy_mean': np.mean(accuracy_scores),
            'accuracy_std': np.std(accuracy_scores, ddof=1), # Bessel's correction
            'training_time_mean': np.mean(training_times)
        }

    return results

results = run_experiments(models, X_train, y_train)
```

The sample standard deviation is computed using Bessel's correction (`ddof=1`), which provides an unbiased estimate of the population standard deviation (see Section D.4.2.1).

To summarize the results in tabular form:

```
df_results = pd.DataFrame.from_dict(results, orient='index')
df_results = df_results.drop(['raw_accuracy_scores'], axis=1)
print(df_results)
```

	accuracy_mean	accuracy_std	training_time
Logistic Regression	0.968686	0.008316	0.027309
KNN	0.971696	0.010683	0.000466
Random Forest	0.971926	0.010893	0.251670
Gradient Boosting	0.967756	0.008047	1.538705
SVM	0.980508	0.008619	0.037445
MLP	0.975640	0.010851	1.173836

The table above provides a comparison of each model's average accuracy, variability (via standard deviation), and training time across 15 evaluation rounds. Among all models, SVM achieves the highest accuracy while also remaining computationally efficient. We will visualize the results and analyze their statistical significance later in this section.

12.3.4.4   Logging

Storing the experimental results in a log file is a simple yet essential practice for ensuring reproducibility and facilitating future comparisons. Logs also serve as valuable documentation, allowing you to track changes and measure progress over time.

The following code snippet saves the experiment results, including the raw accuracy scores, to a CSV file. To make each file unique and traceable, the filename includes a timestamp based on the current date and time:

```
from datetime import datetime

# Create the /logs directory if it doesn't exist
os.makedirs('logs', exist_ok=True)

# Generate a timestamped filename
timestamp = datetime.now().strftime('%Y-%m-%d_%H-%M-%S')
filename = f'logs/digits_results_{timestamp}.csv'

# Write results to a CSV file
with open(filename, 'w', newline='') as file:
    writer = csv.writer(file)
    writer.writerow(['Model Name', 'Raw Accuracy Scores', 'Accuracy Mean',
                    'Accuracy Std', 'Training Time'])
```

```
for model_name, metrics in results.items():
    writer.writerow([model_name, metrics['raw_accuracy_scores'],
                    metrics['accuracy_mean'], metrics['accuracy_std'],
                    metrics['training_time']])
```

12.3.4.5   Visualizing the Results

We now visualize the mean accuracy of each model, averaged over the 15 evaluation runs, using a bar chart with error bars indicating the standard deviation:

```
# Plot accuracy results
accuracies = [metrics['accuracy_mean'] for metrics in results.values()]
std_errors = [metrics['accuracy_std'] for metrics in results.values()]
model_names = list(results.keys())

plt.bar(model_names, accuracies, yerr=std_errors, capsize=5)
plt.ylabel('Accuracy')
plt.ylim([0.9, 1.0])
plt.xticks(rotation=45)
plt.tight_layout()
```

Figure 12.1 shows that the support vector machine (SVM) achieves the highest average accuracy, followed closely by the multi-layer perceptron (MLP). The low standard deviations indicate consistent performance across different random seeds and cross-validation folds.

We also compare the average training time of each model to assess computational efficiency:

```
# Plot training times
training_times = [results[name]['training_time'] for name in model_names]

plt.bar(model_names, training_times, color='red')
plt.ylabel('Training Time (seconds)')
plt.ylim([0, max(training_times) * 1.2])
plt.xticks(rotation=45)
plt.tight_layout()
```

Figure 12.2 reveals large differences in training time. Gradient boosting and MLP are the most time-consuming due to their complex and the number of iterations involved in training. In contrast, logistic regression and KNN are the fastest to train. While KNN has the shortest training time, its prediction phase is typically much slower than other models (not measured here). Interestingly, kernel-based SVM, which is usually considered computationally expensive, exhibits relatively fast training on this dataset.

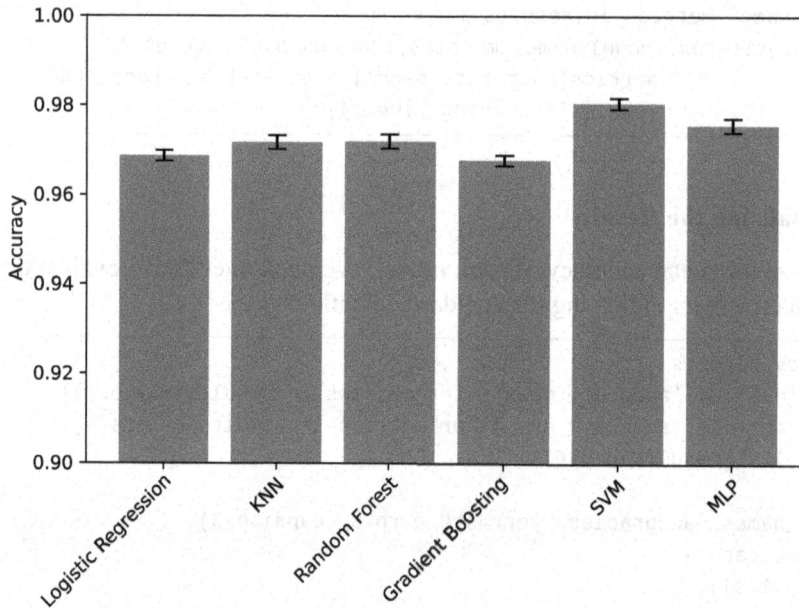

Figure 12.1: Comparison of model accuracies averaged over three random seeds and five-fold cross-validation. Error bars represent the standard deviation across the 15 evaluation rounds. SVM achieves the highest mean accuracy, followed by MLP and random forest.

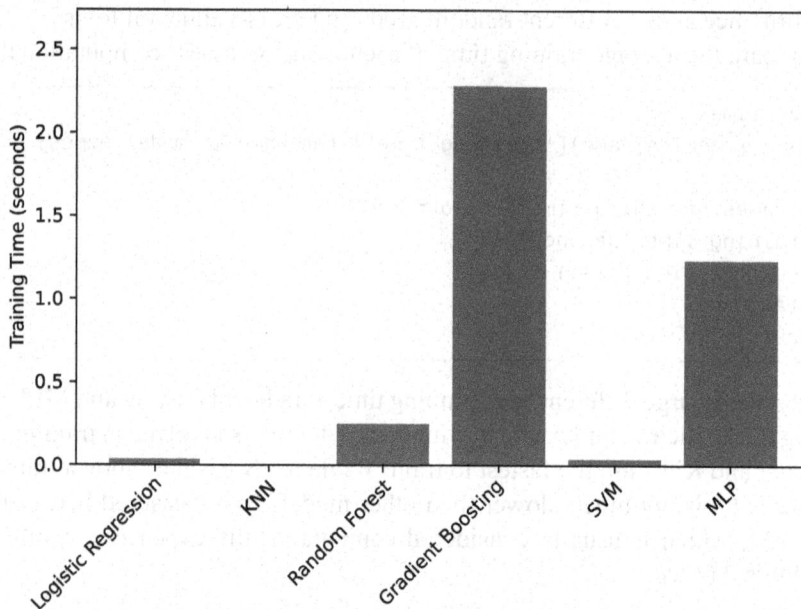

Figure 12.2: Comparison of average training times (in seconds) of the six classifiers, averaged over three random seeds and five-fold cross-validation.

12.3.4.6   Hyperparameter Tuning and Error Analysis

Having identified the top-performing models such as SVM and MLP, the next step is to further enhance their performance through hyperparameter tuning. Techniques such as grid search, random search, or Bayesian optimization can be used to identify configurations that improve predictive accuracy, reduce overfitting, or accelerate training.

Beyond tuning, analyzing model predictions can provide valuable insights into the model's behavior and failure modes:

- Confusion matrices provide a class-by-class breakdown of predictions and can expose systematic errors, such as certain digits being frequently misclassified as others (see the MNIST example in Section 5.8.3.5).

- Class-wise precision, recall, and F1 scores provide granular insights into model performance for each class and are particularly valuable when working with imbalanced datasets.

- Inspecting misclassified examples, particularly those with high loss values or those consistently misclassified across different models, can uncover ambiguous or hard-to-learn patterns in the data.

12.3.4.7   Confidence Intervals

To quantify uncertainty in model performance estimates, we can compute **confidence intervals** based on repeated evaluations. These intervals help determine whether observed differences between models are statistically meaningful or simply due to random variation.

A confidence interval defines a range within which the true value of a performance metric (e.g., mean accuracy) is expected to lie with a specified **confidence level**, typically 95%. For example, if we obtained a 95% confidence interval of [0.974, 0.982] for the model's mean accuracy, then we are 95% confident that the true mean lies within this range. For a detailed discussion on confidence intervals, see Section D.6.

Assuming that the sample mean is approximately normal (e.g., when the sample size is sufficiently large), the confidence interval for the sample mean is given by:

$$\mathrm{CI} = \overline{x} \pm z_{\alpha/2} \cdot \frac{\sigma}{\sqrt{n}}, \tag{12.1}$$

where:

- $\overline{x}$ is the sample mean (i.e., the average model accuracy across evaluation rounds),

- σ is the sample standard deviation,

- n is the number of repeated measurements (i.e., the number of evaluation rounds),

- $z_{\alpha/2}$ is the critical value from the standard normal distribution for the desired confidence level α.

As the number of repetitions n increases, the width of the confidence interval decreases, resulting in a more precise estimate of the true mean.

The function below computes a confidence interval for a given list of accuracy scores:

```python
from scipy.stats import norm

def compute_confidence_interval(scores, confidence=0.95):
    """Compute the confidence interval for a model's accuracy."""
    mean_score = np.mean(scores)
    sem = np.std(scores, ddof=1) / np.sqrt(len(scores)) # standard error of the mean
    z_value = norm.ppf((1 + confidence) / 2)
    margin_of_error = z_value * sem
    return mean_score - margin_of_error, mean_score + margin_of_error
```

We then apply this function to each model's raw accuracy scores:

```python
for name, metrics in results.items():
    lower, upper = compute_confidence_interval(metrics['raw_accuracy_scores'])
    results[name]['confidence_interval'] = (lower, upper)
```

Finally, we summarize the results in a table, displaying each model's mean accuracy followed by its 95% confidence interval in parentheses:

```python
df_results = pd.DataFrame([
    {model: f"{data['accuracy_mean']:.3f} ({data['confidence_interval'][0]:.3f}, "
            f"{data['confidence_interval'][1]:.3f})"
     for model, data in results.items()}
], index=['Accuracy (95% CI)'])

df_results
```

Figure 12.3 shows the 95% confidence intervals for each model. Overlapping intervals (e.g., between SVM and MLP) suggest that the models have comparable performance, while non-overlapping intervals indicate statistically distinguishable results.

12.3.4.8 Statistical Significance Testing

When comparing machine learning models, it is important to assess whether the observed performance differences are **statistically significant** or merely due to random variation [160, 154, 293]. Statistical testing strengthens the validity of your conclusions by accounting for variability across cross-validation folds, repeated runs, or multiple evaluation datasets.

	Logistic Regression	KNN	Random Forest	Gradient Boosting	SVM	MLP
Accuracy (95% CI)	0.969 (0.964, 0.973)	0.972 (0.966, 0.977)	0.972 (0.966, 0.977)	0.968 (0.964, 0.972)	0.981 (0.976, 0.985)	0.976 (0.970, 0.981)

Figure 12.3: 95% confidence intervals for model mean accuracy scores, based on 15 evaluation rounds.

In this section, we demonstrate how to apply common statistical tests in Python. For a detailed overview of hypothesis testing, see Section D.7.

12.3.4.8.1 Comparing Two Algorithms

To determine whether one model consistently outperforms another across repeated evaluations, two widely used tests are:

- **Paired *t*-test:** Assumes that the differences in paired scores are approximately normally distributed (see Section D.7.4.2).

- **Wilcoxon signed-rank test**: A non-parametric alternative that does not assume normality. It is preferred when the sample size is small or the distribution of differences is skewed (see Section D.7.5.2).

Both tests operate on paired results (e.g., accuracy scores on the same cross-validation folds). If the resulting p-value is below a predefined significance level (typically $\alpha = 0.05$), we reject the null hypothesis and conclude that the difference in performance between the models is statistically significant.

The following code performs a paired *t*-test to determine whether the accuracy difference between the SVM and MLP models across 15 evaluation rounds is statistically significant:

```
from scipy.stats import ttest_rel

# Extract the accuracy scores of the two models
scores_svm = np.array(results['SVM']['raw_accuracy_scores'])
scores_mlp = np.array(results['MLP']['raw_accuracy_scores'])

# Conduct paired t-test
t_stat, p_val = ttest_rel(scores_svm, scores_mlp)
print(f'Paired t-test statistic: {t_stat:.4f}, p-value: {p_val:.4f}')
```

```
Paired t-test statistic: 2.5430, p-value: 0.0234
```

Because the p-value is below 0.05 and the mean accuracy of SVM is higher, we conclude that SVM significantly outperforms MLP.

In practice, differences in model accuracy often violate the normality assumption [154], making the Wilcoxon signed-rank test a more appropriate choice in such cases:

```
from scipy.stats import wilcoxon

# Conduct Wilcoxon signed-rank test
w_stat, p_val = wilcoxon(scores_svm, scores_mlp)
print(f'Wilcoxon test statistic: {w_stat:.4f}, p-value: {p_val:.4f}')
```

```
Wilcoxon test statistic: 23.5000, p-value: 0.0413
```

This p-value also falls below 0.05, reinforcing the conclusion that the performance difference is statistically significant.

In general, the paired t-test is more powerful when its assumptions are met, as it takes into account the magnitude of the differences. The Wilcoxon test, by contrast, relies only on the signed ranks of the differences, making it more robust to outliers and deviations from normality, but less powerful than the paired t-test when detecting small but consistent effects.

12.3.4.8.2 Comparing Multiple Algorithms

When comparing more than two models, the standard procedure involves two steps:

1. Perform a **global test** to check whether any statistically significant differences exist among the models.

2. If the global test is significant, conduct **post-hoc tests** to identify which specific pairs of models differ.

Two widely used global tests for comparing the performance of multiple models are:

- **ANOVA (Analysis of Variance)**: Tests whether the mean performance differs significantly across models (see Section D.7.7.1). It assumes that the performance scores are normally distributed and have equal variances across the models (homoscedasticity).

- **Friedman test**: A non-parametric alternative that compares the ranked performance of the models (see Section D.7.7.3). It does not assume normality or equal variances, making it well-suited for machine learning evaluation settings where the number of runs is small or the variance differs across models.

The following code applies the Friedman test to compare the accuracy scores of all models:

```
from scipy.stats import friedmanchisquare

# Extract relevant arrays from the results dictionary
model_scores = {model: data['raw_accuracy_scores']
                for model, data in results.items()}

# Conduct the Friedman test
f_stat, p_val = friedmanchisquare(*model_scores.values())
print(f'Friedman test statistic: {f_stat:.4f}, p-value: {p_val:.4f}')
```

```
Friedman test statistic: 25.2888, p-value: 0.0001
```

Since the p-value is well below 0.05, we conclude that there are statistically significant performance differences among the models. To identify which specific model pairs differ, we apply the **Nemenyi post-hoc test** (see Section D.7.7.4) using the `scikit-posthocs` library:[17]

---

17. https://scikit-posthocs.readthedocs.io; Install using `pip install scikit_posthocs`.

	Logistic Regression	KNN	Random Forest	Gradient Boosting	SVM	MLP
Logistic Regression	1.000000	0.850735	0.872331	0.997944	0.001616	0.239574
KNN	0.850735	1.000000	1.000000	0.591718	0.078461	0.909831
Random Forest	0.872331	1.000000	1.000000	0.624125	0.068976	0.892042
Gradient Boosting	0.997944	0.591718	0.624125	1.000000	0.000254	0.088978
SVM	0.001616	0.078461	0.068976	0.000254	1.000000	0.559106
MLP	0.239574	0.909831	0.892042	0.088978	0.559106	1.000000

Figure 12.4: Nemenyi test results showing pairwise p-values for all algorithm comparisons. Statistically significant differences are indicated by p-values below 0.05.

```
import scikit_posthocs as sp

df = pd.DataFrame(model_scores)
nemenyi_results = sp.posthoc_nemenyi_friedman(df)
nemenyi_results
```

The output is a matrix of pairwise p-values (see Figure 12.4). Pairs with p-values below 0.05 differ significantly. The results show that SVM significantly outperforms both logistic regression ($p \approx 0.002$) and gradient boosting ($p \approx 0.0003$), while the performance differences between other models are not statistically significant.

Notably, this outcome differs from our earlier Wilcoxon test comparing SVM and MLP, which did find a significant difference. The discrepancy arises because the Nemenyi test accounts for multiple comparisons by applying a more conservative significance threshold. This reduces the risk of false positives when evaluating many model pairs simultaneously.

12.3.4.8.3 Critical Difference (CD) Diagrams

To visually summarize the results of pairwise model comparisons, we can use a **critical difference (CD) diagram**. This diagram displays the average ranks of the models along a horizontal axis. Models that are not significantly different from each other are connected by a horizontal bar.

The following code generates the CD diagram using `scikit-posthocs`:

```
# Calculate ranks of the scores and the mean ranks
df_ranks = df_scores.rank(axis=1, method='average', ascending=False)
mean_ranks = df_ranks.mean(axis=0)

# Plot CD diagram
sp.critical_difference_diagram(mean_ranks, nemenyi_results)
```

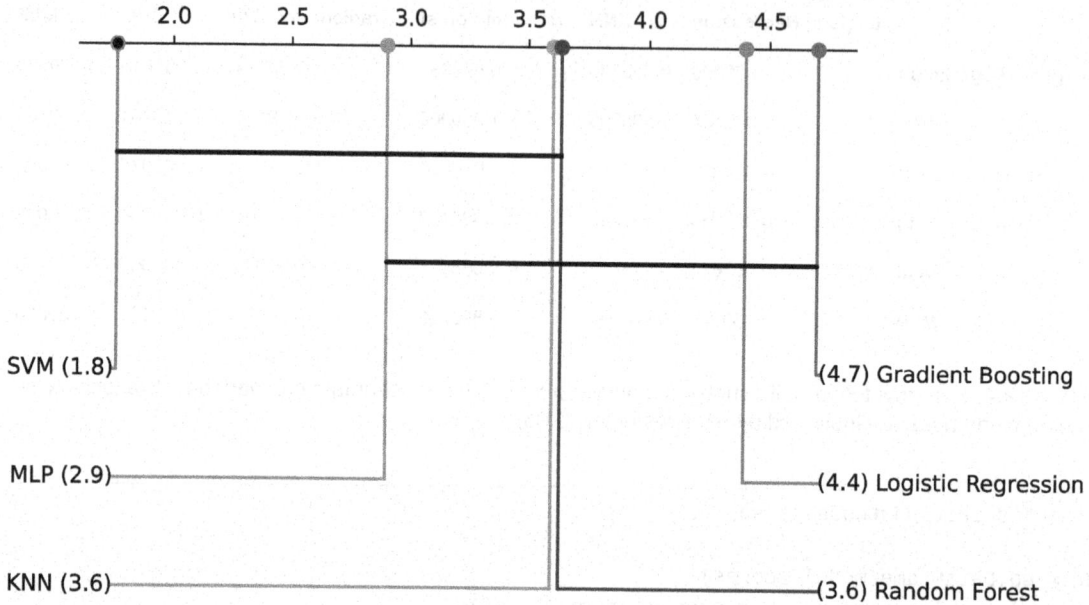

Figure 12.5: Critical difference (CD) diagram comparing the mean ranks of the evaluated models (shown in parentheses next to each model's name). Lower ranks indicate better average performance. Models that are not significantly different are connected by a horizontal bar.

Figure 12.5 shows the resulting diagram. It confirms that the only statistically significant differences are between the SVM model and both logistic regression and gradient boosting.

12.3.4.9   Final Evaluation on the Test Set

To assess the true generalization ability of the models, we now evaluate the top-performing ones on the held-out test set. Specifically, we select the models that achieved the highest cross-validation scores and showed no statistically significant differences among them—namely, SVM, MLP, KNN, and random forest.

Before the final evaluation, each model is retrained on the full training set to make use of all available training data:

```
# Evaluate models that showed no significant difference during cross-validation
selected_models = ['SVM', 'MLP', 'KNN', 'Random Forest']
test_results = {}
for name in selected_models:
    model = models[name]

    # Retrain on the full training set
    if 'random_state' in model.get_params():
        model.set_params(random_state=42)
```

```
    model.fit(X_train, y_train)
    test_accuracy = model.score(X_test, y_test)
    test_results[name] = test_accuracy

# Display the test results
print("Accuracy on the test set:")
for model_name, test_accuracy in test_results.items():
    print(f'{model_name}: {test_accuracy:.4f}')
```

```
Accuracy on the test set:
SVM: 0.9806
MLP: 0.9806
KNN: 0.9750
Random Forest: 0.9722
```

The test results closely mirror the cross-validation scores, with SVM and MLP achieving the highest test accuracy, followed by KNN and random forest.

Importantly, the test set is used only once at this final evaluation step, after all model selection and hyperparameter tuning are complete. Performing any further optimization at this stage would risk data leakage and undermine the role of the test set as an unbiased estimator of generalization performance.

12.4   Research in Machine Learning

Research in machine learning is fast-paced, challenging, and increasingly impactful across both industry and academia. From foundational theory to cutting-edge applications, the field offers a wealth of opportunities for innovation. However, making meaningful contributions requires more than curiosity—it demands strong theoretical foundations, practical skills, a methodical approach to experimentation, and continuous engagement with the latest research developments.

While academic institutions have historically led machine learning research, many of today's most influential breakthroughs come from industrial research labs such as OpenAI, Google Deep-Mind, Meta AI, and Microsoft Research. These organizations leverage vast computational resources and massive datasets to develop state-of-the-art models such as OpenAI's GPT-5 and DeepMind's Gemini 2.5. However, much of this research remains behind closed doors, with limited public access to training data, model architecture, and implementation details—hindering reproducibility, independent validation, and the ability of the broader research community to build upon these advancements.

At the same time, open research communities are actively working to democratize machine learning and promote transparency. Initiatives such as Hugging Face[18] and EleutherAI[19] foster

---

18. https://huggingface.co
19. https://www.eleuther.ai

collaboration by releasing open-source models, datasets, and tools, enabling reproducible research and broader participation.

The rise of preprint servers such as ArXiv[20] has transformed the research landscape by allowing researchers to rapidly share their findings and receive early feedback. Building on this shift toward openness, it has become common in machine learning and AI for conferences and journals to provide open access, with papers freely available online. Platforms like OpenReview[21] go even further by making the peer review process itself publicly accessible, fostering greater transparency and accountability in research.

Given the rapid pace of the field, keeping up with new developments is essential. You can stay current by regularly reading papers from top machine learning venues (see next section), contributing to open-source projects, engaging with online communities on platforms like Kaggle and Reddit, and following leading researchers on social media (see Section 12.6.2).

12.4.1   Conferences and Journals

Following leading conferences and journals is a key way to stay informed about the latest developments in machine learning. Conferences, in particular, offer a fast-paced view of emerging trends, breakthroughs, and ongoing open problems in the field.

Prominent conferences in machine learning include:

- NeurIPS[22] (Conference on Neural Information Processing Systems): Widely regarded as the premier venue for machine learning research, NeurIPS features both foundational theory and cutting-edge applications across machine learning, deep learning, and neuroscience. Founded in 1987 (originally named NIPS, renamed to NeurIPS in 2018), the conference is highly competitive, drawing thousands of submissions each year. In addition to the main proceedings, it hosts a wide range of workshops, tutorials, and competitions that highlight emerging research directions.

- ICML[23] (International Conference on Machine Learning): One of the oldest and most respected conferences in the field, ICML is a leading venue for both foundational and applied research spanning the full spectrum of machine learning. Covered topics include learning theory, optimization, probabilistic modeling, deep learning, and real-world applications, among others. Like NeurIPS, ICML maintains a rigorous peer-review process, with an acceptance rate typically around 20–25%.

- ICLR[24] (International Conference on Learning Representations): Known for shaping the development of deep learning, ICLR focuses on representation learning, neural networks, and large-scale learning systems. It is also notable for its open peer review process, encouraging transparency and community engagement throughout the review process.

---

20. https://arxiv.org
21. https://openreview.net
22. https://neurips.cc
23. https://icml.cc
24. https://iclr.cc

- AISTATS[25] (International Conference on Artificial Intelligence and Statistics): A leading venue at the intersection of machine learning and statistics, AISTATS features high-quality work on probabilistic modeling, Bayesian inference, and statistical learning theory.

- COLT[26] (Conference on Learning Theory): COLT is the premier venue for research on the theoretical foundations of machine learning, covering topics such as statistical and computational learning theory, online learning, generalization bounds, optimization, and complexity analysis of learning algorithms.

In addition to these core machine learning venues, several major conferences in artificial intelligence and related fields also feature a strong emphasis on machine learning. Notable examples include:

- Artificial Intelligence: AAAI[27] (Association for the Advancement of Artificial Intelligence) and IJCAI[28] (International Joint Conference on Artificial Intelligence).

- Data Mining: KDD[29] (ACM SIGKDD Conference on Knowledge Discovery and Data Mining) and SDM[30] (SIAM International Conference on Data Mining).

- Computer Vision: CVPR[31] (Conference on Computer Vision and Pattern Recognition) and ICCV[32] (IEEE/CVF International Conference on Computer Vision).

- Natural Language Processing: ACL[33] (Annual Meeting of the Association for Computational Linguistics) and EMNLP[34] (Conference on Empirical Methods in Natural Language Processing).

- Robotics: ICRA[35] (International Conference on Robotics and Automation), IROS[36] (IEEE/RSJ International Conference on Intelligent Robots and Systems) and CoRL[37] (Conference on Robot Learning).

While conferences offer rapid dissemination of results, journals provide the space for more comprehensive analysis, extended experimentation, and rigorous theoretical development.[38] Several leading journals play a central role in advancing machine learning and artificial intelligence research:

---

25. https://aistats.org
26. https://www.learningtheory.org
27. https://aaai.org/conference/aaai
28. https://ijcai.org
29. https://www.kdd.org
30. https://www.siam.org/conferences-events/past-event-archive
31. https://cvpr.thecvf.com
32. https://iccv.thecvf.com
33. https://aclweb.org
34. https://emnlp.org
35. https://www.ieee-ras.org/conferences-workshops/fully-sponsored/icra
36. https://www.ieee-ras.org/conferences-workshops/financially-co-sponsored/iros
37. https://roboticsconference.org
38. Typical conference papers in machine learning are limited to 6–10 pages (excluding references and supplementary material), whereas journal papers often have no strict page limits.

- JMLR[39] (Journal of Machine Learning Research): Widely regarded as the flagship journal in machine learning, JMLR is an open-access publication that covers all areas of the field. It is known for its rigorous peer review and strong editorial board.

- TPAMI[40] (IEEE Transactions on Pattern Analysis and Machine Intelligence): A top-tier journal for computer vision, pattern recognition, and machine learning. It is frequently cited for both foundational and applied contributions, with a 2024 impact factor of 18.6.[41]

- Nature Machine Intelligence[42]: A high-impact, interdisciplinary journal from the Nature portfolio that publishes cutting-edge research across machine learning, robotics, neuroscience, and the societal and ethical implications of AI.

- TNNLS[43] (IEEE Transactions on Neural Networks and Learning Systems): A prominent IEEE journal covering neural networks, deep learning, and broader machine learning topics.

- MLJ[44] (Machine Learning Journal): Established in 1986 and published by Springer, MLJ is one of the first journals dedicated to machine learning. It covers both foundational and applied work, ranging from classical methods to modern developments in deep learning and deployment.

- FnTML[45] (Foundations and Trends in Machine Learning): A unique journal publishing long-form survey and tutorial-style articles written by leading experts. It is especially valuable for gaining deep, foundational understanding of key topics in machine learning.

- Neural Computation[46]: A leading journal published by MIT Press that focuses on theoretical and computational neuroscience, neural networks, and biologically inspired learning algorithms, bridging the gap between neuroscience and machine learning.

- AIJ[47] (Artificial Intelligence Journal): Established in 1970, AIJ is one of the oldest and most highly cited journals in AI. It covers a broad range of topics including automated reasoning, planning, knowledge representation, machine learning, computer vision, robotics, and natural language processing.

- JAIR[48] (Journal of Artificial Intelligence Research): A leading open-access journal publishing high-quality research across all areas of AI, with a strong focus on both theoretical and applied machine learning.

---

39. https://www.jmlr.org
40. https://www.computer.org/csdl/journal/tp
41. The impact factor is a commonly used metric that reflects the average number of citations in a given year to articles published in the journal during the preceding two years.
42. https://www.nature.com/natmachintell
43. https://cis.ieee.org/publications/t-neural-networks-and-learning-systems
44. https://link.springer.com/journal/10994
45. https://www.nowpublishers.com/mal
46. https://direct.mit.edu/neco
47. https://www.sciencedirect.com/journal/artificial-intelligence
48. https://www.jair.org/index.php/jair

12.4.2   Writing Research Papers

Writing is a core part of conducting machine learning research—it is how ideas are clarified, tested, refined, and ultimately shared with the broader community. A well-crafted paper not only presents novel contributions but also positions them clearly within the existing body of knowledge and the wider research landscape.

Most machine learning papers follow a standard structure with the following parts:

1. **Abstract**: A concise summary of the research problem, the proposed approach, and key results. It should capture the reader's interest and motivate further reading.

2. **Introduction**: Introduces the problem in more depth, motivates the research and explains its significance, identifies gaps in prior work, and provides a high-level overview of the proposed solution.

3. **Related Work**: Reviews relevant literature, identifies the limitations of existing approaches, and positions the current work in relation to them—highlighting its novelty, improvements, or differences.

4. **Methodology**: Describes the proposed method in detail, including mathematical formulations, model architecture, algorithms, training procedures, and underlying assumptions. The description should be sufficiently detailed to enable replication by other researchers.

5. **Experiments and Results**: Describes the experimental setup, including datasets, evaluation metrics, baselines, and hyperparameters. Experimental results are presented using tables and figures, often accompanied by statistical significance analysis. Additional analyses may include comparisons to prior work and ablation studies that assess the contribution of individual components in the model.

6. **Discussion**: Interprets the results, reflects on their significance, and acknowledges limitations. It may also consider potential societal or ethical implications.

7. **Conclusion**: Summarizes the main contributions and findings and suggests directions for future work.

8. **References**: A complete list of cited works, formatted according to the target venue's style.

9. **Appendices** (if applicable): Includes supplementary material such as proofs, additional results, or implementation details, which support the main content but are not essential to the core narrative.

Strong research papers share several key qualities:

- Novelty: Introduces a new idea, insight, or result that meaningfully advances the field.

- Clarity and conciseness: Communicates ideas clearly and efficiently, avoids unnecessary jargon, and presents technical content in a structured, accessible way.

- Sound methodology: Proposes a well-justified, principled approach with clearly stated assumptions, grounded in theory and/or empirical evidence.

- Thorough evaluation: Validates the proposed method across diverse datasets or settings and compares it against strong baselines or prior work.

- Reproducibility: Provides sufficient detail, including code, data, and experimental setup, to enable replication of the results.

- Literature awareness: Demonstrates familiarity with related work and clearly positions the contribution within the existing research landscape.

- Transparency: Reports results honestly, acknowledges limitations, and avoids exaggerating contributions or claims.

- Self-containment: Provides sufficient background and context to ensure the paper is accessible to readers who are not experts in the specific domain.

- Ethical considerations: Reflects on the broader societal implications of the work, addressing issues such as fairness, privacy, potential misuse, and unintended consequences.

In addition to these general guidelines, each conference or journal has its own submission requirements—typically outlined in a "Call for Papers" section on the venue's website—including formatting rules, page limits, ethical disclosures, and, in some cases, guidelines for code and data submissions. These requirements reflect the field's growing emphasis on transparency, reproducibility, and responsible research practices in machine learning.

12.4.3   Open Research Questions

Despite remarkable progress, many foundational and practical challenges in machine learning remain unresolved. The following research questions continue to drive active inquiry and innovation across the field:

- **Large Language Models (LLMs)**: How can we reconcile the strong, human-level performance of recent LLMs on a wide range of tasks, including academic benchmarks (e.g., AP exams), coding problems, and general knowledge questions, with their persistent failures on tasks that demand rigorous symbolic reasoning, such as those posed in the USA Mathematical Olympiad (USAMO) [478, 390], and real-world planning scenarios [634]?[49] Do current scaling laws reliably predict continued improvements in LLM capabilities, or are we approaching fundamental limits—such as data availability, computational resources, or representational capacity—beyond which performance gains begin to plateau? [309, 601, 189]

---

49. As I am writing these lines, OpenAI's experimental reasoning model achieved gold-medal performance at the 2025 International Mathematical Olympiad (IMO), solving 5 out of 6 problems and scoring 35/42. See `https://github.com/aw31/openai-imo-2025-proofs`. Nonetheless, broader evaluations show that models still fall short on generalizable symbolic reasoning tasks [38].

What internal mechanisms allow LLMs to perform complex reasoning and learn new tasks from in-context examples, despite being trained primarily as next-token predictors? [612, 524, 621, 45] How can we make LLMs more controllable, truthful, and aligned with human intent? [297, 366, 110]

- **Artificial General Intelligence (AGI)**: Is it possible to build systems that demonstrate human-level reasoning, adaptability, and autonomy across a wide range of tasks? [226, 80] What theoretical and engineering breakthroughs are needed to make meaningful progress toward AGI? How should we define and measure intelligence in machines? [119, 121] To what extent does scaling of model size, data, and compute bring us closer to AGI? Are current architectures, such as transformers, sufficient for this goal, or do we need fundamentally new paradigms [474]? Can AI systems eventually improve their own capabilities, initiating a process of recursive self-improvement and possibly giving rise to superintelligence behavior? [62, 649]

- **Generalization**: Why do deep neural networks generalize well despite being heavily over-parameterized and often converging to local optima or saddle points—seemingly in conflict with classical statistical learning theory [13, 633, 421]? How can we explain surprising phenomena such as *benign overfitting*, where models that perfectly fit noisy training data still generalize well to new, unseen data? [29, 362, 641] Another puzzling behavior is *double descent*, where test error initially increases with model complexity (as expected), but then decreases again once the model becomes sufficiently expressive to interpolate the training data [436, 141].

- **Robustness**: How can we develop machine learning models that are more robust to the challenges encountered in real-world settings, such as distribution shifts [384, 265], adversarial attacks [233, 5], and noisy or corrupted inputs? [450, 357]

- **Ethics and Fairness**: How can we design machine learning systems that are fair, privacy-preserving, and accountable? What strategies can mitigate algorithmic bias and prevent harmful or discriminatory outcomes? [3, 412, 27, 210].

- **Interpretability and Explainability**: How can we build models that are easier to interpret and explain, especially in high-stakes domains such as healthcare, law, and finance? [501, 386, 85, 445, 50]

- **Causality and Causal Inference**: How can machine learning systems move beyond statistical correlation to model and reason about cause-and-effect relationships? [470, 477, 531] What assumptions are needed to infer causal structure from observational data, and how can we design models that support interventions, counterfactual reasoning, and changes in data-generating processes? [380, 486]

- **Scalable and Efficient Learning**: How can we reduce the computational, memory, and data demands of training and deploying large models, without compromising performance? [87, 225, 66, 640]

- **Data Quality**: How can we improve data quality through better labeling strategies, robust outlier and anomaly detection techniques, and principled dataset design practices that ensure class balance, coverage of edge cases, and alignment with real-world deployment scenarios? [101, 520, 464, 459]

- **Continual and Lifelong Learning**: How can we build models that continuously learn and adapt to new tasks over time, while preserving knowledge from earlier tasks and avoiding catastrophic forgetting? [148, 607, 668]

- **Multimodal Learning**: How can we enable models to learn and act in environments involving multiple data modalities—such as vision, language, sound, and actions—and effectively integrate information across them? [26, 494, 500, 655, 222]

- **Neural-Symbolic Integration**: How can we effectively combine symbolic reasoning (e.g., logic rules, knowledge graphs) with deep learning to support explicit reasoning, generalization from limited data, and interpretable decision-making? Can neural-symbolic systems bridge the gap between statistical learning and human-like reasoning? [214, 652, 127]

- **Theoretical Foundations of Learning**: What are the theoretical limits of what machine learning can achieve? [591, 543, 235] Which learning problems are provably hard or even undecidable? [37, 206, 95] What are the implications of the No Free Lunch theorem for algorithm design and model selection? [630, 482, 666] What classes of functions can different models represent, and under what conditions do they serve as universal approximators? [548, 21, 592] What tradeoffs exist between model expressiveness, generalization, sample complexity, and computational efficiency, and how can we quantify them using theoretical or empirical tools? [444, 237, 24]

These open questions are shaping the future of machine learning and offer exciting opportunities for meaningful, forward-looking research. Many of these topics will be revisited in subsequent volumes of this series, where we explore cutting-edge developments and emerging directions in modern machine learning.

12.5   Machine Learning Competitions

Machine learning competitions offer an engaging and practical way to apply your knowledge to real-world problems, sharpen your problem-solving abilities, and connect with a global community of practitioners. These contests span a wide range of domains—from medical diagnosis and drug discovery to climate modeling, financial forecasting, self-driving cars, and even the deciphering of ancient manuscripts. Many competitions also offer substantial prize money, adding an extra incentive to participate.

In 2024 alone, more than 400 competitions were hosted across over 20 platforms, with total prize pools exceeding $22 million [93]. These competitions vary widely in scope, duration, and difficulty, offering valuable experience for participants at all skill levels—from newcomers to seasoned professionals.

Notable past competitions that have spurred major advances in the field include:

- Makridakis (M) Competitions[50] (1982–): A long-running and influential series that has driven significant progress in time series forecasting. Key innovations emerging from these competitions include the adoption of ensemble and hybrid methods, a stronger emphasis on probabilistic forecasting and uncertainty quantification, and the development of robust, scale-independent accuracy metrics such as MASE and sMAPE. Later rounds of the competition focused on scalability to millions of time series, hierarchical forecasting, and reproducibility through open datasets and transparent evaluation protocols [391, 392].

- DARPA Grand Challenges[51] (2004–2007): A pioneering series of competitions that advanced the field of autonomous driving. Teams were tasked with building self-driving vehicles capable of navigating complex real-world environments, including obeying traffic laws, handling intersections, and avoiding obstacles [577, 590, 82]. These challenges catalyzed breakthroughs in robotics, perception, and control, and played a foundational role in launching the modern autonomous vehicle industry, with many participants later leading major efforts in academia and industry.

- Netflix Prize[52] (2006–2009): A landmark competition that challenged participants to improve Netflix's movie recommendation algorithm by at least 10% [39]. It led to major advances in recommendation algorithms and demonstrated the power of large-scale ensemble methods—the winning solution combined hundreds of models and incorporated two levels of meta-models [580].

- ImageNet Challenge[53] (2010–2017): A large-scale image recognition competition that marked a turning point in computer vision and deep learning [512]. The challenge required classifying 1.2 million images across 1,000 object categories. The 2012 winning model, *AlexNet* by Alex Krizhevsky et al., demonstrated the power of deep convolutional neural networks and is widely credited with launching the modern deep learning era [334].

- ARC Prize[54] (2019–): A grand challenge[55] designed to measure progress toward artificial general intelligence (AGI) using tasks from the Abstraction and Reasoning Corpus (ARC). Each task presents a few input-output examples on colored 8×8 grids, and the objective is to infer the underlying transformation and apply it to new test cases. Solving these tasks requires abstract reasoning, pattern recognition, and strong generalization from limited data. The competition has attracted growing interest, with recent submissions advancing the state-of-the-art in few-shot reasoning, program synthesis, and neuro-symbolic approaches [120, 121].

---

50. https://forecasters.org/resources/time-series-data
51. https://www.darpa.mil/about/innovation-timeline
52. https://www.kaggle.com/datasets/netflix-inc/netflix-prize-data
53. https://www.image-net.org/challenges/LSVRC
54. https://arcprize.org
55. A grand challenge is an ambitious, high-impact scientific or technological problem whose solution would represent a major advance in the field. Such challenges often aim to track long-term progress and typically offer substantial prize incentives.

- Vesuvius Challenge[56] (2023–): An ongoing grand challenge that combines machine learning and X-ray tomography to recover ancient Greek text from carbonized papyrus scrolls buried during the eruption of Mount Vesuvius in 79 CE. Because the scrolls are too fragile to unroll physically, virtual unwrapping and ink detection have become central challenges. In 2024, participants achieved a historic milestone of decoding extended passages from one of the scrolls. The competition has now entered its next stage, offering a $200,000 prize for the first team to successfully read an entire scroll.

- AI Mathematical Olympiad (AIMO)[57] (2024–): A $10 million grand challenge to build a public, open-source AI model capable of solving International Mathematical Olympiad (IMO) gold-level problems. In the second Progress Prize (October 2024–March 2025), participants were provided with 110 challenging National Olympiad–style problems for training, while evaluation was conducted on a separate private set of 50 problems within a 5-hour test window.

The winning solution solved 34 of 50 problems with a state-of-the-art reasoning system built on three components: (1) the OpenMathReasoning dataset (540K problems with 3.2M chain-of-thought traces, 1.7M tool-integrated reasoning traces, and 566K selection traces); (2) tool-integrated reasoning, combining LLMs with Python code execution; and (3) generative solution selection (GenSelect) for choosing the best among candidate solutions. These advances led to the OpenMath-Nemotron models (1.5B–32B parameters), setting new benchmarks for open-source math reasoning systems [432].

12.5.1 Major Platforms

Kaggle[58], founded in 2010, remains by far the most prominent and influential platform for machine learning and data science competitions. With over 22 million users, it hosts challenges spanning nearly every domain of machine learning—from structured data problems and image classification to large-scale language modeling and time-series forecasting—making it a central hub for both applied projects and cutting-edge research. Kaggle also offers a rich ecosystem of datasets, public notebooks, discussion forums, and educational resources, fostering community learning and collaboration.

Other notable platforms include:

- Hugging Face Competitions[59]: A growing platform for open-source machine learning challenges across NLP, vision, audio, and tabular domains. Competitions range from fine-tuning pretrained models and prompt engineering to evaluating generative capabilities, testing robustness and fairness, and contributing to the development of benchmark datasets.

---

56. https://scrollprize.org
57. https://aimoprize.com
58. https://www.kaggle.com
59. https://huggingface.co/competitions

- AICrowd[60]: Specializes in complex, research-oriented challenges in areas such as reinforcement learning, multi-agent systems, robotics, and lifelong learning.

- DrivenData[61]: Hosts machine learning competitions focused on social impact, addressing real-world challenges in public health, education, climate change, disaster response, and more.

- Zindi[62]: An Africa-focused platform hosting machine learning competitions in domains such as agriculture, healthcare, and financial inclusion, while supporting a growing regional data science community.

- CodaLab/Codabench[63]: An open-source platform commonly used for academic competitions and reproducible research. It frequently hosts challenges at major conferences such as NeurIPS, ICLR, and CVPR, targeting frontier research problems in machine learning.

12.5.2   Best Practices

Succeeding in machine learning competitions takes more than just trying different models and tuning them: it requires strategic planning, disciplined experimentation, and efficient workflows. Below are several best practices consistently followed by top competitors:

- Understand the problem and rules: Carefully review the competition guidelines, including the task description, evaluation metric, data constraints, and resource limits. For example, some competitions allow the use of external data, while others restrict participants to the provided datasets only.

- Study past solutions: Reviewing winning approaches from similar competitions can yield valuable insights into effective modeling choices, innovative feature engineering techniques, and practical heuristics.

  A striking example comes from Kaggle's March Machine Learning Mania 2023[64] competition, where the winning submission closely resembled an approach originally shared by the 2018 winner.

- Choose an appropriate environment: Depending on your computational needs and hardware access, decide whether to work locally or on cloud-based platforms such as Kaggle Notebooks[65] or Google Colab[66]. Many recent competitions require GPUs to remain competitive. In some cases, competitions mandate submitting runnable code (not just predictions), which must execute within strict runtime and memory limits to ensure fairness and reproducibility.

---

60. `https://www.aicrowd.com`
61. `https://www.drivendata.org`
62. `https://zindi.africa`
63. `https://codalab.org`
64. `https://www.kaggle.com/competitions/march-machine-learning-mania-2023`
65. `https://www.kaggle.com/docs/notebooks`
66. `https://colab.research.google.com`

- Conduct thorough data exploration: Use exploratory data analysis (EDA) to examine feature distributions, detect anomalies, uncover correlations with the target, and assess overall data quality. EDA is often instrumental in guiding preprocessing choices, feature engineering, and model selection.

  For instance, in Kaggle's Optiver Realized Volatility Prediction Competition[67] (2021), top teams discovered that volatility patterns varied significantly across time intervals. By segmenting the data accordingly and engineering time-dependent features, they were able to substantially improve model performance.

- Perform feature engineering: Well-designed features can dramatically improve model performance—sometimes even more than switching to a more complex model.

  For example, in Kaggle's New York City Taxi Trip Duration[68] competition (2017), the winning team started with basic inputs such as pickup/drop-off coordinates and timestamps. They then engineered additional features—such as the distance between pickup and drop-off, hour of day, and weather conditions (retrieved from an external source)—that significantly improved predictive accuracy compared to models trained on raw inputs alone.

- Handle imbalanced datasets: Many real-world datasets, including those used in competitions, exhibit imbalanced class distributions. Techniques such as oversampling the minority class or adjusting class weights can lead to substantial performance gains.

  For example, in Kaggle's Credit Card Fraud Detection Competition[69] (2018), participants improved fraud detection by oversampling the minority class and carefully tuning class weights—leading to higher recall of fraudulent transactions despite the severe class imbalance.

- Apply data augmentation: For tasks like image or text classification, data augmentation strategies, such as rotating, flipping, or cropping images, or replacing words with synonyms in text, can improve generalization and model robustness.

  For instance, in Kaggle's HPA Single Cell Classification Competition[70] (2021), participants applied advanced augmentation strategies, including geometric transformations and MixUp (interpolating between pairs of examples), to boost performance on a challenging multi-label image classification task.

  Some competitions also permit the use of external data to enrich the provided dataset. For example, in the Netflix Prize competition, the winning team improved predictive accuracy by incorporating movie metadata from IMDb, adding contextual information to the original dataset that contained only user ratings.

- Optimize for the evaluation metric: Align your model's training objective with the competition's evaluation criterion. A mismatch between the training objective and the final scoring metric can lead to suboptimal performance.

---

67. https://www.kaggle.com/competitions/optiver-realized-volatility-prediction
68. https://www.kaggle.com/competitions/nyc-taxi-trip-duration
69. https://www.kaggle.com/mlg-ulb/creditcardfraud
70. https://www.kaggle.com/competitions/hpa-single-cell-image-classification

For example, in the Jigsaw Unintended Bias in Toxicity Classification Competition[71] (2019), the evaluation metric was a custom variant of AUC that emphasized fairness across identity subgroups. Top teams adjusted their loss functions to better reflect this weighted objective, improving their ability to detect toxic content across diverse demographic groups.

- Use pretrained models: For tasks in computer vision and natural language processing, fine-tuning pretrained models instead of training from scratch can dramatically reduce training time and improve performance. This is particularly beneficial when labeled data is scarce, as pretrained weights provide a strong initialization based on prior learning.

  For example, in Kaggle's Google Landmark Retrieval Competition[72] (2020), participants were tasked with building models that, given a query image, could retrieve matching images of the same landmark from a large collection. The winning team fine-tuned an EfficientNet model [574] on higher-resolution inputs and adjusted the loss function to give more weight to images with more reliable labels, leading to significant improvements in retrieval accuracy.

- Use ensemble methods: Combine multiple models to leverage their complementary strengths using techniques like bagging, boosting, and stacking. Ensembles are especially effective in tabular data competitions, where gradient-boosted decision trees (GDBTs) are often combined with deep learning models to boost predictive accuracy.

  For example, in the American Express Default Prediction Competition[73] (2022), participants predicted credit card defaults using anonymized customer data. The winning team used an ensemble that integrated GBDTs with recurrent neural networks (RNNs), capturing both structured tabular features and temporal dynamics to achieve state-of-the-art results.

- Avoid overfitting to the leaderboard: Use cross-validation to evaluate your models rather than relying solely on the public leaderboard. This helps ensure robust generalization, as final rankings are typically based on a hidden private leaderboard.

- Apply post-processing to the predictions: Adjust classification thresholds or calibrate predicted probabilities to better align with the competition's evaluation metric.

  For example, in Kaggle's Histopathologic Cancer Detection Competition[74] (2019), the winning team fine-tuned the classification threshold to better balance precision and recall, leading to a significant improvement in their F1 score.

- Track experiments and iterate effectively: Maintain reproducible workflows by logging experiments, tracking metrics, and documenting key changes. Analyze your model's errors using tools such as confusion matrices, error breakdowns by features[75], or visualizations of misclassified examples to identify patterns and refine your approach.

---

71. https://www.kaggle.com/competitions/jigsaw-unintended-bias-in-toxicity-classification
72. https://www.kaggle.com/c/landmark-retrieval-2020
73. https://www.kaggle.com/competitions/amex-default-prediction
74. https://www.kaggle.com/c/histopathologic-cancer-detection
75. For example, you can group validation samples by feature values (e.g., age groups, transaction size, image brightness) and compute performance metrics within each group to uncover patterns in model performance. This can help identify systematic weaknesses or biases.

12.5.3   Common Tools and Libraries

Examining the tools and frameworks used by winning competition solutions offers valuable insights into current trends in machine learning. The following list summarizes key libraries and model architectures frequently observed in recent competitions [92, 93]:

- **Programming languages and core libraries**: Python remains the dominant language in ML competitions, with over 96% of winning solutions in 2024 written in Python. Core libraries such as NumPy Pandas, and Scikit-Learn are ubiquitous, while Polars is gaining traction for efficient large-scale data processing. In deep learning, PyTorch is by far the most popular framework, and the Hugging Face Transformers library is a standard choice for working with pretrained language models.

- **Tabular data**: Gradient-boosted decision trees (GBDTs), implemented in libraries such as XGBoost, LightGBM, and CatBoost, continue to dominate structured data tasks. These models are often combined with neural networks to leverage their complementary strengths when working with tabular data—for example, tree-based models excel at capturing local feature interactions, while neural networks are better at learning smooth global representations such as embeddings for categorical features.

- **Computer vision**: Convolutional neural networks remain foundational in computer vision tasks, with ConvNeXt widely used for image classification, U-Net for image segmentation, and YOLO for real-time object detection. Diffusion models are increasingly being applied to tasks like image generation and data augmentation. Vision transformers (e.g., ViT, Swin) and hybrid CNN–Transformer architectures are also gaining traction, though they are still relatively uncommon among 2024 competition winners.

- **Natural language processing**: Transformer-based open-source language models such as DeBERTa, LLaMA, and DeepSeek are frequently fine-tuned for tasks like text classification, question answering, and summarization. Retrieval-augmented generation (RAG) architectures are gaining popularity for augmenting language models with contextually relevant information retrieved from external sources during inference.

- **Time series forecasting**: Classical statistical models such as ARIMA are still used for simple univariate forecasting. However, most winning solutions rely on LSTMs, CNNs, or XGBoost models enhanced with handcrafted temporal features such as lagged predictors and rolling statistics. Transformer-based architectures such as Informer, Autoformer, and SAMformer are gaining momentum for long-horizon forecasting, though they are still relatively rare among top entries.

- **LLMs as workflow assistants**: Large language models are increasingly being used throughout the machine learning workflow—not just for NLP tasks. Participants use LLMs to generate and debug code, perform exploratory data analysis (EDA), create synthetic data, and assist with labeling. LLMs also help interpret evaluation results, suggest hyperparameter settings, recommend follow-up experiments, and brainstorm alternative modeling strategies or pipeline designs.

12.6   Additional Resources

This section provides a curated selection of textbooks and online resources to deepen your understanding of machine learning principles and practical techniques and stay current with ongoing
developments in the field. While the primary focus is on supervised machine learning, many
of these resources also cover foundational topics such as optimization, Bayesian methods, and
learning theory that are relevant across all areas of machine learning. Future volumes will provide dedicated recommendations for their respective topics, including deep learning, unsupervised
learning, and large language models.

12.6.1   Recommended Textbooks

The textbooks listed below offer more detailed coverage of topics introduced in this volume. They
are intended for readers seeking to build a stronger theoretical foundation or explore more advanced aspects of supervised learning.

Several of these books are considered classics in the field, written by researchers who played a
foundational role in shaping machine learning. For example, *Statistical Learning Theory* by Vapnik
introduced the VC framework, a cornerstone of machine learning theory, while *Classification and
Regression Trees* by Breiman et al. presented the CART algorithm, which laid the groundwork for
many of the decision tree and ensemble methods developed in the decades that followed.

- **Learning Theory**

  - *Statistical Learning Theory* by Vladimir Vapnik [597]: Develops the theoretical foun-
    dations of VC theory and introduces key principles of learning, including empirical
    and structural risk minimization, generalization bounds, and the VC dimension. The
    book also presents support vector machines (SVMs) as a practical realization of these
    principles. This advanced book is best suited for readers with strong mathematical
    background.

  - *The Elements of Statistical Learning* (2nd ed.) by Hastie, Tibshirani, and Friedman
    [258]: A comprehensive and widely cited reference by leading researchers in the field.
    The book popularized many key methods in both supervised and unsupervised learn-
    ing, including regularization techniques, additive models, and dimensionality reduc-
    tion techniques.

  - *Understanding Machine Learning* by Shalev-Shwartz and Ben-David [542]: A rigor-
    ous introduction that bridges learning theory and practical algorithms, covering topics
    such as VC dimension, PAC learning, SVMs, boosting, and decision trees.

- **Regression and Generalized Linear Models**

  - *Introduction to Linear Regression Analysis* (6th ed.) by Montgomery, Peck, and Vin-
    ing [430]: A detailed and statistically grounded treatment of linear regression. Topics
    include parameter estimation, hypothesis testing, residual analysis, assessment of mul-
    ticollinearity, and extensions such as weighted least squares and nonlinear regression.

– *Applied Logistic Regression* (3rd ed.) by Hosmer, Lemeshow, and Sturdivant [277]: A thorough resource for building, interpreting, and validating logistic regression models. It covers model formulation, coefficient interpretation, variable selection strategies, goodness-of-fit measures, and extensions to multinomial and ordinal logistic regression.

– *Generalized Linear Models* by McCullagh and Nelder [404]: A seminal work that formalized and extended the GLM framework originally introduced by Nelder and Wedderburn [440]. It presents a unified approach to modeling diverse response types using link functions and exponential family distributions.

- **Bayesian Methods**

– *Bayesian Data Analysis* (3rd ed.) by Gelman et al. [219]: A comprehensive guide to Bayesian modeling, inference, and analysis. The book covers foundational topics such as prior specification, Bayesian inference, hierarchical modeling, and variational Bayes, as well as practical tools such as Markov Chain Monte Carlo (MCMC) sampling methods and techniques for Bayesian model comparison.

– *Bayesian Optimization* by Garnett [216]: A modern introduction to black-box function optimization using Bayesian methods. It covers key ideas such as Gaussian processes, acquisition functions, and the exploration–exploitation tradeoff, with applications to hyperparameter tuning, experimental design, and other domains where function evaluations are expensive or noisy.

- **Probabilistic Graphical Models**

– *Probabilistic Graphical Models: Principles and Techniques* by Koller and Friedman [326]: A comprehensive and rigorous reference on probabilistic graphical models. The book provides in-depth coverage of Bayesian networks, Markov random fields, factor graphs, hidden Markov models, and influence diagrams. It explores both exact and approximate inference methods—including variable elimination, belief propagation, and variational inference—and algorithms for learning model structure and parameters.

- **Decision Trees**

– *Classification and Regression Trees* by Breiman, Friedman, Olshen, and Stone [73]: A foundational text that introduced the CART algorithm, a key milestone in statistical learning. It explains the principles of recursive partitioning, splitting criteria, pruning strategies, and model interpretation. The book also addresses practical concerns such as handling missing data, selecting informative variables, and assessing model stability.

- **Ensemble Methods**

– *Ensemble Methods: Foundations and Algorithms* by Zhou [669]: A comprehensive overview of ensemble learning techniques, including bagging, boosting, and stacking. The book provides theoretical insights into why ensembles work, along with practical design choices such as ensemble size, selection of base learners, weighting schemes, and aggregation strategies.

– *Boosting* by Schapire and Freund [527]: An in-depth treatment of boosting theory by the inventors of AdaBoost. The book presents boosting as a form of additive modeling and margin-based learning, and explores its connections to game theory, optimization, and statistical learning theory. It covers key algorithms including AdaBoost, LPBoost, BrownBoost, and LogitBoost, as well as variants for regression and multi-class classification.

- **Support Vector Machines and Kernel Methods**

  – *An Introduction to Support Vector Machines and Other Kernel-Based Learning Methods* by Cristianini and Shawe-Taylor [139]: An accessible and well-structured introduction to the theory and application of support vector machines (SVMs) and kernel methods. Topics include large-margin classification, Lagrange duality, the kernel trick, soft-margin classifiers, generalization bounds, and extensions to multiclass and multilabel classification problems.

  – *Learning with Kernels* by Schölkopf and Smola [533]: A comprehensive exploration of kernel-based learning methods. The book provides a detailed treatment of support vector machines, kernel ridge regression, and Gaussian processes, grounded in the framework of regularization theory and reproducing kernel Hilbert spaces (RKHS). It laid much of the theoretical foundation for modern kernel methods and remains a key reference in the field.

- **Optimization**

  – *Convex Optimization* by Boyd and Vandenberghe [64]: A foundational text exploring the theory and algorithms of convex optimization. It covers topics such as convex sets and functions, duality theory, and optimization algorithms including gradient descent, Newton's method, and interior-point methods. The book combines mathematical rigor with practical examples drawn from signal processing, control, statistics, and machine learning.

  – *Numerical Optimization* (2nd ed.) by Nocedal and Wright [448]: A comprehensive reference on numerical methods for unconstrained and constrained optimization problems. It covers both first-order and second-order optimization methods, including gradient descent, Newton and quasi-Newton methods (such as BFGS and L-BFGS), and conjugate gradient techniques. Advanced topics include trust-region strategies, interior-point methods, linear programming, penalty and barrier formulations, augmented Lagragian methods, and sequential quadratic programming (SQP).

- **Natural Language Processing**

  – *Speech and Language Processing* (3rd ed., online draft) by Jurafsky and Martin [306]: A foundational textbook on natural language processing and computational linguistics. It covers both classical topics—such as finite-state methods, statistical language models, part-of-speech tagging, parsing, and semantics—and modern deep learning approaches, including transformers, contextual embeddings, and pre-trained language models. The book is freely available in an evolving online draft.

- *Foundations of Statistical Natural Language Processing* by Manning and Schütze [395]: A classic textbook that laid the groundwork for statistical approaches to NLP. It covers core techniques such as n-gram language models, part-of-speech tagging, probabilistic context-free grammars, as well as key machine learning methods for NLP, including maximum entropy models, hidden Markov models, and the expectation–maximization algorithm. Though predating the deep learning era, it remains a valuable resource for understanding the statistical foundations of modern NLP systems.

- *Natural Language Processing with Python* by Bird, Klein, and Loper [53]: A hands-on guide to NLP using the Natural Language Toolkit (NLTK) library, written by its creators. It introduces essential NLP tasks such as tokenization, stemming, tagging, parsing, and classification, demonstrating how to implement them in Python.

- **Python Libraries for Machine Learning**

  - *Hands-On Machine Learning with Scikit-Learn, Keras, and TensorFlow* (3rd ed.) by Aurélien Géron [223]: A practical, project-based guide to building end-to-end machine learning systems in Python. Topics include data preprocessing, supervised and unsupervised learning, model evaluation, and hyperparameter tuning using Scikit-Learn, as well as deep learning using TensorFlow and Keras.

  - *Python for Data Analysis* (3rd ed.) by Wes McKinney [409]: Written by the creator of Pandas, this book provides a practical and accessible introduction to data wrangling using Pandas and NumPy. It covers tasks such as data cleaning, transformation, aggregation, visualization, and working with time series, as well as performance optimization and efficient I/O.

12.6.2   Online Platforms and Tools

Beyond textbooks and research articles, online resources and communities can help you stay up to date with recent developments, best practices, and emerging trends in machine learning.

12.6.2.1   Library Documentation

The following websites serve as primary references for widely used libraries and frameworks in machine learning and deep learning:

- Scikit-Learn Documentation[76]

- XGBoost Documentation[77]

---

76. `https://scikit-learn.org`
77. `https://xgboost.readthedocs.io`

- PyTorch Documentation[78]

- Hugging Face Documentation[79]

12.6.2.2   Blogs and Online Publications

The following blogs and websites are widely recognized in the machine learning community. They provide accessible tutorials, research highlights, practical guides, and insights into current trends and real-world applications.

- Machine Learning Mastery[80]: Jason Brownlee's blog featuring hands-on, code-driven tutorials for both foundational and advanced topics in machine learning.

- Towards Data Science[81]: A widely read publication offering accessible tutorials, practical guides, and commentary on current trends in data science and machine learning.

- ML Glossary[82]: A compact and accessible reference with concise visual explanations, code examples, and formulas for key machine learning concepts and algorithms.

- OpenAI Blog[83]: Official updates from OpenAI, featuring model release announcements, performance benchmarks, alignment and safety research, and real-world applications of large language models using tools like ChatGPT and the Assistants API.

- DeepMind Blog[84]: Reports on cutting-edge AI research from Google DeepMind, including advances in large language models (e.g., Gemini), scientific and mathematical discovery (e.g., AlphaFold, AlphaGeometry, AlphaEvolve), and reinforcement learning (e.g., AlphaGo, AlphaZero, AlphaStar).

- Andrej Karpathy's Blog[85]: Posts by Andrej Karpathy, former director of AI at Tesla and founding member of OpenAI, offering technical yet approachable insights on neural networks, LLMs, and building ML systems from scratch.

- Colah's Blog[86]: Essays by Christopher Olah, co-founder of Anthropic, on deep learning theory and mechanistic interpretability, known for their depth and clarity.

---

78. https://pytorch.org/docs
79. https://huggingface.co/docs
80. https://machinelearningmastery.com
81. https://towardsdatascience.com
82. https://ml-cheatsheet.readthedocs.io
83. https://openai.com/news
84. https://deepmind.google/discover/blog
85. https://karpathy.ai
86. https://colah.github.io

12.6.2.3   YouTube Channels

The following YouTube channels combine visual storytelling with technical depth, offering an engaging way to learn complex ideas through animations, lectures, and expert commentary.

- MIT OpenCourseWare[87]: Full university-level courses on diverse topics in machine learning and AI, featuring recorded lectures from live MIT classes, along with accompanying assignments, exams, and lecture notes.

- Stanford CS Channel[88]: Video recordings of Stanford's flagship courses including *CS229: Machine Learning* and *CS224n: Natural Language Processing with Deep Learning*.

- 3Blue1Brown[89]: Visually intuitive animations explaining complex mathematical concepts in areas such as calculus, linear algebra, topology, and probability theory. Its neural networks series is especially popular among visual learners.

- Two Minute Papers[90]: Concise and engaging summaries of recent research papers in AI, machine learning, computer graphics, physics, and science. Each video distills complex ideas into short, digestible episodes.

- StatQuest with Josh Starmer[91]: Friendly and often humorous explanations of statistics and machine learning concepts, delivered with simple visuals and memorable analogies to build strong intuition.

- Lex Fridman Podcast[92]: Long-form interviews with AI researchers, scientists, and public thinkers discussing the technical, philosophical, and ethical aspects of artificial intelligence and related fields.

12.6.2.4   Social Media Influencers

The following researchers and thought leaders actively share insights on social media platforms like X (formerly Twitter) and LinkedIn, where they discuss recent advances, provide expert commentary, and engage in broader conversations shaping the future of AI and machine learning.

- Sam Altman[93]: CEO of OpenAI. Shares updates on OpenAI's development roadmap and reflects on the broader societal implications of artificial general intelligence.

- Andrew Ng[94]: Co-founder of Coursera and DeepLearning.AI, and adjunct professor at Stanford university. Promotes accessible, hands-on AI education and leads initiatives to democratize AI worldwide.

---

87. https://www.youtube.com/user/MIT
88. https://www.youtube.com/@stanfordonline
89. https://www.youtube.com/c/3blue1brown
90. https://www.youtube.com/@TwoMinutePapers
91. https://www.youtube.com/user/keeroyz
92. https://lexfridman.com/podcast
93. https://x.com/sama
94. https://x.com/AndrewYNg

- Geoffrey Hinton[95]: Turing Award recipient and 2024 Nobel laureate in Physics for his foundational work in deep learning. Shares reflections on the future of AI, as well as growing concerns about the risks of artificial general intelligence (AGI).

- Yann LeCun[96]: Turing Award winner and Chief AI Scientist at Meta. As a prominent voice in public debates on AI progress, he contends that current large language models are insufficient for achieving AGI and advocates for hybrid cognitive architectures that combine intuitive perception (System 1) with deliberative planning and reasoning (System 2).

- Fei-Fei Li[97]: Professor at Stanford and co-director of the Human-Centered AI Institute. Advocates for ethical AI, human-centered design, and stronger collaboration between academia and industry in shaping responsible AI.

- Demis Hassabis[98]: CEO of DeepMind. Shares cutting-edge work at the intersection of artificial intelligence, neuroscience, and human cognition, exploring fundamental questions about the nature of intelligence.

12.6.2.5 Author's Website

Visit the author's website at roiyeho.com[99] for updates related to the book, including errata, downloadable slides, code examples, supplementary materials, solutions to selected exercises, and progress on future volumes in this series.

12.7 Looking Ahead to Volume II

Congratulations on reaching this milestone! Completing the first volume means you have built a solid foundation in the principles and practice of supervised machine learning. This is no small feat, and you should be proud of the knowledge and skills you have gained along the way.

In the next volume of this series, we will expand our focus to unsupervised learning and deep learning. Topics will include clustering algorithms, dimensionality reduction, density estimation, anomaly detection, and semi-supervised learning. We will also explore neural networks in depth—from classical perceptrons and feedforward networks to modern deep learning architectures including convolutional and recurrent networks, autoencoders, transformers, and graph neural networks. Building on the foundations developed in this volume, Volume II will equip you with the tools and theoretical background needed to address a broader range of machine learning challenges.

I hope you are as excited for the journey ahead as I am to guide you through it!

---

95. https://twitter.com/geoffreyhinton
96. https://x.com/ylecun
97. https://x.com/drfeifei
98. https://x.com/demishassabis
99. https://roiyeho.com

12.8 Exercises

12.8.1 Multiple-Choice Questions

12.1. Which of the following algorithms are typically sensitive to the scale of the input features?

   (a) Decision tree

   (b) k-nearest neighbors

   (c) Logistic regression

   (d) Random forest

   (e) Support vector machine

12.2. Consider the following learning algorithms and their runtime complexities for training and inference, where n is the number of training samples and d is the number of features. Which of the following statements is true?

   (a) The training time complexity of linear regression using the normal equations is $\mathcal{O}(nd^2)$.

   (b) The inference time complexity of k-nearest neighbors (KNN) can be reduced from $\mathcal{O}(nd)$ to $\mathcal{O}(\log n)$ using KD-trees for nearest neighbor searches.

   (c) The training time complexity of random forests depends linearly on d, n, and the number of trees T.

   (d) The training complexity of support vector machines scales quadratically with n.

   (e) The inference time complexity of gradient boosting is $\mathcal{O}(Th)$ where T is the number of trees and h is the maximum tree depth.

12.3. Which of the following models are likely to overfit on a small, noisy dataset?

   (a) Ridge regression

   (b) Polynomial regression with degree 5

   (c) Decision tree with a maximum depth of 10

   (d) SVM with an RBF kernel

12.4. Which of the following statements about regression algorithms are true?

   (a) Ordinary least squares (OLS) regression assumes that the variance of the errors is constant across all values of the independent variables.

   (b) OLS cannot be solved using the normal equations if there is perfect multicollinearity among the predictors.

   (c) All linear regression problems can be formulated as a system of linear equations.

   (d) The squared loss in OLS can be derived from the maximum likelihood estimation principle under the assumption that the residuals are normally distributed.

12.5. Which of the following classifiers are capable of achieving perfect accuracy on the training data shown in Figure 12.6?

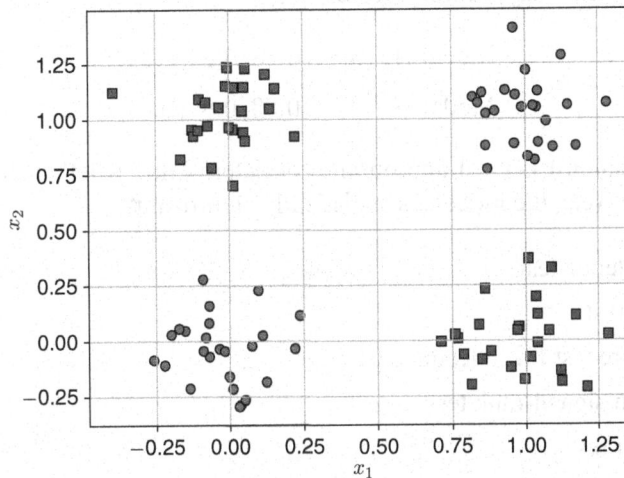

Figure 12.6: Sample dataset with two classes

(a) k-nearest neighbor with $k = 5$

(b) Decision tree with a maximum depth of 2

(c) AdaBoost using decision stumps as base learners

(d) SVM with a polynomial kernel of degree 2

12.6. Which of the following statements about optimization algorithms in machine learning are correct?

(a) Batch gradient descent with a sufficiently small learning rate is guaranteed to decrease the loss function at every iteration for a convex, differentiable objective function.

(b) Stochastic gradient descent (SGD) converges faster than batch gradient descent in terms of number of iterations.

(c) SGD converges to the global minimum for convex and smooth functions if the sum of the learning rates diverges, while the sum of their squares converges.

(d) Newton's method has a quadratic convergence rate for all twice-differentiable, convex functions.

(e) Coordinate descent is guaranteed to converge to the global minimum for strictly convex objective functions.

12.7. A researcher wants to compare the performance of two machine learning models, A and B, on the same dataset. Both models are evaluated using the same 5 folds of cross-validation, producing the following accuracy scores:

$$\text{Model } A: [0.82, 0.85, 0.84, 0.81, 0.83],$$

$$\text{Model } B: [0.81, 0.83, 0.82, 0.80, 0.82].$$

Which statistical test is most appropriate for determining whether the observed difference in accuracy between the models is statistically significant?

  (a) Independent t-test

  (b) Paired t-test

  (c) Chi-square test for independence

  (d) Wilcoxon signed-rank test

  (e) Friedman test

12.8. Which of the following hyperparameter changes are likely to increase bias and reduce variance in their respective models?

  (a) Decreasing the maximum depth of a decision tree

  (b) Increasing the regularization strength λ in ridge regression

  (c) Increasing the number of neighbors k in k-nearest neighbors

  (d) Lowering the learning rate η in gradient boosting

  (e) Increasing the kernel coefficient γ in an SVM with an RBF kernel

  (f) Reducing the number of trees T in a random forest

12.9. A company wants to predict whether customers will churn (cancel their subscription) based on features such as monthly usage, customer support calls, contract type, and payment history. The dataset contains 50,000 samples, with a moderate class imbalance (85% non-churn, 15% churn). Which of the following algorithms is best suited for this task?

  (a) Logistic regression

  (b) k-nearest neighbors

  (c) SVM with an RBF kernel

  (d) Gradient boosting

12.10. A healthcare research team wants to predict whether a patient is at high risk for a particular disease (yes/no) based on patient data such as age, BMI, blood pressure, and cholesterol levels. They also need the predictions to be easily interpretable so that doctors can understand how each feature contributes to the final decision. Which algorithm is most appropriate for this classification task?

(a) Logistic regression

(b) Decision tree

(c) Gradient boosting

(d) SVM with a linear kernel

12.8.2 Theoretical Exercises

12.11. Define each of the following terms or concepts in 1–2 sentences:

- Loss function
- Generative model
- Cross-validation
- Overfitting
- Posterior probability
- Hyperparameter
- Bias–variance tradeoff
- L1 regularization
- Elastic net
- Stochastic gradient descent
- Newton's method
- Cross-entropy loss
- TF-IDF
- Gini impurity
- Cost-complexity pruning
- Bootstrap aggregating (bagging)
- Gradient-boosted trees
- Target encoding
- Soft-margin SVM
- Hinge loss
- The kernel trick

- Radial basis function (RBF)
- Paired *t*-test
- Convex optimization
- Logit
- Confusion matrix
- F1 score
- Epoch
- Feature engineering
- Robust scaling
- Bayesian optimization
- Early stopping
- Feature importance
- Precision and recall
- Area under the curve (AUC)
- Negative log likelihood (NLL)
- Decision threshold
- SMOTE
- Softmax
- Maximum a posteriori (MAP)
- Oblivious tree

12.12. Match each of the models listed below to one of the decision boundaries shown in Figure 12.7. Briefly explain your choice for each match.

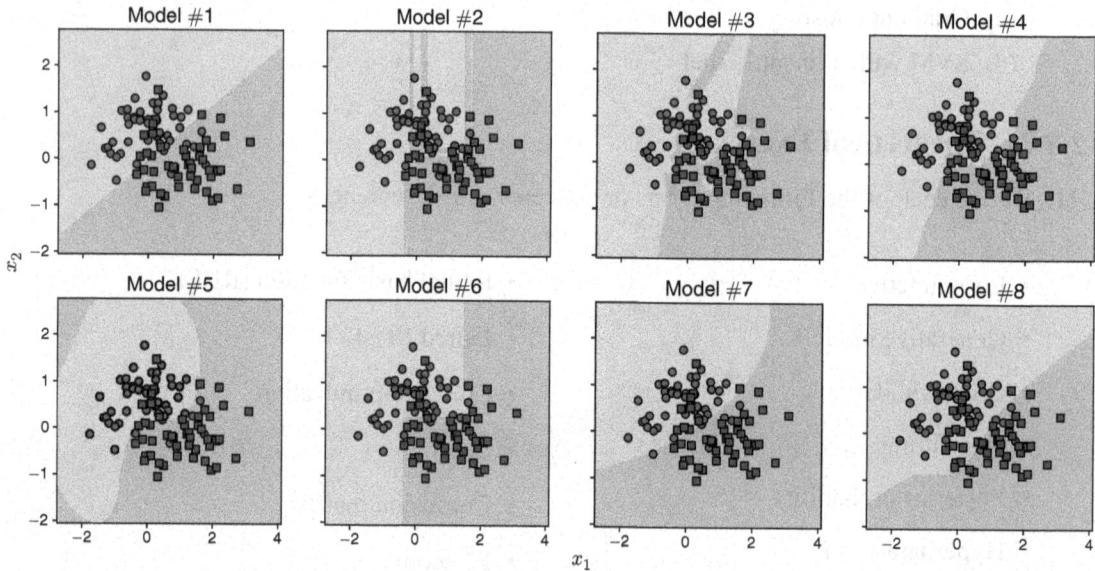

Figure 12.7: Decision boundaries produced by various machine learning models on a two-dimensional dataset.

Model options:

- Logistic regression
- k-nearest neighbor with $k = 1$
- k-nearest neighbor with $k = 10$
- Gaussian naive Bayes
- Decision tree
- Gradient boosting
- SVM with a polynomial kernel
- SVM with an RBF kernel

12.13. You are given a training set with binary labels, where all the examples are unique. You train a classifier on this dataset. Then, you randomly choose three training examples and duplicate them (along with their labels), so they appear twice in the new training set. You train a second classifier of the same type on this updated training set. For each of the following algorithms, determine whether the decision boundaries of the new classifier are necessarily identical to those of the original classifier. Briefly justify each of your answers.

   (a) Logistic regression

   (b) k-nearest neighbors with $k = 1$

(c) k-nearest neighbors with $k = 3$

(d) Decision tree with a maximum depth of 4

(e) AdaBoost with decision stumps

(f) Hard-margin SVM (assuming the dataset is linearly separable)

12.14. You have a training set with binary labels and $d \geq 3$ features. Two of the features, j and k, have a perfect negative linear relationship, i.e., there exist constants $a < 0$ and $b \in \mathbb{R}$ such that, for each example $\mathbf{x}_i$,

$$x_{ik} = ax_{ij} + b.$$

Two classifiers are trained:

- The first classifier is trained on the original dataset with all d features.
- The second classifier is trained on a modified version of the dataset in which the k-th feature has been removed, leaving $d - 1$ features.

For each of the following algorithms, determine whether the training accuracy of the second classifier is necessarily equal to that of the first classifier. Briefly justify your answer in each case.

(a) k-nearest neighbors with $k = 1$

(b) Decision tree

(c) Hard-margin SVM (assuming the dataset is linearly separable)

(d) Soft-margin SVM with $C = 1$ (assuming the dataset is linearly separable)

12.15. You are tasked with building a predictive model for the following real-world scenarios. For each case:

- Select the most appropriate learning algorithm for the task and justify your choice based on relevant criteria such as domain suitability, predictive accuracy, data requirements, computational efficiency, interpretability, and robustness to noise or class imbalance.
- Outline the data preprocessing steps needed (e.g., handling missing values, encoding categorical features, normalization, or feature engineering).
- Describe how the model will be evaluated and tested, including the choice of evaluation metrics and dataset splitting strategy (e.g., train/validation/test or cross-validation).

The scenarios are:

(a) **Fraud detection in financial transactions**. You are building a model to detect fraudulent transactions in a financial dataset. The dataset contains 1 million examples, with only 1% labeled as fraudulent. It includes both categorical features (e.g., transaction type, merchant category, country of origin) and numerical features (e.g., transaction amount, account balance, transaction frequency).

Constraints and challenges:

- The dataset is highly imbalanced, with only 1% of the transactions labeled as fraudulent.
- False positives may inconvenience customers, but false negatives (missed fraud) pose significant financial and reputational risks.
- The model must handle mixed data types (categorical and numerical).
- Real-time predictions are required to flag potentially fraudulent transactions immediately.
- The dataset may contain errors, outliers, or incomplete information, particularly in user-entered fields.
- Interpretability is important, as the system must justify why a transaction was flagged as fraudulent for audits or customer inquiries.

(b) **Hospital length-of-stay prediction**. A hospital system aims to predict the length of stay (in days) for patients admitted through the emergency department. The dataset includes structured information such as demographics (age, gender), vital signs, lab test results, medication history, and comorbidities, as well as unstructured clinical notes written by physicians and nurses during the first 24 hours of admission. Accurate predictions can help optimize resource allocation, such as bed availability and staffing needs.

Constraints and challenges:

- The target variable (length of stay) is continuous and highly skewed—most patients stay 1–3 days, but some may stay significantly longer.
- The dataset includes missing values, especially in lab results and medical history fields, which may not be consistently recorded across patients.
- Some categorical features, such as discharge disposition or admission type, have high cardinality.
- Outliers in length-of-stay (e.g., 30+ days) can disproportionately affect model performance.
- The model must incorporate both structured variables and unstructured text notes to improve predictive accuracy.
- Interpretability is important, as hospital staff need to understand which factors contribute to long predicted stays.
- Prediction speed is not critical, but the model should generalize well across different hospital units and patient populations.

12.16. Based on the runtime complexities of supervised learning algorithms in Table 12.2, identify the most appropriate classification algorithm(s) for each of the following datasets. In addition to training complexity, consider any special requirements specified in each case. Assume binary classification for all scenarios unless otherwise specified.

(a) A dataset with 10 million samples and 10 features.

(b) A dataset with 1,000 samples and 100,000 features.

(c) A dataset with 500,000 training samples and 5,000 features. The task requires real-time predictions with low inference latency.

(d) A dataset with 20,000 samples and 200 features. The task involves classifying inputs into 500 different categories. The model must offer a good tradeoff between training time, accuracy, and scalability for handling many classes efficiently.

(e) A dataset with 100 million samples and 1,000 features. The model must scale efficiently with distributed training across multiple machines.

(f) A dataset with 1 million samples and 500 features. The dataset is highly imbalanced, with only 1% of the samples belonging to the positive class.

(g) A streaming dataset where new samples arrive continuously at a rate of 1,000 samples per minute. The system maintains a sliding window of the most recent 50,000 samples (with 100 features), and the model must support incremental updates to adapt to concept drift.

(h) A small but noisy dataset with 500 samples and 20 features. The model must be robust to outliers and perform well with limited data.

12.17. Explore recent research in supervised machine learning using the following steps:

(a) Select three recent papers that focus on traditional supervised machine learning methods (excluding deep learning). Examples include linear models, kernel methods, decision trees, ensemble methods, optimization techniques, and Bayesian approaches. The papers must have been published within the last three years in top-tier conferences (e.g., NeurIPS, ICML, ICLR, CVPR) or journals (e.g., JMLR, TPAMI).
You may select from the following examples:

- *Learning Curves of Stochastic Gradient Descent in Kernel Regression*, H. Zhang, W. Lin, Y. Liu, and C. Fang, ICML 2025 [660].

- *Computational Efficiency under Covariate Shift in Kernel Ridge Regression*, A. D. Vecchia, A. M. Watusadisi, E. De Vito, and L. Rosasco, ICML 2025 [152].

- *Random Feature Representation Boosting*, N. Zozoulenko, T. Cass, and L. Gonon, ICML 2025 (poster) [672].

- *Convergence and Trade-Offs in Riemannian Gradient Descent and Riemannian Proximal Point*, D. Martínez-Rubio, C. Roux, and S. Pokutta, ICML 2024 [400].

- *Sampling-based Multi-dimensional Recalibration*, Y. Chung, I. Char, and J. Schneider, ICML 2024 [122].

- *Linear Regression using Heterogeneous Data Batches*, Ayush Jain et al., NeurIPS 2024 [290].

- *Learning-Rate-Free Learning by D-Adaptation*, A. Defazio and K. Mishchenko, ICML 2023 [151].

- *Weakly Supervised Regression with Interval Targets*, Xin Cheng et al., ICML 2023 [113].
- *Feature Adaptation for Sparse Linear Regression*, Jonathan Kelner et al., NeurIPS 2023 [315].
- *Binary Classification with Confidence Difference*, Wei Wang et al., NeurIPS 2023 [609].

(b) Read each selected paper thoroughly.

(c) For each paper, write a concise summary (maximum 500 words) that includes:

- The main research objectives.
- The methodology used to address the problem.
- Key findings and their significance for the field or practical applications.
- The strengths and weaknesses of the suggested approach.
- Suggestions for future research based on the paper's contributions.

(d) Write a formal peer review for each paper, following the official NeurIPS Reviewer Guidelines.[100].

12.18. Investigate recent advancements or extensions to a machine learning algorithm discussed in the book by completing the following steps:

(a) Choose a specific model, such as linear regression, decision trees, gradient boosting, support vector machines (SVMs), or Bayesian networks.

(b) Summarize at least three academic papers published within the last five years that propose new algorithms, modifications, or extensions to the chosen model. These may include scalability and efficiency improvements (e.g., distributed training, approximation methods, faster optimization techniques), novel regularization startegies, robustness to noise and outliers, adaptations for online or incremental learning, and extensions to handle complex data types (e.g., graphs, time series, multi-label data).

(c) Implement one of the methods or extensions introduced in the papers. If code is available (e.g., via a GitHub repository), you may consult it for reference, but your implementation should reflect your own understanding and originality. Compare the performance of your implementation with that of the standard version covered in the book, using appropriate evaluation metrics and datasets.

(d) Write a short report summarizing your findings, including:

- A concise description of the selected papers and their contributions.
- Key insights from your implementation and evaluation.
- Practical challenges encountered during implementation and how you addressed them.
- A comparative analysis of the original and extended methods in terms of performance, computational complexity, or applicability to real-world problems.

---

100. https://neurips.cc/Conferences/2025/ReviewerGuidelines

12.8.3 Programming Exercises

12.19. You are tasked with building a predictive model to determine whether a diabetic patient will be readmitted to the hospital within 30 days of discharge. The Diabetes 130-US Hospitals for Years 1999–2008[101] dataset, available from the UCI Machine Learning Repository, contains ten years of clinical care records from 130 hospitals and integrated delivery networks across the US.

The dataset consists of 101,766 hospital records, each corresponding to a patient diagnosed with diabetes. It includes 50 features encompassing patient demographics, lab results, co-morbidities, medication history, and hospital stay details. The target variable is binary: 1 if the patient was readmitted within 30 days, and 0 otherwise.

This prediction task is both clinically and economically important. Poor inpatient care and follow-up can lead to inadequate glycemic control, increasing the risk of complications, morbidity, and early readmissions. Diabetes affects over 25.5 million people in the US, with prevalence continuing to rise. Diabetic patients face a hospital readmission rate of 14.4–22.7%, nearly double that of non-diabetic patients (8.5–13.5%) [509]. These readmissions contribute significantly to healthcare costs and negatively impact patient outcomes and quality of life.

Challenges and constraints:

- Mixed data types: The dataset contains both categorical features (e.g., medication names) and numerical features (e.g., lab results).

- High dimensionality: With 50 input features, effective preprocessing and feature selection are essential to reduce noise and potential redundancy.

- Class imbalance: Early readmissions account for only about 11% of the data, resulting in a roughly 1:8 class imbalance. This requires careful handling to avoid biased predictions.

- Interpretability: For clinical deployment, it is crucial that model predictions can be explained and trusted by healthcare providers.

Design and conduct a systematic comparison between various machine learning algorithms on this dataset using the following steps (see also Section 12.3):

(a) Download the dataset from the UCI Machine Learning Repository. Use the file `diabetic_data.csv` as your primary dataset.

(b) Data exploration:

    i. Calculate basic descriptive statistics, such as mean and standard deviation for numerical features, and frequency counts for categorical variables.

    ii. Identify features with missing or incomplete values, and assess their potential impact on analysis and modeling.

---

101. https://archive.ics.uci.edu/dataset/296/diabetes+130-us+hospitals+for+years+1999-2008

iii. Quantify the degree of class imbalance in the target variable.

iv. Examine the distributions of both categorical and numerical features, identifying any skewness, irregularities, or other notable patterns.

v. Detect outliers in numerical features using statistical methods such as z-scores.

vi. Analyze the correlations among features and between each feature and the target variable. Consider both linear associations (e.g., Pearson correlation) and nonlinear associations (e.g., Spearman rank correlation).

vii. Create visualizations such as histograms, boxplots, and correlation heatmaps to better understand feature distributions and relationships.

(c) Data preprocessing:

i. Convert the target variable from its original three categories: `'NO'`, `'>30'`, and `'<30'` into a binary classification problem:

- Positive class (1): Patients readmitted within 30 days (`'<30'`).
- Negative class (0): Patients not readmitted or readmitted after 30 days (`'NO'` and `'>30'`).

ii. Encode categorical variables into suitable numerical representations.

iii. Handle missing values using appropriate methods such as imputation or removing features with a high percentage of missing values.

iv. Normalize or standardize numerical features to ensure compatibility with algorithms that are sensitive to feature scales.

v. Engineer new features by transforming or aggregating existing ones. For example:

- Create a feature that sums the number of outpatient, emergency, and inpatient visits for each patient to capture overall healthcare utilization.
- Convert age ranges into their midpoint values to provide a continuous numerical representation that can be more effectively processed by machine learning algorithms (e.g., "[50-60]" becomes 55).
- Group similar categories in features like admission type, discharge type, and admission source into broader, clinically meaningful categories.

vi. Drop irrelevant or highly correlated features to eliminate redundancy.

(d) Train–test split:

i. To ensure a fair evaluation and avoid data leakage, split the dataset such that all records associated with the same patient are assigned either to the training set or the test set, but not both. To achieve this, you can use Scikit-Learn's `GroupShuffleSplit`[102] with the `patient_nbr` column as the grouping key.

(e) Algorithm selection:

i. Select at least eight machine learning algorithms for this task, ensuring coverage of diverse model families (e.g., linear models, distance-based methods, tree-based models, kernel-based methods, and ensemble techniques).

---

102. `https://scikit-learn.org/stable/modules/generated/sklearn.model_selection.GroupShuffleSplit.html`

ii. Justify your choices by discussing how each algorithm handles the specific characteristics of the dataset, such as mixed data types, high dimensionality, class imbalance, and interpretability requirements.

(f) Model training: Train each model on the training set using default hyperparameter values and evaluate its performance. To ensure robust and reliable results, account for both variability in the data split and randomness in model training:

    i. Perform group-aware cross-validation using Scikit-Learn's GroupKFold[103] with patient_nbr as the grouping key. This ensures that all records from the same patient appear in the same fold.

    ii. For models with stochastic elements, repeat the entire cross-validation process using multiple random seeds (e.g., 5 different seeds).

(g) Performance reporting:

    i. Compute and report the average values of the following performance metrics across all cross-validation folds and random seeds: accuracy, precision, recall, F1 score, and AUC.

    ii. Report 95% confidence intervals to quantify the variability across folds and seeds:

$$\text{CI} = \overline{x} \pm 1.96 \cdot \frac{\sigma}{\sqrt{ks}},$$

where $\overline{x}$ is the mean performance metric, σ is its standard deviation, k is the number of cross-validation folds, and s is the number of random seeds.

(h) Statistical testing:

    i. Perform the Friedman test on the cross-validation results to assess whether differences in performance across models are statistically significant.

    ii. If the test indicates significant differences, conduct post-hoc pairwise comparisons using the Nemenyi test to identify which models differ significantly.

    iii. Visualize the results using a critical difference (CD) plot.

(i) Hyperparameter tuning:

    i. Optimize the hyperparameters of each model using techniques such as grid search, random search, or Bayesian optimization.

    ii. Compare the performance of each tuned model with its default configuration to assess the impact of hyperparameter tuning.

    iii. Perform statistical testing (e.g., paired t-test or Wilcoxon signed-rank test) to determine whether the performance improvements from tuning are statistically significant.

---

103. https://scikit-learn.org/stable/modules/generated/sklearn.model_selection.GroupKFold.html

(j) Class imbalance handling:

    i. Experiment with different strategies for addressing class imbalance, including oversampling (e.g., SMOTE), undersampling, and cost-sensitive learning (e.g., using class weights or weighted loss functions).

    ii. Evaluate the impact of these techniques on model performance. Use appropriate statistical tests to determine whether the observed changes are significant.

(k) Final model comparison:

    i. For each algorithm, identify the best-performing version based on previous steps (i.e., after hyperparameter tuning and class imbalance handling).

    ii. Compare the best-performing models using key metrics such as accuracy, F1 score, and AUC.

    iii. Record the average training time and prediction time for each model.

    iv. Use the Friedman test to assess whether performance differences among the final models are statistically significant. If significant, conduct post-hoc pairwise comparisons to determine which models differ from each other.

    v. Visualize the final comparisons using a critical difference (CD) plot.

    vi. Report the final test set performance of each model using accuracy, precision, recall, F1 score, and AUC.

(l) Summarize your work in the format of an academic paper using the official LaTeX template from NeurIPS 2025. You can download the template directly from: `https://media.neurips.cc/Conferences/NeurIPS2025/Styles.zip`. The paper should include the following sections:

    i. Abstract and Introduction: Clearly state the problem, describe the dataset, and explain the motivation behind your work. Summarize your approach and main findings.

    ii. Related Work: Briefly review relevant literature, including prior studies that used the Diabetes 130-US Hospitals dataset (e.g., [564, 213]) and broader literature on hospital readmission prediction. Summarize key methods, findings, and insights that influenced your approach.

    iii. Methodology: Describe the full modeling pipeline, including preprocessing, model selection, hyperparameter tuning, and techniques for handling class imbalance.

    iv. Experiments and Results: Present the evaluation results for all models, including performance metrics such as accuracy, F1 score, and AUC; visualizations such as ROC curves, confusion matrices, and critical difference plots; and the outcomes of statistical significance tests. Clearly indicate which models performed best and under what conditions.

v. Discussion and Conclusion: Analyze your findings by discussing the strengths and limitations of each model in the context of this dataset, the impact of hyperparameter tuning and class imbalance handling methods, and any tradeoffs encountered, such as computational cost versus accuracy. Additionally, reflect on the challenges faced during experimentation and explain how you addressed them.

12.20. Choose an ongoing Kaggle competition that interests you and can be addressed using traditional supervised learning algorithms. Follow these steps:

(a) Register for the competition and carefully review the problem description, evaluation metrics, and submission requirements.

(b) Literature research:

   i. Investigate the domain of the problem. Identify common approaches used to solve similar problems by reviewing relevant academic papers, blog posts, and industry reports.

   ii. Explore past Kaggle competitions and forum discussions related to the problem. Review winning solutions to identify effective techniques used in similar tasks.

(c) Data exploration and preprocessing:

   i. Download the dataset(s) provided by the competition.

   ii. Conduct exploratory data analysis (EDA) to understand the data structure, feature distributions, correlations, and potential anomalies.

   iii. Preprocess the data as needed (handle missing values, scale features, encode categorical variables, handle class imbalance, etc.).

(d) Model training and evaluation:

   i. Train at least three supervised learning models on the training data.

   ii. Evaluate performance using cross-validation or a validation split, applying the competition's evaluation metric.

(e) Model optimization:

   i. Improve your model using techniques such as feature engineering, variable transformation, feature selection, or discretization, incorporating domain knowledge where relevant.

   ii. Tune the hyperparameters using grid search, random search, or other optimization techniques.

   iii. Select your best model based on validation performance.

(f) Submission:

   i. Generate predictions on the test set using your best model and submit them to the competition.

   ii. Record your public leaderboard score.

(g) Iteration and improvement:

    i. Review public notebooks, discussion forums, and alternative solutions shared by other participants.

    ii. Refine your pipeline by incorporating new insights and resubmit an improved version.

    iii. Continue iterating—experiment with additional algorithms, advanced feature engineering, ensembling, or domain-specific techniques. Track how each modification affects your performance.

Bibliography

[1] Situational awareness: The decade ahead. `https://situational-awareness.ai`, 2024.

[2] G. Aad, T. Abajyan, B. Abbott, J. Abdallah, S. A. Khalek, A. A. Abdelalim, R. Aben, B. Abi, M. Abolins, O. AbouZeid, et al. Observation of a new particle in the search for the Standard Model Higgs boson with the ATLAS detector at the LHC. *Physics Letters B*, 716(1):1–29, 2012.

[3] M. Abadi, A. Chu, I. Goodfellow, H. B. McMahan, I. Mironov, K. Talwar, and L. Zhang. Deep learning with differential privacy. In *Proceedings of the 2016 ACM SIGSAC Conference on Computer and Communications Security*, pages 308–318, 2016.

[4] A. Abdiansah and R. Wardoyo. Time complexity analysis of support vector machines (SVM) in LibSVM. *International Journal of Computer Applications*, 128(3):28–34, 2015.

[5] A. Abomakhelb, K. A. Jalil, A. G. Buja, A. Alhammadi, and A. M. Alenezi. A comprehensive review of adversarial attacks and defense strategies in deep neural networks. *Technologies*, 13(5):202, 2025.

[6] J. Abramson, J. Adler, J. Dunger, R. Evans, T. Green, A. Pritzel, O. Ronneberger, L. Willmore, A. J. Ballard, et al. Accurate structure prediction of biomolecular interactions with AlphaFold 3. *Nature*, 630(8016):493–500, 2024.

[7] H. A. Abu Alfeilat, A. B. Hassanat, O. Lasassmeh, A. S. Tarawneh, M. B. Alhasanat, H. S. E. Salman, and V. S. Prasath. Effects of distance measure choice on k-nearest neighbor classifier performance: A review. *Big Data*, 7(4):221–248, 2019.

[8] C. Adam-Bourdarios, G. Cowan, C. Germain, I. Guyon, B. Kegl, and D. Rousseau. Learning to discover: the Higgs boson machine learning challenge. `https://higgsml.ijclab.in2p3.fr/documentation`, 2014.

[9] C. C. Aggarwal. *Recommender Systems: The Textbook*. Springer, 2016.

[10] C. C. Aggarwal, A. Hinneburg, and D. A. Keim. On the surprising behavior of distance metrics in high dimensional space. In *Proceedings of the 8th International Conference on Database Theory*, pages 420–434, 2001.

[11] A. C. Aitken. On least squares and linear combinations of observations. *Proceedings of the Royal Society of Edinburgh*, 55:42–48, 1935.

[12] R. Akbani, S. Kwek, and N. Japkowicz. Applying support vector machines to imbalanced datasets. In *Proceedings of the 15th European Conference on Machine Learning*, pages 39–50, 2004.

[13] Z. Allen-Zhu, Y. Li, and Z. Song. A convergence theory for deep learning via over-parameterization. In *Proceedings of the 36th International Conference on Machine Learning (ICML)*, pages 242–252, 2019.

[14] D. Amodei, C. Olah, J. Steinhardt, P. Christiano, J. Schulman, and D. Mané. Concrete problems in AI safety. *arXiv preprint arXiv:1606.06565*, 2016.

[15] A. Andoni and P. Indyk. Near-optimal hashing algorithms for approximate nearest neighbor in high dimensions. *Communications of the ACM*, 51(1):117–122, 2008.

[16] J. D. Angrist and J.-S. Pischke. *Mostly Harmless Econometrics: An Empiricist's Companion*. Princeton University Press, 2009.

[17] A. Ankan and A. Panda. pgmpy: Probabilistic graphical models using Python. In *Proceedings of the 14th Python in Science Conference (SciPy 2015)*, pages 6–11, 2015.

[18] Anthropic. Claude 3.7 Sonnet and Claude Code. https://www.anthropic.com/news/claude-3-7-sonnet, February 2025.

[19] Anthropic. Claude takes research to new places. https://www.anthropic.com/news/research, April 2025.

[20] R. Atallah and A. Al-Mousa. Heart disease detection using machine learning majority voting ensemble method. In *Proceedings of the 2nd International Conference on New Trends in Computing Sciences*, pages 1–6, 2019.

[21] M. T. Augustine. A survey on universal approximation theorems. *arXiv preprint arXiv:2407.12895*, 2024.

[22] M. Ayer, H. D. Brunk, G. M. Ewing, W. T. Reid, and E. Silverman. An empirical distribution function for sampling with incomplete information. *The Annals of Mathematical Statistics*, 26(4):641–647, 1955.

[23] D. Bahdanau, K. Cho, and Y. Bengio. Neural machine translation by jointly learning to align and translate. *arXiv preprint arXiv:1409.0473*, 2014.

[24] Y. Bahri, E. Dyer, J. Kaplan, J. Lee, and U. Sharma. Explaining neural scaling laws. *Proceedings of the National Academy of Sciences*, 121(27):e2311878121, 2024.

[25] P. Baldi, P. Sadowski, and D. Whiteson. Searching for exotic particles in high-energy physics with deep learning. *Nature Communications*, 5(1):4308, 2014.

[26] T. Baltrušaitis, C. Ahuja, and L.-P. Morency. Multimodal machine learning: A survey and taxonomy. *IEEE Transactions on Pattern Analysis and Machine Intelligence*, 41(2):423–443, 2018.

[27] S. Barocas, M. Hardt, and A. Narayanan. *Fairness and Machine Learning: Limitations and Opportunities*. MIT Press, 2023.

[28] K. A. Barry, Y. Manzali, M. Lamrini, F. Rachid, and M. Elfar. Heart disease prediction using weighted k-nearest neighbor algorithm. *Operations Research Forum*, 5(3):76, 2024.

[29] P. L. Bartlett, P. M. Long, G. Lugosi, and A. Tsigler. Benign overfitting in linear regression. *Proceedings of the National Academy of Sciences*, 117(48):30063–30070, 2020.

[30] M. J. Basgall, W. Hasperué, M. Naiouf, A. Fernández, and F. Herrera. SMOTE-BD: An exact and scalable oversampling method for imbalanced classification in big data. In *Proceedings of the VI Jornadas de Cloud Computing & Big Data (JCC&BD)*, pages 1–6, 2018.

[31] S. Bassan, G. Amir, M. Zehavi, and G. Katz. What makes an ensemble (un)interpretable? In *Proceedings of the 42nd International Conference on Machine Learning (ICML)*, pages 3142–3201, 2025.

[32] G. E. Batista, R. C. Prati, and M. C. Monard. A study of the behavior of several methods for balancing machine learning training data. *ACM SIGKDD Explorations Newsletter*, 6(1):20–29, 2004.

[33] E. Bauer and R. Kohavi. An empirical comparison of voting classification algorithms: Bagging, boosting, and variants. *Machine Learning*, 36:105–139, 1999.

[34] T. Bayes. An essay towards solving a problem in the doctrine of chances. *Philosophical Transactions of the Royal Society of London*, 53:370–418, 1763.

[35] B. Becker and R. Kohavi. Adult Dataset. UCI Machine Learning Repository, 1996. DOI: https://doi.org/10.24432/C5XW20.

[36] D. A. Belsley, E. Kuh, and R. E. Welsch. *Regression Diagnostics: Identifying Influential Data and Sources of Collinearity*. Wiley, 1980.

[37] S. Ben-David, P. Hrubeš, S. Moran, A. Shpilka, and A. Yehudayoff. Learnability can be undecidable. *Nature Machine Intelligence*, 4:234–239, 2022.

[38] G. Beniamini, Y. Dor, A. Vinnikov, S. G. Peled, O. Weinstein, O. Sharir, N. Wies, T. Nussbaum, I. B. Shaul, T. Zekharya, et al. FormulaOne: Measuring the depth of algorithmic reasoning beyond competitive programming. *arXiv preprint arXiv:2507.13337*, 2025.

[39] J. Bennett and S. Lanning. The Netflix prize. In *Proceedings of KDD Cup Workshop*, pages 3–6, 2007.

[40] C. Bentéjac, A. Csörgő, and G. Martínez-Muñoz. A comparative analysis of gradient boosting algorithms. *Artificial Intelligence Review*, 54:1937–1967, 2021.

[41] J. L. Bentley. Multidimensional binary search trees used for associative searching. *Communications of the ACM*, 18(9):509–517, 1975.

[42] J. O. Berger. *Statistical Decision Theory and Bayesian Analysis*. Springer, 2nd edition, 1985.

[43] J. Bergstra, R. Bardenet, Y. Bengio, and B. Kégl. Algorithms for hyper-parameter optimization. In *Advances in Neural Information Processing Systems (NeurIPS)*, pages 2546–2554, 2011.

[44] J. Bergstra and Y. Bengio. Random search for hyper-parameter optimization. *Journal of Machine Learning Research*, 13(1):281–305, 2012.

[45] L. Berti, F. Giorgi, and G. Kasneci. Emergent abilities in large language models: A survey. *arXiv preprint arXiv:2503.05788*, 2025.

[46] D. P. Bertsekas and J. N. Tsitsiklis. *Introduction to Probability*. Athena Scientific, 2nd edition, 2008.

[47] D. Bertsimas and J. Dunn. Optimal classification trees. *Machine Learning*, 106:1039–1082, 2017.

[48] A. Beygelzimer, S. Kakade, and J. Langford. Cover trees for nearest neighbor. In *Proceedings of the 23rd International Conference on Machine Learning (ICML)*, pages 97–104, 2006.

[49] C. Bielza, G. Li, and P. Larranaga. Multi-dimensional classification with Bayesian networks. *International Journal of Approximate Reasoning*, 52(6):705–727, 2011.

[50] A. Bilal, D. Ebert, and B. Lin. LLMs for explainable AI: A comprehensive survey. *arXiv preprint arXiv:2504.00125*, 2025.

[51] P. Billingsley. *Probability and Measure*. Wiley, 4th edition, 2012.

[52] S. Bird. NLTK: The natural language toolkit. In *Proceedings of the COLING/ACL 2006 Interactive Presentation Sessions*, pages 69–72, 2006.

[53] S. Bird, E. Klein, and E. Loper. *Natural Language Processing with Python: Analyzing Text with the Natural Language Toolkit*. O'Reilly Media, 2009.

[54] C. M. Bishop. *Pattern Recognition and Machine Learning*. Springer, 2006.

[55] R. Blagus and L. Lusa. SMOTE for high-dimensional class-imbalanced data. *BMC Bioinformatics*, 14:1–16, 2013.

[56] S. L. Blodgett, S. Barocas, H. Daumé III, and H. Wallach. Language (technology) is power: A critical survey of "bias" in NLP. In *Proceedings of the 58th Annual Meeting of the Association for Computational Linguistics (ACL)*, pages 5454–5476, 2020.

[57] A. Blumer, A. Ehrenfeucht, D. Haussler, and M. K. Warmuth. Occam's razor. *Information Processing Letters*, 24(6):377–380, 1987.

[58] S. Bochner. Monotone funktionen, stieltjessche integrale und harmonische analyse. *Mathematische Annalen*, 108:378–410, 1933.

[59] M. Bojarski, D. Del Testa, D. Dworakowski, B. Firner, B. Flepp, P. Goyal, L. D. Jackel, M. Monfort, U. Muller, J. Zhang, et al. End to end learning for self-driving cars. *arXiv preprint arXiv:1604.07316*, 2016.

[60] H. Borchani, G. Varando, C. Bielza, and P. Larrañaga. A survey on multi-output regression. *Wiley Interdisciplinary Reviews: Data Mining and Knowledge Discovery*, 5(5):216–233, 2015.

[61] B. E. Boser, I. M. Guyon, and V. N. Vapnik. A training algorithm for optimal margin classifiers. In *Proceedings of the 5th Annual Workshop on Computational Learning Theory*, pages 144–152, 1992.

[62] N. Bostrom. *Superintelligence: Paths, Dangers, Strategies*. Oxford University Press, 2014.

[63] G. E. P. Box, G. M. Jenkins, G. C. Reinsel, and G. M. Ljung. *Time Series Analysis: Forecasting and Control*. John Wiley & Sons, 5th edition, 2015.

[64] S. Boyd and L. Vandenberghe. *Convex Optimization*. Cambridge University Press, 2004.

[65] A. P. Bradley. The use of the area under the ROC curve in the evaluation of machine learning algorithms. *Pattern Recognition*, 30(7):1145–1159, 1997.

[66] F. Brakel, U. Odyurt, and A.-L. Varbanescu. Model parallelism on distributed infrastructure: A literature review from theory to LLM case-studies. *arXiv preprint arXiv:2403.03699*, 2024.

[67] L. Breiman. Bagging predictors. *Machine Learning*, 24:123–140, 1996.

[68] L. Breiman. Out-of-bag estimation. Technical Report 421, Statistics Department, University of California, Berkeley, 1996.

[69] L. Breiman. Stacked regressions. *Machine Learning*, 24(1):49–64, 1996.

[70] L. Breiman. Arcing classifiers. *The Annals of Statistics*, 26(3):801–849, 1998.

[71] L. Breiman. Pasting small votes for classification in large databases and on-line. *Machine Learning*, 36:85–103, 1999.

[72] L. Breiman. Random forests. *Machine Learning*, 45:5–32, 2001.

[73] L. Breiman, J. Friedman, R. Olshen, and C. Stone. *Classification and Regression Trees*. Chapman & Hall/CRC, 1984.

[74] L. Breiman and J. H. Friedman. Predicting multivariate responses in multiple linear regression. *Journal of the Royal Statistical Society: Series B (Statistical Methodology)*, 59(1):3–54, 1997.

[75] G. W. Brier. Verification of forecasts expressed in terms of probability. *Monthly Weather Review*, 78(1):1–3, 1950.

[76] S. Brin. Near neighbor search in large metric spaces. In *Proceedings of the 21st International Conference on Very Large Data Bases*, pages 574–584, 1995.

[77] C. E. Brodley and P. E. Utgoff. Multivariate decision trees. *Machine Learning*, 19:45–77, 1995.

[78] T. Brown, B. Mann, N. Ryder, M. Subbiah, J. D. Kaplan, P. Dhariwal, A. Neelakantan, P. Shyam, G. Sastry, A. Askell, et al. Language models are few-shot learners. In *Advances in Neural Information Processing Systems (NeurIPS)*, pages 1877–1901, 2020.

[79] M. W. Browne. Cross-validation methods. *Journal of Mathematical Psychology*, 44(1):108–132, 2000.

[80] S. Bubeck, V. Chandrasekaran, R. Eldan, J. Gehrke, E. Horvitz, E. Kamar, P. Lee, Y. T. Lee, Y. Li, S. Lundberg, et al. Sparks of artificial general intelligence: Early experiments with GPT-4. *arXiv preprint arXiv:2303.12712*, 2023.

[81] M. Buckland and F. Gey. The relationship between recall and precision. *Journal of the American Society for Information Science*, 45(1):12–19, 1994.

[82] M. Buehler, K. Iagnemma, and S. Singh. *The DARPA Urban Challenge: Autonomous Vehicles in City Traffic*. Springer, 2009.

[83] M. D. Buhmann. Radial basis functions. *Acta Numerica*, 9:1–38, 2000.

[84] J. Buolamwini and T. Gebru. Gender shades: Intersectional accuracy disparities in commercial gender classification. In *Proceedings of the 1st Conference on Fairness, Accountability and Transparency*, pages 77–91, 2018.

[85] N. Burkart and M. F. Huber. A survey on the explainability of supervised machine learning. *Journal of Artificial Intelligence Research*, 70:245–317, 2021.

[86] J. P. U. Cadavid, S. Lamouri, and B. Grabot. Trends in machine learning applied to demand & sales forecasting: A review. In *International Conference on Information Systems, Logistics and Supply Chain*, 2018.

[87] H. Cai, C. Gan, T. Wang, Z. Zhang, and S. Han. Once-for-all: Train one network and specialize it for efficient deployment. In *International Conference on Learning Representations (ICLR)*, 2020.

[88] M. Campbell, M. Egerstedt, J. P. How, and R. M. Murray. Autonomous driving in urban environments: Approaches, lessons and challenges. *Philosophical Transactions of the Royal Society A: Mathematical, Physical and Engineering Sciences*, 368(1928):4649–4672, 2010.

[89] L. Cañete-Sifuentes, R. Monroy, and M. A. Medina-Pérez. A review and experimental comparison of multivariate decision trees. *IEEE Access*, 9:110451–110479, 2021.

[90] Y. Cao, T. A. Geddes, J. Y. H. Yang, and P. Yang. Ensemble deep learning in bioinformatics. *Nature Machine Intelligence*, 2(9):500–508, 2020.

[91] D. Caragea, A. Silvescu, and V. Honavar. A framework for learning from distributed data using sufficient statistics and its application to learning decision trees. *International Journal of Hybrid Intelligent Systems*, 1(1–2):80–89, 2004.

[92] H. Carlens. The state of competitive machine learning in 2023. `https://mlcontests.com/state-of-competitive-machine-learning-2023`, 2024.

[93] H. Carlens. The state of machine learning competitions in 2024. `https://mlcontests.com/state-of-machine-learning-competitions-2024`, 2025.

[94] N. Carlini, F. Tramer, E. Wallace, M. Jagielski, A. Herbert-Voss, K. Lee, A. Roberts, T. Brown, D. Song, U. Erlingsson, et al. Extracting training data from large language models. In *Proceedings of the 30th USENIX Security Symposium*, pages 2633–2650, 2021.

[95] M. C. Caro. From undecidability of non-triviality and finiteness to undecidability of learnability. *International Journal of Approximate Reasoning*, 163:109057, 2023.

[96] R. Caruana and A. Niculescu-Mizil. An empirical comparison of supervised learning algorithms. In *Proceedings of the 23rd International Conference on Machine Learning (ICML)*, pages 161–168, 2006.

[97] G. Casella and R. L. Berger. *Statistical Inference*. Duxbury Press, 2nd edition, 2002.

[98] C. P. Chai. Comparison of text preprocessing methods. *Natural Language Engineering*, 29(3):509–553, 2023.

[99] T. Chai and R. R. Draxler. Root mean square error (RMSE) or mean absolute error (MAE)?–Arguments against avoiding RMSE in the literature. *Geoscientific Model Development*, 7(3):1247–1250, 2014.

[100] N. Chakrabarty and S. Biswas. A statistical approach to adult census income level prediction. In *International Conference on Advances in Computing, Communication Control and Networking*, pages 207–212, 2018.

[101] V. Chandola, A. Banerjee, and V. Kumar. Anomaly detection: A survey. *ACM Computing Surveys*, 41(3):1–58, 2009.

[102] B. Chandra, R. Kothari, and P. Paul. A new node splitting measure for decision tree construction. *Pattern Recognition*, 43(8):2725–2731, 2010.

[103] C.-C. Chang and C.-J. Lin. LIBSVM: A library for support vector machines. *ACM Transactions on Intelligent Systems and Technology*, 2(3):1–27, 2011.

[104] K.-W. Chang, C.-J. Hsieh, and C.-J. Lin. Coordinate descent method for large-scale L2-loss linear SVM. *Journal of Machine Learning Research*, 9:1369–1398, 2008.

[105] O. Chapelle, B. Schölkopf, and A. Zien. *Semi-Supervised Learning*. MIT Press, 2006.

[106] N. V. Chawla, K. W. Bowyer, L. O. Hall, and W. P. Kegelmeyer. SMOTE: Synthetic minority over-sampling technique. *Journal of Artificial Intelligence Research*, 16:321–357, 2002.

[107] C. Chen, A. Liaw, and L. Breiman. Using random forest to learn imbalanced data. Technical report, University of California, Berkeley, 2004.

[108] H.-L. Chen, C.-C. Huang, X.-G. Yu, X. Xu, X. Sun, G. Wang, and S.-J. Wang. An efficient diagnosis system for detection of Parkinson's disease using fuzzy k-nearest neighbor approach. *Expert Systems with Applications*, 40(1):263–271, 2013.

[109] T. Chen and C. Guestrin. XGBoost: A scalable tree boosting system. In *Proceedings of the 22nd ACM SIGKDD International Conference on Knowledge Discovery and Data Mining*, pages 785–794, 2016.

[110] X. Chen, H. Wen, S. Nag, C. Luo, Q. Yin, R. Li, Z. Li, and W. Wang. IterAlign: Iterative constitutional alignment of large language models. *arXiv preprint arXiv:2403.18341*, 2024.

[111] Y. Chen and Y. Hao. A feature weighted support vector machine and k-nearest neighbor algorithm for stock market indices prediction. *Expert Systems with Applications*, 80:340–355, 2017.

[112] Z. Chen, J. Li, P. Chen, Z. Li, K. Sun, Y. Luo, Q. Mao, D. Yang, H. Sun, and P. S. Yu. Harnessing multiple large language models: A survey on LLM ensemble. *arXiv preprint arXiv:2502.18036*, 2025.

[113] X. Cheng, Y. Cao, X. Li, B. An, and L. Feng. Weakly supervised regression with interval targets. In *Proceedings of the 40th International Conference on Machine Learning (ICML)*, pages 5428–5448, 2023.

[114] H. Chernoff. A measure of asymptotic efficiency for tests of a hypothesis based on the sum of observations. *The Annals of Mathematical Statistics*, 23(4):493–507, 1952.

[115] D. Chicco, M. J. Warrens, and G. Jurman. The coefficient of determination R-squared is more informative than SMAPE, MAE, MAPE, MSE and RMSE in regression analysis evaluation. *Peerj Computer Science*, 7:e623, 2021.

[116] D. M. Chickering. Optimal structure identification with greedy search. *Journal of Machine Learning Research*, 3:507–554, 2002.

[117] H. A. Chipman, E. I. George, and R. E. McCulloch. Bayesian CART model search. *Journal of the American Statistical Association*, 93(443):935–948, 1998.

[118] H. A. Chipman, E. I. George, and R. E. McCulloch. BART: Bayesian additive regression trees. *The Annals of Applied Statistics*, 4(1):266–298, 2010.

[119] F. Chollet. On the measure of intelligence. *arXiv preprint arXiv:1911.01547*, 2019.

[120] F. Chollet, M. Knoop, G. Kamradt, and B. Landers. ARC prize 2024: Technical report. *arXiv preprint arXiv:2412.04604*, 2024.

[121] F. Chollet, M. Knoop, G. Kamradt, B. Landers, and H. Pinkard. ARC-AGI-2: A new challenge for frontier AI reasoning systems. *arXiv preprint arXiv:2505.11831*, 2025.

[122] Y. Chung, I. Char, and J. Schneider. Sampling-based multi-dimensional recalibration. In *Proceedings of the 41st International Conference on Machine Learning (ICML)*, pages 8919–8940, 2024.

[123] P. Ciaccia, M. Patella, and P. Zezula. M-tree: An efficient access method for similarity search in metric spaces. In *Proceedings of the 23rd International Conference on Very Large Data Bases*, pages 426–435, 1997.

[124] D. A. Cieslak and N. V. Chawla. Learning decision trees for unbalanced data. In *Machine Learning and Knowledge Discovery in Databases*, pages 241–256, 2008.

[125] D. Ciregan, U. Meier, and J. Schmidhuber. Multi-column deep neural networks for image classification. In *Proceedings of the IEEE Conference on Computer Vision and Pattern Recognition (CVPR)*, pages 3642–3649, 2012.

[126] F. H. Clarke. Generalized gradients and applications. *Transactions of the American Mathematical Society*, 205:247–262, 1975.

[127] B. C. Colelough and W. Regli. Neuro-symbolic AI in 2024: A systematic review. *arXiv preprint arXiv:2501.05435*, 2025.

[128] R. D. Cook and S. Weisberg. Diagnostics for heteroscedasticity in regression. *Biometrika*, 70(1):1–10, 1983.

[129] G. F. Cooper. The computational complexity of probabilistic inference using Bayesian belief networks. *Artificial Intelligence*, 42(2–3):393–405, 1990.

[130] C. Cortes and V. N. Vapnik. Support-vector networks. *Machine Learning*, 20(3):273–297, 1995.

[131] V. G. Costa and C. E. Pedreira. Recent advances in decision trees: An updated survey. *Artificial Intelligence Review*, 56(5):4765–4800, 2023.

[132] K. Coussement and D. Van den Poel. Churn prediction in subscription services: An application of support vector machines while comparing two parameter-selection techniques. *Expert Systems with Applications*, 34(1):313–327, 2008.

[133] T. Cover and P. Hart. Nearest neighbor pattern classification. *IEEE Transactions on Information Theory*, 13(1):21–27, 1967.

[134] T. M. Cover and J. A. Thomas. *Elements of Information Theory*. Wiley-Interscience, 2nd edition, 2006.

[135] P. Covington, J. Adams, and E. Sargin. Deep neural networks for YouTube recommendations. In *Proceedings of the 10th ACM Conference on Recommender Systems*, pages 191–198, 2016.

[136] R. G. Cowell, A. P. Dawid, S. L. Lauritzen, and D. J. Spiegelhalter. *Probabilistic Networks and Expert Systems: Exact Computational Methods for Bayesian Networks*. Springer, 2007.

[137] D. R. Cox. The regression analysis of binary sequences. *Journal of the Royal Statistical Society: Series B (Methodological)*, 20(2):215–242, 1958.

[138] H. Cramér. *Mathematical Methods of Statistics*, volume 9 of *Princeton Mathematical Series*. Princeton University Press, 1946.

[139] N. Cristianini and J. Shawe-Taylor. *An introduction to support vector machines and other kernel-based learning methods*. Cambridge University Press, 2000.

[140] B. Cui, B. C. Ooi, J. Su, and K.-L. Tan. Contorting high dimensional data for efficient main memory KNN processing. In *Proceedings of the ACM SIGMOD International Conference on Management of Data*, pages 479–490, 2003.

[141] A. Curth, A. Jeffares, and M. van der Schaar. A U-turn on double descent: Rethinking parameter counting in statistical learning. In *Advances in Neural Information Processing Systems (NeurIPS)*, 2023.

[142] D. Dablain, B. Krawczyk, and N. V. Chawla. DeepSMOTE: Fusing deep learning and SMOTE for imbalanced data. *IEEE Transactions on Neural Networks and Learning Systems*, 34(9):6390–6404, 2022.

[143] P. Dagum and A. Galper. Dynamic network models for forecasting. In *Proceedings of the 8th Conference on Uncertainty in Artificial Intelligence*, pages 41–48, 1992.

[144] A. Dal Pozzolo, O. Caelen, R. A. Johnson, and G. Bontempi. Calibrating probability with undersampling for unbalanced classification. In *Symposium on Computational Intelligence and Data Mining*, pages 159–166, 2015.

[145] E. Davis and G. Marcus. Commonsense reasoning and commonsense knowledge in artificial intelligence. *Communications of the ACM*, 58(9):92–103, 2015.

[146] J. Davis and M. Goadrich. The relationship between precision-recall and ROC curves. In *Proceedings of the 23rd International Conference on Machine learning (ICML)*, pages 233–240, 2006.

[147] C. de Boor. *A Practical Guide to Splines*, volume 27 of *Applied Mathematical Sciences*. Springer-Verlag, 1978.

[148] M. De Lange, R. Aljundi, M. Masana, S. Parisot, X. Jia, A. Leonardis, G. Slabaugh, and T. Tuytelaars. A continual learning survey: Defying forgetting in classification tasks. *IEEE Transactions on Pattern Analysis and Machine Intelligence*, 44(7):3366–3385, 2021.

[149] R. Dechter. Bucket elimination: A unifying framework for reasoning. *Artificial Intelligence*, 113(1–2):41–85, 1999.

[150] Google DeepMind AlphaEvolve: A Gemini-powered coding agent for designing advanced algorithms. `https://deepmind.google/discover/blog/alphaevolve-a-gemini-powered-coding-agent-for-designing-advanced-algorithms`, May 2025.

[151] A. Defazio and K. Mishchenko. Learning-rate-free learning by D-adaptation. In *Proceedings of the 40th International Conference on Machine Learning (ICML)*, pages 7449–7479, 2023.

[152] A. Della Vecchia, A. M. Watusadisi, E. De Vito, and L. Rosasco. Computational efficiency under covariate shift in kernel ridge regression. In *Proceedings of the 42nd International Conference on Machine Learning (ICML)*, 2025.

[153] G. E. Delury, editor. *The World Almanac and Book of Facts, 1975*. Newspaper Enterprise Association, 1974.

[154] J. Demšar. Statistical comparisons of classifiers over multiple data sets. *Journal of Machine Learning Research*, 7:1–30, 2006.

[155] L. Deng. The MNIST database of handwritten digit images for machine learning research. *IEEE Signal Processing Magazine*, 29(6):141–142, 2012.

[156] Z. Deng, X. Zhu, D. Cheng, M. Zong, and S. Zhang. Efficient kNN classification algorithm for big data. *Neurocomputing*, 195:143–148, 2016.

[157] M. Denil, D. Matheson, and N. de Freitas. Consistency of online random forests. In *Proceedings of the 30th International Conference on Machine Learning (ICML)*, pages 1256–1264, 2013.

[158] P. Diaconis, S. Holmes, and R. Montgomery. Dynamical bias in the coin toss. *SIAM Review*, 49(2):211–235, 2007.

[159] R. Díaz-Uriarte and S. Alvarez de Andrés. Gene selection and classification of microarray data using random forest. *BMC Bioinformatics*, 7:1–13, 2006.

[160] T. G. Dietterich. Approximate statistical tests for comparing supervised classification learning algorithms. *Neural Computation*, 10(7):1895–1923, 1998.

[161] T. G. Dietterich. Ensemble methods in machine learning. In *International Workshop on Multiple Classifier Systems*, pages 1–15, 2000.

[162] T. G. Dietterich. An experimental comparison of three methods for constructing ensembles of decision trees: Bagging, boosting, and randomization. *Machine Learning*, 40:139–157, 2000.

[163] T. G. Dietterich and G. Bakiri. Solving multiclass learning problems via error-correcting output codes. *Journal of Artificial Intelligence Research*, 2:263–286, 1995.

[164] V. Dignum. *Responsible Artificial Intelligence: How to Develop and Use AI in a Responsible Way*. Springer Nature, 2019.

[165] G. Ditzler and R. Polikar. Incremental learning of concept drift from streaming imbalanced data. *IEEE Transactions on Knowledge and Data Engineering*, 25(10):2283–2301, 2012.

[166] DMLC. Machine learning challenge winning solutions. https://github.com/dmlc/xgboost/tree/master/demo#machine-learning-challenge-winning-solutions.

[167] A. J. Dobson and A. G. Barnett. *An Introduction to Generalized Linear Models*. Chapman and Hall/CRC, 4th edition, 2018.

[168] A. Dogan and D. Birant. A weighted majority voting ensemble approach for classification. In *Proceedings of the 4th International Conference on Computer Science and Engineering*, pages 1–6, 2019.

[169] P. Domingos and M. Pazzani. Beyond independence: Conditions for the optimality of the simple Bayesian classifier. In *Proceedings of the 13th International Conference on Machine Learning (ICML)*, pages 105–112, 1996.

[170] P. Domingos and M. Pazzani. On the optimality of the simple Bayesian classifier under zero-one loss. *Machine Learning*, 29(2–3):103–130, 1997.

[171] G. Douzas, F. Bacao, and F. Last. Improving imbalanced learning through a heuristic oversampling method based on k-means and SMOTE. *Information Sciences*, 465:1–20, 2018.

[172] H. Drucker. Improving regressors using boosting techniques. In *Proceedings of the 14th International Conference on Machine Learning (ICML)*, pages 107–115, 1997.

[173] H. Drucker, C. J. Burges, L. Kaufman, A. Smola, and V. N. Vapnik. Support vector regression machines. In *Advances in Neural Information Processing Systems (NeurIPS)*, pages 155–161, 1996.

[174] T. Duan, A. Anand, D. Y. Ding, K. K. Thai, S. Basu, A. Ng, and A. Schuler. NGBoost: Natural gradient boosting for probabilistic prediction. In *Proceedings of the 37th International Conference on Machine Learning (ICML)*, pages 2690–2700, 2020.

[175] R. O. Duda and P. E. Hart. *Pattern Classification and Scene Analysis*. Wiley, 1973.

[176] S. A. Dudani. The distance-weighted k-nearest-neighbor rule. *IEEE Transactions on Systems, Man, and Cybernetics*, (4):325–327, 1976.

[177] R. Durrett. *Probability: Theory and Examples*. Cambridge University Press, 5th edition, 2019.

[178] P. H. Eilers and B. D. Marx. Flexible smoothing with B-splines and penalties. *Statistical Science*, 11(2):89–121, 1996.

[179] W. S. El-Kassas, C. R. Salama, A. A. Rafea, and H. K. Mohamed. Automatic text summarization: A comprehensive survey. *Expert Systems with Applications*, 165, 2021.

[180] C. Elkan. The foundations of cost-sensitive learning. In *Proceedings of the 17th International Joint Conference on Artificial Intelligence (IJCAI)*, pages 973–978, 2001.

[181] F. Esposito, D. Malerba, and G. Semeraro. A comparative analysis of methods for pruning decision trees. *IEEE Transactions on Pattern Analysis and Machine Intelligence*, 19(5):476–491, 1997.

[182] A. Esteva, B. Kuprel, R. A. Novoa, J. Ko, S. M. Swetter, H. M. Blau, and S. Thrun. Dermatologist-level classification of skin cancer with deep neural networks. *Nature*, 542(7639):115–118, 2017.

[183] R.-E. Fan, K.-W. Chang, C.-J. Hsieh, X.-R. Wang, and C.-J. Lin. LIBLINEAR: A library for large linear classification. *Journal of Machine Learning Research*, 9:1871–1874, 2008.

[184] D. E. Farrar and R. R. Glauber. Multicollinearity in regression analysis: The problem revisited. *The Review of Economic and Statistics*, pages 92–107, 1967.

[185] T. Fawcett. An introduction to ROC analysis. *Pattern Recognition Letters*, 27(8):861–874, 2006.

[186] M. Feffer, M. Hirzel, S. C. Hoffman, K. Kate, P. Ram, and A. Shinnar. Searching for fairer machine learning ensembles. In *Proceedings of the Second International Conference on Automated Machine Learning*, volume 224, pages 17/1–19, 2023.

[187] A. Fernández, S. Garcia, F. Herrera, and N. V. Chawla. SMOTE for learning from imbalanced data: Progress and challenges, marking the 15-year anniversary. *Journal of Artificial Intelligence Research*, 61:863–905, 2018.

[188] M. Fernández-Delgado, E. Cernadas, S. Barro, and D. Amorim. Do we need hundreds of classifiers to solve real world classification problems? *The Journal of Machine Learning Research*, 15(1):3133–3181, 2014.

[189] M. A. Finzi, S. Kapoor, D. Granziol, A. Gu, C. De Sa, J. Kolter, and A. G. Wilson. Compute-optimal LLMs provably generalize better with scale. In *International Conference on Learning Representations (ICLR)*, 2025.

[190] R. A. Fisher. *Statistical Methods for Research Workers*. Oliver and Boyd, 1925.

[191] R. A. Fisher. *The Design of Experiments*. Oliver and Boyd, 1935.

[192] R. A. Fisher. The use of multiple measurements in taxonomic problems. *Annals of Eugenics*, 7(2):179–188, 1936.

[193] W. D. Fisher. On grouping for maximum homogeneity. *Journal of the American Statistical Association*, 53(284):789–798, 1958.

[194] E. Fix and J. L. Hodges. Discriminatory analysis, nonparametric discrimination: Consistency properties. Technical Report 4, USAF School of Aviation Medicine, Randolph Field, 1951.

[195] A. Freitas, A. Costa-Pereira, and P. Brazdil. Cost-sensitive decision trees applied to medical data. In *Proceedings of the 9th International Conference on Data Warehousing and Knowledge Discovery*, pages 303–312, 2007.

[196] Y. Freund and R. E. Schapire. Experiments with a new boosting algorithm. In *Proceedings of the 13th International Conference on Machine Learning (ICML)*, pages 148–156, 1996.

[197] Y. Freund and R. E. Schapire. A decision-theoretic generalization of on-line learning and an application to boosting. *Journal of Computer and System Sciences*, 55(1):119–139, 1997.

[198] J. Friedman, T. Hastie, H. Höfling, and R. Tibshirani. Pathwise coordinate optimization. *The Annals of Applied Statistics*, 1(2):302–332, 2007.

[199] J. Friedman, T. Hastie, and R. Tibshirani. Additive logistic regression: A statistical view of boosting. *The Annals of Statistics*, 28(2):337–407, 2000.

[200] J. Friedman, T. Hastie, and R. Tibshirani. Regularization paths for generalized linear models via coordinate descent. *Journal of Statistical Software*, 33(1):1–22, 2010.

[201] J. H. Friedman. Greedy function approximation: A gradient boosting machine. *The Annals of Statistics*, 29(5):1189–1232, 2001.

[202] J. H. Friedman. Stochastic gradient boosting. *Computational Statistics & Data Analysis*, 38(4):367–378, 2002.

[203] M. Friedman. The use of ranks to avoid the assumption of normality implicit in the analysis of variance. *Journal of the American Statistical Association*, 32(200):675–701, 1937.

[204] N. Friedman, D. Geiger, and M. Goldszmidt. Bayesian network classifiers. *Machine Learning*, 29:131–163, 1997.

[205] N. Friedman and D. Koller. Being Bayesian about network structure: A Bayesian approach to structure discovery in Bayesian networks. *Machine Learning*, 50(1–2):95–125, 2003.

[206] V. Froese and C. Hertrich. Training neural networks is NP-hard in fixed dimension. In *Advances in Neural Information Processing Systems (NeurIPS)*, 2023.

[207] N. Frosst and G. Hinton. Distilling a neural network into a soft decision tree. *arXiv preprint arXiv:1711.09784*, 2017.

[208] R. Fung and K.-C. Chang. Weighing and integrating evidence for stochastic simulation in Bayesian networks. In *Machine Intelligence and Pattern Recognition*, volume 10, pages 209–219. Elsevier, 1990.

[209] M. Galar, A. Fernandez, E. Barrenechea, H. Bustince, and F. Herrera. A review on ensembles for the class imbalance problem: Bagging-, boosting-, and hybrid-based approaches. *IEEE Transactions on Systems, Man, and Cybernetics, Part C (Applications and Reviews)*, 42(4):463–484, 2012.

[210] I. O. Gallegos, R. A. Rossi, J. Barrow, M. M. Tanjim, S. Kim, F. Dernoncourt, T. Yu, R. Zhang, and N. K. Ahmed. Bias and fairness in large language models: A survey. *Computational Linguistics*, pages 1–79, 2024.

[211] J. Gama, R. Fernandes, and R. Rocha. Decision trees for mining data streams. *Intelligent Data Analysis*, 10(1):23–45, 2006.

[212] M. A. Ganaie, M. Hu, A. K. Malik, M. Tanveer, and P. N. Suganthan. Ensemble deep learning: A review. *Engineering Applications of Artificial Intelligence*, 115:105151, 2022.

[213] A. Gandra. Predicting hospital readmissions in diabetes patients: A comparative study of machine learning models. *International Journal of Health Sciences*, 8(3):289–297, 2024.

[214] A. d. Garcez, M. Gori, L. C. Lamb, L. Serafini, M. Spranger, and S. N. Tran. Neural-symbolic computing: An effective methodology for principled integration of machine learning and reasoning. *arXiv preprint arXiv:1905.06088*, 2019.

[215] V. Garcia, E. Debreuve, and M. Barlaud. Fast k nearest neighbor search using GPU. In *Proceedings of the IEEE Computer Society Conference on Computer Vision and Pattern Recognition Workshops*, pages 1–6, 2008.

[216] R. Garnett. *Bayesian Optimization*. Cambridge University Press, 2023.

[217] C. F. Gauss. *Theoria motus corporum coelestium in sectionibus conicis solem ambientium*. Friedrich Perthes and I.H. Besser, 1809.

[218] P. Geladi and B. R. Kowalski. Partial least-squares regression: A tutorial. *Analytica Chimica Acta*, 185:1–17, 1986.

[219] A. Gelman, J. B. Carlin, H. S. Stern, D. B. Dunson, A. Vehtari, and D. B. Rubin. *Bayesian Data Analysis*. CRC Press, 3rd edition, 2013.

[220] S. Geman, E. Bienenstock, and R. Doursat. Neural networks and the bias/variance dilemma. *Neural Computation*, 4(1):1–58, 1992.

[221] S. Geman and D. Geman. Stochastic relaxation, Gibbs distributions, and the Bayesian restoration of images. *IEEE Transactions on Pattern Analysis and Machine Intelligence*, 6(6):721–741, 1984.

[222] Gemini Team, Google DeepMind, G. Comanici, et al. Gemini 2.5: Pushing the frontier with advanced reasoning, multimodality, long context, and next generation agentic capabilities. *arXiv preprint arXiv:2507.06261*, 2025.

[223] A. Géron. *Hands-On Machine Learning with Scikit-Learn, Keras, and TensorFlow: Concepts, Tools, and Techniques to Build Intelligent Systems*. O'Reilly Media, 3rd edition, 2022.

[224] P. Geurts, D. Ernst, and L. Wehenkel. Extremely randomized trees. *Machine Learning*, 63:3–42, 2006.

[225] A. Gholami, S. Kim, Z. Dong, Z. Yao, M. W. Mahoney, and K. Keutzer. A survey of quantization methods for efficient neural network inference. In *Low-Power Computer Vision*, pages 291–326. Chapman and Hall/CRC, 2022.

[226] B. Goertzel. Artificial general intelligence: Concept, state of the art, and future prospects. *Journal of Artificial General Intelligence*, 5(1):1, 2014.

[227] U. Gohar, S. Biswas, and H. Rajan. Towards understanding fairness and its composition in ensemble machine learning. In *Proceedings of the 45th International Conference on Software Engineering*, pages 1533–1545, 2023.

[228] B. A. Goldstein, A. E. Hubbard, A. Cutler, and L. F. Barcellos. An application of random forests to a genome-wide association dataset: Methodological considerations & new findings. *BMC Genetics*, 11:1–13, 2010.

[229] G. H. Golub and C. F. Van Loan. *Matrix Computations*. Johns Hopkins University Press, 4th edition, 2013.

[230] P. Good. *Permutation Tests: A Practical Guide to Resampling Methods for Testing Hypotheses*. Springer, 2nd edition, 2000.

[231] I. Goodfellow, Y. Bengio, and A. Courville. *Deep Learning*. MIT Press, 2016. https://www.deeplearningbook.org.

[232] I. J. Goodfellow, J. Pouget-Abadie, M. Mirza, B. Xu, D. Warde-Farley, S. Ozair, A. Courville, and Y. Bengio. Generative adversarial nets. In *Advances in Neural Information Processing Systems (NeurIPS)*, pages 2672–2680, 2014.

[233] I. J. Goodfellow, J. Shlens, and C. Szegedy. Explaining and harnessing adversarial examples. In *International Conference on Learning Representations (ICLR)*, 2015.

[234] Google Gemini Team. Gemini: A family of highly capable multimodal models. *arXiv preprint arXiv:2312.11805*, 2023.

[235] P. Gourdeau, T. Lechner, and R. Urner. On the computability of robust PAC learning. In *Proceedings of the 37th Conference on Learning Theory (COLT)*, pages 2092–2121, 2024.

[236] I. S. Gradshteyn and I. M. Ryzhik. *Table of integrals, series, and products*. Academic Press, 8th edition, 2014.

[237] R. Grazzi, M. Pontil, and S. Salzo. Bilevel optimization with a lower-level contraction: Optimal sample complexity without warm-start. *Journal of Machine Learning Research*, 24:1–37, 2023.

[238] M. Greenwald and S. Khanna. Space-efficient online computation of quantile summaries. *ACM SIGMOD Record*, 30(2):58–66, 2001.

[239] A. Gretton, K. M. Borgwardt, M. J. Rasch, B. Schölkopf, and A. Smola. A kernel two-sample test. *Journal of Machine Learning Research*, 13:723–773, 2012.

[240] L. Grinsztajn, E. Oyallon, and G. Varoquaux. Why do tree-based models still outperform deep learning on typical tabular data? In *Advances in Neural Information Processing Systems (NeurIPS)*, pages 507–520, 2022.

[241] V. Gulshan, L. Peng, M. Coram, M. C. Stumpe, D. Wu, A. Narayanaswamy, S. Venugopalan, K. Widner, T. Madams, J. Cuadros, R. Kim, R. Raman, P. C. Nelson, J. L. Mega, and D. R. Webster. Development and validation of a deep learning algorithm for detection of diabetic retinopathy in retinal fundus photographs. *JAMA*, 316(22):2402–2410, 2016.

[242] N. Gunasekara, B. Pfahringer, H. M. Gomes, and A. Bifet. Gradient boosted trees for evolving data streams. *Machine Learning*, 113(5):3325–3352, 2024.

[243] C. Guo, G. Pleiss, Y. Sun, and K. Q. Weinberger. On calibration of modern neural networks. In *Proceedings of the 34th International Conference on Machine Learning (ICML)*, pages 1321–1330, 2017.

[244] H. Guo and S. B. Gelfand. Classification trees with neural network feature extraction. In *Proceedings of the IEEE Computer Society Conference on Computer Vision and Pattern Recognition (CVPR)*, pages 183–184, 1992.

[245] R. H. Güting, T. Behr, and J. Xu. Efficient k-nearest neighbor search on moving object trajectories. *The VLDB Journal*, 19:687–714, 2010.

[246] I. Guyon and A. Elisseeff. An introduction to variable and feature selection. *Journal of Machine Learning Research*, 3:1157–1182, 2003.

[247] T. Hagendorff. The ethics of AI ethics: An evaluation of guidelines. *Minds and Machines*, 30(1):99–120, 2020.

[248] R. K. Halder, M. N. Uddin, M. A. Uddin, S. Aryal, and A. Khraisat. Enhancing k-nearest neighbor algorithm: A comprehensive review and performance analysis of modifications. *Journal of Big Data*, 11(1):113, 2024.

[249] A. Halevy, P. Norvig, and F. Pereira. The unreasonable effectiveness of data. *IEEE Intelligent Systems*, 24(2):8–12, 2009.

[250] J. M. Hammersley and P. Clifford. Markov fields on finite graphs and lattices. Unpublished manuscript, 1971.

[251] R. W. Hamming. Error detecting and error correcting codes. *Bell System Technical Journal*, 29(2):147–160, 1950.

[252] H. Han, W.-Y. Wang, and B.-H. Mao. Borderline-SMOTE: A new over-sampling method in imbalanced data sets learning. In *International Conference on Intelligent Computing*, pages 878–887, 2005.

[253] D. J. Hand and K. Yu. Idiot's Bayes—not so stupid after all? *International Statistical Review*, 69(3):385–398, 2001.

[254] J. A. Hanley and B. J. McNeil. The meaning and use of the area under a receiver operating characteristic (ROC) curve. *Radiology*, 143(1):29–36, 1982.

[255] L. K. Hansen and P. Salamon. Neural network ensembles. *IEEE Transactions on Pattern Analysis and Machine Intelligence*, 12(10):993–1001, 1990.

[256] P. Hase and M. Bansal. Evaluating explainable AI: Which algorithmic explanations help users predict model behavior? *arXiv preprint arXiv:2005.01831*, 2020.

[257] D. Hassabis, D. Kumaran, C. Summerfield, and M. Botvinick. Neuroscience-inspired artificial intelligence. *Neuron*, 95(2):245–258, 2017.

[258] T. Hastie, R. Tibshirani, and J. Friedman. *The Elements of Statistical Learning: Data Mining, Inference, and Prediction*. Springer, 2nd edition, 2009.

[259] H. He, Y. Bai, E. A. Garcia, and S. Li. ADASYN: Adaptive synthetic sampling approach for imbalanced learning. In *2008 IEEE International Joint Conference on Neural Networks (IEEE World Congress on Computational Intelligence)*, pages 1322–1328, 2008.

[260] H. He and E. A. Garcia. Learning from imbalanced data. *IEEE Transactions on Knowledge and Data Engineering*, 21(9):1263–1284, 2009.

[261] K. He, X. Zhang, S. Ren, and J. Sun. Delving deep into rectifiers: Surpassing human-level performance on ImageNet classification. In *Proceedings of the IEEE International Conference on Computer Vision (ICCV)*, pages 1026–1034, 2015.

[262] M. A. Hearst, S. T. Dumais, E. Osuna, J. Platt, and B. Schölkopf. Support vector machines. *IEEE Intelligent Systems and Their Applications*, 13(4):18–28, 1998.

[263] D. G. Heath. *A Geometric Framework for Machine Learning*. PhD thesis, The Johns Hopkins University, 1993.

[264] D. Heckerman. A tutorial on learning with Bayesian networks. In M. I. Jordan, editor, *Learning in Graphical Models*, pages 301–354. Springer, 1998.

[265] D. Hendrycks, S. Basart, N. Mu, S. Kadavath, F. Wang, E. Dorundo, R. Desai, T. Zhu, S. Parajuli, M. Guo, et al. The many faces of robustness: A critical analysis of out-of-distribution generalization. In *Proceedings of the IEEE/CVF International Conference on Computer Vision (ICCV)*, pages 8340–8349, 2021.

[266] M. Henrion. Propagating uncertainty in Bayesian networks by probabilistic logic sampling. In *Machine intelligence and Pattern Recognition*, volume 5, pages 149–163. Elsevier, 1988.

[267] N. J. Higham. *Accuracy and Stability of Numerical Algorithms*. SIAM, 2002.

[268] G. E. Hinton, S. Osindero, and Y.-W. Teh. A fast learning algorithm for deep belief nets. *Neural Computation*, 18(7):1527–1554, 2006.

[269] D. Hirata and N. Takahashi. Ensemble learning in CNN augmented with fully connected subnetworks. *IEICE Transactions on Information and Systems*, 106(7):1258–1261, 2023.

[270] J. Hirschberg and C. D. Manning. Advances in natural language processing. *Science*, 349(6245):261–266, 2015.

[271] J. Ho and A. A. Efros. Denoising diffusion probabilistic models. In *Advances in Neural Information Processing Systems (NeurIPS)*, pages 6840–6851, 2020.

[272] T. K. Ho. The random subspace method for constructing decision forests. *IEEE Transactions on Pattern Analysis and Machine Intelligence*, 20(8):832–844, 1998.

[273] W. Hoeffding. Probability inequalities for sums of bounded random variables. *Journal of the American Statistical Association*, 58(301):13–30, 1963.

[274] A. E. Hoerl and R. W. Kennard. Ridge regression: Biased estimation for nonorthogonal problems. *Technometrics*, 12(1):55–67, 1970.

[275] J. H. Holland. *Adaptation in Natural and Artificial Systems*. University of Michigan Press, 1975.

[276] R. A. Horn and C. R. Johnson. *Matrix Analysis*. Cambridge University Press, 2nd edition, 2013.

[277] D. W. Hosmer Jr, S. Lemeshow, and R. X. Sturdivant. *Applied Logistic Regression*. John Wiley & Sons, 3rd edition, 2013.

[278] T. Hothorn, K. Hornik, and A. Zeileis. Unbiased recursive partitioning: A conditional inference framework. *Journal of Computational and Graphical Statistics*, 15(3):651–674, 2006.

[279] A. S. Householder. Unitary triangularization of a nonsymmetric matrix. *Journal of the ACM*, 5(4):339–342, 1958.

[280] C.-J. Hsieh, K.-W. Chang, C.-J. Lin, S. S. Keerthi, and S. S. Sundararajan. A dual coordinate descent method for large-scale linear SVM. In *Proceedings of the 25th International Conference on Machine Learning (ICML)*, pages 408–415, 2008.

[281] X. Hu, C. Rudin, and M. Seltzer. Optimal sparse decision trees. In *Advances in Neural Information Processing Systems (NeurIPS)*, pages 7265–7273, 2019.

[282] P. J. Huber. Robust estimation of a location parameter. *The Annals of Mathematical Statistics*, 35(1):73–101, 1964.

[283] D. A. Huffman. A method for the construction of minimum-redundancy codes. *Proceedings of the Institute of Radio Engineers*, 40(9):1098–1101, 1952.

[284] G. Hulten, L. Spencer, and P. Domingos. Mining time-changing data streams. In *Proceedings of the Seventh ACM SIGKDD International Conference on Knowledge Discovery and Data Mining*, pages 97–106, 2001.

[285] J. D. Hunter. Matplotlib: A 2D graphics environment. *Computing in Science & Engineering*, 9(03):90–95, 2007.

[286] L. Hyafil and R. L. Rivest. Constructing optimal binary decision trees is NP-complete. *Information Processing Letters*, 5(1):15–17, 1976.

[287] J. P. Ioannidis. Why most published research findings are false. *PLoS Medicine*, 2(8):e124, 2005.

[288] O. Irsoy, O. T. Yıldız, and E. Alpaydın. Soft decision trees. In *Proceedings of the 21st International Conference on Pattern Recognition (ICPR)*, pages 1819–1822, 2012.

[289] P. Jaccard. Étude comparative de la distribution florale dans une portion des alpes et des jura. *Bulletin de la Société Vaudoise des Sciences Naturelles*, 37:547–579, 1901.

[290] A. Jain, R. Sen, W. Kong, A. Das, and A. Orlitsky. Linear regression using heterogeneous data batches. In *Advances in Neural Information Processing Systems (NeurIPS)*, 2024.

[291] A. K. Jain, M. N. Murty, and P. J. Flynn. Data clustering: A review. *ACM Computing Surveys*, 31(3):264–323, 1999.

[292] W. James and C. Stein. Estimation with quadratic loss. In *Proceedings of the Fourth Berkeley Symposium on Mathematical Statistics and Probability*, volume 1, pages 361–379, 1961.

[293] N. Japkowicz and M. Shah. *Evaluating Learning Algorithms: A Classification Perspective*. Cambridge University Press, 2011.

[294] N. Japkowicz and S. Stephen. The class imbalance problem: A systematic study. *Intelligent Data Analysis*, 6(5):429–449, 2002.

[295] H. Jegou, M. Douze, and C. Schmid. Product quantization for nearest neighbor search. *IEEE Transactions on Pattern Analysis and Machine Intelligence*, 33(1):117–128, 2010.

[296] J. L. W. V. Jensen. Sur les fonctions convexes et les inégalités entre les valeurs moyennes. *Acta Mathematica*, 30(1):175–193, 1906.

[297] J. Ji, B. Chen, H. Lou, D. Hong, B. Zhang, X. Pan, T. A. Qiu, J. Dai, and Y. Yang. Aligner: Efficient alignment by learning to correct. In *Advances in Neural Information Processing Systems (NeurIPS)*, 2024.

[298] R. Jin and G. Agrawal. Efficient decision tree construction on streaming data. In *Proceedings of the Ninth ACM SIGKDD International Conference on Knowledge Discovery and Data Mining*, pages 571–576, 2003.

[299] T. Joachims. Text categorization with support vector machines: Learning with many relevant features. In *Proceedings of the 10th European Conference on Machine Learning*, pages 137–142, 1998.

[300] T. Joachims. Training linear SVMs in linear time. In *Proceedings of the 12th ACM SIGKDD International Conference on Knowledge Discovery and Data Mining*, pages 217–226, 2006.

[301] A. Jobin, M. Ienca, and E. Vayena. The global landscape of AI ethics guidelines. *Nature Machine Intelligence*, 1(9):389–399, 2019.

[302] J. Johnson, M. Douze, and H. Jégou. Billion-scale similarity search with GPUs. *IEEE Transactions on Big Data*, 7(3):535–547, 2019.

[303] I. T. Jolliffe. A note on the use of principal components in regression. *Journal of the Royal Statistical Society Series C: Applied Statistics*, 31(3):300–303, 1982.

[304] I. T. Jolliffe. *Principal Component Analysis*. Springer Series in Statistics. Springer, 2nd edition, 2002.

[305] M. I. Jordan. *Learning in Graphical Models*. MIT Press, 1998.

[306] D. Jurafsky and J. H. Martin. *Speech and Language Processing: An Introduction to Natural Language Processing, Computational Linguistics, and Speech Recognition with Language Models*. 3rd edition, 2024. Draft version available at https://web.stanford.edu/~jurafsky/slp3.

[307] F. Kamiran, T. Calders, and M. Pechenizkiy. Discrimination aware decision tree learning. In *2010 IEEE International Conference on Data Mining (ICDM)*, pages 869–874. IEEE, 2010.

[308] T. Kansal, S. Bahuguna, V. Singh, and T. Choudhury. Customer segmentation using k-means clustering. In *International Conference on Computational Techniques, Electronics and Mechanical Systems*, pages 135–139, 2018.

[309] J. Kaplan, S. McCandlish, T. Henighan, T. B. Brown, B. Chess, R. Child, S. Gray, A. Radford, J. Wu, and D. Amodei. Scaling laws for neural language models. *arXiv preprint arXiv:2001.08361*, 2020.

[310] S. Kariyappa and M. K. Qureshi. Improving adversarial robustness of ensembles with diversity training. *arXiv preprint arXiv:1901.09981*, 2019.

[311] V. Karpukhin, B. Oguz, S. Min, P. Lewis, L. Wu, S. Edunov, D. Chen, and W.-t. Yih. Dense passage retrieval for open-domain question answering. In *Proceedings of the 2020 Conference on Empirical Methods in Natural Language Processing (EMNLP)*, pages 6769–6781, 2020.

[312] G. Ke, Q. Meng, T. Finley, T. Wang, W. Chen, W. Ma, Q. Ye, and T.-Y. Liu. LightGBM: A highly efficient gradient boosting decision tree. In *Advances in Neural Information Processing Systems (NeurIPS)*, pages 3146–3154, 2017.

[313] M. Kearns and Y. Mansour. On the boosting ability of top-down decision tree learning algorithms. In *Proceedings of the Twenty-Eighth Annual ACM Symposium on Theory of Computing*, pages 459–468, 1996.

[314] J. M. Keller, M. R. Gray, and J. A. Givens. A fuzzy k-nearest neighbor algorithm. In *IEEE International Conference on Systems, Man, and Cybernetics*, page 114–121, 1985.

[315] J. Kelner, F. Koehler, R. Meka, and D. Rohatgi. Feature adaptation for sparse linear regression. In *Advances in Neural Information Processing Systems (NeurIPS)*, 2023.

[316] M. G. Kendall. A new measure of rank correlation. *Biometrika*, 30(1–2):81–93, 1938.

[317] M. Khalilia, S. Chakraborty, and M. Popescu. Predicting disease risks from highly imbalanced data using random forest. *BMC Medical Informatics and Decision Making*, 11:1–13, 2011.

[318] A. Y. Khintchine. Sur la loi des grands nombres. *Comptes Rendus de l'Académie des Sciences*, 188:477–479, 1929.

[319] D. P. Kingma and M. Welling. Auto-encoding variational Bayes. In *International Conference on Learning Representations (ICLR)*, pages 1–14, 2014.

[320] J. F. C. Kingman. *Poisson Processes*. Clarendon Press, 1992.

[321] D. G. Kleinbaum and M. Klein. *Survival Analysis: A Self-Learning Text*. Springer, 3rd edition, 2012.

[322] R. Koenker and G. Bassett Jr. Regression quantiles. *Econometrica: Journal of the Econometric Society*, 46(1):33–50, 1978.

[323] R. Kohavi, A. Deng, B. Frasca, T. Walker, Y. Xu, and N. Pohlmann. Online controlled experiments at large scale. In *Proceedings of the 19th ACM SIGKDD International Conference on Knowledge Discovery and Data Mining*, pages 1168–1176, 2013.

[324] R. Kohavi and C.-H. Li. Oblivious decision trees, graphs, and top-down pruning. In *Proceedings of the 14th International Joint Conference on Artificial Intelligence (IJCAI)*, pages 1071–1077, 1995.

[325] R. Kohavi, D. Tang, and Y. Xu. *Trustworthy Online Controlled Experiments: A Practical Guide to A/B Testing*. Cambridge University Press, 2020.

[326] D. Koller and N. Friedman. *Probabilistic Graphical Models: Principles and Techniques*. MIT Press, 2009.

[327] W. Kong, Z. Y. Dong, Y. Jia, D. J. Hill, Y. Xu, and Y. Zhang. Short-term residential load forecasting based on LSTM recurrent neural network. *IEEE Transactions on Smart Grid*, 10(1):841–851, 2019.

[328] M. Köppen. The curse of dimensionality. In *Proceedings of the 5th Online World Conference on Soft Computing in Industrial Applications*, pages 4–8, 2000.

[329] M. Kosinski, D. Stillwell, and T. Graepel. Private traits and attributes are predictable from digital records of human behavior. *Proceedings of the National Academy of Sciences*, 110(15):5802–5805, 2013.

[330] K. Kowsari, K. Jafari Meimandi, M. Heidarysafa, S. Mendu, L. Barnes, and D. Brown. Text classification algorithms: A survey. *Information*, 10(4):150, 2019.

[331] B. Krawczyk. Learning from imbalanced data: Open challenges and future directions. *Progress in Artificial Intelligence*, 5(4):221–232, 2016.

[332] B. Krawczyk, L. L. Minku, J. Gama, J. Stefanowski, and M. Woźniak. Ensemble learning for data stream analysis: A survey. *Information Fusion*, 37:132–156, 2017.

[333] A. Krizhevsky. Learning multiple layers of features from tiny images. Technical report, University of Toronto, 2009.

[334] A. Krizhevsky, I. Sutskever, and G. E. Hinton. ImageNet classification with deep convolutional neural networks. In *Advances in Neural Information Processing Systems (NeurIPS)*, pages 1097–1105, 2012.

[335] A. Krogh and J. Vedelsby. Neural network ensembles, cross validation, and active learning. In *Advances in Neural Information Processing Systems (NeurIPS)*, pages 231–238, 1994.

[336] F. R. Kschischang, B. J. Frey, and H.-A. Loeliger. Factor graphs and the sum-product algorithm. *IEEE Transactions on Information Theory*, 47(2):498–519, 2001.

[337] M. Kubat and S. Matwin. Addressing the curse of imbalanced training sets: One-sided selection. In *Proceedings of the 14th International Conference on Machine Learning (ICML)*, pages 179–186, 1997.

[338] M. Kukar, I. Kononenko, et al. Cost-sensitive learning with neural networks. In *Proceedings of the 13th European Conference on Artificial Intelligence*, pages 88–94, 1998.

[339] J. Lafferty, A. McCallum, and F. C. N. Pereira. Conditional random fields: Probabilistic models for segmenting and labeling sequence data. In *Proceedings of the 18th International Conference on Machine Learning (ICML)*, pages 282–289, 2001.

[340] T. Lahovnik and S. Karakatič. GATree: Evolutionary decision tree classifier in Python. *Journal of Open Source Software*, 9(100):6748, 2024.

[341] W. Lam and F. Bacchus. Learning Bayesian belief networks: An approach based on the MDL principle. *Computational Intelligence*, 10(3):269–293, 1994.

[342] K. Lang. Newsweeder: Learning to filter Netnews. In *Proceedings of the 12th International Conference on Machine Learning (ICML)*, pages 331–339, 1995.

[343] S. L. Lauritzen. *Graphical Models*. Oxford University Press, 1996.

[344] S. L. Lauritzen and N. Wermuth. Graphical models for associations between variables, some of which are qualitative and some quantitative. *The Annals of Statistics*, 17(1):31–57, 1989.

[345] N. Lay, Y. Tsehay, M. D. Greer, B. Turkbey, J. T. Kwak, P. L. Choyke, P. Pinto, B. J. Wood, and R. M. Summers. Detection of prostate cancer in multiparametric MRI using random forest with instance weighting. *Journal of Medical Imaging*, 4(2):024506, 2017.

[346] Y. LeCun, Y. Bengio, and G. Hinton. Deep learning. *Nature*, 521(7553):436–444, 2015.

[347] Y. LeCun, B. Boser, J. S. Denker, D. Henderson, R. E. Howard, W. Hubbard, and L. D. Jackel. Backpropagation applied to handwritten zip code recognition. *Neural Computation*, 1(4):541–551, 1989.

[348] J. Lee, H.-A. Kao, and S. Yang. Service innovation and smart analytics for industry 4.0 and big data environment. *Procedia CIRP*, 16:3–8, 2014.

[349] A.-M. Legendre. *Nouvelles méthodes pour la détermination des orbites des comètes*. F. Didot, 1805.

[350] E. L. Lehmann and J. P. Romano. *Testing Statistical Hypotheses.* Springer, 3rd edition, 2005.

[351] A. L. Lehninger, D. L. Nelson, and M. M. Cox. *Lehninger Principles of Biochemistry.* W.H. Freeman and Company, 7th edition, 2017.

[352] S. J. Leon. *Linear Algebra with Applications.* Pearson, 9th edition, 2014.

[353] V. I. Levenshtein. Binary codes capable of correcting deletions, insertions, and reversals. *Soviet Physics Doklady*, 10(8):707–710, 1966.

[354] P. Lewis, E. Perez, A. Piktus, F. Petroni, V. Karpukhin, N. Goyal, H. Küttler, M. Lewis, W.-t. Yih, T. Rocktäschel, et al. Retrieval-augmented generation for knowledge-intensive NLP tasks. In *Advances in Neural Information Processing Systems (NeurIPS)*, pages 9459–9474, 2020.

[355] J. Li, S. Ma, T. Le, L. Liu, and J. Liu. Causal decision trees. *IEEE Transactions on Knowledge and Data Engineering*, 29(2):257–271, 2016.

[356] J. Li, A. Sun, J. Han, and C. Li. A survey on deep learning for named entity recognition. *IEEE Transactions on Knowledge and Data Engineering*, 34(1):50–70, 2020.

[357] M. Li and C. Zhu. Noisy label processing for classification: A survey. *arXiv preprint arXiv:2404.04159*, 2024.

[358] W. Li, P. Yi, Y. Wu, L. Pan, and J. Li. A new intrusion detection system based on KNN classification algorithm in wireless sensor network. *Journal of Electrical and Computer Engineering*, 2014(1):240217, 2014.

[359] X.-B. Li. A scalable decision tree system and its application in pattern recognition and intrusion detection. *Decision Support Systems*, 41(1):112–130, 2005.

[360] Z. Li, K. Ren, Y. Yang, X. Jiang, Y. Yang, and D. Li. Towards inference efficient deep ensemble learning. In *Proceedings of the Thirty-Seventh AAAI Conference on Artificial Intelligence*, pages 8711–8719, 2023.

[361] Z. Li, W. Yang, J. Yuan, J. Wu, C. Chen, Y. Ming, F. Yang, H. Zhang, and S. Liu. RuleExplorer: A scalable matrix visualization for understanding tree ensemble classifiers. *IEEE Transactions on Visualization and Computer Graphics*, 2024.

[362] Z. Li, Z.-H. Zhou, and A. Gretton. Towards an understanding of benign overfitting in neural networks. *arXiv preprint arXiv:2106.03212*, 2021.

[363] K. G. Liakos, P. Busato, D. Moshou, S. Pearson, and D. Bochtis. Machine learning in agriculture: A review. *Computers and Electronics in Agriculture*, 147:70–90, 2018.

[364] C.-J. Lin, R. C. Weng, and S. S. Keerthi. Trust region Newton method for large-scale logistic regression. *Journal of Machine Learning Research*, 9(4):627–650, 2008.

[365] C.-Y. Lin. ROUGE: A package for automatic evaluation of summaries. In *Proceedings of the ACL Workshop on Text Summarization Branches Out*, pages 74–81, 2004.

[366] S.-C. Lin, L. Gao, B. Oguz, W. Xiong, J. Lin, W.-t. Yih, and X. Chen. FLAME: Factuality-aware alignment for large language models. 2024.

[367] D. V. Lindley. The philosophy of statistics. *The Statistician*, 49(3):293–337, 2000.

[368] C. X. Ling, Q. Yang, J. Wang, and S. Zhang. Decision trees with minimal costs. In *Proceedings of the 21st International Conference on Machine Learning (ICML)*, pages 69–77, 2004.

[369] B. Liu and R. Mazumder. Randomization can reduce both bias and variance: A case study in random forests. *arXiv preprint arXiv:2402.12668*, 2024.

[370] C. Liu, Y. Chan, S. H. Alam Kazmi, and H. Fu. Financial fraud detection model: Based on random forest. *International Journal of Economics and Finance*, 7(7), 2015.

[371] G. Liu, H. Zhao, F. Fan, G. Liu, Q. Xu, and S. Nazir. An enhanced intrusion detection model based on improved kNN in WSNs. *Sensors*, 22(4):1407, 2022.

[372] T. Liu, A. Moore, K. Yang, and A. Gray. An investigation of practical approximate nearest neighbor algorithms. In *Advances in Neural Information Processing Systems (NeurIPS)*, pages 825–832, 2004.

[373] T.-Y. Liu. Learning to rank for information retrieval. *Foundations and Trends in Information Retrieval*, 3(3):225–331, 2009.

[374] W. Liu, S. Chawla, D. A. Cieslak, and N. V. Chawla. A robust decision tree algorithm for imbalanced data sets. In *Proceedings of the 2010 SIAM International Conference on Data Mining (SDM)*, pages 766–777, 2010.

[375] H. Lodhi, C. Saunders, J. Shawe-Taylor, N. Cristianini, and C. Watkins. Text classification using string kernels. *Journal of Machine Learning Research*, 2:419–444, 2002.

[376] W.-Y. Loh. Improving the precision of classification trees. *The Annals of Applied Statistics*, 3(4):1710–1737, 2009.

[377] W.-Y. Loh. Classification and regression trees. *Wiley Interdisciplinary Reviews: Data Mining and Knowledge Discovery*, 1(1):14–23, 2011.

[378] W.-Y. Loh and Y.-S. Shih. Split selection methods for classification trees. *Statistica Sinica*, 7(4):815–840, 1997.

[379] M. Lopez de Prado. *Advances in Financial Machine Learning*. John Wiley & Sons, 2018.

[380] D. Lopez-Paz, K. Muandet, B. Schölkopf, and I. Tolstikhin. Towards a learning theory of cause-effect inference. In *Proceedings of the 32nd International Conference on Machine Learning (ICML)*, pages 1452–1461, 2015.

[381] G. Louppe and P. Geurts. Ensembles on random patches. In *Machine Learning and Knowledge Discovery in Databases*, pages 346–361, 2012.

[382] C. Lu, C. Lu, R. T. Lange, J. Foerster, J. Clune, and D. Ha. The AI scientist: Towards fully automated open-ended scientific discovery. *arXiv preprint arXiv:2408.06292*, 2024.

[383] J. Lu. Matrix decomposition and applications. *arXiv preprint arXiv:2201.00145*, 2022.

[384] J. Lu, A. Liu, F. Dong, F. Gu, J. Gama, and G. Zhang. Learning under concept drift: A review. *IEEE Transactions on Knowledge and Data Engineering*, 31(12):2346–2363, 2018.

[385] Y. Lu and W. He. SELC: Self-ensemble label correction improves learning with noisy labels. *arXiv preprint arXiv:2205.01156*, 2022.

[386] S. M. Lundberg and S.-I. Lee. A unified approach to interpreting model predictions. In *Advances in Neural Information Processing Systems (NeurIPS)*, pages 4765–4774, 2017.

[387] A. L. Maas, R. E. Daly, P. T. Pham, D. Huang, A. Y. Ng, and C. Potts. Learning word vectors for sentiment analysis. In *Proceedings of the 49th Annual Meeting of the Association for Computational Linguistics: Human Language Technologies*, pages 142–150, 2011.

[388] H. Magureanu and N. Usher. Consensus learning: A novel decentralized ensemble learning paradigm. *arXiv preprint arXiv:2402.16157*, 2024.

[389] P. C. Mahalanobis. On the generalised distance in statistics. *Proceedings of the National Institute of Sciences of India*, 2:49–55, 1936.

[390] H. Mahdavi, A. Hashemi, M. Daliri, P. Mohammadipour, A. Farhadi, S. Malek, Y. Yazdanifard, A. Khasahmadi, and V. Honavar. Brains vs. bytes: Evaluating LLM proficiency in Olympiad Mathematics. *arXiv preprint arXiv:2504.01995*, 2025.

[391] S. Makridakis, E. Spiliotis, V. Assimakopoulos, Z. Chen, A. Gaba, I. Tsetlin, and R. L. Winkler. The M5 uncertainty competition: Results, findings and conclusions. *International Journal of Forecasting*, 38(4):1365–1385, 2022.

[392] S. Makridakis, E. Spiliotis, R. Hollyman, F. Petropoulos, N. Swanson, and A. Gaba. The M6 forecasting competition: Bridging the gap between forecasting and investment decisions. *International Journal of Forecasting*, 41(4):1315–1354, 2025.

[393] S. G. Mallat. A theory for multiresolution signal decomposition: The wavelet representation. *IEEE Transactions on Pattern Analysis and Machine Intelligence*, 11(7):674–693, 1989.

[394] C. D. Manning, P. Raghavan, and H. Schütze. *Introduction to Information Retrieval*. Cambridge University Press, 2008.

[395] C. D. Manning and H. Schütze. *Foundations of Statistical Natural Language Processing*. MIT Press, 1999.

[396] N. Manwani and P. Sastry. Geometric decision tree. *IEEE Transactions on Systems, Man, and Cybernetics, Part B (Cybernetics)*, 42(1):181–192, 2011.

[397] M. Marcus, B. Santorini, and M. A. Marcinkiewicz. Building a large annotated corpus of English: The Penn Treebank. *Computational Linguistics*, 19(2):313–330, 1993.

[398] K. Mardiansyah and W. Surya. Comparative analysis of ChatGPT-4 and Google Gemini for spam detection on the SpamAssassin public mail corpus. *Research Square Preprint*, 2024.

[399] A. A. Markov. Extension of the limit theorems of probability theory to a sum of variables connected in a chain. *Izvestiya Fiziko-Matematicheskogo Obshchestva pri Kazanskom Universitete, 2-ya seriya*, 15:135–156, 1906. In Russian. English reprint in Howard (ed.), Dynamic Probabilistic Systems, Vol. 1 (1971).

[400] D. Martínez-Rubio, C. Roux, and S. Pokutta. Convergence and trade-offs in Riemannian gradient descent and Riemannian proximal point. In *Proceedings of the 41st International Conference on Machine Learning (ICML)*, pages 34920–34948, 2024.

[401] A. M. Martínez and A. C. Kak. PCA versus LDA. *IEEE Transactions on Pattern Analysis and Machine Intelligence*, 23(2):228–233, 2001.

[402] A. McCallum and K. Nigam. A comparison of event models for naive Bayes text classification. In *Proceedings of the AAAI-98 Workshop on Learning for Text Categorization*, pages 41–48, 1998.

[403] J. McCarthy, M. L. Minsky, N. Rochester, and C. E. Shannon. A proposal for the Dartmouth summer research project on Artificial Intelligence. *AI Magazine*, 27(4):12–14, 2006. Originally written August 31, 1955; proposal for the 1956 Dartmouth summer research project.

[404] P. McCullagh and J. A. Nelder. *Generalized Linear Models*. Chapman & Hall/CRC, 2nd edition, 1989.

[405] W. S. McCulloch and W. Pitts. A logical calculus of the ideas immanent in nervous activity. *The Bulletin of Mathematical Biophysics*, 5:115–133, 1943.

[406] D. McElfresh, S. Khandagale, J. Valverde, V. Prasad C, G. Ramakrishnan, M. Goldblum, and C. White. When do neural nets outperform boosted trees on tabular data? In *Advances in Neural Information Processing Systems (NeurIPS)*, 2024.

[407] D. McFadden. Conditional logit analysis of qualitative choice behavior. In P. Zarembka, editor, *Frontiers in Econometrics*, pages 105–142. Academic Press, 1973.

[408] W. McKinney. Data structures for statistical computing in Python. In *Proceedings of the 9th Python in Science Conference*, pages 51–56, 2010.

[409] W. McKinney. *Python for Data Analysis: Data Wrangling with Pandas, NumPy, and Jupyter*. O'Reilly Media, 3rd edition, 2022.

[410] D. Mease, A. J. Wyner, and A. Buja. Boosted classification trees and class probability/quantile estimation. *Journal of Machine Learning Research*, 8(3), 2007.

[411] W. Medhat, A. Hassan, and H. Korashy. Sentiment analysis algorithms and applications: A survey. *Ain Shams Engineering Journal*, 5(4):1093–1113, 2014.

[412] N. Mehrabi, F. Morstatter, N. Saxena, K. Lerman, and A. Galstyan. A survey on bias and fairness in machine learning. *ACM Computing Surveys*, 54(6):1–35, 2021.

[413] M. Mehta, R. Agrawal, and J. Rissanen. SLIQ: A fast scalable classifier for data mining. In *Proceedings of the 5th International Conference on Extending Database Technology*, pages 18–32, 1996.

[414] M. Mehta, J. Rissanen, and R. Agrawal. MDL-based decision tree pruning. In *Proceedings of the 1995 ACM SIGKDD International Conference on Knowledge Discovery and Data Mining*, pages 216–221, 1995.

[415] N. Meinshausen. Quantile regression forests. *Journal of Machine Learning Research*, 7:983–999, 2006.

[416] L. Mentch and S. Zhou. Randomization as regularization: A degrees of freedom explanation for random forest success. *Journal of Machine Learning Research*, 21(171):1–36, 2020.

[417] J. Mercer. Functions of positive and negative type, and their connection with the theory of integral equations. *Philosophical Transactions of the Royal Society of London*, 209:415–446, 1909.

[418] V. Metsis, I. Androutsopoulos, and G. Paliouras. Spam filtering with naive Bayes — which naive Bayes? In *Proceedings of the 3rd Conference on Email and Anti-Spam*, 2006.

[419] J. Miles. R-squared, adjusted R-squared. *Encyclopedia of Statistics in Behavioral Science*, John Wiley & Sons, 2005.

[420] S. Minaee, N. Kalchbrenner, E. Cambria, N. Nikzad, M. Chenaghlu, and J. Gao. Deep learning–based text classification: A comprehensive review. *ACM Computing Surveys*, 54(3):1–40, 2021.

[421] C. Mingard, H. Rees, G. Valle-Pérez, and A. A. Louis. Deep neural networks have an inbuilt Occam's razor. *Nature Communications*, 16:220, 2025.

[422] J. Mingers. Expert systems—rule induction with statistical data. *Journal of the Operational Research Society*, 38(1):39–47, 1987.

[423] J. Mingers. An empirical comparison of pruning methods for decision tree induction. *Machine Learning*, 4:227–243, 1989.

[424] J. Mingers. An empirical comparison of selection measures for decision-tree induction. *Machine Learning*, 3:319–342, 1989.

[425] M. L. Minsky and S. A. Papert. *Perceptrons: An Introduction to Computational Geometry*. MIT Press, 1969.

[426] T. Mitchell. *Machine Learning*. McGraw Hill, 1997.

[427] B. Mitra and N. Craswell. An introduction to neural information retrieval. *Foundations and Trends in Information Retrieval*, 13(1):1–126, 2018.

[428] V. Mnih, K. Kavukcuoglu, D. Silver, A. A. Rusu, J. Veness, M. G. Bellemare, A. Graves, M. Riedmiller, A. K. Fidjeland, G. Ostrovski, S. Petersen, C. Beattie, A. Sadik, I. Antonoglou, H. King, D. Kumaran, D. Wierstra, S. Legg, and D. Hassabis. Human-level control through deep reinforcement learning. *Nature*, 518(7540):529–533, 2015.

[429] J. Močkus. The Bayesian approach to local optimization. In *Bayesian Approach to Global Optimization: Theory and Applications*, volume 37 of *Mathematics and Its Applications*, pages 125–156. Springer, 1989.

[430] D. C. Montgomery, E. A. Peck, and G. G. Vining. *Introduction to Linear Regression Analysis*. John Wiley & Sons, 6th edition, 2021.

[431] H. P. Moravec. The Stanford cart and the CMU rover. *Proceedings of the IEEE*, 71(7):872–884, 1983.

[432] I. Moshkov, D. Hanley, I. Sorokin, S. Toshniwal, C. Henkel, B. Schifferer, W. Du, and I. Gitman. AIMO-2 winning solution: Building state-of-the-art mathematical reasoning models with the OpenMathReasoning dataset. *arXiv preprint arXiv:2504.16891*, 2025.

[433] S. K. Murthy. Automatic construction of decision trees from data: A multi-disciplinary survey. *Data Mining and Knowledge Discovery*, 2:345–389, 1998.

[434] S. K. Murthy, S. Kasif, and S. Salzberg. A system for induction of oblique decision trees. *Journal of Artificial Intelligence Research*, 2:1–32, 1994.

[435] D. Nadeau and S. Sekine. A survey of named entity recognition and classification. *Lingvisticae Investigationes*, 30(1):3–26, 2007.

[436] P. Nakkiran, G. Kaplun, Y. Bansal, T. Yang, B. Barak, and I. Sutskever. Deep double descent: Where bigger models and more data hurt. *Journal of Statistical Mechanics: Theory and Experiment*, 2021(12):124003, 2021.

[437] A. Narayanan and V. Shmatikov. How to break anonymity of the Netflix prize dataset. *arXiv preprint cs/0610105*, 2006.

[438] A. Natekin and A. Knoll. Gradient boosting machines, a tutorial. *Frontiers in Neurorobotics*, 7:21, 2013.

[439] R. Navigli. Word sense disambiguation: A survey. *ACM Computing Surveys*, 41(2):1–69, 2009.

[440] J. A. Nelder and R. W. Wedderburn. Generalized linear models. *Journal of the Royal Statistical Society: Series A (General)*, 135(3):370–384, 1972.

[441] P. B. Nemenyi. *Distribution-free Multiple Comparisons*. PhD thesis, Princeton University, 1963.

[442] J. Neyman. Outline of a theory of statistical estimation based on the classical theory of probability. *Philosophical Transactions of the Royal Society of London. Series A*, 236(767):333–380, 1937.

[443] J. Neyman and E. S. Pearson. On the problem of the most efficient tests of statistical hypotheses. *Philosophical Transactions of the Royal Society of London. Series A*, 231:289–337, 1933.

[444] B. Neyshabur, Z. Li, S. Bhojanapalli, Y. LeCun, and N. Srebro. Towards understanding the role of over-parametrization in generalization of neural networks. In *International Conference on Learning Representations (ICLR)*, 2019.

[445] A.-P. Nguyen, D. L. Moreno, N. Le-Bel, and M. Rodríguez Martínez. MonoNet: Enhancing interpretability in neural networks via monotonic features. *Bioinformatics Advances*, 3(1):vbad016, 2023.

[446] T. Niblett and I. Bratko. Learning decision rules in noisy domains. In *Proceedings of the 6th Annual Technical Conference on Research and Development in Expert Systems*, pages 25–34, 1987.

[447] A. Niculescu-Mizil and R. Caruana. Predicting good probabilities with supervised learning. In *Proceedings of the 22nd International Conference on Machine Learning (ICML)*, pages 625–632, 2005.

[448] J. Nocedal and S. Wright. *Numerical Optimization*. Springer Science, 2nd edition, 2006.

[449] J. R. Norris. *Markov Chains*, volume 2 of *Cambridge Series in Statistical and Probabilistic Mathematics*. Cambridge University Press, 1998.

[450] C. G. Northcutt, A. Athalye, and J. Mueller. Pervasive label errors in test sets destabilize machine learning benchmarks. *arXiv preprint arXiv:2103.14749*, 2021.

[451] R. M. O'Brien. A caution regarding rules of thumb for variance inflation factors. *Quality & Quantity*, 41:673–690, 2007.

[452] T. E. Oliphant. *Guide to NumPy*. Trelgol Publishing, 2006.

[453] S. M. Omohundro. Five balltree construction algorithms. Technical Report TR-89-063, International Computer Science Institute, 1989.

[454] OpenAI. ChatGPT: Optimizing language models for dialogue. `https://openai.com/blog/chatgpt`, 2022.

[455] OpenAI. GPT-4 technical report. *arXiv preprint arXiv:2303.08774*, 2023.

[456] OpenAI. Sora: Creating video from text. `https://openai.com/sora`, 2024.

[457] D. Opitz and R. Maclin. Popular ensemble methods: An empirical study. *Journal of Artificial Intelligence Research*, 11:169–198, 1999.

[458] A. Ororbia, A. Mali, A. Kohan, B. Millidge, and T. Salvatori. A review of neuroscience-inspired machine learning. *arXiv preprint arXiv:2403.18929*, 2024.

[459] W. Orr and K. Crawford. Building better datasets: Seven recommendations for responsible design from dataset creators. *Journal of Data-centric Machine Learning Research*, 1:1–20, 2024.

[460] T. M. Oshiro, P. S. Perez, and J. A. Baranauskas. How many trees in a random forest? In *Proceedings of the 8th International Conference on Machine Learning and Data Mining in Pattern Recognition*, pages 154–168, 2012.

[461] J. Ouyang, N. Patel, and I. Sethi. Induction of multiclass multifeature split decision trees from distributed data. *Pattern Recognition*, 42(9):1786–1794, 2009.

[462] R. K. Pace and R. Barry. Sparse spatial autoregressions. *Statistics & Probability Letters*, 33(3):291–297, 1997.

[463] A. S. Palli, J. Jaafar, M. H. Md Saad, A. A. Mokhtar, H. M. Gomes, A. A. Soomro, and A. R. Gilal. Smart adaptive ensemble model for multiclass imbalanced nonstationary data streams. *Scientific Reports*, 15(1):21140, 2025.

[464] G. Pang, C. Shen, L. Cao, and A. van den Hengel. Deep learning for anomaly detection: A review. *ACM Computing Surveys*, 54(2):1–38, 2021.

[465] A. Papagelis and D. Kalles. GA Tree: Genetically evolved decision trees. In *Proceedings of the 12th IEEE International Conference on Tools with Artificial Intelligence*, pages 203–206, 2000.

[466] K. Papineni, S. Roukos, T. Ward, and W.-J. Zhu. BLEU: a method for automatic evaluation of machine translation. In *Proceedings of the 40th Annual Meeting on Association for Computational Linguistics (ACL)*, pages 311–318, 2002.

[467] B. Park and J. K. Bae. Using machine learning algorithms for housing price prediction: The case of Fairfax County, Virginia housing data. *Expert Systems with Applications*, 42(6):2928–2934, 2015.

[468] A. Paszke, S. Gross, F. Massa, A. Lerer, J. Bradbury, G. Chanan, T. Killeen, Z. Lin, N. Gimelshein, L. Antiga, et al. PyTorch: An imperative style, high-performance deep learning library. In *Advances in Neural Information Processing Systems (NeurIPS)*, pages 8024–8035, 2019.

[469] J. Pearl. *Probabilistic Reasoning in Intelligent Systems: Networks of Plausible Inference*. Morgan Kaufmann, 1988.

[470] J. Pearl. *Causality: Models, Reasoning and Inference*. Cambridge University Press, 2nd edition, 2009.

[471] K. Pearson. Note on regression and inheritance in the case of two parents. *Proceedings of the Royal Society of London*, 58:240–242, 1895.

[472] K. Pearson. On the criterion that a given system of deviations from the probable in the case of a correlated system of variables is such that it can be reasonably supposed to have arisen from random sampling. *Philosophical Magazine*, 50(302):157–175, 1900.

[473] F. Pedregosa, G. Varoquaux, A. Gramfort, V. Michel, B. Thirion, O. Grisel, M. Blondel, P. Prettenhofer, R. Weiss, V. Dubourg, et al. Scikit-learn: Machine learning in Python. *Journal of Machine Learning Research*, 12:2825–2830, 2011.

[474] J. Pei, L. Deng, S. Song, M. Zhao, Y. Zhang, S. Wu, G. Wang, Z. Zou, Z. Wu, W. He, et al. Towards artificial general intelligence with hybrid Tianjic chip architecture. *Nature*, 572(7767):106–111, 2019.

[475] D. Peng, Z. Gui, and H. Wu. Interpreting the curse of dimensionality from distance concentration and manifold effect. *arXiv preprint arXiv:2401.00422*, 2023.

[476] R. Penrose. A generalized inverse for matrices. In *Mathematical Proceedings of the Cambridge Philosophical Society*, volume 51, pages 406–413, 1955.

[477] J. Peters, D. Janzing, and B. Schölkopf. *Elements of Causal Inference: Foundations and Learning Algorithms*. MIT Press, 2017.

[478] I. Petrov, J. Dekoninck, L. Baltadzhiev, M. Drencheva, K. Minchev, M. Balunović, N. Jovanović, and M. Vechev. Proof or bluff? Evaluating LLMs on the 2025 USA Math Olympiad. *arXiv preprint arXiv:2503.21934*, 2025.

[479] A. Pinheiro, H. P. Pinheiro, and P. K. Sen. The use of Hamming distance in bioinformatics. In *Handbook of Statistics*, volume 28, pages 129–162. Elsevier, 2012.

[480] J. Platt. Sequential minimal optimization: A fast algorithm for training support vector machines. Technical Report MSR-TR-98-14, Microsoft Research, 1998.

[481] J. Platt. Probabilistic outputs for support vector machines and comparisons to regularized likelihood methods. *Advances in Large Margin Classifiers*, 10(3):61–74, 1999.

[482] K. Poland, K. Beer, and T. J. Osborne. No free lunch for quantum machine learning. *arXiv preprint arXiv:2003.14103*, 2020.

[483] M. F. Porter. An algorithm for suffix stripping. *Program*, 14(3):130–137, 1980.

[484] L. Prechelt. Early stopping—but when? In *Neural Networks: Tricks of the Trade*, volume 1524 of *Lecture Notes in Computer Science*, pages 55–69. Springer, 1998.

[485] L. Prokhorenkova, G. Gusev, A. Vorobev, A. V. Dorogush, and A. Gulin. CatBoost: Unbiased boosting with categorical features. In *Advances in Neural Information Processing Systems (NeurIPS)*, pages 6639–6649, 2018.

[486] M. Prosperi, Y. Guo, M. Sperrin, J. Koopman, J. Min, X. He, S. Rich, M. Wang, I. Buchan, and J. Bian. Causal inference and counterfactual prediction in machine learning for actionable healthcare. *Nature Machine Intelligence*, 2(7):369–375, 2020.

[487] F. Provost and T. Fawcett. *Data Science for Business: What You Need to Know About Data Mining and Data-Analytic Thinking*. O'Reilly Media, 2013.

[488] F. Quin, D. Weyns, M. Galster, and C. C. Silva. A/B testing: A systematic literature review. *Journal of Systems and Software*, page 112011, 2024.

[489] J. R. Quinlan. Induction of decision trees. *Machine Learning*, 1(1):81–106, 1986.

[490] J. R. Quinlan. Simplifying decision trees. *International Journal of Man-Machine Studies*, 27(3):221–234, 1987.

[491] J. R. Quinlan. *C4.5: Programs for Machine Learning*. Morgan Kaufmann Publishers, 1993.

[492] J. R. Quinlan. Bagging, boosting, and C4.5. In *Proceedings of the Thirteenth National Conference on Artificial Intelligence*, pages 725–730, 1996.

[493] L. R. Rabiner. A tutorial on hidden Markov models and selected applications in speech recognition. *Proceedings of the IEEE*, 77(2):257–286, 1989.

[494] A. Radford, J. W. Kim, C. Hallacy, A. Ramesh, G. Goh, S. Agarwal, G. Sastry, A. Askell, P. Mishkin, J. Clark, G. Krueger, and I. Sutskever. Learning transferable visual models from natural language supervision. In *Proceedings of the 38th International Conference on Machine Learning (ICML)*, pages 8748–8763, 2021.

[495] E. Raff, J. Sylvester, and S. Mills. Fair forests: Regularized tree induction to minimize model bias. In *Proceedings of the 2018 AAAI/ACM Conference on AI, Ethics, and Society*, pages 243–250, 2018.

[496] A. Rahimi and B. Recht. Random features for large-scale kernel machines. In *Advances in Neural Information Processing Systems (NeurIPS)*, pages 1177–1184, 2007.

[497] E. Rahm and H. H. Do. Data cleaning: Problems and current approaches. *IEEE Data Engineering Bulletin*, 23(4):3–13, 2000.

[498] P. Rajpurkar, J. Zhang, K. Lopyrev, and P. Liang. SQuAD: 100,000+ questions for machine comprehension of text. *arXiv preprint arXiv:1606.05250*, 2016.

[499] C. E. Rasmussen and C. K. I. Williams. *Gaussian Processes for Machine Learning*. MIT Press, 2006.

[500] S. Reed, K. Zolna, E. Parisotto, S. Gómez Colmenarejo, A. Novikov, G. Barth-Maron, M. Giménez, Y. Sulsky, J. Kay, J. T. Springenberg, T. Eccles, J. Bruce, A. Razavi, A. Edwards, N. Heess, Y. Chen, R. Hadsell, O. Vinyals, M. Bordbar, and N. de Freitas. A generalist agent. *Transactions on Machine Learning Research*, 2022.

[501] M. T. Ribeiro, S. Singh, and C. Guestrin. Why should I trust you? Explaining the predictions of any classifier. In *Proceedings of the 22nd ACM SIGKDD International Conference on Knowledge Discovery and Data Mining*, pages 1135–1144, 2016.

[502] J. Richiardi, S. Achard, H. Bunke, and D. Van De Ville. Machine learning with brain graphs: Predictive modeling approaches for functional imaging in systems neuroscience. *IEEE Signal Processing Magazine*, 30(3):58–70, 2013.

[503] R. Riess and Z. Sottile. Uber self-driving car test driver pleads guilty to endangerment in pedestrian death case. https://www.cnn.com/2023/07/29/business/uber-self-driving-car-death-guilty, July 2023.

[504] J. J. Rodriguez, L. I. Kuncheva, and C. J. Alonso. Rotation forest: A new classifier ensemble method. *IEEE Transactions on Pattern Analysis and Machine Intelligence*, 28(10):1619–1630, 2006.

[505] R. Rombach, A. Blattmann, D. Lorenz, P. Esser, and B. Ommer. High-resolution image synthesis with latent diffusion models. In *Proceedings of the IEEE/CVF Conference on Computer Vision and Pattern Recognition (CVPR)*, pages 10684–10695, 2022.

[506] F. Rosenblatt. The perceptron: A probabilistic model for information storage and organization in the brain. *Psychological Review*, 65(6):386, 1958.

[507] S. M. Ross. *A First Course in Probability*. Pearson, 9th edition, 2014.

[508] D. Ruano-Ordás, F. Fdez-Riverola, and J. R. Méndez. Using evolutionary computation for discovering spam patterns from e-mail samples. *Information Processing & Management*, 54(2):303–317, 2018.

[509] D. J. Rubin. Correction to: hospital readmission of patients with diabetes. *Current Diabetes Reports*, 18(4):21, 2018.

[510] S. Ruggieri. Efficient C4.5. *IEEE Transactions on Knowledge and Data Engineering*, 14(2):438–444, 2002.

[511] D. E. Rumelhart, G. E. Hinton, and R. J. Williams. Learning representations by back-propagating errors. *Nature*, 323(6088):533–536, 1986.

[512] O. Russakovsky, J. Deng, H. Su, J. Krause, S. Satheesh, S. Ma, Z. Huang, A. Karpathy, A. Khosla, M. Bernstein, et al. ImageNet large scale visual recognition challenge. *International Journal of Computer Vision*, 115:211–252, 2015.

[513] S. Russell and P. Norvig. *Artificial Intelligence: A Modern Approach*. Pearson, 3rd edition, 2016.

[514] A. Saffari, C. Leistner, J. Santner, M. Godec, and H. Bischof. On-line random forests. In *Proceedings of the IEEE 12th International Conference on Computer Vision Workshops*, pages 1393–1400, 2009.

[515] O. Sagi and L. Rokach. Ensemble learning: A survey. *Wiley Interdisciplinary Reviews: Data Mining and Knowledge Discovery*, 8(4):e1249, 2018.

[516] F. Salehi, E. Abbasi, and B. Hassibi. The impact of regularization on high-dimensional logistic regression. In *Advances in Neural Information Processing Systems (NeurIPS)*, pages 11982–11992, 2019.

[517] G. Salton. *Automatic Text Processing: The Transformation, Analysis, and Retrieval of Information by Computer*. Addison-Wesley, 1989.

[518] G. Salton and C. Buckley. Term-weighting approaches in automatic text retrieval. *Information Processing & Management*, 24(5):513–523, 1988.

[519] E. L. Salvador. Use of boosting algorithms in household-level poverty measurement: A machine learning approach to predict and classify household wealth quintiles in the Philippines. *arXiv preprint arXiv:2407.13061*, 2024.

[520] N. Sambasivan, S. Kapania, H. Highfill, D. Akrong, P. Paritosh, and L. M. Aroyo. "Everyone wants to do the model work, not the data work": Data cascades in high-stakes AI. In *Proceedings of the 2021 CHI Conference on Human Factors in Computing Systems*, pages 1–15, 2021.

[521] A. L. Samuel. Some studies in machine learning using the game of checkers. *IBM Journal of Research and Development*, 3(3):210–229, 1959.

[522] B. Sarwar, G. Karypis, J. Konstan, and J. Riedl. Item-based collaborative filtering recommendation algorithms. In *Proceedings of the 10th International Conference on World Wide Web*, pages 285–295, 2001.

[523] F. E. Satterthwaite. An approximate distribution of estimates of variance components. *Biometrics Bulletin*, 2(6):110–114, 1946.

[524] R. Schaeffer, B. Miranda, and S. Koyejo. Are emergent abilities of large language models a mirage? *Advances in Neural Information Processing Systems (NeurIPS)*, pages 55565–55581, 2023.

[525] R. E. Schapire. Using output codes to boost multiclass learning problems. In *Proceedings of the 14th International Conference on Machine Learning (ICML)*, pages 313–321, 1997.

[526] R. E. Schapire. Explaining AdaBoost. In *Empirical Inference: Festschrift in Honor of Vladimir N. Vapnik*, pages 37–52. Springer, 2013.

[527] R. E. Schapire and Y. Freund. *Boosting: Foundations and Algorithms*. MIT Press, 2012.

[528] R. E. Schapire, Y. Freund, P. Bartlett, and W. S. Lee. Boosting the margin: A new explanation for the effectiveness of voting methods. *The Annals of Statistics*, 26(5):1651–1686, 1998.

[529] L. Schlosser, T. Hothorn, R. Stauffer, and A. Zeileis. Distributional regression forests for probabilistic precipitation forecasting in complex terrain. *The Annals of Applied Statistics*, 13(3):1564–1589, 2019.

[530] F. Schlüter. A survey on independence-based Markov networks learning. *Artificial Intelligence Review*, 42(4):1069–1093, 2014.

[531] B. Schölkopf. Toward causal representation learning. *Proceedings of the IEEE*, 109(5):612–634, 2021.

[532] B. Schölkopf, R. Herbrich, and A. J. Smola. A generalized representer theorem. In *Proceedings of the 14th Annual Conference on Computational Learning Theory*, pages 416–426, 2001.

[533] B. Schölkopf and A. J. Smola. *Learning with Kernels: Support Vector Machines, Regularization, Optimization, and Beyond*. MIT Press, 2002.

[534] B. Schölkopf, A. J. Smola, R. C. Williamson, and P. L. Bartlett. New support vector algorithms. *Neural Computation*, 12(5):1207–1245, 2000.

[535] F. Sebastiani. Machine learning in automated text categorization. *ACM Computing Surveys*, 34(1):1–47, 2002.

[536] G. A. F. Seber and A. J. Lee. *Linear Regression Analysis*. John Wiley & Sons, 2012.

[537] A. Segatori, F. Marcelloni, and W. Pedrycz. On distributed fuzzy decision trees for big data. *IEEE Transactions on Fuzzy Systems*, 26(1):174–192, 2017.

[538] F. Seghir, A. Drif, S. Selmani, and H. Cherifi. Wrapper-based feature selection for medical diagnosis: The BTLBO-KNN algorithm. *IEEE Access*, 11:61368–61389, 2023.

[539] E. Seneta. A tricentenary history of the law of large numbers. *Bernoulli*, 19(4):1088–1121, 2013.

[540] R. Sennrich, B. Haddow, and A. Birch. Neural machine translation of rare words with subword units. In *Proceedings of the 54th Annual Meeting of the Association for Computational Linguistics (ACL)*, pages 1715–1725, 2016.

[541] J. Shafer, R. Agrawal, and M. Mehta. SPRINT: A scalable parallel classifier for data mining. In *Proceedings of the 22nd International Conference on Very Large Data Bases*, pages 544–555, 1996.

[542] S. Shalev-Shwartz and S. Ben-David. *Understanding Machine Learning: From Theory to Algorithms*. Cambridge University Press, 2014.

[543] S. Shalev-Shwartz, O. Shamir, K. Sridharan, and N. Srebro. Learnability, stability and uniform convergence. *Journal of Machine Learning Research*, 11:2635–2670, 2010.

[544] S. Shalev-Shwartz, Y. Singer, and N. Srebro. Pegasos: Primal estimated sub-gradient solver for SVM. In *Proceedings of the 24th International Conference on Machine Learning (ICML)*, pages 807–814, 2007.

[545] C. E. Shannon. A mathematical theory of communication. *The Bell System Technical Journal*, 27(3):379–423, 1948.

[546] J. Shawe-Taylor and N. Cristianini. *Kernel Methods for Pattern Analysis*. Cambridge University Press, 2004.

[547] Y.-S. Shih. Families of splitting criteria for classification trees. *Statistics and Computing*, 9(4):309–315, 1999.

[548] T. Shinogi and A. Imiya. Comparison of the representational power of random forests, binary decision diagrams, and neural networks. *Neural Computation*, 34(4):1019–1043, 2022.

[549] H.-Y. Shum, X. He, and D. Li. From Eliza to XiaoIce: Challenges and opportunities with social chatbots. *Frontiers of Information Technology & Electronic Engineering*, 19:10–26, 2018.

[550] R. Shwartz-Ziv and A. Armon. Tabular data: Deep learning is not all you need. *Information Fusion*, 81:84–90, 2022.

[551] B. Siciliano and O. Khatib, editors. *Springer Handbook of Robotics*. Springer, 2nd edition, 2016.

[552] D. Silver, A. Huang, C. J. Maddison, A. Guez, L. Sifre, G. van den Driessche, J. Schrittwieser, I. Antonoglou, V. Panneershelvam, M. Lanctot, S. Dieleman, D. Grewe, J. Nham, N. Kalchbrenner, I. Sutskever, T. Lillicrap, M. Leach, K. Kavukcuoglu, T. Graepel, and D. Hassabis. Mastering the game of Go with deep neural networks and tree search. *Nature*, 529(7587):484–489, 2016.

[553] D. Silver, J. Schrittwieser, K. Simonyan, I. Antonoglou, A. Huang, A. Guez, T. Hubert, L. Baker, M. Lai, A. Bolton, et al. A general reinforcement learning algorithm that masters chess, shogi, and Go through self-play. *Science*, 362(6419):1140–1144, 2018.

[554] A. J. Smola and B. Schölkopf. A tutorial on support vector regression. *Statistics and Computing*, 14:199–222, 2004.

[555] C. Spearman. The proof and measurement of association between two things. *The American Journal of Psychology*, 15(1):72–101, 1904.

[556] P. Spirtes, C. N. Glymour, and R. Scheines. *Causation, Prediction, and Search*. MIT Press, 2nd edition, 2000.

[557] M. Spivak. *Calculus*. Publish or Perish, Inc., 4th edition, 2008.

[558] R. F. Sproull. Refinements to nearest-neighbor searching in k-dimensional trees. *Algorithmica*, 6:579–589, 1991.

[559] A. M. Stefan and F. D. Schönbrodt. Big little lies: A compendium and simulation of p-hacking strategies. *Royal Society Open Science*, 10(2):220346, 2023.

[560] J. Stewart. *Calculus: Early Transcendentals*. Cengage Learning, 9th edition, 2020.

[561] S. M. Stigler. Thomas Bayes's Bayesian inference. *Journal of the Royal Statistical Society: Series A (General)*, 145(2):250–258, 1982.

[562] C. J. Stone. Consistent nonparametric regression. *The Annals of Statistics*, 5(4):595–620, 1977.

[563] M. Stone. Cross-validatory choice and assessment of statistical predictions. *Journal of the Royal Statistical Society: Series B (Methodological)*, 36(2):111–133, 1974.

[564] B. Strack, J. P. DeShazo, C. Gennings, J. L. Olmo, S. Ventura, K. J. Cios, and J. N. Clore. Impact of HbA1c measurement on hospital readmission rates: Analysis of 70,000 clinical database records of diabetes patients. *Journal of Diabetes Science and Technology*, 8(1):95–102, 2014.

[565] G. Strang. *Introduction to Linear Algebra*. Wellesley-Cambridge Press, 6th edition, 2023.

[566] Student. The probable error of a mean. *Biometrika*, 6(1):1–25, 1908.

[567] C. Sun, A. Shrivastava, S. Singh, and A. Gupta. Revisiting unreasonable effectiveness of data in deep learning era. In *Proceedings of the IEEE International Conference on Computer Vision (ICCV)*, pages 843–852, 2017.

[568] S. Sun and R. Huang. An adaptive k-nearest neighbor algorithm. In *2010 Seventh International Conference on Fuzzy Systems and Knowledge Discovery*, pages 91–94, 2010.

[569] R. S. Sutton and A. G. Barto. *Reinforcement Learning: An Introduction*. MIT Press, 2nd edition, 2018.

[570] G. J. Székely and M. L. Rizzo. Testing for equal distributions in high dimension. InterStat, 2004.

[571] R. Szeliski. *Computer Vision: Algorithms and Applications*. Springer, 2010.

[572] Y. Taigman, M. Yang, M. Ranzato, and L. Wolf. DeepFace: Closing the gap to human-level performance in face verification. In *Proceedings of the IEEE Conference on Computer Vision and Pattern Recognition (CVPR)*, pages 1701–1708, 2014.

[573] B. A. Tama, I. M. I. Subroto, and K. Mustofa. Prediction of energy consumption based on neural network techniques. *IEEE Transactions on Sustainable Energy*, 8(3):1216–1224, 2017.

[574] M. Tan and Q. Le. EfficientNet: Rethinking model scaling for convolutional neural networks. In *Proceedings of the 36th International Conference on Machine Learning (ICML)*, pages 6105–6114, 2019.

[575] M. Tang, A. Athreya, D. L. Sussman, V. Lyzinski, and C. E. Priebe. A nonparametric two-sample hypothesis testing problem for random graphs. *Bernoulli*, 23(3):1599–1630, 2017.

[576] S. Tangirala. Evaluating the impact of Gini index and information gain on classification using decision tree classifier algorithm. *International Journal of Advanced Computer Science and Applications*, 11(2):612–619, 2020.

[577] S. Thrun, M. Montemerlo, H. Dahlkamp, D. Stavens, A. Aron, J. Diebel, P. Fong, J. Gale, M. Halpenny, G. Hoffmann, et al. Stanley: The robot that won the DARPA Grand Challenge. *Journal of Field Robotics*, 23(9):661–692, 2006.

[578] R. Tibshirani. Regression shrinkage and selection via the lasso. *Journal of the Royal Statistical Society: Series B (Methodological)*, 58(1):267–288, 1996.

[579] T. M. Tomita, J. Browne, C. Shen, J. Chung, J. L. Patsolic, B. Falk, C. E. Priebe, J. Yim, R. Burns, M. Maggioni, et al. Sparse projection oblique randomer forests. *Journal of Machine Learning Research*, 21(104):1–39, 2020.

[580] A. Töscher, M. Jahrer, and R. M. Bell. The BigChaos solution to the Netflix grand prize. *Netflix Prize Documentation*, pages 1–52, 2009.

[581] H. Touvron, T. Lavril, G. Izacard, X. Martinet, M.-A. Lachaux, T. Lacroix, B. Rozière, N. Goyal, E. Hambro, F. Azhar, A. Rodriguez, A. Joulin, E. Grave, and G. Lample. The LLaMA 3 herd of models. *arXiv preprint arXiv:2407.21783*, 2024.

[582] F. Tramèr, A. Kurakin, N. Papernot, I. Goodfellow, D. Boneh, and P. McDaniel. Ensemble adversarial training: Attacks and defenses. In *International Conference on Learning Representations (ICLR)*, 2018.

[583] L. N. Trefethen and D. Bau. *Numerical Linear Algebra*. SIAM, 1997.

[584] I. Tsamardinos, L. E. Brown, and C. F. Aliferis. The max-min hill-climbing Bayesian network structure learning algorithm. *Machine Learning*, 65(1):31–78, 2006.

[585] G. Tsoumakas and I. Katakis. Multi-label classification: An overview. In *Data Warehousing and Mining: Concepts, Methodologies, Tools, and Applications*, pages 64–74. IGI Global, 2008.

[586] J. W. Tukey. Comparing individual means in the analysis of variance. *Biometrics*, 5(2):99–114, 1949.

[587] J. W. Tukey. *Exploratory Data Analysis*. Addison-Wesley, 1977.

[588] A. M. Turing. Computing machinery and intelligence. *Mind*, 59(236):433–460, 1950.

[589] M. Tweedie. An index which distinguishes between some important exponential families. In *Statistics: Applications and New Directions, Proceedings of the Indian Statistical Institute Golden Jubilee International Conference*, pages 579–604, 1984.

[590] C. Urmson, J. Anhalt, D. Bagnell, C. Baker, R. Bittner, M. Clark, J. Dolan, D. Duggins, T. Galatali, C. Geyer, et al. Autonomous driving in urban environments: Boss and the urban challenge. *Journal of Field Robotics*, 25(8):425–466, 2008.

[591] L. G. Valiant. A theory of the learnable. *Communications of the ACM*, 27(11):1134–1142, 1984.

[592] M. E. Valle, W. L. Vital, and G. Vieira. Universal approximation theorem for vector- and hypercomplex-valued neural networks. *arXiv preprint arXiv:2401.02277*, 2024.

[593] J. E. Van Engelen and H. H. Hoos. A survey on semi-supervised learning. *Machine Learning*, 109(2):373–440, 2020.

[594] A. van Witteloostuijn and J. van Hugten. The state of the art of hypothesis testing in the social sciences. *Social Sciences & Humanities Open*, 6(1):100314, 2022.

[595] V. N. Vapnik. *Estimation of Dependences Based on Empirical Data*. Springer-Verlag, 1982.

[596] V. N. Vapnik. *The Nature of Statistical Learning Theory*. Springer-Verlag, 1995.

[597] V. N. Vapnik. *Statistical Learning Theory*. Wiley, 1998.

[598] V. N. Vapnik and A. Y. Chervonenkis. On the uniform convergence of relative frequencies of events to their probabilities. *Theory of Probability & Its Applications*, 16(2):264–280, 1971. English translation of original Russian work (1965).

[599] A. Vaswani, N. Shazeer, N. Parmar, J. Uszkoreit, L. Jones, A. N. Gomez, Ł. Kaiser, and I. Polosukhin. Attention is all you need. In *Advances in Neural Information Processing Systems (NeurIPS)*, pages 5998–6008, 2017.

[600] A. Verikas, A. Gelzinis, and M. Bacauskiene. Mining data with random forests: A survey and results of new tests. *Pattern Recognition*, 44(2):330–349, 2011.

[601] P. Villalobos, A. Ho, J. Sevilla, T. Besiroglu, L. Heim, and M. Hobbhahn. Position: Will we run out of data? Limits of LLM scaling based on human-generated data. In *Proceedings of the 41st International Conference on Machine Learning (ICML)*, pages 49523–49544, 2024.

[602] S. V. N. Vishwanathan, N. N. Schraudolph, R. Kondor, and K. M. Borgwardt. Graph kernels. *Journal of Machine Learning Research*, 11:1201–1242, 2010.

[603] E.-J. Wagenmakers, M. Lee, T. Lodewyckx, and G. J. Iverson. Bayesian versus frequentist inference. In *Bayesian Evaluation of Informative Hypotheses*, pages 181–207. Springer, 2008.

[604] A. Wald. *Sequential Analysis*. Wiley, 1947.

[605] W. Wallach and C. Allen. *Moral machines: Teaching robots right from wrong*. Oxford University Press, 2008.

[606] L. Wang, C. Lyu, T. Ji, Z. Zhang, D. Yu, S. Shi, and Z. Tu. Document-level machine translation with large language models. *arXiv preprint arXiv:2304.02210*, 2023.

[607] L. Wang, X. Zhang, H. Su, and J. Zhu. A comprehensive survey of continual learning: Theory, method and application. *IEEE Transactions on Pattern Analysis and Machine Intelligence*, 46(8), 2024.

[608] M. Wang, X. Xu, Q. Yue, and Y. Wang. A comprehensive survey and experimental comparison of graph-based approximate nearest neighbor search. *arXiv preprint arXiv:2101.12631*, 2021.

[609] W. Wang, L. Feng, Y. Jiang, G. Niu, M.-L. Zhang, and M. Sugiyama. Binary classification with confidence difference. In *Advances in Neural Information Processing Systems (NeurIPS)*, 2023.

[610] L. Wasserman. *All of Statistics: A Concise Course in Statistical Inference*. Springer, 2004.

[611] D. S. Watkins. Understanding the QR algorithm. *SIAM Review*, 24(4):427–440, 1982.

[612] J. Wei, Y. Tay, R. Bommasani, C. Raffel, B. Zoph, S. Borgeaud, D. Yogatama, M. Bosma, D. Zhou, D. Metzler, E. H. Chi, T. Hashimoto, O. Vinyals, P. Liang, J. Dean, and W. Fedus. Emergent abilities of large language models. *Transactions on Machine Learning Research*, 2022.

[613] L. Weidinger, J. Mellor, M. Rauh, C. Griffin, J. Uesato, P.-S. Huang, M. Cheng, M. Glaese, B. Balle, A. Kasirzadeh, et al. Ethical and social risks of harm from language models. *arXiv preprint arXiv:2112.04359*, 2021.

[614] K. Q. Weinberger and L. K. Saul. Distance metric learning for large margin nearest neighbor classification. *Journal of Machine Learning Research*, 10:207–244, 2009.

[615] G. M. Weiss. Mining with rarity: A unifying framework. *ACM SIGKDD Explorations Newsletter*, 6(1):7–19, 2004.

[616] B. L. Welch. The generalization of "Student's" problem when several different population variances are involved. *Biometrika*, 34(1–2):28–35, 1947.

[617] Y. Wen, D. Tran, and J. Ba. BatchEnsemble: An alternative approach to efficient ensemble and lifelong learning. In *Proceedings of the 37th International Conference on Machine Learning (ICML)*, 2020.

[618] F. Wenzel, J. Snoek, D. Tran, and R. Jenatton. Hyperparameter ensembles for robustness and uncertainty quantification. In *Advances in Neural Information Processing Systems (NeurIPS)*, pages 6514–6527, 2020.

[619] H. White. A heteroskedasticity-consistent covariance matrix estimator and a direct test for heteroskedasticity. *Econometrica*, 48(4):817–838, 1980.

[620] C. Whitrow, D. J. Hand, P. Juszczak, D. Weston, and N. M. Adams. Transaction aggregation as a strategy for credit card fraud detection. *Data Mining and Knowledge Discovery*, 18:30–55, 2009.

[621] N. Wies, Y. Levine, and A. Shashua. The learnability of in-context learning. In *Advances in Neural Information Processing Systems (NeurIPS)*, pages 36637–36651, 2023.

[622] F. Wilcoxon. Individual comparisons by ranking methods. *Biometrics Bulletin*, 1(6):80–83, 1945.

[623] C. Williams and M. Seeger. Using the Nyström method to speed up kernel machines. In *Advances in Neural Information Processing Systems (NeurIPS)*, pages 682–688, 2000.

[624] S. Williamson, K. Vijayakumar, and V. J. Kadam. Predicting breast cancer biopsy outcomes from BI-RADS findings using random forests with chi-square and MI features. *Multimedia Tools and Applications*, 81(26):36869–36889, 2022.

[625] D. R. Wilson. Asymptotic properties of nearest neighbor rules using edited data. *IEEE Transactions on Systems, Man, and Cybernetics*, 2(4):408–421, 1972.

[626] E. B. Wilson. Probable inference, the law of succession, and statistical inference. *Journal of the American Statistical Association*, 22(158):209–212, 1927.

[627] T. Winograd. Understanding natural language. *Cognitive Psychology*, 3(1):1–191, 1972.

[628] T. Wolf, L. Debut, V. Sanh, J. Chaumond, C. Delangue, A. Moi, P. Cistac, T. Rault, R. Louf, M. Funtowicz, et al. Huggingface's transformers: State-of-the-art natural language processing. *arXiv preprint arXiv:1910.03771*, 2019.

[629] D. H. Wolpert. Stacked generalization. *Neural Networks*, 5(2):241–259, 1992.

[630] D. H. Wolpert and W. G. Macready. No free lunch theorems for optimization. *IEEE Transactions on Evolutionary Computation*, 1(1):67–82, 1997.

[631] S. Wu, O. Irsoy, S. Lu, V. Dabravolski, M. Dredze, S. Gehrmann, P. Kambadur, D. Rosenberg, and G. Mann. BloombergGPT: A large language model for finance. *arXiv preprint arXiv:2303.17564*, 2023.

[632] Y. Wu, M. Schuster, Z. Chen, Q. V. Le, M. Norouzi, W. Macherey, M. Krikun, Y. Cao, Q. Gao, K. Macherey, J. Klingner, A. Shah, M. Johnson, X. Liu, Łukasz Kaiser, S. Gouws, Y. Kato, T. Kudo, H. Kazawa, K. Stevens, G. Kurian, N. Patil, W. Wang, C. Young, J. Smith, J. Riesa, A. Rudnick, O. Vinyals, G. Corrado, M. Hughes, and J. Dean. Google's neural machine translation system: Bridging the gap between human and machine translation. *arXiv preprint arXiv:1609.08144*, 2016.

[633] J. Xiao, R. Sun, Q. Long, and W. J. Su. Bridging the gap: Rademacher complexity in robust and standard generalization. In *Proceedings of the 37th Conference on Learning Theory (COLT)*, 2024.

[634] J. Xie, K. Zhang, J. Chen, T. Zhu, R. Lou, Y. Tian, Y. Xiao, and Y. Su. Travelplanner: A benchmark for real-world planning with language agents. *arXiv preprint arXiv:2402.01622*, 2024.

[635] Y. Xie, X. Li, E. Ngai, and W. Ying. Customer churn prediction using improved balanced random forests. *Expert Systems with Applications*, 36(3):5445–5449, 2009.

[636] Y. Xie, Y. Wang, A. Nallanathan, and L. Wang. An improved k-nearest-neighbor indoor localization method based on Spearman distance. *IEEE Signal Processing Letters*, 23(3):351–355, 2016.

[637] W. Xiong, L. Wu, F. Alleva, J. Droppo, X. Huang, and A. Stolcke. Toward human parity in conversational speech recognition. *IEEE/ACM Transactions on Audio, Speech, and Language Processing*, 25(12):2410–2423, 2017.

[638] D. Xu, Y. Shi, I. W. Tsang, Y.-S. Ong, C. Gong, and X. Shen. Survey on multi-output learning. *IEEE Transactions on Neural Networks and Learning Systems*, 31(7):2409–2429, 2019.

[639] J. Xu, J. Liu, Z. Ma, Y. Wang, W. Wang, and E. Ngai. KNN-based collaborative filtering for fine-grained intelligent grad-school recommendation system. In *Heterogeneous Networking for Quality, Reliability, Security and Robustness*, pages 494–508, 2023.

[640] M. Xu, D. Cai, W. Yin, S. Wang, X. Jin, and X. Liu. Resource-efficient algorithms and systems of foundation models: A survey. *ACM Computing Surveys*, 57(5):1–39, 2025.

[641] R. Xu and K. Chen. Rethinking benign overfitting in two-layer neural networks. *arXiv preprint arXiv:2502.11893*, 2025.

[642] W. Yan. Application of random forest to aircraft engine fault diagnosis. In *Proceedings of the 2006 Multiconference on Computational Engineering in Systems Applications*, pages 468–475, 2006.

[643] B.-S. Yang, X. Di, and T. Han. Random forests classifier for machine fault diagnosis. *Journal of Mechanical Science and Technology*, 22:1716–1725, 2008.

[644] X. Yang, L. Tan, and L. He. A robust least squares support vector machine for regression and classification with noise. *Neurocomputing*, 140:41–52, 2014.

[645] Y. Yang, I. Garcia Morillo, and T. M. Hospedales. Deep neural decision trees. *arXiv preprint arXiv:1806.06988*, 2018.

[646] Z. Yang, A. Sudjianto, X. Li, and A. Zhang. Inherently interpretable tree ensemble learning. *arXiv preprint arXiv:2410.19098*, 2024.

[647] Y. Yao, L. Rosasco, and A. Caponnetto. On early stopping in gradient descent learning. *Constructive Approximation*, 26(2):289–315, 2007.

[648] P. N. Yianilos. Data structures and algorithms for nearest neighbor search in general metric spaces. In *Proceedings of the 4th Annual ACM-SIAM Symposium on Discrete Algorithms*, pages 311–321, 1993.

[649] X. Yin, X. Wang, L. Pan, L. Lin, X. Wan, and W. Y. Wang. Gödel agent: A self-referential agent framework for recursive self-improvement. *arXiv preprint arXiv:2410.04444*, 2024.

[650] T. Young, D. Hazarika, S. Poria, and E. Cambria. Recent trends in deep learning based natural language processing. *IEEE Computational Intelligence Magazine*, 13(3):55–75, 2018.

[651] C. Yu, B. C. Ooi, K.-L. Tan, and H. V. Jagadish. Indexing the distance: An efficient method to KNN processing. In *Proceedings of the 27th International Conference on Very Large Data Bases*, pages 421–430, 2001.

[652] D. Yu, B. Yang, D. Liu, H. Wang, and S. Pan. A survey on neural-symbolic learning systems. *Neural Networks*, 2023.

[653] H. Yu and J. Yang. A direct LDA algorithm for high-dimensional data — with application to face recognition. *Pattern Recognition*, 34(10):2067–2070, 2001.

[654] T. Yu and H. Zhu. Hyper-parameter optimization: A review of algorithms and applications. *arXiv preprint arXiv:2003.05689*, 2020.

[655] Y. Yuan, Z. Li, and B. Zhao. A survey of multimodal learning: Methods, applications, and future directions. *ACM Computing Surveys*, 57(7):1–34, 2025.

[656] B. Zadrozny and C. Elkan. Obtaining calibrated probability estimates from decision trees and naive Bayesian classifiers. In *Proceedings of the 18th International Conference on Machine Learning (ICML)*, pages 609–616, 2001.

[657] B. Zadrozny and C. Elkan. Transforming classifier scores into accurate multiclass probability estimates. In *Proceedings of the Eighth ACM SIGKDD International Conference on Knowledge Discovery and Data Mining*, pages 694–699, 2002.

[658] B. Zadrozny, J. Langford, and N. Abe. Cost-sensitive learning by cost-proportionate example weighting. In *Proceedings of the IEEE International Conference on Data Mining (ICDM)*, pages 435–442, 2003.

[659] H. Zhang. The optimality of naive Bayes under zero-one loss. *Machine Learning*, 1(2):3–22, 2004.

[660] H. Zhang, W. Lin, Y. Liu, and C. Fang. Learning curves of stochastic gradient descent in kernel regression. In *Proceedings of the 42nd International Conference on Machine Learning (ICML)*, 2025.

[661] M. Q. Zhang. Identification of protein coding regions in the human genome by quadratic discriminant analysis. *Proceedings of the National Academy of Sciences*, 94(2):565–568, 1997.

[662] N. L. Zhang and D. Poole. A simple approach to Bayesian network computations. In *Proceedings of the 10th Biennial Canadian Conference on Artificial Intelligence*, pages 171–178, 1994.

[663] S. Zhang, X. Chen, X. Ran, Z. Li, and W. Cao. Prioritizing causation in decision trees: A framework for interpretable modeling. *Engineering Applications of Artificial Intelligence*, 133:108224, 2024.

[664] T. Zhang, F. Ladhak, E. Durmus, P. Liang, K. McKeown, and T. B. Hashimoto. Benchmarking large language models for news summarization. *Transactions of the Association for Computational Linguistics*, 12:39–57, 2024.

[665] W. Zhang, Y. Deng, B. Liu, S. J. Pan, and L. Bing. Sentiment analysis in the era of large language models: A reality check. *arXiv preprint arXiv:2305.15005*, 2023.

[666] X. Zhang, H. Gu, L. Fan, K. Chen, and Q. Yang. No free lunch theorem for security and utility in federated learning. *ACM Transactions on Intelligent Systems and Technology*, 14(1):1–35, 2022.

[667] W. X. Zhao, K. Zhou, J. Li, T. Tang, X. Wang, Y. Hou, Y. Min, B. Zhang, J. Zhang, Z. Dong, et al. A survey of large language models. *arXiv preprint arXiv:2303.18223*, 2023.

[668] J. Zheng, S. Qiu, C. Shi, and Q. Ma. Towards lifelong learning of large language models: A survey. *ACM Computing Surveys*, 57(8):1–35, 2025.

[669] Z.-H. Zhou. *Ensemble Methods: Foundations and Algorithms*. CRC Press, 2012.

[670] J. Zhu, H. Zou, S. Rosset, and T. Hastie. Multi-class AdaBoost. *Statistics and Its Interface*, 2(3):349–360, 2009.

[671] H. Zou and T. Hastie. Regularization and variable selection via the elastic net. *Journal of the Royal Statistical Society: Series B (Statistical Methodology)*, 67(2):301–320, 2005.

[672] N. Zozoulenko, T. Cass, and L. Gonon. Random feature representation boosting. *arXiv preprint arXiv:2501.18283*, 2025.

Index

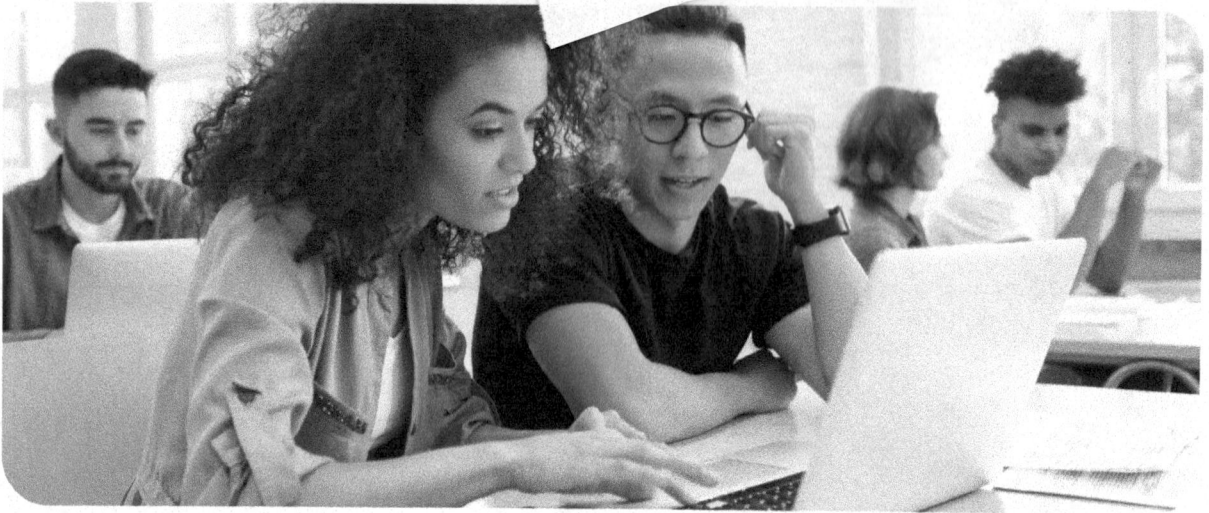

Register Your Product at informit.com/register

Access additional benefits and save up to 65%* on your next purchase

- Automatically receive a coupon for 35% off books, eBooks, and web editions and 65% off video courses, valid for 30 days. Look for your code in your InformIT cart or the Manage Codes section of your account page.

- Download available product updates.

- Access bonus material if available.**

- Check the box to hear from us and receive exclusive offers on new editions and related products.

InformIT is the trusted technology learning source and online home of information technology brands at Pearson, the world's leading learning company. At informit.com you can shop our books, eBooks, and video training. Most eBooks are DRM-free and include PDF and EPUB files.

- Take advantage of our special offers and promotions (informit.com/promotions).

- Sign up for special offers and content newsletter (informit.com/newsletters).

- Access thousands of free chapters and video lessons.

- Enjoy free ground shipping on U.S. orders.*

Offers subject to change.
** *Registration benefits vary by product. Benefits will be listed on your account page under Registered Products.*

Connect with InformIT—Visit informit.com/community

»Pearson   InformIT®

Addison-Wesley • Adobe Press • Cisco Press • Microsoft Press • Oracle Press • Peachpit Press • Pearson IT Certification